LEGAL SYSTEMS OF THE WORLD

LEGAL SYSTEMS OF THE WORLD

A POLITICAL, SOCIAL, AND CULTURAL ENCYCLOPEDIA

Volume III: M–R

Edited by Herbert M. Kritzer

A B C ⬥ C L I O

SANTA BARBARA, CALIFORNIA · DENVER, COLORADO · OXFORD, ENGLAND

Library of Congress Cataloging-in-Publication Data

Legal systems of the world : a political, social, and cultural
encyclopedia / edited by Herbert M. Kritzer.
    p. cm.
Includes index.
    ISBN 1-57607-231-2 (hardcover : alk. paper); 1-57607-758-6 (e-book)
    1. Law—Encyclopedias. I. Kritzer, Herbert M., 1947–
K48 .L44 2002
340'.03—dc21
                2002002659

"Cape Verde" originally published in the *Journal of African Law* 44, no. 1 (2000): 86–95.

Material in "Comoros" and "Djibouti" used with the kind permission of Kluwer Law International.

Material in "European Court of Justice" from Kenney, Sally J. "The European Court of Justice: Integrating Europe through Law." 81 Judicature 250–255 (1998). Reprinted in *Crime and Justice International,* November.

06 05 04 03 10 9 8 7 6 5 4 3

This book is also available on the World Wide Web as an e-book. Visit abc-clio.com for details.

ABC-CLIO, Inc.
130 Cremona Drive, P.O. Box 1911
Santa Barbara, California 93116–1911

CONTENTS

LEGAL SYSTEMS OF THE WORLD

Volume I: A–D

LEGAL SYSTEMS
OF THE WORLD

Volume III

MACEDONIA

COUNTRY INFORMATION

Macedonia is located in southeastern Europe, bordering Bulgaria to the east, Greece to the south, Albania to the west, and Yugoslavia to the north. Part of the border with Yugoslavia lies next to the southern Yugoslav region of Kosovo. According to its 1991 Constitution, the official name of the country is the Republic of Macedonia. However, in its international relations, the name of the country is the Former Yugoslav Republic of Macedonia (FYROM), in accord with an agreement reached at the time of the country's admission to the United Nations in 1993. Most states have recognized Macedonia under this latter name.

The area of Macedonia is approximately 9,800 square miles. Much of Macedonia is mountainous. It does not have a coastline. The capital is Skopje.

Estimates in late 2000 placed the population of Macedonia at 2,030,000. According to the government's figures, 67 percent of the population is made up of Macedonian Slavs, with ethnic Albanians the largest minority group at 23 percent. The Albanian population is concentrated primarily in the west and north, close to Albania and to Kosovo, which also is populated primarily by ethnic Albanians. Other ethnic groups include Turks (4 percent), Roma (2 percent), and Serbs (2 percent). The official language of Macedonia is Macedonian, a south Slavic language written in the Cyrillic alphabet. However, the constitution provides that in localities where a substantial number of residents do not speak Macedonian as their native language, the laws shall establish conditions for the use of the prevalent ethnic group's language as an official language. A goal of the ethnic Albanian population is a constitutional amendment that would recognize Albanian as an official language.

HISTORY

Macedonia became an independent country in 1991, during the disintegration of the former Socialist Federal Republic of Yugoslavia (SFRY). From 1946 to 1991, Macedonia was one of the six constituent Republics of the SFRY.

The existing state of Macedonia occupies a substantial part of a larger geographic region called Macedonia since as far back as the fourth century B.C.E. Slavic tribes began to settle in Macedonia in the sixth century C.E., and from the seventh to the fourteenth centuries the region was ruled at different times by the Byzantine Empire, the Bulgars during periods of the ninth and thirteenth centuries, and the Serbian Empire in the early and middle fourteenth century. This complex history has been a basis for competing modern assertions over the territory of historical Macedonia by Bulgaria, Greece, and Serbia. Beginning in the later fourteenth century, Macedonia became part of the Ottoman Empire for over 500 years. Ottoman control ended as a result of the Balkan wars of 1912–1913, after which the region was divided among Bulgaria, Greece, and Serbia, with almost all of the territory of present-day Macedonia going to Serbia. Following World War I, Serbian Macedonia was incorporated into the Kingdom of the Serbs, Croats, and Slovenes (renamed the Kingdom of Yugoslavia in 1929). Following World War II, Macedonia became a constituent republic within the Socialist Federal Republic of Yugoslavia when it was formed in 1946.

Amid the splintering of the SFRY in 1991, the people of Macedonia in September approved a referendum calling for an independent Macedonia. The legislature adopted a formal declaration to that effect on September 17, 1991, and the current constitution was adopted on November 17, 1991.

Macedonia remained outside the bitter conflicts that marked the breakup of the former SFRY in 1991–1995. However, its economy was severely affected by United Nations trade sanctions against Yugoslavia from May 1992 to November 1995, because some 60 percent of Macedonia's trade prior to that time had been with the republics of Serbia and Montenegro. In addition, Macedonia's economy also suffered from an economic blockade instituted from February 1994 to September 1995 by Greece, which feared that by adopting the name Macedonia and certain state symbols, the new country intended to make claims on the adjacent Greek province of Macedonia. When admitting Macedonia to the United Nations on April 8, 1993, the United Nations General

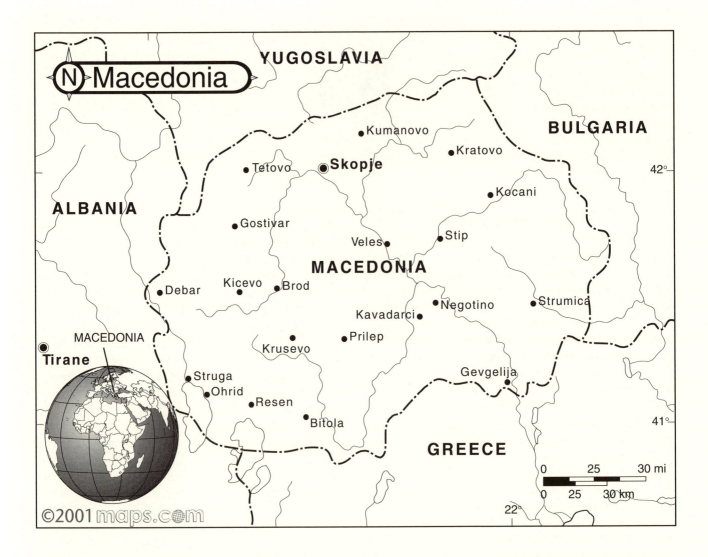

Assembly resolved that the state would be called the Former Yugoslav Republic of Macedonia pending settlement of the differences with Greece over its name. Greece agreed to normalize relations with Macedonia in September 1995 and in so doing promised Macedonia access to the northern Greek port of Thessaloniki, its nearest outlet to the sea. Meanwhile, the mid-1990s witnessed Macedonia's admission into a number of global and European organizations, including its entry in 1995 into the Organization of Security and Cooperation in Europe (OSCE) and the Council of Europe.

Beginning in 1998, the developing crisis in adjacent Kosovo had a deep impact on Macedonia. During the displacement of ethnic Albanians from Kosovo in 1999, several hundred thousand refugees flooded into Macedonia, although most had returned to Kosovo by the end of 2000.

Internally, Macedonia's leaders since independence have sought to introduce a market-based economy and to promote privatization. In 1998, a major change in Macedonian politics took place as the result of parliamentary elections in which a coalition of two opposition parties,

the Internal Macedonian Revolutionary Organization–Democratic Party for Macedonian National Unity (VMRO–DPMNE) and the Democratic Alliance (DA), took 59 of the 120 seats in the Parliament, defeating the governing Social Democratic League of Macedonia (SDSM), which as the successor to the SFRY-era Communist Party had ruled Macedonia since its independence. The winning coalition then joined with several ethnic Albanian parties to form a new government headed by VMRO-DPMNE leader Ljubcho Georgievski as prime minister. The governing coalition's power increased in December 1999 with the election of Boris Trajkovski of the VMRO-DPMNE party as president.

Ethnic tensions between Macedonian Slavs and ethnic Albanians, evident since 1997 amid claimed human rights violations against the latter by the police, controversy over proposed establishment of an Albanian-speaking university in the city of Tetovo, and the Kosovo refugee crisis of 1999, burst into open conflict in February 2001 with the launching of an armed insurgency by the ethnic Albanian National Liberation Army in the northwestern part of the country. Since that time, Macedonian Slav and ethnic Albanian leaders, under intense pressure from foreign diplomats, have sought to negotiate a political solution that will ward off the threat of full-scale civil war. These tensions have been exacerbated by poor economic conditions in the country, where unemployment in mid-2001 was estimated at 37 percent of the workforce. An additional problem facing the government is ongoing concern about the high level of crime, much of which is linked to criminal organizations operating across national borders.

LEGAL CONCEPTS

Macedonia's legal system is based on institutions and normative principles associated with the European continental civil law tradition. Its institutional structure has been strongly influenced in the twentieth century by legal development in Serbia, which in turn had borrowed heavily in the late nineteenth and early twentieth centuries from continental models, especially Austria. Much of the normative base was inherited from the SFRY, although a considerable amount of new legislation has been enacted in the past decade.

The 1991 Constitution established Macedonia as a unitary state based on a single Macedonian citizenship, rather than one recognizing group rights based on ethnicity. The constitution contains an extensive listing of human rights, which correspond in large part to those in the European Convention for the Protection of Human Rights and Fundamental Freedoms (ECHR) and other international human rights instruments to which Macedonia is a party, including the International Covenant on Civil and Political Rights and the International Convention on the Elimination of All Forms of Racial Discrimination. According to the constitution, a citizen of Macedonia may invoke these human rights guarantees in proceedings before the courts. Because Macedonia is a party to the ECHR, individuals who claim that governmental acts violate that convention's provisions have a right to appeal to the European Court of Human Rights if they have exhausted their remedies within the Macedonia legal system. The constitution also includes "respect for the generally accepted norms of international law" among the fundamental values of the constitutional order and states that international agreements to which Macedonia is a party, which cannot be amended by legislation, shall be among the sources of law applied by the courts.

The constitution states that the separation of governmental powers into legislative, executive, and judicial branches is also a fundamental value of the constitutional order. The constitution is the supreme normative source of law, requiring that all legislation and other governmental acts must be in conformity with it. Legislative acts are superior to governmental regulatory acts, and the courts are empowered to judge whether this requirement

is satisfied in specific cases. Judicial precedent is not formally recognized as a source of law.

The power to adopt generally applicable legislative acts is within the exclusive competence of the unicameral Assembly of the Republic of Macedonia, which also has exclusive authority to amend the constitution. Of the 120 seats in the assembly, representatives holding 85 are elected by popular vote, while 35 representatives are chosen on the proportionality principle: the percentage that parties gain from the overall vote. Representatives to the assembly are elected for four-year terms.

Statutes enacted by the assembly since 1991 include the 1995 Law on the Courts, the 1996 Criminal Code, the 1997 Code of Criminal Procedure, and the 1998 Law on Trial Proceedings. The assembly has not enacted a civil code; therefore, the topics typically addressed in such codes are found in a number of separate legislative acts. A significant number of laws affecting private business activity have been enacted since 1991, including laws on trade, commercial companies, public enterprises, and bankruptcy. In addition to law making, the assembly plays a crucial role in the appointment and dismissal of many other public officials, including judges on the Constitutional Court and the courts of general jurisdiction, as well as the public prosecutor.

The executive branch comprises the president, who is directly elected, and a government led by a prime minister who is elected by and responsible to the assembly. The president, who is the head of state, serves for a term of five years. The government, including the prime minister, is responsible for execution of the laws. The assembly may terminate the mandate of the government any time by a vote of no confidence. If a majority of the representatives in the assembly approve a motion of no confidence, the government is obliged to resign.

The administration of governmental affairs is subject to an extensive body of procedural and substantive administrative law, inherited from the SFRY. Except in certain exceptional cases prescribed by law, the courts are empowered to review final administrative determinations for their conformity to the constitution and to legislation.

Judicial functions are performed by the Constitutional Court, a three-tiered system of courts of general jurisdiction, and military tribunals whose jurisdiction is limited to resolution of disputes involving military personnel. Macedonia used to have a separate system of commercial courts for resolution of disputes involving business entities; however, those courts have been abolished and their responsibilities have been transferred to the courts of general jurisdiction. Emergency courts are prohibited by the constitution.

The prosecution of crimes is the responsibility of the public prosecutor, who is required to initiate criminal prosecution if proof exists that a criminal offense has been committed. In certain cases prescribed by law, private individuals may also bring charges for alleged violations of the criminal laws.

The constitution also provides for the post of public attorney to protect the constitutional and legal rights of citizens when violated by bodies of state administration and other agencies with public mandates. Pursuant to this mandate, legislation establishing the Office of the People's Ombudsman was enacted in 1997.

Although the foundations of criminal and civil procedure in Macedonia's court system lie in the civil law tradition, recently enacted legislation (the Law on the Courts, 1995; the Code of Criminal Procedure, 1997; the Law on Trial Proceedings, 1998) has introduced a number of elements associated with the adversarial system. In criminal procedure, the investigating judge is assigned the responsibility for supervising steps taken by the police and prosecutor during the pretrial proceedings. Criminal trials in most cases are conducted by mixed panels of professional judges and lay persons: two judges and three lay persons for serious crimes, and one judge and two lay persons for less serious crimes. Cases involving minor crimes are heard by a single professional judge. During the trial phase, the judges direct the presentation of evidence, examine witnesses, and make the ultimate finding of innocence or guilt. A particular goal of legal reformers since independence has been revision of certain aspects of the procedural rules. The 1997 Code of Criminal Procedure introduced many changes intended to promote adherence to constitutional and international norms and human rights standards. As to civil procedure, the 1995 Law on the Courts and the 1998 Law on Trial Proceedings introduced provisions intended to make civil proceedings more concentrated and to give the parties, rather than just the court, the opportunity and responsibility to gather and manage the presentation of evidence.

As a party to the New York Convention on the Enforcement of Foreign Arbitration Awards of June 20, 1958, Macedonia is required to provide judicial recognition and enforcement of awards rendered by arbitration panels in other countries. Such judicial treatment of foreign arbitration awards is required unless an award was rendered with certain procedural infirmities or its recognition and enforcement would be contrary to the public policy of Macedonia.

CURRENT COURT SYSTEM STRUCTURE

Administration of the judicial system is the joint responsibility of the Ministry of Justice and the Judicial Council, a seven-member body elected by the assembly. Matters such as budget allocation and determination of the number of judicial posts are in the hands of the Ministry of Justice. Therefore, the courts themselves do not make the determinations as to their budgetary and staffing needs. The Judicial Council proposes to the assembly the election and dismissal of judges, monitors judges' performance of their duties and disciplines judges for ethical violations, and proposes two judges to sit on the Constitutional Court. Its members serve for a term of six years, and may be reelected once to an additional six-year term.

The Constitutional Court is vested with the power to decide constitutional questions, including the adjudication of complaints by individuals that a governmental act has violated their constitutional rights and the resolution of disputes between the governmental branches as to the constitutional allocation of powers. The court is empowered to decide constitutional questions referred to it by the courts of general jurisdiction.

The three-tiered courts of general jurisdiction include twenty-seven courts of first instance (municipal courts), three courts of appeal (district courts), and the Supreme Court. They preside over criminal and civil cases and appeals from decisions of administrative agencies. Separate administrative courts do not exist in Macedonia. The Supreme Court is the highest court in the system of courts of general jurisdiction and is vested with the mandate to ensure uniformity in application of the laws by all lower courts. It has twenty-five members, who decide specific cases in smaller panels.

The Chamber of Commerce of Macedonia administers a system of private arbitration of disputes involving foreign businesses. The chamber adopted rules for its Foreign Trade Court of Arbitration in 1993.

STAFFING

The appointment of all judges to the courts of general jurisdiction is performed by the assembly, which must choose from among recommendations by the Judicial Council. All judges appointed to the courts of general jurisdiction are granted life tenure subject to mandatory retirement as specified by law. Justices of the Constitutional Court, who serve a nine-year, nonrenewable term, are also elected by the assembly; however, the nomination of two of the candidates for the Constitutional Court is reserved for the president of the republic, while the Judicial Council also proposes two candidates. The Constitutional Court is composed of nine justices.

Along with the above provisions regarding life tenure or fixed terms of service, the constitution also provides for dismissal of judges by the assembly, acting upon determinations made by the Judicial Council. Judges may be dismissed by the assembly if the Judicial Council concludes that they have permanently lost the ability to carry out their professional duties, have committed a serious disciplinary offense, or have performed their duties in an unprofessional or unethical manner. In addition, a judge is also subject to dismissal if he or she has been found guilty of a criminal offense for which the sentence is at

Legal Structure of Macedonia Courts

Constitutional Court	Courts of General Jurisdiction Supreme Court Courts of Appeal Trial Courts	Commercial Courts Higher Commercial Court First Instance Courts	Military Tribunals

least six months in prison. The grounds for dismissal of justices on the Constitutional Court are narrower: if a justice is sentenced to imprisonment of at least six months for commission of a criminal offense or if he or she has permanently lost the ability to perform the required responsibilities. In the latter case, this determination is made by the other justices of the Constitutional Court, and the assembly and Judicial Council are not involved in the decision.

In July 1996, pursuant to the Law on the Courts, the assembly reviewed the status of all judges in the courts of general jurisdiction. Following the review, some 660 judges were appointed to posts in the court system. Of these, approximately two-thirds had never served as judges before. In response to the great need to train new judges and to educate judges regarding the many new laws, the Macedonian Judges' Association has established an extensive program of continuing education for judges.

The public prosecutor is appointed by the assembly and serves for a six-year term, which is renewable. The assembly is also empowered to dismiss the public prosecutor, although the constitution does not specify any particular grounds upon which such dismissal must be based.

Entry into the private practice of law in Macedonia is governed by legislation enacted in 1992. Licensing and disciplining of attorneys are the responsibility of the Bar Association of Macedonia, which has approximately 1,000 members. Membership in the Bar Association, which was established in 1945, is compulsory for all attorneys. Foreign attorneys may be licensed to practice law in Macedonia if their country grants reciprocal treatment. Macedonia has one degree-granting law faculty, at the University of Saints Cyril and Methodius in Skopje. Approximately 300 law degrees are granted each year.

IMPACT OF LAW

Since independence, improvement in the standing and authority of the legal system has been a goal of many of the system's participants, legal reformers in the political system, and foreign intergovernmental and nongovernmental organizations. Members of the judiciary receive very low salaries and the courts are poorly equipped. According to many observers, public respect for the legal system in Macedonia is not high, particularly among ethnic minorities. Many members of the public view the courts as influenced by other branches of government and unable to provide adequate relief for citizens against illegal actions by other governmental authorities, particularly the police, who are under the authority of the Ministry of the Interior. Also, critics of the courts state that court proceedings often are slow and inefficient.

Determined efforts have been made to increase the public standing of the legal system, and to establish an authoritative place for legal norms and procedures in Macedonian public life. Many new substantive and procedural laws have been enacted, and legal reformers have focused considerable attention on efforts to establish more administrative autonomy for the courts and improve the efficiency of the judicial process. The Macedonian Judges' Association plays a major role in seeking reforms. One of the goals of judges is to transfer decision making over budget allocation from the Ministry of Justice to institutions administered by the judges themselves. Reformers also seek improvements in the work and living conditions of the judiciary, claiming that salaries for judges and court personnel must be increased in order to safeguard against the attractions of bribery. In regard to the work of the police, human rights groups report that widespread efforts have been made within the governmental structure to improve law enforcement standards.

Two questions, both outside direct control of the legal system, can be expected to influence the system's development in the near future: the status of the economy and the degree of success in forging a workable structure for peaceful resolution of ethnic disputes. In regard to the latter question, a key factor will be the identification of a means to reconcile the constitutional commitment to protection of individual rights within a political framework of multiethnic democracy with the demands for group rights advanced by ethnic Albanian organizations.

Peter Krug

See also Arbitration; Civil Law; Civil Procedure; Constitutional Review; Criminal Procedures; European Court and Commission on Human Rights; Government Legal Departments; Human Rights Law; Judicial Independence; Judicial Selection, Methods of; Ottoman Empire; Prosecuting Authorities; Yugoslavia: Kingdom of and Socialist Republic

References and further reading

Brashear, Lydia. 1997. "A Year in the Balkans: Macedonia and the Rule of Law." *Human Rights* 24, no. 1: 18–20.

Glenny, Misha. 2001. "A Tinderbox Determined to Ignite." *The Scotsman* (June 28): 11.

Jurist: The Legal Education Network ["World Law" section], "Macedonia," http://jurist.law.pitt.edu/world/macedonia. htm (accessed September 9, 2001).

Lance, Evelyn B. 2000. "Judicial Reform in Macedonia." *The Judges' Journal* 39, no. 4: 34–36.

Macedonian Business Law Association, http://www.mbla. org.mk (accessed June 18, 2001).

Macedonian Legal Resource Center, http://www.mlrc.org.mk (accessed June 18, 2001).

Pribichevich, Stoyan. 1982. *Macedonia, Its People and History.* University Park, PA: Pennsylvania State University Press.

MADAGASCAR

GEOGRAPHY

Madagascar was once part of the continent of Africa but split apart from it several million years ago. The island now sits some 250 miles east of the continent, separated from it by the Mozambique Channel. Sitting in the Indian Ocean, Madagascar is isolated from Asia and Africa, an isolation that preserved its independence through most of its history. Modern Madagascar may represent the Africa of a bygone era, with its mountains and jungles, but it also reflects its poverty, political instability, and tribal conflict.

As the fourth-largest island in the world, behind Greenland, New Guinea, and Borneo, Madagascar comprises some 600,000 square kilometers of territory. At its widest from east to west, the island stretches for some 360 miles. From north to south, the island ranges some 1,000 miles, or approximately the distance from Chicago, Illinois, to New Orleans, Louisiana. The large landmass, though, contains a fairly small population of 14 million. At the same time, Madagascar ranks low among nations in terms of the per capita income of its residents and its gross domestic product, making it one of the poorest countries in the world.

Although it has no land borders, Madagascar sits close not only to the African mainland but also to several chains of islands that make up independent countries. Directly to the west and on the continent sits the country of Mozambique. To the northwest in the Indian Ocean are the Comoros Islands. Directly north of Madagascar are several clusters of islands that make up the Seychelles, and to the east lies the island nation of Mauritius. There are also two French-controlled islands near Madagascar, Mayotte to the west and Reunion Island to the east.

Though not a part of Africa, Madagascar has some of the same geographic features of that continent. The eastern half of the island is dominated by a mountain range known as the Central Highlands. It is in this region that many of the island's rivers begin their descent to the Indian Ocean. To the west of the Central Highlands sit the central plains, where the capital and largest city, Antananarivo, is located. The western coast is composed of lowlands and rain forests, where many of the country's exotic plants and animals live. The northern reaches of the island are dominated by the Tsaratanna Massif Range, which includes the highest mountain on Madagascar, Mount Ambohitra. At the very northern tip of the island sits the country's largest port and former French naval base, Antsiranana. The southern half of the island ranges from desolate desert areas to river valleys. There major rivers—the Onilahy, the Mangoky, and the Mania—start flowing from the southern Central Highlands and end at the Mozambique Channel. Most of the rivers are not navigable because of the rapids created by the downward flow from the mountains.

The dense jungles and the rugged mountains make land transportation difficult through the island's interior. For that reason, the largest urban areas, other than the capital, are located along the coast. Antananarivo sits in almost the geographic center of the island and is most easily reached by plane because of the limited and poorly maintained roads.

Madagascar is composed of several different ethnic and tribal groups. Although they follow different customs, most of the tribal groups speak the Malagasy language, making communication and cooperation easier. The Sakalava, who live along the western coast, make up the third-largest tribe on the island. The Betsimisarake, who comprise the second-largest ethnic division, live along the eastern coast. But the largest and most dominant tribal group is the Merina, accounting for approximately one-quarter of the island's population. Living in the Central Highlands, the Merina dominated the smaller tribes and were the main force that fought the French during the colonial era. The Merina are likely descendants of Polynesians who migrated to the island thousands of years earlier. Along with the indigenous people, there are some newer immigrants, including Indians, Chinese, and the remnants of the French left over from the colonial period.

Madagascar may be best known for its spectacular scenery and its many unusual or one-of-a-kind animals and plants. Most Malagasy live in rural areas, and agriculture is their main source of income. In fact, agriculture is the primary source of income for the island as a whole. Although socialist agricultural policies eliminated many private farms and all but destroyed the agricultural sector, it has been revived by the lifting of state controls. For this

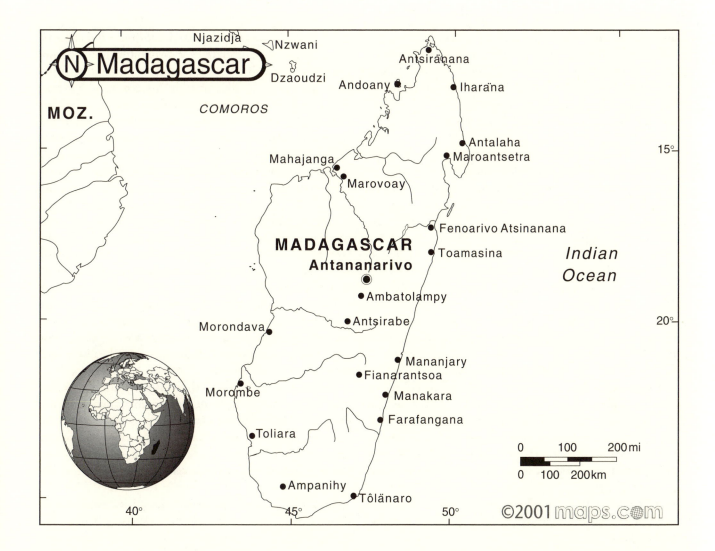

reason, the major export items from the island include coffee, vanilla, and cloves. There are few natural resources on Madagascar, and those that exist are frequently inaccessible or too expensive to extract. The result has been an economically impoverished island with a heavy debt load that has inhibited economic growth.

HISTORY

Because of its geographic position separate from Africa and its distance from the great trading routes of Europe, North Africa, Asia, and the Middle East, Madagascar has been isolated from much of the political and military turmoil of the past centuries. At the same time, it has not benefited from the progress that drove that era.

Madagascar was likely populated both by the peoples of the South Pacific and the Indian Ocean and by those from nearby Africa. The Malagasy language spoken on the island is derived from Polynesian and Malaysian dialect. Additionally, elements of the Bantu language are found on the island. Although the descendants of these South Pacific peoples make up the indigenous population, apparently the first colonizers to use the land were

Arab traders, who constructed small, temporary settlements that they used along with others on the African coast. The first significant attempts at colonization did not occur until after Vasco da Gama pierced the southern Horn of Africa. Yet the Europeans focused on colonizing the African mainland rather than Madagascar, and not until the middle of the seventeenth century did the French plant permanent settlements on the island. But the colonial plans went awry, and a massacre of the French followed; thereafter, they abandoned Madagascar and left it free of Europeans for another century.

As the French dithered, the various tribes on the island fought for dominance. One tribe, the Merina, won the battle. The Merina capital, Antananarivo, was used by the powerful Merina king Andrainampoenemorina to combine several other kingdoms under his control. His son Radama made the tribe the dominant military and political force on the island. Radama also attempted to modernize the country, allowing missionaries to set up schools to teach reading and other basic skills. This move spread literacy across the island. His successor, though—Queen Ranavalona I—ended many of these advances, torturing and killing natives who had converted and limiting her contacts with the West to the slave trade. Her death in 1861 set into motion a process of building closer ties to the Europeans. Direct French intervention in the island followed, with the overthrow and exile of the monarchy and the 1896 declaration that Madagascar was a French colony.

The French, though, were unable to completely control the entire island. The rugged interior of the country and its primitive or nonexistent transportation limited French control to the capital and various coastal outposts, including the major naval base at Diego Suarez at the northernmost tip of the island. The French allowed the Malagasy limited political authority after World War I. The island fell under the control of the Vichy French regime in 1940 and saw an invasion by Allied forces in 1942, for the Allies feared Japanese expansion into the area. After the war, France began granting greater authority to the island's population, making all residents French citizens. A 1947 revolt produced tens of thousands of casualties, mostly Malagasy, but French control was shaken. In the 1950s, France made preparations for granting independence as it saw its North African and Southeast Asian colonies rise up in revolt. Seeking to escape the costly maintenance of the colonies, Charles de Gaulle's government, taking control in 1958, adopted a policy of allowing greater local control. In 1959, Madagascar took its own step, declaring independence from France, and in 1960, the French accepted the inevitable and granted it. On June 26, 1960, Madagascar became an independent nation.

The first president of the country, Philibert Tsiranana, was able to acquire the support of the major ethnic groups in the country, and he developed close ties to the West, including France. He established the first political party in the independent nation, the Social Democratic Party of Madagascar, and included all major ethnic groups within its leadership. Tsiranana presided over a peaceful country during the 1960s, even as it struggled with economic problems and the difficulties associated with forming a democracy. But in the 1970s, political instability grew. A series of violent riots weakened the government, and as violence spread in 1972, civil war threatened to break out across the country. Tsiranana stepped down in favor of General Gabriel Ramanantsoa, who organized a military government. But the economic and political problems worsened as tribal differences between the Merina and other coastal tribes erupted into violence. The situation produced another change in government, this one more permanent. In 1975, Didier Ratsiraka, a military officer, was chosen as leader. Ratsiraka went to work immediately, rewriting many laws and starting the second Madagascar Republic with his election to a seven-year presidential term. Ratsiraka's success at restoring order, though, was followed by his turning the country into a socialist nightmare. He wrote and followed his own "Little Red Book" while initiating economic planning that further impoverished his people. From 1975 to near the end of his first period in office, Ratsiraka crushed democratic freedoms and operated a one-party communist state. During the entire period, the economic health of the country declined, its isolation increased, and the citizens of the island grew more restless. This attitude was exhibited in the results of the 1989 presidential "election," in which Ratsiraka ran as the only candidate and received only 63 percent of the vote, a startlingly low number for the leader of an authoritarian government that could manufacture a 90 percent win. This poor showing and the collapse of communism in Europe suggested Ratsiraka's time in office was limited. A series of demonstrations in 1991 led to an early presidential election in 1992 and the selection of a new president, Albert Zufy. A new constitution was written, and the socialist policies that produced so much misery and deprivation for the people of Madagascar were repealed.

But democracy proved a difficult transition for Madagascar. An impeachment of the president in 1996 followed a move by Zufy to change the constitution and expand presidential power over the prime minister's office. Zufy resigned in September 1996, and in a November election, he lost by a single percentage point to the former president, Ratsiraka. At the turn of the century, Ratsiraka appeared to have learned his lesson, refusing to turn back the clock and return the island to its socialist past.

LEGAL CONCEPTS

Legal concepts within Madagascar have continued to follow a dual approach in dispensing justice. The government abides by a constitution that is specific in its limitations on governmental power and the rights that are to be protected from governmental abuse. These rights include speech, association, religious practice, travel, the owning and disposing of property, and due process at trial. By the 1990s, most of these rights were being upheld in practice by the government. In cases where political rights were restricted, the courts were able to act, overturning convictions of those prosecuted for criticizing the regime. Yet the frequent changes in the constitution has undermined its legal basis. Whereas the 1992 Constitution was seen as a return to a democratic state, changes in 1995 and a major set of changes in 1998 granted more power to the president and appeared to undermine the idea of a government operating under the rule of law.

The poor government record on training and retaining judges has also harmed the rule of law on the island. The judges who serve are poorly paid and easily corrupted by bribes. A burst of criminal activity has overburdened the courts, with the result that many defendants remain in jail for months or years before going to trial. The socialist regime, with its emphasis on a particular economic and political system rather than a neutral legal system, also prevented the rule of law from taking root on the island.

Although the national government is limited by the constitution, there is a recognition in Madagascar that local concerns are best settled by local governments. Under Article 35 of the constitution, the *fokonolona* (local governments) have the authority to protect the rights and property of the citizens within their community. They do this by enforcing tribal law (*dina*) in tribal courts. These courts are manned by local officials and are not under the authority of the central government. Dina law is based in tradition, passed down verbally from village elder to village elder, and can change dramatically from village to village and region to region. As happens with most tradition-based systems, dina law's power over criminal actions was limited by the government, which extended its authority with the spread of government courts. But with the backlog of cases in those courts, dina law has again become dominant in many parts of the country.

Operating under a more informal process, dina law lacks many of the procedures one would find in a regular Madagascar court, and it can issue and then enforce summary judgments, including the immediate execution of a convicted killer. Such drastic actions by the village courts have alarmed the government, which has attempted to influence those courts by educating the judges in basic procedures. The National Assembly passed legislation that would streamline dina into a single code that would apply the same law to all village courts throughout the island.

STRUCTURE OF THE COURTS
The Madagascar judicial structure and its approach to the law resembles the French system of courts in limiting the power of judges to review the constitutionality of laws, instead allowing them only to examine the legality of trials and government decisions. The Council of State also separates the administrative law system from the regular legal system.

Within the Madagascar judiciary, three courts are used to conduct most trials and hear appeals. Local district courts, known as Courts of First Instance, have civil and criminal divisions and hear most minor criminal cases, usually those involving prison sentences of less than five years. They also hear all civil cases without regard to their size. There are a total of eleven such courts throughout the country. The Court of Appeals has dual jurisdiction as a trial and appellate court. The court conducts criminal trials in all cases in which penalties exceed five years in prison. Multiple-judge panels decide these cases. The single Court of Appeals sits in the capital of Antananarivo.

The Madagascar Supreme Court has limited authority in hearing appeals. Based on the country's French colonial background, the Supreme Court can only decide whether a lower court misinterpreted or misapplied the law in its ruling. It cannot declare a law unconstitutional or interpret and apply the constitution in deciding a case. It also has administrative duties over the lower courts in ensuring their proper disposition of cases. In addition, the court administers regulations that apply to judges, and it can move lower-court judges into different districts to help lessen the workload.

Operating outside the regular judiciary and generally recognized as the highest court in the country is the Administrative and Financial Constitutional Court. This court has extensive jurisdiction that exceeds the powers of a constitutional court in most countries. The court is composed of the justices themselves but also the Council of State and the Audit Court. The Constitutional Court is composed of nine members serving six-year terms and is appointed by a combination of all three branches of government. It has a broad array of powers granted under the constitution. The court rules on the constitutionality of treaties, law, and regulations, and it resolves conflicts between the states within Madagascar and between state agencies and territorial governments. In addition, the court is granted the power to decide contested elections.

Several articles of the constitution identify when the Constitutional Court can exercise its authority. Before being placed in the country's official code, all laws are submitted to the country's president. If the Constitutional Court determines that the law is unconstitutional, that law cannot be promulgated or entered as the law of the country. On such a ruling, the president has the choice of taking out the unconstitutional portions of the law and enforcing the constitutional provisions, dropping the law as unenforceable, or sending the law back to the legislature so that it can change the parts that are considered unconstitutional.

In addition, the Constitutional Court has the power to consider the constitutionality of all internal regulations passed by the legislature. It can also be asked for and give an advisory opinion on whether a pending piece of legislation or a presidential decree violates the constitution. Individual Malagasy can appeal to the court, claiming a personal violation of rights by the enforcement of a law. Finally, the Constitutional Court is given a pivotal role in the replacement of an impaired president. If two-thirds of the National Assembly votes that that president is impaired, the Constitutional Court has the power to order the president removed from office. The court can also declare a temporary impairment, but after four months, it must either lift that decision or declare the president permanently impaired and removed from office.

The Constitutional Court also includes the Council of

Structure of Madagascar Courts

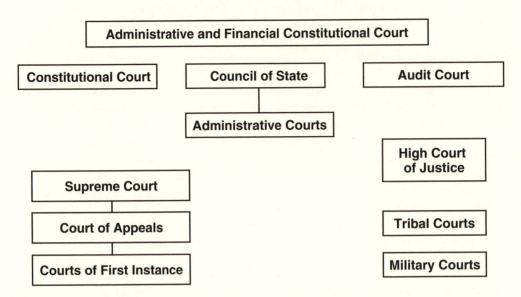

State, resembling the institution used within the French court system. The Madagascar Council of State has the power to overturn regulations written by executive branch agencies on the basis that they violate Madagascar law or the constitution. The council can issue an advisory opinion, stating whether a pending regulation violates the constitution or the law. The court also hears all appeals from the rulings by lower administrative courts.

A final part of the Constitutional Court is the Audit Court. This court has powers beyond traditional judicial duties in that it can examine the financial accounts of all public agencies and can supervise the implementation of the budget of any agency. The court also hears appeals of appropriation decisions (regarding how money is spent) that are issued by lower administrative courts. It also aids the legislature in supervising the spending of money by agencies.

The broad powers granted the Constitutional Court make it a partly judicial and partly legislative body. In looking at pending legislation or overseeing the spending of money, usually the domain of legislatures, the judiciary is drawn into the political process, something that threatens its independence and authority in making constitutional decisions.

SPECIALIZED COURTS

One of the specialized courts operating outside the regular judicial system is the High Court of Justice. This court hears all impeachment actions against high government officials accused of crimes and misdemeanors. The High Court has jurisdiction over the president of the country, cabinet officials of the main departments of government, justices of the Constitutional Court, and justices of the regular Supreme Court. The High Court of Justice conducts trial only after the majority of the National Assembly has voted to try a particular official for a crime. The High Court's decision to remove an official cannot be appealed to any other court.

Early in its existence, the High Court was faced with the pending trial of President Albert Zufy. A two-thirds vote of the National Assembly impeached Zufy on the charges of misappropriating government funds for his personal use. But before the trial could be held, Zufy resigned and called a snap election, which he lost. Since that time, the High Court has not been asked to conduct a trial of an impeached official.

Another set of special courts are also some of the most frequently used courts on the island. Village courts use traditional tribal law (the dina). The village court operates at the local level, in both rural and urban areas, and either as a replacement for a poorly functioning government court or as the only court in existence for an entire region. Village courts use local chiefs or elders to hear and decide disputes, including civil and criminal cases. Independence in 1960 was expected to remove many criminal cases from the control of the village courts because of the harsh and summary punishments carried out under dina law. But with the weakening of central authority and the inability of the government to staff the courts and pay the judges, the village courts have become an integral part of the justice system.

This form of local control of government is recognized in the Madagascar Constitution. According to Article 35, the fokonolona have the authority to protect their citizens' cattle herds, land, and tribal traditions. The village courts are granted jurisdiction over most land issues and all minor criminal issues.

A third type of special court is the military court. Military justice is limited to active-duty military personnel and officers. Few cases are heard by these courts, and the constitution prohibits their use in trying civilians.

SELECTION AND STAFFING

The Madagascar Constitution sets out a complex method of making judicial appointments to the various levels of courts in the country. The Constitutional Court's nine members are appointed to six-year, nonrenewable terms. Three of the nine are chosen by the president, two by the National Assembly, one by the Senate, and three by the Superior Council of Magistrates, an organization composed of appellate and trial court magistrates. Among these nine, a president is chosen to lead the court.

The Supreme Court membership is chosen by the National Assembly and the president. The general prosecutor of the court, the official responsible for arguing cases before it, is also chosen by the president. The High Court of Justice also has nine members, including justices from the other High Courts and members of the Parliament. The president of the Supreme Court and three of his court colleagues serve on the High Court, as do two members of the National Assembly and two members of the Senate. Because the High Court acts only when the National Assembly impeaches an official, its membership, particularly the legislative members, may change from one court meeting to another. In addition, when the High Court is not in session, the members return to their regular business within the government. Judges serving on the Court of Appeals and the Courts of First Instance are appointed by the president unless that power is delegated to the prime minister.

Staffing the courts has proved a problem for the Madagascar government. There are limited facilities for training lawyers; in fact, there is only one law program in the country, forcing most students to receive their law degrees on the African continent or in France. But even those who return to Madagascar with the proper training are less likely to take a job as a government judge. With low or, at times, no pay, the judiciary is not an attractive occupation for the best-trained lawyers.

IMPACT

The Madagascar judiciary is a complex system, with multiple courts performing a variety of tasks, including a village court system that operates in those regions where the government courts cannot. The Constitutional Court, with its array of duties ranging from ruling on the constitutionality of pending legislation to having its Audit Court oversee the appropriation of funds, is as much a political body as it is a judicial one. The regular court system—featuring a trial court and an appellate court as well as the Supreme Court—resembles the judiciary of France, the former colonizing power of the island, with

its emphasis on applying the law rather than interpreting it and the prohibition against the regular courts interpreting the constitution.

The village courts are the most intriguing element of the modern Madagascar judiciary. The failure of the government courts to operate efficiently in dispensing justices to the population, particularly in criminal cases, has forced many citizens to return to tribal courts to settle disputes. This is a sign of regression, as the tribal courts rely on traditional law (the dina), ignore the procedure of more formal courts, and hand down and enforce harsh penalties, frequently without appeal. The use of such courts is a setback in the development of the rule of law and a judicial system in Madagascar.

Douglas Clouatre

See also Administrative Law; Civil Law; Constitutional Review; France; Indigenous and Folk Legal Systems

References and further reading
Allen, Philip. 1995. *Madagascar.* Boulder, CO: Westview Press.
Eveleigh, Mark. 2001. *Maverick in Madagascar.* New York: Lonely Planet.
Feeley-Harnick, Gilliam. 1991. *A Green Estate: Restoring Independence in Madagascar.* Washington, DC: Smithsonian Institution Press.
Gade, Daniel. 1996. *Madagascar.* New York: McDonald and Woodward Publishing.
Green, Rebecca. 1997. *Merina.* New York: Rosen Publishing.
Metz, Helen. 1994. *Indian Ocean: Five Island Nations.* Washington, DC: Library of Congress.
Murphy, Dervla. 1989. *Muddling through in Madagascar.* San Francisco: Overlook Press.
Shores, Christopher. 1996. *Dust Clouds in the Middle East: The Air War for East Africa, Iraq, Syria, Iran and Madagascar, 1940–1942.* New York: Grub Street Press.
Tyson, Peter, and Russell Mittermeier. 2001. *The Eighth Continent: Life, Death and Discovery in the Lost World of Madagascar.* New York: Harper Perennial Press.

MAGISTRATES—CIVIL LAW SYSTEMS

WHAT IT IS

In the civil law tradition (Merryman 1985), the term *magistrate* (*magistrats, magistrati, magistrados*) designates career personnel performing judicial and sometimes also prosecutorial and administrative functions. Broadly speaking, it refers to the judiciary. The defining elements of a civil law judiciary include the following:

- Selection tends to be made on a technical basis through examinations at a young age, usually immediately after university, with little or no emphasis placed on candidates' previous professional experience.
- Training takes place mainly within the judiciary.

- A hierarchy of ranks determines organizational roles. Advancement up the career ladder is competitive, and promotions are granted according to formal criteria combining seniority and merit. Hierarchical superiors have wide discretion in determining merit.
- Magistrates are supposed to be capable of performing all organizational roles associated with their rank (for instance, to be able to adjudicate criminal, bankruptcy, family law, and fiscal cases or, in some cases, even to act as a public prosecutor) and at the same time compete for higher positions. Magistrates are therefore recruited not for a specific position but for a wide set of roles, and in the course of their career they tend to change jobs often. This in turn makes guarantees of independence more problematic because of the influence hierarchical superiors (or in some cases the government itself) have over these moves.
- Guarantees of judicial independence tend to be lower than in common law systems. Judges tend to enjoy a lower degree of internal independence (in relation to other judges).
- A strong effort is made to depoliticize the role of the judge.

In general, civil law judiciaries take on the form of bureaucratic organizations. They are found mainly in continental Europe but also in South America (e.g., Chile) and Asia (e.g., Japan).

HISTORICAL BACKGROUND

The main characteristics of civil law judicial organizations emerged as a consequence of the great reorganization of the state that has taken place in continental Europe since the eighteenth century. In other words, it is a by-product of the process of centralization of political authority brought about by absolutist monarchs. For instance, the effects of the reforms of judicial education and selection instituted by Frederic the Second in Prussia can still be felt, and the Napoleonic reforms of the beginning of the nineteenth century have strongly influenced the organization of the judiciary of all Latin countries. The constitutionalization of political power and the consequent development of judicial guarantees of independence partially weakened the relationship of the judiciary to the crown, but the organizational integration of the judiciary into the structure of public administration was maintained, if not strengthened. The decline of the monarchy in the nineteenth century did not radically alter the situation; it merely transferred the power to exert influence over the judiciary to a parliamentary executive.

The lower level of independence of civil law judges is not the only element that historically distinguishes the

position of these judges from their common law counterparts. In continental Europe, mistrust of the judiciary has always been high, and judicial power has been considered an important power to be checked. This has been the case particularly in France because of the role judges played in the ancien régime. It has meant that a large group of disputes between citizens and the state do not fall under the jurisdiction of ordinary courts but are assigned to special administrative courts, where judges are under greater governmental influence. More important, continental judges tend to act in a subordinate way to the political branches and to the norms they enact. For instance, the original role of the French Court of Cassation was to check the way courts applied the law and to report "wrong" interpretations to the legislature for correction. This role reflects a historical interpretation of the separation of powers principle that assigns a privileged role to the legislature, since it represents the popular will. The implication is that the judiciary has no special reserved domain beyond deciding individual cases. Any form of judicial review of legislation was ruled out, so the legislature emerged in a very strong position (Merryman 1985).

MAJOR VARIANTS

Broadly speaking, civil law judiciaries can be separated into two subtypes. In the Germanic and Scandinavian countries, magistrates are recruited after a long period of training (Mestitz and Pederzoli 1995). In Germany, after completing legal studies at a university, candidates for the legal profession sit the "first state examination." If successful, they are granted status as temporary civil servants, allowing them to carry out their practical training and receive a small salary. During this period, trainees become familiar with the full range of legal roles they may have to perform in the near future: the judiciary (both civil and criminal), bar, civil service, and public prosecution. The final stage of the legal selection process is the "second state examination," covering subject matter similar to the first but with a more practical orientation. It is only after completion of the second state examination that separate selections are made for judges or prosecutors. Therefore, the training is comparable to that for other legal professions (lawyers, civil servants). As a result, the esprit de corps tends to be stronger as well as the relative autonomy from politics, which is in any case related to the predominantly passive posture of the judiciary.

In the Latin countries (France, Italy, Portugal, and Spain) recruitment is made right after university studies, and the separation between the legal professions is deeper. Traditionally, the influence of the executive was stronger. However, since the end of World War II, some significant changes have taken place. First of all, judicial schools have been established in order to improve the education of magistrates. For example, in France, Portugal, and Spain after the initial examination, magistrates undergo a training period of at least two years. The most important innovation, however, has been the institution in these countries of self-governing bodies, or higher councils of the judiciary, composed at least in part of magistrates elected by their colleagues. Although in different forms and degrees, today they all play an increasingly important role in managing magistrates' careers: promotions, transfers, and disciplinary proceedings tend to be entrusted to such bodies. Since in France and Italy a unified corps of magistrates perform both judicial and prosecutorial functions, the higher council there is in charge of both judges and prosecutors, although Italy is much ahead in assimilating the two roles. In Portugal both prosecutors and judges enjoy a separate higher council, but in Spain only judges are managed by the higher council.

The powers and composition of these self-governing bodies are critical factors; obviously, the more extensive their functions, the stronger their role will be and the weaker the minister of justice will be. However, two additional factors are the ratio of judges to nonjudicial members on higher councils and the way judicial representatives are chosen. Judicial independence will inevitably be stronger with a higher ratio of members chosen directly by and from the judiciary. According to these criteria, the Italian judiciary has the highest degree of independence among European civil law countries.

SIGNIFICANCE

Traditionally, the bureaucratic setting of the continental judiciaries was associated with a passive, executory definition of the judicial role: the judge as *la bouche de la loi* (the mouth of the law), as a faithful executor of the legislative will. The judicial hierarchy was there to ensure that actual behavior would conform to the stereotype, and a link with the political system was usually provided through the appointment of higher-ranking magistrates by the executive. In this way, political influence could spread all over the judicial corps.

Recent changes in the institutional setting of courts in Europe have triggered a process of expansion of judicial power. Most European countries have introduced some form of judicial review of legislation. In addition, the reviewing role of the European Court of Justice and the European Court of Human Rights is increasingly felt all around Europe (Cappelletti 1989; Stone 2000). The traditional deference toward parliamentary statutes has been negatively affected: today, judges feel themselves more free to look at them with a critical eye, often engaging themselves in quite a lot of interpretation in order to bring statutes in line with constitutional principles. Moreover, the creation of judicial self-governing bodies has significantly altered the traditional relationship between judges and the political system.

One of the first consequences of creating a higher council of the judiciary is to increase the *external* independence of the judiciary by decreasing the traditional power of the executive. But since no higher council is composed solely of judges, an important role remains for the institution in charge of appointing the nonjudicial members. This duty is often assigned to parliament, which allows political parties to bypass the minister of justice and influence the judiciary directly. The creation of a self-governing body also has consequences for the *internal* independence of the judiciary. Entrusting promotion and appointment of judges to a collegial body where normally all judicial ranks are represented contradicts the traditional hierarchical principle, whereby only higher-ranking judges are entitled to evaluate lower-ranking colleagues. The lower ranks acquire a new power, since they can participate in the process of choosing higher-ranking judges. Moreover, judicial elites have been further weakened by the loss of power of their traditional ally, the minister of justice. As a result, challenges to the very idea of a judicial career by the lower ranks have often been successful: the number of judicial ranks has been reduced, and the influence of senior judges' assessments of lower-ranking judges has strongly declined. In Italy (the most extreme case) promotions have de facto been abolished, at least from the economic point of view, and judicial salaries and rank increase simply based on the number of years of service (Di Federico 1988).

This erosion of hierarchical links is particularly relevant to the general expansion of judicial power. With the creation of higher councils, the reference group of judges has tended to diversify. Traditional members of the reference group, such as senior judges and legal academics (Merryman 1985), have decreased in importance, since they no longer enjoy a monopoly of power over evaluations for judicial promotion. In addition, the professional criteria of the judiciary have begun to shift. Technical legal knowledge (or conformity to the ideology of the judicial elite) is no longer the only important element for promotion. Views of others outside the judicial system (in particular, political parties in parliament) have gained in importance, especially if they can participate in the appointment of members of the higher council. Similarly, the interests of the media and the judiciary increasingly overlap, since judicial (especially prosecutors') actions provide the media with news. In return, the media are able to support and publicize the actions of judges and prosecutors.

Inside the judiciary itself, higher councils tend to increase the role of judicial associations, since they organize the electoral participation of judges. In Italy, where this trend is more developed and no judicial member of the higher council is now elected without the backing of one of these politically oriented groups, decision making in the higher council is heavily dependent on alignments between these associations. As judicial actions gain political significance, a higher council may become the main institution where the judiciary's elected representatives can meet political representatives and develop a new relationship with the political system. Judicial self-governing bodies have thus opened up a new channel of political influence on the judiciary, which can be seen as a consequence of the slow but steady attempt to limit executive power and the consequent strengthening of judicial guarantees in civil law judiciaries.

In general, the extent to which the judiciary intervenes in the political process is conditioned by the evolution of the political system and by the way the judicial system is organized. However, the connections between judges and the political system do influence judges' reference groups, their conception of the judicial role, and therefore their decisions. The creation of judicial self-governing bodies is capable of producing a radical change in the judiciary's traditional hierarchy; this in turn can diversify the judiciary's reference group and place it, at least in part, outside the judiciary. All these processes seem also to support the development of judicial activism: judges and magistrates have been central players in a series of major political controversies throughout the 1990s in almost all Latin European countries.

Carlo Guarnieri

See also Civil Law; Constitutional Review; France; Germany; Italy; Judicial Independence; Judicial Selection, Methods of; Portugal; Prosecuting Authorities; Spain

References and further reading
Cappelletti, Mauro. 1989. *The Judicial Process in Comparative Perspective.* Oxford: Clarendon.
Di Federico, Guiseppe. 1988. "The Crisis of the Justice System and the Referendum on the Judiciary." Pp. 25–49 in *Italian Politics: A Review.* Edited by Robert Leonardi and Piergiorgio Corbetta. London: Pinter.
Jacob, Herbert, Erhard Blankenburg, Herbert M. Kritzer, Doris Marie Provine, and Joseph Sanders. 1996. *Courts, Law, and Politics in Comparative Perspective.* New Haven: Yale University Press.
Merryman, John H. 1985. *The Civil Law Tradition.* 2nd ed. Stanford: Stanford University Press.
Mestitz, Anna, and Patrizia Pederzoli. 1995. "Training the Legal Professions in Italy, France and Germany." Pp. 155–180 in *The Global Expansion of Judicial Power.* Edited by Neal C. Tate and Torbjorn Vallinder. New York: New York University Press.
Pederzoli, Patrizia, and Carlo Guarnieri. 1997. "Italy: A Case of Judicial Democracy?" *International Social Science Journal* 152: 253–270.
Stone, Alec. 2000. *Governing with Judges: Constitutional Politics in Europe.* Oxford: Oxford University Press.

MAGISTRATES—COMMON LAW SYSTEMS

WHAT THEY ARE

Magistrates are judicial officers who establish the basic rules and principles of the society. Magistrates have a variety of titles: in England they are also called justices of the peace, while in the United States they are named associate judges. Many magistrates, or those with similar designations, consider low-level criminal, civil, or administrative conflicts concerning municipalities or boroughs, or disputes between individuals. The limited jurisdictional scope of magistrates' decisions often does not require them to be lawyers. In common law systems, magistrates can render decisions without trial by jury. No universal definition of magistrates exists because of their varying jurisdictional parameters.

Common law systems place the locus and scope of lawmaking authority in the judiciary. Magistrates are often the initial contact between citizens and the judiciary; as such, these judicial officers have an important role in defining judicial authority and the legitimacy of the judiciary in the society. The traditional role of magistrates was to encourage local, individual compliance and obedience with judicial decisions. Magistrates' reliance upon law, combined with their understanding of local customs, facilitates that goal and increases public confidence in the judiciary.

Magistrates in both the United States and England are governed by principles derived from English common law tradition, such as precedent. Precedent, stare decisis (which means in Latin "to stand by things that have been settled"), allows decisions to be consistent with previous rulings and permits the law to follow a predictable course. Magistrates work within the jurisdictional and decisional constraints of their individual court systems, whether on the federal, state, or local level.

Magistrates, as neutral and detached judicial officers, are often required to assess whether a search warrant should be issued based upon findings of probable cause or whether there is an indictable criminal offense. Police officers or prosecutors must provide evidence that will support their conclusion of probable cause or a crime sufficient for an indictment. Magistrates make independent and reasonable judgments based upon the reliability or credibility of police or prosecutor arguments.

HISTORICAL BACKGROUND

The common law tradition establishes that ordinary individuals should participate in the legal process. The magistrate system allows citizens from a broad economic and social cross-section of society, including both men and women, to consider evidence and render fair rulings. In both the United States and countries such as England, magistrates are selected for their ability to exercise good judgment. In this fashion, citizens can be judged by a member of their local community who is also one of their peers. Magistrates' Court has the historical tradition of being a "court of the people." Individual conduct is considered in relation to the fair, average member of the community. This court was supposed to be convenient and nontechnical; moreover, the magistrate's role was to give impartial consideration to all persons or matters before the court.

In 1195, King Richard I introduced lay magistrates, or justices of the peace, to England and Wales by permitting certain knights to preserve peace and keep order in unruly areas. Through the end of the nineteenth century, lay magistrates, holding an unpaid position, usually came from the higher social classes. In England currently, lay magistrates work in the local court systems and come from many segments of society.

In the United States, magistrates are usually elected or appointed at the lowest court level for a specific term of office, two or four years, in a county or municipality. The Mission Statement of the Magistrates of North Carolina aptly characterizes their duties and responsibilities throughout the United States. This statement (1993) says: "The mission of the Magistrate is to protect and preserve the rights and liberties of all of the people, as guaranteed by the Constitution and laws of the United States and North Carolina, by providing a fair, independent and accessible forum and the just, timely and economical resolution of their legal affairs."

Magistrates, as assistant judges, have played a variety of roles in local and national courts. In local courts, they resolve small criminal offenses, in contrast to the regular trial court used for serious crimes, such as substantial misdemeanors and felonies. Magistrates also resolve civil lawsuits involving small sums of money, interpersonal disputes, and minor violations of governmental laws. During the twentieth century, there was a significant movement away from magistrates as lay officials to individuals with legal training. In national courts, magistrate judges have become an important component of U.S. district courts. In both England and the United States, magistrates' ability to establish legal rules based upon local norms and traditions is an essential part of the common law legal process. In this view, the law should serve everyday human needs and should be adapted to meet changing needs. The evolution of law to meet social norms or social needs can lead to public acceptance of this judicial power.

The position of U.S. magistrate was created in 1968 (Public Law 90-578, 28 U.S.C. 631–639) to reform the U.S. commissioner system and provide a new first echelon of judicial officers in the federal judicial system, as well as to alleviate the increasing workload of U.S. district courts. The importance of U.S. magistrates to the operation of the federal courts was recognized in 1990 with a change in their title from "magistrate" to "magistrate judge." Since 1968 various congressional statutes have increased the scope of their authority. For example, in 1996, Congress required that all minor misdemeanors in U.S. district courts be tried before magistrates, to allow U.S. district judges to devote more time to substantive matters in civil and criminal cases of greater significance.

MAJOR VARIANTS

There are substantial differences between the roles played in common law systems by magistrates in the United States and in countries like England. In the United States, magistrates act as assistant judges with jurisdiction over a wide range of civil and criminal cases. In countries like England, magistrates are the judges of the lowest courts, usually called Magistrates' Courts.

In England and similar countries, magistrates are either justices of the peace or stipendiary magistrates and have primarily criminal jurisdiction as well as jurisdiction over juveniles. Magistrates also resolve petty offenses, grant local licenses, and rule upon civil issues of common understanding. Magistrates who are justices of the peace are unpaid lay judiciaries who often lack legal training. Their jurisdiction is usually a single county. They may receive assistance on complex legal issues from stipendiary magistrates. In Great Britain, when cases are appealed from the Magistrates' Court, they may be heard by either the High Court or the Crown Court. In Great Britain there are frequent discussions over discontinuing the use of lay magistrates and replacing them with individuals with legal training.

In England, a stipendiary magistrate—an appointed barrister or solicitor with at least seven years of practice who sits in a Magistrates' Court on a full-time salaried basis—assists lay magistrates in larger jurisdictions. These stipendiary magistrates offer legal interpretations and have judicial authority equivalent to that of lay magistrates. In England, stipendiary magistrates are found mainly in inner (metropolitan) London and large provincial centers.

In U.S. national courts, an important variation of the basic magistrate system is the U.S. magistrate judge, who is part of the U.S. District Court system. Such judges, almost all attorneys, are appointed by district court judges for a specific time period: eight years for full-time magistrates and four years for part-time magistrates. Their duties are specified by that court and consistent with U.S. magistrate statute; the magistrate judges are Article I (of the U.S. Constitution) judges. District court judges assign the magistrate judges a wide variety of duties, ranging from civil trials and trials for criminal misdemeanors to pretrial proceedings such as bail hearings, depending upon the different emphases in district courts. In some U.S. district courts magistrates try the full range of cases, except felonies, heard by a U.S. District Court judge; in others they are restricted by the particular district court to some specific kinds of cases or issues, such as social security administrative hearings. Decisions of U.S. magistrates may be appealed to either the U.S. District Court or to the U.S. Court of Appeals. The vast majority of magistrates' decisions are not appealed to the U.S. District Court.

SIGNIFICANCE

Public acceptance of magistrates' legal rulings is an important foundation of the Anglo-American legal system. In common law systems, magistrates administer justice on the local level. Magistrates in common law systems support a tradition of justice that ordinary citizens can enforce laws on behalf of the people. Magistrates' decisions are responsive to the needs of the community and a key element in the exercise of government power.

Steven Puro

See also Lay Judiciaries; Magistrates—Civil Law Systems
References and further reading

Administrative Office of the United States Courts. 2000. *Judicial Business of the United States Courts: Report of the Director (2000).* Washington, DC: Administrative Office of the United States Courts.
Smith, Christopher E. 1990. *United States Magistrates in the Federal Courts: Subordinate Judges.* New York: Praeger.

MAINE

GENERAL INFORMATION

Maine was admitted to the Union in 1820 as part of the historic Missouri Compromise that paired Maine, a free state, with the slave state of Missouri. The area that thus became the state of Maine had previously been part of Massachusetts. Maine is the largest of the New England states, occupying more than half of the region's territory. Maine's population of 1.25 million ranks thirty-eighth in the nation.

Prosperity came early to Maine because of the booming national market for products such as lumber, ice, and sailing ships. The state's population grew rapidly, doubling from 300,000 to 600,000 between 1820 and 1860. After the Civil War, however, the growth rate of both the state's economy and its population slowed as the demand for Maine's exports declined; it would take another 130 years for the state's population to double again.

With a median household income in 1997 of just under $39,000, Maine ranks thirty-seventh among the states. The state's largest industries are pulp and paper (nearly 90 percent of the state is forested) and tourism.

Agriculture and fishing, once staples of Maine's economy, both declined precipitously during the twentieth century. Today there is much discussion in political circles about the "Two Maines," a reference to the disparity between the state's relatively prosperous southern portion, which has benefited from its proximity to Boston and the rest of New England, and the region of northern Maine, which because of its geographical isolation continues to lag behind economically.

Maine's population is overwhelmingly (over 98 percent) white. Portland, the state's largest city, is something of an anomaly in that regard, because it serves as a major refugee resettlement center. More than forty languages can be heard in the Portland public schools. The state's largest ethnic group is Franco-American, a legacy of the waves of in-migration during the nineteenth century by French Canadians drawn to jobs in the textile mills. Although most of those mills have long since closed, the cities of Waterville, Lewiston, and Biddeford, as well as the St. John Valley in northern Maine, all retain a distinctively Franco-American character. The political influence of Franco-Americans in Maine has been evident mostly at the local level. In fact, no French-surnamed politician has ever won statewide office.

The Republican Party dominated Maine politics from before the Civil War until Edmund Muskie led a mid–twentieth century revival of the Democratic Party. Although party registrations are now fairly evenly split between Republicans and Democrats, fully 40 percent of the state's registered voters are "unenrolled" in any party. In the last quarter-century, Maine has twice elected independent governors: James Longley (1975–1979) and Angus King (1995–present). A striking element of Maine's participatory political culture is its record of consistently high voter turnouts, which are usually among the best in the nation.

EVOLUTION AND HISTORY

Echoing the language of the U.S. Constitution, Maine's constitution (written in 1819) created "one Supreme Judicial Court and such other courts the Legislature may from time to time establish." Throughout the nineteenth and early twentieth centuries, justices of the Supreme Judicial Court traveled around the state, sitting as trial judges and assisted by a small number of lower court judges. Even after the present statewide Superior Court was established in 1929, Supreme Judicial Court justices continued to divide their time about equally between trials and appellate work until the late 1960s. As a legacy of its dual responsibilities, the Supreme Judicial Court even today is commonly referred to as the "Law Court" when it sits to hear appeals from the lower courts. This history of itinerancy also helps explain why the Maine Supreme Judicial Court has the distinction of being one of only two state supreme courts (the other is Louisiana's) with no building of its own. The court's members share office space with Superior Court judges in county courthouses around the state. They usually meet to hear oral arguments and discuss pending cases in the Cumberland County Courthouse in Portland.

CURRENT STRUCTURE

The main task of the Supreme Judicial Court today is to hear appeals regarding lower court decisions on matters of state constitutional or statutory law. In 1998–1999, the court received 752 such appeals (78 percent of which were civil cases, 22 percent criminal) and disposed of 719 cases. As the state's only full-fledged appellate court (the Superior Court does hear some appeals from the District and Administrative courts), the Supreme Judicial Court does not benefit from the significant amount of case screening performed by intermediate appeals courts in some of the more populous states. Thus the Supreme Judicial Court's relatively low reversal rate of 16 percent reflects its responsibility for hearing all appeals, rather than only the most meritorious ones.

This same structural feature also contributes to the court's high level of decision-making consensus, compared with other state supreme courts. Dissenting opinions are filed in only about 10 percent of the Maine Supreme Judicial Court's decisions. Another factor that may help account for this general pattern of agreement among the justices is the relative absence of ideological cleavages in Maine politics.

The Supreme Judicial Court also has a three-judge Sentence Review Panel with the authority to order reviews of appeals from any criminal sentence of more than one year. If granted, such a review is then conducted by the full court, which can adjust the sentence either up or down. In addition, from time to time (on average, about once a year), the court is asked by the governor or the legislature to issue an advisory opinion on some important legal issue. Finally, the Supreme Judicial Court is also responsible for issuing procedural rules for all of the state's courts, for supervising admission to the bar, and for disciplining Maine's lawyers and judges. The court has seven members, currently five men and two women.

One step below the Supreme Judicial Court is the Superior Court, which has branches in each of Maine's county seats (see figure). The sixteen judges (currently fourteen men and two women) of the Superior Court travel among the counties, holding regular court sessions. Superior Court has exclusive jurisdiction over more serious criminal cases (those resulting from grand jury indictments), civil cases involving amounts of more than $30,000, and injunctive relief cases. The court shares jurisdiction with the District Court in lesser criminal cases and in civil cases with damages under $30,000. Divorces

Legal Structure of Maine Courts

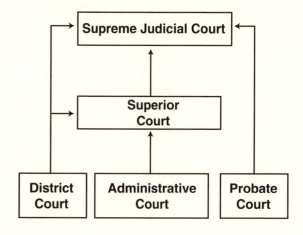

may be filed in either Superior or District court. The Superior Court is the only court in Maine in which jury trials are held. In 1998–1999, 14,605 cases were filed in the Maine Superior Court, 71 percent of which were criminal and 29 percent civil.

Under the Maine constitution, citizens have the right to a jury trial in all criminal cases and in all civil cases except divorces and injunctions. It was once possible for defendants who were convicted in District Court to request a de novo jury trial in Superior Court. In 1982, however, the law was changed to require that criminal defendants formally request a transfer to Superior Court within twenty-one days of entering their plea in District Court. In the absence of such a request, the right to a jury trial is considered waived. About half of the criminal filings in Superior Court result from such requests, though jury trials are ultimately held in less than 5 percent of all criminal cases.

In civil cases, defendants in actions filed in District Court may have the case removed to Superior Court if they wish to have a jury trial. Civil cases filed in Superior Court are held before a judge unless one of the parties requests a jury. As with criminal cases, only a small fraction of civil cases are ever decided by either a jury or a judge. Approximately 95 percent are settled by the parties, withdrawn, or summarily dismissed without going to trial.

The third tier of Maine's judicial system is occupied by the District Court. The statewide District Court system was created in 1961 to replace a patchwork of seventy-five local and municipal courts staffed by part-time judges, most but not all of whom were lawyers. Today, thirty-one judges (twenty-three men and eight women) serve on Maine's District Court. About two-thirds of these are assigned permanently to one of the thirty-three court locations spread among the state's thirteen judicial districts; the other judges serve at-large and are assigned to preside wherever they are most needed.

The District Court is the "workhorse" of the Maine

judicial system, with exclusive or shared jurisdiction over a wide range of legal actions, including divorce, juvenile, small claims, requests for protection from abuse and harassment, criminal matters involving penalties of less than one year in jail or a $1,000 fine, smaller civil cases, and all criminal and civil traffic offenses. In 1997–1998, a total of 260,766 cases were filed in the District Court. Of these, 33 percent were criminal cases, 17 percent were civil cases, and 50 percent were noncriminal traffic violations.

Maine also has three "subject matter courts." In each county there is a Probate Court with responsibility for matters relating to trusts and estates, wills, adoptions, name changes, guardianships, and protective orders. Probate judges serve part-time, for four-year terms. They are the only elected judges in the state.

The Administrative Court was created in 1973 to hear cases involving the suspension, revocation, or refusal of licenses by administrative agencies. Most of the latter involve decisions of the state's Bureau of Liquor Enforcement. Administrative Court judges, who sit exclusively in Portland, may also assist that city's District and Superior courts with domestic relations cases.

Small claims courts, held as special sessions of the District Court, hear cases involving monetary claims of up to $4,500. Appeals may be taken to the Superior Court on matters of law.

In the late 1970s, Maine was one of the first states to make state-sponsored mediation services available in Small Claims Court. Voluntary mediation was soon introduced in some counties for divorce cases as well. A 1984 law made mediation mandatory prior to a court hearing in all contested divorce cases involving minor children. Although mandated mediation was initially opposed by some divorce attorneys, a 1990 survey showed overwhelming support for the program among Maine divorce lawyers. Several pilot projects in Maine have experimented with offering or even requiring the use of alternative dispute resolution services such as case evaluation and mediation in nondivorce civil cases. Despite impressive evidence from these studies that some forms of pretrial ADR can increase rates of settlement and reduce reliance on formal discovery, motions, and judicial hearings, Maine's judicial policy-makers have not yet seen fit to extend mandatory mediation beyond divorce.

STAFFING

With the exception of Probate Court judges, all members of the state's judiciary are appointed by the governor with the advice and consent of the legislature. Judicial appointments at all levels are for seven-year terms, renewable at the governor's discretion. On only four occasions since 1970 has a governor failed to reappoint a judge who sought a new term. In each case the person denied reap-

pointment was a District Court judge appointed during a previous administration. Despite the fact that party organizations in Maine are not particularly strong, many Maine judges have previously participated in politics at some level. Prior to the formation of the Superior Court in 1929, most appointees to the Supreme Judicial Court came directly from private practice. Since that time, well over half have had prior experience on the Superior Court.

THE LEGAL PROFESSION IN MAINE

In 1991, Maine had 3,128 lawyers, one for every 395 citizens, placing it fortieth among the states in number of lawyers but somewhat higher—thirty-fourth—in lawyers-per-capita. The bar was 81 percent male and 19 percent female, a distribution quite close to the overall national figure at the time. Of the 2,342 lawyers in private practice in Maine, 39 percent were in solo practice, 21 percent worked in 2–5 person firms, 18 percent were in 6–20 person firms, and 22 percent belonged to firms with 21 or more members. In comparison to national figures, the legal profession in Maine is notably skewed toward sole and small-firm practitioners.

Each of Maine's sixteen counties has an elected district attorney who is responsible for prosecuting all crimes except homicides committed in the county. Homicides are handled by the state attorney general's office, which also represents the state and its agencies in state and federal courts. The attorney general is one of three constitutional officers (the others being the secretary of state and the state treasurer) who are elected every two years by a majority vote of the Maine Legislature. The office has typically been occupied by successful and well-regarded politicians. Since Maine has no lieutenant governor, the attorney general's position might be expected to be a stepping-stone to either the governorship or national office. In the last half-century, however, only one attorney general has succeeded in achieving higher office in Maine.

The state of Maine has no public defender system. Representation of indigent criminal defendants is provided free through an "assigned counsel" system, in which private attorneys' names are drawn from a list of volunteers who are paid a nominal fee by the state. In civil cases, assistance for low-income persons is available through the Volunteer Lawyers Project of the Maine Bar Foundation, the Cumberland Legal Aid Clinic, operated by the University of Maine School of Law (the state's only law school), and the federally financed Pine Tree Legal Assistance Program. Maine's lawyer population, like many of its other resources, is unevenly distributed around the state. The problem of "access to justice" is particularly acute in sparsely populated areas of northern and eastern Maine.

RELATIONSHIP TO NATIONAL SYSTEM

Only a small number of decisions of the Maine Supreme Judicial Court have been accepted for review by the U.S. Supreme Court. Of these, the most recent case, *Alden v. Maine* (119 S.Ct. 2240) deserves special mention because it is part of the vigorous debate over the doctrine of federalism begun by the court in the 1990s. A group of probation officers seeking overtime pay brought suit against their employer, the State of Maine, under provisions of the federal Fair Labor Standards Act. The Maine Supreme Judicial Court dismissed the lawsuit, holding that the state's sovereign immunity protected it from being sued without its consent. The U.S. Supreme Court agreed, though by a narrow margin of 5–4. Writing for the court, Justice Anthony Kennedy held that the Article I powers that gave Congress the authority to enact the Fair Labor Standards Act did not abrogate the principle of state sovereign immunity. In a lengthy dissent, Justice David Souter challenged the court's understanding of the constitutional status of federalism and argued that under Article I, Congress could allow for federal rights to be enforced in state courts. The same five justices who made up the majority in *Alden* have succeeded in a number of recent federalism cases in reversing the Supreme Court's longstanding pattern of deference to national power.

Richard J. Maiman

See also Alternative Dispute Resolution; Federalism; Mediation; United States—Federal System; United States—State Systems

References and further reading

Coogan, William H. 1987. *A Citizen's Guide to the Maine Courts.* Augusta: Maine Bar Foundation.

Maiman, Richard J., David Karraker, and Al Leighton. 1999. *The Maine Superior Court Alternative Dispute Resolution Pilot Project: Program Evaluation Final Report.* Portland, ME: Edmund S. Muskie School of Public Service.

McEwen, Craig A., Lynn Mather, and Richard J. Maiman. 1994. "Lawyers, Mediation, and the Management of Divorce Practice." *Law & Society Review* 28, no. 1: 149–186.

Palmer, Kenneth. 2000. "Maine's Supreme Judicial Court and the United States Supreme Court: Two Decades of Review." *Maine Bar Journal* 15, no. 2: 140–143.

Palmer, Kenneth T., G. Thomas Taylor, and Marcus LiBrizzi. 1992. *Maine Politics and Government.* Lincoln and London: University of Nebraska Press.

MALAWI

COUNTRY INFORMATION

Malawi is a landlocked country located in southern Africa. Tanzania is on its northern border; Zambia lies to the west and northwest; and it is cupped by Mozambique to the south, southwest, and east. Within Malawi's 118,480 square kilometers are narrow, elongated plateaus, rolling plains, rounded hills, and mountains. Some of the land mass is taken up by the magnificent 24,000-square-kilometer Lake Malawi, which stretches for almost the entire length of the country. Malawi's physical beauty has been described by many observers in the past as the Switzerland of Africa. The comparison can go no further, however. Malawi is a tropical country with a rainy season from November to May, and a dry season from May to November.

Malawi's 10 million citizens include members of various African ethnic groups such as the Lomwe, Sena, Tumbuka, and Yao; people of European and Asian ancestry; and people of mixed ancestry. Approximately half of Malawi's citizens are literate. Malawi schools are operated by the state and by religious and other private organizations. The majority of citizens are members of Protestant religious groups, but there are large numbers of Roman Catholics and some Muslims. A small percentage of the population follows traditional indigenous religious beliefs and practices. English and Chichewa are the official languages, although there are other indigenous languages that are spoken throughout the country.

Malawi is among the world's least developed countries. Approximately half of the population lives below the poverty line and because of a predominantly agricultural economy, most of Malawi's citizens (approximately 90 percent) live in rural areas. The gross domestic product (GDP) is less than $9 billion, and the current rate of growth is approximately 3 percent. Various types of agricultural products account for approximately half of the GDP and about 90 percent of export revenue. Malawi's economy depends on large amounts of economic assistance from multilateral organizations like the World Bank and the European Union, and from individual donor nations.

Lilongwe is the capital city of Malawi. It was built and located in the central part of the country after Malawi became independent. It is now the seat of the national government. Since 1994, Malawi has embraced multiparty democracy.

Its legal system is based on the English common law and on local customary law. Judicial review of legislative acts resides in Malawi's High Court. Malawi has not accepted compulsory jurisdiction of the International Court of Justice. It is a member of the United Nations and the (British) Commonwealth of Nations and has membership in almost forty other international political and economic organizations. Malawi is also a party to many treaties on human rights and economic matters.

HISTORY

The first references to the Malawi people appeared in the records of the Portuguese, the first colonialists in central

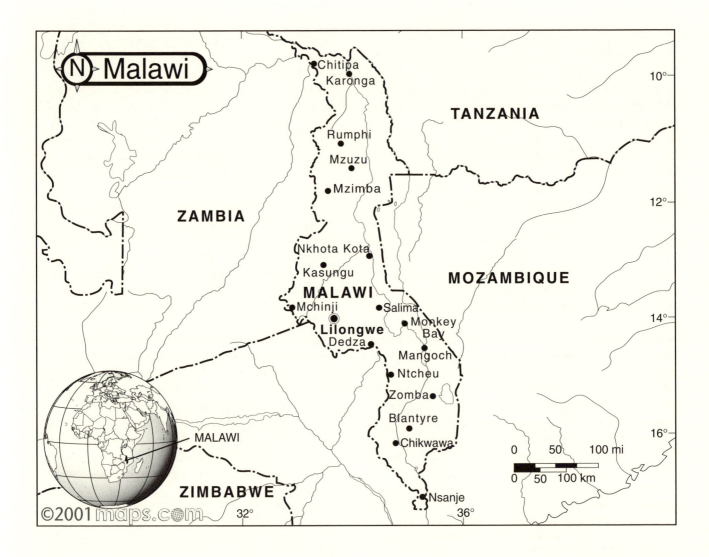

Africa. Between 1858 and 1863, Dr. David Livingstone, the Scottish missionary and explorer, made four journeys into what is now Malawi, as part of a British government–sponsored expedition. These expeditions kindled British interest in the area and this led to the establishment of the Central African Protectorate in 1891. The Central African Protectorate was renamed the Nyasaland Protectorate in 1907. The name Malawi was adopted in 1964 when the Nyasaland Protectorate gained independence from Britain. By 1886 and through a series of agreements between the German, Portuguese, and British governments, Malawi's present-day borders were established. Discontent among the Africans toward the British resulted in an unsuccessful revolt by Rev. John Chilembwe, an American-trained Nyasaland (Malawi) clergyman, in 1915. The movement toward independence gained momentum in the 1950s when, after an absence of thirty years, Dr. Hastings K. Banda, an American- and British-trained physician, returned to Nyasaland to lead the struggle for independence from Britain.

Against the wishes of the majority of the Africans, the Nyasaland Protectorate was joined into a federation with Southern Rhodesia (now Zimbabwe) and Northern Rhodesia (now Zambia) in 1953. The federation was dissolved by Britain in 1963. In 1964, Nyasaland gained independence as the sovereign state of Malawi within the Commonwealth of Nations. On July 6, 1966, Malawi became a republic within the Commonwealth. Under the republican constitution, Dr. Banda retained tremendous economic and political power over the country. This broad personal power created political discontent in the country. During Dr. Banda's regime there were many cases of gross abuses of power, lack of governmental accountability, and misuse and mismanagement of the country's resources. Pressure from internal and external groups led to a referendum on the one-party state in June 1993. The Banda regime lost this referendum and this led to the first multiparty elections in May 1994. A day before the 1994 elections, the Malawi National Assembly adopted a provisional democratic constitution. In the multiparty elections of 1994, the Banda regime lost, ending three decades of political oppression. In February 1995 the National Constitutional Conference was held for the purpose of adopting a new constitution. Rather than replace the provisional constitution, the National Assembly decided in April 1995 to make modest amendments to it to address some of the issues that had been raised at the Constitutional Conference. As amended, the provisional constitution entered into force as a permanent constitution on May 17, 1995.

LEGAL CONCEPTS

Malawi's supreme law is found in its constitution. The constitution provides for a separation of powers into executive, legislative, and judicial branches of government. The constitution is extremely detailed. It covers every conceivable area of Malawi's economic, political, and social life. It, for example, establishes a National Compensation Tribunal whose function is to deal with alleged criminal and civil liability of the Banda regime. The constitution recognizes the right of people and communities to their own cultural identity in accordance with local values, languages, and customs. It addresses problems of the elderly, the disabled, and rural communities. It also advocates the right to a clean and healthy environment for all people. The constitution provides for a Parliament that consists of the National Assembly, the Senate, and the president as head of state. Due to limited resources, the Senate has not yet been established. A constitutional amendment in 1995 provides that until the establishment of the Senate, all legislation shall be enacted by the National Assembly as if the constitution had not made provision for the establishment of the Senate. Of the 53 African constitutions examined by the author, only nine are bicameral. Several African states that were once bicameral have now opted for unicameralism. It is likely, therefore, that the Senate will never be established. An act of Parliament has supremacy over any other law but it is subject to the constitution. Parliamentary sovereignty has therefore been modified in favor of constitutional supremacy, thus departing from the Westminster model. To the extent that Parliament can override a presidential veto after a twenty-one-day cooling-off period, Parliament remains the supreme legislative authority in Malawi.

The constitution calls for the election of the president by a majority of the electorate through direct, universal, and equal suffrage. Each term of the president lasts five years. The constitution prohibits a person from serving more than two five-year terms. A person is qualified to be elected president if the person is a citizen of Malawi by birth or descent, has attained the age of thirty-five years, and, during the seven years preceding the election, has not been convicted by a competent court of a crime involving dishonesty or moral turpitude. The seven-year disqualification was adopted after a very bitter debate at the 1995 Constitutional Conference. The 1994 Provisional Constitution had provided for a lifetime disqualification. One of the major political parties successfully lobbied for a repeal of the lifetime disqualification in order to protect its candidate for the presidency. Additional qualifications are that the person be of sound mind, not be an undischarged bankrupt, and owe no allegiance to a foreign country.

The Malawi Constitution provides for a president, a first vice president, and a second vice president. The first and second vice presidents are not given any specific constitutional powers because their principal duty is to assist the president. They may exercise such functions as are conferred on them by the president or by an act of Parliament. The president may assign ministerial responsibilities to the first and second vice presidents. The vice presidency is very weak constitutionally, thus making it difficult for one of the vice presidents to challenge the authority of the president. The president and the first and second vice presidents serve in their offices for a maximum of two consecutive terms. Each term is limited to five years in length. The president and first vice president may be impeached for serious crimes committed against the constitution or for a breach of the written laws of Malawi. The second vice president can only be removed by the president. The second vice president cannot belong to the same political party as the president and is not in the line of succession. The office of second vice president has been vacant since 1997.

The Malawi Constitution also provides for a Parliament, which consists at present of the National Assembly, a proposed Senate, and the president as the head of state. The National Assembly is directly elected. Its size is not fixed by the constitution but is controlled and determined by the Electoral Commission. The principle behind not fixing the size of the National Assembly is to enable the Electoral Commission to fix the size of the National Assembly and to demarcate constituencies on the basis of population density and geographical features, thereby guaranteeing that all votes cast throughout the country are given fair and equal weight. Some of the powers of the National Assembly include control of Malawi's finances. A practice has developed whereby the National Assembly is acquiring a greater role in the management of the country's finances and a Budget Committee has recently been established to reflect this. The Senate is intended to serve a different purpose. The senators are to be indirectly elected. In the Senate, chiefs, women's organizations, disabled persons, and other special groups are to be represented. The idea behind the Senate is to ensure that all special interests and all regional, ethnic, or religious groups are represented. The Senate has been given equal powers to that of the National Assembly. For example, the Senate has an equal role in the impeachment of the president and the first vice president.

The judicial system is adversarial. There is provision for trial by jury and the government provides modest legal aid for defendants who are unable to hire a private attorney. The Law Society of Malawi, through its Legal Resources Centre established in 1993, also provides legal services to indigents and low-income earners.

All criminal prosecutions (other than courts-martial) are carried out under the auspices of the director of public prosecutions. Under the 1995 Constitution, the director of public prosecutions was required to act independently of any person or authority. This independence was removed by a constitutional amendment in 1998 and the director of public prosecutions now exercises his powers subject to general and specific direction from the attorney general.

The judiciary had been severely subverted and compromised under the Banda dictatorship. The constitution therefore provides for the independence of the judiciary and prohibits the establishment of courts of superior or concurrent jurisdiction with the Supreme Court of Appeal or the High Court. Under the Banda dictatorship, political opponents were tried in traditional courts where judges (traditional chiefs) had no legal training, where there was no legal representation, and where the rules of evidence did not apply. These courts were parallel to the regular courts. The conviction rate in these courts was in most cases 100 percent. With the establishment of civilian oversight over the police through the Police Service Commission, a constitutional requirement that no government or political party shall use the police to promote a political party or undermine another political party, and the establishment of an inspectorate of prisons to monitor prison conditions, the general attitude of the public is that the present legal and penal system is an improvement over the system that prevailed under the Banda regime. With more resources and better training, the system should register more improvements in future.

CURRENT COURT SYSTEM STRUCTURE

The Supreme Court of Appeal is the highest court of record. It is the highest appellate court and has jurisdiction to hear appeals from the High Court and such other courts and tribunals as may be conferred on it by the constitution or by an act of Parliament. The chief justice is appointed by the president, subject to confirmation of a two-thirds majority of the members of the National Assembly present and voting. There can be no less than three other Supreme Court justices. All other judges are appointed by the president on the recommendation of the Judicial Service Commission. The members of the Judicial Service Commission are appointed by the president. The commission consists of the chief justice, who is the chairman, the chairman of the Civil Service Commission, an appeals justice, a legal practitioner, and a magistrate. The powers of the Judicial Service Commission include nominating candidates for judicial offices, exercising discipli-

nary control over judicial officers and recommending the removal of judicial officers. The constitution provides that all magistrates and other judicial officers, who under the constitution are appointed by the chief justice on the recommendation of the Judicial Service Commission, shall hold their office until the age of seventy, unless they are removed for incompetence or misbehavior. All other judicial officers, including the chief justice, hold their offices until the age of sixty-five years unless they are removed for incompetence or misbehavior.

The High Court is the second highest court in the land. It has unlimited original jurisdiction to hear and adjudicate any civil or criminal disputes under the law. It also has original jurisdiction over constitutional questions. The High Court consists of such judges, being not less than three, as prescribed by an act of Parliament. Parliament may also establish subordinate courts to be presided over by professional magistrates and lay magistrates. A person cannot be appointed a judge unless that person is entitled to practice as a legal practitioner, advocate, or solicitor and has been entitled to so practice for not less than ten years.

Although the constitution grants Parliament the power to establish traditional and local courts, these have not yet been constituted. However, in the rural areas (over 90 percent of the people live in rural areas), there are traditional mechanisms of varying degrees of formality that are used to resolve disputes under customary law. Some of these mechanisms operate under the auspices of local chiefs.

SPECIALIZED JUDICIAL BODIES

The constitution provides for an industrial relations court, subordinate to the High Court, which has original jurisdiction over labor disputes and other issues that involve employment. The composition of this court is left to Parliament. Parliament also has the power to set up traditional and local courts that are presided over by lay persons or chiefs. The constitution also establishes the Office of Ombudsman. The ombudsman has the power to investigate cases where it is alleged that a person has suffered an injustice and there is no apparent reasonable remedy through a court proceeding. The ombudsman operates independently of any person or authority in Malawi. He serves a term of not more than five years. He has extensive investigative powers and may initiate proceedings in the High Court against any person or authority in Malawi for noncompliance with requests made in connection with his investigative powers. He has the power to make annual reports to the National Assembly. The reports shall detail all complaints made to his office, remedies afforded, and recommendations as to how such grievances should be handled in future. The ombudsman is granted the same privileges and immunities as enjoyed

Legal Structure of Malawi Courts

```
┌─────────────────────────────────────────────┐
│           Supreme Court of Appeal             │
│                                               │
│   Supreme Court of        Appellate Jurisdiction │
│       Record            Civil Law   Criminal Law │
│                          Constitutional Law      │
└─────────────────────────────────────────────┘

┌─────────────────────────────────────────────┐
│                 High Court                    │
│                                               │
│         Unlimited Original Jurisdiction       │
│                                               │
│ Civil Law  Criminal Law  Constitutional Law  Judicial Review │
└─────────────────────────────────────────────┘

┌───────────────────────────────────┐
│          Magistrates' Courts        │
│                                     │
│     Unlimited Original Jurisdiction │
│                                     │
│         Civil Law   Criminal Law    │
└───────────────────────────────────┘

┌───────────────────────────────────┐
│     Traditional or Local Courts     │
│            Customary Law            │
└───────────────────────────────────┘
```

by members of Parliament. He is also paid a salary out of the Consolidated Fund.

The constitution also establishes a Law Commission. The Law Commission has the power to review and make recommendations in connection with the amendment of laws. The Law Commission consists of a permanent law commissioner, who is appointed by the president on the recommendation of the Judicial Service Commission. The law commissioner must be a legal practitioner or a person who is qualified to be a judge. The Law Commission is an independent entity, much like the ombudsman, in that it exercises its function and powers independently of any other person or authority.

The constitution also establishes a Human Rights Commission. The primary function of the commission is to investigate violations of human rights that are guaranteed by the constitution or any other law. The Human Rights Commission consists of the law commissioner, the ombudsman, and persons nominated by other organizations. These persons are nominated by organizations that in the absolute discretion of the law commissioner and the ombudsman are representative of Malawi society and are concerned with the promotion of the rights and freedoms guaranteed in the constitution.

Another specialized body established under the constitution is the National Compensation Tribunal. The tribunal has been established to redress the excesses of the Banda dictatorship. The tribunal shall cease to exist ten years from its establishment. It has jurisdiction to entertain claims with respect to alleged civil and criminal liability of the Banda regime. The chairman of the tribunal must be a judge appointed by the chief justice on the recommendation of the Judicial Service Commission. The chairman is assisted by such additional members and by such assessors and other experts as are appointed in accordance with an act of Parliament. The tribunal may engage in informal arbitration and also has the power to submit a case to the ordinary courts. Its decisions are subject to review by the High Court. In its proceedings the tribunal is required to apply the same standards of proof as are required in the ordinary courts unless the tribunal otherwise determines in the interest of justice in any particular case or class of cases. Its proceedings must conform to standards of justice as set out in the constitution and to the principles of natural justice.

Through an act of Parliament, an Anti-Corruption Bureau has been established. The purpose of the bureau is to investigate suspected cases of corruption by public officials and to refer cases where it appears that corruption has taken place to the director of public prosecutions for possible prosecution.

One of the most important specialized bodies established under Malawi's new democratic dispensation is the Electoral Commission. The commission is chaired by a judge who is appointed by the president on the recommendation of the Judicial Service Commission. The other members of the commission, being not less than six, are appointed by the president as provided for under the Parliamentary and Presidential Elections Act. Members of the commission are appointed with respect to every general election. The commission, which is required by law to act independently, has responsibility over presidential, parliamentary, and local elections. Among its responsibilities are organizing and directing voter registration, devising voter registers and ballot papers, the printing and distribution of ballot papers, establishing and operating polling stations, and overall management of the electoral process in order to guarantee its security. A member of the commission may be removed by the president on the recommendation of the Public Appointments Committee on the grounds of incapacity or incompetence. The general feeling by Malawi and international election observers is that the first democratic elections in 1994 were conducted competently and fairly. There has been considerable controversy with respect to the 1999 elections and the results of the presidential election and some parliamentary constituencies are being challenged in the courts. The perception by many Malawians outside the governing party is that the commission is biased in favor of the government and that the commission was unable to prevent massive electoral fraud. If democracy is to survive in Malawi, ways must be found to guarantee the integrity of the Electoral Commission and the electoral process.

STAFFING

During the British colonial administration, the legal profession was divided into barristers and solicitors, as was the case in Britain. Today, the legal profession is fused into one and lawyers are referred to as legal practitioners, advocates, or solicitors. Legal practitioner is the most widely used term.

Lawyers are trained at the Faculty of Law of the University of Malawi. There are also a number of lawyers who have been trained in the United Kingdom and other commonwealth countries. To be admitted to the Malawi bar, a person must hold a law degree from the University of Malawi or other commonwealth country and must pass an examination set by the Law Society of Malawi. Private law practice tends to be more lucrative and therefore more attractive than government service in the Ministry of Justice and other government agencies in spite of the security of tenure and income that come with service in the government. There is at present no continuing legal education.

Judges and other members of the judiciary may be appointed from the bar, the bench, or the civil service. Once selected, a judicial officer enjoys security of tenure until the prescribed age for retirement. Thus a judicial officer's salary and allowances may not be reduced without that officer's consent. A judicial officer may be removed from office only for incompetence or misbehavior, and then only after a motion for such removal has been debated in the National Assembly, has been passed by a majority vote of all the members of the National Assembly, and has been submitted to the president as a petition for the removal of the judge in question. The constitution requires that the entire procedure for removal must be in accordance with the principles of natural justice.

There is no formal training for judicial officers, although periodically national seminars are held at which judicial officers are able to interact and exchange ideas. There are also some external opportunities for judicial officers to improve their skills. Under the auspices of the Commonwealth Secretariat, for example, Malawi judicial officers have the opportunity to participate in conferences and workshops overseas organized by the Commonwealth Magistrates and Judges Association. Within Africa itself, there have been held periodic judicial seminars to which Malawi judicial officers have been invited. These seminars enable Malawi judicial officers to discuss matters of mutual interest with their counterparts in other African countries. The Commonwealth Lawyers Association attracts lawyers from all the commonwealth countries at the periodic commonwealth law conferences that the association organizes. At these conferences other commonwealth groups such as the ministers and attorneys general of the commonwealth, and presidents and officials of commonwealth bars and law societies, have conducted workshops in areas of interest to these groups. One of the significant events at the commonwealth law conferences is the Commonwealth Law Moot competition, which is administered by the Commonwealth Legal Education Association and is open to all commonwealth law students. These events do have a positive impact on the legal skills of commonwealth lawyers and law students, including those from Malawi. Recently, the Association of American Law Schools has taken an interest in legal education in Africa and several members of the Malawi law faculty, including the dean, have participated in workshops on legal education in the United States.

IMPACT

During the thirty-year Banda dictatorship, the judiciary was subverted and compromised. A very timid judiciary abdicated its role as the buffer between the government and the people. Suspected opponents of the regime were either detained for long periods of time without trial or were driven into exile. In one instance, a political opponent of the regime was detained without trial for twenty-nine years! The regime's lack of respect for the rule of law resulted in the public's complete contempt of the legal and judicial system.

The advent of multiparty democracy in 1994 is beginning to have an impact on the public perception of the legal system and the judiciary. Although some of the members of the judiciary are carryovers from the Banda era, the framework that should enable the judiciary to define its role in a democratizing society is now in place. The appointment of new judges, some of whom are rather inexperienced, will help to improve the manner in which the judiciary is perceived by the public.

There is emerging a new attitude toward the rule of law by the Malawi people. There seems to be a recognition that societies that adhere to the rule of law and respect human rights tend to create conditions that are attractive to foreign private capital—a necessary condition for economic and human development. At the moment, Malawi people may be divided into those that operate in the commercial sector and those that operate in the noncommercial sector. The former are governed by modern commercial laws, including regional and international rules, while the latter are generally governed by customary rules and informal mechanisms for settling disputes. To some extent then, attitudes toward law are dictated by where one is placed in the social and economic structure. These attitudes will also be shaped by whether the government is able to eradicate poverty and reduce corruption. Hungry people do not have the luxury of theorizing about the rule of law. If the government is able to reverse or at least stop the economic decline, reestablish security within the country, and contain official corruption, prospects for a viable internal legal order are good.

In 1995, Malawi adopted a democratic constitution. At least at the formal level, there is now a framework for an orderly democratic political structure. The question now is one of management. Strategies must be devised for transforming old undemocratic institutions and practices into democratic ones. The first democratic presidential and parliamentary elections in 1994 were declared free and fair by international observers. Five years later, the presidential and parliamentary elections were declared "substantially free and fair" by the international observers. This regression in the management of the elections is a cause for concern because democratization cannot be effected if Malawi is unable to build self-sustaining mechanisms that guarantee free and fair elections. There were serious problems of preelection intimidation and voter registration fraud as well as vote-counting irregularities. The reelection of the incumbent president was challenged by the opposition and the case is still in the courts. Local government elections as provided for in the 1995 constitution have now been scheduled for November 2000, but the establishment of the Senate has been postponed indefinitely due to lack of funds. In the end then, what role the law will play in the political and social life of the country will depend on whether the government is able to implement economic policies that produce enough resources to finance democratic institution building.

A. Peter Mutharika

See also Adversarial System; Appellate Courts; Common Law; Criminal Law; Customary Law; Human Rights; Judicial Independence; Judicial Review; Legal Aid; Legal Professionals —Civil Law Traditions

References and further reading
Africa Watch. 1990. *Where Silence Rules: The Suppression of Dissent in Malawi.* New York: Africa Watch.
Amnesty International. 1994. *Malawi: A New Future for Human Rights.* London: Amnesty International.
Cullen, Trevor. 1994. *Malawi: A Turning Point.* Edinburgh: The Pentland Press.
Law Society of England and Wales. 1992. *Human Rights in Malawi.* London: Law Society of England and Wales.
MacCracken, John. 1977. *Politics and Christianity in Malawi 1875–1940.* Cambridge: Cambridge University Press.
Mutharika, A. Peter. 1995. "The Presidency and the Vice-Presidency, The Structure and Role of Parliament (National Assembly and Senate) and the Relationship between Branches of Government under the Constitution." Working paper presented at the National Constitutional Conference, Lilongwe, Malawi, February 19–23.
———. 1996. "The 1995 Democratic Constitution of Malawi." *Journal of Africa Law* 40, no. 2: 205–220. London: Oxford University Press.
Williams, Trevor. 1978. *Malawi: The Politics of Despair.* London: Cornell University Press.

MALAYSIA

GENERAL INFORMATION

Location, Size, and Topography

Malaysia is in Southeast Asia. It is divided into two separate landmasses referred to as West Malaysia and East Malaysia. West Malaysia is on the Malay Peninsula and is bordered by Singapore to the south and Thailand to the north. To the west, across the Straits of Malacca, lies the Indonesian island of Sumatra, while the South China Sea lies to the east. East Malaysia is on the northern third of the island of Borneo, with part of Indonesia to the south and the country of Brunei nestled between the two states of West Malaysia (Sabah and Sarawak). The 120,000 square kilometers of West Malaysia contain coastal plains both east and west of a central ridge of mountains. East Malaysia's 200,000 square kilometers consist primarily of low-lying forests and rivers in the state of Sarawak and coastal plains rising to mountains in the state of Sabah. The equatorial location of both East and West Malaysia and the moderating influence of surrounding oceans yield warm weather with little seasonal variation. Daily temperatures in low-lying areas range from lows of roughly 24 degrees to highs of up to 35 degrees Celsius (with cooler temperatures prevailing in the highland areas). Exposure to both northeast and southwest monsoon seasons makes for a predominantly wet climate, with average annual rainfalls of 2,500 millimeters or more. The warm, wet weather supports a tropical rainforest that covers about four-fifths of Malaysia.

Population, Capital City, and GDP

Malaysia has a population of approximately 23.8 million. Roughly 1.8 million people live in the capital city of Kuala Lumpur, which is more or less centrally located on the western coastal plain of West Malaysia. The gross domestic product (GDP) of Malaysia was estimated to be U.S.$89.7 billion in 2000, providing an estimated per capita GDP of U.S.$3,852.

Culture and Language

The country has three main racial groups: Malay, Chinese, and Indian. The Malays constitute about 58 percent of the population, the Chinese 28 percent, and the Indians 7 percent. There are also aboriginal groups, who make up about 2 percent of the population (this percentage being much higher in West Malaysia). The official language is the local Malay language (Bahasa Melayu). Several dialects of Chinese are spoken, including Cantonese, Mandarin, Hokkien, Hakka, Hainanese, and Foochow. Indian languages include Tamil, Malayalam, and Punjabi. Several indigenous languages are also spoken, particularly the Iban and Kadazan languages of the

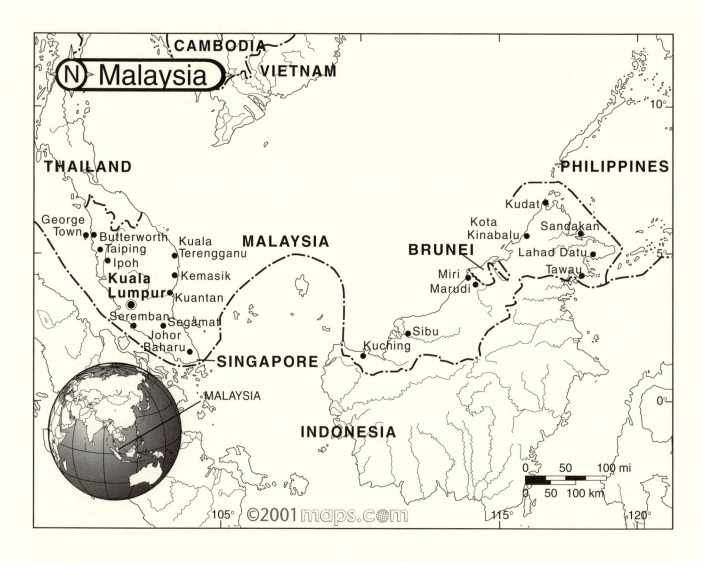

indigenous groups of East Malaysia. Much of the population has a knowledge of English. The literacy rate is estimated to be about 84 percent.

Religion
The Malay population is predominantly Muslim. Those of Indian decent primarily practice Hinduism, although there is also a small Sikh population. The Chinese practice primarily Buddhism, Confucianism, or Taoism. There is also a segment of the population who follow Christianity.

Type of Legal System
As a former British colony, the country has maintained an English common law tradition. However, that tradition lies alongside both an Islamic law system (administered through the Syariah courts) and the customary law (or "Adat" law) of various aboriginal groups.

HISTORY
Sarawak's Niah caves were the site of one of the oldest finds of modern man (estimated to be as much as thirty-five thousand years old). There is evidence of human habitation in peninsular Malaysia dating back ten thousand years. Over the years people appear to have migrated to the area from various places, and, by the time of the first European arrival in the sixteenth century, there were well-established fishing and agrarian communities along the coasts and the rivers in low-lying floodplains. Nomadic hunting and gathering communities were also present farther inland. The customs of these communities were among the original sources of customary law in Malaysia.

Prior to the European arrival there was also a well-established trading system with people from China, India, and Arabia. By 1400 C.E., the Malay state of Malaka was an important port at which merchants from China arrived on the northeast monsoon winds to trade with merchants from Arabia and India, who arrived on the winds of the ensuing southwest monsoon. These trade connections brought various influences to the region. Early on, Hinduism had a pronounced effect on Malay customs and customary law. Later the influence of Islam came to dominate, having a significant impact on Malay customary law and ultimately leading to its becoming an important element of the modern-day laws of Malaysia.

In 1511, Malaka fell to the Portuguese, and it remained in Portuguese control for 130 years until the Dutch wrested it from them in 1641. The Dutch controlled Malaka until 1824, except for brief periods of British control from 1795 to 1801 and from 1807 to 1818. The British then took control, pursuant to the Anglo-Dutch treaty of 1824. This expanded British influence in the region, which had earlier been established by British settlements in Penang (1876) and Singapore (1819).

Initially the British, like the Portuguese and Dutch before them, did not extend their influence inland on the peninsula. However, as the nineteenth century progressed, and British rubber and tin interests on the peninsula increased, the British came to exercise greater political control over the peninsular Malay states. By the Treaty of Pangkor in 1874, the British brought the rulers of the peninsular Malay state of Perak under the supervision of a British resident. Similar arrangements were made with other Malay states, and by 1914 the southern portion of the Malay Peninsula included the British Straits Settlements of Singapore, Melaka, and Penang; the British protectorate of the Federated Malay States of Negeri Sembilan, Pahang, Perak, and Selangor; and the unfederated Malay states of Johor, Kedah, Kelantan, Perlis, and Terenganu (also being British protectorates, in which the sultans ruled subject to the advice of a British advisor). For the Malay states the effect of the treaties was that, though nominally legally sovereign, they were under British control, except for Malay custom and Islamic matters. On the island of Borneo, James Brooke obtained Sarawak by concession from the Sultan of Brunei in 1841, and by 1865 British companies were operating in Sabah (or British North Borneo) as a result of concessions from the Sultan of Brunei and the Sultan of Sulu. These concessions were later transferred to the Chartered Company of British North Borneo. With British control over the areas that now constitute Malaysia came British common law.

The Japanese invaded the Malay Peninsula and Borneo late in 1941, and they retained control until the British re-established their authority in 1945. The British then proposed a Malayan Union under British control for the Malay states on the peninsula, with Singapore, Sarawak, and British North Borneo (Sabah) as separate Crown colonies. This met with considerable opposition, and, instead, the Federation of Malaya—consisting of the nine peninsular Malay states along with Penang and Melaka—was formed. Under the Federation of Malaya arrangement, the British committed themselves to preparing for the independence of the federation. A royal commission, headed by Lord Reid, was set up to develop a constitution for the country, and the federation became formally independent on August 31, 1957. The constitution followed a Westminster style of parliament and drew on the earlier federal constitutions of other former British colonies (particularly India). In 1963, Singapore, Sarawak, and Sabah joined the federation to form the country of Malaysia. In 1965, Singapore separated, leaving the nine peninsular Malay states, the former Straits Settlements of Penang and Melaka, and the northern Borneo states of Sabah and Sarawak constituting the country of Malaysia, operating under a federal constitution.

LEGAL CONCEPTS

The Constitution

Malaysia has a federal system in which the powers of government are divided between the federal government and state governments. The division of powers is set out in the federal constitution. While the constitution provides for a federal system, it is one with a strong central government. The federal government's list of powers includes external affairs, defense, internal security, police, civil and criminal law and procedure and the administration of justice, citizenship, finance (including currency, banking, bills of exchange, foreign exchange, capital issues, and stock and commodity exchanges), trade, commerce and industry, shipping, navigation and fisheries, communications and transport, federal works and power, education, health, and labor and social security. The state's list of powers includes such things as matters of the Islamic religion in the state, land tenure, compulsory acquisition of land, licenses for mining, agriculture and forests, municipal government, and public works for state purposes. There is also a list of concurrent powers concerning such matters as sanitation, drainage and irrigation, fire safety, housing, and culture and sports. Where otherwise valid federal and state laws conflict, the federal law is paramount.

Each state also has a constitution that must contain certain provisions, as required by the federal constitution. The constitution provides for the supremacy of the federal constitution. It also establishes Malaysia as a federation, a constitutional monarchy, and a parliamentary democracy. It provides for Islam as the religion of the country but also guarantees freedom of religion. The constitution sets out the framework for the parliamentary, executive, and judicial branches of government.

The federal constitution stipulates certain rights and freedoms, including the right to liberty of the person, to be informed of the grounds of arrest, to legal counsel, and to be released after arrest without unreasonable delay. The rights and freedoms also include the prohibition of slavery and forced labor; protection against retrospective criminal laws and repeated trials; the right to equality before the law and equal protection under the law; freedom of movement; prohibition of banishment; freedom of speech, assembly, and association; freedom of religion; and the right not to be deprived of property without adequate compensation. Some of these rights and freedoms are stated in absolute terms. Others are subject to certain qualifications. For instance, Parliament is given authority to pass a law imposing restrictions on the right to freedom of speech "as it deems necessary or expedient in the interest of the security of the Federation."

The federal constitution may be amended by an act of Parliament that, subject to limited exceptions, requires the support of not less than two-thirds of the total number of members of both houses of Parliament. Certain amendments to the constitution also require the consent of the Conference of Rulers.

Heads of State
The federal constitution created a federal head of state known as the king (or "Yang di-Pertuan Agong"). The king is elected by the Conference of Rulers. The executive authority of the federation is vested in the king and is exercised by him, the cabinet, or any minister authorized by the cabinet. When the king exercises executive authority he must do so according to the advice of the cabinet or a minister acting under cabinet authority. When the constitution requires the king to act upon advice, the king must accept that advice and act in accordance with it.

The head of state in each of the nine Malay states is the ruler of the state. The ruler is the sultan in seven of the Malay states, the Yang di-Pertuan Besar in Negri Sembilan, the raja in Perlis, and the governor in Melaka, Penang, Sabah, and Sawarak.

The Conference of Rulers
The Conference of Rulers consists of the rulers of the nine formerly independent Malay states and the governors of Penang, Melaka, Sabah, and Sarawak. The conference (without the four governors) elects the king. The Conference of Rulers must be consulted upon the appointment of the judges of higher courts (see "Staffing," below). They must also be consulted on the appointment of the auditor general and members of the Election Commission. Certain amendments to laws—such as restrictions on freedom of speech, assembly, or association; constitutional provisions concerning citizenship; the structure or powers of the Conference of Rulers; parliamentary privileges; the national language; or quotas and privileges in favor of Malays or the natives of Sabah and Sarawak—also require consultation with the Conference of Rulers. Further, no law directly affecting the privileges, position, honors, or dignities of the rulers can be passed without the consent of the Conference of Rulers.

Parliament and State Legislatures
The federal Parliament, as provided in the federal constitution, consists of a lower house (the House of Representatives, or Dewan Rakyat) and an upper house (the Senate, or Dewan Negeri). The Senate consists of seventy members, made up of two members from each state elected by the legislative assembly of the state, two members for the Federal Territory of Kuala Lumpur, and one each representing the Federal Territories of Labuan and Putrajaya, appointed by the king, as well as forty other members appointed by the king. The term of a senator is limited to three years, and a senator cannot hold office for more than two terms, either continuously or otherwise.

The House of Representatives consists of 194 members who are elected by the general public in each of 194 constituencies. Constituency boundaries and the conduct of elections are dealt with through an Election Commission appointed pursuant to the federal constitution. The 194 members are made up of 182 who come from the various states and 12 who represent the Federal Territories of Kuala Lumpur, Labuan, and Putrajaya. Elections occur at least every five years, inasmuch as, pursuant to the constitution, Parliament is automatically dissolved after five years and elections must be held within sixty days of the dissolution of Parliament. Elections can occur sooner, if the king accepts the advice of the prime minister to dissolve Parliament prior to the expiry of the five-year period. In addition to making laws, Parliament authorizes the levy of federal taxes and the spending of federal money.

State legislatures have only one chamber—the state legislative assembly. State legislative assemblies consist of members elected in state general elections and pass laws coming under the state list of powers.

The Executive
The executive consists of the cabinet assisted by the public service, the police force, and the armed forces. The prime minister presides over the cabinet. The prime minister is appointed by the king and is an elected member of the House who, in the opinion of the king, is likely to command the confidence of a majority of the members of the House of Representatives. Since independence in 1957, the person who has commanded such confidence has been the leader of the United Malays National Organization (UMNO), the biggest party in the coalition known as the Barisan Nasional (formerly called the Alliance). The king, on the advice of the prime minister, appoints the other members of the cabinet. The king, on the advice of the prime minister, may also appoint deputy ministers and parliamentary secretaries. Cabinet ministers (other than the prime minister), deputy ministers, and parliamentary secretaries may be members of either the House of Representatives or the Senate.

Cabinet ministers are assisted by a public service. The appointment, promotion, transfer, discipline, and dismissal of members of the public service are the responsibility of the Public Services Commission, established under the constitution. A member of the commission cannot be a member of either house of Parliament or of a state legislative assembly, nor a member of the public service or a trade union. There is a federal police force, the appointment, promotion, and discipline of whose members are the responsibility of the Police Force Commission, established under the constitution. The constitution also establishes the Armed Forces Council, which, under the general authority of the king, is responsible for the command, discipline, and administration of the armed forces (except for matters relating to the operational use of the armed forces).

Legislative Process

Bills, other than money bills, may originate in either house of Parliament. Money bills dealing with taxation or expenditures can originate only in the House of Representatives. In the normal process, a bill introduced in the House of Representatives goes through a first reading, second reading, a committee stage, and a third reading. It is then referred to the Senate, where it goes through a similar process. When a bill has been passed by both houses and agreement reached on any amendments, it is presented to the king for his assent. The king has up to thirty days to assent to a bill. If the bill is not assented to within that time, it is deemed to have become law.

Sources of Law

The four main sources of law in Malaysia are written law, common law, Islamic (or Sharia) law, and customary law. Written law consists of the federal and state constitutions, enactments of the federal Parliament and state legislatures, and subsidiary legislation (regulations and rules). Subsidiary legislation is made by a body or person authorized to do so under acts of the federal Parliament or a state legislature.

English common law and rules of equity have been formally adopted under the Civil Law Act of 1956. The common law consists of the English common law and rules of equity as developed by the courts of Malaysia, subject to conflicting provisions of written law and subject to such qualifications as local circumstances make necessary. There are some statutes that largely codify elements of the common law, such as the Contracts Act of 1950, the Sale of Goods Act, and the Specific Relief Act.

Malaysian courts follow the principle of stare decisis. Courts follow previous decisions made in cases before the courts. Decisions of the High Courts are binding on subordinate courts. Decisions of the Court of Appeal are binding on the High Courts and subordinate courts, and decisions of the Federal Court are binding on the Court of Appeal and all other lower courts (on the court structure, see "Current Court System Structure," below). Decisions of the Privy Council in England are binding with respect to appeals that arose from Malaysia. However, appeals to the Privy Council in criminal law matters were abolished in 1978, and appeals to the Privy Council on all other matters were abolished in 1985. Decisions of the House of Lords in England are not binding, but they are often referred to.

Islamic law has its base in the Holy Quran, interpretations of it attributed to the prophet Muhammad, laws agreed to by lawyers in ancient times, commentaries by ancient and modern scholars, and in custom. In the multiracial context of Malaysia, Islamic law is applied only to Muslims in matters of personal law, such as marriage, divorce, guardianship, and inheritance.

Customary law in West Malaysia has its origins in ancient Malay customary law, Hindu law, and Islamic law. In East Malaysia customary law consists of Malay customary law applicable to Malays, native customary law applicable to non-Malay natives, and Chinese and Hindu customary law codified in state statutes. These laws are administered by Native Courts.

The Rule of Law

The principle of the rule of law is applied in Malaysia generally following English administrative law as developed in Malaysian courts. Decisions by administrators and tribunals must be within the scope of the discretion or jurisdiction granted. They must conform to the principles of "natural justice" (that is, procedural fairness or "due process").

A notable exception to the rule of law was a constitutional immunity granted to the rulers that protected them against both criminal and civil proceedings. This immunity was removed in 1993 with the qualification that proceedings against the king or rulers must be brought in a special court and only with the consent of the attorney general.

Internal Security

Another significant feature of Malaysian law is the concern for internal security reflected in constraints on the otherwise constitutionally protected freedom of speech, controls on assemblies, and, most significantly, in the Internal Security Act. The Internal Security Act allows a police officer to arrest and detain a person without charge or warrant for up to sixty days, where the detention "is necessary with a view to preventing him from acting in any manner prejudicial to the security of Malaysia or any part thereof or to the maintenance of essential services therein or to the economic life thereof." The minister responsible for internal security can extend the period of detention by order, each order having a duration of up to two years. The minister in charge of printing presses and publications may also ban the printing and circulation of publications that are deemed prejudicial to the national interest, public order, or security. Furthermore, there are wide powers of arrest and detention for persons suspected of trafficking in dangerous drugs. In addition, there are extensive powers to control assemblies in public or private places that are "likely to be prejudicial to the interest of the security of Malaysia . . . or to excite a disturbance of the peace."

The Death Penalty
The death penalty is a feature of Malaysian law used in relation to offenses such as murder, the trafficking of dangerous drugs, the possession of unlicensed firearms in a security area, or the discharge of a firearm in the commission of an offense with intent to cause death or injury to any person.

Affirmative Action and the New Economic Policy
Since 1957 the federal constitution has provided for Malay quotas in the civil service. Further quota regimes were provided pursuant to a New Economic Policy (NEP) adopted in the aftermath of race riots in 1969. These policies were directed at ameliorating the relatively weaker position of Malays in the economy. While they may be of diminishing significance, these policies continue to be a feature of the Malaysian legal and political system.

CURRENT COURT SYSTEM STRUCTURE
The court system is principally federal. Both state and federal laws are enforced in the federal courts. The only state courts are the Syariah courts, which administer Islamic law, and the Native Courts in Sabah and Sarawak, which deal with customary law. The main trial-level courts are the High Courts. In addition there are Sessions Courts and Magistrates' Courts. The High Courts and inferior courts have such jurisdiction and powers as may be conferred by or under federal law. They also have no jurisdiction in respect of any matter within the jurisdiction of the Syariah courts.

High Courts
There are two High Courts, one in peninsular Malaysia, known as the High Court in Malaya, and the other in East Malaysia, known as the High Court in Sabah and Sarawak. Except for matters falling in the jurisdiction of the Syariah courts, these courts have an unlimited original jurisdiction within their territory. They can also hear appeals from Sessions Courts and Magistrates' Courts.

Court of Appeal
The appellate courts are the Malaysian Court of Appeal (or Mahkamah Rayuan) and the Federal Court (Mahkamah Persekutuan). The Court of Appeal is composed of the president of the Court of Appeal and ten other judges. It hears appeals from decisions of the High Court and has such other jurisdiction as may be conferred by federal law.

Federal Court
The Federal Court is composed of the chief justice of the Federal Court, the president of the Court of Appeal, the chief judges of the High Courts, and seven other judges appointed by the king on the advice of the chief justice of the Federal Court. The Federal Court has jurisdiction to hear appeals from decisions of the Court of Appeal or the High Court and such other jurisdiction as conferred by federal law. The Federal Court has jurisdiction to determine whether a law is invalid on the grounds that it was a matter over which Parliament—or a state legislature, as the case may be—has no power to make laws. In addition, the king may refer any question regarding the effect of a provision of the constitution to the Federal Court. The Federal Court also has jurisdiction to determine disputes between states or between the federation and any state. Where any question as to the effect of the constitution arises in proceedings before another court, the Federal Court has jurisdiction to determine the question and to remit the case to the other court to be disposed of in accordance with the Federal Court's determination.

Sessions Courts
A Sessions Court has criminal jurisdiction to try all offenses that are not punishable by death. It also has jurisdiction in civil cases concerning motor vehicle accidents, landlord and tenant cases, and other cases involving amounts of up to ringgit (RM) 250,000, and it can hear cases involving higher amounts if the parties consent. However, civil disputes involving matters such as requests for specific performance, rescission of contract, injunctions, declaratory decrees, or enforcement of trusts are outside the jurisdiction of the Sessions Court.

Magistrates' Courts
First-class Magistrates' Courts hear lesser criminal offenses with penalties generally limited to up to ten years in prison or punishable by fine only. They can impose sentences of up to five years in prison, fines of up to $10,000, whipping of up to twelve strokes, or a combination thereof. A Magistrates' Court can also hear civil cases involving amounts of up to RM25,000. First-class Magistrates' Courts also hear appeals from Pengulu Courts. Second-class Magistrates' Courts hear civil cases involving amounts of up to RM3,000 and criminal cases involving offenses with penalties of up to twelve months in prison or punishable by fine only. They can impose sentences of up to six months, fines of up to RM1,000, or a combination thereof.

Pengulu's Courts
Pengulu Courts exist in West Malaysia and deal with cases involving all Asian parties who speak and understand the Malay language. They deal with civil cases in-

volving amounts of up to RM50 and minor offenses punishable by fines of up to RM25.

Juvenile Courts

Offenses committed by juveniles (between the ages of ten and eighteen) are tried in Juvenile Court, unless a capital offense is involved. The court consists of a magistrate sitting with two advisors (one of whom, where practicable, is to be a woman). The magistrate decides the case, while the advisors advise only on the sentence. A prison sentence is a last resort, the usual sentence being to send the person to an approved school.

Syariah Courts

Syariah Courts are state courts that are quite separate from the federal courts, which have no jurisdiction over any matter within the jurisdiction of the Syariah Courts. They have jurisdiction over Muslims in matters of personal and family law, such as betrothal, marriage, divorce, maintenance, guardianship, adoption, legitimacy, succession, and charitable and religious trusts. Their jurisdiction in criminal matters is limited to that provided for in federal law and is generally restricted to offenses by Muslims against Syariah law where the offense is punishable by no more than three years in prison, a fine of up to RM 5,000, whipping not exceeding six strokes, or a combination thereof.

Native Courts

In Sabah and Sarawak, customary laws are applied by Native Courts. The jurisdiction of these differs somewhat between Sabah and Sarawak, but in general it extends to situations in which both parties are natives; cases involving religious, matrimonial, or sexual matters where one party is native; and other cases in which jurisdiction is conferred by written law.

Other Courts

In addition there are courts-martial that deal with persons doing military service; they have no jurisdiction in civil law matters concerning civilians or military service personnel, and no criminal jurisdiction over civilians. The minister responsible for the Industrial Relations Act may refer disputes between employers and trade unions to an Industrial Court, and a director general of labor may be called upon to settle disputes over employee wages.

Several statutes provide for arbitration, and the Arbitration Act of 1952 sets out rules for domestic arbitration. There is also a Regional Center for Arbitration in Kuala Lumpur that provides facilities for arbitration of international commercial transactions.

Legal Structure of Malaysia Courts

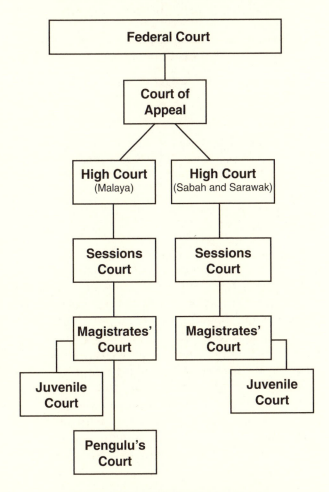

SPECIALIZED JUDICIAL BODIES

Specialized judicial bodies of note are the tribunal constituted for the removal of certain judges, the special court created for proceedings involving the king or the rulers, and the Human Rights Commission.

A special tribunal is set up wherein the prime minister represents to the king that a judge of the Federal Court, the Court of Appeal, or a High Court ought to be removed on the grounds of a breach of the code of ethics, or because of inability—from infirmity of body or mind or any other cause—to properly discharge the functions of his office. The tribunal is to consist of not less than five persons who hold or have held office as a judge of the Federal Court, the Court of Appeal, or a High Court, or persons who have held similar offices in any part of the Commonwealth. The king may, on the recommendation of the tribunal, remove the judge from office. In 1988 three judges were removed from the Supreme Court (later renamed the Federal Court) pursuant to the recommendations of two such tribunals.

When the constitutional immunity of the rulers from court proceedings was removed in 1993, it was done pursuant to a compromise with the rulers whereby proceed-

Structure of Malaysian Courts

Syariah Court Structure (Example)

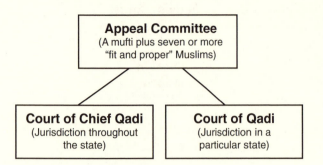

```
        ┌─────────────────────────────┐
        │     Appeal Committee        │
        │ (A mufti plus seven or more │
        │   "fit and proper" Muslims) │
        └─────────────────────────────┘
           ╱                    ╲
┌──────────────────┐   ┌──────────────────┐
│ Court of Chief   │   │  Court of Qadi   │
│ Qadi             │   │ (Jurisdiction in a│
│ (Jurisdiction    │   │  particular state)│
│ throughout       │   │                  │
│ the state)       │   │                  │
└──────────────────┘   └──────────────────┘
```

Note: Actual Syariah court structures may vary from state to state.

ings against them, or the king, would be held in a special court. The special court consists of the chief justice of the Federal Court (who presides as chairperson), the chief judges of the High Courts, and two other persons, appointed by the Conference of Rulers, who hold or have held office as a judge of the Federal Court or a High Court. The court has jurisdiction to try offenses committed in the federation by the king or a ruler, and all civil cases by or against the king or a ruler of a state.

A Human Rights Commission created in 1999 has the power to inquire into allegations of infringements of human rights and, upon finding an infringement, to refer the matter to the relevant authority with recommendations.

STAFFING

Lawyers

A person who has a bachelor of laws (or equivalent degree) from certain prescribed universities in Malaysia, Singapore, the United Kingdom, Australia, New Zealand, or Ireland, or is a barrister-at-law in England, or has passed the Certificate in Legal Practice examinations, can be admitted as an advocate and solicitor if he or she is a citizen or permanent resident, is eighteen years of age or more, is of good character, has satisfactorily served a prescribed period of study in Malaysia, and has passed (or is exempt from) the Bahasa Malaysia Qualifying Examination. In the past many lawyers had received their legal education in England, but that became less common as new law schools were created in the country.

The Judiciary

The king appoints the judges of the High Courts, the Court of Appeal, and the Federal Court. However, the king must act on the advice of the prime minister and must also consult the Conference of Rulers. Except in the case of the appointment of the chief justice of the Federal Court, the prime minister, in determining the advice to be given the king, must consult with the chief justice of the Federal Court. For an appointment to the Court of Appeal, other than the president of the Court of Appeal, the prime minister must also consult the president of the Court of Appeal. For an appointment to a High Court, the prime minister must consult the chief judge of that High Court. To be qualified for appointment, candidates must have been in the legal service for a period of ten years.

Sessions Court judges are appointed by the king upon the recommendation of the chief judge of the relevant High Court. First-class magistrates are appointed by the relevant state authority (and by the king in federal territories) on the recommendation of the relevant chief judge of the High Court. Sessions Court judges and first-class magistrates must be members of the legal service. Second-class magistrates must be fit and proper persons.

A typical core legal concept in common law jurisdictions is the independence of the judiciary. Mechanisms directed at providing a degree of judicial independence in Malaysia include security of tenure (to age sixty-five), a prohibition against the alteration of remuneration and other terms of office (including pension rights) during the tenure of a judge, and a restriction against discussion of the conduct of a judge in either house of Parliament or in a state legislature. A measure of security of tenure is provided for judges of the Federal Court, Court of Appeal, and High Court in that they can be removed only for a breach of a judicial code of ethics, or on the grounds of inability, from infirmity of body or mind or any other cause, to properly discharge the functions of his or her office—and then only upon the recommendation of a special tribunal (see "Specialized Judicial Bodies," above).

IMPACT OF LAW

The English common law and court system provide a legal infrastructure for commerce that has been successful in other economically well developed countries. At the same time, the application of customary and Syariah law in personal matters reflects local conditions and may thus serve local acceptance of the law much better than alien concepts of English law. The application of Syariah law through separate Syariah courts, but limited to Muslims in its application, provides a compromise between the importance of Islam among the Malays and the multiracial nature of Malaysian society.

Constitutional constraints on certain fundamental liberties and on the jurisdiction of courts give relatively more power to the executive branch of government than one might expect to find in other Westminster-style parliamentary systems. This may reflect so-called "Asian values," which are said to place greater weight on societal interests over individual interests than do so-called "Western values."

Legal Structure of Malaysia Courts

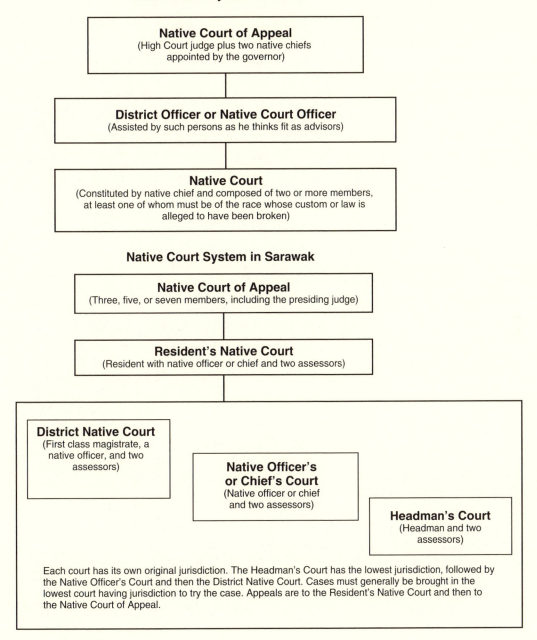

Native Court System in Sabah

Native Court of Appeal
(High Court judge plus two native chiefs
appointed by the governor)

District Officer or Native Court Officer
(Assisted by such persons as he thinks fit as advisors)

Native Court
(Constituted by native chief and composed of two or more members,
at least one of whom must be of the race whose custom or law is
alleged to have been broken)

Native Court System in Sarawak

Native Court of Appeal
(Three, five, or seven members, including the presiding judge)

Resident's Native Court
(Resident with native officer or chief and two assessors)

District Native Court
(First class magistrate, a
native officer, and two
assessors)

**Native Officer's
or Chief's Court**
(Native officer or chief
and two assessors)

Headman's Court
(Headman and two
assessors)

Each court has its own original jurisdiction. The Headman's Court has the lowest jurisdiction, followed by
the Native Officer's Court and then the District Native Court. Cases must generally be brought in the
lowest court having jurisdiction to try the case. Appeals are to the Resident's Native Court and then to
the Native Court of Appeal.

The 1957 Federal Constitution constituted a compromise between the Malays (who feared domination by the non-Malays who controlled the economy), non-Malays (who feared political domination and the risk of not being citizens in the country they had made their home), and the Malay rulers (who feared a loss of their position). Since 1957 the social dynamics of the country have changed. Malays are a much more significant part of the economy, arguably in part because of the NEP. Thus the Malays may now have economic interests more in common with those of other races. Attitudes toward the Malay rulers appear to have altered, as suggested by constitutional changes concerning the rulers in 1983, 1993, and 1995. Thus the original constitutional compromise may be less significant than it was in the past.

Mark Gillen

See also Common Law; Customary Law; Islamic Law; Legal Pluralism
References and further reading
Ahmad, Sharifah Suhana. 1999. *Malaysian Legal System.* Kuala Lumpur: Malayan Law Journal.
Crane, Cheryl, Mark Gillen, and Ted McDorman. 1998. "Par-

liamentary Supremacy in Canada, Malaysia and Singapore." Pp. 155–217 in *Asia-Pacific Legal Development.* Edited by Douglas M. Johnston and Gerry Ferguson. Vancouver: U.B.C. Press.

Current Law Journal Legal Network. www.cljlaw.com (accessed May 18, 2001).

Gillen, Mark. 1995. "The Malay Rulers' Loss of Immunity." *U.B.C. Law Review* 29: 163–197.

Gillen, Mark, and Ted McDorman. 1991. "The Removal of the Three Judges of the Supreme Court of Malaysia." *U.B.C. Law Review* 25: 171–197.

Ibrahim, Ahmad. 1992. *Towards a History of Law in Malaysia and Singapore.* Kuala Lumpur: Dewan Bahasa Dan Pustaka.

Ibrahim, Ahmad, and Ahilemah Joned. 1995. *The Malaysian Legal System.* 2d ed. Kuala Lumpur: Dewan Bahasa Dan Pustaka.

Lee, H. P. 1995. *Constitutional Conflicts in Contemporary Malaysia.* Kuala Lumpur: Oxford University Press.

Malaysian Bar Council. www.jaring.my/bar-mal/ (accessed May 9, 2001).

Malaysian Civil Service Link. mcsl.mampu.gov.my (accessed May 29, 2001).

Malaysian Judiciary. http://www.kehakiman.gov.my (accessed May 11, 2001).

Suffian, Tun Mohamed. 1989. *An Introduction to the Legal System of Malaysia.* 2d ed. Petaling Jaya: Penerbit Fajar Bakti.

Yatim, Rais. 1995. *Freedom under Executive Power in Malaysia: A Study of Executive Supremacy.* Kuala Lumpur: Endowment Sdn. Bhd.

MALDIVES

COUNTRY INFORMATION

Mala is a Sanskrit word meaning a garland. The Republic of Maldives—essentially an archipelago—is located in south Asia. Situated in the Indian Ocean, about 400 miles to the southwest of Sri Lanka, and set vertically across the equator, it comprises a group of about 1,200 low-lying coral islands clustered in double rows forming a chain. It thus derives its name from its unique geographical structure. These 1,200 islands grouped into twenty-six atolls cover an area of 298 square kilometers.

The total population of this island country is around 278,000 persons spread over 199 islands. For administrative reasons, these islands are marked into twenty units, also called atolls, and are each headed by an atoll chief *(Atholhuvarin).* Male is the capital island and houses about one-quarter of the population. Male also remains the political, administrative, and commercial center of the island nation.

Fisheries and tourism comprise the two major sectors of the Maldivian economy, with the latter being a major source of foreign exchange. Although Maldives is a popular tourist destination, it fortunately does not suffer from trafficking in women or prostitution, ills that gen-erally afflict tourist resorts elsewhere in the world. Maldives is poor in mineral resources and has limited potential in the agricultural sphere. Although Maldives has basically a planned economy, President Ghayoom's administration has since the 1980s adopted free-market-oriented policies and encouraged foreign investment. More recently, the administration has prioritized sustainable development and environmental protection.

Maldives boasts one of the highest literacy levels in the South Asian Association for Regional Cooperation (SAARC) region, especially among women. However, underemployment and unemployment of women in particular remain a problem. Social, cultural, and topographical reasons have hindered women from traveling to Male, the capital island, and taking up secondary education. This has impeded their full and active participation in the organized sectors of the economy and confined them to house or child care and traditional work areas, including fish processing, agriculture, and handicraft production.

Historical sources suggest that the islands were formed more than 2,400 years ago, and according to foreign travelogues, the islands were inhabited as early as 1900 B.C.E. However, despite occupying a strategic location in the Indian Ocean—a frequently traversed shipping zone—the island nation has had a distinctly homogeneous and very cohesive society with one culture, one language (Dhivehi), and one religion (Islam). The language Dhivehi is a dialect of Sinhala (the national language of Sri Lanka) and its script is derived from Arabic. The people of Maldives are racially homogeneous and are predominantly of Sri Lankan and Indian origin.

HISTORY

According to historical sources the people of Maldives embraced Islam in as early as 1153. Through most of its recorded and known history, Maldives has, except for a few spells, remained independent. Maldives does not share with its neighboring countries in the region—India, Pakistan, and Sri Lanka—a history of direct British colonial rule. Although by the late nineteenth century the British had established their total dominance over the whole of the Indian Ocean area, Maldives never became an actual protectorate of the British Empire and continued to enjoy autonomy in its internal affairs. Under an agreement undertaken between the Maldivian sultan and the governor of Ceylon in 1887, Maldives enjoyed the status of a protected state without actually transforming into a protectorate. The British government was in charge of only its external affairs and this too ended when Maldives achieved total independence on July 26, 1965.

Maldives is an Islamic republic. Its government is organized on the presidential model with an indirectly

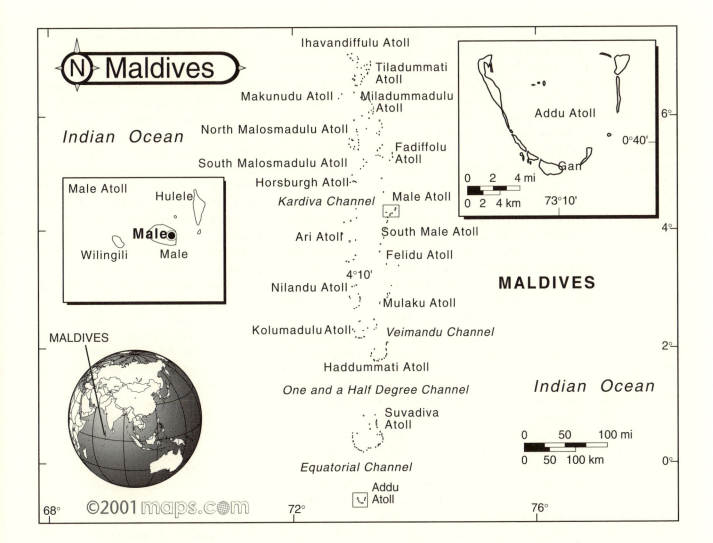

elected president as the head of state and government. It also has a parliament (Majlis) comprised of fifty members. While forty-two members of parliament are elected, the president nominates the remaining eight members. Male, the capital island, and the twenty administrative atolls have two representatives each in the Majlis. The term of office of both the president and elected members of parliament is five years. The president appoints all the important officials including judges, the attorney general, and the atoll chiefs. Hitherto, the atoll chief had a religious function of leading the Friday prayers. But today he is in charge of the atolls and functions under the overall supervision of the Ministry of Atolls Administration. This ministry is responsible for the land management and overall administration of the atolls and islands. The constitution requires the head of the state to be a Sunni male; women are barred from contesting and holding this position only. Universal adult franchise exists in Maldives and women are eligible to vote in all elections (including that of the election of the president) and to stand for election to all other public positions. Although women enjoy the right of full participation in activities at the international level, their actual participation remains nominal. Currently only three out of the fifty members in the Majlis are women, of whom two are nominated members.

LEGAL CONCEPTS

The Republic of Maldives is a Muslim nation. It has a written constitution that has been in force since January 1, 1988. The constitution designates Maldives as a "democratic republic based on the principles of Islam" and under the terms of Article 156, law includes the norms and provisions of *sharia* established by the Qur'an. As a natural corollary, the Maldivian legal system is based on the Islamic *sharia* law, although given its limited colonial heritage, the influence of English common law in some matters including commercial law is discernible. For instance, under Maldives's legal system, all persons are presumed to be innocent until proven guilty. The constitution guarantees to all citizens important civil and political rights, including the right to defend oneself with the services of a lawyer, freedom from ex post facto laws, freedom from double jeopardy, right to inviolability of residential dwellings and premises, freedom of movement, right to property, and freedoms of expression, assembly, and to form associations. All citizens have a duty imposed by the constitution to be loyal to the state and to obey the constitution and law of Maldives that necessarily includes *sharia* law.

Matters of criminal law, civil contracts, and company law are governed by laws enacted by the parliament that are in turn based on *sharia* law. However, it is the *sharia* law that exclusively governs all personal law matters such as marriage, divorce, family, child custody, and inheritance. As per the precepts of *sharia* law, men are regarded to head their households. They have a right to unilaterally divorce their spouses on any grounds or for no reasons at all and by the use of a simple verbal formula. They also have a right to practice polygamy; they have the freedom to marry up to four wives. It is true that polygamy exists in Maldives but this practice is not widespread. Although women too can divorce their spouses, their rights in this regard are sharply restricted. Unlike their male counterparts, they cannot employ the verbal formula to divorce their partners. They are required to apply to the family courts and demonstrate that they have good causes, such as ill treatment or lack of maintenance by their spouses, in order for their divorce applications to succeed. Furthermore, it is up to the discretion of the judges to decide whether women should be granted a divorce. The normal procedure followed by the family courts' judges in divorce applications is to first interview both sides in the dispute, followed by attempts to reconcile the warring partners for a period of three months, after which they arrive at a final decision. Under Maldivian Law 10/95, a women can be granted a divorce on the grounds of a prolonged absence by her husband. In cases where a man is abroad and refuses to divorce his wife, the court can grant a divorce to the woman provided a period of six months has elapsed since she filed her divorce application. In the event that a divorce is granted, any property that has been registered as joint property is divided equally between the husband and wife. Property acquired by a couple during the marriage is also, in the case of a divorce, equally divided between the partners by the court. In dividing this type of property, the court also takes into account a woman's (intangible) contributions such as child care and house care. Following a divorce, the husband is legally bound to provide for his wife's maintenance for the duration of the *idda* period. The *idda* period is equivalent to three monthly menstrual cycles for a woman who is not pregnant and in the case of a pregnant woman, until she gives birth to a child. The amount that a woman receives for child support and her maintenance from her divorced spouse is also governed by the *sharia* law. Maldives has one of the highest divorce rates in the world, with 59 percent of the total number of marriages ending in divorce.

The constitution categorically states that Islam is the state religion and that the president is the supreme authority to propagate the basic tenets of Islam. Thus there is no clear demarcation between state and religion and the head of the state is required to perform both secular and religious functions. Men and women are granted equal rights but within the framework of the Islamic *sharia* and subject to such limitations that it imposes on women. According to Maldives Law 14/72, the testimony of men and women has equal weight in all matters and circumstances except those specified in the Qur'an. For instance, in matters relating to inheritance, the testimony of two women is required to equal that of one man. Despite the limitations imposed by *sharia* in certain spheres that impede the emancipation of women, there are some progressive features that deserve mention. In Maldives, automatic citizenship is granted to children born to Maldivian mothers and foreign fathers, and women can obtain a passport and travel without the need for prior permission of their husbands or male guardians. A new Family Law Bill codifying the *sharia* law has been drafted and is due to receive the force of law very soon.

CURRENT STRUCTURE

A Magistrates' Court, popularly called Island Court, is present in each inhabited island. It is headed by a *ghazi* (magistrate) and tries criminal matters. The High Court of Maldives is situated in Male and comprises five judges, including the chief justice. It is independent of the Ministry of Justice in both financial and administrative matters and has its own budget. It decides a wide range of cases, including politically sensitive cases. Under the constitution the qualifications for a High Court judge are that he must be a Sunni Muslim and in the opinion of the president has the necessary education qualifications and the competence to discharge the duties and responsibilities of a judge. Male also has a civil court, criminal court, family court, and children's court that fall within the administrative jurisdiction and control of the Ministry of Justice. Appeals from these courts lie to the High Court of Maldives. However it is the High Court that decides to take up for hearing any case from the lower court if it is of the opinion that it is in the interests of justice to do so. At a minimum, two judges are required to preside over each sitting. There are eight other lower courts in Male that deal with theft, debt, and property cases. In criminal matters, the police department, which falls under the Ministry of Defense and National Security, is responsible for undertaking investigations. Once the investigating task is complete, the department forwards the case to the attorney general's office. The attorney general is the prosecuting authority on behalf of the state in Maldives. The president remains the final source of appeal in

Structure of Maldives Courts

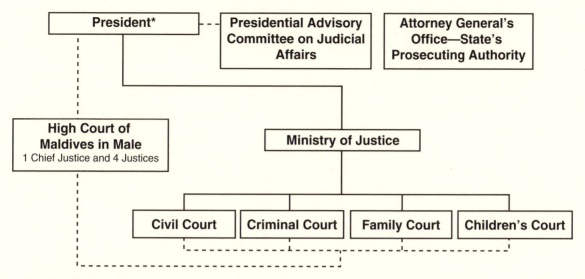

*The President exercises his appellate powers in consultation with the Presidential Advisory Committee on Judicial Affairs.

Note: Maldives is divided into twenty administrative units called atolls. Each atoll has an Islands Court. According to article 39 of the Constitution, the president is the highest authority of the administration of justice.

- - - - Lines of judicial review

all cases. He decides all appeals in consultation with the Presidential Advisory Committee on Judicial Affairs. Jury trials are nonexistent in Male. Most trials are public trials. The judges are required to be Muslims and are in office so long as they enjoy the confidence of the president. The High Court's decisions are reported in the Government Gazette.

SPECIALIZED JUDICIAL BODIES

Maldives's historical background has rendered unnecessary the establishment of specialized judicial bodies such as the Truth and Reconciliation Commission in South Africa. Maldives is a United Nations member state and has ratified two significant international treaties. They are the Convention on the Rights of the Child and the Convention on the Elimination of All Forms of Discrimination, although it has entered significant reservations to the latter. It has not accepted the jurisdiction of the International Court of Justice. Although there are no specific human rights–oriented groups in the island nation, mention must be made of Fashaan, a nongovernmental organization that has been active in espousing the cause of women's emancipation in Maldives and urging the government to ease the legal barriers that impact women's emancipation

LEGAL PROFESSION

In Maldives, although there are no disparities in the enrollment numbers of male and female students up to grade ten, a smaller number of women candidates go in for secondary education. Maldives has no university and therefore students are compelled to go abroad for tertiary studies. Although the government provides scholarships for this purpose, few women apply for them. Generally speaking, the legal profession is not a very popular one in Maldives. A large proportion of students have a career in science and technology as their first option, followed by a career in commerce, with a stint in social sciences and law being the last choice. In order to be eligible to study law, students need to complete their A levels (equivalent to grade twelve). The Institute of Sharia and Law and the Institute of Islamic Studies are located in Male, where the students can pursue their studies. The law program in Maldives is for three years on the successful completion of which students obtain their first degree in law and are eligible to practice law.

Very few women opt for programs in law and consequently the legal profession in Male is a male-dominated one. The Ministry of Justice is responsible for the regulation and administration of the legal profession. As of November 29, 2000, Male had 108 lawyers in total. Law students from Maldives who opt to go abroad generally choose English-speaking countries such as Canada, England, India, and Sri Lanka for higher studies. For instance, the present attorney general has a doctoral degree from Canada and the dean of the law institute in Male has pursued higher legal studies in England.

IMPACT

Maldives is an Islamic republic wherein the powerful influence of *sharia* law encompasses the entire governmental structure, legal edifice, education system, and indeed impacts the very way of life of the people, especially women, in the island nation. Furthermore, as per the constitution the president is both the supreme authority to propagate the tenets of Islam and the highest authority for administering justice. The judges hold office during his pleasure. Thus, Maldives clearly does not have an independent judiciary. In this scenario it is arguable that the judiciary is potentially a weak institution to make a positive impact on any matters, including interpretation of laws and/or legal reform. Women have a subordinate role in society and any measures for achieving their total emancipation in accordance with Maldives's international obligations and international standards is clearly linked to reform of *sharia* law. And the initiative to achieve that can only emanate from the president, the people's Majlis, and to a limited extent from civil society.

Vijayashri Sripati

See also Commercial Law (International Aspects); Family Law; Government Legal Departments; International Court of Justice; Juvenile Justice; Legal Education; Probate/Succession Law; Prosecuting Authorities; Qadi (Qazi) Courts

References and further reading

Ellis, Royston, and Gemunu Amarasinghe. 1995. *Guide to Maldives.* Chalfort, St. Peter, England: Bradt.
Initial Reports of States Parties Submitted by States Parties under Article 18 of the Convention on the Elimination of All Forms of Discrimination against Women: Maldives. January 28, 1999. CEDAW/C/MDV/I.
Maloney, Clarence. 1980. *People of the Maldive Islands.* Bombay: Orient Longman.
The President's Office, Republic of Maldives, http://www.presidencymaldives.gov.mv./v2/body.phtml (accessed August 15, 2001).
Robinson, Francis, ed. 1989. *The Cambridge Encyclopedia of India, Pakistan, Bangladesh, Sri Lanka, Nepal, Bhutan and the Maldives.* Cambridge: Cambridge University Press.

MALI

GENERAL INFORMATION

Located in the midst of West Africa, Mali has served as a connection between North Africa and sub-Saharan Africa. Sitting in the midst of the Sahara Desert, Mali stretches over 450,000 square miles. Its more than ten million people are divided among several tribal groups. Bordered by seven countries, it is a mix of the Islamic north and the tropical south of Africa. Mali has its longest border to the east and north, that with the Islamic nation of Mauritania. Directly to the north of Mali sits Algeria, a country fighting an Islamic insurgency and suf-

fering from political instability. Directly to the west is the Niger, while to the south and west is Burkina Faso, a country with which Mali fought a border war in 1983. To the south, Mali has shorter borders with the Côte d'Ivoire, Guinea, and Senegal.

Mali is divided between the arid and desert north and the more tropical south, where much of the population lives. The northern reaches of the country along the Algerian and Mauritanian borders are flat and barren, with the occasional hilly region. The main geographic feature of this portion of Mali is the Valle du Tilemsi, a valley running from near the Algerian border southward to the River Niger. There are no rivers or waterways in the north, which is traversed only by ancient trails used for centuries by Arab traders.

In the south, the River Niger serves as the main geographic feature and the boon to the economy. Stretching from the Niger border and flowing west then south through Mali, the river supports much of the agriculture of the country and sustains much of the urban life in Mali. In addition to the Niger, several smaller rivers run through the southern reaches. These include the Bani, the Bagoe, and the Baoule. In the western portion of the country, bordering Guinea and Senegal, hills rise up, with two rivers, the Bafing and the Babule, which run north to south.

Much of the population and commercial activity in the country are located along the Niger, with the country's largest and oldest cities sitting on its banks. On the eastern reaches of the river, near the country of Niger, the city of Gao, an ancient trading center and city of West African empires, has approximately sixty-five thousand residents. Moving west along the Niger and at the northernmost point in Mali sits the ancient and mysterious city of Tombouctou, or Timbuktu. This city no longer dominates Mali, being one of its smallest cities, with a population under forty thousand.

As the Niger turns south it runs past the cities of Mopti and Segou. Finally, as the Niger prepares to enter Guinea, it passes by the largest urban area of Mali, composed of more than one million people, or 10 percent of the country's population. Bamako is the capital and main economic center of Mali. Its status is aided by the easy navigability of the Niger, allowing for rapid movement of goods through the midsection of the country. The northern reaches of Mali are isolated by their distance from the Niger.

Development projects along the Niger and other rivers have produced other waterways, including a series of lakes. These include Lakes Fagaibine, Niangay, and Debo. Many of these projects were completed during the first decades of Mali independence, when a socialist-oriented government attempted to isolate the country from its neighbors and the West. These policies, along with the

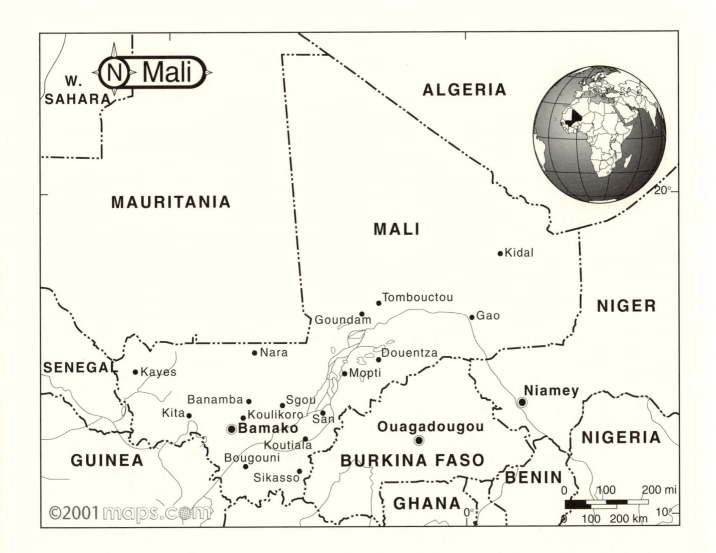

wide and empty expanses, prevented the country from advancing economically. By the turn of the twentieth century Mali was one of the ten poorest countries in the world, with a per capita income of less than three hundred dollars a year.

Agriculture is the main source of income, with more than 70 percent of the population growing their own food. The population struggled with starvation after independence, and exports were limited. The rise of a democratic government in the early 1990s led to a free market system being developed and new exports, particularly gold, being shipped from the country. While it is unlikely that Mali will ever regain its position as a major transit point for trade in West Africa, new government policies will likely improve the livelihood of a people who fight the encroaching Sahara Desert while sitting at the crossroads of the commercially valuable Niger River.

HISTORY

Through the centuries of civilization in western Africa, Mali has served as a transit point for goods and invading armies from such empires as Ghana and the Songhai.

Mali's own Malinka Empire existed along the northern reaches of the Niger River from the twelfth through the fourteenth centuries. That empire was conquered by the Songhai Empire during the fifteenth century. But even with that change in power, the city of Timbuktu remained a major assembly and stopping point for traders bringing goods from the western coast and hoping to sell them throughout western and central Africa. Timbuktu was used by salt traders who used camels to transport their wares from the Sahara to the Niger River, whence they could be sent along the Niger either south to the empires near the Atlantic coast or into central Africa. The caravans of the Sahara earned Timbuktu its romantic reputation as an exotic and isolated city in the midst of Africa.

Several centuries would pass before those Europeans telling the stories would visit Timbuktu and remain safely in the city. Permanent settlements were begun by the French, who were building a colonial empire across the African continent stretching from the British Sudan to the Atlantic coast in present-day Mauritania. The French named the Mali region the Soudan, after the British colony in East Africa. The French colonials ruled with a less than strict hand, mainly introducing French law and language into the region and drafting citizens of West Africa into the French Army during the two world wars. Trade and commerce continued, though the French did put an end to the open slave trade. French control of much of West Africa made it easier for traders to move through the region, causing many areas to become more economically interdependent. At the same time, French West Africa served as one of the few territories controlled by the Free French during World War II.

But that period also showed the French weakness, and with the Fourth Republic being established after the war, many West African countries sought a measure of independence from France. Political agitation occurred in Mali, as it did in its neighbors. The start of the French Fifth Republic in 1958 witnessed a change in the status of West Africa. Many of the territories were granted greater independence, and by 1960 many countries were breaking away from the French. Mali was one, however, that attempted to maintain the economic benefits of a West Africa without borders. It did so by joining a confederation with Senegal, its neighbor to the west. The confederation was to allow the two countries to maintain open trade while having separate political systems. The Senegalese, though, thought that they were the senior partners, and in August 1960 the confederation was broken. On September 22, 1960, Mali declared full independence from France.

Having earned its independence from Europe, however, the Mali government proceeded to shackle itself to socialist economic policies that separated the country from France and its trade and impoverished ordinary citizens. The political and economic situation went from bad to worse in 1968 with a military coup. More than twenty years of political dictatorship and economic mismanagement followed, earning Mali the status of a pauper nation dependent upon aid from the Soviet Union and occasionally the International Monetary Fund. Human rights and constitutional government were ignored during a brief war with neighboring Burkina Faso in 1983, which only deepened the misery. The collapse of the Soviet Union and belief in socialism offered a ray of hope. The rise of free market economies in the countries south of Mali heightened public dissatisfaction with the government and led to a series of revolts and demonstrations. Another military coup followed, leading to a new constitution and elections in 1992. Presidential and legislative elections were conducted with multiple parties competing for seats. The new democratic government put into place free market policies that allowed for foreign investment and for regular citizens to own property and advance their lives. Through the 1990s political and economic progress in

the country moved slowly forward, and while a single party grew to dominate the national government, several parties took control of local and regional governments. Mali has renewed ties with the United States, seeking U.S. investment in the suddenly active gold mines. It has also traded more with France, hoping to utilize long dormant ties with the former colonial power. In doing so, Mali has seen living standards begin to creep forward while political institutions begin to create a democratic society.

LEGAL CONCEPTS

Mali's legal system has undergone three periods of growth. During its precolonial period, the law in the region was tribally or community based. Rules governing society and relationships involving property and politics were handed down orally from generation to generation. Few of the procedures found in Western courts were used in tribal courts. Chiefs were responsible for handing down rulings on the basis of testimony in hearings. Trial by ordeal was also used, with a defendant in a criminal case undergoing a form of torture or a dangerous act to determine his guilt or innocence.

The arrival of the French saw many of these tribal traditions swept away and replaced by the fixed code of France. Written law was introduced throughout West Africa and remained as the sole legal code in many of the countries upon their gaining independence. Criminal, civil, and commercial law was dictated by the traditions of the Napoleonic Code and provided some stability in countries in which political instability had reigned. Mali was one such country.

The coming of independence marked the beginning of the third period of growth. The new Mali government began to rewrite some of the laws governing the old French territory. These laws enforced socialist ideals by refusing to protect private property and allowing for the confiscation of that property. Yet political instability prevented a complete replacement of all French law. That allowed most citizens of Mali to be protected at the local level by judges familiar with the French code and willing to enforce it in a neutral fashion. The lack of a written Mali code, particularly in civil and commercial matters, ensured that Western ideals were advanced in court rulings. Unfortunately many of the political protections and legal protections in criminal trials found in the 1962 Mali Constitution and the Napoleonic Code were ignored by the central government. Military rather than civilian courts became the favored forum for trying those who challenged the military government, and the rule of law was weakly defended.

The overthrow of the military government in 1991 was followed by the writing of a new constitution. The 1992 version protected the same civil liberties and political rights found in most Western constitutions. The difference between the 1992 and 1962 constitutions was that the later version included an independent judiciary that could enforce those rights against government violations. National and local officials were forced to permit criticism of the government, ownership of property, and regular trial procedures before imprisoning someone. In addition, the French legal code remained in force unless specifically overruled by Mali law. Hence the new Mali regime had a legal system in place and needed only to build the institutions to enforce those laws.

STRUCTURE

Because of the introduction of French legal ideas into most West African colonies, when the countries became independent they adopted much of the French judicial structure. The Mali judicial system is one that has close ties to the French approach to the law. The court structure divides the power to interpret the law from the power to determine whether a law is unconstitutional. A Constitutional Court is granted the judicial review power to determine whether a law is void because it violates a specific part of the constitution.

The justices on the Constitutional Court hear cases at the request of the president of Mali, from members of the Mali legislature or lower court judges facing a constitutional issue in a pending case. The Constitutional Court does not hear appeals from ordinary citizens.

In addition to the Constitutional Court, Mali has a regular court system with three levels of courts. The courts of First Instance are the national trial courts. These courts are spread throughout each of Mali's eight regions and Bamako, the capital. Single judges hear criminal, civil, and administrative cases. They are able only to apply and interpret the law in the case before them. Their decisions can be appealed to the Mali Appeals Court. Located in Bamako, the Appeals Court has multiple judges sitting in court hearing and again deciding whether the lower court had misapplied the law. The Appeals Court cannot rule on the constitutionality of the law.

The highest court in the regular judicial system is the Mali Supreme Court. The Supreme Court hears appeals from the lower Appeals Courts. It rules on the legality of the lower court decision. One of its major rulings came in the mid-1990s when it overturned the legislative elections because of mismanagement. New elections were called, and the court oversaw that these were run within the confines of the law. The Supreme Court has the final say in a legal case unless a constitutional issue has been raised by a litigant in the lower court. The Supreme Court has no authority over decisions handed down by the Constitutional Court, and that court cannot overrule the legal interpretation of the Supreme Court.

Legal Structure of Mali Courts

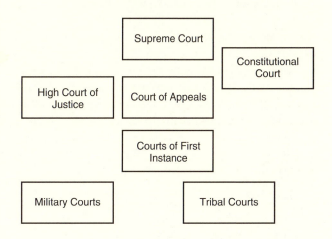

SPECIALIZED COURTS

Mali has a dual system of courts. The main legal system is run by the government and includes trial and appellate courts. Along with that system is the more informal tribal court system, which functions throughout the country. These tribal courts operate at the local level and differ among the different tribal groups living in Mali. They were once the sole means of settling legal disputes in Mali but were replaced by the French courts and law. In modern Mali, these tribal courts hear most minor cases involving civil disputes and family disagreements. Because these disputes are based on tradition handed down through the tribes, the Mali government has allowed the courts to operate without much interference. In addition, the tribal courts recognize the ethnic differences among the tribes, and by respecting those differences, the modern Mali government has maintained a level of peace among them.

The tribal courts operate at the village level, with local chiefs or elders serving as judges. The methods of hearing and deciding disputes differ among the groups, but most hear cases within a public place and with each side presenting its arguments. Tribal courts operate on the theory of maintaining harmony within a small community. Hence individual rights are less likely to be respected and clear-cut victories for one litigant over another are less likely to be handed down by the chief. Appeals are limited because most of the village court decisions deal with small civil claims. Tribal courts, though, do allow citizens to ignore them and have their case heard in a regular government court.

Another specialized court operates under government authority. The High Court of Justice has the specific function of trying high executive officials for treason. The High Court replaced military courts, which conducted treason trials in the past in secret hearings. The High Court is composed of a mix of Supreme Court justices and members of the legislature. The court has only the power to remove officials, not prosecute them for their misdeeds.

Another set of specialized courts are the military courts. Prior to the 1992 Constitution, with a military dictatorship in control, military courts heard criminal cases involving those accused of political crimes. The military courts were more likely to find a defendant guilty and hand down a harsh sentence. With the 1992 Constitution, however, military courts were returned to their normal place in adjudicating cases involving active-duty members of the Mali military.

SELECTION AND STAFFING

The Mali judicial system has suffered from a lack of qualified lawyers and judges. The extreme poverty in the country and the political instability of the government have limited the opportunities for most Mali students to pursue a career in law. The main university in the capital city of Bomako provides limited legal training to the few students who can attend. Those with sufficient means can attend other West African universities in countries such as Ghana and Sierra Leone. An even smaller number of students obtain legal training in French or U.S. universities.

With a limited number of properly trained lawyers, the appointment of judges has focused on political qualifications. The previous military government sought judges who would be politically loyal to the government, while the new democratic government focuses on membership in the ruling party.

The Mali Ministry of Justice, working with the Mali president, appoints judges and is granted the power to remove them. The requirements for selection to the Supreme Court and the Court of Appeals are prior judicial experience, while appointment to the lower trial courts requires a judge to have a law degree.

The tribal courts are populated by political leaders either at the local or the tribal level. These judges are chosen based upon political knowledge, leadership abilities, and familiarity with the law. There is little formal training of tribal judges, with traditions being passed down orally from one judge to another.

IMPACT

The new Mali democracy has been successful in constructing institutions that respect most constitutional limitations on their power. The democratic freedoms enjoyed, though, are based on the self-restraint of the government, rather than a fully functioning judiciary. The single critical ruling in favor of democratic values made by the judiciary was the Supreme Court's ruling calling for new parliamentary elections because of fraud and mismanagement in the original elections. The independence of the courts is limited by the lack of well-trained and experienced judges and attorneys, and the ability of the government to influence judges through appointment and removal.

The powers granted to the courts under the constitution are broad and intended to make judges a partner in governing the country. The Constitutional Court has the power of judicial review in being able to strike down legislation that is considered a violation of the constitution. The regular court system operates under the French model, restricting itself to interpreting and applying the law and determining if it was properly applied by a lower court.

Although judicial institutions exist and the constitutional protections of political rights and liberties from governmental intrusion are on the books, the Mali court system struggles to aid in the development of a democratic society. Economic problems and less than a decade of democracy in the country present obstacles to political and legal stability. But with the new 1992 Constitution, Mali appears to be moving in the right direction for the first time in its forty-year history.

Douglas Clouatre

See also Burkina Faso; Civil Law; France; Indigenous and Folk Legal Systems; Judicial Review

References and further reading
Bengin, R. James, John Staatz, and David Robinson, eds. 2000. *Democracy and Development in Mali.* Lansing: Michigan State University.
Gardner, Brian. 1988. *The Quest for Timbuktu.* New York: Harcourt Brace.
Hopkins, Nicholas. 1982. *Popular Government in an African Town: Kita, Mali.* Chicago: University of Chicago Press.
Jenkins, Mark. 1997. *To Timbuktu.* New York: Morrow.
Kiss, Agi. 2001. *The Road through Mali.* Westport, CT: Westview.
McIntosh, Roderick. 1998. *The Peoples of the Middle Niger.* New York: Blackwell.
McKissack, Pat, Patricia McKissack, and Fredrik McKissack. 1995. *The Royal Kingdoms of Ghana, Mali and Songhai.* New York: Henry Holt.
Treach, Richard. 1982. *Forbidden Sands: A Search in the Sands.* Chicago: Academy.

MALTA

COUNTRY INFORMATION

The Republic of Malta is located in the center of the Mediterranean Sea, just south of Sicily and about 300 kilometers east of Tunisia. Its territory of roughly 316 square kilometers (about one-tenth the size of Rhode Island) consists of the largest island, the Island of Malta (246 square kilometers), and the smaller islands of Gozo (67 square kilometers) and Comino (2.59 square kilo-

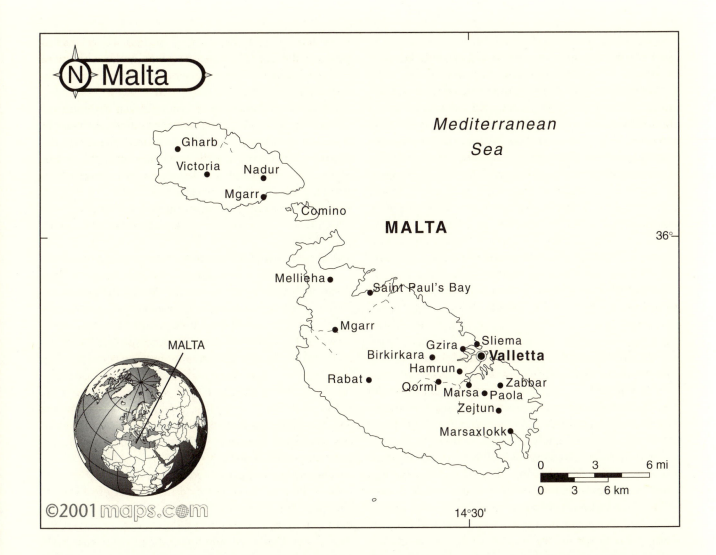

meters), as well as tiny outlying islets. Although the country is centrally administered, it is divided into three regions comprising sixty-seven local councils and thirteen electoral districts. The Maltese islands are hilly, and their coastline is heavily indented. Malta's ethnic heritage is diverse, reflecting the nation's history at the crossroads of competing empires, and combines Arab, Sicilian, French, Spanish, Italian, and English elements. Ninety percent of the 394,583 Maltese (an estimate as of July 2001) live in towns, concentrated in the capital, Valetta (7,172), Rabat, and Sliema. The principal languages are Maltese and English. More than 90 percent of the Maltese follow Malta's state religion, Roman Catholicism.

Despite the fact that Malta is one of the world's most densely populated areas, with very few natural resources, a limited water supply, and no domestic energy sources, the island benefits from a favorable geographic location, mild climate, and a well-educated, productive labor force. The per capita gross domestic product (GDP) is $14,300, and unemployment stands at 4.5 percent (2000 estimate). As of 1999, GDP composition by sector was 25.5 percent industry, 3 percent agriculture, and 71.7 percent services. The country's industrial output includes clothing, semiconductors, shipbuilding and repair, construction, and textiles. Chief agricultural crops are potatoes, grapes, cauliflower, and tomatoes. Current major export goods include clothing, machinery, and transport equipment. A major source of income is tourism. In preparation for membership in the European Union (EU), Malta has gradually deregulated its industrial sector, modernized agricultural production, and improved its environmental policies. Significant problems remain, however, especially in the areas of intellectual and industrial property rights, as well as infrastructure and public administration. Nonetheless, Malta is among the best-prepared candidates for EU membership.

The Republic of Malta is a constitutional parliamentary republic within the Commonwealth. President Guido de Marco has been head of state since 1999. Since the last national elections in September 1998, Prime Minister Edward Fenech-Adami from the Nationalist Party, which favors Malta's entry into the European Union, has headed a majority government (as of December 2001).

HISTORY

The historical record for what is now the Republic of Malta dates back to the first millennium B.C.E., when first the Phoenicians and then the Carthaginians and Romans used the islands as trading and military posts because their strategic location in the center of the Mediterranean made control over their territory highly desirable. From 870 to 1090 C.E., the Maltese Islands were under Arab rule, which left its imprint on Maltese life, customs, and language, followed by four centuries of rapidly changing domination by Normans, Germans, Sicilians, and French.

By a decree dated March 23, 1530, the Holy Roman Emperor Charles V ceded the Islands of Malta and Gozo to the Sovereign Military Order of St. John, whose knights heavily fortified the islands in subsequent centuries, in recognition of their enormous strategic value, and provided the new cities with an adequate water supply, gardens, a hospital, law courts, a theater, and a library. For the first time, serious studies in the Maltese language, hitherto a spoken language only, were undertaken.

The rule of the knights ended in 1798, when, with the arrival of the French under Napoléon Bonaparte, the islands fell under French rule and, after the Napoleonic Wars, officially became part of the British Empire in 1814. Until 1849, when the island was granted a constitution providing for limited elections, the Maltese had no say in the administration of their homeland. In subsequent decades, however, the situation improved gradually as the British reorganized the law courts, granted freedom of the press, opened primary schools in every village, and expanded the transport system. Rising discontent after World War I—in which Malta had staunchly supported the British and served as a hospital and army base—over unemployment, the political situation, and bread prices led to riots against the British government.

In 1921 Malta was granted the Amery-Milner Constitution, which institutionalized Malta's autonomy over internal affairs and established male suffrage and a bicameral legislature. After a period of political-religious conflict between the government and the church, gubernatorial autocracy was reimposed, which lasted throughout World War II, during which the Maltese heroically defended their islands and withstood prolonged German attacks.

After the war, a dual system of government was reintroduced, guaranteeing universal adult suffrage and Maltese autonomy over internal matters. After prolonged disagreements over the islands' political future, the elected Maltese government entered into negotiations with Britain over the independence of the archipelago. In a referendum, the Maltese voted for independence, and the Republic of Malta became a sovereign state on September 21, 1964.

Under the 1964 Constitution, Malta became a parliamentary democracy within the Commonwealth, with Queen Elizabeth II as the pro-forma sovereign of Malta. In 1974 the constitution was revised and vested executive authority in a Maltese president. Almost immediately after independence, Malta became an active participant in international affairs. In 1987, Malta declared its neutrality; it started membership negotiations with the European Union in 1990. The last decade has witnessed aggressive modernization programs by the government, especially in the areas of agriculture, industry, and infrastructure, in order to meet strict EU admission criteria. The elections of 1998 returned the right-of-center Nationalist Party under Fenech-Adami to power.

The Maltese political system is dominated by the Nationalist Party and the socialist Malta Labour Party, which have alternated in the government of the island republic since the middle of the last century. The Constitution of 1964 (revised in 1974) is the supreme law of the land and establishes the separation of powers. The legislative power is vested in a unicameral legislature, the House of Representatives. The sixty-five to sixty-nine delegates, depending on the margin of victory by the winning party, are elected by popular vote from thirteen electoral districts for five-year terms on the basis of proportional representation.

The executive is composed of the president of the Republic, the prime minister, and the cabinet of ministers. The president is elected for a term of five years and appoints the prime minister as well as the members of the cabinet upon recommendation of the prime minister. He or she may dissolve the House of Representatives and, with the consent of two-thirds of the representatives, appoints judges.

The judiciary consists of a four-level system of civil and criminal courts. The Constitutional Court stands at the apex as the highest court of appeal. Ranked below are the Court of Appeal and the Court of Criminal Appeal; the Civil Court: First and Second Halls; the Criminal Court; the Courts of Magistrates; the Gozo Courts; the Small Claims Tribunal; and the Juvenile Court. Specialized judicial and semijudicial bodies are the National Audit Office and the ombudsman.

LEGAL CONCEPTS

The Maltese legal system combines elements of Roman civil law; the Napoleonic Codes, especially in civil law; and English common law, particularly in criminal procedure, certain areas of criminal law, public law, and merchant shipping. It firmly establishes the rule of law; the separation of powers; an independent judiciary; and comprehensive guarantees of civil, political, economic, and social rights. Human rights reports show government compliance with almost all constitutional provisions.

Legal Structure of Malta Courts

Constitutional Court (Highest Court of Appeal in Constitutional and Human Rights Matters)	

Court of Appeal (Civil, Family, Commercial, Administrative Jurisdiction)	Court of Criminal Appeal (Criminal Jurisdiction)

Civil Court: First and Second Hall (Civil, Family, Administrative, Commercial Jurisdiction)	Criminal Court (Criminal Jurisdiction)

Courts of Magistrates for Gozo (Inferior and Superior Civil and Commercial Jurisdiction)	Courts of Magistrates (Minor Civil and Criminal Jurisdiction)

Juvenile Court	Small Claims Tribunal

Few attempts by officials to influence the judicial process are known, although corruption remains a general problem. Structural difficulties, such as lack of funding, understaffing, and a substantial backlog in civil cases, need to be resolved. Sporadic incidents of ethnic discrimination against the country's small Muslim minority and gender discrimination remain a problem.

The Constitution of Malta is the supreme law of the land. All domestic laws must conform to constitutional provisions. International treaties, once ratified, become part of domestic law and are enforceable through domestic courts. As a member of the United Nations, the Council of Europe, and the Council on Security and Cooperation in Europe (CSCE) and as a candidate for EU membership, Malta has accepted compulsory jurisdiction of the International Court of Justice (ICJ), with reservations, and the European Court of Human Rights, recognizing the right to individual petition. It is a party to a large number of international treaties, including the Universal Declaration on Human Rights, the International Covenant on Civil and Political Rights, the European Convention on Human Rights, the Biodiversity Convention, and the Nuclear Test Ban Treaty.

The Maltese Constitution guarantees and protects all basic civil and political rights, among others, the right to life, equality, nondiscrimination, due process, privacy, fair remuneration, pay equity, and social security, as well as freedom of conscience and worship, expression, assembly, association, and movement. Anyone who claims that his or her rights have been violated by an official organ may request a review of that particular decision by a court or the ombudsman (see below). Every convicted person has the right to appeal a court ruling, and every accused enjoys the presumption of innocence and has the right to assistance of counsel. Every accused who does not understand or speak English or Maltese has the right to an interpreter.

CURRENT STRUCTURE

The judicial structure of the country is laid down in Chapter VIII of the Constitution of the Republic of Malta. The Constitution provides for the independence of courts as well as the independence and impartiality of judges (Article 39). All judges are bound by the law, and only courts are allowed to decide on the guilt of an accused person and the penalty for criminal and civil offenses (Article 39). The judiciary of the Republic of Malta consists of the Constitutional Court; the Court of Appeal; the Court of Criminal Appeal; the Criminal Court; the Civil Court: First and Second Halls; the Courts of Magistrates; the Gozo Courts; the Juvenile Court; and the Small Claims Tribunal.

Article 95 establishes a Constitutional Court, composed of three judges, as the highest court of appeals and the final arbiter of the constitutionality of laws, official acts, and alleged violations of human rights. It has original jurisdiction over questions of elections and election law.

The Court of Appeal hears appeals from special tribunals, the First Hall of the Civil Court, and the Court of Magistrates in civil matters, whereas the Court of Criminal Appeal, consisting of three judges, hears appeals from the Criminal Court and from judgments delivered by the Court of Magistrates as a Court of Criminal Judicature.

The Criminal Court is composed of one judge who sits with a jury of nine persons to try offenses exceeding the competence of the Courts of Magistrates as Courts of Criminal Judicature. Its counterpart, the First Hall of the Civil Court, hears all cases of a civil or commercial nature exceeding the jurisdiction of the Courts of Magistrates and all claims of violations of human rights. The Second Hall hears cases involving family law and the confirmation of testamentary executors.

The Courts of Magistrates, or so-called inferior courts, are presided over by a single magistrate and hear both minor civil and criminal cases, specifically claims not exceeding 1,000 Maltese liri and offenses punishable with up to six months' imprisonment. The Court of Magistrates for Gozo has inferior and superior civil and commercial jurisdiction in cases comparable to those heard by the Maltese First Hall of the Civil Court.

Established by an act of Parliament, the Small Claims Tribunal, overseen by an adjudicator such as a lawyer, handles money claims of less than 100 Maltese Liri and decides on the basis of law and equity. The proceedings are generally informal. Minor infringements of the law, such as minor traffic offenses and littering, have been depenalized and are heard by appointed commissioners of justice, even in the absence of the accused.

SPECIALIZED JUDICIAL BODIES
Malta has established a small number of specialized and semijudicial bodies.

The Juvenile Court consists of a single magistrate and hears charges against persons under the age of sixteen years. The court is assisted by two persons (a quasi-jury), one of whom is always a woman, but is not bound by their advice.

The ombudsman is an independent officer of parliament appointed by the president, with the approval of two-thirds of all the members in the House of Representatives. Charged with enhancing the protection of citizens against improper treatment by state officials, he or she is empowered to investigate complaints against the police, government authorities—with the exception of elected officials, the judiciary, and several other specialized bodies—statutory boards, and local councils. Although the ombudsman has no power to sanction the offending authorities, only to make recommendations for a resolution of the complaint and to make the case public, almost all recommendations have so far been accepted and the complaint resolved to everyone's satisfaction. The current office holder, Joseph Sammut, was elected in 1996.

The National Audit Office is an independent controlling body entrusted with overseeing the management of state property, state finances, and the fulfillment of the state budget. The Land Arbitration Board strives to resolve land disputes.

STAFFING
All sixteen judges and the chief justice, as well as the country's sixteen magistrates, are appointed by the president of the republic for unlimited terms, with the advice of the prime minister and the consent of the House of Representatives. The minimum qualifications for a judicial appointment are that the person be a citizen of Malta and have practiced law for a minimum of seven years (for magistrates) or twelve years (for superior court judges). The mandatory retirement age is sixty-five years for superior court judges and sixty years for magistrates. Both superior court justices and magistrates are independent and enjoy immunity from prosecution for criminal offenses for the time of their tenure. A justice or magistrate may be removed from office by the president only "on the ground of proved inability to perform the functions of his or her office or proved misbehavior" (Article 97), if two-thirds of all of the members of the House of Representatives agree.

The University of Malta's Faculty of Laws offers legal training in civil, criminal, commercial, comparative, international, and European law, and confers bachelor's, master's, and doctoral degrees. Malta's approximately 550 lawyers—"advocates"—are qualified to practice after a six-year course of study and one year of practical training, usually completed concurrently with the final year of studies, after which lawyers may set up their own practices. Most Maltese law firms are small and practice in all fields, although shipping, finance, and European law are increasingly important.

IMPACT
Malta's institutions are democratic and function smoothly. Civil, political, economic, social, and cultural rights are generally respected, although some concerns remain about the efficiency of public administration, the implementation of the country's policies with respect to the treatment of asylum seekers, and gender equality. Domestic violence, in particular, remains a problem. There has been significant progress, in particular with the adoption of the new Asylum Act, but efforts are still needed with respect to data protection, immigration, visa policy, and judicial cooperation. Also, special attention will have to be devoted to the backlog of civil law cases. Furthermore, the enforcement of intellectual and industrial property rights has to be significantly reinforced to make the country attractive for large-scale investment.

Since its application for membership in the European Union, almost all government policies have been directed toward reforming Malta's economy and infrastructure, which were marred by inefficiency and corruption, to meet EU membership criteria. Although the country lags behind some of its competitors for membership in conforming to EU standards, especially in agriculture, environmental protection, and regional policy, it has been judged by the European Commission, as late as November 2000, to be among the best-placed candidates to meet the strict European Union standards.

Sylvia G. Maier

See also Common Law; Napoleonic Code; United Kingdom
References and further reading
Attard, Joseph. 1988. *Britain and Malta: The Story of an Era.* Valletta, Malta: PEG.
Council of Europe. 1995. *Administrative, Civil and Penal Aspects, Including the Role of the Judiciary, in the Fight against Corruption.* Proceedings, Valletta, Malta, June 14–15, 1994.
Frendo, Henry. 1999. *The Origins of Maltese Statehood—A Case Study of Decolonisation in the Mediterranean.* Valletta, Malta: PEG.
———, ed. 1993. *Maltese Political Development 1798–1964: Selected Readings.* Valletta, Malta: Ministry of Education and Human Resources.
Frendo, Henry, and Oliver Friggieri, eds. 1994. *Malta: Culture and Identity.* Valletta, Malta: Ministry of Youth and the Arts.
Hull, Geoffrey. 1993. *The Malta Language Question: A Case History in Cultural Imperialism.* Valletta, Malta: Said International.

Mula, Charles. 2000. *The Princes of Malta: The Grand Masters of the Order of St. John in Malta, 1530–1798.* Valletta, Malta: PEG.

Official Website of the Government of Malta. http://www.magnet.mt (accessed December 14, 2001).

Sant, Alfred. 1995. *Malta's European Challenge.* Malta: SKS, Information Department, Malta Labour Party.

MANITOBA

Manitoba is the fifth-largest of ten provinces in the Canadian federal system and has roughly 3 percent of the national population. As in other provinces, Manitoba's population is largely urban and heavily concentrated within the provincial capital of Winnipeg.

JURISDICTION

A federal-provincial division of powers obtains in Manitoba, as in the other provinces. With regard to criminal law, the Canadian constitution in practice is a little complicated. Criminal law (most of which is found in the Criminal Code of Canada) is reserved to the exclusive jurisdiction of the Parliament of Canada. As the courts have defined it, criminal law is a prohibition plus a penalty directed to an appropriate public purpose and the federal power has been treated as free standing, which means that by making certain activities criminal the national government can regulate matters that are otherwise within provincial jurisdiction. However, the provincial government can also create prohibitions-plus-penalties (technically "offenses" rather than "crimes"), although these must be clearly ancillary to the province's substantive heads of power and they cannot infringe on federal powers. These offenses often overlap with, or even duplicate, federal criminal laws, but the Supreme Court's very relaxed approach to paramountcy has prevented this from being a problem in practice. Both federal "crimes" and provincial "offenses" are handled by the same courts; the Canadian system is a single rather than a double pyramid. Civil law is largely a matter of provincial legislative jurisdiction—contracts, personal property, landlord-and-tenant, labor relations, and so on—although the federal Parliament enjoys jurisdiction over many labor and commercial issues relating to the essential elements of railway and airplane transportation or radio (and, more recently, telephone) communication.

Most of the judicial pyramid is under provincial jurisdiction. The provincial legislature establishes and maintains the Provincial Courts and sets the procedure for civil matters, although the federal Parliament has authority over criminal procedure. The question of the prosecution power is curiously clouded; until the 1970s, provincial Crown prosecutors exercised prosecutorial discretion under federal criminal law statutes, but a string of Supreme Court of Canada decisions cast this situation in doubt before settling on a de facto concurrent power. Thus, *most* such prosecutions are conducted by provincial employees, but *some* are carried out by federal Crown prosecutors. The policing power is almost exclusively in the hands of the provinces (sometimes delegated to cities or municipalities), although this is complicated by the fact that eight provinces have contracted with the federal police force (the Royal Canadian Mounted Police) to act as a provincial police force; only Ontario and Quebec operate their own provincial police.

THE ABORIGINAL JUSTICE ISSUE

The biggest challenge facing the Manitoba justice system is the aboriginal issue. Aboriginal peoples (the currently accepted term in Canadian usage is *First Nations*) constitute a larger percentage of the population in Manitoba than in any other province in Canada—just over 12 percent. About 60 percent of these individuals are "status Indians" (under the terms of the Canadian Constitution and the relevant federal legislation), which is to say that they are descendants of charter aboriginal communities that have entered into agreements that create specific rights and entitlements, usually including reserve land. However, aboriginal reserves in Manitoba (as in the rest of Canada) face major problems, with high levels of poverty and unemployment, a heavy reliance on government assistance, and a variety of social problems, including alcoholism, drug addiction, and suicide. As a result, many status Indians live off the reserve, typically in large urban centers (which in Manitoba means Winnipeg). Because they tend to lack the education, the skills, and the experience that would allow them to integrate successfully into the broader society, they live in marginal and often miserable circumstances. The entirely predictable consequence is that they are dramatically overrepresented among the ranks of criminal defendants and prison inmates—comprising at least 50 percent of that population, more than four times their share of the general population. This situation has been aggravated by a lack of cultural understanding and sometimes by overtly discriminatory behavior as well. A major Aboriginal Justice Inquiry was established in 1988, and its 1991 report led to the creation, also in 1991, of the Aboriginal Justice Implementation Commission, which is still in operation.

THE LEGAL PROFESSION

The legal profession in Canada is defined on a provincial basis. Provincial law societies are the self-governing entities that control access to the profession and police its practices. The Law Society of Manitoba derives its authority from the Law Society Act. Its central body is made up of the sixteen benchers who are elected by the profession on the basis of six different electoral districts, one of which (Winnipeg) elects ten of the benchers.

There are also four lay benchers, a faculty bencher (currently, the dean of the law school), and a student bencher, as well as the Manitoba and Canadian justice ministers, who are ex officio benchers.

To be admitted to the practice of law, one must have a law degree from a recognized university. In practice, most Manitoba lawyers receive their degrees from the province's only law school at the University of Manitoba. They must then serve two years of articles and pass a bar exam set by the Law Society of Manitoba. Only members of that organization may practice law in the province, and the society has the power to suspend or disbar members who are found to have violated the rules of the profession.

As of March 31, 2000, there were 1,720 active members of the Manitoba bar, working in 146 law firms. About a quarter of them were women, and more than 80 percent of them worked within the city of Winnipeg. About half of them practiced at least some criminal law, including the 50 Crown prosecutors and 30 staff lawyers with Legal Aid Manitoba.

THE COURTS

The Canadian court system in general, of which the Manitoba court system is a fairly standard example, has two curious features. The first is that there is a single hierarchy of trial and appeal courts to deal with both federal and provincial laws, rather than two separate hierarchies. The second is that the judges in some provincial courts are appointed by the federal government, a uniquely Canadian device that has historically caused far fewer practical problems than one might have anticipated.

The lowest level of the Manitoba court system is the Provincial Court of Manitoba. This "purely provincial" court was established, in Manitoba as in the other Canadian provinces, during the 1970s, replacing the former Magistrates' Court but differing from it in several significant ways. First, although there were a number of lay magistrates, only lawyers in good standing with at least five years of experience can become provincial judges. Second, the Provincial Court, unlike the Magistrates' Court, is a court of record, such that appeals are conducted on the record and not by trial de novo. Third, unlike the Magistrates' Court, the Provincial Court has a chief judge, with general administrative and governmental liaison responsibilities. Fourth, there now exists a Judicial Council for Provincial Judges, including judicial members and a bencher from the law society, that sits as a discipline committee; without its recommendation, a provincial judge cannot be removed from office.

Judges of the Provincial Court are appointed and paid by the provincial government (after screening by the nonpartisan Judicial Council), retiring at age seventy. They serve "on good behavior" (the corresponding term for magistrates was "at pleasure") and can only be removed for cause after a formal inquiry process dominated by judicial members. As of 2001, there were thirty-nine provincial judges, including a chief judge, and the workload of the Provincial Court is primarily in the area of criminal law. There are six different locations in which provincial judges are resident, but in addition, they operate fifty different circuits to serve dozens of nonurban locations.

The jurisdiction of the Provincial Court includes:

- Offenses under provincial legislation and municipal bylaws
- Summary conviction ("misdemeanor") offenses under federal legislation, defined as offenses for which the maximum penalty is six months in prison and/or a fine of $2,000
- Preliminary hearings for indictable offenses ("felonies") under federal legislation
- Trials for indictable offenses in which the accused has chosen trial by provincial judge
- Trials for young offenders accused of any federal or provincial offense (unless successful application has been made to remove the matter to adult court)
- Concurrent jurisdiction with the Court of Queen's Bench on child protection and family matters except for divorce

Provincial judges sit alone and without a jury. The fact that the accused can (and often does) elect trial by provincial judge for serious indictable offenses means that it is incorrect to think of provincial judges as dealing only with minor matters; in fact, this is less true of Canada's system than of any other court system in the world.

The next level of courts in Manitoba is the Court of Queen's Bench. This is one of the "Provincial Superior Courts" in Section 96 of the Constitution Act 1867. It is unusual because, though it is a provincial court (and therefore established and maintained by the provincial legislature under the authority of Section 92.14), its judges are appointed and paid by the government of Canada, retiring at age seventy. Each province has a Section 96 trial court; the terminology for this court varies, but *Queen's Bench* is the most common designation.

As a general rule, "purely provincial" lower-court judges are rarely elevated to the Provincial Superior Court. The major explanation is political—the appointments are made by two different levels of government. It is also sometimes suggested that the distinction between the two sets of courts is best described in terms of specialization (criminal and family matters for the "purely provincial" court, mainly civil matters for Provincial Superior Court), although some would still maintain that the distinction is one of merit (the better lawyers wait for and would not settle for less than the higher court).

There are currently thirty-three Queen's Bench justices, who hold regular hearings in eleven different locations. The Provincial Superior Trial Courts are courts of general jurisdiction with extensive responsibilities covering both civil and criminal cases. On criminal matters, they hear indictable offenses (that is, felonies) if the accused has not elected trial by the lower "purely provincial" court; this can include jury trials, which are more common than they were in the 1970s. On civil matters, which constitute a majority of the caseload, they deal with major lawsuits (those over the small claims limit). In Manitoba, unlike in many other provinces, small claims (that is, lawsuits involving less than $7,500) are under the jurisdiction of the Court of Queen's Bench; they are initially heard and decided by a hearing officer, with appeal lying to the Court of Queen's Bench. The court also has an extensive family law jurisdiction, exclusive in most of the province and concurrent with the Provincial Court in some part of the province on some matters.

The Provincial Superior Courts are the longest-standing courts in Canada, the core around which the other courts have been constructed. The case law still acknowledges them as the courts with the power to rule on the constitutionality of statutes and bylaws, the legality of administrative tribunals, and the determination of violation and remedy under the Canadian Charter of Rights and Freedoms. They are also the courts of appeal for decisions rendered by the Provincial Court (except for indictable offenses, for which appeal lies directly to the Court of Appeal); ever since the establishment of the Provincial Court, these are appeals "on the record" rather than by trial de novo, and they constitute only a small part of the Queen's Bench caseload. Unlike the lower court, the Court of Queen's Bench is a generalist bench, and the typical judge will, over any reasonable period of time, preside over trials involving all types of cases.

In the past, one would have explained the central position of the Provincial Superior Trial Courts by the fact that they were the only courts to enjoy a constitutionally entrenched judicial independence. Section 99 of the Constitution Act of 1867 stipulates that they hold office "on good behavior" and are removable only by an action of both the Senate and the House of Commons (something that has only happened once in Canadian history). However, judicial independence now enjoys a firmer constitutional status. For one thing, a guarantee of an "independent and impartial tribunal" is part of the Canadian Charter of Rights and Freedoms; for another, recent Supreme Court decisions have suggested judicial independence is a "constitutive constitutional principle" that is exemplified rather than constituted by Section 99 and the charter. Either way, it is now less accurate than before—and therefore less relevant to relative status—to suggest that any one set of courts enjoys a more firmly established degree of judicial independence than the others.

Legal Structure of Manitoba Courts

Court of Appeal of Manitoba

Court of Queen's Bench of Manitoba

Hearing Officers
(Small Claims)

Provincial Court of Manitoba
Criminal Division   Family Division
Youth Division

At the highest level of the Manitoba court system is the Court of Appeal of Manitoba. In constitutional terms, this court is also a Provincial Superior Court, which means that the court is established and maintained by the province but its judges are appointed and paid by the government of Canada. The Court of Appeal currently consists of seven judges, five men and two women; there are also two supernumerary justices of the court—that is, appellate court judges who are approaching the age of retirement and have opted to serve only part-time. The court conducts its hearings only in Winnipeg. Like the other Canadian Courts of Appeal, the Manitoba court has chosen to deal with the growing caseload by sitting in panels—normally three and rarely, for unusually serious matters, five—with a regular, monthly rotation of panels.

Like the other provincial appellate courts, the Manitoba Court of Appeal is required by its governing legislation to receive "reference questions" from the provincial government. In other words, it issues "advisory opinions" responding to hypothetical questions framed by the provincial government that do not arise out of concrete cases by the normal appeal process. These questions are often narrowly technical, but they can be politically freighted. The most significant example was a 1987 reference on whether the sections of the federal criminal code dealing with prostitution violated the charter's protection of the right to freedom of expression. The example demonstrates the blending of federal and provincial responsibilities—the provincial government asked the federally appointed judges of a provincial court about the constitutionality of a piece of federal legislation.

Based on such criteria as Supreme Court reversal rates or citation frequencies, the Manitoba Court of Appeal ranks toward the middle of the provincial appellate courts.

It has an unusual distinction: between the wars, its chief justice, John Prendergast, was pressured into resigning on the grounds that the provincial legal society felt that a string of reversals at the hands of the Supreme Court had severely compromised the appellate court's credibility. At the other extreme, probably the most highly regarded chief justice ever to serve in Manitoba was Samuel Freedman, who was on the court in the 1970s.

The pinnacle of the Manitoba court system, the Manitoba Court of Appeal, is an intermediate appellate court within the Canadian system, with its decisions subject to appeal to the Supreme Court of Canada. This is true of *all* Court of Appeal decisions: Under the Canadian Constitution, the Supreme Court is a "General Court of Appeal for Canada," and there is no Canadian counterpart to the U.S. principle that a state Supreme Court is the final court on matters of purely state law. The convention of Supreme Court appointments in Canada is that most Supreme Court judges are elevated from provincial Courts of Appeal, with a "prairie provinces" seat rotating between Alberta, Saskatchewan, and Manitoba. The most recent Manitoban to hold that seat was Brian Dickson, who was appointed to the Supreme Court in 1973 and served as chief justice from 1984 to 1990; he had previously served on the Manitoba Court of Appeal for six years.

Peter McCormick

See also Alberta; British Columbia; Canada; Federalism; Judicial Review; New Brunswick; Newfoundland and Labrador; Northern Territories of Canada; Nova Scotia; Ontario; Prince Edward Island; Quebec; Saskatchewan
References and further reading
"The Aboriginal Justice Implementation Commission." http://www.ajic.mb.ca/ (accessed January 9, 2002).
"Court Processes: Manitoba's Court System." http://www.gov.mb.ca/justice/court/court.html (accessed January 9, 2002).
Gall, Gerald. 1995. *The Canadian Legal System.* Toronto: Carswell.
"The Law Society of Manitoba." http://www.lawsociety.mb.ca/ (accessed January 9, 2002).
McCormick, Peter. 1994. *Canada's Courts.* Toronto: James Lorimer.
McCormick, Peter, and Ian Greene. 1990. *Judges and Judging: Inside the Canadian Judicial System.* Toronto: James Lorimer.
Russell, Peter. 1987. *The Judiciary in Canada: The Third Branch of Government.* Toronto: McGraw Hill–Ryerson.

MARSHALL ISLANDS

COUNTRY INFORMATION

The Republic of the Marshall Islands (RMI) lies in the north-central Pacific Ocean. The country is made up of twenty-nine atolls and five low-lying islands, which lie in two parallel archipelagoes: the western Ralik (sunset) and eastern Ratak (sunrise) chains. RMI shares maritime boundaries with Kiribati (south), Nauru (southwest), the Federated States of Micronesia (east), and the Commonwealth of the Northern Mariana Islands (northeast). Its land area of some 170 square kilometers consists mainly of low coral limestone. RMI also claims a 12-mile territorial sea, a 24-mile contiguous zone, and a 200-mile exclusive economic zone, which extend over 1.2 million square kilometers. The population, estimated at 60,000 people, is mainly indigenous Micronesians. RMI faces the problem of overpopulation and about 48 percent of the population is under the age of fifteen. The literacy rate is high, reportedly at 93 percent. The country's gross domestic product (GDP) of $105 million is supplemented annually by $65 million in U.S. aid. The GDP per capita is $1,670. Most of the population lives in the two main urban centers: the capital, Majuro (19,664), and Ebeye (9,311). English is the official language, but two major Marshallese dialects from the Malayo-Polynesian family and Japanese are also spoken. The climate is generally hot and humid yearlong, with the wet season from May to November. The average temperature is about 81° F to 82° F.

HISTORY

The original inhabitants of the RMI were Micronesians who arrived about 2000 B.C.E. to 500 B.C.E. Thereafter, the islands had long and colorful associations with Europeans, then Japanese and Americans. The country owes its name to the British naval captain William Marshall, who sailed through the area in 1788. Although the Treaty of Tordesillas (1494) ceded the Marshall Islands to Spain, it was Germany that annexed the islands and declared a protectorate in 1886. In 1920 the League of Nations granted a mandate over the islands to Japan, which had captured the islands from Germany in 1914. When Japan withdrew from the league in 1934, it retained possession of the islands and fortified them as part of its own preparations for the next war. After the Allied occupation in 1944, the United States gained effective control and from 1946 to 1962 the U.S. maintained an active nuclear-testing program on some of the islands in the Marshalls group. In 1947 the United Nations granted the United States a security trust over the Marshall Islands and five other Micronesian entities, which became known as the Trust Territory of the Pacific Islands (TTPI). The TTPI entities were referred to as *districts*.

After four decades under U.S. administration, the road to self-determination began in 1965 with the formation of the Congress of Micronesia, with representatives from all of the districts. When the Congress declined to approve a greater Micronesian political entity, the Marshall Islands set up its own Political Status Com-

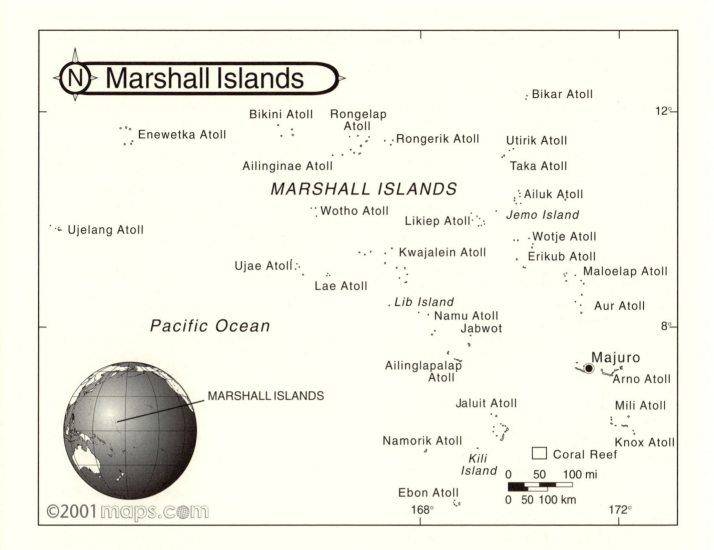

mission to negotiate separately with the U.S. The formation of the government took place in 1979, and in 1983 voters and the Nitijela (the lower house of the bicameral legislature) in the RMI approved the Compact of Free Association with the United States. In 1990, the UN Security Council terminated the RMI's trusteeship status and in 1991 RMI joined the United Nations. The main issue at independence was compensation arising from the effects of the former U.S. nuclear-testing program. Attempts by U.S. authorities to clean up the affected islands have not been altogether successful and compensation claims continue as a result of that program. In response, the U.S. established a trust fund for affected islanders. Under the 1983 Compact of Free Association, a further trust fund of $150 million was set up to provide $270 million in compensation payments over the fifteen-year life of the compact, which expires in 2001. Apart from providing for compensation, the fund also established a Nuclear Claims Tribunal, which, from 1991 to 1995, awarded $43.2 million to 1,196 claimants for health conditions presumed to be caused by radiation. The tribunal projects that it will have $100 million in personal injury

claims by 2001, when the compact ends, but it was only granted $45 million.

The legal system of the RMI is essentially modeled on the U.S. legal tradition. After World War II the basic structure of government in broad terms was set out under the 1947 Trusteeship Agreement between the United Nations and the United States. Two categories of legislation were also enacted locally. The first was orders by the Trust Territory administering authorities and laws passed by the Congress of Micronesia. These were published as the Trust Territory Code in 1952 and 1970 with supplements. A further publication of the Trust Territory Code in 1980 was not adopted as positive law. The second category of laws was passed by the Marshall Islands District Congress (renamed in 1968 as Nitijela, "gathering of wise or powerful people") between 1958 and 1978. These were published as the Marshall Islands District Laws 1975–1978. Case laws were also an important source of laws. These included American common law, as expressed in the Restatements of the Common Law, and decisions of the High Court of the trust territory as published in the Reports of the Trust Territory of the Pacific

Islands for the period from 1951 to 1988. According to the High Court "decisions of Trust Territory courts do not have stare decisis . . . effect in the courts of Marshall Islands" today (*Langijota v. Alex* 1990).

From independence, the basic laws of the country are the Constitution of 1978 and the Compact of Free Association 1983. On July 12, 1978, the Marshall Islands electorate voted against the adoption of a Micronesian constitution. Instead, the Constitutional Convention (convened in 1977) adopted the draft of the constitution on December 21, 1978, which was approved by a referendum on March 1, 1979, and entered into force on May 1 of the same year. Although the Marshallese electorate and the Nitijela approved the compact in September 1983, it only entered into force on October 21, 1986, after U.S. congressional approval. Its fifteen-year duration expired in 2001, so negotiations for its renewal are in progress. The RMI's international legal capacity is constrained by the terms of the compact, which limits the capacity of the RMI to enter into foreign relations (section 123) and grants the government of the United States full authority and responsibility for security and defense of the islands (section 311). The main source of laws of the country today are legislation that consists of applicable preindependence laws enacted by the Congress of Micronesia, Marshall Islands District laws, and postindependence laws passed by the Nitijela. All these are compiled and codified in the Marshall Islands Revised Code 1988, which consist of two volumes. As well, subsidiary legislation and the common law are continued in force as part of the existing law by the constitution. Judgments of the Supreme Court and the High Court of the Marshall Islands undoubtedly are published in the Marshall Islands Law Reports.

Customary law is an integral part of the lives of Marshall Islanders, especially those who live in the rural areas. The constitution and legislation provide for the continued existence of customary laws. The constitution defines customary law to mean "any custom having the force of law in the Marshall Islands; and includes any Act declaring the customary law" (art. 14, sec. 1). Although the constitution does not say how custom is to acquire the force of law, apart from declarations by the Nitijela, the Supreme Court has stated that the courts can also declare customary law. The Nitijela has enacted several pieces of legislation, especially in connection with customary rights of succession to chiefly titles. Although the constitution is the supreme law, it also says that its provisions relating to fundamental rights shall not invalidate "the customary law or any traditional practice concerning land tenure or any related matter." This is a reflection of the significance of the islanders' customary land tenure systems. Another interesting feature on maintenance of customary law is the creation of the Council of Iroij, which is made up of traditional chiefs. A Customary Law Commission was set up in 1989 to study, collect, and publish materials on customary law in order to assist the Nitijela in its constitutional task of codifying customary law.

LEGAL CONCEPTS

The constitution is the supreme law and any other law that is contrary to it is void to that extent. That document upholds the separation of powers between executive, legislative, and judicial branches of government. It also provides for a bill of rights, which catalogs basic civil and political rights such as freedom of thought, speech, religion and association, due process and fair trial, freedom from slavery and servitude, freedom from cruel and unusual punishment, freedom from discrimination, rights to health, education, and legal services, guarantees of private property and just compensation, and so on. Breaches of constitutional rights are actionable before courts of law.

Among other former TTPI states, the RMI is unique in that its political system incorporates both the presidential and Westminster models. It has a bicameral system made up of the Council of Iroij (upper house) and the Nitijela. The former is made up of twelve paramount chiefs (Iroijlaplap) who are nominated to represent their respective islands. The council, whose functions are merely advisory, is empowered to review legislation affecting customary law or any traditional practice including land tenure and to express its opinion on matters of national concern. The Nitijela is comprised of thirty-three senators who are elected by universal suffrage of voters eighteen years or older and represent twenty-four electoral districts. Members serve four-year terms: the last elections were held in November 1999. The speaker presides over the meetings of the Nitijela and the clerk is in charge of the administrative business of the legislature.

The Nitijela is the main law-making body of the country. Legislative bills are usually passed by the majority of the members after three readings. After its passage, a bill becomes law after being signed by the clerk and speaker. Special legislative procedures exist for some matters such as compensation related to the U.S. nuclear-testing program, qualifications of judges, and amendments to the constitution. Constitutional amendments for certain specified matters can only be done if the proposed amendment has been submitted to the people by a constitutional convention and has been approved by two-thirds of the votes validly cast in a referendum. The constitution also guarantees a system of local government, for purposes of which twenty-four local atoll governments have been set up. These have power to make ordinances over their geographical areas but such laws must not contradict national laws or executive instruments.

The executive government is vested in the cabinet, which now is made up of eleven members who are selected by the president from among the members of Nitijela. The president is elected by the Nitijela for a four-year term and heads both the state and the government. The current president, Kessai Hesa Note, assumed office on January 3, 2000. Amata Kabua, a traditional paramount chief in his own right, became president after independence and remained in office through several elections. There have been no political parties since independence, but two informal groups emerged after the 1991 general elections. These are the Kabua Party (Amata Kabua) and United Democratic Party, which is associated with the current speaker of the Nitijela, Litokwa Tomeing.

The Constitution of the RMI creates various offices to assist in the administration of the country. A chief secretary who is also the chief administrative and advisory officer of the government heads the Public Service. The attorney general is in charge of the administration of justice, gives legal advice on matters referred to him by the cabinet, conducts legal proceedings on behalf of the republic, and ensures that the laws are faithfully executed. The secretary of finance oversees the financial affairs of the country. A three-member Public Service Commission (PSC) is the employing authority for the public service and has the general oversight and control of its organization and management. The Judicial Services Commission (JSC) is made up of the chief justice of the High Court (chairman), the attorney general, and another member. It is responsible for making recommendations to the cabinet for the qualifications and appointment of judges of the High Court and Supreme Court and for making appointments and removal of judges of subordinate courts.

CURRENT COURT SYSTEM STRUCTURE

The judicial system of the RMI is modeled on the U.S. system with modifications to take into account local circumstances. These consist of the Supreme Court, the High Court, the Traditional Rights Court, district court, and community court. The Supreme Court and the High Court are the superior courts whose members are appointed by the cabinet with approval of the Nitijela. Judges who are citizens of the Marshall Islands hold office during good behavior until they reach seventy-two years of age, whereas expatriate judges serve on two-year contracts. The Supreme Court is the final court of record and is comprised of the chief justice and two associate justices. It hears appeals from the High Court and deals with questions concerning the interpretation of the constitution as referred to it by the High Court. The decision of the majority prevails in particular cases. The High Court consists of the chief justice and associate justices. It has original unlimited jurisdiction over civil and criminal matters. As well, it deals with specified matters (probate, admiralty, and maritime) and has appellate jurisdiction over subordinate courts as well as power to review actions of government agencies. The High Court normally consists of a single judge, except that a three-person bench will be convened to deal with any case that involves either a substantial question of constitutional law or any other matter of public importance. Any person who is accused of committing an offense punishable by three or more years in prison is entitled to trial by a jury of four persons.

The Traditional Rights Court (TRC) is made up of panels of three or more judges who are selected by the JSC so as to include a fair representation of all classes of customary land-owning units. The jurisdiction of the court is limited to the determination of questions relating to titles or to land rights or to other legal interests depending wholly or partly on customary law and traditional practice. Cases usually come before it by way of referrals from other courts. Although substantial weight is given to the TRC's determinations, they are not binding. The district court is made up of a presiding judge and associate justices who are appointed by the JSC. It has original concurrent jurisdiction with the High Court over civil matters whose value does not exceed $5,000 and criminal matters in which the penalty does not exceed a fine of $2,000 or imprisonment for a term of three years or both. The district court also hears appeals from the community court. The community court operates in each local government area. It is made up of a presiding judge and associate justices who are appointed by the JSC. It has original concurrent jurisdiction with the High Court over civil matters whose value does not exceed $100 and over criminal matters in which the penalty does not exceed a fine of $200 or imprisonment for a term of six months or both. Special mechanisms have been set up parallel to the judicial system for dealing with claims, whether by the government or by private citizens, for loss or damage arising out of the U.S. nuclear-testing program. Initial claims are made to a one-member Special Tribunal and on appeal to a three-member Nuclear Claims Tribunal. Appeals from decisions of this latter body go to the Supreme Court.

Despite the constitutional guarantee for judicial independence, the relationship between the judicial and other branches of government have often been uneasy. Since 1989, many local and expatriate chief justices have resigned their posts because of perceived interference by politicians through legislative or administrative means. For example, the U.S. Department of State's *Country Report on Human Rights Practices for 1998* reported that the president and his cabinet ministers publicly criticized the foreign High Court chief justice harshly, on the government radio station, following the judge's declaration concerning a constitutional interpretation with which the government disagreed.

Legal Structure of Marshall Islands Courts

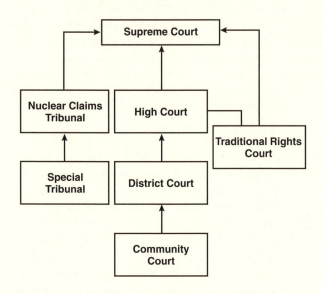

There is no law school in the Marshall Islands. Many of the local lawyers trained in the U.S. and a few others have obtained their legal qualifications in neighboring Pacific island countries such as Australia, New Zealand, Papua New Guinea and, since 1995, the University of South Pacific Law School at Vanuatu. Prior admission to the bar is necessary in order to practice law in the Marshall Islands. The legal qualifications to practice are similar to those for the U.S. The Marshall Islands has about twenty-one practicing lawyers and a bar association exists locally.

IMPACT OF LAW

The system of constitutional democracy that the Marshall Islanders have chosen for themselves implies a recognition of the paramount place of the rule of law. The political and judicial mechanisms were borrowed from Western institutions but these have been modified in order to suit local circumstances. This is necessary because the society is changing and the country has to co-exist in the modern internal community where, with the emergence of market integration, the rule of law is seen as essential for attracting investment and conducting trade. The main difficulty now is reconciling traditional norms and institutions with the modern system.

Yolisaguyau Tom'tavala

See also Common Law; Constitutionalism; Customary Law; Judicial Independence; Legal Pluralism

References and further reading
CIA, "The World Factbook 2000—Marshall Islands," http://www.odci.gov/cia/publications/factbook/geos/rm.html (accessed January 18, 2001).
Embassy of the Republic of the Marshall Islands to the United States of America, "RMI Online—The Internet Guide to the Republic of the Marshall Islands," http://www.rmiembassyus.org/ (accessed January 18, 2001).
Hezel, Francis X. 1995. *Strangers in Their Own Land.* Pacific Islands Monograph Series 13. Honolulu: University of Hawai'i Press.
Johnston, Giff. 1991. "A Case of Justice versus Tradition?" *Islands Business* (April): 16–18.
Jonge, Alice de. 1993. *The Constitution of the Marshall Islands: Its Drafting and Current Operations.* The University of New South Wales Centre for Pacific Studies, Pacific Studies Monograph No. 8. Sydney: Centre for Pacific Studies.
Zorn, Jean. 1993. "The Republic of the Marshall Islands." Pp. 100–139 in *South Pacific Islands Legal Systems.* Edited by Michael A. Ntumy. Honolulu: University of Hawai'i Press.

MARXIST JURISPRUDENCE

POLITICAL THEORY OF LAW

Marxism may have paid the price for its success in achieving its declared objective of transcending the division between theory and politics. Its adoption as the official theory of the communist movement early in the twentieth century was to lead to claims that the policies pursued by the Soviet state incorporated Marxist theory. One result was that the legal system developed in the Soviet Union was claimed to embody the Marxist theory of law. Whether such legal systems were in any sense Marxist is complicated by the fact that Karl Marx himself bequeathed no elaborated theory of law. Marx never dedicated sustained attention to law; hence any account of his views on law must be constructed from the scattered but extensive fragments. These cannot simply be stitched together to form a composite theory because his remarks were made in many different contexts (Cain and Hunt 1979).

The legal system of the Soviet Union was primarily a product of making permanent the "dictatorship of the proletariat." For Marx, this phrase never expressed anything more than the limited contention that after seizing political power through revolutionary means, the new workers' state would have to secure that power by dictatorial means. Rendered permanent in Soviet law under Joseph Stalin, it produced a highly centralized and repressive legal system.

There were many other aspects of Marx's formulations on law that do not fit into the mold that was constructed in the Soviet Union. In order to avoid any suggestion that these elements can be fitted together to make a coherent whole, they are here treated as a set of discrete themes. It should further be noted that a certain caution should be exercised in using a terms such as *Marxist jurisprudence;* it is probably more accurate to suggest that Marx's views are closer to a sociology of law than to a jurisprudential theory.

Marx's writings on law exhibit a number of general themes:

1. Law is superstructural.
2. Law and state are closely connected; law exhibits only a relative autonomy from the state.
3. Law gives effect to the prevailing economic class relations.
4. The content and procedures of law manifest the interests of the dominant class(es).
5. Law is ideological.
6. Legal rights obscure the primacy of socioeconomic interests.

LAW AND LEGAL SUPERSTRUCTURE

To locate the place of law within society Marx drew on the imagery of "base" and "superstructure" that distinguished between the "economic structure of society," which forms the base, and "a legal and political superstructure . . . to which correspond definite forms of social consciousness." Law is assigned to the "superstructure," which "reflects" the base. Thus it is the economic structure that determines the character and content of the law.

The notion of base-superstructure relies on an analogy involving an imagery of society as a building in which the economy provides the foundation for the edifice of legal, political, social, and cultural institutions. The base-superstructure metaphor runs the risk of committing Marxism to an "economic determinism," in that it attributes causal priority to the economic base. There was a "weaker" version of this idea of causation, in which the "base" is pictured as prescribing the boundaries or limits for the different elements of the superstructure. This softer version of "determination" was most clearly stated by Friedrich Engels in his "Letter to Bloch":

> According to the materialist conception of history, the ultimately determining factor in history is the production and reproduction of real life. Neither Marx nor I have ever asserted more than this. . . . The economic situation is the basis, but the . . . juridical forms, and especially the reflections of all these real struggles in the brains of the participants in political, legal, philosophical theories exercise their influence upon the course of the historical struggles and in many cases determine their form in particular. (Engels 1975, 394–395; emphasis in original)

This version of the determination thesis is often referred to as the "theory of relative autonomy" of law. Thus law, though superstructural, can have causal effects by reacting back upon the economic base, which still retains causal priority, but only "in the last instance."

LAW AND STATE

Marx's account of law emphasizes the intimate connection between law and the state. Law is first and foremost a mechanism of state power giving effect to the state's monopoly on the legitimate means of violence. It may also exhibit a significant degree of autonomy and separation from the state. The state is both within and outside the law. The core of the modern democratic state lies in the varieties of the idea of a state based on law (*Rechtsstaat*), which are epitomized by constitutional doctrines of the rule of law, through which law and state mutually prescribe their fields of competence.

It is within the law-state relationship that the important question of the relationship between law and coercion arises. Marx stressed the repressive character of law in order to redress the blindness of much liberal jurisprudence that had played down the role of legal repression. But in reacting against the omissions of liberal theory, Marxists came perilously close to simply reversing liberalism's error by equating law with repression. The really difficult problem is to grasp the way in which repression is present in the course of the "normal" operation of modern legal systems. The repressive role of criminal law is most readily apparent, but a wider range of legal procedures are coercive and where they are deployed systematically set up patterns of repression.

ECONOMIC RELATIONS AND THE LAW

Law plays a key role in the production and reproduction of capitalist economic relations. A number of key legal relations form part of the conditions of existence for capitalism, without which it could not function. Most important, law provides and guarantees a regime of property and of contractual exchange. The expansion of the forms of capital and their circulation require such a regime that protects the multiple forms in which capital circulates as legal interests.

Legal relations have distinctive effects, the most important of which is the extent to which legal relations actually constitute economic relations. The most significant example is the formation of corporations with limited liability; these are legal creations in that it is the ability to confer a legal status that limits the liability of participants and thus makes the corporation a viable vehicle for the cooperation of diverse capitals.

It is important to stress the complex interactions that exist between legal and economic relations. Legal doctrines and processes must make provision for the interrelations of capital through commercial law, insurance, banking, and other financial services. For Marx, these mechanisms function as background conditions that constitute the framework within which economic relations are conducted. Law also provides the central conceptual apparatus of property rights, contract, and other legal relations that play the double role of both constituting a coherent framework for economic activity and providing important components of the ideological conceptions of rights, duties, and responsibilities that are persistent elements in the public discourses of political and economic life.

LAW AND CLASS RELATIONS

Law facilitates the reproduction of class relations by sustaining and legitimating patterns of social inequality and subordination. The aggregate effects of law work to the systematic disadvantage of the least advantaged social classes. In addition, the content and procedures of law constitute an arena of struggle within which the relative positions of social classes change over time. These two theses are neither incompatible nor contradictory; they are both true at one and the same time. The first thesis that law disadvantages the disadvantaged operates at all levels of legal processes. Substantive inequalities that disadvantage the working class and other subordinate social categories are embedded in the content of legal rules. But law is also an arena of struggle. Social interests are translated into rights claims, and some of these are protected as legal rights. Conflicting interests are fought out in terms of opposing rights claims. Such conflicts are not equally protected within the legal process. Not all claims are so readily capable of translation into the form of individual rights; the result is that those interests congruent with existing rights categories are more likely to succeed than claims not matching these characteristics. Claims not grounded in individual or property claims fare less well before law courts than those that are consistent with the dominant model of capitalist legal rights.

IDEOLOGY AS LAW AND LAW AS IDEOLOGY

Law is ideological in a double sense; law itself is an ideological product and is itself a major carrier of ideology. Law is created within an existing ideological field in which the values associated with social relations are continuously asserted, debated, and struggled over. Law is a major bearer of ideological messages that, because of the general legitimacy accorded to law, serve to reinforce and legitimate the ideology that it carries.

Ideology is not falsity or false consciousness; nor is it a direct expression of economic interests. Rather ideology involves competing frames of reference through which people think and act. The dominant ideology is the prevailing influence that forms the common sense of the period and thus appears natural, normal, and right. The key project of every dominant ideology is to cement together the social formation under the leadership of the dominant class. The content of legal rules embody ideological messages. Law as an ideological process provides authoritative legitimation of the norms that it articulates and

enforces. Modern democratic law involves a legitimacy that is impersonal, as well as formal legitimation of social relations through which "law" becomes increasingly equated with "reason." The legitimation of social order appeals to law simply because it is law and as such provides the grounds for the obligations of obedience imposed upon citizens.

THE CRITIQUE OF RIGHTS

In his earliest writings, Marx addressed issues within contemporary German legal philosophy. The abiding legacy of this engagement was Marx's unqualified critique of rights. The rights of human beings could be nothing other than the ahistorical rights of the isolated and abstract legal subject. He retained this position; as late as 1875 he condemned talk of "equal rights" in the draft program of the German Social Democrats as "obsolete verbal rubbish." His alternative insisted that political claims be advanced and struggled for as interests rather than as rights.

Much of the subsequent history of Marxist theory of law has engaged with the problem of rights. In one direction, the early Soviet jurist Evgeny Pashukanis (1980) sought to elucidate the interconnection between the legal form and the commodity form. Pashukanis viewed the contract and the legal rights it created as the expression of commodity exchange. His most important contention was that law is irredeemably bourgeois. Thus he rejected the idea of "socialist law" and proposed that socialism should usher in the withering away of law and with it all reliance on rights.

Marxists in the West have generally taken a more sympathetic view of rights. In the interwar period, German scholars in the critical theory tradition defended the place of strategies of legal reform within the socialist project (Renner 1972). More recently, Marxist scholarship has been concerned to reinstate the role of rights and justice within a radical political tradition (Buchanan 1982; Collins 1982; Poulantzas 1978).

Alan Hunt

See also Soviet System

References and further reading
Buchanan, Allen E. 1982. *Marx and Justice: The Radical Critique of Liberalism.* London: Methuen.
Cain, Maureen, and Alan Hunt. 1979. *Marx and Engels on Law.* New York: Academic Press.
Collins, Hugh. 1982. *Marxism and Law.* Oxford: Oxford University Press.
Engels, Frederick. 1975. "Letter to Bloch (21/9/1890)." Pp. 394–396 in *Marx-Engels Selected Correspondence.* Moscow: Progress.
Pashukanis, Evgeny. 1980. *Pashukanis: Selected Writings on Marxism and Law.* Edited by P. Beirne and R. Sharlet. New York: Academic Press.
Poulantzas, Nicos. 1978. *State, Power, Socialism.* London: New Left Books.

Renner, Karl. 1972. *The Institutions of Private Law and Their Social Functions.* Edited by Otto Kahn-Freund. 1949. London: Routledge.

MARYLAND

GENERAL INFORMATION

Maryland is located on the eastern seaboard of the United States in the Mid-Atlantic region. The state is 9,775 square miles in size, and consists of a mixture of scattered cities and suburbs. The total population is about 5.1 million, and the state is demographically diverse, with about 27 percent African American, 3 percent Hispanic, and 68 percent Caucasian.

The Eastern Shore, which is separated from the western part of the state by the Chesapeake Bay, is used extensively for agricultural and livestock purposes, with poultry at the top of farm production values. Although agriculture remains the largest single land use in Maryland, with around 35 percent of total land area, it directly supports only a small number of people. In 1994, the services sector, with 29.9 percent of the total, was the largest employer in Maryland, followed by retail trades (19.5 percent), government (19.1 percent), and manufacturing (8.5 percent). More recently, technology industries have grown exponentially, and by 1998 they provided nearly 150,000 jobs in the private sector. Baltimore, the largest city, had a 1990 population of 736,014.

Maryland was established in 1632 when King Charles I of Britain granted a charter to Lord Baltimore. The first meeting of the General Assembly convened in St. Mary's City in 1634, and in 1694 the capital was moved to Annapolis, the site, some ninety-eight years later, of the historic Annapolis Convention, where delegates' discussions about changing the Articles of Confederation evolved into a draft of the U.S. Constitution. Maryland, one of the original thirteen colonies to declare its independence from Britain in 1776, later became the seventh state of the United States.

EVOLUTION AND HISTORY

The Maryland judicial system has undergone many changes through the years under four different constitutions. The first, of course, was ratified in 1776; the second came in 1851, and the last two were written during the Civil War era—1864 and 1867. In addition, in fall–winter 1967–1968, a constitutional convention met to draw up a revised charter, but the voters rejected the proposed document in the May 1968 election. During Maryland's colonial history, courts served as the administrative agencies of local government. Later, boards of commissioners were created to take on administrative responsibilities, and the courts assumed the more traditional role of the judicial branch. The first court system was a four-tiered judiciary, with the Court of Appeals as the highest appellate court, an intermediate appellate court, and district courts; the fourth level consisted of limited jurisdiction tribunals presided over by justices of the peace. Specialty courts were also established as needed to resolve recurring issues. For example, orphans' courts probated estates and wills, and chancery courts were created in some areas to handle equity cases.

In 1805 the intermediate appellate courts were abolished, and under the Constitution of 1851 county courts became circuit courts, and towns and cities were allowed to create an array of minor municipal and justice of the peace courts. In 1966, by constitutional amendment, the Maryland General Assembly was given the authority to re-establish an intermediate appellate court, and subsequently the Court of Special Appeals came into being. Although Maryland's citizens turned down the opportunity to adopt a new state charter in 1968, a number of constitutional amendments were adopted shortly thereafter, calling for a major overhaul of the court system. Thus, in 1971, the district courts began operation replacing the hodge-podge of justice of the peace courts, municipal courts, and people's courts. The orphans' courts remained, but they were removed from the state judicial system to become part of county government. As a result of these changes, the state of Maryland again has a four-tiered court system: Court of Appeals, Court of Special Appeals, circuit courts, and district courts (see figure).

CURRENT STRUCTURE

Legal Profession and Legal Training

The Maryland lawyer population in September 2000 was around twenty-eight thousand active lawyers. Legal education in the state is provided by two law schools, at the University of Maryland at Baltimore and at the University of Baltimore, both in Baltimore City. In addition, many of the graduates from law school programs in the District of Columbia, such as Howard University, Georgetown University, George Washington University, American University, and Catholic University, take the Maryland bar exam and practice in the state.

Legal Aid Services

In civil cases, the Maryland Legal Services Corporation (MLSC) provides legal representation and advice to poor individuals and families. Created by the General Assembly in 1982, it provides grants to nonprofit organizations, which in return provide civil legal services to eligible persons. These grants are made possible by the Interest on Lawyer Trust Account (IOLTA), which was also established by the General Assembly to accumulate interest

Structure of Maryland Courts

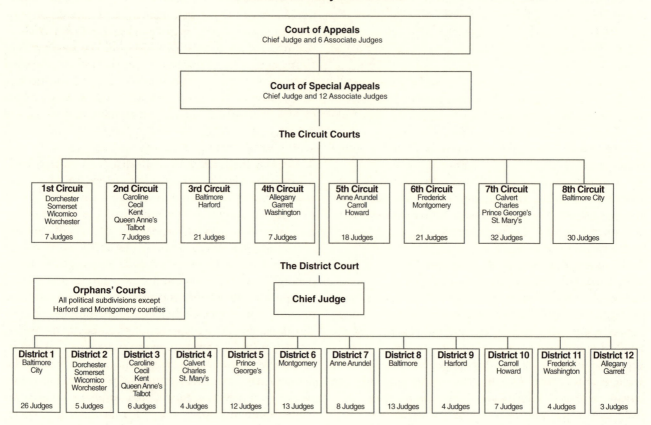

| **Court of Appeals** |
| Chief Judge and 6 Associate Judges |

| **Court of Special Appeals** |
| Chief Judge and 12 Associate Judges |

The Circuit Courts

1st Circuit	2nd Circuit	3rd Circuit	4th Circuit	5th Circuit	6th Circuit	7th Circuit	8th Circuit
Dorchester Somerset Wicomico Worchester	Caroline Cecil Kent Queen Anne's Talbot	Baltimore Harford	Allegany Garrett Washington	Anne Arundel Carroll Howard	Frederick Montgomery	Calvert Charles Prince George's St. Mary's	Baltimore City
7 Judges	7 Judges	21 Judges	7 Judges	18 Judges	21 Judges	32 Judges	30 Judges

The District Court

| **Orphans' Courts** | **Chief Judge** |
| All political subdivisions except Harford and Montgomery counties | |

District 1	District 2	District 3	District 4	District 5	District 6	District 7	District 8	District 9	District 10	District 11	District 12
Baltimore City	Dorchester Somerset Wicomico Worchester	Caroline Cecil Kent Queen Anne's Talbot	Calvert Charles St. Mary's	Prince George's	Montgomery	Anne Arundel	Baltimore	Harford	Carroll Howard	Frederick Washington	Allegany Garrett
26 Judges	5 Judges	6 Judges	4 Judges	12 Judges	13 Judges	8 Judges	13 Judges	4 Judges	7 Judges	4 Judges	3 Judges

from client trust funds. All privately practicing attorneys in Maryland are required by law to place all eligible client trust funds into an IOLTA account. The interest earned on these accounts is payable to the MLSC solely for the charitable purpose of helping poor citizens with legal services. In 1996–1997, the MLSC provided legal advice or representation to a total of 73,874 low-income individuals.

Administrative Hearings

Maryland's businesses and citizens may not always agree with the actions taken by state government. If settlement conferences and mediation fail to resolve these disagreements, they may be heard by an administrative judge. In states following the "central panel" model, administrative law judges for all state agencies are provided by a single independent state agency; in other states, each agency provides its own administrative law judges. Before 1990, Maryland was one of the latter states, as many executive-branch agencies employed hearing examiners to adjudicate hearings. However, in response to increasing load and complexity, the state legislature decided it would be better to create a centralized office. Thus the Office of Administrative Hearings (OAH) came into existence as an independent agency under the executive branch of government, reporting directly to the governor.

Some states do allow agencies to provide their own administrative law judges, even when that agency is a party in the dispute. This system has been criticized as open to political pressure and manipulation. Because of this problem of conflict of interest, Maryland has adopted the "central panel" model, or the OAH, for such disputes, so that an unbiased administrative law judge hears all contested cases.

Judicial System

The Maryland judicial system currently is composed of district courts, circuit courts, the Court of Special Appeals, and the Court of Appeals, arranged in a single four-tiered hierarchy (see figure).

The district courts of Maryland, which are at the base of the system, were created as a result of a 1970 constitutional amendment, thus replacing the miscellaneous municipal courts. The jurisdiction of the district courts extends into both criminal and civil cases but is limited, with both monetary and time-imprisonment restrictions. They have exclusive jurisdiction on all criminal cases and motor vehicle and boating violations, when the imprisonment term is less than three years and the fine is less than $2,500. They also have exclusive jurisdiction in all civil cases, including all landlord and tenant cases, replevin actions (to recover personal property claimed to have been unlawfully taken), and other claims in which the dollar amount involved is less than $2,500. The district courts also share concurrent jurisdiction with the circuits in civil cases in which the claim is higher than $2,500 but less than $25,000 and in certain criminal cases. The district court system is divided into twelve geographic regions of varying size. Six districts consist of a single county each; these are the state's largely urban counties (covering the city of Baltimore in the north and its metropolitan area, and the Washington, D.C., suburban counties). Three other districts have two counties each, and the remaining three districts are composed of three to five counties. All of the districts have at least three judges, and the largest (with twenty-three) is in Baltimore City. A chief judge presides over each court and, with the approval of the chief judge of the Court of Appeals, appoints administrative judges within the district. No jury trials are held at the district level, and a party who wishes to place a case before a jury panel must proceed to the circuit courts.

The Maryland circuit courts, consisting of 143 judges, represent the next level in the judicial hierarchy. They have original jurisdiction in a broad range of categories, including all trials by jury, and civil and criminal cases with penalties above the limits for the district court. The circuit court also hears appeals from the district court, from the orphans' courts in some instances, and from certain administrative agencies such as the departments of Personnel, Taxation and Assessment, and Zoning. Losing parties in cases before the circuit court may, in turn, request permission from the Maryland Court of Special Appeals to review the decision.

The courts are arranged into eight geographical units. Each of the first seven circuits is composed of two or more counties, while the jurisdiction of the Eighth Judicial Circuit extends only to the city of Baltimore.

The Maryland Court of Special Appeals, consisting of thirteen members, including a chief judge and twelve associates, sits in Annapolis, the state capital. It was created by constitutional amendment in 1966, in response to the rapidly growing caseload and the consequent backlog of the Court of Appeals, the state's highest tribunal. Members of the Court of Special Appeals are appointed by the governor, confirmed by the Senate, and stand for election on their records without opposition for ten-year terms. According to a 1994 constitutional amendment, appointments are made so that there is one member from each of the regions represented by the seven appellate judicial circuits, and the remaining six members are selected from the state at large. A presiding chief judge is designated by the governor. Those who wish to seek a second term face a retention election before the voters in the region they were selected to "represent."

The court originally had limited jurisdiction to hear only criminal cases, hence the designation Court of "Spe-

cial" Appeals. However, the court's jurisdictional reach has been expanded so that now it has exclusive initial appellate authority over any reviewable decision by a lower court, and it generally also hears appeals taken directly from the circuit and orphans' courts. In addition, the court considers applications for review in matters such as habeas corpus appeals, continued hospitalization of insane or incompetent defendants, appeals from criminal guilty pleas, and denial of victim rights.

The judges of the court usually sit in panels of three. However, a hearing or rehearing before the court en banc (all thirteen judges) may be ordered in any case by a majority of the full contingent of judges.

In order to facilitate efficient flow in the civil caseload, the court makes extensive use of prehearing conferences. These conferences consist of a panel of judges who attempt to identify cases that might be good candidates for settlement discussions among the parties. Moreover, a prehearing may result in outright dismissal, limitation of the issues, or remand for additional trial court action. Otherwise, a case will be scheduled for a more thorough review, perhaps including oral arguments.

In some criminal cases, the General Assembly has granted, by statute, discretionary power to the court, allowing the judges to decide whether to place the case on the regular docket or to deny the appeal. Most of the docket, however, consists of direct appeals from lower courts.

The Maryland Court of Appeals, consisting of seven judges, is the state court of last resort. It was established by the first constitution of 1776 and has been located in Annapolis since 1851. The court has exclusive jurisdiction in several very special types of case, including death penalty convictions and legislative redistricting. Since 1975, the Court of Appeals has determined its own docket with discretionary review power whereby the justices decide whether to grant review under the writ of certiorari. The vast majority of requests for review represent appeals from either a circuit court or the Court of Special Appeals. If certiorari is not granted to a circuit court case, the appeal may then be filed with the Court of Special Appeals. The decision is final, however, in the event of a denial of certiorari in an appeal from the Court of Special Appeals.

In addition, the court creates procedural rules that govern the practice of law within courts across all jurisdictions of the state system of courts, and the court has the power to govern such things as the admission of attorneys into the practice of law on recommendation of the State Board of Law Examiners.

STAFFING

Before 1971, Maryland governors could directly appoint judges, without submitting their names for approval by the Senate. However, dissatisfaction, especially among members of the organized bar, led to the adoption of a set of reforms generally known as "merit selection" procedures. In 1970 a statewide judicial nominating commission was established by executive order, with the purpose of recommending nominees to the governor for appointment to the appellate courts. As structured since 1999, the nominating commission consists of seventeen members—a chairperson appointed by the governor; eight laypersons, including one from each appellate judicial circuit and one from the state at large; and eight lawyers, including one member each elected by lawyers from the seven appellate judicial circuits and one lawyer appointed by the governor.

In addition, there were also eight regional nominating commissions created to perform the same function with respect to trial court vacancies. In 1988, the commission system was restructured so that each county with a population of 100,000 or more would have its own nominating board. There are currently sixteen commission districts. Each nominating board has thirteen members consisting of a mixture of laypersons and lawyers, and a chairperson who is appointed by the governor.

In the case of a judicial vacancy, the Administrative Office of the Courts notifies the appropriate nominating commission and bar associations and makes an announcement in the *Daily Record*. The commission chair also advertises the vacancy. The commission then meets to consider the applications and supporting information, and interviews are conducted with the applicants. By secret ballot, the commission members create a short list of the three "legally and professionally most qualified" for judicial office; the list is forwarded to the governor, who then makes an appointment from among the names provided.

District court judges, who must be lawyers, are appointed by the governor and confirmed by the Senate for ten-year terms and may be reappointed. Circuit court judges, who must also be lawyers, are initially appointed in the same manner. However, the appointee must run for a fifteen-year term at the next regularly scheduled general election. And, unlike other judges in the state system, circuit court members can face opposition. Although it has occurred very infrequently, the name of any qualified member of the bar may be placed on the ballot to challenge an incumbent appointee in the election.

For both the Court of Special Appeals and the Court of Appeals, the chief judge is selected by the governor. Members are initially appointed by the governor and confirmed by the Senate for ten-year terms. A second term requires approval by the voters in an uncontested retention election.

Wayne V. McIntosh

See also Appellate Courts; Judicial Selection, Methods of; Maryland; Trial Courts; United States—Federal System; United States—State Systems

References and further reading
Boyd, Laslo V. 1987. *Maryland Government and Politics.* Centreville, MD: Tidewater Publishers.
Maryland Legal Services Corporation. "I.O.L.T.A. Interest on Lawyer Trust Accounts." Annual Report, July 1, 1996, to June 30, 1997.
Maryland Manual (1996–1997). 1996. Edited by Diane P. Frese. State Archives of the State of Maryland. Baltimore: United Book Press.
Miller, R., and S. Darnley. 1990. *Understanding Maryland Government.* Annapolis, MD: Educational Consultants in the Humanities Association.
State of Maryland. "Office of Administrative Hearings Packet." 1996. Md. AH 1. 2:00A /996.

MASSACHUSETTS

GENERAL INFORMATION

Massachusetts is the most populous of the New England states, in the northeastern portion of the United States. New York borders it to the west, Vermont and New Hampshire to the north, Rhode Island and Connecticut to the south, and the Atlantic Ocean to the east. The total estimated population is around 6,100,000. Of the total population, roughly 5 percent are Black, nearly 4.8 percent Hispanic, less than 1 percent Native American, and about 90 percent are White. Boston, the capital and largest city, is located in the easternmost portion of the state. Massachusetts lies within about 8,257 square miles.

Massachusetts is traditionally industrial. The predominantly urban population lends well to diverse manufacturing in the densely populated state. Many of the industries, including printing, publishing, and jewelry, date back to before the American Revolution. Besides industrial sectors, Massachusetts remains strong in agricultural arenas. Dairy and commercial fishing remain among the strongest in the country.

Massachusetts is historically the capital of higher education in America. Noted universities are Harvard, the Massachusetts Institute of Technology, Brandeis, Tufts, Amherst College, Williams College, and the University of Massachusetts at Amherst.

On February 6, 1788, Massachusetts became the sixth of the original thirteen states to ratify the U.S. Constitution. The state has been the site of numerous historical events in United States history, including battles of the Revolutionary War, Shay's Rebellion, Paul Revere's Ride, and the Boston Tea Party.

EVOLUTION AND HISTORY

The coast of Massachusetts was most likely *discovered* by Norsemen in the eleventh century and was settled by Europeans in the sixteenth and seventeenth centuries. The history of Massachusetts is replete with factors that have been integral in shaping the current governmental structure of the United States. In 1635, the Boston Latin School was founded, with Harvard University established one year later. By 1647, a law was passed requiring elementary schools in towns of fifty or more. While these were not free schools, they are considered the beginning of what is known as organized or popular education in the United States.

With England spending much of its time fighting France in the eighteenth century, Massachusetts was able to live under more relaxed laws. In 1764, the Sugar Act virtually abolished foreign trade, most of which Massachusetts depended upon, specifically concerning gold. In 1765, the Stamp Act taxed out of the colony most of the remaining funds. Although the Sugar Act was repealed in 1766, other repressive measures were enacted.

In 1770, the Boston Massacre occurred when British soldiers fired upon a crowd of citizens. In 1773, Samuel Adams helped inspire the Boston Tea Party and in 1775 Paul Revere embarked on his famous ride with the first shot of the Revolutionary War in Concord; the "shot heard round the world." On March 17, 1776, the Battle of Bunker Hill occurred and the British evacuated. The first blood of the war was shed in Massachusetts, yet the troops won a major battle.

John Adams, later the second president of the United States, wrote the Massachusetts Constitution, which was ratified on June 15, 1780. The Constitution of Massachusetts is the oldest written constitution still in effect. The commonwealth, as it is known, has historically been progressive in enacting laws. Civil rights laws as well as laws preventing the exploitation of women and minors were introduced at an early stage. Ironically, suffragettes Susan B. Anthony and Lucy Stone both hailed from Massachusetts, yet the commonwealth was still debating the full enfranchisement of women when the Nineteenth Amendment to the U.S. Constitution was ratified in 1920.

Notable Massachusetts citizens include presidents John Adams, John Quincy Adams, Calvin Coolidge, and John F. Kennedy, as well as famous jurists Oliver Wendell Holmes and Louis Brandeis.

CURRENT STRUCTURE

Massachusetts history remains unique to the world. The highest state court in Massachusetts, the Massachusetts Supreme Judicial Court, is the oldest appellate court in continuous existence in the Western Hemisphere. The Massachusetts judicial system is arranged hierarchically into three main levels, with the lowest level containing specialized courts.

The trial court is the first of three levels of the commonwealth's judiciary. Within the trial court are seven court departments:

1. Boston Municipal Court
2. District Court
3. Housing Court
4. Juvenile Court
5. Land Court
6. Probate and Family Court
7. Superior Court

The Boston Municipal Court (BMC) includes most criminal offenses that do not require the imposition of a state prison sentence. The BMC may conduct probable cause hearings, contract and tort actions, and small claims cases. A total of eleven justices sit in the BMC. The district court serves all of the commonwealth, except Boston. This totals sixty-nine court divisions. The district court has jurisdiction over felonies and misdemeanors that do not involve more than two and one-half years in state prison. There are 168 justices in the district court. The housing court handles landlord/tenant issues and cases that affect the health, safety, or welfare of persons inhabiting property that is regulated by local cities and towns under state and local codes. There are five divisions of the housing court with a total of six justices. The juvenile court has jurisdiction over delinquency, guardianship, and the termination of parental rights. The juvenile court has six divisions with thirty-three justices in counties throughout the state. The land court has jurisdiction over matters regarding title and real property as well as the Registry of Deeds and zoning issues. The land court has one division with four justices. The probate and family court has jurisdiction over family-related matters such as divorce, paternity, custody, and adoption. The probate and family court has fourteen divisions with a maximum of forty-nine justices at any given time. The superior court has jurisdiction over the highly serious matters such as murder, armed robbery, and rape, as well as cases where damages exceed $25,000. There are fourteen divisions with seventy-six justices within the superior court. Following the trial court is the appeals court.

The Massachusetts Appeals Court and the Supreme Judicial Court share jurisdiction over most cases. However, most appeals are filed within the appeals court first. The appeals court sits with a rotating panel of three judges. The appeals court also runs a single justice session throughout the year that reviews attorney's fees awards and motions of civil and criminal sentencing appeals. The single justice session, which rotates through the appeals court, is designed to evaluate variables within court decisions such as attorney's fees to be certain that fairness and equality are present. The court has a chief justice, twelve associate justices, and four recall justices.

The Massachusetts Supreme Judicial Court, which sits in Boston, is the highest state court of the commonwealth. There are seven justices, including the chief jus-

Legal Structure of Massachusetts Courts

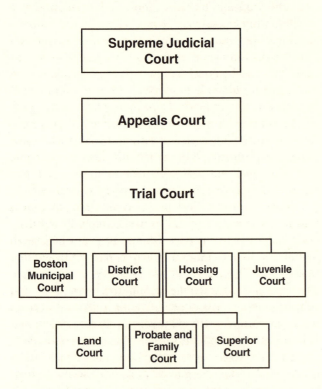

tice. Full court sittings of the Supreme Judicial Court are usually held for all counties in Boston in the first week of each month from September to May as designated by the court.

NOTABLE FEATURES OF LAW AND LEGAL SYSTEM

Massachusetts is one of twelve states in the United States that do not impose the death penalty. Current efforts by the Republican governor Paul Celucci to create a death penalty in the commonwealth have fallen short in both the state legislature as well as in the court of public opinion. Massachusetts history, driven by rebellion, allows it to wear, as a badge of honor, the fact that Massachusetts has not imposed capital punishment since 1947 and abolished the death penalty in 1984. One of the most famous cases in Massachusetts history is, in fact, the death penalty case of Sacco and Vanzetti. The two men, who were painted as Italian anarchists, were executed in 1927 after being convicted of murder. However, subsequent data shows that the men were most likely not guilty of the charges. The case undoubtedly remains an infamous case in American jurisprudence and touches upon the intermittent failures, whether revisionist or not, of the juridical system in the United States.

The jury system is well established in the U.S. Constitution and is guaranteed in the Massachusetts Constitution as well. The American judicial system stresses the importance of a trial by jury and the commonwealth is

no exception. In 1980, the Massachusetts Supreme Judicial Court decided the case of *Commonwealth v. Bastarache,* which involved a defendant convicted of manslaughter. The court found that persons between the ages of eighteen and thirty-four were being excluded from the juror selection process. The court determined that underrepresentation of any group could not continue. *Bastarache* helped initiate the one day/one trial jury system to be implemented in all fourteen judicial districts. When *Bastarache* was decided, the one day/one trial jury system was functioning as a pilot program only in Middlesex County. The case changed the jury system. The case helped establish the Office of the Jury Commissioner (OJC) of Massachusetts. The result has been an effort to gain a higher juror yield as well as accentuate a diverse jury pool. Currently in the commonwealth, fifty-eight courts utilize jurors in fourteen judicial districts. Massachusetts has a fairly expeditious judicial system for jurors, showing that 85 percent of the jurors complete their service in one day and 95 percent finish in three days.

The Committee for Public Counsel Services (CPCS) is a fifteen-member body established by the Massachusetts General Laws to oversee the legal representation to indigent persons in the commonwealth. Of the nearly 300,000 cases annually, around 2,400 private attorneys, appointed by various courts, provide legal representation. The CPCS also oversees the operation of a state department comprised of 126 public attorneys and administrators that provide legal services to various indigent parties. The CPCS has thirteen regional offices with attorneys in various counties and specific courts.

Massachusetts is among the states where all judicial vacancies are filled by gubernatorial appointments. The governor's appointments are subject to confirmation by the Executive Council, a constitutional body composed of eight members elected from councilor-districts as well as the lieutenant governor. Each appointee is selected from a panel of at least three candidates recommended by a Judicial Nominating Committee established by the governor.

A Judicial Nominating Council (JNC) is in place, in accordance with the constitution, to advise the governor on the appointment of judges, clerk-magistrates, and clerks of the court. The JNC is made up of twenty-five members divided into four regions, loosely based by grouping counties. The JNC solicits, interviews, evaluates, and recommends candidates to fill vacancies in the courts in their respective regions. There is a special nominating council established for the selection of judges to the Supreme Judicial Court, signifying the importance of the highest state court. Nominees are further evaluated by a Joint Bar Screening Committee comprised of Massachusetts county bar association members. Qualifications for judgeships entail what the JNC terms "a wide variety of factors," including education, professional experience, law practice, employment history, business involvement, civic community involvement, conduct, and health. By statute, all judges are appointed for life but must retire no later than age seventy. In rare instances, the removal of a judge is done by the governor with consent of the Executive Council upon address of both houses of legislature. The specific process by which judges are nominated is public yet there are no specific qualifications that would exclude certain individuals.

STAFFING

In the year 2000, there were 363 total judges. There are 393 total judges in the commonwealth designed to hold adjunct positions as well as interim positions. The Massachusetts Constitution contains all information pertaining to the selection, requirements, ages, and salaries of judges. There are eleven district attorneys, consistent with the regions and counties. There is a district attorneys' association designed to act as a service for the citizens of the commonwealth as well as a connection for the numerous districts. Each district attorney is elected. The total number of licensed attorneys to practice law in Massachusetts is 53,412. There are 43,080 after filtering through the active practice status. Active practice status entails grouping attorneys who are retired or inactive, as well as judges and clerks who are lawyers but cannot practice law within the Commonwealth of Massachusetts.

There are a total of seven American Bar Association–accredited law schools in the state. They include Boston College, Boston University, Harvard, New England School of Law, Northeastern, Suffolk, and Western New England College of Law. The data amounts to: 349 full-time faculty and 436 part-time faculty, roughly 179 of which are women; 2,369 Juris Doctorates granted per year; and 6,980 total law students in the commonwealth. It should be noted that Harvard University Law School, established in 1817, is the oldest continuously operating law school in the United States.

RELATIONSHIP TO NATIONAL SYSTEM

Massachusetts sits within the jurisdiction of the First Circuit Court of Appeals. The First Circuit is the federal appellate court, one step below the United States Supreme Court. The First Circuit entails Maine, Massachusetts, New Hampshire, Puerto Rico, and Rhode Island.

Aaron R. S. Lorenz

See also Capital Punishment; Incarceration; Judicial Independence; Juries; Juvenile Justice; Judicial Selection, Methods of; Small Claims Courts; Trial Courts; United States—Federal System; United States—State Systems
References and further reading
Commonwealth of Massachusetts. 1999. *Massachusetts Facts: A Review of the History, Government, and Symbols of the Commonwealth.* Boston: Citizen Information Service.
Cushing, John D. 1984. *A Bibliography of the Laws and Resolves of the Massachusetts Bay, 1642–1780.* Wilmington, DE: Massachusetts Historical Society.
Davis, William T. 1900. *The History of the Judiciary in Massachusetts.* Boston: The Boston Book Company.
Kaufman, Martin, John W. Ifkovic, and Joseph Carvalho, eds. 1988. *A Guide to the History of Massachusetts.* New York: Greenwood Press.
Silverman, Robert A. 1981. *Law and Urban Growth: Civil Litigation in the Boston Trial Courts, 1880–1900.* Princeton, NJ: Princeton University Press.
Wilkie, Richard, and Jack Tager, eds. 1991. *Historical Atlas of Massachusetts.* Amherst: University of Massachusetts Press.

MAURITANIA

GENERAL INFORMATION

The Islamic Republic of Mauritania is situated in northwest Africa and encompasses an area of 1,030,700 square kilometers; it borders on Senegal and Mali to the north and east, Algeria in the far northwest, and the disputed territory of Western Sahara in the northwest. The country also has an Atlantic coastline of over 400 kilometers, which constitutes an important economic resource because of its abundant fisheries. Mauritania's approximately 2.5 million inhabitants (as of 1999) fall into three fairly well defined ethnic-racial groups, each of which accounts for roughly one-third of the total population. The socially and politically dominant group is the so-called White Moors, or "Beydanes"; they are of Arab-Berber extraction and are the most light skinned of the country's people. Secondly, the Black Moors, as their name suggests, are much darker complexioned but consider themselves Arabs; they are descended from non-Arab black Africans who, beginning in the sixteenth century, were captured and enslaved by invading Arab tribes. Finally, the country also hosts a minority of black Africans with no history of servitude, who traditionally resided in the fertile Senegal River Valley in the south and who do not play a prominent role in Mauritania's political life. All Mauritanians, regardless of ethnicity, are Muslim.

One of Mauritania's most glaring weaknesses is its narrow economic base, which, since its independence from France in 1960, has been based on the export of iron ore deposits in the north as well as on the fisheries along the coast. Alternative means of livelihood, such as agriculture and animal husbandry, have been in steep decline for decades because of droughts and the resultant desertification. Among many other impoverishments, the majority of the population lacks access to clean water, electricity, and medical care. The average per capita annual income in 2000 was only $440, although newly discovered de-

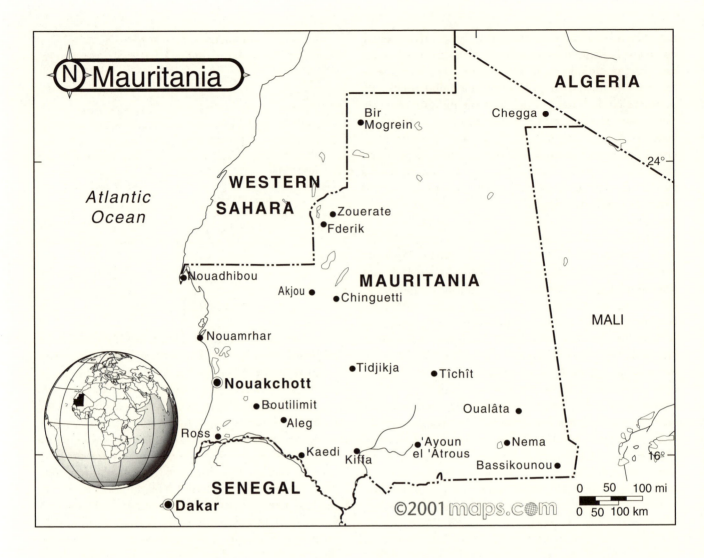

posits of iron ore in northern Mauritania and the discovery of offshore oil contributed to improving economic prospects, with increases in the gross domestic product (GDP) in the 1990s often reaching 4 to 5 percent per annum. High debt levels impelled the government to adhere to a program of fiscal "restructuring" dictated in large part by the International Monetary Fund (IMF), steps that included freer convertibility of the national currency and the privatization of some public functions. While rather successful in purely economic terms, this was politically controversial, as it entailed a relative loss of control by the state over the economy, in turn illustrating some of Mauritania's problems as it attempted to reconcile a highly traditional society with an array of modernizing influences.

HISTORY

Although the history of Mauritania as a separate nation begins only in November 1960 with the granting of independence by France, an indigenous people, known as the Bafour, had inhabited the territory as hunter-gatherers until about 2500 B.C.E., when they were displaced by

Berbers, who developed beneficial trade relationships with the black African kingdoms to the south. This state of affairs lasted until about 1000 C.E., when Islamic warriors advanced from the east to establish the Almoravid Empire, which extended throughout the North African region and was itself eclipsed in the early 1200s by the migration of Arab tribes. Subsequently, a series of wars between these Arabs and the Berbers—ending in 1674—permanently ensured the ascendancy of the Arabs and the subordination of the remaining Berber tribes. A three-tier hierarchy (which persists to this day) was established: warrior tribes headed the new order, while religious/monastic groups *(zawaya)* stood between the warrior Arabs and the lowest caste, the *zenaga,* or tributaries/vassals. Slavery was instituted mainly among the black Africans who had not fled south in time to escape the Arab invasions.

After a few hundred years of relative tranquility, the French government, which had previously occupied neighboring Senegal, made a decision in 1899 to occupy Mauritania as well—a task that was not accomplished until 1909, after considerable armed resistance. But having shown little interest in developing its Mauritanian colony, Paris showed some willingness to grant autonomy and then independence to the country after World War II; free elections starting in the late 1940s brought to power Mokhtar Ould Daddah, the territory's only lawyer and a member of an important religious tribe. From November 28, 1960, to July 10, 1978, Ould Daddah governed the country with a firm but generally benevolent hand through his chosen political group, the Parti du Peuple Mauritanien (Mauritanian People's Party—PPM). Over his nearly two decades in office, Ould Daddah nationalized the country's iron mines, introduced a new national currency, the ouguiya, and collaborated with Morocco in the mid-1970s to annex the former Spanish colony of Western Sahara, despite the opposition of the international community and the Polisario Front, a Western Saharan nationalist group that demanded full independence for the territory. The resulting guerrilla war with Polisario nearly demolished Mauritania's economy and paved the way, in July 1978, for Ould Daddah's overthrow at the hands of the country's small military officer corps, headed by Lieutenant Colonel Mustapha Ould Mohammed Salek. Salek's inability to reach a peace agreement in Western Sahara led to his own displacement in 1979–1980 by Lieutenant Colonel Mohamed Khouna Ould Haidallah, who signed an agreement with Polisario and withdrew from Western Sahara but was unable to improve the poor condition of the Mauritanian economy.

On December 12, 1984, another officer, Colonel Maaouiya Ould Sid'Ahmed Taya, overthrew Ould Haidallah and promised a new and more responsive regime. Despite some initial successes in curbing corruption and generating economic growth, ethnic tensions steadily grew in the late 1980s and generated a brutal government counterreaction, with serious human rights violations being committed mostly against the minority black African population between 1987 and 1990. After Mauritania was ostracized from much of the world community for these abuses, as well as its perceived support for Iraq during the 1990–1991 Gulf crisis, President Ould Taya decided to drastically change tactics and embrace multiparty democracy and a generally pro-Western foreign policy. Free elections in early 1992 having awarded the civilian presidency to Ould Taya, the Mauritanian Second Republic was founded on April 18. A series of elections from 1992 to 2000 continued to award nearly total power to President Ould Taya's Parti Républicain, Démocratique et Social (Republican and Social Democratic Party—PRDS), generating domestic and international skepticism about the sincerity of the head of state's commitment to democratic norms. Such qualms were intensified by Ould Taya's periodic imprisonment of certain opposition leaders and by his censorship of the country's independent newspapers.

LEGAL CONCEPTS

Mauritania is a unitary republic with one national legal system, which is largely a hybrid between traditional Malekite Islamic jurisprudence and modern, French-influenced civil law. Administratively, the country is divided into twelve *régions* and one special district covering the capital city of Nouakchott and its suburbs. Each region, in turn, was divided into a total of fifty-three *départements* (in Arabic, *moughataas*). Each department is run by a governor responsible to the central authorities in Nouakchott. Below this level there are 207 *arrondisements* administered by popularly elected mayors, pursuant to a democratic reform carried out by President Ould Taya in 1986 and continued after the further democratization of Mauritania in 1991–1992. In 2001 the overwhelming majority of the regions, departments, and arrondisements were controlled by Ould Taya's PRDS political party.

The supreme law of Mauritania is the Constitution of the Second Republic, approved by popular referendum on July 12, 1991. Consisting of 103 articles, this document, in addition to declaring Islam the official religion of the state and Arabic the official language (but with other languages accorded a degree of recognition), guarantees to all citizens basic human rights including those of speech, travel, privacy, and association; provides that all persons accused of a crime shall be presumed innocent until proven guilty; and asserts that the sanctity of the home and correspondence shall be respected by government officials. On the other hand, Article 18 states that all Mauritanians have an obligation to protect the independence of the country and, in a broadly worded provision, that "treason, espionage, and going over to the enemy as well as all infractions committed with prejudice to the security of the state shall be punished with all the rigor of the law." Many of the remaining provisions deal with the powers and responsibilities of the president of the republic and the bicameral Parliament in enacting legislation. Articles 81 through 88 provide for the Constitutional Council, which consists of six members chosen by the president, the president of the National Assembly, and the president of the Senate, for a term of nine years. The council examines all "organic" laws for their conformity to the constitution, and no appeals are permitted from any of their decisions. Four further articles (89–92) establish, in broad outline, Mauritania's judicial system, and Articles 94–97 describe two bodies with purely consultative status, the High Islamic Council and the Economic and Social Council. Both councils operate largely at the behest of the president, with only limited interactions with Parliament and other state agencies.

Although the preamble to the 1991 Mauritanian Constitution describes Islam as "the sole source of law," the underlying reality is considerably more complicated.

Structure of Mauritanian Courts

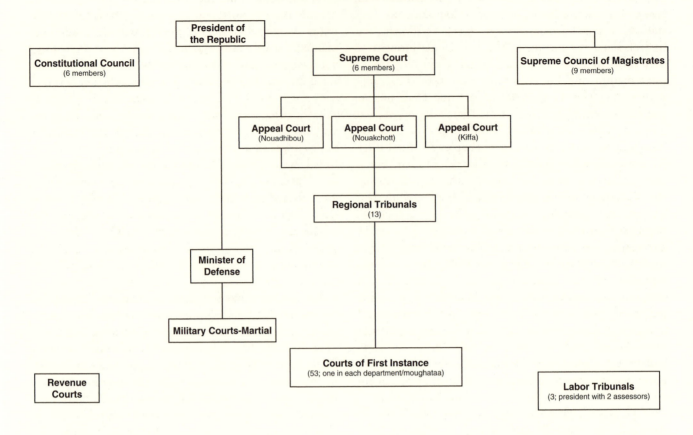

Criminal law, for example, has been officially "modern" since the legal reforms carried out by the French in 1946, except for the brief and intensely controversial experiment with the *sharia* in the early 1980s. Similarly, commercial, nationality, administrative, and some other legal areas were almost entirely Western-derived. The only real areas of Islamic jurisprudence were to be found in family law, inheritance, and other personal status questions addressed by either the Koran or the accounts of the statements and practices of the prophet Mohammed (*hadiths*). The overt sexual discrimination of the *sharia*—that is, according a woman's testimony only half the weight of a man's, among other disabilities—is found only within the strictly Islamic sector, with men and women treated equally in all other areas. Reflecting this duality of legal systems, it is frequently the case that judges and magistrates have training in both Islamic and modern civil/criminal law; several courts (including the Courts of First Instance in each department) have both Islamic and "ordinary" panels.

Since 1992, Mauritania has also attempted to blend the consensus-based Islamic dispute resolution of an earlier time with Western practice: an ombudsman of the republic, for example, attempts to mediate between citizens and government agencies. In addition, a separate criminal justice system for juveniles exists, with no child under the age of twelve being criminally liable, and with defendants between thirteen and eighteen years of age receiving generally more lenient treatment than adults charged with similar offenses.

CURRENT STRUCTURE

At the apex of Mauritania's judicial structure in 2001 is the Supreme Court, composed of six members chosen for a fixed term of years by the National Assembly (the lower house of Parliament) and the Senate, whose chief justice is a magistrate appointed by the president of the republic for a five-year term. The membership of the Supreme Court (or High Court of Justice, as it is sometimes called) is divided between jurists specializing in Islamic law and secular law, although the chief justice must be versed in both areas. The Supreme Court also retains a financial counselor, consistent with its role as overseer of public administration and its original jurisdiction over state-owned property, in addition to its appellate responsibilities.

Below the Supreme Court there are three appeals courts, located in Nouakchott, the commercial center of Nouadhibou, and the inland city of Kiffa. These panels hear appeals on the merits from both regional and departmental lower courts, although they also have original jurisdiction over felonies. Each Court of Appeal is further split into two chambers, one handling only civil and commercial cases and the other, a "mixed" chamber with competence over Islamic, criminal, and other law. One step below the Courts of Appeal, thirteen tribunals, one in each region of the country, have original jurisdiction over misdemeanors and hear appeals from the departmental courts. Finally, fifty-three tribunals, one in each department, hear domestic relations, inheritance, and divorce cases, as well as those civil cases that do not involve amounts greater than 10,000 ouquiyas (at the 2000 exchange rate, about U.S.$41). Each departmental court has a president and jurists with training in both Islamic and secular law. Wrongful assertions of jurisdiction by these courts, as well as any variations from due process, are appealed to either the three appeals courts or the Supreme Court. All proceedings, in whatever Mauritanian court, are open to the public and international human rights observers. All defendants in criminal cases, regardless of their ability to pay, are guaranteed legal counsel and also have the right (evidently respected in practice) to call witnesses and confront their accusers. In a significant development in 1999, a requirement that three judges preside over each trial was abolished, freeing many more jurists to hear cases and substantially shortening pretrial detention periods.

SPECIALIZED JUDICIAL BODIES

Although not courts in the strict sense of the word, in that they do not hear specific cases and controversies, the Constitutional Council and the Supreme Council of Magistrates are noteworthy because of their close relationship with the legal process. The Constitutional Council, with six members appointed by the executive and legislative branches, hears challenges to presidential and parliamentary elections, announces the results of national referenda, and decides on the constitutionality of basic laws and parliamentary rules. In most cases, the council is required to render a judgment within thirty days of submission.

The Supreme Council of Magistrates, by contrast, takes a more active role in the administration of justice. The council is made up of nine members: the president of the republic, the minister of justice, the president and senior vice president of the Supreme Court, three magistrates, and one representative each from the National Assembly and the Senate. Its annual review evaluates the courts' adherence to both law and due process, reassigns magistrates to different jurisdictions as needed, and makes rules for the training of judges and other judicial personnel—a process that gathered much added momentum in the late 1990s.

There are three other branches of the judiciary in Mauritania, and their limited jurisdictions places them outside the confines of the four-tiered regular court structure. Revenue Courts hear matters pertaining only to taxes and fees, while the three Labor Tribunals in the country deal with disputes between employers and workers on issues such as wages, benefits, working conditions, and unionization. Each Labor Tribunal has one presiding neutral judge, who is assisted by two assessors, one each representing the interests of employers and workers. There is no appeal from its decisions. Finally, military courts-martial, convened from time to time, judge offenses committed by members of the country's still-influential military establishment. These tribunals have very little publicity attached to them and are under the direct purview of the army chief of staff (*chef de l'état major*) and the minister of defense, both of whom answer to President Ould Taya in his constitutional role as commander-in-chief of all Mauritanian armed forces.

STAFFING

In view of the country's small and largely undereducated population, short history as an independent nation, and (until 1992) lack of experience with democratic institutions, the Mauritanian judiciary from 1960 until well into the 1990s was distinguished by uneven training (there were no law schools in the country) and a decided lack of autonomy from the executive branch of government. This was not surprising, given the long periods of either one-person civilian rule (Mokhtar Ould Daddah's presidency from 1960 to 1978) or military governance (1978–1992), in which presidential fiat, not legislative formulation/enactment or judicial review, was the decisive political factor. There were, to be sure, some attempts to improve the quality of individuals employed by the judiciary beginning in the 1960s and 1970s, but these had only a limited effect on account of the authoritarian character of the state and the scarcity of human and financial resources. Additional measures to upgrade the judicial branch were undertaken in the 1990s, including overseas specialized training for about 30 of the 224 total personnel by 2000. Lawyers in private practice, who had received their educations mostly abroad and who were concentrated in Nouakchott and a few other towns, were also the recipients of continuing legal education.

Whether intended for judges or attorneys, the primary motivation behind these reform efforts was negative public perception, including the belief that magistrates and others could abuse their power with little restraint and that citizens were basically at their mercy.

A major example of this occurred in July 1996, when six magistrates were among fifty-five or so people, included the Nouakchott public prosecutor and an adviser to the Court of Appeal, arrested and charged with complicity in a drug-trafficking scheme. More than a dozen police officers were also implicated. Underscoring the impunity with which these judicial officers had acted, only the arrest and interrogation of Osmane Baidy, reputedly a leading drug dealer in Mauritania, provided information that led to the arrests. The magistrates, for their part, were treated relatively leniently, as two were acquitted, two more given suspended jail sentences, and two others incarcerated for two to three years.

Mauritanian lawyers not associated with the Ould Taya regime, and especially those concerned with governmental conduct in the area of human rights, have three organizations to which they may belong. The first, the Conseil de l'Ordre des Avocats (Council of the Order of Lawyers—COA), functions as the formal Mauritanian Bar. A second group, the Association des Juristes Mauritaniens (Association of Mauritanian Jurists—AJM) is a voluntary group of attorneys seeking to uphold professional standards; it was founded on August 21, 1984. Finally, the country's Lique Mauritanienne des Droits de l'Homme (Mauritanian Human Rights League—LMDH) is the primary vehicle for attorneys and others to interact with the courts and government in human rights cases, which have been increasingly frequent after the mid-1990s. The LMDH was founded on April 13, 1986, and is sometimes the object of official intimidation because of its stance against arbitrary detention, maltreatment, and trial proceedings that do not meet international standards.

IMPACT

As a country with poorly developed formal institutions, and one in which the structure of society was still essentially tribal, Mauritania's legal system by 2001 was largely a tool of the authorities in serving their policies of limiting dissent and maintaining a formally pluralistic political party structure in which all real power was firmly in the hands of President Ould Taya and his backers in the PRDS and the security forces. Ordinary Mauritanians had ample reasons for believing that the courts were at best irrelevant to their daily lives and certainly little impediment to the untrammeled exercise of state power. For example, during the crisis atmosphere of the late 1980s under Comite Militaire de Salut National (CMSN) military rule, the courts actively served the interests of the state without any independence: the State Security Section of the Special Court of Justice, which operated under a broad and unreviewable grant of authority from the governing junta, held its proceedings in the closed precincts of the J'reida army barracks several miles north of Nouakchott. The three presiding judges were all military officers and were not even required to have had any legal education. They rendered their decisions with little or no input from defense counsel and with no appeals allowed from their frequently harsh verdicts. Serious additional charges were often filed against defendants on the very day of their trials, and defense lawyers, when they were allowed, were never able to prepare adequately. In addition, military courts often utilized a greatly expanded definition of the legal doctrine of *flagrant-delit* (literally, being "caught in the act" of committing an offense by a law-enforcement officer) in cases of conspiracy or other inchoate crimes. This also meant that no preliminary hearing before a magistrate was required, even in capital cases.

After the 1992 inauguration of the Mauritanian Second Republic, matters improved considerably, although the powers of the government to detain prisoners incommunicado for limited times and to restrict the flow of information were still extravagant, at least when compared with Western countries. President Ould Taya and his obedient Interior Ministry could still imprison opposition leader Ahmed Ould Daddah several times during the 1990s, and reportedly also did so in early 2001 to another popular politician and one-time presidential candidate, Mohamed Lemine Ch'Bih Ould Cheikh Malanine, on unfounded charges of being an agent of Libya. Press censorship was another area in which the advocates of free expression had achieved little by way of appeal to the judiciary, and legal limits on the discretion of the Ministry of the Interior were often not observed in practice. The judicial branch showed a fair degree of independence, however, in the fall of 1995, when, after a large-scale roundup of suspected members of the pro-Iraq Arab Baath Socialist Party and a demand for strict sentences for some of the defendants by the prosecution, it dismissed most of the charges and freed all the accused, citing insufficient evidence. Likewise, a trial court acquitted Ahmed Ould Daddah and a fellow opposition political activist in March 1999 after they had been charged with "incitement to violence and attacking public order" in connection with questions concerning an alleged agreement with Israel to stockpile nuclear wastes.

In spite of these positive signs of independence and at least a degree of respect for the rule of law, Mauritania's legal apparatus had not succeeded in garnering widespread public confidence. The citizenry, instead, opted whenever possible for informal or tribally based dispute resolution processes. In sum, the general unpopularity of the government of Mauritania was mirrored fairly closely in public perceptions of the courts and the legal system in general. Further evolution of these perceptions was dependent mainly upon whether President Ould Taya or his eventual successor would make further moves in the direction of genuine democracy.

Anthony G. Pazzanita

See also Administrative Tribunals; Appellate Courts; Civil Law; Commercial Law (International Aspects); Constitutional Law; Constitutional Review; Corporal Punishment; Criminal Law; Family Law; Government Legal Departments; Islamic Law; Judicial Independence; Judicial Misconduct/Judicial Discipline; Judicial Review; Juvenile Justice; Labor Law; Magistrates—Civil Law Systems; Qadi (Qazi) Courts; Trial Courts

References and further reading
Amnesty International. 1989. *Mauritania 1986–1989: Background to a Crisis: Three Years of Political Imprisonment, Torture and Unfair Trials.* New York: Amnesty International.
Calderini, Simonetta, Delia Cortese, and James L. A. Webb, Jr. 1992. *World Bibliographical Series: Mauritania.* Oxford: Clio Press.
Gerteiny, Alfred G. 1967. *Mauritania.* New York: Praeger.
Handloff, Robert E., ed. 1990. *Mauritania: A Country Study.* Washington, DC: U.S. Government Printing Office.
Human Rights Watch/Africa. 1994. *Mauritania's Campaign of Terror: State-Sponsored Repression of Black Africans.* New York: Human Rights Watch.
Ould-Mey, Mohameden. 1996. *Global Restructuring and Peripheral States: The Carrot and the Stick in Mauritania.* Lanham, MD: Littlefield Adams Books.
Pazzanita, Anthony G. 1996. *Historical Dictionary of Mauritania.* 2d ed. Lanham, MD: Scarecrow Press.
Salacuse, Jeswald W. 1969. *An Introduction to Law in French-Speaking Africa. Volume I: Africa South of the Sahara.* Charlottesville, VA: Michie Company.
U.S. Department of State. 1995–2001. *Country Reports on Human Rights Practices.* Washington, DC: U.S. Government Printing Office.

MAURITIUS

COUNTRY INFORMATION

Mauritius is situated in the southwest of the Indian Ocean, 800 kilometers east of Madagascar. It consists of the principal island (Mauritius) and three small islands (Agalega, Rodrigues, and Saint Brandon). Although volcanic in origin, volcanic activity has completely ceased. It has an area of 1,864 square kilometers and, apart from a gap on the steep south coast, is surrounded by coral reefs that enclose lagoons and sandy beaches. Inland, it rises from the coastal plain to a central plateau at 670 meters, bordered by three mountain ranges with peaks in excess of 800 meters. It has numerous rivers and waterfalls. The country has no indigenous population. Its 1.2 million inhabitants are a mix of ethnic groups: Indo-Mauritian (68 percent); Creole (27 percent); Sino-Mauritian (3 percent); and Franco-Mauritian (2 percent). Literacy of the total population over fifteen is approximately 83 percent. From an original agricultural economy, Mauritius has developed into a diversified economy with growing industrial, financial, and tourist sectors and a low unemployment rate. It has a gross domestic product (GDP) of some $12 billion. The population below the poverty line is estimated at 10 percent. The majority religion is Hindu (52 percent), with the balance largely Catholic (26 percent) and Muslim (17 percent). The country has a mixed legal system combining elements of French civil law and English common law. While the official language is English, French and Creole are commonly and widely spoken.

Mauritius has a maritime climate: tropical with the risk of cyclones during summer (November to April); subtropical during winter (June to September). The capital is Port Louis, with 120,000 inhabitants. The currency is the Mauritius rupee: MUR28.2 per U.S.$1 (April 2001).

HISTORY

The island was for a long period unknown and uninhabited, although visited by Arabs and Malays as early as the tenth century. In 1511 it was discovered by Portuguese explorers, who were probably the first Europeans to land on the island. The Portuguese, who gave the name Mascarenes to the islands now known as Mauritius, Rodrigues, and La Réunion, showed no further interest. In 1598 a Dutch naval squadron visited the island and named it Mauritius in honor of Prince Maurice Van Nassau, *Stathouder* of Holland. This was followed in 1638 by the establishment of the first Dutch settlement. After several further attempts, settlement proved to be commercially unsuccessful and the Dutch abandoned the island in 1710. During the Dutch period sugarcane, domestic animals, and deer were introduced.

France took possession of the island in 1715, initially as a port of call on the route to India, and named it Isle de France. French colonization began in 1721. At first the island was administered by the Compagnie des Indes (the French East India Company), but from 1767 it was in the charge of officials appointed by the French government. During the French period the sugar industry was developed, relying heavily on slave labor introduced from Africa and Madagascar. The French also established Port Louis as a naval base and ship-building center. The Napoleonic period saw the island being used by the French as a base from which to harass British maritime communications with India. In 1810 a British expeditionary force captured the island and placed it under military administration. By the Treaty of Paris, 1814, France ceded full sovereignty over the island to Britain and its former name, Mauritius, was restored. After the capture, the British government gave and honored a political undertaking to preserve the religion, laws, and customs of the inhabitants.

British colonial administration from 1814 was responsible for rapid social and economic changes. A significant event was the abolition of slavery in 1835 and the payment of £2 million compensation to sugar planters for the loss of their slaves. The abolition of slavery had far-reaching socioeconomic and demographic repercussions. The sugar planters turned to India, from where they brought in large numbers of indentured laborers to work in the sugarcane fields. These Indian immigrants, both Hindu and Muslim, brought about profound changes in the fabric of society. They were later joined by a small number of Chinese traders. During the British period the

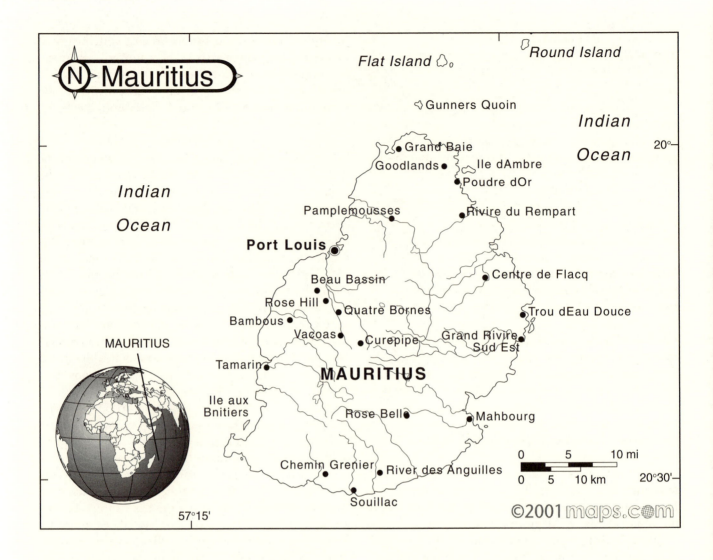

Mauritius

Flat Island 〇₀

Round Island

Gunners Quoin

Indian

Ocean

20°

Grand Baie

Goodlands ●   ● Ile dAmbre

● Poudre dOr

Indian

Ocean

Pamplemousses   Rivire du Rempart

Port Louis ●

Beau Bassin   Centre de Flacq

Rose Hill ●   ● Quatre Bornes

Bambous ●

Vacoas ●   Curepipe   Grand Rivire

Sud Est

Trou dEau Douce

Tamarin   MAURITIUS

Ile aux
Bnitiers

Rose Belle ●   ● Mahbourg

Chemin Grenier   River des Anguilles

Souillac

MAURITIUS

0   5   10 mi

0   5   10 km

20°30'

57°15'

©2001 maps.com

sugar industry thrived and the island flourished largely due to exports of sugar to Britain. Also during this period the means of communication were extended and improved and an adequate infrastructure developed.

As a dependent territory of the United Kingdom Mauritius was administered by a governor who retained wide executive powers. In 1825 a Council of Government was established that, after the adoption of the Constitution of 1885, included not only official and nominated members but also a minority of members elected on a limited franchise. Negotiations for a more liberal regime, in which the social-democratic Mauritius Labor Party, founded in 1936, played a leading role, resulted in the adoption of the Constitution of 1947, which extended the franchise to all adults who could pass a simple literacy test. It also replaced the Council of Government with a Legislative Council on which the elected members were in a majority. Constitutional conferences held in London in the 1950s resulted in the adoption of universal adult suffrage. Further constitutional conferences in 1961 and 1965 paved the way for Mauritius to achieve independence.

In 1968 Mauritius adopted a new constitution based on the British parliamentary model and became an independent state within the British Commonwealth. That constitution, which was monarchical in form, was replaced by the present republican constitution in 1992 substituting a president for the British queen as head of state and making various consequential amendments. In addition to the Labor Party, Mauritius has two other principal political parties, the Militant Socialist Movement (MSM) and the Mauritian Militant Movement (MMM).

Mauritius is a member of a group of over seventy African, Caribbean, and Pacific (ACP) countries that have entered a partnership agreement with the European Union (EU). This, the Cotonou Agreement 2000, provides a framework for economic and trade cooperation between the EU and the ACP countries. The principal benefit is preferential access for ACP products to EU markets on a nonreciprocal basis. Under the terms of this agreement, the EU has undertaken for an indefinite period to purchase and import at guaranteed prices specific quantities of cane sugar from Mauritius.

LEGAL CONCEPTS

The Republic of Mauritius is a sovereign democratic state. Its constitution is the supreme law of the land and any laws inconsistent with it are void. While legislation is the primary source of law, Mauritius follows the common law tradition and recognizes case law as a major source of law. A law reporter system (*Mauritius Reports*) has been published continuously since 1861. As well as providing for the legislative, executive, and judicial branches of government, the constitution also guarantees human rights, created the office of ombudsman, established Service Commissions and the Public Service, and contains provisions relating to citizenship and national finance.

Under the constitution, the power to make laws for Mauritius is vested in its Parliament. But, subject to that, its law and legal system remain a unique mixture of the legal traditions of both its former colonial rulers. The French Code Civile, Code de Commerce, and Code Pénal provide the framework of Mauritian private, commercial, and criminal law respectively. But aspects of family law and the law relating to bankruptcy, banking, corporations, and criminal evidence and procedure all follow English models. Mauritian commercial law is influenced by its association with the EU through participation in the Cotonou Agreement. Subject to the written constitution, public law generally, including the system of judicial review of administrative action, follows the English common law mold. The Mauritian courts refer to the relevant French and English legal authorities for guidance but do not regard themselves as bound by them.

The constitution gives pride of place to the protection of fundamental rights and freedoms of the individual. It contains a series of detailed provisions dealing with the right to life, the right to personal liberty, protection from slavery and forced labor, protection from inhuman treatment, protection from deprivation of property, the right to a fair trial, protection of freedom of conscience, protection of freedom of expression, protection of freedom of assembly and association, protection of freedom to establish schools, protection of freedom of movement, and protection from discrimination. These rights and freedoms are subject to respect for the rights and freedoms of others and for the public interest.

The unicameral Parliament of Mauritius consists of the president and a national assembly with seventy members. Sixty-two of the assembly's members are chosen in general elections by universal adult suffrage and secret ballot. The right to vote is granted at eighteen years. There are twenty-one electoral districts; twenty for Mauritius returning three members each and one for Rodrigues returning two members. The eight additional seats are allocated by an independent Electoral Supervisory Commission to the most successful unelected candidates in such a way as to achieve communal balance without disturbing the political outcome of the election.

The head of state and commander-in-chief is the president of Mauritius, who is elected by the National Assembly. The president appoints the prime minister, who must be the member of the National Assembly who in the president's judgment is best able to command the support of the majority of the members of the assembly. Acting on the advice of the prime minister, the president appoints the deputy prime minister and other ministers from the members of the assembly. The president also appoints as leader of the opposition the member of the assembly who in his judgment commands the support of the opposition parties. The present president is Cassam Uteem (MMM). The present government, which came into power after the general election held in September 2000, is an alliance of the MMM and the MSM with Aneerood Jugnauth (MSM) as prime minister.

Responsibility for the conduct of government business and the administration of government departments lies with the prime minister and the other ministers who together form the Cabinet. While executive authority is vested in the president, that authority is exercised in accordance with the advice of the Cabinet, which retains collective responsibility for such advice. The president's authority to dissolve Parliament and initiate a general election is exercised in accordance with the advice of the prime minister who may so advise at any time. But if the assembly passes a resolution of no confidence in the government and the prime minister does not resign, the president shall remove him from office and dissolve Parliament. The Parliament will also stand dissolved five years after the previous general election, if not dissolved earlier.

The power to make laws for the peace, good order, and government of Mauritius is vested in its Parliament. That power is exercised by bills passed by the assembly and assented to by the president, which then become acts of Parliament. The president may only withhold his assent to a bill that has been passed by the assembly in order to request the assembly to reconsider it. He is then obliged to assent to the bill after reconsideration whether or not it has been amended. While a simple majority of the assembly is sufficient to pass ordinary bills, bills to amend the constitution require special procedures and majorities. A bill to amend the constitutional status of Mauritius would require the assenting votes of not less than three-quarters of the electorate in a referendum and all of the members of the assembly. Treaties to which Mauritius is a party are not a direct source of law and may be applied by the courts only if they have been incorporated by an act of Parliament.

Judicial authority is vested in the Supreme Court, which functions at both trial court and appellate levels. It also has jurisdiction to determine breaches and questions of interpretation of the constitution, to enforce fundamental rights and freedoms, and to decide questions as to membership of the National Assembly. It has a supervisory jurisdiction over subordinate courts and tribunals and over the legality of executive and administrative acts. A final appeal from the Supreme Court lies to the Judicial Committee of the Privy Council in the United Kingdom in specified instances. The retention of this right of appeal, to what was historically the final court of the British Empire, recognizes the need for a detached and independent final tribunal to resolve sensitive legal issues that may arise in a small and closely knit community.

The attorney general is a member of the National Assembly and of the Cabinet and is the principal legal adviser of the government. He also presides over a group of barristers known as state counsel who conduct criminal prosecutions. Principal responsibility for initiating criminal prosecutions is vested in the director of public prosecutions, who must have the same qualifications for appointment as a judge of the Supreme Court. Appointments as state counsel are the responsibility of the Judicial and Legal Service Commission, which is presided over by the chief justice. Appointment to public offices generally is the responsibility of the Public Service Commission. Similarly, the Police Service Commission appoints the commissioner of police and other members of the police force. The independence of these commissions is underwritten by the constitution.

The ombudsman is appointed by the president after consulting the prime minister, the leader of the opposition, and any other leaders of parties in the National Assembly. His independence is safeguarded by the constitution. At the request of an individual or of a minister or other member of the assembly or on his own initiative, he may investigate allegations of injustice resulting from maladministration by government departments, the police, the Prison Service, and other authorities prescribed by Parliament. He may also investigate allegations of fraud or corruption against ministers, members of the National Assembly, and other public officers. The ombudsman has wide powers of investigation and authority to demand documents and information. Where the ombudsman substantiates an allegation of maladministration, he may make appropriate reasoned recommendations for remedial action. He may draw to the attention of the prime minister, other ministers concerned, and the National Assembly any failure to take adequate action in a reasonable time. In relation to an allegation of fraud or corruption, he must make a report to the president, which will then be forwarded to the prime minister and the National Assembly.

CURRENT COURT SYSTEM STRUCTURE

Judicial authority in Mauritius, subject to the possibility of appeal to the Judicial Committee of the Privy Council in the United Kingdom, is vested in the Supreme Court by the constitution. The Supreme Court is composed of the chief justice, the senior puisne judge, and a number of puisne judges as prescribed by Parliament, currently seven. The president appoints the members of the court: the chief justice on the advice of the prime minister, the senior puisne judge on the advice of the chief justice, and the puisne judges on the advice of the Judicial and Legal Service Commission. Following English practice, they are appointed from the ranks of barristers of at least five years' standing. Judges of the Supreme Court enjoy security of tenure until retirement age. This is subject to a procedure of removal on grounds of infirmity or misbehavior. There are in addition a number of inferior courts, the intermediate court, the district courts, and the industrial court, with specific and limited jurisdiction. Magistrates, appointed by the Judicial and Legal Service Commission, staff these: two or three in the case of the intermediate court and one in the other two cases. Magistrates are appointed by the Judicial and Legal Service Commission from persons with at least three years' standing as barristers. While the official language of the courts is English, persons with insufficient command of English may use French, Creole, or other languages. Interpretation and translation services are provided.

The Supreme Court has unlimited civil jurisdiction. It can hear any civil action as a trial court, including, at the choice of the plaintiff, cases that fall within the limited civil competence of the Intermediate and district courts. The Supreme Court has exclusive jurisdiction over divorce cases and forms special divisions for bankruptcy and admiralty matters. In all of these instances a single judge usually sits, although more may be assigned to cases perceived as complex and important. Decisions of the court in civil cases may be appealed to a three-judge bench of the Supreme Court, which is then styled the court of appeal. The court of appeal, sitting with two judges, also hears civil appeals from the Intermediate and district courts.

Minor criminal offences are tried by district courts that sit in various locations throughout Mauritius. The intermediate court, which sits in Port Louis, has jurisdiction over most serious crimes (excluding homicide). Neither of these courts sits with a jury. Very serious crimes, particularly murder, are tried by the assize court, consisting of a single judge of the Supreme Court sitting with a nine-member jury. Criminal appeals from the intermediate court and the district courts go to a court of appeal of two Supreme Court judges. Appeals from the assize court go to a three-member court of appeal presided by either the chief justice or the senior puisne judge.

In addition to its trial court and appellate jurisdictions over civil and criminal cases, the Supreme Court has review powers of two kinds: review of constitutionality and

Legal Structure of Mauritius Courts

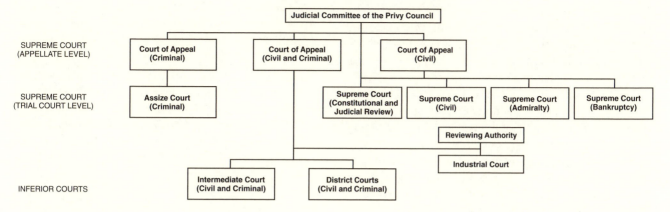

review of legality. In respect to the former, it may consider any question of whether authorities or persons have performed their functions in accordance with the constitution. The court has wide powers to make declarations that the constitution has been contravened and to grant appropriate remedies. In respect to the latter, it has jurisdiction to determine whether public authorities have acted within their legal competence. When they have failed to do so, illegal acts will be declared void and illegal omissions will be required to be remedied. While both of these jurisdictions function within the framework of the constitution, the substantive and procedural rules for review are largely common law in nature and continue to rely significantly on the practice of the English High Court.

A final appeal from civil, criminal, and review decisions of the Supreme Court goes to the Judicial Committee of the Privy Council in cases set out in the constitution. There is an appeal as of right from final decisions on the interpretation of the constitution and on the enforcement of fundamental rights and in respect to claims above a certain financial limit. There is an appeal by leave of the Supreme Court from final decisions in civil cases and in cases that raise issues of great general or public importance. Appeals in any civil or criminal matter may also lie with the special leave of the Judicial Committee.

The constitution empowers the president, acting on the advice of an independent Commission on the Prerogative of Mercy, to grant to convicted persons, as appropriate, a pardon, respite in the execution of punishment, substitution of a lesser punishment, or remission of the whole or part of a punishment or penalty.

SPECIALIZED JUDICIAL BODIES

The industrial court has exclusive jurisdiction over cases arising under labor and factory laws. Its proceedings have an informal nature. In addition to its judicial authority, the court has a conciliatory role aimed at achieving an amicable settlement between the disputing parties. All decisions of the court are subject to scrutiny by a reviewing authority, the chief justice, or his delegate. The reviewing authority has wide powers to quash, revise, or remit for a further hearing. The decisions of the court are not binding until this review has been completed. Decisions of the industrial court may be appealed to a two-member court of appeal.

The constitution provides for an Electoral Boundaries Commission and an Electoral Supervisory Commission, both appointed by the president on the advice of the prime minister in consultation with the leader of the opposition. Members of the assembly, candidates for public office, and public officials are excluded from membership of these bodies. The task of the Boundaries Commission is to carry out an independent review of the boundaries of electoral districts in light of demographic changes and to make recommendations for alterations in the boundaries. The aim is to ensure that the number of inhabitants in each electoral district is as nearly equal as possible. The Supervisory Commission is responsible for the registration of electors and for supervising the elections of members of the assembly. In addition, any bill before Parliament and any secondary legislation proposing changes in the law relating to these matters must be referred to the Supervisory Commission for comment.

STAFFING

The legal profession, reflecting Anglo-French influences, has three distinct branches: notaries, attorneys, and barristers. Notaries are responsible for drawing up and attesting documents required for transactions relating to the transfer of real property, the administration of decedents' estates, matrimonial property, and corporations. Attorneys, equivalent to English solicitors, are general legal practitioners whose principal functions are to give advice and to prepare cases and brief barristers for the argument of cases in the superior courts. They may also plead cases in the lower courts. Barristers are essentially advocates and enjoy a comprehensive right of audience in all Mauritian courts. The number of notaries is fixed by law, currently at forty-five. Each notary practices individually with a supporting staff. There are no legal limits on the numbers of attorneys and barristers. There are at present about 160 attorneys and over 140 barristers, the latter mostly based in Port Louis, the seat of the principal courts.

Legal education has undergone far-reaching changes in recent years. Traditionally notaries and attorneys were trained by apprenticeship and qualified by passing examinations set by a committee responsible to the chief justice. There was no requirement for formal legal training, although a small minority studied for a law degree in England or France. At that time, admission as a barrister was conditional on having first qualified as a barrister in England. This involved a four-year program of legal studies in England, three studying for a law degree and one preparing for English bar examinations. In the early 1980s these arrangements were subjected to a wide-ranging review on the recommendations of which the present system of legal education is based. In 1985 a School of Law was established at the University of Mauritius with provision for a three-year program leading to the degree of bachelor of laws (LL.B.). Those intending to enter any of the branches of the legal profession must now first obtain that degree. Thereafter, they undertake a fourth year of vocational training under the auspices of the Council of Legal Education. That in turn is followed by one further year of practical training for intending barristers and two years for intending notaries and attorneys. After the completion of the relevant program a license to practice is granted.

IMPACT OF LAW

Mauritius is a mature, sophisticated, and stable democracy that has functioned peacefully for over thirty years. Governments of changing political allegiance have uneventfully succeeded each other following regular general elections. The multiracial nature of its population has not resulted in serious confrontation or violence. An essential factor in all of this has been respect for the rule of law and for the rights and freedoms of the individual. The law, legal system, and administration of justice in Mauritius have played a key role in guaranteeing this state of affairs. An independent, skilled, and respected judiciary, aided by an able legal profession, has progressively developed the law from its mixed colonial origins into a distinctive Mauritian legal order that has shown its adaptability and responsiveness to contemporary demands and challenges.

John W. Bridge

See also Barristers; Civil Law; Common Law; Constitutional Review; England and Wales; France; Judicial Review; Juries; Napoleonic Code; Notaries; Privy Council; Solicitors; United Kingdom

References and further reading
Angelo, Anthony H. 1970. "Mauritius: The Basis of the Legal System." *Comparative and International Law Journal of Southern Africa* 3: 228–241.
Boolel, Vinod. 1996. "The Influence of the European Convention on the Constitutional Law of Mauritius." *European Human Rights Law Review* 2: 159–170.
Bridge, John W. 1997. "Judicial Review in Mauritius and the Continuing Influence of English Law." *International and Comparative Law Quarterly* 46: 787–811.
Brown, L. Neville. 1996. "Mauritius: Mixed Laws in a Mini-Jurisdiction." Pp. 209–223 in *Studies in Legal Systems: Mixed and Mixing.* Edited by Esin Örücü, Elizabeth Attwooll, and Sean Coyle. The Hague: Kluwer Law International.
Colom, Jacques. 1994. *La Justice Constitutionnelle dans les États du Nouveau Commonwealth: Le Cas de L'Île Maurice.* Paris: Economica.
De Smith, Stanley A. 1968. "Mauritius: Constitutionalism in a Plural Society." *Modern Law Review* 31: 601–622.
The Government of Mauritius: Official Web Portal, http://ncb.intnet.mu/govt/ (accessed April 25, 2001).
Manrakhan, Jagadish. 1994. *A Reading of the Law at Réduit.* University of Mauritius: Éditions de l'Océan Indien.
Mauritius Constitutional Conference. 1965. Cmnd. 2797. London: Her Majesty's Stationery Office.
Napal, D. 1962. *Les Constitutions de l'Île Maurice.* Port Louis: The Mauritius Printing Company Limited.

MEDIATION

WHAT IT IS

Mediation is a process in which a third party (usually neutral and unbiased) facilitates a negotiated consensual agreement among parties to a dispute, transaction, or public policy matter without rendering a formal decision. Most commonly, mediation occurs when two parties to a dispute seek the assistance of a neutral third party to help them resolve or settle the conflict between them. Increasingly, however, mediation is used even when parties have lawyers (such as in mediation programs that are attached to formal courts) and when there are more than two parties. Because mediation is designed to help the parties craft their own solutions to problems, the animating ideas of mediation are voluntariness, consent, self-determination, and negotiated rather than decisional modes of resolution. In addition, the techniques of facilitated negotiation or mediation are increasingly being used in situations other than traditional two-party legal disputes, in such situations as complex multiparty public policy disputes (such as environmental siting, budget allocations, municipal governance situations), international treaties on peace and trade, and the formation of transactions and entities. For example, the idea of "partnering" has been applied to use mediation techniques for communication and problem solving when large construction projects are planned and the parties construct a consensual process for dispute resolution before any actual disputes occur. Mediation processes are also used to facilitate "public conversations" on difficult public policy topics, such as abortion, affirmative action, and social welfare policy, which may not produce a negotiated "outcome" other than further understanding of value differences.

Mediation is intended to be a facilitated communication process in which the neutral third party structures communication so that parties may share information about their interests, needs, and objectives (rather than stated oppositional "positions") in order to solve problems between or among them. As facilitators of communication, mediators ask questions of the parties, ask them to directly negotiate with each other, and unlike in a court or more formal setting, the mediator may meet privately with the parties (in what are called caucuses) to determine what the parties really want but may be afraid to disclose with the other party present. Thus, in economic terms, mediation is intended to reduce information asymmetries and prevent "waste" from occurring when the parties fail to share important information with each other because of fears of strategic manipulation by the other side. Increasingly, some mediators are inclined to offer their own suggestions for solutions to problems, and thus the role of the mediator as a "pure" facilitator or as more active "evaluator" has become more controversial and, some would say, has moved closer in some contexts to the role of an arbiter.

Much mediation is conducted privately, with parties contracting for its use either before a dispute has ripened or a transaction is planned or during the "eruption" of a dispute. In addition, mediation is now recommended and in some cases required by courts when a formal legal complaint is filed. Various forms of mediation, such as "shuttle diplomacy," are also used in the international arena to attempt resolution of international and nation-state conflicts, and some forms of mediation are also used to resolve international trade and commercial disputes as well. So mediation as a process is developing in parallel but sometimes different forms in the public and private sectors, within particular national cultures, and also within multinational domains as a pluralist legal process that can be used across legal jurisdictional boundaries.

HISTORICAL BACKGROUND

Mediation is probably as old as humankind itself. Even in primitive and ancient societies, the "triad" of two parties and one neutral was one of the oldest forms of dispute resolution. Although different societies and cultures used the "third party" in different ways, ranging from a "neutral" who facilitated a consensual solution made by the parties to a deeply embedded-in-the-community "wise elder" who imposed a solution on the parties (closer to arbitration or adjudication) to a "panel" of neutrals (as in

African moots) who helped determine what was best for the community as well as the parties, the idea of going to a third party for help in dispute resolution seems to be a human universal. Different cultures place different values on the purpose of mediation—to resolve disputes between conflictual parties, to secure community harmony for others affected by a dispute or conflict, or even, in its use in Maoist China, as a process of political rectification in dispute resolution.

Modern use of mediation is motivated by several different (and sometimes conflicting) themes or values. Like some forms of commercial arbitration, mediation is used when the disputing or transacting parties share a community or life world and therefore have common norms to apply to their dealings and problem solving. Thus, mediation is now commonly used in ethnic communities, neighborhoods, industry-specific contracts, labor-management relations, and family matters. One of the most eloquent elaborators of the modern mediation concept, Lon Fuller, a legal philosopher, suggested that mediation was a way for parties in a relationship "to reorient themselves to each other," thereby indicating that mediation is a particularly appropriate method of dispute resolution when there is an ongoing relationship between the parties (or when, as in the case of divorce, the parties are ending a relationship with ongoing consequences for others, such as their children).

Others have suggested that mediation may be appropriate even when the parties do not have ongoing relationships but might craft a better solution to their problem than a more formal institution might give them. Legislatures write laws for the general population that might not be appropriate in particular cases, and courts can only resolve past disputes and have limited remedial power over future dealings of the parties. Judicial systems are limited to monetary damages and some injunctive relief. Mediation allows parties to craft their own individualized solutions to problems and conflicts, including arrangements and indeed "rules" for the future; thus, mediation provides the possibility of both "better" or Pareto-optimal solutions (where both parties are made as well off as possible without further harm to the other) to conflicts and problems and the possibility of flexible and future-oriented governance for the parties. Because of the consensual nature of decision making, the flexibility of process, and the possibility of involvement of not just the immediate parties but all stakeholders in a problem, mediation processes are increasingly being used in a variety of governmental, policy, and legal processes in which multiple parties have an interest in situations with multiple issues. Mediators serve as facilitators of democratic consensus-building processes by developing process rules, managing mutual information sharing, and helping the parties brainstorm possible solutions for evaluation and consensual (not necessarily majoritarian) adoption and implementation.

For many engaged in the formal litigation system, mediation has been recently encouraged because of a belief that it will not only provide better-quality solutions to litigated problems but because it is thought to provide cheaper and faster resolutions to problems and thus provide more efficient justice for the litigating parties, as well as greater speed and less cost for the judicial system as a whole. Attempts to empirically measure these claims of greater efficiency have been mixed at best.

The modern use of mediation, at least in U.S. courts, can be dated from an important speech delivered by Professor Frank Sander of the Harvard Law School in 1976 at the Pound Conference on the Causes of Popular Dissatisfaction with the Administration of Justice, at which the idea of a "multidoor courthouse" was first proposed. Mediation was described as one of the processes that a screening clerk would recommend to parties seeking a more consensual, relationship-preserving method for resolving disputes. Some twenty-five years later, many U.S. courts (now followed by courts in the United Kingdom, Canada, Australia, and other common law justice systems) have instituted variations on the multidoor courthouse to include mediation in a "menu" of different choices that parties might have in processing their disputes. In addition to caseload reduction, the hope is that mediation will increase access to justice by affording more people more forums for dispute resolution, both within the courts and without, and will provide a forum in which not everyone will have to be represented by a lawyer.

KEY CONCEPTS AND USAGE

Mediation is based on an ideology of voluntariness and consensual decision making. The parties to a dispute or transaction are considered the principal actors. Decisions are generally not to be rendered by the third party, who is not a judge (or even an arbitrator). Instead, *the third party facilitator* is, in most cases, supposed to be neutral and unbiased with respect to both the parties and the subject matter of the dispute or transaction. The *third party neutral* is supposed to facilitate communication between the parties by managing conversational rules or by asking parties to explore underlying needs, interests, and goals, as opposed to stating or demanding legal positions. Mediation is designed to seek party-developed solutions to disputes, problems, conflicts, or transactions with maximum party participation. The result or outcome of a mediation is a consensual agreement that is legally a contract or, in a few specialized cases, may be entered as a court order or judgment. Most mediation agreements still require court enforcement if they are not adhered to, though the empirical evidence, such as it is, suggests that compliance with mediated agreements is higher than with court orders in contested cases.

There are a variety of issues and controversies sparked by the use of mediation, including whether mediation is possible when the parties have unequal bargaining power or resources, whether mediation privatizes important public justice concerns and "hides" negotiated agreements from public view in important matters, and whether mediation practice should be limited to particular professional domains such as law or psychology since the work of mediators often involves predicting what a court would do or facilitating the communication patterns of human beings. Thus, mediation is a multidisciplinary practice with an eclectic theoretical foundation that spans several possible domains. In recent years, there has been a call for more regulation of mediation practice, in terms of who is considered qualified to mediate, what conflicts of interests or ethics rules should be applied, and whether mediators should be made accountable or liable for the agreements over which they preside. Whether the effectiveness of mediation as a process (as measured by party satisfaction, outcome durability, fairness, or efficiency) can be established by empirical study remains unsettled as a variety of studies at local, regional, national, and international levels seek to operationalize and study the different measures of "success." Since high-quality solutions may actually take more time and expense to accomplish (especially in the new complex multiparty-multi-issue forms of mediation), the goals of fairness, durability, and efficiency may be somewhat contradictory to each other.

Mediators themselves are engaged in debates about whether mediation must always be *pure facilitated mediation* or whether it is appropriate, in the name of providing reality testing to the parties, for the mediators to evaluate or predict legal or likely outcomes for the parties so they can decide what solution makes the most sense for them. These debates about the proper role of the mediator implicate concerns about the "essential" process integrity of different kinds of legal processes in a continuing effort to keep mediation separate from other forms of legal process like adjudication, arbitration, or dyadic negotiation. Different schools of practice emphasize different elements of the mediation process. For example, *transformative mediation* emphasizes the recognition by parties of each other's needs and empowerment, favoring the relationship-preserving aspects of mediation, whereas others focus more on the *task orientation* of dispute settlement. For some, the key values of mediation are party participation and democratic control of a process that affects the parties. Since for some proponents, mediation is seen as a social movement to enhance democratic and party participation and legitimacy of outcome, as well as a process that is intended to promote peaceful and more harmonious relations between parties, use of mediation in other than these consensual and voluntary settings is seen as a possible distortion of the motivating ideal.

INSTITUTIONAL ELEMENTS

Because of the hope that mediation might speed case processing time and reduce caseloads, mediation has been appended to the formal processing of cases in many courts. Some courts require all parties to consider some form of alternative dispute resolution before going to trial; others simply recommend some attempt at one of the alternatives to trial. Where mediation is formally located in the courts (as in some U.S. states and most U.S. federal courts), there is some court oversight in the form of training of mediators, ethical standards and rules, and some empirical evaluation of settlement rates. Many mediators are concerned, however, that use by formal institutions of a process that was intended to be flexible and seek solutions that may be beyond what a court could do will co-opt the essence of this process.

Most mediation is still conducted in private settings, including commercial and trade settings, labor management, and family and divorce. In some settings where contracts require people to use more rigid forms of arbitration, many are now advocating that mediation, a more flexible and voluntary process, should be tried first in a "tiered" system of dispute resolution. Because of the many settings in which mediation is used, including training young people to learn "peer mediation" to manage their own conflicts with friends and in schools, a great variety of people perform mediational roles in community and nonprofessional settings, as well as in highly specialized settings that may require some subject matter expertise (such as international trade, health care, construction disputes, and intellectual property). There are also choices about whether mediation should be specified in advance, as in a contract, as the dispute resolution mechanism of choice, or whether parties should wait until a dispute has ripened to consider what form of dispute resolution they seek to utilize.

Mediation is now often thought to provide a transparent enough process that it is considered especially effective in international and cross-jurisdictional settings. Parties can set their own ground rules for participation, select their own third-party facilitators, and elaborate their own decision rules (majority, supramajority, consensus) for different kinds of disputes. In the international arena, mediation is now seen as a particularly appropriate form of process when there are conflicts about what forum or what law ought to apply in a particular situation. However, there is concern that mediation is somewhat "ethnocentric" in that it privileges "talking" as a way of resolving conflicts and thus may grant great power to particular individuals, groups, or cultures that are more self-disclosing or oral in tradition.

It is unlikely that any particular single institution can control mediation since it is now practiced in formal legal institutions, in many private and nongovernmental settings, and across many disciplines with a full range of participants. A great variety of professional associations have begun to develop regulatory frameworks, including ethics, qualification, and credential requirements, and some political entities, state legislatures, and courts have promulgated rules and standards about how mediation can be practiced, but for the most part the practice of mediation remains relatively unregulated, with easy entry by those who would mediate or be mediated.

Those who strongly support mediation as a process hope that it will continue to be used as a flexible, voluntary, conciliatory (as contrasted to adversarial) process that will improve relations between parties, provide forums for international peace and efficient relations, and provide better solutions to both individual and large social problems where more formal institutions have failed.

Carrie Menkel-Meadow

See also Adversarial System; Alternative Dispute Resolution; Arbitration; Civil Procedure; Legal Pluralism; Moots; Neighborhood Justice Centers; United States—Federal System; United States—State Systems

References and further reading

Bush, Robert Baruch, and Joseph P. Folger. 1994. *The Promise of Mediation*. San Francisco: Jossey-Bass.

Fuller, Lon. 1971. "Mediation: Its Forms and Functions." *Southern California Law Review* 44: 305–339.

Greenberg, Melanie, John Barton, and Margaret E. McGuinness. 2000. *Words over War: Mediation and Arbitration to Prevent Deadly Conflict*. Lanham, MD: Rowman and Littlefield.

Grillo, Trina. 1990–1991. "The Mediation Alternative: Process Dangers for Women." *Yale Law Journal* 100: 1545–1610.

Menkel-Meadow, Carrie. 2001. *Mediation: Theory, Practice and Policy*. Aldershot, U.K.: Ashgate.

Moore, Christopher. 1986. *The Mediation Process: Practical Strategies for Resolving Conflict*. San Francisco: Jossey-Bass.

Nader, Laura. 1993. "Controlling Processes in the Practice of Law: Hierarchy and Pacification in the Movement to Re-Form Dispute Ideology." *Ohio State Journal of Dispute Resolution* 9: 1–25.

Riskin, Leonard. 1996. "Understanding Mediators' Orientations, Strategies and Techniques: A Grid for the Perplexed." *Harvard Negotiation Law Review* 1: 7–51.

Sander, Frank. 1976. "The Varieties of Dispute Processing." 70 F.R.D. (Federal Rules Decisions) 79.

MERCOSUR

See Dispute Resolution under Regional Trade Agreements

MERIT SELECTION ("MISSOURI PLAN")

Merit selection is the term most commonly used to refer to a method of selecting state court judges through a nominating commission process. The merit selection plan is designed to stress professional qualifications, reduce the influence of politics in the judiciary and the judicial appointments process, and eliminate the need for campaigning and fund-raising by attorneys seeking judicial office. Under a merit selection system, a bipartisan or nonpartisan commission of lawyers and laypersons recruits, investigates, and interviews applicants for judicial vacancies. Following a thorough review of the qualifications of applicants, the commission generally votes to recommend three to five of the most highly qualified nominees to the appointing authority (usually a state governor) for final appointment. Following a short initial term in office, judges are subject to one of two methods that provide for possible removal from the bench, the most common of which is a nonpartisan retention election, in which voters are asked only whether a particular judge should be retained in office. In the alternative, nominating commissions reevaluate sitting judges and recommend reappointment or removal, subject to confirmation by the appointing authority.

Most states utilizing merit selection plans use the system for all levels of courts, though a number of states apply variations of the plan in certain situations, such as for interim vacancies or for specific levels of courts. Typically, in states with histories of judicial elections, merit selection plans are implemented through a state constitutional amendment process. Other states have codified the use of nominating commissions into state statutes, and fewer still have implemented limited nominating commissions through the use of executive orders. A variant of merit selection is also used in some instances for selecting nominees for vacancies on the federal courts of the United States.

HISTORICAL BACKGROUND

During the colonial era, leaders of the American Revolution attacked the system of royal appointment of judges. The Declaration of Independence stated that the king had "made judges dependent on his will alone, for the tenure of their offices, and the amount and payment of their salaries." The original thirteen states provided for appointment of judges either by the legislature or by the governor and his council. But in 1832, in a development partially born of the populist movements of the Jacksonian era, the state of Mississippi initiated the practice of judicial elections. By the Civil War, twenty-four of thirty-four states had established an elected judiciary. From that point forward, every state admitted to the Union adopted popular election of some or all judges.

Elective systems proved to have serious faults, with political machines selecting judges often perceived as corrupt and incompetent. By the end of the nineteenth century, several states adopted nonpartisan judicial elections, an ineffective reform in states where political party leaders continued to select judicial candidates. Critics of all elective systems for judges, most notably Roscoe Pound, began to advocate a "merit plan," through which a commission would nominate potential judges for their professional qualifications, not their political affiliations. Origins of the plan are usually traced to Albert M. Kales, one of the founders of the American Judicature Society. In 1940, Missouri became the first state to adopt a nonpartisan nominating commission plan for appellate judges and trial court judges in St. Louis and Kansas City (with trial court judges in the rest of the state remaining under a system of partisan elections). Over the next fifty years, thirty-one states and the District of Columbia adopted a nominating commission system for initial or interim vacancies on some or all levels of court.

State constitutions generally contain specific provisions relating to judicial selection. Since most states' judicial selection plans relied upon popular elections, reform efforts triggered formal constitutional amendment processes, which almost invariably require voter approval. Between 1940 and 1980, seventeen of twenty-nine states that voted on the issue of merit selection approved a merit plan. The reasons for the success of merit plans in some states and not others during this time are numerous. In addition to issues of ballot wording, the issues at stake in a proposed constitutional amendment are not always uniform. Some merit plans were bundled together with other reforms, whereas other proposals attempted to implement merit plans alone. Perhaps most important, the political cultures between and within states with respect to public attitudes toward the judiciary and concerns about judicial accountability exhibit considerable variance. For example, support for merit selection plans historically has varied considerably between urban and rural areas, the latter having stronger traditions of judicial elections.

THE 1980S AND 1990S

Although the debate over the role of politics in judicial selection has received much attention, voter attitudes toward merit selection have cooled off significantly since 1980, in stark contrast to the first forty years after the adoption of the Missouri Plan. Since 1980 only three states (Rhode Island, Connecticut, and Utah) have approved a full merit selection plan via constitutional amendment. In 1988, New Mexico voters approved a "hybrid" plan that incorporates aspects of the merit plan and popular elections. Most proposed amendments in support of the merit plan have failed to reach the ballot;

those that have, such as the 2000 proposal to extend merit selection to all levels of courts in Florida, more often than not go down to resounding defeats. Although no states using constitutional or statutory merit plans for appellate courts have reverted to popular elections or other appointment-based schemes, merit selection as a political proposition appears to be losing steam. Hybrid systems such as situational merit selection plans may present the best opportunity for reformers to initiate nominating commission elements into the judicial selection process.

THE NOMINATING COMMISSION PROCESS

Although a number of judicial selection systems utilize particular aspects of the merit selection plan, such as gubernatorial appointments or retention elections for judges, a selection plan taken as a whole cannot be accurately described as merit selection in the absence of a formal nonpartisan or bipartisan nominating commission (see figure). The use of a nominating commission assumes that there are measurable differences in appointment outcomes between "pure" gubernatorial or legislative appointive schemes and systems with a separate nominating commission that makes recommendations for appointments.

Although the function of nominating commissions is the same across states, there is considerable variance in the rules creating and governing commissions. The most common model uses an "independent" commission created by a constitutional amendment or statutory provision. Any such codification of the nominating commission addresses at least three specific areas relating to the composition of the commission: length of fixed terms of office for commissioners; who appoints or elects the members and chair of the commission; and the balance of lawyers, judges, and nonlawyer members. Typically, lawyer members are elected or appointed through state and county bars. Judge members are usually elected by the state bar or serve by virtue of tenure and frequently include the presiding chief justice. Nonlawyer members are generally appointed by the governor, the state legislature (exclusively or in an advise and consent role with the governor), or county or local officials.

The converse of the nominating commission established by rule of law is the "dependent" commission created by executive order. Typically, these commissions exist in states with histories of appointing judges. Under a dependent commission, the current governor appoints all members, and there are no fixed terms of service. In the absence of state statutes, the specifics of a dependent nominating commission may vary from one administration to the next. The lack of systematic structure over time is the dependent commission's vulnerability as well as its strength: although governors can alter the nominating commission process in highly partisan or ad hoc ways—if not eliminate it altogether—it is also far easier to implement initially than a system requiring formal state constitutional amendments. Dependent commissions have a "work in progress" characteristic that renders them easier to implement and revise or amend over time. They are also malleable enough for improvements and experiments with different processes, such as a rule requiring that the commission members represent the diversity of the jurisdiction on which a judge will be called upon to serve.

Judicial nominating commissions are charged with several important responsibilities, including posting notices of judicial vacancies; recruiting, investigating, and interviewing applicants; deliberating and voting on the slate of nominees; and transmitting names and supporting documentation to the appointing authority. In order to winnow the applicant pool, most commissions make initial cuts based on written applications, although some commissions grant interviews to all applicants who meet minimum statutory requirements for judicial service. In addition to conducting personal interviews with some or all applicants, commissions generally perform background and reference checks in order to identify those who may be disqualified by prior bar disciplinary findings or criminal records, as well as to verify positive qualifications. Following complete interviews and investigations, commissions meet in private to deliberate and vote upon the final slate of nominees. Generally, commissions nominate three to five of the most highly qualified applicants and transmit those names and supporting documentation to the appointing authority (usually the governor) for appointment. The governor then may conduct additional interviews and background and reference checks before selecting an appointee.

Although nominating commission systems are designed to reduce or eliminate the influence of certain types of political considerations in the judicial selection process (such as partisan patronage), some scholars, participants, and other observers have criticized the process as secretive or elitist, favoring well-connected white males over women, people of color, or attorneys working outside large or prestigious law firms. Although social scientific evidence suggests that in the aggregate, no one selection scheme as an institution systematically favors or disfavors particular groups, the persisting perception of exclusivity can threaten the legitimacy of commissions and dissuade nontraditional attorneys from applying. Although nominating commissions under the merit plan do not include the ultimate appointing authority, governors may apply "litmus tests" to nominees in making appointments, leading some members of the commission to favor particular types of nominees over others. Moreover, in states that use nominating commissions only for interim

American Judicature Society's Model Merit Selection Plan

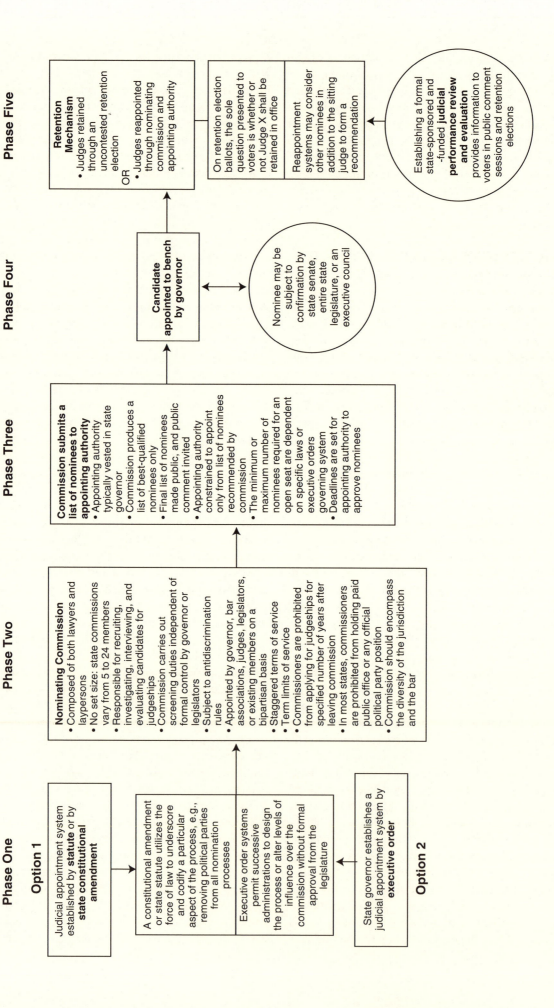

Phase One | **Phase Two** | **Phase Three** | **Phase Four** | **Phase Five**

Option 1

Judicial appointment system established by **statute** or by **state constitutional amendment**

A constitutional amendment or state statute utilizes the force of law to underscore and codify a particular aspect of the process, e.g., removing political parties from all nomination processes

Executive order systems permit successive administrations to design the process or alter levels of influence over the commission without formal approval from the legislature

Option 2

State governor establishes a judicial appointment system by **executive order**

Nominating Commission
- Composed of both lawyers and laypersons
- No set size: state commissions vary from 5 to 24 members
- Responsible for recruiting, investigating, interviewing, and evaluating candidates for judgeships
- Commission carries out screening duties independent of formal control by governor or legislators
- Subject to antidiscrimination rules
- Appointed by governor, bar associations, judges, legislators, or existing members on a bipartisan basis
- Staggered terms of service
- Term limits of service
- Commissioners are prohibited from applying for judgeships for specified number of years after leaving commission
- In most states, commissioners are prohibited from holding paid public office or any official political party position
- Commission should encompass the diversity of the jurisdiction and the bar

Commission submits a list of nominees to appointing authority
- Appointing authority typically vested in state governor
- Commission produces a list of best-qualified nominees only
- Final list of nominees made public, and public comment invited
- Appointing authority constrained to appoint only from list of nominees recommended by commission
- The minimum or maximum number of nominees required for an open seat are dependent on specific laws or executive orders governing system
- Deadlines are set for appointing authority to approve nominees

Candidate appointed to bench by governor

Nominee may be subject to confirmation by state senate, entire state legislature, or an executive council

Retention Mechanism
- Judges retained through an uncontested retention election
  OR
- Judges reappointed through nominating commission and appointing authority

On retention election ballots, the sole question presented to voters is whether or not Judge X shall be retained in office

Reappointment systems may consider other nominees in addition to the sitting judge to form a recommendation

Establishing a formal state-sponsored and -funded **judicial performance review and evaluation** provides information to voters in public comment sessions and retention elections vacancies, a nominee's potential "electability" may weigh heavily on the nomination and appointment process.

Two additional critical elements of any merit selection plan are the initial length of terms for judges and whether the nominating commission is utilized for all vacancies. For example, ten states use a form of nominating commission to fill interim vacancies but do not do so for selection for open seats. States characterized as "merit plan" systems also exhibit considerable variance in the initial length of term for appointed judges, with most falling in the range of one to three years, up to a maximum of twelve years. To illustrate the importance of the length of term before retention or reappointment, consider that a judge reaching the state supreme court in her fifties would likely serve out the remainder of her career standing for retention only once or twice, with a ten-year term length. Advocates of lengthening initial judicial terms argue that judges who face frequent retention or reappointment pressures, such as every six years or more frequently, are more likely to face significant political pressures, including the need to raise campaign funds.

The final phase of the merit selection plan is a formal mechanism designed to incorporate concerns for public accountability as well as the maintenance of professional standards. Under the reappointment system, nominating commissions reappoint judges in much the same way as the initial appointment process—including the option to remove the sitting judge in lieu of competing nominees. In contrast, in retention elections, voters ultimately decide whether a sitting judge, identified only by name and level of court, should be retained in office.

It is important to clarify that although retention elections are a key feature of most merit plans in practice, they are not a universal feature of all merit plans per se. Moreover, there are a number of states that make use of retention elections independent of nominating commission appointment schemes. The merit selection plan operates on the assumption that there are observable differences between systems that utilize retention elections combined with a "pure" gubernatorial appointment scheme, systems that combine retention elections with contested judicial elections for open seats, and systems that utilize retention elections in concert with a nominating commission.

In recent years, retention elections have come under barrages of criticism on two fronts: the first is that the process renders otherwise good judges vulnerable to attack from single-issue interest groups. From a behavioral standpoint, judges may "run scared" and alter or shade their decision-making processes in accordance with popular preferences. The second is that, given that retention election defeats across all levels of courts are in fact extremely rare, retention elections effectively rubber-stamp judges into a de facto life tenure appointment. (However,

proponents of the merit plan argue that as a normative value, an underlying purpose of the merit plan is to filter the best candidates and ensure them a considerable degree of security in their tenure.) As is the case with judicial elections generally, voter turnout issues and low levels of information on which to base a decision can cast retention elections in a negative light. Because all but two states conduct judicial elections at the same time as all other elections, the "roll-off" rates, whereby voters ignore the portion of the ballot dealing exclusively with judicial or retention elections, are generally high. Moreover, in states with a large judicial retention ballot, the process of paying particular attention to individual judges can be cumbersome; frequently, political and legal organizations advocate automatic "yes on all" retention votes rather than attempt to guide voters in differentiating between individual judges.

In response to these criticisms, six states with merit selection plans have implemented official state-sponsored and -funded judicial performance evaluation programs. Designed primarily to increase the levels of objective information available to voters in retention elections, performance evaluations address both critiques of retention elections to some degree. A coherent negative evaluation from a state-sponsored group theoretically should carry far more weight than assorted and disjointed bar or interest group evaluations and be more effective in removing incompetent judges. Focusing on a judge's overall performance also ensures judges' tenure will not be viewed on the basis of one unpopular ruling. Additionally, there is a feedback component as evaluations highlight necessary areas for improvement for individual judges and perhaps the judiciary taken as a whole. These evaluations seek to systematically collect information from a wide range of sources, including appointed and elected legal actors as well as nonlawyers who come into contact with a particular judge, on a myriad of topics involving a judge's legal, personal, and managerial skills. The evaluation committee then disseminates the information to the widest audience possible depending on resources; some states send the results to all registered voters. Because performance evaluations carry the weight of an official state-sponsored mechanism, it is important above all that the system is fair and consistent to all parties and is reliable from a social scientific methodological standpoint.

POLITICS AND MERIT SELECTION
Much ink has been spilled over the most appropriate method for selecting state court judges. Beginning with the debates at the first constitutional convention and continuing to the present day, supporters of elective systems and appointive systems alike have vigorously argued over the comparative benefits and flaws of each system.

MERIT SELECTION IN THE UNITED STATES

Merit selection states at all levels

Alaska, Colorado, Connecticut, Delaware, District of Columbia, Hawaii, Iowa, Maryland, Massachusetts, Nebraska, New Hampshire, New Mexico, Rhode Island, Utah, Vermont, Wyoming

States that use merit plans only to fill interim (midterm) vacancies

Idaho, Kentucky, Minnesota, Montana, Nevada, North Dakota, West Virginia, and Wisconsin

States that utilize merit plans only for appellate courts or courts of last resort

Arizona, Florida, Indiana, Kansas, Missouri*, New York, Oklahoma, South Dakota, Tennessee, Indiana*, Kansas*

*Missouri, Indiana, and Kansas have splits at the circuit court level due to "local control" measures over judicial selection methods. Thus, there is considerable turnover among methods over time. As of 2001, in Kansas seventeen of thirty-one circuits used merit selection; in Indiana, just two counties (Lake and St. Joseph); in Missouri, four counties (Jackson, Clay, Platte, and St. Louis).

Indeed, although intended to remove judges above the political fray, merit selection plans clearly have the potential to affect political systems as well as legal institutions. The ongoing debate reflects the fundamental tension created by competing desires for a judiciary that is independent and impartial yet accountable to the people it serves. Scholars who have attempted to "prove" which system produces the best judges have been continually frustrated by the subjective nature of their inquiry. At the beginning of the twenty-first century, the stakes appear to be higher than ever, with political parties, interest groups, political action committees, and other third parties giving unprecedented attention and money to both competitive and noncompetitive retention elections for judges. As state courts are increasingly involved in contentious political, economic, and social issues, debates surrounding the selection of state judiciaries will remain at the forefront of both law and politics.

Seth S. Andersen
Joel F. Knutson

See also Judicial Independence; United States—Federal System; United States—State Systems

References and further reading

Ashman, Allan, and James J. Alfini. 1974. *The Key to Judicial Merit Selection: The Nominating Process.* Chicago: American Judicature Society.

Aspin, Larry. 1999. "Trends in Judicial Retention Elections, 1964–1998." *Judicature* 83, no. 2: 79–86.

Baum, Lawrence. 1994. *American Courts: Process and Policy.* Boston: Houghton Mifflin.

Dubois, Philip. 1990. "Voter Responses to Court Reform: Merit Judicial Selection on the Ballot." *Judicature* 73, no. 5: 238.

Esterling, Kevin M., and Seth S. Andersen. 2000. "Diversity and the Judicial Merit Selection Process: A Statistical Report." *Research on Judicial Selection, 1999*: 1–39.

Watson, Richard A., and Rondal G. Downing. 1969. *The Politics of the Bench and the Bar: Judicial Selection under the Missouri Nonpartisan Court Plan.* New York: John Wiley.

MEXICO

GENERAL INFORMATION

Mexico is the northernmost country in Latin America, bordering the United States to the north, the Pacific Ocean to the west, the Caribbean Sea to the east, and Guatemala to the south. Mexico is the most populous Spanish-speaking country in the world and the second most populous country in Latin America, after Portuguese-speaking Brazil. The nation's 98.1 million citizens are 60 percent mestizo (Indian-Spanish), 30 percent a complex mix of approximately fifty indigenous ethnic groups, and 9 percent persons of European ancestry. The average life expectancy for men is seventy-three years and for women seventy-seven years. Literacy rates are estimated at approximately 89.6 percent, although that figure varies by region. Mexico joined Canada and the United Sates in the North American Free Trade Agreement (NAFTA) in January 1994, which phases out all tariffs over a fifteen-year period. Mexico's economy has grown at an annualized rate of 2.3 percent in 1994–1999. The capital, Mexico City, is often classified as the world's largest metropolitan area and is home to approximately 21 million people (1997 census). About 70 percent of the people live in urban areas. The country is majority Catholic (89 percent), 6 percent Protestant, and 5 percent other. Some 26.5 percent of Mexicans were classified as living in poverty, 20 percent in extreme poverty. The country's legal system is based on European civil law. Spanish is the official national language, but there are more than sixty indigenous languages spoken throughout the country. The climate varies from tropical to desert.

HISTORY

Highly advanced cultures, including those of the Olmecs, Mayas, Toltecs, and Aztecs ruled what is today Mexico

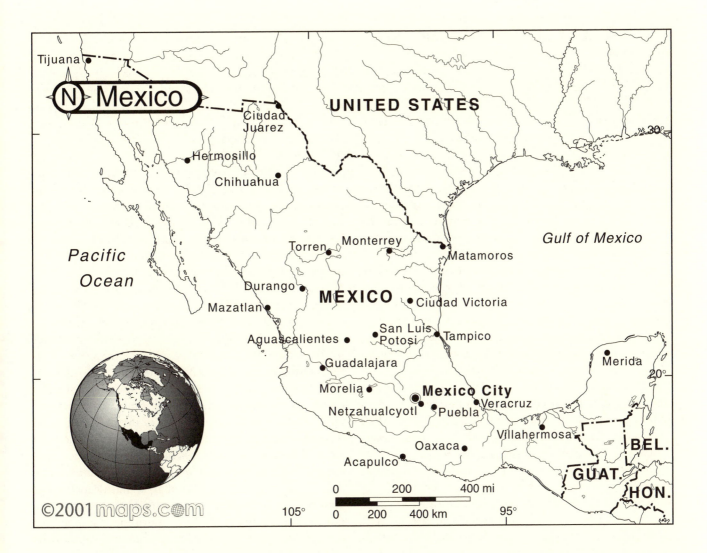

and parts of Guatemala for more than a thousand years before the Spanish arrived. During that time, a complex oral legal tradition emerged in Mexico whereby traditional authority (Aztec and Mayan authority in the south) resolved conflicts. In 1519–1521, Mexico was conquered by Spain, remaining a Spanish colony for nearly three hundred years. Spanish law governed disputes exclusively in private law, commerce, property, family inheritance, and obligations among those of European ancestry in colonial Mexico. Nevertheless, the Spanish Crown also kept the customary indigenous law and legal institutions that did not go against established Spanish customs or church doctrine, under the concept of *usos y costumbres* (use and customs). The movement toward Mexican independence started in 1810, when a war for independence was launched.

Mexico achieved independence in 1821 and adopted its first constitution in 1824. The 1824 Constitution provided for a federal republic consisting of nineteen states, four territories, and a federal district. Mexico is therefore a federal political system. Internal armed conflict ensued between the conservative and liberal ele-ments of the newly independent Mexican state, and the 1824 Constitution was not implemented. In 1857 a new constitution was adopted by the liberal element that had ascended to power. The 1857 Constitution included such democratic rights as the separation of powers, the equality of all citizens before the law, the principle of innocence until proven guilty, freedom of expression and of the press, the protection of private property, the abolition of special privileges for the clergy and the military, and agrarian reform. The 1857 Constitution also consolidated judicial review around the *amparo* (habeas corpus) suit, a limited but nonetheless initially effective form of individual rights protection. At the same time, however, the independence of the judiciary in practice remained limited in the area of electoral law. The principle of judicial abstention from electoral and political matters by the Mexican Supreme Court was well consolidated by the turn of the century and remained that way until judicial reforms in 1994. After the triumph of the 1910 Mexican Revolution, the 1857 Constitution was replaced by the current Mexican Constitution of 1917.

Mexico's severe social and economic problems erupted in a revolution that lasted from 1910 to 1920 and gave rise to the 1917 Constitution. The 1910 Revolution toppled the longstanding dictatorship of General Porfirio Díaz (1877–1911). It is estimated that by 1910 almost 97 percent of the arable land in Mexico was in the hands of no more than one thousand families, while 2 percent belonged to small land holdings and 1 percent belonged to municipalities.

In 1917 a constitution was promulgated with the intent of creating a liberal-democratic system in Mexico. Nevertheless, the chaos of the revolution (diverse regional leaders competing for power, political assassinations, economic crises) did not provide the social conditions for the consolidation of a democratic regime. In 1929, formed under a different name, the Institutional Revolution Party (PRI) emerged as a coalition of interests and as a vehicle for keeping political competition in peaceful channels. What began in 1917 as a constitutional settlement deteriorated into a unique Mexican-style authoritarianism in which unwritten law, as opposed to written laws contained in the constitution, came to endow the executive branch of government with almost unlimited powers and functions. Between 1920 and 1994, Mexican presidents had enormous powers based on unwritten law, including the ability to choose their own political successor, to act as a constituent power with the authority to make amendments to the constitution, and to act as chief legislator, inasmuch as historically senators and legislators have not legislated. A Mexican president could also establish himself as the ultimate authority in electoral matters (since electoral material did not fall under the aegis of judicial review); designate state governors, members of PRI majorities in Congress, and most state representatives and mayors; remove governors, mayors, and legislators at the federal and state levels; impose his viewpoint on one or both houses of Congress; assume jurisdiction in judicial matters; impose his authority over state governors; and hold sway over municipal government. For almost seventy-one years, Mexico's national government has been controlled by this authoritarian regime in which the official party, the PRI, won every presidential race until the July 2000 elections and most gubernatorial and mayoral races until the mid-1990s.

In 1939 a rightist political party called the PAN (Partido Acción Nacional) was created by those who objected to the nationalization of the private property of the church, to land reform, to the government's expropriation of the holdings of foreign oil companies, and to its nationalization of such basic industries as fertilizers, telephones, electricity, airlines, steel, and copper. Thereafter, ruling PRI elites decided that limited but controlled electoral competition with weak political opposition parties was preferable to strict one-party hegemonic rule, as long as fraud and other extralegal tactics guaranteed large PRI electoral majorities.

A series of political pacts and electoral reforms took place in 1977, 1989, and 1996, resulting in the loss of PRI control from the federal administration of elections. By 1997 a new generation of non-PRI affiliated intellectuals, professors, journalists, and citizens administered elections under an autonomous Federal Electoral Institute (IFE). The July 2, 2000, election victory of Vicente Fox Quesada of the opposition Alliance for Change coalition (including the PAN and the Mexican Green Party, PVEM), in what are considered to have been the freest and fairest elections in Mexico's history, ended the PRI's seventy-one-year hold on the presidency.

NAFTA-induced reforms to the constitution ended the inalienability of Indian lands in Mexico. The question of trading the earth is a high priority to the indigenous peoples of Mexico and has prompted the demand for the return of unallocated state lands that were taken from indigenous peoples. On the day that NAFTA went into effect (January 1, 1994), the EZLN—the Emilio Zapata National Liberation Army—initiated an armed uprising in the poor, southern Mexican state of Chiapas. A series of formal talks between the government and the EZLN broke off in 1996, when the Zedillo government refused to agree to constitutional reforms, including the right of collective ownership of land and property and political autonomy for indigenous communities standing outside the existing Mexican Constitution. Although incoming president Fox pledged his political support for constitutional reforms promoting greater indigenous rights, many legislators still oppose the idea of collective property rights for indigenous communities.

The impartial administration of justice in Mexico is hindered for a number of reasons. Budgetary constraints have historically hampered the extension and development of courts. Poverty means that few can afford an attorney. Low salaries for judicial policemen ($300 per month) and regular policemen ($200 per month) open the door to corruption and inefficiency in policing. Especially sensitive is the job of the judicial police force, which belongs to the general prosecutor's office in every state.

The flow of drugs from Mexico into the United States by organized crime is also a major obstacle to the impartial administration of justice, especially along the U.S.-Mexican border. For example, according to extradition documents submitted by the government of Mexico in San Diego, California, in 1997, key family members of the Tijuana Cartel dispensed an estimated $1 million weekly in bribes to Mexican federal, state, and local officials, who ensure that the movement of drugs continues unimpeded to the gateway cities along the southwestern border of the United States. Every year there are violations of due process rights; torture; disappearances; and the murder of independent labor organizers, opposition political party activists, opposition indigenous leaders, peasants, reformist political elites, independent lawyers, clergy and laity who defend indigenous populations or support liberation theology, journalists, human rights activists, gays, and whistle-blowers, carried out by covert government agents.

LEGAL CONCEPTS

As in most countries, Mexico's supreme law is found in its constitution. That document provides for the separation of powers into executive, legislative, and judicial branches of government. It also provides for basic and fundamental human rights, including free speech, presumption of innocence, the right to an attorney in criminal matters, rights to health protection, guarantees of private property, protections for labor, freedom of belief and religion, freedom of contract, and so on. Article 4 officially recognizes the rights of indigenous peoples to their own cultural identity in accordance with local languages, cultures, means, customs, resources, and specific forms of social organization, and it promises to guarantee them effective access to the jurisdiction of the state.

Article 71 of the 1917 Constitution states that legislation is the only source of law. Virtually all legislation, federal or state, dates from this postrevolutionary period; in the case of conflict, federal law is paramount. The *usos y costumbres,* or customary treatment of indigenous legal issues under administrative courts, applies where there is no applicable law. In judicial and agrarian proceedings, Article 4 states that indigenous practices and judicial customs shall be taken into account in the terms that the law establishes. The proposed COCOPA constitutional reforms of 1996 would have raised indigenous rights to the level of formal constitutional guarantees of legal pluralism, including the right to self-governing political communities, the right to traditional systems of production, and the right to manage and operate their own development projects. However, with the failure of the San Andréas accords, custom remains a secondary source for law.

The president serves a six-year term and may not hold office a second time. There is no vice president; in the event of the removal or death of the president, a provisional president is elected by Congress. The current president, Vicente Fox, assumed office on December 1, 2000. The Congress is composed of a Senate and a Chamber of Deputies. Consecutive re-election is prohibited. Senators are elected to six-year terms, and deputies serve three-year terms. In the lower chamber, three hundred deputies are directly elected to represent single-member districts, and two hundred are selected by a modified form of proportional representation from five electoral regions created for that purpose across the country. The two hundred proportional representation seats were originally created to help smaller parties gain access to the chamber.

Election of the president requires a majority of the popular votes cast. There are no second-round elections. The constitution forbids a sitting president from being re-elected. The Mexican Constitution empowers both the executive and the legislative branches to initiate legislation, but only the Chamber of Deputies can initiate bills concerning taxes and the recruitment of troops. However, in practice, the executive has (until 1997) initiated almost all legislation and certainly all legislation of any consequence. A new bill must pass both chambers by a majority vote. The president has the power of veto, but not a line-item veto. The president's veto can be overridden by Congress with a two-thirds majority vote in each chamber. The historical twentieth-century domination of the Mexican president over weakened legislative and judicial branches began to change in 1997. The rise in the number of deputies and senators elected to the Chamber of Deputies and Senate (at the federal level, and in various states) has led to a rapid increase in the amount of legislation initiated by the opposition in the 1997–2000 period.

The Supreme Court is composed of eleven justices and one chief justice. The president nominates the candidates for the Supreme Court, and the Senate can approve the nomination with a two-thirds majority. There are no elected judges in Mexico. The president also has the power to remove a Supreme Court justice with the approval of the Senate and the Chamber of Deputies. Supreme Court judges were originally appointed with life tenure. However, the 1994 judicial reforms altered the Supreme Court nomination process, to make the judiciary more politically independent of the PRI regime. Since 1994 candidates must be law-school graduates with ten years' experience, preferably in the judicial system, and they cannot have held a political position for at least a year before the appointment. The 1994 reform changed life tenure to a staggered fifteen-year fixed term, on the argument that fifteen years is sufficient to protect judicial independence for incumbent presidents, and has the advantage of allowing for healthy renewal of the highest tribunal. The current membership on the court was established in 1994. Every four years the court names one of its members president. The current chief justice is David Góngora Pimental, elected in January 1999. Circuit judges and district judges are appointed by the Supreme Court to four-year terms. Circuit judges and district judges may be reappointed or promoted to a position at the end of the four-year term, but they may be dismissed only for bad conduct. The 1994 judicial reforms also strengthened the Supreme Court by extending the reach of its powers of constitutional review by increasing the scope of its decisions. Previously, the Supreme Court's review of legislation had been sharply restricted; the court could declare a law unconstitutional only in regard to the individual in question.

With respect to state judiciaries, a high degree of influence is exerted by regional politics on state courts—including the appointment of judges by the incumbent governor. At the state level, tenure is almost nonexistent. In the Federal District Superior Court, for example, among forty-nine superior judges only seven have tenure. Their decisions lack all precedent force, and they are not even published in most of the states.

A separate set of federal and state administrative courts exist for deciding election matters. The permanent Federal Electoral Tribunal (TRIFE) is the highest legal court for deciding matters of elections and is located in Mexico City. Five regional electoral tribunals process election disputes only during election years. Prior to the 1996 electoral reforms, electoral magistrates were appointed by the president and approved by the Chamber of Deputies. At the request of the opposition parties, the 1996 reforms required the Supreme Court to propose candidates for the permanent and regional electoral tribunals. A two-thirds Senate vote is required for confirmation. The members serve a single eight-year term. The essential function of the electoral tribunals is to hear questions of potential fraud and other violations of political rights relating to elections. Although as of 2000 TRIFE was independent of former ruling party control, in many states where the political influence of the PRI remained strong, standoffs occurred over election results and lines of legal authority between the federal electoral court, state electoral courts, and PRI, even after the July 2, 2000, win of the presidency by the opposition PAN.

The 1917 Constitution formally recognizes an attorney general that presides over the Office of the General Prosecutor and supervises all criminal prosecution. The attorney general is named by the president and removed by the president only for just cause. Until the 2000 election of Vicente Fox, all of Mexico's attorney generals except one (1994–1996, from the PAN) have been members of the PRI. In actual practice, the functions of the office have historically been subordinate to the powers of the president under the metaconstitutional norms of twentieth-century Mexican authoritarianism. The executive branch has absorbed those segments of the administration of justice linked to criminal proceedings; the executive has controlled the appointment of all kinds of judges and justices; the president has been the top official in safety matters; and he has commanded the biggest corps of police in Mexico City, as well as dictating general policy to all the security bodies through the Commission on Public Safety. The prison system has been in the hands of the president; he has enjoyed the power to pardon anyone sentenced and thus to eliminate most judicial penalties. With such strong powers, the president has historically been the chief administrator of justice, so that all criticisms concerning the administration of justice are also leveled against his performance and his bureaucratic apparatus. The lack of autonomy and insufficiently strong internal oversight within the criminal justice system has led to corruption. A recent report noted that only 6.6 percent of the labor force within the Office of the General Prosecutor was evaluated by an internal commission as "legal, honest, efficient, professional, loyal and impartial." Various waves of reforms have been proposed to eradicate corruption, to promote morality and honesty, and to reduce the influence of drug traffickers in the administration of justice. In 1994 the Mexican Congress passed penal code reforms to criminalize money laundering, to establish some controls on chemical diversion, and to modernize investigative techniques, including surveillance, witness protection, and prosecution for criminal association and conspiracy.

During the period of intense democratization (1997–2000), a number of reforms aimed at reducing corruption and improving the administration of justice were implemented. The left opposition party won the mayoral post in Mexico City in 1997 and doubled the pay for new judicial police in Mexico City to about $1,000, a middle-class salary. New entrance requirements have been implemented to break the link between the police and criminality, including two years of college, an extensive background check, and no previous police experience. Nearly half of Mexico City's thirty-two hundred judicial police are now products of the new system. The incoming Fox administration proposed in December 1999 to eliminate the Office of the General Prosecutor altogether, and to redistribute its criminal justice functions to a new Justice Department and a new Department of Public Security. Under the Fox proposal, the Office of the General Prosecutor would be reconstructed as a general investigatory body dedicated exclusively to the investigation of crime and without judicial police. In April 2000, a new National Program to Combat Corruption went into effect. It includes the development of a new ethical code for civil servants, and the certification by federal agencies that they are successfully trying to combat corruption. The Fox administration also plans to elaborate a new set of juridic norms to regulate, coordinate, and make more public the way Mexico's intelligence and security agencies handle the public surveillance of citizens.

Treaties concluded by the executive and approved by the Senate achieve national status after their official domestic publication. Mexican courts consistently equate treaties with legislative acts, affirm their incorporation into national law, and hold that they are binding throughout the land.

Nevertheless, while Mexican judges are bound to give primacy to constitutional treaties over state laws, they are also bound to give primacy to the constitution over international treaties. Hence, in the case of normative conflict, the traditional Mexican system would grant an injunction against the unconstitutional norms, without annulling an international treaty beyond the concrete cases brought to the courts.

According to a 1994 opinion poll, 72 percent of the population in Mexico City distrust the police. A report from the Human Rights Commission of the United Nations listed Mexico among the countries in which torture is widely practiced by the military and police. Inefficiency, lack of access to justice, corruption, case overload, and budgetary constraints are commonly named both as complaints by justices and as complaints against the justice system. The Mexican Supreme Court heard 18,241 cases between 1997 and 1999. In contrast, the U.S. Supreme Court heard only 261 in that same period. One federal judiciary counselor noted that people have to walk for seventy hours to reach the nearest court in the mountainous regions of the Mexican state of Oaxaca. The Fox administration increased the judiciary's budget by 77 percent in 2001, a sizable increase from the traditional 0.67 percent of the budget allocated to the judiciary.

CURRENT COURT SYSTEM STRUCTURE

Mexico is a federal system, and there are two separate judicial systems. Nationally, there is a three-tiered federal judiciary consisting of an appointed Supreme Court, sixteen circuit courts, and sixty-eight district courts (as well as the courts of the federal district). In addition, there are special courts for labor and fiscal matters, although any structured and organized overall system of administrative courts is lacking. The states each have their own Supreme Courts and a great number of elected justices of the peace. Except in the area of labor disputes, Mexican state legislatures can organize their own state tribunals in the areas of civil law, penal law, and administrative law. Beyond those areas, the states' power to legislate is quite limited. Local judges must always adjust their rulings to adhere to the federal constitution, even when state law runs contrary. This is called the principle of "diffuse control of the constitution."

The Supreme Court is the highest body within the judicial branch, serving not only as the forum of last resort but also as the administrative and budgetary oversight institution for all courts. The Supreme Court meets in plenary session for cases involving jurisdictional issues, constitutional issues, and agrarian issues. The Supreme Court divides and meets in panels. There are four panels: crim-inal, civil, administrative, and labor. A special office—the Federal Judicial Council—investigates acts of corruption, incapacity, and negligence among judges and serves to ensure compliance with established norms. In addition to the Supreme Court, there are the following tribunals in Mexico, among others:

1. Federal tribunals (federal circuit courts, federal district courts), to review controversies that arise out of laws or acts of state or federal authorities that violate individual guarantees
2. The State Supreme Court (primarily for review from state tribunals)
3. State tribunals (for civil law, penal law, and administrative law)
4. Federal administrative courts (to provide judicial oversight to administrative decisions and dispute resolution), including:
5. Federal Electoral Court (an administrative court to adjudicate election disputes)
6. Federal District Court (an administrative court to deal with controversies arising from the government of the federal district)
7. Federal Tax Court (an administrative court that reviews fiscal controversies between an individual and the government)
8. The Labor Board of Conciliation and Arbitration (an administrative court to resolve controversies arising from labor disputes)
9. Superior Court for Land Reform (an administrative court to deal with land reform disputes)
10. Military tribunals (limited to military crimes by military personnel)

The Mexican federal judiciary is based on a three-tiered system. The Supreme Court has final appellate jurisdiction over all state and federal courts. There are circuit courts that serve as federal appellate courts. The circuit courts are divided into single judge courts and collegiate courts. There are district courts and jury courts, which are the federal courts of the first instance.

The constitution gives federal courts jurisdiction over controversies that arise out of laws or the acts of state or federal authorities that violate individual guarantees; controversies between states or a state and federal authorities; all matters involving federal laws and treaties; all cases in which the federal government is a party; all cases involving maritime law; and all cases that involve members of the Diplomatic and Consular Corps. The federal judiciary has a great share of the judicial power vis-à-vis state judiciaries.

Among the most important cases the federal courts hear are "*amparo* suits" (*juicio de amparo*). The *amparo*

Structure of Mexican Courts

Federal Circuit Courts	Federal Administrative Courts
Federal District Courts	Tax, Agrarian, Labor, Electoral, Military

State Supreme Courts
State Tribunals— Penal, Civil, Family, Administrative

Notary Public

suit is an original Mexican institution without an exact equivalent in the common law tradition. The word *amparo* literally means favor, aid, protection, or shelter. Legally the word encompasses elements of several legal actions of the common law tradition: writ of habeas corpus, injunction, error of mandamus, and certiorari. There are five types of *amparo* suits: (1) *amparo* in defense of individual rights such as life, liberty, and personal dignity; (2) *amparo* against laws (defending the individual against unconstitutional laws); (3) *amparo* in judicial matters (examining the legality of judicial decisions); (4) administrative *amparo* (providing jurisdiction against administrative enactments affecting the individual); and (5) *amparo* in agrarian matters (protecting the communal *ejido* rights of peasants). The *amparo* suit may be either direct (initiated in the Supreme Court, in collegiate circuit courts) or indirect (initiated in a district court and brought up by the previously mentioned courts).

There are several federal judicial bodies that are not part of the regular court structure. The most important are the Federal Tax Court, labor courts, and military courts. The Federal Tax Court is an administrative court with jurisdiction over controversies arising in fiscal matters between an individual and the government. The Tax Court's responsibilities and structure are covered by the Fiscal Code and the Organic Law of the Tax Court. The labor courts are administrative courts with jurisdiction over claims by workers who allege that their rights under the Federal Labor Code have been violated, disputes over collective bargaining, and strike-related matters. Labor courts' responsibilities and structure are covered by the Federal Labor Law. The Superior Court for Land Reform (an administrative court) was created to deal with the difficult question of the backlog of land reform cases compiled for more than fifty years, whose resolution was supposed to be in the hands of

the Ministry of Land Reform before the court's creation. The military courts' responsibilities and structure are covered by the Organic Law of the Military Courts.

SPECIALIZED JUDICIAL BODIES

The constitution was modified in 1992 to create an independent National Human Rights Commission (CNDH). State governments were also required to create human rights commissions. The head of the CNDH is appointed by the president, although the appointment has to be ratified by the Senate, which also has to accept the president's resignation. The initiative to create the CNDH was undertaken by President Salinas in January 1992; it gave citizens a new option for protecting individual rights. From May 1993 to May 1994, the commission received more than twenty-four complaints a day at its office in Mexico City alone. As the offices spread throughout the country, the daily number of complaints rose to seventy-two. Some 70 percent of the claims before the commission came from poor people who could not afford the services of lawyers to engage in a lawsuit. The most common complaints included violations of prisoners' rights, abuse of authority by government officials, illegal detention by the judicial police, delay by the agents of the general prosecutor in bringing the accused before the courts, refusal to render health services at public institutions, false accusations and indictments, medical malpractice, denial of the constitutional right of petition, and torture. In 1993–1994 the report of the incumbent president of the commission states that fifty-three recommendations were issued against agents who practiced torture, generally in an attempt to extract a confession. Only seven of such cases were brought to trial. The role of the CNDH has been weakened by two factors: first, the CNDH cannot discuss issues related to political rights, electoral, labor, or federal judicial matters; and second, its recommendations are not mandatory. The CNDH remains an administrative commission with juridic personality but without punitive legal powers.

In addition to the Federal Electoral Tribunal (the administrative court that adjudicates election disputes), the Mexican Constitution recognizes the Federal Electoral Institute (IFE) as an administrative public organ with juridic autonomy and its own budget. The IFE is in charge of regulating all aspects of elections, including civic training and education, drawing electoral boundaries, regulating the rights and prerogatives of interest groups and political parties, registering and maintaining voter lists, the preparation of election day, the regulation of poll watching, the computation of election results, and so forth. The IFE council president and eight council members are selected at the same time to seven-year terms by a two-thirds Chamber of Deputies vote. Additional council members with voice but not vote include those proposed from the legislative power, representatives of the political parties, and an executive branch member. The IFE has a high operating budget. Previously, elections were controlled by the PRI-controlled executive branch under the aegis of the Interior Ministry with a built-in conflict of interest. Therefore the 1996 electoral reforms that brought about the 1997 autonomy of the IFE from the previous ruling party are seen as the legal cornerstone underpinning Mexico's democratization and transition to clean elections. Yet the IFE's authority is limited: the federal electoral code does not give the IFE the authority to regulate either the private media or government expenditures during campaigns. In the past, both have been used to the unfair advantage of particular candidates. Nor does the electoral code give the IFE sufficient tools or powers to easily carry out some responsibilities within its mandate, such as monitoring campaign spending. Some concerns remain about its ability to fully guarantee fair elections in rural areas in which widespread poverty, significant political violence, and the historical practice of vote buying occur. The IFE does possess the legal powers to confer financial penalties upon political parties who violate campaign spending limits.

The NAFTA created an Advisory Committee on Private Commercial Disputes, providing investors who feel wronged by the actions of a signatory country or its state-owned enterprises access to a well-defined arbitration proceeding. This proceeding largely incorporates the rules and procedures developed by the International Center for Settlement of Investment Disputes; chapter 19 provides for resolution of dumping disputes by a binational panel.

STAFFING

There is no exact statistic for practicing attorneys in Mexico. Registration in the most important bar association—the Mexican Bar Association (Barra de Abogados)—is voluntary, and only a small percentage of practicing lawyers belong. Membership tends to be dominated by older, well-established lawyers who also do part-time teaching and writing. Currently, the Mexican Bar Association has about eighteen hundred members. The federal judicial branch of government has approximately 735 judges plus support staff working on its behalf. This includes 11 Supreme Court ministers, 6 counselors to the Federal Judicial Council, and about 718 federal circuit and district judges.

A 1995 constitutional amendment formalized the process of recruiting federal circuit and district judges. This law now allows the newly established Federal Judicial Council to appoint federal district and circuit judges after a competitive examination based on the principles of "excellence, objectivity, impartiality, professionalism and independence." Circuit and district judges must have

at least five years of professional practice. About two hundred circuit judges and three hundred district judges have been nominated in the last five years under the new law. Until 1994, an informal federal career existed in which young recruits would ascend the internal hierarchy of judicial posts up to the position of clerk at the Supreme Court. From there, they could be appointed at the proposal of one of the justices. The Federal Judicial Council has the power to appoint, assign, remove, suspend, or transfer judges, and thus there is no legal concept of tenure for federal judges. The Supreme Court retains the right to limited review of the council's decisions. Informal judicial career or direct appointment of the state governor remains the norm for state judges.

In terms of training, the Mexican law student is able to practice law after obtaining a law school diploma and after receiving a state license certificate recognizing the diploma. Legal training consists of a five-year degree relying on lectures, horn books, and oral exams. There is no bar examination as a prerequisite to practice. To acquire a state certificate, however, six months to one year of community service either through legal aid or government agencies is required. This apprenticeship requirement allows the prospective new attorney to gain practical experience and provides assistance to entities in need of legal assistance. The typical law school faculty consists of three to six full-time academics and from twenty to fifty part-time teachers who are active practitioners. The largest law school is the national law school, Universidad Nacional Autónoma de Mexico (UNAM), one of the oldest universities in the hemisphere. The majority of federal judges and prosecutors are graduates of the UNAM. Most Mexican states also offer law degrees—that is, Universidad Nacional Autónoma de Puebla, Universidad Nacional Autónoma de Sonora, Universidad Nacional Autónoma de San Luis Potosí, and so forth. Mexican universities also offer master's and doctoral degrees in law, with an emphasis on upgrading and modernizing specialized areas of law for Mexican legal practitioners.

IMPACT OF LAW

The Mexican justice administrative system is a fundamental institution in society. The desire for a greater rule of law has emerged across diverse sectors of society as Mexico undergoes a transition to democracy. Yet the justice system is in the process of change brought on by Mexico's market integration into NAFTA, rising crime rates, the drug traffic, problems with corruption within the police, and a sense of insecurity and fear felt by citizens that inhibits them from lodging formal complaints against authorities. Private citizens consistently rank crime, security, and poverty as the top national issues of concern. As a result, the rule of law is seen as essential to ensure a stable and efficient legal system. Under the

Zedillo administration, reforms to grant the judicial system more power and autonomy were begun. The election of the first opposition president, Vicente Fox, promises to further extend the autonomy of the judicial system and to treat various legal and social problems that contribute to legal instability through long-term reforms. Fox began his first one hundred days in office by calling upon those working within Mexico's legal institutions to reconceptualize their roles and to take into account social aspects of legal issues in order to "recover the credibility and confidence of society." Systematic reform will be a long-term process.

Sara Schatz

See also Administrative Tribunals; Civil Law; Constitutional Law; Constitutional Review; Indigenous and Folk Legal Systems; Judicial Independence; Judicial Review; Judicial Selection, Methods of; Legal Education; Native American Law, Traditional

References and further reading
Ávalos, Francisco A. 2000. "The Mexican Legal System." Littleton, CO: F. B. Rothman.
Cicero, Jorge. 1997. "International Law in Mexican Courts." *Vanderbilt Journal of Transnational Law* 30 (November): 1035–1082.
Domingo, Pilar. 2000. "Judicial Independence: The Politics of the Supreme Court in Mexico." *Journal of Latin American Studies* 32: 705–735.
Drumbl, Mark A. 1998. "Amalgam in the Americas: A Law School Curriculum for Free-Markets and Open Borders." *San Diego Law Review* 35, no. 4 (fall): 1053–1090.
Fix-Fierro, Héctor. 1998. "Judicial Reforms and the Supreme Court of Mexico: The Trajectory of Three Years." *U.S.-Mexico Law Journal* 6 (spring): 1–22.
Gessell, Jeffrey N. 1997. "Customary Indigenous Law in Mexico." *Georgia Journal of International and Comparative Law* 26, no. 3: 643–671.
Guitron, Julian. 1994/1995. "Mexico: A Decade of Family Law, 1983–93." *Louisville Journal of Family Law* 33 (spring): 45–70.
Herget, James E., and Jorge Camil. 1978. *An Introduction to the Mexican Legal System.* Buffalo, NY: William S. Hein.
Hoester, V. 1998. "The NAFTA and the Complete Integration of the Legal Profession: Dismantling the Barriers to Providing Cross-border Legal Services." *U.S.-Mexico Law Journal* 6 (spring): 71–80.
Mayer-Serra, Carlos Elizondo. 1996. "Constitutionalism and State Reform in Mexico." Pp. 41–58 in *Mexico after Salinas.* Edited by Monica Serrano and Victor Bulmer-Thomas. London: University of London, Institute of Latin American Studies.
Melgar Adalid, Mario. 1998. "Mexican Justice toward the 21st Century: The Federal Council of the Judicature: Formation, Branches, and Operation." *U.S.-Mexico Law Journal* 6 (spring): 23–34.
Oropeza, Manuel González. 1996. "The Administration of Justice and the Rule of Law." Pp. 59–78 in *Mexico after Salinas.* Edited by Mónica Serrano and Víctor Bulmer-Thomas. London: University of London, Institute of Latin American Studies.

Schatz, Sara. 1998. "A Neo-Weberian Approach to Constitutional Courts in the Transition from Authoritarian Rule: The Mexican Case (1994–97)." *International Journal of the Sociology of Law* 26, no. 2 (June): 217–244.
———. 1999. "Delayed Transitions to Democracy and the Struggle for Political Citizenship Rights: The Case of Mexico." *Studies in Law, Politics and Society* 19: 165–199.

MICHIGAN

GENERAL INFORMATION

Serving more than 9.9 million people, the legal system of Michigan has authority over the eighth most populous jurisdiction in the United States, one that is more populous than 65 percent of the national legal systems of the world. The state of Michigan encompasses 96,700 square miles divided into two distinct areas separated by the Great Lakes and the Straits of Mackinac, and it is organized into fifty-seven counties, which establish jurisdictional boundaries for most trial courts and for the state's prosecutors. About 45 percent of the population is located in the three-county Detroit metropolitan area, which is the hub of legal activity in the state and is home to 56 percent of the state's lawyers.

What is now Michigan was part of the Northwest Territory, an area of more than 250,000 square miles that would later become five states and part of a sixth. Governed successively under the Ordinance of 1784 and the more important Northwest Ordinance of 1787, Michigan's legal system predates the U.S. Constitution.

EVOLUTION AND HISTORY

The Northwest Ordinance, drafted principally by Thomas Jefferson, established a structure of government for Michigan that included distinct executive, legislative, and judicial bodies. More important, it included statements of rights well beyond those that would be incorporated into the original U.S. Constitution of 1787, including religious tolerance, trial by jury, habeas corpus, the right to bail, protection against cruel or unusual punishment, the sanctity of contracts, and security against deprivations of liberty or property except by a jury of one's peers or the law of land. Notably, the ordinance called for government to encourage schools and education and to protect Indian lands and rights. Slavery and involuntary servitude were prohibited throughout the territory.

Those features largely endured in each of Michigan's four constitutions. The original statehood constitution, that of 1835, was a spare document consisting mainly of a greatly expanded bill of rights and a clearly articulated separation of powers. A mandate for education and the reservation of certain funds for schools and a university, the authorization of county offices, and the prohibition of slavery completed it.

The prolix Constitution of 1850 reflected the Jacksonian impulse by providing for the election of most public officials, regulating corporations and railroads as well as taxation and government finance, and embedding local government arrangements in the basic law. This second state constitution slightly modified the tripartite separation of powers by giving constitutional status to the University of Michigan. Oddly, it weakened individual liberties by dissolving the Bill of Rights and scattering its limitations on government power throughout the document. A significant innovation, persisting to the present day, mandated a popular vote at sixteen-year intervals on convening a new constitutional convention.

The Constitution of 1908—at more than twenty-two thousand words about three times the length of the U.S. Constitution—continued the trend toward embedding numerous legislative policies in the fundamental law and constitutionally elaborating the structure of local government. It reassembled and elaborated individual rights and liberties in a new Declaration of Rights. Voter initiation of constitutional amendments was a modest step toward Progressive-style direct democracy; within five years, further amendments would introduce referendum, initiative, and the recall of elected officials.

Despite several efforts, no constitutional convention was mandated by voters until 1961, because of resistance from conservatives and rural communities that feared a new constitution would shift political power to the urban centers of southeast Michigan by mandating apportionment of the legislature on a one-person, one-vote basis. A convention was called by referendum in 1961, the convention deliberated in 1961–1962, and the present constitution was approved by voters in 1963 by a slim margin of 7,000 votes out of more than 1.6 million cast.

CURRENT STRUCTURE

The 1963 Constitution preserved most of the features of earlier constitutions. It substantially strengthened the governor by limiting the number of principal departments to twenty, authorizing him to appoint department heads who would serve at his pleasure unless rejected by a majority of the entire Senate within sixty days, and vesting in him the power to reorganize the executive branch or shift functions between departments unless his actions were vetoed by both houses of the legislature. Many constitutional provisions earmarking tax revenues for specific purposes and limiting the state's taxing authority were eliminated, largely in response to the fiscal crises that had occurred in the 1950s during recessions in the automobile industry.

The movement for civil rights for blacks in the 1950s and early 1960s spurred the convention to add an equal protection clause to the constitution, to prohibit discrimination because of religion, race, color, or national origin, and to create a Civil Rights Commission with investigatory, rule-making, and adjudicative powers. Responding to the McCarthy era in American politics, the convention also imposed procedural limitations on legislative investigations.

The Civil Rights Commission became the third agency with separate constitutional status. Although the legislature may prescribe its procedures, the commission's basic constitutional authority may not be diminished by legislation. In 1940, by initiative, the voters created a constitutional Civil Service Commission and vested it with sweeping independent authority over employees in executive and administrative agencies. The commission's power and its independence from legislative oversight were largely preserved in the 1963 Constitution, although the legislature was empowered by a two-thirds vote to uniformly reduce the compensation increases authorized by the commission.

The Constitution of 1963 extended the sweeping constitutional autonomy of the regents of the University of Michigan, established in the 1850 Constitution, to the governing boards of the state's other public universities. A university governing board has been defined by the judiciary as "the highest form of juristic person known to law, a constitutional corporation of independent authority, which, within the scope of its functions, is co-ordinate with and equal to that of the legislature." The courts have rejected legislation to regulate admissions, curriculum, the composition or structure of the faculty, tuition rates, investment policies, the expenditure of funds (including state appropriations), and the method for selecting university presidents (including the application of the state's open meetings act).

The Michigan legal system was substantially affected by the 1963 Constitution's changes in the judicial branch, especially by the mandate for a consolidated judiciary that vested the "judicial power of the state . . . exclusively in a single court of justice" with the Supreme Court at its head (see figure). The court retained its longstanding authority to issue prerogative and remedial writs and its appellate authority, subject to rules that it would make. In addition to the court's long-established "general superintending control" over the courts, the new constitution also created an "administrator of courts . . . to aid in the administration of the courts of [the] state," who would "perform administrative duties assigned by the [supreme] court." And the Supreme Court's constitutional power to issue general rules regulating "the practice" in all courts was extended to make rules of "procedure" as well.

The Supreme Court has held that the constitution vests in it all of the necessary rule-making, administrative, and superintending authority necessary to govern the judiciary. It has decided also that circuit courts have

Structure of Michigan Courts

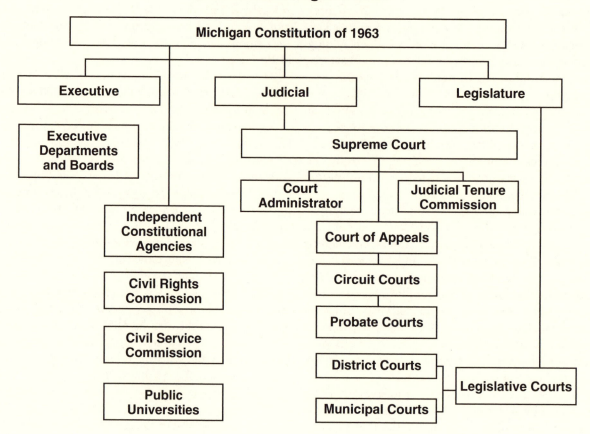

the authority to appoint staff and expend funds for the conduct of court business and to compel counties to pay those expenses, subject to Supreme Court review of the reasonableness of such expenditures. And the court has broadly construed its constitutional authority over practice and procedure, holding, for example, that court rules of evidence, procedures for selecting jury instructions, and authority to set aside accepted pleas prevail over conflicting statutes.

In recent years, between 2,250 and 3,000 petitions have been filed annually in the Supreme Court. Between 55 and 60 percent are criminal matters, the rest civil. About 3.5 percent of cases are disposed of by order and opinion, and another 4.5 percent by order alone. About 2 percent of petitions are withdrawn or dismissed, and the remainder—about 90 percent—are denied, making final the decision of the lower court.

The 1963 Constitution added a Court of Appeals, partly in response to a new constitutional right of criminal defendants to appeal convictions. Panels of the court sit in districts of roughly equal population, drawn along county lines. In recent years the court's twenty-eight judges, sitting in four districts, have disposed of between 7,700 and 12,600 cases annually. About 60 percent of the cases filed with the court are civil matters, and about

40 percent of the court's decisions are by opinion, the remainder being by order.

The circuit courts, organized along county lines, are constitutionally vested with original jurisdiction and appellate jurisdiction from inferior courts, subject to exceptions adopted by the legislature. The Supreme Court has mandated family divisions within the circuit courts, staffed in part by judges of the Probate Court, to handle domestic relations cases, including divorce, paternity disputes, support litigation, and personal protection orders. Between 61 and 70 percent of circuit court filings in recent years have been family and juvenile matters, and about equal proportions of the remaining cases are civil and criminal matters. About 9,000 appeals from inferior courts are filed annually with circuit courts.

The legislature's creation of the Family Division in the Circuit Court greatly reduced the caseload in the constitutionally mandated probate courts. Although now limited largely to cases involving guardianships, conservatorships, commitments of the mentally ill, and the administration of estates and trusts, probate courts nonetheless had between 84,000 and 87,000 filings annually in the late 1990s. There is a probate court in all but ten Michigan counties, where pairs of counties have voted to share a probate judge.

In recent years, the district courts, created as courts of limited jurisdiction by the legislature, have had about 410,000 criminal filings, 2.4 million traffic filings, and 435,000 civil filings, including small claims matters. The handful of remaining municipal courts, with jurisdiction similar to that of the district courts, had about 32,000 filings annually.

In conjunction with the legislature, the Supreme Court has created mediation centers across the state, and those centers resolve 90 percent of the cases submitted to them. It has also created drug courts within existing courts, which are special dockets for drug users that provide judicially supervised treatment, mandatory drug testing, and various rehabilitation services.

STAFFING

The Supreme Court consists of seven members who serve eight-year terms, except that a justice appointed to the court by the governor to fill a vacancy serves only until the next election. Two justices are elected by the voters of the state on a nonpartisan ballot in the November general election in each even-numbered year (one in the eighth year). By law, nominations of Supreme Court candidates are made by the political parties at their conventions. A sitting justice may be placed on the ballot for re-election by filing an affidavit requesting to be slated as an independent candidate. The judges of other courts, both statutory and constitutional, serve six-year terms, are both nominated and elected on the nonpartisan ballot, and stand for election in the even-numbered years. Judicial vacancies throughout the state are filled by the governor.

No person may be elected or appointed to the Supreme Court or any other judicial office after reaching age seventy. Supreme Court justices and other judges may be removed by impeachment by a majority of the House of Representatives and conviction by two-thirds of the Senate. Unlike other civil officers, judges may be removed by the governor on a concurrent resolution of two-thirds of the members of each house of the legislature for reasonable cause that would not be sufficient grounds for impeachment. An amendment to the 1963 Constitution creates a Judicial Tenure Commission that, operating under rules established by the Supreme Court, may recommend the disciplining of judges to the Supreme Court; and the court may censure, suspend, retire, or remove a judge.

Prosecutors are elected by the voters in each of the fifty-seven counties; and the state, under the supervision of the Supreme Court, maintains public defender services in all courts.

The Supreme Court's constitutional power over court practice has been construed as authority to regulate the practice of law, including admissions to the bar. Membership in an integrated state bar association is mandatory, and the Supreme Court oversees the development of rules for the practice of law. Attorney discipline is undertaken by the Attorney Discipline Board, which operates under the supervision of the judiciary.

In 2000, Michigan's legal system was served by approximately 31,000 resident attorneys, one for every 320 state residents. This represented a two-decade increase in the number of attorneys from 18,000 in 1981, about one for every 515 Michigan residents. Despite the growth in the number of lawyers, 86 percent of Michigan's attorneys reported to the state bar that they had all the work they could handle (59 percent) or more than they wanted (27 percent). Michigan lawyers are overwhelmingly recruited from the state's five law schools, including public law schools at the University of Michigan and Wayne State University and a private law school affiliated with Michigan State University.

There is considerable evidence that the Michigan judiciary has become increasingly affected by partisan and electoral politics. Studies of the Supreme Court, whose members are nominated by party conventions, have shown that many cases are decided by justices voting largely along party lines. And while political parties and their allied interest groups have long been active in promoting the election of Supreme Court candidates, the trend toward electoral partisanship has accelerated in recent years, with justices sometimes campaigning at party meetings, fundraising events, and presidential campaign rallies. The two major parties have helped their respective Supreme Court nominees to raise large amounts of campaign money; interest groups have contributed generously; and so-called independent expenditures by parties and allied interest groups in behalf of endorsed candidates have increased significantly. Campaign expenditures for three Supreme Court seats in 2000 were estimated at $15 million.

The same level of partisanship has not been evident in campaigns for lower court judges. However, Democrats, labor unions, and black political leaders made a systematic effort in the mid-1990s to defeat some lower-court judges in Detroit who had been appointed by a Republican governor; and some of those judges were unseated. Even without party nominating arrangements, there appears to be an increase in the number of incumbent lower-court judges who are challenged and in the number of contests for vacant judgeships. Campaign expenditures in many contested lower-court races have escalated significantly.

Despite the increased electoral competition in judicial races, Michigan's 1963 Constitution makes it difficult to defeat sitting judges. The constitution mandates that they be designated on the ballot as judges or justices of their respective courts when seeking to retain their seats. For large numbers of voters who have little information about judicial candidates, these designations are determinative.

RELATIONSHIP TO THE NATIONAL SYSTEM

The Michigan Constitution of 1963 was written during the expansion of federal constitutional rights and liberties fashioned by the U.S. Supreme Court under Chief Justice Earl Warren. Although Michigan's constitutional convention maintained and expanded the Declaration of Rights and added for the first time an equal protection clause, there was sentiment in the convention to regard state guarantees of individual rights and liberties as equivalent to those ensured by the U.S. Constitution. As a result, the Michigan judiciary has largely interpreted state constitutional guarantees to be the same as their counterpart federal rights. Recent decisions of the U.S. Supreme Court diminishing the scope of some federal constitutional rights and liberties and declining to expand the scope of others have been regarded as precedents for the interpretation of the Declaration of Rights. Michigan has therefore not participated in the modern movement toward judicial federalism in which state judiciaries give independent and broader meaning to state constitutional guarantees of individual rights and liberties.

David Adamany

See also Appellate Courts; Constitutional Law; Federalism; Judicial Selection, Methods of; Trial Courts; United States—Federal System; United States—State Systems

References and further reading

Bateman, Brent. 1999. "Partisanship on the Michigan Supreme Court: The Search for a Reliable Predictor of Judicial Behavior." *Wayne Law Review* 45, no. 2A (summer): 357–390.

Brauer, Kurt. 1998. "The Role of Campaign Fundraising in Michigan's Supreme Court Elections: Should We Throw the Baby Out with the Bathwater?" *Wayne Law Review* 44, no. 2A (summer): 367–393.

Christoff, Chris. "Some Voters Skipped Supreme Court Contest," *Detroit Free Press,* at http://www.freep.com/news/mich/court24_20001124.htm

Fino, Susan P. 1996. *The Michigan State Constitution: A Reference Guide.* Westport, CT: Greenwood Press.

Michigan Supreme Court. 2001. *Michigan's Courts: Striving for Excellence.* Michigan's One Court of Justice, 2000 Annual Report. Lansing: Michigan State Court Administrative Office.

MICRONESIA, FEDERATED STATES OF

GEOGRAPHY

The Federated States of Micronesia (FSM) is located in the central Pacific. It occupies the major part of that group of Micronesian islands called the Carolines. The FSM consists of hundreds of islands and atolls, which span over 3 million square miles of ocean and lie between 0° to 14° north latitude and from 136° to 166° east latitude. The geography is varied, ranging from isolated reefs and atolls barely above sea level to dramatic peaks of several hundred meters. The major landmasses are Pohnpei, Kosrae, and Yap, and the total land area is 700.8 square kilometers. The country has hot and wet tropical climate (Ngaire and Ngaire 1989, 69).

BRIEF POLITICAL HISTORY

The islands that now make up FSM were ruled successively by Spain, Germany, Japan, and the United States. In 1565, Spain claimed Micronesia with the aim of acquiring territory and converting heathens to Christianity. In the 1800s, the Germans visited the territory, but unlike the Spanish, they concentrated on trade, copra, and mining. Additionally, the Germans attempted to convert the customary land-tenure system into a freehold system. Micronesia fell under another colonial power in 1914 when the Japanese took over from the Germans. Four years later, the League of Nations mandated Micronesia to Japan. Under Japanese rule Micronesia saw more economic development in the ensuing twenty-four years than was witnessed during the two previous colonial administrations. In 1944, through the Pacific campaign, Micronesia was again annexed by the United States, which was primarily interested in it as a military installation; as such, all development on Micronesia was centered around that need. In 1947, Micronesia was turned into a trust territory, with the exception of Guam. This political arrangement stayed in place until 1986, when the UN Trusteeship Council approved the Compact of Free Association between FSM and the United States.

THE FEDERAL SYSTEM

Unlike many of the Pacific states, the FSM is a federal republic, with a federal system of government similar to that of the United States. There are three branches of government—the executive, headed by the president; the legislature, composed of secretaries from the different departments; and the judiciary, headed by the chief justice of the Supreme Court. The states operate within this structure. There are four states in FSM—namely, Yap, Truk, Pohnpei, and Kosrae—and they have their own governors, executives, legislatures, and judiciaries (Ngaire and Ngaire 1989, 70). Broadly, the FSM federal system reflects the U.S. constitutional system, wherein the powers of national and state governments are provided under the respective constitutions. However, there are three major differences. First, the constitutions in FSM provide potential roles for traditional leaders. Second, the way power is divided between the national and state governments in FSM is different from that in the United States. Finally, the powers and duties of the FSM national executive and legislative branches sometimes overlap in ways that would be considered a violation of

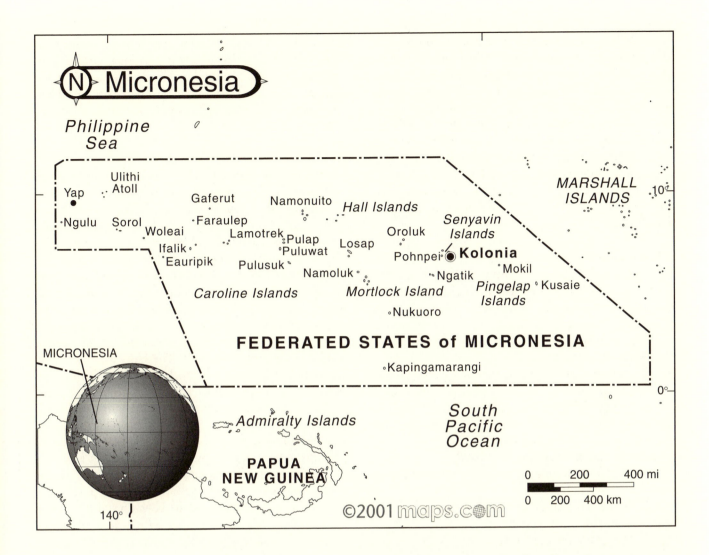

the separation of powers doctrine in the United States (Zorn 1993, 463).

SOURCES OF LAW

FSM Constitution

The FSM Constitution went into effect on May 10, 1979, and by its own terms, it is the supreme law of FSM. Any act of the government that conflicts with the FSM Constitution is invalid to the extent of the conflict (Article 2, Section 1). Other sources of law also exist in FSM and are recognized by the constitution. These include state constitutions, legislation (local, state, and national), treaties, the traditions of the people, the decisional law of the Micronesian courts (common law), and certain statutes of the trust territory. These laws are only valid to the extent that they do not conflict with the FSM Constitution (Zorn 1993, 466). Like any constitution, the FSM Constitution provides the framework for government to operate and guarantees the rights of citizens.

The power to review laws and determine the extent of conflict between the different sources of law resides with the FSM Supreme Court. In exercising its power of judicial review, the court interprets the constitution according to the Judicial Guidance Clause in the FSM Constitution. This clause requires courts to conform their decisions to the provisions of the constitution itself, to customs and traditions of Micronesia, and to any social and geographic configurations of the FSM. Amendments of the constitution may be made through a constitutional convention, by popular demand, or by Congress. Proposed amendments become part of the constitution if approved by 75 percent of votes cast in at least three of the four states. Furthermore, every ten years, Congress must, pursuant to section 2 of Article 14 of the constitution, ask voters whether they require a convention to be established to consider any revision or amendment of the constitution. The most recent convention was held in 2001.

State Constitutions

State constitutions are also an important source of law in FSM. Each of the states (Pohnpei, Yap, Kosrae, and Truk) has a state constitution, and each state constitution is, by its own terms, the supreme law of that state (subject only to the FSM Constitution). Any state law that is inconsistent with the state constitution will be invalid to the extent of the inconsistency. State courts also have the power to review state and local legislation and to overturn those laws that violate the state or federal constitution. Unlike the FSM Constitution, which exists only in English, the state constitutions are rendered in both English and a local language (Zorn 1993, 467). An amendment of a state constitution begins with a proposal, which must be approved by either 25 percent of the registered voters in that state or a resolution by passed by 75 percent of the legislature.

National Legislation
National legislation is made by the Congress of FSM. Pursuant to Article 9 of the FSM Constitution, the National Congress is vested with powers to make laws

1. To regulate national defense
2. To ratify treaties
3. To regulate immigration, nationalization, and citizenship
4. To impose duties and tariffs
5. To impose income taxes
6. To issue and regulate currency
7. To regulate banking, foreign and interstate commerce, insurance, bankruptcy, and patents and copyrights
8. To regulate navigation and shipping
9. To establish usury limits
10. To provide for a postal system
11. To acquire and govern new territory
12. To govern the national capital area
13. To regulate marine resources
14. To regulate the national public service
15. To impeach and remove the president, vice president, and Supreme Court justices
16. To prescribe penalties for national crimes
17. To override a presidential veto by not less than a three-fourths vote of all state delegations

The scope of Congress's law-making authority is limited by the constitutional requirement that the national government has only the powers expressly delegated by the FSM Constitution (as just listed). However, both Congress and states have the power to appropriate public funds, borrow money on public credit, promote education and health, and establish systems of social security and public welfare (Zorn 1993, 468).

State and Local Legislation
Another source of law is legislation enacted by individual states for themselves and local bodies within their boundaries. Such laws apply only to those individual states. The states may make laws on all matters other than those exclusively delegated to the national government, subject only to the state and national constitutions. If any state or local legislation is inconsistent with the FSM Constitution, that legislation will be invalid to the extent of its inconsistency.

Treaties
Treaties are considered a major source of law in FSM, although normally they would not be considered as such. Particularly important is the Compact of Free Association with the United States, which establishes the U.S. obligation to defend the FSM, establish military facilities, and financially support the FSM. Treaties in general are negotiated by the president and must be ratified by two-thirds of the national legislature. For major treaties such as the Compact of Free Association, which delegate significant powers of government to another nation, there must also be approval of three-quarters of all state legislatures (Zorn 1993, 469). The FSM has diplomatic relations and has entered into bilateral and multilateral treaties with other nations as well. These treaties, however, do not have the force of law unless ratified by FSM.

Customary Law
"The customary norms and dispute settlement processes of the peoples of Micronesia are the earliest and most enduring sources of law in the FSM, but the position of custom as a source of law in the FSM's new legal system is ambiguous" (Zorn 1993, 469). However, unlike those of its Melanesian neighbors Vanuatu and the Solomon Islands, in which custom is recognized as a separate body of law, the federal and state constitutions in FSM recognize custom as a source of common law and legislation. Customary principles therefore become law only to the extent that they are considered when enacting legislation or common law; they are not a separate body of law.

Trust Territory Laws
These are the laws that governed the country when it was still a U.S. trust territory. The federal and state constitutions, however, provide that only those trust territory laws that have not been amended or repealed may continue in force, to the extent that they are not inconsistent with the constitution. Today, only a few such laws are in place.

Common Law
Common law is the body of case law developed in jurisdictions apart from FSM. When FSM was still a trust territory, the U.S. common law applied to it. At independence, however, the FSM Constitution and the state constitutions did not receive the common law of the U.S. or trust territory courts. Article 11 of the constitution

provides that judicial decisions of the FSM must be consistent with the "Constitution, Micronesian customs and traditions, and the social and geographical configuration of Micronesia" (Zorn 1993, 470). The intention is to fashion a uniquely Micronesian common law, looking first at the constitution and then at custom. If neither is appropriate, then the common law of other jurisdictions can be used, including the U.S. common law and that of other trust territory courts.

KEY GOVERNMENT STRUCTURES

National Government
The FSM Constitution establishes a tripartite system of government, with executive, legislative, and judicial branches. These branches exist at the national level as well as in the states.

Head of State
At the head of the national government is the president, who is both chief executive and head of state. The president receives ambassadors, conducts foreign policy and national defense, and, with the consent of Congress, appoints U.S. ambassadors to operate overseas missions. More general duties include implementing the provisions of the constitution and all national laws and granting pardons.

Executive
This branch is established under Article 10 of the FSM Constitution. The president is the head of the executive branch and is assisted by a vice president. Under the constitution, both can be appointed for a term of not more than two years. However, unlike the U.S. model, in which everyone votes for the president, the FSM system approximates the Westminster system, with the president being chosen by a majority of Congress.

Legislature
The Congress of FSM is vested with the legislative powers of the national government. Article 9, Section 8, attempts to apportion congressional constituencies so that there will be representation of both people and states. It provides that one member be elected at large from each state and additional members elected from congressional districts in each state apportioned by population. State members serve for four years, and district members serve for two years. A member of Congress must be at least thirty years old, not have been convicted of a felony, and may not hold public office or employment.

The legislature's main function is to make law. For a bill to become law, it must pass two readings on separate days, after which it is presented to the president. If the president disapproves it, it is returned to the Congress

Legal Structure of Micronesia Courts

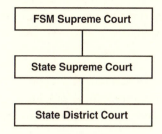

within ten days (or thirty days if Congress has less than ten days left in that session) for relevant alterations. However, Congress may, with a vote of three-fourths of its members, override presidential disapproval of a bill.

Apart from making laws, Congress also has the power to remove the president, vice president, or justice of the Supreme Court for charges of treason, bribery, or conduct involving corruption. Congress also has the power to establish committees for researching and investigating legislation. Finally, as alluded to earlier, Congress, together with the president, has the power to ratify treaties; however, in treaties that delegate major powers to another government (such as the Compact of Free Association), a further requirement of approval by two-thirds of the states is required (Zorn 1993, 476).

Judiciary
Pursuant to Article 11 of the constitution, the judicial power of the national government vests in the Supreme Court. The Supreme Court is to have both a trial and an appellate division and such inferior courts as established by statute. The Supreme Court is made up of a chief justice and not more than five associate justices, who are to be appointed by the president with approval of at least two-thirds of Congress. A justice of the Supreme Court must have a law degree or extraordinary legal ability gained through at least five years of legal practice.

Article 11, Section 2, declares that the Supreme Court is the highest court in the nation and thus has original and exclusive jurisdiction in matters involving disputes between states, foreign officials, admiralty and maritime cases, the FSM Constitution, national laws or treaties, and other domestic laws. The chief justice is the administrative head of the national judicial system and may make rules governing the national courts, divide the Supreme Court and other inferior courts into geographic areas, assign judges among the divisions, and establish rules of procedure and evidence. Additionally, the chief justice governs the admission to practice and discipline of attorneys.

State Governments
Like the national government, state governments consist of an executive, a legislature, and a judicial branch. A

governor, who is elected by the people, heads the executive. Although the states are sovereign entities, power over foreign relations resides with the national government and the president as the FSM's head of state.

Executive

All the states have a governor, who is vested with executive authority. The constitutions of Yap and Pohnpei provide that no person may serve for more than two consecutive terms of eight years. All the states also have a lieutenant governor, who would become governor if that office is vacated. As chief executive officer of the state, the governor is responsible for execution of the laws of the state. Additionally, like the president, the governor has the power to grant reprieves and pardons. The governor is also responsible for appointing the chief officers of the executive departments, subject to the approval of the legislature.

Legislature

All four states have legislatures that are responsible for making the state laws. The composition of the legislature differs from state to state. In Pohnpei, there are twenty-three members; in Yap, Kosrae, and Truk, there are ten senators. The number of legislatures each state has depends on the population as well as the social configuration of the state.

The legislatures meet regularly to make laws as outlined by the state constitutions. To become law, a bill must pass two readings of the legislature on two separate days. After the bill is passed by the legislature, it is presented to the governor for consideration. If the governor approves the bill, it is passed as law, but if the governor disapproves the bill, it must be returned to the legislature with objections. However, similar to national legislation, the legislature can override the governor's veto (but by a lesser majority of two-thirds of the membership).

State legislatures additionally have the power to conduct investigations, hold public hearings, subpoena witnesses and documents, and administer oaths. They are also empowered to impeach and remove the governor and lieutenant governor and other officials for misconduct. Members of state legislatures are also privileged from arrest during and while going to or returning from legislative sessions (Zorn 1993, 478).

Judiciary

In Pohnpei, Article 10 of the state constitution vests the judicial power in the Pohnpei Supreme Court and in such inferior courts as may be established by statute. The Pohnpei Supreme Court consists of a chief justice and up to four associate justices. The court is divided into a Trial and an Appellate Division. Each justice of the Pohnpei Supreme Court is a member of both the Trial Division and the Appellate Division. A single justice may hear a case in the Trial Division, but no less than three may form an appellate panel. The Trial Division justice must not sit on appeal.

In Yap, the State Court may have a chief justice and at least two associate justices. The State Court also has a Trial and an Appellate Division. As in the Pohnpei case, one judge may sit for the Trial Division, but not less than three must sit for appeals. The Trial Division has original jurisdiction, and the Appellate Division has jurisdiction to hear all cases heard in the Trial Division. Justices of the State Court are appointed by the governor, with the advice and consent of the legislature, and they serve for six years. Yap law also provides for a court in each municipality. Such courts would be presided over by judges knowledgeable in custom, with an aim of settling minor disputes arising in the municipality before they get to the State Courts. The jurisdiction of the Municipal Court is limited to civil cases involving residents of the municipality and certain criminal offenses. If the Trial Division of the State Court considers the case beyond the jurisdiction of the Municipal Court, the Trial Court will order the case to be tried in the Trial Court (Zorn 1993, 479–480).

CIVIL LAW AND PROCEDURE

The civil procedure of the national courts is governed by Article 11 of the FSM Constitution, together with the Judiciary Act of 1979 (FSM Code, Title 4). In addition to the powers laid down in these provisions, Article 11, Section 9, of the FSM Constitution further provides that the chief justice can establish rules of civil procedure. These rules are similar to U.S. rules of procedure and as such lack the flexibility of custom. The state courts are, however, more flexible, applying customary means of settling disputes. All the other fundamental rules or procedure are in line with the adversarial system. In FSM national and state courts, the party seeking redress carries the onus of bringing the action to court, plus the burden of proving the case on a preponderance of evidence.

Torts

In FSM, tort law is a matter for the state courts rather than the national courts. Other civil matters that are regulated by state legislation include commercial law, personal property, contracts, wills and succession, and family law. The only two situations in which the national courts will hear tort cases is when there are conflicts of jurisdiction between states and when the national government is a party to the case. The common law provides the basis for tort law, but the courts often resort to custom as well. This has yielded different results on certain issues (Zorn 1993, 512).

The courts in FSM have developed the law on torts to reflect the country's circumstances. An example is the FSM Supreme Court stance that contributory negligence as mandated by the American Law Institutes Restatement will not be applied in FSM; instead, the less harsh rule of comparative negligence will be used. Similar developments also occur in state courts. The Pohnpei Supreme Court imposed a duty on the owner, seller, or controller of machinery to educate Pohnpeians about its dangers before selling such machinery. The Pohnpei Supreme Court also held that in collecting damages, multiple defendants are not jointly and severally liable but should pay according to the extent of injury caused to the plaintiff. In tort claims, the national government is not immune in certain cases. These include:

- Claims for recovery of any tax erroneously collected
- Claims for damages arising from improper administration of the law
- Claims on an express or implied contract
- Claims for recovery of up to U.S.$20,000 for loss of property, injury, or death resulting from the negligence of a public officer

Contracts
In most other jurisdictions of the Pacific, contract law is based on common law. This is true for FSM as well, although the common law there basically means the law developed by the courts from interpreting the constitution and FSM customs. As with torts, one observes some tension between judges who are inclined to either constitution or custom. On the one hand, FSM Supreme Court judges accept too readily that since a contract arises in a business context, custom must be excluded. On the other hand, state court judges are more familiar with customary contract principles and are swayed toward using custom. However, both the constitution and custom accept that common law should provide the guide for contracts law.

Family Law
Family matters in FSM remain in the exclusive jurisdiction of the states, yet none of the states has enacted family law legislation. Perhaps this is because citizens may choose to marry and divorce under statute or custom. According to custom, parties may marry when they are mature, and maturity is judged by behavior rather than age. In FSM, marrying involves a process of gift giving, feasts, ceremony, and eventual residence, after which the marriage is considered to have taken place. If the parties choose to marry under statute, the male must be over eighteen and the female over sixteen. Title 39 of the Trust Territory Code, which applies to states until it is revoked by new family laws, further requires that the marriage ceremony must be performed by a member of the clergy and witnessed by two persons.

The arrangement for divorce is similar; that is, it can

be effected either under custom or statute. According to most Micronesian societies, a separation or divorce may occur whenever one of the spouses renounces the other. The grounds for divorce according to custom include violence, desertion, and adultery. If a party chooses to dissolve the marriage under statute, more stringent limitations are imposed. The court will grant an annulment only if the marriage was illegal when entered into or voidable (meaning, in the legal sense, legal until declared void prospectively—the declaration does not have retrospective effect). If the parties have resumed cohabitation, the court may also refuse annulment. The grounds for divorce under statute include (1) adultery, (2) cruelty, (3) desertion for one or more years, (4) habitual drunkenness, (5) a prison sentence of three or more years, (6) leprosy, (7) separation without cohabitation for two consecutive years, and (8) willful failure of the husband to provide support (Zorn 1993, 506).

CRIMINAL LAW AND PROCEDURE
Until 1991, the national courts had jurisdiction over major crimes while states had jurisdiction over minor crimes. However, in 1991, this provision of the constitution (Article 9, Section 2) was amended so that jurisdiction of the national court now encompasses matters inherently national in character. This distinction has nonetheless remained blurry, and the FSM Criminal Code further defines felony and misdemeanor offenses. According to the code, a felony is punishable by more than one year of imprisonment, while a misdemeanor is punishable by imprisonment of not more than thirty days. Murder has no statute of limitation. For crimes attracting imprisonment of more than ten years, the statutory limitation period is six years; the limitation for any felony is three years, for a misdemeanor two years, and for a petty misdemeanor six months. The National Criminal Code requires courts to look at custom when deciding criminal cases. Despite this stipulation, however, the FSM Supreme Court has refused to consider a traditional Pohnpeian forgiveness ceremony in determining criminal liability. The court has also held that customary punishments can only go toward mitigating a sentence.

Recently, states have acquired exclusive jurisdiction over all crimes except those of an inherently national character. This, it is believed by some, could lead to a greater use of customary practices and procedures in dealing with criminal offenses in issues determining liability (where customary obligations as to retribution, for example, are often set up as potential defenses) as well as mitigation in penalties. This should be no surprise given the states' inclination to use custom to settle disputes.

Criminal procedure rights are provided pursuant to Article 11, Section 9, of the constitution. The FSM Supreme Court has also adopted rules of criminal procedure similar to the U.S. Federal Rules of Criminal Procedure. Under Title 12, a person may not be arrested without a warrant unless there is likelihood of a breach of peace or if the offender is in the act of committing a criminal offense. During arrest, only reasonable force may be applied by the law enforcement officer, and the usual rights of persons apply, which include:

- Right to counsel
- Right to see family members and employer
- Right to be released or charged within a reasonable time
- Right to remain silent
- Right to be informed of all of one's rights before questioning

In addition, any person arrested for a criminal offense other than murder is entitled to be released on bail before conviction. Arrested persons also have the right to have, in advance of trial, a copy of the charges, as well as the right to present a witness of their choice and give evidence on their own behalf if they so choose.

Bob Hughes
Phillip Tagini

See also Common Law; Customary Law; Federalism; Legal Pluralism

References and further reading

Douglas, Norman, and Ngaire Douglas. 1989. *Pacific Islands Yearbook*. 16th ed. New North Ryde, New South Wales: Angus and Robertson.
Zorn, Jean G. 1993. "Federated States of Micronesia." Pp. 462–517 in *South Pacific Legal Systems*. Edited by M. Ntumy. Honolulu: University of Hawai'i Press.

MILITARY JUSTICE, AMERICAN (LAW AND COURTS)

Military justice is that system of laws, courts, and legal procedures dealing with members of the armed forces that has evolved in the United States from the revolutionary era. The first "articles of war" were based on the British code known by the same term. Revised by John Adams and Thomas Jefferson in 1775 and 1776, they endured until after World War II with only minor changes. Two underlying problems in U.S. military justice were not resolved until 1950, when Congress adopted the Uniform Code of Military Justice (UCMJ). These were the issue of appellate procedure and the relationship of civilian authority over military justice.

In terms of due process, military law differs substantially from its civilian counterpart, although these differences have diminished over the years. Within the military, emphasis on individual rights and liberties shifts to an insistence on rank, discipline, and obedience, along with the understanding that the mandatory obedience to an order may well mean certain injury or death. Moreover, as part of the military context, basic rights such as freedom of speech or press are subordinated to the military mission. Historically, the commander has had almost total authority over the men in his command. In terms of courts-martial, he usually selected members of the court who were inferior in rank. He could accept or reject the verdict. If unsatisfied with it, he could order the court to "reconsider." Moreover, a long-established tradition within the military encouraged harsh sentences to be handed down by a court-martial, only to be reduced by the commander as a sign of mercy, forgiveness, and another opportunity for the accused to redeem himself.

By the Revolutionary Era, the right of an appeal to a higher civilian court had already become a staple in the American colonies. But it had no counterpart in the military. Yet military courts-martial probably represented the earliest American federal judicial trials, as they predate the adoption of the U.S. Constitution by more than a decade. We are so accustomed to the long-established system of appellate courts at both state and federal levels that it might be a surprise to learn that they are of relatively recent vintage in military law. The framers probably anticipated some sort of tension concerning the issue of civilian control over the military. Thus, while the president is indeed the commander-in-chief, his army is clothed, fed, paid, equipped, and governed by congressional fiat.

Although in theory, as commander-in-chief, the president could review all court-martial verdicts, in reality the growing demands of his office made any systematic and thorough review impossible. Abraham Lincoln probably "reviewed" more court-martial records than all of his predecessors. But given the nature of the other demands upon his time, thorough review was impossible. By contrast, in a civilian appellate trial, judgment is based upon a thorough consideration of the lower court record. Traditionally, in U.S. law such consideration involved strict scrutiny of that record for errors of law.

The question can be raised as to the extent that the military had any such procedure. Military justice requires promptness; proper appellate consideration requires time for unhurried judicial reflection. Further, military justice could not assume the availability of an appellate courtroom in a fixed location, as is true in civilian life. With the army or whatever branch of the military that it served, to a great extent military justice had to follow the personnel subject to it. There has always been an underlying tension between the success of the military mission and the requirement that military justice follow proper procedures.

It may have been the awareness of the unique characteristics of military life that contributed to a lack of involvement and interest from civilian authorities concerning military justice, with the exception of the episodic presidential review just noted. But it appears that such a paucity of interest resulted more from tradition than from congressional intent. While the U.S. Supreme Court did indeed hear a number of cases concerning military actions during the Civil War era, with one notable exception that tribunal always declined to intervene. In 1858 by a vote of 8 to 1, for example, and with no formal dissent submitted, the court held that a court-martial verdict "when confirmed . . . is altogether beyond the jurisdiction or inquiry of any civil tribunal whatever" (*Dynes v. Hoover*). The court cited no authority for this broad conclusion, somehow accepting as a given that military law was not subject to civilian oversight.

What appears to be an exception, the famous case of *Ex Parte Milligan* (1866), concerned the trial of a civilian by a military commission. While the High Court declined to sustain military authority in this case, and while it denied congressional authority to set up military commissions when civilian legal tribunals were in operation, in fact the decision said nothing about military authority over its own personnel. In no way did it change the reality that military law provides for no formal appellate review of a court-martial beyond the commander involved, who usually is neither an attorney nor interested in matters of legal procedure.

Yet the same needs that historically led to civilian appellate courts existed in military justice. Although Congress did on occasion intervene in behalf of some unfortunate with influential political connections, neither Congress nor the chief executive was equipped in any judicial sense to get at the "truth." In 1889 one retired colonel actually proposed a military court of appeals—not, it should be emphasized, a court of military appeals. The former would be located within the military justice system, while the latter would, presumably, be outside and probably more independent in its conclusions. Suggested again during World War I, it was endorsed—for a third time—in 1948. This time, the proposal received a sympathetic response from Congress.

With the several military branches now unified, at least to some extent, into a Department of Defense, a rationale no longer existed for separate bodies of laws governing the army and navy. Further, with the legacy of World War II still fresh, as well as a number of outrageous miscarriages of military justice identified, Congress in 1950 approved a proposed new uniform code of military justice, one that ultimately consisted of more than 140 separate articles. Several of them established two separate appellate courts. One, the intermediate level of appellate review, was located within the military, and its judges were to be selected by the chief lawyer of each service, the judge advocate general. Moreover, that official determined the number of years that these judges would serve. Almost invariably drawn from officers in the JAG corps, although civilians were eligible for appointment, Senate confirmation was not required.

In contrast, the highest appellate court was to consist of three judges (now five), appointed from civilian life by the president and confirmed by the Senate. Unlike federal district and circuit court judges, they have never been granted life tenure, but rather serve for limited terms, currently set at fifteen years. Although the president may reappoint a judge to this tribunal, in actuality that has been extremely rare since 1951. Created in 1950, the U.S. Court of Appeals for the Armed Forces has the primary job of reconciling military law with the constitutional rights of U.S. citizens who choose to enlist in the armed forces. The question, easy to raise but extremely difficult to resolve, concerns the extent to which the military mandate can supersede them. When confronting such issues, the court must draw on several sources that govern military law. Highest in importance is, of course, the U.S. Constitution, followed by the federal statute that comprises the Uniform Code of Military Justice. In addition, a large number of military regulations have evolved in the last half-century. In theory drafted by the president as commander-in-chief, but in reality prepared by the military and endorsed by the president, this Manual for Courts-Martial sets forth a massive collection of instructions and procedures. They have much the same relation to military justice as federal statutes have to constitutional law. Finally, there is now a substantial body of military justice case law, consisting of more than half a century of decisions handed down by the U.S. Court of Appeals for the Armed Forces (USCAAF).

While the U.S. Supreme Court has been able to hear certain appeals from USCAAF since 1983, in reality it rarely does. With few exceptions, USCAAF functions as the ultimate expositor of military law. For the most part, when the High Court hears a military justice appeal, almost invariably it has sustained the government's position. The one famous exception to that trend was the decision in the case of *O'Callahan v. Parker* (1969). In this case, a divided court denied the right of the military to court-martial a soldier who had committed an offense while on leave, off post, and allegedly not connected to the military mission. The decision included some unfavorable comparisons between military justice and its civilian counterpart from Justice Douglas. Almost immediately, however, the court began a retreat from its holding, and in 1987 (again by a narrow margin) it overruled *O'Callahan* and dramatically expanded the reach of military justice (*Solorio v. United States*).

Intentionally or not, outside of USCAAF civilian courts have continued to observe the tradition of very limited, if at all existent, interference with the administration of military justice. Yet there have been, even within this narrow framework, some important changes. The commander may still select members of a court-martial, but he cannot select the military judge, and on paper at least, he is forbidden to interfere in any way with the independence of that tribunal. Further, he cannot direct that reconsideration of a verdict take place. In a general court-martial, counsel representing the defendant must be an attorney, as must be the military judge. Federal rules of evidence are in effect, and indeed in a few instances military law has even gone beyond its civilian counterpart. The military equivalent of a grand jury proceeding, for example, is much more thorough and fairer than what commonly occurs in a civil court.

Yet the tensions between military judicial standards and what is acceptable in the world of civilian justice remain, and indeed may be incapable of resolution. It is difficult for a civilian attorney to accept a judicial proceeding in which the prosecuting authorities can appoint and remove the judges. Moreover, the courts, especially the U.S. Supreme Court, have repeatedly insisted that U.S. members of the armed services do not lose their constitutional liberties when they enlist. But specifics have been lacking, and the tendency has been to proclaim this generalization even while consistently declining to apply it in the given instance. The challenge for U.S. military law and justice as it enters the twenty-first century is to ensure that its all-volunteer armed services receive the best and fairest system of justice possible under military law. They have volunteered to go to their deaths if necessary, and they deserve no less.

While the U.S. military justice system should not be seen as an archetype for military justice systems in other countries, the same types of issues confronted by the development and operation of the U.S. system are generally present elsewhere. These issues include (1) the role of civilian oversight of military justice, in terms of either command structures or civilian appellate processes; (2) the integration of military justice into the military's general command structure; (3) the role of military justice both in terms of internal discipline and as a parallel to civilian criminal courts as applied to military personnel; and (4) the jurisdiction, or lack of jurisdiction, of military courts over civilians. The resolution of these issues in each country turns on the specific legal and political situation of the country.

Jonathan Lurie

See also Adversarial System; Constitutional Law; Criminal Law; Judicial Independence; United States—Federal System

References and further reading

Gilligan, Francis, and Frederic Lederer. 1991. *Court-Martial Procedure.* Charlottesville, VA: Michie.
Lurie, Jonathan. 1992. *Arming Military Justice: The Origins of the United States Court of Military Appeals, 1775–1950.* Princeton: Princeton University Press.
———. 1998. *Pursuing Military Justice: The History of the United States Court of Appeals for the Armed Forces.* Princeton: Princeton University Press.
———. 2001. *Military Justice in America: The U.S. Court of Appeals for the Armed Forces, 1775–1980.* Lawrence: University Press of Kansas.
Moyer, William F., Jr. 1972. *Justice and the Military.* Washington, DC: Public Education Institute.

MINNESOTA

GENERAL INFORMATION

Minnesota, one of the fifty states of the United States, bears a Sioux name meaning "sky-tinted water." Within its borders are the sources of three major river systems, including the Mississippi, and more than ten thousand lakes. Its central location in the Northern Plains has figured prominently in its economic and political history. The State of Minnesota came into being on May 11, 1858, even though its legal system had begun to take shape decades before.

The Northwest Territory Act of 1787 established the first courts to claim jurisdiction over what would become the Territory of Minnesota in 1849. Under the terms of the Territorial Act of 1849, Congress created and President Zachary Taylor appointed a three-person Supreme Court. The chief justice and two associate justices were all lawyers from other states and were paid an annual salary of $1,800. Each also served as a district (trial) judge in a different area in the territory. They then gathered to sit as the Supreme Court to review their own decisions. Finally, in 1857, the U.S. Congress approved legislation to authorize statehood, and the first Minnesota constitution was adopted.

Perhaps the most celebrated court case in Minnesota history is *Jay M. Near v. State of Minnesota ex rel Olson,* decided by the U.S. Supreme Court in 1931 by the narrowest of margins. The opinion of the court, written by Chief Justice Charles Evans Hughes, struck down the Minnesota Public Nuisance Law of 1925 as an unconstitutional prior restraint upon publication of the *Saturday Press,* owned by the petitioner, Jay M. Near. In the fall of 1927, Near had published allegations that the mayor of Minneapolis and the chief of police were protecting, rather than combating, organized crime in the city. That issue of the paper was removed from the newsstands by order of the police chief. Near was then charged under the 1925 state law with publishing a "malicious, scandalous and defamatory newspaper." Hennepin County District Judge Mathias Baldwin agreed, citing Near as a "public nuisance" and enjoining him from any future publication of the *Saturday Press.* The Minnesota Supreme Court unanimously affirmed Baldwin's restraining order. Finally, in June 1931, the U.S. Supreme Court lifted the injunction on both First and Fourteenth Amendment grounds.

Today, Minnesota ranks twentieth among the fifty states in population, with about 4.8 million residents. Just over 90 percent are white. Political history provides an explanation for this proportion. In 1819 a U.S. military post, Fort Snelling, was established for defense of the frontier against Native Americans. That military presence provided an incentive for several thousand northern European immigrants, mostly Scandinavian and Irish, to settle in the area during the 1850s. Their cultural legacies have remained dominant for nearly 150 years, even though significant increases in numbers have occurred during the 1980s and 1990s, especially among Asian Americans and African Americans.

Minnesota's economy is one of the most diverse and dynamic in the United States. For example, the value of agricultural commodities produced in the state ranks sixth in the nation. More than 75 percent of the country's iron ore is extracted from the state, a reflection of the storied heyday of the Mesabi Iron Range a century ago. Computer and medical technology have also achieved a significant presence in the Minnesota economy.

There are many other comparative indicators of the state's economic health and the quality of life of its residents. For example, Minnesota consistently ranks among the highest ten states in personal income and the proportion of its adult population that have earned a college degree. Minnesota is perennially among the top five states in high school graduations, the top three in the proportion of residents who own a home, and the top two in life expectancy.

EVOLUTION AND HISTORY

Law and politics in Minnesota continue to reflect the impact of the Progressive movement, dating from the first quarter of the twentieth century. Centered in the Midwest, Progressivism stimulated mass political participation to enhance the accountability of public officials to their constituents. Turnout among Minnesota's eligible voters in presidential and statewide elections continues routinely to reach 65 to 70 percent, far above the national average. Similarly, allegations of official misconduct have been quite rare for several decades. Proof of such misbehavior is even less common.

The development of a legal system may well date from the arrival in the town of Mendota of the first practicing attorney in 1835, Henry Hastings Sibley. The first case on record decided by a Minnesota state court came in 1858. The lawsuit involved the defendant's stray cow, which had wandered onto the plaintiff's property. The plaintiff sued for payment of $2 in pasture fees, a claim that the court rejected.

Other notable events in the evolution of the legal system include a provision of the 1858 Constitution that created a Supreme Court, the jurisdiction of which was confined to appeals from other courts. In 1881 the Minnesota Supreme Court was enlarged from three to five members (it is currently at seven), and in 1883 judicial terms of office were reduced from seven to six years (currently the same). Then within less than a decade, the Minnesota Legislature created the juvenile courts in 1917 and conciliation courts in 1919, and in 1921 first authorized the Supreme Court to establish qualifications for admission to the Minnesota bar.

After World War II, a series of significant reforms occurred, directly affecting the practice of law and the conduct of judges. In 1947 the state legislature authorized the Supreme Court to create uniform Rules of Civil Procedure. In 1955 the Supreme Court adopted the American Bar Association Canons of Professional Ethics. By 1969 the Supreme Court had established a Commission on Judicial Responsibility. Two amendments to the state constitution were approved by Minnesota voters in 1972 and 1982, respectively. The first provided for the creation of the Minnesota Commission on Judicial Standards (now known as the Board on Judicial Standards). The second brought the Intermediate Court of Appeals into being.

Also in 1982, the state legislature passed the Court Unification Act, which reorganized into a single system of district (trial) courts what had been separate county, municipal, and probate courts. Beginning in 1983, the Minnesota Court of Appeals was organized. In 1991 the Minnesota Supreme Court became the first in the United States to be staffed by a majority of female jurists. Then in 1998 the first female chief justice was seated in the Supreme Court's center chair.

CURRENT STRUCTURE

The court system in Minnesota has been organized into three tiers or levels since 1983, as shown in the accompanying figure.

More than 250 trial judges preside in the district courts. These courts have been organized since 1959 for administrative efficiency into ten judicial districts across the state's eighty-seven counties. A trial court is located in each county's seat of government. More than two million cases are filed in these courts every year. Each of the two most populous counties constitutes a distinct judicial district, while in more sparsely populated areas in the state as many as eighteen counties compose a single district. The jurisdiction of the district courts is divided by subject matter—family, juvenile, probate, civil, criminal, and conciliation. All proceedings are recorded, in the event that a verdict is appealed.

Family cases involve such disputes as dissolution of marriage, child support, and adoption. Juvenile cases,

Legal Structure of Minnesota Courts

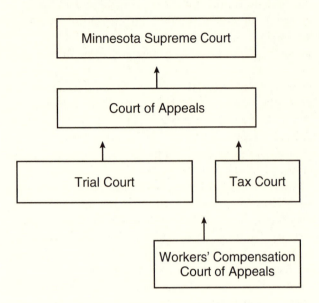

raising such legal matters as traffic offenses, delinquency, and truancy, involve alleged offenders under the age of eighteen. The disposition of disputes over estates takes place in probate courts. All types of civil cases—disputes between private citizens, government agencies, corporations, or other organizations—are considered in district courts. Criminal cases, prosecutions by the state against individuals, corporations, or other organizations accused of committing violations, also begin in this court. Criminal violations run the gamut from minor traffic violations to murder in the first degree. Under the provisions of the Minnesota Constitution, no appeal can be made from a "not guilty" verdict on a criminal charge.

Most cases in District Court can be tried before a judge alone—a bench trial—or before a judge and jury. Six persons constitute a jury in civil cases and misdemeanor criminal cases, while twelve persons compose a jury in criminal cases involving felony charges. Jury verdicts must be unanimous in all criminal cases but may be rendered by "substantial majority" in civil cases.

Conciliation cases, more commonly known as small claims, involve litigants seeking a monetary settlement of a dispute in an amount less than $7,500. No attorneys appear to represent clients. The parties serve as their own advocates. No juries hear these cases. If a litigant seeks a reversal of a judge's decision, the case goes for review to the District Court. This procedure is an exception to what is otherwise exclusively the trial jurisdiction of the District Court.

Since November 1983, the Minnesota Court of Appeals, now composed of sixteen judges, has decided cases sitting in panels of three. These judges travel to cities throughout the state to hear oral argument in appeals, as

a matter of constitutional right, from the final decisions of trial courts, administrative agencies, and local governments. Oral arguments are open to the public without exception.

About twenty-five hundred appeals are brought before the Court of Appeals every year. Some 95 percent go to final judgment there. Minnesota law requires that the Court of Appeals reach a disposition within ninety days of a scheduled conference or oral argument on a case. This statutory deadline is the most stringent imposed on any appellate court in the United States.

The Minnesota Supreme Court, composed of seven justices, has appellate jurisdiction from decisions of the Court of Appeals and from two specialized courts, the Workers' Compensation Court of Appeals and the Tax Court. Unlike the Court of Appeals, the Supreme Court considers cases only as a collective body. Since 1983, the court has had the discretion to select cases for appellate review from among the nearly one thousand that appear on its docket each year.

In addition to deciding important cases about constitutional issues and public policy questions, the Supreme Court oversees the operation of the legal system in Minnesota. In that administrative capacity the court supervises all other state courts. A chief judge in each of the ten judicial districts is responsible for implementation of standards established by the Supreme Court and for reporting the results.

The Supreme Court also regulates the practice of law in Minnesota in a number of ways. For example, a bar examination is offered to law school graduates twice annually, under the auspices of the Supreme Court. Successful applicants are subsequently admitted to the Minnesota bar. Continuing legal education, required of all active lawyers in the state, is a responsibility of the high court. The court also has the authority to impose sanctions on sitting judges, as well as on practicing attorneys who have engaged in unethical, unprofessional conduct. The most severe forms of disciplinary action at the court's disposal include removing judges and disbarring attorneys.

NOTABLE FEATURES OF
THE MINNESOTA LEGAL SYSTEM

In 1976 the Minnesota Office of Administrative Hearings was established by the Minnesota Legislature. As an independent state agency, the office provides an impartial hearing process for citizens who disagree with government policy in any of nine areas identified in the Administrative Procedures Act: health, human rights, human services, labor and industry, natural resources, pollution control, public utilities, transportation, and veterans' affairs. Disputes about local government personnel and licensing actions and, since 1987, controversies over child support are also considered. The office numbers among twenty-five "central panel" hearing agencies across the United States.

All hearings are conducted by twelve full-time and fifty-five part-time administrative law judges in ways similar to courts of law. In 1982 workers' compensation judges also became a part of the Office of Administrative Hearings. Currently, thirty-seven of them decide disputes arising in workers' compensation benefit proceedings. All of these judges within the office are executive, not judicial, officials. All must be lawyers with extensive legal backgrounds.

STAFFING

The Minnesota Constitution stipulates that judges be "learned in the law." In practice, that means "currently licensed to practice in Minnesota." The constitution also provides that judges "shall be elected by the voters from the area in which they are to serve." For district court judges, that means voters within one of the state's ten judicial districts. For judges of the Court of Appeals and justices of the Supreme Court, it means a statewide electorate. State statutes prescribe a term of six years for all judges serving in the judicial branch, with no limits on re-election. Minnesota Supreme Court rules prohibit candidates from seeking, accepting, or using endorsement by a political party. Similarly, judicial candidates may not attend partisan gatherings or publicly discuss any disputed political or legal issue.

Most judges in Minnesota voluntarily retire from the bench prior to the expiration of their term. Under the constitution, the governor may make appointments to fill these vacancies. An appointed judge may then seek election to a full six-year term at the first general election occurring more than a year after appointment. The frequency with which this practice occurred inspired the Minnesota Legislature to establish a Commission on Judicial Selection in 1989. Currently composed of forty-nine members, the commission makes recommendations to the governor to fill vacancies in the district courts. At least three but no more than five candidates' names are forwarded to the governor, from which list he may, but is not required, to choose. Vacancies on the appellate bench are also filled by gubernatorial appointment without involvement by the commission. Members of the commission are not compensated for their service.

Formal legal education, culminating in the award of a degree to successful students, has been available in Minnesota since the late nineteenth century. The University of Minnesota Law School, the first in the state, has been in continuous operation since 1890. The William Mitchell College of Law, known originally as the St. Paul College of Law, celebrated its centennial in 2000. The Hamline University School of Law was established in 1972. These three schools combine to enroll about 750 new students each year. The University of St. Thomas Law School opened its doors to first-year students in 2001. All are located in the Twin Cities of Minneapolis and St. Paul.

The legal profession in Minnesota, as in other areas of the United States, has experienced dramatic demographic change since about 1970. For example, the number of attorneys more than quadrupled, from about five thousand in 1965 to more than twenty-two thousand in 1999. Only about a hundred women practiced law in Minnesota in 1970, representing less than 2 percent of the profession. By 2000 about seventy-five hundred did so, constituting some 34 percent of lawyers in the state. Just as significant has been the national leadership of Minnesota lawyers over the years in promoting legal reform—in setting professional standards, in preserving judicial independence, in simplifying procedure, and in serving indigent clients and criminal defendants.

RELATIONSHIP TO THE NATIONAL SYSTEM

Seven judges serve in federal district court for the District of Minnesota. Trials raising federal claims are conducted in Duluth, Minneapolis, and St. Paul. Appeals of trial verdicts go to the Eighth Circuit Court of Appeals. Appeals from decisions of the circuit courts may go to the Supreme Court of the United States in Washington, D.C.

Federal bankruptcy court, with offices in Duluth, Fergus Falls, Minneapolis, and St. Paul, considers bankruptcy petitions. Four judges serving appointed terms of fourteen years staff the federal bankruptcy bench in Minnesota.

Steven H. Hatting

See also Administrative Law; Judicial Selection, Methods of; Juries; Juvenile Justice; Probate/Succession Law; Small Claims Courts; Trial Courts; United States—Federal System; United States—State Systems

References and further reading
Minnesota State Bar Association. 1983. *The First 100 Years: 1883–1983.* Minneapolis: North Central Publishing.
———. 1997. *Judicial Elections Task Force Report and Recommendations.* Minneapolis: Minnesota State Bar Association.
———. 1997. *Women in the Legal Profession Task Force: Report.* Minneapolis: Minnesota State Bar Association.
———. 1999. *For the Record: 150 Years of Law and Lawyers in Minnesota.* Minneapolis: Minnesota State Bar Association.
Minnesota Supreme Court. 1989. "Task Force for Gender Fairness in the Courts: Final Report." *William Mitchell Law Review* 15: 825.
———. 1993. "Task Force on Racial Bias in the Judicial System." *Hamline Law Review* 16: 477.
———. 1997. *Joint Committee on Legal Aid Funding and Services: Report.* St. Paul: Minnesota Supreme Court.
Research Department, Minnesota House of Representatives. 1996. *The Minnesota Judiciary: A Guide for Legislators.*

MISSISSIPPI

GENERAL INFORMATION

Mississippi achieved statehood in 1817 as the twentieth state admitted to the Union and was readmitted in 1870. It ranks thirty-second in size and thirty-first in population. The estimated population in 1998 was 2,752,092, with a density of 58.7 persons per square mile. Mississippi's largest ethnic group is black (37 percent). Mississippi is rural and considered one of the Bible Belt states in the southern United States. Alabama lies along the eastern border of Mississippi, with Tennessee on the north and Louisiana on the west. The southern boundary touches the Gulf of Mexico, with the Mississippi River along the western boundary.

Mississippi is more than its stereotype of being one huge cotton plantation. There are at least six distinctive regions in regard to its economic, political, and social features. Mississippi's newer chicken, catfish, and casino industries complement the established cotton and forestry resources. With the state's development of the grain-fed, pond-raised process, catfish consumption has spread worldwide and Mississippi ranks first in world production. Mississippi continues to be a rural agricultural state, although the state's new economic development efforts resulted in attracting an automotive plant, which will be similar to those in Tennessee and Alabama.

Unfortunately, Mississippi is distinctive from the other states by typically being ranked as the worst in the nation in important factors, such as health care in 2000. In quality of education and teacher salaries, Mississippi and Arkansas regularly alternate as fiftieth. At times, Mississippi has improved its ranking only to fall into an economic slump that again throws the state behind the others.

EVOLUTION AND HISTORY

Mississippi's roots are a political culture that some have described as "traditionalistic," in which Mississippi's heritage provided a hierarchical political arena with the old-family elites retaining power. Government's function was to maintain the status quo for a stable social order so there was no need for large and costly government. Power was derived from patron-client relationships, which resulted in a high level of political corruption. This corruption was not viewed as a betrayal of the public trust, but as an appropriate way to maintain the traditional order. The state has been gradually transforming from that traditionalism, with the slowest movement occurring in the judiciary. Mississippi is one of the most communal states in the Union, and hometown identity carries great importance.

Mississippi's traditionalism may explain the state's having four constitutions in quick succession because they were responses to major historical events. The Constitution of 1817 was a conservative document reflecting class and therefore the judges were selected by the legislature and could serve, with good behavior, until age sixty-five. Jacksonian democracy resulted in the Constitution of 1832, which, while reflecting class, also resulted in Mississippi's being the first state to popularly elect all of its judges. The Constitution of 1869 was a Reconstruction document in which black and Republican participation was very high. Selection of judges shifted to gubernatorial appointment with Senate approval. White Democrats wrote the Constitution of 1890, which reflected race as revealed in its *understanding clause* as a suffrage literacy requirement. The constitutionality of this clause was upheld in 1898 by the U.S. Supreme Court in *Williams v Mississippi* (170 US 213). Amendments in 1912 and 1915 resulted in returning the state to an elective judiciary.

CURRENT STRUCTURE

Mississippi's judicial branch has experienced recent alterations that have moved it toward a more professional legal orientation, for example, the creation of an intermediate appellate court and provision for court administrators. However, critics continue to point out the problems with the existence of the justice court, which provides common sense solutions and a separate chancery court.

Mississippi's complex organization and jurisdiction of its courts may be seen in the accompanying figure. At the lower level of the hierarchy are four limited jurisdiction courts (having limited authority over cases): justice court, municipal court, county court, and youth court. (Youth court is not shown because it is an adjunct of county court or a division of chancery court.) The general jurisdiction trial court of law for the state is the circuit court, with questions of equity (disputes that the rule of law cannot resolve) reserved for the chancery court. The state has two appellate courts: the court of appeals and the Supreme Court, which is the highest state court.

A *justice court* (formerly justice of the peace) is located in every county and is not a court of record, which means if an appeal is made the case must be tried anew (de novo) to establish a record in the circuit court (county court if one exists). Because each subdivision in a county may have a justice court judge, in 2000 there were 191 judges for the 92 courts. They have authority over civil actions up to the amount of $2,500, criminal law misdemeanors (penalty of less than one year in jail), and a committing role for serious crimes. Trial by jury is statutorily permissible, but rare.

The *municipal court* may have as many as three judges if the city's population is over 10,000 and only one judge for smaller cities. In 2000, there were about 223 courts with approximately 300 judges. They exist at the political whim of the mayor and/or board, which makes both

Structure of Mississippi Courts

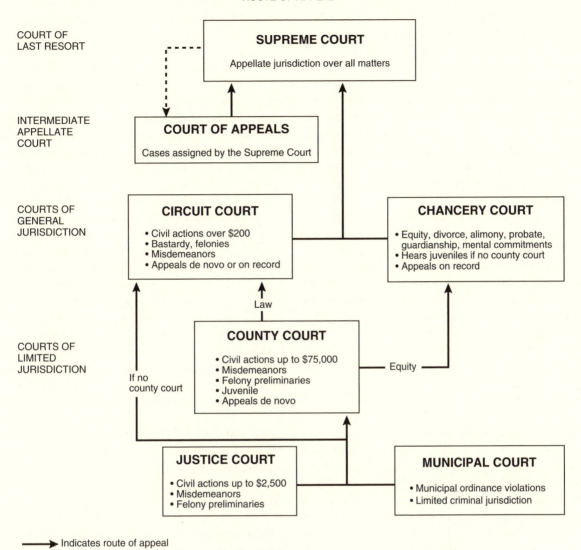

ROUTE OF APPEAL

COURT OF LAST RESORT

SUPREME COURT
Appellate jurisdiction over all matters

INTERMEDIATE APPELLATE COURT

COURT OF APPEALS
Cases assigned by the Supreme Court

COURTS OF GENERAL JURISDICTION

CIRCUIT COURT
- Civil actions over $200
- Bastardy, felonies
- Misdemeanors
- Appeals de novo or on record

CHANCERY COURT
- Equity, divorce, alimony, probate, guardianship, mental commitments
- Hears juveniles if no county court
- Appeals on record

Law

COURTS OF LIMITED JURISDICTION

COUNTY COURT
- Civil actions up to $75,000
- Misdemeanors
- Felony preliminaries
- Juvenile
- Appeals de novo

If no county court

Equity

JUSTICE COURT
- Civil actions up to $2,500
- Misdemeanors
- Felony preliminaries

MUNICIPAL COURT
- Municipal ordinance violations
- Limited criminal jurisdiction

→ Indicates route of appeal

Source: Mississippi Judiciary Directory and Court Calendar (Jackson: Mississippi Secretary of State, 2000), p. iv.

numbers volatile. Municipal judges have the authority to hear cases involving violations of city ordinances as well as other minor offenses. They have the same role as the justice court judge in performing the function of a committing official and the route for appeals is the same.

Larger counties may have a *county court,* which may have more than one judge. In 2000, nineteen counties were financially responsible for a county court and there were twenty-four judges. The judges have authority in civil actions with a value up to $75,000, misdemeanor cases, and felony (punishment of one or more years in prison) preliminaries. Under conditions of a circuit court heavy workload, both civil and criminal cases may be transferred to this court except capital punishment cases. Youth court is an adjunct of county court, so juvenile matters are under

its jurisdiction and the civil proceedings are closed to the public. If the child is under thirteen years old, no criminal prosecution is permitted. Appeals may be made to the Supreme Court. Adult defendants in county court have the right to a twelve-person jury and can appeal to the appropriate court, circuit, or chancery. De novo appeals from justice court and municipal court may be heard.

Circuit court has authority over major criminal and civil cases and is organized in districts of one to seven counties. The average number is four and the number of judges varies from one to four. In the year 2000, Mississippi had twenty-two districts with a total of forty-nine judges. The civil cases must have a value of over $200 and the court has additional jurisdiction over issues of bastardy and misdemeanors. The felony cases may have a twelve-person jury and require a unanimous decision. Jury trials in civil cases require only nine of the twelve jurors to agree. This court accepts de novo appeals of cases from justice court and municipal court and appeals of cases on the record from county court.

Chancery court's judges are named chancellors because the English king's chancellors provided justice when law could not. In 2000, there were twenty chancery districts with forty-five chancellors. These districts do not coincide with the circuit court's. Chancery court has authority over issues of equity, divorce, alimony, probate, guardianship, and mental commitments. If no county court exists in a chancery court district, juvenile cases are presented to the chancellors, who often assign them to a youth court referee.

In Glick and Vines's (1973, 12) study on state courts, Mississippi was ranked fiftieth in legal professionalism based on many factors, including its confusing court structure; for example, the court system continues a separate chancery court but lacks an intermediate appellate court. The state continued without an intermediate appellate court until one was created statutorily in 1993 to fulfill its function of aiding the reduction of backlogged Supreme Court cases. Another reform in 1995 changed the election of judges to a nonpartisan ballot for all judges, excluding justice court judges.

The *court of appeals* in Mississippi was created as a deflective court (as in Iowa) in 1993 after a study. The Supreme Court receives all notices of appeal and briefs and deflects those it deems appropriate, which is approximately 75 percent of the appellate cases. The 1999 Annual Report of the Supreme Court indicated that 57 percent of the court of appeals cases heard on the merits were civil and 43 percent were criminal. One of the ten judges is appointed as the chief judge by the Supreme Court chief justice. Cases are heard by rotating panels of three containing either the chief judge or one of the two presiding judges. An opinion is circulated to all of the judges, who then vote, with their decision being final in most cases, even though an appeal may be made by writ of certiorari to the Supreme Court.

Approximately 10 percent of the cases disposed of in 1999 were related to administrative law and were filed by the Worker's Compensation Commission, the Employment Security Commission, and the State Personnel Board, among other agencies. These three named agencies have their own administrative law judges, while the other agencies use in-house hearing officers. This is the court of last resort for workers' compensation cases. In July 1998 the court of appeals successfully began to operate under the legislatively mandated 270-day rule in regard to the time limit in which a case must be completed.

The *Supreme Court* has appellate jurisdiction over all matters. The 1999 Annual Report of the Supreme Court indicated that 73 percent of its cases on the merits were civil and 27 percent were criminal. By statute, certain cases must be retained by the Supreme Court: death penalty, utility rates, annexations, bond issues, elections contests, and trial cases that held a statute unconstitutional. Also the Supreme Court typically keeps cases involving a question of first impression, urgent issues of great public importance, substantial constitutional questions, and cases involving inconsistency or conflict in decisions between the two courts. The court has nine justices, with a chief justice and two presiding justices who are determined by seniority. Cases are heard in rotating panels of three justices, with one member being the chief justice or a presiding justice. The decision of the panel is considered to be a decision of the whole court in that if one justice dissents, the case is circulated to all of the justices. Capital murder cases must be heard by the whole court. These cases are placed at the top of the docket and can prevent other cases from being heard promptly.

A 1992 statute created the Administrative Office of the Courts (AOC) and designated the chief justice the administrative head of the Mississippi courts. The AOC consists of a director and staff to oversee the administration of the trial court system. Because Mississippi courts historically were underfunded, it also has the role of being the liaison between the legislature and courts to encourage adequate funding.

NOTABLE FEATURES OF LAW/LEGAL SYSTEM

Traditionally the office of attorney general is housed in the executive branch, but since its first constitution Mississippi provides for the attorney general in the article that establishes the judiciary.

Two notable features may cause attorneys and their clients problems. Only Mississippi, Tennessee, and Arkansas have not consolidated their chancery and circuit courts. Equity cases in the other states are heard in the general jurisdiction law court, either on specified days by all judges or by a specified judge within that court. The other important feature is that Mississippi has ten counties with more than one county seat. The effect is that lawyers must be alert to not file papers in the wrong court or courthouse and may have to drive long distances to get to the correct court.

In 1837, Mississippi was the first state to establish a woman's right to her property (Chickasaw Susan Allen) through a case, *Fisher v. Allen,* that adopted Chickasaw custom. Ironically, not until 1968 were women in Mississippi allowed to serve on juries.

STAFFING

In 1995, Mississippi was ranked forty-eighth based on its population per lawyer ratio of 531 to 1. By 2000, Mississippi had approximately 235 judgeships that required a law degree. The pool for these positions consisted of 6,978 active lawyers, of whom almost 20 percent were female and 7 percent were black. A wide range in the number of lawyers practicing in a county exists; for example, in 2000 there were 0 in Issaquena County and 2,014 in Hinds County, which includes part of the capital. Twenty-three percent of the counties in the state had fewer than ten active lawyers.

By law, active attorneys must be admitted to the bar and be members of the Mississippi Bar Association. The Magnolia Bar Association is predominately black in membership. The state is affiliated with many national legal professional associations, such as the Mississippi Women Lawyers Association. For other legal personnel, there are the Mississippi Association of Legal Assistants and the Mississippi Association of Legal Secretaries.

Mississippi has two accredited law schools, the University of Mississippi School of Law, established in 1854, and a private school, Mississippi College School of Law, located in Jackson. From 1878 to 1880 Rust College supported a private black law school. Another short-lived private law school was at Millsaps College before World War I.

Mississippi judges must be attorneys, with the exception of justice court judges. Since 1975, justice court judges have the minimum requirement of a high school degree or equivalent, but one person lacking that qualification still serves. The number of justice court judges with a law degree has remained fairly constant, at about 7 out of approximately 190 judges.

Since 1995 all of the judicial positions have been filled by nonpartisan election, with the exception of the justice court judges, who still run on a partisan ballot, and municipal judges, who are appointed by the governing authority. This change was accomplished when two-party competition began to spread from other offices to the judiciary with the first known Republican elected to the Supreme Court in 1992. Although the Supreme Court has long been under an elective selection process, there is the perception that Mississippi has an appointive system. Often justices resigned effective during their term of office so that replacements could be appointed by the governor. Since the early 1980s governors have adopted nominating committees similar to the merit plan. Under this process, the state's first woman and first black person were appointed to the Supreme Court. Vacancy appointments also produced a Supreme Court with two women serving together for the first time from April 1999 through December 2000.

The qualifications for trial and appellate court judges are the same as those for the circuit and chancery court judge—at least twenty-six years old and a qualified elector who has five years' experience as an attorney-at-law. Below the level of the court of appeals, all of the judges have four-year terms and the judges for the appellate courts serve eight-year terms. New judges have training sessions as well as continuing legal education requirements. The Mississippi Judicial College provides those training programs. The Mississippi Judicial Performance Commission was established to investigate complaints and take actions ranging from a "do-right" letter to a judge to recommendations to the Supreme Court for removal from office. Attorneys are disciplined through investigations of complaints by the Mississippi Bar Association.

Mississippi Legal Services, which consists of five agencies, has the primary goal of providing civil legal assistance to low-income and senior citizen residents. In 1999 the most frequent types of cases completed were family, consumer, and administrative in nature. There were only thirty-four legal services attorneys in the state in 2000. Therefore, Legal Services Corporation provided Mississippi a grant to create a statewide legal service information Website.

RELATIONSHIP TO NATIONAL SYSTEM

Mississippi is under the Voting Rights Act of 1965, which impacted judicial elections. In the federal case *Kirksey v. Allain* (the case became *Martin v. Mabus*) the districts for circuit, chancery, and some county courts were challenged on the basis that they had not been precleared by the U.S. Justice Department, they were not equal in population size, lines had been drawn to dilute black voting strength, and multimember districts were used that also diluted black voting strength. In 1987, only one circuit court judge was black and none of Mississippi's chancellors were black. A three-judge panel ruled that judicial elections were under the Voting Rights Act of 1965 and halted thirty-three trial judges' elections. The election was held in December 1989 after Attorney General Moore announced a settlement and declared that his office would no longer contest to the bitter end civil rights cases, which appeared to be a losing cause.

The issue of desegregation still impacts many legal aspects in the state. In 1975, Jake Ayers, Jr., and others began a lawsuit charging that there was a dual university system that was segregated. In 1987, U.S. District Court of Northern Mississippi Judge Neal Biggers, Jr. dismissed *Ayers v. Allain*. In 1992, the U.S. Supreme Court remanded this case (now *United States v. Fordice*) to Judge Biggers to remedy the presence of vestiges of segregation. Governor Musgrove initiated joint secret settlement meetings. After the legislature approved the settlement's monetary provisions, senior status Judge Biggers signed off on February 15, 2002. Commentators wonder whether the litigation is over since Mrs. Ayers may appeal this settlement and Judge Biggers hinted that if the legislature exceeds the monetary settlement a case may arise.

Diane E. Wall

See also Capital Punishment; Equity; Iowa; Lay Judiciaries; Legal Aid; Judicial Selection, Methods of; Probate/Succession Law; United States—Federal System; United States—State Systems

References and further reading

Annual Report of the Supreme Court, Executive Summary, 1999. http://www.mssc.state.ms.us/StateJudiciary (accessed November 8, 2000).

Carson, Clara N. 1999. *The Lawyer Statistical Report: The U.S. Legal Profession in 1995.* Chicago: American Bar Foundation.

Gates, Jimmie E. 2000. "New Service Offers Legal Help Online." *Jackson Clarion-Ledger* (November 27): 1B.

Glick, Henry Robert, and Kenneth N. Vines. 1973. *State Court Systems.* Englewood Cliffs, N.J.: Prentice-Hall.

Krane, Dale, and Stephen D. Shaffer. 1992. *Mississippi Government and Politics: Modernizers versus Traditionalist.* Lincoln: University of Nebraska Press. See especially Diane E. Wall, "The Antiquated Judicial System," pp. 154–175.

Landon, Michael de L. 1979. *The Honor and Dignity of the Profession: A History of the Mississippi State Bar, 1906–1976.* Jackson: University Press of Mississippi.

Mississippi Bar Association. 2000. "Membership Data and Label Rental Fees." Jackson: Mississippi Bar Association.

Mississippi Secretary of State. 2000. *Judiciary Directory and Court Calendar.* Jackson: Mississippi Secretary of State.

Skates, John Ray, Jr. 1973. *A History of the Mississippi Supreme Court, 1817–1948.* Jackson: Mississippi Bar Foundation.

Wall, Diane E. 1987. "Judicial Incumbency: The Case of Mississippi Supreme Court, 1932–1985." *Southeastern Political Review* 15: 111–135.

MISSOURI

GENERAL INFORMATION

Missouri is an important industrial and farming state in the Midwest region of the United States. The state's name comes from an Indian expression meaning "the town of the large canoes," and its nickname is "The Show-Me State." Missouri is the twenty-first largest state in the union, spanning 69,709 square miles. Its location borders two great rivers, the Mississippi and the Missouri, and has made it a center of water, land, and air transportation. The 1996 U.S. Census update reported that Missouri had 5,358,692 people and ranked sixteenth in population among the fifty states and the District of Columbia. By 2000 it became the seventeenth most populous, with 5.5 million people.

Some 88 percent of Missourians are white, and approximately 11 percent are black. The major population groups are German, Irish, English, French, and Scotch-Irish. Some two-thirds of the people in Missouri live in urban areas. Kansas City has the state's largest population (443,878), and St. Louis ranks second (368,215). These two cities rank among the nation's chief transportation, grain, and livestock centers.

Currently, most Missouri workers are employed in nonmanufacturing industries, especially the service sector, which includes government, health care, and retail trade. The state's factories turn out large numbers of automobiles, especially in the St. Louis area, and engage in manufacturing activities such as meat-packing and fertilizer production, which are related to Missouri's large farm output. Missouri ranks among the leading producers in the United States of beef cattle, corn, hogs, and soybeans.

Missouri is the home of famous Americans, including Harry S. Truman, the thirty-third president of the United States; Mark Twain, the creator of Tom Sawyer and Huckleberry Finn; Walt Disney, the famous motion picture producer; and one U.S. Supreme Court justice, Charles E. Whittaker (1957–1962).

EVOLUTION AND HISTORY

Many tribes of Indians known as mound-builders lived in the Missouri region long before Europeans and Spaniards arrived. The Indian tribes built large earthwork mounds that still may be seen in various sections of the state, but mainly what is now east-central Missouri.

Missouri was part of the Louisiana Purchase, bought from France by the United States in 1803. In 1812, Congress organized the Missouri Territory with a population greater than twenty thousand; it was settled mainly by Southerners who brought black slaves with them. Missouri's application in 1819 for admission to the Union as a slave state caused a nationwide dispute between slavery and antislavery sympathizers. This dispute was not settled until 1820, when Congress passed the Missouri Compromise. Under that legislation, Missouri entered the Union as a slave state on August 10, 1821, with a population of 66,586 people, including slaves.

In 1857 the U.S. Supreme Court issued the historic Dred Scott decision: *Dred Scott v. Sanford.* The court ruled that Scott, a Missouri slave, was deemed to be "property" and did not have rights of national citizenship. The ruling greatly increased ill feeling between the North and the South. Meanwhile, many Missourians who lived near the western border of the state feared that the newly organized Kansas Territory would become a free state. As more antislavery families settled in Kansas, scattered warfare broke out between Missourians and Kansans. This warfare began prior to and continued through the U.S. Civil War (1861–1865). Kansas became a free state in 1861.

Missouri became the center of national interest in 1861, as the nation wondered if it would remain in the Union or join the Confederacy. A state convention in February and March voted to remain in the Union. Most Missourians wanted to stay neutral, however, if war should come.

By the early 1960s, most public schools in Missouri were desegregated. The state constitution had provided for segregated schools, but in 1954 the Supreme Court of the United States ruled that compulsory segregation of public schools was unconstitutional. In recent years Missouri, like other states, has encountered financial challenges in funding education, health and welfare programs, environmental programs, and new bridges and highways. In 1986, Missouri began a state lottery to increase its revenue for public education. In 1994 voters amended the constitution to permit riverboat gambling. The socially conservative values of a Bible Belt state and the acceptance of gambling revenues continue to be hotly contested topics.

LEGAL PROFESSIONALS AND LEGAL TRAINING

Most of the attorneys who take the bar examination in Missouri are educated in one of four law schools: University of Missouri, Kansas City, School of Law; University of Missouri School of Law, Columbia; Washington University School of Law, St. Louis; or Saint Louis University School of Law. The Missouri Bar Association says that there are approximately twenty-five thousand attorneys licensed to practice in the state of Missouri. The Missouri Bar, under Rule 15, requires that attorneys complete fifteen hours of continuing education on an annual basis in order to renew their licenses.

LEGAL AID AND CRIMINAL DEFENSE SERVICES

Legal assistance is available to those individuals or groups who "are faced with economic barriers in obtaining legal representation" from Missouri Legal Services, a private nonprofit law firm. Offices are located in six main locations and satellite offices around the state. Legal Services receives funds from state public defender appropriations and private fund-raising efforts. Many of its services are provided by volunteer lawyers. It provides legal advice and representation in civil matters to individuals and families earning less than 125 percent of the federal poverty level, and for the elderly earning less than 187 percent of the poverty level. Family law, rights to government services and benefits, and landlord-tenant disputes are the main categories for legal assistance. Legal Services of Eastern Missouri has established special programs for underserved populations who meet income guidelines, such as immigrants residing in Missouri and seeking asylum in the United States (Immigration Law Project). Legal Aid Services lists its services on the World Wide Web through the Missouri Bar Association at www. mobar.org. Public defender offices provide legal services in criminal matters for individuals with the same income levels as those served by Legal Services.

THE MISSOURI JUDICIARY

General Structure

The Missouri courts system receives its judicial power from the Missouri Constitution:

Article V., Section 1. The judicial power of the state is vested in a Supreme Court, a court of appeals consisting of districts as prescribed by law, and circuit courts. Judges must retire by the age of 70.

Missouri Circuit Courts

The circuit courts were created on December 15, 1826, by an act of the Missouri General Assembly. They were so named because one judge would travel a "circuit" between courthouse locations by horseback to hear cases in the designated area.

Missouri circuit courts, the only trial courts in the state, are courts of original civil and criminal jurisdiction—that is, the courts closest to the people. The overwhelming number of cases begin in the circuit court. Within the circuit court, there are three levels of jurisdiction: circuit, associate, and municipal. Missouri's counties and the city of St. Louis are organized into forty-five judicial circuits, with each circuit consisting of one to five counties. Each circuit has at least one circuit judge; the General Assembly approves additional judges according to personnel and caseload considerations. Circuits with more than one judge are divided into separate courtrooms (or "divisions"). In a multiple-judge circuit, a presiding judge is selected from among the judges. The court, through the presiding judge, is responsible for the administration of the circuit and hires administrative personnel—such as a court reporter, juvenile officer, and circuit clerk—to conduct these administrative tasks. In 1997 the Office of State Court Administrator started a Family and Juvenile Court Division to comply with state statutory mandates as they apply to juvenile services. Cases heard in the circuit courts include criminal and civil cases, juvenile cases, family law issues, probate, and small claims.

On January 2, 1979, as a part of Missouri's Unified Judicial System, all courts of limited and general trial jurisdiction were reorganized into a single trial court under the circuit court.

Under this Unified Judicial System there are two main subdivisions: the Associate Circuit Division, which considers matters heard by magistrates prior to 1979 and can hear all cases filed before the circuit court; and the Municipal Division. The Municipal Division hears ordinance violations and must be created in cities with more than 400,000 persons. Other cities can create municipal divisions or allow the circuit court to hear these matters. Circuit court subdivisions may include a juvenile division.

Legal Structure of Missouri Courts

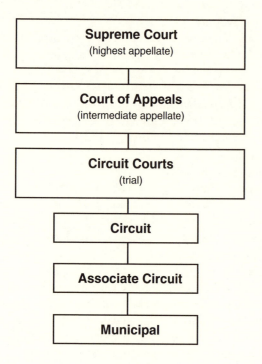

Circuit courts may add "specialized" courts and may appoint commissioners to address issues that require particular legal expertise. For example, in Jackson County (Kansas City area), the circuit court appoints a number of judicial commissioners for family court, drug court, and the Probate Division. The commissioners serve four-year terms and are required to meet the same qualifications as associate circuit judges. Appeals from the commissioners' decisions proceed to a circuit judge, and then to the Missouri Court of Appeals. Appeals of circuit and associate circuit judge decisions go directly to an appellate court—either the Missouri Court of Appeals or Missouri Supreme Court. These commissioners and specialized courts are found mainly in jurisdictions with large populations and heavy caseloads.

Once appointed, circuit judges must have their names placed on the ballot every six years, and associate circuit judges every four years, to allow the electorate to vote to retain them.

To be eligible to serve as a circuit judge, individuals must have been a citizen of the United States for ten years, a qualified voter for three years preceding selection, not less than thirty years of age, and a resident in the circuit for at least one year. Associate circuit judges must be qualified voters of the state, be at least twenty-five years old, and have such other qualifications as required by law. Both types of judges must be licensed to practice law in Missouri. Currently, 175 associate circuit judges are authorized by state statute.

Administration and Staffing of the Missouri Judiciary

The Supreme Court supervises and directs the Office of States Courts Administrator, the administrative support arm of the Missouri state court system. The OSCA's mission is "to provide exceptional administrative support to all courts as they endeavor to deliver fair, effective, and expeditious justice to the citizens of this state." The Supreme Court appoints a state courts administrator and other staff to aid in the administration of the courts throughout the state. For its own administrative matters, the Supreme Court must appoint a clerk of the Supreme Court and may appoint other staff. Each administrative appointee serves at the pleasure of the court; General Assembly rules control their salaries. The staffing practices of circuit courts have been discussed previously.

Courts in a Technological World

Courts in the state of Missouri and the Missouri Bar Association tout their capability to stay in touch with the people they serve through technology. Extensive information can be found on websites of the Missouri Judiciary, the Missouri Bar Association, and the Legal Services Offices. For example, there are information for clients, instructions from the Supreme Court to attorneys who deal in family law regarding custody agreements between parents, and links for lay persons to conduct legal research. The Missouri Judiciary website at www.osca. state.mo.us contains this message: "Welcome to the Missouri Judiciary website, source of instant access to information on state courts as they strive to deliver prompt, independent justice."

RELATIONSHIP TO NATIONAL SYSTEM

Two of the ninety-four U.S. district courts are located in Missouri, with main locations respectively in St. Louis (Eastern District) and Kansas City (Western District). Cases appealed from either of these courts are heard by the Eighth Circuit of the U.S. Court of Appeals. If further appeals are taken, the U.S. Supreme Court uses discretionary authority whether or not to hear the case. If state law or the state constitution conflicts with the U.S. Constitution, cases may go directly from state court to the U.S. Supreme Court, mainly from the Missouri Supreme Court.

Missouri has been the source of major U.S. Supreme Court decisions throughout its history. In 1857, as noted earlier, *Dred Scott v. Sanford* decided that Negro slaves were not citizens with rights to sue in national courts because of the unconstitutionality of the Missouri Compromise. Many historians credit this decision as a key starting point for the American Civil War, 1861–1865. Strong conservative Catholic sentiments have generated several key reproductive rights cases, especially *Webster v. Reproductive Health Services* (1989), which established new state restrictions on women's rights to an abortion. The Supreme Court gave partial support to the Missouri law but did not overturn the key precedent—*Roe v. Wade* (1973).

An early "right-to die" case was *Nancy Cruzan v. Director, Missouri Department of Health* (1990). Could an individual in a vegetative state have life-support devices removed, even if that decision led to the individual's death? The Supreme Court refused to follow common law doctrines for a right to die and required that Nancy Cruzan's parents establish a right to refuse medical treatment with "clear and convincing" evidence of her wishes to withdraw life-sustaining interventions. The parents re-petitioned the Missouri trial court with such evidence, and it allowed Nancy Cruzan's feeding and hydration tubes to be withdrawn. The Cruzan decision led Missouri to pass state legislation for health care surrogates; other states emphasized use of "advance directive" and "living will" laws to resolve questions of refusal of medical treatment.

Steven Puro

See also Judicial Selection, Methods of; Merit Selection ("Missouri Plan"); United States—Federal System; United States—State Systems

References and further reading
Bailey, Thomas A., and David M. Kennedy. 1994. *The American Pageant: A History of the Republic.* 10th ed. Lexington, MA: D.C. Heath.

Chen, Stephen. 1986. *Missouri in the Federal System.* 3d ed. Lanham, MD: University Press of America.

Dunne, Gerald T. 1993. *The Missouri Supreme Court: From Dred Scott to Nancy Cruzan.* Columbia: University of Missouri Press.

Hardy, Richard J., et al., eds. 1995. *Missouri Government and Politics.* Rev. ed. Columbia: University of Missouri Press.

McCandless, Carl A. 1949. *Government, Politics, and Administration in Missouri.* St. Louis, MO: Educational Publishers.

Parrish, William E. 1992. *Missouri: Heart of the Nation.* 2d ed. Arlington Heights, IL: Forum.

MISSOURI PLAN

See Merit Selection ("Missouri Plan")

MOLDOVA

COUNTRY INFORMATION

An independent republic that was part of the Soviet Union until 1991, Moldova is situated in eastern Europe. Its western border is the Prut River, and it is landlocked, bordered by Romania to the west and Ukraine in all other directions. Its gross domestic product (GDP) for 1998, including that of Transdniestria, was approximately $1.8 billion, or slightly more than $410 per capita.

Transdniestria (population 670,000—two-thirds of whom are Russians and other Slavs) is situated along the eastern border of Moldova, a narrow sliver of land between the Dniester River and the Ukrainian border. A Soviet-style state, it has proclaimed itself an independent republic. No country recognizes it, although Russia sympathizes. In 1992, over 1,000 persons were killed in a civil war. Russian troops remain in Transdniestria to guard Soviet-era weapon stockpiles and border posts.

Moldova is the most densely yet least populated of the former Soviet republics (130 persons/square kilometer, or 336 persons/square mile). Its population, approximately 4.3 million (1998), is declining. Its geographic area is 33,800 square kilometers (13,200 square miles)—slightly smaller than Taiwan and slightly larger than the Netherlands.

Moldova is divided into *uyezds* (districts), cities, and villages. Two or more villages may unite in a *comuna*, a territorial unit. Some cities are recognized as municipalities and divided into sectors. A *uyezd* is a regional territorial unit that includes villages and cities (municipalities). Gagauzia in southern Moldova has autonomous status.

Moldova's population is heterogeneous. Ethnic Moldovans comprise about two-thirds of Moldova's population, and Ukrainians and Russians each comprise about 13 percent. Gagauz, Bulgarians, Belorussians, Gypsies, and others comprise the remainder. The Gagauz are a Christian people who speak a Turkish language. They are concentrated in the southwestern part of Moldova and have attained autonomy. Orthodox Christianity is the dominant religion in Moldova. The country has a civil legal system.

HISTORY

Before the common era, Scythians occupied the land that now comprises Moldova. Thracian tribes pushed the Scythians east over the Prut and Dniester Rivers. Dacians were among the strongest Thracian tribes. Dacian king Decebalus united the Thracian tribes in the first century B.C.E. from the Tisa River in the west to the Dniester River in the north and east to the Danube River in the south. Customs, orders of kings, and other laws formed Dacian law. The Dacians yielded to Roman conquest in 105 B.C.E. and accepted Roman culture and Christianity. Gradually, Roman law replaced local law. The Romanian language, which is quite similar to the Moldovan language, is distinctly Latin in character. In the third century B.C.E., barbarian tribes (Huns and Goths) invaded, and the Romans retreated, but the Huns and Goths did not remain. Local chiefs administered justice and exercised political power.

The land now comprising Moldova was subject to several migrations and invasions into and from Europe over the next several centuries, notably by the Avars, Bulgari-

ans, and Magyars. Bogdan, a Romanian, founded the principality that came to be Moldavia. It encompassed more than present-day Moldova, including land west of the Prut River. In the early fifteenth century, the Turks invaded. Stephen the Great (Stefan cel Mare) successfully fought many battles against the Turks. In 1511 his successor, Bogdan the Blind, and Bayazid II entered a treaty by which the Porte (empire) recognized Moldavia as a free and independent country, allowed Moldavia to rule and govern itself according to its ancient laws and institutions, and agreed to protect and defend Moldavia's territorial integrity. In return, Moldavia agreed to pay monetary tributes to the Porte annually.

Moldavia's administrative scheme resembled the Byzantine imperial scheme and prevailed from the fifteenth to nineteenth centuries. A prince who received his investiture from the sultan ruled, and his authority was absolute. The prince appointed a council of twelve, the divan, which received and decided appeals of judicial matters. In the mid–seventeenth century, Moldavia adopted the Justinian Code, which princes modified to reflect local conditions and customs. In practice, the prince interpreted the code, and his will became law. Moldavians could not appeal a prince's decision. A unan-

imous decision of the divan delayed implementation of a prince's decision but did not reverse it. A Foreign Department heard cases in the first instance involving foreign subjects. A boyar (nobleman) and two judges presided in the presence of an officer of the foreign consulate to which the foreign party was attached. Local law was paramount, subject to the prince's confirmation. If the prince withheld confirmation, an appeal to the grand vizier in Constantinople or to the prince's own judgment was available. Bias against the foreign party was such that the role of the foreign consulate's officer often became that of attorney. There were other departments in the principality (police, treasury, criminal, etc.) that reported to the prince and followed his instructions.

Three classes of persons lived in Moldavia: boyars, tradesmen, and peasants. Boyars were landowners and eventually assumed the power to elect the divan. Already in 1749, Constantine Mavrocordat in Moldavia abolished slavery among the peasantry, but not among the Gypsies. Nevertheless, peasants owed tribute to the boyars; although ostensibly free, peasants had to work for the landowners. Princes owed tribute to the Porte. They could not interfere with the ecclesiastical council, and the church became a powerful force. The church metropolitan (the head of the church) served on government councils, and the clergy was exempt from taxation. Monasteries acquired considerable property through contributions and bequests.

In the eighteenth century, the Turks began placing princes of Greek origin (*phanariots*) on the Moldavian throne. Because *phanariots* had to pay a bribe for such appointments, they taxed oppressively. Corruption at all levels of government thrived and was a significant problem for the occupying Russians in the nineteenth century.

From the time of Peter the Great, Turkey and Russia fought for control of key transportation routes, such as the mouth of the Danube River, the Black Sea, and the Bosporus Straits. Because Moldavia lay between the two countries, one of them usually occupied Moldavia. Through the Treaty of Kutchuk Kainardji (1774), Turkey obtained Moldavia, but Catherine II obtained the right to protect and intervene on behalf of Christians in the Ottoman Empire, a privilege to interfere in the internal affairs of Christian nations that had been absorbed into the Ottoman Empire. Under the terms of another treaty (1788), Russia obtained the territory between the Bug and Dniester Rivers, a portion of which is now Transdniestria. In 1812 Turkey and Russia signed the Peace of Bucharest, by which Turkey ceded eastern Moldavia, that is, land between the Prut and Dniester Rivers, to Russia. Russia renamed this area Bessarabia and occupied it for 106 years.

Russia appointed a provisional governor but was too weak from its war with France to govern without substantial reliance on the local population. A Supreme Council, whose members were both elected and appointed, exercised supreme administrative and judicial powers and ruled by majority vote. The tsar and appointed governors—only one of whom was not Russian—actually governed Bessarabia. Russia's Bessarabian Statute of 1818, an effort to allow local autonomy and establish order, accomplished little. In 1828, Nicholas I initiated a change to a purely Russian system, including Russian laws, and that same year a statute established the administrative system of Besarabskaia Oblasti, which unified Bessarabia's administrative system with the Russian Empire's. The Romanian language was excluded from public life.

Under Nicholas I and succeeding tsars, Russian penal laws applied, including the Russian Criminal Codes of 1846 and 1885. With regard to civil law, existing Moldavian laws applied, but Bessarabian civil legislation was not codified and was often outdated and ineffective. An 1828 statute provided that when Bessarabian civil legislation was inadequate, Russian legislation would apply. A decree transforming Besarabskaia Oblasti into Besarabskaia Gubernia of the Russian Empire (1873) cost Bessarabia its autonomous status in the Russian Empire.

After the Russian Revolution of February 1917, the provisional government was concerned that Bessarabia might unify with Romania and impede Russia's war efforts. As Russia's war effort faltered, Bessarabia's drive for independence gained momentum. Neighboring Ukraine achieved independence. Some in Ukraine had an interest in annexing Bessarabia because many Moldavians lived in Ukraine. The Russian Revolution of October 1917 brought further chaos to Bessarabia.

On October 20, 1917, a congress of all Moldavians in Russia assembled in Chisinau and declared Bessarabia's territorial and political autonomy. The congress created the Council of the State (Sfatul Tarii) pending election of a Constituent Assembly. The Sfatul Tarii in turn appointed a Council of Directors to act as a provisional government. On December 2, 1917, Bessarabia became the Moldavian Democratic Republic.

Russia signed a separate peace with the Central Powers. Much of its army, sympathetic to the Bolsheviks, dispersed and moved to places such as Moldavia. The Sfatul Tarii requested military assistance from Romania to restore order. Moldavians, some with substantial landholdings, opposed Bolshevism. On January 24, 1918, the independence of the Moldavian Republic was declared. On March 27, 1918, the Sfatul Tarii voted that the Moldavian Democratic Republic join Romania.

Moldavia was part of Romania until June 27, 1940. Romania treated Moldavia as an outpost and invested little, assuming that any investment in Moldavia would be usurped by a foreign power.

The Soviet Union opposed Romanian incorporation of Moldavia and never recognized it. The Soviet Union established the Autonomous Moldavian Soviet Socialist Republic (AMSSR) as part of the Ukrainian SSR on October 12, 1924. The Soviet Union considered this republic to extend east of the Dniester River. The AMSSR was an instrument of Soviet political action against Romania.

During World War II, Joseph Stalin agreed with Adolf Hitler to stay out of Romania in exchange for the return of Moldavia, which Stalin received on June 27, 1940. On August 2, 1940, the Moldavian Soviet Socialist Republic (MSSR) was created. During the war, Romania, in alliance with Germany, overran Moldavia. Only in 1944, through the Soviet-Romanian Armistice Convention, was the Soviet Union's claim to Moldavia reestablished; it was later reaffirmed in the Romanian Peace Treaty of 1947.

The Soviet Union endeavored to strengthen its base of power in the MSSR and to isolate it from Romanian influence. Beginning with the decree of the Supreme Council of the Soviet Union of December 14, 1940, Soviet laws became applicable. Non-Moldavians assumed offices within the party and the state (including Leonid Brezhnev in the 1950s). They pursued communist indoctrination and integration into the Soviet economy, which included collectivization of agriculture. Russians and Ukrainians migrated in, and Moldavians migrated out. Soviet propaganda also focused on establishing the Moldavian language as separate from the Romanian language. The Cyrillic alphabet was reintroduced.

Moldova's first significant move toward independence from the Soviet Union was the Moldavian Supreme Soviet's adoption on August 31, 1989, of a language law that declared Moldovan based on Latin script to be the state language. The Moldovan Parliament did not actually declare independence until August 27, 1991. The country was renamed the Republic of Moldova.

One result of in-migration of substantial minorities has been a lack of unity concerning Moldova's future—whether as an independent country, as part of Romania, or as a member of the Commonwealth of Independent States. Russians in Transdniestria and Orthodox Christian Turks in the south (Gagauz) have resisted unification with Romania and pursued their own independence movements.

Transdniestria retains the Soviet model. It is home to much of Moldova's industry and wields economic clout in its relations with Chisinau. Gagauzia does not have such clout; it is one of Moldova's poorest regions. The Gagauz have demonstrated less resistance to initiatives of the Moldovan government. In 1991 and again in 2000, Moldova adopted citizenship laws that were not based on ethnicity to help mollify minorities who fear reunification with Romania. It now appears Moldova will continue as an independent country. In 1994, Gagauzia achieved special autonomous status within Moldova. Gagauzia may enact its own laws so long as they are consistent with legislation of the Republic of Moldova. Transdniestria does not have the same special status.

LEGAL CONCEPTS

Moldova's constitution provides that the Republic of Moldova is a sovereign, independent, unitary, and indivisible state. National sovereignty rests in the people, who exercise it directly or through representative bodies. No private person, group, political party, or political authority may exercise state power on its own behalf. The Republic of Moldova is a democratic state governed by the rule of law, where a person's dignity, rights and liberties, and free development, as well as justice and political pluralism, are supreme and guaranteed values. Democracy embodies political pluralism incompatible with dictatorship and totalitarianism. The state may not establish an official ideology.

Moldova's constitution guarantees the right to possess private property as well as intellectual property, including the pecuniary and moral interest arising in connection with intellectual creations. The state shall guarantee the right to possess property in all forms not contradicting society's interests.

Respect for and protection of the human person is the state's foremost duty. All citizens are equal before the law and authorities, notwithstanding race, nationality, ethnic origin, language, religion, sex, views, political choice, property status, or social origin. Foreign citizens and stateless persons have the same rights and duties as citizens, except as provided by law. Rights and liberties can be abridged only by law and only in cases that concern, for example, the protection of national security, public order, public health or morals, or the rights of citizens. They may also be abridged to carry out a criminal investigation or to prevent the consequences of natural calamities or technological accidents. The state is to ensure the right of an individual to know his or her rights and obligations; it must publish laws and other normative acts and ensure their availability. Public authorities must guarantee that citizens receive information regarding societal matters and issues of private concern. The right of a person to information cannot be abridged. An individual is entitled to take lawful measures to vindicate violation of his or her rights and liberties and to have effective legal remedies rendered by competent judicial authorities. An individual has the right to legal defense counsel.

Legislative, executive, and judicial powers are separate and interact. The constitution vests legislative power in Parliament, executive power in the president and government, and judicial power in judicial authorities. The constitution is the supreme law of the Republic of Moldova. Any law or normative act contradicting the constitution has no legal effect. Moldova's constitution requires it to comply with the United Nations Charter and treaties to which Moldova is a party and to establish relations with other countries on the basis of generally recognized principles and norms of international law. A law contrary to provisions of an international treaty to which the Republic of Moldova is a party must yield; a constitutional provision must be revised before yielding to provisions of an international treaty.

CURRENT STRUCTURE

Specialized Judicial Bodies
Moldova's constitution and its Law on Judicature provide for the following judicial authorities: (1) *uyezd,* sector, and municipal courts; (2) tribunals; (3) an Appellate Chamber; and (4) a Higher Judicial Chamber. By statute, economic and military courts have been created and currently function. The Law on Administrative Court provides that administrative courts are to be created, whose main task will be to exercise judicial control of public authorities. The Constitutional Court plays a distinct role in Moldova's judicial system.

Trial Courts
Trial courts operate in *uyezds,* sectors of cities, and municipalities. They examine all cases that do not fall within

Legal Structure of the Republic of Moldova Courts

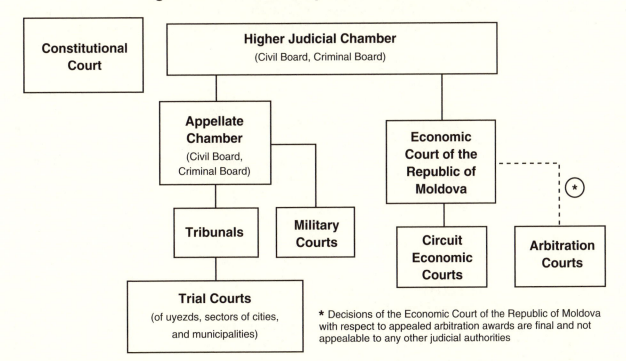

* Decisions of the Economic Court of the Republic of Moldova with respect to appealed arbitration awards are final and not appealable to any other judicial authorities

the competence of other judicial authorities. Their jurisdiction extends to cases involving people; cases involving the actions of local public authorities, enterprises, institutions, and organizations, as well as their officials whose actions violate the law, abuse power, or encroach upon citizens' rights; and various cases involving the declaration of rights or status of individuals.

Tribunals

A tribunal operates in a particular circuit embracing a certain number of courts and consists of one or several boards. Boards are formed from the tribunal's judges. Deputies of the tribunal's chairpersons preside. A tribunal examines cases involving actions of municipal public authorities, municipal enterprises, and institutions and organizations, as well as those of their public officials, committed in violation of law or abuse of power and encroaching upon citizens' rights; cases involving intellectual property (except trademark disputes, which fall within the competence of trial courts); cases involving environmental pollution; and petitions concerning the recognition and enforcement of foreign court decisions. Tribunals act as appellate courts with respect to decisions of trial courts and examine suits appealed by way of "extraordinary procedure."

Economic Courts

Economic courts are specialized courts authorized to examine economic disputes arising out of relations among legal persons or natural persons registered as entrepreneur–natural persons. Economic courts include circuit economic courts, the Economic Court of the Republic of Moldova, and the Higher Judicial Chamber when it examines economic disputes.

Military Courts

Military courts are specialized courts administering justice in the military. Military courts include military courts, the Appellate Chamber, and the Higher Judicial Chamber. Military courts hear civil suits involving damages caused by military crimes and cases involving military discipline and rank.

Appellate Chamber

The Appellate Chamber examines petitions concerning actions of central authorities and their officials committed in violation of law or as an abuse of power that encroaches on citizens' rights. The Appellate Chamber also acts as an appellate judicial authority with respect to the decisions of the tribunals and military courts and, within the limits of its competence, in cases appealed by way of "extraordinary procedure." The Appellate Chamber consists of civil and criminal boards formed from the Appellate Chamber's judges. Deputies of the Appellate Chamber's chairperson preside.

Higher Judicial Chamber

The Higher Judicial Chamber is the highest judicial authority. It consists of the chairperson, two deputies who act as chairpersons of the civil and criminal boards respectively, and twelve judges. The Higher Judicial Chamber examines cases and hears appeals within its competence from the Appellate Chamber. The Higher Judicial Chamber also examines suits appealed by way of "extraordinary procedure," including petitions filed to enforce the law and to reverse court decisions.

Constitutional Court

The constitution declares the Constitutional Court to be the sole authority of constitutional judicature. It is independent of any other public authority. The Constitutional Court consists of six judges appointed for six years. Parliament, the president, and the Higher Magistrates' Council each appoint two judges. The court passes on the constitutionality of laws and treaties, construes the constitution, states positions on initiatives to revise the constitution, confirms the results of republican referenda as well as parliamentary and presidential elections, determines the existence of circumstances justifying the dissolution of Parliament or the suspension from office of the president or the interim office of the president, passes on exceptional nonconstitutional cases submitted by the Higher Judicial Chamber, and decides matters dealing with the constitutionality of a party.

Arbitration Courts

The Law on Arbitration provides for the creation of arbitration courts authorized to examine any disputes, with the exception of those falling within the competence of other authorities. To date, only the International Arbitration Court under the Chamber of Commerce and Industry of the Republic of Moldova has been created and functions.

Key Players

Parliament

The constitution declares Parliament, a unicameral body comprised of 101 members, to be the supreme representative body of the people and the sole law-making authority. Members of Parliament are elected for four-year terms. It is divided into parliamentary groups (blocs), each comprising members of one party. The permanent bureau and other parliamentary organs comprise members from the different blocs. If necessary, special and investigative commissions can be created. Parliament may pass laws; declare the holding of referenda; construe laws and ensure the uniformity of legal regulations; approve internal and external policies; approve military doctrine; exercise parliamentary control over executive power; ratify, suspend, or abrogate treaties; approve and control the public budget; exercise control over aid to foreign countries and aid from foreign sources; elect and appoint public officials; approve orders and medals; declare the partial

or general mobilization of the armed forces; declare a state of emergency, martial law, or war; examine and initiate hearings on matters of societal interest; suspend the activity of local public authorities; and pass bills of amnesty.

The President

The constitution declares the president to be the head of state. The president serves a four-year term and is limited to two consecutive terms. The president may promulgate laws and adopt decrees, nominate the government, attend meetings of Parliament and address Parliament on issues of national concern, dissolve Parliament, negotiate and conclude treaties and submit them to Parliament for ratification, accredit and withdraw diplomatic representatives of the Republic of Moldova, act as the commander-in-chief of the armed forces and on prior approval of Parliament declare partial or general mobilization, undertake measures to repel aggression and declare a state of war, award state medals and titles of honor, award supreme military ranks, resolve matters of citizenship and political asylum, appoint public officials, grant pardons, request referenda on matters of national concern, award higher ranks to civil servants, and suspend acts of the government that contradict legislation pending a final decision of the Constitutional Court. When the office of president becomes vacant, or the president has been suspended from office or is temporarily unable to discharge his or her duties, the responsibility of the office passes to the chairperson of Parliament or the prime minister, in that order.

Government

The constitution requires the "government" to exercise general control over public administration. The government answers to Parliament. The government consists of the prime minister, the first vice prime minister, other vice prime ministers, other ministers, and others designated by law. The Law on Government authorizes the government to implement laws and presidential decrees; control ministries, departments, and other authorities; control the activity of executive local public authorities; implement economic and social programs; administer authorities for the protection and security of the country and citizens; ensure the implementation of the country's internal and external policy; and adopt resolutions and ordinances. The Law on Government entitles and, if necessary, requires members of the government to participate in the meetings of Parliament (or the work of its commissions) and to express opinions regarding matters being discussed.

Ministries, Departments, Services (Agencies) and Inspectorates, and Governmental Commissions

Ministries   The constitution gives power to ministries to implement the government's policies and ordinances.

Ministries are the central branch authorities of the republic. A minister presides over a ministry and is personally responsible for the performance of the ministry's tasks.

Departments Parliament creates departments to administer, coordinate, and control areas of national economy not within the competence of ministries. The government appoints a general director to preside over a department.

Services (Agencies) and Inspectorates The government creates services and inspectorates to control the implementation of laws and other normative acts. It appoints directors to preside over services and inspectorates.

Commissions The government may create permanent and temporary (ad hoc) commissions to study existing problems and work out appropriate solutions.

Public Prosecution Office

The Public Prosecution Office is an independent authority in the system of judicial authorities. It represents the general interests of society, defends legal order and citizens' rights and liberties, administers and conducts criminal prosecutions, and maintains criminal charges in judicial bodies in accordance with law. The system of prosecution offices includes the General Prosecution Office, regional (circuit, city or municipal, and *uyezd*) prosecution offices, and specialized (military, environmental, transport, penitentiary) prosecution offices.

Court of Audit

The constitution vests the power to control the accumulation, administration, and use of public financial resources in the Court of Audit, which also administers the use of public property. It is the supreme authority of financial control and is independent in exercising its powers. The Court of Audit consists of seven members; the chairperson and deputy preside. The Court of Audit must annually submit to Parliament a report on the administration and use of public financial resources.

Higher Magistrates' Council

The Higher Magistrates' Council is an independent authority created to establish and administer the judicial system. The constitution provides that one of the Higher Magistrates' Council's main duties is to appoint, transfer, and promote judges as well as to impose disciplinary measures on them. The Higher Magistrates' Council consists of eleven member-magistrates whose term of office is five years. The minister of justice, the chair of the Higher Judicial Chamber, the chair of the Appellate Chamber, the chair of the Economic Court, and the general prosecutor are member-magistrates of the Higher Magistrates' Council. Of the remaining six member-magistrates, three are elected by secret ballot by the united boards of the Higher Judicial Chamber,

and three are elected by the Parliament from accredited professors.

Parliamentary Advocates and Human Rights Center

The Law on Parliamentary Advocates establishes parliamentary advocates and the Human Rights Center. Parliamentary advocates assist in vindicating citizens' rights, improving human rights legislation, and familiarizing the population with law. They may file suit with a judicial authority or petition relevant public authorities to initiate disciplinary, administrative, or criminal proceedings against officials who violate human rights. Parliament appoints three parliamentary advocates to five-year terms. The Human Rights Center is composed of parliamentary advocates and their accompanying service personnel. It is an independent public institution whose main function is to assist parliamentary advocates.

Army

The military forces of the Republic of Moldova protect the state in case of armed aggression and ensure the inviolability of the country's borders and airspace. The military forces consist of regular forces and a trained military reserve. The president, Parliament, and government exercise superior administrative control of the military forces within the limits of their competence. The Defense Ministry is the central public authority exercising direct control of the military forces.

Police

The Law on Police declares the police to be an armed law enforcement public authority founded on the basis of strict compliance with law to protect the life, health, rights, and liberties of citizens and the interests of society and the state from criminal and other unlawful acts. The police are part of the Ministry of Internal Affairs. State police exercise powers throughout Moldova; municipal police exercise powers within the limits of an administrative unit.

STAFFING

Attorneys

Any citizen of the Republic of Moldova who knows the Moldovan language and has a law degree and a clean reputation may practice law as an attorney. The Ministry of Justice grants licenses to practice law, and attorneys must pass the qualification exam. Persons who have experience working as a judge, or as a lawyer for at least five years, or who have received a scientific degree in jurisprudence are exempt from the qualification exam. Those who have a law degree but who do not have legal experience and persons who have legal experience of less than three years may practice law as an attorney after one to two years of training and subsequent passage of the qualification exam.

Notary Office

The Law on Notarial Activity provides that notarial activity may be practiced by physical persons (individuals) in the name of the state. A notary may draft and execute legal documents; certify acts executed by a notary, an interested person, a lawyer, or the order of a judge or a public authority (various contracts, wills, powers of attorneys, etc.); certify inheritance procedures, certain facts, signatures, and the date of submission of documents; accept documents for safekeeping; protest bills of exchange (promissory notes); certify copies of documents, translate documents and certify the accuracy of a translation; and issue certified copies of notarial acts. Notaries may also provide legal advice on matters unrelated to the contents of drafted or executed acts. Persons who have a law degree, have one year of specialized training or two years of specialized experience, and have passed a qualifying examination may engage in notarial activity.

Prosecutors

The constitution declares that Parliament appoints the prosecutor general on the proposal of the chairperson of Parliament. The prosecutor general appoints lower prosecutors. Prosecutors serve five-year terms. Any citizen in satisfactory health who has a law degree, possesses necessary professional and relevant moral qualities, and has not been convicted may serve as a prosecutor. Regional and specialized prosecutors must be at least twenty-five years old. Persons who have graduated from higher educational institutions but who have no practical legal experience shall be trained at the prosecution office for one year. The prosecutor general may reduce the term or exempt a person from training. A prosecutor may not hold another remunerated public or private position, except for teaching or scientific research.

Judges

The constitution provides that the president appoints judges of all judicial authorities on the proposal of the Higher Magistrates' Council. Parliament appoints judges of the Higher Judicial Chamber on the proposal of the Higher Magistrates' Council. Judges of all judicial authorities (including the Constitutional Court) are magistrates and members of the magistrates corps. Any citizen of Moldova who is twenty-five years old and has a law degree can serve as a magistrate. Additionally, a judge of a military court must be a professional officer. A candidate for the office of judge must have at least two years of legal experience. Persons who have been judges for five, seven, and fifteen years may be appointed as judges of tribunals, the Appellate Chamber, and the Higher Judicial Chamber, respectively. Persons who have been judges at least five or seven years may be appointed as judges of circuit economic courts or the Economic Court of Moldova, re-spectively. Persons with less than two years of legal experience must take an examination to be admitted for training as a judge. Training occurs in court and lasts one year, at which time the trainee must pass a qualification examination. Persons who have served as judges for five years or more are exempt from the qualification exam, provided they were not discharged from the office more than five years ago. The constitution provides that judges who have passed the qualification exam receive initial five-year appointments. The second term lasts until the judge reaches age sixty-five. The constitution also provides that judges are to be independent, impartial, and irremovable.

Judges of the Constitutional Court

The constitution declares that a judge of the Constitutional Court must have at least fifteen years of legal experience. An appointee to the Constitutional Court cannot be older than sixty-five. During their terms of office, judges of the Constitutional Court are irremovable, independent, and answerable only to the constitution.

IMPACT

The Republic of Moldova was a part of the Soviet Union until 1991. Its constitution prescribes many safeguards of human rights and the rule of law, and its laws are crafted in accordance with international standards. Nevertheless, the country suffers from a legal tradition, even predating Soviet times, that did not embrace the rule of law. Corruption and poverty are serious problems that inhibit the development of the rule of law. Moreover, the status of Transdniestria remains a serious problem, both legally and politically.

William P. Kratzke
Iurie Lungu

See also Civil Law; Ottoman Empire; Romania, Soviet System

References and further reading
Fischer-Galati, Stephen. 1975. "Moldavia and the Moldavians." Pp. 415–433 in *Handbook of Major Soviet Nationalities.* Edited by Zev Katz. New York: Free Press.
Forter, Norman L., and Demeter B. Rostovsky. 1931. *The Roumanian Handbook.* London: Simpkin Marshall.
IMF Staff Country Report No. 99/110, *Republic of Moldova: Recent Economic Developments,* available at http://www. imf.org/external/country/MDA/index.htm (cited October 23, 2001).
Jewsbury, George F. 1976. *The Russian Annexation of Bessarabia 1774–1828.* New York: Columbia University Press.
King, Charles. 1994. "Moldovan Identity and the Politics of Pan-Romanianism." *Slavic Review* 53: 345.
———. 2000. *The Moldovans.* Stanford, CA: Hoover Institution Press.
Library of Congress Country Study, available at http://lcweb2. loc.gov/frd/cs/mdtoc.html (cited October 23, 2001).
Moldovan Parliament's website: http://www.parliament. md/en/ (cited October 23, 2001).
Moldova's official website: http://www.Moldova.net (cited October 23, 2001).

Popovici, Andrei. 1931. *The Political Status of Bessarabia.* Washington, DC: Ransdell.

"Poverty in Eastern Europe: The Land That Time Forgot." 2000. *The Economist* (September 23): 27–30.

Wilkinson, William. 1820. *An Account of the Principalities of Wallachia and Moldavia.* London: Strahan and Spottiswoode.

MONACO

COUNTRY INFORMATION

The Principality of Monaco lies in western Europe on the coast of the Mediterranean Sea, about 15 kilometers (9 miles) east of Nice and 8 kilometers (5 miles) west of the Italian border. Monaco's territory occupies a collection of densely clustered hills, with a headland that looks southward over the Mediterranean. It is surrounded by the French Department of the Alpes-Maritimes. The principality covers a total area of 1.95 square kilometers of land and 71.1 square kilometers of territorial sea.

As of July 2000, Monaco had a population of 31,693, consisting of French (47 percent), Monégasque (16 percent), Italian (16 percent), and other (21 percent) nationals. While French is the official language, English, Italian, and Monégasque are also spoken. Some 90 percent of the population is Roman Catholic.

As there is no agricultural land in Monaco, the Monégasque economy is mainly based on a strongly developed service sector, including banking; an industrial sector; and real estate and construction activities. Tourism is also an important source of income, providing an estimated 25 percent of total government revenue in 1991. The state has no income tax and no business taxes, and it thrives as a tax haven both for individuals who have established residence and for foreign companies that have set up businesses and offices in the country. The state retains monopolies in a number of sectors, including tobacco, the telephone network, and the postal services. Living standards are high—roughly comparable to those in prosperous French metropolitan areas. The electorate comprises only Monégasque citizens over twenty-one years of age. The death penalty was abolished in 1962.

HISTORY

Monaco's history is closely related to its position on a natural harbor, which made it strategic territory to control for both political and commercial interests. In 1191, the coast of Monaco was put under the feudal system and subordinated to the Republic of Genoa. A struggle for power had arisen between two parties in the Genoese Republic—the Guelphs and the Ghibellines. In 1295, the Ghibellines won authority over Genoa and expelled the Guelphs from the city. Among the Guelphs were members of the Grimaldi family. On January 8, 1297, François Grimaldi, disguised as a Franciscan monk, gained entry to the fortress of Monaco held by the Ghibellines. The fortress was seized, and the Grimaldi family established its authority over Monaco. Since 1297, the Principality of Monaco has been ruled by the hereditary monarchy of the Grimaldi dynasty.

Beginning in 1297, the descendants of François Grimaldi entered into various treaties with the neighboring countries of Spain and France. These involved a garrison from either nation being installed in Monaco in return for protecting the Monégasques. The most enduring of these treaties was the Treaty of Péronne, concluded by the prince of Monaco and King Louis XVIII of France in 1641. This form of protection, which allowed the prince of Monaco full internal sovereignty over his three communes—Monaco, Menton, and Roquebrune—was upheld until 1793, when, in the period following the French Revolution, the communes were attached to France. After the deposition of Napoleon in 1814, the prince of Monaco regained his rights over the principality with the same conditions that had existed under the Treaty of Péronne.

Following the second deposition of Napoleon, the Kingdom of Sardinia persuaded the Congress of Vienna that the Monégasque coast should not be left under French protection. The Congress decided that Monaco, Menton, and Roquebrune would be brought under the protection of the king of Sardinia, with conditions similar to those embodied in the Treaty of Péronne. In 1848, due to dissatisfaction with the level of taxation, the communes of Roquebrune and Menton declared themselves free cities. Each commune held plebiscites, which revealed overwhelming support for their incorporation into the French Empire.

On February 2, 1861, the prince of Monaco entered into a treaty with France, under which he abandoned his rights over Menton and Roquebrune for the sum of 4 million francs and France's protection of Monaco. The treaty further provided that the prince of Monaco would not ally his principality with any power other than France and would neither seek nor accept the protection of any power other than France. On July 19, 1918, a final treaty was signed between France and Monaco, based on France's protective friendship. This is the basis of the present Franco-Monégasque relationship.

From 1867 on, Monaco started to develop its economy and to strengthen its financial resources by opening a casino and encouraging luxury tourism. On February 8, 1869, all direct taxation was abolished. During World War I, Monaco declared its neutrality. Similarly, when World War II broke out, it declared itself neutral, but it was nonetheless bombed and occupied, first by the Italians and later by the Germans.

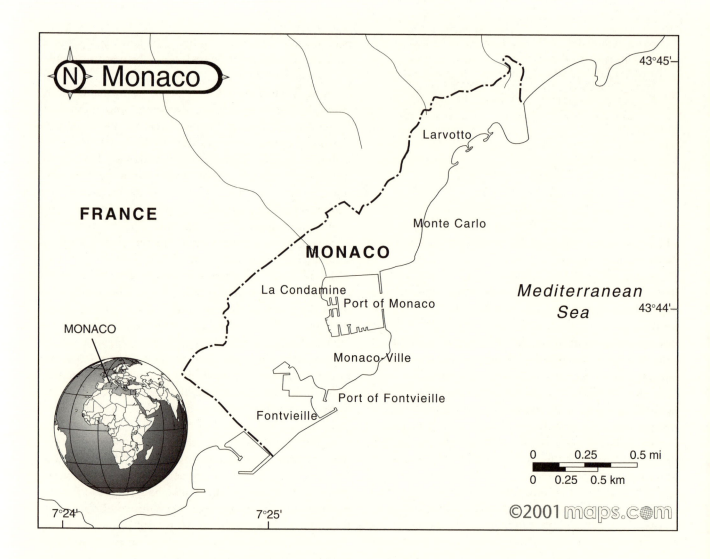

In 1962, Monaco's refusal to impose income taxes on its residents and on international businesses with established headquarters in Monaco led to a severe crisis with France. The French implemented a number of coercive measures, including refusing to register French citizens in Monaco who, after five registered years in Monaco, could have been exempt from paying French taxes; no longer granting visas to foreigners wishing to take up residence in Monaco; withdrawing its national decision not to consider Monégasque citizens foreigners in France; and banning the importation of Monégasque pharmaceutical products into France, which led to dismissals in Monaco's pharmaceutical industry. Each of these steps was taken legally and in accordance with the respective conventions between France and Monaco governing the specific subject matter.

The French applied these forms of pressure between October 1962 and April and May 1963, until a compromise was eventually reached between the prince and the French government. Under the arrangement, French citizens in Monaco were to be taxed by France at French rates, and Monaco imposed taxes on Monégasque companies conducting more than 25 percent of their business outside Monaco.

The French influence over much of Monaco's functioning is pervasive and enshrined by the Monégasque Constitution. In addition, the French laws and regulations on war materiel are automatically in force in Monaco. Similarly, Monégasque laws in relation to pharmacies, arms and munitions, and insurance are to be harmonized as far as possible with the corresponding French legislation. The strong French presence in Monaco's governance has, in the past, led to other nations' querying Monaco's statehood and its capacity as a separate legal nation. In 1924, for example, the United Kingdom opposed Monaco's application to join the League of Nations on the grounds that to admit Monaco would be to accord France another vote. By 1948, however, the Executive Board of the United Nations Educational, Scientific, and Cultural Organization (UNESCO) recommended that Monaco be admitted to UNESCO on the basis that its position as a sovereign state had not been prejudiced by the limitation of its freedom of action to which Monaco had agreed (under the treaties between France and Monaco).

In 1993, Monaco joined the United Nations. It is currently a member of numerous international organizations, including the Economic Commission for Europe, the International Atomic Energy Agency, the International Telecommunications Satellite Organization, the International Criminal Police Organization, the Organization for Security and Cooperation in Europe, the United Nations Conference on Trade and Development, UNESCO, and the World Health Organization.

LEGAL CONCEPTS

Monaco is a hereditary and constitutional monarchy, which respects the law and fundamental rights and freedoms (Article 2 of the constitution). The succession to the throne is secured by the direct and legitimate descendants of the prince regnant, with priority given to male descendants. In 1918 and 1919, for fear that German relatives of the Grimaldi family would make claims to the throne should Prince Louis II, then without heirs, die in battle during World War I, France and Monaco entered into agreements that provide for Monaco's incorporation into France should the reigning prince die without leaving a male heir. Prince Louis II, who became the ruler of Monaco in 1922, died in May 1949 and was succeeded by his grandson, Prince Rainier III, the current prince regnant.

The first constitution of the Principality of Monaco was promulgated in 1911. Under the Monégasque Constitution, Monaco observes the separation of executive, legislative, and judicial powers (Article 6). Executive power is exercised under the authority of the prince by the four-member Council of Government (Articles 3, 43, and 44). The prince represents the principality in its relations with foreign powers and signs and ratifies treaties.

A new constitution, introduced in December 1962, abolished the formerly held principle of the divine right of the ruler and stipulated that the National Council, which had previously been selected by a panel, be elected by universal adult suffrage.

CURRENT STRUCTURE

The Executive

The executive consists of the prince and the government. The government itself consists of the minister of state, who must be French, and three government councillors (Article 43). Each of the members of government is appointed by the prince.

The Minister of State

The minister of state must be a French national. He or she carries a preponderant vote in the Government Council. Since the 1961–1962 dispute between France and Monaco over fiscal matters, the minister of state's countersignature has been required on sovereign orders.

Government Councillors

There are three specific positions within the Government Council in addition to the minister of state. The first is councillor for the interior, a position that must be held by a French national; the second is councillor for finance and economy; the third is councillor for public works and social affairs (the latter two being positions held by Monégasque nationals). Each of the government councillors is appointed by the prince and can be dismissed by the prince. The government is therefore not responsible to the Monégasque Parliament (Article 50).

In the executive sphere, there are also a number of subject-specific commissions and councils whose role is to assist the government and be available for consultation on matters related to their specific areas of expertise. One example is the Crown Council, which, under Article 77 of the constitution, is to be consulted on the conclusion of international treaties, on the dissolution of the National Council, on the naturalization or reintegration of former nationals, and in relation to the granting of pardons and amnesty. The Crown Council, whose opinion is not binding on the government, consists of seven Monégasque nationals who are each appointed by the prince for three years. Three of its members are proposed by the National Council.

Another important council in the executive hierarchy is the State Council. It consists of twelve members, appointed by the prince after consultation with the minister of state and the director of judicial services. The State Council receives draft laws, decrees, and orders from the prince and minister for state for study (Article 52).

The executive has the power to produce sovereign orders and ministerial orders. Sovereign orders are deliberated in the Government Council before being countersigned by the minister of state and presented to the prince for approval. Ministerial orders need not have been deliberated by the Government Council. They are signed by the minister of state and promulgated in the absence of any objection from the prince within ten days of his receiving them.

Under this model, a French national, in the role of the minister of state, has significant power of veto and involvement in the executive arm of Monégasque governance. This influence over the exercise of executive power in Monégasque society is tempered somewhat by a restriction on the minister of state's role in the legislative process.

Legislative

The Monégasque legislature consists of two bodies—the prince and the National Council. The National Council is composed of eighteen members who are elected by universal and direct suffrage for a period of fifteen years (Article 53 of the constitution). To be eligible for election, a person must be a Monégasque citizen over the age of twenty-five. A person cannot be a member of both the National Council and the Government Council. Under Article 74, the prince can dissolve the National Council after consultation with the Crown Council. On such a dissolution, new elections will be called.

The National Council has the right to approve a budget and to give approval for laws to be promulgated, but it has no right to initiate new laws. That exclusive right lies with the prince (Article 66). Article 66 further provides, however, that new laws must be adopted by both the prince and the National Council, which provides a check on the prince's power. Additionally, draft proposals of new laws can be submitted to the prince for his formal initiation.

Thus, the legislative process commences with the prince, who initiates the law. The laws are deliberated in Government Council until they receive the minister of state's signature. The proposed law is then submitted to the National Council, which has a right of amendment. The National Council can vote for or against the law. If it is approved by a majority, the law will be promulgated by the prince.

It can thus be seen that although the minister of state can bar the submission of a draft law to the National Council, once a proposed law has been submitted to that body the law can be amended and promulgated without having to be reapproved by the minister of state. In this way, the French influence on Monégasque law is limited to a degree.

Constitutional Stability
Articles 94 and 95 of the constitution deal with proposed constitutional amendments. Under Article 94, the constitution can be amended by mutual agreement between the prince and the National Council. Article 95 allows the National Council, with the approval of two-thirds of its members, to propose a partial or total constitutional amendment. Such a proposal may, however, be disregarded by the prince or the government. Otherwise, any proposed amendments to the constitution follow the same legislative deliberation and procedure as other laws. Again, this provides the French with some influence over how Monaco is governed.

SPECIALIZED JUDICIAL BODIES
Monaco's Civil Code dates from December 21, 1880, and while not identical to the French Civil Code, it is similar to it. The principality has an elaborate judicial system, with several specialized commissions and tribunals. Judicial power is held by the prince, who, under

Articles 5 and 88 of the constitution, is deemed to have delegated it to the courts and tribunals, which administer justice in his name. The organization of the legal system is similar to that of France. The curial hierarchy splits into three categories at the level of first instance: civil, penal, and administrative.

There is one Justice of the Peace, the civil Court of First Instance, criminal courts of first instance, a Court of Appeal, and the Supreme Tribunal. In addition, there are specialized tribunals for specific subject matters.

Under Article 6, Paragraph 1, of the Franco-Monégasque Convention of July 28, 1930, the majority of judges in the Monégasque courts and tribunals must be French nationals seconded from the French judicial administration. An exception to this is made for the Criminal Tribunal. Under the convention, the French judges cannot have a permanent appointment in the Monégasque judiciary. The independence of the judges is guaranteed by the constitution (Article 88).

Civil and Commercial Law
At the base level of the hierarchy sit three specialized tribunals of first instance: the Labour Tribunal, the Arbitration Commission on Rents, and the Arbitration Commission on Commercial Rents. If a matter does not fall within the specialized jurisdiction of these tribunals, a civil dispute can be taken before the Tribunal of First Instance and from the tribunal to the Court of Appeal (Articles 21[1] and 22 of the Code of Civil Procedure). Subject to monetary limits of jurisdiction, certain disputes concerning civil and commercial law can be brought before the Justice of the Peace. Before giving judgment, the Justice of the Peace will attempt to reconcile the parties.

Criminal Law
The present Criminal Code dates from September 28, 1967. As with the Civil Code, the Criminal Code is not entirely identical to the French Penal Code. In criminal procedures, there are three different tribunals of first instance: the Justice of Peace, the Correctional Tribunal, and the Criminal Tribunal. The Criminal Tribunal is composed of three French magistrates and three lay Monégasques (Article 25 of the Code of Criminal Procedure). While an appeal against sentences handed down at first instance by the Correctional Tribunal can be lodged before the Court of Appeal, no further appeal lies against the verdict of the Criminal Tribunal (Article 24).

Appeal Courts
Sitting above both the criminal Correctional Tribunal and the civil tribunal of first instance is the Court of Appeal. Above the Court of Appeal lies the Court of Judicial Revision, which can reverse any judgment of last instance that violates the law (Article 23 of the Code of

Legal Structure of Monaco Courts

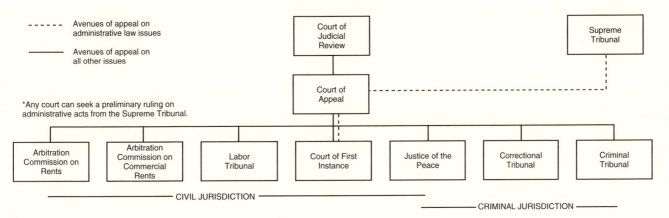

Civil Procedure and Article 30 of the Code of Criminal Procedure).

Administrative Law

A separate hierarchy of courts relates to administrative proceedings. Any decision or sovereign order emanating from any administrative authority taken with the view to implementing legislation can be the subject of an action brought before the Supreme Tribunal. The Supreme Tribunal is composed of five judges and two substitutes who are appointed by the prince and proposed by the National Council, the State Council, the Crown Council, the Court of Appeal, and the Tribunal of First Instance (Article 89 of the Constitution). The judges are appointed for four years and have to be confirmed in office if they are presented for a second time after this period. No further appeal lies against a judgment from the Supreme Tribunal.

Any court or tribunal can ask the Supreme Tribunal for a preliminary ruling on the validity of an administrative decision or sovereign order. Similarly, if the action or failure to act of an administrative authority does not fall within the direct competence of the Supreme Tribunal, a legal action can be brought before the Tribunal of First Instance. From there lies the possibility of appeal to the Court of Appeal with the Supreme Tribunal as a final court of cassation (Article 90[B][ii]).

The Supreme Tribunal has further competences, including the constitutionality of the rules of procedure of the National Council and of legislated law (Article 90[A]). Under Article 90(A)(ii), however, a law can only be annulled by the Supreme Tribunal if it violates the fundamental rights and freedoms embodied in the constitution. Any person whose fundamental rights and freedoms are violated by a law can bring an appeal for annulment of that law before the Supreme Tribunal. Similarly, if the infringement of a constitutional human right by a Monégasque law has been invoked by a party

to a matter being heard by any other court of tribunal, the Supreme Tribunal's jurisdiction to hear such matters must be invoked.

STAFFING

As discussed earlier, the judiciary consists of French judges seconded to the Monégasque system. The decision handed down by the European Commission of Human Rights on June 28, 1993, in the case of *JM v. France* is authority for the proposition that the judges are acting in a Monégasque capacity and not as functionaries of France. This independence is also guaranteed by the constitution.

There are no schools of law in Monaco, and accordingly, the Monégasque legal tyro must head abroad to study. There are a number of recognized law faculties in France and other French-speaking states and provinces (such as Belgium and Quebec). With their (usually French) foreign training and due to the fact that many of the practitioners within Monaco's legal system are "borrowed" from its Gallic neighbor, the Monégasque legal profession is nearly indistinguishable from the French, save for the slightly different hierarchy and the contents of its Civil and Penal Codes, as described earlier.

IMPACT

For the people of Monaco and for the nation as a whole, surely none of the country's laws have had more impact than the tax laws. The minimal tax burden imposed on citizens and long-term residents has lured the wealthy to Monaco, which gives it an image as a glamorous haven and playground for the rich and famous and ensures its prosperity.

Also extremely influential are the series of treaties and conventions between France and Monaco. Indeed, Monaco's close alliance with its neighbor has raised questions about its status as an independent nation. Perhaps the prevailing atmosphere within the European Union for microcommunities to assert their rights to self-determination will encourage Monaco to loosen its ties with France. That may prove extremely difficult, however, given the degree to which France is enmeshed in Monaco's governing infrastructure at all levels.

Fiona Murray

See also Civil Law; France; International Law; Magistrates—Civil Law Systems

References and further reading

Blaustein, Albert P., and Gisbert H. Flanz, eds. 1971. *Constitutions of the Countries of the World: Monaco.* Dobbs Ferry, NY: Oceana Publications.

Central Intelligence Agency, "World Fact Book 2000: Country Listing—Monaco," http://www.odci.gov/cia/publications/factbook/ (cited May 18, 2001).

Duursma, Jorri. 1996. *Fragmentation and the International Relations of Micro-States: Self-Determination and Statehood.* Cambridge: Cambridge University Press.

Gale Force, "Monaco On Line," http://www.monaco.mc/ (cited May 18, 2001).

Robert, Jean-Baptiste. 1973. *Histoire de Monaco.* Paris: Presses universitaires de France.

MONGOLIA

COUNTRY INFORMATION

Mongolia is a landlocked country in Central Asia bordered by the Russian Federation to the north and the People's Republic of China to the south, east, and west. Mongolia is almost three times the size of France and over twice the size of Texas, and it is the nineteenth largest country in the world. The size of the territory is 1.6 million square kilometers (604,800 square miles). It is mostly plateau, broken by mountains in the northwest. The Gobi Desert, located in the southern region, features mountain ranges across 3,000 square miles.

High altitude, about 1,600 meters above sea level, exacerbates the semiarid continental climate. Six months of the year are below freezing (October–March). January temperatures average about –25°C, but a low of –40°C is often recorded. Some of the highest barometric pressures in the world have been recorded in Mongolia. It has the coldest capital in the world, with severe weather conditions that result in a higher percentage of budget expenditures being allocated to heating. Twelve percent of the health budget and 20 percent of the education budget is spent on heating.

Mongolia has one of the lowest population densities in the world: 2.4 million people, according to the census held in January 2000, living in an area of 1.6 million square kilometers. About 70 percent of the population is under thirty-five years old. In 1925 the population was 684,000. Since 1994 Mongolia has been divided into twenty-one provinces (*aimags*) and one municipality (capital city Ulan Bator), with appointed governors and elected local assemblies. The resident population of Ulan Bator is 632,900, with 91,400 in Darkhan, and 68,000 in Erdenet. The principal language is Mongolian. There is no state religion, but Buddhist Lamaism is being encouraged for worship.

In 1989 Mongolia joined the Group of 77. In February 1991 it became a member of the Asian Development Bank, as well as the IMF and the World Bank. In 1994, the European Union announced the inclusion of Mongolia in TACIS, the EU's program of technical assistance to the Commonwealth of Independent States. In 1997, Mongolia became a member of the World Trade Organization. In 1998 it became a member of ASEAN Forum.

Mongolia's economy was disrupted in 1990–1991 by the collapse of command economies in the USSR and eastern European countries, and by the first steps toward privatization and a market economy in Mongolia itself. However, during 1993 Mongolia's economy stabilized: prices were liberalized, there was a reduction in inflation, levels of current expenditure were reduced, and a new exchange rate mechanism was implemented. The first indications of economic growth were recorded in 1994. The Democratic Alliance coalition government, elected in June 1996, initiated a wide-ranging program of economic reforms. At the end of that year the government announced a four-year economic program including restructuring of the banking system, thereby averting the risk collapse in the sector and reforms of the taxation system. In August 1997, it was reported that all government-owned commercial assets and public enterprises were to be privatized, except those considered essential for the country's economic security. A significant reduction in the rate of inflation, growth in gross domestic product (GDP), and an increase in reserves of foreign exchange were the main economic achievements recorded in recent years. GDP per head is $394 (1997) in comparison with Kazakhstan at $1,361; China at $733; Malaysia at $4,517; Russia at $3,053; and Thailand at $2,539.

The economy of the country is shaped by the dominance of the agricultural sector and a dependency on the production of minerals. Agriculture (including forestry) contributes an estimated 31.0 percent of GDP. Animal herding is the main economic activity and is practiced throughout the country. Livestock numbers (sheep, goats, horses, cows, and camels) reached a new record of 33 million at the end of 1998. Mongolia has significant, largely unexplored mineral resources and is a leading producer and exporter of copper, molybdenum, and fluorspar concentrates. It is the second largest exporter of cashmere in the world. Main commodities for export are copper, gold, and cashmere.

Mongolia is dependent on the importation of 100 percent of its petroleum products. Mongolia imports electricity and petroleum products from the Russian Federa-

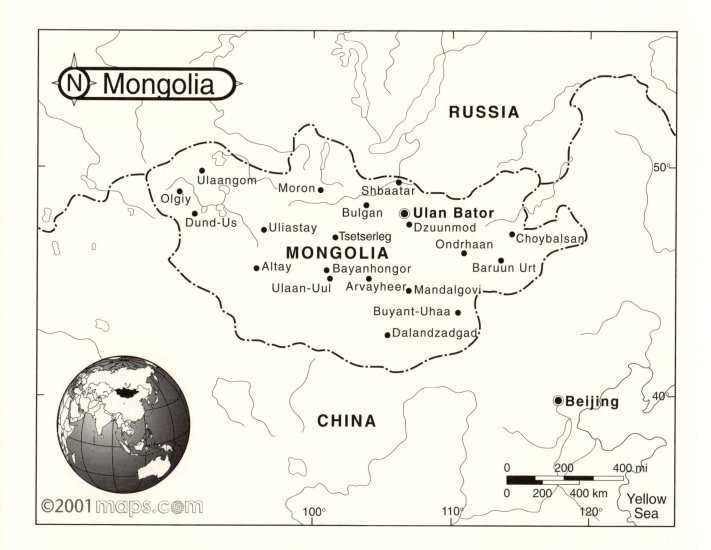

tion. However, the discovery of petroleum reserves in late 1994 raised the possibility that Mongolia might become increasingly self-sufficient in energy requirements.

The social welfare system is comprised of the social security scheme, which is noncontributory and provides a basic level of benefits, and the social insurance scheme, to which those in formal employment contribute. Unemployed persons are entitled to receive benefits, provided that they have contributed to the scheme for at least two years. Of total current expenditure by all levels of government, 11.8 percent goes for health and 16.0 percent for social security.

Ten-year general education is compulsory, beginning at six years of age. Students may attend vocational technical schools from sixteen to eighteen years of age. Current expenditure on education by all levels of government averages 17.5 percent. The adult literacy rate is about 90 percent. The gender map of Mongolia is unique. About 70 percent of all lawyers and 65 percent of all judges are women. Ninety percent of medical students and the majority of the student bodies in other universities are women.

HISTORY

From the twelfth century, unified Mongolia, under the famous ruler Genghis Khan, had been subject to customary law. The Mongol empire was one of the biggest in the world with a sophisticated system of administration, taxation, and laws. The heritage of statehood and law of Mongolia are treasured in the codified written laws of the Great Zasag (Great Governance of Genghis Khan), Halh Djouram, and many other laws.

After the disintegration of the empire, Mongolia broke into a number of separate, often-warring tribes (khanates). In the late seventeenth century, Mongolia came under the control of the Manchu Dynasty of China. But in 1911, Mongolia declared its independence. With support from czarist Russia, Mongolia gained autonomy as a feudal Buddhist monarchy, but Russia accepted Chinese suzerainty over the country in 1915.

In 1920, Mongolian nationalists led by D. Sukhbaatar appealed to the new Soviet regime for assistance, and in March 1921 they met on Soviet territory to found the Mongolian People's Revolutionary Party (MPRP) and established a Provisional People's Government. In November

1924, after the death of Bogdo Khan, the Mongolian People's Republic (MPR) was proclaimed. Thus, Mongolia became the world's second communist state. This marked the beginning of the period of Soviet domination. The MRP became increasingly dependent on the USSR for support. The government conducted campaigns to collectivize the economy and to destroy the power of the nobility and Buddhist priests.

In 1989, following the collapse of the communist regime in Eastern Europe, the Mongolian Democratic Union was established. The reformers won and the entire MPRP Central Committee stepped down. Mongolia, along with other postcommunist countries, embarked on a radical and comprehensive reform in all spheres of the nation's political, legal, economic, and social life.

The constitution was adopted by the People's Great Hural (Parliament) on January 13, 1992, and came into force on February 12 of that year. It proclaims Mongolia to be an independent sovereign republic, which ensures for its people democracy, justice, freedom, equality, and national unity. It recognizes all forms of ownership of property, including land, and affirms that a "multistructural economy" will take account of "universal trends of world economic development and national conditions."

Supreme legislative power is vested in the unicameral seventy-six-member State Great Hural, elected by universal, free, direct suffrage by secret ballot for four years, with a chairman and vice chairman elected from among the members. The State Great Hural recognizes the president on his election and appoints the prime minister and members of the cabinet. Decisions of the State Great Hural are taken by a simple majority. A presidential veto of a decision of the State Great Hural can be overruled by a two-thirds majority of the State Great Hural.

The president, who is directly elected for a term of four years, is the head of state and commander in chief of the armed forces. Presidential candidates are nominated by parties with seats in the State Great Hural.

The government cabinet is the highest executive body and organizes and ensures the nationwide implementation of the constitution and other laws. It works out guidelines for economic and social development as well as elaborates and implements comprehensive measures on sectoral development.

The Supreme Court, headed by the chief justice, is the highest judicial organ. The overall judicial system consists of the Supreme Court, Aimag and Capital City Courts, Soum, Inter-soum, and district courts. According to the constitution, specialized courts such as criminal, civil, and administrative may be formed. Judicial independence is protected by the General Council of Courts. The prosecutor general, nominated by the president, serves a six-year term.

LEGAL CONCEPTS

Traditional Law before the 1920s

Mongolia's history spans more than 2,000 years of emerging statehood and legal development. It was in the twelfth century B.C.E. that the first unified Mongolian state was created by Genghis Khan. Genghis Khan promulgated the Great Zasag (also known as Yasa), or Great Governance, the customary law governing the Mongolian nation at this time. The Great Zasag law has been documented extensively by the Persian historian Rashid Ad-Din. The main features of the law are as follows:

- The law confirmed the basis of the Mongol kingdom as an Empire and that the *zarlig* (ordinance) of the Great Khan Genghis was an indisputable norm—law. "If my ordinances will be followed verbally and not followed by the actions, openly or in a conceived way, this will turn out to be a stone thrown into the water, or an arrow in the grass";
- The law confirmed the highest power to the khan and to the Great Huruldai (Assembly), which consisted of the representatives of the military chief commanders of the khan;
- The law approved the administrative division of the state into the western, eastern, central, and southern parts and structured the nomadic people into groups of ten thousand, one thousand, one hundred, and ten;
- The military structure of the empire was the same as an administrative structure, and unified military duty for all men between fifteen and sixty years of age was introduced;
- The criminal system and definition of main crimes were covered extensively;
- The principles of a taxation system were introduced with punitive measures for nonpayment of taxes;
- Principles of international relations, including the principles of peaceful relations with other kingdoms and states, respect for representatives of other states, special privileges of Mongol ambassadors and declaration of wars only by the decision of Great Huruldai, were stated in the law;
- Family law and the principles of law of wills were covered;
- The norms governing religion and state confirmed respect for all religions and the separation of church from the state; and
- The importance of "five cattle"—horses, cows, sheep, goats, and camels—in the lives of nomadic Mongols and the protection of pastureland were confirmed by the law.

Between the fall of the Great Empire of the Mongols and 1911, a number of laws played an important role in the evolution of the legal norms and principles established in the fourteenth century during the reign of Kublai Khan, the grandson of Genghis Khan, ruling the Yuan dynasty. They were the Nevterhii Huul (Clear Law), which confirmed the supremacy of Mongols over the Chinese and other nations, as well as Halh Djouram and a number of others, which are representative of the feudal period of Mongolian legal history.

After the disintegration of the empire in the eighteenth century, the Manchu dynasty ruled over China and Mongolia, placing the first foreign-ruled statehood that lasted for two hundred years. While Mongols always considered themselves distinct from agriculturalists to the south, during these two centuries Mongolia became legally and administratively part of China. The Manchu dynasty fell in the Chinese revolution of 1911. By 1921 Mongolia was a theocratic monarchy with Buddhism as the dominant religion, and Bogdo Khan was the religious and secular leader.

Socialist Law 1924–1990

In 1921, Mongolia declared its independence under Mongolian revolutionaries, the Mongolian People's Party (MPP). In 1924, after the death of Bogdo Khan, Mongolia became the Mongolian People's Republic and MPP changed its name to Mongolian People's Revolutionary Party (MPRP). From these times Mongolia became increasingly closely connected with the Soviet Union. What followed was a period of sixty-five years of legal enactments to establish Mongolia as a socialist society in law and economy. The legal system of this period was defined as Soviet.

According to William E. Butler the extent to which early Mongolian leadership was influenced by Soviet Marxist-Leninist ideology is still debated, but all sides agree that the Soviet Union played a decisive role in bringing the revolution to fruition in Mongolia and in shaping Mongolian legal institutions. Soviet influence on the legal system was nearly total. Legal change in Mongolia closely followed parallel developments in the Soviet Union. The 1940 Mongolian Constitution was closely modeled on the 1936 Soviet one, and revisions in 1944, 1949, 1953, and 1959 reduced the differences even further. The socialist legal system was derived out of the Russian system, which had preceded it, and was based generally on the Roman-German (civil or continental) legal system. Socialist legality saw law as a means to an end, namely the building of a communist society. There was no inherent virtue in the law, apart from its role in building socialism.

Transition to Democracy and Building a New Legal System

In the period after the democratic revolution and before the adoption of the new constitution in 1992, the first standing legislature, State Baga (Small) Hural (Parliament), was established through the amendment to the former 1960 Constitution of the People's Republic of Mongolia. This event signaled the start of the legal reform process. Within a period of eighteen months the State Baga Hural adopted fourteen new laws and made amendments to thirty-six laws in force. Those were the important laws such as the Business Entities and the Privatization Law that laid the fundamental principles of democracy and the market economy.

In 1990, a twenty-member Constitutional Drafting Commission was created. The commission began examining the constitutions of more than one hundred different nations. Four separate drafts of a new constitution were circulated among the Constitutional Drafting Commission. The final draft was circulated to a number of international constitutional experts for comments. The new constitution was adopted on January 13, 1992, by the second annual session of the national assembly, The People's Great Hural. The Constitution of 1992 is Mongolia's supreme law of the land, which can be amended only by a three-quarters majority of the Parliament members. In addition to laying down Mongolia's new constitutional framework, the constitution enshrines a number of basic human rights and fundamental freedoms, reflecting the influence of both the American Bill of Rights and European constitutions.

After the adoption of the Constitution of 1992, systematic measures were taken to implement its provisions. Since 1992 Mongolia has passed the fundamental stage of legal reforms and entered what may be defined as the period of major change. Firstly, Mongolia passed all the laws established by the constitution. According to the constitution, thirty-four different areas of the law needed regulation, all of which were covered during this six-year period. These were fundamental laws defining the structure and powers of the three branches of government, such as the law on the president, parliament, judiciary, government, prosecutor's office, police, and so on. The law on the administrative and territorial units and their governance was adopted to determine the legal status of territorial units and served as a basis for restructuring legal institutions.

At present, more than 500 laws regulating important branches of economic and social life have been adopted. Major laws regulating the economy were a revised civil code, taxation law, foreign investment law, companies law, cooperatives law, securities law, law on international commercial arbitration, law on state (central) and municipal property, foreign exchange law, and so on.

As a result of the adoption of the new democratic con-

Structure of Mongolian Courts

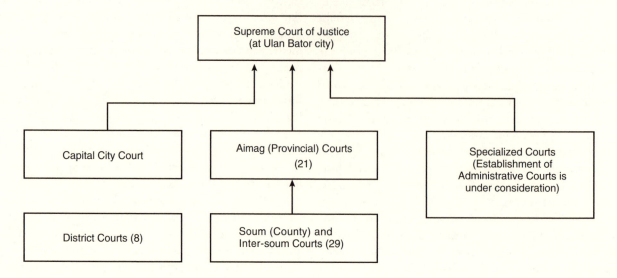

stitution in 1992 and a comprehensive set of legislative reforms in the following years, it can be said that Mongolia has embarked on developing a totally new legal system. This newly built system has the main characterisitcs of the Roman-German (continental or civil) law traditions, but has a strong influnce of the Anglo-American (common) law elements as consequence of the world globalization trends, particularly with regard to business and commercial laws.

CURRENT STRUCTURE

The new, democratic Constitution of Mongolia formalized the distribution of powers between the judicial, executive, and legislative branches of the state, enshrining the Mongolian judiciary's independent status. The basic judicial system of Mongolia consists of three levels of courts:

- at the apex or cassational level is the Supreme Court of Mongolia;
- at the appeal level there are the Aimag (provincial) courts and the Capital City Court; and
- at the first instance level there are the Soum (county), Inter-soum courts, and district courts.

According to Article 5 of the Judiciary Act of Mongolia, the State Great Hural of Mongolia is invested with the power to establish, modify, and dissolve courts on the basis of a proposal by the General Council of Courts, which is a body responsible for ensuring the independence of the judiciary, made upon consultation with the Aimag and Capital City governors in respect to the Aimag, Capital City, Soum, Inter-soum, and district courts, and with the Supreme Court in respect to the specialized courts. The size of the jurisdiction area, the loca-

tion and population density, and the case rates are to be taken into consideration when establishing a new court.

The ordinary courts in Mongolia are as follows.

The Supreme Court

The Supreme Court is the highest judicial organ in the country. It consists of the chief justice and sixteen justices. The president of Mongolia appoints justices of the Supreme Court upon their presentation by the General Council of Courts to the State Great Hural. By the nomination from the Supreme Court the president again appoints a chief justice from among the members of the Supreme Court for a term of six years. The Supreme Court is divided into civil cases chamber and criminal cases chamber. The presiding justices of the two respective chambers are appointed by the president upon the proposal of the chief justice for a term of six years. The jurisdiction of the Supreme Court includes the power to:

- examine and consider cases or disputes decided by Aimag, Capital City, Soum, Inter-soum, and district courts through cassational proceedings;
- examine and consider cases or disputes decided by Aimag and Capital City courts through appeal;
- examine and hear cases or disputes in the first instance within its jurisdiction;
- examine and consider decisions of courts concerning capital punishment through cassational proceedings;
- issue official interpretations on the application of laws except for the constitution and other powers provided by law.

Judicial Research Center

There is a Judicial Research Center, attached to the

Structure of Mongolian Courts—Civil Cases

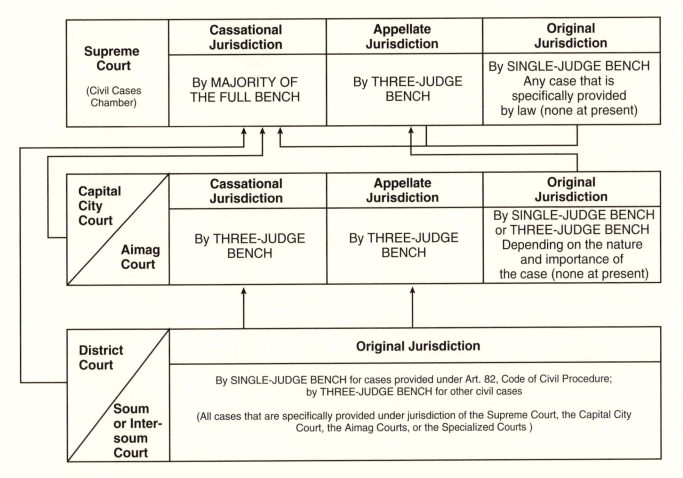

Supreme Court (Civil Cases Chamber)	Cassational Jurisdiction	Appellate Jurisdiction	Original Jurisdiction
	By MAJORITY OF THE FULL BENCH	By THREE-JUDGE BENCH	By SINGLE-JUDGE BENCH Any case that is specifically provided by law (none at present)

Capital City Court / Aimag Court	Cassational Jurisdiction	Appellate Jurisdiction	Original Jurisdiction
	By THREE-JUDGE BENCH	By THREE-JUDGE BENCH	By SINGLE-JUDGE BENCH or THREE-JUDGE BENCH Depending on the nature and importance of the case (none at present)

District Court / Soum or Inter-soum Court	Original Jurisdiction
	By SINGLE-JUDGE BENCH for cases provided under Art. 82, Code of Civil Procedure; by THREE-JUDGE BENCH for other civil cases (All cases that are specifically provided under jurisdiction of the Supreme Court, the Capital City Court, the Aimag Courts, or the Specialized Courts)

Notes: 1. Where a COURT in deciding cases finds that the law to be applied is not in conformity with the constitution, then court proceedings shall be suspended and it shall refer its opinion to the SUPREME COURT, and if the latter considers that the opinion has grounds, then it submits a matter to the CONSTITUTIONAL COURT.
2. The SUPREME COURT shall examine and make decisions related to the protection of law, human rights, and freedoms provided under it, which are transferred to it by the CONSTITUTIONAL COURT and by the prosecutor general.

Supreme Court, which renders advice on the theoretical legal issues arising in the application and interpretation of laws by the Supreme Court and which provides information to it by submitting proposals on judicial statistics and legal practice.

Aimag (Provincial) Courts and the Capital City Court

Aimag (provincial) courts and the Capital City Court are composed of a chief judge and fellow judges, who are appointed by the president on the proposal of the General Council of Courts. The chief judge is appointed for a term of six years. There are twenty-one Aimag courts and a single Capital City court with a staff of 107 judges. The jurisdiction of these courts includes the power to:

• examine and consider cases or disputes decided by the Soum, Inter-soum, and district courts through appeal or supervision

• examine and hear cases or disputes in the first instance within its jurisdiction
• other powers provided by law

Soum (County), Inter-soum, and District Courts

Soum (county), Inter-soum, and district courts are courts of first instance and are composed of the chief judge and judges, who are appointed by the president on the proposal of the General Council of Courts for a term of six years. There are twenty-nine Soum and Inter-soum courts and eight district courts, with a total of more than 200 judges. The jurisdiction of these courts is to examine and hear cases or disputes in the first instance. These courts shall not examine and hear cases or disputes that are within the jurisdiction of the Supreme Court, the Aimag courts, the Capital City Court, and specialized courts.

Structure of Mongolian Courts—Criminal Cases

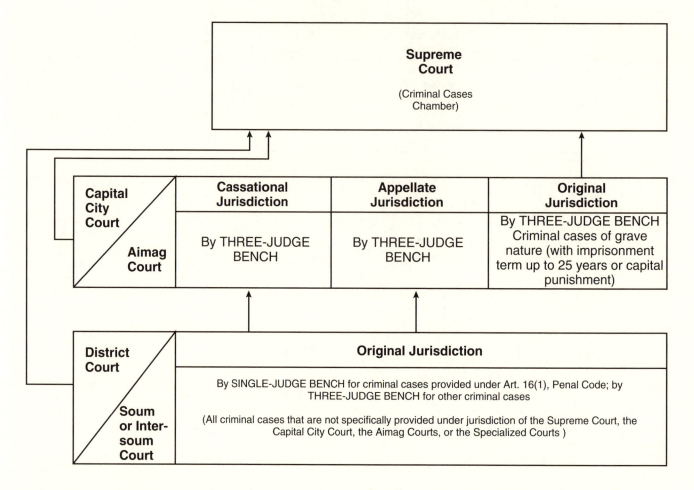

General Council of Courts

Under Article 49 of the constitution it is provided that the General Council of Courts (Judicial Service Commission) shall function for the purpose of guaranteeing the independence of the judiciary. Further, it shall, without interfering in the activities of courts and judges, deal exclusively with the selection of judges from among lawyers, protection of their rights, and other matters pertaining to the insurance of conditions guaranteeing the independence of the Mongolian judiciary. Thus, this body performs a role of the Judicial Service Commission in Mongolia. The organization and procedure of activities of the General Council of Courts are regulated by the Law on Courts, 1993.

SPECIALIZED JUDICIAL BODIES

Constitutional Tsets (Court)

The constitutional tsets (Court), established for the first time in 1992, supervises the implementation of the constitution and makes judgment on violations of its provisions. There are a total of nine members, each serving six-year terms. Three each are nominated by the State Great

Hural, by the president, and by the Supreme Court. The chairman is elected from among members for a three-year term majority of votes. The constitutional court may decide to take a case on its own initiative, or on the basis of individual petitions from citizens, the State Great Hural, the president, the prime minister, the Supreme Court, or the prosecutor general. If the constitutional court finds that statutory laws, decrees, or other decisions by the State Great Hural or the president or government decisions or international treaties violate the constitution, it submits its decision to the State Great Hural, and if not accepted then the constitutional court reexamines it and makes a final decision. Laws, decrees, instruments of ratification, and other decisions in question found unconstitutional by the constitutional court are considered invalid.

Specialized Courts

It is stated in the Constitution of Mongolia that specialized courts, such as civil, criminal, or administrative courts, may be established according to the categories of respective cases. The activities and decisions of such courts shall be under the supervision of the Supreme

Court. Thus specialized courts may be in the form of first instance and appeal courts. These courts shall be composed of the chief judge and other judges. And it shall have jurisdictional power to examine and make decisions on cases and disputes specifically provided by law. At present no particular specialized court has yet been established in Mongolia. However, since 1999 a draft law on the establishment of administrative courts has been under the consideration of the State Great Hural.

Arbitration Tribunal

The Arbitration Tribunal of Mongolia, operating under the aegis of the Mongolian Chamber of Commerce and Industry, was originally established in 1961 to resolve trade disputes between Mongolian state enterprises and those of other COMECON (Council for Mutual Economic Assistance) former socialist countries. In 1991, arbitration court expanded to consider all commercial disputes involving foreign trade, regardless of the nationality of the disputants. A new Law on Foreign Arbitration was entered into force on December 15, 1995.

National Human Rights Commission

The Law on the National Human Rights Commission of Mongolia of December 7, 2000, establishes the National Human Rights Commission as an institution mandated with the promotion and protection of human rights and charged with monitoring the implementation of the human rights provisions in the Constitution of Mongolia and the international treaties to which Mongolia is a state party. In its operation, the commission adheres to the principles of the rule of law, independence, protection of human rights and freedoms and legitimate interests, justice, and transparency. It is apparent from the legislation establishing the commission that the institution was established in conformity with the Principles Relating to the Status of National Institutions (the Paris Principles). The commission officially began its operations after the adoption of the said law and upon the appointment of its members by Parliament on January 11, 2001.

STAFFING

Since the socialist period there have been broadly three groups of lawyers making up what could be called the legal profession in Mongolia: those who adjudicate cases and formal disputes in the courts of justice, the judges; those who supervise over the inquiry into the investigation of cases and the execution of punishment and represent the state in the court proceedings, the public prosecutors; and those who provide legal advice to the general public and represent individuals in the courts, the advocates. These groups have separate organizational structures, regulations, and rules of ethics and different professional admission requirements. Despite the differences

between these groups, however, there seems to be great fluidity in the Mongolian legal profession, and its members do not expect to stay on one branch of it for their entire career. Rather, they move easily between roles as judges, public prosecutors, advocates, and government or private sector legal advisors, as well as to less strictly legal roles such as the police officers or tax inspectors.

Legal education in Mongolia is provided in the School of Law, National University of Mongolia, and about twenty other private law schools. Education for a lawyer is generally completed at the undergraduate level. The curriculum is of a general nature, covering a broad spectrum of legal subjects, and is completed in five years. Master's and doctoral degrees can be also pursued at the later stages.

At present, no uniform national system for selection and credentialing of lawyers exists in Mongolia. However, efforts are under way to consider and establish such a system.

IMPACT

Today, the poor economy continues to be a scourge to the country. Partly this is the result of weakness in the enforcement of laws. Laws passed during the previous years of reforms are still being criticized for their broadness, because they fall short of fully addressing every aspect of real-life requirements, and for their vagueness, which renders them susceptible to contradictory interpretations. These realities necessitate a refined look at the body of law and its further development.

The growing incidence of poverty is of great concern to the society in general, especially in the light of a rise in the number of vulnerable groups, such as street children, low-income female-headed households, low-income women, herders, those residing in remote areas, and the urban poor. This presents a daunting challenge for the state as well as the civil society organizations, to raise the critical awareness and knowledge of these disadvantaged people about their rights and the newly emerging laws.

The main constraints of ordinary citizens' access to the legal system are a lack of knowledge of rights and the law, the reluctance of people to assert their rights in the courts, and the complex nature of both criminal and civil justice systems. The 1992 Constitution of Mongolia declares nondiscrimination on the basis of one's nationality, language, sex, social status, social origin, religion, or political views. In accordance with this fundamental principle all other laws are not discriminatory toward women, the disabled, or any other group of population, although some of them contain provisions that affect certain groups in adverse ways. In some cases laws and ministerial policies contradict each other.

Another major constraint is that public servants, who are the law enforcers and administrators, have poor knowledge of existing legislation or lack legal qualifications to effectively carry out their duties. There is an absence of national institutions, from the legal system to the tax collection system to NGOs, that are sufficiently robust to play the role such institutions would play in more mature market economies. In addition, purely geographical considerations influence the state of legal literacy, because of the vast territory and sparse population.

And lastly, because of the inefficiency and inefficacy of the Mongolian court system, a judicial reform program is being implemented focusing on improving the court administration and on providing judicial training.

G. Bayasgalan

See also Customary Law; Soviet System

References and further reading

Asian Development Bank. 1995. *Developing Mongolia's Legal Framework: A Needs Analysis.* Metro Manila, Philippines: Asian Development Bank.

Bohanon, Richard L., and William Plouffe, Jr. 1999. "Mongolian Bankruptcy Law: A Comparative Analysis with the American Bankruptcy System." *Tulsa Journal of Comparative and International Law* 7: 1–117.

Butler, William E. 1982. *The Mongolian Legal System: Contemporary Legislation and Documentation.* The Hague: Nijhoff.

Dylykov, S. D. 1965. *Halh Djouram: Memorial of the Mongolian Feudal Law of XVIII Century.* Nauka: General Editorial Staff of Eastern Literature, Moscow.

Ginsburg, Tom. 1994. "The Transformation of Legal Institutions in Mongolia, 1990–93." *Issues and Studies, A Journal of Chinese Studies and International Affairs* 30, no. 6 (June): 77–113.

"The Legal Reform Program of Mongolia." 1998. Resolution of the State Great Hural. *Ardyn Erkh* newspaper (January 22).

Pradahn, Sanjay. 1998. *Reinvigorating State Institutions: Evaluation and Development.* The Institutional Dimension, World Bank.

Riazanovski, Valentin A. 1965 (1937). *Fundamental Principles of Mongol Law.* Bloomington: Indiana University Press.

Weller, Steven, and Heike Gramchkov. 2000. *Towards an Independent Judicial System in a Democratic Mongolia.* Report, National Center for State Courts, USAID AEP 5486-I-00–6031–00. Ulan Bator, Mongolia.

MONTANA

GENERAL INFORMATION

Montana gained statehood as the forty-first state in 1889, entering the Union in the company of Washington, North Dakota, and South Dakota. Geographically, Montana is the nation's fourth largest state, covering a land area of approximately 145,878 square miles. Bounding Montana on the north are the Canadian provinces of Saskatchewan, Alberta, and British Columbia; on the east are North Dakota and South Dakota; on the south are Wyoming and Idaho; and on the west is Idaho. Montana's pre-2000 census population was estimated to be 882,800, enough people to provide the state only one member in the U.S. House of Representatives.

The vast terrain of Montana stretches across the Northern Rockies and Great Plains. The pioneers, who joined ten indigenous Indian tribes in Montana territory, developed the state into a place of distinctive political culture and institutions. In a rough sense, Montana can be said to possess three geographic and cultural regions.

The western region of Montana lies between the Bitterroot Mountains on the west and the Continental Divide of the Rocky Mountains on the east. The region's weather is tempered by moist Pacific winds, and its economy has been shaped by its mineral and timber riches, a moderate climate conducive to cattle raising and fruit growing, and world-class tourist destinations. Using traditional descriptors of political culture, the western region's outlook has tended to be individualistic and permissive.

Montana's northern region tracks the Missouri River drainage east of the Rocky Mountains and has been called the "Highline" since the Great Northern Railroad opened it to settlement in the 1890s. The climate is that of the northern Great Plains, and as such temperatures tend to be extreme and rainfall limited. The hard work of the early wheat farmers—"sodbusters"—has yielded today's "Golden Triangle," one of the richest grain-producing areas of the world. The political culture of the northern region has been moralistic and regulatory.

The southern region of the state is defined geographically by the Yellowstone River and its tributaries flowing out of Wyoming and eastward to their confluence with the Missouri River at the North Dakota border. The Yellowstone Valley, like the Highline, has a continental climate. Its abundant hay crops have supported cattle and sheep ranching, and oil fields and vast deposits of low-sulfur coal have diversified the area's economy. Early development was furthered by the completion of the Union Pacific, Northern Pacific, and Milwaukee railroads. The political culture of the southern region has been a hybrid of the other two regions.

From the perspectives of geography and culture, therefore, Montana is a surprisingly diverse state. Its well-known features of Western ruralism and sparse population belie substantial differences among its regions and residents. One of the state's mottos, the "Treasure State," draws attention to Montana's natural resource wealth and development. The more recent motto, "Big Sky Country," represents the desire of some to emphasize environmental preservation and tourism. The state's inability to resolve this ambivalence has resulted in substandard economic performance. The Corporation for Enterprise Development in 2000 gave Montana a grade of D in each of three rated areas of the state's economy: performance, development capacity, and business vitality. Some negative specifics included Montana's lowest rank among all the states in annual pay, fourth lowest in digital networks, and sixth lowest in teacher salaries. High rankings for Montana were in the areas of quality of education, recent job growth, and air quality.

EVOLUTION AND HISTORY

The state's geographic and cultural diversity has produced a distinctive political-legal system. Its hallmarks have been populism, progressivism, party competition, and citizen participation. The populism was evident in 1884. Not waiting for an invitation from the U.S. Congress, the people of the territory submitted a putative statehood constitution. After it was rejected, the statehood charter of 1889 was presented and accepted. The 1889 Constitution was characteristic of its peers in its distrust of government and resulting goal of "damage control." Such negativism was increasingly found to be dysfunctional as the state confronted the modern challenges of civil rights, public participation, and environmental protection.

In 1972, Montanans wrote and ratified a new state constitution. Its principal themes of responsive and accountable government are manifested throughout—for example, in its legislative and executive articles. The legislature is a large bicameral body with one hundred representatives and fifty senators, all from single-member districts. The governor is empowered to preside over an integrated executive branch. Only the judicial article of the 1889 Constitution was left largely untouched. In the local government article the state's 56 counties and 127 municipalities are given a range of structural options and enabled to adopt home-rule powers.

There can be no doubt that the 1972 Montana Constitution sustained and to a degree enhanced the participatory nature of the state's politics. Party competition, one measure of democratic health, continues to score high. In sixty-five election outcomes between 1946 and 1996 (state house, state senate, and governor), the Democrats won 51 percent of the time and Republicans won 48 percent of the time. In the more recent period of 1982 to 1996, the Republican success rate was 55 percent, pointing to a possible emerging Republican dominance in the state. Election turnout in Montana continues to be high, as measured by the participation of the voting-age population. From 1976 to 1996, Montana was ranked in the highest turnout category of 60 to 70 percent, usually a full 15 percent above the national figure. Direct democracy also marks Montana as a highly participatory state. Since 1972, Montana voters have passed upon an average of about eight ballot measures in each statewide election.

CURRENT STRUCTURE

Montana's 1972 Constitution authorizes a three-level state judiciary (see figure). At the lowest level are courts of limited jurisdiction. In 1999 their kinds and numbers included eighty city courts, seventy justice of the peace courts, and four municipal courts. The jurisdiction of these courts is to some degree exclusive but extensively overlapping. Municipal court judges must be lawyers, and they receive their positions through election. Justice of the peace and city court judges do not have to be lawyers. Judges in justice courts are elected to four-year terms, while city court judges may be elected or appointed. A Commission on Courts of Limited Jurisdiction oversees the municipal, city, and justice courts and conducts required training courses for their judges. In 1999, Montana's courts of limited jurisdiction had a total caseload of 282,254 filings, of which about 45 percent were criminal.

Montana's fifty-six district courts are at the second level of the state's judiciary. These courts are organized into twenty-one judicial districts and are staffed by thirty-seven district judges. The original jurisdiction of these courts includes felonies and civil and probate cases. Their limited appellate jurisdiction extends to the state's courts of limited jurisdiction. District court judges must be lawyers, and they attain their positions ordinarily by nonpartisan election to six-year terms or, in case of vacancies, by appointment by the governor, who is assisted by the Judicial Nominating Commission. In 1999 the state's twenty-one judicial districts disposed of 34,629 cases. The range in dispositions per judge was from 388 to 1,215.

At the top of the Montana judicial system is the Montana Supreme Court, on which serve seven justices. They, like the district court judges, attain their positions ordinarily through nonpartisan election or, in the event of a vacancy, by gubernatorial appointment. Their term of office is eight years. The Montana Supreme Court is the only state tribunal with solely appellate jurisdiction (in 1999 and 2001, the Montana Legislature rejected a reform measure for an intermediate appellate court). As a result, the Montana Supreme Court has a high nondiscretionary docket: 709 filings in 1999. By the end of 1999, the Montana Supreme Court had disposed of 669 cases, issued 341 formal opinions, and maintained a backlog of 557 pending cases. Increasingly, the Montana Supreme Court is deciding cases without the use of oral argument. Besides resolving disputes through the normal appellate decision-making process, the Montana Supreme Court, with the assistance of the clerk of the Supreme Court, also administers a program of appellate mediation.

In addition to the constitutionally required judicial system, Montana also uses many administrative tribunals (for example, for state government personnel appeals,

Legal Structure of Montana Courts

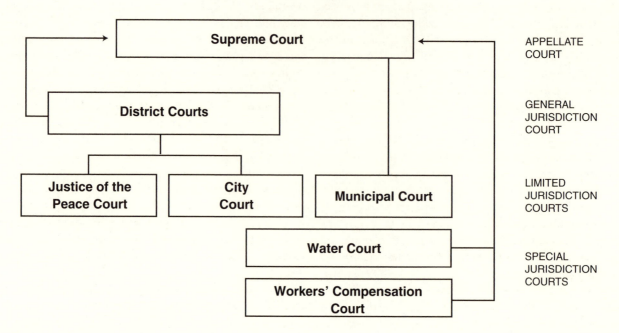

and for tax adjustment) and two courts of special jurisdiction, the Workers' Compensation Court and the Water Court. The legislatively created Workers' Compensation Court resolves disputes arising under workers' compensation and occupational disease legislation. Its judge is appointed by the governor to a six-year term and in 1999 received 270 petitions, conducted 57 trials, and issued 108 decisions.

The Montana Water Court was created by the Montana Legislature in 1979 and given exclusive jurisdiction over the adjudication of existing water rights in the state. The chief water judge is appointed by the chief justice of the Montana Supreme Court and is assisted by one water judge in each of the state's four water divisions and by special water masters. The Water Court also has authority to review reserved water rights compacts negotiated between the state, the federal government, and the state's seven tribal governments.

NOTABLE FEATURES OF LAW/LEGAL SYSTEM
Legal commentators have praised Montana's 1972 Constitution as one of the world's most progressive modern governmental documents. Its Declaration of Rights contains many rights that are either implicit or not mentioned in the U.S. Constitution. For example, among its fundamental guarantees are individual privacy, a right to attend public meetings, a right of access to government records, and a right to a clean and healthful environment. Also of note in the Declaration of Rights is an expansive individual dignity clause that prohibits both state and private actors from discriminating on account of race,

color, sex, culture, social origin or condition, or political or religious ideas.

Other notable features of the current constitution are a waiver of sovereign immunity (with liability caps imposed by the legislature), the creation of a trust fund from the proceeds of the state's coal severance tax, which in 1998 had a balance of about $630 million, the provision of a right of equal educational opportunity, the recognition of the "distinct and unique cultural heritage of the American Indians," a mandate that each local government provide its voters an opportunity every ten years to review its structure, and a requirement that the state electorate be given the opportunity every twenty years to vote on holding a new constitutional convention. The constitution also allows Montana's lawmakers to legalize gambling and lotteries, and the legislature subsequently created a public policy controversy in the state by the breadth of its authorization.

The Montana Supreme Court has enhanced the notable features of the state's constitution through its use of the independent and adequate state grounds doctrine. By deciding cases solely on the basis of Montana constitutional law and isolating those decisions from the federal constitutional decisions of the U.S. Supreme Court, the Montana Supreme Court has given some state constitutional rights an interpretation more expansive than that given to the analogous federal rights by the U.S. Supreme Court. For example, the Montana Supreme Court has ruled that the right of equal educational opportunity requires state equalization of school funding, and that the right of privacy prohibits the state from criminalizing homosexual relations.

STAFFING

As discussed above, the judges of Montana district courts and the justices of the Montana Supreme Court can come to their offices by way of either nonpartisan election or appointment. While there has been greater elective competition for positions on the Supreme Court than for judgeships in district courts, appointment has been a significant route to both courts. The constitution provides that the governor has the duty of appointing a replacement to an open seat on the courts. The governor's nominee is selected from a list of three to five attorneys made available by the Judicial Nomination Commission. The Montana Senate must confirm the appointment. The name of the appointed judge or justice appears on the next election ballot, whether or not an opponent has filed for the position. This review procedure allows voters to pass on the performance of the appointed judge or justice, regardless of the existence of a challenger. Whenever a judge or justice is rejected by the electorate in an uncontested election, the gubernatorial appointment and senatorial confirmation procedure is used.

Montana judges can be disciplined by the Judicial Standards Commission, a constitutional body composed of two district court judges, one attorney, and two lay members. The commission's authority includes censure, suspension, and removal of a judicial officer. In 1999 the commission received thirty-nine complaints and had six pending complaints. Action taken in 1999 included thirty-two dismissed complaints, one private reprimand, one public reprimand, and eleven complaints held over.

Concerning the regulation of lawyers, Montana has an integrated bar under the control of the state Supreme Court. Accordingly, the Supreme Court is in charge of admitting lawyers to the practice of law and overseeing their discipline. In 2000, some 2,550 lawyers had "practicing" status, and there were about 160 "nonpracticing" members of the bar. Two bar examinations each year are the basis for admitting approximately one hundred lawyers annually. In 1998 the Montana Supreme Court did away with the option of being admitted to the practice of law by motion of an existing bar member. The Commission on Practice, established by the Montana Supreme Court, reviews complaints alleging unethical conduct by Montana lawyers. In 1999 the commission had a caseload of 218 new complaints and 146 pending complaints. That year the commission's disciplinary actions consisted of twenty-two admonishments, one license suspension, and no disbarments.

RELATIONSHIP TO NATIONAL SYSTEM

One of the principal ways in which Montana has been related to the federal judicial system is through litigation arising from the state's seven Indian reservations and tribal governments. These are the Flathead (Salish and Kootenai tribes), Blackfeet, Rocky Boy's (Chippewa and Cree tribes), Fort Belknap (Gros Ventre and Sioux tribes), Crow, Northern Cheyenne, and Fort Peck (Assiniboine and Sioux tribes). The assertion by the tribal governments of their civil and criminal jurisdiction has resulted in alleged conflicts with the authority of Montana state and local governments. In recent years, federal courts have been asked to rule in Montana-based cases dealing with such issues as tribal regulation of nonmember hunting and fishing on reservation lands, tribal regulation of docks and breakwaters on Flathead Lake, and tribal court jurisdiction over non-Indians engaged in reservation activities. Montana, just like many other Western states, has been the source of interesting and important litigation that has given the U.S. Supreme Court the opportunity to chart the complicated contours of American Indian law.

James J. Lopach

See also Native American Law, Traditional; United States—Federal System; United States—State Systems

References and further reading

Lopach, James J., ed. 1983. *We the People of Montana: The Workings of a Popular Government.* Missoula: Mountain Press Publishing Company.

Lopach, James J., Margery Hunter Brown, and Richmond L. Clow. 1998. *Tribal Government Today: Politics on Montana Indian Reservations.* Rev. ed. Niwot: University Press of Colorado.

Montana Department of Revenue. *Biennial Report, July 1996 to June 1998.*

Montana Supreme Court. 1999. *Annual Report.*

MOOTS

GENERAL DEFINITION

A moot is a traditional social gathering for the purposes of discussing existing laws, enacting new ones, or, most commonly, resolving disputes. Although many scholars have focused their historical or ethnographic studies of moots on this last purpose, it would not be correct to say that moots are used only for resolving disputes, even if that function is perhaps the most important when moots are considered cross-culturally. Moots are most often found within customary legal systems and represent an important aspect of customary legal procedure, although moots are usually not the only type of legal procedure available to customary legal actors, particularly with respect to dispute resolution. In most customary legal systems, a moot is the first procedural stage and is considered a preferable and more informal method for resolving local disputes than are later procedural stages, which are usually more formal and coercive.

Moots have been used at many different levels of society, from the smallest level, the village or hamlet, to much larger levels, including even the maximal political level, as with the *Althing* of Iceland, which served as a moot for the entire Icelandic polity. But most commonly moots were used at the smaller levels, especially during and after the colonial era, when Anglo-American common law and continental civil law were forcibly imposed on many areas around the world that were already regulated by customary legal systems. In these cases, the use of moots to discuss laws and resolve disputes at the regional and maximal levels was brought to an end.

Many observers have noted that moots are held in the open air in a location that has special significance for the community because of this function. Indeed, moots are sometimes described as "open-air assemblies." Some moot-places assume a sacred, quasi-religious nature. It is thought that because moots are typically held in a public place invested with special significance, and in the open air, moots can be described as socially open, participatory, and even democratic events. This point leads to an interesting question, which, unfortunately, cannot be definitively answered but nevertheless should be considered: to what extent have small rural communities been—governed as they have traditionally been by customary law—essentially democratic because of the prevalence and importance cross-culturally of the moot as the primary forum for community politico-legal affairs?

Although moots serve as the first and the preferred form of dispute resolution in communities where they exist, in many places moots also serve what we can call legislative functions. Many communities throughout history have not made a functional distinction between lawmaking, law-enforcing, and law-interpreting activities. The reason appears to be quite practical, as opposed to theoretical or ideological: sharp task specialization, including that in political and legal spheres, is associated with the rise of large, socially complex polities. But history shows that this correlation between the size of communities and the extent of differentiation between the various legal functions is not a perfect one. Again, to return to the example of the Icelandic *Althing* (which I will describe in more detail below), this great open-air moot, held every summer, performed legislative, executive, and judicial functions—a culture-bound distinction to be sure—for the entire Icelandic nation.

HISTORICAL BACKGROUND

Because moots are found in many parts of the world, and throughout recorded history, it is not possible to isolate and describe a specific historical trajectory for the moot as a legal procedure. As I have already said, moots were likely the key politico-legal forum within communities even before recorded history, and therefore it would not be possible to identify a time when moots were first used by communities to formalize communal rights and obli-

gations and to resolve disputes. Nevertheless, it is useful to identify the earliest known descriptions of moots in order to establish certain historical parameters for their use and importance. If the Bible can be taken to reflect actual historical practices, we can start with the Book of Joshua, which describes a large-scale, open-air moot in which "Joshua gathered all the tribes of Israel to Shechem, and called for the elders of Israel, and for their heads, and for their judges, and for their officers." And in the New Testament, from the Book of John, we read that "when Pilate there heard that saying, he brought Jesus forth, and sat down in the judgment seat in a place that is called the Pavement, but in the Hebrew, Gabbatha." Most commentators have argued that this encounter took place at an open-air "court of justice," which also served as the site of less formal moots.

Turning to early India, the *Náradiyá Dharma-sastra* invalidates disputes resolved through secret or nighttime proceedings and admonishes people to resolve their disputes in the open air, during the daytime, and with full public participation. Indeed, many anthropologists have observed how in areas of rural India today disputes are settled during the *panchayet,* in which disputants, their families, and sometimes all other members of the community meet to discuss the ongoing dispute and decide on ways to resolve it.

Finally, we can turn to the Roman historian Tacitus. In his ethnographic history of the early Germans, the *Germania* (completed in 98 C.E.), Tacitus describes in detail the multipurpose Assembly of the Germans, which was composed of all free men of the community. Even though chiefs played prominent roles during the functioning of the Assembly, all men present (presumably women were excluded, although that is not clear) took part in judicial and legislative decision-making. Tacitus emphasizes that these moots were perhaps the best expression of the participatory and roughly democratic nature of early German society.

Moving from the early historical record to more recent times, it is worth considering the ways in which moots have been transformed by significant political developments. Perhaps the single most important political development in this regard—a development that was, moreover, significant for all customary legal procedures—was the imposition of the Anglo-American common law and legal systems derived from the Roman civil law during the second wave of colonialism, which began in earnest after the mid–nineteenth century. As I have mentioned, to the extent that moots were used as legal forums at regional and national levels in the precolonial era, this practice was ended after the coming of the Europeans, who replaced the regional and national moots with either common law or civil law courts. This had the effect of actually increasing the importance of the community moots, because such events became more than simply the first and preferred method for resolving local disputes. During and after the colonial era, they also became symbols of local resistance and cultural continuity in the face of colonial abuses.

Further, colonialism also had the effect of sharpening the distinctions between customary law and the law of the colonial administration for people in communities who had not considered their legal systems in that light before. The result was that, after independence, many new nation-states consciously adopted the legal systems of the former colonial powers; customary legal procedures such as the moot, thereafter to be found mostly in rural areas, came to be seen as barriers to national development.

MAJOR VARIANTS

In view of the diversity in the way that moots have been used and shaped throughout history, it is difficult to trace precise patterns of regional or historical moot variants. Nevertheless, one can find some significant differences in the form and content of moots across time and region. In order to illustrate this, I will describe three well-known and well-documented moots—from early Britain, from early Iceland, and the Kpelle moots of current-day Liberia in Africa.

In 1072 an important open-air moot was held on Pennenden Heath, in Kent in England, only six years after the Norman Conquest. At issue were conflicting rights over land, and the parties were the powerful Bishop of Bayeux and the Archbishop of Canterbury. Over the course of three days men who were considered learned in customary English law from the surrounding district were called on to testify about the competing claims. During the moot, witnesses were called on to assist with the judgment, but the moot proceeded through open discussion by all present without the use of formal limiting procedures. At the end of three days, the archbishop was able to recover rights to archbishopric lands, and the judgment was ratified by the new English king—even though it went against the Bishop of Bayeux, who happened to be his brother.

In Iceland after 930 C.E., the *Althing* served as a national moot, a forum that was a national version of the many local *Things*. The *Althing* was held at *Thingvalla*, which was a plain of lava divided into several important subparts, including the Hill of Laws and the Court of Laws. This famous moot was directed by specific individuals, and there was more of an element of control over the proceedings than we have seen in the early English example. During each case, both sides presented their arguments while the gathered crowd of freemen surrounding the area expressed their approval or disapproval with each side through shouts or applause. At the end of the presentations the chiefs in attendance agreed among themselves which side had presented the better argument, and a decision was reached.

Finally, we turn to the moots of the Kpelle of Liberia. These moots are used by the Kpelle to resolve disputes that are thought by the Kpelle to require less formality. During this Kpelle *berei mu meni saa*, the parties come together accompanied by kinsmen on each side. In addition, neighbors of the disputants also participate in the moot. The participants do not utilize formal principles to resolve disputes during these moots; rather, they attempt to reach a result that is satisfying to both sides. These moots are typically held on a Sunday in the home of the person who has initiated the proceeding. There will be a mediator present, who will have been selected by the one who has called the moot. The mediator will be someone who is both related to the complainant and someone recognized for his skill in resolving disputes. The session is ended after the mediator pronounces a judgment of fault, after both parties, and anyone present, have spoken. The person found to be at fault will then offer a formal apology, which takes the form of symbolic gifts. The winning party will then reciprocate with a smaller symbolic gift, so as to show that he accepts the apology in good faith.

SIGNIFICANCE

The moot is always an important legal and political institution in societies in which it is found. Many scholars believe that moots are important because they serve to restore local harmony by reaching results that are acceptable to the entire community. Although moots are most commonly found in customary legal systems around the world, at the turn of the twenty-first century some common law and civil law countries were experimenting by making moots an "alternative dispute resolution" proceeding that parties could have recourse to in certain circumstances.

Mark Goodale

See also Alternative Dispute Resolution; Customary Law; Iceland; Mediation

References and further reading

Gibbs, James L. 1963. "The Kpelle Moot: A Therapeutic Model for the Informal Settlement of Disputes." *Africa* 36, no. 1: 1–11.
Gomme, George Laurence. 1880. *Primitive Folk-Moots: Or, Open-Air Assemblies in Britain.* London: Sampson Low, Marston, Searle and Rivington.
Lunt, W. E. 1956. *History of England.* New York: Harper and Brothers.
Nader, Laura, and Harry F. Todd, eds. 1978. *The Disputing Process: Law in Ten Societies.* New York: Columbia University Press.
Renteln, Alison Dundes, and Alan Dundes, eds. 1995. *Folk Law: Essays in the Theory and Practice of Lex Non Scriptum.* Vols. 1 and 2. Madison: University of Wisconsin Press.
Tacitus. 1970. *The Agricola and the Germania.* London: Penguin.

MOROCCO

GENERAL INFORMATION

Considered part of the Maghrib, or "where the sun sets," Morocco is the westernmost of the Arab states. The country stretches to the Mediterranean in the north, where it borders Algeria and extends along the Atlantic coast of Africa. To the east it borders the sub-Saharan state of Mauritania. The country's exact size and internationally recognized boundaries remain in dispute, as it continues to lay claim to the Western Sahara, the former Spanish colony to its south. Hence any geographic description of the country must take into account Morocco proper and the Western Sahara region.

Morocco proper comprises the northern half of the country and is divided by several chains of the Atlas Mountains. Along the Atlantic coast are lowland plains, while to the east, along the Algerian border, is a mixture of mountains and plateaus. The southern portion of Morocco proper forms the northern reaches of the Sahara desert. Within Morocco, the river system serves as the major source of water for a growing population and the agricultural sector. The Sibou is the largest river; it stretches from the Atlas Mountains down to the coast, where it runs into the Atlantic near the capital city of Rabat.

To the south is the former Spanish colony known as the Western Sahara. When the Spanish left in 1975, a war began over control of the territory. The more than 280,000 square kilometers of land is mountainous in the north, where the Atlas Mountains extend from Morocco. The major portion of the region, or the Rio de Oro, is flat and composed mainly of desert. Most of the inhabitants of the region live along the coast, where agriculture is possible and the unrelenting heat of the interior is cooled by the ocean.

Not including the sparsely inhabited Western Sahara, Morocco is one of the fastest growing of the North African states, with more than thirty million people living in the country by 2000. They are a mix of Arabs and Berbers, with a small Jewish population. More than one-third of the population is under the age of fourteen, and more than 95 percent of the population is under the age of sixty-five. The population explosion in the country has occurred in the main cities in the country and may serve as a boon to the economy or as a future source of instability.

The Moroccan economy is based mainly on the extraction and export of natural resources and the sale of artisan goods to Western tourists. The rise and fall in the price of those commodities has placed pressure on the economy. Export earnings have also fluctuated in the prime commodity of Morocco, phosphate, as those resources located in disputed territory came under military attack.

The agricultural sector of Morocco has been in a steady decline. Much of the farming was basic and on small plots of land. It produced food for use by the farmers and their family, but little for export. A smaller amount of land was farmed in large plots using irrigation and modern machinery. The subsistence type of farming was unable to keep up with the growing population, forcing the country to import food. The only growth in agriculture was in the fishing industry. Much of the fish was canned and exported abroad, but that did little to help the ever-growing dependence on food imports.

Mineral exports constituted an even greater portion of Morocco's earnings. The largest such export was phosphate, with Morocco placing second only to the United States in its production. While phosphate mines are located throughout the country, the largest sources are in the eastern and northern reaches of the disputed Western Sahara territory. The difficulty in moving the mined product to be shipped became apparent when the transportation network was attacked by rebels. The Moroccans depended upon an extensive conveyer-belt system to move the phosphate across trackless desert. The interruption of that system by Polisario rebels limited export. Only with successful defensive measures taken by the military was phosphate production brought back to normal levels.

Morocco has also developed large natural gas resources, used only for domestic consumption. Unlike many of its North African neighbors, Morocco contains no significant oil reserves. Instead it must import most of its energy, creating economic distress when the prices rise.

The relative political and economic stability of Morocco has made it a tourist attraction for Westerners and bolstered one of its biggest markets. Craftsmen in the major cities produce carpets, leather goods, metal ware, and pottery for sale. Most of these items are produced by artisans in small shops or marketplaces, with their main customers being tourists. Tourism provides considerable earnings to the country, with the Atlantic beaches and the larger cities of Rabat, Casablanca, and Marrakech serving as the major destination for tours.

HISTORY

Some of the earliest inhabitants of the Moroccan region were members of the Berber tribes who migrated from sub-Saharan Africa and the desert regions of Asia. The area bordering the Mediterranean and Atlantic was later controlled by a series of empires, including the Carthaginians and the Romans. The latter empire was in a constant low-level war with the Berbers, who were able at times to cut communications between the Roman province of Mauretenia (which included the Morocco region) and the East African Roman provinces. The regions served a limited economic role for the empire and had even less military and political importance. For most of the Roman occupation the Berbers were unaffected by

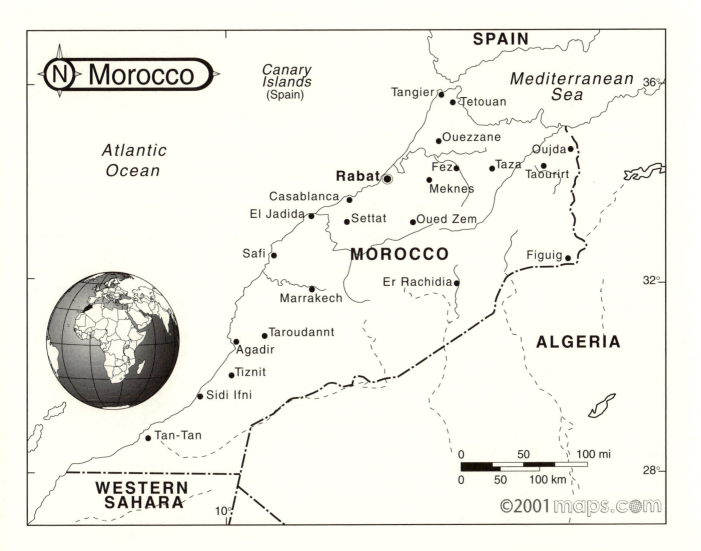

the empire's culture, or the subsequent disintegration of central control caused by the invasion and conquest by the Vandals in 429.

With the end of Roman control, the Berbers faced an invasion from the east by the armies of Islam. While the Arab armies were eventually able to conquer the territory, they had difficulty in exerting political and religious control over the population. In fact, by the eleventh century, the Berbers set aside tribal differences and constructed an empire that stretched from Spain to modern-day Tunisia. It was during this period that the peoples living in the Moroccan region established a national identity.

The collapse of the empire in Spain during the fourteenth and fifteenth centuries produced political chaos and intermittent civil wars. At the same time, Morocco was the sole North African state to escape direct colonization by the Europeans. This can be explained by the ability of the Moroccan sultans to play one major power off of another by granting trading privileges to Moroccan ports to several European states. This made colonization by a single power difficult, as it would limit the privileges granted to the other. At the same time, this strategy produced intense

competition among the major European powers as they sought leverage in expanding their privileges.

During the early years of the twentieth century, there were several disputes that almost expanded into a general European war. The French, with British support, claimed Morocco as their sphere of influence. Their main rival on the continent, Germany, protested, and did so with a show of force by German Kaiser Wilhelm II, who rode a white horse down Moroccan streets as a sign of the country's interest in Morocco. By 1912, though, France had established political preeminence in Morocco, while allowing the sultan to remain as a figurehead ruler.

Morocco remained a partly autonomous part of French West Africa and part of the Vichy Regime until liberated in 1942. After the end of World War II, Morocco was swept up in the same independence movement that was affecting French Algeria. Independence came in 1955, with Mohammed V as king. He ruled only five more years, and after his death in 1961 his son, Hassan II, assumed the throne and started to build Morocco into a modern and semiconstitutional state that was one of the most Western oriented of all Arab states.

Hassan faced several coup attempts during his first ten years of rule. In combating rebels in the military, he clamped down on the armed forces, taking personal control over them. He conducted several purges of military officers and named loyal generals to key positions. By the mid-1970s the main threat to Moroccan stability was the economic and political crises created by the departure of the Spanish from their Western Saharan colony on Morocco's southern border. Morocco claimed the entire territory as its own but was able to occupy only the northern third. By 1980 the Moroccan military, enhanced in size to control the new territory, was in a life and death struggle with the Polisario rebel group, fighting for Western Saharan independence. At the same time Morocco contended with Western diplomatic pressure to reach a peaceful end to the battle, even if it meant granting the Western Sahara its freedom. Pressed by the economic drag of the war and the threat of political isolation from the West, Morocco created a defensive shield around the most economically viable portion of the area. This lessened the level of military conflict while allowing Morocco to maintain a low political profile on the issue.

With the military issue all but resolved, many of the economic problems associated with the war also lessened. King Hassan turned the government's attention inward. He was able to effectively guide his country through a period of Arab radicalism and political turmoil that struck most of the Middle East. In doing so he balanced the demands of the Muslim population with his desire to enhance ties with the West. He moved closer to a democratic system with the ratification of the 1996 Constitution, which included the formation of more representative institutions. His death in 1999 brought his son to power and produced uncertainty as to whether the young king could hold together Moroccan society.

With few natural resources and a lack of a manufacturing base, Morocco has been forced to borrow money from Western banks. While the country has been able to repay the debt, it has done so only after financial crises linked with its war in the Western Sahara.

LEGAL CONCEPTS

Under its modern governing system, Morocco has been a traditional monarchy with slow movement in the direction of a constitutional monarchy. Hassan II (1961–1999) started the country toward a constitutional system. He was responsible for the writing of three constitutions, one in 1970, another in 1972, and the last in 1996. He was personally involved in overseeing the development of new institutions, including an elected house of the legislature and a marginally independent judiciary. At the same time Hassan retreated from personal rule, while maintaining oversight powers for such duties as choosing judges.

Hassan's first move toward democratizing government power involved the creation of a partly elected House of Representatives. With two-thirds of its members elected by a select group of voters and one-third appointed by the monarch, the chamber was to provide a democratic voice in the passage of legislation. Yet the House had limited legislative powers, which included writing civil service reform, privatization of certain government-owned industries, and composing a criminal code. Their sessions were limited to two a year, lasting no more than a total of four months. In addition, the king had the power to overturn legislation while all bills were routed through the Supreme Court's Constitutional Chamber for its approval. That chamber, filled with the king's handpicked judges, could declare any bill unconstitutional and void.

The king also oversaw the establishment of a judicial branch that began to take a few short steps toward independence while maintaining the monarchy and the traditions of French colonial power. The 1996 Constitution protects rights such as private property, public participation in government, speech, and religion. At the same time, those rights can be limited under the law by a decree from the monarchy or under emergency declarations. The judiciary has only limited functions and structures for upholding the constitutional order.

CURRENT STRUCTURE

The Moroccan judiciary and legal culture have been affected by the French legal system. As a civil law country, the power of the lower courts is limited to interpreting and applying the law as written by the national legislature. At the same time, the Muslim character of the country requires a separate Islamic system that utilizes a more common law approach, in which judges have power of interpretation that allows them to change the law so as to meet the immediate needs of society. Additionally, the government courts began to integrate traditional religious and indigenous law into the legal framework.

At the time of independence, Morocco had a variety of legal systems functioning alongside the official judicial system. Along with Moroccan courts there existed Islamic *sharia* courts, Jewish rabbinical courts, and customary Berber courts. With the departure of the French and the consolidation of power in the national government, these separate systems were either melded into the regular courts or saw their jurisdictions and subject matter shrink.

The rabbinical courts of Jewish law were the first judicial system folded into the Moroccan courts. The declining Jewish population made a separate system unnecessary. Instead, the trial courts in Morocco were pledged to enforce Jewish law within rabbinical sections. Judges within these sections would decide personal issues and family law.

Legal Structure of Morocco Courts

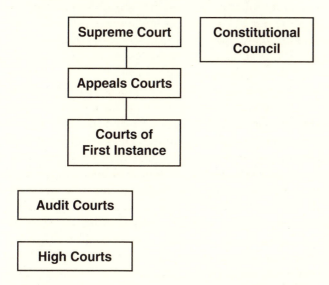

Berber law, passed down from generation to generation in an oral tradition, was the next to be consolidated within the Moroccan system. Some of these traditions surrounding family disputes and personal property were retained by the Moroccan courts, but most other Berber legal customs were replaced. Islamic *sharia* law became the law for the Berbers, most of whom were Muslim. While Islamic courts grew in the population they served, the Moroccans continued to limit the law's scope. All criminal cases and large civil cases were handled in government courts under the French Napoleonic Code.

The declining importance of Islamic law was generally accepted by the population—unlike other countries, such as Iran and Algeria, where revolts followed such decisions. The tight control exercised by the monarchy and the relative prosperity of the country helped Morocco in its quest to change its legal system.

The main lower trial courts in the regular Moroccan judicial system are the courts of first instance. They hear all criminal cases and all nonfamily civil cases. The first instance courts are staffed with magistrates appointed by the king and make their decisions in the name of the monarchy. They enforce legislatively made law under a structure resembling the French civil law culture.

The decisions of these lower courts could be appealed to one of several regionally located appellate courts. Under the 1972 Constitution, appellate court decisions could be appealed to the Supreme Court, which was the highest court in the land. That changed with the 1996 Constitution and the changes making the Supreme Court one of only two high courts in Morocco.

The original Moroccan Supreme Court under the 1972 Constitution had five subdivisions. Four of the five—the criminal, civil, administrative, and social divisions—hear appeals from litigants who lost their case in the lower appeals courts. All of the divisions lack judicial review powers to declare lower court decisions or laws unconstitutional. Instead, the Supreme Court divisions must examine the procedure used by the lower courts and their adjudication of the law. If a mistake is found, the justices can overturn the lower court verdict and call for a new trial.

The fifth division of the Supreme Court was known as the Constitutional Chamber. This chamber had judicial review powers that could be used within a somewhat constricted jurisdiction. The Constitutional Chamber was granted the power to settle disputes between the executive branch and the Parliament over the constitutionality of laws. The court could also exercise abstract review powers in examining a pending piece of legislation and determining whether it would violate the constitution. Finally, the Constitutional Chamber decided election disputes and determined the winner in such elections.

In addition to the Supreme Court, Morocco also has a Special High Court that conducts trials of government officials formally accused of crimes under a parliamentary vote. Military courts became important during the 1960s and 1970s as they were used to try officers who had attempted to overthrow the monarchy.

While government officials are considered under the control of the constitution and the courts, the king is considered above those institutions. His decisions cannot be reviewed, much less struck down by a court. As part of his democratization efforts, though, Hassan began to develop competing institutions and to identify those rights that would be protected from governmental intrusion. By the mid-1990s, Morocco was set to take a large step toward modeling itself after the Western democracies.

As Western ties expanded, so did King Hassan's determination to Westernize Morocco and enhance the power of institutions beyond the monarchy. In 1996 a new constitution was ratified. It expanded suffrage rights for ordinary Moroccans while forming new institutions to complement the monarchy.

The constitution reformed the House of Representative so that all of its members were elected by the Moroccan citizenry. The House was joined by a House of Counsellors, whose members were appointed by the king. Both chambers were given a constitutional role to play, in serving in the new judicial institution created under the constitution.

SPECIALIZED JUDICIAL BODIES

The 1996 Constitution created several special judicial bodies that existed outside the regular court system. The newly created Constitutional Council took the place of the Constitutional Chamber within the old Moroccan Supreme Court. Its twelve members were divided into those selected by the monarchy and those selected by the people's elected representatives. Six of the members served with the king's approval. Three members were appointed by a majority vote of the House of Representatives, and three were appointed by a vote of the House of Counsellors. All of the members served a nine-year non-renewable term and could not be removed except for malfeasance in office. The divided method of selection provided a degree of independence in carrying out its central role within the constitutional system.

Under Article 81 of the constitution, the council acts like a constitutional court, separate from the regular judiciary. The council does not hear appeals from litigants seeking to overturn a lower court decision. Those are heard by the Moroccan Appeals Courts or the Supreme Court. Instead, the members of the Constitutional Council determine the validity of parliamentary elections and have the power to overturn an election if irregularities are found. The council also has the power to consider the constitutionality of pending legislation before the Parliament. The council will examine the legislation at the request of the king, the prime minister, the president either of the House of Representatives or the House of Counsellors, or one-quarter of the membership of either house of Parliament.

The council studies the pending bill and rules on the constitutionality of the legislation. Once the council rules that a bill is unconstitutional, its decision is considered binding on the other branches of government. The bill cannot pass the Parliament without changes that meet the concerns of the council. Because it has the final say on the constitutionality of a pending law, the council need not hear individual challenges to that law. In addition, the power to review constitutionality is limited to the council and cannot be exercised by the regular courts in the Moroccan judiciary.

An Audit Court was also established under the 1996 Constitution. Its members were given supervisory power over the budgets of the national government and all local units of government. It also conducted oversight of all departments, auditing their books to ensure that public funds were spent properly.

The 1996 Constitution moved Morocco in the direction of a democratically elected legislature and a partly independent judiciary, which could use constitutional rights as a check on government power. While the monarch retained final power, the formation of the institutions suggested that instead of an absolute monarchy, the country was destined to move toward a constitutional monarchy.

STAFFING

Morocco has a training program both for lawyers studying government law and for those seeking to follow a career in Islamic law. There are universities in the main cities of the country, though Rabat contains the largest and most proficient law school. Upon achieving a law degree, lawyers can seek a career in private practice or attempt to move toward a judicial career. Judicial appointments, though, require some political contacts.

One of the changes wrought by the 1996 Constitution was the method of selecting members of the judiciary. The Supreme Council of the Magistracy was given this job. The members of the council include the king, who is its presiding officer, the justice minister, the Supreme Court president, the Supreme Court's prosecutor general, two magistrates from lower courts of appeals, and four lower trial court magistrates. Each member of the council has been appointed to his position either by the king or by the council itself. Every judge in Morocco must be nominated by the council and appointed by the king. Once appointed, a magistrate could not be removed except by an extraordinary vote of Parliament for malfeasance in office. But the system, with the king at its helm, ensures that all appointments will be made under the watchful eye and approval of the monarch.

IMPACT

As one of the more Westernized of the Arab and Muslim countries, Morocco has maintained close economic and political ties to Europe and the United States. At the same time it has developed political and legal institutions that could serve as a check on monarchical power in the country. The advent of a constitutional council, acting as a legal check on the power of the legislature and the monarch, created a limited mechanism for the rule of law. At the same time it made the constitution preeminent in protecting rights and creating an indirect form of judicial review.

The Morocco that King Hassan II passed on to his son at the start of the twenty-first century was politically stable and was turned toward a form of government responsible to a constitution rather than the whims of a king. Future events will determine whether a strong and independent judiciary can function within a Muslim country, or if Western-style legal institutions are doomed to failure in the Middle East.

Douglas Clouatre

See also Appellate Courts; Civil Law; Constitutional Review; Criminal Law; Customary Law; Judicial Selection, Methods of; Napoleonic Code; Trial Courts
References and further reading
Hart, David M. 2000. *Tribe and Society in Rural Morocco.* Portland, OR: Frank Cass.
Munson, Henry. 1993. *Religion and Power in Morocco.* New Haven: Yale University Press.
Nelson, Harold. 1985. *Morocco: A Country Study.* Washington, DC: University Press.
Pennell, C. R. 2000. *Morocco since 1830.* New York: New York University Press.

Waltz, Susan Eileen. 1995. *Human Rights and Reform: The Changing Face of North African Politics.* Berkeley: University of California Press.

Ziba, Mir-Hosseini. 1993. *Marriage on Trial: A Study of Islamic Law.* New York: I. B. Tauris.

Zoubir, Yahia, and Daniel Volman. 1993. *International Dimensions of the Western Sahara Conflict.* Westport, CT: Praeger.

MOZAMBIQUE

GENERAL INFORMATION

The Republic of Mozambique lies on the east coast of Africa, bordered by South Africa and Swaziland to the south, Zimbabwe, Zambia, and Malawi to the west, and Tanzania to the north. Bisected by the Zambezi River and covering 801,590 square kilometers, the country comprises varied terrain of coastal lowlands, central plateaus, and mountains along the western border. The climate varies from tropical to subtropical.

Much of the population of seventeen million follows traditional African customary beliefs, though there are about five million Christians, the majority being Roman Catholics, and four million Muslims. The population is overwhelmingly young (44.8 percent are fourteen years of age or under) and rural (71.4 percent). While Portuguese is the official language, a number of African languages, such as Emakhuwa, Xichangana, Elomwe, Cisena, and Echuwabo are widely spoken. Adult illiteracy remains high, at approximately 60 percent (men 45 percent; women 77 percent). Social welfare remains poor, with an average life expectancy of approximately forty-three years and an infant mortality rate of 145.7 per thousand births. Most Mozambicans live in traditional huts, without electricity, piped water, or sanitation. Modern brick housing accounts for only 10.08 percent of homes. The average number of births per woman is 5.9, and the population growth is estimated at 2.3 percent. In 1991 there were only 435 physicians in the country (37,141 inhabitants per physician). Diseases such as malaria (three million cases in 2000), cholera, and AIDS are pandemic.

Agriculture remains the mainstay of the economy, contributing 33 percent of GDP in 1998 and employing 81 percent of the economically active population. Fishing is the principal export industry, mainly shrimp and prawn, while the principal cash crops include cotton, cashews, sugar cane, and copra. The main subsistence crop is cassava. Industry contributes approximately 18 percent of GDP and employs only 6 percent of the economically active population. Manufacturing is limited to processing agricultural commodities, while mining is limited to coal, salt, and more recently bauxite, graphite, and aluminum. However, significant deposits of natural gas, iron, marble, manganese, uranium, titanium, gold, and other ores and precious stones are known to exist and may be exploited in the future. The country's largest project to date is the construction of the MOZAL aluminum smelter. Electricity is derived mainly from hydroelectric power, particularly from the Cohora Bassa plant on the Zambezi River. Recent improvement and the repair of these facilities will result in the capacity to export electricity to its neighbors. Principal export markets include Zimbabwe, South Africa, Portugal, Spain, India, the United States, and Japan, while imports primarily derive from South Africa, the United States, Japan, and Portugal.

While exports and production remain below levels achieved in the 1970s, the country's recent growth was one of the highest in Africa. GDP increased in real terms by an average of 5.7 percent per year from 1990 to 1998, and 10 percent in 1999. This followed a period of economic stagnation in the 1980s as war and drought took its toll, requiring massive emergency food imports and foreign aid. Those problems were exacerbated by rigid, centrally planned economic policies. Central to the economic turnaround has been the conservative fiscal and monetary policies of the government. The robust economic recovery of the 1990s was, however, threatened in February 2000 when Mozambique suffered massive flooding in the southern and central regions. This resulted in further foreign aid packages and a deferral of all payments due on the country's foreign debt, estimated at U.S.$5,991 million in 1997. The flooding had the effect of dampening growth, which was 2.1 percent in 2000, and resulted in an increase in inflation, measuring 12.7 percent. Mozambique remains one of the poorest countries in the world, with an average annual per capita income of U.S.$222 in 2000.

The continued restoration of the country's infrastructure, structural reform, and liberalization of the economy bode well for the future. While the 2000 floods had a dramatic effect on the economy, prospects of foreign assistance for infrastructure reconstruction are likely to stimulate economic growth.

HISTORY

The history of the law and the judicial system of implementing law are reflected in a consideration of the political turmoil of the past forty years. While Portugal's colonial administration of Mozambique was recognized at the Berlin Congress in 1884–1885, Portugal had, in fact, had varying degrees of influence and control since the fifteenth century. The state became a single economic and administrative unit only in 1941, following the demise of the influence of the British-chartered companies that were granted concession throughout southern Africa. In 1952 the colony of Mozambique became an overseas province and therefore constitutionally incorporated into Portugal.

In the 1960s nationalist groups began to form, fore-

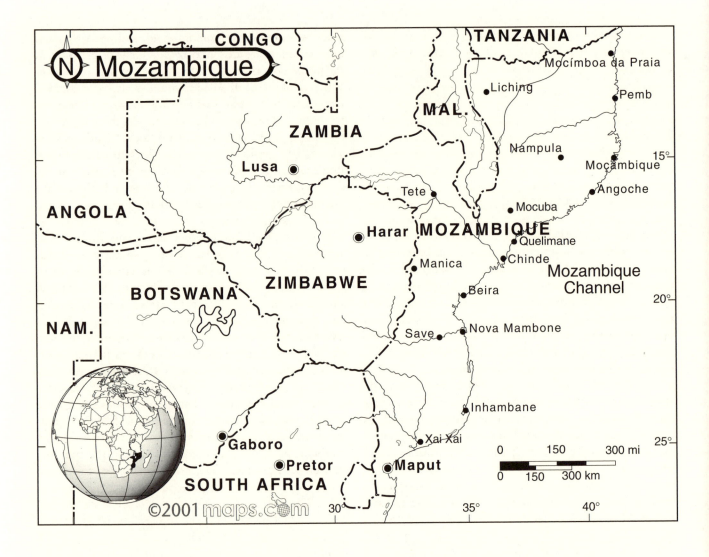

most of which was the Frente de Libertação de Moçambique (Frelimo), led by Eduardo Mondlane until his assassination in 1969 by Portuguese agents. Frelimo took up armed resistance to Portuguese rule, and the following ten years witnessed the increasing expansion of Frelimo influence and a war characterized by atrocities by both belligerents. Following the coup in Lisbon in 1974, talks were undertaken in Zambia between the new Portuguese government and Frelimo to end the decade-long war and grant independence. The white minority attempted to challenge the agreement reached and to establish a white provisional government. That attempt failed, and after a period of transitional government, full independence was achieved on June 25, 1975. Samora Machel, Mondlane's successor, became the first president of the People's Republic of Mozambique. In 1977, Frelimo was reconstituted as a political party governed by Marxist-Leninist principles, and elections were held at all levels of government. Most of the 250,000 whites migrated to Portugal or South Africa, leaving a paucity of educated professionals and experienced administrators.

The speed at which Portugal transferred the administration of Mozambique to Frelimo resulted in political and administrative chaos. This included total disruption in the administration of justice. In an attempt to consolidate its control, Frelimo embarked on a strategy of limiting opposition and controlling the population. That strategy included widespread nationalization, including that of the legal profession; suppression of religious groups and activities; the creation of a National Service for Public Security (SNASP—Serviço Nacional de Segurança Popular) with extensive powers to limit antistate activities; and the establishment of "re-education" camps. To fill the void left by the collapse of the colonial court system, a new system of People's Tribunals, based on the concept of popular justice, was established.

Resistance to the one-party state came from the Resistência Nacional Moçambique (Renamo), which developed from a relatively isolated resistance movement into a formidable insurgency force that caused persistent disruption to rail, road, and petroleum pipeline links. The civil conflict between Frelimo and Renamo was to last for sixteen years, fueled by the inextricable links to conflicts in its neighboring states and the Cold War.

Reduction of the Soviet influence in Africa in the 1980s ushered in a period of ideological change and constitutional reform. In 1983, Machel re-established links with the United States and developed closer ties with the West. In 1984, Mozambique was admitted to the IMF and World Bank. The process of liberalizing the economy fell to Mário Machungo, who was to become the prime minister in 1986, after the creation of the post by the constitutional reforms. Although the country was established as a socialist state at independence, by 1981 the deepening economic crisis in Mozambique forced Machel to announce that many small businesses would return to private ownership. At the same time, numerous reforms were made in an attempt to combat the inefficiency, corruption, and incompetence endemic in the government administration, the military, and the police.

In late 1986, Machel was killed in an air accident, and the minister of foreign affairs, Joaquim Alberto Chissano, was appointed president. Chissano continued with economic liberalization policies and succeeded in establishing increased aid from the West. Domestic economic growth, however, continued to be hampered by the ongoing conflict with Renamo. In 1987, Chissano succeeded in reviving the Nkomati Accord, the agreement with South Africa that each state would not aid the resistance movement in the other state. This contributed to an agreement with South Africa and Portugal to rehabilitate the Cohorra Bassa hydroelectric plant, the improvement of road and rail links between the states, and the opening up of the South African labor market to Mozambican migrant mine workers.

From 1979 to 1990, two separate legal systems existed in Mozambique. While civil and criminal jurisdiction, with its judiciary and police force, was administered by the Ministry of the Interior, the state security system was run by the military and the SNASP. This system was established to deal with security issues resulting from the continued conflict with Renamo. In particular, the disruption of vital services by Renamo led to the promulgation of new laws on crimes against the security of the state that broadened the range of crimes carrying the death penalty, which had been reintroduced in 1979. Now many nonpolitical and nonviolent crimes, such as hoarding and smuggling, were punishable by death. Public flogging was also reintroduced for a range of crimes, such as robbery and black marketeering.

By the late 1980s a military stalemate had developed, owing much to the decline in military support from third states. The global shift to neoliberal economics and democratization opened up the prospect of a negotiated settlement. In 1989, Frelimo renounced its Marxist-Leninist orientation, opened party membership to all Mozambicans, announced the drafting of a new constitution, engaged in reconciliatory discussions with the

Catholic Church, and sought to enter into negotiations with Renamo. An important precursor to ending the conflict was reached in 1990, when Frelimo announced its commitment to a multiparty system and proposed the holding of elections in 1991. This initiated a round of direct talks with Renamo commencing in Rome. On November 30, 1990, a new constitution was adopted, which enshrined the principles of political pluralism, a free-market economy, private property rights, and freedom of the press and included an extensive section on the role of the courts and the protection of human rights. The official name of the country was altered to the Republic of Mozambique. In December 1990, direct talks resulted in an agreement on a partial ceasefire. Unfortunately, a general peace agreement was reached only in October 1992, after protracted and difficult negotiations that led to an agreement on issues such as the constitution of Renamo as a political party and the holding of elections based on proportional representation. The agreement provided for the demobilization of troops, surrendering of weapons, and the creation of a National Defence Force composed of equal numbers of troops from both parties, which would be overseen by the UN Operation in Mozambique (ONUMOZ). This proved to be a difficult and protracted operation, as was the process of repatriating 1.5 million refugees from neighboring states, the resettlement of between four and five million internally displaced persons, and the integration of eighty thousand former combatants into civilian life. Considerable foreign aid was made available for those processes.

After protracted negotiations concerning election laws, the first multiparty presidential and legislative elections were held in October 1994. Chissano secured an outright majority over Renamo's nominee Afonso Dhlakama in the presidential elections, while Frelimo secured 129 of the 250 seats in the assembly. Renamo secured 112 seats, while the electoral coalition of smaller parties secured 9. No opposition party member was appointed to the subsequently formed government under Prime Minister Pascoal Mocumbi. While irregularities did occur in the elections, the results were accepted by all parties. The same, however, cannot be said for the municipal elections (consisting of 23 cities, 116 other district capitals, and 394 administrative posts). Held in June 1998, the elections were boycotted by sixteen opposition parties, including Renamo; with a low voter turnout of only 14.6 percent, it prompted unsuccessful demands for the annulment of the results and undermined the legitimacy of the elected representatives.

In September 1999 presidential and legislative elections were again held, with results similar to those of the elections in 1994 (Chissano being elected president, and Frelimo securing 133 of the 250 seats). This time Dhlakama did not accept the result, alleging widespread fraud, though international monitors ruled that the vote had been free and fair despite some technical difficulties. The Supreme Court, exercising the function of the Constitutional Council that had yet to be established, rejected Renamo's appeal against the results.

While a generalized feeling of war fatigue prevails in the population, the acute tensions and distrust that exist in the political arena mean that renewed conflict is a continual threat. In November 2000, demonstrations organized by Renamo spilled over into violent clashes with police leaving forty dead, including seven police officers.

Poverty and the isolation of rural communities have meant that the benefits of peace have yet to reach all Mozambicans. The fact that Mozambique remains one of the most aid-dependent states in the world subjects it to continual third-party demands, and the construction of a viable, sustainable economy remains delicately poised. There are, however, promising indications. A recent World Bank report on private sector development has hailed the privatization program as the most successful in Africa. Concerns have, however, been raised regarding the extent to which all the population, rather than an elite, are benefiting from privatization and economic liberalization.

LEGAL CONCEPTS

In 1990 the people's assembly unanimously approved the new constitution, which declares Mozambique to be an independent, sovereign, unitary, and democratic state of social justice. Holding that Frelimo had drafted the constitution without its participation, Renamo did not immediately accept it and has sought to modify the constitution on numerous occasions. In particular, Renamo criticized the separation of powers provisions.

Although under the 1975 constitution the Supreme People's Tribunal, as well as other courts established by law, was declared subordinate to the People's Assembly, the rule of law is entrenched in the new constitution and the judiciary declared independent. The new constitution contains numerous human rights provisions, including the prohibition of torture, the abolition of the death penalty, and the principle of nondiscrimination. Similarly, democratic rights were introduced, including the right to vote (electing representatives by universal, direct, secret, and periodic suffrage), to a free press, to form political parties, to own property and to compensation for the taking of property, and to strike; as well as the freedom of assembly, association, and religion. Chapter IV of the constitution provides for the guarantees of rights and freedoms of Mozambicans and provides that "all citizens shall have the right of recourse to the courts against any act which violates their rights recognised by the Constitution and the law," and that "individual rights and freedoms shall be guaranteed by the state." To give effect to these ideals, the right to habeas corpus was introduced;

the use of preventative imprisonment, though permitted, was greatly curtailed; ex post facto laws were prohibited; and defendants were given the right to defense and to legal assistance and aid. Only in time of war, emergency, or siege, and subject to limitations of duration, may these freedoms and guarantees be limited. While the new constitution entrenches these many democratic and human rights, the extent to which they are observed in practice is, however, questionable.

The organs of state consist of a president, an assembly, a council of ministers, an independent judiciary, and a Constitutional Council. The president, who is elected by the majority vote of the people for a five-year term and limited to three consecutive terms, is the head of government and commander-in-chief of the armed forces. While eligible to stand for re-election in 2004, Chissano has indicated that he will not seek a third term, believing that, inasmuch as he was already president in 1990 when the constitution was adopted, to do so would be to violate the spirit of the law. The president is given broad powers in directing governmental activity, national defense, and foreign relations. These powers include the power to call general elections, dissolve the assembly, convene and preside at sessions of the council of ministers, appoint the prime minister, and promulgate laws and order their publication. The president may return a bill to the assembly for re-examination but must promulgate the law if the assembly then approves the bill by a two-thirds majority. The president is also empowered to appoint, exonerate, and dismiss the attorney general and deputy attorney general of the republic, and appoint the president and deputy president of the Supreme Court, the president of the Constitutional Council, and the president of the Administrative Court. These appointments are subject to ratification by the assembly. The assembly, the highest legislative body of the state, is made up of between 200 and 250 deputies elected to a five-year term, while the council of ministers is the government of the state.

While the constitution provides for an independent judiciary, the executive (and by extension Frelimo) dominates the judiciary, which lacks adequate resources and is chronically understaffed, plagued by corruption, and largely ineffectual.

The nascent legal system of Mozambique is emerging from a complex mix of African customary law, Portuguese colonial codes, and norms arising from the postindependence legal system based on popular justice. The new constitution provides that existing laws shall, insofar as they are not inconsistent with the constitution, remain in force until expressly revoked or altered, the effect of which was that many of the colonial Portuguese codes continue to apply, particularly in areas such as business and commerce. With the dearth of qualified legal professionals following independence and the ensuing conflict, many of these laws remained unaltered for many years, and some continue to apply in theory if not in practice.

The dismantling of the colonial state apparatus included the dismantling of the legal system and the introduction of a system based on popular justice, with the People's Tribunals as the center of judicial activity. The functioning of the tribunals is underpinned by the concepts of popular participation and informalism and the central dispute resolution mechanisms of mediation and conciliation. In the postindependence state, the tribunals are also concerned with social engineering, particularly with regard to the development of national unity. In this regard, traditional and customary African law is regarded as oppressive and therefore has been abolished as a recognized source of law in the courts. From the activities of these tribunals have emerged new norms in areas of immediate social intercourse. These include, for example, the endorsement of de facto unions as the basis for family law.

However, as the lay judges are granted a wide discretion, underpinned by the guiding concept of "good sense and justice," customary African law continues to subsist. This system has, however, resulted in an uneven development of norms throughout the country.

Although ownership of land is vested in the state, and it cannot be sold, mortgaged, or otherwise encumbered or alienated, the state grants title and conditions for the use of land to individuals or collectives for up to fifty years. In doing so, the state does recognize rights acquired through inheritance or occupation. This reflects the ideal that the use and enjoyment of land are the rights of all Mozambicans as well as a universal means for the creation of wealth and social well-being. This legacy of the socialist era has, however, spawned corruption and inhibited growth and investment, since land cannot be used as collateral for finance. Consequently, land rights are currently a politically sensitive area.

Despite constitutional provisions regarding the equality of men and women in all spheres, the civil and commercial codes contradict one another and the constitution. In terms of family law, wives and daughters require male approval for all legal undertakings, such as entering into a lease, obtaining loans, starting a business, or contracting for goods and services. While a new land law introduced in 1997 permits women to exercise rights over land, ignorance of the law and entrenched traditional practice continue to undermine women's rights.

In terms of business law, much has been influenced by demands for private-sector development by external agencies. With the lack of qualified lawyers following independence, little was done to alter the existing Portuguese codes, and by the early 1990s the legislation covering company law, corporate finance, and bankruptcy was still largely based on those outdated codes, together with supplementary legislation relating to the planned economy of the late 1970s. The inadequate capacity of the legal and judicial system has hampered economic development in Mozambique, and a concerted effort has been made to address this issue. Frelimo's commitment to a democratic society and a free-market economy in the 1990s and the World Bank's requirement for private sector development have necessitated a complete revision of the business law, a process that has been ongoing since the launch of the World Bank's 1992 Development Credit Agreement on Capacity Building: Public Sector and Legal Institutions Development Project. This project includes the provision of funds to strengthen and develop the legal reform process, particularly in business law, and to conduct seminars and workshops in areas of proposed legislative amendment, such as in corporate law, banking law, and mortgages and securities law. This has begun to bear fruit with recent tax and customs reforms and the introduction of legislation governing investment. By 1997, however, the project report found that Mozambique still lacked a comprehensive reform process, resulting in serious deficiencies in the legal system. While some of the problems have been addressed, it was concluded that the donor aid in this sphere was not commensurate with the magnitude and character of the system's difficulties.

Given the inadequacies of the system, it is not surprising that recourse to the judicial system for commercial disputes is rare. In 1999 the government recognized alternative dispute resolution and introduced legislation to govern arbitration between domestic and international companies based on the UNCITRAL model. For purely domestic disputes, the legislation is considerably wider and includes provision for arbitration in noncommercial matters. In 1998, Mozambique acceded to the New York Convention on the Recognition and Enforcement of Foreign Arbitral Awards.

Freedom of the press in Mozambique has made great progress. While state-owned media generally reflect the views of the ruling party, particularly TV Mozambique, reporting has become increasingly transparent, particularly with regard to Radio Mozambique, whose coverage is regarded as generally fair and unbiased. Since 1992 numerous periodicals and broadcasters have been licensed, and their criticism of the government has largely been tolerated.

The constitution provides for the right of free association and the right to strike. The 1991 labor law implements these rights and, in particular, forbids retribution against strikers, hiring of substitute workers, and lockouts. In 1991 the main national trade union (OTM) purportedly severed its political links with Frelimo, though doubts remained as to its independence, resulting in 1998 in the formation of the Confederation of Free and Independent Trade Unions. Specific labor disputes are generally arbitrated through special workers' committees, formally recognized by the government. Current trade union concerns relate to fears that free trade zones created in 1998 would result in less favorable labor rights because of government incentives offered to foreign investors. On the other hand, foreign investors are concerned with the introduction of legislation limiting the number of foreign workers in the country, forcing them to employ unqualified nationals for key management positions. Forced and bonded labor in rural areas remains a concern, as does child labor.

CURRENT STRUCTURE

There are two complementary formal justice systems in Mozambique: the civil/criminal system and the military system. The highest judicial organ of Mozambique is the Supreme Court, which administers the civil/criminal system and which has jurisdiction throughout the national territory as a court of original and appellate jurisdiction. Although the Ministry of Defence administers the military courts, the Supreme Court may hear appeals from these courts. The Supreme Court is composed of professional judges who are appointed by the president after consultation with the Supreme Council of the Judiciary and elected judges who are chosen by the assembly. The latter have jurisdiction in primary trial court matters only, and matters of law may be dealt with only by the professional judges.

The lower courts consist of provincial and district courts, which deal with civil and criminal matters, as well as the local customary courts and traditional authorities arising from the previous forms of popular tribunals, which tend to deal mostly with domestic issues and some petty crimes. While there are provincial courts in all provinces, few are staffed by trained judges, despite the fact that the Judicial Magistrates Statute requires a law degree. District courts have yet to be established in all districts.

The Administrative Court controls the legality of administrative acts and supervises the legality of public expenditure. In fulfilling this mandate, the court adjudicates contentious matters arising from administrative acts and procedures and appeals against decisions by organs of the state, its office holders, agents, and employees. Apart from the Supreme Court and other courts of justice, the constitution also provides for courts-martial, customs courts, fiscal courts, maritime courts, and labor courts.

The judiciary has been criticized as being corrupt, biased, and unproductive. In the provincial courts of Mozambique, a backlog of cases has developed, with reports that cases dating back to 1982 have yet to be resolved. The professionalism of judges has also recently been called into question, in the 2001 report of the Human Rights and Development Association, Mozambique's leading human rights body. The increasing pressure to cleanse the judiciary has resulted in twenty-four judges being expelled since 1995.

Structure of Mozambican Courts

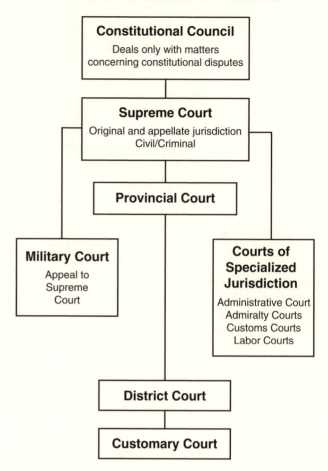

The Office of the Attorney General includes the Office of the Public Prosecutor, a hierarchically organized magistracy that represents the state before the courts and that controls the legality and duration of detentions, initiates criminal prosecutions, enforces criminal sentences, and ensures the legal defense of minors and of absent or incapacitated persons. The Office of the Attorney General has, unfortunately, suffered from pervasive corruption and a general lack of professionalism and dedication among its staff. In 2001 a new attorney general was appointed, who vowed to overhaul the system and embarked on a major shake-up of provincial offices. This has included the institution of disciplinary and criminal proceedings against staff. The level of corruption that existed is exemplified in the warrant of arrest for the previous attorney general in connection with the country's biggest fraud case, involving the theft of U.S.$14 million from the Commercial Bank of Mozambique at the time of its privatization. The fight against corruption has recently turned violent; a leading deputy attorney general heading corruption investigations was shot in 2001.

The police and correctional services in Mozambique are, unfortunately, in a deplorable state. A 2001 Human Rights and Development Association report revealed that police were operating under very poor conditions. For example, the Maputo Provincial Command has only two operational vehicles. The police have also been criticized for lack of professionalism, arbitrary abuse of power, indiscriminate use of firearms, and arbitrary detentions. Reversing the trend in previous years, 2000 saw an increase in the number of reports of police abuse, including torture, extrajudicial executions, and deaths in detention. Reports of detainees being denied legal representation and long periods of detention before charges are brought are numerous. This is as much a result of citizens not knowing their constitutional rights as the inadequacy of police training. Resources are also wholly inadequate for providing appropriate legal representation. The National Police Affairs Commission, created to ensure that the police operate within the terms of the constitution, has proved ineffective. Attempts have been made recently to address these problems. In 1999 higher standards for the police were imposed, including entrance qualifications, compulsory human rights training, and higher salaries. In September 1999 a police service academy was opened for training of mid- to high-ranking officers.

In 2000 a UN Development Program report revealed that prisons were extensively overcrowded and conditions deteriorating. The Maputo central prison, built to house 800, currently contains 2,407 prisoners, while in Zambesia, the central prison, built to house 90, currently holds 686, of whom 446 are still awaiting trial. Conditions in the maximum security prison have deteriorated to the extent that the sewerage system no longer functions and the roof is close to collapse. Corruption is also clearly evident in the number of escapes from prison, apparently with the connivance of prison guards. In May 1999, an interministerial review committee was established to investigate the problem of the high percentage of detainees in prisons that were awaiting trial, often for extended periods, and it appears that some releases resulted.

SPECIALIZED JUDICIAL BODIES

The Constitutional Council is an organ with special jurisdiction on legal questions arising from or related to the constitution, including the power to adjudicate the constitutionality and legality of legislative and regulatory acts of the state organs, settle conflicts of jurisdiction between organs of sovereign authority, and pronounce upon the legality of referenda. It also has the power to supervise the electoral process. The president, president of the assembly, prime minister, and attorney general have standing before the council. There is no appeal against decisions of the Constitutional Council. The council has, however, yet to be established, as its functions are exercised on an interim basis by the Supreme Court.

STAFFING

Given Mozambique's tumultuous political history, it is not surprising that the provision of legal education, the emergence of a private legal profession, and the development of a viably independent judiciary are relatively new phenomena. Although the first university, Universidade de Lourenço Marques, was established in 1963, the provision of legal education remained abroad and primarily the domain of white Portuguese. With the flight of white professionals after independence in 1975, only about twenty-five lawyers remained in the country and an urgent need arose to establish a postindependence judicial infrastructure. A central concept in this reconstitution of the legal profession was its nationalization.

In January 1975, the university was reconstituted as the Eduardo Mondlane University, with provision for legal education. The latter proved a challenging task, given the lack of legal expertise, the constitutional uncertainties at independence, and the difficulties associated with revising and nationalizing the Portuguese codes that prevailed. These problems were compounded by the difficulty in finding promising students, given that illiteracy rates in 1975 stood at approximately 95 percent. The shortage of qualified legal personnel led to a shortening of the period of full-time education to two years and the immediate employment of students as judges and prosecutors. The political turmoil of the 1980s led to the closure of the law school from 1983 to 1987, resulting in a further dearth of legal professionals. The development of the People's Tribunals staffed by lay members of the community filled the void to some extent, though qualified professionals were still required to explain new legislation and overcome the problems of reporting, in light of the high illiteracy rates.

By 1991 the number of legally qualified professionals had risen to only ninety. This modest increase was a result of the World Bank's 1989 project to strengthen the legal and judicial capacity of Mozambique, which included the provision of on-the-job training schemes in legal drafting and research, particularly for the Legal Department of the Ministry of Finance, and the reopening of the law school in August 1987. The reopening of the school had much to do with pressure from those students who were forced to interrupt their studies in 1983. In 1988 the first intake of ninety new students were admitted, and the average yearly intake has remained at around one hundred. There has been a steady increase in the number of students qualifying in law, and the law school today consists of 770 students and 39 professors. Unfortunately, the university lacks the funds to increase its capacity further, resulting in the establishment since 1996 of three private law schools catering to 150 students each year.

In 1992 a World Bank project was initiated that has a primary aim of building and maintaining capacity in key public institutions and the strengthening of the legal infrastructure. In particular, funding was provided for expanding legal education, preservice and in-service training for lawyers, the creation of computerized legal databases and library collections, and improving the public administration of legal institutions. This program has achieved some success, though many problems remain. There are currently about eight hundred lawyers in Mozambique, and their numbers are expected to rise to about twenty-two hundred over the next ten years. Many of the increasing number of law graduates enter the more lucrative private sector, resulting in a continued dearth of professionals in the public sector. This includes legal education, where approximately 70 percent of teaching staff at the university are in part-time private practice. Those who do enter the public sector are appointed as judges or prosecutors after a short-term training course organized by the Supreme Court and the Attorney General's Office. There are a total of about 160 judges throughout the country.

Supreme Court nominations are prepared by the Higher Judicial Magistrates' Council (CSMJ—the body responsible for overseeing professional behavior among magistrates), which is generally constituted by Frelimo party members. The list of nominations is presented to the president, who then presents his choices to the assembly for approval. No assembly approval is needed for other judicial appointments. Judges of the Supreme Court must be over thirty-five years of age. They hold appointments for life, except for removal upon impeachment or in cases of mental disability, notorious lassitude, or other infamous official behavior.

IMPACT

The 1990 Constitution introduced an extensive section on human and democratic rights, but these remain remote from Mozambican realities. While partial adherence to the rule of law for orderly political competition has provided the framework within which Mozambique has achieved some success in terms of political stability, difficulties in building a comprehensive legal system in Mozambique have resulted in considerable credibility problems in Mozambique's ethnically and linguistically heterogeneous population. These difficulties have arisen not only because some of the laws and procedures are obsolete, having originated in the colonial era, but also because of endemic levels of corruption and incompetence at all levels of the judiciary, police force, and correctional services. It is reported that many victims of crimes do not seek police assistance because of the usual demands for bribes to investigate the matter. Dissatisfaction with the police and the judiciary and rising levels of crime have resulted in continuing mob and vigilante killings. The centralization of legal expertise and institutions in Maputo has also resulted in considerable regional imbalance and

differentiation in legal practice. These symptoms led the incumbent attorney general to declare, in early 2001, that "the Mozambican legal system is sick!" The cure currently being administered is a reconcerted effort to reform the judiciary, streamline and simplify regulations, improve enforcement mechanisms, reduce government bureaucracy, and improve salary and training for government officials.

Craig Forrest

See also Administrative Tribunals; Alternative Dispute Resolution; Civil Law; Constitutional Law; Customary Law; Human Rights Law; Indigenous and Folk Legal Systems; Lay Judiciaries; Portugal

References and further reading
Gunderson, Aase. 1992. "Popular Justice in Mozambique: Between State Law and Folk Law." *Social and Legal Studies* 1, no. 2: 257–282.
Hall, M., and T. Young. 1991. "Recent Constitutional Developments in Mozambique." *Journal of African Law* 35, nos. 1 and 2: 102–115.
Hanlon, Joseph. 1996. *Peace without Profit: How the IMF Blocks Rebuilding in Mozambique.* Portsmouth, NH: Oxford and Heinemann.
Harvey, Charles, and Mark Robinson. 1995. *The Design of Economic Reforms in the Context of Political Liberalization: The Experiences of Mozambique, Senegal and Uganda.* Discussion Paper 353. Brighton: Institute of Development Studies, University of Sussex.
Landua, Luis. 1998. *Rebuilding the Mozambique Economy: Assessment of a Development Partnership.* Washington, DC: International Bank for Reconstruction and Development.
McQueen, Norrie. 1997. *The Decolonisation of Portuguese Africa: Metropolitan Revolution and the Dissolution of Empire.* London and New York: Longman.
Newitt, Malyn. 1995. *A History of Mozambique.* London: Hurst.
Penvenne, J. M. 2000. "Confronting Leviathan: Mozambique since Independence." *International Journal of African Historical Studies* 33, no. 1: 198–200.
Pitcher, M. A. 1996. "Recreating Colonialism or Reconstructing the State? Privatisation and Politics in Mozambique." *Journal of Southern African Studies* 22, no. 1: 49–74.
Sachs, A., and G. H. Welch. 1990. *Liberating the Law: Creating Popular Justice in Mozambique.* London: Zed Books.
Seidman, Ann, Robert B. Seidman, and Theodosio Uate. 1999. "Assessing Legislation to Serve the Public Interest: Experiences from Mozambique." *Statute Law Review* 20: 1–34.
Seleti, Yonah. 2000. "The Public in the Exorcism of the Police in Mozambique: Challenges of Institutional Democratization." *Journal of Southern African Studies* 26, no. 2: 349–364.
Synge, Richard. 1997. *Mozambique: UN Peacekeeping in Action, 1992–1994.* Washington, DC: U.S. Institute of Peace Press.

MYANMAR
See Burma

N

NAFTA

See Dispute Resolution under Regional Trade Agreements

NAMIBIA

COUNTRY INFORMATION

Namibia, formerly called Southwest Africa, is a country of 824,292 square kilometers (318,261 square miles). It is located in the southwestern part of Africa along the Atlantic Coast and shares borders with Angola to the north, Botswana to the east, and South Africa to the south. A small northeastern strip of the territory extends the country's boundaries to Zambia, touching on the Zambezi River. Three topographic zones form the Namibian landmass. A coastal plain 1,600 kilometers in length and with a width ranging from 65 to 160 kilometers stretches from north to south along the Atlantic frontier. Known as the Namib Desert, this region is dry, with mountains of sand dunes forming beautiful scenery in place of vegetation cover. The average annual rainfall is less than 100 millimeters. Going from the Namib Desert toward the interior of the country, the topography rises into a plateau range dotted with mountains of various heights. Further east, the topography slopes to yet another desert, the Kalahari.

Namibia has an ethnically and racially diverse population, estimated to be 1.77 million in 1999. Of that number, whites made up around 5 to 6 percent, and blacks accounted for 94 to 96 percent. The major ethnic groups of the country are the Ovambo (who make up 50 percent of the population), the Kavango (9 percent), the Herero (7 percent), and the Damara (7 percent). With a population density of two inhabitants per square kilometer, Namibia appears to be sparsely populated. That is a misimpression, though, because the deserts that make up the eastern and western parts of the country are uninhabitable; consequently, most of the population is concentrated on the plateau. Over half of the country's inhabitants and two-thirds of the black population living on the plateau reside in its northern third because that area is better drained. The small white population lives on and controls the remaining two-thirds of the plateau to the south, which is also well drained.

Namibia has done relatively well economically as compared to other countries in Africa. Per capita gross domestic product (GDP) was $4,300 in 1999. The economy's performance on the index of growth has been mixed. After a poor showing during the early 1980s, the economy was on the way to recovery in the mid-1980s. However, economic growth was very inconsistent throughout the 1990s. The economy grew at 5.1 percent in 1991, but that rate fell to 3.5 percent in 1992 and 2 percent in 1993. In 1994, it registered a 6.6 percent growth, but again, the rate fell over subsequent years—to 3.3 percent in 1995, 2.9 percent in 1996, and 1.8 percent in 1997.

Namibia's economy, like that of most Third World countries, is highly dependent on primary products, mainly in the areas of mining, agriculture, and fishing. Mining contributed 13 percent of the country's GDP in 1997, down from 50 percent in 1980. That sector also employed 7,700 people in 1998, as compared to 21,000 in 1977, and made up 60 percent of the country's total exports in 1997. Agriculture's share of GDP was 10.5 percent in 1997, up from 7.3 percent a decade earlier. In the same year (1997), it employed 44 percent of the labor force. Because of the fragile nature of the land, livestock dominates the bulk of agricultural activities. Manufacturing accounted for around 13.7 percent of GDP in 1997. Most of the activities in this sector involve producing basic goods for the domestic market and processing the country's main primary products for export—minerals, fish, and meat. Although the fishing sector had experienced significant decline before independence in 1990 due to overexploitation, the new government of Sam Nujoma moved to reinvigorate it in order to diversify the economy and tap the country's special advantages in that area. Namibia's principal exports are diamonds, uranium, zinc, tin, lithium, silver, copper, beef, mutton, goat, and fish. The unemployment rate in 1997 was around 22 percent in a labor force of 500,000, while inflation was 8 percent.

Despite the fact that Namibia's economy seems not to have the numerous problems found in many other coun-

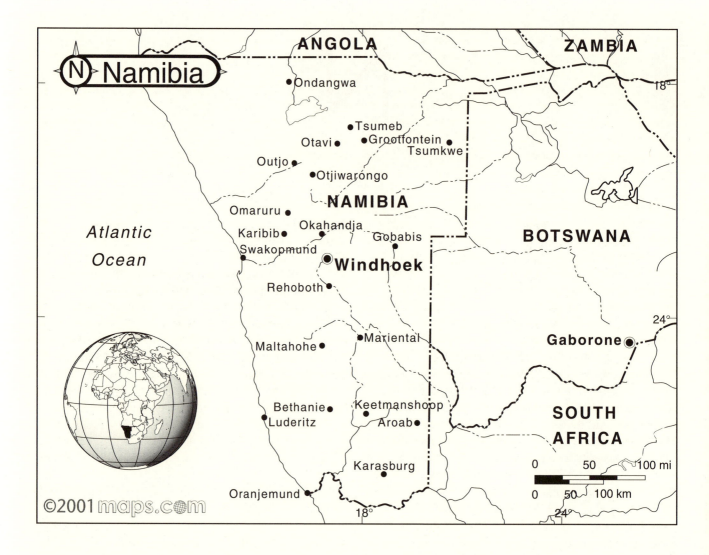

©2001 maps.com

tries in Africa, all is not well. In the area of income, for example, the GDP per capita, which is $3,500, is a misleading figure. In addition to earning less than whites, blacks have been forced out of their lands by white ranchers in two-thirds of the south and central plateau region, and they have had to leave farming and ranching work to pursue cheap wage work on white commercial ranches and in the mines. In addition, absentee landlords (most of whom live in South Africa) own more than half of Namibia's commercial farms; unemployment among blacks is much higher than among whites; and demobilized former warriors from the independence struggle have not been completely integrated in the workforce. The economy is also heavily dependent on South Africa. The return of Walvis Bay, the country's only port, by South Africa in 1994 and the introduction of a new Namibian dollar to replace the South African rand have been steps toward easing such dependence. Still, South African firms dominate Namibia's economy, and roads and rail services connecting Namibia to the world go through South Africa. Meanwhile, the new government of Sam Nujoma, who had adhered to a socialist ideol-

ogy during the liberation struggle and promised to undertake massive land redistribution, has abandoned the socialist agenda in favor of a market economy built on attracting private investments—and been too slow in pursuing the latter.

HISTORY

Namibia is a country of many ethnic groups, all of which settled the country at different times. The San, who are the original inhabitants of the territory, had no statelike organization. Instead, they were organized around kinship groups, with hunting and gathering as their principal livelihood. By 1000 C.E., the San had been joined by other groups, among them the Ovambo and Herero. The Ovambo, the largest of the new groups, were farmers. They came from the Okavango region of southeastern Angola and settled in Namibia in the better-drained and wooded northern plateau area. Unlike the San, the Ovambo had developed highly organized political institutions to regulate their society. The Herero, who were mainly a pastoral people with a clan-based social organization, penetrated Ovambo-settled areas and installed themselves to the south in the central plateau region. The Mbanderu, another group related to the Herero, settled to the southeast, toward northwestern Botswana. Migration from the south in the mid- to late 1600s completed the dynamics of indigenous African settlement in Namibia. The main group from the south was the Nama, a Khoikhoi-speaking pastoral people who were being pushed northward from their land in the western cape region of South Africa by Boer trekkers during the later part of the seventeenth century.

By 1884, when Germany laid claim to the area now known as Namibia, various groups having different modes of social and political organization and engaging in a variety of occupations inhabited the territory. To further its aims of extending its hegemony to the hinterland, Germany would later exploit the ethnic rivalry between the pastoral Herero and their Nama counterparts over control of pasture areas in the central plateau. In addition, conflicts flared between the Herero and the German settlers and traders who seized their pasture lands and engaged in cattle-trading schemes that increasingly depleted the Herero herds. Finally, in 1904, the Herero rose up against the German traders and settlers and killed over 100 of them. In the ensuing fight, all but 16,000 Herero were killed, out of a total population of 80,000. Most of the Herero then fled into the harsh Kalahari, where only a few would survive. Similar conflicts between German settlers and traders and the Nama also caused a significant loss of lives among the latter group. At the end of these wars, Namibia became an uncontested German colony. Thereafter, German political structures were instituted in the territory, and the exploitation of its resources was put in motion. German rule was particularly harsh, characterized by forced labor, land seizure, wrenching taxation, and inhuman treatment of blacks.

German control of Namibia was, however, short-lived. With the outbreak of World War I, newly independent South Africa invaded the area, defeated the Germans, and took control of the territory. South Africa's control was a much welcomed relief for the blacks, who thought their situation would improve considerably. That control was formally agreed to by the League of Nations under the Mandate Agreement. The Mandate Agreement required South Africa and other countries that were given control over the former colonies of the defeated powers to promote the development and welfare of the indigenous peoples—a step toward independence for the territories.

However, rather than follow the Mandate Agreement, South Africa ruled Namibia as a colony. It exploited Namibia's resources, used the territory as a market for South African products, and failed to build infrastructures that would link Namibia to the outside world—or make it independent of South Africa. In fact, all connections between Namibia and the wider world, such as roads, railways, and air and sea transport, went through South Africa. Further, South African farmers and commercial ranchers moved into the central and southern plateau areas and completed the task that German settlers had started by evicting all but a few indigenous pastoral inhabitants; these individuals were pushed into small enclaves where they could no longer meaningfully engage in pastoral life. Deprived of their traditional economic activities, black Namibians came to depend on wage labor on white ranches, mines, and farms. When the National Party came to power in South Africa in 1948 and began to aggressively pursue an official policy of separate development for the races in South Africa—the policy known as apartheid—it regarded Namibia as a South African province and instituted apartheid there as well, despite protests and agitations from black Namibians.

As South Africa moved to institutionalize apartheid and other repressive policies, the United Nations, which replaced the League of Nations, refused to grant South African authorization to annex Namibia, as it had repeatedly requested. In retaliation, South Africa refused to comply with the UN demand to transfer the status of its administration to that of a UN trust territory, which was what all League of Nations mandates had become after World War II. In response to the absence of action by South Africa in regard to Namibia's status, the UN took a number of decisions designed to force it out of the territory. In October 1966, the UN General Assembly revoked South Africa's mandate over Namibia. The following year, the United Nations appointed the Council for Namibia to serve as a transitional government for the territory, and in 1969, the UN Security Council called on South Africa to withdraw from the territory altogether. These actions did not, however, seem to have any impact on South Africa, as in 1969, it declared Namibia as its fifth province. It then moved full-swing to convert most of the native reserves into *bantustans* (tribal homelands), as it had in South Africa proper. In the 1970s, it began to undertake what it considered its own political reforms in the territory. But in 1973, the United Nations recognized the Southwest African People's Liberation Organization (SWAPO) as the authentic representative of the Namibian people. This action was followed by the appointment of a UN commissioner for Namibia in the same year.

SWAPO was an offshoot of the Ovamboland People's Organization (OPO) and had been formed in 1957 by migrant workers demanding better conditions. It became involved in activist activities against the introduction of apartheid in Namibia. In 1960, the OPO reconstituted itself into a political organization after realizing that only political change would accomplish its goals. Its strategy, which was military, political, and diplomatic, intensified during the 1970s and 1980s. Its military engagement of South Africa's forces and death squads kept the pressure on that country for over twenty years, while its diplomatic activities kept the Namibian question alive internationally.

The collapse of the Portuguese colonies in Africa changed the context of South Africa's rule in Namibia. When a civil war erupted in Angola after the withdrawal of Portugal, the Popular Movement for the Liberation of Angola (MPLA)—whose control of Angola was being challenged by the Union for the Total Independence of Angola (UNITA)—brought in Cuban troops to help in its war efforts. UNITA was getting its support from South Africa and the Western powers. As SWAPO intensified its military activities against the South African defense forces, South Africa started launching attacks against SWAPO bases in Angola. These attacks were also meant to destabilize the Angolan government, in support of UNITA. As Western governments made calls for the withdrawal of Cuban troops from Angola, South Africa increasingly justified its presence in Namibia as necessary to contain communist expansion in southern Africa, even though the United Nations passed Resolution 435 calling for UN-supervised elections in the country. However, delays by South Africa led to no movement on this front until action was forced by an event in 1987. That event was the encirclement of South African troops in Cuito Cuanavale, a town in southeastern Angola where Angola's air defense systems were installed—systems that could be used to prevent South African aircraft from delivering supplies to UNITA forces. Faced with this predicament, South Africa agreed to a cease-fire brokered by the United States and the Soviet Union. As part of the agreement that was negotiated, South Africa committed to withdrawing from Namibia. In exchange, Angola agreed to send Cuban troops home. Further, UN-supervised elections would be held in 1989 to elect a constituent assembly, which would then write a constitution in preparation for independence, slated for March 1990. The assembly would also select the country's first president. In the election, SWAPO won 57 percent of the votes cast, and its leader, Sam Nujoma, became Namibia's first president.

LEGAL CONCEPTS

Namibia has a republican constitution and a unitary system of government vested in a bicameral legislature (the National Assembly and the National Council); an executive branch headed by the president, who is both head of state and head of government; and an independent judiciary headed by the Supreme Court. The governmental system fuses parliamentary and presidential features, similar to those of France. The constitution requires the popular election of the president, who must appoint his or her cabinet from among members of the National Assembly; these ministers are then responsible to the assembly and to the president. The National Council is viewed

as a means of providing equality among the regions, but it also plays the important role of giving the National Assembly a second chance to reexamine legislation. Election to the National Assembly is by proportional representation, based on party lists from a national constituency. Members are elected to five-year terms. Members of the National Council, by contrast, are selected from among the thirteen Regional Councils. Each Regional Council selects two members of the National Assembly, who serve six-year terms. Although unitary, the political system is very decentralized administratively. The constitution makes provisions for the creation of the Regional Councils, whose members are elected. However, the Regional Councils have no independent power and act only to implement matters delegated to them by the president or by acts of the National Assembly within their regions. Nevertheless, they also select from among their members, as mentioned, two individuals to represent their regions in the National Council, and they serve the important function of making demands for their regions within the national institutions. As leader of government business in the National Assembly, the prime minister (PM) performs the role that PMs traditionally perform in parliamentary systems—that is, the role of spokesperson for ruling party, defending and pushing the state's agenda through Parliament. There is also an independent ombudsman, an autonomous position that, until the recent wave of democratization around the world, had not featured prominently in governmental organizations.

The constitution adopted in 1990 by the Constituent Assembly (which became Namibia's first National Assembly) is officially the supreme law of the country. Viewed from the perspective of constitutional governments, Namibia's constitution could be considered as a standard document of its type, but it also reflects the circumstances under which the state came into existence and the aspirations of the people. It provides for a secular democratic state, with guarantees of the basic rights of citizens. One whole chapter of the constitution, containing some twenty articles, is devoted to the rights that citizens enjoy under the constitution. Although one can see similarities here with the U.S. Constitution, Namibia's experiences under the apartheid system of South Africa make what could be referred to as its own Bill of Rights more than a copycat document. Among the various rights enumerated are: due process rights; property rights; privacy rights; the right to education; and freedom of speech, religion, movement, press, and association. It also guarantees the protection of citizens from discrimination of all types, including apartheid (the discrimination against which the founders fought), as well as the protection of life, human dignity, and so forth. Reflecting a commitment to forever guard the country from the experiences it suffered under apartheid, the constitution allows no amendment or repeal of the articles of the Bill of Rights. The constitution is also noted for the goals it sets for the state, including the economic principles the state should pursue.

Although SWAPO controlled the Constituent Assembly when the constitution was being written, the final product was surprisingly moderate ideologically, given SWAPO's socialist bent. For example, it commits Namibia to the principles of a mixed economy made up of public, private, joint public-private, cooperative, and small-scale family-type ownerships. And to cement SWAPO's relationship with its base, the constitution also emphasizes the state's commitment to the welfare of the people, with reference to legislation and actions that would be directed toward promoting equality of opportunity for women, ensuring the health and strength of workers, encouraging the formation of independent trade unions, protecting workers' rights, promoting citizens' access to public facilities, and so on. The importance given the role of the state in the economy is much different than might have been expected, given the trend that was already taking place in Africa as the World Bank forced governments to privatize their economies.

The separation of powers, judiciary review, and an independent and impartial judiciary are concepts vaguely applicable to the Namibian political system, but they have not yet been tested in practice. The very fact that cabinet ministers must be appointed from within the National Assembly eliminates the existence of a separation of executive and legislative powers. Thus, the separation of powers exists only between the judiciary and the legislature and between the executive and the judiciary. The judiciary is empowered to rule on constitutional issues and to issue an opinion on a constitutional interpretation of a bill by the president. The constitution also provides for an independent and impartial judiciary. However, this principle is being challenged in a case currently under way: The argument is being made that the independence of the judiciary is threatened by the fact that politicians in the Ministry of Justice are responsible for transferring judges. The implication is that officials in the Ministry of Justice, which is part of the executive branch of government, could use their power to transfer judges as a means to punish or reward judges whose decisions they like or do not like. A ruling on the case has not been issued. However, it is likely that the decision will endorse these arguments, as a similar challenge in South Africa succeeded.

Namibia's legal system is based on a complex mixture of South African law and, through it, Roman-Dutch law; British common law practices; and indigenous African customary and common law. Because the bulk of Namibia's colonial experiences were under South African colonialism, postcolonial Namibia draws on the common law of South Africa for direction. Meanwhile, South Africa itself looks for guidance on the common law and practices of the Roman-Dutch and English systems. This reflects the importance of the 150-plus years of Dutch control until 1806, which was followed by 100-plus years of British control that lasted until 1910. However, despite statutory recognition of the importance of the principles of English common law in regard to evidence and mercantile issues, Roman-Dutch common law is authoritative in South Africa. In another twist, English common law is followed in the Cape Province on matters of insurance and shipping. This might be explained by the fact that the majority of the whites in the Cape Province are English, while in the rest of South Africa, the white population is dominated by those who trace their origins to Holland. Because this second group also controlled South Africa when it became independent, the tendency was to lean toward Dutch common law practices.

Namibia's legal practices and constitution recognize the common and customary laws of the country's indigenous peoples. Precedent in the recognition of the customary laws and practices of indigenous Africans already exists in South Africa (and, for that matter, in other parts of Africa colonized by the British). But the recognition of indigenous people's customary and common law practices in postcolonial Africa should also be seen as a desire by leaders of the new states to restore some elements of the eroded influences of those very laws. For Namibia, that could be interpreted as only one element in the recognition of indigenous dispute resolution mechanisms and regimes and the interest in reconciling them with the efforts to build a new Namibia—after more than a century of efforts to destroy such regimes under foreign control. The establishment of the Council of Traditional Authorities, which advises the president on traditional matters, is another effort to reconcile the activities of the modern state and those of the various groups within its borders. But efforts to recognize and enhance common and customary laws and institutions only take place to the extent that they do not conflict with national laws and institutions. When conflicts do arise, the National Assembly is empowered to invoke its supremacy over all other laws except the constitution and enact measures that take precedence over the customary and common law practices.

The final foundation of Namibia's legal system is the National Assembly. It is given the foremost role in law making and empowered to "initiate, approve, or decide to hold a referendum." Several other key roles for this body are stipulated in the constitution as well. Furthermore, although the constitution does not discuss the impeachment of the president or the circumstances under which impeachment would take place, the National Assembly could invoke certain of its powers to impeach the country's president. For example, it is empowered to "take such steps as it considers expedient to uphold and defend the Constitution and the laws of Namibia and to advance the objective of Namibian independence." It is also authorized to "receive reports on the activities of the Executive, and to require senior officials to appear before it to account for, or explain any of their acts, and programs from time to time."

CURRENT STRUCTURE

Namibia is a very young country in terms of the duration of its independence and hence the duration of its constitution, having had an independent constitution only since 1990. For that reason, any discussion of the justice sector is necessarily limited. Essentially, the structure and functioning of this sector are a holdover from the colonial era (in this case, the South African system), reinforced by the 1990 Constitution. The principal provisions in the constitution regarding the administration of justice address the court system, the selection of judges, the attorney general, the prosecutor general, the powers of the courts, and the ombudsman. The court system in Namibia is organized with the Supreme Court at the top, the High Court below the Supreme Court, and Magistrates' Courts below the High Court.

Unlike the High Court and the Supreme Court, which are established by the constitution, Magistrates' Courts are established by acts of Parliament in various districts. The High Court is presided over by the judge president and has original jurisdiction to hear cases of criminal, civil, and constitutional matters; it sits in different regions on a rotating basis. It also serves as an appellate court on cases from the Magistrates' Courts. The Supreme Court is the highest court in Namibia. It sits in Windhoek, is presided over by the chief justice, and hears appellate cases from the High Court on civil, criminal, and constitutional matters, including those that involve the rights guaranteed under Chapter 3 of the 1990 Constitution. The Supreme Court also has the responsibility of dealing with matters referred to it by the attorney general and other matters authorized by Parliament. In exercising his or her power to appoint and dismiss key members of the judiciary and the legal system—including judges, the prosecutor general, the ombudsman, and others—the president makes such decisions on the recommendation of the Judiciary Services Commission. The commission is composed in such a way as to enable the president to benefit from expert legal opinion, as opposed to purely political opinions. Its members include the chief justice, a judge appointed by the president, the attorney general, and two members appointed by the legal professional organization. Representing the state's interest in the High Court or the Supreme Court is the prosecutor general, whose position is constitutionally mandated and confined to criminal matters.

Judges in the Supreme and High Courts are appointed

Legal Structure of Namibia Courts

Supreme Court (Appellate)		
Civil	Criminal	Constitutional

High Court Original/Appellate Jurisdiction		
Civil	Criminal	Constitutional

Lower Courts Magistrates' Courts

by the president of the republic, acting on the recommendations of the Judiciary Service Commission. On appointment, judges serve in office until the retirement age of sixty-five. Past that age, they can continue in office only if the president extends their tenue, which he or she has the constitutional powers to do. However, the constitution limits the presidential extension of a judge's tenure to five years. Parliament could also extend the retirement age of judges beyond sixty-five or seventy years of age. The constitution also makes provisions for the removal of judges from office. Such removal can only be done by the president, again acting on the recommendations of the Judiciary Service Commission, after an investigation establishes either that the judge in question is mentally incapacitated or that he or she has engaged in gross misconduct under Paragraph 3 of the 1990 Constitution.

SPECIALIZED JUDICIARY BODIES

Namibia's experiences under apartheid, together with the rampant corruption, mismanagement of public funds, and civil rights abuses so prevalent in many African societies, seemed to have pushed the state to take an extra step to prevent a repetition of such occurrences. In addition to an independent judiciary, the Namibian Constitution creates an independent ombudsman charged with investigating abuses of power; violations of rights; and excessive exploitation, degradation, or overutilization of natural resources. The ombudsman refers his or her findings to the prosecutor for prosecution in court. The record on prosecutions based on complaints made to the ombudsman is limited, but the number of complaints that have been made against different agencies is significant, given the size of Namibia. A total of 663 complaints were received in 1998, more than in previous years. The agencies against which such complaints were made were also more diversified; they included local government agencies, parastatals, and central government agencies. It is difficult to determine the level of independence of the ombudsman, since no particularly controversial cases have emerged to test that independence. Two cases might have given a measure of the independence of the ombudsman—one involving the role of torture in SWAPO's bases in Angola during the liberation struggle and a second calling for Namibia to create a truth commission similar to that in South Africa. However, neither of these cases has been pursued. Thus, there is little to go by beyond the stated objectives of the ombudsman and the number of complaints it receives.

STAFFING

Staffing in the legal system of Namibia remains a major issue for the country, due to the impact of South Africa's colonial policy. That policy created many imbalances in terms of the distribution of facilities and human resources, recruitment, training, protection, access to the profession, and other personnel-related issues. Since gaining independence, the Namibian state has moved to change and reform the system of the administration of justice to make the legal system more effective and fair.

Until 1990, legal services were concentrated in white areas of Namibia, and public sector practitioners in these areas, such as judges, magistrates, and prosecutors, were mainly whites. Since 1990, the legal infrastructure has been extended to formerly underserved areas, which are primarily black parts of the country. Actions were also taken to be more inclusive in employment practices by recruiting black and women magistrates and judges. For example, the number of black resident magistrates, only twelve in 1990, increased to twenty-five in 1996. Similarly, the number of black magistrates has also increased, from eighteen in 1990 to thirty-six in 1994 and fifty-five in 1996. The new government has also emphasized the recruitment of women. In 1995, 40 percent of the prosecutors, attorneys, legal drafters, legal advisers, and heads of offices were women.

Another provision undertaken in the area of staffing involved legal education. Until the mid-1990s, members of the legal profession in Namibia were trained in South Africa. The establishment of a law faculty at the University of Namibia changed that and forced Namibia to structure its own legal education. Such training now features a five-year program, after which the graduate is awarded the LL.B. degree. In addition to providing a formal legal education, the faculty of law at the University of Namibia houses a Training Center to provide further education for working members of the legal profession, including magistrates, prosecutors, and other lower-level legal employees. The center also trains new recruits into the legal profession from the university as well as those from foreign law schools.

The merger of the two previously separate domains of the advocate and the attorney was also undertaken. But in 1995, Parliament passed the Legal Practitioners Act (Act 15 of 1995). This act enables attorneys to move to the private sector and practice law; it also enables advocates to move from the private sector to the public sector. In addition, it widens the pool from which judges can be appointed.

Another matter involving staffing changes had to do with the recognition of graduates of foreign law schools who sought to practice in Namibia. Previously, those who received their training somewhere besides South Africa were not allowed to practice in Namibia. This was changed in 1991 under the Attorneys Amendment Act (Act 17 of 1991) and the Admission of Advocates Amendment Act (Act 19 of 1991).

IMPACT

The impact of the legal system in Namibia is difficult to measure, given the absence of any independent surveys on that issue and the newness of the state. Therefore, what is offered here necessarily focuses on a comparison with the system prior to independence. Before all the changes that have been discussed occurred, Namibia was a country in which the rule of law could hardly be considered to exist. Legal services were distributed to the advantage of certain segments of the society, and the majority of the citizens were deprived of various legal protections and rights. In the postindependence period, however, all the changes embedded in the new constitution and its legal provisions have completely reordered Namibian society in a fundamental way. This reordering has opened up opportunities in unprecedented ways. On the negative side, the new legal system seems unable to deal adequately with the recent wave of crimes. Ultimately, only time will tell how effective and consistent the state will be in upholding the principles and actions it has undertaken in regard to its current legal system.

Moses K. Tesi

See also Angola; Botswana; Common Law; Customary Law; Legal Education; Legal Professionals—Civil Law Traditions; South Africa; Zambia

References and further reading

Cliffe, Lionel, Ray Bush, Jenny Lindsay, Brian Mokopakgosi, Donna Pankhurst, and Balefi Tsie. 1994. *The Transition to Independence in Namibia.* Boulder, CO: Lynne Rienner.

Forest, Joshua Bernard. 1998. *Namibia's Post-Apartheid Regional Institutions.* Rochester, NY: University of Rochester Press.

July, Robert W. 1992. *A History of the African People.* Prospect Heights, IL: Waveland Press.

Leys, Colin, and John Saul, eds. 1995. *Namibia's Independence Struggle and Its Aftermath: The Two-Edge Sword.* London: James Currey.

Lindeke, William A. 1995. "The Political Economy of Namibia Development." *Journal of African Policy Studies* 1, no. 1.

Naldi, Gino. 1995. *Constitutional Rights in Namibia.* Windhoek, Namibia: Juta and Co.

Shillington, Kevin. 1995. *History of Africa.* New York: St. Martin's Press.

Van Wyk, D., M. Wiechers, and R. Hill, eds. *Namibia Constitutional and International Law Issues.* Unisa, Namibia: Verloren van Themat Centre for Public Law Studies.

Weiland, Heribert. 1999. "Elections as a Cornerstone of Democracy: The Namibia Experience." *Journal of African Policy Studies* 5, nos. 2 and 3.

Werner, Wolfgang. 1993. "A Brief History of Land Dispossession in Namibia." *Journal of Southern African Studies* 19, no. 1.

World Bank. 1989–2000. *World Development Report.* Various issues. New York and Oxford: Oxford University Press.

NAPOLEONIC CODE

The French Civil Code, or Code Napoléon, promulgated on March 21, 1804, has been considered an important foundation and example for modern civil law systems throughout the world. Napoléon Bonaparte took on the arduous task of revising France's outmoded and confusing legal system inherited from the monarchy and the Revolution.

HISTORY

The legal system of France before the code was similar to a patchwork of various, disingenuous regional laws with strictly defined territorial divisions. The written laws in place in the south were taken from the ancient Roman law, modeled on the Code of Justinian and to a lesser extent, the Theodosian Code (the word *code* comes from the Latin, *codex,* meaning a book made of tablets or leaves bound at one edge). The passage of time allowed for this region of France, known as *le pays de droit écrit* (country of written law), to maintain the key elements of the ancient Roman law through decision by regional courts. In the north, several and varied regional customs dominated. This *pays de droit coutumier* (country of customary law) borrowed mainly from feudal Frankish and Germanic institutions. At its zenith, no fewer than sixty-five general customs were in force, the most prevalent being the *coutume de Paris* and the *coutume de Normandie.* The French monarchy also participated through royal *ordonnances,* some of which dealt with private or civil law. Marriage and family law was dealt with almost exclusively by the Roman Catholic Church and canon law. Early attempts in the sixteenth and seventeenth centuries failed to unify these sources of law, especially the regional customs, into one national codification. The powerful French monarchy ruling at the time believed that such reform would empower the nation too strongly and undermine the privileges traditionally bestowed upon the kings and queens of France.

In the late eighteenth century, the hope of a codified system of private law was more immediately buttressed by the liberties achieved through the Declaration of the Rights of Man and Citizen in 1789; the declaration listed the inalienable rights of every French person. It and the Constitution of 1791 directed that the codification of private law in France would be the best way to promote the ideals set forth by the French Revolution as well as to ensure the continued stability and cohesion of the nation. Several ambitious lawmakers and legal scholars arose from this postrevolutionary period to attempt national codification. One, Jean-Jacques-Régis de Cambacérès, led the creation of a draft civil code and proposed such an innovation to the newly created National Constituent Assembly. This code was considered radically innovative in the realm of family law (e.g., equality between father and mother vis-à-vis power over the children, common authority over marital assets between spouses) but relied on old French law of the ancien régime for laws of property and obligation (the written law of the south proved very comfortable for the law of obligations and contracts).

It was not until 1799 that the beginnings of the great 1804 code first came to shine. Napoléon himself understood that unifying the nation under a single system of private law codification would not only help the people of France but would also solidify his political prowess in the Republic. Napoléon sought to create the most cohesive, efficient, and logical collection of principles of law in the world, taking France from its former ways to remedy the chaotic situation that prevailed.

Napoléon's commission of four jurists for this *projet* was headed by François-Denis Tronchet, considered the defender of the old French law, particularly the historical north regional custom, *la coutume de Paris.* Jean-Marie-Etienne Portalis, another jurist, gained significant recognition as a philosopher and learned jurist. Coming from the Roman law–enriched south of France (Aix-en-Provence), Portalis is considered the most prolific and important contributor (next to Bonaparte himself) of the code. Félix-Julien-Jean Bigot de Préameneu, a former advocate and judge, and Jacques Maleville, the commission's recording secretary, completed this quartet, bringing strong opinions of both the customary law of northern France as well as the written laws of southern France to Napoléon's grand attempts at unification. Napoléon was known to be very involved in the meetings of the drafters.

Napoléon sought a code that would be both open and systematic, and that was indeed produced: open in the sense that a truly functional code could not speak of every situation; it must speak in general but concrete legal principles and allow the judge to fill in the lacunae (gaps) of these general principles. Judges should not create law when they do this; rather they should show the parties at hand the intent of the lawgiver, the legislator.

In this journey, judges would be allowed to resort to the code article in question, its context in relation to the code as a whole, the decisions of courts, and opinions and comments of learned jurists. The code was to be systematic, in that it would start with a clean legal slate, as Napoléon and Cambacérès passed legislation that abrogated all previous French laws bearing on the subject matter of the proposed civil code. The code would be systematic as well in its innovation of a sequence of continuously numbered articles regulating all areas of the private law of France. That is to say, it would be limited systematically and sequentially to the law of persons, the law of things, and the modes of acquiring ownership or rights in things.

PARADIGMATIC CONCEPTS

The classifications and divisions of the code serve as necessary first steps in the analytical task of fashioning a legal remedy for the wide array of factual situations in which disputes arise. The ideas of Napoléon and his commission ensured that this general conceptual framework would last via the aid of the judiciary as well as legal academics and commentators.

The division of the law of "persons" into different legal institutions of the family such as marriage, tutorship, adoption, divorce, and so on proved to be innovative in its own right. Equality of the sexes, however, took many years to come to fruition. The Napoleonic Code vested strong authority and rights of disposition of marital property in the husband, as well as almost exclusive authority over the children in the father. Although these concepts seem arcane to the modern-day student, the law of persons in the code was not known for its substantive declarations but was more known for its conceptual framework. Most importantly, the code brought marriage into the realm of state regulation and out of the hands of the church. This emancipation from ecclesiastical control was evident in the requirement for an engaged couple to register with a regional civic official, for a religious minister lacked the power to bind the couple into the legal bond of matrimony. Further, by placing the law of persons first in his sequencing division, Napoléon made a statement that the rights of the French people are based on law (i.e., the civil code) first and foremost and not on mere rules of natural reason. By including in Book I on Persons several articles on the classification of persons, the drafters of the code meant for these classifications to have some bearing on problems that could be encountered in Book III on Things and the different modes of acquiring the ownership of things. This reading of code articles in pari materia (*pari* means "like" or "similar"; hence, reasoning on one subject matter to give it some meaning on the basis of its close resemblance with another similar subject matter) was crucial to the vitality and growth of Napoléon's 1804 code.

The classification of things in the code's second book was also crucial to the code's book on modes of acquiring ownership in things. Ownership as the most exclusive right in things was highly dependent on that thing's proper classification. The code's division into things immovable and movable continues in the major civil law systems of the world today. The various subclassifications of ownership in things were expounded as well in this second book of the code. Although the right of owners allows them exclusively to use, to receive the fruits of, and to dispose of that property, legal concepts such as usufruct and servitude limited ownership and the rights of the owner. A usufructuary could have limited rights of use of a thing and its fruits but could not dispose of it; a servitude allowed someone to encumber an owner's thing with limited rights relative to the utility of the thing in question. Importantly, the Napoleonic Code created a classification of rights in things that would have significant effects in a person's control of that thing: "Real rights" generally would follow the thing itself no matter how many times it would change ownership, while "personal rights" had a bearing on the persons directly involved in a particular transaction.

The third book of the code is considered the most important because it breathes life into the reason for codification by linking the first two books to the rights and obligations for which they were classified in the first place. Such a method of acquiring ownership of things concerns what rights a person has in a particular thing. This method could range from the obvious methods of acquisition of ownership (e.g., by death of a parent or succession, by a donation) to the more abstract methods, which would require much assistance from the judiciary to fill in the gaps of the code's generalities (e.g., the law of delicts or torts).

With respect to obligations, Book III of the code divided such right-acquiring devices into those that would be conventional (arising with an explicit agreement) and those obligations that would arise without any explicitly formed agreement but would bind a person because of strong societal norms and expectations. Along these lines, the code has been said to have solidified in civil law the Roman categories of contract, quasi-contract, delict, and quasi-delict. Although the freedom to contract is not expressly spelled out, it is an underlying and fundamental principle in several articles. The latter classification would be the basis for civil law systems' rules of delicts, which were the precursor for common modern-day legal rules involving personal injury, defamation, and general laws of torts, among others in several civil law jurisdictions. Article 1382, for example, states: "Every act whatever of man that causes damage to another obliges him by whose fault it happened to repair it." The sweeping language of this article covers *any* act capable of causing harm or injury to another without an illustrative list or an establishment of legal characterizations. The article is drafted in a way that leaves the court with a great freedom of decision, further establishing a strong link between the role of the legislator in a civil law system and the role of the judge as one who aids the lawgiver or legislator by giving substance to the general framework of the legislator's statement on behalf of the people. Finally, Book III of the Napoleonic Code regulates a number of specific contractual obligations concerning partnership, the law of mandate (principal and agent in the common law realm), mortgage, and prescription (time limitations on actions).

KEY ELEMENTS

The division and classification of persons and things and the rights relative to these groups serve as the springboard for the principal element of legal reasoning and analysis in the Napoleonic Code and throughout the civil law world. The division creates, particular to specific legal concepts, a deductive logical ladder—one that states a general premise in one or two broad articles and continues with gradual progressions of specificity. All the while, however, the code is left general enough not to render any article superfluous or irrelevant and not to be outdated too quickly. Moreover, the general articles allow judges to fashion a remedy from the legislator's intent. Broad articles allow much freedom in this kind of judicial analysis, and although the cases themselves do not create new law separate from the code, a consistent line of reasoning by the judiciary can be relied on as *jurisprudence constante* (constant, consistent jurisprudence). Such a consistency can aid individual judges when they interpret these broad articles of the code in subsequent, similar matters.

Another special and dynamic feature of the code is that its structure lends itself to several legal methods of reasoning, transcending a restrictive use of individual books of the code. For example, an action for wrongful death in a code-based system is considered as an obligation arising without agreement. This action could be brought, to extend the example, for the death of an infant whose stillborn birth was the result of the negligence of the attending physician. If it is assumed that Article 1382, in Book III, does not sufficiently define the concept of *person* or *man,* then the classifications of persons in the articles of Book I on Persons could be read in pari materia with the action given by Article 1382. On the opposite end of the analytical spectrum, when a particular article creates a listing found to be exhaustive (either by express legislative decree in the article or by justified judicial reasoning), that article is to be given a reasoning *ratio legis stricta,* or strictly construed to the terms expressed. This ability to use the various books and divisions of the code in furtherance of solving particular and personal disputes was a major force in its continued vitality throughout the world, from almost immediately after its early-nineteenth-century inception up to the beginning of the twenty-first century.

BREADTH OF USE

The timing of the Napoleonic Code's promulgation in 1804 lent itself very well to a wide dissemination of its use. Practically speaking, Napoléon Bonaparte's power was close to its apex in 1804; thus, the parts of the European continent under French control were bound by the code (e.g., Belgium, Luxembourg, parts of western Germany, northwestern Italy, and Monaco, among others). Later conquests by Napoléon led to the introduction of the code into more Italian territory, the Netherlands, and much of the remainder of western Germany and Switzerland.

As the nineteenth century progressed, the code was voluntarily adopted in several European and Latin American countries. Many South and Central American countries remained true to the code's format and divisions but gave it some modification. Bolivia, Chile, Ecuador, Colombia, Uruguay, and Argentina have all adopted the arrangement of the code as well as having borrowed much of its substance. The code was introduced into Haiti and the Dominican Republic in the early part of the nineteenth century and is still in force there. Although the introduction of Germany's Civil Code in 1900 and the Swiss Code in 1912 somewhat reduced the influence and effect of the Napoleonic Code on other parts of the world, countries such as Brazil, Mexico, Peru, and Greece based their civil codes on comparative methods borrowed from these early-twentieth-century codes, with a heavy influence as well from the Napoleonic Code.

The Province of Quebec in Canada still relies on the Napoleonic Code's format and analytical framework, as does the State of Louisiana in the United States. Louisiana's 1808 Digest and 1825 Code and its revised 1870 Code (still in force today) stay incredibly true to Napoléon's original 1804 code. Both Quebec and Louisiana are surrounded by a separate and distinct legal system, the common law system, and have had to modify their commercial laws to survive as part of their respective federation. But Quebec's and Louisiana's private law is still strongly linked to the Napoleonic Code, and legal scholars and commentators in these regions fight to keep the link strong, all the while giving their civil codes a contemporary face.

Alain A. Levasseur
Gregory R. Bordelon

See also Canon Law; Civil Law; Contract Law; Customary Law; France; Judicial Review; Law and Society Movement; Natural Law; Private Law; Roman Law; Tort Law

References and further reading

Atias, Christian. 1985. *Le Droit civil.* Edited and translated by Alain A. Levasseur. 1987, retitled *The French Civil Law: An Insider's View.* Paris: Presses Universitaires de France.

David, René. 1974. "The Civil Code in France Today." *Louisiana Law Review* 34: 910 et seq.

Halpérin, Jean-Louis. 1992. *L'Impossible Code Civil.* Paris: Presses Universitaires de France.

———. 1996. *Le Code Civil.* Translated by David W. Gruning and Alain A. Levasseur. 2001, retitled *The Civil Code.* Paris: Dalloz Publishers.

Levasseur, Alain. 1969. "Code Napoléon or Code Portalis?" *Tulane Law Review* 43: 762–774.

———. 1970. "On the Structure of a Civil Code." *Tulane Law Review* 44: 693–703.

NATIVE AMERICAN LAW, TRADITIONAL

Traditional Native American law encompasses the traditional and customary dispute resolution systems of the over 600 indigenous nations, tribes, and bands of what is now the United States. It is distinct from Native Hawaiian law, which encompasses the traditional and customary legal systems of Hawai'i that culminated in the dynasty of Kamehameha I. It is also distinct from American Indian Law, which encompasses the 367 treaties, as well as federal laws and court decisions that define the sovereign-to-sovereign relationship between Native American tribes and the United States.

PARADIGMATIC CONCEPTS

Although anthropologists identify eleven distinct cultural zones ranging from the northeast to California and the Alaska panhandle, a few generalizations can be made safely about some central concepts of traditional Native American law. First is the *tribe* as the basic unit of social organization. Common bonds of ancestry, kinship, language, culture, religion, and authority united the people; in many native languages, the name of the tribe itself means "the people."

Tribes provided for themselves in one of two ways. Either they were agricultural, and were seminomadic or rooted to a specific area, or they were hunters, fishers, and gatherers, moving nomadically across a wide area with the seasons. Tribes, especially among the nomadic hunting societies of the west, were often composed of numerous *bands,* which were themselves groupings of extended families. In the rooted agricultural tribes of the east and southwest, *clans* of extended intergenerational families defined society: the Iroquois had eight clans, the Apache sixty-two. Kinship structure was crucial, as membership—and power—in the clans generally was matrilineal, passing from mother to child. Among the western nomadic hunter/gatherer tribes, clans were rare. When present, as among the seven clans of the Missouri River valley–dwelling Ponca, they were patrilineal. Power resided with the men.

Tribes united in a federation or association, or linked by common language, culture, or religion, acted as a *nation.* Prominent examples of American Indian nations include the Haudenosaunee (Iroquois), the Ani-Yun-Wiya (Cherokee), the Diné (Navajo), and the Lakota (Sioux).

KEY ELEMENTS OF LAW

Formal and *informal* legal systems evolved together to minimize conflict in society. Patterns of conflicts and disputes emerged in response to how the tribe organized economically to provide for its needs. The focus of law was not on defining legal parameters of power or realizing abstract concepts of justice, but rather on efficient *dispute resolution* aimed at maximizing group values and therefore survival. The primary manifestation of law in tribes was *judicial* rather than *legislative.* Law to the individual was about responsibility rather than rights. Legal systems focused not on statutorily defined notions of individual rights but rather on the person's *obligation* as a member of a family, clan or band, tribe, and nation. They also adapted to the prevalence or incidence of murder, rape, and theft, as well as the need to accommodate marriage, adoption, and divorce. Legal systems with few exceptions emphasized private, familial, or clan-based means of dispute resolution for transgressions that did not harm the group as a whole. Punishment emphasized the restoration of social harmony, whether through formal or informal rituals of retribution, ostracism, or restitution. Crimes against the group as a whole were generally punished at a larger public level.

Religion was also used to reinforce obligation by creating incentives and punishments to observe group norms. Traditional tribal society rarely divided along such European lines as the secular from the sacred, or the public from the private. While there was a great variety of religious belief, ritual, and dogma, common threads emphasized concepts of natural harmony, as well as the use of religious ritual to reinforce legal concepts of individual responsibility and communal welfare. Religion also augmented such social concepts as shame, honor, deviance, and taboo as informal means of social control.

HISTORICAL DEVELOPMENT BEFORE AND DURING THE EUROPEAN CONQUEST

Agricultural Tribes of the East, Southwest, and Pacific Coasts

A number of similar features characterize the legal systems of the forest and coastal dwelling tribes of the Great Lakes, Atlantic, Gulf, and Pacific coasts, and the mesa-dwelling tribes of the desert southwest. First was economic: they were farmers, supplementing their diets by hunting, fishing, and trapping. Second was kinship: strong matrilineal clans had primary responsibility to enforce the law. Third was political organization: while the eastern tribes featured a plethora of formal political confederacies, the tribes of the southwest and the Pacific coast tended to be village-based with weak or nonexistent national associations. While religion was a key feature for defining social norms and reinforcing legal obligation among eastern tribes, particularly the Cherokee and Iroquois, it was synthesized to an even greater degree among the southwestern tribes such as the Hopi and Navajo.

The Ani-Yun-Wiya (Cherokee)—literally the "real people"—are centered on the Great Smoky Mountains and provided for economically by agriculture, supplemented by hunting. Politically, the many Cherokee towns were semiautonomous, allied with a weak national council composed of the town leaders from the five regions. Although lacking coercive powers, the council addressed national concerns by forging consensus. Kinship structure was crucial, as strong matrilineal clans retained the judicial function, resolving disputes, enforcing norms, and implementing punishments.

Murder created a debt of blood; the clan of the victim had the right to avenge the death. The ill will created by clan-based punishment systems was countered by the religious ritual of the Great New Moon Feast in the autumn, where the village and its members would be ritualistically cleansed, and family hearths relit from a common flame to emphasize unity. This religious ritual was also reinforced by religious tradition that emphasized the *harmony ethic,* creating powerful social norms against giving offense and public argument. Followers of this norm were accorded honor and status; transgressors were to be shunned and mocked. Among their neighbors the Choctaws, offering a willing substitute could pay the blood debt, as could offering up oneself for adoption, as murder was defined broadly to include both accidental death as well as the suspicion of using witchcraft to cause someone's death. Dueling was also allowed, but by custom ended with the death of both participants.

Although they were neighbors to the Cherokees and Choctaws, the Muscogee (Creek) legal and political system had a number of markedly different features. The Creek confederacy was made up of five tribes in approximately one hundred *talwa* (towns). The *talwa* were divided between *red towns* responsible for war-making and *white towns* responsible for civil affairs. Strong social norms prohibited the shedding of blood in white towns. Conflicts between towns were settled in often-vicious ball games. *Miccos,* who together formed a national council, led the towns. Disputes within a *talwa* that could not be resolved led often to the creation of new villages; such a division would then render the old dispute ended.

The formal and informal legal systems of the southern nations stood in distinct contrast with the Haudenosaunee (Iroquois)—literally, the People of the Longhouse—whose domain centered around the eastern Great Lakes and whose influence stretched as far north as Hudson Bay and south to Virginia. The Longhouse People—the Mohawk, Oneida, Onondaga, Cayuga, Seneca, and later the Tuscarora in 1722—were farmers, hunters, and trappers. The Ne Gayaneshagowa (Great Binding Law/Peace) of the five nations, given in probably the 1400s by the Mohawk prophet Deganawidah in conjunction with the Onondaga leader Hiawatha, governed the Iroquois.

The Iroquois had (and to this day still have) powerful matrilineal clans. The power of the women in Iroquois society derived in large part from the division of labor. Men hunted, trapped, conducted diplomacy, and waged war, while women husbanded the extensive crops of corn, raised the children, and managed the villages. Unlike nomadic tribes where the men were part of daily village life, the Haudenosaunee women had to run the society essentially for themselves while the men were away for weeks or months at a time.

Before the Great Binding Law, the clans were responsible for enforcing law, especially the blood debt from murder. Murder was avenged in one of three ways. Murder could be avenged by taking the life of the murderer or a member of his family. The victim's family could adopt a replacement for the deceased, either the murderer himself or a member of his family. Or they could accept some form of restitution from the murderer. What was radical about the Great Binding Law was that it took the enforcement of law out of the hands of the clans and their informal norms and placed it into the hands of the nation as a whole. It fostered strong social norms toward the willing acceptance of adoption or restitution over the desire for revenge.

The Great Binding Law was essentially designed to prevent warfare between the five nations and among the eight clans. It contained distinct sections describing processes for such civil law issues as adoption, marriage, and immigration, as well as more conventional political issues such as war, peace, and the impeachment of chiefs who violated community norms. Powerful mechanisms of what can only be called checks and balances were placed in formal structure to accomplish the former. Powerful norms emphasizing restitution and the resumption of harmony over retribution were to accomplish the latter. Religious belief and ritual augmented this emphasis on restitution. The late-eighteenth-century Seneca prophet Ganeodigo (Handsome Lake) began a religious movement emphasizing the Gaiwiio (the Good Word), melding key beliefs of the Quakers with traditional Iroquois spirituality. This religious tradition, also known as the Code of Handsome Lake, created a series of processes, structures, and, most importantly, rituals for ensuring the resolution of disputes.

Among the agricultural and seminomadic tribes of the desert southwest and California, the village was the primary unit of social organization. Autonomous villages were united by language, religion, and culture but not federated politically or legally. Village life was structured by matrilineal clans as well as by *moieties,* social fraternities that organized activity for medicine/ healing, hunting, religion, comedy and storytelling, and war. Dispute resolution centered on village headman and clan leaders, who would meet together to mediate intervillage disputes. Like the Cheyenne and the Iroquois, the southwestern tribes are marked by the integration of religion and political life, with the leader often being considered a priest. Religion provided a powerful reinforcement to social norms. Among the Apache, for example, shamans were believed to have the power to bless or curse individuals based on their behavior; flouting social norms would bring down a curse on an entire family. Taboos reinforced social norms and legal obligations.

The tribes of the Pacific Northwest provide a stark contrast. They were primarily fishermen and hunters, yet they were not nomadic, and according to some accounts had the greatest population density outside of Mesoamerica. Unlike any other in North America, the northwestern tribes generally had class-based societies, valued the accumulation of material wealth and property, and were organized in a patriarchical manner, with property descending from the father to the eldest son. Tribal life centered in autonomous villages, with confederations rare and short-lived, and intervillage war common. Many also practiced slavery, holding debtors and war captives in bondage. Murder was an offense against the victim's family, who had the right to seek retribution. However, the class and standing of both victim and perpetrator mitigated the revenge; a wealthy high-standing perpetrator would be held to a lesser punishment for killing an individual with lesser standing, and higher-class individuals had the option to make restitution instead of being punished.

Hunting and Gathering Tribes of the Great Plains, Basin, and Plateau

A number of similar features characterize the legal systems of those whose economic structures were completely reliant on nomadic hunting. The nomadic existence created a different social structure than the eastern and southwestern agricultural tribes. Since during times of peace the men were not separated from the camp for extended periods of time, women played a much less prominent political and social role. Clans as among the agricultural tribes were generally nonexistent. However,

like the agricultural tribes, religion played a crucial role in defining society and hence laws. Intertribe confederacies as among the eastern tribes were nonexistent, yet, like the east and the south, there was a powerful nation whose social, legal, and political structure characterized life on the plains.

The Lakota (Sioux) Nation, centered on their sacred ground of the Black Hills, dominated the plains, with their influence felt from Canada to Texas. The Oceti Sakowin (the seven council fires, or allies, as the Lakota referred to the extended nation) are composed of three tribes: the Lakota (Teton Sioux), the Dakota (Santee Sioux), and the Nakota (Yankton Sioux). The traditional basic unit of the Lakota was the band; the Teton Sioux are composed of seven bands, and the Santee four. The bands of the Yankton, Santee, and Teton would assemble en masse in the summer for political, religious, and social gatherings.

The band was composed of numerous *tiyospaye,* camps of roughly thirty households each. In times of peace the *tiyospaye* would move autonomously, rejoining the larger band at the changing of the seasons; during war they moved in a coordinated fashion. The camp was led by a *wakinunsa* (shirt-wearer), one of whose primary responsibilities was dispute and conflict resolution. While kinship was a dominant feature of Lakota society, there were no clans as in the east, and women rarely played an active political or legal role.

Law among the Lakota *tiyospaye* was defined and enforced by three organized societies. The *akicitas* were the police societies, which kept order when the camp was traveling and during the buffalo hunt. Transgressors of hunt rules could be beaten or even have their horses taken away; in rare extreme cases punishment could be death or banishment. Order and cohesion were crucial during these two events, and the police society chosen for that season had wide latitude to cajole as well as to use force and discipline to ensure the smooth operation of both activities. The police societies, besides punishing smaller offenses, also worked with the *wakinunsa* to negotiate settlements between families. Also important were the warrior societies, which organized young men for offensive and defensive war.

The third organization that dominated Sioux society was the *naccas,* the civil societies. The *naccas* of the *tiyospaye* organized the hunts, determined the timing and order of camp movements, and selected the police society for the season. The *naccas* from the different *tiyospaye* formed the leadership of the bands in the *naca ominicia,* the tribal council. The council was led by *wicasa itancans,* one of whose primary functions was the resolution of disputes and the punishment of crimes that could not be settled or punished by the families involved. The *wicasa yatapikas* (supreme national council) met when the bands congregated for the summer festival, including the rituals of the Sun Dance. Also known as the *owners* of the nation, one of their primary responsibilities was to resolve disputes and punish crimes between bands or tribes, as well as offenses that threatened national unity.

Dispute resolution and punishment were decentralized; solutions were sought at a level as close to the dispute as possible. Families were in theory entitled to revenge for murder, but powerful social norms encouraged the acceptance of restitution or adoption of a replacement, as the ill will created by vendetta would be destructive to the unity required for nomadic village existence. Punishment for lesser offenses was often meted out socially, through mockery or ostracism.

Features of the legal systems of the Lakota nation were common throughout the Great Plains. The Assiniboine, Comanches, Crows, Mandans, Pawnee, and Ponca all shared similar band structures; use of soldier, police, and civil societies; and family-centered dispute resolution that emphasized restitution over retribution in punishment. Unlike the Lakota, however, they did not have strong national councils. The Ponca, along with the U'Ma'ha (Omaha) and Pawnee, were also partially agricultural, residing in the fertile Missouri River valley.

Banishment as a punishment for murder was a central feature of Cheyenne society, as the murderer was considered to be forever impure. Cheyenne social organization had many features common to the plains nomadic hunters—bands, tripartite warrior, police, and civil societies, and male-dominated political and social life. Yet the Cheyenne are worth noting at length for the extent to which religion, law, and politics were synthesized.

The leader of the Cheyenne was also its religious leader: the Sweet Medicine Chief, named after the Cheyenne prophet Sweet Medicine, who, like Deganawidah for the Iroquois, created the code that united the Cheyenne. The Sweet Medicine Chief is the intercessor for the Cheyenne with the Creator. Sweet Medicine's Law has the features of a covenant; if the Cheyenne follow the law and keep the covenant, the Creator would provide for them. The ark of this covenant was the Sweet Medicine Bundle, which contained arrows and feathers and was kept by the Chief. The principal crime was murder of another Cheyenne; the murderer was considered to be impure for having broken the covenant, and was punished by being banished from the group following a ceremony in which the Sweet Medicine Bundle was purified by replacing the arrows and feathers. Banishment on the High Plains was akin to a death sentence; however, if the individual survived at least a year, he could ask for reinstatement, which required the assent of the victim's family. If allowed, however, the murderer was always to be shunned as an outsider.

The tribes of the Great Basin and Plateau, such as the Yakima, Nez Perce, Colville, Coeur d'Alene, and Shoshone, shared many aspects of the social organization of the Plains tribes. Organized in small villages that belonged to loosely confederated bands, they traveled seasonally to hunt, fish, and gather food. They did not have clans, or the complex tripartite societies of the Plains tribes, nor strong national leadership traditions. Dispute resolution centered in the village and extended family, and murder was answered with vengeance, adoption, or restitution, but generally without the strong social norms encouraging the latter.

Stephen G. Bragaw

See also Customary Law; Gypsy Law
References and further reading

Deloria, Vine, and Clifford M. Lyttle. 1983. *American Indians, American Justice.* Norman: University of Oklahoma Press.
Harring, Sidney. 1994. *Crow Dog's Case: American Indian Sovereignty, Tribal Law, and United States Law in the Nineteenth Century.* New York: Cambridge University Press.
Johansen, Bruce Elliot, ed. 1998. *The Encyclopedia of Native American Legal Tradition.* Westport, CT: Greenwood Press.
Llewellyn, Karl N., and E. Adamson Hoebel. 1941. *The Cheyenne Way: Conflict and Case Law in Primitive Jurisprudence.* Norman: University of Oklahoma Press.
O'Brien, Sharon. 1989. *American Indian Tribal Governments.* Norman: University of Oklahoma Press.
Wallace, Anthony F. C. 1969. *The Death and Rebirth of the Seneca.* New York: Vintage Books.

NATURAL LAW

INTRODUCTION

How do the laws of the state differ from the dictates of a successful, well-organized robber-gang? Is the difference that law has some connection with justice (St. Augustine)?

Natural law theory states that law has some necessary connection with morality (or justice) and reason. The instinct that law and justice are intertwined appears at the start of the Western legal tradition. In the Greek play *Antigone,* the heroine disobeys the king's command that her brother's body be left unburied—there is an order to the way of living that mortal commands cannot alter, even upon pain of death. More strikingly, Socrates announces that one must disobey an immoral command to do wrong. He then kills himself in obedience to the law, as one has a duty to obey the law.

The existence of such a connection is controversial, and rejected by "legal positivists," who see law as merely a set of commands, or customary rules, or a technique of social regulation, or who find "morality" and "reason" to be too vague. Even those accepting the connection dispute its essence and consequences. Nevertheless the "connection thesis" colors natural law's answers to vital questions: What is the nature of law—rules or commands? What is law's purpose—to impose peace, or to establish justice, or to provide tools for rulers? As well as the specific rules and commands of a particular state (the *positive* or *civil law*), is there a natural law that is valid everywhere (Aristotle)? Does law have any necessary moral content (for example, human rights), or may it have any content whatsoever? Should we obey the law? When may we disobey the law?

FOUNDATIONS: FROM ANCIENT GREECE TO AQUINAS

Early Greeks thinkers did not distinguish sharply between natural occurrences and purposeful human activity. Both natural and human events were seen in terms of "rightness," an idea close to "fate." (This metaphysics carries over into one widely discredited interpretation of natural law—that one ought to do what one's *nature* indicates is one's natural end or goal.)

Plato and Aristotle develop the idea of natural law. Both stress that laws must not serve selfish interests but rather the common good. For Plato, the perfect ideal law can be perceived only by the highly trained, intellectual "guardian" elite.

Aristotle's more mundane conception discusses ideas of the state, the good life, and equity (as well as citizenship, and commutative and distributive justice). The state is a self-sufficient union that provides through its laws for the common pursuit of the human good; that is, the state promotes the "good life." A practically reasonable man of some experience who has lived in a sound state can apprehend what is good for human flourishing given our nature (slavery and patriarchy are natural; communism and usury unnatural). Strict positive laws cannot always ensure human flourishing, as its requirements cannot be predicted accurately in advance. Therefore, equity must be invoked to "perfect" the law or "complete" it in specific cases to reach the right result.

The Romans also wrote about natural law. The orator Cicero adopts Greek Stoic ideas (with their conception of human equality and a meaning to the world identified with "reason"). He describes a natural law instilled at birth, unalterable, unamendable, overriding, and known to all men by reason. The idea is potentially dangerous—Cicero believed that positive laws requiring a fair trial should yield to the unwritten law that the safety of the people is all.

Sixth-century Roman law compilations contain several conceptions of natural law. Nature instills the "law of nature" in all creatures, including animals. The example of mating and marriage is given. But the texts also identify a separate "law of peoples": these are rules that "natural reason" makes for all humanity. This appears to be a set of rules common to all peoples, but really only meant those simplified rules of Roman law that Romans applied to foreigners. Similarly the idea of natural law is not very exalted, as it usually simply agreed with the positive rules of Roman civil law. Where it did not, then the Romans accepted the violations (for example, slavery).

St. Paul referred to the law that all men, even heathens, can understand, and the early church married Stoic and Christian ideas of divine world order, human equality, and dignity (as all are children of God). Church law recognized the distinction between the law of man and God's *higher* natural law (Gratian's *Decretum* ca. 1140). This higher law provided the possibility to criticize the human law, but the church usually accommodated "unnatural" institutions such as slavery.

"Scholastics," notably St. Thomas Aquinas, synthesized the issues in the thirteenth century. Law is a rule for guiding action, intended for the common good, made by a superior and duly published. There are four types of law—human positive law, the natural law, God's secret law, and His revealed law. While the natural law was promulgated by God, it could (borrowing from Aristotle) be grasped by all people who reflected upon the question of what is good for human beings (for example, protection of life, sociability, the education of children). In this way it was still vague, and its details needed to be completed by the more specific positive human law. This explains why we should obey the positive law. Positive law also provides sanctions to encourage obedience to the law. However, a positive law that violates natural law is a corruption of law. It should nevertheless be obeyed unless the evil of obeying it is greater than the social disturbance that would follow from disobedience.

FROM THE MIDDLE AGES TO MODERN TIMES

In the fragmentation of natural law theory after Aquinas, three general trends are distinguishable. First, there are moves toward a secular natural law. Second, there is a growing faith in the ability of "reason" to yield precise answers about the governance of human conduct. Third, there is increased emphasis on the individual.

Law of Nations

As a reaction to colonial expansion, and wars of religion and state aggrandizement, the philosophers of the "Spanish School" and writers such as Grotius, Pufendorf, and Vattel developed rules for the conduct of states in times of war and peace—what we now call international law. They revived the old "law of peoples" idea, distinguished from the natural law and civil law. Despite his manifest debts to the older tradition, the Dutchman Grotius is often described as the father of modern natural law: he discusses rights as individual faculties and the development of a logical system; and he asserts that the natural law would be valid even if we wickedly denied God's existence.

Rational Law

Lawyers have often immunized the law from external criticism by praising it as inherently "rational." When Britain's king James I asserted that law was based on reason and so, having reason, he could judge, Chief Justice Coke disagreed. Coke replied that English law concurred with reason, but it was an *artificial reason* comprehensible only to the legal elite!

The claim that law accorded with reason took on a new dimension in the seventeenth and eighteenth centuries. The categories of Roman law had often been used to understand the legal rules in civil law countries (more weakly and indirectly in common law countries). Now, some writers, animated by the pursuit of reason, devised rational structures for these concepts. They provided organizing principles that the drafters of the nineteenth-century codes used to structure legal categories.

Hobbes

Hobbes uses nature in various ways. He identifies "natural laws" with facts about human psychology (individuals recoil from pain, and pursue pleasure). He constructs, in an almost mathematical manner, a political theory based on these. He describes the idea of a "state of nature"—a prepolitical world in which individuals are in a war against each other. To avoid eternal war, people confer supreme power on a sovereign whose command (irrespective of its content) is law. His natural laws lead to positivism.

Liberal Natural Law and Natural Rights

In periods when law was revered, political dissent often had to be expressed in terms of law. Despite its conservatism, natural law always had a radical potential. Aquinas argued for constitutional mixed government; Coke held that the rational law limited the king's powers (the "rule of law" prohibition on arbitrariness). Some Scholastics believed that a ruler who ignored the common interest could be deposed; sixteenth-century French monarchomachists advocated tyrannicide. The Spanish School of the sixteenth and seventeenth centuries condemned Spain's exploitation of Native Americans.

Most famously, Locke united the state of nature with a limited radicalism. He thought that men emerge from a prepolitical state, agreeing to create a limited political authority that had to respect the "natural rights" of liberty, property, and security, in order to be legitimate. In extreme cases (the 1688 British Revolution) the people could replace a tyrant.

The idea of natural rights—overriding individual claims that are not created by positive law, but inhere in

one by virtue of one's status as a human being—became commonplace with American independence and the 1789 French Revolution (see Tom Paine's *The Rights of Man* or the 1789 French *Declaration of the Rights of Man and Citizen*).

Yet at this time natural law and natural rights theories were widely attacked. Natural law was criticized for its uncertain content, its logical fallacies, its naïve idealism, its excessive individualism, its antihistorical character, and its tendency to defend the interests of some social groups rather than others without good reason (Kant, Rousseau, Burke, Bentham, Hegel, Marx). The scientific study of law and modern liberalism demanded that law and morality be separated (Bentham, Kant, later Hart and Kelsen). The nineteenth century saw the triumph of legal positivism.

NATURAL LAW TODAY

Following the horrors of state absolutism in World War II, the natural law claim that law could not be separated from justice reemerged. The war crimes trials punished people for obeying the unjust commands of state authorities; the United Nations proclaimed the *Universal* Declaration of Human Rights; and some writers insisted that truly evil commands are not laws (Radbruch).

We now have a law of international human rights that all states must respect. Recently this has led to special war crimes tribunals, trials of state leaders for violating human rights, and even a treaty for a permanent International Criminal Court. Modern constitutions (now regarded as *higher law*) contain catalogues of (natural) human rights, which are entrusted to courts for their protection (for example, the U.S. Supreme Court, or the German Federal Constitutional Court). Sometimes even when a text makes no mention of human rights, a court has decided they were implicitly protected (for example, the European Court of Justice). These rights often affect sensitive issues (euthanasia, political financing, labor relations, and so forth). As judicial power expands, some writers see judges as "prophets" of a better law while others condemn them as antidemocratic Platonic "guardians." Meanwhile, actions of civil disobedience and protest also reinforce the claims of justice over state power, and pose the question of the duty to obey the law. All these phenomena have reignited vigorous debates over natural law or natural rights in modern jurisprudence.

Finnis revives Aristotle and Aquinas: all people can appreciate that certain goods are intrinsically valuable—that is, objectively good (life, sociability, knowledge, play, aesthetic experience, practical reasonableness, speculation about the infinite). People can practically reason about these goods—they understand that it is wrong to act deliberately against them; that it is wrong to deny anyone these goods; and that they need to cooperate to obtain them in a well-ordered community. Law is a means for the cooperative achievement of these goods for all, as well as embodying the good of sociability itself.

Other theories reject a strong conception of objective values in favor of basic human rights and the rule of law. Dworkin holds that law is a practice of interpretation; the best interpretation of law justifies law by upholding individual rights (especially equality). Alexy believes that law needs a theory of legal reasoning, which must borrow from general notions of how to reason. This leads to the idea of respect for other participants in a rational dialogue and ultimately to human rights. Fuller thinks that law's purpose—the guidance of the life of rational beings—implies respect for the rule of law (arbitrary laws cannot provide guidance).

Today, even legal positivists regularly talk about moral issues in legal practice. Hart acknowledges that there are rules that one regularly finds in all societies designed to ensure survival of the fragile human character (this use of the term implies nothing about "rightness" or "legality"). Perhaps the time has come to replace the disagreement between "natural law" and "legal positivism" with a less doctrinaire discussion over the role of morality in law.

Any study of this role should remember the varied and controversial history of natural law. Natural law has been invoked by sexists, but also by egalitarians; intellectual elitists have favored it, but so have believers in universal rights. We are left with more questions than when we started: can natural law be reconciled with democracy and pluralism? How to demonstrate what is "rational" or "moral" (and not just a rationalization of intuition and power interests)? What role do morality and reason have in legal systems that are sometimes violent, often corrupt and unjust, and always the site of struggle?

Rory O'Connell

See also Ancient Athens; Constitutional Review; Equity; Human Rights Law; International Criminal Court; International Law; Judicial Review; Legal Positivism; Legal Realism; Napoleonic Code; Roman Law

References and further reading
Aquinas, St. Thomas. 1959. *Selected Political Writings.* Oxford: Basil Blackwell.
D'Entreves, A. P. 1994. *Natural Law: An Introduction to Legal Philosophy.* New Brunswick: Transaction.
Dworkin, Ronald. 1986. *Law's Empire.* London: Fontana.
Finnis, John. 1980. *Natural Law and Natural Rights.* Oxford: Oxford University Press.
———. 1991. *Natural Law.* Dartmouth: Ashgate.
George, R. P. 1994. *Natural Law Theory: Contemporary Essays.* Oxford: Clarendon Press.
Kelly, John. 1992. *A Short History of Western Legal Theory.* Oxford: Clarendon Press.
Rommen, Heinrich. 1964. *The Natural Law.* St. Louis: Herder.
Weinreb, Lloyd. 1987. *Natural Law and Justice.* Cambridge: Harvard University Press.

NAURU

GEOGRAPHY

Nauru is one of the smallest democracies in the world and is located in an isolated part in the world's biggest ocean—the Pacific. It is situated 41 kilometers south of the equator at 166°56' east longitude. Its closest neighbors are Banaba (Ocean Island), 300 kilometers to the east, and Kiribati and Tuvalu, some 500 kilometers to the northeast. Nauru is about 4,000 kilometers north of Sydney and 4,457 kilometers west of Honolulu. A small, raised atoll surrounded by reefs, it has an area of 8 square miles; at low tide, the island's circumference is 15 kilometers. The terrain is made up largely of phosphate-bearing rock, which covers three-fifths of the entire island. The highest point of the plateau is 70 meters. The current population of Nauruans in Nauru is 3,400.

POLITICAL HISTORY

For an unknown number of centuries, Nauru was uninhabited. The first inhabitants were probably castaways who drifted there from some other islands. After that, Nauru witnessed a succession of migrants, settlers, and administrators. The first of these outside contacts was Capt. John Fearn, who discovered Nauru. Captain Fearn named the island "Pleasant Island" because of its attractive appearance and the warmth of its people. The island was known by that name for the next eighty-eight years, during which there was very little contact with Europeans.

In the middle of the 1800s, Nauru saw another wave of migrants, this time as the beachcombers from the whaling ships. Around 1930, with the expansion of the European and U.S. whaling industries, Nauru became a port of call where food and other supplies could be obtained. It was also in the path of the sperm whale that was highly sought after in the European and U.S. markets.

Most of the beachcombers conformed to the way of life on the island and were helpful as intermediaries with traders from visiting ships. Some, however, such as the Irish convict John Jones, were hostile to the islanders. Such individuals introduced guns, which led to a stockpiling of firearms by the locals; this, in turn, resulted in an increase in massacres both between locals themselves and against visitors on trading ships. Given the insecurity of this situation, German traders requested that the island be incorporated within the German Marshall Islands Protectorate.

In 1886, under the Anglo-German Convention, the island was formally allocated as a German sphere of influence and renamed "Nauru," a corruption of the local name "Naoero." Two years later, the first German administrator was sent to Nauru from the nearby Marshall Islands. On January 21, 1888, Germany granted exclusive rights to Jaluit Gesellschaft, a German company, to

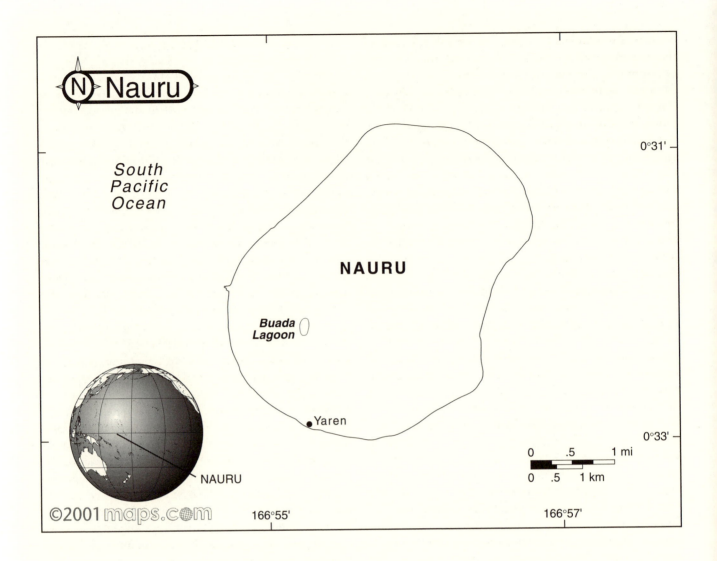

procure and trade in products from Nauru. The British Pacific Islands Company discovered phosphate deposits on Nauru two years later, and in 1906 and 1907, it entered into agreements with Jaluit Gesellschaft and acquired rights from that company to exploit the island's phosphate deposits.

Between World War I and Nauru's independence in 1968, two more imperial powers arrived on the island: the Australians and Japanese. During World War I, Nauru was occupied by Australian troops under an arrangement with the British to protect British concerns in the Pacific Islands Company. In 1919, under the Versailles Treaty, German surrendered its overseas territories, including Nauru, to the Allied forces. In that same year, the Nauru Island Agreement was signed between Australia, Great Britain, and New Zealand, giving Australia a mandate to administer Nauru for the next five years.

During World War II, the Japanese bombed Nauru, occupied the island, and deported 1,201 Nauruans to Truk Island. On January 31, 1946, the Japanese surrendered the island to an Australian force, which looked after the island until the UN Trusteeship Agreement was approved in November 1947. Political advancement of Nauruans began in 1951 when the Nauru local government was formed. Under the enabling act (the Nauru Local Government Ordinance of 1951), nine members were elected to the Nauru Local Government Council from eight electoral districts. The nine council members later appointed a head chief to preside over all meetings. Nauru was governed under this arrangement until 1965.

In 1965, with pressure from Nauru and the United Nations, a further agreement between the United Kingdom, Australia, and New Zealand was reached to increase local participation in the island's administration. The Nauru Act of 1965 established Nauru's Legislative Council and Executive Council. The Legislative Council consisted of fifteen members and dealt with the "peace, order and good governance of the island," as well as phosphate ownership and royalties. The Executive Council was composed of an administrator (appointed by Australia), two elected members, and two official members of the Legislative Council, appointed by the governor-general of Australia.

In 1966, the United Nations passed a resolution recommending independence for Nauru and recognizing the sovereignty of the Nauru people over the phosphate on the island. Following talks with the United Kingdom, Australia, and New Zealand, the Nauru Independence Bill was introduced in the Australian Parliament. This bill called for the Nauru Legislative Council to pass an ordinance assigning responsibility for drawing up a new constitution. Accordingly, the Legislative Council passed the Constitutional Convention Ordinance in November 1967, which was assented to on November 27. In January 1968, the Nauru Constitutional Convention had its first meeting; in a later meeting, it adopted a constitution and declared that this document would take effect on January 31, 1968. Under the provisions of the first constitution, the people of Nauru elected a head chief and eighteen members of the Legislative Assembly, as well as members of the Council of State and other bodies necessary to run the government at independence. Nauru became a politically independent republic on January 31, 1968. Since then, it has been functioning on a Westminster model of government, with a Parliament, an executive, and a judiciary.

SOURCES OF LAW

Nauru Constitution
One of the main sources of law in Nauru is the national constitution, adopted in 1968 by the Constitutional Convention that was created by the Legislative Assembly. In Nauru, the constitution is the supreme law, and any laws inconsistent with the constitution will be void to the extent of the inconsistency. The constitution can be amended, and a special procedure for this is laid down in Article 84 of the document. Salient features of this provision include the following:

- An interval of ninety days or more must pass between the introduction of the bill and the passing of the bill
- The bill must be passed by not less than two-thirds of the total number of members of Parliament

A number of provisions in the constitution cannot be amended unless two-thirds of the voters of the island approve the amendment through a referendum. Such provisions include the following:

- Schedule 5—on the rules for amending the constitution
- Articles 1 and 2—on the independence of Nauru and the supremacy of the constitution
- Articles 3 to 15—on fundamental rights
- Articles 16 and 17—on the president of Nauru and executive authority of the cabinet

- Articles 26 and 27—on the establishment and powers of Parliament
- Articles 58, 59, 60, and 65—on government finances
- Article 71—on citizenship
- Article 85—on existing laws at time of independence

The constitution, being the supreme law, also provides for the application of other sources of law, such as legislation, common law, and customary law.

Legislation
Similar to other Pacific jurisdictions, Nauru has four kinds of legislation. First, there are acts of Parliament passed since independence in 1968. Second, there is subsidiary legislation, including regulations made under various parent acts of Parliament. The power to make these laws is delegated to various government agencies by enabling acts, and if there is a conflict between an act of Parliament and a subordinate act, the act of Parliament prevails. Third, there is preindependence legislation in force immediately before Nauru's Independence Day. These laws are provided for under Section 85 of the constitution. Fourth, Section 4(1) of the Customs and Adopted Laws Act of 1971 adopts certain statutes of general application in force in England on January 31, 1968. Additionally, the Criminal Code of Queensland, Australia, as in force on July 1, 1921, still applies in Nauru.

Common Law
Like most of the countries in the South Pacific, Nauru also adopted the principles of common law and equity from England. This adoption was done pursuant to Section 4(1) of the Customs and Adopted Law Act of 1971, which provides that Nauru will adopt the principles of common law and equity applicable in England on January 31, 1968, to the extent that such principles are consistent with the circumstances of Nauru. The principles of common law and equity adopted from England are therefore persuasive in Nauruan courts.

Customary Law
Like most countries in the South Pacific, Nauru has expressly taken a position about the application of customs. Section 3 of the Adopted Laws Act (1971) provides that "the institutions, customs and usages of the Nauruans . . . shall be accorded recognition by every court, and have full force and effect of law, to regulate the matters specified in the Act." The customs and usages of the Nauruan people may be applied in cases involving the following issues:

- Title to and interests in land, except leasehold
- Disposition of property, both real and personal, either inter vivos or, on death, by will or intestacy
- Any matter affecting Nauruans only

However, where customary principles come into conflict with the constitution or legislation, customs will be abrogated.

THE KEY GOVERNMENT STRUCTURES

Head of State
The Constitution of Nauru does not create a head of state office. This is, however, implicit in Article 16 of the constitution, which establishes the office of the president; as a matter of practice, the president is treated as the head of state. The procedure for electing a president is provided by Article 16 of the constitution.

Executive
The cabinet exercises the executive power in Nauru, for the constitution grants the cabinet the power of "general direction and control of the government of Nauru." The cabinet of Nauru comprises the president, who is elected by Parliament, and four or five ministers appointed by the president. Ministers cease to hold office when a new president is elected, when removed by the president, or on resignation. Parliament may remove the cabinet and president through a motion of no confidence. Such a vote must carry a vote of at least one-half of the total numbers of members of Parliament. If Parliament fails to choose a new president within seven days, Parliament itself is dissolved.

Legislature
Similar to the executive, the legislature of Nauru reflects the Westminster system, with the general power to make laws for the peace, order, and good government of the nation. There are eighteen elected members of Parliament, chosen from among the constituencies, and a speaker of the house, who is not an elected member. Members of Parliament must satisfy certain requirements. No person can be a member of Parliament unless he or she is a citizen of Nauru and at least twenty-one years of age. Other factors that could disqualify a person from becoming a member of Parliament are: bankruptcy, insolvency, insanity, conviction for a criminal offense punishable by death or one year or more of imprisonment, and holding an office in the government of Nauru or its agents.

The life of any Parliament is three years. It may also convene to have an election before its three-year term is up if the president dissolves Parliament before the prescribed time runs out. A quorum is half the total number of members of Parliament, and bills are passed with a simple majority of Parliament. However, certain laws can only be passed by a two-thirds majority (discussed earlier).

Legal Structure of Nauru Courts

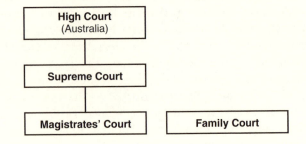

Judiciary

Supreme Court
The Supreme Court of Nauru is established as a superior court by the constitution. This court has original jurisdiction to hear any case concerning the interpretation of the constitution. It also gives advisory opinions on any questions that may arise in the cabinet concerning the interpretation or effect of the constitution. Parliament may provide for an appellate division of the Supreme Court, consisting of one or two judges. The constitution also provides that appeals from the decisions of the Supreme Court may be taken to another country.

The Courts Act of 1972 provides for the positions of registrar and deputy registrar of the Supreme Court. The registrar is responsible for administering court matters, such as filing suits and setting hearing dates. As of 2001, there was one judge sitting at the Supreme Court of Nauru. The judges of the Supreme Court are appointed by the president and must have been entitled to practice as a barrister or solicitor in Nauru for at least five years.

District Court
The District Court is established under the Courts Act of 1972. Its main aim is to hear cases arising from within the district. The District Court has jurisdiction to hear contract or torts cases not exceeding $A3,000. However, it has a very limited jurisdiction in dealing with criminal issues. The small size of the community means that matters of a criminal nature are best left to the Supreme Court. Similar to the requirement for appointing judges for the Supreme Court, candidates must be entitled to practice as barristers and be able to plead in a court of law before they can be appointed as magistrates. The president appoints the magistrates after consultation with the chief justice.

Family Court
Nauru is the second country in the Pacific (along with Fiji) to have a specialized Family Court. The Nauru Family Court was established by the Family Court Act of

1973. The court consists of the resident magistrate and other members appointed by the president. The Family Court has jurisdiction to hear maintenance cases pursuant to the Maintenance Ordinance of 1959–1967 and adoption cases under the Children Ordinance of 1965–1967. The proceedings in the Family Court are held in camera and not open to the public.

THE CIVIL LAW AND PROCEDURE

Many elements of Nauru civil law and procedures are adopted from the English system; they include family law, property law, contract law, tort law, wills and succession, commercial law, labor law, and public law. In civil cases, the private individual initiates proceedings. The procedure for raising claims is prescribed in the Civil Procedure Act of 1972. The burden of proof in civil claims is the civil burden—that is, a balance of probabilities.

THE CRIMINAL LAW AND PROCEDURE

Nauru has adopted the Queensland Criminal Code as the main legislation governing offenses on the island. In the Queensland Criminal Code, the offenses are divided into the following categories:

- Offenses against public order, including treason, inciting to mutiny, assisting escaping prisoners of war, and sedition
- Offenses against the executive and legislative power, such as interfering with the head of state and Parliament, giving false evidence, refusing to give evidence as a witness before Parliament, and bribing or receiving bribes from a member of Parliament
- Unlawful assemblies and breaches of peace, including rioting, smuggling arms, forcible entry, challenge to a duel, threat of violence, and unlawful prosecutions
- Offenses against the administration of law and justice, including disclosure of official secrets; corruption and abuse of office; corrupt and improper practice in elections; selling and trafficking in offices; judicial corruption; perjury or fabrication or destruction of evidence; corrupting, deceiving, or preventing a witness from attending a hearing; conspiracy to bring false accusations or to defeat justice; attempting to pervert justice; escaping, rescuing, and obstructing officers of court; offenses relating to currency; and offenses relating to posts and telegraphs
- Acts injurious to the public in general, including offenses against religious worship; offenses against sexual morality, including indecent treatment or abuse of children; indecent acts; incest; attempts to procure abortions; obscene publications and exhibitions; nuisance and misconduct relating to corpses; and offenses against public health
- Offenses against persons, including assault; homicide covering willful murder; murder; manslaughter; aiding suicide; and assault and abduction of females, including rape, bigamy, and kidnapping
- Offenses relating to property, including stealing or theft; stealing with violence, such as robbery, burglary, and housebreaking; obtaining property by false pretenses and cheating; and receiving stolen or fraudulently obtained property
- Offenses involving forgery and counterfeiting of trademarks and other documents, fraudulent debtors, and offenses relating to business associations

Section 37 of the constitution, however, provides that "nobody can be charged for an offence that is not defined by, and the penalty for which is not prescribed by, a written law." In addition to the due process requirement provided by Section 37, Part 5 of the Criminal Code provides freedom from criminal responsibility for offenses committed in the following situations:

- Where a person makes an honest claim of right in property-related offenses is excused by Section 23
- Where a person does not have the requisite intention to commit an offense, that person is not criminally responsible
- Where there is mistake of fact—in circumstances prescribed under Section 25
- Where an offense is committed in an emergency (but this does not affect the defenses of provocation and self-defense)
- Where a person pleads and proves insanity
- Where the person is a minor under seven years of age
- Where a person is under the age of fourteen, he or she will not be criminally responsible for the offense of rape

In Nauru, criminal procedure is regulated by the Criminal Procedure Act (1972). The act protects the rights of persons charged with an offense as guaranteed by the constitution of Nauru. Offenders are prosecuted by the Prosecution Office and must prove the guilt of the person charged beyond a reasonable doubt.

Phillip Tagini

See also Common Law; Customary Law
References and further reading
Deklin, T. 1993. "Nauru." Pp. 142–157 in *South Pacific Islands Legal Systems*. Edited by M. Ntumy. Honolulu: University of Hawai'i Press.
Douglas, Norman, and Ngaire Douglas. 1989. *Pacific Islands Yearbook*. North Ryde, New South Wales: Angus and Robertson Publishing.

Mehra, N. 1990. *Practice and Procedure of the Parliament of Nauru.* Nauru: Parliament of Nauru.

Ntumy, M., ed. 1993. *South Pacific Islands Legal Systems.* Honolulu: University of Hawai'i Press.

NEBRASKA

GENERAL INFORMATION

Nebraska is located in the so-called heartland of the United States. It is known as a heartland state because of its central Great Plains location, its heavy reliance on a traditional agriculturally based economy, and a culture that emphasizes basic values. Nebraska, like most of its neighboring plains states, is changing at an incremental rate. For instance, the 2000 census showed that the population in Nebraska grew from 1,578,385 in 1990 to 1,711,263 in 2000. The 2000 census further indicated that a significant part of that growth has been along a central corridor (marked by large railroad lines and Interstate 80), and around its two main urban centers, Omaha and Lincoln, on the eastern edge of the state. Nebraska covers 77,358 square miles. Ethnic homogeneity in this vast state has been punctuated by a great increase in diversity. Historically, numerous small towns settled by waves of European immigrants characterized Nebraska. Settlers were drawn to Nebraska as part of the general execution of Manifest Destiny: some intended to settle here, while others fell into Nebraska as they were headed to California, Oregon, or Utah. Recent immigrants have enriched the diversity of the state. For example, the Hispanic population grew at an annual rate of 155 percent in the 1990s. Increasing numbers of Asian Americans and African Americans will continue to add diversity to the ethnic composition of Nebraska.

Nebraska is known as the "Cornhusker State" and for good reason, as the foundation of the economy is linked to agriculture. While Nebraska continues to have a strong agricultural economy, small manufacturing, meat processing, and a variety of other businesses including insurance and high tech have recently prospered. Diversification of the economy has reduced the dependence on agriculture and ensured a higher degree of economic prosperity. Once the entire economy of the state was linked to agriculture, and when the farm economy was poor the state's economy was also poor. That is no longer the case; the recent downturn in farm prices has not slowed the state's economic growth, and it has had little effect on the communities along the central corridor and within the metro areas of Lincoln and Omaha.

The state has a quality system of higher education, and it is fortunate to have two very fine law schools at the University of Nebraska and Creighton University. Both schools provide extensive service to the legal profession as well as to the citizens of Nebraska. Law clinics can be found at both schools, and both schools provide appropriate resources to practicing attorneys.

As of 1995, Nebraska had 4,651 lawyers. In terms of the ratio of the number of lawyers to the state's population, Nebraska ranked twenty-third among U.S. states. About 19 percent of Nebraska's lawyers are women, and 70 percent are in private practice. Lawyers who wish to practice in Nebraska must be members of the Nebraska Bar Association.

EVOLUTION AND HISTORY

Nebraska's political history contains many fascinating characters and features. Some characters of note include the great populist and presidential candidate William Jennings Bryan, the prominent progressive George Norris, the brilliant legal scholar Roscoe Pound, and the Wall Street genius Warren Buffet. Nebraska remains the only state, thanks to George Norris, to operate a nonpartisan unicameral legislature. The structure of the court system, however, is fairly typical.

This is not to say that the judiciary has not issued landmark cases of national consequence. The infamous *Meyers v. Nebraska* (1923) illustrates a case in which the Nebraska court was swayed by the anti-German sentiment of the post–World War I era. More recently, the judiciary was confronted with the issue of partial birth abortion in *Stenberg v. Carhart* (2000), resulting in the state attorney general's arguing (and losing) before the U.S. Supreme Court. Aside from the landmark cases percolating from the Nebraska judiciary, the mechanics of the Nebraska court system are rather typical.

CURRENT STRUCTURE

Nebraska's court structure is similar to that of most other sparsely populated states. The accompanying figure illustrates the similarities in that the number of kinds of courts is limited, the structure is simple, most courts are trial courts, and the appellate system is streamlined and quite easy to follow. Furthermore, specialized courts are few and far between in Nebraska.

The workhorses of the Nebraska judicial system are the county courts and the district courts. County courts are found in many of Nebraska's ninety-three counties, and they work to address most of the day-to-day matters of the state's citizens in their small claims division. County courts in Nebraska have original jurisdiction in most minor criminal and civil cases, perform preliminary hearings for most criminal cases, handle traffic matters and juvenile cases (except when the legislature has established juvenile courts in the counties), and enforce most municipal ordinances. Superior to the county courts are the district courts.

Legal Structure of Nebraska Courts

Nebraska Supreme Court
Chief Justice and 6 Judges
Highest Appellate Court:
- discretionary appeals from the Court of Appeals
- mandatory appeals in:
    + capital cases
    + cases concerning constitutionality of statutes
- may hear cases removed from or that have bypassed the Court of Appeals by a petition of further review. Original Jurisdiction: specified cases

Court of Appeals
6 Judges
Panels of 3 judges hear appeals throughout state
Intermediate Appellate Court:
- trial court appeals except those heard by Supreme Court pursuant to:
    + mandatory jurisdiction
    + direct appeal status
    + removal procedures
    + bypass procedures

Separate Juvenile Courts
8 Judges
Serving in 3 counties (Douglas, Sarpy, and Lancaster)
Jurisdiction: county court, juvenile, and domestic jurisdiction

District Courts
53 Judges
Serving 12 districts
Trial court of general jurisdiction:
- felony cases
- domestic relations cases
- civil cases more than $15,000
When serving as an appellate court:
- county court appeals
- administrative agency appeals

Workers' Compensation Courts
7 Judges
Judges hear cases throughout the state
Jurisdiction: occupation, injury, and illness cases

Administrative Tribunal
Each board, commission, department, officer, division, or other administrative office or unit of the state government authorized by law to make rules and regulations
(not a part of the state court structure)

County Courts
59 Judges
Serving 12 districts
Jurisdiction:
- domestic relations cases
- misdemeanor cases, including traffic and municipal ordinance violations
- preliminary hearings in felony cases

* Source: Nebraska State Court Administrator's Office.
1 A 54th district judge was to be added July 1, 2000.
2 A ninth juvenile judge was to be added July 1, 1999.

Nebraska's district courts are found in twelve judicial districts across the state. Within the twelve districts are fifty-four individual courts. These courts have some appellate jurisdiction; judges may hear appeals from county courts and the separate administrative tribunals found in some agencies. Most often, Nebraska district courts do not hear cases on appeal; they are quite busy hearing cases where they are the trial court and have original jurisdiction. District courts handle major civil and criminal cases, and they serve as the trial court for many of the more serious domestic relations cases. District courts exclusively handle all capital punishment cases in the trial phase.

The relatively new (established in 1991) Nebraska Intermediate Court of Appeals is composed of two panels of three judges. The judges rotate through the panels under the direction of a chief judge who is appointed from the panel of judges by the state Supreme Court. Even though the Nebraska Intermediate Court of Appeals is relatively new, it has steadily increased its caseload as well as gaining acceptance in judicial circles as a highly important court. A good number of cases, especially prisoner complaints and appeals, go directly to the Intermediate Court of Appeals unless the Supreme Court decides to hear the case first. Just as state Supreme Court chief justice William Hastings had desired when he proposed the new court in 1987, the court of appeals has helped eliminate the high court's backlog of cases.

Nebraska's Supreme Court consists of six judges and a chief justice. Each judge comes from one of six judicial districts in the state. The chief justice is selected at large and represents, in a manner of speaking, the entire state. While most of the high court's cases come through its appellate jurisdiction, it does have original jurisdiction in cases in which the state is party to revenue and civil disputes. The high court's original jurisdiction extends to a small list of other matters, but its most visible role is when death penalty appeals come to it.

Nebraska also has a few separate juvenile courts. These courts handle cases in Nebraska's urban counties: Douglas, Sarpy, and Lancaster. In total, there are nine juvenile court judges in Nebraska, and they handle most matters relating to neglected, dependent, and delinquent children. Outside of the metro-area counties, juvenile matters are handled by county court judges, in addition to their other duties.

Nebraska does have one special court, the Workers' Compensation Court. This court meets in the state capital, Lincoln, and its sole purpose is to administer and enforce the Nebraska Workers' Compensation Act. Administering and enforcing normally means that the court hears cases when worker claims for benefits have been made.

Court administration in Nebraska is largely left to the courts themselves, and the Nebraska Supreme Court takes the lead in these matters. Of course, this is not unlike the role that the U.S. Supreme Court (especially its chief justice) takes in the administration of the federal courts. There is also a state court administrator, who oversees most of the judicial selection activities in Nebraska.

STAFFING

The selection of judges is modeled after the Missouri Plan. Being a Missouri Plan (or "merit plan," as most judges and the bar prefer to call it) state, Nebraska also has a Judicial Resources Commission, charged with determining when judicial vacancies have occurred. The commission also makes recommendations to the unicameral legislature about redistricting. The Judicial Resources Commission is composed of a district judge, a county judge, a Supreme Court judge, six members of the Nebraska bar, and seven governor-appointed citizens. Another commission, the Judicial Nominating Commission, is more directly related to Nebraska's "merit plan" for judicial selection and retention. The nominating commissions listen to candidates for new positions once the Resources Commission finds a vacancy. There are numerous commissions, because a local one is called each time a vacancy has occurred. Each commission includes four bar-appointed lawyers and four nonlawyers appointed by the governor. The duty of the commission is to present two names from the list of the applicants to the governor, who then will select the judge to fill the vacancy.

Retention elections are consistent with Nebraska's populist political culture, in which elections heightened democratic governance. Despite this electoral mechanism, very few judges have lost a retention election. Still, if voters perceive poor judicial behavior, they may vote not to retain the judge.

A third commission has been established by the legislature to help ensure ethical behavior on the part of judges. The Commission on Judicial Qualifications, like the other panels described above, has appointees who by law must come from a variety of citizen groups. Three judges are appointed by the chief justice of the Nebraska Supreme Court to the Judicial Qualifications Commission. Likewise, the bar appoints three lawyers, and the governor appoints three citizens. Members of this commission serve four-year terms and meet to determine whether they should recommend to the Supreme Court that a judge be reprimanded, disciplined, censured, or suspended. Punishment for judges may come if they are found to have: (1) willfully engaged in misconduct, (2) failed to perform their duties, (3) exhibited habitual intemperance, (4) been convicted of a crime of moral turpitude, (5) been disbarred, or (6) been engaged in conduct that harms their office or the conduct of justice.

It is important to note that the Nebraska Supreme Court controls the admission and discipline of attorneys.

The Nebraska Bar Association in turn asserts only general influence over the judiciary. The bar has viewed the Nebraska courts and the activities of its officers as working well. No doubt the bar does raise issues of importance to the workings of the judiciary. Greater questions of fairness and justice, as well as racial and gender issues, challenge actors in the judicial arena. It was not until the close of the twentieth century that the Nebraska Bar Association had a woman as the president of the bar. The 1999–2000 president of the bar and first woman ever elected to serve as the president of the bar did heighten the awareness of diversity issues. The bar also indicated that Nebraska's pool of practicing attorneys did not represent minorities because most attorneys are white. Given the increasing minority population and the call for gender and racial equality, the court staff could indeed become more diverse.

NOTABLE FEATURES

It is the general consensus that the Nebraska courts as a whole are well-established parts of the Nebraska governmental process. A closer examination shows that justice from the Nebraska bench requires reform every so often. The inclusion of an Intermediate Court of Appeals meant that efficiency within the realm of appellate actions was greatly improved.

Further, issues of fairness will not go away, regardless of the court system. Today there is a challenge for the judiciary to embrace diversity and issues raised by discrimination (a good example of a festering issue is the administration of the death penalty in Nebraska). Discrimination in death penalty cases is not solely based on race; it also seems to be related to income. Currently, every person on death row in Nebraska was represented by a public defender. The correlation between income and capital punishment is serious enough that the legislature proposed both a study of it and a moratorium on the use of capital punishment. The governor signed the law funding and requiring the study but vetoed the moratorium. Ultimately the task is on the judiciary to preserve the integrity of justice in Nebraska. Of course, there are other issues that will allow the courts to make a profound mark on the efficacy of the administration of justice in Nebraska.

In fine populist tradition, the citizens of the state of Nebraska typically assume that they serve as the ultimate judges. The citizens have come to expect fair treatment from all Nebraska institutions, especially the courts. After all, the state motto is "Equality Before the Law."

Peter Longo
John L. Anderson

See also Capital Punishment; Judicial Selection, Methods of; Juvenile Justice; Trial Courts; United States—Federal System; United States—State Systems

References and further reading
Kristensen, Douglas A. 1992. "The Nebraska Court of Appeals: Finally an Opportunity for Prompt Justice." *Creighton Law Review* 25: 469–486.
Miewald, Robert D. 1984. *Nebraska Government and Politics.* Lincoln: University of Nebraska Press.
Miewald, Robert D., and Peter J. Longo. 1993. *The Nebraska State Constitution: A Reference Guide.* Westport, CT: Greenwood Press.
Miller-Lerman, Lindsey. 1993. "The Nebraska Court of Appeals." *Creighton Law Review* 27: 146–157.
Nebraska Blue Book. 2000. www.state.ne.us.

NEIGHBORHOOD JUSTICE CENTERS

Neighborhood justice centers (NJC) are court-deferral programs designed to mediate minor civil and criminal disputes between parties who had (or continue to have) ongoing relationships (for example, family members, neighbors, or landlords and tenants). In most jurisdictions, mediation is mandatory on filling a domestic civil complaint. In others, a judge will order the parties to go to mediation as part of the court's ruling. The location of NJCs varies from inside court buildings along with other deferral programs to distinctly separate locations, such as neighborhood centers and office buildings.

NJCs were established in the early 1980s as part of a worldwide reform movement called "alternative dispute resolution" or "access to justice." According to the reformers, mediation by lay citizens trained in the skills of labor mediation promised efficiency via specialized forums for particular kinds of problems and the rational allocation of judicial resources. Reformers also claimed that mediation was a consensus-building process that parties preferred to the adversarial model of adjudication. There is, however, little sound empirical evidence to support this claim; indeed, what was once a "voluntary" service has been made largely mandatory because parties were not willing to voluntarily go to NJCs. In the United States, the legal profession's interest in rationalizing, streamlining, and fine-tuning the judicial system to cope more effectively with a wide range of problems was a theme in court administration and court reform throughout the twentieth century. The U.S. Attorney General's Office created pilot NJCs, which then served as models for local bar associations and community groups to replicate. Within a decade of their development, NJCs became as prevalent as small claims courts in the U.S. court system. These court-related mediation programs are the most typical kind of NJCs.

The term "neighborhood justice center" is also a generic term for mediation programs not affiliated with courts or focused on rationalizing dispute processing.

Neighborhood justice has been part of broader social transformation experiments in Cuba, Chile, and Portugal since the 1974 revolution, where the public theater of the lower courts is seen as a powerful socialization experience. In the contemporary U.S. movement, there is talk of "community empowerment," the creation of a new sense of community through self-governance or neighborhood control, decentralized judicial decision making, and the substitution of community members for professional dispute resolvers. Proponents of this type of program turn to socialist experiments conducted under revolutionary conditions for inspiration, deliberately taking on the social transformation agenda that accompanied these movements. Advocates view community mediation as completely independent of the judicial system and locate its authority in the local neighborhood rather than the state.

Another kind of neighborhood justice center is those that emphasize "personal growth and development" and view mediation as a process of consensual dispute settlement that "empowers" individuals, permits them to take greater control over their own lives by enhancing their personal skills in dealing with conflict, and endows them with techniques that they can apply to other situations. These neighborhood justice centers use psychological approaches instead of labor-mediation approaches in their dispute process training sessions. There are also religiously inspired mediation programs that argue that learning to settle differences through sharing ideas and talking will diminish dependence and improve spiritual well-being.

Local programs typically spin off from a single ideological project, but there are interesting mixes among them. Some programs emphasize social and personal transformation; others advocate increased efficiency as well as greater personal satisfaction. While the court-related NJCs espouses a close working relation with the judicial system, the social transformation neighborhood justice programs may reject all ties with it. The personal growth programs may cooperate with the state judicial system but derive their ideological inspiration from the helping professions rather than the judicial system. To some extent, however, a therapeutic approach to problem solving is already well entrenched in the judicial system.

Comparative studies of informalism reveal much sharper and deeper political divisions over the meaning of community mediation than those apparent in the U.S. experience. For example, in the former Soviet Union, China, Cuba, Chile, and Portugal, "popular justice" has been associated with periods of upheaval and revolution. Informalism was harnessed to the task of reshaping society according to a new, revolutionary vision. In the early postrevolutionary years, the Cuban government viewed local justice as a form of public theater to be carried out on the streets with a clear articulation of the new moral order. Similarly, in Portugal after the 1974 revolution, popular justice played a role in social transformation. The 1971 proposal in Chile to establish neighborhood courts was promoted by Salvador Allende's recently elected party, designed to establish a nationwide system of elected, neighborhood, lay-staffed courts, framed in the critique that the poor had no access to the existing legal system and that the professional judiciary was part of the legal order that discriminated against the poor. However, in other Third World countries, neighborhood justice reforms have been designed to promote modernization by pulling marginal and obstreperous elements into the center.

The terms of debate over neighborhood justice in the United States are not as stark: The underlying political meanings are more subdued and camouflaged. In the U.S. context, it is harder to find sharp divisions between self-government and state power, working-class control and professional control, or the use of legal metaphors and relationship metaphors. Although the three ideological projects discussed earlier are analytically distinct, the boundaries between them are ambiguous, with considerable borrowing of ideas and central symbols. Indeed, the use of symbols in the community mediation movement lies in their very ambiguity—in the multiplicity of interpretations that are possible and are mobilized as resources for the reform movement and within local programs.

Christine B. Harrington

See also Alternative Dispute Resolution; Mediation
References and further reading
Able, Richard, ed. 1982. *The Politics of Informal Justice.* Vols. 1 and 2. New York: Academic Press.
Auerbach, Jerold S.1983. *Justice without Law?* New York: Oxford University Press.
Harrington, Christine B. 1985. *Shadow Justice: The Ideology and Institutionalization of Alternatives to Court.* Westport, CT: Greenwood Press.
Harrington, Christine B., and Sally Engle Merry. 1988. "Ideological Production: The Making of Community Mediation." *Law and Society Review* 22: 709–735.
Hofrichter, Richard. 1987. *Neighborhood Justice in Capitalist Society: The Expansion of the Informal State.* Westport, CT: Greenwood Press.
Milner, Neal, and Sally Merry, eds. 1993. *The Possibility of Popular Justice.* Ann Arbor: University of Michigan Press.
Nader, Laura, and Harry L. Todd, eds. 1978. *The Dispute Process: Law in Ten Societies.* New York: Columbia University Press.
Pipkin, R. M., and J. Rifkin. 1984. "The Social Organization in Alternative Dispute Resolution: Implications for Professionalization of Mediation." *Justice Systems Journal* 8: 204–207.
Tomasic, Roman, and Malcolm Feeley, eds. 1982. *Neighborhood Justice: Assessment of an Emerging Idea.* New York: Longman.
Yngvesson, Barbara. 1993. *Virtuous Citizens, Disruptive Subjects: Order and Complaint in a New England Court.* New York: Routledge.

NEPAL

COUNTRY INFORMATION

Nepal, home of some of the tallest mountains in the world and part of the Himalaya mountain range, is a small country situated between India to the south and Tibet and China to the north. To many, Nepal conjures up images of majestic mountains and historic climbs up Mount Everest, the highest mountain peak in the world. But within its approximately 54,912 square miles, Nepal's terrain is quite varied. In the northern regions, the terrain is mountainous. The central region or Hill region contains the capital, Kathmandu, and is characterized by terraced hills and valleys. In the southern region, known as the Tarai, the terrain is flat and fertile, and the climate is tropical. Outside of the Tarai region, the climate varies depending on altitude, with mountainous peaks in the arctic or subarctic climatic zones.

Nepal is one of the poorest countries in the world. It is home to approximately 24,702,119 inhabitants. Of those, almost half live below the poverty line. Eighty percent of the population relies on agriculture for its livelihood. The gross domestic product (GDP) is about $27.4 billion. The literacy rate among males age fifteen and over is 40.9 percent, and the rate among females age fifteen and over is 14 percent.

Approximately 89.5 percent of the population is Hindu, 5.3 percent Buddhist, 2.7 percent Muslim, and the remaining 2.5 percent practice other religions, including Christianity. The three major ethnic groups can be divided by geographic origin: Indo-Nepalese, Tibeto-Nepalese, and indigenous Nepalese. Although the caste system is no longer officially recognized in Nepal, caste discrimination still occurs.

Since 1992, approximately 96,000 refugees from nearby Bhutan have been living in seven refugee camps established in Nepal by the United Nations High Commissioner for Refugees. An estimated 2,000 Tibetans also seek refuge in Nepal each year.

HISTORY

Lumbini, which is in the Tarai region of Nepal, was the birthplace of the Buddha in 563 B.C.E. Nepal's history as a kingdom goes back over 1,500 years. The earliest kingdom, that of the Licchavis, began in the late fifth century C.E. This opened the door for a series of successive kingdoms and the development of the Kathmandu Valley as an important focal point of social and political activity.

Modern Nepal began to take shape in 1559, when Dravya Shah founded the House of Gorkha, a hereditary monarchy. Gorkha slowly expanded its territory in the seventeenth and eighteenth centuries until it clashed with the British East India Company over the annexed territories, which were territories administered by the British East India Company in the border region south and west of the Gorkha empire. The Anglo-Nepalese War (1814–1816) took its toll on Nepal and its Gorkha-led army. Although the resulting treaty, the Treaty of Sagauli, stripped Nepal of some territory in the Tarai region, the British East India Company found the territory difficult to govern and later returned some of the land, creating roughly the same boundaries Nepal has today.

Beginning in 1846 and continuing until 1950, Nepal entered a period of successive dictatorships led by Rana prime ministers, descendants of the house of Rana. During the Rana period, the government functioned as a landed aristocracy despite calling itself a constitutional monarchy. The Rana prime ministers maintained control by cultivating a strong relationship with the army.

A shift occurred in 1950, when a small revolt resulted in the demise of the Ranas and the restoration of the monarchy. The revolution involved armed struggle and political demonstrations, including demonstrations of 50,000 people in Kathmandu. Shortly after the revolt, the monarch, King Tribhuvan Bir Bikram Shah, assumed control of the executive functions of government and the armed forces. Political parties were active but not powerful, and the country maintained the semblance of a democracy for nine years, during which a number of successive governments struggled against the power of the monarch.

In 1961, political parties became illegal, and King Mahendra Bir Bikram Shah Dev established a four-person committee to recommend changes to the constitution. In 1962, the new constitution was adopted. It placed enormous power in the hands of the king and established the *panchayat* system, which was a council system of governance at the village, district, and local levels. Although perhaps envisioned as a democratic institution, in practice, the *panchayat* system operated as a tool of the monarchy.

Leaders of the political parties, many of whom had been exiled to India, began to agitate for multiparty politics in Nepal in the late 1980s, and the demand for a multiparty system gained momentum. In February 1990, the pro-democracy movement was formally established and support grew for an end to the *panchayat* system. Bowing to political pressure and unrest, in April 1990, the government lifted the ban on political parties, the prime minister resigned, and other changes in the government structure indicated that democracy was dawning in Nepal.

In November 1990, the king approved a newly drafted constitution, which placed more power in the hands of the people. In May 1991, general elections were held, the *panchayat* system was dismantled, and a new bicameral Parliament was formed. May 1992 ushered in elections at the village and municipality levels. The new constitution also ensured that the military was not at the disposal of the king but was subject to parliamentary authority.

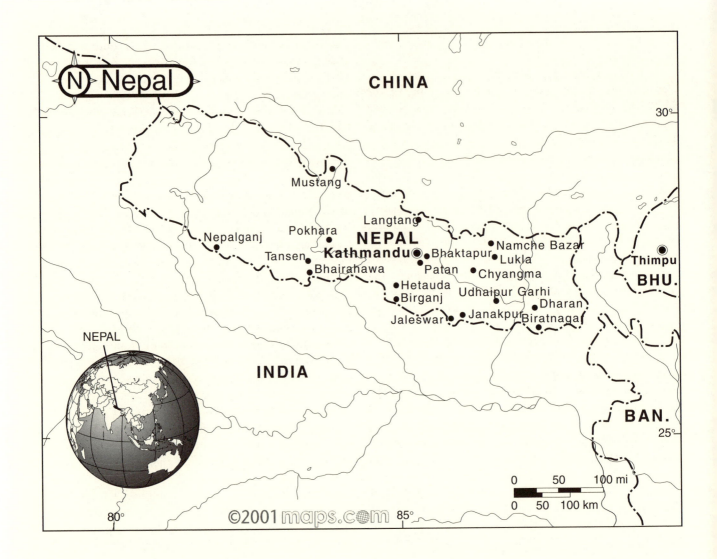

LEGAL CONCEPTS

The legal system has its roots in both English common law and Hindu traditions. One of the most salient laws in Nepal is the National Code or Muluki Ain, which means the law of the land. The 1,400-page Muluki Ain is a single legal text that was compiled in 1854, incorporating all of the then-existing socioreligious texts, which were primarily Hindu. It represents a blend of customary law and common law. The 1854 Muluki Ain included provisions addressing civil and criminal law, revenue collection, relations between landlords and peasants, intercaste disputes, and marriage and family law. Since 1854, courts in Nepal have applied the Muluki Ain.

The Muluki Ain of 1854 contained hierarchical categories of people, or castes, that privileged certain groups over others. The Brahmin or Chetri, the warrior caste, were at the top of the hierarchy; the Tibeto-Burman tribal communities dominated the middle. The Untouchable groups were at the bottom of the caste system. The Muluki Ain imposed corporal punishment and high fines on the lower castes but exempted higher castes from more serious punishment.

The most recent amendments to the Muluki Ain occurred in 1963. The 1963 version prohibited discrimination based on caste, creed, or sex and included a uniform family law applicable to all religious communities. More recent amendments reflect the influence of common law principles borrowed from neighboring India. In some areas of law, the Muluki Ain continues to govern.

The 1990 Constitution marked the beginning of true democracy in Nepal by shifting power from the king to the people. In Nepal, the constitution is the supreme law of the land, and all laws inconsistent with it will be declared void. The 1990 Constitution creates a system of checks and balances and divides power among three separate branches of government: the executive, the legislative, and the judiciary. The legislative branch consists of a bicameral Parliament made up of the king, the House of Representatives, and the National Assembly.

According to the constitution, executive power is vested in the king and the Council of Ministers. The leader of the majority party in the House of Representatives is appointed prime minister by the king. The Council of Ministers consists of the prime minister, a deputy prime minister, and other ministers appointed from among the parliamentarians.

The House of Representatives consists of 205 members, who are elected for five-year terms. The number of seats in the House per election district is equal to the ratio of the population in that district to the national population. For purposes of election to the House of Representatives, at least 5 percent of the total number of candidates from any political party must be women. Anyone eighteen years of age and over is entitled to vote.

The National Assembly consists of sixty members, ten of whom are nominated by the king. Another thirty-five members of the National Assembly are elected by the House of Representatives on the basis of proportional representation; at least three of the thirty-five must be women. The remaining fifteen members, three members from each of five regions, are elected by an electoral college consisting of elected village and local authorities. At least every five years, parliamentary elections are held.

Any issue before either house of Parliament is subject to a majority vote of the members present and voting. Members may introduce bills in either house of Parliament, with the exception of finance bills, which may only be introduced in the House of Representatives. Once either of the houses passes a bill, it is submitted to the other House. If it passes in the second House, it is submitted to the king for assent. If the second House rejects the bill or passes it with amendments, it is sent back to the House where it originated.

Although bills are submitted to the king for assent, the king does not have veto power. If the king sends a bill back for further discussion and it passes a second time, the king must give his assent within thirty days. Article 71 of the 1990 Constitution further delineates the procedure for passage of bills in Parliament and provides several exceptions to these rules.

The judicial branch in Nepal consists of three tiers of courts: the Supreme Court, the appellate courts, and the district courts. The Supreme Court is the highest court, and all other courts, except the military court, are subordinate to it. The Supreme Court consists of the chief justice of Nepal and up to fourteen other judges. The chief justice serves a term of seven years. The king appoints the chief justice on the recommendation of the Constitutional Council, and the other Supreme Court judges on the recommendation of the Judicial Council.

The Constitutional Council consists of the prime minister, chief justice, speaker of the House of Representatives, chair of the National Assembly, and leader of the opposition in the House of Representatives. The Judicial Council consists of the chief justice, the minister of Justice, the two senior-most judges on the Supreme Court, and one distinguished jurist nominated by the king. Eligibility to serve on the Supreme Court is limited to those who have worked as an appellate judge or the equivalent for at least ten years, have practiced law as an advocate or senior advocate for at least fifteen years, or have been a distinguished jurist for at least fifteen years.

Article 88 of the constitution provides that any Nepali citizen may petition the Supreme Court to have a law, in whole or in part, declared void if it is inconsistent with the constitution. The Supreme Court also has appellate jurisdiction. The Supreme Court may not, however, interfere with the decisions and proceedings of the military court except to determine whether or not the military court has jurisdiction. The king may request that the Supreme Court offer its opinion as to the interpretation of the constitution or other complicated legal questions.

The 1962 Constitution provided that the king had supreme judicial authority and could order the Supreme Court to revise its decision on a given matter. This is no longer true under the 1990 Constitution. Now, the Supreme Court's decisions are binding. This includes the government and all inferior courts. Under the new constitution, however, the king retains the power to suspend, commute, or remit any sentence imposed by any court, including special courts and military courts.

The king appoints the attorney general on the recommendation of the prime minister. The attorney general is the chief legal advisor to the king's government, and the attorney general advises the government on constitutional and other legal matters. The Attorney General's Office represents the government in any suits involving the rights or interests of the government. The eligibility requirements for the attorney general are the same as those for the Supreme Court.

The 1990 Constitution guarantees a number of fundamental rights and freedoms. One of the most significant rights guaranteed by the 1990 Constitution is the right to form political parties. The ban on political parties prior to 1990 was, in fact, one of the primary causes of the political agitation that led to the promulgation of the new constitution. Article 112 of the 1990 Constitution prohibits the imposition of restrictions on political parties or organizations.

The constitution guarantees the right to equality before the law and equal protection of the laws. The constitution specifically prohibits discrimination on the grounds of religion, race, sex, caste, tribe, or ideological conviction. The nondiscrimination provision, however, specifically allows for affirmative action programs and a provision guaranteeing equal pay for men and women.

Despite the constitution's prohibition of discrimination, members of lower castes and women still face significant discrimination in Nepal. Although not unique to Nepal, violence against women, including domestic violence and dowry violence, impairs women's enjoyment of equal rights. In addition, women continue to struggle for legal rights such as equal inheritance rights and rights to property within the family.

Unlike the 1962 Constitution, the 1990 Constitution prohibits capital punishment. The new constitution also guarantees freedom of expression and peaceful assembly; freedom of association, including the right to form unions; freedom of movement; freedom to practice any profession or occupation; and freedom of the press. Each of these rights, however, is subject to exceptions or limitations in the constitution that purport to preserve the sovereignty of the kingdom, the peaceful relations among castes or communities, or public health and morality.

According to the constitution, no one may be punished for an offense that was not a crime when the act was committed. There is also a prohibition against double jeopardy, meaning that no one may be prosecuted and punished twice for the same offense. No one may be compelled to testify against himself or herself. There is also a prohibition against physical or mental torture and cruel, inhuman, or degrading treatment. Once in custody, a person must be informed of the basis of the arrest and must not be denied the right to consult with a lawyer.

Other rights enshrined in the constitution include the right against preventive detention, the right to information, the right to property, the right to preserve one's culture, the right to religion, the right against exploitation, the right against exile, the right to privacy, and the right to constitutional remedy.

Although the 1962 Constitution contained a right against exploitation, the 1990 version includes a clause specifically prohibiting children from working in factories, mines, or any other hazardous employment. This is undoubtedly in response to the growing recognition of the problem of child labor throughout the developing world and in Nepal in particular. Several nongovernmental organizations, including the World Organization Against Torture, Anti-Slavery International, and the Child Workers in Nepal Concerned Center, have documented the problem of child labor in Nepal.

The right against exploitation is also intended to combat another problem that tragically affects children in Nepal: the practice of trafficking in human beings. Human Rights Watch estimates that there are 20,000 Nepali women and girls in Bombay who have been coerced to travel to India to work as prostitutes in brothels (Global Report, 1995). Many of these women and girls, some as young as ten years old, are kept in debt bondage for years and subject to risk of infection of HIV/AIDS or other sexually transmitted diseases.

In Article 26, the constitution articulates a commitment to providing free legal aid to indigent people. In practice, however, free legal representation is not routinely provided due to resource constraints. Remuneration for appointed lawyers is almost nonexistent. Although the Legal Advice and Consultancy Center (LACC) and other nongovernmental organizations provide legal services, there are significant unmet legal needs among the poor.

According to the Nepal Treaties Act of 1990, if Nepalese law conflicts with an international treaty to which Nepal is a party, the treaty provision controls. Nepal is a party to a number of human rights treaties, including: the International Covenant on Civil and Political Rights; the International Covenant on Economic, Social, and Cultural Rights; the International Convention on the Elimination of All Forms of Discrimination Against Women; the International Convention on the Elimination of Racial Discrimination; the Convention Against Torture, and Other Cruel, Inhuman or Degrading Treatment or Punishment; the Convention on the Rights of the Child; and numerous International Labor Organization conventions.

CURRENT COURT SYSTEM STRUCTURE

The Supreme Court of Nepal is the highest court in the country. The appellate courts are under the Supreme Court, and the district courts are under the appellate courts. There are seventy-five district courts and eleven appellate courts. All lower court decisions are subject to appeal; even acquittals in criminal cases are subject to appeal.

An independent judiciary is one of the bedrock principles of a democratic society. The Supreme Court of Nepal has demonstrated its independence by striking down unconstitutional legislation. It has, for example, stricken provisions of the 1991 Citizenship Act and the 1992 Labor Act. The Supreme Court, however, is hampered by a significant backlog of cases. According to some estimates, there are 15,000 active cases at the Supreme Court level, resulting in a delay of more than ten years on a given case.

In each administrative district, the chief district officer is charged with maintaining political stability and order. The powers of the chief district officer are quasi-judicial and are subject to appeal before the appellate, and in some cases district, courts. The chief district officer often summons the parties to a dispute to appear before him or her and attempts to mediate. In the case of less serious crimes, the chief district officer might make a ruling and impose a small penalty, all of which would be subject to appeal. In the case of an individual seeking a divorce, the local or regional development committee is charged with attempting reconciliation. If the attempted mediation has failed, the case may be referred to the local district court.

SPECIALIZED JUDICIAL BODIES

Military personnel are tried before military courts and are immune from prosecution in civil courts. The 1992 Children's Act requires the government to establish a

Legal Structure of Nepal Courts

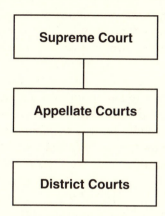

Supreme Court

Appellate Courts

District Courts

juvenile court, but the government has not yet implemented this provision. The constitution provides that special courts and tribunals may be established for the purpose of hearing special types of cases as long as they are not established for the purpose of hearing one particular case.

In 1996, the Parliament enacted a bill creating a Human Rights Commission. The Human Rights Commission theoretically has the authority to investigate human rights violations, but as of February 2000, the commission had not yet been established. In July 1999 the Supreme Court issued an order directing the government to immediately establish the commission. Approximately two months later, the government convened a task force, which in December 1999 issued recommendations on the establishment of the commission.

STAFFING

There are two levels in Nepalese legal education: the certificate level and the diploma level. The certificate level prepares students to be legal assistants or to be midlevel judicial administrators. Students may continue their legal studies beyond the certificate level and move to the diploma level. Government statistics from 1998 indicate that the number of law students in Nepal has declined slightly in recent years, dropping from 6,380 students in 1994–1995 to 3,928 students in 1996–1997. Tribhuvan University Institute of Law is one of the primary legal education institutions.

A national bar association, called the Nepal Bar Association, is actively involved in the community and has a number of committees, including an examination conducting committee and a publications committee. A Supreme Court Bar Association consists of members of the bar who frequently practice before the Supreme Court. Members of the bar are vocal in advocating for institutional changes within the judiciary, such as better documentation of judicial precedents and codification of

laws, activation of a law reform commission, improved judicial training, and increased budgetary allocations for the judiciary. Advocating for the establishment of a judicial training academy in Nepal, the Joint Registrar of the Supreme Court estimated that approximately 10,000 legal professionals, including quasi-judicial officials in the public and private sectors, would benefit from such an academy. Members of the bar have also joined representatives of nongovernmental organizations and legal educators in discussions and symposia designed to improve legal education in Nepal and foster the development of clinical legal education.

IMPACT

Charges of corruption are widespread within the judiciary in Nepal. Very few people deny the existence of corruption, but many differ as to the best approach to combat it. Some observers blame the low pay of judges and other judicial staff. A study conducted by the Institute of Legal Research and Resources found that 3 percent of lawyers, 8 percent of government attorneys, 26 percent of police, and 1 percent of judges were involved in extracting bribes from criminal suspects.

The 1990 Constitution ushered in great progress in Nepal. The democratic functioning of government has instilled a sense of optimism in the potential of representative government and the potential of law to effect social progress. Although much progress is yet to be made in Nepal, recent political and legal reforms are cause for optimism.

Johanna Bond

See also Judicial Independence; Legal Aid
References and further reading
Government of Nepal. 1998. *Nepal in Figures 1998*. Library of Congress Microfiche Collection, 98/62664.
Human Rights Watch. 1995. *Global Report on Women's Human Rights* 230.
"Judicial Academy Vital for Legal Education." 2000. *Kathmandu Post*, Sept. 1.
Kingdom of Nepal. 1999. Ministry of Information and Communication, Dept. of Information.
Library of Congress. 1993. *Nepal and Bhutan*. Country Studies, Federal Research Division, Library of Congress.
Thapa, Dhruba Bar Singh. 1984. "The Legal System of Nepal." In *Modern Legal Systems Cyclopedia*, vol. 9. Edited by Kenneth Robert Redden. Buffalo, NY: W. S. Hein.
United Nations. 1994. Core Document forming part of the Report of States Parties: Nepal. 14/06/94.HRI/CORE/1/Add.42.
U.S. Dept. of State. 2000. "1999 Country Reports on Human Rights Practices: Nepal." http://www.state.gov/www/global/human_rights/1999_hrp_report/nepal.html (accessed November 25, 2001).
World Factbook 2000—Nepal, at http://www.odci.gov/cia/publications/factbook/geos/np.html (accessed November 25, 2001).

NETHERLANDS

COUNTRY INFORMATION

The Kingdom of the Netherlands consists of the Netherlands, the Dutch Antilles, and Aruba. The Charter of the Kingdom *(Statuut van het Koninkrijk der Nederlanden)* specifies that the three parts of the kingdom have their own power of legislation. Therefore, this contribution is limited to the Netherlands, located in Western Europe. The country is bordered by the North Sea, Belgium, and Germany. Although small (41,532 square kilometers), it has a long coastline (450 kilometers) and always has been closely linked to the sea, which is both the country's friend and its foe. Situated in the originally swampy area around the deltas of the rivers Rhine, Meuse, and Schelde, most of the country consists of land reclaimed from the sea by building dikes and draining polders. In fact, about half of the country is below sea level, often as much as 5 meters. This became horribly apparent when, in 1953, a combination of high tide and severe storm flooded large parts of the western provinces, drowning 1,835 people. This disaster led to the building of even more dikes along the seashore. Small floodings in 1992 and 1994 and the threat of larger ones along the rivers have now led to the major strengthening of river dikes.

The Dutch climate is mild. The weather is much influenced by the relatively warm Gulf Stream through the North Sea, causing cool summers and mild winters.

Sixteen million rather wealthy people inhabit this flat country. The Dutch are the tallest in the world, supposedly because of good nutrition. Life expectancy at birth is seventy-eight years for women and seventy-five for men. After large-scale immigration in recent decades from the former colony Suriname and countries around the Mediterranean—notably Morocco, Turkey, Greece, and Italy—minority ethnic groups now comprise about 10 percent of the population. Although the country is a Protestant nation, the largest religious group is Roman Catholics (about a third), and a quarter of the population is Protestant; other religious groups each have less than 5 percent. The official language is Dutch. Although the capital is Amsterdam, The Hague (in Dutch called both Den Haag and 's-Gravenhage) is the seat of government.

The Netherlands is a modern industrialized nation with much natural gas and petroleum. Even though the country is among the most densely populated in the world, it succeeds in being a large exporter of agricultural products. A highly mechanized agricultural sector employs no more than 4 percent of the labor force but provides large surpluses for the food-processing industry and for exports. Thus the Netherlands ranks third worldwide in value of agricultural exports, behind the United States and France. The central position of the country guarantees an important role for transport and foreign trade in the economy, in which both the Harbor of Rotterdam (the largest in the world) and Schiphol Amsterdam Airport (much larger than strictly necessary for such a small country) play an important role. Most trade, however, is within the European Union, that is, 78 percent of the export and 61 percent of the import.

The Netherlands is a member of the European Union and is participant to almost all relevant treaty organizations. Please note that the Netherlands is often referred to as Holland, but Holland in fact is only the western, but admittedly the most prosperous and the most populated, part of the country.

HISTORY

The Netherlands became independent from Spain in 1579. In those days the country was larger, also including parts of the present Belgium and Luxembourg. The 80-year war against Spain led to what we now call the Golden Age of the Netherlands. Trade and art flourished. After a steady decline, the French occupied the country in 1795.

Prior to the French occupation (1795–1813) of the Netherlands, the country was a federal republic that consisted of rather autonomous provinces and consequently had a judicial system that resembled a hodgepodge. Although Roman-Germanic law provided a generally accepted legal framework, customary law governed much of legal decision making. The French not only brought the system of codification to the Netherlands, but also left the country with a uniform, hierarchical structure of courts.

The history of the present-day Dutch legal system really started during the occupation in 1811 when the Netherlands was incorporated in the French Empire. This gave the country a unified legal system in which law was codified. After independence the first Dutch Constitution stipulated that all Dutch law should be incorporated in codes.

In 1814 the country became a constitutional monarchy and was unified with the present-day Belgium. In 1831, however, Belgium seceded and formed a separate kingdom. During the nineteenth century, industrialization in the Netherlands was much slower than in the rest of Western Europe, resulting in the saying, "Everything comes twenty years later in the Netherlands."

The country remained neutral during World War I. That war in fact brought relative wealth to the country, because the Dutch kept on trading with all combating parties. During World War II the Netherlands was occupied after a ten-day war with Germany in May 1940. The occupation lasted until May 1945, although the Allied forces in the second half of 1944 liberated the southern part. That winter, supplies became so scarce in Holland that it is still called the Hungerwinter.

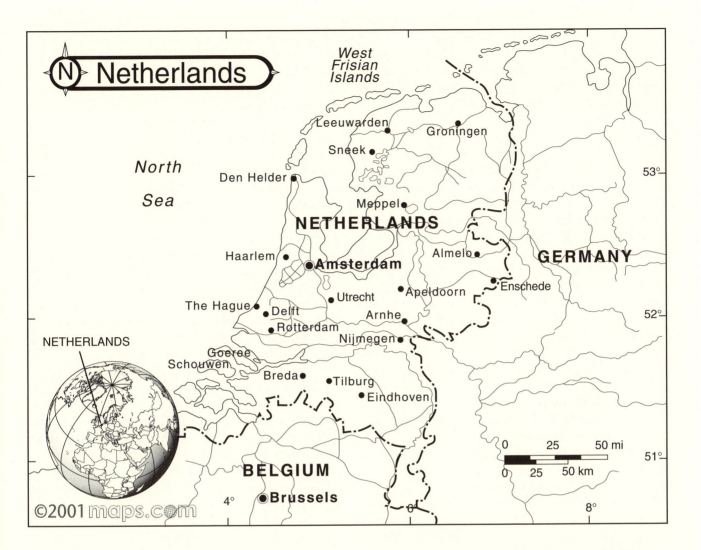

Especially during the first half of the twentieth century, Dutch society was strongly divided in so-called *zuilen,* parts of society that are divided according to religious and political denominations. The most important *zuilen* in which Dutch society was divided were Catholics, Protestants, Socialists, and Humanists (an extensive discussion is given in Kossmann 1978, 567–574). To ensure a stable society, the government system was built on negotiation and compromise among the denominations, rather than antagonism between the *zuilen.* Although the *zuilen* became less and less important in the decades after World War II, the compromising nature of Dutch society has remained. This form of "pacificatory democracy" (Kossmann 1978, 569) requires, among others, a cabinet to appoint both political allies and allies of the opposition to important offices. If a cabinet did not, it could likewise expect the present opposition to fill every important vacancy with their own allies when the opposition came into power. But, more important, appointment of allies of the opposition is an essential part of the compromising structure that ensures a stable government, even with incompatible political and religious

zuilen. This produces a tendency to depoliticize political questions (Lijphart 1975). The custom to appoint allies of the opposition is thus firmly established in the Netherlands in appointments to, for instance, mayors, commissioners of the queen (*commissarissen der Koningin;* the governors in each province), or members of the Raad van State (State Council; comparable to the French Conseil d'Etat). The compromising nature is also notable in labor relations, where labor unions and employer organizations work together instead of being antagonistic parties. It also can be found in law, as will be shown below.

LEGAL CONCEPTS

Constitution

The Netherlands is a constitutional monarchy where neither the constitution nor the monarch is very important. The constitution is of little importance for two reasons. First, the constitution itself bans judicial review of acts of Parliament to the constitution. Thus any interpretation of the constitution is left to Parliament itself and citizens cannot challenge law on constitutional arguments in court. Second, treaties supersede the constitution. This is most important for the European Convention on Human Rights. The decisions of the European Court of Human Rights, therefore, are binding in the Netherlands and are now the vehicle by which most of the typical constitutional rights are enforced.

The monarch, presently Queen Beatrix, is of little importance either. This is also caused by a provision in the constitution, which says that the king is immune and the ministers are accountable. The monarch only plays a rather modest role in the formation of a new Cabinet of Ministers after an election for Parliament.

The roots of the Dutch Constitution (Grondwet) lie in the *Trias Politica,* the separation of the legislative, administrative, and judicial powers. Though the first constitution in 1814 has been changed and enlarged many times, still several concepts of the *Trias Politica* remain. However, constitutions stemming from the *Trias Politica* can have different forms, for example the French and the American constitutions. The original Dutch Constitution resembled the French version of the idea of separation of powers, in which the democratic element of political decision making was dominant. In essence, majority rule determined political questions and therefore also the outcome of the legislation process. The question of constitutional incompatibility had to be decided by the Parliament itself, not by the judiciary; the judiciary merely was the *bouche de la loi,* that is, should strictly apply legislation without its own interpretation.

Thus, contrary to the American version where the division of powers has led to a system of checks and balances, the French and the Dutch versions have led to a *separation* of powers. That might be one of the reasons that in the nineteenth century little emphasis was given to possible mistakes of the executive or the legislator. One could not imagine that these bodies would make mistakes or take decisions that were unjust or disproportionately disadvantageous for individuals or groups of citizens. Dominant legal doctrine considered democratic decision making the best guarantee against these kinds of failures.

The Dutch Constitution prescribed codification of the law that resulted in the civil code of 1838 and the criminal code of 1881. These codes, as revised, are still in force today. Shortly after World War II, a fundamental recodification of the civil code was undertaken. The *Nieuw Burgerlijk Wetboek* (New Civil Code) came into force in portions in the last two decades. The basic idea of extensive codification in the Netherlands—as, for instance, in Germany—was that each and every thinkable subject could be incorporated in a code, and thus the role of the judge was no more than to apply a rule of law to a specific case (*le bouche de la loi* after Montesquieu 1834/1748). The body of legislative rules was paramount and any development of the law through precedents was out of the question. See, however, the developments discussed below.

Government

Legislative power is exercised by the Crown (in fact the Cabinet of Ministers) and Parliament (Staten-Generaal), which is comprised of two chambers. The seventy-five members of the First Chamber (Eerste Kamer) or upper house are indirectly elected through the twelve provincial councils; the 150 members of the Second Chamber (Tweede Kamer) or lower house are directly elected by popular vote. All serve a four-year term, but the cabinet can dissolve any or both of the chambers to bring about new elections at any time. New bills can be proposed by the cabinet or by the Second Chamber—the latter happens not very often. The First Chamber may only approve or reject the bills without amending them.

Because of the system of proportional elections, Dutch Parliament is comprised of many different parties. Usually between twenty and thirty different political parties partake in elections. At present, nine different parties are represented in the First and Second Chambers together. The largest parties never attract much more than 30 percent of the votes. Dutch governments therefore are always coalition government of two or more parties.

In the legislative process the Council of State also plays a role. The council is composed of the monarch, the heir apparent, and appointed councilors. The advice on legislation of the Council of State is compulsory.

National and International Law

Since World War II Dutch law is more and more intertwined with international law, international treaties, and the law and case law of supranational institutions. This development has largely restricted Dutch political autonomy, not only because many important decisions are no longer made in The Hague but in Brussels as a result of the Dutch membership of the European Union, but also because the government and the legislator are bound by the case law of some international courts. The fact that the interpretation of many treaties is reserved for independent international courts had a rather unexpected impact on Dutch politics, especially in the field of fundamental human rights.

A major step to the internationalization of law was made in the 1953 change of the constitution, in which it was explicitly stated that national law should not be applied if this is incompatible with a self-executing provision of a treaty. Thus the constitution made it possible to review national law, including constitutional law, against standards established by certain provisions of treaties, and no distinction was made between treaties that entered into force before or after the enactment of national law.

Though this prevalence of treaties was properly taught in the law faculties in the decades that followed, it was of no great practical importance. In that period the Supreme Court tried to avoid any reference to international law by giving an interpretation—sometimes rather widely—of a comparable constitutional provision that corresponded to the international treaty. The year 1980 was a turning point, partly due to the spin-off of the academic courses. By then the Supreme Court began to review national law to international law openly, especially to the European Convention of Human Rights. Please note that the Netherlands has no constitutional court.

After 1980 many citizens started to use the right to appeal individually to the European Courts of Human Rights for alleged violation of the Convention, which resulted in judgments of the European Court in which Dutch national law was considered to be in conflict with specific provisions of that Convention. International and supranational law, as interpreted by the European Court or the EC Court, has a considerable influence on national law, for instance by prohibiting the legislator to make any rule that is in conflict with that interpretation. So, one of the major components of the judicialization of politics could be found in the restrictions of government authority by the development of the international and supranational law and the case law of the international courts.

Constitutional Review

As mentioned earlier, the Dutch Constitution stems from a tradition in which there is no supremacy of the judiciary over the legislator. An important argument for the so-called inviolability of acts of Parliament was that Parliament itself, as the representatives of the people, was best equipped to judge if a certain act of Parliament was incompatible with the constitution. This opinion had many strong adherents in the first half of the last century. Nevertheless the discussion is revived from time to time.

The discussion on the judicial review was fed by the increasing influence of international law on case law of the Supreme Court and the lower courts. Nowadays we find ourselves in a peculiar situation: An act of Parliament can be declared incompatible with self-executing provisions of international treaties, but not with the constitution. This holds even when in the treaty and in the constitution essentially the same principle is included in about the same words. This is an inconsistency that is impossible to explain to non-Dutch scholars (Kortmann 1990, 336).

Another argument in favor of the ban on judicial review, the argument that Parliament itself is able to maintain a certain degree of quality in its legislative function, has become less convincing during the last years. Decreasing dualism between government and Parliament and the speed and pressure under which some drafts have passed Parliament have occasionally resulted in a legislative botch job. A notorious example is the so-called Harmonization Act of 1988, in which rights of university students were curtailed in a retrospective manner. Ultimately an appeal to the judge failed, because the Supreme Court upheld the principle that an act of Parliament is inviolable. The Court, however, underwrote that some aspects of the Harmonization Act were in conflict with general, though unwritten, rules of law and announced that it would not exclude a sort of judicial review in the future (Van Koppen 1992).

Civil Law

The Dutch Supreme Court has come far from the *bouche de la loi* ideology of the nineteenth century. The Supreme Court always had some influence on the law, merely by the interpretations of statutes given in the Court's decisions. These interpretations, of course, set precedents, both for the Court itself and for lower courts. But the important task of looking after the uniformity of the law has gradually been overshadowed by the Court's function in developing the law. Starting with the hallmark decision in *Lindenbaum v. Cohen* (1919; *see* Van Koppen 1990), the Supreme Court has taken up the role of deputy-legislator. That very decision—in which the Supreme Court widened the definition of tort from a mere breach of written rights or duties to breach of duty of care—for instance, made a bill with the same subject superfluous.

In recent years the Supreme Court gave new interpretations to existing statutes or formulated new rules for unforeseen problems, making legislation unnecessary, even on issues where a clear political majority in Parliament would have produced legislation relatively swiftly. More important, the Court produced case law on issues, such as the right to strike, euthanasia, and abortion, where the strongly divided Parliament was unable to pass legislation. Supreme Court decisions play such an important role in these matters because of some of the peculiarities of Dutch politics.

For a long time the Dutch government has been built on a coalition of two or three, sometimes even five, political parties. No party has ever reached a majority in Parliament. When one of the coalition parties agrees with the opposition on a hot issue and could join with the opposition into a majority vote on such an issue, that party yet has to consider the opinion of the coalition partner in order to avoid the risk of breaking up the coalition. So even if there is a majority in the Parliament as a whole for a political choice on a certain issue, it is not sure that that choice will be made. More often the decision on these issues is postponed and the Supreme Court has to fill the gap.

The permanent coalition character of Dutch government also introduces compromise in the content of legislation, because clear-cut legislation on controversial issues would often risk the cooperation in the coalition. This means that the compromise mostly is of a diffuse and vague nature. Statutes, then, often need extensive interpretation before they can be applied in practice, giving the judiciary an important role in such controversial matters.

In the last four decades coalition parties became even more involved with each other by the introduction of the so-called *regeeraccoord* (government agreement), an extensive written document on all major and many minor political issues. The agreement not only binds members of the cabinet, but also members of the parliamentary majority. Voting against any government proposal covered by the agreement is considered a breach of political contract and endangers the coalition. The government agreement, made in covert negotiations, in fact binds members of Parliament to cabinet decisions and thus turns the traditional dualism between cabinet and Parliament into a monistic ruling by the cabinet. This enables the government to run bills through Parliament on sheer political force, sometimes producing acts of low quality. In such political circumstances the Supreme Court receives a new function: guardian of the quality of the law (Van Koppen 1990).

Criminal Law

When the Dutch criminal code was adopted by Parliament in 1886, the importance of prison as the primary sanction was paramount. Fines were meant for the most minor cases. The Dutch criminal system has always been quite lenient, although in recent decades the average sentence severity has been nearing the European average. After World War II, punishment has gradually been reformed. After expanding the possibilities of financial, rather than prison, punishment, suspended sentences have become possible, and a major shift has occurred toward community service as a principal penalty for less serious crimes.

After World War II new crimes were introduced in the code—for instance drug-related crimes, environmental crimes, and discrimination—while others have been decriminalized—for instance homosexual behavior, abortion, and, most recently, euthanasia.

Criminal procedure is done in an inquisitorial system. Professional judges, either on a three-judge panel or sitting alone, determine both guilt and the sentence. There is no lay element in Dutch criminal procedure. The Dutch system is characterized by an emphasis on the pretrial phase. In the pretrial phase the police conduct investigations. These are done under the formal heading of a public prosecutor (*officier van Justitie*). In major crime cases further investigations can be done by a judge commissioner (*rechter-commissaris;* comparable to the French *juge d'instruction*). The involvement of a judge commis-

sioner is compulsory when the suspect is detained in custody, and if certain investigative acts are done, as phone tapping and house searches. The police, prosecution, and judge commissioner thus build a dossier, which is the central element in Dutch criminal procedure.

The grounds for pretrial detentions in the Netherlands are the danger of the suspect or the interest of the investigation. Suspects can be detained, first by the police for three days, then by a short continuation by the judge commissioner, and thereafter by the court, deciding in closed chambers. Together these continuations cannot take longer than 106 days, after which the trial should start, at least formally. If pretrial detention of the suspect is no longer deemed necessary, he or she is released. There is no system of bail in the Netherlands.

Prosecutors have almost omnipotent powers to dismiss cases outside of court through the use of the conditional or unconditional waiver and by offering the suspect a transaction. To a limited extent the police have the same power. There is no plea bargaining.

Suspects have a right to legal council. If the suspect may be deprived of liberty and cannot afford an attorney, the state pays for legal counsel. The attorney, however, has no automatic right to be present at suspect or witness interrogations by the police, but has such a right for interrogations by the judge commissioner. The attorney also has the right to ask the prosecutor or judge commissioner to add documents to the dossier. Dutch attorneys seldom conduct their own investigations or have a private detective do it for them.

The emphasis on the dossier is quite notable during the trial stage. Most trials are not more than a quick review of the dossier, especially if the suspect has confessed. Trials can be as short as half an hour and trials longer than a full day are very rare. In most trials no witnesses are heard, since their statements are in the dossier in the form of a sworn statement by police officers or a report by the judge commissioner of his or her interrogations. The prosecution can call witnesses; the defense has to ask the prosecution to call witnesses on its behalf. The prosecution can refuse to call certain or all witnesses, even with the argument that such is not in the interest of the defense. This decision can be appealed to the court, but if granted will cause an adjournment of the trial.

The purpose of the Dutch trial is to discover the truth and to a much lesser extent to secure a fair trial. Based on the dossier, questioning is done by the court, while the prosecution and attorneys can ask supplementary questions. Cross-examination does not exist.

During trial the suspect does not have to take a formal position of pleading guilty or not guilty. In all cases the court has to review the evidence, even after the suspect has confessed, although in the latter kind of case evidence tends to generate little discussion during trial.

The Dutch trial is a one-phase trial; there is no separate sentencing hearing. All documents that are relevant for the sentence, as for instance reports on the suspect by psychiatrists and psychologists and the suspect's rap sheet, are part of the dossier and are thus known to the judge while determining guilt.

Dutch courts have wide discretion in imposing sentences. For each crime and misdemeanor there is a specific maximum—for instance, twelve years' imprisonment for involuntary manslaughter—but there is a general minimum for all, namely one day in jail or a 15-guilder fine. The court can even declare a suspect guilty without punishment. That was common in recent years for doctors who were formally charged with murder for committing euthanasia and were found guilty.

In sentencing, the court can choose between penalties and measures. Penalties include imprisonment, jail detention, community service, and fines. Life imprisonment is only rarely given and only for murder or manslaughter with aggravating circumstances. Community service, introduced in 1989, can be given if the defense asked for it and only instead of prison terms of less than six months. Sentences can be suspended wholly or in part under conditions set by the court. The death penalty was abolished in the Netherlands in 1870.

Measures can be imposed upon suspects even if the suspect has been acquitted. They include seizure of objects from the suspect, confiscation of the profits of a crime, and an order for detention in a psychiatric hospital for a period of up to one year if the individual presents a danger to him- or herself, to others, or to property.

If the court deems the suspect insane, no punishment shall follow, but the suspect can be committed to a psychiatric prison for compulsory treatment. If the suspect is deemed partly insane, both a prison term and compulsory treatment can be sentenced.

CURRENT COURT SYSTEM STRUCTURE

Courts for Civil and Criminal Cases

The Dutch court system is organized in four layers (see figure). The lowest level, the cantonal court (*kantongerecht*), hears petty offenses and small claims. In addition, the cantonal court has original jurisdiction for some specific civil cases, regardless of amount of controversy, among which are cases on tenancy and labor. The trial court (*arrondissementsrechtbank*) hears all other criminal and civil cases. The trial court also hears appeals from decisions of the cantonal courts in its district. Decisions of the trial court sitting as a court of first instance are appealable to the court of appeal (*gerechtshof*). In ordinary appeals the cases are dealt with de novo. The sixty-one cantonal courts, the nineteen trial courts, and the five courts of appeal are structured hierarchically.

As a rule, two stages of appeal are possible in each procedure: after the decision in the first instance, appeal to the next higher court is possible, and the second decision is subject to appeal in cassation to the Supreme Court. As in the first appeal, leave to appeal in cassation to the Supreme Court is not required. In an appeal in cassation, however, the facts as determined by the lower courts are not reviewable; the Supreme Court can only decide on issues of law.

Both criminal and civil cases are tried by professional judges; a jury is unknown in the Netherlands. Cantonal court judges sit alone and as a rule they try both criminal and civil cases. In the trial courts and the courts of appeal, specialized divisions exist, in which three judges sit en banc. Due to the heavy caseload, however, the exception of an *unus iudex* (a single judge) in the trial courts has recently come to be the rule. At the Supreme Court five justices usually sit on a case, but the number can be reduced to three where appropriate.

Supreme Court

The Supreme Court (Hoge Raad der Nederlanden), as any Dutch court, announces all of its decisions as unanimous and judges are obliged to maintain secrecy on their deliberations. As in most other countries, no leave to appeal is necessary and the Supreme Court has no control over its docket. Public prosecution at the Supreme Court is represented by one procurator-general and fifteen assistant procurators-general. Both justices and procurators-general are appointed for life (i.e., until the age of seventy) and are fully independent of the government. The independence of procurators-general is justified on the grounds that they may have to prosecute members of Parliament and cabinet members before the court. Such a prosecution, however, has never been instituted.

The procurators-general play a role in both criminal and civil cases. In all civil cases and many criminal cases, a procurator-general renders an opinion before the Court itself starts deliberations. These opinions are published together with the decision of the Court. Thus, the opinions of the procurators-general in which they disagree with the later decision of the Court (about 30 percent of the cases) are the nearest the Dutch come to dissenting opinions.

The Supreme Court is divided into three divisions: the civil division, the criminal division, and the so-called third division. The latter, established in 1919, has jurisdiction in tax cases and expropriation cases. Unlike the civil and criminal divisions, the third division is split into two fixed panels, which divide cases depending on the statute involved. The third division as a whole, however, meets weekly at lunch to ensure unity of decision making. The full court rarely meets, unlike for example the German Bundesgerichtshof or the French Cour de Cassation.

Since the Supreme Court cannot consider the facts of

Structure of Netherlands Courts

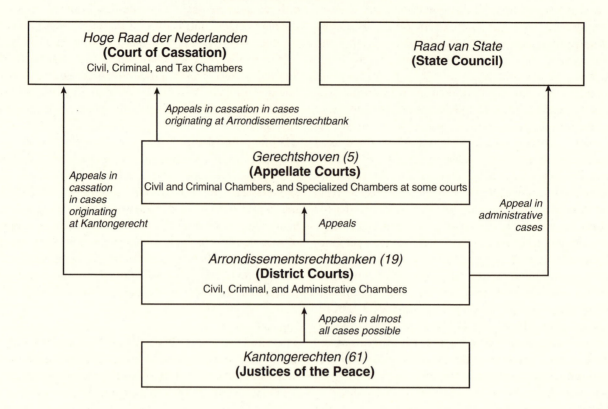

the case, the Court refers cases to a lower court after reversal, if the facts of the case need further consideration. These cases may be referred to the court that gave the decision that was appealed or another court at the same level.

SPECIALIZED JUDICIAL BODIES

Special chambers of trial courts deal with most special legal cases. There are, for instance, special chambers for juvenile cases and for minor economic offenses. Only for administrative cases, there exist specialized judicial bodies. A case against a government decision—local, provincial, or central—always has to start with a complaint with the body that issued the decision. To that second decision, in most cases, appeal is possible to the administrative chamber of the trial court. After that decision, appeal is possible to the department of administrative decisions of the State Council (Afdeling Bestuursrechtspraak van de Raad van State). At this level, however, there are also other specialized appellate bodies, as for instance the Central Council of Appeal (Centrale Raad van Beroep) for civil servant cases and social insurance cases.

STAFFING

Judges and Prosecutors

There are two courses to becoming a judge. The first is participation in the judges' training, which also is the training for public prosecutors. Immediately after completing a university law degree, one can apply for a position in the training, which takes six years. The training includes courses and apprenticeships of two years each at a trial court and at a public prosecutor's office. Trainees also serve an apprenticeship outside the court system, usually in an attorney's office. After these six years, one can apply to a vacancy, either at a trial court or as a prosecutor. The second course to becoming a judge is called the outsiders. An outsider becomes a judge by applying to a position at a trial court after at least six years of experience in the field, usually as an attorney, a university professor, or at the Ministry of Justice. A committee must pass all applicants.

Positions as vice president or president of a trial court, as cantonal judge, and as justice in an appellate court are always filled with applicants who have been trial court judges prior to that. Judges retire at the age of seventy.

Next to full-time judges in all trial and appellate courts, many so-called judge-replacers or justice-replacers hear cases. These are lawyers who work as, for instance, attorneys or university professors and serve as judges part-time. Usually outsiders serve as judge- or justice-replacers for some years before becoming full-time judges. An advantage of the system of judge- and justice-replacers is that it ensures that the judiciary keeps in touch with other parts of society. Thus, the discussions between legal academics and judges are quite open. A disadvantage is that sometimes serving as a judge-replacer involves a conflict of interest. For that reason, attorneys are not appointed as judge-replacers in their own district.

Supreme Court

According to law the Second Chamber of Parliament has an almost decisive influence on the appointments to the Supreme Court, because it is the Second Chamber's competence to put forward a list of three nominees, from which the Crown (i.e., the cabinet) has to choose. In practice, however, cooptation takes place. When there is a vacancy in the Supreme Court, the Court draws up a list of six candidates, who are recommended to become justices. Thereupon the Parliament puts, without any discussion or public attention, the first three candidates of that recommendation list on the list of nominees, of which the number one always is appointed by the Crown (*see* Van Koppen 1990).

All justices appointed after World War II had a very low political profile, as opposed to the appointments in the nineteenth century. No specific strategy or political prevalence can be discerned, when we set aside that lawyers with extreme points of view do not have a chance to be appointed. Nevertheless it is not ruled out that in private the sitting justices, when they have to draw up the list of candidates, take into account the recommended lawyers' political affinity and philosophy of life in order not to depart too much from the proportional composition of the Lower House of Parliament. This could explain why the Supreme Court succeeded up till now effectively in maintaining this cooptation system.

Bar

To become an attorney, one has to have a university law degree and start with a three-year apprenticeship at a law firm combined with courses given by the Dutch Bar Association.

IMPACT OF LAW

Probably the most notable characteristic of the Dutch judiciary and its decision making is the absence of any overt or covert political influence. That does not mean that the compromising nature of Dutch political life is not discernible in legal decision making as well. There is a tendency toward forms of mediation in any stage of procedures instead of adjudication. There is also a tendency for judges to interpret what the legislator has meant with a legal rule or to base a decision on what contracting parties intended to accomplish rather than to follow the letter of the law or the contract. For this very reason, Dutch contracts are much shorter than, for instance, American contracts, since judges tend to ignore what is written down in favor of what was meant anyway.

The compromising nature of Dutch society also is notable in a typical phenomenon that is called *tolerating policy* (*gedoogbeleid*). In many instances illegal situations are tolerated for all kinds of policy reasons, to such an extent that local government sometimes even issues a *tolerating permit* for situations that are, strictly speaking, quite illegal. Until recently, for instance, prostitution and brothels were formally forbidden, but widely tolerated. Recently, prostitution became formally allowed and government regulated. Another example is the Dutch drugs policy. Formally both hard and soft drugs are forbidden. In practice, however, the selling of soft drugs is tolerated in coffeehouses to such an extent that in Dutch *coffee shop* is a word to denote a place where you can buy drugs. These coffee shops can have a certain amount of drugs in stock. In some larger cities, houses that sell hard drugs are also tolerated. That, of course, leaves the problem of where the managers of these houses must buy their drugs, often in quantities that far exceed what is usually tolerated. This problem is simply ignored.

Peter J. van Koppen

See also Appellate Courts; Constitutional Review; Contract Law; Criminal Procedures; European Court and Commission on Human Rights; Inquisatorial Procedure; Judicial Review

References and further reading
Hartkamp, A. S., and Marianne M. M. Tillema. 1995. *Contract Law in the Netherlands.* The Hague: Kluwer.
Kortmann, C. A. J. M. 1990. *Constitutioneel Recht.* Deventer, the Netherlands: Kluwer.
Kortmann, C. A. J. M., and Paul P. T. Bovend'Eert. 1993. *The Kingdom of the Netherlands: An Introduction to Dutch Constitutional Law.* Deventer, the Netherlands: Kluwer.
Kossmann, Ernst Heinrich. 1978. *The Low Countries, 1780–1940.* Oxford: Clarendon.
Lijphart, Arend. 1975. *The Politics of Accommodation: Pluralism and Democracy in the Netherlands.* 2d ed. Berkeley: University of California Press.
Montesquieu. 1834/1748. *De l'esprit des lois.* Paris: Lebigre.
Tak, Peter J. P. 1999. *The Dutch Criminal Justice System: Organisation and Operation.* The Hague: Wetenschappelijk Onderzoeken Documentatiecentrum.
Van Erp, J. H. M., and E. H. Hondius, eds. 1995. *Netherlands Reports to the Fourteenth International Congress of Comparative Law, Athens, 1994.* The Hague: T. M. C. Asser Institute.
Van Koppen, Peter J. 1990. "The Dutch Supreme Court and Parliament: Political Decisionmaking versus Nonpolitical Appointments." *Law and Society Review* 24: 745–780.
———. 1992. "Judicial Policymaking in the Netherlands: The Case by Case Method." *West European Politics* 15: 80–92.

NETHERLANDS ANTILLES AND ARUBA

GEOGRAPHY, HISTORY, AND HUMAN RESOURCES

The Dutch Caribbean counts six islands. Curaçao, Aruba, and Bonaire are situated 30 to 80 kilometers off the Venezuelan coast. Located 880 kilometers further north are Saba, Sint-Eustatius (also called Statia), and the southern part of Sint-Maarten (St. Martin's northern part belongs to France), some 345 kilometers east and southeast of San Juan, Puerto Rico. The six islands were known as Curaçao and subordinated areas during the colonial period. Subsequently, they were named the Netherlands Antilles (NA). To end the colonial past definitively, the NA and Suriname (Dutch Guyana) were granted full autonomy in internal affairs in 1954. Suriname became totally independent in 1975. Aruba separated politically from the NA to gain its own autonomy in internal affairs in 1986 (status aparte). Today, the Kingdom of the Netherlands consists of three political entities: the Netherlands, the Netherlands Antilles (five islands), and Aruba.

When Columbus discovered the Leeward Islands, Saba, Sint-Maarten, and Sint-Eustatius, during his second quest to America in 1493, the islands were no longer inhabited by the original Indian population formed by Arawak and Carib tribes. Alfonso de Ojeda, the discoverer of Curaçao (1499), found some fifteen Indian villages. The origins of the Indians living on Curaçao probably date back to the year 3000 B.C.E. The Spanish crown declared Curaçao, Aruba, and Bonaire to be of no use in 1513, labeled them as islas inutiles, and rendered them to the hands of Indian hunters. Hardly any Indians were left on Curaçao a few years later: Most of them were transported as slaves to plantations in what is now known as Haiti and the Dominican Republic. The same thing happened to the Aruban Indians. A Holland-based trade company called the West Indian Company (WIC) set sail for Curaçao and Bonaire in 1634, and took control of both islands from the Spaniards; Aruba was taken two years later. The three Leeward Islands came into Dutch possession by 1640. France and Holland made a treaty to share Sint-Maarten in 1648; the northern part is French and the southern part is Dutch since then. The WIC controlled the islands until 1792, when it ceased to exist. From then on, the islands fell under the direct authority of the Dutch government.

Aruba, Bonaire, and Curaçao (ABC) are the biggest islands, with a surface area of 444 square kilometers, 193 square kilometers, and 288 square kilometers respectively. These islands belong to the Lesser Antilles for the coast of Venezuela. The smaller islands, Saba, Sint-Eustatius, and Sint-Maarten, occupy an area of 13, 21, and 34 square kilometers respectively, and are part of the greater group of Leeward Islands.

The NA and Aruba have a tropical climate, fairly constant throughout the year. However, the climate of the ABC islands shows significant differences compared with the climate on Sint-Maarten, Sint-Eustatius, and Saba as islands located within the Atlantic hurricane belt. The ABC islands have a tropical climate but a rather low degree of humidity. The average temperature is 27.5° C. Most of the rain falls in the last two months of the year. The three smaller islands are less arid than the ABC islands due to a higher annual rainfall; the average temperature is about 25° C. Most rain falls from May till December.

The language is not uniform on the six Dutch Caribbean islands. The language usually spoken on Curaçao, Aruba, and Bonaire is Papiamentu, which is a mixture of Spanish, Portuguese, Dutch, English, French, and some Arawak-Indian and African influences. Papiamentu is one of the few Creole languages of the Caribbean that has survived to the present day. It is the spoken language among the local people of Curaçao, Bonaire, and Aruba. The official language is Dutch. On the other islands, the common language is English.

The total population of the six islands of the NA and Aruba (1998) was estimated at 300,599 in 1996 (Curaçao 152,700; Aruba 93,424; Bonaire 14,169; Sint-Maarten 36,231; Sint-Eustatius 2,609; Saba 1,466).

The ethnic composition of the population is diverse. Approximately 85 percent is black in the NA, while the other 15 percent is white with a very small Asian minority. Eighty percent of the population of Aruba is of mixed white-Indian descent; the other 20 percent is black. Saba is half black and half white. Sint-Maarten is 70 percent inhabited by people who were not born on the island. Aruba is for the greater part Roman Catholic, and for the remaining part Protestant. Curaçao and Bonaire are predominantly Roman Catholic; the remainder are Protestant, Jewish, or Muslim. Sint-Maarten is 40 percent Roman Catholic; Saba is 70 percent Roman Catholic. Sint-Eustatius is 30 percent Methodist, and there are also Anglicans, Seventh Day Adventists, and Jehovah's Witnesses. Animistic religions have hardly any visible influence. The average life expectancy is seventy-seven years; on Curaçao and Aruba there is one doctor for 500 and 870 inhabitants, respectively, and one dentist for every 3,333 and 4,270 inhabitants, respectively. Literacy is almost 100 percent. Education is comparable with the system in the Netherlands: Curaçao and Aruba have their own universities; the Saba University School of Medicine offers medical training to students from all over the world.

The NA do not have abundant natural resources. Though oil is not locally produced, oil processing and shipping are important for the Antillean economy. On Curaçao, calcium phosphate is extracted, and limestone and salt are mined on Bonaire. The importance of agriculture is marginal because of the poor quality of land

and the shortage of water. Fishing, mining, and agriculture account for less than 1 percent of GDP.

The NA and the Aruban economies thrive mainly on income generated in the tourism sector, the oil refining and shipping sector, the financial services centers, and on funds granted to them in the form of development aid. The economies are open and vulnerable to influences from the world market. The general income per capita is high for the region. In 1997 it amounted to U.S.$10,800 per head in the NA, and U.S.$16,600 per head in Aruba. These figures, however, cannot camouflage the fact that the Antillean national debt rose to 73 percent of the GNP in 1997 (41 percent for Aruba), resulting in a shortage of financial reserves to cover for three months of import (five months for Aruba). In order to avert a collapse of the economy, the NA started an adjustment program in July 1996 with the assistance of the International Monetary Fund and the Dutch government.

With the exception of Sint-Maarten and Aruba, where the tourism sector is the biggest employer, the government fulfills this role for the other islands. Thirty-seven percent of the working population of Curaçao works for the government on the Antilles (more than 50 percent on Saba). Unemployment rates differ per island. On Aruba there is a need for personnel from outside the island, whereas on the NA 18 percent of the working population is unemployed, a severe problem especially among the island's youth. Since 1998, many persons have left Curaçao to find a better future in the Netherlands.

LEGAL HISTORY

The constitutional history of the Antilles has much in common with the history of Suriname (the former Dutch Guyana). Until 1816, there existed only one Council of Justice and Police with jurisdiction in all criminal, administrative, and civil affairs. A separation between the executive and the judiciary was effected in 1815. The six Antilles and Suriname were administratively unified in 1828, a situation that lasted until 1845. In that year, the Antilles were placed separately under the administration of a governor-general and a colonial council, who ruled the islands on behalf of the Dutch king. With the abolition of slavery in 1863, the labor engine of the colonial economy came to a standstill. A government regulation enacted in 1865 gave the Dutch Parliament more control in colonial matters. Many models were proposed to modernize the constitutional relation between the Netherlands and the islands from 1920 on. Democratization started with the first elections in 1937, and a full-grown parliamentary system was introduced in 1950. A new legal document, named the Statute of the Kingdom of the Netherlands, was enacted in 1954 to mark the end of the colonial period. The former colonies were granted full autonomy in internal affairs, although

supervision was not totally excluded. The constitution of the NA, in its turn, provides for a certain degree of autonomy for separate islands of the NA. As the island autonomy was in practice much more restricted than the constitutional provisions foresaw, complaints about dominance by Curaçao as the biggest island became stronger. Finally, the Dutch government had to permit Aruba to leave the constitutional structure of the NA in 1986. The island of Sint-Maarten is making efforts to follow the Aruban example.

The Antillean law system has its roots in the continental civil law tradition. The Antillean constitution contains provisions for the legislative power and the judiciary. Magistrates find their guiding principles in the codified laws and to a lesser extent in precedents in jurisprudence.

The law of the Dutch Republic—Roman-Dutch law of Continental origin—was declared valid and applicable in the colonies in 1629. The local authorities also had the power to enact legislation for internal affairs. The Government Regulation of 1865 paved the way for the introduction of a large-scale codification by promulgating the principle of concordance in Article 138. Concordance meant that the law in the colonies had to resemble as much as possible the laws of the Dutch motherland. Colonial ordinances were expected to meet this requirement. Concordance was especially applied in the fields of civil and commercial law. Probably the most important date from a legal-historical point of view was midnight between April 30, and May 1, 1869. At that hour the new codification for Curaçao and the other five islands came into force. Roman-Dutch law was abandoned and the islands fell from that time under a legal regime very much the same as in the Netherlands. The French-inspired codification of 1869 included a civil code, a commercial code, a code of civil procedure, a notary public law, a criminal code, a code of criminal procedure, and general provisions of legislation. A separate bankruptcy regulation was introduced in 1931. The Islands Regulation of 1951 introduced autonomous hemispheres for the islands, while it reserved restricted powers for the National Antillean administration. Excluded from interference by the islands are: the civil and commercial law, the civil procedure, criminal law and criminal procedure, the notary public office, the jurisdiction in administrative and fiscal affairs, and the composition and authority of the judiciary. Further, the police, postal services, the interisland traffic, the labor legislation, and the prison system are also exempt from island authority.

Though the principle of concordance has never been applied strictly (it is first and foremost important for civil and commercial law affairs), it has so far not completely been abandoned. As a consequence of concordance, the Antillean legal profession has access to Dutch legal literature and jurisprudence. Besides, concordance facilitates law finding in Antillean and Aruban cases by the Dutch Supreme Court.

LEGAL CONCEPTS

The NA and Aruba derive their constitutional status from the Charter of the Kingdom of the Netherlands. This charter comprises a kind of federal structure, with the Netherlands, the NA, and Aruba as partner countries. These three countries should be autonomous in the representation of domestic interests while attending to common affairs on the basis of equal partnership and assisting each other. In legal terms, the federal structure of the charter is of an inviolable nature, as the Dutch Constitution is not allowed to interfere in this structure. Alterations in the charter can only be implemented with consent of each country.

The charter labels the following topics as common affairs: defense, international relations, nationality, order of knights, nationality of ships, supervision of general regulations about migration between the countries, general conditions for immigration of foreigners and extradition. Other affairs can be considered as common affairs with the assent of all partners. Each country has to realize human rights, legal certainty, and good governance, and the federal structure should guarantee the solution of problems in cases of negligence.

The charter leaves room for all kinds of cooperation between separate partners outside the field of common affairs. Well-known examples of tripartite cooperation are: the framework for avoidance of double taxation in the relationship between the Netherlands and its overseas partners, and the Coast Guard for the NA and Aruba as an instrument in the war on drugs in Caribbean waters. The NA and Aruba have a bipartite agreement for mutual cooperation. As this agreement is mainly drafted in terms without obligations, the need to install a constitutional court to settle disputes between the NA and Aruba was never really felt. The most substantial element of this agreement is the Joint Court of Appeal of the NA and Aruba.

The preface of the charter puts forward the principle of equal partnership between the Netherlands, the NA, and Aruba. However, consideration of the decision-making procedures in the federal structure can only lead to the conclusion that Dutch politicians play a dominant role. The federal government of the charter is in fact no more than the Dutch government with the obligation to consult the representatives of the NA and Aruba. These representatives lack authority to veto federal decisions that could ultimately harm Antillean and Aruban interests. Consequently, the NA and Aruba have always been reluctant to consider proposals from the Dutch side to extend the number of common affairs. On the other hand, they could not fully ignore pressures in the field of their internal affairs considering their dependence on Dutch financial support.

The federal structure of the charter is incomplete since it was designed as a temporary arrangement toward independence day. For that reason, a federal Parliament to control administrative decision making and a constitutional court to settle disputes between federal partners have never come to pass.

The charter prescribes for the NA and Aruba a system of government with ministers being responsible to the Parliament. The governor of each country represents the Dutch queen as head of state. As such, he has a ceremonial role in public life in which he should refrain from political statements. His yearly address to Parliament (state of the union) falls completely under the responsibility of the ministers of the cabinet. Besides his role as head of state, the governor has to play a role as supervisor of the federal government. In this last role, he should not avoid confrontations with politicians in power. This contradictory role creates a complicated situation in which the role as head of state is the easiest one to play.

The constitution of the NA is a dated document since it was amended only slightly after its genesis in 1955. Thus, freedom of expression is only guaranteed as it is related to the printing press, and the right to privacy is still unknown. The poor catalog of human rights is in legal practice not significant since the court is forbidden to evaluate acts of Parliament in light of this catalog. Fortunately, Antillean citizens can refer to the European Human Rights Treaty in court in cases of infringements of their rights by the legislature. New human rights insights from Europe can in this way have their impact on Antillean law.

The Antillean Ministerial Council is presided over by the prime minister, who is at first responsible for coordination within the government. As governments are usually dependent on coalitions of parties, the role of the prime minister is indispensable. Moreover, the parties in the coalition usually stand for interests of different islands so that tensions in the cabinet are never far away.

The Antillean Council of Advice has to support the government in legislative and administrative affairs. It has to function as a think tank superior to party politics. Unlike its Dutch equivalent, the Council of State, the Antillean Council of Advice has never played a role in the adjudication of justice in administrative matters.

The Antillean Parliament has twenty-two members. Seats are preserved for different islands:

- Curaçao 14 seats
- Bonaire 3 seats
- Sint-Maarten (Dutch part) 3 seats
- Sint-Eustatius 1 seat
- Saba 1 seat

Consequently, election campaigns are restricted to separate islands and Parliament functions more as an island representation than as a nationwide people's representation.

The Antillean Parliament decides about proposals for new laws that are usually submitted by the government. Besides law making, Parliament has to control the government in the execution of its tasks. Ministers have to account for themselves and their civil servants to Parliament. If a majority in Parliament supports a vote of no confidence, a minister has to resign.

The Antillean Audit Commission has to support parliamentary control with reports about bookkeeping, budgetary discipline, and efficiency. Reports of the Audit Commission should play a significant role in parliamentary debates.

The Aruban constitution, which was enacted in 1986, has a more modern look than its Antillean equivalent. The human rights catalog is more elaborate. Moreover the court is permitted to assess acts of Parliament in the light of constitutional human rights.

In essence, the Aruban constitutional order has the same features as the Antillean one. As Aruba is but one island instead of an archipelago, the twenty-one parliamentary seats are not geographically bound. Political parties are easy to establish. However, the good governance debate may lead to political parties that have to comply with varying requirements to ensure transparency in politics.

Administration of justice in civil and criminal cases is a common affair of both the NA and Aruba. The court of appeal is thus named the Joint Court of Appeal of the NA and Aruba. Including the president of the joint court, the maximum number of judges is twenty. A further ten deputies may be appointed. Individual members of this court can be instructed by the court president to decide first-instance cases. This means that judges of the joint court may work in the NA as well as in Aruba. Cases in appeal are brought before the Joint Court of Appeal, that is, a board of some members of the court. After a decision in appeal, a civil or criminal case can be brought over the ocean to the Supreme Court in The Hague in the Netherlands. The Supreme Court is not allowed to evaluate fact finding in previous stages of the process but it can correct possible misjudgments in law application (cassation).

Judges are not elected but are appointed for life; normally this means that they end their career when they reach the age of sixty-five. Persons who are at least thirty years old, have Dutch nationality, and hold a law degree from a university in the NA, Aruba, or the Netherlands may apply for a position in the NA and Aruba judiciary, which is separate from the Dutch judiciary. Application procedures are guided by the president of the Joint Court of Appeal, and a list of recommendations is composed by the complete joint court. This list is discussed in a joint meeting of the NA and Aruban ministers. The names of

the candidates for a judicial position are then sent to the federal government of the charter, where the appointments are effected. Because of a shortage of local candidates, the majority of judges are experienced Dutch professionals, who are stationed for approximately three years in the NA and Aruba. If they stay too long, they have to face regression in their employee status and are no longer allowed to proceed with their career in the Netherlands.

When Aruba separated from the NA in 1986, Dutch politicians pled for a common attorney general for both the NA and Aruba. As both countries saw public prosecution as an internal affair, a common attorney general proved to be out of the question. The federal kingdom government therefore appoints a separate attorney general for each country to guide public prosecution. To prevent political interference in public prosecution affairs, the Joint Court of Appeal has said that the attorney general can be allowed to evaluate orders from his political superiors. He should put these orders to a legal test with attention to principles of a proper administration, including a proper process. Ultimately, the Joint Court of Appeal has the final say in this matter.

Lawsuits are rather simple in the NA and Aruba. Cases in first instance are discussed in the court of first instance. The name *court of first instance* suggests a separate organization with its own magistrates. However, the president of the Joint Court of Appeal instructs individual judges to decide cases in first instance by themselves. Cases in appeal are brought before the Joint Court of Appeal, that is, a board of some members of this court who have not been involved in the case in first instance. Dissenting opinions in public are prohibited as the principle of secrecy in consultations prevails.

In criminal cases, the public prosecution has the power to refrain from legal proceedings for policy reasons, although interested parties can make their complaints to the Joint Court of Appeal. The revision of the code for criminal procedure in 1997 ended the dominance of the examining magistrate in the phase prior to public trial in favor of the public prosecution. Yet dossiers are built up before the trial and the trial is mostly used to get clarification about obscurities in written documents. Juries are unknown in Antillean and Aruban criminal procedure. Although society asks for more severe penalties, the application of the death penalty is no point for discussion. The death penalty article is, however, never removed from the criminal code.

Very recently, the NA and Aruba have modernized their civil code after the Dutch model with some minor adaptations due to local circumstances. In terms of family law, these adaptations are too superficial. The notion of a core family (one spouse and children) still dominates the legal structure although Caribbean men often have different sexual relationships and paternities in addition to marriage or life companionship. However, the jurisprudence of the European Court for Human Rights has caused a breakthrough: Since 1985 the legal position of extramarital children who are officially recognized by their father is equal to the position of marital children.

In spite of the new civil code, modernizations of Dutch company law in the last decades did not have their reflection in Antillean and Aruban company law. The argument is that modern Dutch company law is too much influenced by guidelines from the European Union, whereas Antillean and Aruban company law should reflect the proximity of the United States. To add to the confusion, it must be noted that the competition on the world market for offshore financial services has its impact on Antillean and Aruban company law. This market asks for simply structured companies that can be established fast. Thus, the Aruban Exempt Corporation and the Antillean Private Corporation show similarities to the International Business Corporation of the Cayman Islands.

Judicial review of administrative action is regulated in the NA and Aruba by different regulations—the Antillean Act on judicial review will come into force soon. The Antillean procedure differs from the Aruban procedure on two major points:

- A procedure to raise objections to persuade the administration has to precede the judicial process (NA); the litigant may choose to omit the objection procedure (Aruba).
- Appeal to the Joint Court of Appeal is possible after a decision in first instance (NA); appeal is not possible (Aruba). The above-mentioned procedures for judicial review are not applicable in cases to be decided by specialized tribunals. Cases concerning civil servants, tax matters, social security, and supervision over the financial sector are thus determined by separate rules for judicial review.

In administrative law, administrative legislation has to be applied. This legislation is not very well elaborated in the NA and Aruba. As a consequence, the judge has to take refuge with principles of proper administration as he knows them from Dutch handbooks (motivation of decisions, weighing of interest, keeping promises, principle of equality, and so on). Moreover, as most judges are temporarily engaged from the Netherlands, Dutch doctrine can easily be followed. However, the Joint Court of Appeal decided recently that the principle of keeping promises must be judged from the Caribbean perspective that Caribbean officials very easily raise expectations.

Social security laws are not well developed in the NA and Aruba, although the Aruban economy could make higher allowances possible. For that reason, unemploy-

Structure of Netherlands Antilles and Aruba Courts

Supreme Court of the Netherlands
The Hague, the Netherlands
Review of civil and criminal court decisions. Cassation may be brought by one of the parties to a case or may be brought by the Supreme Court's Procurator General.

↑ CASSATION

Joint Court of Appeal
of the Netherlands Antilles and Aruba
Willemstad, Curaçao
Keeps sessions in Curaçao and Aruba, and may keep session on the other four islands (St. Maarten, Bonaire, St. Eustatius, and Saba). Appeal of verdicts and judicial decisions of the Court of First Instance. Supervision of the proper administration of justice and prosecution. Disciplinary proceedings in medical affairs, public notary affairs, and affairs concerning members of the bar and bailiffs.

↑ APPEAL

Court of First Instance
Willemstad, Curaçao, and Oranjestad, Aruba
The Court of First Instance of Curaçao has jurisdiction over the other four islands (St. Maarten, Bonaire, St. Eustatius, and Saba). Sessions may be kept in any of these four islands. The Court has jurisdiction over all civil and criminal affairs that do not fall within the jurisdiction of another court. The Court also has jurisdiction in military affairs.

Administrative justice falls either within the jurisdiction of the judiciary or within the jurisdiction of special tribunals, in which members of the judiciary also take part:

1. Civil servants' tribunal and tribunal of appeal in civil servants' affairs
2. Tribunal of appeal in tax affairs
3. Five social security tribunals

ment on Curaçao without financial support from relatives forces the unemployed to emigrate to the Netherlands.

CURRENT STRUCTURE

In the last decades, the war on drugs and the fight against corruption have put the judicial system under severe pressures. The judicial apparatus became overburdened and the Curaçao prison became notorious for its inhuman conditions, especially after visits from European human rights authorities. The Dutch government has thus given financial support to build a new prison to meet modern standards for detention. In its turn, the

Antillean government puts effort in the detection of corruption under the prison guards to prevent alarming escapes. In 1998, the dean of the Antillean bar asked attention for the continuous economy measures of the Antillean government and made a plea for a judicial system as a common affair under the charter of the kingdom.

The practice of temporal transfers of Dutch judges to the NA and Aruba entails differences in legal positions for different types of judges. A stay in the tropics is for temporarily transferred judges a step in their career at home. Judges who are locally recruited in the Dutch Caribbean have fewer career possibilities and are totally dependent on local politics for a rise in salaries. Recently, these judges had to threaten the Antillean government with legal action for an alleviation of austerity measures.

Many Dutch Caribbean lawyers have their businesses outside litigation in the courtroom. Although exact figures are not available, most lawyers' offices will make highest profits in legal advice for the protection of assets of rich foreigners. Especially the defense of poor suspects is considered an ungrateful occupation due to the petty compensation from the government.

As interests involved in litigation became more important, cases ended more and more in a definitive judgment of the Dutch Supreme Court despite costs of litigation. The overburdening of the Supreme Court (with Dutch and overseas cases) has already led to a plea for a limitation of cases to be decided. What the effect will be for the flow of Antillean and Aruban cases is still unclear.

Although the constitutional subsistence of the Antillean archipelago is insecure due to fragmenting forces, the Joint Court of Appeal will stay a solid institution. History has shown that the separation with Aruba in 1986 left the position of the joint court unchallenged. The awareness on the islands in the Dutch Caribbean that autarchy in the adjudication of justice can lead to disasters is great.

However, fragmentation of the Antillean archipelago will have a negative impact on the level of legal education as the sense of urgency for cooperation in this field is missing. Another problem will be that laboriously traceable differences in legislation on different islands will contribute to the overburdening of the Supreme Court.

H. F. Munneke
A. J. Dekker

See also Civil Law; Constitutional Law; European Court and Commission on Human Rights; Federalism; Napoleonic Code; Netherlands

References and further reading
Bakker, J., and R. van der Veer. 1999. *Nederlandse Antillen en Aruba: Mensen, politiek, economie, cultuur, milieu.* [The Netherlands Antilles and Aruba: People, Economy, Culture, Environment.] Amsterdam: Koninklijk Instituut voor de Tropen.
Cijntje, D. E., et al., eds. 1999. *Netherlands Antilles Business Law: Legal Accounting and Tax Aspects of Doing Business in the Netherlands Antilles.* The Hague: Kluwer Law International.
Munneke, H. F. 2001. *Recht en samenleving in de Nederlandse Antillen, Aruba en Suriname: Opstellen over recht en sociale cohesie.* [Law and Society in the Netherlands Antilles, Aruba, and Suriname: Essays on Law and Social Cohesion.] Nijmegen: Wolf Legal Publishers.
Rijn, A. B. van. 1999. *Staatsrecht van de Nederlandse Antillen.* [Constitutional Law of the Netherlands Antilles.] Deventer: W. E. J. Tjeenk Willink.
http://www.electionworld.org/aruba.htm (accessed September 11, 2001).
http://www.electionworld.org/netherlandsantilles.htm (accessed September 11, 2001).
http://encarta.msn.com/find/search.asp?search=aruba (accessed September 11, 2001).
http://encarta.msn.com/find/search.asp?search=netherlands+antilles (accessed September 11, 2001).
http://www.odci.gov/cia/publications/factbook/geos/aa.html (accessed September 11, 2001).
http://www.odci.gov/cia/publications/factbook/geos/nt.html (accessed September 11, 2001).

NEVADA

GENERAL INFORMATION

Nevada is located in the western United States. It is bordered by California on the west, Arizona on the southeast, Utah on the east, and Idaho and Oregon on the north. The state's landmass is 110,540 square miles, making it the seventh largest in the country. Concomitantly, it is one of the most sparsely populated, with only two million people, 20 percent of whom are Hispanic (constituting the fifth largest concentration in the United States), 7 percent African American, 5 percent Asian, and 1 percent American Indian.

Referred to as the Silver or Sagebrush State, Nevada is unique. In 1931 it became the first and, for many decades the only, state to allow casino gambling. The Silver State is also the only state to allow legalized prostitution by county option in the fifteen rural counties, but not in Clark County (Las Vegas) or Washoe County (Reno), where that option is by state statute not available.

Nevada is also notable for the large amount of land within its borders (87 percent) owned or controlled by the federal government. In some rural counties the federal government controls up to 97 percent of available land. This partially explains why almost all of Nevada's population lives in two major urban areas. Of its two million people, approximately 70 percent reside in Clark County in southern Nevada and another 20 percent live in the Reno–Carson City area in the northern part of the state, making Nevada one of the most highly urbanized states in the Union.

EVOLUTION AND HISTORY

The beginnings of a judicial structure in the state can be traced to the Compromise of 1850, which created the territories of Utah and New Mexico. The northern 90 percent of present-day Nevada was included in the former and the southern 10 percent was part of the latter.

In 1861, with tensions running high between the Mormon-dominated Utah government and the non-Mormons living in what would later become Nevada, Congress created a separate Nevada Territory with a supreme court, three district courts, probate courts, and justices of the peace. Each of the three district courts, which held trials in major cases, was staffed by a territorial judge appointed by President Abraham Lincoln. The three sat together as a group to constitute the territory's supreme court for the purpose of hearing appeals from the district courts. Probate judges and justices of the peace, who held trials on minor legal matters, were elected.

By 1863 the inhabitants of Nevada Territory were as resolute in ridding themselves of these federally appointed judges as they had previously been in disencumbering themselves from Utah's Mormon-dominated judiciary. The sad state of the judiciary was a motivating force in the territory's inhabitants' calls to Congress in 1863 and again in 1864 to give them statehood. In August 1864 all three Territorial Supreme Court justices resigned amid allegations of wrongdoing, and Nevada Territory operated with no judiciary until statehood was approved on October 31, 1864.

The Nevada state judicial system was structured very much like its territorial predecessor. The major trial courts, or courts of general jurisdiction, were the district courts. The minor trial courts, or courts of limited jurisdiction, were the justice courts, staffed by justices of the peace. The state constitution also allowed for the creation of municipal courts in the incorporated towns and cities to enforce municipal ordinances.

At the pinnacle of the Nevada state judiciary was the Nevada Supreme Court. Like its predecessor, the Nevada Territorial Supreme Court, the state's highest court consisted of three justices. Unlike the territorial high court, however, the justices did not concurrently serve on the district courts.

Although the basic court structure remains the same today as it was when Nevada became a state in 1864, this superficial resemblance masks both major and minor changes that have occurred since that time. For example, during the Progressive era of the early twentieth century, the legislature changed the method of judicial selection from partisan to nonpartisan elections.

The 1970s were a period of tremendous change for the Nevada court system. In 1976 and 1978, respectively, the terms of district court judges and justices of the peace were extended from four to six years. A 1976 amendment to the state constitution provided for a unified state court structure under the direction of the chief justice of the Nevada Supreme Court, who, as administrative head of the state court system, had authority over judges' workloads and assignments. Also added to the state constitution in 1976 were provisions establishing a Commission on Judicial Selection and a Commission on Judicial Discipline.

One final noteworthy change in the evolution of the state's judiciary is the composition of the state Supreme Court. The state constitution provided for three justices to serve on that court with the proviso that the legislature could increase that number to five. As a result of the Supreme Court's increased workload, the legislature chose this option in 1967. In yet another 1976 amendment to the state constitution, the voters approved a change removing any cap on the number of justices, leaving this entirely to the legislature. The amendment also allowed the high court, if it had more than five members, to preside over appeals in panels rather than as a single group. As a result of the court's increasing workload and difficulty in deciding cases in a timely manner, the state legislature increased the number of justices to seven effective in 1999. In that way the court could meet in two panels of three justices each, not including the chief justice, and hear twice as many cases as previously.

CURRENT STRUCTURE

As noted, the Nevada state judiciary currently looks very much as it did upon statehood in 1864. The courts of limited jurisdiction are the justice courts and municipal courts; the courts of general jurisdiction are the district courts; and the state's sole appellate court is the Nevada Supreme Court.

The justice courts are staffed by justices of the peace who serve in the fifty-five geographical townships across the state. As courts of limited jurisdiction, they hear minor civil ($7,500 or less) and criminal (misdemeanor) cases. Additionally, these courts hold preliminary hearings in felony cases to determine if there is sufficient evidence to forward a serious criminal case to the District Court for trial.

Municipal courts are established by the city council or city charter in the eighteen incorporated areas of the state. They are also courts of limited jurisdiction and hear cases involving violations of city ordinances. As is the case with the justice courts, the vast majority of the municipal courts' dockets consist of traffic and eviction cases.

The courts of general jurisdiction, the district courts, are established in nine judicial districts across the state and hear more serious civil (over $7,500) and criminal (felony) cases. A third function of these courts is to hear appeals from the justice and municipal courts. Because all justice courts and some municipal courts are courts of record, the District Court's review of these cases is limited to questions of fairness and procedure only. However, appeals from a municipal court that is not a court of record require the appellant to receive a trial de novo—that is, an entirely new trial—in District Court. A special division of the District Court, called Family Court, handles family law issues such as divorce, child support, child custody, adoption, and termination of parental rights.

The sole appellate court in the state judicial system is the Nevada Supreme Court, which is required to hear all appeals that are properly brought to it. In addition, it has a modicum of original jurisdiction through its constitutionally granted power to issue writs. With the exception of major cases, which are heard by all the justices sitting en banc, appeals to the Supreme Court are decided by one of two panels of three associate justices. The chief justice does not sit on either of these panels.

NOTABLE FEATURES OF LAW/LEGAL SYSTEM

In the year 2000, there were 5,901 attorneys practicing in Nevada, providing a population-to-attorney ratio of approximately 339:1. There would likely be even more attorneys in the state if Nevada had opened its law school before it did. Although a private law school opened, languished, and then quickly closed in Reno in the 1980s, there was no state-financed law school in Nevada until 1998. In the fall semester of that year, a state law school opened on the campus of the University of Nevada, Las Vegas. Prior to that time, prospective attorneys were forced out of state to more expensive private law schools, or to compete for the relatively few positions open to out-of-state residents in other states' law schools. Because many could not afford private school fees or out-of-state tuition at the state schools, and because many potential law students could not, for various reasons, leave the state, Nevada's lack of a law school worked to keep the attorney population artificially low.

The law school at the University of Nevada, Las Vegas, is the only one operating in the state. It offers a standard three-year, full-time program and a four-year, part-time program, both of which lead to a juris doctor degree. Attorneys in the state must graduate from an ABA-accredited school of law in order to take the bar exam, which they must pass in order to practice in Nevada.

Two elements of Nevada's legal system are representative of the frontier era in which the state's constitution was written. By 1864, Nevada mining interests had so corrupted state government, including the judiciary, that drafters of the constitution felt compelled to implement institutional structures that would provide some justice to the new state's citizens. One of these structures is the requirement that in civil cases only a three-fourths verdict from a jury is necessary to make a decision. This was

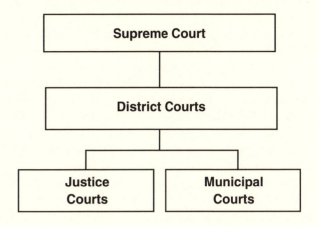

Legal Structure of Nevada Courts

needed in light of the mining companies' habit of bribing a juror to hang the jury if one of the ubiquitous mining cases haunting the courts was going to go badly for the company. The three-fourths requirement would, at the very least, require the companies to bribe more than one juror.

Similarly, there was substantial debate at the constitutional convention over the size of the Nevada Supreme Court. Some thought that five justices would be harder to corrupt than three, while others concluded that it would be difficult to find five honest men to serve on the court. Consequently, the drafters compromised by establishing a three-justice court and giving the legislature the option to raise it to five.

STAFFING

Although all state judges were initially chosen by partisan election, the state legislature adopted nonpartisan elections in 1915 in an effort to take the politics out of judicial selection. All Nevada state judges, with the exception of a few municipal court judges, are now chosen by nonpartisan election.

Justices of the peace serve six-year, staggered terms. The state constitution requires only that they be "qualified electors." A "qualified elector" is anyone at least eighteen years old who has been a resident of the state for six months and a resident of the election district for thirty days. State statute further restricts the office to those with a high school diploma (or its equivalent), which allows for the selection of lay (or nonlawyer) justices of the peace. However, the legislature has required that, in some instances, a justice of the peace must be an attorney. Under this law, a justice of the peace must be a lawyer in counties with a population of 400,000 or more when the particular township in which this justice will preside has a population of 100,000 or more. The attorney requirement also applies to counties with a population less than 400,000 when the particular township has 250,000 or more. Given these strictures, the attorney requirement applies only to the areas in and around Las Vegas and Reno.

Municipal court judges are selected by either nonpartisan election or city council appointment, as determined by the city council or city charter. Those who are elected serve four-year terms of office, while those who are appointed serve at the pleasure of the city council. State statute requires these judges to be citizens of the state, a resident of the city for one year, and a "qualified elector." The cities may also add to these qualifications, such as by requiring municipal court judges to be lawyers.

District court judges serve six-year, nonstaggered terms of office. The state constitution mandates that one need only be a "qualified elector" in order to be a district court judge. However, statute requires judges to be at least twenty-five years old, an attorney licensed to practice law in Nevada, and a two-year resident of the state.

Justices of the Nevada Supreme Court must meet the same eligibility requirements as district court judges. They also serve six-year terms, although staggered. The justice who is in the last two years of his or her term takes over the position of chief justice. When more than one are in the last two years of a term, the state constitution establishes that the eligible justices choose by lot, typically a coin toss.

Should a judge leave the bench in midterm, the method of selecting a replacement will vary depending upon the court. A vacant justice of the peace position will be filled by the county commission of the county in which the township is located, while a municipal court vacancy will be filled according to the rules in the city charter, typically a city council appointment. Midterm vacancies on the Supreme Court or District Court are filled by the use of a modified merit plan. The Commission on Judicial Selection, consisting of three lawyers appointed by the state bar, three laypeople appointed by the governor, and the chief justice or an associate justice selected by the chief justice, will evaluate applications from those wishing to fill the vacancy and will send the governor a list of three names of acceptable candidates. The governor must choose one of these three individuals to fill the position; he cannot go off the list. The person selected will then serve only until the next general election, at which time the judge must run in a nonpartisan race for the remainder of the term. If the vacancy is on the Supreme Court, the seven-member "permanent" commission will make its recommendation to the governor. If the vacancy is on the District Court, the commission will consist of the seven permanent commissioners plus two temporary commissioners: an attorney appointed by the state bar and a layperson appointed by the governor, both of whom must live in the judicial district for which that judge is being selected. The members of the permanent commission actually serve four-year, staggered terms of office, while the two temporary commissioners serve only until the list of nominees has been sent to the governor.

Because virtually all state judges in Nevada are chosen by nonpartisan election, the voters may choose to remove them at regularly scheduled elections. In addition, those suspected of wrongdoing may be removed by a recall election initiated by the voters prior to the expiration of the judge's term. Judges may also be sanctioned by the Nevada Commission on Judicial Discipline, which may reprimand or censure judges, require additional education, or even remove them from the bench. Supreme Court justices and judges of the District Court may also be impeached by the state legislature. This process requires the State Assembly to vote impeachment charges for misdemeanor or malfeasance in office by a simple majority of the total membership. After a trial in the State Senate, a two-thirds vote of the total membership would be necessary for conviction and removal from office. A method of legislative removal short of impeachment is also provided for in the state constitution. The legislature may, for "any reasonable cause," remove a Supreme Court justice or District Court judge upon the vote of a two-thirds majority of the total membership of each house.

Michael W. Bowers

See also Federalism; Lay Judiciaries; Merit Selection ("Missouri Plan"); Small Claims Courts; Trial Courts; United States—Federal System; United States—State Systems

References and further reading

Alverson, Bruce, et al. 2000. *Nevada Law Summary.* Las Vegas: Alverson, Taylor, Mortensen, Nelson, and Sanders.
Bowers, Michael. 1993. *The Nevada State Constitution: A Reference Guide.* Westport, CT: Greenwood Press.
———. 1996. *The Sagebrush State: Nevada's History, Government, and Politics.* Reno and Las Vegas: University of Nevada Press.
Driggs, Don W., and Leonard E. Goodall. 1996. *Nevada Politics and Government: Conservatism in an Open Society.* Lincoln: University of Nebraska Press.
Neilander, Dennis. 1997. "The Judicial Branch." Pp. 31–51 in *Towards 2000: Public Policy in Nevada.* Edited by Dennis L. Soden and Eric Herzik. Dubuque, IA: Kendall/Hunt Publishing Co.

NEW BRUNSWICK

GENERAL INFORMATION

One of the fourteen political units comprising Canada (nine other provinces, three territorial governments, and the federal or national government), the province of New Brunswick covers 28,345 square miles and has a population of 729,630. It is the largest in landmass (and second in population) of the three maritime provinces, the others being Nova Scotia and Prince Edward Island. New Brunswick links this region to the United States through its border with Maine.

With approximately 85 percent of the province's land covered by forest, it is not surprising that forestry, with its accompanying pulp and paper industry, makes one of the most significant contributions to the economy. Mining, potatoes, commercial fishing, the food and beverage industry, and tourism are also important. More recently, call centers and other information technology businesses have been attracted to the province.

The population of New Brunswick is split almost equally between urban and rural dwellers. The largest city, Saint John (population 72,500), is the most highly industrialized; it is also the major port. Moncton, with a population of nearly 60,000, is the most fully bilingual and the fastest-growing city. The capital city, Fredericton, located on the St. John River, is the smallest of the three major cities, with 46,500 people. Edmundston (population 11,000) and Bathurst have among the highest proportion of Acadian residents in the province (for example, 40 percent of the 14,500 people in Bathurst are francophone). Edmundston is dependent on pulp and paper, and Bathurst on mining. The newest city, Miramichi, was established on January 1, 1995, out of Chatham and Newcastle and other smaller communities; it has a population of 21,500.

Almost two-thirds of the New Brunswick population speak English as their first language. Slightly more than one-third of the population are Acadians, whose first language is French. Members of each primary language group are clustered in different parts of the province, with Acadians in the north and southeast of the province, English-speakers in the west and south.

The first inhabitants of the province were the Mi'Kmaq, whose territory is in what is now Nova Scotia, Prince Edward Island, and the Gaspé Peninsula (they also inhabited part of Newfoundland); the Malecite, whose territory extends to what is now New England; and the Passamaquoddy in the south of the province. Today 10,250 aboriginal persons, comprising fifteen First Nations (mainly Maliseet and Mi'kmaq), live on the twenty-five reserves and off-reserve. There has been a gradual increase in "self-government" in the First Nations Communities. For example, under a 1997 tripartite policing agreement entered into by the Mi'kmaq (Micmac) Indian Island First Nation, New Brunswick, and Canada, an aboriginal member of the RCMP–First Nation Community Policing Service provides policing services to the reserve. In recent years the First Nations have asserted land claims and other aboriginal rights under treaties and Section 35 of the Constitution Act of 1982, including claims to a share in the province's natural resources, especially logging and the lobster fishery. The claims of off-reserve aboriginal peoples also require resolution. More recently, the emergence of claims by self-identified Acadian Métis has created controversy.

The First Nations' earliest contact with Europeans was likely with Basque fishermen sometime in the 1400s in the most northeasterly portion of the province. The first European settlers, as opposed to seasonal or occasional visitors, were French who in 1604 established a short-lived settlement on the border of what is now New Brunswick and Maine at the mouth of the St. Croix River. Known as Acadia, the area was the subject of dispute between France and Great Britain until France ceded it to the British in 1713. Beginning in 1755 the British expelled Acadians unwilling to swear allegiance to Britain, and they did not return until after the end of the Seven Years War in 1763. Many Acadians settled permanently in Louisiana.

After the American Revolution, fourteen thousand United Empire Loyalists (including black Loyalists and slaves) fled into the portion of Nova Scotia that became New Brunswick. The period of Anglophone dominance lasted until well into the twentieth century. Louis J. Robichaud, the first elected Acadian premier (in 1960—an Acadian had inherited the premiership from a resigning premier in 1923), established a program of equal opportunity involving a redistribution of resources from the better-off areas to the poorer areas of the province, which benefited the economic situation of Acadians and began the process of bilingualism.

The province became (and remains) the only officially bilingual province in Canada with the enactment in 1969 of the Official Languages Act. The 1981 Act to Recognize the Equality of the Two Official Linguistic Communities in part provided for separate English-language and French-language school districts (there are currently twelve Anglophone and six francophone school districts). Bilingualism in the New Brunswick legislature and courts was entrenched in the Constitution Act of 1982, and in 1992 the Canadian Charter of Rights and Freedoms was amended to entrench the equality of the two linguistic communities, including the right to distinct educational and cultural institutions.

The only concerted opposition to linguistic dualism has come from the Parti-Acadian, which promoted a separate Acadian province in the late 1970s, and from the Confederation of Regions Party, founded in 1989, which, despite becoming the official opposition in 1991, no longer has a serious presence in the province. The liberals and the progressive conservatives have support among both major language groups. It is of interest that the only two bilingual place-names in Canada are New Brunswick/Nouveau-Brunswick and Grand Sault/Grand Falls, a town in New Brunswick. A mark of how significant the Acadian community has become is that Moncton was selected as the site of the Sommet de la Francophonie, held in September 1999 and attended by fifty-two countries.

Other major ethnic groups are the Irish and Scots, who arrived in large numbers at the beginning of the nineteenth century. The Scots' influence is reflected in the fact that New Brunswick adopted an official tartan in 1959. Today, although the province has a less diverse population than some other parts of Canada, it is populated by people who have emigrated from countries around the world and their descendants. For example, there are nearly nineteen hundred people who identify themselves as having origins in East and Southeast Asia, more than nine hundred whose origins are Arabic, and New Denmark is home to the largest group of persons of Danish descent in North America.

EVOLUTION AND HISTORY

New Brunswick was part of Nova Scotia until 1784, when, in response to pressure from the Loyalists, it was made a separate province named for George III's ancestral seat, Brunswick, in Germany. In 1867 the province joined with Nova Scotia and Canada (now Ontario and Quebec) to form the new Dominion of Canada, with the enactment by the U.K.'s Parliament of the British North America Act of 1867. A New Brunswick case, *R. v. Chandler* (1868), established the courts' judicial review jurisdiction to determine that each level of government remained within its sphere of competence under the act.

Although talk about a maritime union that began prior to confederation has never reached fruition, there is a commitment to economic and educational cooperation among the maritime provinces.

New Brunswick was slow in extending full political rights to all its residents. For example, nonaboriginal women received the provincial vote only in 1919 and the right to run in elections in 1934, making New Brunswick the second last province to extend this right, while aboriginal people living on a reserve were not permitted to vote in provincial elections until 1963.

CURRENT STRUCTURE

The lieutenant governor, representing the queen in New Brunswick, is appointed by the federal government; there is a single fifty-five-member legislative assembly. (Until 1892, New Brunswick also had an upper house, the legislative council, although responsible government had been instituted by 1848.) The province has ten members each in the House of Commons and Senate at the national level.

New Brunswick has a two-tier court system composed of the inferior courts and the superior courts, both of which are provincial courts by virtue of section 92(14) of the Constitution Act of 1867, which gives the provinces

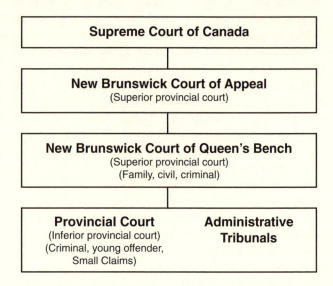

Legal Structure of New Brunswick Courts

Supreme Court of Canada

New Brunswick Court of Appeal
(Superior provincial court)

New Brunswick Court of Queen's Bench
(Superior provincial court)
(Family, civil, criminal)

Provincial Court
(Inferior provincial court)
(Criminal, young offender, Small Claims)

Administrative Tribunals

jurisdiction over "the administration of justice in the province."

The initial level of the Superior Court is called the Court of Queen's Bench, with which the county or district courts were amalgamated in 1979. Twenty-two judges (including the chief justice) are appointed to trial and family divisions in eight judicial districts. Eight judges are to be named to the Family Division, but they are ex officio judges of the Trial Division. The Queen's Bench has inherent jurisdiction, as well as jurisdiction over matters assigned to it by particular statutes, and its judges hear serious criminal, divorce, and other family cases, among other matters. Only the Superior Court has jurisdiction with respect to determining the constitutionality of legislation if that is the only issue raised.

There are six full-time judges, including the chief justice of New Brunswick, on the Court of Appeal, which sits in Fredericton. In addition to hearing appeals from the lower courts, the Court of Appeal may hear references brought by the provincial cabinet about the constitutionality of provincial or federal legislation. Appeals from the Court of Appeal are to the Supreme Court of Canada.

Superior Court judges for New Brunswick are chosen from the bar of New Brunswick. The independence of Superior Court judges is guaranteed by the combination of appointment by the governor-general of Canada, the fixing and provision of salaries by Parliament, and removal by the governor-general on address of the Senate and House of Commons as set out in sections 96 to 100 of the Constitution Act of 1867, which applies to all superior courts in Canada. In reality, the federal minister of justice selects Superior Court judges from those recommended by provincially based committees, and the prime minister recommends the successful candidate to the governor-general.

The Provincial Court deals with the majority of legal

disputes, including many criminal charges, municipal by-laws, and highway traffic offenses, among other matters. Its jurisdiction is determined by statute. The Provincial Court is designated as a youth court for the purpose of the federal Young Offender Act. Provincial judges are responsible for matters performed by other judicial officers elsewhere, including receiving information, signing search and arrest warrants, conducting bail hearings, and the like. There are twenty-six provincially appointed judges who must be a member of the bar of New Brunswick and have been a member in good standing of a bar of any province for ten years at the time of appointment. There is a judicial appointments committee that makes recommendations to the minister of justice from among applicants, but, as with the federal process, there is criticism that it is too political, as well as criticism that there are insufficient women at all levels of the courts. Judges must retire at seventy-five, subject to removal for misconduct. In October 2000, the province accepted the recommendations of its Judicial Remuneration Commission to pay provincially appointed judges $141,202. The establishment of the commission satisfied the requirements for judicial independence set out by the Supreme Court of Canada in the Provincial Judges Reference (1997). Complaints about judges' conduct may be made to the provincial Judicial Council, which may issue reprimands or determine that a judge should be removed from office; the cabinet is bound by the determinations of the council.

There is a registrar for both the Queen's Bench and Court of Appeal who must be a barrister of ten years' standing, a clerk for each judicial district for the Trial Division, and an administrator for the Family Division (these last may be the same person). There is a chief sheriff and a sheriff in each judicial district responsible, for example, for jury management, conducting auctions, escorting prisoners, and seizing goods.

The Small Claims Court was established in January 1999 to deal with enforcement of debts and recovery of possession of personal property worth up to $6,000. Adjudicators, who must be practicing members of the Law Society, sit on the court, and the registrar and clerks of the Court of Queen's Bench serve as the registrar and clerks.

Disputes about benefits and services, such as workers' compensation, and certain areas of law, such as labor relations and human rights, are adjudicated by a system of administrative tribunals; only a small number of those decisions would eventually be determined by the courts on judicial review. A "rentalsman" is responsible for some landlord-tenant matters, including mediating disputes that arise between landlords and tenants.

NOTABLE FEATURES OF LAW/LEGAL SYSTEM

New Brunswick is a totally common law jurisdiction, a feature it shares with all other jurisdictions in Canada, except Quebec, which has a civil law system. There have been no claims to extend linguistic and cultural duality to the legal system.

New Brunswick delivers legal aid to accused criminals through the private bar and a duty counsel system at the province's courthouses. The only civil legal aid is delivered by staff solicitors to persons, primarily women, who have suffered domestic abuse. Parents whose children are the subject of a Crown application for guardianship or temporary custody may also be able to obtain legal aid. New Brunswick's legal aid system is one of the most limited in the country.

STAFFING

There are just over thirteen hundred lawyers (active and nonpracticing), of whom approximately 28 percent are women. There are few aboriginal lawyers or lawyers from racialized communities.

Although required to have at least two years' undergraduate education, most entrants have acquired an undergraduate degree before beginning the three-year course of studies leading to the bachelor of law degree, or LL.B. Candidates must also complete articles with a member of the bar and the bar admission course before they can be called to the bar of the province.

New Brunswick has two law schools. The English-speaking school, established in Saint John in 1892, moved to Fredericton in 1959 and has been located on the main campus of the University of New Brunswick since 1968. The French-speaking L'École de Droit was established in 1978 at the Université de Moncton, itself founded in 1964 and the largest francophone university in Canada outside Quebec. Both faculties are common law faculties.

RELATIONSHIP TO NATIONAL SYSTEM

New Brunswick would be left geographically isolated from the rest of Canada in the event of Quebec separation; scenarios in response include a renewed impetus to maritime union and closer connections with the eastern seaboard provinces of the United States. There is also concern about the continued viability of the Acadian community in the event of Quebec independence.

Patricia Hughes

See also Appellate Courts; Canada; Federalism; Judicial Selection, Methods of; Legal Aid; Legal Education; Nova Scotia; Small Claims Courts; Trial Courts

References and further reading
Andrew, Sheila M. 1996. *The Development of Elites in Acadian New Brunswick, 1861–1881.* Montreal and Kingston: McGill-Queen's University Press.
Bell, D. G. 1992. *Legal Education in New Brunswick: A History.* Fredericton: University of New Brunswick.
Fanjoy, Emery M. 1990. "Language and Politics in New Brunswick." *Canadian Parliamentary Review* 13: 2–8.

Gould, G. P., and A. J. Semple. 1980. *Our Land: The Maritimes.* Fredericton: Saint Annes Point Press.

New Brunswick Government. "About New Brunswick." http://www.gov.nb.ca.

Statistics Canada. "Population by Ethnic Origin, 1996 Census" and "Population by Aboriginal Group, 1996 Census." http://www.statcan.ca.

Wilbur, Richard. 1989. *The Rise of French New Brunswick.* Halifax: Formac Publishing.

NEW HAMPSHIRE

GENERAL INFORMATION

The state of New Hampshire is located in the Northeastern United States. It lies north of the state of Massachusetts, west of the state of Maine, east of the state of Vermont, and south of the Canadian province of Quebec. The state is 8,969 square miles in size, making it the forty-fourth largest state in the nation. Its current population (as of the 2000 census) is 1,235,786, and it is the forty-first most populous state in the United States.

One of the original thirteen states, New Hampshire has never had a strong agricultural economy. Its rocky soil is poor by regional standards, although it produces significant quantities of dairy products and maple syrup. The state is, however, blessed with abundant water resources, a seventeen-mile Atlantic seacoast, trees, and natural beauty. These resources provided the state with three of the major bases of its economy throughout the nineteenth and most of the twentieth centuries—industry, fishing, and tourism. In the eighteenth and the early nineteenth centuries, the abundance of lumber provided the raw materials necessary for a shipbuilding industry. Later in the nineteenth century, the abundance of flowing rivers provided power for mills throughout the state, and New Hampshire remained a major producer of paper, textiles, shoes, and other goods throughout much of the twentieth century. In the past few decades, many of these industries have largely been eliminated by competition with foreign production.

New Hampshire's tourist industry, however, remains strong. The state has a long tradition of serving as a resort area for residents of its more populous neighbors to the south. In the nineteenth century, much of this was the province of large resort hotels in the White Mountains. Today's summer tourists, however, head for the ocean beaches in the southeastern area of the state, the swimming and fishing areas of the state's lakes region, and the amusement parks scattered throughout the state. The fall season sees massive numbers of tourists heading for the White Mountains in the north-central part of the state to witness the changing colors of the leaves.

The past few decades have seen a remarkable transformation in the southern part of New Hampshire. Many of the cities there, especially Manchester and Nashua, have been growing dramatically. This has resulted from an increase in the high-technology and white-collar industries in those areas, and from an increasing integration of this area with the rapidly growing economy of the Boston area. As a result, much of this region of the state has gone from having a rural or small-town character to that of an urban or suburban area. The change in the population base of the state has also been reflected in the state's politics. Up until the last decade, conservative Republicans held a virtual monopoly on political power at the state level. In the past decade, however, the Democratic Party has become competitive within the state, and a significant moderate wing of the Republican Party has also emerged.

New Hampshire plays a unique role in U.S. presidential politics. Since 1920, the state has held the first presidential primary in the nation. Locals often brag that, since 1952, candidates have not been able to become president without first winning the New Hampshire primary, but that claim has been undermined by the primary defeats of Bill Clinton in 1992 and George W. Bush in 2000. Nonetheless, the state's primary continues to play a role in winnowing out nonviable candidates.

EVOLUTION AND HISTORY

New Hampshire is one of the original thirteen colonies that formed the United States. British colonists settled at what is now the town of Rye in 1623, and New Hampshire was declared a royal colony in 1679. The colony became a hotbed of revolutionary sentiment, and the royal governor was expelled in 1775. New Hampshire was the only one of the thirteen colonies not to be invaded during the Revolutionary War, but New Hampshire soldiers fought in many of the major battles of that war.

New Hampshire's first state constitution was enacted in 1776, but that document proved to be short-lived. The state constitution that is currently in effect was enacted in 1784, although it has been revised almost continuously since then. Amendment can occur in two ways. Under the first method, each of the two houses of the legislature must pass a proposed change by a three-fifths vote of the entire membership. Once that occurs, the proposed change must be approved by two-thirds of the voters in a general election. The second method is by constitutional convention. A majority vote of both houses of the legislature may call such a convention at any time; if the legislature does not call for a convention in any ten-year period, it may be called for by a majority of voters in a general election. Delegates to the convention are chosen by popular election, and proposals approved by a three-fifths majority of the delegates must also be approved by two-thirds of the vote in a general election before becoming effective. Amendments alter the text of the existing constitution, rather than being appended at the end.

As enacted in 1784, the state constitution laid out the basic institutions of government that exist today. The constitution provides for a bicameral "General Court" (legislature), consisting of a Senate and a House of Representatives. The Senate is constitutionally limited to twenty-four (originally twelve) members, while the House has always been a much larger body. Despite the relatively small size of the state, the New Hampshire House of Representatives currently has the largest number of members (four hundred) of any state legislative chamber in the United States.

The executive branch is divided as well. In addition to the governor (originally called the president), the constitution provides for a popularly elected five-member council, commonly referred to as the Executive Council. "All judicial officers, the attorney general, and all officers of the navy, and general and field officers of the militia" must be nominated by the governor and approved by the council.

New Hampshire's judiciary has had a complicated constitutional evolution. At the time of the Revolutionary War, the existing colonial Superior Court was essentially kept intact, to become the new state's high court. Perhaps because they took the existence of this court for granted, the drafters of the 1784 Constitution do not seem to have given much thought as to how best to preserve the independence of the judiciary. Despite the fact that the constitution provided that "for the security of the rights of the people . . . the judges of the supreme judicial court should hold their offices so long as they behave well," the constitution also provided the legislature with plenary powers to organize the courts. That power was used several times in the nineteenth century to "reorganize" the courts following shifts in the partisan composition of the legislature, largely replacing the entire existing court system. It was not until 1966 that the constitution was amended to clearly provide for the continuing existence of the Supreme Court and "a trial court of general jurisdiction known as the superior court, and such lower courts as the legislature may establish."

Despite the lack of a clear legal provision for an independent judiciary in the 1784 Constitution, the practice of judicial review of legislative statutes appeared fairly early in New Hampshire history. The inclusion of a bill of rights in the 1784 Constitution provided the courts with a rationale for finding statutes unconstitutional. This appears to have happened as early as 1786, when several judges found that a statute allowing justices of the peace to try civil cases involving debts of ten pounds or less (the "Ten Pound Act") violated the constitutional right to a jury in civil trials. In response, the legislature met to consider impeaching the judges, but instead repealed the law.

Several notable legal and political figures have hailed from New Hampshire. Two U.S. Supreme Court justices, Levi Woodbury (1789–1851) and current justice David Souter, are from the state. Lawyer and statesman Daniel Webster (1782–1852), perhaps the greatest courtroom advocate of his day, was born in New Hampshire. In addition to serving as a U.S. congressman and senator from Massachusetts, and twice as secretary of state, Webster won several landmark cases before the U.S. Supreme Court. These include *Dartmouth College v. Woodward* (1819), which invalidated New Hampshire's attempt to abrogate Dartmouth College's royally granted charter, and *McCulloch v. Maryland* (1819), which ratified the federal government's power to establish a national bank and denied states the power to tax such federally created entities. Franklin Pierce (1804–1869) was elected fourteenth president of the United States, serving from 1853 to 1856. He was a New Hampshire politician who attracted national attention for his heroics in the Mexican War. His administration is notable primarily for its failure—it foundered on the issue of slavery in the Kansas territory, and he was not renominated by the Democratic Party.

CURRENT STRUCTURE

Legal Profession and Legal Training
As of 2001, 3,021 active lawyers resided in the state. Admission to the bar requires graduation from a law school and passage of the state's bar exam. One law school is located in the state—the Franklin Pierce Law Center in Concord.

Most criminal prosecutions in the state are handled by the county attorney's offices. The one major exception to this rule is that all homicide cases in the state are handled by the state's Department of Justice. Representation for indigent criminal defendants is provided by the New Hampshire Public Defenders. This is a state-funded private corporation maintaining nine offices throughout the state.

Judicial System
New Hampshire has two levels of trial courts. District courts have jurisdiction over misdemeanor criminal cases, preliminary hearings in felony cases, traffic violations, juvenile cases, and domestic violence issues. In addition, these courts have jurisdiction over civil cases without juries, including small claims cases. In two of the state's ten counties, district courts also hold jury trials. There are thirty-seven district courts in New Hampshire (see figure).

Superior courts are at the next higher level. These are trial courts of general jurisdiction. These courts have original jurisdiction over felonies, divorces, and civil jury

Legal Structure of New Hampshire Courts

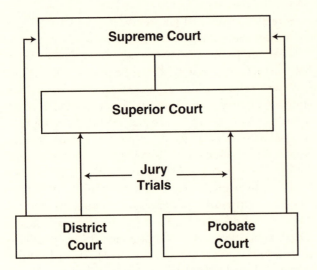

trials. Some cases tried in district court can be appealed de novo to a superior court. In addition, some appeals from administrative agency decisions can be heard in a superior court, of which there are eleven in the state.

New Hampshire is one of the few states with no intermediate court of appeals. The state's five-member Supreme Court, located in Concord, handles all appeals from superior courts and most from district courts, as well as most appeals from administrative agencies. Because this court has a discretionary docket, no appeal by right exists in the New Hampshire court system. The Supreme Court, as a response, does a very thorough review of the motions for certiorari and chooses to fully review a relatively large number of cases (approximately eight hundred). In addition to its appellate responsibility, the Supreme Court is charged with the constitutional duty to issue advisory opinions whenever required to do so by "each branch of the legislature as well as the governor and council." Finally, the chief justice is constitutionally designated as the "administrative head of all the courts." As such, he must, "with the concurrence of a majority of the supreme court justices, make rules governing the administration of all courts in the state and the practice and procedure to be followed in all such courts."

In addition to this basic structure of trial courts and the Supreme Court, the state has a probate court in each of the ten counties. These courts have jurisdiction over trusts and estates, wills, adoption, termination of parental rights, guardianships, and involuntary commitments. The state has also created a pilot program to provide family courts in two of the state's ten counties (Rockingham and Grafton). These courts handle adoptions, divorces, child custody, child support, juvenile justice, and domestic violence.

Administrative Hearings and Appeals

Administrative adjudications are heard by officers of the agencies with jurisdiction over the matters involved. The proper venue for appeal of agency actions varies according to statutes. Most administrative appeals are heard by the Supreme Court. Some actions, specified by statute, may be appealed to the Merrimack Superior Court, which is located at Concord. All state agencies are represented in court by the state's Department of Justice.

NOTABLE FEATURES OF LAW/LEGAL SYSTEM

New Hampshire is a common law state. Until the past decade, the courts were not viewed generally as strong, independent institutions. In the past decade, however, the state's Supreme Court has invalidated the state's system of school funding, which was based almost entirely on property taxes that were collected and spent locally. As a result, the state has had to implement a new statewide property tax arrangement to address the court's demand that tax burdens in support of schools be distributed more equitably. This has drastically increased the visibility of the court in the state's politics.

The judicial branch of government has generally been charged with policing its own conduct. The Judicial Conduct Committee is, in fact, a committee of the Supreme Court (superior court justices are designated to sit on the committee in matters involving Supreme Court justices). In 1999, however, the Supreme Court was rocked by a complicated scandal involving, among other issues, improper influence exercised by one of the justices over the judicial handling of his own divorce, and the participation of justices in cases from which they had formally recused themselves. As a result of this scandal, one justice resigned, another retired, and the chief justice was impeached but acquitted. As of this writing, there are currently several proposals for reform of the laws involving the discipline, appointment, and tenure of judges, but it is unclear what reforms will be instituted.

STAFFING

All judicial officers are appointed by the governor and the Executive Council. Once appointed, judges serve "during good behavior" until the constitutionally mandated retirement age of seventy years. There are two ways to remove judges. The first method is impeachment and conviction by the legislature. The second is the bill of address, which allows for removal by the governor of any judicial official with the approval of a majority of both houses of the legislature and the executive council.

RELATIONSHIP TO NATIONAL SYSTEM

The single federal district court in the state is located in Concord. Cases from that court can be appealed to the First Circuit Court of Appeals, located in Boston, Massachusetts. Cases from that court can be appealed to the U.S. Supreme Court, as can New Hampshire Supreme Court decisions involving questions of federal law.

Daniel Krislov

See also Appellate Courts; Common Law; Constitutional Review; Judicial Independence; Judicial Review; Judicial Selection, Methods of; Massachusetts; United States—Federal System; United States—State Systems

References and further reading
Heffernan, Nancy Coffey, and Ann Page Stecker. 1996. *New Hampshire: Crosscurrents in Its Development.* Rev. ed. Hanover, NH: Library of New England.
Lambert, Richard M. 1985. "The 'Ten Pound Act' Cases and the Origins of Judicial Review in New Hampshire." Unpublished M.A. thesis, University of New Hampshire.
New Hampshire Judiciary Website, http://webster.state.nh.us/courts/.
Page, Elwin L. 1959. *Judicial Beginnings in New Hampshire.* Concord, NH: Evans Printing Co.

NEW JERSEY

GENERAL INFORMATION

New Jersey is a state in the Middle Atlantic region of the United States. It is the fifth smallest state (21,277 square kilometers) but the most densely populated (about 89 percent of the total population live in urban areas), with three-quarters of the people living in northern New Jersey. According to the 2000 census there are 8,414,350 people living in New Jersey. Caucasians compose the largest share at 6,261,187 (included in this number are Hispanics/Latinos, who may be either white or black). There are 5,557,209 white not including Hispanic/Latino individuals; 1,211,750 African Americans; 1,117,191 Hispanic/Latino; 524,356 Asians; and smaller numbers of other groups.

New Jersey is known as the Garden State because of its many rich farmlands that are among the nation's leading producers of peaches, cranberries, and blueberries. It is also called the breadbasket to New York and Philadelphia. More recently, manufacturing has become the largest contributor (about one-third) to New Jersey's economy. It leads the nation in the production of chemicals, and one-sixth of all drugs manufactured in the United States come from New Jersey.

The Dutch were the first European settlers to establish a permanent settlement in New Jersey (1660). The area was later brought under British control (1664), and the British claimed title until New Jersey became one of the original thirteen colonies to declare its independence in 1776. It was in New Jersey where many famous Revolutionary War battles took place, including the famous battle for Trenton, which was secured when George Washington and his troops crossed the Delaware River on Christmas night of 1776.

Fearing the possibility of underrepresentation, New Jersey at the Constitutional Convention proposed a plan of government in which the legislature would be unicameral, with equal representation among the states. Eventually the convention adopted a bicameral system with two houses: the Senate emulating the New Jersey plan of two senators per state, and the House of Representatives being based on population. Satisfied that they would be properly represented, New Jersey was the third state to ratify the Constitution of the United States in 1787.

EVOLUTION AND HISTORY

New Jersey has had three different constitutions during its history as a state. The first was adopted in 1776, having been hastily drafted during the Revolutionary War period. It was influenced by the animosity toward the previous royal governors, who had been appointed by the king of England, therefore giving most of the control over the government to the legislature. It provided minimal separation of powers. The legislature selected the governor, and he had very little power. The second constitution, adopted in 1844, still gave most power to the legislature. However, the governor was now elected by the people but could serve only one three-year term.

The third and current constitution was drafted at a convention in 1947 and became effective in 1948. This constitution developed a tripartite system of government with a clear separation of powers. It created a strong governor and strong Supreme Court. Under this constitution the governor serves a maximum of two successive four-year terms and exercises both broad powers of appointment and line-item veto power. The governor appoints all statewide judges and justices, all county prosecutors, the attorney general, and most other high-level officials. All appointments require approval by the state senate. The governorship in New Jersey is often referred to as one of the strongest in the nation. No state official other than the governor is elected by all the voters of the state.

New Jersey, unlike many states, does not have a system of initiative or referendum to alter the constitution. In order for a constitutional amendment to be placed on the ballot, the legislature must vote in favor of the amendment by a three-fifths majority in both houses in one year, or by a majority of both houses in two successive years. It then must be approved by a majority of the voters. As of 2000, there were fifty-five amendments to the current constitution.

Under the 1947 Constitution, the legislature initially was divided into the Senate, consisting of one senator from each of the twenty-one counties, and the Assembly, composed of members chosen from the counties on the

Legal Structure of New Jersey Courts

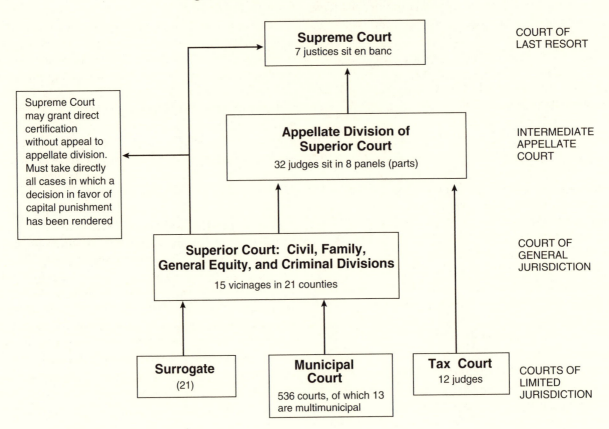

Supreme Court
7 justices sit en banc

COURT OF LAST RESORT

Supreme Court may grant direct certification without appeal to appellate division. Must take directly all cases in which a decision in favor of capital punishment has been rendered

Appellate Division of Superior Court
32 judges sit in 8 panels (parts)

INTERMEDIATE APPELLATE COURT

Superior Court: Civil, Family, General Equity, and Criminal Divisions
15 vicinages in 21 counties

COURT OF GENERAL JURISDICTION

Surrogate
(21)

Municipal Court
536 courts, of which 13 are multimunicipal

Tax Court
12 judges

COURTS OF LIMITED JURISDICTION

---

basis of population. Subsequently, after the decisions of the U.S. Supreme Court mandating one person one vote, the legislature was restructured by a constitutional amendment in 1966 into a Senate of forty members and an Assembly of eighty members. All districts are based on population, so that today the various Senate and Assembly districts cross county lines.

Prior to this constitution, the legal system in New Jersey was complex and confusing, with an outdated sixteen-person court of Errors and Appeals at its apex. Law and equity were rigidly separated, and the system led to delays and complexities. The new constitution provided for a streamlined system with a seven-member Supreme Court led by a chief justice with significant powers over the entire system.

CURRENT STRUCTURE

Legal Profession and Legal Training

There were 70,264 lawyers admitted to practice in New Jersey in 1999. Of these, 54,581 were active practitioners. However, it should be noted that a number of these lawyers practice in New York City, Philadelphia, or elsewhere, or are corporate counsel for many of the large corporations headquartered in New Jersey.

There are numerous state, county, and specialty bar associations. There are three law schools in the state: two public law schools—Rutgers University School of Law in Newark and Rutgers University School of Law in Camden—and one private law school, Seton Hall University School of Law. Admission to the bar is controlled by the Supreme Court, which is also responsible for lawyer discipline. The Institute for Continuing Legal Education is responsible for running a training program in which all new members of the bar are required to participate. The institute also runs many programs for legal education of the practicing members of the bar. There is, however, no mandatory continuing legal education requirement in New Jersey.

Legal Services and Criminal Defense Services

There is a large Public Defender's Office in New Jersey funded by the state, with approximately four hundred lawyers. It handles the defense of indictable criminal cases for defendants who are unable to afford private counsel. In New Jersey the state constitution grants a right to indictment by a grand jury in all offenses that are punishable by a sentence of more than six months. Each county has a Public Defender's Office with a central office in Trenton. In cases in which there is a conflict of interest or special situation, the public defenders may pay outside counsel. The Public Defender's Office also provides counsel in cases dealing with mental health issues, issues arising out of Megan's Law (the law dealing with community notification of the existence of sex offenders living therein), and child abuse issues.

Additionally, municipalities are required by law to provide a municipal public defender to represent defendants in the municipal court for nonindictable offenses when those defendants are unable to afford counsel and the offenses carry the possibility of incarceration, heavy fines, or loss of privileges such as the right to drive.

Civil cases for individuals who cannot afford private counsel are often handled by Legal Services offices. There are fifteen Legal Services programs: fourteen local field programs providing direct services in all twenty-one counties, and a statewide coordinating office. In 2000 there were 203 attorneys working in those offices. In 2000 there were also well over 1,200 private and corporate attorneys who took pro bono cases on referral from Legal Services. Legal Services receives funding from federal, state, and local governments, as well as significant amounts from interest on lawyers' trust funds and some small proportion from private sources. The total funding in 1999 was about $29 million. Specialized legal services are also provided by other groups, including a number of community health law projects, an education law center, as well as free legal services that are available through the clinical programs of the three law schools.

Administrative Hearings

In 1978 the Office of Administrative Law (OAL) was created by the legislature to conduct administrative hearings. (Previously each agency had its own full- and part-time hearing officers.) The OAL has full-time state employees within the executive branch who are designated "administrative law judges." These judges are responsible for conducting hearings in contested cases and preparing a recommended report and decision. The report and decision then go to the head of the administrative agency for final decision. The head of the agency can adopt, reject, or modify the decision of the administrative law judge. Therefore, while hearings are carried out by a semiautonomous administrative agency, the final decision remains with the agency, which has the statutory jurisdiction to set and enforce regulatory policy. Decisions of the head of the agency can be appealed to the Appellate Division of the Superior Court. Administrative law judges are appointed by the governor with the consent of the Senate for five-year terms.

Judicial System

The statewide judicial system is composed of a Supreme Court and a Superior Court, which is divided into three divisions including Appellate Division, Law Division, and Chancery Division. The Law Division is further divided into civil and criminal parts, and the Chancery Division is divided into family part and general equity. There is also a tax court, which is not a constitutional court but was created by the state in 1979 to handle specialty tax cases. All of these judges are appointed for seven-year terms by the governor, with advice and consent of the Senate. If reappointed, they are on the court until the constitutionally required retirement age of seventy. Judges, however, are allowed to serve on recall at the request of the chief justice after retirement.

Once a judge is appointed to the Superior Court, the chief justice determines the division and county in which the judge will sit. Generally new judges are assigned to one of the trial courts. New Jersey ascribes to a system of rotation, so that judges are regularly transferred from one division or part to another. After some years of experience, some judges will be assigned to the Appellate Division. With rare exceptions, once judges are assigned to the Appellate Division they no longer rotate.

There is a Superior Court in each of the twenty-one counties in New Jersey, with the smaller counties grouped together to create vicinages. There are fifteen vicinages in New Jersey. The eleven larger counties constitute their own vicinages. The remaining ten counties are grouped into four vicinages: (1) Atlantic County and Cape May; (2) Morris and Sussex; (3) Somerset, Hunterdon, and Warren; and (4) Gloucester, Cumberland, and Salem. Each vicinage in New Jersey has an assignment judge selected by the chief justice. This judge is the administrative head in the vicinage and works in conjunction with the chief justice in administering the system.

In the trial courts some cases are tried by the judge alone, and in other cases by a jury. The New Jersey Constitution provides that in all criminal cases the defendant has the right to a jury trial. (Defendants do not have a right to a jury trial in quasi-criminal cases in which the potential punishment is six months or less.) In all civil cases the New Jersey Constitution provides that the right to a jury trial "shall remain inviolate." This has been interpreted to mean that there is a right to a trial by jury in those cases in which there was a right to a jury trial at common law. The Chancery Division does not have trials by jury because it deals with equitable issues that were tried without a jury at common law. New Jersey permits the trial of a legal issue without a jury if it is being decided as part of an issue in which equitable relief is requested and the legal issue is ancillary to the equitable issue. New Jersey requires a unanimous twelve-person jury in criminal cases. In civil cases it requires a verdict of five jurors when six are deliberating and ten jurors when twelve are deliberating.

There is an automatic right of appeal in all cases to the Appellate Division. The judges of the Appellate Division are combined into eight four-judge parts but hear cases in panels of two or three. There is a presiding judge of the Appellate Division who, in addition to appellate duties, is the administrative judge of the division. Each part also has a presiding judge. Presiding judges are determined by seniority within the Appellate Division. The appeal is based on the record developed below. There is a right to appeal from the actions of the Appellate Division to the Supreme Court in any case in which there is a constitutional issue involved or there was a dissent in the Appellate Division. In other cases the parties can request certification to the Supreme Court. Under the capital punishment statute in New Jersey, all capital cases in which the jury decides in favor of the death penalty go directly to the Supreme Court and are not reviewed by the Appellate Division. The death penalty was reenacted in 1982, and the New Jersey Supreme Court upheld its constitutionality in 1987. As of 2000 there had been no executions under the statute.

In addition to the statewide system, there are local municipal courts. The municipal court judges are appointed by the governing body of the local municipality. Some of the larger cities have full-time municipal judges and most of the smaller municipalities have part-time municipal judges. The municipal courts handle the largest number of cases. They hear quasi-criminal cases called disorderly persons offenses or petty disorderly persons offenses wherein the possible penalty is six months or less. These include simple assault, petty theft, and driving offenses including drunk driving. Cases dealing with violations of municipal ordinances are also handled in the municipal court.

An appeal from the municipal court goes to the Law Division, where it is considered de novo, which means that the Law Division judge rehears the case and makes a new finding of fact, and does not simply review the case on the record.

Since the adoption of the new constitution in 1947, the New Jersey Supreme Court has gained a national reputation as a progressive, independent, and liberal court. Its decisions have led the nation in breaking new ground in many areas. Early on it decided the Karen Anne Quinlan case, the first major right-to-die case in the country. In that case the court permitted the father of a comatose daughter to disconnect her life support systems, even though it would cause her death. It was one of the first states to hold that the system of providing funding for public schools in the poorer urban districts that primarily relied upon local property taxes was unconstitutional and mandated increased spending by the state in behalf of schools in those areas. In the *Mount Laurel* decisions it decided that municipalities had a constitutional obligation to provide their fair share of low- and moderate-income housing within their areas. It has also relied upon its own state constitution in a large number of cases to grant greater individual rights to its citizens than the U.S. Supreme Court had granted. This freedom to be innovative is the result of many factors, perhaps most importantly the method of judicial appointment and the strong support in New Jersey for the concept of judicial independence. The state has also been bolstered by the high quality of the justices who have been appointed.

John B. Wefing

See also Appellate Courts; Capital Punishment; Constitutional Law; Judicial Independence; Judicial Selection, Methods of; Juries; Legal Aid; Neighborhood Justice Centers; Trial Courts; United States—Federal System; United States—State Systems

References and further reading
Connors, Richard J., and William J. Dunham. 1984. *The Government of New Jersey.* Lanham, MD: University Press of America.
Fitzgerald's Legislative Manual. 2000. Trenton: State of New Jersey.
Tarr, G. Alan, and Mary Cornelia Aldis Porter. 1988. *State Supreme Courts in State and Nation. New Jersey: The Legacy of Reform.* New Haven: Yale University Press.
Wefing, John B. 1998. "The New Jersey Supreme Court 1948–98: Fifty Years of Independence and Activism." *Rutgers Law Journal* 29: 701.
Williams, Robert F. 1990. *The New Jersey Constitution: A Reference Guide.* New Brunswick, NJ: Rutgers University Press.

NEW MEXICO

GENERAL INFORMATION

New Mexico is located in the southwest region of the United States. It is bounded by Arizona, Utah, Colorado, Oklahoma, and Texas. The state has been labeled the "land of enchantment" because of its austere physical beauty and fascinating diversity of peoples and cultures. New Mexico ranks fifth in size among the fifty United States, with a land area of 78 million acres (121,666 square miles). Much of the land is publicly owned. The federal government, the State of New Mexico, and the twenty-two Indian tribes combined own 55 percent of the land, leaving only 35 million acres in private hands.

The Rio Grande Valley traversing the center of the state from north to south is the defining feature of New Mexico's geography. The valley has been the central locus of New Mexico's people, history, and economy. It defined the transportation routes and the population settlement patterns. Outside the valley, New Mexico shares the same topographical features, varied climate, and general aridity of the other Rocky Mountain states.

Throughout most of New Mexico's 400-year history, the Hispanic population and culture have been concentrated in the northern half of the state. Also resident in this region are the Navajo, Jicarilla Apache, and most of the Pueblo Indian tribes.

East of the central mountains lie the broad level plains that form the western reaches of the Great Plains and connect New Mexico with Texas and Oklahoma geographically and culturally. Ranching, irrigation farming, and mineral extraction (especially oil and gas) dominate the economy of the east and south.

New Mexico was colonized by the Spanish beginning in 1598, with the purpose of Christianizing the settled Indians and providing a "defense in depth" of New Spain against enemy intruders. The area was the northernmost province of the Spanish Empire—remote, sparsely populated, deliberately xenophobic (foreigners were forbidden entry), and organized to conduct military operations. It remained closed to foreigners until the Mexican Declaration of Independence ended Spanish rule in 1821. New Mexico became part of the Republic of Mexico, but it remained a remote, peripheral province little touched by the turbulence in Mexico City. However, during the Mexican period, trade with the United States flourished and U.S. immigration began. The U.S. period was ushered in by General Stephen Kearny's conquest of New Mexico in 1846.

The descendants of the Spanish colonists and the Indians made up the majority of people in New Mexico throughout the nineteenth and well into the twentieth centuries. However, by 1950, Anglo (white, not Hispanic) immigration produced an Anglo majority that lasted through 1990. The 2000 census put New Mexico's population at 1,819,046, with an ethnic composition of 48 percent white (not Hispanic), 40 percent Hispanic (any race), 8 percent American Indian, 2 percent black, and less than 1 percent Asian. New Mexico is the first state in which no single racial or ethnic group constitutes a majority of the population; everyone belongs to a minority group. Females are 51 percent of the population, and the median age is thirty-four years. Personal income per capita is low at $22,000, making New Mexico the forty-eighth state by this measure. Thus, New Mexico's culture is not that of a homogeneous, white middle class but instead is a "mosaic" of diverse cultures. Further, the population is more female, younger, and poorer than those of its neighboring states.

The New Mexico economy is preindustrial and underdeveloped. It is based on agriculture, mineral extraction, and expenditures of the federal government. The gross state product was $45 billion in 1997, with only 64 percent of the civilian labor force employed in private, nonagricultural occupations. Manufacturing employs less than 8 percent of the workforce, while trade employs 20 percent and services 19 percent. Twenty-three percent of all workers are employed by the government at either the federal, state, or local level.

Spending by the federal government has always been important in the New Mexico economy. But it became the major component of the state's economic growth during and after World War II, with heavy federal spending at military installations and on defense-related research and development in New Mexico facilities.

EVOLUTION AND HISTORY

New Mexico's relative poverty and public sector–dominated economy have put a premium on the skillful pursuit of politics at all levels of government. In fact, the practice of politics in New Mexico has been refined to a virtual art form. Politics is a game that is played for material stakes, with finesse and intensity. The Hispanic New Mexicans quickly adapted to a new political system after the U.S. conquest in 1846. New Mexico was governed by military governors under martial law until 1850, when it was granted territorial status by the Congress as part of the great Compromise of 1850. With the establishment of civil government, the law-making process was American and Anglo-Saxon. The majority of legislators were Hispanic, and the leaderships of both the Democratic and Republican Parties were representative of both cultural groups. Statutes governing descent and distribution of property, marital and family matters, and the control of land and water promptly became a blend of the continental and the common law. Consequently, the law, political institutions, and political process of New Mexico bear the stamp of both the Spanish and the Anglo-American cultures.

New Mexico did not achieve statehood until 1912. Two years earlier, Congress directed Arizona and New Mexico to write constitutions and get them ratified in citizen referenda. In New Mexico, a Republican-dominated convention wrote a "sane and conservative" document after cutting a deal with the Hispanic delegates to include strong civil rights protections for the citizens of Spanish descent. The constitution was approved by New Mexico voters and by the U.S. Congress in 1911 and became effective with the state's admission to the Union in 1912. The 1910 Constitution remains the basic law of New Mexico, although it has been amended more than 200 times. The most important change affecting New Mexico law and the judiciary came in 1988 with the voters' approval of an amendment establishing a new judicial selection process (Hain, Garcia, and St. Clair 1994).

Prior to 1988, the New Mexico Constitution provided that *all* judges be elected in partisan elections. Judicial vacancies occurring between general elections were filled by the governor. In practice, most judges obtained office by gubernatorial appointment, and few were defeated in elections (usually, the incumbents were unopposed in either primary or general elections). In the 1988 general election, a constitutional amendment was approved that created a new judicial selection process that is a hybrid of the "merit plan" and partisan election. The new procedure applies to the selection of judges for the appellate, district, and Metropolitan Courts. The Magistrates', Municipal, and Probate Courts were not affected. The amendment provided for fifteen judicial nominating commissions, one each for the thirteen judicial districts, the appellate courts, and the Metropolitan Court, which recommend qualified applicants to the governor for appointment to the bench, followed by a partisan election at the next general election. This selection system will be described in detail.

CURRENT STRUCTURE

The structure of the New Mexico court system is similar to that of the other forty-nine states. There are trial courts and appellate courts. The trial courts are divided into those of limited jurisdiction and those of general jurisdiction. The lowest level of courts is the Municipal Courts and the county Magistrates' and Probate Courts. These are limited-jurisdiction courts in which the judges need only be qualified electors. In counties with a population over 200,000 (there is only one—Bernalillo County, containing the city of Albuquerque), the Magistrates' and Municipal Courts are combined into a Metropolitan Court. The Metropolitan Court judges must be lawyers, unlike those of the other three limited-jurisdiction courts. The judges in these courts all serve four-year terms, although the method by which the Metropolitan Court judges gain their seats on the bench differs from the other three, as will be described.

The trial court of general jurisdiction is the District Court. The District Courts have original jurisdiction in all matters and causes not excepted by the New Mexico Constitution and appellate jurisdiction in all cases originating in the inferior courts. The District Court judges must be lawyers with at least six years of experience in the practice of law; they must also be at least thirty-five years old and reside in the district for which they are elected or appointed. There are thirteen judicial districts with a total of seventy-two judges. The term of District Court judges is six years.

The New Mexico appellate courts are the Court of Appeals and the Supreme Court. The Court of Appeals has ten judges, and the Supreme Court has five justices. The members of both courts serve eight-year terms, must be lawyers with ten or more years of experience in the practice of law, must be at least thirty-five years old, and must have resided in New Mexico for at least three years immediately preceding the assumption of office (New Mexico Constitution, Article 6).

The Court of Appeals has mandatory jurisdiction in civil, noncapital criminal, and juvenile cases. It has discretionary jurisdiction in interlocutory decision cases and administrative agency appeals. The Supreme Court is the court of last resort and has superintending control over all inferior courts and attorneys licensed in the state. The court has mandatory appellate jurisdiction over criminal matters in which the sentence imposed is life in prison or the death penalty, appeals from the Public Regulation Commission, appeals from the granting of writs of habeas corpus, appeals in actions challenging nominations, and removal of public officials. It has discretionary jurisdiction over all other appeals from the state courts and certified questions from the federal courts.

STAFFING

Legal Profession

In 2000, there were 4,730 practicing attorneys in New Mexico, ranking the state thirty-second nationally by population-attorney ratio. Some 3,080 attorneys are in private practice. Attorneys are required to have a degree from a law school accredited by the American Bar Association and pass the New Mexico bar examination in order to practice in the state. Legal training in the state is provided by the University of New Mexico School of Law.

Judicial Selection

The 1988 amendment to Article 6 of the New Mexico Constitution established the process that applies to the selection of judges for the appellate, district, and Metropolitan Courts. The magistrates and probate judges are elected in partisan elections, while the municipal judges are elected in nonpartisan elections (as are all municipal officials). The amendment created judicial nominating commissions to make recommendations to the governor for appointments to the appellate, district, and Metropolitan Courts. The composition of the commissions varies slightly, depending on the specific court for which judicial nominees are to be selected. The Appellate Judges Nominating Commission consists of: the chief justice of the Supreme Court or his or her designee from the Supreme Court; two Court of Appeals judges appointed by the chief judge of that court; one lawyer and one nonlawyer appointed by the governor; one lawyer and one nonlawyer appointed by the speaker of the House of Representatives; one lawyer and one nonlawyer appointed by the president pro tempore of the Senate; and four members of the New Mexico state bar "representing civil and criminal prosecution and defense," appointed by the state bar president and the judges on the commission. The dean of the University of New Mexico Law School chairs the commission but votes only in the event of a tie. The constitution requires that the appointments to the commission be made such that the two largest political parties are equally represented. Additional appointments may be made by the president of the state bar and

Legal Structure of New Mexico Courts

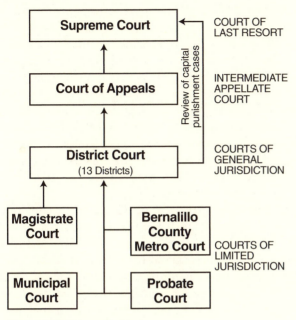

(Arrows indicate appeal routes)

the judges on this committee in order to achieve the partisan balance. These additional members will all be lawyers, since the constitution requires that "these additional members of the state bar shall be appointed such that the diverse interests of the state bar are represented." The dean of the law school is designated as the final arbiter of whether such diverse interests are represented.

The District Court Judges Nominating Committee for each judicial district is appointed in the same manner as the appellate commission, except that one of the Court of Appeals judges is replaced by the chief judge of the District Court or his or her designee, and the lawyer and nonlawyer members appointed by the various officials must be residents of the judicial district.

The Metropolitan Court Judges Nominating Committee is again composed like the appellate commission, except that the two Court of Appeals judges are replaced by the chief judges of the applicable District Court and the Metropolitan Court and the nonjudge members must be residents of the judicial district in which the Metropolitan Court is located.

When a vacancy occurs in any of the courts covered by the judicial nominating procedures, the applicable commission has thirty days within which to solicit, accept, and evaluate applications for the judicial position and to submit to the governor the names of the persons a majority of the commission recommends as qualified for the office. Immediately after receiving the commission nominations, the governor may make one request for additional names. If a majority of the commission finds that

there are more qualified applicants to be recommended, additional names may be submitted. The governor must appoint a person from the final list of nominations within thirty days after receiving the list. If the governor fails to make an appointment, then the chief justice of the Supreme Court must fill the vacancy by selecting someone from the commission's list of nominees. This provision has been invoked only once in the first ten years of the selection system's operation. In 1999, Governor Gary Johnson refused to appoint the one nominee given to him by a District Court nominating commission, and the appointment was made by Chief Justice Joseph Baca (no minimum or maximum number of names is prescribed by law, but the commissions customarily recommend two to four names per vacancy). The person appointed to the judicial office serves until the next general election. The judge must win a partisan election to continue in office. The judge must declare a party identification and win his or her party's nomination in a primary election. If the appointed judge is defeated in the general election, the winning candidate assumes the office and serves for the full term. At the end of the prescribed term, the incumbent judge who has won a partisan election is subject to a nonpartisan retention election and may serve as long as the voters choose to retain him or her. If the voters reject the incumbent judge in the retention election (the judge must be affirmed by at least 57 percent of the voters), he or she must vacate the office on January 1, following the general election. The vacancy is then filled by gubernatorial appointment, using the judicial nominating procedure.

In the first ten years of the current judicial selection system, eighty-one judges were appointed to fill vacancies. Fifty-eight survived the partisan election and went on to serve the full term of office. Nine judges were defeated in primary elections, and nine lost in the general elections. The other five judges either resigned before the election or failed to get on the ballot for some other reason. Once having won a partisan election, the judges face only periodic retention elections. Two judges have failed to win 57 percent of the vote in retention elections.

The New Mexico judicial selection system appears, on the surface, to be a rather bizarre aberration of the merit selection system. However, the "New Mexico Plan" is a logical result of the evolution in the actual practice of judicial selection in New Mexico over the forty years prior to 1988. The nominally partisan election system had become a "voluntary merit selection" process. Most judicial vacancies were filled by gubernatorial appointment, following a screening of all applicants by a committee of the state bar association and informal legislative input. Subsequently, the appointed judge would stand for election at the end of the term to which he or she was appointed. The hybrid system created by the 1988 constitutional amendment is the result of political compromise between the proponents of a pure nomination-appointment system and the proponents of a partisan election system.

Gilbert K. St. Clair

See also Judicial Selection, Methods of; Merit Selection ("Missouri Plan"); United States—Federal System; United States—State Systems

References and further reading

Dixon, Eric D. 1989. "A Short History of Judicial Reform in New Mexico." *Judicature* 73: 48–50.

Hain, Paul, F. Chris Garcia, and Gilbert K. St. Clair, eds. 1994. *New Mexico Government.* 3d ed. Albuquerque: University of New Mexico Press.

Romero, Leo M. 2000. "Judicial Selection in New Mexico: A Hybrid of Commission Nomination and Partisan Election." *New Mexico Law Review* 30, no. 2: 177–225.

Winters, Glenn R. 1952. "The New Mexico Judicial Selection Campaign: A Case History." *Judicature* 35: 166–170.

NEW SOUTH WALES

GENERAL INFORMATION

The state of New South Wales, with a population of over 6.4 million people, houses more than a third of Australia's total population of around 18.5 million people. Over 4 million of its people live within 100 kilometers of its largest city, Sydney. Around 2 percent of its population consists of Aborigines, the indigenous people of Australia, and 25 percent of its people were born in countries other than Australia.

New South Wales has a land area of 801,600 square kilometers, and the topography ranges from sandy beaches to the Great Dividing Range to fertile farmland. In fact, over 65 percent of New South Wales is farmland. The region's economy is capitalist and relatively affluent, with the main industries including agriculture, mining, and tourism. Around one-third of Australian manufacturing takes place in New South Wales.

EVOLUTION AND HISTORY

Australia was originally settled by a mix of soldiers, convicts, and camp followers. On January 26, 1788, the British First Fleet, under Capt. Arthur Phillips, landed first at Botany Bay and then at Sydney, the future capital of New South Wales. Many of the first and later settlers were convicts. Their offenses varied, though many were transported for reasons that would now be considered minor. Their sentences also varied, although, in reality, the sentences equated to life, since going home was almost impossible. When the First Fleet arrived in Sydney, civil and criminal courts had already been established by letters patent called the Charter of Justice of 1787. These courts would soon be found inadequate because of a lack of legal practitioners and an increased demand for commercial and civil justice from the growing population.

The men from the First Fleet, however, were not the first settlers to the land that would become New South Wales. Many experts believe that the aboriginal peoples who occupied various parts of Australia, including New South Wales, came across the sea from Southeast Asia around 50,000 years ago. In the area that is now considered Sydney, there were 3,000 Aborigines when the new British settlers arrived. The Aborigines were not able to unite quickly enough to face the European colonizers, and the British drove many Aborigines away, either through force or disease. Other Aborigines left voluntarily, moving to more remote areas.

Although the indigenous peoples of New South Wales had a set of complex legal systems in place, the indigenous legal systems were not recognized by the British settlers. The settlement of New South Wales was initially a military establishment, and its purpose was to house convicts. As a result, its institutions mirrored that purpose and were more orientated toward maintaining order than ensuring rights. Law officers were appointed to deal with civil and criminal cases, but they were not necessarily trained in the law. In addition, the head law officer, the deputy judge advocate, was subordinate to the governor, so any protection through separation of powers was denied. Finally, the right to a trial by jury was not recognized in any court. The settlers utilized this imported law structure to strip the indigenous peoples of their land and homes.

In the beginning, the new colony was completely dependent on Britain for supplies. Over time, New South Wales became less and less dependent on Britain for food, but the colony faced instability over the huge socioeconomic gulfs in its citizenry. Citizens were divided into three tiers: officers and their families, soldiers and free settlers (and emancipated convicts), and convicts. The quality of life for each group was vastly different, with the lowest group (convicts) living in squalor. Captain Phillips believed that new free settlers had to be attracted with incentives in order for New South Wales to prosper. The new settlers could use the convicts as a labor force, and he allowed the officers to pay them in rum (they were called the Rum Corps). The new arrangement helped spur the economy, but the corps became increasingly corrupt. Britain responded to the increasing corruption by sending Lt. Col. Lachlan Macquarie to clean up the corps.

Macquarie became governor of New South Wales and began the restructuring of the colony. He initiated a plan that would foster the colony's growth, including new roads and towns. In addition, he ordered that convicts who had served their time should have rights as citizens, and he began appointing them to public positions. During Macquarie's term as governor, Ellis Bent was appointed deputy judge advocate. Bent, who actually possessed legal training, often clashed with Macquarie over matters of law and ended up withdrawing from court. His withdrawal, however, would lead to the appointment of John Thomas Bigge, a former chief justice of the English colony of Trinidad, to investigate conditions of the colony of New South Wales in a royal commission of inquiry.

Although Bigge's report, the *Report on the Judicial Establishments of New South Wales,* dismissed the notion of trial by jury, it did disclose enough trouble in the New South Wales justice system to lead the government to undertake an overhaul of the administration in the region. New letters patent, known as the Third Charter of Justice, were created in 1823. The report would also lead to New South Wales dispensing with the old British system of instituting criminal proceedings with a grand jury. Instead, it would adopt an attorney general in the New South Wales Act of 1823 and provide the office with the powers of prosecution. This position would become increasingly important in the new government. In addition, the new Third Charter of Justice established the Supreme Court of New South Wales, with both civil and criminal jurisdictions; it also gave the chief justice a high rank in the government and provided for the admission of legal practitioners.

The first attorney general was Saxe Bannister. He was appointed in October 1823 and was sworn in at the first sitting of the Supreme Court in 1824. Bannister insisted that the right of trial by jury was implicit in the New South Wales Act of 1823, and the first chief justice, Francis Forbes, agreed. Together, these two secured the right of jury trial for New South Wales citizens.

As the settlers began to spread out and explore the rest of Australia, New South Wales started to expand. The British began to see it as a place to make money, rather than simply a place to send unwanted convicts. The last convict ship from Britain arrived in 1848. The other colonies were either claimed by Britain (for example, Western Australia and Tasmania) or carved from New South Wales, with South Australia being the first in 1834. In 1843, the first partially elective council was established. In 1857, all white males were given the right to vote (women would not gain that right until 1902, and Aborigines had no right to vote until 1967).

The discovery of gold in the 1850s changed the social and economic structure of the colony significantly by attracting miners from all over the world who stayed and settled in the country. In addition, the Industrial Revolution was taking place in Britain, and the demand for mineral resources grew, which helped spur the Australian economy even further. In the 1890s, the calls for federation of the colonies grew louder, until New South Wales became a part of the new Australian nation in 1901.

CURRENT STRUCTURE OF THE JUDICIAL BRANCH

Australia has a federal system of government, with elements of both the U.S. and the Westminster systems. On the one hand, the High Court of Australia has extensive jurisdiction over federal matters and is modeled closely on the Supreme Court of the United States. On the other hand, state courts continue to be courts of general jurisdiction and can decide federal as well as state matters (unless some federal court is given exclusive jurisdiction over a certain issue). The Parliament has also frequently delegated more federal jurisdiction to state courts—unlike the U.S. Congress, which has a similar power but rarely uses it. In addition, unlike the U.S. Supreme Court, the Australia High Court is a general appeals court for the various state Supreme Courts.

Australian government and law are divided into three levels: the commonwealth government, with authority derived from a written constitution; the state government, with residual powers; and the local government. At the federal level, government and the courts are concerned with defense, trade and foreign affairs, telecommunications, currency, and postage. The state level primarily deals with schools, health services, crimes, and transportation issues, but the Parliament can legislate for the peace, welfare, and good government of the state in all matters not specifically reserved to the commonwealth government. Finally, the local government regulates libraries, planning, building approval, parks, sports areas, and community services.

New South Wales has a three-tiered state court system as well: local courts, district courts, and the Supreme Court (which includes the Court of Appeal and the Criminal Court of Appeal). Most of these courts have both civil and criminal jurisdiction. Whereas the commonwealth rules for courts were created, for the most part, in one stroke at the joining of the states, the New South Wales system of courts developed gradually and in a sometimes complex manner. As discussed earlier, the Supreme Court of New South Wales was brought into existence by the Third Charter of Justice in 1823. This charter and later acts, culminating in the Supreme Court Act of 1970, provide the framework for the modern courts.

THE SUPREME COURT

The highest court in the state is the Supreme Court of New South Wales. Theoretically, the Supreme Court has unlimited jurisdiction with regard to state law. The Supreme Court Act of 1970 specifically provided that this court has "all the jurisdiction which may be necessary for the administration of justice in New South Wales." In practice, the Supreme Court exercises general jurisdiction with regard to civil matters and only hears the most serious of criminal offenses. In addition, the Supreme Court is divided into several "divisions" that operate independently and specialize (the Common Law Division, the Court of Appeal, and the Commercial Division) (Morison 1980, 115). Although New South Wales originally separated common law courts and equitable courts, either remedy is generally available to judges today. If there is a conflict between common law and equitable rules, however, equitable rules prevail.

As for federal jurisdiction, since about 1960 the Supreme Court has been divested of jurisdiction in several areas by commonwealth acts. This divestment has included a wide range of family matters that now technically fall under federal jurisdiction; however, the Jurisdiction of Courts (Cross-Vesting) Act of 1987 allows state Supreme Courts to share jurisdiction (Crawford 1993, 135) with federal courts.

All judges are appointed in Australia. Federal judges are appointed by the commonwealth government, and state judges are appointed by the state government. Tenure of the judicial appointment varies, depending on the level of the judicial appointment. In the federal courts of Australia, Section 72 of the constitution provides that judges are appointed by the governor-general and serve during good behavior until the age of seventy. The retirement age for judges at the state level is seventy-two. Removal of a judge requires that the governor-general receive the agreement of both Houses of Parliament and that removal must be grounded on proved misbehavior or incapacity. Section 72 does not apply to state courts; however, New South Wales passed the Judicial Officer's Act in 1986, which makes the requirements for removal of state court judges similar to those of federal judges, with one exception. In addition to the requirements of the federal process, Parliament can only consider removing a judge once the Conduct Commission of the Judicial Commission has reported that a matter "could justify parliamentary consideration of . . . removal" (Crawford 1993, 65). Magistrates in local courts usually have less protection from removal than state court judges.

There are forty-one judges on the Supreme Court, although the court also makes use of "reserve" or "auxiliary" judges (those judges who have recently retired) as needed. A Supreme Court justice must meet one of the following criteria: (1) be a member of the Industrial Commission, (2) be a barrister of at least five years' standing or a solicitor of at least seven years' standing, or (3) have a combination of the last two qualifications extending over seven years. In addition, the Supreme Court may appoint masters who can decide minor judicial matters, including interlocutory appeals and taxation of costs (setting the amount of the winner's costs that the loser must pay).

Matters coming before the Supreme Court will usually be heard by one judge. However, the Supreme Court of New South Wales also acts almost as its own intermediate appellate court. It has original jurisdiction in some civil matters (especially those exceeding $A750,000) and in serious criminal matters. Unlike other courts, the Supreme Court can choose to hear civil cases for any dollar amount, although it reserves the right to remit cases to lower courts and often does so. It also has jurisdiction to hear appeals from the District Court and, in some cases, from Local Courts. In that regard, its discretion to hear cases is limited. A right to one appeal is generally accepted. The full court, however, acting as the Court of Appeals, has wide discretion to hear (or not to hear) appeals from virtually any lower court and from one-judge decisions in the Supreme Court. The Supreme Court also acts as an intermediate appeals court for the High Court of Australia.

THE DISTRICT COURTS

The District Courts of New South Wales can hear three categories of cases: civil, criminal, and appeals against decisions made by government officials. The types of civil matters heard by the District Courts include personal injury, damage to property, contract disputes, and debt-recovery cases. In general, the District Courts can handle cases in which the amount being claimed is up to $A750,000. They can also handle cases in which the amount of money in question is higher if both parties to the case agree. One exception to this rule is that the District Courts have unlimited jurisdiction in claims for damages in personal injury cases arising out of motor vehicle accidents. The District Courts also utilize optional arbitration in civil matters, and they can hear appeals against decisions made by government officials in their official capacity.

The types of criminal cases that are heard in the District Courts include: offenses against the person, assaults, sexual assaults, offenses relating to property, offenses involving drugs, and offenses involving fraud. They cannot, however, handle cases involving murder or treason; rather, these cases must start in the Supreme Court. Criminal matters almost always begin in the Local Court and then are transferred to the District Courts for trial, sentencing, or as an appeal against a decision of a magistrate in the Local Court. District Courts can also hear some appeals against decisions made by magistrates in the Local Court, but the right to appeal is generally a matter of discretion for the judge.

Jury trials are most likely to be found in District Courts. The use of jury trials has been in decline all over Australia, but they are still found in many criminal and some civil cases. Generally, juries consist of twelve members for serious offenses. The subject of jury trials, however, has been hotly debated in New South Wales, especially for civil cases and highly complex litigation requiring specialized knowledge. Jury trials can cause delays and cost vast amounts, in terms of both money and resources expended. But proposals to do away with jury trials are met with resistance and are said to be undemocratic.

LOCAL COURTS

There are 160 Local Courts in New South Wales. They are presided over by magistrates. The types of matters that they can deal with include certain limited criminal issues that can be decided without a jury. These criminal matters are called summary offenses and include traffic infractions, minor stealing, offensive behavior, and minor assaults. The Local Courts also hear matters concerning juvenile prosecution and care, civil actions to recover amounts up to $A40,000, some family law issues, and coronial (i.e., coroner) inquiries. In addition, magistrates are responsible for hearing applications for restraining orders, and in conducting committal proceedings, they decide if there is enough evidence to go forward on more serious criminal cases.

OTHER COURTS

There are several other types of courts in New South Wales. For example, the Compensation Court has jurisdiction over claims for worker's compensation disputes and is also in charge of assessing a worker's fitness for employment. The Industrial Relations Commission of New South Wales presides over cases that involve industrial disputes (including employment conditions and wages, wrongful dismissal, registration of trade unions and the altering of their rules, and unfair contracts). The Administrative Decisions Tribunal reviews particular types of administrative decisions and has both original and appellate jurisdiction in various administrative claims. The Land and Environment Court of New South Wales deals with both civil and criminal enforcement in regard to environmental planning and protection.

THE LEGAL PROFESSION AND LEGAL AID

The legal profession in Australia is organized and regulated primarily by each state. Lawyers admitted to practice in any state are also eligible to practice in federal courts. Generally, there is also state-to-state cooperation, so that a person admitted to practice in one state will also be accepted by another. In New South Wales, the legal profession is mostly divided into barristers and solicitors. Barristers generally "confine themselves to advocacy, drafting and giving legal opinions," and appearing in court, whereas solicitors are more concerned with "general advice to clients . . . preparation for litigation [and] non-litigious matters" (Crawford 1993, 72). There is a long history of dividing the two types of practice, but the overall trend has been toward the commingling of duties.

Legal assistance for socially and economically disadvantaged people in New South Wales is provided by the Legal Aid Commission of New South Wales. The commission provides both representation and other legal services, including free legal advice and alternative dispute resolution programs. The commission receives both state money (for state matters) and commonwealth money (for commonwealth matters) and operates as an independent statutory body. In addition, the commission works in partnership with private lawyers.

Legal advice is offered for free to the general public. For most representation services, people must meet jurisdiction, means, and merit tests. Jurisdiction tests determine the areas of law in which the commission is authorized to provide representation for clients. These include the broad areas of family law, civil law, administrative law, veterans' matters, criminal law, mental health matters, children's matters, and prisoners' matters. Means tests are required in most cases and take into account an applicant's income and assets. In many instances, applicants are required to pay a portion of their own legal fees. Merit tests are used by both the state and commonwealth governments in all civil cases and in criminal appeals to determine whether the applicant has a reasonable prospect of success and whether the spending of legal aid funds would substantially benefit the applicant or the community. Merit tests do not apply in the following areas: initial criminal law matters, children in the children's court, disabled persons appearing before the Guardianship Tribunal, and separate representation of children in family court proceedings.

SPECIAL ISSUES

The Appointment of Judges

As discussed earlier, all Australian judges are appointed at present. Judges are selected by appointment rather than some other selection method (for example, election) primarily because appointment is seen to give, combined with long tenure, a large amount of judicial independence. Although there appears to be very little controversy surrounding the choice of appointment as a selection mechanism, controversy in recent years has surrounded the criteria and method used in the appointment process. To begin with, very few scholars or practitioners seem to know exactly what criteria are used in the appointment of judges. The current system of appointing judges is largely a mystery; the executive (the governor-general through the attorney general) has complete control and is not required to follow any guidelines. The attorney general will often solicit opinions of esteemed legal counsel, but this is often done in an unorganized fashion and is a very informal process. Some sectors of the legal profession have called for a more open and organized appointment process. Other have argued that appointments should be made by the use of a nonpolitical

Legal Structure of New South Wales Courts

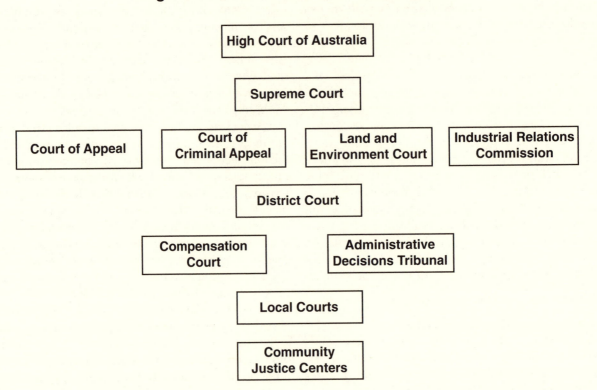

judicial appointments board (although this would require an amendment to the constitution).

In addition, many in the legal system are now calling for the appointment of a more representative bench. Proponents believe that the judicial system is tainted if it is seen to be discriminatory and that ethnicity and gender should be considered in the appointment process in order to bring about a judicial system that is more proportionally representative of various groups in the community. Opponents suggest that the appointment of judges should be based entirely on merit in order for the community to have confidence in its ability to deliver justice.

Aborigines and the Law

Aboriginal people have only been included in Australia's population statistics since 1967. As of 1996, 352,970 people identified themselves as being of indigenous origin in Australia. In New South Wales, approximately 111,000 people consider themselves to be of aboriginal origin. Recently, although Aborigines faced discrimination under the Australian political system, there has been movement toward increased political inclusion and returning some of the land that the British colonists appropriated. In 1992, the High Court issued a decision overturning the assumption that, for legal purposes, Australia was uninhabited when the colonists arrived and that those settlers could therefore lay claim to any and all land they came upon. In 1994, the Native Title Act was created, setting up a system for deciding land claims by Aborigines through the Native Title Tribunal. Questions remain as to how successful title claims by Aborigines will be, but the Legal Aid Commission in New South Wales offers aid to indigenous peoples wishing to put forward claims. Aborigines have also been involved in a significant amount of lawsuits against the government for discriminatory practices, including suits against the commonwealth for its practice of taking children out of their aboriginal homes and placing them with white families in the 1960s. Although these cases have not fared well in the federal courts, the issue of compensation for the victims of this policy is still debated in the justice system.

The New South Wales Law Reform Commission

As discussed, the origins of law in New South Wales are varied and often complex. The resulting justice system can be somewhat confusing. In 1959, the government realized that reform was needed in order to increase efficiency and economy in the administration of justice. Looking to Great Britain, the New South Wales Law Reform Commission was created in 1967 with the purpose of streamlining the law. The Reform Commission aims to eliminate defects, repeal obsolete laws, consolidate, simplify, and sponsor needed reforms in the law. It is concerned with both procedure and the fusion of law on the books. Over the years, the Reform Commission has varied between extreme activity and being stalled by political fights. Many of its recommendations have drawn fire, although many more have been accepted. Today, the Reform Commission is in a period of revitalization.

Joy A. Willis
Reginald Sheehan

See also Appellate Courts; Australia; Civil Law; Common Law; Equity; Judicial Review; Judicial Selection, Methods of; Juries; Legal Aid; Legal Education; Trial Courts

References and further reading
Australian Government, "Australia's Legal System," http://law.gov.au/auslegalsys/ (cited August 15, 2001).
Bennett, J. M. 1974. *A History of the Supreme Court of New South Wales.* Sydney: Law Book Company.
Crawford, James. 1993. *Australian Courts of Law.* Melbourne: Oxford University Press.
Gleeson, Murray. 1999. "Access to Justice—A New South Wales Perspective." *University of Western Australia Law Review* 28, no. 2: 192–198.
Graycar, Regina. 1998. "Compensation for the Stolen Children: Political Judgements and Community Values." *University of NSW Law Journal* 4, no. 3: 253–258.
Kendall, Christopher N. 1997. "Appointing Judges: Australian Judicial Reform Proposals in Light of Recent North American Experience." *Bond Law Review* 9: 175–198.
McWilliams, Evelyn. 1999. "What Sort of Judges Do We Want? And How Should We Choose Them?" *Law Society Journal* 37, no. 7: 53.
Morison, W. L. 1980. *The System of Law and Courts Governing New South Wales.* Melbourne: Butterworths.
New South Wales Government, "Lawlink," http://www.lawlink.nsw.gov.au (cited April 5, 2001).
Parker, Christine. 1997. "Justifying the New South Wales Legal Profession, 1976 to 1997." *Newcastle Law Review* 2, no. 2: 1–29.

NEW YORK

GENERAL INFORMATION

New York is the United States' third largest state and one of its most diverse. Its population has been hovering around 18 million for the past few decades. A medium-sized state with an area of about 49,000 square miles, New York extends from the Atlantic Ocean on the east to Lake Erie on the west. Its most important fault line historically has been that separating New York City (which is made up of five boroughs, each of which is a county) from the rest of the state ("upstate"). Traditionally the City, which is the nation's financial, legal, and cultural center as well as home to some of its mass media giants, has been more Catholic, Jewish, African American, and Hispanic than the predominantly white Anglo-Saxon Protestant upstate. The City remains the preserve of the Democratic Party despite several Republican mayors; upstate is a Republican stronghold that contains some

Democratic enclaves. At present, the suburban New York City counties of Westchester, Rockland, Nassau, and Suffolk are of great importance both politically and economically, and comprise a region distinct from the City with its large numbers of recent immigrants and apartment dwellers and from the less economically prosperous remainder of the state outside the City.

LEGAL PROFESSION AND LEGAL TRAINING

There are fifteen law schools in the state, including two, Columbia and New York University, with a national reputation. It has considerably more than 100,000 practicing lawyers and one of the highest ratios of lawyers to total population in the country. Many of these attorneys are solo practitioners or work for small firms or corporations, but a significant number are partners or associates in some of the nation's most renowned and largest law firms.

STRUCTURE OF COURT SYSTEM

One would expect that a state with so many top-notch lawyers and law firms would have a streamlined judicial system. Instead, according to Judith Kaye, in 2000 the chief judge of the New York Court of Appeals, "New York now holds the dubious distinction of having the most complicated, incomprehensible court structure in the Union." (Kaye 2000, 1) Though called a unified court system, in some ways this billion-dollar-plus-per-year operation that handles over 4 million filings per annum is anything but.

Court of Appeals

The Court of Appeals, the state's highest court, is the descendant of the Court for the Trial of Impeachments and the Correction of Errors created by New York's first constitution, that of 1777. That court consisted not only of judges but also of the members of the state senate and the lieutenant governor. The Constitutional Convention of 1846 converted it into today's Court of Appeals, half of whose members were elected statewide and half of whose members were selected from the misleadingly named Supreme Court, a trial court. In the Constitutional Convention of 1867–1868, the Court of Appeals was made a seven-person tribunal whose chief judge and six associate judges were elected statewide. The court still consists of this septet. Their terms are fourteen years (unless they reach the mandatory retirement age of seventy before the fourteen years are up), but there are no limits to the number of terms for which they and other judges in the state can serve. However, thanks to a 1977 state constitutional amendment, Court of Appeals judges are now selected by the governor from a list prepared by a bipartisan Commission on Judicial Nomination whose members are picked by him, the chief judge, and legislative leaders. His choices are subject to confirmation by the state senate.

Legal Structure of New York Courts

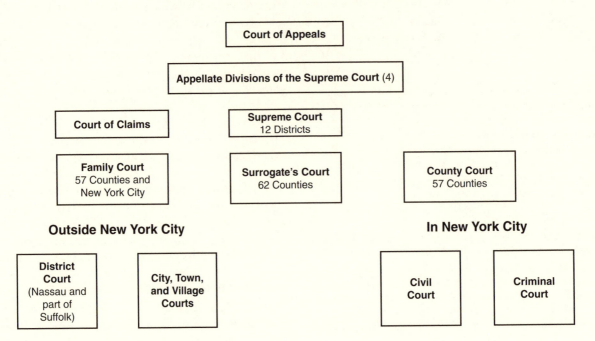

The court hears appeals in both civil and criminal cases and is basically free to shape its docket. (In turn, the United States Supreme Court hears appeals from some of its decisions.) In civil cases the entire court decides whether to accept an appeal; in criminal cases a single judge does. In 1998 it resolved 197 appeals, affirming more results below than it reversed. In the majority of cases before it, it will hear oral argument and hand down its decision six to eight weeks afterward. At least 80 percent of its cases are decided without dissenting or even concurring opinions. The chief judge appoints a chief administrator for the courts, whose aides and subordinates have the responsibility of moving trial court judges to the tribunals where their services are most needed.

The court has for many years been among the three or four most prestigious state courts in the country. Some of its pioneering decisions are required reading for law students. For example, in *Lawrence v. Fox* (1859), it held that Lawrence could sue Fox for the $300 that Holly had given Fox to pay a debt from Holly to Lawrence but that Fox had not bothered handing to Lawrence. Under the law in many jurisdictions at the time, Lawrence could not have recovered from Fox because he was not a party to the contract between Holly and Fox. And in *MacPherson v. Buick Motor Co.* (1916), a leading consumer protection case, it held that a driver who bought a car from a local dealer and who was injured in an accident because of the vehicle's defective wheel could sue the manufacturer for negligence even though it was not a party to the

contract for the purchase of the car. *MacPherson* was authored by Judge (later Chief Judge) Benjamin N. Cardozo, one of America's greatest jurists, who in 1932 was appointed to the United States Supreme Court by President Herbert Hoover even though the president was a Republican and the judge a Democrat. Cardozo's poetic masterpiece *The Nature of the Judicial Process* is still used in college and law school classes to illustrate the point that judges do make law, albeit within limits. In the early 1990s the Court was criticized by some New York public officials for being too soft on criminals, but even in those years about 75 percent of its decisions in criminal cases were pro-prosecution.

Town and Village Courts

If one drives too fast through a rural area or small town in most of the state he will be taken not before a Cardozo but before a town or village judge who in other states would be termed a magistrate or justice of the peace. The chances are that this judge will not be a lawyer even though her duties include the arraignment of suspects in serious as well as minor cases. She will actually try minor cases. There are 2,300 of these mostly part-time judges sitting in 1,000 courts throughout the state. Unlike all other New York courts from the Court of Appeals on down (which have a total of about 1,200 judges), the town/village tribunals are financed locally rather than by the state. The town/village judges are elected for four-year terms by the voters in the area over which they have jurisdiction.

Courts Limited to New York City

The structure of the court system in New York City differs from that in the rest of the state. There are no town or village courts in this metropolis. The lowest court for civil cases in the City is called civil court, whose members are elected for ten-year terms. Each of the five boroughs has its own civil court branch. Civil court tries civil cases involving amounts of less than $25,000 (as of 2000). Its busy housing part hears disputes between landlord and tenant, and in its small claims part arbitrators (usually local lawyers) handle civil suits involving $3,000 or less (as of 2000). More often than not, neither side in small claims will be represented by a lawyer. The author of this entry, without employing an attorney, once successfully sued the local phone company there for $150 for damage done to his car by one of its vehicles: The defendant did not even bother to send a representative to the hearing!

Individuals arrested in the City usually first go before its criminal court (which has a branch in each borough) for an arraignment in which the judge—appointed by the mayor for a ten-year term—makes sure that the defendant is aware of the charges against her and that she is advised of her right to a lawyer. She may be denied bail or released on bail or on her own recognizance. The court will ensure that she has a free lawyer in case she is indigent—even if she is charged with no more than a minor misdemeanor. Depending on the locale of the branch before which she appears and/or the assignment system used by its clerks, that attorney may be a private lawyer reimbursed from public funds or an individual employed by an organization such as the Legal Aid Society. (Some counties outside the City provide a public defender to represent indigents.) Criminal court can try misdemeanor cases itself. Within a few days of arraignment, it sometimes will hold a preliminary hearing (which the defendant may waive) in a felony case to determine whether there is reasonable cause to believe that the defendant committed the crime. If the answer is in the affirmative, he will be bound over to the grand jury. Whether the offense is a felony or a misdemeanor, the odds are very high that he will plead guilty to a lesser charge at some point between arraignment and trial.

State Supreme Court

The New York State Supreme Court has been the state's major trial court since colonial days. The state is divided into twelve judicial districts, each of which has a subdivision of the court. For example, Kings and Richmond Counties (i.e., the New York City boroughs of Brooklyn and Staten Island) comprise the Second Judicial District. The Supreme Court justices (the only jurists in the state who have this title) are selected in partisan elections for fourteen-year terms by the voters of their respective judicial districts. Sometimes both major parties will support

the same candidate, in which case she is a sure winner. Though quite a few of the candidates for Supreme Court have been faithful political servants of one party or the other—for example, a recently elected Second Judicial District justice had for many years been chairperson of the Richmond County Democratic Party—they are these days also competent lawyers who (like candidates for any judicial position above the town/village level) are carefully screened by one or more bar associations. (Politics also plays a role in the nomination of individuals to fill other judicial posts. For example, the current Richmond County surrogate was a Republican New York City council member; and a recently elected Staten Island civil court judge is the brother of a Republican state assemblyperson.)

In New York City and a few other metropolitan areas, the Supreme Court tries felony cases after the defendant has been indicted by a grand jury, which will usually indict if the district attorney handling the case asks it to do so. Often the indictment will be handed down quickly after arrest, thus ending the chances for a preliminary hearing. (If the defendant waives the grand jury stage, she will be prosecuted under an *information* filed by the district attorney.) Everywhere in the state, the Supreme Court handles civil suits involving substantial sums of money as well as, for example, mortgage foreclosures, requests for injunctions, and divorce, separation, and annulment proceedings. However, if one wants to sue the State of New York for money damages, he must bring suit in the court of claims, a special statewide court whose judges are appointed by the governor for nine-year terms with the advice and consent of the state senate. The subdivisions of the Supreme Court in New York City are extremely busy but the number of Supreme Court justices in a particular judicial district is capped by the state constitution at one for every 50,000 residents of that district. So to prevent these subdivisions from falling too far behind on their work, judges from the court of claims or lower courts frequently are made acting Supreme Court justices. In 2000 there were almost as many acting as regular Supreme Court justices in the City.

County, District, and City Courts

In areas where the Supreme Court does not handle felony cases county courts do; and there is one of these in every county outside New York City. Their judges are elected in partisan contests by the voters of their county and serve for ten years. They have jurisdiction over some civil cases where (as of 2000) amounts of up to $25,000 are involved. However, in Nassau and the western part of Suffolk Counties, district courts have been set up to handle misdemeanors and civil suits for less than $15,000 (as of 2000); in sixty-one cities there are city courts with basically the same powers as the district courts; and town and village courts, where they exist, function as small claims courts. District court judges are chosen in partisan elections; city court judges may be selected this way or picked by local authorities. District court judge terms are six years; those of full-time city court jurists are ten years. In some areas, the county court can hear appeals from the town, village, and city courts.

Family Court

New York City and the fifty-seven counties outside the metropolis each have a family court that deals with, among other things, child support, juvenile delinquents, persons in need of supervision, and spousal abuse. Family court judges serve ten years. They are elected by voters of the county, except that the New York City mayor appoints the judges of that City's family court. At present that court and the City's criminal court are overwhelmed with work. Their dockets swelled between 1990 and 2000 but the number of their judges has for political reasons remained constant.

Surrogate's Court

Each of the state's sixty-two counties, including the five New York City boroughs, has a surrogate's court whose main function is to hear cases involving the administration of decedents' estates. Surrogates are elected for fourteen-year terms by the voters of the county. In some counties, the county court judge also serves as the family and/or surrogate's court judge. The political parties very much want to win the surrogate elections, for the surrogate has patronage in the form of *guardianships* to protect, for example, the interests of children. These guardianships are not infrequently doled out to lawyers faithful to the surrogate's party. Sometimes these pay only a few hundred dollars; but a former New York City mayor received one worth $25,000 from a Manhattan surrogate whom he had supported in a tight primary. The newspapers from time to time make disapproving noises about this type of political favoritism, but it is perfectly legal.

Intermediate Appellate Courts

The state does not have a single intermediate court for appeals cases. Rather, it is divided into four judicial departments, each of which has an appellate division of the Supreme Court to hear appeals in civil and criminal cases. The appellate division justices are Supreme Court justices whom the governor has promoted. Most serve as appellate division justices for five years or until the expiration of their term in office as a Supreme Court justice, whichever is shorter. The busiest appellate divisions are in the First and Second Departments, covering New York City and its suburbs. To relieve the burden on them, Appellate Terms of the Supreme Court have been set up in these departments to hear appeals in relatively minor civil

and criminal cases. The chief administrator of the state courts designates which Supreme Court justices will sit as appellate term justices.

PROPOSALS FOR COURT REFORM

The court maze described above is not only difficult for the public to understand but may, as well, seriously inconvenience litigants. For example, a wrangling married couple will see their divorce suit handled by Supreme Court but may have to argue in family court about who gets custody of the children and who has to provide for their support. To simplify matters, Chief Judge Kaye has proposed that the Supreme Court, the court of claims, the county courts, the family court, and the surrogate's court be merged into one Supreme Court and that the lesser trial courts, that is, the New York City civil and criminal courts, the district courts, and the city courts, be combined into one statewide district court. However, the enactment of these reforms will require an amendment to the New York State Constitution. They thus must be passed first by one legislature and then by the first regular session of the next legislature—and then be approved in a referendum by a majority of the voters voting on them.

RELATION TO NATIONAL SYSTEM

Four federal judicial districts are located in the state, including the district court for the Southern District of New York, which handles some of the nation's most important civil and criminal cases. Decisions from these courts can be appealed to the U.S. Second Circuit Court of Appeals.

REMEDIES FOR JUDICIAL MISCONDUCT

Judges in New York State as elsewhere are only human beings, and occasionally one will abuse his position. A 1977 state constitutional amendment therefore created a Commission on Judicial Conduct. This body receives and hears complaints about judicial misconduct and then conducts hearings. After the hearing it may exonerate the judge, admonish or censure him, or even remove him from office subject to his appeal to the Court of Appeals from any adverse decision. For example, it recently censured a veteran Supreme Court judge who asked his secretary whether she liked sex and then tried to kiss her. But this man is the exception: The vast majority of judges in New York State are highly competent.

Daniel Kramer

See also Criminal Procedures; Judicial Selection, Methods of; Juvenile Justice; Magistrates—Common Law Systems; Small Claims Courts; United States—Federal System; United States—State Systems

References and further reading
Bergan, Francis. 1985. *The History of the New York Court of Appeals, 1847–1932*. New York: Columbia University Press.

Chief Administrator of New York State Courts. 1998. *Twenty First Annual Report.* New York: New York State Office of Court Administration.

Kaye, Judith S. 2000. "Time Has Come to Streamline Court System." *New York Law Journal* (May 1): S1.

Lawrence v. Fox. 1859. 20 N.Y. 268.

League of Women Voters of New York State. 1990. *The Judicial Maze: The Court System in New York State.* Albany, NY: League of Women Voters of New York State.

MacPherson v. Buick Motor Co. 1916. 217 N.Y. 382, 111 N.E. 1050.

New York State Bar Association. n.d. *The Courts of New York.* Albany, NY: New York State Bar Association.

Sterk, Stewart E. 1998. "The New York Court of Appeals: 150 Years of Leading Decisions." *Syracuse Law Review* 48: 1391–1451.

"Structure of the Courts." 2001. *New York Law Journal.* http://www.nylj.com/links/structure.html (accessed November 25, 2001).

NEW ZEALAND

GENERAL INFORMATION

New Zealand is situated in the Southwest Pacific Ocean and is made up of two main islands and a group of smaller islands. The total landmass is 270,500 square kilometers, similar to that of Japan or the British Isles. The more densely populated North Island is separated from the South Island by the Cook Strait. The weather is changeable, but overall the climate is mild. New Zealanders are enthusiastic participants in outdoor activities of all sorts. The economy is oriented to primary production.

The 3,800,000 inhabitants are 74 percent of European heritage, 15 percent indigenous Mäori, 6 percent Pacific Islander, and 5 percent Asian. The largest religion is Christianity, although other religions are growing rapidly. Some 85 percent of the population is urban. Auckland, on the North Island, has more than 1,000,000 inhabitants. It has the largest Pacific Islander population of any city in the world.

HISTORY

Mäori have inhabited New Zealand for more than a thousand years. Captain James Cook landed in 1769 and claimed New Zealand for Britain, but little attention was paid to this claim for a number of years. In the early part of the nineteenth century, small trading settlements grew up as Europeans dealt with Mäori and engaged in whaling. The law played very little part in constraining the behavior of settlers or sailors. Such control as there was came from the British colonial presence in New South Wales, and on a few occasions trials took place in New South Wales, Australia, for crimes committed in New Zealand.

In 1840, Captain William Hobson was authorized to negotiate with Mäori to acquire sovereignty for Britain. On February 6, 1840, about fifty Mäori chiefs signed the Treaty of Waitangi, and about five hundred more signatures were obtained by October 1840. Although the precise effect of the treaty remains a matter of debate, it recognized the sovereign authority of the British Crown over New Zealand.

Following the Treaty of Waitangi, disharmony developed between the European settlers and Mäori. Sporadic incidents of violence occurred over the following decades, culminating in the intense fighting of the 1860s. The next few decades saw the confiscation of Mäori land and the forced resettlement of many tribal members.

Upon the initial colonization of New Zealand, English common law was applicable. All relevant English statutes were also in effect. The British Parliament retained the power to legislate for New Zealand. However, as New Zealand moved from its initial status of a dependent colony to a largely independent state, the practical and theoretical ability of the British law-making power lessened. New Zealand gained full control over its constitution in 1947, and any theoretical possibility of the British Parliament enacting a law governing New Zealand ended in 1986. In 1988 the New Zealand Parliament clarified which English statutes were still in effect in New Zealand. The list specified such seminal constitutional legislation as the Magna Carta of 1297, the Petition of Right of 1627, and the Bill of Rights of 1688.

Insofar as the common law is concerned, the twentieth century saw New Zealand judges exhibit a growing independence of thought in their treatment of the law as laid down by English judges. As will be seen, the English Judicial Committee of the Privy Council is the ultimate appellate body in the New Zealand hierarchy of courts. By virtue of the doctrine of precedent, judgments of the Privy Council are binding on New Zealand courts when there is no reason to conclude that the particular judgment is not applicable to conditions in New Zealand. Although that is the theoretical position, New Zealand courts have in practice shown themselves adept at circumventing the apparent conclusions of the Privy Council in earlier judgments. Although the judgments of the House of Lords and English Court of Appeal are often referred to by New Zealand courts and treated with respect, they are not binding precedents.

The process by which New Zealand achieved its current unfettered power to legislate its own laws began in 1854 with the sitting of its first General Assembly, marking the start of representative government. Women were granted the right to vote in 1893. Although the legislature was formerly made up of the elected House of Representatives and an appointed Legislative Council, the council was abolished in 1950. General elections are held

at least every three years, but there are occasions when the prime minister has ordered an election before the expiration of the three-year period. Although there are municipal and regional council governments, the main lawmaking power rests with the Parliament, which sits in the capital city of Wellington and legislates for the whole country. For much of the twentieth century, governments were formed from one of the two dominant political parties, National and Labour.

Reform of the electoral system has introduced a form of proportional representation (MMP) similar to that in operation in Germany. Each voter casts two votes, one for a candidate in the voter's electorate and one for the preferred political party. New Zealand has a remarkably high level of voter participation, with 90 percent voter turnout. The members of the House of Representatives are composed of the most popular candidate from each electorate and representatives from political parties in numbers dependent upon the level of support shown by voters for that party throughout the country.

The first election under MMP in 1996 fulfilled predictions that the new system would see more minor political parties represented in Parliament and the need for coalitions among political parties to achieve the support necessary to secure the passage of legislation. The 1999 election saw the Labour Party assume the dominant role in Parliament. Labour, in coalition with various less powerful parties on the left of the political spectrum, has raised the taxes of higher-income earners and has embarked on a program of social reform.

LEGAL CONCEPTS

New Zealand's British heritage is reflected in the lack of any single written constitution. The "unwritten" constitution can be found in various sources, including parliamentary conventions, the common law, New Zealand statutes, and various other instruments ranging from English statutes such as the Magna Carta to, arguably, the Treaty of Waitangi. There is general acceptance of such core concepts as the rule of law, the separation of powers, and parliamentary supremacy.

New Zealand is nominally a constitutional monarchy, with the English Crown as the titular head of government, represented through the governor-general, who is appointed for a term of five years. The actual head of government is the prime minister, being the leader of the political party that, in coalition with other minor parties, holds the most seats in the House of Representatives. Helen Clark has been prime minister since the 1999 election. All legislation passed by the New Zealand Parliament must receive royal assent through the governor-general, but that is a mere formality. Assent has not been withheld since 1895.

There is some support to further reduce New Zealand's symbolic ties with the British Crown. There remains a continuing debate whether there should be an end to appeals to the Privy Council in London.

The executive arm of government, under the control of the prime minister and her cabinet of government ministers, sets government policy and effectively controls which legislation comes before the House of Representatives for consideration. Although Parliament is composed of a single House of Representatives, some scrutiny of proposed legislation is ensured by the requirement that virtually all government bills be considered by a select committee as part of the legislative process. A vast amount of regulation-making power is delegated to numerous subordinate administrative bodies.

Although jury trials are potentially available in most classes of civil litigation, their use is in practice limited to defamation suits and claims against state agencies for one form or another of outrageous conduct. In the context of criminal proceedings, jury trials are common. Trials for serious crimes (such as murder, sexual violation) must be by jury. No jury trial is possible for the least serious of offenses. For most criminal offenses, the Crown will have the option of proceeding by way of a jury trial or a "summary trial" in front of a judge alone. With very few exceptions, where the maximum potential punishment is imprisonment for more than three months and the Crown has chosen to proceed by way of a summary trial, the accused has the right to elect to have the case tried by a jury. A jury consists of twelve people selected at random from the electoral roles; their verdict must be unanimous, or a new trial will be held in front of a fresh jury.

The procedure in the majority of civil and criminal proceedings in New Zealand is typically that of the adversary system. In civil proceedings, pretrial discovery is available and includes mandatory disclosure to opposing parties of all relevant documents. Pretrial oral examination of opposing parties is not provided for, but questions may be put in writing. The information that a party wishes to offer from witnesses will be set out in a statement provided to the other side before trial. Thus when a witness is called to the witness box at trial, it will be mainly for the purpose of cross-examination on the pretrial statement. Subject to various alterations by statute, New Zealand applies the basic concepts from the English common law of evidence. The losing party in a civil lawsuit will be ordered to pay a substantial portion of the actual legal costs of the winning party. Legal aid in the form of state-funded representation by a lawyer is available in civil litigation, subject to various criteria. In many cases, a legally aided litigant will be expected to repay the legal aid grant from any funds recovered in the litigation. A legally aided person who loses a lawsuit will not normally be ordered to pay the costs of the winning party.

In keeping with its historical ties to Britain, New Zealand criminal proceedings are taken in the name of the Crown against an accused person. Police prosecutors will present the case for the Crown in the majority of summary trials. In the prosecution of more serious offenses, however, the police will normally represent the Crown at the preliminary hearing, at which the court determines if there is a sufficient body of evidence against an accused to justify a subsequent trial by jury. If, as is usual, the court determines that the jury trial will take place, the prosecution will thereafter be conducted by a lawyer representing the Crown. Crown lawyers will be involved from the commencement of the prosecution of the most serious crimes.

Recent years have seen a substantial growth in the right of an accused to obtain pretrial disclosure of the evidence possessed by the Crown. Legal aid is available for people charged with relatively serious offenses who cannot afford their own lawyer. A range of punishments are available to a sentencing judge, including imprisonment, community service, periodic detention (one day per week of supervised labor in the community), home detention, and probation. There is no death penalty, and early release on parole is all but automatic.

New Zealand has ratified numerous international treaties and instruments, including the International Covenant on Civil and Political Rights. Although that process alone has not made any of the provisions of these international instruments enforceable in New Zealand courts, there are occasions when judges have relied upon international instruments as an aid in the interpretation of a New Zealand statute. Ratification of an international instrument has on occasion been followed by the enactment of a New Zealand statute designed to manifest the internationally recognized rights into the local laws of New Zealand. The Human Rights Act exemplifies this process. The act prohibits discrimination on a wide number of grounds, including sexual orientation, age, religious belief, race, disability, political opinion, and marital status. The act provides special procedures to bring about the end to particular instances of discriminatory practices and to provide compensation to the victims of discrimination.

New Zealand's Bill of Rights is a relatively weak piece of legislation. The Bill of Rights purports to protect a wide spectrum of rights, including the right to refuse medical treatment; freedom of thought, expression, and religion; protection against unreasonable search and seizure; the right of silence; and the right to counsel. However, the Bill of Rights is subject to other legislation. Thus if another statute infringes upon any rights set out in the Bill of Rights, effect will be given to that other statute. Nonetheless, the Bill of Rights has achieved a practical importance in cases in which effect can be given to one of the guaranteed rights without overriding another statute. Thus there have been numerous cases where courts have excluded evidence that the police have obtained through a breach of the Bill of Rights. The Court of Appeal has also approved of actions for compensation against the state taken by persons whose rights under the Bill of Rights have been infringed.

The New Zealand Parliament has been increasingly willing to legislate over a broad variety of topics. Parts of the field of contract law are closely controlled by a series of statutes. Because of the application of the doctrine of precedent, any reading of such statutes must be supplemented by an investigation of the binding interpretations of individual statutory provisions rendered by the higher courts in rulings made in individual lawsuits. In other fields, such as tort law, some large areas have been left relatively undisturbed by legislation. New Zealand has provided the common law world with some leading examples of recovery for pure economic loss (that is, financial loss not connected to damage to person or property of the claimant).

Other notable legislation includes the Ombudsman Act, which follows the Swedish lead of establishing an independent official to investigate and make recommendations arising out of a grievance reported by a citizen who has encountered a difficulty in dealing with some aspect of government administration; the Citizens Initiated Referenda Act, which requires the government, upon receipt of a petition of 10 percent of the electorate, to hold a nonbinding referendum on a particular topic; the Māori Language Act, making Māori an official language and permitting the giving of oral evidence in court in the Māori language; the Privacy Act, which defines a right of privacy and establishes procedures to redress reported invasions of privacy; the Official Information Act, which sets out a mechanism whereby the public can gain access to information held by the government; the Health and Disabilities Commissions Act, which provides mechanisms for enforcing compliance by health care providers with a code of rights for consumers; the Resource Management Act, which utilizes sustainable management as the guiding principle in the management of the environment; and the Companies Act and the Securities Act, which make insider trading a civil wrong but not a criminal offense and which leave takeover activity largely unregulated.

One of the most notable features of New Zealand law is the accident compensation system, by virtue of which all personal injuries are compensated in prescribed amounts regardless of the cause of the injury. Since the system commenced in 1974, the level of payable compensation has been eroded by continuing governmental fiscal restraint measures. There is a complete ban on any lawsuits for compensation for personal injuries suffered in New Zealand (although suits for punitive damages are still possible). Thus the victim of an automobile accident, medical misadventure, or even an intentional assault is limited to the benefits payable under the accident compensation system.

The 1840 Treaty of Waitangi purported to guarantee various rights to the Māori, such as their undisturbed possession of their lands and "treasures." The latter term has been interpreted to include language and culture. At the date of the treaty, Māori had a well-developed system of customary law. One of the factors behind the unrest that began shortly after the signing of the treaty was the dissatisfaction felt by Māori on account of the lack of recognition given to their concepts of property and land tenure. Māori lost significant holdings of communal land through questionable purchases by non-Māori and government moves to individualize land title. Although the treaty has been used by the courts as an aid in the interpretation of some legislation, it has never been generally incorporated into New Zealand domestic law. A number of individual statutes have referred directly to the treaty. These references have specified that the statute should be interpreted in accordance with the principles of the treaty or interpreted having regard to the special relationship between Māori and their ancestral land.

CURRENT COURT SYSTEM STRUCTURE

The Judicial Council of the Privy Council in London remains the ultimate appellate court in the New Zealand judicial system. Appeals to the Privy Council come from the New Zealand Court of Appeal, the highest of the domestic courts. A handful of appeals in civil proceedings are taken to the Privy Council each year. There is a right of appeal in any case in which the judgment of the Court of Appeal involves NZ $5,000 or more. Permission is required for appeals to the Privy Council from a Court of Appeal judgment in a criminal proceeding. Such criminal law appeals are all but unheard of.

The Court of Appeal consists of a president, currently Sir Ivor Richardson, and six permanent members. Dame Sian Elias, current chief justice of New Zealand, is an additional member of the Court of Appeal, as well as being the head of the High Court. The Court of Appeal usually sits with three members on the bench, but larger quorums will sit in a case of greater public importance. It is common for members of the High Court to sit with per-

Legal Structure of New Zealand Courts

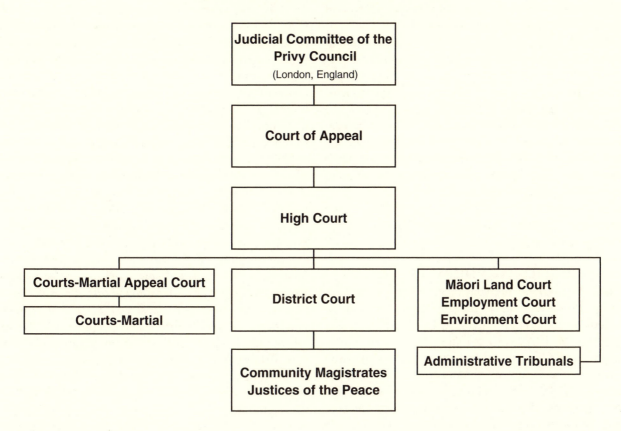

manent members of the Court of Appeal in routine appeals in criminal matters.

The High Court hears trials of the most serious criminal offenses and trials in civil cases involving claims exceeding $200,000. In addition to the chief justice, there are thirty-six High Court judges. Appeals from the High Court are heard by the Court of Appeal.

The bulk of criminal proceedings are heard in the District Court, which also tries civil claims involving less than $200,000. Appeals from District Court go to either the High Court or the Court of Appeal, depending on the nature of the proceeding. There are 120 members of the District Court, some of whom sit in the specialist divisions, the Family Court and the Youth Court. Additionally, there are other courts that have their own procedure and appellate structure. Most important are the Māori Land Court, which hears disputes over claims to Māori Land, the Employment Court, and the Environment Court (see figure).

At the bottom end of the hierarchy of courts are community magistrates and justices of the peace. These officials are not legally trained but perform administrative functions and preside over hearings involving the least serious criminal offenses, such as traffic offenses. Civil disputes involving less than $7,500 may be heard by a Disputes Tribunal, presided over by an official who may not

be legally trained and who is directed by legislation to decide disputes according to the substantial merits and justice of the case.

Legislation establishes and regulates courts-martial and the Courts-Martial Appeal Courts. A court-martial has jurisdiction over military personnel who are charged with any one of the numerous listed offenses relating to conduct as a member of the armed forces, or any of the offenses applicable to the general New Zealand public. Court-martial jurisdiction exists regardless of where the offense occurs.

There are numerous administrative tribunals, which are responsible for determining a wide spectrum of citizens' rights. The Commerce Commission can grant authorizations to engage in otherwise prohibited anticompetitive business conduct. The Human Rights Commission investigates claims and promotes settlements between opposing parties. If a contested hearing is necessary, it will take place before the Complaints Review Tribunal, a body established to hear similar disputes referred from other administrative bodies, such as the Privacy Commission or the Health and Disabilities Commission. Other tribunals with which ordinary citizens may well have contact include the Tenancy Tribunal, the Taxation Review Authority, and the Liquor Licensing Authority. The law relating to judicial review of administrative decisions is highly developed in

New Zealand. In the case of some tribunals, there is provision for appeals to the regular courts upon questions of law raised by the decision of the tribunal.

Although the most common form of dispute resolution is adversarial, there are examples in which alternative dispute resolution techniques are a practical component of the judicial system. Commercial arbitration is common. Mediation is a part of all proceedings in the Employment Court. Likewise in Family Court proceedings, disputing parties must engage in the mediation process, and lawyers acting for the parties are under a statutory duty to promote reconciliation in disputes other than those involving the division of property. New Zealand has been a world leader in using family group conferences to facilitate meetings between young offenders and victims.

SPECIALIZED JUDICIAL BODIES

Beyond the specialist divisions of the standard court hierarchy already mentioned, the most important specialized judicial body is the Waitangi Tribunal, established by legislation in 1975. This tribunal investigates claims brought by Māori to redress grievances arising from breaches of the Treaty of Waitangi. Except in respect to claims for land held by government-controlled corporations, the tribunal is limited to making recommendations. However, some of these recommendations have been acted upon by the government. There have been instances in which large compensation packages and transfers of Crown land have occurred.

STAFFING

Judges appointed to the courts in the standard hierarchy must have held a lawyer's practicing certificate for seven years. Appointment is meant to be on merit rather than as a result of political affiliation. A wide spectrum of the legal profession and the community is consulted during the process of appointing a judge. Once appointed, a judge cannot be removed from office until reaching retirement age (sixty-eight), being found guilty of serious misconduct, or upon losing the capacity to act.

Except for special cases, such as lay advocates in Employment Court, a person must be qualified as a lawyer to practice law in New Zealand. Qualification comes through successfully obtaining a law degree from one of New Zealand's five law schools and completion of a three-month professional training course. More than half of the students currently studying law are women. Foreign lawyers wishing to practice in New Zealand must pass a special examination and may be ordered to undergo further university training, although there are special dispensations for Australian lawyers.

The legal profession is self-governing. All lawyers belong to the New Zealand Law Society, which has enacted a code of ethics and disciplines its members. There are some 8,150 lawyers holding practicing certificates, of whom 33 percent are women. Among lawyers, 84 percent are in private practice, 7 percent are employed by the government, and 5 percent are employed in the corporate sector. Community law centers provide free legal advice and assistance to the public in fields of law not normally catered for by private law firms. New Zealand has the third highest number of lawyers per general population in the world (one lawyer per 540 people).

IMPACT OF LAW

New Zealand's is a heavily regulated society, and the law has a real effect on the daily lives of the country and its residents. There is little evidence of corruption in the public service or law enforcement agencies. The recent change to a form of proportional representative government has served to spread power among a wider band of the political spectrum. Many law reform initiatives come from the government-funded Law Commission. Important topics for possible future law reform include calls for an autonomous legal system for Māori, and—in keeping with overwhelming public support in a 1999 referendum—tougher sentencing for violent offenders.

Richard Mahoney

See also Adversarial Systems; Alternative Dispute Resolution; Arbitration; Common Law; Customary Law; Judicial Review; Juries; Legal Aid; Mediation; Parliamentary Supremacy

References and further reading
Cooke, Robin Q. C., ed. 1969. *Portrait of a Profession: The Centennial Book of the New Zealand Law Society.* Wellington: A. H. and A. W. Reed.
Durie, E. T. 1996. "Will the Settlers Settle? Cultural Conciliation and the Law." *Otago Law Review* 8: 449–465.
Joseph, Philip. 1993. *Constitutional and Administrative Law in New Zealand.* Sydney: Law Book Company.
McDowell, Morag, and Duncan Webb. 1995. *The New Zealand Legal System: Structures, Processes and Legal Theory.* Wellington: Butterworths.
New Zealand Law Commission. 1999. *Evidence: Reform of the Law; Code and Commentary.* Report 55, vols. 1 and 2. Wellington.
New Zealand Official Yearbook, On the Web 1999, http//www.stats.govt.nz/ (accessed August 1, 2000).
Orange, Claudia. 1987. *The Treaty of Waitangi.* Wellington: Allen and Unwin.
Robertson, Bruce, ed. 1992. *Adams on Criminal Law.* Wellington: Brookers.
Robson, J. L., ed. 1967. *New Zealand: The Development of Its Laws and Constitution.* London: Stevens and Sons.

NEWFOUNDLAND AND LABRADOR

GENERAL INFORMATION

Newfoundland has had five centuries of European settlement but only about two centuries with a formally constituted judicial system.

Newfoundland, which became the tenth province of Canada on March 31, 1949, is the ninth most populated province, with 538,823 people as of 2000, and the seventh largest in area at 405,720 square kilometers (156,649 square miles). It is the country's easternmost province; it has both a smaller island portion, Newfoundland, and a larger mainland portion, Labrador. In 1990 the provincial House of Assembly passed legislation to change the official name of the province to "Newfoundland and Labrador," but the legislation took about ten years to be proclaimed.

Newfoundland and Labrador has a variety of First Nations peoples and European descendants. There are the Inuit and Montagnais-Naskapi (also known as the Innu) in Labrador; the Micmac of Conne River in the island portion, the French and Scots on the west coast, originating from elsewhere in Atlantic Canada; and of course the Irish and English, who emigrated from southern Ireland and southwestern England, respectively.

That which drew many of these groups was the fishery, which dominated the island's economy until the late 1800s and generated a distinct society and settlement pattern. For centuries the population was scattered in remote coastal villages, called "outports." Only in the last century or more has economic diversification (farming, mines, pulp and paper, wartime defense, and, latterly, service industries) resulted in the movement of population to larger interior centers.

EVOLUTION AND HISTORY

The general history of Newfoundland and Labrador comprises several phases, the divisions of which are difficult to delineate with perfect clarity, but are essentially as follows: presettlement (before explorer John Cabot's landfall in 1497); a fishing station—at least officially (early 1500s–late 1700s, early 1800s); colonial status (1825–1931), which saw the grant of representative government in 1832, and recognition of responsible government in 1855; a brief status as a dominion within the British Commonwealth of Nations (1931–1934); a finances-related relinquishment of responsible government under a British-appointed Commission of Government (1934–1949); and confederation with Canada, 1949–present (actually a misnomer, since it involved joining the Canadian federation).

On the other hand, the legal and judicial history is much less complicated to describe, and occurred in three major phases.

1. 1497–1791: Three centuries of rudimentary justice: The economy, specifically the transient cod fishery, determined the rudimentary justice system of the first legal period. After Cabot, there developed an important migratory and seasonal fishery and along with it a customary practice of having justice administered by the "fishing admiral." The master of the first ship to visit any port was deemed to be the admiral, and would decide all disputes relating to fisheries and civil matters, as well as allot fishing grounds and maintain order. A short-lived attempt to regularize law enforcement—the first North American Vice Admiralty Court (held in Trinity in 1615)—had little subsequent effect, and the effective voice in the administration of justice remained the fishing admiral. Subsequent efforts were made to set bounds on the application of customary law and to establish a local infrastructure for rudimentary legal services, all within the context of British policy (which included various legislation in the late 1600s, as well as King William's Act of 1698 and Palliser's Act of 1775), which discouraged permanent settlement on the island, long considered a detriment to a successful fishery.

2. 1791–1949: A stable colonial/dominion/commission judicial system: In 1791, Newfoundland and Britain began a process of stabilizing the (nascent) colony's legal system, delineating a clear judicial hierarchy, and, by stages, elaborating a lower court system. The informality of the Newfoundland judicial infrastructure had led to certain legal challenges, and the British Parliament responded with the first Newfoundland Judicature Act of 1791. The act established a Court of Civil Jurisdiction consisting of a chief judge (Judge John Reeves being the first) together with two assessors. Still, the worries about implying permanency of population were so great that this, and a successor court, the Supreme Court of Judicature of the Island of Newfoundland, begun the next year, 1792, were to have effect for one year only. The Supreme Court was renewed annually and finally made permanent in 1809, at which time its geographical remit was extended to include Labrador. This Supreme Court was presided over by a chief justice, had jurisdiction in both civil and criminal matters, and, together with the surrogate courts that the governor could create in order to serve the outlying areas of the province in suits of a civil nature, constituted the superior court of the province.

The modern Newfoundland and Labrador judiciary began to take shape with the Judicature Act of 1824, a result of the growth of a sedentary population, a powerful local governance reform movement, and some egregious misapplications of justice (for example, the famous Butler and Landergan case of 1820).

Interestingly, local judicial reform occurred before political reform. The Judicature Act of 1824 and the Royal Charter of 1825 issued in pursuance of it created the Supreme Court of Newfoundland, to be presided over by a chief justice and two assistant judges. They respectively combined all civil and criminal jurisdiction in Newfoundland "as fully and as amply" as the jurisdictions of several separate courts in Great Britain. There was appeal to the king in council from the Supreme Court. As a replacement for the system of surrogate courts of the 1792 act, there were to be created three districts, each with its own circuit court. The Judicature Act instituted a Court of Civil Jurisdiction for Labrador. There were also courts of sessions, held at the governor's direction. The Supreme Court was sworn in during January of 1826. Newfoundland was thus given a court with a full range of powers, a court that continued to function, with minor alterations by successive judicature acts, for the next 150 years (until 1974), when a period of structural modernization began. The early judicial reform predated, and some say influenced, the granting of representative government in 1832 and responsible government in 1855.

3. 1949–present: A provincial judicial model: The third period of evolution of the judiciary begins with Newfoundland joining the Dominion of Canada as a province in 1949. Immediate changes were slight; much of the preconfederation structure remained in place. The major difference was that now Newfoundland would be open to whatever reform tides beset the other jurisdictions in Canada. These were to be substantial later in the century.

All British North America Acts, 1867 to 1946 (hereafter called the BNA Acts, but after 1982 renamed the Constitution Acts) were to apply to Newfoundland as if she had been a province of Canada since the union (1867). Newfoundland was to retain its courts of civil and criminal jurisdiction, and its system of legal officers, until altered. The governor-general (that is, the federal cabinet) was thereafter to appoint judges of the Newfoundland superior, district, and county courts, as per section 96 of the BNA Act. The Newfoundland District Courts Act of 1949 created a system of district courts in seven judicial districts, along the Canadian provincial model.

This model lasted a quarter-century. Thereafter came some basic structural changes, many engendered by the structural renewal taking place in other Canadian provinces. The Judicature (Amendment) Act of 1974 created the Court of Appeal and the Trial Division as separate divisions of the Supreme Court; previously, the Supreme Court heard appeals from itself sitting in the first instance as a trial court. The Unified Family Court Act of 1977 created a Unified Family Court, an innovative special division of the Supreme Court with comprehensive jurisdiction over family matters. The Judicature Act of 1986, now merged the district courts—created after confederation—with the Supreme Court. This is as far as Newfoundland and Labrador's legal and judicial odyssey has progressed.

CURRENT STRUCTURE

In order to understand the current structure of the courts in Newfoundland and Labrador, one has first to understand the relevant sections of the Constitution Act of 1867. Section 101 enables the federal Parliament to create "a general court of appeal for Canada" as well as additional federal-level courts. This is the constitutional basis for the creation of the Supreme Court of Canada and other federal courts. On the other hand, the provinces, by virtue of S. 92(14) of the same act, are given a general jurisdiction over "the administration of justice in the province" as well as "the constitution, maintenance, and organization of provincial courts, both of civil and criminal jurisdiction," despite the fact that criminal law is allocated to the federal authorities by section 91(27). Procedure in civil matters is allocated to provincial courts, but procedure in criminal matters falls under federal jurisdiction.

The Constitution Act of 1867, by virtue of S. 129, expressly continued the three-tier hierarchical pattern of courts that the uniting provinces had had at the time of confederation: (1) "superior" courts, (2) county or district courts, and (3) "provincial" (inferior) courts, sometimes known as Magistrates' Courts. The superior courts were to be appointed and paid by the federal authority, according to Ss. 96–100 of the 1867 act, and the provincial courts were to be appointed and paid by the provincial authority, according to 92(4). By the end of the twentieth century, the county/district courts had been amalgamated into the superior court level in nine provinces, including Newfoundland (see above), thus increasing the size of the superior courts.

Newfoundland and Labrador thus has a two-tier system, composed of the Supreme Court and the Provincial Court. The Judicature Act (above) continues the Supreme Court and vests it with all criminal and civil ju-

Structure of Newfoundland and Labrador Courts

Supreme Court of Canada

Federal Court of Canada

Supreme Court of Newfoundland (Court of Appeal)

The provincial government creates this court but the federal government appoints and pays its judges. This court is constituted by Provincial Statute (the Judicature Act). The court sits in the city of St. John's, but may sit in other locations in the province, as the court requires.

Judges

The judges of the Court of Appeal are appointed by the federal governor in council. The Court of Appeal consists of the chief justice of Newfoundland and five other judges, called judges of appeal. There are three supernumerary judges of appeal.

Jurisdiction

Appellate jurisdiction in civil and criminal appeals; jurisdiction and power to hear and determine appeals respecting an order or decision of a judge of the Trial Division. It may also hear references from the lieutenant governor in council.

Appeals

Trial Division, Unified Family Court, Provincial Court.

Supreme Court of Newfoundland (Unified Family Court)

The provincial government creates this court but the federal government (through the assigning of Trial Division judges) appoints and pays the judges. The court holds sittings in premises located within the Avalon and Bonavista Peninsulas as the chief justice of the Trial Division may direct.

Judges

The judges of the Unified Family Court are appointed by the federal governor in council and assigned to this court by the chief justice of the Trial Division. There are two judges in the United Family Court.

Jurisdiction

Dissolution and annulment of marriage, judicial separation, matrimonial property, guardianship, custody and access, interspousal Criminal Code offenses, formation of marriage, maintenance, adoption, declarations of legitimacy, child protection, and other matters associated with families.

Appeals

None.

Supreme Court of Newfoundland (Trial Division)

The provincial government creates this court but the federal government appoints and pays its judges. This court is constituted by Provincial Statute (the Judicature Act). Each judge appointed to the Trial Division serves in one of six judicial centers: Corner Brook, Gander, Grand Bank, Grand Falls, Happy Valley–Goose Bay, and St. John's.

Judges

The judges of the Trial Division are appointed by the federal governor in council. The Trial Division consists of twenty judges, one of whom is the chief justice of the Trial Division and the other nineteen of whom are called judges of the Trial Division. One or more of the nineteen are appointed by the chief justice to the Unified Family Court.

Jurisdiction

Civil: Probate and guardianship, divorce and matrimonial actions, all outside the Avalon and Bonavista Peninsulas.
Criminal: Indictable offenses under the Criminal Code tried by a judge and jury, or judge alone.

Appeals

From Provincial Court, and administrative tribunals and designated boards.

Provincial Court of Newfoundland

The provincial government creates this court and appoints and pays its judges. This court is constituted by Provincial Statute (Provincial Court Act, 1991). The lieutenant governor in council (LGIC) may divide the province into Provincial Court districts and appoint provincial court judges to them; however, this does not affect said judges' jurisdiction throughout the province.

Judges

The LGIC, on the recommendation of the Minister of Justice and attorney general, officially appoints provincial court judges. No person may be recommended by the minister without the recommendation of the Judicial Council of the Provincial Court of Newfoundland. The LGIC shall appoint a Provincial Court judge as Chief Judge.

Jurisdiction

Criminal: All Criminal Code offenses (both summary conviction offenses and indictable offenses); offenses under provincial statutes; offenses under federal statutes.
Civil: Civil actions up to $3,000; some exceptions apply.
Family: Outside St. John's and surrounding areas, adoption, spousal and child support, neglected children, delinquency, affiliation.

Appeals

None.

risdiction vested upon it by the Judicature Act of 1824, the Royal Charter of 1825, and by law in force in the province. The Supreme Court has three divisions, an appeal division, called the Court of Appeal; the Trial Division; and the Unified Family Court. The Court of Appeal consists of the chief justice of Newfoundland and Labrador and five other judges, called judges of appeal. There are three supernumerary judges of appeal. The court has jurisdiction to hear appeals in both civil and criminal matters from the Trial Division, the Unified Family Court, and the Provincial Court (for indictable offenses). It may also hear references from the lieutenant governor in council (meaning, by convention, the provincial cabinet). References are requests for opinions of the court that have no judicial import, but that generally have political impact.

The Supreme Court of Newfoundland and Labrador (Trial Division) consists of twenty judges, one of whom is designated the chief justice of the Trial Division (who comes after the chief justice of Newfoundland and Labrador in precedence). The court sits in six judicial centers around the province but, in order to facilitate the flexible assignment of judges on a case basis to where they are needed, there are no geographical boundaries identified with the centers. It has unlimited jurisdiction in criminal matters conferred on it by the federal criminal code and hears cases involving indictable offenses under the code, to be tried by a judge alone or by a judge and jury. It has jurisdiction over most civil actions and generally in financial matters over $3,000 (although it can adjudicate small claims, too). It shares matters of family law (jurisdiction over nullity, judicial separation, corollary relief, divorce, matrimonial property, custody, access, and guardianship) with the Unified Family Court; the latter, a specialized family law court and a division of the Supreme Court, Trial Division, exercises jurisdiction in a specified area around the capital of the province, St. John's (the Avalon and Bonavista Peninsulas), and the former in all other areas of the province. The Trial Division hears criminal appeals from summary convictions in Provincial Court, civil appeals from the Provincial Court (Family Division and Small Claims Division), and appeals and judicial review hearings from decisions of administrative boards and tribunals in the province.

The Provincial Court is constituted by provincial statute (the Provincial Court Act, 1991) and is headed by a judge called the chief judge, whose function it is, among other things, to coordinate and apportion the work of provincial judges. It handles all summary conviction offenses under federal and provincial statutes, and indictable offenses unless these are excluded by the criminal code (for example, murder). It hears civil actions under $3,000, and has concurrent jurisdiction with the Supreme Court (Trial Division) over many different family matters outside of the Avalon and Bonavista Peninsulas involving marriage, support, maintenance, child welfare, legitimacy, paternity, adoption, and interspousal criminal code offenses (except for divorce, which is always heard in Supreme Court); youth criminal matters involving young offenders; and traffic matters.

There are many administrative law forums in the province. The Bar Admission Course in Administrative Law of the Law Society of Newfoundland lists close to forty-five of them. The most high-profile are those associated with or issuing from the Human Rights Commission, the Labour Relations Board, and the Workplace Health, Safety and Compensation Commission.

STAFFING

Staffing of the legal system refers to matters such as the qualifications, tenure, recruitment, vetting, selection, and training of key actors like judges and lawyers. The qualifications for provincial superior, district, and county courts are set out in Ss. 97 and 98 of the Constitution Act of 1867 and maintain that appointments will be made only from persons who are members of the bar of that particular province. As for provincial court appointments (involving provincially appointed and provincially paid judges), the Newfoundland Provincial Court Act of 1991 specifies that a judicial appointee must be a member in good standing of both a provincial bar (for at least ten years) and the Law Society of Newfoundland.

The tenure of federally appointed judges is such that they shall hold office "during good behaviour" (in effect a permanent appointment, unless removed for cause by the governor general on address of the Senate and House of Commons) until the compulsory retirement age (amended to seventy-five years old, according to the new S. 99[2] of the Constitution Act of 1867). Section 12 (1) of the Provincial Court Act of 1991 mandates that every judge shall retire upon attaining the age of sixty-five years.

Vetting is done differently for the different levels of court. Regarding "section 96 judges" (that is, federal appointments to the provincial superior court), a list of names is submitted by an independent official, called the commissioner for federal judicial affairs, to a seven-member independent advisory committee set up in each province and territory, who are broadly representative of the bench, the bar, and the general public. Advising the minister, committees assess candidates in one of three categories—"recommended," "highly recommended," or "unable to recommend" for appointment. The minister of justice is ultimately responsibility for appointments. Before recommending such an appointment to the cabinet, the minister may consult with senior members of the judiciary and the bar, and the appropriate provincial attorneys general/ministers of justice. The governor-general, acting on the advice of the federal cabinet, makes the official federal judicial appointment. The federal prime minister chooses the chief justice in Newfoundland and Labrador, as well as in other provinces.

In the case of provincial judges, the vetting is done by a six-member statutory body, the Judicial Council of the Provincial Court of Newfoundland, whose job it is, in addition to its investigatory and disciplinary functions, to consider all applicants for judicial appointment and make a recommendation to the minister with respect to those applicants. The Judicial Council can consider prospective names from any source, in addition to those suggested by the minister of justice and attorney general.

Judges are already trained lawyers by the time they come to the bench, but there is now a venue for continuing education. The Canadian Judicial Centre is a federal-provincial, jointly funded institution established in 1987 to provide judicial education for both federal and provincial judges at all levels of court.

The basic training of Newfoundland and Labrador lawyers takes place on the mainland; there is no law school in the province. The standard course of studies takes three years. After graduation, the student serves a twelve-month period of articles of clerkship with a practicing lawyer, taking the Newfoundland Bar Admission Course within that period, and after articling and successfully finishing the course and the Bar Admission Examinations, is called to the bar of the province. Thus the individual becomes a member of the Law Society of Newfoundland. Once called to the bar, the lawyer becomes both a barrister and solicitor.

Christopher Dunn

Special thanks for the invaluable help of Christopher P. Curran, then Acting High Sheriff of Newfoundland, and Frank O'Brien, Director of Legal Education, Law Society of Newfoundland, who gave access to specialized material and whose expert knowledge aided immensely in the preparation of this piece.

See also Appellate Courts; Canada; Criminal Law; Federalism; Judicial Selection, Methods of; Magistrates—Common Law Systems; Trial Courts; United Kingdom

References and further reading
English, Christopher, and Christopher P. Curran. 1991. *A Cautious Beginning: The Court of Civil Jurisdiction, 1791: Commemorative Essay.* St. John's: Jesperson Press.
Green, J. Derek, and Christopher P. Curran, eds. 2000. *T. Alex Hickman: Speeches and Writings from a Life in the Law.* Paper presented by the Hickman Symposium Committee at the Symposium "The Independence of the Bench and Bar: Ancient Principles, Modern Challenges." November 17.
"Judicature" and "Judicature—Family Law." 1991. Pp. 143–146 and 137–142, respectively, in *Encyclopedia of Newfoundland and Labrador.* St. John's: Harry Cuff Publications.
Law Society of Newfoundland. 2000. *2000 Bar Admission Courses (Administrative Law, Civil Procedure, Family Law).* St. John's: Law Society of Newfoundland.
"Newfoundland and Labrador." 1999. Pp. 1628–1636 in *The Canadian Encyclopedia.* Toronto: McClelland and Stewart.
Newfoundland Law Reform Commission. 1989. *Legislative History of the Judicature Act 1791–1988.* Cat. No. NLRC-IWD4. St. John's: Law Reform Commission.
Pearce, Mona B. 1993. "Newfoundland Court System." Organization Chart. St. John's: Department of Justice, Province of Newfoundland and Labrador.

NICARAGUA

GENERAL INFORMATION

Nicaragua is located in Middle America, between the Caribbean Sea and the North Pacific Ocean; it borders Honduras to the north and Costa Rica to the south. Its territory covers roughly 130,000 square kilometers (50,450 square miles), which makes it slightly smaller than Wisconsin and slightly larger than New York State. It is divided into three distinct geographic regions: extensive Atlantic coastal planes, central interior mountains, and narrow Pacific coastal plains interspersed with volcanoes and two freshwater lakes of modest size. The country's 4.9 million inhabitants (1999 estimate) include a mixture of European, Amerindian, and African ancestries. Mestizos (mixed European and indigenous) constitute 69 percent of the population; Europeans constitute 17 percent; and African and indigenous, 9 and 5 percent, respectively. As in many other countries in Latin America, racial classifications are based as much in culture as in genetics. An indigenous person who migrates to a large urban setting, learns Spanish, and wears Western clothing becomes a mestizo even if that person has no trace of European ancestry; examples of this phenomenon can be seen in the indigenous suburbs of Masaya (Monimbo) and Leon (Subtiava). The term *indio* often has sociocultural connotations and no relation to an individual's race; for the most part, only indigenous peoples on the Atlantic (eastern) coast retain tribal customs and languages, and remain ethnically distinct. In the mid- and late 1980s, indigenous peoples in Nicaragua began to assert their political and social presence, and since 1988, Nicaragua has served as permanent secretariat of the Parliament of the Indigenous Peoples of the Americas.

Culturally, Nicaragua reflects the dual Ibero-European and indigenous majority. Spanish is the official language, although English and some indigenous dialects are spoken on the Atlantic coast. Close to 85 percent of the population is Roman Catholic, and the other 15 percent evangelical Protestant, Anglican, or Moravian. Nicaragua's population is concentrated mostly on the Pacific lowlands and the adjacent interior highlands; close to 54 percent live in urban areas. As in other countries in Latin America, poverty in Nicaragua seems to be more prevalent

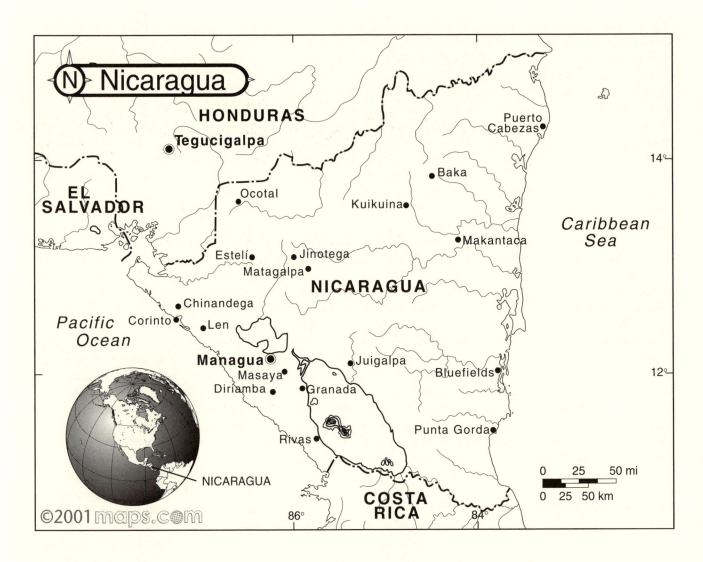

map: ©2001 maps.com

among indigenous groups in the rural areas. However, with the increase in urban migration since the 1972 earthquake, large urban slums have appeared in the larger cities of the Pacific coast.

Nicaragua's $2.3 billion economy (as of 2000) is composed by sector as follows: agriculture (32 percent of GDP), industry (24 percent of GDP), and services (44 percent of GDP). The economy grows at an annual rate of 5 percent, and the annual inflation rate is 10 percent. Nicaragua's per capita GDP is only $495, which places it in second place among the poorest countries in the Western Hemisphere. Indeed, more than 50 percent of Nicaraguans live in dire poverty. Nicaragua's natural resources include arable land, livestock, fisheries, gold, and timber. Its main exports are coffee, seafood, beef, sugar, industrial goods, gold, bananas, and sesame, all of which are exported, primarily to the United States, the European Union, the Central American Common Market, and Mexico. Major imports include petroleum, agricultural supplies, and manufactured goods, which arrive from the United States, the Central American Common Market, Venezuela, and the European Union. Nicaragua

began implementing free-market reforms in 1991, following twelve years of economic free fall under the Sandinista government. Since then, some 351 state enterprises have been privatized; inflation has been reduced from 13,500 percent to 12 percent; and foreign debt has been cut in half. Expansion of the economy began in 1994 but leveled off in 2001, as a result of a fall in prices of its main export commodities in world markets, as well as the global economic downturn.

HISTORY

Nicaragua—or more properly, the Republic of Nicaragua—took its name from Chief Nicarao, the leader of a tribe that, at the arrival of the Spanish in 1504, inhabited the isthmus of Rivas, the western coast of present-day Lake Nicaragua, and the Gulf of Nicoya, in present-day Costa Rica. The first urban Spanish colonial settlements were founded in 1524, with the resulting emergence of the cities of Granada and León. In 1821, Nicaragua, along with four other Central American provinces, proclaimed independence from Spain. The five independent colonies for a brief period joined the Mexican Empire but later seceded, maintaining the federation of United Central American Provinces until 1838. Since then, Nicaragua has been truly an independent republic, the political life of which has been shaped by a deep and long-standing rivalry between the Granada-based conservatives and the León-based liberals. Such rivalry has often resulted in civil war and in the intervention of foreign figures in Nicaragua's domestic affairs. For example, in 1855 the liberals invited William Walker to join their struggle against the conservatives; a year later, Walker proclaimed himself president and ruled the country for another year, until he was overthrown in 1857 by a coalition of liberals and conservatives. The latter ruled Nicaragua until 1893, when the liberals, led by José Santos Zelaya, seized the presidency.

Zelaya's sixteen-year regime saw the resolution of a dispute with Britain over Nicaragua's Atlantic coast, the reincorporation of that region into Nicaragua, and a good-faith attempt to resolve issues surrounding an interoceanic canal and other property interests of U.S. citizens and corporations. When the latter failed, however, the U.S. government gave political support to the conservatives and intervened militarily to protect U.S. lives and property. The United States maintained troops in Nicaragua continuously from 1912 until 1933, with a brief nine-month hiatus in 1925–1926. In 1927 the United States brokered an agreement to end the ongoing quarrel between conservatives and liberals, but it was rejected by liberal renegade Augusto Cesar Sandino, who retreated to the mountains. U.S. Marines based in Nicaragua engaged in battle with Sandino and his guerrilla fighters until 1933, when U.S. troops left permanently. Sandino was later assassinated.

In 1936, while heading the newly formed National Guard, Anastasio Somoza Garcia became president, thus beginning a dynasty that ruled Nicaragua, with some interruptions, for more than four decades. In 1979, a massive civil and military uprising led by the Sandinista Front for National Liberation (FSLN) ousted the government of Anastasio Somoza Debayle and replaced it with an authoritarian dictatorship of decidedly Marxist tendencies. During that period of time (1979–1990) Nicaragua's relations with the United States deteriorated dramatically, amid allegations that the Sandinista government was massively nationalizing the private sector, was confiscating private property without just compensation, supported guerrilla movements in other Central American countries, and maintained close ties to known world terrorists and drug traffickers. The United States suspended aid to Nicaragua in 1981 and in 1985 imposed an embargo on all U.S.-Nicaragua trade, while providing military and financial aid to the Nicaraguan Resistance, otherwise known as the Contras. With mounting domestic and international pressure, particularly after the 1987

Central American peace agreement designed and negotiated by Oscar Arias, the Sandinista regime reached an agreement with the Contras, as a result of which presidential elections were held in February 1990. Violeta Chamorro, the widow of a prominent Nicaraguan journalist and member of one of the more traditional political families, won the election, under a political coalition named UNO. During Chamorro's government, which lasted close to seven years, considerable progress was achieved in the consolidation of democratic institutions, the reprivatization of state-owned enterprises, and the reduction of human rights violations. General elections for the presidency, the legislature, and municipal governments were again held in October 1996, with the resulting installation in January 1997 of liberal president Arnoldo Aleman, the former mayor of Managua.

In 1998, Hurricane Mitch caused death to more than nine thousand people and widespread damage in excess of $10 billion, leaving close to two million people homeless. Municipal elections held in November 2000 resulted in significant gains for President Aleman's Liberal Constitutionalist Party of municipal offices in several areas of the country; they also resulted in significant victories for the Sandinista Party, as it captured the mayoralties of several of the larger urban areas, including Managua. The presidential and legislative elections, held again in November 2001, resulted in a defeat for the Sandinista candidate and the election of Enrique Bolanos, a prominent figure in the business community who had served as vice president under Aleman.

LEGAL CONCEPTS

Nicaragua is a unitary republic composed of fifteen administrative divisions, or *departamentos;* two autonomous regions; and 145 municipalities. All laws follow the civil law tradition and are national. They are promulgated by the national assembly, which is the unicameral legislative branch of government, with subsequent ratification by the executive; they become effective upon publication in *La Gaceta,* the official governmental record. Municipal governments throughout the country may also promulgate regulations, but their applicability is limited to the jurisdiction of that particular municipality. The four branches of Nicaraguan government—legislative, judicial, executive, and electoral—are based in the country's capital of Managua (pop. 1.7 million), which is located in the Pacific region.

Nicaragua is a constitutional, participative, and representative democracy, wherein the political constitution is the supreme law of the land. International treaties are incorporated into Nicaraguan ordinary law automatically, unless they require a constitutional amendment because they affect a particular constitutional provision. With that exception, and except in cases in which national sovereignty, national defense, the state's financial obligations (including international trade and other commercial treaties), international integration obligations, or basic human rights are affected, the executive may ratify a treaty without prior approval from the legislative branch. The current political constitution dates back to 1987, but it was revised substantially in mid-1995 and again in early 2000 to provide for a more even distribution of power among the four government branches. The 1995 amendments reflect the compromises reached between the executive and legislative branches as a result of which the legislature emerged with greater independence and power. Among these were the ability to override a presidential veto with the vote of a simple majority and the ability to thwart the presidential pocket veto of a bill. In addition, terms of office for both the president and members of the legislature were limited to five years, and elections for both branches are held concurrently. The 2000 amendments, promulgated as Law 330 of January 9, 2000, and published in *La Gaceta* on January 18, 2000, addressed certain territorial and nationality issues, reaffirmed certain international obligations, provided for a procedure for the impeachment of and deprivation of constitutional immunity from the president and other public officials, provided for new requirements to hold public office in all four branches, and reformed the Supreme Electoral Council.

The national assembly consists of ninety deputies elected from party lists drawn at the national and subnational levels (*departamentos* and autonomous regions). In addition, after the 2000 constitutional reforms, defeated presidential and vice presidential candidates also serve a five-year term as deputies, as do the outgoing president and vice president if they were elected by popular vote. In the 1996 elections, the Liberal Alliance, a coalition of five political parties and sectors of another two, won forty-two seats, while the Sandinista Front won thirty-six. Nine other political parties and alliances won the remaining fifteen seats, for a total of ninety-three deputies serving in the national assembly from 1996 to 2002. These figures include the defeated presidential candidate and former Sandinista president Daniel Ortega Saavedra. There are a total of nineteen parties represented, independently or as part of a coalition. However, as a result of the 2000 electoral rules, the Supreme Electoral Council (CSE) recognized legal status and authorized participation in the national elections of November 2001 for only three parties. These are the Liberal Constitutional Party (PLC), the Sandinista Front for National Liberation (FSLN), and the Nicaraguan Party of the Christian Path (CNN).

Traditionally, the executive branch in Nicaragua has had broad governmental powers, which often led to imbalance among the four branches. But as a result of the constitutional amendments of 1995 and 2000, such powers have now been more equitably distributed, with resulting gains for the legislative branch. The executive is composed of one president and one vice president. President Aleman's initial vice president, Enrique Bolanos, resigned in 2000 to become the presidential candidate for the PLC. The president of Nicaragua is chief of state, head of government, and chief of the armed forces. His or her immunity may be taken away by a vote of two-thirds in the national assembly. The president is supported by a council of twelve cabinet divisions or ministries, each one of which has one minister and two vice ministers appointed by the president.

The Supreme Electoral Council (CSE) is a coequal branch of government, responsible for the organization and holding of elections, plebiscites, and referendums. The CSE is led, after the 2000 constitutional amendments, by seven magistrates and three alternates elected to terms of five years by the national assembly. This gives rise to the possibility that the dominant parties in the legislative branch will exert great influence on the CSE and could lead to the overpoliticization of electoral institutions.

The judicial branch of government is led by the Supreme Court, which supervises the functioning of a largely ineffective and overburdened system of lower courts—trial and appellate. The number of Supreme Court magistrates was increased from seven to twelve in the 1995 constitutional amendments. The magistrates are elected by the national assembly for seven-year terms. The 2000 constitutional amendments provided new eligibility requirements for the position of magistrate, most of which deal with nationality and residency.

The Political Constitution of 1987, as amended, guarantees freedom of speech and other basic political rights, including privacy, freedom of religion, press, movement, assembly, and due process. In addition, it guarantees the right to property in a multiplicity of forms (public, private, associative, cooperative, and communal), as well as political, social, and ethnic pluralism and diversity. In Nicaragua there is no state censorship, and diverse opinions and perspectives are expressed openly and freely among all sectors of civil society, including media and academia. The constitution guarantees specific percentages of the national budget to each of the four branches of government. It also declares the independence of the judicial and electoral branches, and it recognizes independent agencies of government, such as the Office of the Superintendent of Banks and Other Financial Institutions, the Office of the General Comptroller of the Republic, and the Ombudsman for Human Rights. Holders of those offices are elected by majority vote in the national assembly.

Certain constitutional guarantees may be suspended by the president in consultation with his cabinet, but only on national security, national economy, or national emergency grounds, and in accordance with the Law of Emergencies. Other constitutional guarantees can never be suspended. Any citizen may challenge the constitutionality of a law, and may through a Recurso de Amparo avoid the applicability of a particular constitutional provision. The right of habeas corpus is also reaffirmed; this has been more frequently used in cases of illegal detention, but may also be applicable in a much wider range of circumstances. The constitution may be modified by legislative initiative of the president or of one-third of the national assembly. Partial constitutional modifications require a 60 percent vote in the national assembly, but a total constitutional modification requires two-thirds. Usually, legislative process for any matter other than a constitutional amendment may be initiated by members of the National Assembly, the president, any magistrate of the Supreme Court or the Supreme Electoral Council, or any citizen, provided that the latter is supported with verifiable signatures of five thousand individuals, and provided further that such citizen-initiated legislative process does not concern organic laws, taxation, international obligations of the state, amnesties, or indictments. All laws are promulgated by the president, and become effective upon publication in *La Gaceta*. The president may not use veto powers to amend any constitutional modification law.

One of the more significant advances achieved in the 1987 political constitution was the recognition of Nicaragua's indigenous peoples and the reaffirmation of their rights, privileges, and immunities. Article 180 of the constitution recognizes their right to live and develop under diverse social and political structures according to their cultural and historic traditions. The constitution also recognizes their right to communal land tenure, their right to exploit natural resources, and their right to preserve their culture and dialects, religions, and customs. It is their constitutional right to employ, whenever the law permits, their own dialects as an official language.

CURRENT STRUCTURE

Justice administration in Nicaragua rests with the Supreme Court of Justice, the appellate tribunals, and district and local courts, all of which form the judicial power. Chapter V of the Political Constitution of 1987, as amended in 1995 and 2000, and more specifically Articles 158 through 167, provide for the functions of the judicial branch. In addition, the Organic Law of the Judicial Power of the Republic of Nicaragua, known as Law 260 and published in *La Gaceta* number 137 on July 23, 1998, provides for the organization and operation of the judicial branch. The Supreme Court also oversees the property of public registries. Military tribunals oversee misconduct and other affairs purely within the jurisdiction of the armed forces. The constitution guarantees allocation of no less than 4 percent of the national budget to the Supreme Court.

Twelve magistrates of the Supreme Court are elected by simple majority in the national assembly and serve seven-year terms. The twelve magistrates elect among them one president and one vice president of the judicial power, who serve one-year terms subject to unlimited reelection until the end of their terms. The Supreme Court has four subject matter panels denominated *salas,* which include civil, criminal, constitutional, and administrative review. Each *sala* is composed of no fewer than three magistrates elected for that purpose among the twelve magistrates of the Supreme Court; each magistrate may serve in one or two *salas.* Quorum is set at two-thirds of magistrates assigned to a particular *sala.* Constitutional review is reserved exclusively for the Supreme Court.

The Supreme Court appoints magistrates to the nine appellate tribunals distributed across the country as follows: Las Segovias (for Nueva Segovia, Madriz, and Esteli), Occidental (for Chinandega and Leon), Managua (solely for the department of Managua and the National District), Sur (for Masaya and Carazo), Granada (for Granada and Rivas), Central (for Chontales, Boaco, and Rio San Juan), Norte (for Jinotega and Matagalpa), Atlantico Norte (for the RAAN), and Atlantico Sur (for the RAAS, el Rama, and Nueva Guinea). Additional geographic circumscriptions may be designated from time to time by the Supreme Court. Appellate tribunals are divided into three *salas:* civil, criminal, and administrative review (usually labor-related). Magistrates in appellate tribunals serve for a period of five years. Some tribunals have five magistrates (one president, two assigned to civil and two to criminal *salas*); others have six magistrates (three for civil and three for criminal *salas*). As part of ongoing legal reform, the subject matter jurisdiction of the appellate tribunals will be expanded to include cases currently adjudicated by specialized bodies and which deal with property, labor, and administrative review.

The Supreme Court also appoints trial courts that are staffed by one judge and are divided into district and local courts. Their appointment is indefinite and may be ended only for cause. At least one district or local court is located in each *departamento* and autonomous region. In some instances they hear trials of cases on all subject matters, and are therefore known as Juzgado de Distrito Unico; in other instances, their subject matter jurisdiction is limited by the Supreme Court, and they are therefore called juzgado local. The apparent duplicity in trial courts has been subject to long-standing criticism because it leads to inefficiency and lack of uniformity in the administration of justice. It is expected that ongoing legal reforms will address these issues and propose the creation of a single trial court system, providing, if necessary, for more than one branch of the trial court in any given *departamento* or *region autonoma.*

Structure of Nicaraguan Courts

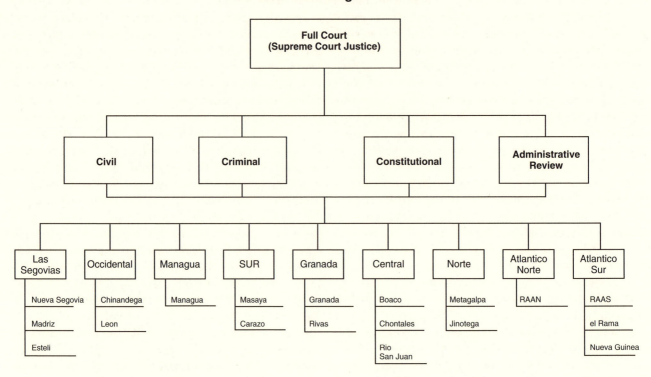

SPECIALIZED JUDICIAL BODIES

The Supreme Court oversees the public registries for real and nonreal property that are established in each *departamento* and autonomous region. These have in the past provided for administrative and judicial review of disputes, particularly with respect to the devolution of private property that was confiscated by the Sandinista government from 1979 through the late 1980s. However, with ongoing legal reforms, the review functions of these bodies are expected to go to the district or local courts.

Other judicial bodies include military courts, which oversee misconduct and other issues that arise under the internal codes of the Nicaraguan armed forces. There is evidence of paramilitary courts for civilians that have been in operation at different periods of history. In addition, the two autonomous regions on the Atlantic coast establish, from time to time, other judicial bodies that interpret indigenous laws and regulations. The Organic Law of the Judicial Power and the Political Constitution of 1987, as amended, both recognize these indigenous courts or tribunals, and give complete deference to the indigenous governments to dictate the substantive and procedural content of the laws and regulations, as well as the administrative functions of the courts and tribunals, so long as they do not come into conflict with other provisions of the political constitution.

STAFFING

For a country of its size and territorial extension, Nicaragua has relatively few judicial officers. There are 12 magistrates of the Supreme Court of Justice, 42 magistrates of the appellate tribunals, and 230 local and district court judges. In addition, a significant number of judicial consultants, or *peritos judiciales,* are appointed from time to time from a roster maintained by the Supreme Court. These judicial consultants assist trial and appellate courts in a variety of tasks, including the signature of warrants, deeds, and certain court orders, in addition to the holding of minor evidentiary hearings. Because not everyone on the roster serves, at least concurrently, as *peritos judiciales,* their current number is not available. The Ministry of Justice has not released the number of prosecutors or public defenders.

All judicial officers are appointed or elected, as the case may be, from a roster created by the commission of the judicial profession, which in turn is appointed by the twelve magistrates of the Supreme Court. Discipline of judicial officers is carried out by the Supreme Court, upon recommendation of its Commission for Disciplinary Regime.

Legal education in Nicaragua, like higher education in general, is undergoing significant changes. The oldest law faculty dates back to the mid-nineteenth century and has functioned continuously in Leon. In the twentieth century two other law schools emerged in Managua, and until the mid-1980s these were the only law schools in the entire country. Since then, however, a number of private, often start-up institutions of higher education granting law degrees have emerged. Neither the private bar nor the judicial power regulates legal education, and therefore the quality of legal training varies widely.

IMPACT

For many decades, the judicial system in Nicaragua was subject to heavy criticism and was perceived not to be impartial, transparent, efficient, or free of bureaucracy. These criticisms increased during the Sandinista regime, when a number of legal reforms created a myriad of quasi-judicial bodies. Since the mid-1990s, however, a number of projects have led to the creation of a judicial college and the study of mechanisms to improve the administration of justice. Among these are proposed organic reforms to the structure of the courts, as well as the transformation of the Ministry of Justice into a public ministry. It is anticipated that the trial system (*juicio oral*) will also gradually be adopted. All of these reforms will undoubtedly contribute to public confidence in the judicial branch, with the resulting strengthening of the democratic institutions and principles of Nicaragua.

Harold O. M. Rocha

See also Civil Law; Human Rights Law; Indigenous and Folk Legal Systems; Magistrates—Civil Law Systems; Nicaragua; The Spanish Empire and the Laws of the Indies

References and further reading

Belaunde, F., F. Fernandez Segado, and R. Hernandez Valle, eds. 1992. *Los Sistemas constitucionales Iberoamericanos.* Madrid: Editorial Dykinson.

Buitrago, Edgardo. 1993. *Resumen esquematico de las constituciones de Nicaragua.* Managua: Konrad-Adenauer-Stiftung.

Chamorro, Violeta. 1996. *Dreams of the Heart: The Autobiography of President Violeta Barrios de Chamorro of Nicaragua.* New York: Simon and Schuster.

Clavero, Bartolome. 1994. *Derecho indigena y cultura constitucional en America.* Mexico, D.F.: Siglo Veintiuno.

Constitucion Politica de Nicaragua. 2001.

Escobar Fornos, Ivan. 1996. *Constitucion y derechos humanos.* Managua: Universidad Centroamericana.

Mainwang, Scott, and Mathew S. Schugart, eds. 1997. *Presidentialism and Democracy in Latin America.* Cambridge: Cambridge University Press.

NIGER

COUNTRY INFORMATION

Niger is a landlocked state in Africa, bordering on Nigeria and Benin in the south, Algeria in the southeast, Libya in the north, Mali in the west, and Chad in the east. It is a vast and arid state (except along the Niger River) that historically has been the gateway between north and sub-Saharan Africa. With an area of 1,267,000 square kilometers, Niger is perceived as the largest state in West Africa. The population, according to 2001 estimates, is 10,355,156. The population growth rate is 2.8 percent (2000 estimate), and the population density in 1993 was 6.6 persons per square kilometer. The population is rela-

tively small compared to the size of the country, due to the arid nature of Niger.

The climate is hot and humid and is characterized by low and uncertain rainfall. The average annual rainfall ranges from 31 inches (79 centimeters) in the south to less than 4 inches (10 centimeters) in the northern area. Rainfall in the south lasts from June to October. The population is more concentrated in the south because of the frequent rain; by contrast, most of the northeastern region is uninhabitable because of its aridity. Average temperatures in Niger are high throughout the year and range between 81°F and 84°F.

Rated by the United Nations as the second-poorest country in Africa after Sierra Leone, which is ravaged by civil war, Niger has an economy centered on subsistence agriculture, animal husbandry, reexport trade, and uranium, which has been the major export since the 1970s. Agriculture is the cornerstone of Niger's economy. About 90 percent of the people depend on agriculture for a living (either as subsistence farmers or pastoralists). The main crops are millet, peanuts, sorghum, beans, cowpeas, rice, and cassava. Cowpeas and cotton are cultivated for export. Livestock raising—sheep, goats, poultry, donkeys, and cattle—is the principal agricultural activity. In the early 1990s, the annual livestock population included 5.4 million goats, 3.4 million sheep, and 1.8 million cattle. Fishing is done in Lake Chad and the River Niger, and the catch is locally consumed.

Industry and commerce employ 6 percent of the labor force, while the government employs 4 percent. The gross national product (GNP) of Niger, according to 1997 World Bank estimates, was equivalent to U.S.$200 per head, while the gross domestic product (GDP) in 1999 was U.S.$640 million.

Almost 6 percent of the GDP comes from mining, with uranium as the major export. In 1992, 80 percent of Niger's export earnings were derived from uranium exports. The figure declined to 62 percent in 1995 and increased to 75 percent (still less than the 1992 number) in 1997. With Niger accounting for one-tenth of the total output from the mining of uranium in the world, it is ranked third in this category after Canada and Australia. Other natural resources include coal, iron ore, tin phosphates, gold, and petroleum.

Niger has one of the lowest literacy rates in the world. Schooling is free and mandatory for children between the ages of seven and fifteen, but with the shortage of teachers, coupled with the wide dispersion of the population, only about 25 percent of primary-school-aged children receive an education. In the early 1990s, some 368,700 pupils attended primary school annually, while 74,300 pupils were enrolled in secondary schools.

The main ethnic groups include the Hausa, who make up 56 percent of the population; the Djerma, 22 percent;

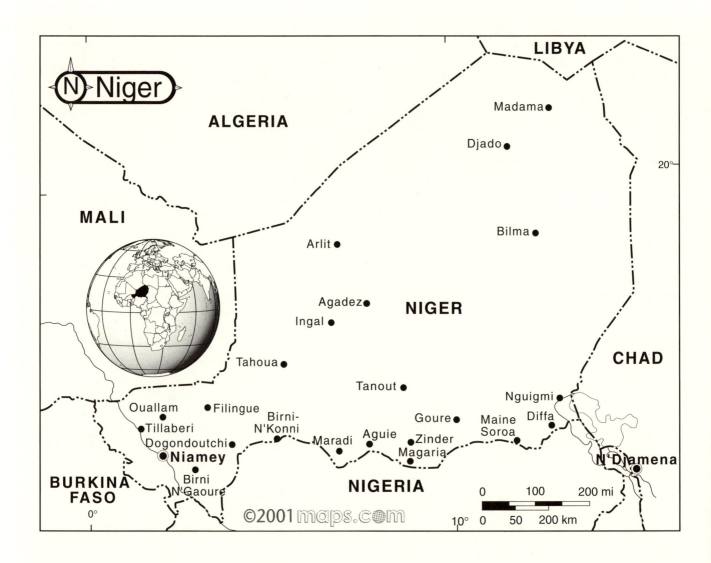

the Fula, 8.5 percent; the Tuareg, 8 percent; the Beri Beri (Kanouri), 4.3 percent; and the Arab, Toubou, and Gourmantche, 1.2 percent. The official language is French, but a wide variety of languages are spoken by the different ethnic groups on a daily basis. The great majority of Niger's people are Sunni Muslims (80 percent). Most of the rest adhere to traditional religious beliefs, and some are Christians.

HISTORY

Lying on the caravan route from North Africa to the Hausa states during the Middle Ages, Niger served as an important strategic and economic crossroads between North and West Africa. It was part of the ancient Empires of Mali, Songhai, and Karnem Bornu. In the nineteenth century, the Fulanis conquered the area under Usuman dan Fodio and imposed Islam as the dominant religion.

European influence in Niger began between the eighteenth and nineteenth centuries when the Scottish explorer Mungo Park explored the River Niger. Later, in 1850, German explorers Heinrich Barth and Eduard Vogel made their entry into the region. During the Europeans' scramble for Africa that culminated in the Berlin Conference (1884–1885), which partitioned Africa among the major powers of Europe, France gained control over Niger. The French occupied it in 1890 and then made it a military territory in 1900, an autonomous territory in 1922, and an overseas territory in 1946. In 1958, Nigerien voters approved the French Constitution and voted to make the territory an autonomous republic within the French community. On August 3, 1960, Niger withdrew from the French community and proclaimed its independence. Its first president was Hamani Diori, the leader of Parti Progressiste Nigerien (PPP).

In the early 1970s, Niger was hit by severe drought, causing widespread food shortages and serious losses in terms of livestock production. Diori's government was accused of misappropriating food aid intended for drought victims. The aftermath of this accusation was a bloodless coup d'état, masterminded by the armed forces' chief of staff, Lt. Col. Seyni Kountché, in 1974.

Kountché immediately established the twelve-man Conseil Militaire Supérieur (CMS), with himself as chairman, to govern the country. He also suspended the constitution and dissolved the National Assembly. In 1983, Kountché created the National Council for Development (CND), made up of 150 members who were freely elected from different social and professional groups in Niger's seven regions. The CND was a purely consultative rather than legislative body.

Six years after the coup, Kountché granted the CND the mandate to draft a preconstitutional document called the "national charter." In 1987, the draft charter was massively approved by 99.6 percent of the people in a referendum. Five months after the referendum, Kountché died after a protracted illness and was succeeded by the armed forces' chief of staff Ali Saibou as the chairman of CMS.

Saibou gave the CND a mandate to draft a new constitution. It was finally ready in 1988, and it was overwhelmingly approved by 99.3 percent in a national referendum in 1989. Saibou created a new party—the Mouvement National pour une Société de Développement (MNSD)—and lifted the ban on all political activities.

In the wave of economic, social, and political chaos in the late 1980s and early 1990s, the National Conference of All Nigeriens was convened to discuss ways and measures to redress Niger's institutional, social, economic, and political problems. The conference stripped Saibou of all executive powers. However, he retained the title of head of state, with only a ceremonial role, pending the drafting and enactment of a new constitution. The army and police came under the control of the fifteen-man Haut Conseil de la République (HCR), established by the National Conference. The HCR, which functioned as an interim legislature, ensured the effective implementation of the resolutions of the National Conference and supervised the drafting of the constitution of the third republic.

The draft national constitution was approved by a vote of 89.9 percent on December 26, 1992, in a national referendum. Legislative and presidential elections followed in 1993, and Mahamane Ousmane emerged victorious as president of the third republic.

In January 1996, Ousmane's government, which since its inception had grappled with political, social, and economic problems exacerbated by the devaluation of the franc (CFAF) in 1994, was overthrown by a military coup d'état led by Ibrahim Bare Mainassara. Mainassara formed the twelve-member Conseil de Salut National (CSN), suspended the 1992 Constitution, dissolved Parliament, outlawed all political organizations, and imposed a state of emergency.

To pave the way for a return to civilian rule, Mainassara created two independent consultative bodies, the Conseil de Sages (Council of the Wise) and the coordinating committee of the National Forum, with the mandate to study and submit proposals for a constitutional change, revise the electoral code, and amend the charter that governed political parties. The proposals for the draft new constitution were submitted and approved by 92.3 percent in a national referendum in 1996.

In July 1996, Mainassara emerged victorious in the presidential election that was characterized as flawed after the Commission Electorale Nationale Indépendent (CENI) was dissolved by the military government. Opposition parties cried foul, but the Supreme Court did not hesitate to validate the result, comfirming Mainassara as the president of the fourth republic. On assuming office, Mainassara restored CENI and went ahead to organize and manage a legislative election, which was boycotted by three major opposition parties.

On April 9, 1999, Mainassara was overthrown in a bloody coup d'état by members of his presidential guard, led by Maj. Daouda Mallam Wanké. Wanké and his cohorts initially described the death of Mainassara as an "unfortunate accident." They later changed that description to a "tragic accident" and finally to the bolder description of "coup d'état." The military junta created the military Conseil de Réconciliation Nationale (CRN), with Maj. Daouda Malam Wanké at its head. The 1996 Constitution, all political activities, and all organizations were suspended. The CRN also dissolved the National Assembly. A twenty-one-point set of guidelines was signed to function as a constitutional document during the transition period. In May 1999, a new constitution was drafted by a consultative council of state elders appointed by the CRN and submitted to a referendum that approved the measure on July 18, 1999, by an 89.57 percent vote.

LEGAL CONCEPTS

Today, Niger is in its Fifth Republic. It is also a unitary state with a multiparty system. Administratively, it is divided into seven regions (*départements*) and thirty-five districts or counties (*arrondissements*). Each département is headed by a *préfet* (divisional officer), while the arrondissement is headed by a *sous préfet* (district officer).

The constitution of the Fifth Republic provides for a semipresidential system of government in which the president of the republic is elected for a five-year term by direct, universal suffrage. The president is eligible for reelection just once. The constitution also provides for the single-chamber, eighty-three-member National Assembly; members are elected for five-year terms as well. The president appoints the prime minister from the majority party in Parliament. The prime minister is the head of government and is responsible to the legislative National Assembly, which is competent to remove the prime minister by a vote of censure. In case the security of Niger is threatened, the president may (after consultation with the prime minister, the president of the National Assembly, the president of the Supreme Court, and the president of the Constitutional Court) declare a state of emergency.

Although the constitutions of the first, second, third, and fourth republics provided for the principle of separation of power between the executive and legislative branches and the executive and judiciary branches, the strong bureaucratic and centralized nature of the various regimes in Niger have made it difficult to strengthen the judiciary through this principle. The judiciary (with the exception of the Supreme Court, which on occasion has asserted its independence) has been subject to executive influence. This paradigm shift from the constitutional provisions has led to the failure to forge a coherent, responsible, and independent judiciary, as previewed by the constitution.

According to legal hierarchy in Niger, the constitution is the supreme law of the land. It defines the state of Niger, establishes its sovereignty, guarantees the rights of its people, and proclaims their attachment to democratic and human rights principles. International treaties negotiated, signed, and ratified by the president of the republic become law immediately on publication. However, international treaties can only have the force of law if they are not contrary to Niger's constitution. Next to the constitution and international treaties in the legal hierarchy are the laws adopted by the National Assembly and promulgated by the president of the republic. The promulgation of any law adopted by the National Assembly has to be done fifteen days from the date of transmission by the president of the National Assembly to the president of the republic. However, the fifteen-day limit for promulgation of any law adopted by the National Assembly is reduced to five days if the assembly declares such a promulgation a matter of urgency. The president of the republic may then ask the National Assembly to deliberate on the law again before the deadline for its promulgation. In such a case, the National Assembly cannot refuse the president's request. However, if the assembly votes for the law with an absolute majority, the president of the republic promulgates it in accordance with the procedure of urgency.

Furthermore, a significant portion of the laws in Niger's statute books are in the form of subsidiary legislation—that is, they are rules and regulations that have the force of law made by the president (in the form of presidential decrees), administrative body of public officers such as the prime minister (prime ministerial order), ministerial order and prefectorial orders, and orders issued by mayors of a particular municipality.

Niger's legal system is based on the French civil law system and indigenous customary law. Traditional chiefs do act as mediators and counselors, and they have authority in customary matters as well as modern laws when they are designated as auxiliaries to local administrators. When the government produces legislation that is a codification of the custom of the people, traditional chiefs (who are regarded as guardians and custodians of the custom) are pivotal in the smooth implementation of such legislations. An example in this light is the Rural Code that was adopted in 1993 (Ordinance No. 93-015 of March 1993), dealing with land tenure.

Since almost the entire population of Niger is Muslim, most Nigeriens submit to social and cultural practices that have Islamic inspiration. Thus, Islam also provides a framework of law (*sharia*) that is applied through moot (arguments presented before local community elders and a legal officer) at the local level. The courts, administrative authorities, and chiefs use the Qur'an as a normative reference to check the validity of statements given by the litigants. It is believed that lying under oath subjects the perjurer to certain unpleasant supernatural sanctions, such as leprosy or impoverishment.

CURRENT STRUCTURE

Niger's system of justice is administered in the name of the people of Niger. The constitution of the Fifth Republic guarantees fundamental human rights, freedom of association, freedom of religion, freedom of speech, and freedom of press. It also prohibits torture and other cruel, inhuman, or degrading treatment or punishment. Arbitrary arrest and detention without charges in excess of forty-eight hours are condemned by the constitution and other laws. If police fail to find sufficient evidence within the detention period, the prosecutor gives the case to another officer, and a new forty-eight-hour detention period begins. The State Security Law gives police power to detain criminals and ensure that identity documents are in order. Detention often lasts months or years; some people wait as long as eight years to be charged. The police search must be backed by a warrant issued by a judge. However, police may search without a warrant if they have a strong suspicion that a house or a specific location shelters criminals or stolen property. The law provides defendants with the rights to counsel, to be fully present at their trials, to question witnesses, to examine the evidence against them, and to appeal any verdicts against them, first to the Court of Appeal and then to the Supreme Court. It also provides for the right to a lawyer once an individual is in detention. Minors have the right to counsel at public expense. Bail is available for all crimes that carry a penalty of less than ten years of imprisonment. Civil and criminal cases that are not political acts are tried publicly. If the criminal or civil cases involve political acts, they are tried in camera. The judiciary may review executive actions in cases in which administrative decisions were challenged. But the judiciary does not have power to review legislation enacted by Parliament or another central legislative organ.

The Supreme Court is the highest court in Niger. It comprises three chambers—the judicial chamber, the administrative chamber, and the account and budgetary chamber. The court reviews only the application of the law and constitutional questions. Its president is appointed by a presidential decree.

Next to the Supreme Court is the Court of Appeal, which reviews questions of facts and law. The court sits at Niamey. Defendants may appeal verdicts first to an appellate court and then to the Court of Appeal if they are not satisfied.

The Constitutional Court established after the National Conference and enshrined in the constitution of the Fifth Republic has jurisdiction in constitutional and electoral matters. It reviews the constitutionality of laws and ordinances, as well as the conformity of international treaties with the constitution. Election irregularities can only be declared by the Constitutional Court. The court is composed of seven members who are at least forty years of age and who are appointed for six-year, nonrenewable terms. The Constitutional Court elects its president for a three-year term, which can be renewed. The function of the members of the Constitutional Court is incompatible with other public offices. The court's members enjoy immunity from arrest or prosecution except in case of flagrante delicto. In such a case, the president of the court must give his or her accord to such an arrest or prosecution.

The High Court of Justice sits in the capital, Niamey. It is competent to try the president of the republic in cases of high treason. It is also competent to try other past or present state officials. It is composed of seven permanent members and three rotating members who are all deputies. These members are elected by the National Assembly. The court elects its own president.

The Assize Courts (Cours d'Assises) sit at Niamey, Maradi, Tahoua, and Zinder. They have the jurisdiction to try persons sent to them by the Chambre d'Accusation of the Court of Appeal. There are also District Magistrates' Courts or Courts of First Instance (Tribunaux de Première Instance), Justices of Peace (Justices de Paix), and Labor Courts (Tribunal de Travail). The District Magistrates' Courts sit at Niamey (with subdivisions at Dosso and Tillabéri), Maradi, Tahoua (with subdivisions at Agadez, Arlit, and Birni-N'Konni), Diffa, and Zinder. The Court of First Instance tries simple offense cases and trivial civil cases. Justices of Peace sit at Tillabéri, Ouallam, Dosssso, Madaoua, Tessaoua, Gouré, N'Guigmi, Bilma, and Birn-N'Gaoure. These courts hear police offense cases, certain misdemeanor cases, and cases that involve customary law. Labor Courts function at Niamey, Zinder, Maradi, Tahoua, Birni-N'Konni, Agadez, Dosso, and Diffa. They hear minor labor disputes involving employers and employees but do not have the jurisdiction to hear collective-bargaining cases.

SPECIALIZED JUDICIAL BODIES

With the advent of the National Conference held in March 1991, Niger political and judicial institutions were set aside. The Haut Conseil de la République (HCR) established by the National Conference, functioned as the executive, legislative, and judicial body. It examined key political issues that had affected Niger from the preindependent to the postindependent era. The HCR advocated retribution against those who mishandled the Tuareg rebellion. It also held those responsible for the persistent corruption and power greed that plagued Niger's society before the National Conference. At the same time, the HCR called for a healing of Niger's wounds and envisioned a new road ahead.

The constitution of the Fifth Republic, Article 33, created the National Commission on Human and Fundamental Rights, composed of nineteen members, to defend and promote human rights in Niger. The commission has jurisdiction to summon anyone suspected of committing a human rights violation for questioning and may impose penal sanctions of up to six months of imprisonment and/or fines for those found guilty.

The freedom and independence of the media, including the press, are guaranteed by the Supreme Communication Council, an independent administrative authority. The council monitors media ethics and the fair access of political parties, associations, and citizens to official information and communication media.

The right to be tried in an ordinary court using established legal procedures can be modified in certain circumstances. During a state of emergency, for instance, the judiciary is deprived of its power, as the rule of law is no longer observed. On such an occasion, the Court of State Security, which sits in Niamey and operates out of the normal legal framework, is competent to try cases (political cases such as those of individuals accused of destabilizing the security of the state) that are not within the jurisdiction of the High Court. Thus, the court incorporates a martial court. The Court of State Security can also review the sentences of those already in detention. However, information regarding the rules, the procedures, and the right of the defendant to counsel is not available to any defendant held by the Court of State Security.

STAFFING

The judiciary depends on resources from the government. The Ministry of Justice has long been called the "poor relation" because it possesses neither adequate financial resources nor sufficient human resources to discharge its function properly. With the advent of democracy in the 1999s, there has been some improvement in the material resources made available to the judiciary, although human resources are still insufficient.

To become a practicing lawyer, one has to be admitted to the Niger Bar Association (Ordre des Avocat du Niger), created by Ordinance No. 76-40 of December 24, 1976. Prior to becoming a member of the bar, one must have graduated from a law school with a J.D. or LL.B. degree, undergone a pupillage or apprenticeship with a practicing attorney, and obtained a certificate of apprenticeship; in addition, a prospective member must not be an ex-convict, must not have a history of bankruptcy, and must be a Nigerien national. Former magistrates with at least five years of seniority, law professors, and court clerks (*greffiers*) with a License en Droit (LL.B. or J.D.) are also eligible to practice law without meeting the requirement of apprenticeship.

Judges undergo professional training in all areas of law or in the main areas of law (civil, penal, and administrative law). Newly appointed judges are given practical experience, under the supervision of a senior judge, for at least a year. Until 1992, students who obtained a master's degree in law specializing in the judiciary were directly admitted to the National Legal Service Training College in Paris to undergo eighteen months of theoretical and practical training. Since September 1994, candidates with a master's degree in law have had to take a test before being allowed to enroll for a training course lasting two years.

The government appoints state prosecutors and also appoints and promotes presiding judges, based on good conduct, experience, integrity, and particular ability. The Judiciary Act provides judges with security in tenure. However, if the requirements of service require it, judges can be transferred by the appointing authority with the consent of the Judicial Service Commission, which must give the reason for its decision. There is no specific tenure for judges except those of the Constitutional Courts, who are appointed for six-year, nonrenewable terms. Judges are civil servants just like any other state employee and are entitled to retire after thirty years of service or at the age of fifty with a pension. The pension paid to judges is based on their salary, without additional benefits. Judges are also graded according to seniority and merit as *magistrat du première classe, deuxième classe, troisième classe* (first-class magistrate, second class, third class), and so on. Foreign lawyers can appear in Nigerien courts for specific cases.

IMPACT

Since independence, Niger has suffered under austere military rule and periods of civil unrest that have had serious repercussions on its legal system. The various military governments have spared no effort in disregarding the constitution whenever there was a coup d'état. Their motive has been nothing other than to consolidate and safeguard personal rule. The constitution has been revised and redrafted several times.

The judiciary has been critized for not maintaining its independence, partly because judges sometimes fear reassignment or having their financial benefits reduced if they render a decision that is unfavorable to the government. This situation has, of course, affected the justice system. In addition, the justice system encounters numerous technical difficulties in relation to staffing and as a result of Niger's constant descent into political chaos.

However, Niger's justice system enjoys a fairly good reputation among the public. In particular, the Supreme and Constitutional Courts have distanced themselves from the influence of the government, which explains why both politicians and private citizens always turn to these courts for redress.

Peter Tesi

See also Civil Law; Judicial Independence; Legal Professionals—Civil Law Traditions; Magistrates—Civil Law Systems; Sierra Leone
References and further reading
Charlick, Robert B. 1991. *Niger: Personal Rule and Survival in the Sahel.* Boulder, CO, and San Francisco: Westview Press.
Englebert, Pierre. 2000. "Niger." Pp. 795–817 in *Africa South of the Sahara, 2000.* 29th ed. London: Europa.
Fuglestad, Finn. 1983. *A History of Niger: 1850–1960.* Cambridge: Cambridge University Press.
Lund, Christian, and Gerti Hesseling. 1999. "Traditional Chief and Modern Land Tenure Law in Niger." Pp. 135–151 in *African Chieftaincy in a New Socio-Political Landscape.* Edited by E. Adriaan, B. van Rouberoy van Nieuwall, and Rijk van Dijk. Leiden, the Netherlands: African Studies Center.
Ramsay, F. Jeffress. 1999. *Global Studies: Africa.* 8th ed. Guilford, CT: Dushkin/McGraw-Hill.
Spriggs, Karyl Terese. 2000. "The Legal System of the Republic of Niger." Pp. 6.380.3–6.380.15 in *Modern Legal Systems Cyclopedia—Africa.* Edited by Kenneth Robert Redden and Brock William Emerson. Buffalo, NY: Hein.
United Nations Economic and Social Council. 1996. "United Nations Standards and Norms in the Field of Crime Prevention and Criminal Justice: Use and Application of the Basic Principles on the Independence of the Judiciary." Report of the secretary general presented to the Commission on Crime Prevention and Criminal Justice, Fifth Session, Vienna, May 21–31, 1996. UN Doc. E/CN.15/1996/16/Add.4, March 20, 1996.
U.S. Department of State. 2000. "1999 Country Reports on Human Rights Practices: Niger." U.S. Department of State. http://www.state.gov/www/global/human_rights/1997_hrp_report/niger.html (accessed January 4, 2002).

NIGERIA

COUNTRY INFORMATION

Nigeria is one of the largest countries in Africa, with a population of approximately 120 million people. Located in West Africa and covering a total area of 923,768 square kilometers, it is bordered by francophone African countries such as the Niger Republic to the north, the Benin Republic to the west, Cameroon to the east, and the Chad Republic to the northeast. To the south of Nigeria is the vast Atlantic Ocean. The country is composed of over 250 different ethnic groups, the most prominent being the Hausa-Fulani, Yoruba, Igbo, Kanuri, Tiv, Idoma, Urhobo, Itrekiri, and Ibibio. Although Christianity and Islam remain the dominant religious identities in the country, several ethnic communities practice traditional African religions. English is the major official language, a vestige of its history as a British colony.

Nigeria is a predominantly agricultural country: About 75 percent of the people live in rural areas, most of whom are involved in peasant agricultural production. The country is also a major oil producer, with earnings from this sector contributing some 97 percent of the national income. However, in spite of its huge resource base, Nigeria remains one of the world's most underdeveloped nations. About 39 percent of adults are illiterate, 33 percent of the people have no access to health services, and 51 percent are without access to safe water. As of 1998, the gross domestic product (GDP) per capita was barely $256, and the annual rate of inflation was about 11 percent. The poverty and underdevelopment of the country have been reinforced over the years by incessant military incursions into the political process, the imposition of authoritarian rule, and high levels of corruption and resource mismanagement by the elites.

Nigeria has a federal system of government and is composed of thirty-six states and the Federal Capital Territory. Local governments are relatively autonomous. The country's legal system has been influenced not only by English common law but also by *sharia* (Islamic law) and customary law. The impact of these diverse sources of legal principles and doctrines has made Nigeria's legal system very complex.

HISTORY

Prior to the colonial conquest of the African continent and the subsequent subordination of its people to imperial domination, the territory that came to be known as Nigeria was essentially composed of centralized kingdoms and empires, such as the Sokoto Caliphate, the Kanem-Borno Empire, the Benin Kingdom, the Oyo Empire, and the Kwararafa Kingdom, as well as the city-states of the present Niger-Delta area. While ethnic groups such as the Hausa-Fulani in the north and the Yoruba in the southwest had institutions of political power, groups such as the Tiv and Igbo were highly decentralized sociopolitical communities in which age groups played a central role in social and political organization. The intervention of the British colonialists in the late nineteenth century and the subsequent subjugation of the kingdoms and empires mentioned earlier led to fundamental transformations, especially in the organization of political power and modes of control within the colonial state. In the north and southwest, where centralized political institutions had existed (such as the emirate system and the obaship—leadership—among the Hausa-Fulani and Yoruba ethnicities, respectively), indirect rule was introduced as an administrative machinery; among the Igbo, a system of warrant chiefs had to be created for purposes of colonial administration, especially in the areas of taxation, justice, and law and order. These regional and ethnic variations, as will be discussed, affected the evolution of Nigeria's legal system, especially at the level of customary law.

The development of Nigeria's complex legal system was also shaped by patterns of external influences, especially the European/Christian influence from the south and the Arab/Islamic influence from the north. Prior to the imposition of colonial rule, the ancient empires in the north (such as the Sokoto Caliphate and the Kanem-Borno Empire) had extensive trade and diplomatic linkages with the Arab kingdoms of North Africa and the Middle East. This interaction led to the rapid penetration and spread of Islam, including its legal systems, into the northern part of Nigeria. By contrast, colonial penetration from the south by European traders, explorers, and missionaries led to the spread of Christianity as the dominant religious practice in the southern part of Nigeria.

To a large extent, these patterns of external influences subsequently affected the court systems that evolved in the northern and southern portions of the country. Even after Lord Lugard, the governor-general, amalgamated the northern and southern protectorates in 1914 to form Nigeria, the legal systems in the two regions continued to reflect the historical, political, and religious experiences of the people. Thus, the Islamic legal system of *sharia* was used for the administration of justice among the Muslims in the north (especially in civil matters such as divorce, custody of children, and inheritance), whereas the notion of justice in the south was heavily influenced by the European criminal code.

It is pertinent to note that although the British colonial administration in Nigeria introduced English law into the country, it did not entirely reject existing local laws and customs, which until then had been the basis for administering justice among the people. The system of indirect rule used by the British colonial authorities provided the political framework for the administration of

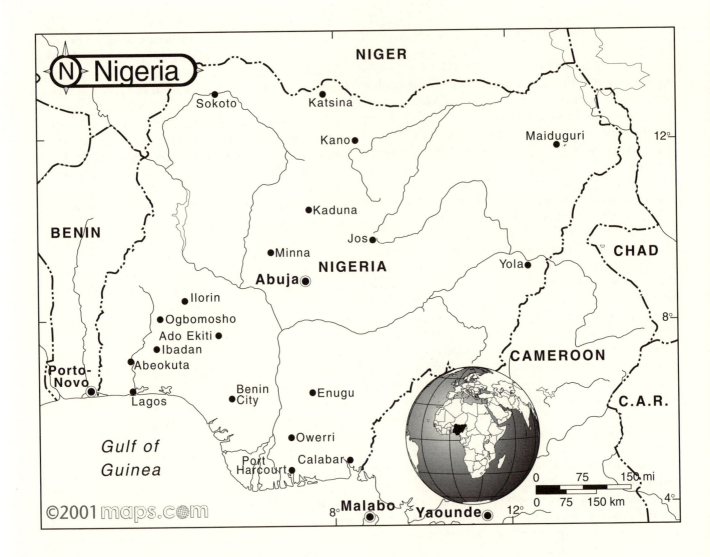

justice according to the principles of both English law and customary law. Between 1900 and 1913, the colonial administration, through the Protectorate Courts Proclamation, established the Supreme Court, Provincial Courts, and Native Courts. The Native (or Customary) Courts were divided into four major categories, labeled A, B, C, and D. Further legal reforms between 1933 and 1943 abolished the Provincial Courts and introduced High Courts and Magistrates' Courts.

The 1954 Constitution was a turning point in the evolution of Nigeria's legal system because it introduced a federal structure in the country, with three governmental regions established—the North, East, and West—and given their own legislatures. Among other things, the constitution provided for the Federal Supreme Court, the High Court in Lagos and each of the three regions, Magistrates' Courts, and Customary Courts. On September 30, 1960, the Sharia Court of Appeal was introduced for the northern regions to accommodate the Muslims.

When Nigeria attained independence on October 1, 1960, it functioned under a parliamentary system of government, which continued until January 15, 1966, when the military intervened and abolished the established regions as well as the constitution. Through Decree 34 of 1966, the military also abolished the federal system of governance and introduced a unitary state. This move to centralize power provoked yet another coup in July 1966, and through Decree 9, the military reverted to federalism, giving the regions their autonomy. In 1967, Nigeria plunged into a violent ethnoregional civil war, which culminated in the death of hundreds of thousands of its citizens, especially the Igbo, who declared a secession. Through another decree, the regime of Gen. Yakubu Gowon divided the regions that existed at that point—North, East, West, and Mid-West—into twelve states, thereby reintroducing federalism as the central principle of state governance in postcolonial Nigeria.

Although Gowon and his regime restored some measure of political stability following the end of the fratricidal civil war in 1970, his failure to restore civilian democratic rule in 1975 as promised led to his overthrow in a bloodless coup that ushered into power the Murtala Obansanjo regime, which held the reins of power between 1975 and 1979. Obansanjo handed over power to a democratically elected government in October 1979. The 1979 Constitution was drafted by a fifty-member committee, called the Constitution Drafting Committee (CDC), appointed by the military regime. The government that came to power was essentially a presidential system with a separation of powers between the executive, legislature, and judiciary. Alhaji Shehu Shagari was elected president under the 1979 Constitution. Corruption, nepotism, interparty thuggery, and factional conflicts ultimately led to the collapse of the second republic in 1983, thereby subjecting the Nigerian state once again to military dictatorship.

From 1983 to 1999, Nigeria was subjected to military authoritarian rule characterized by gross abuses of human rights, communal and religious conflicts, repression and marginalization of minority ethnic groups, corruption, and the erosion of state legitimacy. As the nation's political crises intensified, its economic dislocation deepened, with social infrastructures collapsing and indebtedness to creditors reaching over $30 billion. Strikes by labor, protesting low wages and harsh structural adjustment measures, were met with violent repression. Both the Babangida regime (from 1985 to 1993) and the Abacha regime (from 1993 to 1998) failed to open up the political space through democratic reforms or upholding the rule of law, which ultimately led to Nigeria being ostracized by the comity of nations. After human rights activist Ken Saro Wiwa and eight others were hanged in 1995 by the Abacha regime, Nigeria was suspended from the Commonwealth, and sanctions were imposed by the European Union and Canada.

During the era of military rule in Nigeria, the judiciary as a third arm of government atrophied. The era was characterized by corruption of justice even within the judiciary, the use of ouster clauses in passing decrees, the use of military tribunals instead of the court system, denial of the accused person's right to legal representation, judicial killings, and executive lawlessness. The military, which monopolized both executive and legislative powers at the federal center, also controlled its appointees (the military governors) at the state level. The military governors in turn appointed civil servants from time to time as sole administrators in the local governments. However, with the introduction of the 1999 Constitution and the return to democratic rule on May 29, 1999, Nigeria embraced principles upholding the rule of law, respect for human rights, autonomy of the judiciary, and the separation of executive and legislative powers.

From the foregoing historical exegesis, it can be discerned that Nigeria's law has been derived from a number of diverse sources, namely:

1. Nigerian legislation, which consists of ordinances, acts, decrees, and edicts passed by different levels of government within the country
2. English law, which consists of the following:
   The received English law comprising:
       The common law
       The doctrines of equity
       Statutes of general application in force in
           England on January 1, 1900
       Statutes and subsidiary legislation on specified
           matters
   English law made before October 1, 1960, and
       extending to Nigeria
3. Customary law
4. Judicial precedent
5. Islamic law (*sharia*)

LEGAL CONCEPTS

Although Nigeria, as a former British colony and a member of the Commonwealth of Nations, began its system of governance at independence with the parliamentary model, its civil war experience and the subsequent collapse of the first republic under military hegemony gave way to the adoption of a presidential system characterized by a separation of powers between the executive, the legislature, and the judiciary. The 1999 Constitution, though inspired by the military, provides for fundamental human rights, such as the right to the dignity of the human person; personal liberty; freedom of thought, conscience, and religion; freedom of expression and the press; freedom from discrimination; and the right to acquire and own property anywhere in Nigeria.

Section 131(2) of the 1999 Constitution establishes the office of the president of the federal republic. The president, who is also the head of state and chief of the armed forces, is elected through popular vote. The constitution provides in Section 134(1) that a candidate shall be deemed to have been duly elected if he or she receives (1) the majority of all votes cast in the elections, and (2) no less than one-quarter of the votes cast in each of at least two-thirds of all the states in the federation and the Federal Capital Territory. This requirement is designed to ensure that the person who emerges as Nigeria's president not only commands support in terms of the total votes cast but also has acceptability throughout the country, among the diverse ethnoreligious and cultural groups spread across the thirty-six states of the federation. The constitution empowers the president to appoint the justice of the Supreme Court as well as presidential ministers and heads of parastatals, subject to the ratification of the National Assembly.

At the level of the legislature, the 1999 Constitution provides a bicameral National Assembly, with the Senate being the upper house and the House of Representatives the lower house. The Senate has about 109 members, and the House of Representatives has over 300. Both the president and the members of the National Assembly are elected for terms of four years. Elections at the national, state, and local levels throughout the federation are organized by the Independent National Electoral Commission (INEC); petitions on elections are handled by the Election Tribunals established under Section 285(1) of the 1999 Constitution.

To ensure national unity and integration of the diverse ethnic and religious groups in the federation, Section 14(3–4) of the 1999 Constitution reinforces the federal character principle by stating that the composition of the government of the federation or any of its agencies and the conduct of its affairs shall be carried out in such a manner as to reflect the federal character of Nigeria, thereby promoting national loyalty as well as a sense of belonging.

The person who will serve as attorney general and minister of justice is appointed by the president, subject to the ratification of the National Assembly. This individual is responsible for overseeing the Justice Ministry and supervising criminal prosecutions. The National Judicial Council—which is composed of the chief justice of the federation, five retired justices of the Supreme Court, five judges of state, five members of the Nigerian Bar Association, one Grand Kadi, the president of the Court of Appeal, and one president of the Customary Court of Appeal—is responsible for recommending to the president of the republic individuals to be appointed to the Supreme Court, the Court of Appeal, the Federal High Court, and so forth. The council selects those individuals from a list submitted by the Federal Judicial Service Commission.

Recognizing that Nigeria is a member of the international community, the constitution stipulates respect for international law as well as treaty obligations. Nigeria is a signatory to the Universal Declaration of Human Rights; the African Charter on Peoples and Human Rights; the Commonwealth Harare Declaration on Democracy and Good Governance; the Convention on the Rights of Children; the International Convention on the Elimination of All Forms of Racial Discrimination; the International Pact on Economic, Social and Cultural Rights; the International Pact on Civil and Political Rights; and the Beijing Convention on Women's Rights.

One important aspect of Nigeria's legal system, which has generated a good deal of controversy as well as sectarian violence in recent years, is the issue of extending *sharia*, the Islamic legal system, as state law covering both civil and criminal cases. Section 10 of the 1999 Constitution declares that the government of the federation or of a state shall not adopt any religion as the state religion. In spite of this clause, the government of Zamfara State in the northwestern part of Nigeria declared *sharia* the fundamental legal principle in the state as of November 1999. Directives against such action by the federal government notwithstanding, several states in the north—where Muslims predominate—enacted laws introducing *sharia* as the state religion. Christians, who constitute a minority in most northern states, continue to insist that the introduction of the *sharia* legal system to cover both civil and criminal cases is unconstitutional and a threat to communal coexistence and the political stability of the postcolonial Nigerian state. The *sharia* controversy led to violent sectarian conflict in Kaduna State in January and May 2000, leaving thousands of innocent people dead and property worth millions of naira destroyed. The crisis shook the very foundations of Nigeria's nation-building project, thereby threatening the consolidation of its nascent democracy.

CURRENT COURT SYSTEM STRUCTURE

As indicated earlier, the diverse pattern of external religious, economic, political, and cultural influences that affected Nigeria in its formative years shaped, in a fundamental way, the structural evolution of the country's legal system. The penetration of the Islamic religion into the northern part of Nigeria and its subsequent incorporation into the sociocultural and political values of a majority of the ethnic communities in the region meant that the Islamic legal code of *sharia* has some measure of legitimate raison d'être—insofar as it covers civil matters between Muslims. However, in the southern part of Nigeria, where Christian missionary activities and Western education exerted an enormous influence on the people, Christianity rather than Islam remains the dominant religious practice. In addition, to ensure the smooth administration of justice at the local level, the colonial administration allowed the Customary Courts to operate. In sum, therefore, the complexity of the legal system in Nigeria can be attributed not only to the divergent external colonial influences but also to the ethnic and cultural differences among the populace.

As shown in the figure, the structure of the court system in northern Nigeria incorporates both the Alkali Courts and Area Courts I, II, and III, which handle minor civil and criminal cases at the local level within the community. Also, since there is a large Muslim population in this part of the country, the constitution provides for the establishment of Sharia Courts at the state level where required. According to Section 277 of the 1999 Constitution, the Sharia Court of a state shall, in addition to such other jurisdiction as may be conferred on it by the law of the state, exercise appellate and supervisory jurisdiction in civil proceedings involving questions of Islamic personal law, such as issues of divorce, child custody, and inheritance.

By contrast, the structure of the court system in southern Nigeria incorporates Customary Courts A, B,

Structure of Northern Nigerian Courts

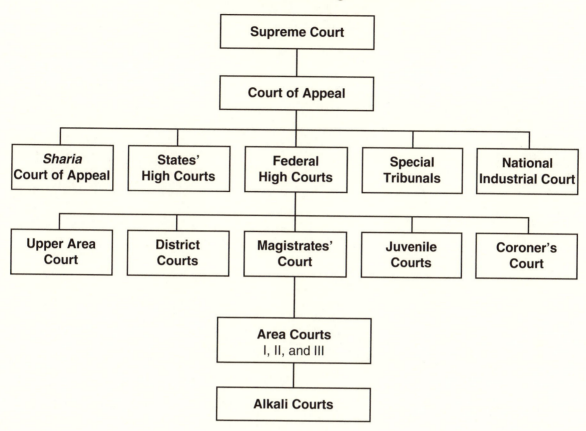

C, and D, as shown in the next figure. Customary Courts have jurisdiction over cases relating to customs as well as traditions in the areas of land matters, marriage, succession, inheritance, and the like. Like the Alkali and Area Courts in northern Nigeria, the Customary and Magistrates' Courts are courts of first instance that handle both criminal and civil matters, depending on their status, jurisdiction, and competence. Magistrates' Courts are spread throughout the country, irrespective of the north-south dichotomy, and they handle criminal matters. The 1999 Constitution also provides for the establishment of States' High Courts across the country. The High Courts hear civil and criminal matters. They are also appellate courts and courts of original jurisdiction. Appeals lie from the High Court to the Court of Appeal. Within each state of the federation, the chief judge, at the apex of the judicial division, exercises administrative as well as supervisory control over the courts.

At the top of the legal system of Nigeria is the Supreme Court, headed by the chief justice, who is appointed by the president on the recommendation of the National Judicial Council and confirmed by the Senate. The 1999 Constitution provides for the appointment of twenty-one Supreme Court justices by the president, again subject to Senate confirmation. Furthermore, it stipulates that to be the chief justice of Nigeria or a justice of the Supreme Court, an individual must have been qualified to practice as a legal practitioner in Nigeria for at least fifteen years.

In terms of its functions and powers, the Supreme Court, to the exclusion of every other court, has original jurisdiction in any dispute between the federal government and a state or between states if and insofar as that dispute involves a question (whether of law or fact) on which the existence or extent of a legal right depends. Further, the Supreme Court has original jurisdiction as may be conferred on it by any act of the National Assembly. The Supreme Court is also the only court in the land with jurisdiction to hear and determine appeals from the Court of Appeal. Decisions of the Court of Appeal are heard by the Supreme Court in issues such as:

- Decisions in any civil or criminal proceeding before the Court of Appeal in which the basis of the appeal involves questions of law alone;
- Decisions in any civil or criminal proceeding on questions as to the interpretation or application of the constitution;
- Decisions in any criminal proceeding in which a

Structure of Southern Nigerian Courts

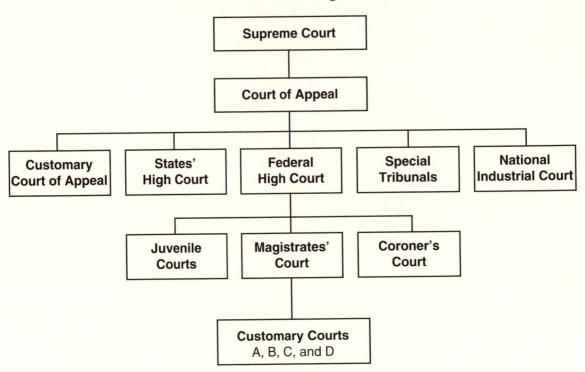

person has been sentenced to death by the Court of Appeal in affirming a death sentence imposed by any other court;

- Decisions on any questions relating to the following:

    Whether any person has been validly elected to the office of president or vice-president under the constitution;

    Whether the term of office of the president or vice-president has ceased;

    Whether the office of the president or vice president has become vacant

There are other types of courts within the Nigerian system, as well. The National Industrial Court, for example, handles issues of trade disputes, collective bargaining, and industrial relations. Established in 1976, this court is composed of a president and four judges appointed by the president of the country on the advice of the National Judicial Council. Juvenile Courts exclusively handle cases involving infants or young offenders, and their emphasis is on counseling, rehabilitation, and protection of young delinquents from being arraigned. The Coroner's Court is empowered to carry out investigations into cases of mysterious, violent, or unnatural deaths. An inquest is usually set up when a prisoner or an accused person dies suddenly in a jail cell or while under police custody. However, if a criminal proceeding has been instituted against the suspect, the coroner must suspend the investigation.

SPECIALIZED JUDICIAL BODIES

Since attaining independence in 1960, Nigeria has suffered under military dictatorships for thirty years. During the era of authoritarian rule, the military more often than not set up judicial bodies to sustain its coercion of civil society. Special military tribunals, for instance, were constituted during the Babangida and Abacha regimes to try people involved in what the government described as "civil disturbances" that threatened public peace and security. It was under one such tribunal that Ken Saro Wiwa and eight other Ogoni activists were hanged to death in 1995.

Apart from military tribunals, administrative tribunals were also used during the military regimes to investigate instances of communal conflicts and violence. They were usually fact-finding bodies constituted by the executive arm of government at the federal or state level; their charge was to ascertain the circumstances that necessitated setting up the tribunal and to proffer solutions. The experience in Nigeria suggests that, more often than not, administrative tribunals are really governmental strategies to avoid making the decisions needed to resolve societal problems, especially in the case of sharp ethnic and religious divisions.

The military regimes also established courts-martial to try officers involved in mutinies, coups, or other forms of treason. There was no appeal from the decision of a court-martial, since the abrogation of the right to appeal the decision of a court-martial by Degree 9 of 1985. Considering the deeply divided nature of the Nigerian military, courts-martial became weapons in the hands of autocratic rulers between 1955 and 1998 and were used to eliminate any form of opposition. Several innocent army officers were executed, detained, or tortured as the result of decisions issued by courts-martial initiated by military dictators.

Following the return to democratic rule on May 29, 1999, the civilian regime of Chief Olusegun Obasanjo established the Human Rights Violations Investigation Commission, which was empowered, among other things, to ascertain or establish the causes, nature, and extent of human rights violation or abuses, and investigates cases of mysterious deaths and assassinations committed in Nigeria. The commission is also to identify the persons, authorities, or institutions involved in such abuses and recommend measures that may be taken, whether judicial, administrative, legislative, or institutional, to redress past injustices and prevent or forestall future violations or abuses of human rights.

Although the commission is yet to finalize its investigations, preliminary findings from its public hearings suggest that there were gross abuses of human rights in Nigeria during the military era. Victims of such abuses were not only military personnel but also individuals from the media, labor, and academia, as well as prodemocracy activists who insisted on a return to the rule of law and good governance within a democratic framework.

Another important legal transformation in Nigeria's new democratic disposition is the establishment of the Independent Anticorruption Commission, aimed at checking corrupt practices in the country's body politic. The bill enacted by the National Assembly, which went into effect in 1999, empowers the commission to receive and investigate any report of conspiracy to commit, attempt to commit, or commission of a corrupt practice and, in appropriate cases, to prosecute the offenders. The bill also provides that the prosecution for an offense under the act shall be initiated by the attorney general of the federation in any superior court of record so designated by the chief judge of a state or the chief judge of the federation capital territory.

STAFFING

Judges are usually appointed through a prescribed procedure by the president or governor, acting on the recommendation of the National Judicial Commission. They must be learned in law (or the Islamic legal system, in the case of the Sharia Courts), and have been in the legal profession for at least fifteen years in the case of the superior courts or ten years in the case of local courts. Once appointed, they cannot be removed without cause, and they hold office until the age of seventy. However, should they commit grievous offenses, judges can be disciplined or relieved.

The Nigerian Law School in Lagos has been the main institution for training legal practitioners in the country. Recently, more campuses were established in Abuja, Kano, and Enugu to accommodate the large number of students completing their basic law course at several Nigerian universities. In addition, the Institute for Advanced Legal Studies in Lagos offers further training for legal practitioners. The Nigerian Bar Association is the only central professional union for legal practitioners in the country.

IMPACT: LAW AND DEMOCRATIZATION

At the root of the dilemmas of the postcolonial Nigerian state are not only its ethnoreligious cleavages and deeply embedded cultural pluralism but also the complexity of its legal system as well as the decades of military autocracy that exacerbated human rights abuses and eroded the institutional capacity of the state itself over the years.

The judiciary, which is supposed to be autonomous in terms of administering and dispensing justice, upholding the rule of law, and defending citizens' rights, was fundamentally subverted and compromised under military rule. During the controversy over the annulment of the June 12, 1993, presidential election results, for instance, judges from different parts of the country issued conflicting opinions about the military annulment of the election results. Instead of upholding justice by ruling on the legality of the election results and its winner, the judiciary compromised its autonomy and ultimately legitimated the subversion of a free and fair election in Nigeria's democratic transition.

With the enthronement of a democratic social order on May 29, 1999, Nigeria once again emerged from the clutches of military autocracy. The current democratic environment, which is anchored in the doctrine of the separation of powers, promises a brighter future for Nigeria's judiciary and the legal system in general. Similarly, the inauguration of the Human Rights Violation Investigation Commission and the Independent Anticorruption Commission indicates that the present regime is returning Nigeria to the path of justice—guaranteeing the human rights of its citizens, upholding the rule of law, and ensuring transparency and accountability in governance. The establishment of three additional law school campuses suggests that the civilian regime, unlike its military predecessors, is determined to strengthen not only the training of legal personnel but also the judiciary. A well-equipped and autonomous judiciary is essential for the sustenance of democratic rule, thereby fostering a political and economic environment capable of attracting foreign investment. Whether Nigeria will sustain the current momentum of democratization and return to the rule of law remains a major challenge for this potentially great country in sub-Saharan Africa.

Dauda Abubakar

See also Administrative Tribunals; Appellate Courts; Civil
Law; Constitutional Review; Criminal Procedures; Customary
Law; Human Rights Law; Islamic Law; Juvenile Justice
References and further reading
Ake, Claude. 1996. *Democracy and Development.* Washington,
    DC: Brookings Institution.
Beckett, Paul, and Crawford Young, eds. 1997. *Dilemmas of
    Democracy in Nigeria.* Rochester, NY: University of
    Rochester Press.
Dada, Tunde. 1998. *General Principles of Law.* Lagos: Folarin
    Nigeria.
Diamond, Larry, Oyeleye Oyediran, and Alex Aboyega, eds.
    1997. *Transition without End: Nigeria Politics and Civil
    Society under Babangida.* Boulder, CO: Lynne Rienner.
Elias, Taslim. 1971. *Nigerian Land Law.* London: Sweet and
    Maxwell.
———. 1990. *Judicial Process in the Newer Commonwealth.*
    Lagos: University of Lagos Press.
Federal Government of Nigeria. 1999. *Independent Anti-
    Corruption Commission Bill.* Lagos: Federal Government
    Press.
Joseph, Richard. 1956. *The Nature of African Customary Law.*
    Manchester, England: Manchester University Press.
———. 1987. *Democracy and Prebendal Politics in Nigeria:
    The Rise and Fall of the Second Republic.* New York and
    Cambridge: Cambridge University Press.
———. 1996. "Nigeria: Inside the Dismal Tunnel." *Current
    History* 95, no. 601: 193–200.
Obilade, Ayo. 1979. *The Nigerian Legal System.* London:
    Sweet and Maxwell.
Osaghae, Eghosa. 1998. *Crippled Giant: Nigeria since
    Independence.* London: C. Hurst.
Young, Crawford. 1976. *The Politics of Cultural Pluralism.*
    Madison: University of Wisconsin Press.

NOMINATING COMMISSION PLAN
See Merit Selection ("Missouri Plan")

NORTH CAROLINA

GENERAL INFORMATION

North Carolina is a state in the southeastern United
States, bordered by the state of Virginia to the north, the
Atlantic Ocean to the east, the states of South Carolina
and Georgia to the south, and Tennessee to the west.
North Carolina contains 52,669 square miles and ranks
twenty-eighth in size among the states. The state is physically diverse from east to west, with a lengthy coastline
in the east, flowing into a flat coastal plain, then a rolling
Piedmont plateau region bounded by forested Ap-
palachian Mountains in the west.

North Carolina was the eleventh most populous U.S.
state in 2000, with 8,049,313 residents. State population
grew 21 percent between 1990 and 2000. In 2000, 72

percent of North Carolinians were white, 22 percent
black, and 1 percent Native American. Five percent of
the population was Hispanic; Hispanic population increased by more than 400 percent between 1990 and
2000. Tobacco, textiles, and furniture dominated the
North Carolina economy well into the twentieth century.
While the state is among the top agricultural producers
in the United States, farming is a decreasing portion of
North Carolina's economy. Technology, trade, finance,
and tourism are expanding parts of the economy.

EVOLUTION AND HISTORY

During the sixteenth century, English, French, and Spanish explorers visited the Carolina region, where more
than thirty different Native American tribes were living.
English influence increased throughout the seventeenth
century, and in 1663, King Charles II of England made
eight of his supporters the Lord Proprietors of Carolina.
The Lord Proprietors promulgated taxes, established
local governments, and appointed officials, including a
governor. Today's legal and judicial systems are influenced by the Lord Proprietors. The Lord Proprietors
called their court system the "General Court." They appointed "justices" to oversee the courts and "justices of
the peace" to try basic criminal and civil matters.

North Carolina was one of the original thirteen English colonies in North America. It became the twelfth of
the original thirteen states when it ratified and consented
to the first U.S. Constitution in 1789. In 1861 it seceded
from the Union and joined the Confederacy in the U.S.
Civil War. North Carolina returned to the Union in
1868.

Over nearly two centuries as a state, North Carolina
developed a two-tier court system. One tier contained a
Supreme Court as the appellate court and a Superior
Court as the general jurisdiction trial court. Both of these
courts were funded by the state and were uniform
statewide. In the lower tier, local courts handled trial of
matters not in the jurisdiction of the Superior Court. In
the 1950s, North Carolina's cities and counties operated
and funded more than 250 such lower courts. Types of
courts, kinds of judicial officials, court jurisdiction, and
funding levels varied widely from location to location.
Clerks of court and justices of the peace worked on a fee
basis. For instance, a justice of the peace might receive a
fee for finding a defendant guilty, but not for a finding of
innocence. Judicial officials could hold other offices as
well; for example, a justice of the peace might also be a
law enforcement officer.

Judges became elected officials as part of post–Civil
War reforms in 1868. This may have been the most important change in North Carolina's court system between
the Colonial period and the mid-twentieth century. Between 1955 and 1970, North Carolina's courts changed

extensively, as a result of constitutional and legislative reforms. These reforms grew out of the work of the Committee on Improving and Expediting the Administration of Justice in North Carolina. It was created by the North Carolina Bar Association after a call for reform by Governor Luther Hodges in 1955. In 1962, North Carolina voters approved a constitutional amendment creating the court system recommended by the committee and in place today; this system began to operate in 1966. Hallmarks of the new system are operation from the state level and uniformity across the state. Administration and budgeting of the court system are centralized. All court employees and officials are paid by the state. An Administrative Office of the Courts, under the direction of the chief justice, administers the system; it also presents a single court system budget to the General Assembly (the state legislature). A new trial court, called the District Court, replaced local courts and received jurisdiction over some matters formerly held by the Superior Court. Magistrates replaced justices of the peace and other local judicial officials. The committee also recommended a new appellate court, the Court of Appeals, which was created in 1967.

CURRENT STRUCTURE

North Carolina's court system is called the General Court of Justice. Defined by the state constitution and a body of state statutes, it is composed of the District Court Division, the Superior Court Division, and the Appellate Division. District and Superior Court officials generally are organized and operate within districts across the state established by statute. The District and Superior Court Divisions mostly do trial work, while the two courts of the Appellate Division handle appeals from those divisions as well as some executive agencies. As in most states, North Carolina executive agencies retain authority to adjudicate some disputes over agency action. The Office of Administrative Hearings provides administrative law judges as independent hearing officers in these matters, called contested cases. Contested case decisions may be appealed to the agency, then into the General Court of Justice, as noted below.

The District Court Division
The two basic officials of this division are the District Court judge and the magistrate. In 2000, North Carolina had 225 District Court judges and about 700 magistrates. The chief justice appoints one judge in each district as a chief District Court judge. That judge is responsible for assigning district judges to sessions of court, assigning and supervising magistrates, assigning small claims cases to magistrates for trial, and working with the other chief District Court judges to create a uniform statewide schedule of fines for magistrates to use.

This division's work is varied and complex. It handles more cases than any of the others, and it has jurisdiction in civil, criminal, and juvenile matters. District Court and Superior Court have concurrent jurisdiction over civil matters. If the amount in controversy is $10,000 or less, a case typically starts in the District Court; the Superior Court is the proper division for cases with amounts in controversy greater than $10,000. A civil trial before a District Court judge may have a jury if requested by the parties, but typically it does not, and the judge decides the case. Civil cases involving amounts of $4,000 or less are sometimes assigned to a magistrate for trial as a "small claims" action. This category includes actions by landlords to evict tenants. Magistrates decide civil cases without the assistance of a jury. Their decisions may be appealed to the District Court, where there is a complete new trial.

Some civil matters are handled by District Court judges, regardless of an amount in controversy. These include family law matters, such as divorce, custody, and support of children; juvenile matters, such as the disciplining of delinquent juveniles or resolving allegations of neglect and abuse; and the involuntary commitment of the mentally ill. In some districts pilot family courts have been established to deal with multiple issues of particular families by assigning them to the same judge and providing more intensive case management than is normal.

The bulk of the District Court's criminal work is administering and trying misdemeanor cases, which include traffic cases. Criminal trials in District Court are always without juries. District Court judges hold preliminary hearings to determine whether probable cause is present for felony matters to proceed to a grand jury for indictment. Magistrates issue search and arrest warrants and set bail. They also accept guilty pleas (1) to minor misdemeanors and infractions (noncriminal violations of law, typically traffic offenses); (2) to certain traffic, littering, alcohol, and related violations; and (3) in worthless-check cases for checks of $2,000 or less. In many of these kinds of cases, magistrates set fines based on a uniform statewide schedule established by the state's chief District Court judges. As with civil decisions, a magistrate's ruling may be appealed to the District Court for a complete new trial. In addition to their civil and criminal duties, the magistrate performs some quasi-judicial functions formerly discharged by justices of the peace, such as performing marriage ceremonies.

The Superior Court Division
The Superior Court has civil and criminal jurisdiction. The Superior Court typically handles civil cases in which the amount in controversy is greater than $10,000. Cases tried only in Superior Court include those involving constitutional issues, eminent domain actions, requests for

Structure of North Carolinian Courts

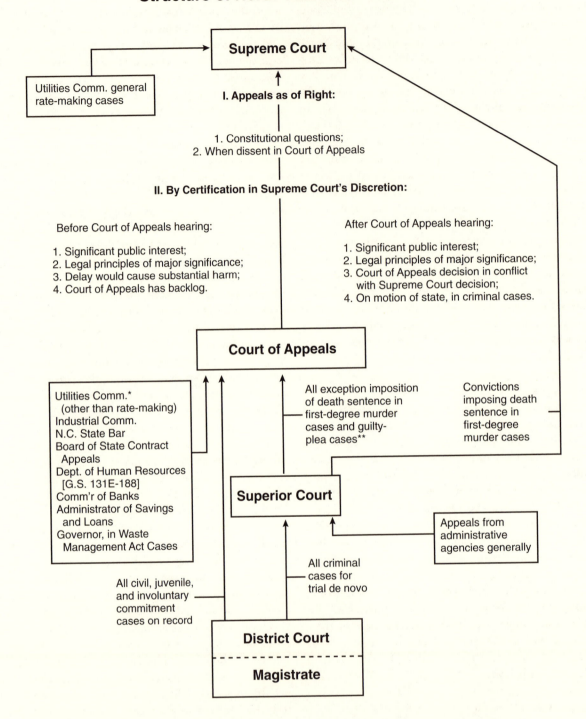

Supreme Court

Utilities Comm. general rate-making cases

I. Appeals as of Right:

1. Constitutional questions;
2. When dissent in Court of Appeals

II. By Certification in Supreme Court's Discretion:

Before Court of Appeals hearing:

1. Significant public interest;
2. Legal principles of major significance;
3. Delay would cause substantial harm;
4. Court of Appeals has backlog.

After Court of Appeals hearing:

1. Significant public interest;
2. Legal principles of major significance;
3. Court of Appeals decision in conflict with Supreme Court decision;
4. On motion of state, in criminal cases.

Court of Appeals

Utilities Comm.*
 (other than rate-making)
Industrial Comm.
N.C. State Bar
Board of State Contract
 Appeals
Dept. of Human Resources
 [G.S. 131E-188]
Comm'r of Banks
Administrator of Savings
 and Loans
Governor, in Waste
 Management Act Cases

All exception imposition of death sentence in first-degree murder cases and guilty-plea cases**

Convictions imposing death sentence in first-degree murder cases

Superior Court

Appeals from administrative agencies generally

All civil, juvenile, and involuntary commitment cases on record

All criminal cases for trial de novo

District Court

- - - - - - - - - - - - - - - - - - - -

Magistrate

* Appeals from the agencies must be heard by Court of Appeals before Supreme Court can hear them.
** Post conviction-hearing appeals and reviews of valuation of exempt property under G.S. Ch. 1C are final with the Court of Appeals.

injunctions, and appeals from contested case decisions by state executive agencies. A civil case may be tried by a jury or the presiding judge, as requested by the parties.

Felony criminal cases are tried in Superior Court before a jury of twelve. About a third of criminal cases in Superior Court are appeals of misdemeanor convictions from District Court. This involves a completely new trial and always is heard by a jury. The jury decides guilt or innocence, and the judge sentences convicted defendants.

The state constitution requires that Superior Court judges rotate, or ride the circuit from one district to another within a particular region designated by law. In recent years, this has meant that Superior Court judges are assigned to particular judicial districts for a six-month period and then rotate to other districts in the next time period. This system descends from the days of the Lord Proprietors, when lack of both judges and court business necessitated circuit riding.

The clerk of Superior Court is responsible for all clerical and record-keeping functions of the District and Superior Courts. The clerk also acts as a judge. The clerk's jurisdiction includes determining the validity of wills and supervising the administration of estates of decedents, minors, and incompetents. The clerk hears special proceedings such as adoptions and has powers to carry out some magistrate functions. Most appeals of clerk decisions are to the Superior Court. Clerks have assistants and deputies to carry out their various functions.

In 2000 there were 105 Superior Court judges. There are 100 clerks of Superior Court, one for each county. Regular Superior Court judges are elected in districts. The governor is authorized by statute to appoint special Superior Court judges who are not tied to particular districts. Each Superior Court district has one senior resident Superior Court judge, with administrative responsibilities within the district.

The Appellate Division

The Court of Appeals and the Supreme Court compose this division. Both courts resolve questions of law, rather than questions of fact. Cases come to them from trial courts, with a record of what happened there. The Court of Appeals is an intermediate appellate court, and the Supreme Court is the highest court in the jurisdiction. The Court of Appeals is the first level court of appeal for some state executive administrative agencies, such as the Industrial Commission, which resolves employment matters such as disagreements over workers' compensation. Two kinds of appeals bypass the Court of Appeals and go directly to the Supreme Court: (1) Superior Court first-degree murder convictions in which the defendant is punished by the death penalty, and (2) general rate-making cases from the state Utilities Commission. Appealing parties have a right to have two kinds of cases automatically heard by the Supreme Court on appeal from the Court of Appeals: (1) appeals involving a constitutional question, and (2) cases with a dissenting opinion in the Court of Appeals. All other appeals are permissive; upon request the Supreme Court may decide to hear arguments in such cases.

Twelve judges comprise the Court of Appeals. They hear cases in panels of three. The Supreme Court has a chief justice and six associate justices. They sit as a group to hear arguments in cases appealed from lower courts. Both courts hear most of their cases in Raleigh, the state capital.

NOTABLE FEATURES OF LAW/LEGAL SYSTEM

North Carolina is notable for its unified, statewide, and state-operated court system. Most of the court system's funding is provided by the state, similar rules and courts are in place across the state, and employees and officials are paid by the state, rather than by local governments. In addition to the judicial officials discussed above, this system organizes and employs prosecutors, public defenders, guardians ad litem (persons who serve as advocates for a child in a court proceeding), trial court administrators, and court reporters. For so many judicial functions to be state-based rather than locally controlled is unusual in the United States.

STAFFING

Judges of the District, Superior, and Appellate Courts must be lawyers. They serve full-time and may not practice law privately. Judges of the Court of Appeals and Supreme Court are elected to eight-year terms in statewide partisan elections. Superior Court judges are nominated by the voters of their district and elected in statewide nonpartisan races for eight-year terms. District Court judges are nominated and elected for four-year terms by the voters of their district in partisan elections. The governor fills vacancies in judgeships. Since the late 1960s many bills have been introduced in the General Assembly to change how judges are selected, but the only significant amendment to date has been changing selection of Superior Court judges from partisan to nonpartisan elections in the 1990s.

Judges are expected to follow the Code of Judicial Conduct. They are subject to review for improper behavior by a Judicial Standards Commission. Upon a recommendation from that commission, the Supreme Court may discipline or remove judges. Judges must earn thirty hours of approved continuing legal or judicial education each year. At least twenty hours must be continuing judicial education. Every judge in the trial division must attend an orientation provided by the Administrative Office of the Courts within their first year after appointment or election. The General Assembly may impeach judges. North

Carolina has a mandatory retirement age of seventy-two for judges.

Magistrates need not be lawyers. They are appointed for two-year terms by the senior resident Superior Court judge on nomination by the clerk of Superior Court. They are supervised by the chief District Court judge in judicial matters and the clerk of court in clerical matters. Magistrates are not under the jurisdiction of the Judicial Standards Commission; however, they may be disciplined or removed for misconduct by a Superior Court judge. Magistrates must attend a two-week training course during their first term. All magistrates appointed after July 1, 1994, must either be college graduates or have an associate degree and four years of experience in a related field. Magistrates meet several times annually for continuing education. There is no mandatory retirement age for magistrates.

A clerk of Superior Court is elected for a four-year term in each county. A clerk need not be a lawyer. In the event of misconduct or mental or physical incapacity, the senior resident Superior Court judge of the clerk's county may remove the clerk after notice and hearing. Clerks and their assistants have several continuing education events each year.

In 2000, 18,118 lawyers possessed a certificate of license to practice law in North Carolina. Lawyers are authorized to practice by passing the state bar exam or showing that they have for four of the past six years been licensed for full-time practice in another jurisdiction. In order to sit for the bar exam, candidates must be graduates of an American Bar Association–approved law school. Lawyers are subject to disciplinary action by the state bar. Active members of the bar must take twelve hours of continuing legal education approved by the state bar in each calendar year. A portion of these hours must be devoted to the topic of ethics or professional responsibility. A variety of public and private organizations offer continuing education.

Thomas H. Thornburg

See also Judicial Selection, Methods of; Juries; United States—Federal System; United States—State Systems

References and further reading
Brannon, Joan. 2000. *The Judicial System in North Carolina.* Raleigh, NC: Administrative Office of the Courts.
Commission for the Future of Justice and the Courts in North Carolina. 1996. *Without Favor, Denial or Delay: A Court System for the 21st Century.* Raleigh, NC.
Drennan, James C. 1998. "The Courts." Pp. 903–926 in *County Government in North Carolina.* Edited by A. Fleming Bell, II, and Warren Jake Wicker. Chapel Hill: Institute of Government, University of North Carolina.
Orr, Douglas M., Jr., and Alfred W. Stuart, eds. 2000. *The North Carolina Atlas: Portrait for a New Century.* Chapel Hill: University of North Carolina Press.
Powell, William S. 1989. *North Carolina through Four Centuries.* Chapel Hill: University of North Carolina Press.
Thornburg, Thomas H. 2000. *An Introduction to Law for North Carolinians.* Chapel Hill: Institute of Government, University of North Carolina.

NORTH DAKOTA

GENERAL INFORMATION

The state of North Dakota, one of the fifty U.S. states, is the northernmost plains state, bordered by Montana to the west, South Dakota to the south, Minnesota to the east, and the Canadian provinces of Manitoba and Saskatchewan to the north. It spans about 70,704 square miles and consists primarily of agricultural land dotted with small to medium-sized towns. The state has a current population of approximately 642,200 people, meaning that it is the forty-seventh most populous state. The largest cities by population are Fargo (approximately 74,100 people) and the state capital, Bismarck (approximately 49,200 people). The vast majority of the population is white (95 percent), with 3–4 percent Native American and 2–3 percent African American, Asian, and other.

North Dakota's land is mostly agricultural, and so is its economic base. Farming is the state's largest industry, as more than 25 percent of the state population is employed either by agriculture directly or in agriculture-related businesses. Agricultural production and manufacturing make up more than 37 percent of the state's total economic productivity. North Dakota is first among the fifty states in production of durum wheat, spring wheat, barley, sunflowers, pinto beans, all dry edible beans, flaxseed, and canola.

North Dakota was the home for various Native American tribes for hundreds of years before European settlement, including the Lakota, Assiniboine, Cheyenne, Mandan, Hidatsa, Arikara, Chippewa, Cree, Blackfeet, Crow, and others. The visit by travelers Meriwether Lewis and William Clark in 1804 marked the advent of U.S. migration to the region—the capital city of Bismarck was founded only eight years later. The land that would become North and South Dakota gained territorial status in 1861, but political considerations and battles between U.S. settlers and Native Americans (General George Custer left from Fort Mandan in Dakota for his ill-fated march to Little Big Horn) delayed statehood until 1889. During territorial days, the railroads brought waves of immigrants, primarily from Scandinavian countries and Germany, with lesser numbers of Scots, Irish, and English, the backbone of North Dakota's population ever since.

EVOLUTION AND HISTORY

North Dakota's politics have often been fractious, dominated by battles between populist and progressive forces on one side and advocates for state economic development on the other. The populist influence was seen in the construction of the judiciary under the 1889 Constitution. The judicial branch consisted of a state Supreme Court, district courts, county courts, justice of the peace courts, and such municipal courts as provided by law. In other words, the court system was relatively decentralized, in keeping with populist local control. Changes came slowly, but eventually North Dakota's judiciary moved toward unification. In 1959, the legislature abolished justice of the peace courts. In 1976, the legislature revamped the judicial article of the state constitution, unifying the court system under the state Supreme Court. District courts were retained, as well as any other courts provided by law. By 1983, the legislature had replaced the multilevel county court structure with a uniform system of county courts throughout the state. In 1991, however, the legislature decided to abolish the county courts altogether (effective in 1995) and to transfer the workload to the district courts. The only minor step toward increasing judicial bureaucracy was the creation of a Court of Appeals in 1987, with statewide, but very limited, jurisdiction. (Although most of this entry will focus on the state's primary legal system, it should also be mentioned that there are four tribal judicial systems in North Dakota as well.)

CURRENT STRUCTURE

The Legal Profession and Training

There are nearly 1,900 attorneys licensed to practice in North Dakota, although this figure includes out-of-state attorneys as well. About 1,300 are currently active. North Dakota is a "closed-bar" state, meaning that a lawyer must join the state bar association in order to practice full-time in the state. The only law school approved by the American Bar Association in North Dakota is the University of North Dakota Law School, located in Grand Forks.

Legal Aid and Criminal Defense Services

Prosecution of criminal cases is primarily the function of state's attorneys. These officers are elected in each county for four-year terms. Criminal defendants who cannot afford an attorney can get one appointed by a judge from a list maintained by the Indigent Defense Council, a state-funded organization supervised by the state Supreme Court. Lawyers sign up for two years at a time; around thirty-five total are presently on the list. The lawyers are paid a flat fee, and eligible clients have incomes of less than 125 percent of the federal poverty level.

In civil cases, legal representation for the indigent is provided from two main sources. First, the state bar association arranges representation for over 2,000 clients per year (pro bono or reduced fee) through a graduated set of programs. Persons with incomes of less than 125 percent

of the federal poverty line can get pro bono representation, with the state bar association individually arranging for a private practice attorney to step in. Persons with incomes of less than 187 percent of the poverty line can receive reduced-fee legal assistance from a lawyer who has signed up ahead of time with the state bar association. Lawyers may also put their names on a state bar association list for full-fee representation.

Second, Legal Assistance of North Dakota provides civil legal assistance to low-income clients as well. The major case categories include family law, social security, housing, consumer, and individual rights. Persons with incomes of less than 125 percent of the federal poverty line are eligible. The organization handles about 3,000 cases per year through staff attorneys, or more commonly, contracted lawyers.

Administrative Hearings

Regarding administrative hearings under the state's Administrative Agencies Practices Act (as well as a few other agency hearings), North Dakota partially follows the "central panel" model, in which one executive branch agency, the Office of Administrative Hearings (OAH), provides administrative law judges (ALJs) to several different state agencies. The major agencies that are required to use OAH include the Department of Human Services, the Agriculture Department, the attorney general (liquor licensing), the Board of Nursing, the Board of Medical Examiners, and the Department of Public Instruction, although over forty-five agencies have requested OAH ALJs since 1991.

Those agencies that are not required to use OAH are the Job Service North Dakota (unemployment compensation hearings), Department of Transportation (implied consent and driver's license suspension hearings), Workers Compensation Bureau (WCB), Public Service Commission (PSC), insurance commissioner, Industrial Commission, labor commissioner, and state engineer (except for two types of hearings for which the agency must use OAH). Some agencies, though, such as the PSC, WCB, insurance commissioner, Industrial Commission, etc. voluntarily use OAH ALJs for some or all of their hearings. The agencies that do not use OAH typically have their own, in-house hearing officers instead of employing attorneys in private practice. The Industrial Commission uses attorneys from the attorney general's office when not requesting OAH ALJs.

OAH uses full-time ALJs to conduct most agency hearings. However, it has authority to contract with attorneys in private practice to act as temporary ALJs to conduct hearings, and OAH uses temporary ALJs for many workers compensation hearings (by agreement with the bureau) and for some other types of hearings on an "as needed" basis.

Only when OAH was established in 1991 was there an effort to institute a full "central panel" model (i.e., in which all agencies would be required to use OAH). There have been no comprehensive efforts since, although deliberations are ongoing regarding the balance between agency flexibility and "universality." One unique feature of OAH's authority is its ability to conduct hearings for agencies without issuing a decision. In other words, the law only requires that the hearing be conducted by an independent ALJ if any agency so requests. If the ALJ acts as a "procedural" hearing officer, the agency head, instead of the hearing officer, then issues the decision. The agency head (not a subordinate) must be present at the hearing, however; usually only boards and commissions use this authority. Otherwise, if the ALJ is acting as a "substantive" hearing officer, the ALJ would issue a recommended decision. Appeals from final agency actions are heard in the district courts.

Judicial System

The North Dakota judicial system currently is headed by the Supreme Court, with supervisory authority over the Court of Appeals, district courts, municipal courts, and small claims courts (see figure).

Small claims courts are limited in jurisdiction to disputes involving less than $5,000. Even though the statutory basis for the small claims courts is separate, district court judges preside over the small claims courts as well. Judges are allowed to appoint referees to develop the factual record and engage in independent investigation of the facts. The legislature intended to allow individual claimants to seek justice without paying high attorney fees in these courts, but the most common users have been businesses collecting on debts and bad checks. There are no appeals from the decisions of the small claims courts.

Municipal courts number around seventy-five and are responsible for dealing with alleged violations of municipal ordinances, unless a juvenile is a defendant. These courts have no jurisdiction over state law issues. The bulk of these courts' dockets come from traffic violations and fine collections. Municipal court decisions can be appealed for a de novo trial in district court. However, noncriminal traffic cases cannot be appealed beyond the district court.

District courts are the primary trial courts in North Dakota for both civil and criminal cases. They have original jurisdiction over all state law issues and original jurisdiction in any case where a juvenile is a defendant, regardless of the source of the alleged violation. Appeals from administrative agency decisions are heard in the district courts. In 1999, approximately 143,300 cases were filed in the district courts, and about 155,700 were disposed there, a slight increase from the previous year.

Legal Structure of North Dakota Courts

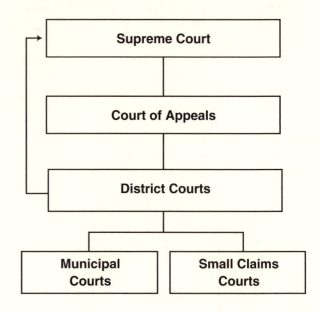

The legislature decides how many district court judgeships to fund, but the Supreme Court itself is responsible for dividing the state into districts and distributing judges to those districts. Currently, the Supreme Court has divided the state along county lines into seven districts, featuring multiple judges in each district for a total of forty-three (in 1999). Each district has a presiding judge, who has additional administrative and supervisory duties. Only three counties each are included in the two east-central districts featuring Grand Forks and Fargo, but the more rural districts comprise six to eleven counties. In fact, in contrast to most other states, the number of district judgeships has declined over time, mostly because of the state's decreasing population.

The district courts are not centrally located in one courthouse. Judges are expected to travel around the district, hearing cases in the county in which they originated—a vestige of the older county court system. The counties are responsible for the physical upkeep of the courtrooms. Consequently, each county also provides a clerk to handle administrative matters, except for the least populous counties, where the recorder of deeds is assigned the task.

As noted above, the *Court of Appeals* is a relatively recent creation, constituted in 1987 by the legislature. The court usually plays a minor role in the judicial system, though, as appeals usually go directly from the district courts to the Supreme Court. The Court of Appeals will only hear cases if the Supreme Court dockets over 250 cases in a year. Since its inception, the court has disposed of only sixty-seven cases (as of 1999) and, in the 1999 term, did not hear a single case. The legislature provides no separate funding for this court.

The North Dakota *Supreme Court* is the state's court of last resort. The court, composed of five justices as provided in the state constitution, has both adjudicative and administrative responsibilities. The court is headed by a chief justice, who is elected by a majority of the Supreme Court justices and district court judges for a five-year term, unless his or her term in office expires first. The chief justice represents the court at official state functions, presides over court conferences, and serves as the administrative head of the state judiciary.

The Supreme Court has been delegated rule-making power by the state legislature regarding judicial operations and procedures. This power includes promulgating codes of procedure and licensing and disciplining attorneys. Also, the court must decide how many judicial districts the state needs and draw the boundary lines between judicial districts. For each of these tasks, the court relies on the assistance of various boards and commissions, including the Disciplinary Board of the Supreme Court, Judicial Conduct Commission, Joint Procedure Commission, Joint Commission on Attorney Standards, Judicial Planning Committee, Juvenile Policy Board, Legal Counsel for Indigents Commission, and others. Furthermore, the court employs both a clerk and administrator. The clerk supervises the assignment and calendaring of cases, distributes the court's opinions, and decides occasional procedural matters. The administrator oversees the court's budget and prepares reports on the state judiciary's workload, among other duties.

In its adjudicative capacity, the Supreme Court exercises both original and appellate jurisdiction. The court only hears cases in original jurisdiction, though, that are of great statewide importance. Otherwise, the court's docket is appellate, and essentially mandatory—most appeals are of right. Consequently, the court's caseload is large, at least compared with the U.S. Supreme Court, typically including well over 200 cases per year orally argued. The North Dakota Supreme Court is required to issue a written opinion in each case (although about one-third of appeals are disposed of by order), and dissenting opinions must be allowed. There are concurring or dissenting opinions in approximately one-fifth of the cases disposed of by full opinion. Also unlike U.S. Supreme Court appeals, in 22 percent of the cases a party appeared *pro se* (without a lawyer), in keeping with North Dakota's populist tradition.

One relatively uncommon feature of the North Dakota Supreme Court's constitutional authority is that four out of the five justices must agree in order to declare an act of the legislature unconstitutional. This provision is likely a result of the populist heritage placing greater faith in elected politicians than relatively independent (albeit still elected) judges. This provision can play a role in legislative-judicial interactions, such as when the court

voted 3–2 in 1994 to void the state system of funding public schools as violating the "uniform(ity)" required by the state constitution (Article 8, Section 2) in *Bismarck Public School District #1 v. State* (511 N.W.2d 247). Since the supermajority was not reached, the system could constitutionally continue.

Civil cases comprise around 70 percent of the court's docket, and 30 percent are criminal appeals. Workers compensation cases and family law issues such as divorce, child custody or support, marital property, and alimony together accounted for 22 percent of the workload. Other notable civil case areas include employer-employee disputes, oil and gas cases, real property cases, and paternity contests. The most common criminal appeals involved drug convictions, sexual offenses, miscellaneous statutory felonies, and postconviction relief proceedings.

STAFFING

Judges in North Dakota are selected by a variety of mechanisms, most of which are tailored to fit the state's unique characteristics. Municipal court judges are elected for four-year terms on a nonpartisan basis. These judges do not have to be attorneys, except in cities with over 5,000 population. Even this requirement can be waived if no lawyer is available to serve. In part because of a small population, municipal judges do not have to be residents of the towns they serve, and judges can preside over multiple courts concurrently. Vacancies are filled by city governing boards. District court judges are elected on a nonpartisan ballot for six-year terms. They must be attorneys and state residents. A typical campaign can cost between $20,000 and $40,000 to run, although a strong majority of these elections are uncontested. In case of a vacancy, the governor appoints a judge with the assistance of the judicial nominating commission (discussed below). One uncommon feature of North Dakota law is that either party to litigation can remove up to one judge from his or her case without cause. This is true even if it means that another district judge will have to assume jurisdiction in a different county than regularly assigned. Judges for the court of appeals can be sitting district court judges, retired district court judges, or retired Supreme Court justices.

North Dakota's original constitution, adopted in 1889, provided for only three justices of the state Supreme Court, serving six-year terms. By 1908, however, caseload pressures led the legislature to increase the court membership to five. In 1930, the judicial term was lengthened to ten years. Justices, who must be attorneys, are elected on a nonpartisan ballot for the ten-year term. Frequently, however, justices will not serve the full term, in which case a replacement must be selected. The new justice will fill out the rest of the term, even if there are intervening general elections. Around half of North

Dakota's Supreme Court justices have initially been selected as interim appointments.

The replacement process starts with the Judicial Nominating Commission, composed of nine members, six permanent and three temporary. The governor, chief justice, and president of the state bar association each select two permanent members and one temporary member. The temporary members are selected only if a district judgeship is vacant; in this case, these temporary members must reside in the vacant district. If a Supreme Court justice must be replaced, only the permanent members participate. These members will send a list of two to seven names to the governor. The governor can make a recommendation from the list, ask for a new list, or call a special election instead.

Matthew H. Bosworth

See also Administrative Tribunals; Appellate Courts; Judicial Selection, Methods of; Juvenile Justice; Legal Aid; Merit Selection ("Missouri Plan"); Pro Se Cases; Small Claims Courts; United States—Federal System; United States—State Systems

References and further reading
Hoberg, Allen C., director, Office of Administrative Hearings, personal communication, December 4, 2000.
Kramer, Marcella. 1988. *A Historical Sketch of the Dakota Territory and North Dakota Supreme Court.* Bismarck: North Dakota Supreme Court.
Melone, Albert, Loren Braud, and Brucer Ough. 1975. *North Dakota Lawyers: Mapping the Social-Political Dimensions.* Publisher's Social Science Report Series No. 1. Fargo: North Dakota Institute for Regional Studies.
North Dakota Supreme Court. 1999. *Annual Report.* Bismarck: North Dakota Supreme Court. Also available at http://www.court.state.nd.us/court/news/AnnualReport1999/ (cited September 14, 2000).
Omdahl, Lloyd B. 1999. *Governing North Dakota 1999–2001.* Grand Forks, ND: Bureau of Government Affairs.
Robinson, Elwyn B. 1995. *History of North Dakota.* Fargo: North Dakota Institute for Regional Studies.
VandeWalle, Gerald W. 1995. *State of the Judiciary Message.* Bismarck: North Dakota Supreme Court.

NORTH KOREA

COUNTRY INFORMATION

North Korea, formally known as the Democratic People's Republic of Korea, is located on the northern part of the Korean Peninsula, which is at the juncture of the northeast Asian continent and the Japanese archipelago. It shares a border with China to the north at the Yalu and Tumen Rivers (1,433 kilometers) and with Russia to the northeast (17 kilometers). Its southern border (241 kilometers) at the thirty-eighth parallel divides it from South Korea (formally known as the Republic of Korea). Approximately 2,495 kilometers of coastline edge the Yellow and East Seas on the west and east, respectively. Located between 38° and 43° degrees north latitude and between 124° and 130° degrees east longitude, North Korea occupies 120,410 square kilometers (about the size of the state of New York or Louisiana). Only 18 percent of the land is arable; 80 percent consists of mountains and uplands. The country has a humid continental climate, with four distinct seasons and heavy precipitation in summer.

North Korea has approximately 22 million inhabitants (homogeneously Korean, with a negligible number of ethnic Chinese and Japanese), 2.3 million of whom reside in its capital, Pyongyang. The national language is Korean, and the literacy rate is as high as 99 percent due to its well-organized, eleven-year compulsory public education system. However, North Korea's gross domestic product (GDP) is only U.S.$22.6 billion, and its per capita income is no more than U.S.$1,000 (these figures are ambiguous due to the lack of transparent state management). In addition to its relatively low GDP, natural disasters since 1995 and the collapse of other communist countries have exacerbated its subsistence economy and driven the majority of its population into extreme poverty and famine. The country's legal system is based on old Soviet legal theory, which was strongly influenced by the civil law system.

HISTORY

Ancient Korea was divided into three kingdoms and not unified until 668 C.E. by the Silla Dynasty, a rule that lasted until the end of the ninth century. After a brief regression into a three-kingdom division early in the tenth century, the peninsula was once again unified by the Koryo Dynasty in 936 C.E., replaced by the Chosun (or Yi) Dynasty in 1392 C.E. It fell to violent Japanese imperialism at the turn of the twentieth century. Each dynasty was quite successful in maintaining centralized control of the peninsula. In particular, the Chosun Dynasty achieved a high degree of centralization based on neo-Confucianism. One distinct aspect of neo-Confucianism is the emphasis on hierarchical order elaborated by ruling Confucian scholars. A sense of domination-subordination was the essence of a hierarchy that was carefully defined into orderly classes in terms of various criteria. Benevolence was the grace of superiors, while unconditional obedience was required of inferiors. Family, not individual, was considered a social unit in society. All organization, including that of the state, was conceived as a large family, with paternalism prevailing at every corner.

Japanese colonization of the peninsula followed the Chosun Dynasty from 1910 until liberation in 1945, a period characterized by strong Korean resistance to harsh Japanese rule. The Japanese defeat in World War II liberated Korea, but the circumstances of demilitarizing the existing Japanese forces by both Soviet and U.S. troops led to the establishment of a temporary partition of the

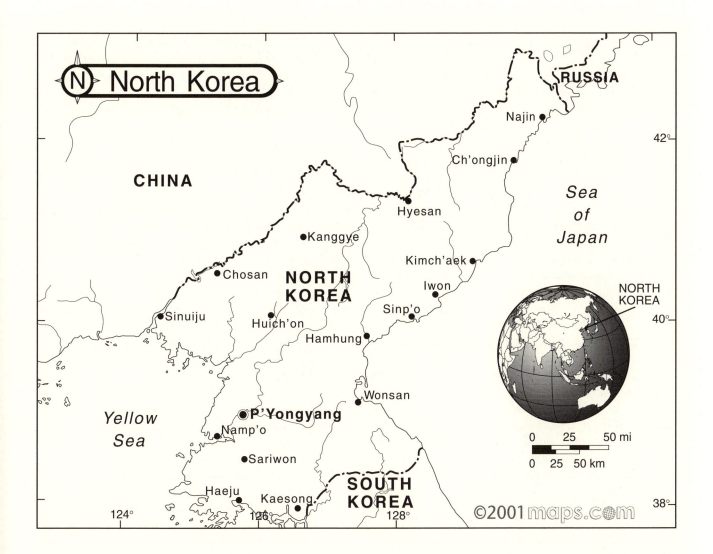

peninsula at the thirty-eighth parallel. As a result of this foreign involvement, the ideological confrontation of the Cold War descended on the region, and this temporary partition led to a historical mishap that would give rise to the existence of two hostile nations.

In the heightening Cold War atmosphere, the United Nations failed to reach an agreement to establish one united government. This led to the inauguration of separate North and South Korean governments in 1948. While the South was founded on the basis of Western democracy, the North adopted the Soviet model of communism. Taking advantage of the incipient, fragile, and unstable democratic plurality of South Korean society, North Korea staged a blitzkrieg against the South in 1950 in order to create a unified government under communism. A three-year fratricidal war ensued, resulting in millions of casualties, and ended only after U.S.-led UN intervention led both sides to reach an armistice by dividing the North and South with the current truce line (the demilitarized zone, or DMZ). At present, no peace treaty has been established to replace the armistice, and the DMZ remains one of the most tense and heavily armed border areas in the world. This internecine civil war between the North and the South has been a significant obstacle in efforts for the two sides to restore a sincere dialogue. However, the collapse of the communist bloc and the Cold War system provided the two with a favorable environment for dialogue in the 1990s, with the world-shocking North-South Summit in June 2000 being the ultimate achievement of the dialogue thus far.

After the division of the Korean Peninsula in 1945, North Korean leader Kim Il Sung, who was fully supported by the Soviet Union at the beginning of state foundation, had consolidated his power by purging his opponents in Stalinist fashion. His record as a resistance fighter against Japanese occupation troops contributed to his commanding political legitimacy as a hero of North Korea. As he solidified his leadership, he practiced a dictatorship unparalleled in any other society in the world. Confrontation with the South contributed to sustaining and strengthening tensions for the sake of his domestic rule. His success in maintaining the totalitarian dictatorship can be attributed to the buildup of pervasive security forces, indoctrination of the people with a "cult of personality," and isolation of the entire populace from the outside world. The success of his near half-century of one-man rule was further evidenced by the easy succession of his heir-appointed son, Kim Jong Il, on his death in 1994.

Under a planned economy, North Korea has conducted orthodox Marxism-Leninism by state and collective ownership. Autarky as a principle has limited the nation to trading only with brethren communist states. The apparatuses that enabled Kim Il Sung to effectively maintain his one-man rule were the Korean Workers' Party's supremacy over government organizations and his so-called *juche* (self-reliance) ideology. North Korean leadership also fully facilitated the Confucian tradition and the Japanese colonial legacy that still remained pervasive in Korean thinking and behavior.

The Korean Workers' Party has functioned as the power base of North Korean leaders. It is perceived, without question, as the sole representative of the people's will, and it has unlimited authority. Party control is reinforced by party elites' interlocking membership with important people in the government and military. Its control is pervasive and reaches into the everyday lives of residents through indoctrination and surveillance. Isolation from the outside world, a rationing of all necessities, and restrictions of individual freedoms reinforce the party's firm grip over its populace.

The juche ideology, the backbone of party guidance and state philosophy, was formulated to justify Kim's dictatorship and the succession to his son by emphasizing peculiar aspects of the North Korean environment. The ideology, advocated as a creative application of Marxist-Leninist principles, also served as a justification for demanding from the populace unlimited loyalty to Kim's leadership. This later developed into a cult of personality surrounding Kim Il Sung and Kim Jong Il, officially supplanting all other philosophical and religious beliefs in the state.

After the collapse of the communist bloc and its members' reform toward a market economy, North Korea found its own survival, economically and politically, in peril. The normalization of South Korea's relationship with the Soviet Union and China in the early 1990s furthered the feeling of vulnerability in the North. The death of its "great leader" Kim Il Sung in 1994 and the following natural disasters made matters more problematic as they pushed North Korean society into mourning, poverty, and famine.

All of this compelled the extremely rigid, isolated, and closed communist society to open negotiations with South Korea and other Eastern powers and to employ a more flexible foreign policy. The dilemma of the North Korean leadership lies in the conflict between the necessity of having a flexible policy for survival and the possibility that the policy itself will undermine the absolute rule of the new leader, Kim Jong Il. However, in spite of its repeated proclamation to remain a staunch socialist state, no alternative other than foreign collaboration has appeared to resuscitate its devastated economy.

LEGAL CONCEPTS

The Democratic People's Republic of Korea, the official government of North Korea, was launched in 1948 with the inauguration of a new constitution modeled after Soviet Stalinism. This constitution was later replaced by the 1972 Constitution, which, among other things, eliminated the characteristic of collective leadership and provided Kim Il Sung with a presidency that would successfully solidify his absolute rule. Essentially, the Supreme People's Assembly (SPA), the highest legislative organ with state sovereignty, was given the power to elect the president to a four-year term (with limitless reappointment), a position that Kim Il Sung was the first to assume and that he held until his death. As president, he became head of state, supreme commander of the armed forces, and chairman of the National Defense Commission (NDC). The presidency also gave him the authority to implement law and policy as the top state executive.

The 1992 amendment to the constitution was made in preparation for the succession of his son. The key change was that the authority to command the armed forces was transferred to the chairman of the NDC, who was also elected by the Supreme People's Assembly. Predictably, the president's successor, Kim Jong Il, was elected as the chairman of the commission. In addition, the 1992 revision provided the legal ground for economic cooperation with foreign states, deemed necessary to help North Korea overcome its economic plight after the collapse of the communist bloc. It was also quite natural that the once prevalent Marxist-Leninist underpinnings were replaced by its juche idea to justify the North Korean version of socialism.

The latest constitutional revision took place in 1998, in an attempt to cope with the country's unfavorable domestic situation and the rapidly changing international environment. The 1998 Constitution abolished the presidency and the Central People's Committee, which was in charge of policymaking and supervised the policy implementation of the Administration Council. Instead, their authorities were transferred to the Supreme People's Assembly Presidium and the cabinet. More significant still, by extending the concept of national defense, the NDC became the highest state organ, with Kim Jong Il assuming the NDC chairmanship. From a legal standpoint, the SPA, composed of representatives from the general public (serving five-year terms), is the highest state organ that entertains sovereign legitimacy as a legislative body. One of its responsibilities is the election of important state officials (the chairman of the NDC and SPA Presidium, premier of the cabinet, chief procurator, chief justice, and so forth). However, the de facto supremacy of the NDC over other state organs and the system's abnormal structure better reflect the power and character of leader Kim Jong Il.

Although the constitution provides the principle of democratic centralism, the principle of democratic representation is no more than a superficial façade to justify totalitarian rule. The highest representative body, the Supreme People's Assembly, consists of representatives from the populace, one for every 30,000 people, chosen by means of universal, equal, direct, and secret vote. However, these representatives are carefully screened by the party before being forwarded to a popular vote. Because of this, the citizens' right to change the government by freely selecting their representatives is obstructed. As a principle, centralism does not embrace the separation of powers. According to socialist legal theory, state authority based on absolute majority rule is inherently monolithic and limitless. The idea of a limited government does not exist in a society that negates the rule of law. There are no checks and balances among state organs but only divisions of labor to implement delegated authority from above. The ultimate authority resides in the party, which is the supreme guiding body. Under these circumstances, the SPA is no more than a puppet acting on party demand. Never has there been a dissenting vote against proposals or candidates presented before the SPA. There are other political parties besides the ruling Korean Workers' Party, but they are government-sponsored, impotent, and obedient, in place only to provide the illusion of democracy.

The most powerful figure pulling the strings in North Korea is the general secretary of the Korean Workers' Party, Kim Jong Il. Since the party is the suprastructure above all government organizations, primary authority resides in his capacity as general secretary. The 1998 Constitution enables Kim Jong Il to manage state affairs behind the curtain, delegating ceremonial and functional roles to the chairman of the SPA Presidium, the cabinet, and others.

Although the North Korean Constitution has extensive provisions for individual freedoms and fundamental rights, North Korea is still viewed as one of the worst countries in terms of human rights protection by the United Nations, Amnesty International, and other such organizations. Obstacles in North Korea make direct monitoring of human rights violations difficult, though a significant volume of information does exist from the testimony of defectors, visitors, North Korean workers abroad, and the like. Regardless of these obstacles, it is not hard to make assumptions about the harsh conditions in terms of human rights, considering North Korea's asphyxiating control over society and the unre-

strained power of the state. In the constitution, Article 63 provides that the rights and duties of citizens are based on the collectivist principle of "one for all and all for one," a principle used to legitimize the unlimited sacrifice and subordination of individuals exacted by the state. The interests of the whole always take precedence, and individuals have no right to assert themselves. Acts that offend the heightened and pervasive collective consciousness are conceived as "political" crimes and accompanied by severe penalty. "Repressive law," as Emile Durkheim suggests, prevails.

In spite of elaborate guarantees, constitutional provisions concerning citizens' rights and freedoms cannot serve as a checking mechanism on the arbitrary exercise of the powers of public organs directed against the interests of individuals. Execution, disappearance, torture, arrest, and detention without appropriate judicial process are typical examples of human rights violations. The arbitrary interference of the public authority in private life is also routine. Unfortunately, citizens do not have meaningful ways to correct or remedy such violations. Other important freedoms (such as those of speech, press, assembly, association, and movement) are protected on paper but not in practice. The media and education are also centrally controlled, and they serve as important organs of state propaganda.

The other aspect that significantly restricts individual freedom is inherent in the centralized command economy of the socialist system. The means of production are owned by the state and social cooperative organizations. The state rations food, clothing, and housing to people. Other necessary services, such as education, medicine, legal assistance, and job allocation, are also provided by the state. The state is the sole allocator of resources, and no tax is levied on the citizens. Private property is limited to consumer products distributed by the state and acquired by transactions. Under this kind of economic system, the freedom of the individual is extremely limited. Moreover, workers are not allowed to exercise their collective rights. Citizens can only entertain their property ownership or freedom of contract by default from state intervention. Transactions among public entities and between public entities and citizens are so-called public contracts devoid of individual initiative or choice. Recently, peasant markets, the only exception to controlled marketing, have appeared in order to make up for the scarcity of everyday necessities, such as fresh vegetables and poultry items. In light of the current conditions, the government acquiesces in their existence.

The planned economy inevitably diminishes active participation on the part of individuals, due to a lack of personal incentive. To prevent laxity, the state reinforces ideology education and indoctrination. And unavoidably, the restraint on individual freedoms increases. This kind

Legal Structure of North Korea Courts

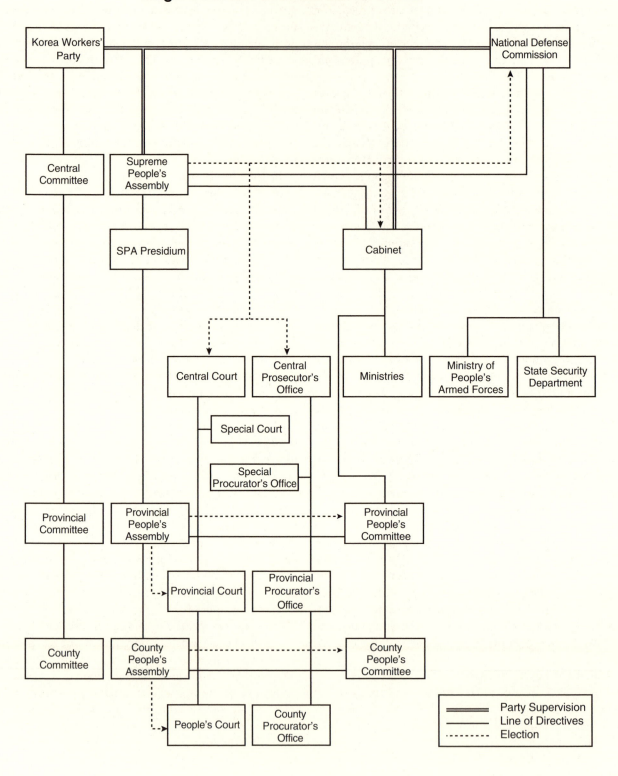

of vicious circle has inescapably resulted in the decline of productivity and has forced the authorities to turn to foreign investment despite the autarky beliefs of the regime. Isolation from the old socialist countries with whom they used to exchange products has accelerated the need for foreign trade and investment.

Since its first joint venture law in 1984, North Korea has enacted many relevant laws for foreign investment, and it designated a free economy and trade zone in the early 1990s. However, its poor infrastructure and bureaucratic red tape, let alone the xenophobic attitude that preserves political stability, have failed to attract foreign investment; only a limited engagement on the part of South Korean businesses and sympathetic Japanese Koreans exists. Despite this failure, one redeeming aspect is that the 1998 Constitution included and modified several provisions that may possibly enable the society to employ a market economy to some extent.

CURRENT JUDICIAL STRUCTURE

Courts in North Korea are separate and independent, as are the Procurator's Offices inasmuch as they are not part of the cabinet but separate entities unto themselves and on the same level as the courts. The current 1998 Constitution provides for the Procurator's Offices and courts in the same subchapter. Unlike previous constitutions, however, the order was reversed by locating the former ahead of the latter.

There are several kinds of courts in North Korea, all of which exist under a three-tiered system: the Central Court, the Provincial or Municipal Court (directly under central authority), and the People's Court. In addition, there is the Special Court, which is composed of the Military Court and the Railroad Court. Although there are three tiers of courts, only one appeal is permissible as a rule. Very rarely is a second appeal ever granted. On the basis of the democratic principle of communism, there is no single-judge court; three people usually take part in the decision-making process. At the first level, one judge and two people's assessors participate in the decision making, while the appellate level consists of three judges. In an appellate review, even in a civil case, the procurator takes part and expresses his or her opinion. It is also important to note that the participation of people's assessors, who are elected laypersons, is a characteristic of the socialist judicial system. These individuals take part in the first-level trial to reflect comrade consciousness, but in principle, they only participate in the process for two weeks a year.

The Central Court is the highest appellate court for appeals from the Provincial or Special Courts. It also exercises broad original jurisdiction over important cases as provided by law or at its own discretionary initiative. It examines extraordinary appeals presented before it from the chief justice of the Central Court or the chief of the Central Procurator's Office. While the three-judge bench of the Central Court presides over extraordinary appeals from the lower courts, the grand bench reviews extraordinary appeals that emerge from the three-judge court of the Central Court itself. The Provincial Court hears appeals from the People's Court, which has general jurisdiction over most civil and criminal cases. The Provincial Court also has original jurisdiction over important cases, such as crimes against the state or grave crimes against individuals. Besides civil and criminal cases, arbitration among social entities is an important jurisdiction of the courts in order to facilitate a planned economy.

The chief justice of the Central Court is elected by the Supreme People's Assembly, while other judges and assessors of the Central Court are selected by the SPA Presidium. The judges and assessors of lower courts are elected by the corresponding Local People's Assembly and serve five-year terms, like those of other elected bodies. The judges of the Special Courts are appointed by the Central Court. Assessors of the Military Court are elected by soldiers of the unit concerned, and those of the Railroad Court are chosen by employees.

In the Court Organization Act, Article 15 does not require a judge (let alone the people's assessor) to have any prior qualifications except ideological enthusiasm and loyalty to party policy. Formal legal education or practical legal training is not a requirement, although most judges do have such backgrounds. This situation speaks for itself in terms of the court's true role in protecting the socialist system. Although the Court Organization Act provides for independent decision making, the court serves as a tool to educate people to cherish their socialism under party direction. The protection of the public and fair trial by law cease to exist in this kind of system. De jure as well as de facto, no state organ is free from the party's control and supervision. In this regard, court decisions are no more than the expression of the party's ideas and policies.

There is also a three-tiered, hierarchical order for prosecution: the Central Procurator's Office, the Provincial Procurator's Office, and the County Procurator's Office. As in the court system, there is also a Special Procurator's Office. The chief of the Central Procurator's Office is appointed by the Supreme People's Assembly, with the same term as that of the SPA member, while other procurators are appointed by the Central Procurator's Office. Procurators have broad authority and discretion over judicial procedure, as is often found in repressive societies. In addition, other law enforcement agencies, such as the State Security Departments and the Ministry of Public Security, play important roles.

STAFFING

The lawyers in North Korea are also quite different from those in Western society. The Lawyers' Association is a state-controlled public entity like any other organization in the country. Although North Korean lawyers do many of the things that lawyers in Western society do—legal consultation, document drafting, and legal representation are but a few examples—the fundamental difference between the two is that lawyers in North Korea work for the interest of the state and not for the interest of their clients. A client's interest is incidentally protected as lawyers faithfully carry out their role. Instead of being vigorous advocates for their clients, lawyers tend to educate their clients and persuade them to feel remorse and to confess.

No private business pursues the individual's interest in North Korea, and the legal practice is no exception in this regard. Legal service is assigned to individual lawyers by the association, and lawyers receive fixed salaries from the state. Article 20 of the Lawyer's Act provides qualifications for lawyers: Those who are qualified as legal professionals (probably graduates of law schools, but this is not a certainty), those who have worked in the legal field for no less than five years, and those who have passed the bar examination after obtaining some legal education are eligible to become lawyers. In this sense, lawyers in North Korea can be called professionals.

Although most North Korean lawyers are aptly educated, legal education has not been a subject of serious attention. Only a few colleges, including Kim Il Sung University, have law departments. The graduates are normally assigned to relevant positions in law enforcement agencies, courts, lawyers' offices, academic institutes, and party offices. After a few years of apprenticeship, they become recognized professionals.

Unfortunately, no statistics on the legal profession are available. Even the number of judges of the Central Court is unknown. There may be as many as several hundred judges, while it is estimated that approximately 1,000 lawyers are working at about 200 offices throughout the country. Each district office is known to have about 5 lawyers.

IMPACT OF LAW

According to Marxist theory, law is perceived to be an instrument to realize the objectives of the ruling class. In a socialist state created by means of a proletarian revolution, law is a weapon used to establish and maintain a proletarian dictatorship and a socialist ideology. Justice is realized not by law but by politics. Law is not autonomous and independent from politics but dependent on politics. As the state has no limit on its authority, state action practiced in the name of the people is ipso facto legitimate, and thus, there is no limit to the means by which the law can be used to enforce state goals. There is no place for the concept of natural law or inalienable rights. In this regard, the political role of the law is especially emphasized in an extremely political, security-conscious society like North Korea. Therefore, security agencies entertain broader authority and discretion in order to effectively control society. The role of the law as a means to check the arbitrary exercise of public power is minimized and negligible. Obeying instructions or orders of the authorities is all that is necessary. Laws or legal decisions need not be publicized, but they typically are; however, this is strictly done for the purpose of propaganda directed toward the outside world, not for the protection of citizens.

What's more, a citizen's behavior is evaluated in terms of political perspective. The overwhelming influence of the party without a legal basis reinforces the political nature of the society. Any departure from official ideology is perceived as a political crime, which is accompanied by harsh punishment. Punishment is given on the basis of a subjective interpretation of one's character and not of the objective consequence of one's action. This kind of operation of justice inevitably produces a large number of political prisoners and prisoners of conscience. However, if North Korea intends to expand its engagement with foreign countries for trade and investment, the importance of law should be emphasized in order to enhance predictability and the protection of foreign parties. Otherwise, North Korea will fail to secure foreign trust and thus encounter only a hollow response to its open-door policy.

Dae-Kyu Yoon

See also Constitutional Law; Marxist Jurisprudence; South Korea; Soviet System

References and further reading
Amnesty International. 2000. *Annual Report: Korea (Democratic People's Republic of)*. http://www.web.amnesty.org/web/ar2000web.nsf/countries/ 3b9aea5470f38e63802568f 20055293b?OpenDocument (accessed January 4, 2002).
Choi, Chongko. 1996. *North Korean Law [Bukhanpop]*. Seoul: Pakyoung-sa.
Choi, Dal-kon, and Shin Young-ho. 1998. *Introduction to North Korean Law. [Bukhanpop-ipmun]*. Seoul: Se-Chang.
North Korea Law Society. 1997–1999. *North Korea's Law and Practice Review. [Bukhanpop-yongu]*. Vols.1–4. Seoul: North Korean Law Society.
Savada, Andrea Matles, and William Shaw, eds. 1994. *North Korea: A Country Study*. Washington, DC: Federal Research Division, Library of Congress.
U.S. Department of State, Bureau of Democracy, Human Rights, and Labor. 1999. *Democratic People's Republic of Korea Report on Human Rights Practices*. http://www.state.gov/www/global/human_rights/1999_hrp_report/northkor.html (accessed December 11, 2001).

NORTHERN IRELAND

COUNTRY INFORMATION

Northern Ireland, part of the United Kingdom, is located on the northeastern segment of the island of Ireland. It is bounded by the Republic of Ireland on the south and west, the Irish Sea on the east, and the North Channel on the north. The country's 5,400 square miles contain both highland and lowland regions, as well as several large lakes and rivers. Lough Neagh, with an area of roughly 150 square miles, is the largest lake in the United Kingdom. The climate in Northern Ireland is temperate, with generally mild temperatures and damp conditions year-round. Correspondingly, agriculture has played a large role in the nation's economy, along with manufacturing. However, industries such as telecommunications and computers have grown substantially since 1990. Overall, the economy in Northern Ireland is linked to that of England, as most exports are sold there. Furthermore, Great Britain provides a great deal of funding to Northern Ireland in the form of governmental grants. Recently, the European Union has set aside substantial funding in the areas of economic development and north-south cooperation.

Northern Ireland has a population of 1,700,000; the vast majority are of English, Scottish, or Irish ancestry. The legal system is based on the common law, although there are a few differences between English and Northern Irish law and procedures. The official language of Northern Ireland is English. However, there has been a trend recently encouraging the use of Gaelic. Regarding religion, the most recent survey reported that 54 percent of the population are Protestants and 42 percent are Roman Catholics. Most of the Protestants are descended from English or Scottish settlers, while the Roman Catholics are predominantly Irish. This division in religious affiliation has been the primary factor in the nation's history and politics since the founding of the country. This schism has resulted in the sectarian conflict and violence that have plagued the nation almost continually.

HISTORY

Northern Ireland emerged as a semiautonomous nation with the passage by the English Parliament of the Government of Ireland Act of 1920. This law divided Ireland into separate regions, North and South, each with a separate Parliament, although both would remain under the dominion of the United Kingdom. However, the terms of the act were not sufficient to the South, and conflict between Irish nationalists and the British ensued. In 1921, the Anglo-Irish Treaty was signed, which gave the South the status of an independent country but retained English control over the North. Thus, the South became known as the Irish Free State (later the Republic of Ireland), while Northern Ireland remained as part of the United Kingdom. Indeed, the Ireland Act of 1949 mandated that no change could be made in the border between the North and the South without the consent of Northern Ireland's Parliament. In essence, these acts reinforced the status of Northern Ireland as a substate of the United Kingdom, although the Republic of Ireland never fully accepted the arrangement.

Following the division of Ireland, separate Parliaments were set up in each nation. In Northern Ireland, a Parliament was established at Stormont. Most domestic matters were allotted to the Stormont Parliament, but issues such as defense and trade were reserved for the English Parliament at Westminster. This division of power continued until March 1972, when the Northern Ireland Parliament was suspended and direct rule by the Westminster Parliament was instituted. Since 1972, there have been several attempts to reintroduce devolution of powers back to a Northern Irish government, but these have been unsuccessful, and direct rule has been the norm. Under direct rule, the Westminster Parliament retains ultimate law-making authority, and the implementation of those laws has been accomplished through the Northern Ireland Office and the Secretary of State for Northern Ireland. However, as will be discussed, significant changes were proposed for the governance of Northern Ireland in the Good Friday Agreement of 1998.

The difficulty, of course, in achieving a political compromise in Northern Ireland stems from what is referred to as "the Troubles." This term pertains to the enduring conflict between the two communities that inhabit Northern Ireland: the Irish, who are Roman Catholic and overwhelmingly tend to support a political union with the Republic of Ireland and an end to ties with the United Kingdom, and the English and Scottish, most of whom are Protestant in religion and largely favor retaining the alliance with Britain. What has made this problem so intractable is the fact that the Protestants (or unionists, as they are known) are the majority population of Northern Ireland, while the Catholics (or republicans) comprise a minority. Thus, by sheer force of numbers, the unionists have been able to dominate political affairs for most of Northern Ireland's history. The minority republicans have felt excluded from politics and discriminated against in social affairs. In the late 1960s, a civil rights movement by the Catholics succeeded in gaining attention for the plight of the republicans, and many reforms were instituted. At the same time, though, the movement created a backlash by the unionists, and acts of terrorism by paramilitary groups on both sides ensued. When the violence continued, the British government sent in troops to maintain order. Most republicans felt that the security forces represented an oppressive force, and the conflict escalated. When the Northern Irish government was ineffective in ending the violence, England suspended the Stormont Parliament and instituted direct rule. The conflict has continued largely unabated since then, with tragic costs in human life. Although there have been many attempts to bring about a peaceful solution in the last thirty years, none have been successful.

Without a doubt, the most significant political and legal change in Northern Ireland in decades (and the best chance to end the conflict) transpired in 1998. Multiparty talks were held in Belfast regarding new political arrangements between England, the Republic of Ireland, and Northern Ireland. These negotiations concluded in April 1998 and became known as the Good Friday Agreement. One month later, referenda were conducted in both the Republic of Ireland and Northern Ireland regarding the proposed agreement. There was a clear majority in both countries: Northern Ireland voted 71.1 percent in favor, and the Irish Republic voted 94.3 percent in favor. Following the referenda, legislation to formally implement the new arrangements was introduced in the Westminster Parliament and was subsequently passed. The Northern Ireland Act of 1998 is the title of the legislation that executes the provisions of the Good Friday Agreement.

The new accord contained many wide-ranging and significant provisions and also dealt with several important constitutional issues. The first was the consent principle: The people of Northern Ireland shall have the ultimate power, through the political process, to decide the fate of the country. There is a binding obligation by both the British and Irish governments to honor the will of the people as to the status of the nation. As such, provisions are made for future polls on the issue to be held, although any such polls must be at least seven years apart. Finally, the Irish Republic agreed to hold a referendum to amend its constitution to remove the territorial claim over Northern Ireland. This referendum was, in fact, passed by vote of the Irish people, and Articles 2 and 3 of the Irish Constitution were removed.

The Good Friday Agreement also provided for the creation of a new Northern Ireland Assembly, which will be largely responsible for legislation affecting Northern Ireland. The new assembly will contain 108 members, elected through a proportional representation system. Procedures exist so that neither unionist nor nationalist parties can dominate the assembly. Committee chairs and other key posts are assigned in proportion to party strength. Also, any decisions made by the assembly must have the support of both unionists and republicans. Specifically, for a key decision to be passed by a simple majority, there must be majority support for the measure among both unionist and nationalist blocs.

Ten departments will be created: Enterprise, Trade and Investment; Regional Development; Culture, Arts and Leisure; Social Development; Environment; Finance and Personnel; Education; Higher and Further Education, Training and Employment; Health, Social Services and Public Safety; and Agriculture and Rural Development. The assembly will elect a first minister and deputy first minister and appoint ten ministers to head the new departments. These twelve ministers will comprise the Executive Committee, which will meet to discuss common issues and create an agenda and budget. Following the devolution of power to the Northern Ireland Assembly, the Secretary of State for Northern Ireland will remain accountable for all matters not allocated to the assembly. The assembly can legislate in those areas not allocated to it with the approval of the British Secretary of State for Northern Ireland.

In addition, several councils will be created. A North/South Ministerial Council including ministers from both Ireland and Northern Ireland will meet twice a year to discuss cross-border issues. A British-Irish Council comprising members from all United Kingdom governments and Ireland will meet biennially to discuss issues such as agriculture, health, the environment, and transportation. Six North/South Implementation bodies were created to assist in the implementation of the new policies.

Human rights and equality were also addressed by the Good Friday Agreement. A Northern Ireland Human Rights Commission was created to advise the assembly on human rights issues. This commission has launched an effort to create a bill of rights for Northern Ireland, which will entrench (as much as possible in a parliamentary supremacy system) fundamental rights for citizens of Northern Ireland. Also, an Equality Commission will be created; its duties will be monitoring and enforcing equality issues. Finally, a Victims of Violence Commission will be created to study ways to provide support for those harmed as a result of the political conflict.

Security issues were also addressed by the agreement. A comprehensive review of the criminal justice system was carried out; this review made a number of suggestions for reform. The British government affirmed the principle of devolving criminal justice issues to Northern Ireland. There was an agreement by both governments to release paramilitary prisoners. Perhaps most contentiously, the participants to the agreement made a commitment to the total disarmament of all paramilitary forces, and the Independent Commission of Decommissioning was to be created. Finally, the British government provisionally agreed to reduce the number of troops and security forces in Northern Ireland and terminate emergency powers.

On the whole, the Good Friday Agreement represents a very ambitious attempt to solve an apparently intractable problem and provide a transition to a new democratic society in Northern Ireland. Some progress has been made in implementing the agreement since its adoption. The new Northern Ireland Assembly was established (although suspended briefly), elections were held, and members of the body were chosen. However, the most difficult element in the agreement's implementation has certainly been the decommissioning of weapons. Although some paramilitary groups have made good-faith efforts to decommission, other groups—both republican and unionist—have refused to honor the pledge, and several deadlines for decommissioning have passed without success. As of this writing, it is not possible to predict whether the issue of decommissioning weapons will prove to be an insuperable obstacle to implementation of the Good Friday Agreement as a whole.

As part of the United Kingdom, the legal system in Northern Ireland shares most of the same concepts and structures as those in England. Northern Irish law is based on the same common law concepts that developed in Britain, and the period of direct rule beginning in 1972 acted to further reconcile Northern Ireland and English law. As will be analyzed, the structure of courts in Northern Ireland has followed the British model. Court procedures and practices have also tended to resemble English customs. Overall, since the birth of the country in 1920, there has been a steady process of legal assimilation with the English. To be sure, there are differences between England and Northern Ireland in the content of certain laws, but there is much more similarity than difference between the two systems.

The major changes that will likely affect the Northern Ireland legal system in the near future are, undoubtedly, the increasing influence of European law and legal institutions, which will be discussed, and also the new legal and political structures arising from the Good Friday Agreement. The new legal doctrines prescribed by transnational courts should have the effect of modernizing some of the social legislation in Northern Ireland. The result of the Good Friday accord and its new political arrangements, assuming that all come to pass, will be to remove the country from direct rule and allow for a new and exclusively Northern Irish jurisprudence to develop. If fully implemented, there will be a unique (for the United Kingdom) bill of rights that will provide guarantees of fundamental human rights and equality. The new democratic institutions will allow for the Northern Irish to fully develop their own domestic policies and legal structures.

LEGAL CONCEPTS

Consistent with other United Kingdom countries, the most important source of law in Northern Ireland is legislation. The English Parliament provides much of the law for Northern Ireland as a province of the United Kingdom; Northern Ireland is represented in the House of Commons with eighteen seats. However, from 1921 until 1972, Northern Ireland had its own Parliament at Stormont, until direct rule from Westminster was imposed in 1972. Direct rule provisionally ended with the adoption of the Good Friday Agreement of 1998. The Good Friday accord created a power-sharing arrangement incorporating the new Northern Ireland Assembly and devolved certain powers to the assembly. As noted earlier, political conflict has prevented full implementation of the new governing arrangements. However, if the conflicts can be resolved, then the influence of the assembly as a source of law should equal or surpass that of the Stormont Parliament in the past.

Northern Ireland is unique in the United Kingdom in that it possesses a written constitution, found in the Government of Ireland Act of 1920 and other statutes. However, Northern Ireland's constitution is not supreme in the sense that the U.S. Constitution is thought to be. Rather, the Northern Irish constitution has acted as a limiting factor at times and not as a primary source of law.

Another primary source of law is the common law, or law created by judges. Unlike in civil law legal systems, judges in common law systems have the ability to rule on new points of law through statutory interpretation or by creating entirely new legal doctrine. These new principles are binding on future decision makers through the doctrine of precedent. That is, a lower court is compelled to follow the legal principle that has been established by a higher court in the past. This practice is often referred to by the Latin phrase *stare decisis,* or "let the decision stand." In practice, however, stare decisis is not followed rigidly. Still, in the Northern Irish legal system, the doctrine of precedent is as strong as it is anywhere in the common law world.

A final source of law is the emerging jurisprudence of the European Union (EU) and the European Convention on Human Rights. The United Kingdom is a member of the European Union and as such is bound by EU law and the decisions of the European Court of Justice, which makes legal decisions on EU treaties and legislation. Indeed, each member of the EU agrees that EU law supersedes national law. The decisions of the European Court are final, and they can overrule decisions by the courts in the member states. Thus, when EU law conflicts with a national law, the European Court can void the national law.

The United Kingdom has also, through the Human Rights Act of 1998, incorporated the European Convention on Human Rights into the domestic law of England, Scotland, Wales, and Northern Ireland. The European Convention arose out of a broad effort to promote social and economic progress among European countries after World War II. It codifies a number of civil and political liberties and attests to the desire of its signatories to achieve "a common understanding and observance" of those rights. The European Court of Human Rights

(ECHR) is the judicial organ of the European Convention. Although the ECHR's docket was relatively empty at its onset, the body has now become a major force in the judicial protection of human rights, as all signatories to the European Convention have filed declarations agreeing to the ECHR's jurisdiction. Approximately half of the signatories have incorporated the treaty into domestic law (including the United Kingdom), thus allowing individuals to invoke the convention and the ECHR's judgments in national judicial proceedings.

A recent example of how the ECHR is serving as a source of law in the United Kingdom relates to the ECHR cases of *Lustig-Prean and Beckett v. the United Kingdom* and *Smith and Grady v. the United Kingdom*. In both of these cases, the plaintiffs were discharged from the British armed forces on the basis of their sexual orientation. In *Lustig-Prean and Beckett,* the ECHR found that the policy of excluding gays and lesbians from serving in the military violated Article 8 of the European Convention. In *Smith and Grady,* the ECHR held that the policy also contravened Article 13 of the European Convention, which grants individuals the right to a remedy when their human rights (as defined by the convention) have been violated. Based on both of these rulings by the ECHR, the United Kingdom removed all restrictions on homosexuals serving in the armed forces. Although not all ECHR and European Court of Justice cases have such dramatic effects, this example shows that both EU and European Convention law will likely serve as increasingly large sources of jurisprudence in Northern Ireland and the United Kingdom as a whole.

The perception of the general public as to the effectiveness and fairness of the legal system and the administration of justice seems to be sharply divided along sectarian lines. Catholics appear to view the Northern Irish legal system to be systematically biased against them and correspondingly give low marks as to the performance of the system. Protestants, by contrast, unsurprisingly do not judge the system as harshly and tend to perceive it as being relatively effective and just.

Overall, the legal professions in Northern Ireland appear to be entering a time of transition. One commentator explains that the bar in Northern Ireland continues to be heavily influenced by British notions of legal positivism and aversion to political activism. At the same time, there are concerns about the composition of the judiciary, in terms of both gender equality and balance between Catholic and Protestant judges. However, the provisions of the Good Friday Agreement as well as the Human Rights Act of 1998 present an opportunity for the bench and legal professions to significantly transform both procedures and attitudes. The following years should see a new focus on new democratic structures, human rights, and equality in the legal system.

CURRENT STRUCTURE

There are three levels in the court system of Northern Ireland: the Supreme Court of Justice, the County Courts, and the Magistrates' Courts. Because Northern Ireland is part of the United Kingdom, the final court of appeal is the English House of Lords. A litigant in the Court of Appeal may appeal to the House of Lords in certain circumstances. In criminal cases, an appeal can be made to the House of Lords if the High Court certifies that the point of law under appeal is of general importance and the Lords deem that the case is suitable for disposition. In civil cases, either the Court of Appeal or the House of Lords must give its permission for a case to proceed to further appeal before the Lords. In practice, only a few criminal or civil cases per year are appealed to the House of Lords.

The Supreme Court consists of three court structures: the Court of Appeal, the High Court, and the Crown Court. The judges on the High Court and the Court of Appeal are appointed by the monarch, who relies on the recommendation of the lord chancellor. Certainly, the most significant judicial officer in Northern Ireland is the lord chief justice, who is the president of the three courts and also acts as the chief administrator.

The Court of Appeal is the highest appellate court within Northern Ireland, and it hears appeals on points of law from the Crown Court in criminal matters and from the High Court in civil cases. The Court of Appeal may also hear appeals on a point of law from the County Court or Magistrates' Court. The judges on the Court of Appeal are the lord chief justice and three lords justices of appeal. However, only three of these judges sit when hearing a case. In some cases, there may be a two-judge panel or even a single judge for minor matters.

The High Court of Justice hears exclusively civil cases. It is the trial court for certain cases, and the court also hears appeals from the County Courts. The High Court is divided into three divisions. The Queen's Bench Division handles tort, contract, and admiralty cases as well as all other cases not specifically allocated to another division. The Chancery Division deals with wills and estate cases, bankruptcy claims, and other business matters. The Family Division handles divorce, adoption, custody, and other domestic relations cases and also matters involving mental patients. The High Court is staffed by the lord chief justice and seven other judges.

The Crown Court hears serious criminal cases on indictment. Crimes that must be tried on indictment include murder, rape, and robbery—these are known in the U.S. system as felonies. Before a case can be tried in the Crown Court, there must first be a committal proceeding in a Magistrates' Court. This is essentially a preliminary hearing in which the magistrate determines that there is sufficient evidence to bind the defendant for a full trial. Judges from several different courts may preside over a

Structure of Northern Ireland Courts

Superior Courts

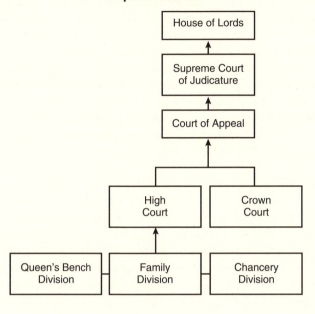

```
              House of Lords
                    ↑
           Supreme Court
           of Judicature
                    ↑
           Court of Appeal
                    ↑
      ┌──────────────┬──────────────┐
   High                        Crown
   Court                       Court
      ↑
┌───────────┬────────────┬────────────┐
Queen's Bench    Family      Chancery
 Division       Division     Division
```

Inferior Courts

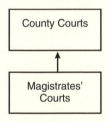

```
   County Courts
         ↑
   Magistrates'
     Courts
```

Crown Court proceeding. Either the lord chief justice, a Court of Appeal judge, a High Court judge, or a County Court judge may try cases in the Crown Court. However, for certain offenses, only a High Court or Court of Appeal judge may preside. Except for Diplock court cases (which will be discussed), there will always be a twelve-person jury sitting to determine the accused's guilt or innocence.

The next level of the Northern Irish court system is the County Courts, which have both civil trial and criminal appellate jurisdiction. The County Court may hear appeals in criminal cases from the Magistrates' Court; however, the vast majority of cases heard in the County Courts are civil in nature. The primary limitation on actions that may be heard in the County Courts is financial. For example, contract and tort cases must involve damages of less than £15,000; libel or slander cases must involve damages of less than £3,000. Various other civil matters, such as applications for adoption, are also heard in the County Courts. Judges in the County Courts typically come from the barristers' ranks. At least ten years of experience as a barrister or solicitor is required for appointment to the County Court bench, although deputy County Court judges can acquire standing as a full County Court judge after three years. Appeals from the County Courts are heard in the High Court, although an appeal of a point of law may be taken to the Court of Appeal.

The Magistrates' Courts handle the majority of minor criminal cases as well as some civil matters. On the civil side, the Magistrates' Courts handle domestic relations matters (although not divorces), small debt cases, and eviction proceedings (known as "ejectment"). In criminal cases, the Magistrates' Courts try summary criminal offenses (similar to misdemeanor crimes in the U.S. legal system) and also conduct preliminary investigations for indictable offenses. The Magistrates' Courts are staffed by resident magistrates, who are solicitors or barristers with at least seven years of experience. Appeals from the Magistrates' Courts are made to the County Court.

The juvenile courts of Northern Ireland try summary offenses for minors of ages between ten and sixteen. If a crime is committed by a minor under the age of ten, no criminal responsibility will attach. The bench for these courts consists of three members—one resident magistrate and two lay members. At least one of the lay members must be a woman. The jurisdiction of the juvenile court includes any criminal offense committed by a minor except homicide. Also, the juvenile court may hear matters involving the safety of a juvenile or cases involving allegations of inadequate parental care.

There are several specialized courts in Northern Ireland. The coroners' courts investigate suspicious or unexplained deaths. If the coroner (who must be a barrister or solicitor with at least five years of experience) determines that the death was not due to natural causes, he or she may hold an inquest. The purpose of an inquest is to ascertain the cause of death; it is a legal proceeding most resembling a trial under the inquisitorial system. There are also election courts, the purpose of which is to resolve contested elections. These courts are staffed by two judges from the High Court and two from the Court of Appeal. The election court only meets if, following an election, a petition is presented alleging that some law or rule has been broken.

There is a system for military justice in Northern Ireland. Courts-martial implement military law for those in the armed forces. However, most ordinary criminal offenses committed by military personnel during peacetime are tried by the ordinary courts. A court-martial may be held if the offense occurred overseas or if the crime only involved members of the armed forces and not any civilians. Serious offenses of this nature may be tried before either a District Court-Martial or a General Court-Martial. A District Court-Martial consists of three military officers who try a case involving enlisted soldiers and noncommissioned officers; this court-martial may impose a punishment of imprisonment of up to two years. A General Court-Martial consists of five officers who may try any member of the armed forces and levy any sentence that is authorized by military law. There are no juries in courts-martial, and defendants are represented by advocates from the Office of the Judge Advocate General. A losing defendant may request to appeal the decision to the Courts-Martial Appeal Court. This court usually sits in London and serves the entire United Kingdom. Three judges decide these appeals.

Finally, there are administrative bodies known as tribunals, which adjudicate a variety of disputes. Created by legislation, these tribunals are quasi-legal institutions that rarely follow the standard rules of evidence and procedure. Rather, these bodies provide a faster and more efficient means by which to settle controversies in certain areas of policy. Standing tribunals include the Social Security Appeal Tribunal, the Lands Tribunal, the Mental Health Review Tribunal, and the Fair Employment Tribunal, among others. The right of judicial review to a court for tribunal decisions generally exists—but not in all cases. For most matters, a citizen wishing to appeal a tribunal decision must apply to the High Court for permission within three months of the tribunal proceeding.

SPECIALIZED JUDICIAL BODIES

Although not really a specialized tribunal, one of the most interesting elements of Northern Irish jurisprudential practice is the Diplock courts, created to deal with terrorism. Put most simply, Diplock courts are nonjury, felony criminal trials, used only for certain offenses that have a connection to terrorism. The reason for the law creating these courts, which are quite atypical within common law legal systems, is to prevent intimidation of jurors by removing these cases to the sole discretion of the judge. The Diplock system had its genesis in a 1972 parliamentary commission on terrorist violence chaired by Lord Diplock. The commission found that traditional jury trials for terrorist offenses presented not only the problem of possible juror intimidation but also the chance of an unjustified acquittal of criminal defendants. For these reasons, the Emergency Provisions Act of 1973 was enacted, providing for several significant deviations from traditional trial procedure and evidentiary rules.

First, if a criminal suspect is accused of committing a terrorist act, then there is no right to an immediate bail hearing. The law provides that some degree of "physical maltreatment" is allowed in order to secure a confession from the accused. After an arrest has been made, the director of public prosecutions conducts an investigation to determine if a trial should proceed. The prosecutor has the discretion to schedule the case as a Diplock trial if he or she believes that the charge is terrorism related. Offenses that may be tried in a Diplock court are murder, rioting, robbery, arson, aggravated burglary, crimes involving firearms and explosives, and membership in certain organizations. There is an additional step before a case can be tried in a Diplock court. After the initial determination to try the accused in a Diplock hearing, the case file is forwarded to the attorney general of the United Kingdom, who reviews the evidence as to whether a Diplock trial is warranted. If the decision is made that a Diplock trial shall proceed, the case is scheduled, typically in the Crown Court. The case is tried solely by the presiding judge, without a jury. The judge may not issue a summary decision, though. He or she is required to explain and provide reasons for the decision. There is automatic right of appeal for those convicted under the Diplock statute.

STAFFING

As in England, there are two types of legal professionals: barristers and solicitors. Solicitors act as generalists and assist the public in a variety of matters, usually outside of the courtroom. Solicitors have the right to appear before the Magistrates' Courts and County Courts, but barristers have the exclusive right to appear before the higher courts. Typically, solicitors perform legal work for the public in matters of property, family law, estates, and minor criminal charges. Solicitors in Northern Ireland tend to be organized in firms, although there are solo practitioners.

Barristers, by contrast, are not allowed to form partnerships or firms and thus work exclusively as solos. Barristers act as advocates in the higher courts and also provide expert advice on legal matters requested by a solicitor. Also, the barrister is required to draft the pleadings for cases heard in the High Court. A client does not initially retain a barrister; rather, the client first engages the solicitor, then the solicitor contacts the barrister if necessary and negotiates the fee. An experienced barrister may apply to become a Queen's Counsel; this is known as "taking silk" and is a highly respected position.

There are several routes available to become a barrister or solicitor. The most typical method is to study law as an undergraduate student and then complete the professional course offered by the Institute of Professional Legal Studies at Queen's University. Nonlaw graduates must take a preliminary course of study for two years, leading to the Certificate in Academic Legal Studies. Admission to the institute course is competitive and requires an admissions examination. The course of study varies depending on whether the student intends to become a solicitor or barrister. For prospective solicitors, there is a two-year program that combines an apprenticeship under a practicing solicitor with academic study at the institute. At the end of the two-year period, the student is granted a restricted practicing certificate, which mandates that he or she may work only as an assistant solicitor for two years. For prospective barristers, an academic course of study at the institute is required for the first nine months, then they are "called to the Bar" and serve what is known as a "pupillage," or apprenticeship, under an experienced barrister for an additional year.

In certain situations, the requirements may be waived. Most commonly, legal professionals who are licensed in other jurisdictions may be admitted as solicitors or barristers. Also, those individuals who have worked as a law clerk in a solicitor's office for at least seven years may be granted a waiver from some of the usual requirements.

The judiciary in Northern Ireland comes primarily from the ranks of the barristers. In the Supreme Court, only barristers with at least ten years of experience may be appointed as judges. These judges are required to retire when they reach the age of seventy-five. In the lower courts, both barristers and solicitors may be appointed as judges. These officials must retire at age seventy-two. There are also lay judges known as justices of the peace who adjudicate minor matters and conduct procedural hearings; these officials typically have no formal legal training. Interestingly, the justices of the peace are granted a lifetime appointment.

IMPACT

Because of the continuing political conflict, law and courts have played a fundamental role in Northern Ireland. Yet, at the same time, the legitimacy of the courts (especially in the criminal justice system) has been questioned by the Irish Republican forces. These paramilitary groups have consistently questioned the neutrality of the Northern Irish judiciary based on the perceived dominance of Protestant members in it. This has contributed to the sense of alienation that many Catholics have felt toward the legal system. One group of commentators has suggested that Northern Ireland's legal system is a "colonial" model, in that the deep divisions in society shape the perceptions of the judicial structure and its effectiveness. However, even with the duality that exists, it is difficult to dispute the importance of law in contemporary Northern Irish society.

Most important, the impact of the legal system has been seen in the continuing effort by legislators and judges to mitigate the political violence and conflict. Politicians, lawyers, and judges have strived to use the rule of law to end the conflict and its consequences. The Emergency Provisions Act and the Diplock system represent one manifestation of this effort, as do attempts to institute antidiscrimination laws. Most recently, of course, the Good Friday Agreement is the most ambitious attempt to completely transform the polity to one based on the values of democratic equality and human rights. Whether this effort will be completely successful is not certain, but the agreement does represent, at the very least, a remarkable attempt to use the rule of law to end the long and bitter conflict.

David Weiden

See also Administrative Tribunals; Barristers; Common Law; England and Wales; European Court and Commission on Human Rights; European Court of Justice; Ireland; Magistrates—Common Law Systems; Scotland; Solicitors; United Kingdom

References and further reading
Boyle, Kevin, Tom Hadden, and Paddy Hillyard. 1975. *Law and State: The Case of Northern Ireland.* Amherst: University of Massachusetts Press.
Dickson, Brice. 1993. *The Legal System of Northern Ireland.* Belfast: SLS Legal Publications.
Hachey, Thomas E., Joseph M. Hernon Jr., and Lawrence J. McCaffrey. 1996. *The Irish Experience: A Concise History.* Armonk, NY: M. E. Sharpe, Inc.
Harvey, Colin J., ed. 2001. *Human Rights, Equality and Democratic Renewal in Northern Ireland.* Oxford: Hart.
Jackson, John, and Sean Doran. 1995. *Judge without Jury: Diplock Trials in the Adversary System.* New York: Oxford University Press.
Lustig-Prean and Beckett v. the United Kingdom, 29 European Court of Human Rights 548 (1999).
Mitchell, Paul, and Rick Wilford, eds. 1999. *Politics in Northern Ireland.* Boulder, CO: Westview Press.
Northern Ireland Office, "Political Development since 1987," http://www.nio.gov.uk (cited December 1999).
O'Leary, Brendan. 1999. "Academic Viewpoint: The Nature of the Agreement." *Fordham International Law Journal* 22: 1628–1667.
Rasnic, Carol Daugherty. 1999. "Northern Ireland's Criminal Trials without Jury: The Diplock Experiment." *Annual Survey of International and Comparative Law* 5: 239–257.
Rose, Richard. 1971. *Governing without Consensus: An Irish Perspective.* London: Faber and Faber.
Smith and Grady v. the United Kingdom, 29 European Court of Human Rights 493 (1999).
Ward, Alan J. 1994. *The Irish Constitutional Tradition: Responsible Government and Modern Ireland, 1782–1992.* Washington, DC: Catholic University of America Press.

NORTHERN TERRITORIES OF CANADA

GENERAL INFORMATION

Canada's three huge northern territories constitute that part of Canada lying north of the 60th parallel and west of Hudson's Bay. Canada claims that the North Pole is its true northern boundary, but the three territories govern the landmass, not the ocean.

The Yukon Territory is located in northwestern Canada. It borders Alaska to its west and the Arctic Ocean to its north. The Yukon consists almost entirely of forest and mountains, and it is drained mainly by the mighty Yukon River, which then traverses Alaska to the Bering Sea. Many internal valleys are perpetually frozen bogs called muskeg. Although the Yukon comprises an area of approximately 483,450 square kilometers, the population of the Yukon is only 31,305. Two-thirds reside in the capital city, Whitehorse.

Nunavut is the newest territory. Nunavut, pronounced "Noo-na-voot" and written as Nunavut in both English and French, means "our land" in Inuktitut, the language of the Inuit, formerly called Eskimos. Unlike the other territories, the word *territory* is not part of Nunavut's official name. It occupies the Arctic islands north of Hudson's Bay and the mainland on the coast of Hudson's Bay. There are some mountains in the northern islands, but the mainland territory consists of tundra—low-lying, level rock pockmarked by small lakes. The entire area is devoid of substantial vegetation. Its area is 1,994,000 square kilometers, and its population is 27,100. Unlike the other territories, most of the population is spread about the territory in small or traditional settlements. Iqaluit (formerly Frobisher Bay) has 4,200 residents.

The third territory, ironically called the Northwest Territories despite the fact that it is a single territory and is not Canada's most westerly jurisdiction, lies between the first two. It shares wooded mountains with Yukon to the west and tundra with Nunavut to the east. There are several huge freshwater lakes, notably Great Bear Lake, one of the largest in the world, and the McKenzie River, which flows north to the Arctic. To the south, the NWT includes a portion of an ancient, mineral-rich mountain chain called the Canadian Shield. The landmass is 1,171,918 square kilometers. The population is 42,083, one-third of whom reside in the capital city, Yellowknife. Inuvik, a settlement near the Arctic Ocean, is the second town in size, with a population of 4,000.

EVOLUTION AND HISTORY

All three territories have a significant aboriginal population. Aboriginals account for about 20 percent of the Yukon population, about half the people of the NWT, and 85 percent of the residents of Nunavut. The major native population of the Yukon is the Slavey peoples, so named because Europeans discovered, on their arrival, that the local population had been enslaved by the coastal nations. The Dene Nation, formerly called Wood Crees and one of the largest Indian groups in North America, dominates the NWT. Almost all the people of Nunavut are Inuit.

Yukon

In 1896 gold was discovered on Bonanza Creek, which is a tributary of the Klondike River. The Klondike Gold Rush resulted in the population surging to 25,000. As a result of this prosperity, the Yukon was made a separate legal entity in 1898. An international rail link to the sea was built between Skagway, Alaska, and Whitehorse. But the gold rush did not last, and by 1921 the population of the Yukon had fallen to 4,157. The territory remained dormant until construction of the Alaska Highway during World War II,

which for the first time enabled overland access from the rest of North America. As a result of this increased access and new development, government services were expanded. After the war there was a mining boom, but, as the century closed, mining was again in decline. In 1953, Whitehorse replaced Dawson as the capital city of the Yukon Territory.

The Northwest Territories

The NWT (the acronym is now commonplace) was so named when Canada in the nineteenth century took over the vast lands of the pioneer fur trader the Hudson's Bay Company. Over time, three provinces and one new territory were carved out, and the modern NWT is what remains.

The NWT also has had some mineral development. The world's first radium mine was opened near Yellowknife in the 1930s. At first the ore had to be flown out because there was neither rail nor road connection. The NWT became the land of the "bush pilots." After World War II, a summer rail and river barge connection to southern Canada was established, and gold and other mines were opened. Later, road and rail networks were extended into the territory, but the most popular winter route for truckers today remains the "ice highway" across Slave Lake—Canada's only public thoroughfare for motor vehicles built simply of ice. The main mining town, Yellowknife, is the capital.

Nunavut

Nunavut, by comparison, has had virtually no resource development, and it continues to be connected to southern Canada only by air—and canoe or dogsled. The Inuit had been until very recently left free to practice their traditional style of living. They lived nomadically in scattered camps and had no formal government, although there were camp bosses—an informal system of management that served them well. But in the 1950s, NATO radar bases were established in the area. The resulting influx of southerners began to cause a breakdown of traditional life, and the Canadian government became concerned for the health and well-being of the aboriginal people. In what has come to be a controversial program, Canada in the 1960s encouraged the Inuit to move from their nomadic existence into villages. Soon afterward, the people began to agitate for self-government. In a 1982 plebiscite, 56 percent of voters elected to split the NWT and create Nunavut. In 1992 the Canadian Parliament approved the Nunavut Land Claims Act, and, on April 1, 1999, Nunavut officially became a territory. On February 15, 1999, it had its first general election. But the principal industry remains tourism and native crafts, including the famous soapstone carvings. In the first year of operation—1999–2000—the federal government provided $552.6 million of Nunavut's budget of $610.107 million.

CURRENT STRUCTURE

The territories are not provinces. They do not have the independent constitutional status of a province under the Canadian Constitution. Legally they are merely creations of the Canadian Parliament. Recently, however, Canada has made them near-provinces. By virtue of federal legislation, each territorial government is responsible for almost all of the same administrative and legislative matters that fall under the jurisdiction of Canadian provinces. They may enact laws dealing with property and civil rights, including education, health, welfare, and other social services, although such programs are often funded through financial assistance from the federal government. As with the provinces, the federal government maintains legislative power over criminal law, native peoples, navigable waters, banking, foreign affairs, and many other topics. A major exception to the provincial model is the administration of natural resources, which remains under the federal government.

The structure of government in the territories very much resembles that of a province. An appointed resident commissioner represents the federal Canadian government in a way similar to the lieutenant governor of a province. An elected legislative council resembles a provincial legislature, and an executive committee of that council acts as the executive, following the traditional model for parliamentary government. The Royal Canadian Mounted Police provide police services for all three territories. As with other Canadian governments, the power of the territorial councils is limited by the Canadian Charter of Rights and Freedoms.

COURTS

Canada has established and appointed full-jurisdiction courts in all three territories, and each has constitutional protection from summary dismissal. The judges may be removed from office only by a joint address to the Commons and Senate of Canada, an indignity to which no Canadian judge in history has been subjected.

The Supreme Court of the Yukon Territory is a superior court of record, which has full civil and criminal jurisdiction throughout the Yukon. It is composed of two resident judges appointed by the Canadian government. They are assisted from time to time by several nonresident deputy judges, who are judges or retired judges from other Canadian superior courts. The Supreme Court is assisted by the Territorial Court, which has a limited criminal and civil jurisdiction.

The Supreme Court of the Northwest Territories is similarly a superior court of record, which has full civil and criminal jurisdiction throughout the territory. It has three judges resident at Yellowknife. It has long been the practice of the Supreme Court of the Northwest Territories to travel to the remote communities in which cases arise. The arrival of the "Court plane," complete with judge, officials, lawyers, and, sometimes, the prisoner, is a common feature of life in "the North," as Canadians generically refer to all the northern territories. The Supreme Court is assisted by the Territorial Court, which has a limited criminal and civil jurisdiction.

Nunavut is unique in Canada in that it has only one trial court, the Nunavut Court of Justice. Amendments to the Criminal Code of Canada that apply only to Nunavut permit the court to deal with all matters arising under the criminal code. In addition the court deals with infractions of other statutes applying to Nunavut, and it handles all civil cases arising in the territory. In other words, the Nunavut Court of Justice is a superior court of record with full civil and criminal jurisdiction throughout the territory. The two judges of that court reside at Iqualuit, and they perform all judicial functions because the new territory adopted a unified trial-court system. They are assisted from time to time by several nonresident deputy judges, who are judges or retired judges from other Canadian superior courts. Although the judges of the Nunavut Court of Justice reside and hear cases in Iqualuit, they also sit in the remote and extremely small communities scattered throughout the territory.

In addition, there exist in each territory several administrative tribunals with a judicial function. The Worker's Compensation Boards in each territory are a noteworthy example. As is the case with most provinces, suits by employees against employers or fellow employees for on-the-job injuries are banned, and in their place the board offers a scheme of compensation paid from rates imposed on employers.

NOTABLE FEATURES OF LAW/LEGAL SYSTEM

General Law

In general, each territory has adopted laws and procedures found in all common law systems. Also, the statute law found in other provinces has largely been duplicated.

The Law and the Aboriginal Peoples

In recent decades, Canada and the local governments have come to see a need to settle outstanding land claims of the northern aboriginal peoples, and to help them to establish institutions that will serve them in the modern age. Indeed, Canada refused to permit a major pipeline development along the McKenzie River Valley for this reason. The first new venture to deal with this need was the 1994 Yukon First Nations Land Claims Settlement Act, which affirmed an agreement with the native people that provided an umbrella for specific settlements with each aboriginal band or nation named in the statute. It also established several joint native-government boards to administer laws respecting land use planning, the management of heritage resources and place names, and fish and wildlife management. The Yukon also enacted legislation to permit a large measure of local government for native lands. Under this umbrella, most nations have settled their land claims and become accustomed to native government on their traditional lands.

A similar settlement is under negotiation in the NWT.

With the creation of Nunavut, the new attitudes have achieved full flower. Canada's Inuit people have in large measure achieved the self-government they sought, and they are now engaged in an effort to establish a form of government that best suits their unique situation. Its land settlement with Canada yields the Inuit title to 355,842 square kilometers, including mineral rights to 35,257 square kilometers.

Also, the territories have attempted to implement programs that incorporate aboriginal traditions and values into the justice system. Although these schemes vary among the different communities, they typically focus on restorative justice: the restoration of harmony in the community by allowing the victim to be heard and by having the accused accept responsibility for his or her actions. In the Yukon, programs offer assistance to the Territorial and Supreme Court with sentencing recommendations and with proposals for the reintegration of offenders into the community. Often, when aboriginal citizens are diverted from the mainstream justice system to these programs, they become accountable to their community in a way that is meaningful to them. The Royal Canadian Mounted Police have the option of utilizing the traditional justice system or referring the offenders to these special programs.

As in the Yukon, it is the practice of the Nunavut Court of Justice to ask some elders of the community to sit with the court when it is dealing with criminal charges. The elders do not discuss the cases with the judges, but they are usually asked if they wish to speak when the court is hearing submissions as to sentence. Their comments may be directed to the accused or to the judge. Either way, the judge has the benefit of the views of the elders of the community in which the offense has taken place.

Legal Profession
The legal professions in all three territories are "fused," and all lawyers can both go to court and do solicitor's work. In common with the provinces, the bar is self-governing and can regulate entry of new lawyers as well as discipline existing lawyers, even to the ultimate remedy of disbarment. There are more than one hundred lawyers in active practice in Whitehorse, and almost that many in Yellowknife. There are far fewer in Iqualuit, and hardly any in any other community in the North. Many "southern" lawyers come to the North to appear for specific

Structure of Canadian Northern Territory Courts

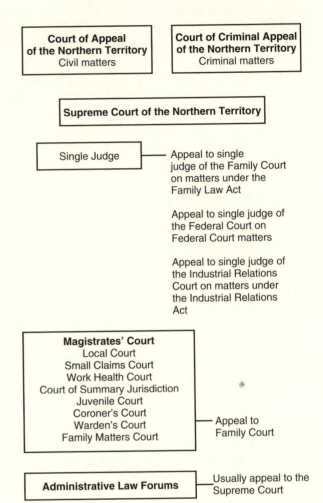

clients in specific cases, and the rules make that relatively easy. A legal aid scheme operates in each territory, so that lawyers in private practice may seek assistance to enable them to act for impecunious clients in both criminal and civil cases. These schemes are perennially short of funds.

RELATIONSHIP TO NATIONAL SYSTEM
Canada has also created three courts of appeal, one for each territory. The Court of Appeal of the Yukon consists in the main of the judges of the Court of Appeal of the nearest province, British Columbia. The courts of appeal of NWT and of Nunavut consist of judges selected from the courts of appeal of the provinces of Alberta and Saskatchewan. In addition, all the superior court judges from all the territories are ex officio members of all the appeals courts. The Yukon Court of Appeal sits in the Yukon or at Vancouver, British Columbia. The NWT Court of Appeal and the Nunavut Court of Appeal can sit in Alberta, but ordinarily sit, respectively, at Yellowknife and Iqualuit.

Decisions of the Territorial Court in the Yukon and

NWT may be appealed in some cases to the Supreme Court and in others to the Court of Appeal. The decisions of the Supreme Court in all three territories are subject to appeal to the appropriate Court of Appeal.

One can, with leave, appeal from any decision of the three courts of appeal to the Supreme Court of Canada.

Roger P. Kerans
Brent Mescall

See also Canada; Customary Law; Native American Law, Traditional

References and further reading
The Canadian Indian: Yukon and Northwest Territories. 1973. Ottawa: Information Canada.
Eber, Dorothy. 1997. *Images of Justice: A Legal History of the Northwest Territories as Traced through the Yellowknife.* Montreal: McGill-Queen's University Press.

NORTHERN TERRITORY OF AUSTRALIA

GENERAL INFORMATION

The Northern Territory is located in the central and north-central part of Australia and is home to just under 200,000 people. At 1.4 million square kilometers in size, its vastness is sometimes difficult for visitors to fathom.

The Northern Territory is a multitude of paradoxes. Because of the vast and rugged terrain to be crossed and the harsh conditions experienced there, the territory was colonized more recently than other places in Australia. In some cases, this has allowed aboriginal groups to retain their language and culture to a greater degree than in other parts of Australia. As a result, many aboriginal people in the Northern Territory speak English as a third, fourth, or fifth language. Also, many Aboriginals continue to live by their traditional laws and culture.

Aboriginal people make up 27.5 percent of the Northern Territory population; this compares with just 3.2 percent in the state with the next highest proportion of Aboriginals. Their struggle to regain ownership of their land is not yet complete. They now own 42 percent of the territory's land, but there are further areas under claim.

Partly because of its geographic closeness to Asia, the Northern Territory is also a melting pot of people from different cultures. Many nonaboriginal "Territorians" also speak English as a third or fourth language.

Natural resources are said to underpin the Northern Territory's economic growth, which was calculated at 5 percent in 2000. Its future growth and prosperity are projected to depend heavily on the continued development of the mining, petroleum, and agribusiness sectors. The collective value of production from the territory's resource industries was $1.98 billion in 1998, making it the largest sector of the Northern Territory economy. These industries are based on extensive petroleum, mineral, land, water, marine, and natural resources.

EVOLUTION AND HISTORY

The Macassan influence from Indonesia is thought to have been the most significant contact aboriginal people of the Top End of the Northern Territory experienced prior to European colonization. The Macassans visited the north coast of the territory predominantly to trade trepang or sea slug. A reportedly convivial commercial and cultural exchange occurred between the traders and the Yolgnu (the aboriginal people of North East Arnhem Land). It follows that, in addition to their own customary law, the Yolgnu had developed principles of commercial and contract law. This is evident today in the language of the Yolgnu, which includes numerous words from Bahasa Indonesia (the Indonesian language). One of these is the word for "money"—*rupia*, phonetically the same as the Bahasa Indonesian word *rupiah*.

On the arrival of the European colonizers in 1788, the whole of Australia was declared to be *terra nullius*. Literally meaning "empty land," this declaration allowed the British colonizers to disregard the existing laws and apply the laws of England "so far as applicable." This practice extended to the aboriginal people of the Northern Territory, and they became bound by the laws of England, although they were unaware of it at the time. A Federal Court challenge to the doctrine of *terra nullius* by the Yolgnu failed in 1971. According to Justice Blackburn in *Milirrpum v. Nabalco* (1971) (17 FLR 141), the Yolgnu had "a subtle and elaborate system highly adapted to this country. . . . If ever a system could be called 'a government of laws, and not of men' it is shown in the evidence before me." However, the court found that there was no formal legal structure of a kind then recognized by English law. More than 200 years later, the principle of *terra nullius* was rejected by the High Court of Australia in *Mabo v. Queensland (No. 2)* (175 CLR 1).

In 1901, Australia became a federation, with six states and numerous territories. At that time, the area that is now known as the Northern Territory was part of the state of South Australia and was known as the Northern Territory of South Australia.

The Northern Territory was surrendered by South Australia and handed back to the control of the Commonwealth under the Northern Territory Acceptance Act of 1910, thereby becoming a territory in its own right. The Northern Territory (Administration) Act provided for an administrator appointed by the governor-general to administer the territory on behalf of the Australian government. Under Section 122 of the Australian Constitution, the Commonwealth has the power to make laws "for the government of any territory surrendered by any state to and accepted by the Commonwealth." This so-called plenary power was interpreted at the time by the High Court as disparate: It allowed the Commonwealth to pass a law without regard to the other sections of the constitution, unless expressly provided. This was demonstrated in the case of *R v. Bernasconi* (1915) (19 CLR 629), which held that the right to a trial by jury in Section 80 of the constitution did not apply to the Northern Territory.

The local population had an ongoing grievance regarding the lack of representation and the continued governance of the territory by the Commonwealth in Canberra. Decisions were argued to have been irrelevant and uninformed, coming as they did from thousands of kilometers away. Pressure for representative government led to gradual concessions by the federal government, including the designation of an elected representative in the federal Parliament.

Until the Commonwealth Electoral Act was amended in 1959, the territory's sole member in the House of Representatives could participate in house debates but could not vote. The 1959 amendment allowed the member to vote on issues related to the Northern Territory. Since the further amendment to the act in 1968, the member representing the Northern Territory has the same voting rights as other members of the House of Representatives. Under Section 4 of the Senate (Representation of Territories) Act, two senators are elected from the Northern Territory to serve in the Australian Senate. The number of Northern Territory members of the House of Representatives increased to two before the federal election in November 2001.

The Northern Territory had no guarantee of representative democracy like that held by the states. The Northern Territory (Administration) Act of 1947 established the Northern Territory Legislative Council. The first Legislative Council consisted of thirteen members—seven official members (government department heads) and six elected members. The administrator of the Northern Territory was the president of the Legislative Council. By 1974, the number of elected representatives had gradually increased to eleven, and the nonofficial membership of the Legislative Council was repealed. The number of official members remained at seven.

In 1974, the Legislative Council was replaced by a fully elected, nineteen-member Legislative Assembly representing the nineteen electoral divisions in the Northern Territory. Currently, there are twenty-five elected representatives in the Legislative Assembly.

In 1978, the Northern Territory (Self-Government) Act (Cth) was passed under Section 122 of the Commonwealth Constitution. This act allows the Northern Territory to legislate in a style similar to that of a state, with some limitations. For example, the Commonwealth has retained the power to make laws about the mining of uranium and some other substances, aboriginal land rights, and Commonwealth national parks.

CURRENT STRUCTURE

Although there were some preliminary discussions about the formation of a "native court" to be presided over by aboriginal tribal elders, the Northern Territory's judicial structure did not develop in that direction. A number of administrative law forums were established under Northern Territory and Commonwealth legislation. Commonwealth tribunals, such as the Social Security Appeals Tribunal and the Administrative Appeals Tribunal, deal with administrative review of some Commonwealth legislation. Among the many tribunals established under Northern Territory legislation are the Escort Agency Licensing Appeals Tribunal, the Land and Valuation Tribunal, the Motor Accidents Compensation Appeals Tribunal, the Lands and Mining Tribunal, the Police Arbitral Tribunal, and the Mental Health Review Tribunal. Other legal forums include the Anti-Discrimination Commission, the Liquor Commission, and the Legal Practitioner's Complaints Committee.

The Magistrates' Courts include the Court of Summary Jurisdiction with criminal and civil jurisdiction; the Family Matters Court, the Small Claims Court, and the Local Court with jurisdiction in civil matters; the Juvenile Court; the Work Health Court; the Coroners' Court; and Wardens' Courts constituted under mining legislation. These courts are constituted by a stipendiary magistrate, except for the Court of Summary Jurisdiction, which may be constituted by a magistrate or two or more justices of the peace. A stipendiary magistrate is a magistrate who receives a salary. Justices of the peace are not paid for their services to the courts and may not have legal qualifications. Again, the Magistrates' Court may exercise some federal jurisdiction, such as in the Family Matters Court; however, these cases may be transferred to the Federal Court.

There is a limited right of appeal from the Magistrates' Court and the Court of Summary Jurisdiction to the Supreme Court. The Supreme Court of the Northern Territory exercises civil and criminal jurisdiction. Appeals from the Supreme Court lie to the Court of Appeal of the Northern Territory for civil matters and to the Court of Criminal Appeal for criminal matters. Both appellate courts are constituted by three judges of the Supreme Court of the Northern Territory. Applications for leave to appeal from the Courts of Appeal can be made to the High Court of Australia. Appeal from the Supreme Court lies to the Full Court of the Federal Court on some federal matters and to the Full Court of the Family Court on family matters.

Although the Northern Territory Supreme Court has some federal jurisdiction, the Federal Court will generally hear matters involving Commonwealth law. The Federal Court's jurisdiction includes matters involving native title, bankruptcy, industrial disputes, actions under the Trade Practices Act of 1974, family law, copyright, and patent. Appeals from the Federal Court are made to the Full Court of the Federal Court and then to the High Court.

NOTABLE FEATURES OF THE LAW/LEGAL SYSTEM

Given the large percentage of aboriginal people in the Northern Territory population, it is not surprising that many notable features of the territory's legal system are associated with issues involving these individuals. Aboriginal and Torres Strait Islander people are overrepresented in the criminal justice system: They make up 27.5 percent of the population but represent 77 percent of the prison population. A historical legal issue that continues today is the regularity with which aboriginal people appear in court without interpreters, whether as plaintiffs, witnesses, victims, or offenders. Although there were early Australian cases discharging accused Aboriginals because interpreters could not be provided, the lack of interpreters for aboriginal people in court was highlighted in the High Court in 1934 and continues to date.

More recently, much attention has been paid nationally and internationally to the Northern Territory's mandatory sentencing laws. In 1997, legislation was passed amending the Sentencing Act, which provided for a mandatory minimum jail sentence for certain property offenses. Given the already high number of aboriginal people in the Northern Territory prisons, this law has been criticized by national and international groups. Minor amendments to this law have been made as a result of this pressure, but the law remains substantially unchanged.

STAFFING

A prospective lawyer in the Northern Territory attends a university for a minimum of four years to complete the Bachelor of Laws degree. He or she then undertakes "practical legal training," to acquire the training needed to be admitted as a barrister and solicitor of the Supreme Court and therefore obtain a practicing certificate from the Northern Territory Law Society.

Practical legal training can be obtained in one of three ways:

1. The prospective lawyer can complete a twelve-month "Articles of Clerkship" with an approved organization. This is usually a private law firm but may be the Attorney-General's Department, the Northern Territory Legal Aid Commission, the North Australian Aboriginal Legal Aid Commission, or the Northern Land Council.

Structure of Northern Territory of Australia Courts

Court of Appeal Civil matters	Court of Criminal Appeal Criminal matters

Supreme Court of the Northern Territory
Single Judge

Appeal to single judge of the Family Court on matters under the Family Law Act	Appeal to single judge of the Federal Court on Federal Court matters	Appeal to single judge of the Industrial Relations Court on matters under the Industrial Relations Act

Magistrates' Court
Local Court, Small Claims Court, Work Health Court, Court of Summary Jurisdiction, Juvenile Court, Coroners' Court, Wardens' Court, Family Matters Court—Appeal to Family Court

Administrative Law Forums
Usually appeal to the Supreme Court

2. He or she can complete a combination program, serving an "Articles of Clerkship" for six months and a "Judges Associate" for twelve months. Judges' associate positions are available with the judges of the Supreme Court of the Northern Territory.

3. He or she can complete a graduate diploma in legal practice with a university or college. This provides for a combination of practical and theoretical study.

Under Section 5 of the Magistrates Act, the minimum eligibility requirement for appointment as a magistrate is being admitted to practice in the High Court or a Supreme Court in a state or territory or in New Zealand, Papua New Guinea, or Great Britain. Section 7(1) of the Northern Territory Magistrates Act provides that a magistrate appointed under Section 4(3) holds office until the age of sixty-five.

Judges of the Supreme Court are appointed by the administrator. Section 32 of the Supreme Court Act provides that the administrator may appoint a person who is under seventy to be the chief justice or a judge of the court if that person either:

• Is or has been a judge of a court of the Commonwealth, a state, or a territory, or
• Has been enrolled as a legal practitioner of the High Court or of the Supreme Court of a state or

territory of the Commonwealth for at least ten years

Tenure for judges of the Supreme Court extends until the age of seventy, according to Section 38 of the Supreme Court Act.

RELATIONSHIP TO THE NATIONAL SYSTEM

The Northern Territory's relationship with the national legal/court system has some unique aspects. First, as mentioned, Section 122 of the constitution has the potential to limit the autonomy of the territory in a manner not experienced by the states. The most dramatic illustration of this occurred in 1997. The Commonwealth Parliament used its power under Section 122 of the constitution to pass the Euthanasia Laws Act of 1997, amending the Northern Territory (Self-Government) Act to remove the power of the territory's Legislative Assembly to make laws with respect to euthanasia and assisted suicide. This amendment meant that the territory's Rights of the Terminally Ill Act of 1995 was ineffective from the date on which the Commonwealth act commenced. The voting on the Commonwealth legislation was a so-called conscience vote, meaning that it was not along party lines.

Second, because of the "disparate" approach taken by the High Court in the interpretation of Section 122, there is some question about the extent to which the rights and guarantees that are enjoyed by other Australians are enjoyed by territory residents. And third, the relationship between the Northern Territory and the Commonwealth is unique because the territory is moving toward becoming a state within the federal structure. It has long been proposed that at some future time, the territory would become a fully autonomous state and no longer at the mercy of Section 122 and the interference of the Commonwealth. In 1999, a controversial statehood convention was held. The Northern Territory government held the view that the territory would achieve statehood by 2000. Many "Territorians" complained that the convention itself was not representative of the territory community, but the convention went ahead and adopted a draft constitution for the new state. Later that year, a referendum narrowly rejected a proposal for statehood for the Northern Territory.

Fiona Hussin

See also Australia; Constitutional Law; Customary Law; Federalism; Indigenous and Folk Legal Systems; Magistrates—Common Law Systems; Solicitors

References and further reading

Australian Bureau of Statistics. 1996. *Census of Population and Housing.* Canberra.
Blundell, Helena. 2000. "A Long Fight for a Basic Human Right." *Alternative Law Journal* 25, no. 5: 219–222.
Castles, Alex. 1982. *An Australian Legal History.* Sydney: Law Book Company.
Horan, Christopher. 1997. "Section 122 of the Constitution: A 'Disparate and Non-Federal' Power?" *Federal Law Review* 25, no. 1.
Libby, Stuart, and Jeremy McArdle, eds. 1993. *The Law Handbook.* Darwin: Community Legal Service, NT Legal Aid Commission.
Northern Territory Government, "A Brief History of Administration," http://www.nt.gov.au/ntg/information/administation_history.shtml (cited December 11, 2000).

NORTHWEST TERRITORIES
See Northern Territories of Canada

NORWAY

GENERAL INFORMATION

The Kingdom of Norway is located in extreme northern Europe, forming the western part of the peninsula known as Scandinavia. Norway borders Sweden, Finland, Russia, the Arctic Ocean, the Atlantic Ocean, and the North Sea. Much of the country is rugged, with high plateaus, steep fjords, difficult mountains, and fertile valleys. More than fifty thousand islands lie off its much-indented coastline. It covers 125,050 square miles (386,000 square kilometers), and its 1999 population was said to be 4,438,547. Nearly half of its population lives in the far south of the country, in the capital region around Oslo. Norway's main industries include timber, fishing, and oil and gas from the North Sea.

Because of the country's isolation, Norway's population is generally quite homogeneous, with only very small Sami (Lapp) and Finnish-speaking minorities. In recent years, however, Norway has also become home to increasing numbers of immigrants, foreign workers, and asylum-seekers from around the world. The country has a very high standard of living and an extensive social welfare system. Norway has one of the highest life expectancy rates in the world, and its literacy rate approaches 100 percent. Norway is also well-known as one of the top nations in the world in the number of books printed per capita, even though Norwegian is one of the world's smallest language groups.

Norway's legal system is a hybrid of the customary law, common law, and civil law traditions. Constitutional customary law uses current legal customs and practices as its foundation, giving them status equal to that of the constitution itself. Norway's legal system is very similar to the ones found among its Nordic neighbors (Denmark, Sweden, Finland, and Iceland). The Nordic legal systems

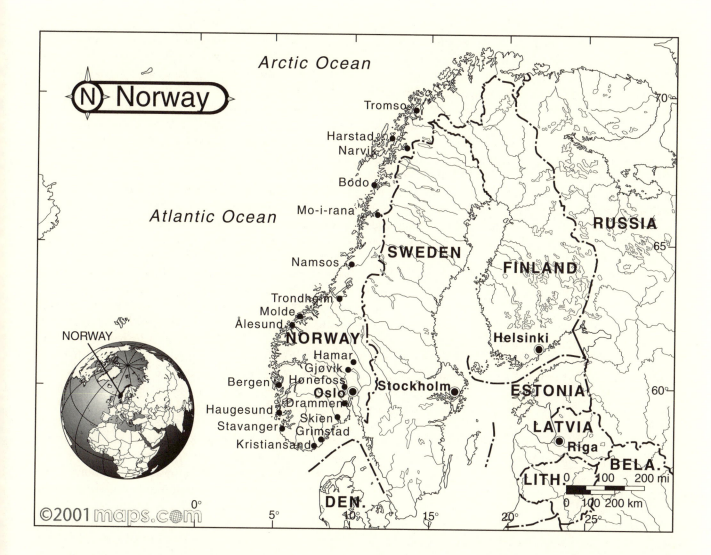

Within the map image: "Arctic Ocean", "Norway", "Atlantic Ocean", "Tromso", "Harstad", "Narvik", "Bodo", "Mo-i-rana", "SWEDEN", "RUSSIA", "FINLAND", "Namsos", "Trondheim", "Molde", "Ålesund", "NORWAY", "Hamar", "Gjøvik", "Helsinki", "Bergen", "Hønefoss", "Oslo", "Stockholm", "ESTONIA", "Drammen", "Haugesund", "Skien", "Stavanger", "Grimstad", "LATVIA", "Kristiansand", "Riga", "NORWAY", "BELA.", "LITH.", "DEN.", "©2001 maps.com", "100 200 mi", "0 100 200 km"

form a third family of European legal traditions, drawing on both common law and civil law roots.

HISTORY

The Viking period of the ninth to eleventh centuries led to the unification of the area now known as the Kingdom of Norway. The Vikings began Norway's economic interdependence with other countries, as they traded with and plundered the coasts from the British Isles to the Mediterranean Sea to North America. Around 1387 the nation came under the control of the Danish Crown, a union that would last for centuries. In 1814, as a result of Denmark's loss in the Napoleonic Wars, Norway was separated from Denmark and was instead combined into a loose federation dominated by Sweden and the Swedish Crown. The current constitution of Norway, however, was adopted on May 17, 1814, and Norwegians consider that date to be the date of the beginning of their independent, modern nation.

The union with Sweden lasted until 1905, when the Swedish monarch formally recognized Norwegian independence. In 1905, Norwegians elected their own king, and King Hakon VII ruled Norway until his death in 1957. His son, King Olav V, reigned from 1957 until 1990. Olav's son, King Harald V, took over the crown in 1991. Thus Norway's legal system has been clearly influenced by the experiences of its Danish and Swedish neighbors.

Judicial independence has long been a foundation of the Norwegian legal system. The 1814 Constitution guarantees an independent judiciary, but the roots of judicial independence began much earlier in Norwegian history. A national legal code was compiled in the 1270s, with a new codification adopted in 1687. In the 1700s, when the nation was under the control of the Danish king, the courts were even then independent and largely functioned outside of the monarch's power. As noted above, the current Norwegian Constitution was adopted on May 17, 1814. Drawing from then-popular European intellectual currents and the ideals expressed in the American and French constitutions, the Norwegian constitution established a constitutional monarchy based on such principles as popular sovereignty, the separation of powers, individual rights, and the balanced distribution of power between the government and the courts. The 1814

Constitution also created the independent Norwegian Supreme Court, as well as establishing the foundations for the current legal system.

Much like their American counterparts, the Norwegian courts in a variety of cases beginning around 1860 declared that the courts themselves would have the power to determine the constitutionality of the actions of other political actors. In Norway, as well as in the United States, this concept is called "judicial review." By 1890, the courts' power of judicial review was generally accepted among Norwegian academics and politicians. Today all of the regular courts can exercise the power of judicial review. Through the years, judicial review has become part of the constitutional customary law, with the same status as the judicial powers spelled out in the constitution. Although today the courts usually give great deference to decisions of the legislature, through constitutional customary law they retain the ability to overturn legislation that they feel is unconstitutional. When the Supreme Court hears a constitutional case, it sits in plenary session. Judicial review exercised under the concept of constitutional customary law today also includes the right of the regular courts to strike down laws that violate the European Convention on Human Rights. Throughout its history, the Norwegian Supreme Court has used its judicial review powers far less often than has the Supreme Court of the United States. In general, the Norwegian courts are very cautious in exercising judicial review.

The regular courts also retain the ability to decide whether administrative decisions are in compliance with statutory rules and human rights principles. There are no special administrative courts in Norway, although there is a special Ombudsman for Civil Administration to whom an appeal may be lodged by those who feel that they have suffered a wrong on the part of the administrative bureaucracy. The Norwegian Ombudsman for Civil Administration was first created in 1963, long after similar offices had been created in other Nordic countries. The office of ombudsman is basically a go-between or liaison between the citizens and their government. Beginning in 1952, when the Ombudsman for Military Affairs was introduced, Norway has created a variety of specialized ombudsman offices. The opinions of the Norwegian Ombudsman for Civil Administration are not binding on affected governmental agencies, but they are generally followed nonetheless. Since the ombudsman settles many grievances between individuals and governmental agencies, the courts tend to hear fewer administrative law cases than might otherwise be expected. Thus, although the courts in Norway retain the power to overturn administrative actions, they exercise that power far less often than do their American counterparts.

The judicial system in Norway is consequently a hybrid of the customary law, common law, and civil law traditions. Some of the current legal rules in Norway are the product of judicial decisions, while others have been codified. The Norwegian penal code was first adopted in 1902, replacing the prior 1842 code. A modern civil procedure code was adopted in 1915, but these procedures have almost constantly been updated. Other parts of the law, such as tort law, are based largely on court decisions. Still other aspects of the law are based on the concept of constitutional customary law.

Norway has long depended on its economic relations with foreign countries, both during independence and during the unions with Denmark and Sweden. Therefore it has been quite natural for Norway to adopt many commercial statutes that are identical to those of the other four Nordic countries, making many commercial-transaction laws uniform throughout Scandinavia. Domestic relations laws have also been standardized throughout much of the Nordic countries. In the 1990s, the country amended many of its other laws in anticipation of potential membership in the European Union (EU). In 1994, however, a national referendum rejected EU membership, just as the voters had rejected European Community membership in an earlier referendum in 1972. Nevertheless, Norway has transformed many of its business laws to accommodate EU legal rules because Norway remains a part of the European Economic Area (EEA), which is affiliated with the European Union. Since Denmark, Sweden, and Finland are now part of the European Union, and since many commercial laws were already uniform throughout Scandinavia, most commentators feel that Norway would not have to make many changes in its laws if it were to join the European Union at some time in the future.

LEGAL CONCEPTS

Norwegian courts have long been independent, and today the legal system is an eclectic blend of elements of the Anglo-American common law tradition and the Continental European civil law tradition. Comparative legal research has a long tradition in Norway, with the country often purposefully adapting foreign legal rules from both common law and civil law societies. In part because of its history, Norwegian law also borrows heavily from the legal rules of the other Nordic countries.

The Norwegian legal system is based in large part upon the notion of constitutional customary law, which complements the provisions of the 1814 Constitution. This principle encompasses the notions of a "common sense of justice" and the "fairness of the result," giving Norwegian law the ability to evolve as societal norms change. Using the concept of constitutional customary law, for example, Norway has evolved into a representative parliamentary democracy with a relatively weak constitutional monarchy without having to amend its 1814

Constitution, even though the constitution calls for a separation of powers system with a strong monarch. The new parliamentary democracy system began in the 1880s, and since then the Storting (the Norwegian Parliament) decides the composition of the cabinet, while the cabinet decides the actions of the Crown. The principle of constitutional customary law thus allows both the courts and the Storting to modernize the interpretation of various provisions of the 1814 Constitution without changing the actual text.

Statutory law, customary law, constitutional law, and judge-made law all exist as equally legitimate sources of law in Norway. Although all the regular courts in Norway have the power to determine the constitutionality of various governmental actions, Norwegian judges have traditionally been very cautious in exercising this power. In deciding cases before them, the courts engage in both interpretation of the law and the application of existing law. When the courts merely apply existing law, Norway's legal system looks more like part of the civil law tradition. When the judges interpret the written constitution or declare a practice to be part of constitutional customary law, however, the Norwegian legal system tends to resemble more the common law tradition. Drawing on the civil law tradition, much of the law today is codified, although judicial decisions remain the foundation for many areas of the law, such as tort law. But because Norwegian law encompasses the notion of constitutional customary law, the Norwegian legal system remains quite flexible. This approach to the law allows the governmental system and the legal system to evolve as the society's notions of "a common sense of justice" change.

CURRENT STRUCTURE

The Norwegian judiciary system consists of a regular three-tier hierarchy of courts plus some specialized courts that handle specific areas of the law. The Supreme Court is at the top of the hierarchy, followed by the High Court Appeals Division, with the district courts serving as the courts of first instance for most cases (see figure). In an attempt to promote mediation and arbitration as alternatives to going to court, Norway has also established Conciliation Boards, which attempt to settle civil disputes before they proceed to the courts of first instance. All the regular courts can hear civil, criminal, administrative, and constitutional cases. Low-income persons can obtain the assistance of a legal aid attorney in Oslo at public expense, or, outside of the capital region, the government will pay the fees of private attorneys.

At the apex of the court system is the Supreme Court of Norway. The Supreme Court has a chief justice and eighteen associate justices. All vacant judgeships are announced for public competition. Nominees to the court are recommended by the minister of justice and are then appointed by the king for a life term. In 1892, Norway abolished the requirement that all justices on the court be members of the state-recognized Lutheran Church. Although women have been eligible to be judges since 1915, the first female justice was appointed to the Supreme Court in 1968.

The Supreme Court is usually divided into three five-member panels and a three-member panel. Two of the larger panels hear individual cases, while members of the third large group are free to pursue individual research projects, teach, give speeches, and generally pursue their own specialized interests. The smaller panel serves as the Appeals Selection Panel, which decides which cases the court will hear and which ones it will dismiss. Membership on the various panels rotates among all judges on the court. All nineteen justices meet en banc for extraordinary cases, such as those challenging the constitutionality of statutes, when the court overturns its previous rulings, or when the chief justice feels that special circumstances warrant having the entire court hear a case. Years can sometimes pass between plenary meetings of the court, although the Supreme Court heard four cases en banc in 1996 alone.

Article 88 of the Constitution of 1814 established the authority of the court in a single sentence: "The Supreme Court pronounces judgment in the final instance." The chief justice of the Supreme Court ranks third among governmental officials, right after the prime minister and the president of the Storting. The Supreme Court Act of 1815 contained the original rules for the organization and competence of the court. This act has been modified numerous times, but the procedural and jurisdictional rules for the Supreme Court continue to be defined by statute. Until 1995, the Supreme Court heard appeals from all criminal proceedings in the courts of first instance. Today, criminal appeals first go to the High Court Appeals Division. Decisions of the Supreme Court, as well as decisions of the Appeals Selection Panel, are printed in the law journal called *Norsk Retstidende*, edited by the Norwegian Bar Association. This journal series was first published in 1836.

The High Court Appeals Division functions as the intermediate appellate court for appeals of both civil and criminal cases from the courts of first instance. There are six such appellate courts in the country, ranging in size from eight to twenty-two judges, including a chief justice on each court. An appeal concerning procedural questions or questions of law might be handled by written proceedings alone, although generally the court also hears oral arguments. The court usually meets as a three-judge panel, although at the discretion of the court, two to four lay jurors may assist the court. The votes of the lay jurors count equally with those of the judges.

Legal Structure of Norway Courts

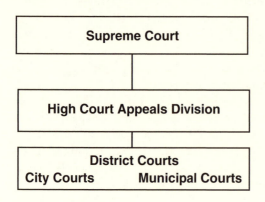

District courts, also called city courts or municipal courts, are the courts of first instance for major criminal or civil cases. These courts also serve as appellate courts that review the decisions of the Conciliation Boards. There are ninety-nine district courts, some having only a single judge, while the municipal court in Oslo has almost thirty judges. Rural courts often have a deputy judge or apprentice judge to assist the single regular judge. Usually a single judge hears the case at this level, although in some instances two lay jurors also vote. The votes of the jurors and the judge are equal, so that the two jurors can override the decision of the professional judge. District courts can also attempt to get the parties to settle their dispute, without regard to any previous mediation efforts before the Conciliation Boards.

The Conciliation Board promotes mediation of civil disputes and hears actions before they are heard in court. These boards consist of three lay judges elected by the county or city council for four-year terms. There are more than five hundred such boards in Norway today. Practicing lawyers cannot serve on the boards, and no attorneys are allowed to represent the parties. If the parties cannot agree on a settlement in a mediation case, the case may proceed to court. The board may also serve as an arbitrator, if the parties request that it do so. Arbitration decisions may be appealed to the district courts.

SPECIALIZED JUDICIAL BODIES

In addition to the regular courts, Norway has various special tribunals that deal with specific areas of the law. These special tribunals include the Labor Court, the Land Apportionment Court, the Guardianship Court, and the Social Security Court. Conciliation boards, designed to promote mediation and arbitration in civil cases, are discussed in more detail above.

Separate military courts have existed in Norway since medieval times. These courts operate under the Military Penal Code of 1902 and the Military Criminal Procedure Act of 1900 (as heavily amended in 1954).

STAFFING

All vacant judgeships are announced for public competition. Judges are appointed by the king for life terms upon the recommendation of the minister of justice. All judges must be Norwegian nationals and financially solvent. Women have been eligible to be judges since 1915. Judges are chosen from the bar, and there are no special educational degree programs for potential judges such as one finds in most of the European civil law countries. There is no regular promotion system for judges, and higher court judges can come from various legal fields including private attorneys, government attorneys, or lower court judges. Judges serve life terms, although there is a mandatory retirement age of seventy. Judges have the right to retire at full pension at age sixty-seven.

Law schools in Norway are government funded and are regulated by the Ministry of Church and Education. A law degree is roughly equivalent to an undergraduate degree in the United States. For the first year and a half, law students take courses and examinations in philosophy, logic, and psychology. The next three to five years focus on specific legal courses. There are very few elective courses in Norwegian law schools, and all the students must pass the same examinations. Students, however, can move through the courses and examinations at their own pace. The Ministry of Justice grants admission to the bar. There is no special bar examination, but the law student must serve a two-year apprenticeship between law school and admission to the bar. The minimum age for lawyers is twenty. Admission to the bar allows the lawyer to appear before any court except the Supreme Court.

The Ministry of Justice also has the authority to revoke a law license in cases of conduct unworthy of the profession, or in which the attorney has acted in such a way as to lose the trust necessary for the profession. The license may also be revoked because of neglect of professional duties. The Appeals Selection Panel of the Supreme Court hears appeals of revocation decisions.

A license to practice before the Supreme Court requires a minimum of an additional year of practice after being admitted to the regular bar. For admission to practice before the Supreme Court, the lawyer must also successfully argue three test pleadings, which require the lawyer to demonstrate a knowledge of both substantive and procedural rules used in the Supreme Court. Sometimes it can take several years before a lawyer is approved to practice before the Supreme Court. All litigants in cases before the Supreme Court must be represented by an attorney, even though Norway does not require that litigants in other courts be assisted by counsel.

An attorney general advises the executive branch on civil matters and represents the state in civil litigation. The attorney general is appointed by the king and has a staff of attorneys. This office is entirely separate from the

Ministry of Justice, and this office does not do any work for the legislative branch. This office should not be confused with the attorney general in the United States, because the Norwegian counterpart of the U.S. attorney general is the Ministry of Justice.

IMPACT

In part because of the civil law tradition's influence in Norway, for Norwegians the law is a highly particularized mechanism for the resolution of a specific type of dispute. The average citizen in Norway is much less attuned to the law as a political process than are persons in the United States, for example. Law in Norway is thought of in technical and administrative terms, but not necessarily as a political process. Although Norway has a highly developed conception of the rights of individuals, Norwegians generally turn to the political and administrative institutions to protect those rights, rather than using the courts to do so.

Public opinion in Norway does not separate the courts from the other institutions of government. Norwegians tend not to think of the courts separately from the rest of the governmental structure, as Americans are likely to do. In the United States, there is broad support among the population for the legal system and for the police, but less support for other governmental institutions. In Norway, on the other hand, the support for the legal system among the populace is generally the same as public support for the government as a whole. In other words, Norwegians see the courts as just another component of the broader governmental system.

Since Norway is in many ways a consensus-driven society, the notion of constitutional customary law gives the Norwegian legal system the ability to evolve as the political consensus changes. Thus the governmental structure has changed radically in Norway without there having been correspondingly radical changes to the 1814 Constitution. The legal system has also adapted to the extensive welfare state system now in place in Norway without the friction found during, for example, the New Deal era in the United States. Judges in Norway are naturally considered lawmakers as well as law-interpreters. Although they have broad interpretive powers, judges in Norway are much more cautious in exercising these powers than are many of their American counterparts. The eclectic legal system in Norway seems to serve that society well.

Mark C. Miller

See also Civil Law; Common Law; Customary Law; Denmark; Judicial Review; Sweden

References and further reading
Christensen, Tom, and B. Guy Peters. 1999. *Structure, Culture, and Governance: A Comparison of Norway and the United States.* Lanham, MD: Rowman and Littlefield.
Husa, Aakko. 2000. "Guarding the Constitutionality of Laws in the Nordic Countries: A Comparative Perspective." *American Journal of Comparative Law* 48: 345–380.
Rieber-Mohn, Georg. 1998. "The Dissolution of Core Values: Development of Crime and Society in Postwar Scandinavia with an Emphasis on Norwegian Circumstances." *Brigham Young University Law Review*: 1629–1643.
Rognes, Jorn. 1998. *Mediation in the Norwegian Land Consolidation Courts.* Madison: Land Tenure Center, University of Wisconsin–Madison.
Ryssday, Rolv. 1981. "The Relationship between the Judiciary and the Legislative and Executive Branches of the Government in Norway." *North Dakota Law Review* 57: 527–539.
Sollie, Finn. 1957. *Courts and Constitutions: A Comparative Study of Judicial Review in Norway and the United States.* Baltimore, MD: Johns Hopkins University Press.
Sverdrup, Ulf. 1998. "Norway: An Adaptive Non-Member." Pp. 149–166 in *Adapting to European Integration: Small States and the European Union.* Edited by Kenneth Hanf and Ben Soetendorp. New York: Addison Wesley Longman.
Tschudi-Madsen, Stephan, ed. 1998. *The Supreme Court of Norway.* Oslo: H. Aschehoug and Co.

NOTARIES

Notaries are a particular group within the province of legal professions. They are drawers of special documents—called "notarial deeds"—by rule legally provided with probatory force and available for public inspection. The term *notary* comes from an ancient Greek and Latin word, *not* (which means "known"), and *arius* (which means "agent" or "carrier"). Since the time of Cicero, "notaries" were those able to write *notae* or *notulae*—that is, to draw documents for public purposes.

Notarial deeds are about the recording of wills as regards relevant sociolegal transactions, particularly those concerning private property (contracting, inheritance, real estate matters, and so forth). The writing and undersigning of such deeds according to given legal standards provide formal-official certainty and security as regards the legal status of goods and relationships in space and time. It is presupposed that legal efficacy of notarial deeds spans centuries.

As the quest for certainty and security is an everlasting issue of any sociolegal system, notarial functions always existed—albeit in different fashion—in any society, preliterate societies included. Hence, one might sort out "functional equivalents"—that is, recording of wordings, oaths, declarations, and so forth—in societies based on oral traditions also. Given certain conditions, even today one might swear to God—that is, before reliable witness—to make a statement valid. By contrast, only in writing-based societies can one find what we now call—following Roman law legacy—"notaries" as trustworthy expert agents. This occurred first in Middle and Far Eastern countries. The existence of "writers" of that type (*scriba*) is documented well before the rise of Rome, in early civilizations such as those of Mesopotamia and Egypt, India, and China.

The distinction between notarial functions, notarial deeds, and notaries as a particular legal profession is a long-lasting issue in the history of any sociolegal system in the world. Notarial functions provide given statements with an aura of truthfulness—that is, convert mere utterances into truth-bearing assertions. Notarial deeds maintain, like a legal fiction, the image of actual performativity and authenticity of given communicative interactions even when they are not under direct observation. Notaries are socially reliable professionals: they say nothing, by rule, about the truth of what is being told them, but provide it with a binding social significance.

We owe to Roman law the establishment of notaries as a key element of Western/Westernized political, social, and cultural systems. This occurred at the time in which Roman notaries—mere scriveners (stenographers or chirographers) often lacking legal education—became involved in the recording of commercial transactions between old and new Roman citizens—that is, when the enlargement of Roman citizenship, enforced by Emperor Antoninus, compelled Rome to adopt (Eastern) usage of certifying transactions by means of written papers implying "local knowledge" (for example, about social value of foreign or domestic goods) and proper technical skills. The innovation was so radical that even their name changed: notaries were labeled *tabelliones,* and, as such, they became an organized group, provided with legal expertise, paid according to a tariff system, working in their own offices (called "stations") nearby public archives or the Forum.

From Emperor Iustinianus up to the early Middle Ages, the Roman legal system became increasingly centralized and bureaucratized. Notaries—called *scriptores,* tabelliones, or *notarii*—turned into public functionaries, enrolled within a state-controlled guild system. At a technical/symbolical level they were provided with a seal—a visible sign of the force of law—with a proper notarial deed (called *instrumentum, acta,* or *charta*) and with specific legal training (about *ars dictandi* and *ars notaria*). However, the most relevant change they endured occurred at politico-institutional levels as a consequence of the disintegration of the Roman Empire. The division of the empire between western and eastern emperors, followed by the schism between Christian-Roman-Catholic and Christian-Orthodox Churches, on the one hand, and the increasing detachment of temporal (empire) from spiritual (church) power, on the other, gave rise to two classes of notaries: those loyal, respectively, to Roman and Roman-Byzantine legal settings. In turn, the settlement of a variety of kingdoms on the part of Germanic tribes within the former Roman Empire's western territory put to the fore another class of notaries, concerned with a spurious mix of Roman and German law. Because of their expertise in both legal systems, they often performed judiciary functions also. Later on, Italian city-states also began to claim notaries for their own, thus challenging the legal authority of either the (German-ruled) Holy Roman Empire or the Roman Catholic Church. At this stage, conditions were ripe, in western Europe, for a veritable war for notaries' "investiture" between the two "universal powers," in order to establish a unique politico-institutional hegemony over the whole European normative realm. The war began in 1291 (Philip the Handsome's ordinance stating the king's power to create king's notaries) and ended in 1512 with the defeat of the Pope (bill—*Reichnotariatordnung*—enforced by the Emperor Maximillian at the Diet of Cologne).

The 1291–1512 war for notaries' "investiture" left a deep mark on the whole political, social, and cultural system in Europe. In fact, it opened the way to two other conflicts: the schism between Roman Catholic and Protestant Churches and the wars for dynastic supremacy among royal families to build up centralized nation-states and colonial empires.

In England, the religious schism fostered by the king gave rise to the establishment of the English common law system, as opposed to continental European legal systems. This political move not only detached English notaries from continental (Roman law) notarial tradition but also prevented the spread of civil law codification. As a result, English notaries experienced an irreversible professional decline, losing a great deal of their social attributes and functional competence, which in fact, since then, have been taken on by solicitors. In Germany, in turn, the religious schism concurred to deepen the fragmentation of regional socio-institutional orders. So much so that, at the beginning of the nineteenth century, the situation was as follows: in Prussia, Brunswick, Bremen, Lubeck, and Hanover, notaries and lawyers were fused together (*Anwaltnotariat*); in Bavaria, by contrast, notarial and lawyering functions were strictly detached; in Prussian Renania and Hamburg, the French Napoleonic notary model was enforced (*Nur-Notariat*), while in Baden and Wurttemberg two special systems were created (respectively, *Amstnotariat* and *Bezirknotariat*) in which notarial and judiciary powers were mixed. Given the institutional and moral confusion produced by schismatic movements, it is by no means fortuitous that—in relation to papal Counter-Reformation policy—a number of ethical codes were published to re-establish a behavioral common ground for practice. One of the most refined examples of such codes is included in a *Compendio de contratos publicos,* first edited in 1652 in Granada by Pedro Melgarejo Manrique for the kingdom of Castilla's notaries. The book had seventeen subsequent editions in one hundred years.

Wars for dynastic supremacy among European royal families to create strong nation-states and colonial empires had long-lasting effects on notaries also. An emblematic case in continental Europe is that of the Basque country's notaries. Since the fourteenth century, Basque notaries' main function has been—and still is—to shelter the Basque people from foreign pressures. In Euskera (the Basque language) notaries are called *baratari,* a term derived from the verb *baratu,* which means "to stop" or "to halt." Accordingly, Basque notaries are the agents that, by knowing the language spoken by the people and their local rules (written in three different bureaucratic styles), witness sociolegal transactions (land transfers, dowry arrangements, and so forth) to prevent the exploitation of local resources. Equally emblematic cases can be found outside Europe. In North America, for example, one still finds civil law notarial models in Louisiana and Quebec, while in any other state of the United States and Canada, notaries as a professional group do not exist, and basic notarial functions are performed by lawyers.

In the West, a further epochal turning point occurred just after the French Revolution. Under the leadership of a notary like Robespierre, Gothic law and age-old professional guilds were abolished in the name of Enlightenment principles. Therefore, as soon as he acquired the power, Napoleon was able to reset the whole system of professions according to new legal standards. Professional Law of 25 Venteuse, Year XI (that is, March 16, 1803) constituted French notaries as civil (that is, state) servants granted with territorial and functional monopoly to perform a public service in private contexts. The service was about authentification, certification, and recording of wills and statements of private citizens (bequests, contracts, constitutions of corporations, and so forth) by means of acts having the same binding authenticity, publicity, and executivity (that is, all the probative force) of judicial decisions. Besides, the above law excluded the mixing of notaries' status-role and functions with those of any other legal profession, put notaries under the disciplinary control of the judiciary, and set up a compulsory enrollment system. The importance of this reform is due to the fact that it fitted organically with a broader socioinstitutional mainstream based on two pillars: nation-oriented state-building and state-centered sociolegal theorizing, both fostered to reduce legal pluralism through positivization and codification—that is, to enhance legal formalism. Hence, also supported by the long-lasting impact of postrevolutionary ideals, throughout the nineteenth century French notaries were a reference point for continental European civil law countries and their extra-European colonies (in particular, those of Latin America, such as Mexico and Venezuela) struggling for national independence and formal-legal "rationalization" of national settings. Altogether these trends exacerbated, in turn, age-

old structural and cultural cleavages between civil law and common law notaries, while reinforcing everlasting claims for a "pure" (organic) state-centered notarial system.

Given the above historical legacy, one finds three notarial models in contemporary Western/Westernized society: a (pure) "state" (civil law) model, a "common law" model, and a "Latin-type" (civil law) model. With reference to either national patterns or country-specific professional traits, each model includes various submodels.

State notaries embody basic patterns of a long-lasting authoritarian/autocratic legal tradition, typical of Western state form since the Byzantine era. They are civil servants acting as state organs. They work within either the judiciary or the administrative system and are provided with official power of either control over private transactions and individual rights or tutelage over general public issues enhanced by the state. Their deeds are veritable "public acts," formally similar to those produced by the state bureaucracy. In Germany, state notaries were set up by Hitler in 1937 and abolished after the fall of the Nazi regime. In Portugal, Salazar abolished Latin-type notaries and established state notaries in 1957 (the so-called Bureaucratic model). In the USSR, czarist state notaries were abolished by Lenin in 1917. In his turn, Khrushchev set up the so-called Soviet model in the late 1950s. The Soviet model was also enforced in the eastern European Soviet Bloc. After the fall of the Berlin Wall, Poland, East Germany, Hungary, Rumania, and Russia turned toward the Latin-type model.

Common law notaries are not state agents at all, but rather selected citizens, appointed by an official authority and granted a personal license to certify, attest, and record—under their own "hand and seal"—the way in which oaths, affidavits, declarations, acknowledgments, and so forth have been performed by private parties. Their deeds are not "public acts" in that they have no probatory force, but provide mere documentary evidence of the recorded performance. Up to the last decade in England and Wales, there were four types of common law notaries: district, general, ecclesiastic, and scriveners. District notaries were abolished in 1990. General and ecclesiastic notaries are enrolled within a common guild ("faculty") still chaired by the Archbishop of Canterbury by virtue of a royal concession given as early as 1533. General and ecclesiastic notaries are almost always primarily solicitors performing notarial functions whenever requested. The volume of their notarial duties and fees is quite low. At present, general notaries can act anywhere in England, including the city of London, which was previously strictly reserved to scriveners only. Ecclesiastic notaries perform notarial functions as chancellors in ecclesiastic courts or as secretaries in Episcopal offices. In turn, scriveners are just notaries (that is, they are not solicitors) and practice successfully full-time, being expert in foreign languages and rules about any sort of commercial transaction. They have been enrolled in an independent guild ("society") and their number has been stable at around twenty-five to thirty members over the centuries. Indeed, they had a statutory monopoly of notarial work within the city of London from 1373 to 1999.

In England, as in any other common law country in the world, notaries represent a marginal legal profession in any respect. For example, in the United States notarial functions are performed by lawyers, and few people, even lawyers, have any idea of what notaries actually were, are, or do.

Latin-type (civil law) notaries are so called because they are typically set up in either European Latin countries or extra-European countries characterized by Latin sociocultural imprintings. They differ from the above-mentioned models, as they are either public officers or (private) professionals. They act as public officers as far as notarial functions and status-role are concerned. However, within this framework, they act as private professionals as regards work organization, personal responsibility (for example, for malpractice), and earnings (from clients' remuneration only). This Janus-headed structuration was first enforced in Italy in 1913, as a refinement of the French model. Since then, Latin-type notaries are typically enrolled in a compulsory guild, practice under the supervision of the judiciary, and have monopolistic power over the production of so-called original notarial deeds. Yet, due to their expertise, they are not involved in drawings and recordings only, but can deal also with legal counseling and negotiation in any legal issue. In countries such as Italy, they can now act in court in certain matters as well. Surely, they are the most compact, prestigious, wealthy, and powerful group within civil law legal professions. At present, the Latin-type model is enforced, according to quite homogeneous standards, in forty-two countries in the world. The International Union of Latin-type Notary—I.U.L.N.—set up in 1948, includes notaries of continental Europe, Central and South America, Francophone areas of North America, Northern and Central Africa, and Far Eastern Asia (Japan) influenced by French, Spanish, or German legal culture. In Asia, countries such as China, Laos, Indonesia, and Vietnam are inclined toward the model, as they have established formal contacts with the union. Under the aegis of the European Affairs Commission, since 1957 the same union has become a reference point for "revising" or "harmonizing" eastern European Slavonic and Middle-East Arabic notarial models. Even European common law countries are now turning toward the Latin-type model, as the presence of English general notaries as "observers" since the 1980s, and full admission of scrivener notaries in 1998 within the union, demonstrate. Two needs explain the move toward such an alignment: to upgrade the legal status of common law notarial acts, given the changes that have occurred in economic and legal systems worldwide, and to catch up with cultural standards according to EU agreements on mutual recognition of professional expertise. At present, notaries embodying or close to the Western civil law tradition are active in seventy-nine countries in the world. By contrast, notaries in common law countries are almost nonexistent. Due to Western pressure, classic Islamic, Brahmanic, and Confucian notarial models are undergoing a sort of "resetting" process. In these cases, however, local patterns play a relevant role still. In an Islamic country such as Morocco, for example, official notaries (called *adul* or *adala*) are, by rule, professional witnesses in court. Their number is important also: the same statement recorded separately by three notaries is seriously considered by the court. Not by chance, to prevent conflicts of interest in case of divorce, even in the present time, every marriage (transfer of bridewealth and so forth) is, by rule, registered before two notaries.

All that has been said makes clear that—contrary to current ideology—one can hardly claim a "globalization of law" at a worldwide level at present. In any case, the thousand-year-old history of notaries shows that: (1) "globalization" in the province of law has never occurred, for a core dimension of law is its symbolic structure/function as a truth-bearing device, and (2) the power-knowledge nexus that a legal profession embodies cannot but reflect, first and foremost, historical conflicts for, and space-time relativity of, given political hegemony.

Vittorio Olgiati

See also Civil Law; Common Law; Legal Pluralism
References and further reading

Basedow, Jürgen. 1991. "Zwischen Amt und Wettbewerb: Perspektiven des Notariats in Europa." *RabelsZ* 11: 409–435.
Dunford, Antony, ed. 1999. *The General Notary*. Woodbridge: Notaries' Society.
Halpérin, Jean Louis. 1996. *Avocats et notaries en France: Les professions judiciaires et juridiques dans l'histoire contemporaine.* Paris: LGDJ.
Olgiati, Vittorio. 1994. "The Latin-type Notary and the Process of European Unification." *International Journal of the Legal Profession* 1, no. 3: 253–268.
Shaw, Gisela. 2001. "Notaries in England and Wales: Modernizing a Profession Frozen in Time." *International Journal of the Legal Profession* 7: 141–155.

NOVA SCOTIA

GENERAL INFORMATION

Nova Scotia is one of the Canadian Atlantic provinces on the eastern seaboard of Canada; it comprises the peninsula of Nova Scotia proper and the adjoining island of Cape Breton. The province is 55,490 square kilometers (21,425 square miles) in size, with a population of roughly 900,000. Halifax is the provincial capital as well as the largest urban center, with a greater metropolitan population of around 250,000; the next largest city—Sydney, in Cape Breton—has a population of roughly 30,000, highlighting the sharp contrast between the metropolitan center of the province and its largely rural outlying regions.

The economy has historically been reliant on primary natural resource development and some secondary heavy industrial manufacturers. Agriculture, fishing, forestry, coal mining, and steel production were the backbone of the Nova Scotian economy throughout the twentieth century, but most of those industries, especially coal and steel, have been in decline, while the fishing and forestry sectors experienced grave problems over the 1990s respecting overutilization and unsustainable development. The discovery of offshore oil and natural gas in the 1980s is heralding the development of a new energy sector within the province, and, as the economy is changing, the industries of the "new economy" are also emerging. Both Halifax and Sydney are becoming homes to a host of information and high-technology firms active in a wide array of secondary manufacturing and tertiary service-delivery and management-information programming. As these new economic sectors evolve, they are joined with vibrant tourism and cultural industries as the public and private sectors develop partnerships to promote the province's spectacular land and seascapes, as well as its unique blend of Aboriginal, French Acadian, Anglo-Celtic, and African–Nova Scotian ethnic heritage.

EVOLUTION AND HISTORY

The land area of Nova Scotia was originally the territory of the Mi'kmaq nation, whose people first came into contact with French and then English explorers and settlers in the seventeenth and eighteenth centuries. By 1758 all of Nova Scotia was under English control, and the British government signed a number of peace treaties with the Mi'kmaq nation respecting land and economic rights. Those treaties were given official recognition in the Royal Proclamation of 1763.

As a British colony, Nova Scotia produced a legal and judicial system under the aegis of the English common law. Thus it has the characteristic structure of a professional bar, an independent judiciary, a precedential system of litigation and legal reasoning, and a reliance on a unitary court structure culminating with an appeal to the Judicial Committee of the Privy Council in London.

Nova Scotia and Quebec were the two major British North American colonies to remain loyal to the United Kingdom during the American Revolution. In 1848, Nova Scotia made Canadian and British political and legal history, becoming the first colony in the British Empire to be granted responsible government, marking a

turning point in the development of the Canadian liberal democratic tradition. The other major constitutional reform affecting the British North American colonies in the latter years of the nineteenth century was the Canadian Confederation of 1867. The Constitution Act of 1867 marked the birth of the Canadian federal state, with provinces such as Nova Scotia being given major roles to play in the fields of natural resource development, education, social policy, and the management of civil law and judicial administration. The development of criminal law, by virtue of the Constitution Act, remains an exclusive federal responsibility.

The Constitution Act also mandated a unique and rather complex system of interlocking federal and provincial responsibilities respecting the establishment and administration of courts within each province. The court system remained unitary, with each province possessing, generally, a set of base-level, general-jurisdiction provincial courts dealing with most all criminal and civil matters. These so-called provincial courts existed within the sole jurisdiction of the provinces, administered by them and with judges appointed by the provincial governments. Above these courts stood a series of general jurisdiction county and district courts, likewise administered by the provincial government but with their judiciary appointed by the federal government. Then above those courts would stand the Supreme Court of the province, and, above it, the Provincial Court of Appeal. All these courts possessed a federally appointed judiciary, but with all such courts being administered by the provincial government. Thus the Constitution Act struck a fascinating balance of federal and provincial responsibilities within a unitary court structure. The system remains unitary in that there is only one system of courts within each province, but the differing orders of government divide responsibilities for judicial appointments, with the federal government claiming the appointment power for the more superior courts. Yet this federal advantage is balanced by provincial responsibilities for the judicial administration of all courts domiciled within the province, inclusive of those with a federally appointed judiciary. In keeping with the unitary nature of the system, appeals from the Provincial Court of Appeal would lie to the Supreme Court of Canada, and then, until 1949, to the Judicial Committee of the Privy Council.

This federal-provincial division of responsibilities has remained largely unchanged since 1867, with some notable developments occurring only in the last quarter of the twentieth century. In 1975 a separate Federal Court of Canada was created to address all federal administrative law litigation arising throughout the country, with this court having regional offices, including one in Nova Scotia. The 1980s and 1990s also witnessed the amalgamation of the Nova Scotia county courts into the Nova Scotia

Supreme Court, and the creation of a separate family branch of both the Provincial and Supreme Courts. With respect to case law, the most significant development within the Nova Scotian legal system in the latter decades of the twentieth century was the emergence of aboriginal constitutional claims seeking to reinvigorate the old treaty rights of the Mi'kmaq nation. A number of these cases, especially *Marshall v. The Queen* (1999, 2000), have been successful in reaffirming the ongoing validity of the eighteenth-century treaties and in allowing the courts to tailor the treaties to meet twenty-first-century realities.

CURRENT STRUCTURE

At the base of the Nova Scotia judicial structure stand a number of special function courts overseen either by provincially appointed judges or part-time adjudicators (see figure). These courts are the Nova Scotia Small Claims Court, the Nova Scotia Probate Court, and the Nova Scotia Summary Proceedings Court. The former deals with civil disputes with a monetary value of up to $10,000 Canadian and is designed to allow plaintiffs and respondents to represent themselves at trial; this court is overseen by part-time adjudicators selected from the ranks of the local bar and appointed to varying terms of service. The latter courts are designed to address a plethora of minor disputes involving motor vehicles, by-laws and regulatory enforcement, and minor criminal and civil matters. These courts are overseen by a mix of provincially appointed judges and justices of the peace.

Above these courts stands the Nova Scotia Provincial Court. This court, overseen by a chief judge and twenty-six provincially appointed judges, possesses exclusive jurisdiction over all summary offenses under provincial statutes and federal acts and regulations, as well as holding jurisdiction to conduct trials involving intermediate criminal and civil matters as defined by the criminal code and other relevant civil legislation. The Provincial Court also possesses jurisdiction to hold preliminary inquiries into the most serious criminal charges in which an accused has elected trial within the Supreme Court. All criminal proceedings commence in Provincial Court, and fully 95 percent of all criminal prosecutions are heard by Provincial Court judges.

A special part of the Nova Scotia Provincial Court is the Nova Scotia Family Court, also staffed by provincially appointed judges, providing a forum for disputes related to the family, including maintenance, custody and access, family violence between spouses or between parent and child, and child protection matters. It is also a youth court, hearing matters involving persons aged twelve to fifteen and charged under the federal Young Offenders Act or the provincial Young Persons Summary Proceedings Act.

Standing above these provincial courts is the Nova Scotia Supreme Court. This court consists of the chief justice of Nova Scotia, an associate chief justice, and twenty-three justices, all of whom are federally appointed; the administration of this court, however, and all other "superior" courts, remains a provincial responsibility. The judges of the Supreme Court sit independently in eighteen locations across the province, holding general jurisdiction in both criminal and civil matters arising within the province. As a matter of course, proceedings in the Supreme Court are reserved for the most serious of criminal infractions, as defined by the criminal code, and the most involved, complex, and high-monetary-value civil proceedings. In dealing with these matters, this court alone is empowered to conduct jury trials, though in both criminal and civil adjudication such trials are becoming exceedingly rare.

The Supreme Court also possesses jurisdiction with respect to disputes emanating from departments of the provincial government, as well as provincially established regulatory agencies, boards, and commissions. This field of law is becoming increasingly important within Canadian society, and the administrative law caseload of the Nova Scotia Supreme Court has grown dramatically in the past quarter-century, reflecting both the increase in state activity within the fields of socioeconomic policy as well as a greater litigiousness among the Canadian public.

A special part of the Supreme Court is its Family Division. This branch of the court hears appeals from the Nova Scotia Family Court, while also possessing original jurisdiction with respect to divorce matters and the more serious criminal charges under the federal Young Offenders Act.

At the apex of the judicial hierarchy is the Nova Scotia Court of Appeal. This court consists of the chief justice and nine other senior justices, two of whom are supernumerary. The Court of Appeal sits in Halifax and operates as a general jurisdiction appellate body, with most of its work involving serious criminal, civil, and administrative law litigation. In recent years it has also had to address important constitutional law matters respecting aboriginal treaty rights. This court exists as the highest court in the province, with appeals lying, by leave, to the Supreme Court of Canada. Given that such leaves are rarely granted, with the Canadian Supreme Court hearing only some 100 to 125 cases per year drawn from across the country, the logical and practical result is that the Court of Appeal for each province tends to become the de facto final adjudicative forum for most all legal disputes in the province, saving and excepting only those raising the most troubling questions of national legal significance.

Finally, a last component element of the Nova Scotia judicial structure is the Federal Court of Canada and its regional trial division sitting in Halifax. This court operates fully within federal jurisdiction, with judges appointed by the federal minister of justice and with its ad-

Structure of Nova Scotian Courts

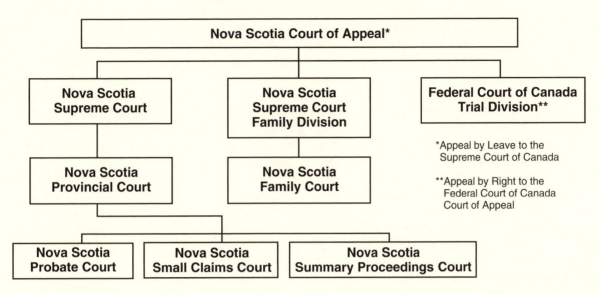

ministration being a responsibility of the federal Department of Justice. The court acts as a federal administrative law court, hearing disputes arising from the decision-making of federal departments and agencies, boards, and commissions applying federal rules and regulations within Nova Scotia. Appeals from this court lie to the Federal Court of Canada, Court of Appeals, domiciled in Ottawa, with a final appeal, by leave, to the Supreme Court of Canada. As such, the Federal Court of Canada trial division within the province is not a part of the judicial hierarchy of the province but a separate entity altogether.

STAFFING

As highlighted above, both the federal and provincial orders of government share responsibility for appointing judges to the courts. Both sets of governments, moreover, share a generally similar approach to judicial appointment. To be eligible for either a federal or provincial judicial appointment, a person must be a member in good standing with the Nova Scotia Barristers' Society with a minimum of ten years' legal experience. The actual appointment process tends to be generally informal, in that there are no American-style selection processes or confirmation hearings. Ordinarily, when a judicial vacancy occurs the relevant minister of justice will establish a committee of advisory officials to consult with the chief judge or chief justice, other members of the judiciary, the chair of the Barristers' Society, and other members of the bar. Leading candidates will be vetted confidentially, and the final decision-making authority rests with the relevant minister of justice and related prime minister or premier.

Once appointed, a judge holds the judicial position, on good behavior, until mandatory retirement at sev-

enty-five, with removal only for cause based upon a vote of censure in either the provincial legislature or federal Parliament, as the case may be. In any and all cases of alleged judicial misconduct, the matter will first be addressed by the Nova Scotia Judicial Council, consisting of the chief justice and chief judge of the province, and other senior members of the bench and bar. The Judicial Council can issue a wide array of findings, ranging from absolution through advice, recommendations for improved behavior, reprimands, and suspensions, all the way to recommendations to the relevant minister of justice for removal.

THE LEGAL PROFESSION AND LEGAL EDUCATION

There are currently some two thousand practicing and nonpracticing lawyers registered with the Barristers' Society of Nova Scotia. As is the case across Canada, the legal profession is not divided into separate ranks of barristers and solicitors; all lawyers are trained to fulfill both duties should they wish. The Barristers' Society itself is a self-governing regulatory body overseeing the administration of the legal profession in the province. The society, founded in 1825, exists under an act of the provincial legislature and is responsible for such main duties as bar admissions and licensing; the establishment of professional ethical standards, and the exercise of professional discipline; the maintenance of a members' insurance system; and the regulation of trust accounts. Legal education in the province is centered upon the Dalhousie University Law School, founded in 1883 and located in Halifax. While "Dal Law" is considered small by Canadian national standards, with 34 faculty and a total undergraduate student population of 441 as of the academic year

2000/2001, this law school nonetheless has a national reputation as one of the leading institutions of higher legal education in the country. In keeping with this reputation, some half of all students admitted to the Dalhousie Law School routinely come from outside Nova Scotia, mainly from other Canadian provinces but with a small minority deriving from other countries. On average, the law school will offer some 150 placements for first-year students and will graduate some 150 students per year. The school offers the standard undergraduate legal curriculum taught from the common law perspective, while also offering a graduate program (of about 25 students) with emphases on maritime law, feminist jurisprudence, and human rights. The law school is also generally noted for its unique Indigenous Black and Mi'kmaq Program (offering specialized recognition and assistance to members of these minority groups), as well as its specialization in Marine and Environmental Law. The school also has two exchange programs with American law schools: the University of Maine Law School, in Portland, and Loyola University in Chicago.

RELATIONSHIP TO NATIONAL SYSTEM

As observed above, as flowing from the structural logic of the Constitution Act of 1867, there are close institutional and administrative linkages between the federal and Nova Scotian governments respecting the organization and working of the courts in Nova Scotia, as in every other Canadian province. The general unitary system necessitates close cooperation between federal and provincial departments of justice regarding the staffing and administration of the courts, and this interrelationship is now also being observed in the growing contacts between federal and provincial court administrators concerned with judicial administration. The Association of Canadian Court Administrators brings together officials and judges from both federal and provincial orders of government involved with the management of Canadian courts, and this organization is helping to forge national, federal, and provincial linkages at the all-important management and operational level with respect to the development of case-flow management systems and general court operational best practices.

David Johnson

See also Administrative Law; British Columbia; Canada; Common Law; Federalism; Indigenous and Folk Legal Systems; Native American Law, Traditional; New Brunswick; Ontario; Quebec; Saskatchewan; United States—Federal System; United States—State Systems

References and further reading
Dyck, Rand. 1995. *Provincial Politics in Canada.* 3d ed. Toronto: Prentice Hall Canada.
Gall, Gerald. 1990. *The Canadian Legal System.* 3d ed. Toronto: Carswell.
Hogg, Peter. 1999. *Constitutional Law of Canada: 1999 Student Edition.* Toronto: Carswell.
McCormick, Peter, and Ian Greene. 1990. *Judges and Judging.* Toronto: Lorimer.
Russell, Peter. 1987. *The Judiciary in Canada: The Third Branch of Government.* Toronto: McGraw-Hill Ryerson.

NUNAVUT

See Northern Territories of Canada

OHIO

GENERAL INFORMATION

Ohio was admitted to the United States in 1803, the seventeenth state to enter the Union. Originally part of the Northwest Territory, Ohio is bounded on the north by Lake Erie and Michigan, on the east by Pennsylvania and West Virginia, on the south by Kentucky, and on the west by Indiana. It is 41,330 square miles in size, with approximately two-thirds of the state still existing as farmland. Currently ranking seventh among the fifty states in terms of population, Ohio had roughly 11.4 million people in 2000. Still, growth in the state's population in recent years has been well below the national average.

The area that is now Ohio was originally settled by mound-building indigenous people who disappeared about 400 C.E. European explorers found the area inhabited by numerous Native American tribes, including the Miami, Shawnee, Wyandot, and Delaware. The first permanent white settlement was established in Marietta in 1788, although earlier mission settlements of Native Americans existed in the 1770s at Schoenbrunn and Gnadenhutten in present-day Tuscarawas County, in the northeastern part of the state.

There has been no single dominating cultural influence on the state. Germans were historically the largest group of immigrants, particularly in the nineteenth century, but in later years, large waves of immigrants from eastern and southeastern Europe were attracted to Ohio's cities. African Americans constitute approximately 10 percent of the state's population, most of whom are concentrated in the cities. For example, nearly half of Cleveland is African American, and in the public schools of Cleveland, Cincinnati, Dayton, and Youngstown, racial minorities are majorities of the public school population. Much of the black population came to Ohio during the great migration from the South in the 1920s.

The state is divided geographically and culturally between north and south. Columbus is the capital and is centrally located. Forty percent of the state is in Appalachia, an economically poor region of the United States spreading to the eastern and southern areas of Ohio. This part of the state has limited agricultural op-portunities and virtually no industrialization. It is largely rural and has the counties with the highest rates of unemployment. Northeastern Ohio is the most heavily industrialized part of the state. Manufacturing represents the largest single segment of the state's employment and remains the most important economic activity. Rapid industrialization occurred in Ohio following the Civil War. The state's north-south division has led to the evolution of different political cultures within the state. The Democratic Party has historically been strong in the northeastern part of the state, with the rest of the state deemed more consistently Republican.

Eight U.S. presidents have been elected from Ohio, earning it the nickname "the mother of presidents." The most recent of these individuals, William Howard Taft, also served as chief justice of the U.S. Supreme Court in the 1920s. Eight associate justices also have ties to Ohio. The last Ohioan to serve on the Court was Potter Stewart, whose tenure ran from 1958 to 1981.

EVOLUTION AND HISTORY

Ohio was the first state carved out of the Northwest Territory. New York, Connecticut, and Virginia all lay claim to the land after the American Revolution, but with the ratification of the Articles of Confederation, their claims were ceded. Still, the tract of land ceded by Connecticut in 1786 had its legal title retained by Connecticut. Unable to establish a civil government, Connecticut sold the land in 1795. Not until 1800 was the federal government recognized as having authority over the land, which had just 1,000 settlers due to the controversy.

The first constitution was adopted in 1803 with statehood. Perceived deficiencies in the organization and functioning of the judiciary were a major impetus for constitutional revision. The basic structure of Ohio's current court system was established in 1851 when the second constitution was ratified. The entire judicial system was revised in the new constitution. The Ohio Supreme Court was given five judges in place of four and was relieved of the cumbersome requirement of holding court annually in each county of the state.

A system of District Courts with appellate jurisdiction was also set up in the 1851 Constitution, each composed of Common Pleas judges and one Supreme Court justice. Separate Probate Courts were authorized, and the clerks of Common Pleas Courts were made elective positions. So, too, were the judges' positions, replacing the method of legislative appointment in place since 1803.

The 1851 Constitution continues to be in effect. However, in 1912, home rule was granted to villages and cities, changing governmental relations. While Ohio remains a unitary government, the home-rule charter is an example of the state willingly altering its unitary character to become a union of home-rule local governments. The Modern Courts Amendment of 1968 changed some of the specifics of judicial organization (for example, it eliminated separate Probate Courts), but the basic structure remains intact.

CURRENT STRUCTURE

There are three levels of constitutional courts in the Ohio system. The Ohio Supreme Court is the court of last resort in the state court system, and it has statewide jurisdiction. Although primarily a court of appellate jurisdiction, the state Supreme Court does have limited original jurisdiction through its power to issue certain extraordinary writs, including the writs of habeas corpus, mandamus, quo warranto, prohibition, and procedendo. Most cases are appealed from the twelve Courts of Appeals. Automatic appeals from some statewide agencies such as the Board of Tax Appeals and the Public Utilities Commission are also heard. One chief justice and six justices are elected to six-year terms in statewide elections.

The intermediate appellate courts are called Courts of Appeals. There are twelve appellate districts in the state, with their geographic size ranging from one to seventeen counties. These appellate cases are heard by three-judge panels. The number of judges per district ranges from four to twelve and depends on the size and caseload of the district. The caseloads vary widely across districts. In the 1998 calendar year, 222 new cases per judge in one district was the high, as compared to a low of 128 new cases per judge in another district. Like the Ohio Supreme Court, these courts can assert original jurisdiction in issuing the above-named writs. The district judges are also elected to six-year terms. As of 2001, there were sixty-six district judges in the state.

Courts of Common Pleas exist in each of Ohio's eighty-eight counties. These are primarily trial courts, although some appeals from city and state administrative agencies may be heard in these courts. All felony cases are adjudicated in these courts; most other criminal and civil disputes are heard there, as well, except for those given exclusively to the legislatively created courts that will be discussed. There has been a 125 percent increase in Common Pleas Court filings since 1979. The Modern Court Amendment passed by voters in 1968 grants Common Pleas Courts the option of forming multicounty partnerships to maximize efficient delivery of judicial services to the public.

The General Division also has jurisdiction in civil disputes involving $15,000 or more. The General Division exists in each county; Probate, Domestic Relations, and Juvenile Divisions may also exist within each court. In seven counties, for example, the General and Probate Divisions are combined. Probate Divisions handle administration of the estates of the deceased and guardianships of minors, as well as adults deemed incompetent to handle their own affairs. Until 1968, separate Probate Courts were constitutionally required. Domestic Relations Divisions have jurisdiction over divorces, dissolutions, and child custody. Juvenile divisions specialize in cases involving alleged delinquency offenses by those under eighteen years of age. Paternity actions are usually heard by this division, as well. There were a total of 375 Common Pleas judges as of this writing.

Judges are elected to the specific divisions of the court established for their county by the Ohio Revised Code. Seven Common Pleas judges within the state are known as the "Magnificent Seven," as they hear cases in all four divisions. More typical are the judges noted earlier that have Probate and General Divisions combined. In metropolitan areas such as Cleveland, the four divisions are distinct, with judges running for specific seats within a division. In Ohio, judges do not rotate among the divisions but rather are elected to a particular division.

In addition to this three-tiered system of constitutional courts, several courts of limited jurisdiction have been created by statute. Municipal Courts handle most traffic and other misdemeanor offenses and can hear civil actions involving up to $15,000. Currently, there are 118 Municipal Courts and 203 municipal judges. Appeals from Municipal Courts are heard by the Courts of Appeals. By law, each Municipal Court must also have a Small Claims Division that hears civil cases where less than $1,000 is at stake. The County Court system was created in 1958 when the system of justices of the peace was abolished. County courts serve the geographic areas within a county that are not within the jurisdiction of a Municipal Court. As of this writing, there are 49 County Courts and 55 county judges. The trend in recent years has been to develop Municipal Courts that exercise countywide jurisdiction.

In cities or villages that do not have their own Municipal Court, Mayors' Courts are legally required. In these courts, the mayor of the city or village decides cases and collects fines involving violations of municipal ordinances and traffic offenses. There are currently approximately 428 Mayors' Courts. Unlike all other courts in Ohio, there is no legal requirement that the presiding officer in these courts, the mayor, be an attorney. These

Structure of Ohio Courts

SUPREME COURT
Chief Justice and Six Associate Justices

Original jurisdiction in select cases; court of last resort on state constitutional questions and questions of public or great general interest; appeals from Board of Tax Appeals and Public Utilities Commission; regulates practice of law and disciplines judges and lawyers

COURTS OF APPEALS
12 Courts, 68 Judges
Three-Judge Panels

Original jurisdiction in select cases; appellate review of judgments of Common Pleas, Municipal, and County Courts; appeals from Board of Tax Appeals

COURTS OF COMMON PLEAS
88 Courts, 376 Judges*

General Division

Civil and criminal cases; appeals from most administrative agencies; felony DUI cases

Domestic Relations Division

Divorces and dissolutions; support; custody of children of divorcing or divorced parents

Probate Division

Probate: Estates, trusts, guardianships; adoption, and mental illness cases; marriage licenses

Juvenile Division

Offenses involving minors; abuse, neglect, and dependency; most paternity actions; custody and support of children of unmarried parents

MUNICIPAL COURTS
118 Courts, 203 Judges

Misdemeanor offenses; traffic cases; most DUI cases; civil actions up to $15,000

COUNTY COURTS
47 Courts*, 55 Judges

Misdemeanor offenses; traffic cases; civil actions up to $15,000

COURT OF CLAIMS
Judges Assigned by Supreme Court
Three-judge panel upon request

All suits against the state for personal injury, property damage, contract, and wrongful death; compensation for victims of crime

MAYORS' COURTS
Approximately 428 Mayors; Misdemeanor offenses; traffic cases
Note: Mayors' Courts are not courts of record

*Numbers current as of January 2001

courts have been the subject of debate for many years. A recent commission in Ohio has recommended that their role be assumed by trial courts. The U.S. Supreme Court declared these courts unconstitutional in 1972 insofar as the mayor is responsible for managing village finances and also has the power to lay and collect fines through which much of a village's revenue is generated. The power to both raise and spend village funds and to act as both executive and judge was seen as violating separation of powers.

There is some concern that Ohio has too many trial courts with confusing and overlapping jurisdictions, which, among other things, may encourage "judge shopping" by lawyers. The caseload of all Ohio courts has been in excess of three million cases annually in recent years.

NOTABLE FEATURES OF LAW/LEGAL SYSTEM
Not all essential court functions are funded at the state level in Ohio. Accordingly, there are some disparities across counties in terms of access to justice and the scope and level of adjudicative services provided. Ohio has

adopted the doctrine of inherent appropriation power. This doctrine of judicial autonomy has been interpreted to conclude that withholding funds by the legislature would serve to usurp the judicial power, violating the principle of separation of powers.

As of 1968, the Ohio Supreme Court was given the authority to prescribe rules governing practice and procedure in all courts in Ohio. This power of superintendence was part of the Modern Courts Amendment (Ohio Constitution, Article 4, Section 5[B]). Since the early 1990s, each court in Ohio has also been required to develop and file with the Ohio Supreme Court a case-management plan. The state has embraced the alternative dispute resolution movement in recent years. The number of court and community mediation programs has grown from 11 in 1991 to 121 programs in 44 counties in 1999.

STAFFING

There were 30,361 attorneys practicing in Ohio according to data published in 1994. Nearly 72 percent of these lawyers are engaged in private practice, and less than 1 percent are classified under "legal aid/public defender." In 1975, the Ohio Public Defender Commission was created. It has nine members and appoints a state public defender who functions in the criminal justice system only. Some counties, usually the more urban counties, have paid offices as well, and the state shares the cost of operating these county offices. If there is no county office, the judge assigns counsel, and the state pays half the cost. The primary mechanism for providing civil legal services to low-income individuals is currently Ohio's eighteen local or regional aid societies. These are funded primarily by court-collected filing fees from civil cases and funds generated by the interest earned on trust accounts held by attorneys or title agents. A legal needs assessment in 1991 found that only one of six low-income Ohioans with legal problems was able to secure professional legal advice or representation.

Legal education is provided in nine law schools throughout the state. Publicly supported schools include the Ohio State University, the University of Akron, the University of Cincinnati, Cleveland-Marshall College of Law (attached to Cleveland State University), and the University of Toledo. The private institutions of Capital University in Columbus, Case Western Reserve University in Cleveland, the University of Dayton, and Ohio Northern University in Ada provide three-year programs leading to the juris doctor degree, as well.

As of 2001, there were 702 active judges serving in the constitutional and legislative courts. An additional 130 retired judges can serve on assignment by the chief justice when they are needed. Ohio's method of recruitment of judges is rather unique and is indicative of incremental change over Ohio's history. Originally, judges were se-

lected by the legislature. Partisan elections replaced that method with the new constitution of 1851. At the beginning of the twentieth century, reformers argued that partisan elections were inappropriate for seemingly neutral governmental actors such as judges. In 1911, nonpartisan general elections replaced partisan general elections. However, partisan primaries determine which candidates will appear on the nonpartisan general election ballot. The Missouri Plan method of merit-based selection was defeated at the polls by voters in 1938. Subsequent attempts to place on the ballot a constitutional amendment requiring merit selection failed in 1979 and again in 1987.

In the event of an in-term judicial vacancy, the governor makes an interim appointment. Voters decide in the next general election whether that appointee or an opponent will complete the term. Governors have discretion as to whom they will consult on these appointments; recent governors have varied in this selection process. Some have contacted bar associations, while others have deferred to party leaders. There is some support for creating a more standardized process.

Terms of office for Ohio judges are six years. With the exception of the presiding officer in the Mayors' Courts, Ohio judges must be engaged in the practice of law for at least six years prior to their candidacy or appointment as judge. As of 1968, an amendment to the Ohio Constitution prohibits persons over the age of seventy from seeking judicial office.

Judges can be removed from office by the state legislature. They can be impeached by a majority vote in the House of Representatives and convicted by a two-thirds vote of the State Senate. Alternatively, a concurrent resolution passed by a two-thirds vote of both chambers can remove a judge from office as well.

RELATIONSHIP TO NATIONAL SYSTEM

Two of the nation's ninety-four federal trial courts are located in Ohio. The U.S. District Court for the northern district sits in Cleveland, and the U.S. District Court for the southern district sits in Columbus. Ohio is part of the Sixth Circuit among the U.S. Courts of Appeals. The Sixth Circuit is headquartered in Cincinnati, Ohio.

Several significant decisions of the Warren Court era (1953–1969) originated in Ohio. Much of the "Warren Court revolution" centered on expanding the rights of the criminally accused. *Mapp v. Ohio* (1961) provided the vehicle by which the exclusionary rule binding on federal law enforcement since 1914 was made applicable to state authorities as well. *Terry v. Ohio* (1968) allowed for an exception to the search warrant requirement so that police officers could "stop and frisk" suspects. And *Sheppard v. Maxwell* (1966) sought to balance the interests of a free press against the right to a fair trial. Sam

Sheppard, a prominent Cleveland-area physician accused of murdering his wife, was acquitted in his second trial after the U.S. Supreme Court decision. His case was sufficiently notorious to inspire the television series *The Fugitive.*

Lauren Bowen

See also Judicial Selection, Methods of; United States—Federal System; United States—State Systems

References and further reading

Amer, Francis Joseph. 1932. *The Development of the Judicial System of Ohio: 1787–1932.* Baltimore, MD: Johns Hopkins University Press.

Duncan, Robert M., and Susan L. Eagan. 2000. "A Changing Landscape: Ohio Courts Futures Commission." http://www.sconet.state.oh.us/publications/futures (accessed October 2001).

Marshall, Carrington T. 1934. *A History of the Courts and Lawyers of Ohio.* New York: American Historical Society.

Ohio Commission on Racial Fairness. 1999. *Report of the Ohio Commission on Racial Fairness.* Columbus: The Supreme Court of Ohio.

The Ohio Courts Summary. 2000. Columbus: The Supreme Court of Ohio.

Paschen, Stephen H. 1997. *Order in the Court: The Courts and Practice of Law in Akron, OH, 1787–1945.* Akron, OH: Summit County Historical Society.

Sheridan, Richard G. 1990. *Governing Ohio: Administrative, Judiciary and Other Operations.* Cleveland, OH: Federation for Community Planning.

Supreme Court of Ohio. http://www.sconet.state.oh.us/ (accessed October 2001).

OKLAHOMA

GENERAL INFORMATION

Oklahoma entered the United States as a state in 1907, the forty-sixth state to do so. It is surrounded by six states—Kansas (north), Missouri (northeast), Arkansas (east), Texas (south), New Mexico (west), and Colorado (northwest)—created out of what was formerly Louisiana Territory. Of the fifty states, Oklahoma is ranked eighteenth in size.

Although Oklahoma is known for its oil, gas, and coal production, it is also a major producer of iodine for the nation. Its major manufacturing sector is in the production of transportation equipment and industrial machinery equipment. The state, however, has a strong agricultural base as well. Oklahoma is normally second in the nation in production of winter wheat. It is fourth in cattle and calf and pecan production. Thirty-four million acres are devoted to farmland.

According to the 2000 census Oklahoma's population was approximately 3.5 million people.

The name *Oklahoma* is derived from the Choctaw language meaning "Land of the Red People." The area now

called Oklahoma was originally set aside by the U.S. government for the relocation of Native Americans, and was called Indian Territory. When it became known that some land in Indian Territory was not assigned to Native Americans, that land was opened to whites for settlement. The result was a splitting of the state into an eastern half and a western half. The existence of the Twin Territories raised questions about the formation of the state of Oklahoma.

EVOLUTION AND HISTORY

Of the five civilized tribes that were relocated to Oklahoma Territory, all but the Seminoles adopted tribal constitutions. While there were attempts to create a unifying single government among these tribes, those efforts failed. When whites living in Oklahoma Territory sought statehood, the question remained as to whether Indian Territory should also seek statehood or whether the two should be united into a single state.

In an attempt to preempt single statehood, the leaders of the Five Civilized Tribes held a convention to write a constitution for Indian Territory. The Sequoyah Convention produced a constitution, but Congress refused to recognize it. On June 16, 1906, Congress passed the Oklahoma Enabling Act providing for the uniting of the Twin Territories into a single state.

In 1906 elections were held for delegates to a constitutional convention to be held in Guthrie. The result of those elections was a landslide for the Democratic Party. Of the 112 twelve delegates elected, 99 were Democrats, 12 were Republicans, and 1 was an Independent.

Shortly after these elections the Constitutional Convention convened in Guthrie. It elected William H. Murray ("Alfalfa Bill") president of the convention. The delegates selected Peter Hanraty, a labor union leader, as vice president. The delegates met from late November 1906 until mid-March 1907. Two other weeklong sessions were held, with the delegates finishing their work in July.

September 17, 1907 (the same month and day the Framers of the U.S. Constitution adjourned), was set as the day for voting on ratification of the proposed constitution. President Theodore Roosevelt did not like the proposed Oklahoma constitution. He sent William Howard Taft, his secretary of war, to Oklahoma to argue against ratification of the document. He was met by two-time Democratic candidate for president, William Jennings Bryan.

Taft's major criticism of the proposed constitution was that at nearly 50,000 words in length, the constitution was not really a constitution at all. To Taft it resembled more a legal code than it did a governing document. Bryan defended the document, calling it the best of all state constitutions and even better than the U.S. Constitution. The residents of Oklahoma seemed to agree with Bryan. The constitution carried the vote in every county with over 70 percent of the entire state voting for ratification.

What was notable about the constitution was the faith it placed in the voters. It provided for many of the devices advocated by the leaders of the Progressive Movement: the direct primary, the initiative, the referendum, and the regulation of trusts.

Just as the Guthrie delegates' distrust of the legislature resulted in a lengthy article in the state constitution relating to the state legislature, likewise, the judicial article was longer than most state constitutions relating to the judicial branch. The original judicial article provided for partisan elections to select members of the state's Supreme Court (with six-year terms).

Likewise, the voters were given the authority to elect members of the state's district courts (to four-year terms).

Several landmark U.S. Supreme Court decisions originated in Oklahoma or Oklahoma courts. Two cases dealing with civil rights and precursors to *Brown v. Board of Education* came from Oklahoma: *Sipuel v. Board of Regents of the University of Oklahoma* (1948) and *McLauren v. Oklahoma State Regents* (1950). Both cases involved the refusal of the University of Oklahoma to admit African Americans. Although the U.S. Supreme Court refused to overrule its "separate but equal" doctrine, it did begin stressing the "equal" portion of the doctrine.

It was also a case from Oklahoma in which the U.S. Supreme Court struck down the use of the "grandfather clause" in application of literacy tests for purposes of voting (*Guinn v. United States,* 1915).

The precedent setting *U.S. v. Jack Miller* (1939), in which the U.S. Supreme Court ruled on the meaning of the Second Amendment right to keep and bear arms, also originated in Oklahoma.

The first case in which the U.S. Supreme Court hinted that it would recognize the right to privacy came in a case from Oklahoma involving an Oklahoma law providing for the sterilization of those with three felony convictions involving certain crimes (*Skinner v. Oklahoma,* 1942).

In the area of women's rights, the landmark case of *Craig v. Boren* (1976), in which the U.S. Supreme Court created the "heightened scrutiny" test for gender discrimination cases, originated in Oklahoma.

CURRENT STRUCTURE

The original article in Oklahoma dealing with the judicial branch (Article 7) was repealed in 1967. The new article retained the Supreme Court, the Court of Criminal Appeals, and district courts. Justices of the peace and magistrates (of county courts) were abolished. The method for selecting judges was also modified.

Presently, the courts of Oklahoma include the following: Supreme Court, Court of Criminal Appeals, district courts, the Senate (when acting as a court of impeach-

Legal Structure of Oklahoma Courts

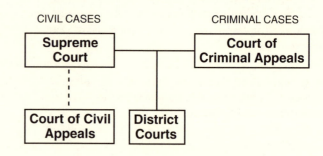

ment), the Court on the Judiciary, the Workers' Compensation Court, the court of tax review, and the court of civil appeals. The legislature created the Court of Civil Appeals in 1968, consisting of six judges. In 1982 the legislature increased the size of this court to twelve. In 1977 the legislature created the Workers' Compensation Court (formerly the State Industrial Court). The court of tax review, a specialized court, hears cases dealing with taxes levied by the state or a subdivision of the state.

While most states typically have a three-tiered court system (trial court, intermediate court, and highest court), Oklahoma has basically a two-tiered system, with the unique characteristic of having two courts of last resort (the only other state with such a system is Texas).

Supreme Court

The Supreme Court was created in the original constitution ratified in 1907. It is the head of the state's judicial system. Article 7, section 2 of the constitution stipulates that the Supreme Court will consist of nine members unless the number is changed by the legislature. Presently, there are nine members on this court.

The Supreme Court is the court of last resort for all civil cases initiated in Oklahoma courts. Any appeal from this court would be to the Supreme Court of the United States (providing the case raised a "federal question"). In addition to appellate jurisdiction, the Supreme Court has original jurisdiction, which extends to a "general superintending control" over all inferior courts and all agencies, boards, and commissions created by the legislature.

Court of Criminal Appeals

Formerly called the Criminal Court of Appeals, this court was renamed the Court of Criminal Appeals in 1957 by the legislature, and this name was retained in the amendments to the constitution reorganizing the judicial branch adopted in 1967. This court can only hear criminal cases. Just as the Supreme Court is the court of last resort for civil cases, the Court of Criminal Appeals is the court of last resort for criminal cases. Any appeal from this court would be to the U.S. Supreme Court (assuming it raised a federal question). In 1987 the size of the court (then three) was increased to five.

Court of Civil Appeals

The state legislature first created this court (called, then, the Court of Appeals) in 1968 with a membership of six judges. This court can hear only civil cases and only those the state's Supreme Court assigns to it. In 1982 the legislature increase the size of this court to twelve.

Decisions of this court (unless appealed to the Supreme Court) are final, but do not create a precedent that must be followed by other Oklahoma courts. However, a majority of the Supreme Court can, if asked to do so, issue a writ of certiorari instructing the Court of Civil Appeals to send a case it has decided up to it for review. If the Supreme Court follows the decision of the Court of Civil Appeals, the ruling does establish a precedent.

District Courts

In matters of state law, the district courts are Oklahoma's trial courts. They can hear both civil and criminal cases. The number of district courts and the number of judges serving on these courts (district judges, associate district judges, and special judges) are determined by the state legislature. There are presently twenty-six judicial districts with seventy-seven district courts manned by seventy-three district judges, eighty associate district judges, and eighty-five special judges.

The authority of special judges to hear cases is more restricted than that of district judges and associate district judges.

Municipal Courts

Municipal courts in Oklahoma are restricted in jurisdiction to hearing only cases dealing with city ordinances. Furthermore, only in cities with a large population can municipal courts' rulings be appealed to the Court of Criminal Appeals. Decisions in the other municipal courts, if appealed, must be heard in district courts in de novo proceedings.

Workers' Compensation Court

This court was formerly called the State Industrial Court. Its name was changed in 1977. The court, as its name indicates, adjudicates disputes involving workers' compensation. Nine judges serve on this court. Its rulings can be appealed, if made within twenty days of the issuance of a ruling, to the state's Supreme Court.

Court on the Judiciary

This court was created in 1966. Article 7-A of Oklahoma's constitution is devoted to this court. Its purpose is to rule on the removal or compulsory retirement of Oklahoma's judges.

The Court on the Judiciary is divided into the trial division and the appellate division. The trial division is composed of nine judges, eight of which are senior district court judges and one an active member of the Oklahoma Bar Association, for two-year terms. The trial division conducts trials to determine whether a judge should be removed from office. The appellate division of this court is composed of nine judges, for two-year terms. This group takes appeals of decisions by the trial division. The appellate division has the authority to affirm, modify, or reverse the judgment of the trial division.

In addition to the actions of the Court on the Judiciary, judges may be removed from office if convicted of a felony by a court of competent jurisdiction, or may be removed through the impeachment process.

NOTABLE FEATURES OF LAW AND LEGAL SYSTEM

Oklahoma is one of only two states that has two courts of last resort: the Supreme Court and the Court of Criminal Affairs. This is due to the fact that Oklahoma's court system is, unlike most states, basically a two-tiered system. After the trial court, civil cases can only be appealed to the Supreme Court and criminal cases can only be appealed to the Court of Criminal Appeals. This allows Oklahoma's appellate judges to specialize in either civil or criminal law.

Also notable about the judicial branch in Oklahoma is the creation, in the 1960s, of a Court on the Judiciary. This court was created as a reaction to scandal occurring in the judicial branch. While the Court on the Judiciary has not been that active since its creation, it has resulted in the disciplining of more judges than in the entire history of the state prior to the court's creation.

STAFFING

Supreme Court

The method used for selecting members of the Supreme Court is the Missouri Plan. When there is a vacancy on the court, the governor appoints a member from a list of three names supplied by the Judicial Nominating Commission (described below). If the governor fails to select a name within sixty days of the vacancy, the chief justice of the Supreme Court is authorized to make the appointment. Following the appointment, the justice (only members of this court are referred to as justices; all others are referred to as judges) will face the voters at the next general election in a nonpartisan retention election (if at least one year has passed since being appointed). The justice, in other words, runs against his own record of performance as a justice, not against another opponent. After the initial retention election, each justice must face the voters again, in a retention election, every six years with no limit on the number of times a justice can be elected.

Court of Criminal Appeals

The judges of the Court of Civil Appeals are selected by the Missouri Plan in the same manner as justices of the state's Supreme Court.

District Courts

District court judges and associate district court judges differ in name only. They each have four-year terms, and they are elected in nonpartisan competitive elections. Special judges are appointed by district judges, and they have no set term (serving at the pleasure of the district judges).

Workers' Compensation Court

Nine judges serve on this court. They are selected by the Missouri Plan.

Court on the Judiciary

The trial division of this court is composed of nine judges, eight of which are senior district court judges and one an active member of the Oklahoma Bar Association. The appellate division of this court is composed of nine judges. Members of both divisions have two-year terms.

Legal Profession in Oklahoma

According to the latest statistical report on the legal profession in Oklahoma, the state ranked nineteenth in the ratio of number of lawyers in the state to the state's population. That is approximately one lawyer for every 335 residents. The aggregate data are 9,716 lawyers, of whom 7,219 were in private practice.

Oklahoma presently has three law schools: the University of Oklahoma College of Law, the University of Tulsa College of Law, and the Oklahoma City University School of Law. To practice law in Oklahoma a person shall be at least eighteen years of age and "have good moral character, due respect for the law, and fitness to practice law." Another requirement is passing the state's bar examination (with some exceptions as specified in state law).

Danny M. Adkison

See also United States—Federal System; United States—State Systems

References and further reading
Adkison, Danny M., and Lisa McNair Palmer. 2001. *The Oklahoma State Constitution.* Westport, CT: Greenwood Press.
Evans, Charles B., and Clinton Orrin Bunn. 1908. *Oklahoma Civil Government.* Ardmore, OK: Bunn Brothers.
Hamilton, Ann, ed. 2001. *Oklahoma Almanac: 2001–2002.* Oklahoma City: Oklahoma Department of Libraries.
Lawler, James J., and Robert L. Spurrier, Jr. "The Judicial System." In *Oklahoma Politics and Policies.* Edited by David R. Morgan, Robert E. England, and George G. Humphreys. Lincoln: University of Nebraska Press.
League of Women Voters of Oklahoma. 1966. *Study of the State Constitution* (Parts I and II). Washington, DC: League of Women Voters Education Fund.
The Oklahoma State Courts Network. www.oscn.net (accessed November 25, 2001).

OMAN

COUNTRY INFORMATION

Oman is one of the most economically underdeveloped of the Persian Gulf states, which include Saudi Arabia, Kuwait, Qatar, Bahrain, and the United Arab Emirates. It also contains one of the few absolute monarchies remaining in the world. Although it practices *sharia* law based on the ancient teachings of the Koran, Oman has promoted economic and educational opportunity for its citizens and is one of the strongest supporters of the West in the Arab world. Such contradictions make Oman one of the most intriguing countries found in the Middle East region.

The unusual nature of Oman is reflected in its borders and the differing sizes the country has been given. Estimates of Oman's land area range from 200,000 to 300,000 square kilometers. The differing estimates are produced by the shifting sands that comprise the country's border with Saudi Arabia, Yemen, and the United Arab Emirates. The longest of those borders, the one with Saudi Arabia, stretches across the Rub Al Khali, a trackless and nearly impenetrable desert. Attempts to clearly identify the boundary are swept away by the shifting sand. Instead the maps of Oman show straight lines that may or may not mark the extent of Omani territory. The same border disputes surround Oman's northern boundary with the United Arab Emirates and their southern border with Yemen. For these reasons, the exact extent of Omani territory may always be disputed.

Because of the hostile climate in the country's interior as temperatures rise well above 100° F, most of the population inhabits the coastal areas of the country. The main cities in Oman are located in the northern region on the Gulf of Oman. This includes the largest city and capital, Muscat. The cities are isolated from the interior by the Hajar mountain range. The other populated section of Oman is in the southern Dhofar region bordering Yemen. There the city of Salalah serves as the district capital and was the home of the sultan who ruled much of Oman during the mid-twentieth century.

Because of the desert interior and the mountain ranges of the north, much of the communication and trade in Oman occurs by sea. Yet the isolation of the major pop-

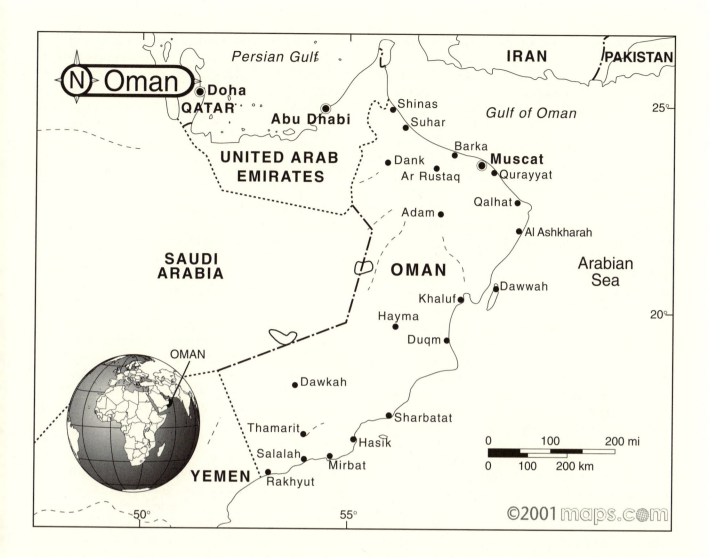

ulation centers also protects from overland attacks and has helped in ensuring political stability in the country.

The northernmost portion of Oman is separated from the rest of the country by the United Arab Emirates. Situated on the tip of the Musundum Peninsula, the town of Al Khasab fronts the strategic Straits of Hormuz, through which a significant portion of the world's oil supply passes before reaching the safety of the open sea. The control of this strategic portion of real estate makes Oman a major player in the Middle East. It has not always been so. While Oman served as a major post for European and Indian traders, it did not play an important political, religious, or military role in the Middle East until the 1980s.

HISTORY

Some of the earliest inhabitants of what is modern Oman were found in the coastal city-state of Magan. Located on the Gulf of Oman near the present capital of Muscat, Magan was a major trading stop for the Mesopotamians and the various empires of India. The southern region of Dhofar was a major producer of frankincense, which was a valuable commodity in the Roman Empire. The Persians later moved across the Gulf of Oman and dominated the southern gulf region, conquering the north coastal areas of Oman. Later the Omanis were able to defeat the Persians, with the Al Azd tribe freeing the territory after a series of battles.

The defeat of the Persians was soon followed by an invasion from the Arabian Peninsula itself. Islamic armies conquered the region and established themselves as the dominant force in Arabia. In Oman itself an Islamic sect known as the Ibadi took root. The Ibadi tended to be stricter in their beliefs than other Muslims while allowing other sects to practice within the community. Modern-day Ibadi followers continue to practice a fundamentalist form of Islam, banning such activities as drinking, dancing, and smoking, and supporting the imposition of severe penalties including death for such acts as adultery and theft.

The economic strength of Oman during the nineteenth century allowed it to establish trading enclaves in Asia and Africa. Omani traders established political control of the island of Zanzibar off the coast of the current country of Tanzania in East Africa. The island served as port of call for Arab ships and was part of the flourishing slave trade of the region. Omani power was weakened, then ended, with the arrival of European explorers and eventual German and British intervention in the area.

The Omanis also established control of the city of Gwadar in modern-day Pakistan. This provided another port of call for traders. Control of the area lasted into the 1950s and had effects on the composition of the Omani population. Because of the spread of Omani power, the country saw immigration from its colonial possessions. Hence members of the Omani military include native Africans and Baluchis from Pakistan.

Because of its presence on the main trading routes to India and the Middle East, the Omani coast became a target of European powers. The Portuguese were the first to establish permanent bases on Omani territory including Muscat and the Straits of Hormuz. The Dutch followed, establishing their control over the Persian Gulf during the seventeenth century and replacing the weakening Portuguese. In turn, by the eighteenth century it was the British who conquered the mini gulf states and such Omani outposts as Muscat. The British suppressed both the piracy and slave trading that made up much of the commerce of the region, hence turning the area into a colony dependent upon Britain for its trade. Yet the British were concerned only with maintaining a port and did not extend their control much beyond the borders of Muscat.

The British allowed the sultan to remain as a figurehead while the interior of the country was ruled by an imam or religious leader. That arrangement changed with the ascension of the Sultan Al Bu Said in 1932. Said attempted to move the country away from close contact with the West, leaving Muscat and spending his life in the southern city of Salalah. At the same time he used the British to quell a rebellion in the interior of the country and defeat the imam. This gave the sultan control of most of the Omani territory. Once secure in power the sultan began restricting Western access to the country, limiting the number of outsiders allowed in. Simultaneously he banned alcohol, tobacco, dancing, singing, and films among his people. Education was forbidden for women and even for male students there were only three schools in the entire country. The sultan went so far as to arrest his own son when he returned from Britain after finishing his college education.

The sultan ruled for thirty-eight years until 1970. At that time the British role in the Persian Gulf was winding down, with control being passed to local authorities. The sultan's isolationism led the British military to conspire with his son to overthrow him. The British commanders of the Omani troops were able to convince the soldiers to support the son's revolt. The coup was successful; the sultan was dispatched to retirement in Britain and his thirty-year-old son ruled over Oman. As the country was modernized by Qaboos and the military became self-sufficient, the British role declined and its officers were replaced by Omani officers.

The new sultan, Qaboos, moved quickly to remove the limits on his people, built schools, and allowed all Omanis to attend. Religious-based bans on most social activities were lifted, as were the restrictions on the entrance of Westerners into the country. Qaboos, though, held on to most of the absolute powers exercised by his father.

Under Sultan Said, Oman was an economic backwater with most Omanis continuing the centuries-old traditions of herding animals as their main source of economic activity. The country's infrastructure was limited to a few hundred miles of paved roads and a single power plant located outside Muscat, able to provide a limited amount of electricity for part of each day. Upon becoming sultan, Qaboos attempted to reinvigorate the economy and needed money to do it. As part of his plan, he, much like his Persian Gulf neighbors, used oil revenues to generate foreign currency. Most of the oil production is centered in the southwestern region of the country near the desert border with Saudi Arabia. The Omani production, though, has been limited to 100,000,000 barrels a year, well below the major producers such as Iran and Saudi Arabia. The oil fields are also a significant distance from ports, making transportation difficult. But Oman's distance from the volatile Persian Gulf region and the threatened bottlenecks made it a more dependable source of oil.

Much of the money generated by oil experts was used by government to build such necessities as schools, roads, ports, and hospitals. The relative backwardness of the country was transformed and modern conveniences such as fresh water, electricity, and inexpensive transportation became ordinary to many Omanis. But the benefits provided by the oil windfall were limited as the government controlled the earnings and the small amount of oil produced. In addition, few Omanis were able to work in the oil fields and hence received no benefits from lucrative jobs. The only major natural resource exports from the country were copper and limestone. Although there were large deposits of these, their production was again limited.

The tiny amount of rainfall has also hampered agricultural advancements. Most of the food produced for Omani consumption comes from livestock, including goats, sheep, and cattle. The main exports have been dates, and most of the food grown is consumed by the farmers. This has forced Oman to import most of its food, except for meat, and placed a burden on its economy. The modernization of the country under Sultan Qaboos has also lured many Omanis to the cities and away from traditional agricultural duties.

One area of food production that flourished in Oman was fishing. Omanis had always been proficient fishermen but the archaic methods limited their catches. Under the new government an agreement was reached between Oman and foreign industries. These professional companies were allowed to fish within Oman's territorial waters in return for a significant portion of their catch as payment.

The extraction of resources and agriculture represent the old Omani way of life. The new economic wave focused on light industry and tourism. The industry was limited to providing the material necessary for building an Omani infrastructure. The government subsidized industrial parks to start new businesses.

The warm climate and wide-ranging beaches of Oman also provide opportunities for attracting tourists. New hotels and attractions were constructed and the old constraints on the number of foreigners allowed into the country were relaxed. Yet Omani tourism and industry composed only a small portion of the country's economy.

The continued growth of the Omani economy relies on the country's openness to the West and ability to attract foreign investment through tourism. The over thirty years of Qaboos rule has witnessed the modernization of a country that had been at least a century behind the rest of the world.

LEGAL CONCEPTS

Oman continues to operate one of the few absolute monarchies in the world. An absolute monarchy allows for few competing institutions, whether they be public or private. The new sultan was faced with running a government with few advisors and even less structure. Oman lacked a constitution and a parliament. Few people had experience in making decisions, much less implementing them. Sultan Qaboos proceeded to create intermediate institutions, including several councils that drew a portion of the population into the decisions made by government. A Council of Ministers was formed and while the sultan held multiple posts including defense, foreign affairs, finance, and prime minister, the others were allowed to operate their departments with little interference from the sultan. The State Consultative Council filled the gap that had opened between the people and the government. The council, composed of members selected from all of the Omani region, provided advice and ideas on how the government was to function. Yet he retained absolute power to issue decrees.

As with other institutions of government, the Omani judiciary was rudimentary and dependent upon traditional *sharia* law. Because *sharia* law was derived from the Koran and authoritative interpretations of it, the government had limited control over the subject of the law or the verdicts reached in the courts.

Sharia law was enforced in Islamic courts under the watchful eye of a *qadi* (*qazi*) or judge. A *qadi* was trained in *sharia* law at an Islamic law school and was not considered a government employee. *Qadis* were given discretion in reaching a decision, occasionally arriving at a compromise rather than abiding by a strict adherence to the law.

The small steps taken by the sultan in the 1980s were seen as an attempt to loosen central political control to a degree while maintaining a strong hand in the continued economic development of Oman. The greatest changes in the political structure of the country came during the 1990s.

In 1996, the government took another step toward a constitutional system with the publication of the White Book. While not referred to as a constitution, the document included a description of the government institutions, their role and power, and the checks placed on government actions. This basic law included the rights of Omani citizens such as compensation for the government taking of private property, the right of ownership of property, the freedom to work in an occupation of one's choice, equality in public employment, and the development of educational resources. The basic law also prohibited government discrimination on the basis of gender, race, religion, or sect. Those charged with crimes were considered innocent until proven guilty while retaining a right to counsel in certain cases, having a right to know of the charges and the right to appeal in most ordinary cases. Finally the White Book protected freedom of expression and freedom to practice religion, and provided protection from searches in the home.

The White Book's guarantees go further than any other Islamic country in protecting the basic rights found in most Western constitutions. The sultan has taken the lead toward the free exercise of religious beliefs. He has allowed a Catholic church, a Protestant church, and a Hindu temple to be built on his personal property. Omanis and visitors are allowed to worship without civil penalties or threat of persecution. In addition, Christian missions have been allowed to function, though it is against the law to proselytize as it is illegal for a Muslim to convert to another religion. Those of non-Muslim faiths are not restricted in traveling about or in and out of the country.

CURRENT STRUCTURE

Part 6 of the White Book details a portion of the judicial institutions that function in Oman. Prior to the 1970s, Oman was run according to traditional Muslim law or the *sharia*. This law was practiced by Islamic trained judges or *qadis* (*qazis*) who were not appointed by the government and who were accountable only to the religious authority in Oman. By 1984, the Omani government was restricting the jurisdiction of the *sharia* courts, preventing them from hearing criminal cases and most civil cases. Yet in taking away these court's powers, the government was faced with establishing a court system of its own to settle the same disputes. In the period between the weakening of the *sharia* courts and the formation of a constitution, the Omani court system developed along the lines of most Western regimes.

At the lowest level of the judiciary is the court of first instance. Judges in these courts hear criminal misdemeanor cases. Directly above these courts are the criminal courts in which felony and other serious criminal cases are heard. Decisions handed down by these courts can be appealed to the single court of appeals located in Muscat. This court has functioned as the last source of appeals. A Supreme Court was supposed to be created, but by 2000 no such court had been formed or justices appointed.

A commercial court system exists separately from the criminal courts. Commercial courts decide labor, tax, and bankruptcy cases. The lowest level within this system is the summary courts, which hear cases involving disputes under $15,000. Those cases involving under $5,000 are unappealable. The five summary courts are located in the major cities and towns of Oman to make it easier for individuals to have their cases heard without being forced to travel long distances. Appeals of these decisions go to the commercial appeals court located in Muscat.

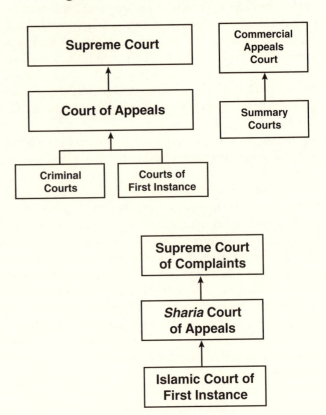

Legal Structure of Oman Courts

SPECIALIZED JUDICIAL BODIES

As the Omani court system has been constructed, it has replaced the once-dominant *sharia* courts. While these courts continue to function, they do so with a much reduced jurisdiction. The judges in these courts decide most cases involving family issues of divorce, marriage, inheritance, and adoption. A total of forty-six *sharia* courts are scattered throughout the country. The *sharia* system is run by the Ministry of Justice. The ministry oversees the decisions and the judges appointed to the courts. In *sharia* law, the courts of first instance are run by a single judge or *qadi* (*qazi*). Decisions handed down by these courts can be appealed to the Muscat *sharia* Court of Appeals. A three-judge panel from this court renders a decision that can be further appealed to the Supreme Committee for Complaints. The committee serves as a part judicial and part political body. It is composed of the grand mufti or chief religious leader of Oman, the minister of Justice, and two other Islamic trained judges. The committee considers whether *sharia* law was properly followed. The presence of the minister ensures that the government has some say in whether a sentence was acceptable to the political authority.

The formation of the formal judicial structure as outlined in the White Book led to a further weakening of the *sharia* law. A 1997 Personal Status law had government identify certain requirements for marriage and divorce. It banned marriage under eighteen without the consent of both parties. In 1999, another decree reformed the judicial structure with the creation of the first Omani Supreme Court and more lower courts with special jurisdictions. It also stated that judges were independent of the government, though in reality government officials have broad powers to influence judges.

Another specialized court is the State Security Court. This special court heard cases involving national security or criminal cases that government wanted handled quickly. In these courts, many legal rights do not exist. Defendants cannot use counsel to defend them, there is no public hearing, procedures are limited, and the right to appeal does not exist. These state security trials represent the authoritarian side of Omani law and the tendency of some government officials to favor expediency over established procedures.

The creation of these courts produced a need for specially trained judges and lawyers. To build a functioning judicial system, Sultan Qaboos changed established Oman policy of limiting education to a few. Instead universities became a symbol of the modernization and Westernization of the country.

STAFFING

One of the greatest failings of the old Omani regime was the limitations it placed on education. Prior to 1970 in

Oman, there were only three secondary schools in the country and no universities. The three schools were restricted to males and provided only limited instruction in religious teaching. The distrust of educational institutions and Western education in particular was demonstrated by the house arrest of the future sultan Qaboos when he returned from his university studies in Great Britain. The overthrow of the old sultan in 1970 changed those policies.

His son, Sultan Qaboos, financed new schools, built a university system, and provided scholarships for Omanis to study in their home country or abroad. Legal education became one of the fastest growing parts of the university system. The major Omani law school operates in Muscat, the capital. Because of the dual system of Omani law, both secular law and Muslim *sharia,* the law school provides a program of studies in both systems though all students are expected to receive a grounding in secular Omani law.

The University of Oman is composed of 6,000 undergraduate and graduate students, over half of whom are women, a rarity in most Islamic countries. A specialized education in the law is provided by the Higher Judicial Institute operated in the town of Nizwa. The institute takes successful law graduates and trains them as judges or legal advisors and prepares them for government service. The institute allows the Omani government to develop law within the country and without the aid of Western legal advisors whose presence might prove politically controversial.

Lawyers who graduate from the law school can be appointed to a government court by the sultan or can acquire an appointment at a *qadi* (*qazi*) to a *sharia* court if they studied Islamic law. While the number of lawyers and qualified judges is small, it is a growing segment of the population as Oman attempts to modernize into a Western-style nation with independent judges and courts.

IMPACT

The Omani legal system stretches back just over a generation. The rise to the throne of Sultan Qaboos witnessed a revolution in the country. No longer a sleepy backwater, Oman became a center of calm and modernization in a region known for its volatility and preference for tradition.

Among all of the institutions developed by Qaboos one of the most dramatic was the judiciary. He moved the country away from traditional *sharia* law that limited Oman's economic and social growth. As the law became secularized there arose a strong need for trained lawyers and judges. The establishment of law schools and university training in the law reversed his father's policy of restricting education to the most elementary levels.

The advancement of Omani law also saw the erosion of *sharia* law as judges were granted power over marriage, divorces, and family law. But unlike other Persian Gulf countries, Oman suffered none of the political instability that followed government intrusion into matters once controlled by the Muslim faith. Qaboos also moved forward in the publication of a White Book in which individual rights were protected by government acting through the judiciary. While the court system and judges did not enjoy the same independence and power of Western courts, they represent one of the most advanced judicial systems within the Persian Gulf region. Oman has created the institutions that might later produce a constitutional monarchy, although Sultan Qaboos has yet to surrender his absolute powers. It is clear, though, that the institutions and traditions established under the sultan's rule will last far beyond his personal reign.

Douglas Clouatre

See also Commercial Law (International Aspects); Islamic Law; Judicial Review; Legal Education; Qadi (Qazi) Courts

References and further reading
Clements, F. A. 1980. *Oman: The Land Reborn.* London: Longman Publishing.
Cordesman, Anthony. 1997. *Bahrain, Oman, Qatar and the U.A.E.: Challenges of Security.* Boulder, CO: Westview Press.
Joyce, Miriam. 1995. *Sultanate of Oman: A Twentieth Century History.* Westport, CT: Praeger Publishing.
Kostiner, Joseph, ed. 2000. *Middle East Monarchies.* Boulder, CO: Lynne Rienner Publishers.
Rigsbee, W. Lynn, and Calvin H. Allen. 2000. *Oman under Qaboos: From Coup to Constitution 1970–1996.* London: Frank Cass Publishing.
Riphenburg, Carol. 1998. *Oman: Political Development in a Changing World.* Westport, CT: Praeger Publishing.
Townsend, John. 1977. *Oman: The Making of a Modern State.* New York: St. Martin's Press.
Vine, Peter. 1995. *The Heritage of Oman.* London: Immel Publishing.
Zahlen, Rosemarie. 1998. *The Making of the Modern Gulf States.* Berkshire, UK: Ithaca Press.

ONTARIO

GENERAL INFORMATION

Ontario, second largest of Canada's ten provinces, is located in the east-central region of the country. Its territory covers 1.1 million square kilometers (413,000 square miles), bounded by Quebec on the east, Manitoba on the west, Hudson Bay and James Bay on the north, and the St. Lawrence River and the Great Lakes to the south. With a population of over 11 million, it is the most populous province in the country. Over 80 percent of the population lives in cities or towns, with the majority in southern Ontario, particularly in Toronto and the surrounding regions.

Ontario has the most productive economy of any province in Canada. In the field of manufacturing, it produces 52 percent of Canada's manufactured goods and 80 percent of manufactured exports. Agriculture and the service industries are also key components of the province's economy. Ontario is the third largest trading partner of the United States, which is aided by the proximity of so many Americans to the province—over 100 million live within a day's drive.

The population of Ontario is extremely diverse, as the province is the prime destination for the majority of immigrants who arrive in Canada. More than sixty different cultural groups call the province home, and the languages spoken reflect this diversity. Chinese, Italian, German, Portuguese, Indo-Iranian, and Greek are among the major languages spoken in the province, although over 7.6 million Ontarians speak English as their first language. The French-speaking population is the largest in Canada outside of Quebec, with the majority living in the east and north of the province. There are more than 167,000 First Nations people in Ontario; they speak Iroquoian and Algonquian.

EVOLUTION AND HISTORY

In the sixteenth, seventeenth, and eighteenth centuries France claimed much of central Canada as its own. The British won control of New France after the Seven Years War (1756–1763) and the Treaty of Paris (1763), which brought a halt to hostilities. In 1791 the Constitutional Act was proclaimed, which divided the province of Quebec into Upper Canada and Lower Canada, modern-day Ontario and Quebec respectively. The act gave each region a lieutenant governor, an appointed Executive Council, an appointed Legislative Council, and an elected House of Assembly. In 1791, the first act of the new Upper Canada House of Assembly was to recognize the English common law as the law of Ontario (prior to this date, the French civil law system predominated). This is generally recognized as the date of reception of the English common law in Ontario.

In 1838 Lord Durham was appointed governor-general of British North America, and he recommended union of the two colonies, Upper Canada and Lower Canada, into a Province of Canada—Canada East (Quebec) and Canada West (Ontario). This attempt at a union proved short-lived. Eventually, the representatives of Canada East and Canada West joined with Nova Scotia and New Brunswick in negotiations for a broader union, which led to Confederation in 1867.

Ontario and Canada both have a parliamentary system of government based on the British model (although whereas the federal Parliament has retained an upper House of Lords, Ontario has a single, elected legislature). In 1867, the Constitution Act, 1867 (formerly known as

the British North America Act) established two different levels of government: federal and provincial. The constitution divided (sometimes in overlapping fashion) all legislative authority between the two levels of government, giving to the federal level powers of a national character (defense, trade, commerce, and so on) while giving to the provinces matters of local concern (municipal government, education, and so on). Due in part to the unique situation of Quebec's separate linguistic, cultural, and legal heritage, the constitution also gave provinces legislative authority over civil rights and property as well as the administration of justice. For this reason, each province has its own civil justice system and its own system of judicial administration.

In Ontario, the courts have undergone many reorganizations since Confederation, most significantly in 1881, when the Judicature Act consolidated the then-existing courts of Chancery, Queen's Bench, and Common Pleas into the High Court of Justice, thus fusing the courts of equity with the common law courts.

In 1982, the Canada Act (UK) patriated the Canadian Constitution, giving Canadian legislators the power to amend laws without permission from the British Parliament, and also contained the Constitution Act, 1982, which, among other provisions, contained a Charter of Rights and Freedoms, with which all federal and provincial government laws and actions must comply. Section 52(1) of this act makes the constitution the supreme law of Canada, and empowers courts to strike down laws or actions that are inconsistent with its provisions.

CURRENT STRUCTURE

All provinces in Canada have a superior court of general jurisdiction, with both a trial and appellate division. Section 96 of the Constitution Act, 1867 provides that appointments to the trial and appellate division of the provincial courts are to be made by the governor-general, the executive branch of the federal government (which, as a practical matter, puts the control over such federal judicial appointments in the hands of federal cabinet and prime minister). In Ontario, the trial court is known as the Superior Court of Ontario, and the appellate court is known as the Ontario Court of Appeal. These superior courts have unlimited jurisdiction and can administer the law in any manner they see fit, except where limited by statute.

The court of appeal is the highest court in Ontario. The chief justice of Ontario is president of the court and responsible for general supervision. There is an associate chief justice and fourteen other justices. It deals exclusively with appellate issues and justices sit in, at minimum, panels of three. Selection of judges to sit on the court of appeal bench, as indicated above, is made by the federal government.

Legal Structure of Ontario Courts

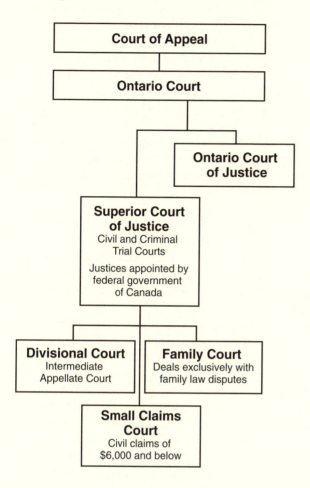

On September 1, 1990, all Ontario courts (except for the court of appeal) were merged into a new body called the Court of Ontario (formerly the Ontario Court of Justice). The Court of Ontario consists of two divisions: the aforementioned Superior Court of Ontario and the Ontario Court of Justice.

The chief justice of the Superior Court is president of the court and there is also an associate chief justice. Additionally, a structure was created that divided the province into eight regions, each with a senior judge responsible for administering the judiciary within his or her region. The Superior Court is the primary trial court for civil matters, and has jurisdiction over monetary disputes exceeding $6,000. Proceedings are heard by either a single judge or a judge and jury. There are two other branches of the Superior Court in addition to the trial level: the divisional court and the small claims court.

The divisional court has a limited appellate jurisdiction over interim orders made by a judge, and final orders where the order concerns payment of less than $25,000. The divisional court also deals with review of matters relating to government agency or board decisions. Judges sit in panels of three at the divisional court level, and all

judges of the Superior Court are also members of this level, as well as the small claims court. Claims up to $6,000 in small claims court can be heard by provincial judges, whereas those up to a lesser amount can be heard by deputy judges who are lawyers appointed by the regional senior judge. Any action dealing with the recovery of personal property or payment of money under a fixed monetary rate, which is periodically increased, falls under the jurisdiction of this court.

The Ontario Court of Justice, the second division of the Court of Ontario, is a provincially appointed court. Traditionally referred to as an inferior court, these provincially appointed judges are more limited in power than the federally appointed Superior Court judges. Less serious criminal law trials and preliminary hearings occur at this level, as do trials for offenses under provincial statutes. Family law matters such as adoption, support and custody, and criminal offenses by youths are also heard in the Ontario Court of Justice.

JUDICIAL APPOINTMENTS

As indicated above, judges of the Ontario Superior Court and the Ontario Court of Appeal are appointed by the federal executive (formally, the governor-general, but only on the advice and direction of the prime minister and cabinet). In 1988, an informal judicial selection process, which involved private recommendations to the office of the minister of Justice, was replaced by a system of direct application by the prospective judge to the federal Office of the Commissioner for Judicial Affairs. The federal Judges Act lists two minimum qualifications for judicial appointments: the prospective appointee must be a member of the bar of one of the provinces (thus licensed to practice law) and must have practiced law, or served in an equivalent capacity, for a minimum of ten years prior to appointment. Provincially appointed judges in Ontario are appointed by the provincial executive (formally the lieutenant governor, but only on the advice and direction of the premier of Ontario). In 1988, the Ontario Judicial Appointments Advisory Committee was formed. The purpose of the committee was to regularize and apply consistent standards to the selection of Ontario judges. Its thirteen members are composed mostly of nonlegally trained citizens, and it advises on provincial judicial appointments to the Ontario Court of Justice. Recent reforms have taken away some of the committee's powers, and it no longer meets for every appointment and its recommendations need not be followed by the premier.

ADMINISTRATIVE AGENCIES

An additional level of adjudicative decision making in Ontario is represented by administrative and regulatory agencies. They deal with various matters, including disputes relating to labor relations, professional discipline, social assistance, land-use planning, environmental regulation, human rights, and securities regulation, just to name a few. These tribunals or agencies are typically by the provincial government so that an expert body might deal more informally with conflicts for which the courts would not be appropriate. These tribunals hear disputes of first instance and, in some circumstances, appeals of decisions from other bodies that deal with similar issues. There are more than forty boards, commissions, and regulatory and administrative agencies currently in the province and they deal with thousands of different applications and decisions every year that would otherwise have to be heard in courts. Each governs to some extent its own rules and procedures. Most of these administrative decision makers have the statutory authority to make findings of law and some also have the power to interpret and apply the constitution.

LEGAL AID

Ontario has recently undergone a major change in the delivery of legal aid services. Originally, the system was voluntary in nature, beginning in 1951, but this did not sufficiently meet the public demand for legal aid services. In 1967 the Ontario Legal Aid Plan was introduced, wherein legal aid certificates were given to private sector lawyers who would work for clients and then be remunerated by the government. Additionally, Ontario funded a network of neighborhood and issue-specific legal clinics and provided duty counsel lawyers for those without representation in criminal court matters. While funded by the province, the legal aid system was administered by the Law Society for Upper Canada. In the 1990s, this system met with fiscal and administrative problems and a new quasi-independent provincial agency was established under the 1998 Legal Aid Services Act, called Legal Aid Ontario.

The new system also provides for a variety of different methods of legal aid, including certificates, legal aid lawyers, duty counsel, and community legal clinic programs. In order to qualify for aid in Ontario, the local legal aid office applies a financial test based on income and assets and may ask the client to make a contribution to their legal fees. These certificate programs are currently available in forty-eight communities throughout the province and offer assistance on a variety of legal issues such as criminal, family, and immigration law. There are seventy community legal clinics that offer advice and representation, examples of which include the Advocacy Centre for the Elderly and Justice for Children and Youth. Other services, such as duty counsel who assist those with criminal proceedings, family court, and some immigration matters, and legal aid societies within the six Ontario law schools are also under the umbrella of the new Legal Aid Ontario program.

STAFFING

In 1999, there were 26,626 practicing lawyers in Ontario. Legal training in Ontario is a shared responsibility between law schools and the provincial law society. The Law Society of Upper Canada, which was founded in 1797, is responsible for ensuring that legal services are provided by qualified and competent lawyers. It approves law school programs, operates bar admission courses, and also offers continuing education programs to lawyers. In order to be admitted to the bar in Ontario a candidate must hold a law degree from a recognized law school and serve an articling term under the tutelage of a qualified member of the law society.

The articling term was twelve months in Ontario but is currently being reduced to ten months, and typically entails working with a lawyer or law firm or serving as a clerk to a judge. A candidate must also pass the bar admission course, which covers a skills phase, professional responsibility, and substantive/procedural issues, to be admitted to the Ontario bar.

There are six law schools in Ontario, with Osgoode Hall Law School of York University, and the University of Toronto's Faculty of Law being particularly highly regarded. The University of Western Ontario and the University of Windsor serve southwestern Ontario, and Queen's University and the University of Ottawa are located in the eastern part of the province. Additionally, there are ten other common-law law schools in Canada from which one could receive the Bachelor of Laws degree, which is a prerequisite for being admitted to the bar in Ontario.

NOTABLE FEATURES OF THE ONTARIO JUSTICE SYSTEM AND ITS RELATIONSHIP WITH THE CANADIAN JUSTICE SYSTEM

The division of powers between the federal and provincial governments in Canada has produced unique challenges for Ontario's justice system. For example, the Constitution Act, 1867 gives the power over criminal law to the federal government while giving power over the administration of justice to the provinces. Therefore, in Ontario, the Superior Court of Ontario, which is staffed by federally appointed judges, adjudicates prosecutions brought by Ontario Crown prosecutors for violations of the federally legislated Criminal Code of Canada.

In family law, the federalism tension is one of overlapping jurisdiction between the Court of Ontario on the one hand and the Federal Court of Canada (created to adjudicate disputes arising under federal legislation) on the other hand. The Constitution Act, 1867 gives the federal government jurisdiction over marriage and divorce, while giving the provinces jurisdiction over marriage. Both federal and Ontario legislation has been passed dealing with questions of spousal support, custody of children, and related issues upon the breakdown of marriage, and for many years, spouses could pursue remedies in both provincial and federal courts. Under a federal initiative, some provinces, including Ontario, established unified family courts, which allow Superior Court judges to apply both provincial and federal laws in this area. This began as a limited pilot project, but is now being expanded to most major population centers in Ontario.

The civil justice system in Ontario is currently undergoing significant restructuring. Recent changes to the Ontario Rules of Civil Procedure now provide for a simplified procedure for civil litigation seeking modest recovery (under $25,000), and also mandatory mediation of civil claims in order to facilitate the early settlement of litigation. The Ontario government is considering significant changes in legislation relating to limitation periods, the regulation of paralegals, and contingency fees (apart from class actions, contingency fees are not permitted in Ontario). A final, notable feature of Ontario's justice system is its ambitious adoption of new technologies in a program called *integrated justice*. The goal of this program will be to create a seamless and paperless justice system. A pilot project involving the e-filing of civil claims in Toronto was successfully launched in 1998.

Lorne Sossin

See also Canada
References and further reading
Benidickson, Jamie. 1996. "From Empire Ontario to California North: Law and Legal Institutions in Twentieth Century Ontario." 23 Manitoba L.J. 620–53.
Ontario Law Reform Commission. 1995. *Rethinking Civil Justice* and *Study Paper on Prospects for Civil Justice.* Toronto: Ontario Law Reform Commission.
Watson, Garry, et al., eds. 1999. *The Civil Litigation Process: Cases and Materials.* Toronto: Emond Montgomery. A Civil Procedure text with cases and commentaries that focus on the civil justice system in Ontario.
Zemans, Fred, and Patrick Monahan. 1997. *A Blueprint for Publicly Funded Legal Services.* Report of the Ontario Legal Aid Review. Toronto: Queen's Printer.

OREGON

GENERAL INFORMATION

Oregon is located in the Northwest Pacific Coast region of the United States of America. Situated between 42° north and 46° north, Oregon is bordered by the state of Washington to the north, Idaho to the east, California and Nevada to the south, and the Pacific Ocean to the west. It is the tenth largest American state in land area, measuring 251,180 square kilometers—475 kilometers, north to south; 604 kilometers, east to west. Oregon is composed of four highly diverse geographical regions (west to east): the Pacific Coast, the Willamette Valley,

the Cascade Mountains, and the Columbia Plateau basin and range region. Several characteristics distinguish Oregon from the national whole.

First, Oregon's population grew explosively during the late 1980s and throughout the 1990s. Between 1990 and 1999, the state's population increased from 2,842,321 to an estimated 3,316,154, a 1.8 percent annual growth rate, twice the national rate. Rapid growth has placed debates over sustaining environmental integrity and managing growth high on the states' political agenda. Complicating the debate is an urban/rural split, with most population and economic growth concentrated in the Willamette Valley.

Second, Oregon presently has ten federally recognized Native American tribes. Oregon's Native American population is estimated at 38,496 according to the 1990 census. Although each tribe and organization has its own individual history, value system, government, language, and ties, all Oregon Natives share common concerns. On the regional level, for example, the Columbia River Intertribal Fish Commission represents tribes in Washington, Oregon, and Idaho on fishery issues. Statewide, many intertribal organizations deal with specific issues such as education, health, legal matters, aging, alcoholism, and adoption. Since congressional adoption of the 1988 federal National Indian Gaming Regulatory Act, nine of the ten Native American tribes have opened gaming centers on trust land.

Third, driven by dwindling resources and global trends, Oregon's economy is undergoing uneven diversification. From the period of European settlement in the mid-nineteenth century until the last decades of the twentieth century, the state's economy was primarily extractive, based on abundant natural resources. For a century and a half, fertile agricultural lands, expansive timber stands, and rich ocean stocks supported farming, lumbering, and fishing. After World War II, cheap hydroelectric power attracted the metals and paper industries. The economic picture began to change fundamentally in the 1980s. Real interest rates soared and home-buying plummeted. A change in federal land management in the early 1990s drastically reduced timber harvests on federal land in Oregon. At the same time, salmon stocks collapsed. The resulting sharp economic downturn reduced Oregon's per capita income to only 90 percent of the national average, while unemployment rates ran ahead of national levels.

Intensive governmental and private efforts at diversification have been partially successful. Presently, Oregon's economic base includes high technology, forest products, agriculture and food processing, tourism, primary and fabricated metals, and transportation equipment. High technology was particularly encouraged during the 1990s. It grew from 22 percent of manufacturing employment in

1990 to 28 percent in 1997. Economic diversification has increased the wages, employment, and population in the state's more urban counties, especially those in the Willamette Valley. But most rural areas continue to grow slowly in employment and population, their wages have lagged far behind those of the urban areas, and they continue to rely heavily on natural resource industries.

Fourth, land-use management has become a defining political issue. Of the more than 61 million acres of land within Oregon's borders, almost 53 percent is owned by the federal government, mainly under the control of the United States Department of Agriculture Forest Service and the Bureau of Land Management. Because the economy is still tied closely to forestry, agriculture, and tourism, conservation of farmland, forests, and water resources is essential. Pressures generated by a growing population, the divisive urban/rural split, and the expansive federal presence seriously complicate management efforts. Today, many urban communities are faced with problems associated with rapid growth and sprawl, while rural towns languish. Planning processes have been initiated to bring local governments together with state and federal agencies to address concerns that transcend the boundaries of any one community—for instance, fire hazards, transportation, water and air quality, and economic development. These processes have been coordinated by Oregon's Department of Land Conservation and Development and the Department of Economic and Community Development.

Oregon's legal system, like the U.S. national system, is grounded historically in common law derived from centuries-old Anglo-American jurisprudence. Most of these common law antecedents have been superseded by the national and state constitutions and federal and state statutes. The original Oregon Constitution, consisting of eighteen articles, was framed by a convention of sixty delegates. The convention met on the third Monday in August 1857 and adjourned on September 18 of the same year. On November 9, 1857, the constitution was approved by the vote of the people of Oregon Territory. The Act of Congress admitting Oregon into the Union was approved February 14, 1859, the date the state's constitution went into effect. Oregon's biennial legislature, called the Legislative Assembly, adopts statutes that are organized by subject matter in a set of volumes called Oregon Revised Statutes (ORS).

Within its borders, Oregon has a unified system of state trial and appellate courts, known as the Oregon Judicial Department. It also has locally funded, limited-jurisdiction municipal courts, county courts, and justice of the peace courts; national (federal) courts; and tribal courts. Federal courts, although located within Oregon (as in all other states), are not part of the state's judicial system. Under the federal system of government created by the American national constitution, sovereignty is divided between the national and state governments. Consequently, a dual court system—more precisely, fifty-one discrete judicial systems—exists.

Generally speaking, Oregon courts have jurisdiction to hear matters arising under ORS and the state constitution, while federal courts have jurisdiction to hear cases and controversies arising under congressional statutes and the national constitution. However, complicating matters, under Article 6 (the Supremacy Clause) of the national Constitution, the federal Constitution and all congressional statutes and treaties take precedence over state constitutional and statutory provisions. All federal questions arising in Oregon under these national laws are heard in federal courts. Further muddying the general picture, defendants in Oregon criminal cases may seek relief in federal courts, via writs of habeas corpus. Oregon's judicial branch of government deliberates on state civil, criminal, and constitutional issues. Oregon judges review the actions of the executive and legislative branches of state government for compliance with the Oregon Constitution.

As illustrated in the accompanying figure, the integrated Oregon judicial system is composed of three levels.

CIRCUIT COURTS

Oregon's circuit courts are the state's trial courts of general jurisdiction. Until 1998, Oregon had other state trial courts called district courts, which had limited jurisdiction over smaller civil cases and lesser crimes. Effective January 15, 1998, district court jurisdiction, authority, powers, functions, and duties were transferred to circuit court (ORS chapter 658 Or Laws 1995). Circuit court judges are elected on a nonpartisan ballot for a term of six years. They must be citizens of the United States, members of the Oregon State Bar, residents of Oregon at least three years, and residents of their judicial district at least one year (except Multnomah County judges, who may reside within ten miles of the county). As of January 1, 1999, there were 163 circuit judges serving the thirty-six Oregon counties. The circuit judges are grouped in twenty-six geographical areas called judicial districts. The circuit courts have juvenile jurisdiction in all counties except Gilliam, Grant, Malheur, Sherman, and Wheeler, where the county court exercises juvenile jurisdiction except for termination of parental rights proceedings, over which the circuit court has exclusive jurisdiction. The circuit courts also exercise jurisdiction in probate, adoptions, guardianship, and conservatorship cases in all except the five counties above. The chief justice of the Oregon Supreme Court appoints the presiding judge in each judicial district. To expedite judicial business, the chief justice may assign any circuit judge to sit in any judicial district in the state, and the chief justice may ap-

Legal Structure of Oregon Courts

Supreme Court has original jurisdiction in mandamus, quo warranto, habeas corpus.

The Supreme Court also reviews death penalty cases, ballot title challenges, and judge/attorney disciplinary matters.

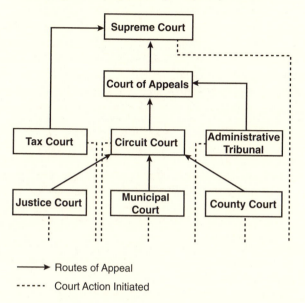

→ Routes of Appeal

----- Court Action Initiated

point members of the Oregon State Bar as circuit judges pro tempore. Since the 1990s, political debate has swirled around the need for new circuit judge positions, particularly in the Portland metropolitan area, and the Legislative Assembly's resistance to creating and funding them.

TAX COURT

In 1961 the Oregon legislature created the tax court to encourage uniform application of tax laws. The tax court is a special court that has limited jurisdiction to hear only cases that involve Oregon's tax laws, including income taxes, corporate excise taxes, property taxes, timber taxes, cigarette taxes, local budget laws, and property tax limitations. The Oregon Tax Court has two divisions—a regular division, presided over by a single judge, and the magistrate division. The regular division judge serves a six-year term and is elected on the statewide, nonpartisan judicial ballot. The regular division judge appoints a presiding magistrate and (presently) four other magistrates to hear cases in the magistrate division. The magistrate division tries or mediates all tax appeals, unless the tax court judge designates the case for the regular division. Trials in the magistrate division are informal proceedings. Statutory rules of evidence do not apply and the trials are not reported. A party may appeal from a magistrate's decision to the judge of the tax court by filing a complaint in the regular division, except in cases filed as small claims. Decisions in small claims procedures are final and may not be appealed. Appeals from regular division decisions go directly to the Oregon Supreme Court.

COURT OF APPEALS

The court of appeals was created in 1969 as a five-judge court. The state legislature expanded membership to six judges in 1973 and to ten in 1977. Judges are elected on a statewide, nonpartisan basis for six-year terms. They must be U.S. citizens, members of the Oregon State Bar, and qualified electors of their county of residence. The chief justice of the Supreme Court appoints a chief judge from among the judges of the court of appeals. The Oregon Court of Appeals has the heaviest caseload of any state intermediate appellate court. The court of appeals has jurisdiction over all civil and criminal appeals, except death penalty cases and appeals from the tax court, and for review of most state administrative agency actions. To manage the heavy caseload, the court divides the judges into three departments of three judges each to hear appeals. The chief judge is not a member of any one panel and may substitute for a member of any department who is not available or has a conflict of interest. Each department is assigned a group of cases. The department evaluates the trial record and the parties' written briefs and oral arguments that describe and analyze claims that the trial court erred. In some cases, the department will agree to affirm the trial court without writing a formal opinion (AWOP). In other cases, after the department votes on whether to affirm or reverse the trial court or remand the case to the trial court for more work, one member of the department drafts an opinion that explains the result and the department's reasoning. A department member who disagrees may draft a dissenting opinion. The department reviews the draft opinion(s) in conference with the chief judge before deciding whether to adopt or revise the decision and draft opinion. Once a department adopts an opinion, it circulates the draft opinion to all judges on the court for comment. In some cases, the full court considers the case in a full court conference when three judges who have reviewed the draft opinion request that the full court consider the case. A party aggrieved by a decision of the court of appeals may petition the Supreme Court for review within thirty-five days after the court of appeals decision is issued. The Supreme Court has discretion whether to review the case. A petition for review is allowed whenever three or more Supreme Court judges vote to allow it. The Supreme Court has authority to appoint a Supreme Court judge, a circuit court judge, or a tax court judge to serve as a judge pro tempore of the court of appeals.

SUPREME COURT OF OREGON

The Supreme Court of Oregon is composed of seven justices elected by nonpartisan statewide ballot to serve six-year terms. Justices elected to the Supreme Court must be U.S. citizens and members of the Oregon State Bar, and must have resided in the state three years. The members of the court elect one of their colleagues to serve as chief justice for a six-year term. The Supreme Court was created by, and its role is defined by, Article 7 of the Oregon Constitution (amended 1910). It is the only Oregon court created by provisions of the Oregon Constitution. The Oregon Supreme Court is primarily a court of review; that is, it reviews the decisions of the court of appeals in selected cases. The Supreme Court has discretion as to which cases it will review. When the Supreme Court decides not to review a case, the court of appeals' decision becomes final. In addition to its review function, the Supreme Court hears direct appeals in death penalty cases and tax court cases, and may accept original jurisdiction in mandamus, quo warranto, and habeas corpus proceedings. Furthermore, the Supreme Court has the responsibility for the admission of lawyers to practice law in Oregon and the power to reprimand, suspend, or disbar lawyers upon investigation and trial by the Oregon State Bar.

The state court administrator position was created by the 1971 legislature. This officer assists the chief justice in exercising administrative authority and supervision over the courts of the state. Specific duties include: supervision of the accounting system for the state courts, preparation of the consolidated budget for the state courts and management of that budget, collection and compilation of statistics relating to the courts in Oregon, establishment and supervision of a statewide automated information system, supervision and management of the indigent defense services program budget, and preparing and maintaining a continuing long-range plan for the future needs of the courts. In addition, the state court administrator supervises staff responsible for daily management of the records of all cases on appeal to the Court of Appeals and Supreme Court, publication of the Oregon Reports, Oregon Reports Court of Appeals, and the tax court opinions, as well as advance sheets for the opinions of all three courts.

Outside the state-funded system of courts, locally funded county, justice, and municipal courts exist. Only six counties now have county court judges who retain any judicial authority. Such authority is limited to juvenile and probate matters. Justice courts are a remnant of territorial days when each precinct of the state was entitled to one. Thirty justice courts currently administer justice in nineteen counties. They have jurisdiction within their county concurrent with the circuit court in all criminal prosecutions except felony trials. They also have jurisdiction over traffic, boating, wildlife, and other violations occurring in their county, and small claims/civil jurisdiction where the amount claimed does not exceed $2,500, except in actions involving title to real property, false imprisonment, libel, slander, or malicious prosecution. Most incorporated cities have a municipal court. They have jurisdiction over violations of the city's ordinances and concurrent jurisdiction with circuit courts over criminal cases occurring within the city limits or on city-owned property. Typical cases adjudicated are minor traffic infractions, certain minor liquor and drug violations, parking violations, and infringements such as animal and fire violations.

James C. Foster

See also California; Federalism; Idaho; Judicial Selection, Methods of; United States—Federal System; United States—State Systems; Washington

References and further reading

Drukman, Mason. 1997. *Wayne Morse: A Political Biography.* Portland, OR: Oregon Historical Society.

Lichatowich, Jim. 1999. *Salmon without Rivers: A History of the Pacific Salmon Crisis.* Washington, DC: Island Press.

Robbins, William G. 1997. *Landscapes of Promise: The Oregon Story, 1800–1940.* Seattle: University of Washington Press.

Robbins, William G., ed. 2001. *The Great Northwest: The Search for Regional Identity.* Corvallis: Oregon State University Press.

Robbins, William G., Robert J. Frank, and Richard E. Ross, eds. 1983. *Regionalism and the Pacific Northwest.* Corvallis: Oregon State University Press.

Schwantes, Carlos Arnaldo. 1996. *The Pacific Northwest: An Interpretive History.* Revised and enlarged edition. Lincoln: University of Nebraska Press.

Walth, Brent. 1994. *Fire at Eden's Gate: Tom McCall and the Oregon Story.* Portland: Oregon Historical Society.

OTTOMAN EMPIRE

GENERAL INFORMATION

Founded in the early fourteenth century, the Ottoman Empire lasted for roughly six centuries before World War I and a subsequent internecine war brought about its collapse. At the height of its power, the Ottoman Empire stretched from Algeria to Persia, from the Balkans to the Arabian peninsula, and included parts of Russia, the Caucuses, Hungary, all of Asia Minor, and much of the Middle East. Ruled by Turkish sultans, the empire was made up of a diversity of conquered peoples, the vast majority of whom were Muslim, although there were significant, and tolerated, Jewish and Christian populations. While the empire was neither a strictly secular nor strictly religious state, Islam played a great role in the government and administration of the state, and in establishing the powers of the sultan. By 1923 the empire had been replaced by the Republic of Turkey and a number of smaller states.

HISTORY

Originally a nomadic people, Turks emerged from Central Asia in the eleventh century to raid western lands. Eventually settling in Asia Minor and adopting Islam as their religion, the most powerful of the Turkic tribes was the Seljuks, who dominated Anatolia for nearly two and a half centuries. Sultan Osman I, first ruler of the Ottoman Empire, consolidated the power of local Turks after the defeat of the Seljuks by the Mongols in the late thirteenth century. Osman moved to expand the empire to western Asia Minor, following which he and his successors sought to conquer southeastern Europe, the lands controlled by the dying Byzantine Empire. By the mid-fourteenth century, with the conquest of Constantinople by Mehmet II, the power base of the Ottoman Empire was firmly established in Anatolia and the Balkans.

The golden age of the empire lasted for nearly ninety years (1481–1566) and was brought about much through the efforts of Mehmet's grandson, Selim I, and great-grandson, Suleyman the Magnificent. Selim expanded the empire's holdings to include the religious sites of Islam, taking the title of caliph upon his conquest of Mecca, thereby displacing the centuries-old Baghdad caliphate and ruling in both religious and secular spheres. Suleyman, the most powerful of all Ottoman sultans, further consolidated the religious power acquired by his father, solidly marrying it to his political power. Under Suleyman, also known as the Lawgiver, monies from the expanded empire's control of trade routes were used to build public and religious works throughout Ottoman lands, increasing imperial influence. Yet his long reign set the scene for the empire's decline, as numerous successors were unable to rule with the power and authority of Suleyman. Weaknesses within the Ottoman Empire were countered by the growing strength and influence of west European states. As the empire grew weaker at its core, provinces began to exercise more independence. Attempts at central reform, culminating in the Tanzimat program of the nineteenth century, were marginally successful, prolonging a decline that was to last until the empire collapsed and the sultanate was abolished in 1923.

LEGAL CONCEPTS

The most controversial subject within the history of Turkish law is the general structure of Ottoman law and its customary (*örfi*) and religious (*sharia*) characteristics: the first a result of individual orders (*ferman*) and laws (*kanun*) of the sultan, the second having its origins in the Koran and the books of Islamic law (*fikih*). With the establishment of the Ottoman Empire, a new and original law system was not created, as the founders of the empire adopted a legal system that was uniform with other Islamic and Turkic states (for example, that of the Seljuk Empire). Throughout the six centuries of the empire, using the broad discretion and implementation authority of the sultans that existed under Islamic law, amendments were made to this legal system, allowing for its evolution.

Because of the nature of the law-making tradition within the Ottoman Empire, and the discretionary power of the sultans, there was no systematic method of legal evolution in specific fields of law until the Tanzimat period. There was, in fact, no written or official document that could have been interpreted as a constitution for the empire. Only the *Teskilat-i Esasiye Kanunnamesi* (Constitutional Law) existed, solely regulating the structure of the state. Not until 1876 did another document approach fulfilling the role of a constitution within the Ottoman Empire—the *Kanun-i Esasi* (Essential Law).

The lack of constitutionally defined limits, however, did not mean that there were no restrictions on the ability of the sultans to make law. Ottoman sultans often took great care to avoid making laws that interfered in areas already regulated by *sharia* and *sharia* principles. *Sharia* focused on the fields of individual law, family law, inheritance, possession law, and commercial law. *Örfi*, the customary law of the sultans, was first exercised during the reign of Mehmet II, and contrary to its name had little to do with the traditions and customs of the Ottoman culture. Rather, customary law dealt with the fields of constitutional law, administrative law, and tax law. Despite the fact that customary and religious law focused on different areas of law, the function of both together remained essentially the same—the maintenance of the state and the power of the sultan.

Outside of *sharia* and *örfi* laws, other sources of law were found in the *fetvas* (religious decrees) issued by muftis (Islamic legal advisors), who were appointed by the sultan and possessed both extensive religious and legal knowledge. The role of *fetva* was twofold. First, the muftis provided *fetvas* to judges (*kadi*) on specialized points of law when the judges' knowledge was not sufficient, in some instances leading to resolution of disputes before final legal action was taken. Second, at times, the parties appearing in court supported their claims by submitting a *fetva* issued in their favor. Before the Tanzimat reforms and the establishment of a systematic appeals process, the presence of the muftis in locations far from the central administration, coupled with the opportunity to have a knowledgeable legal and religious authority with the power to issue *fetvas*, compelled judges to act in compliance with the law.

STRUCTURE AND EVOLUTION

From the thirteenth to the mid-nineteenth centuries, the structure of the legal system and the fundamental laws of the Ottoman Empire remained essentially the same. The religious (*sharia*) courts were the lowest and most common courts for dispute settlement. These courts were staffed by one judge (*kadi, qadi*) and a number of assistants, depending on the size of the region in which a court had jurisdiction. In theory, panel courts were not common. However, given the special role of muftis in the legal process, and the presence of *ssühüd* (witnesses) observing court proceedings, the effect was to increase legal authority at any given time within a single court.

Until the Tanzimat reforms, there was no systematic appeals process under Ottoman law. In such cases in which rulings in *sharia* courts were unsatisfactory, the *Divan-i Hümayun* (Imperial Council), headed by the *Veziriazam* (grand vizier), generally acted as an appellate authority. The Imperial Council also functioned as a specialized court to settle disputes outside the authority of the *sharia* courts. Beyond the *Divan-i Hümayun,* there were different councils (*veziriazam divan*) also headed by the grand vizier that acted as civil courts. Under the guidance of the grand vizier, the *Cuma* (Friday) and *Çarsamba* (Wednesday) divans were held to address specific disputes that could not be settled by the Imperial Council and the unsettled disputes of residents of Constantinople, respectively. *Kazasker divans* (Soldiers' Councils) were specialized councils for administrative personnel and military staff. The Rumeli (European) and Anadolu (Asian) *Kazasker* were the highest authorities in the empire, with the title of judge, reporting directly to the grand vizier.

Inasmuch as the Ottoman Empire was greatly influenced by the Western world during the nineteenth century, important changes in all aspects of Ottoman life occurred, including law. The Tanzimat reforms of the mid-nineteenth century brought about the most comprehensive and systematic changes that the legal system of the Ottoman Empire had experienced. In addition to the *sharia* courts, a number of new and specialized courts were established. *Ticaret* (commercial) courts were founded in every province of the empire to address business concerns, as well as *Nizamiye* (order) courts, to oversee civil and criminal cases. *Suray-i Devlet* (High Committee of State) courts were established to resolve administrative disputes, and the *Cemaat* (society) courts and *Konsolosluk* (consulate) courts were formed to address the needs of non-Muslim citizens in the areas of inheritance and family law, and foreigners, respectively. The appellate system also expanded under the Tanzimat reforms with the creation of the *Meclis-i Tetkikati Seriye* (Inspection Parliament) to act as the appeals court for *sharia* courts, and the *Divan-i Ahkami Adliye* (Justice Council), functioning as the point of appeals for both the *Nizamiye* courts and the *Ticaret* courts.

The "legislative" aspect of the legal system also came under the sweep of the Tanzimat reforms. Beginning in 1840, appointed committees, the most important of which were the *Meclis-i Vala-yi Ahkam-i Adliye* (Justice Parliament) and the *Meclis-i Tanzimat* (Tanzimat Parliament), the latter focusing on law-making reforms, approved a series of changes in the Ottoman system. These committees facilitated the establishment of more formal codified laws, the application of which soon followed. Laws addressing every subject from criminal codes to inheritance to deed registry were updated and placed into uniform practice. Still, given the significant reforms that took place during the mid-1800s, particular fields of law were neglected until a much later date, laws regarding family matters being one example. The first law creating formally recognized family rights and obligations was not enacted until the beginning of the twentieth century, with the creation of the *Hukuk-i Aile Kararnamesi* (Family Law Decree).

During the height of Western influence within the Ottoman Empire, several other changes were made, in addition to the law-making reforms. Between 1850 and 1880, a number of codes and laws were adapted from foreign examples, primarily French, and enacted within the empire. The *Ticaret Kanunnamesi* (Commercial Code of 1850), the *Ceza Kanunu* (Criminal Law Code of 1858), the *Usul-i Muhakemeyi Ticaret Nizamnamesi* (Commercial Procedural Law of 1861), the *Ticaret-i Bahriye Kanunnamesi* (Maritime Law of 1863), the *Usul-I Muhakemat-i Cezaiye Kanunu* (Criminal Procedural Law of 1879), and the *Usul-i Muhakemat-i Hukukiye Kanunu* (Procedural Judicial Law of 1879) were all implemented, and worked to establish a formalized legal process. A final example of Western influence was codified in 1879 with the enactment of the *Mehakim-i Nizamiye Teskilati Kanunu* (Procedural Law of Sharia Court Organization), creating the first office of the state prosecutor.

SPECIALIZED JUDICIAL BODIES

Until the time of Suleyman, expatriates and foreigners were treated the same as imperial subjects under Ottoman law. The advent of the Capitulations (trade privileges) to France in the sixteenth century created special *Konsolosluk* (consulate) courts to address any type of civil, criminal, and commercial dispute of French citizens within the empire, independent of the Ottoman legal process. With the growing weakness of the Ottoman court, these privileges were subsequently extended to all the foreign citizens within the empire, granting foreigners great leeway in their personal and professional affairs.

Recognizing the need to meet the concerns of the growing non-Muslim population of the empire, *Cemaat* (Society) courts were established, dealing solely with family law, inheritance, and individual law, outside of the established legal process.

STAFFING

Within the empire, sultans had special authority and duties in the judicial system, both as a function of Islamic law and their rights as rulers of the empire, using their judicial powers at their own discretion. However, as the

Structure of the Ottoman Empire

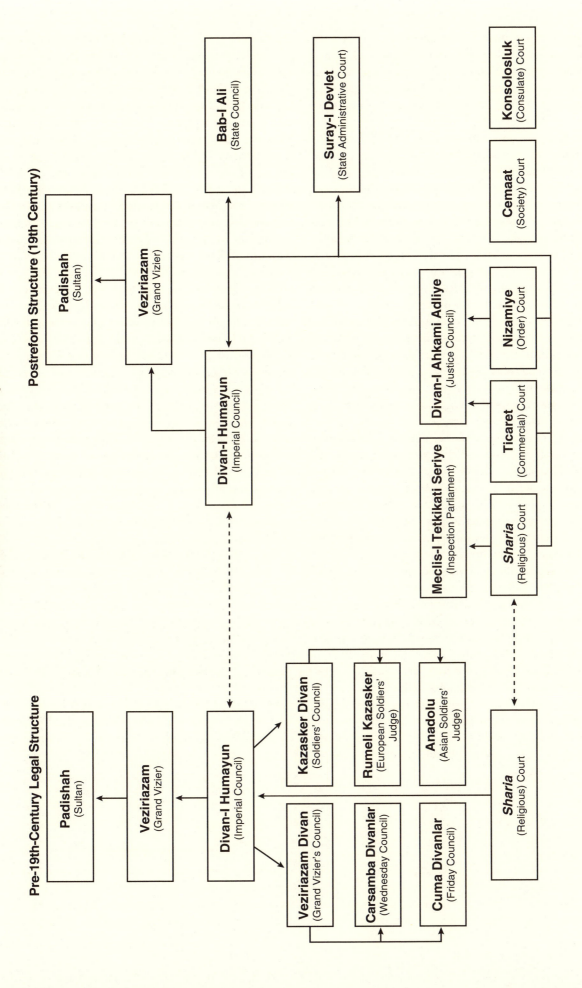

Postreform Structure (19th Century)

Padishah
(Sultan)

Veziriazam
(Grand Vizier)

Bab-I Ali
(State Council)

Suray-I Devlet
(State Administrative Court)

Konsolosluk
(Consulate) Court

Cemaat
(Society) Court

Divan-I Humayun
(Imperial Council)

Divan-I Ahkami Adliye
(Justice Council)

Meclis-I Tetkikati Seriye
(Inspection Parliament)

Nizamiye
(Order) Court

Ticaret
(Commercial) Court

Sharia
(Religious) Court

Pre-19th-Century Legal Structure

Padishah
(Sultan)

Veziriazam
(Grand Vizier)

Divan-I Humayun
(Imperial Council)

Kazasker Divan
(Soldiers' Council)

Rumeli Kazasker
(European Soldiers' Judge)

Anadolu
(Asian Soldiers' Judge)

Veziriazam Divan
(Grand Vizier's Council)

Carsamba Divanlar
(Wednesday Council)

Cuma Divanlar
(Friday Council)

Sharia
(Religious) Court

empire expanded, this power was devolved to judges, the persons who became legally responsible for settling disputes under Ottoman law. Judges were educated in *medrese*, law schools affiliated with religious institutions, and appointed by the central Ottoman administration for a certain term. The original term of appointment was three years, later changed to two years, and by the seventeenth century, reduced to a single year. Judges whose terms of duty had expired were required to reside in Constantinople until another appointment was made.

Given the powers of the sultan, even in the post-Tanzimat period, the judicial branch was nevertheless separated from the executive branch. Outside of the judiciary, judges did not have a hierarchical relationship to follow when reporting cases or outcomes. They were independent government officials, who judged both *örfi* and *sharia* disputes, and whose responsibilities and authority covered civil and criminal cases as well. Judges also performed some administrative functions along with their judicial duties. Acting in the capacity of inspectors, judges monitored businesses and trading institutions. They provided notary services and prepared sale, rent, powers of attorney, and pledge agreements. Assisting judges in the courts were *naib* (deputies), who visited places of crimes or events; *sühud* (witnesses), who were elected among the respected citizens of the society to serve at the trial as an observer; *kassam* (distributors), who assisted the judge in distributing inherited property; and *katip* (stenographers), who dictated trials. Professional attorneys-at-law, in the Western sense, did not exist in the Ottoman legal system, leaving parties to follow up court rulings on their own or through a representative.

The *Veziriazam* (grand vizier), as the most powerful official after the sultan, acted as a representative in the areas where the sultan was authorized. Furthermore, he was the highest official in the judicial system, yet could be replaced at the whim of the sultan. *Kazasker* courts were originally established during the Tanzimat reforms to settle the disputes of the military class, and their officers sat as the highest-ranked judges in the Ottoman legal system. The *Nisanci* (legal interpreters), chosen from among the educated class until the sixteenth century, were permanent members of the Imperial Council and involved with customary law, in addition to their other administrative duties.

IMPACT

Fundamental to the Ottoman legal system were inherent contradictions within the system. The basic law of the Ottoman Empire, *sharia* (religious) law, depended on Islamic codes and was not particularly flexible. The exercise of *örfi* (customary) law, through the use of *ferman* and *kanun* by the sultanate, led to laws restricted only by the precepts of *sharia,* but beyond that was used at the discretion of the sultan. Further development of the Ottoman legal system was led, in fact, by areas of greatest need to the government—public law and tax law. However, because of poorly defined legal precepts, there was an inadequate number of both educated judges and courts in which to try cases, creating an inefficient and weak legal system.

By far the greatest impact within the Ottoman system of law was the Tanzimat reforms of the nineteenth century. The reform movements created new specialized courts, new laws regarding trade, family, civil law, and immovable property, and liberalized the regime, which affected all levels of Ottoman society. However, because these reform efforts were not a result of the internal dynamics of the empire, and the newly adopted laws were heavily influenced by Western laws, contradictions emerged between tradition and religion on the one hand, and modernization and progress on the other, preventing even reform of the legal system from meeting the needs of Ottoman society.

Buket Ö. Cox

See also Customary Law; Islamic Law; Turkey
References and further reading
Aydin, M. Akif. 1996. *Islam ve Osmanli hukuku aristirmalari (Islam and Ottoman Law Research)*. Mecidiyekoy, Istanbul: Iz.
———. 1999. *Turk Hukuk Tarihi (Turkish Law History)*. Istanbul: Beta.
Gerber, Haim. 1994. *State, Society, and Law in Islam: Ottoman Law in Comparative Perspective*. Albany: State University of New York Press.
Imber, Colin. 1996. *Studies in Ottoman History and Law*. Istanbul: Isis Press.
Lewis, Bernard. 1997. *The Middle East: 2000 Years of History from the Rise of Christianity to the Present Day*. London: Phoenix Giant.

P

PAKISTAN

COUNTRY INFORMATION

Originally part of the Indus Valley civilization, later colonized by the British, and an independent country after the partition of India, the Islamic Republic of Pakistan is located in south Asia, bordered by India on the east, Iran and Afghanistan on the west, and China on the north. The nation was created after the 1947 separation of British India into the Islamic state of Pakistan (with two sections, West Pakistan and East Pakistan) and the largely Hindu India. After a war with India in 1971, East Pakistan seceded and became the separate nation of Bangladesh.

Pakistan occupies over 800,000 square kilometers of territory, with a coastline of over 1,000 kilometers. Pakistan's climate is mostly hot and dry but is more temperate in the north and northwest regions. The country's natural resources include extensive natural gas reserves, limited petroleum supplies, coal, iron ore, copper, salt, and limestone. Earthquakes and extensive flooding from heavy rains along the Indus are frequent.

Pakistan's population is estimated at over 140 million. The Pakistani people comprise a diverse set of ethnic groups: Punjabi, Sindhi, Pashtun (Pathan), Baloch, and Muhajir (immigrants from India at the time of partition and their descendants). Consistent with this diversity, Pakistanis speak several languages, including Punjabi, Sindhi, Siraiki (a Punjabi variant), Pashtu, Balochi, Hindko, Brahui, and Burushaski. Urdu is the official language, and English is the lingua franca of the Pakistani elite and most government ministries. Literacy rates are low, especially for girls and women. Islam is the state religion of Pakistan, and 97 percent of the population is Muslim. Christians and Hindus are thus small minorities.

Pakistan is a poor country, with a growth rate just over 3 percent and a gross domestic product of $282 billion, with $35 billion in foreign debt. Over a third of the population lives below the poverty line. State-owned enterprises account for nearly half of the gross national product.

Pakistan encounters chronic conflicts with its neighbor, India, especially over the status of Kashmir and the water resources of the Indus River. Because the separation of the two countries in 1947 was never fully resolved, Pakistan and India have fought in three wars. International concern over the conflict has intensified since, in response to Indian nuclear weapons testing, Pakistan conducted its own nuclear tests in 1998.

LEGAL SYSTEM

Pakistan is a democratic federal republic; however, coups and the imposition of martial law have periodically undermined democratic institutions. The legal system of Pakistan is based on the English common law, with provisions to realize its commitments as an Islamic state. The 1973 Constitution, as amended in 1985, provides for a parliamentary system, with a president serving as the head of state and a popularly elected prime minister as the head of government. The bicameral legislature, the Majlis-i-Shoora (Council of Advisers), consists of the Senate (upper house) and the National Assembly (lower house). The executive is the most powerful branch of government. For example, the Eighth Amendment to the constitution gives the president broad discretion to dissolve the National Assembly.

The constitution, which came into force on April 10, 1973, was suspended on July 5, 1977, and restored with amendments on December 30, 1985. The government suspended the constitution again on October 15, 1999, when a bloodless coup deposed elected Prime Minister Nawaz Sharif and Gen. Pervez Musharaff assumed power as the chief executive. On June 20, 2001, General Musharaff further consolidated his power by appointing himself president and the formal head of state. The general simultaneously effectuated the formal dissolution of the National Assembly and four regional assemblies.

COURT SYSTEM

The Pakistan legal system combines feature of an Islamic legal system based on *sharia* (Islamic law) with a Western system based on English common law. The institutional structure of the court system reflects a formal separation of powers between the judiciary and the executive branches of government. However, politically motivated limits on judicial independence have undermined this principle in practice. Even though many courageous

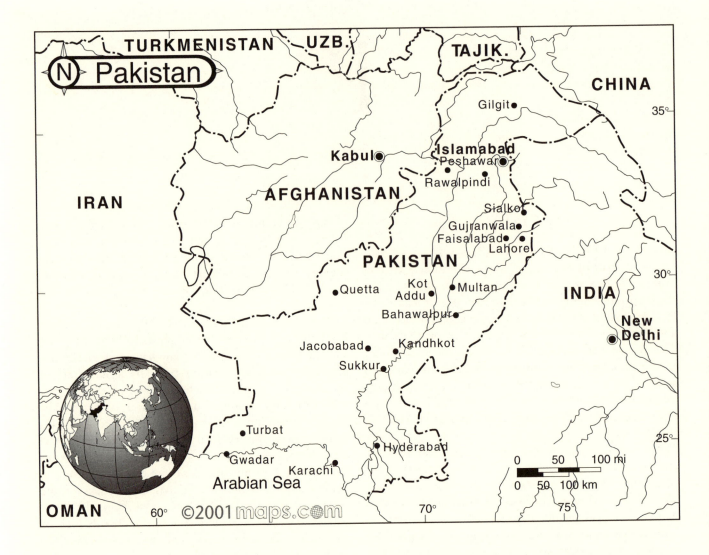

judges have remained faithful to their own independence, the courts have struggled to reconcile foundational legal principles with the exigencies of political forces.

The judiciary consists of the Supreme Court, the Provincial High Courts, and (under their jurisdiction and supervision) District Courts that hear civil cases and Sessions Courts that hear criminal cases. The magistracy deals with cases brought by the police. The Supreme Court has original, appellate, and advisory jurisdictions and is the highest court in the land.

Accordingly, ultimate judicial power rests with the Supreme Court, which comprises a chief justice and thirteen judges. There is a high court in each of the four provinces, each with a chief justice and a number of other judges (that number is determined by law or fixed by the president).

The Supreme Court, to the exclusion of every other court in Pakistan, has the jurisdiction to pronounce declaratory judgments in any dispute between the federal government and a provincial government or between any two or more provincial governments. The Supreme

Court may also decide cases dealing with fundamental rights. The seat of the Supreme Court is at Islamabad.

The president appoints the chief justice of Pakistan and also appoints other judges after consultation with the chief justice. To be eligible for appointment as a judge of the Supreme Court, a candidate must be a citizen of Pakistan and a High Court judge with at least five years of experience or a High Court advocate with fifteen years of experience. The chief justice and judges of the Supreme Court may hold office until the age of sixty-five.

There is a High Court in each of the four provinces. A chief justice presides in each High Court; however, the number of judges varies by province. Including their chief justices, the Lahore High Court of the Punjab, the High Court of Sindh, the Peshawar High Court of North West Frontier Province, and the High Court of Balochistan have fifty, twenty-eight, fifteen, and six judges, respectively.

The principal seat of the Lahore High Court is in Lahore, and it has three benches, at Bahawalpur, Multan, and Rawalpindi. The principal seat of the High Court of Sindh is in Karachi, with a bench at Hyderabad and another at Sukkur. The principal seat of the Peshawar High Court is in Peshawar, and it has two benches, at Abbottabad and Dera Ismail Khan. The principal seat of the High Court of Balochistan is in Quetta, with a bench at Sibi. Each high court may have more benches at other places as the governor, on the advice of the cabinet and in consultation with the chief justice of the High Court, may determine.

A judge of the High Court is appointed by the president after consultation with the chief justice of Pakistan, the governor of the province, and the chief justice of the High Court in which such an appointment is to be made. To be eligible for the High Court, the candidate must be a citizen of Pakistan, at least forty years of age, an advocate of the High Court or a judge for ten years, and a district judge for at least three years. A judge of a High Court may hold office until the age of sixty-two.

A High Court has both original and appellate jurisdiction. A High Court also has the power to withdraw any civil or criminal case from a trial court and try it de novo. The High Court has extensive appellate jurisdiction for appeals from judgments, decisions, decrees, and sentences passed by the civil and criminal courts.

In every district of a province, the District Court is the principal court of original jurisdiction in civil matters. Sessions Courts for criminal law matters also sit under the supervision of the District Court.

District Court judges are selected by competitive examination, and once selected, they become part of the provincial civil service. Within each District Court, civil judges are promoted first to the status of additional district and session judge before rising to the position of district and session judge. A district and session judge presides in each district. The number of districts varies for each province: thirty-five in Punjab, twenty-two in North West Frontier Province, twenty in Sindh, and twenty-two in Balochistan.

LEGAL PROFESSION

The British never introduced the barrister-solicitor distinction in colonial India; thus, contemporary Pakistan does not follow the British model in this regard. Under the Legal Practitioners and Bar Councils Act (1973), law graduates must meet a variety of requirements to practice in the courts as advocates. For practice in the District Courts, law graduates must undergo a six-month apprenticeship with a senior advocate and interview with the Enrollment Committee of the Provincial Bar Council of two elected members of the Council and a judge of the high court, who chairs the committee. For practice in the high court, an advocate must have two years of experience in the District Court and satisfy the requirements of the same Enrollment Committee. For admission to practice in the Supreme Court, an advocate must have ten

Legal Structure of Pakistan Courts

Supreme Court
(Islamabad)
Original, Appellate, and Advisory Jurisdiction

Provincial High Courts
(Punjab, Sindh, North West Frontier Province, and Balochistan)
Federal *Sharia* Court (Islamabad)
(Circuits in Lahore, Karachi, Peshawar, and Quetta)

District (civil) and Sessions (criminal) Courts, Magistracy and Special Courts and Tribunals

years of High Court experience and satisfy the requirements of the Supreme Court Enrollment Committee consisting of two members of the national Pakistan Bar Council and one Supreme Court judge, who chairs the committee.

THE CONSTITUTION AND CODES

The constitution provides many legal guarantees consistent with a self-limiting democratic state, including the right to bail and to counsel, the right of habeas corpus, the right of cross-examination, the right of representation, the right of being informed of charges, the right of appeal, and the prohibition of double jeopardy.

Pakistan's penal code is based on the Indian Penal Code of 1860, with extensive amendments made during both the pre- and postindependence periods. The death penalty is legal in Pakistan. In February 1979, Zia ul-Haq issued new laws that punished rape and adultery, theft, and the consumption of alcohol with severe punishments, including stoning and amputation; however, such penalties were not upheld by the Federal Shari'at Court and were discontinued in 1994. The Pakistani civil justice system functions in accordance with the Civil Procedure Code of 1908. As in many other former British colonies, several problems impede the effective and fair operation of the civil justice courts, including backlog and delay and private corruption.

EMERGENCY PROVISIONS

Emergency provisions are a peculiarity of the Pakistani and Indian Constitutions. The British colonial constitutional provisions and penal codes gave the authorities ample scope for overriding regular legal procedures in the case of persons suspected of political agitation or making threats to the public order. Pakistan has perpetuated and strengthened these provisions and codes through the Security of Pakistan Act and Section 144 of the Code of

Criminal Procedure, which permits a magistrate to prohibit meetings of five or more persons, forbid the carrying of firearms, and impose "preventive detention" on anybody thought likely to disturb public order.

SPECIAL LEGAL CONCEPTS: THE *SHARIA*

The judicial system also applies Islamic legal tenets and values, known as the sharia. Under traditional Islamic law, *usal-al-fiqh* (human comprehension of the *sharia*) comprises the principles of jurisprudence. The Qur'an, the Islamic holy book, and the Sunnah, the sayings and doings of the prophet Muhammad, are two main sources of Islamic law. Jurisprudential scholars establish principles of *ijtihad* (literally, effort), based on a science of independent reasoning and interpretation. If scholarship is in agreement, the consensus, *ijma,* is considered a third source of law. The fourth source is the process of analogic reasoning known as *qiya.*

Pakistan implemented a complete code of Islamic laws and instituted the Federal Shari'at Court, a court of Islamic law, in the 1980s. During that period, the Pakistani government announced its commitment to the development of an Islamic economy. The movement intensified efforts to enforce the prohibition against economic practices outlawed by Muslim theology, such as *riba* (interest). For example, in a landmark decision in 1992, the Federal Shari'at Court (which will be described), drawing on a remarkable book-length survey of distinguished experts, held nearly two dozen major statutes to be "un-Islamic," based on the failure to adhere to the prohibition against interest. Given the severe consequences for the banking system of full compliance with the ruling, the decision is still in limbo on appeal and unlikely to be implemented.

SPECIAL COURTS, BODIES, AND TRIBUNALS

In addition to the ordinary courts, there is the Federal Shari'at Court. This court has eight Muslim judges, including the chief justice; four of the judges are qualified to be High Court judges, and three are *'ulama* (scholars versed in Islamic law). Other courts exercise civil and criminal jurisdiction. Special courts and tribunals deal with specific types of cases, such as drug offenses, income tax appeals, and traffic offenses.

The Federal Shari'at Court has both original and appellate jurisdiction. The court may examine and decide whether a law is repugnant to the injunctions of Islam as laid down in the Qur'an and Sunnah of the Holy Prophet. On finding a violation of Islamic law, the president (in the case of a federal law) or the governor (in the case of a provincial law) is required to take steps to amend the law to bring it into conformity with the injunctions of Islam. The court also has exclusive jurisdiction to hear appeals from the decision of criminal courts under *hudood* law (laws pertaining to intoxication offenses), theft, *zina* (unlawful sexual intercourse), and *qazf* (false imputation of *zina*). The principal seat of the Federal Shari'at Court is at Islamabad, but it conducts circuits in Lahore, Karachi, Peshawar, and Quetta.

In addition to the Federal Shari'at Court, special courts and tribunals are constituted to try specific cases, including trial of offenses in banking, customs, traffic, corruption, commerce, drugs, labor, insurance, tax, and other specialized areas. Appeals from the special courts lie to the High Courts, except in the case of the Labor Courts and Special Traffic Courts, which have separate forums of appeal.

Preliminarily successful pilot projects in judicial mediation in Lahore and Multan were shut down after the 1999 coup, but efforts are under way to reopen, institutionalize, and broaden the use of mediation as an alternative to protracted trials in family and commercial disputes.

At the federal level, the Law and Justice Division acts as an advisory and consultative body to the federal government, ministries, and attached departments. Similarly, the Law Department in each province deals with provincial legal matters. The division is responsible for legislative drafting, handling litigation involving the government, the appointment of government law officers (including staffing the attorney general's office), and the administration of the Federal Judicial Academy, founded in 1988.

The ombudsman (*wafaqi mohtasib*) is an ancient Islamic concept, and many Islamic states have established the Office of *mohtasib,* drawing on the concept of *hisab* (accountability) established by the prophet Muhammad, to prevent injustice against the citizenry. The Institution of Ombudsman, a nonpartisan office, was formally established in 1983; the ombudsman is appointed by the president for a nonrenewable term of four years. The chief purpose of the *wafaqi mohtasib* is to diagnose, investigate, redress, and rectify any injustice done to a person through maladministration on the part of a federal agency or a federal government official. The primary objective of the office is to institutionalize a system for enforcing administrative accountability.

FUNDAMENTAL LEGAL ISSUES

As Pakistan's legal system evolves further into the twenty-first century, legal decision makers will be forced to navigate a difficult course between conflicting historical commitments and contemporary policy decisions. Pakistan is a democratic republic prone to coups and national security interventions based on emergency rule. It is a common law country with a constitutional tradition of separate powers and civil rights, yet it is committed to Islamic traditions of heavily regulating certain forms of private economic activity and the differential legal treatment of women. Independence of the judiciary is difficult to maintain in the face of military rule. Islamic restrictions on certain mechanisms of international finance (for example, interest) create impediments to global economic integration. The elevation of women to their full potential and equal status will be difficult to achieve if the obstacles to rape prosecution are not removed (such as the requirement of having four adult Muslim witnesses or the fact that if the rape prosecution is not successful, the woman will be prosecuted for illicit sexual activity and false accusation). Conflicts emerging from these diverse characteristics of the legal system, its traditions, and modern practices are not always irreconcilable; however, the profound tensions and predicaments they create for legal decision makers are undeniable.

Hiram E. Chodosh
Tassaduq Hussain Jilani

See also Common Law; Constitutional Law; Family Law; India; Islamic Law; Judicial Independence; Judicial Selection, Methods of; Legal Professionals—Civil Law Traditions; Mediation

References and further reading
Gledhill, Alan. 1967. *Pakistan: The Development of Its Law and Constitution.* 2d ed. London: Stevens and Sons.
Haider, Nadya. 2000. "Islamic Legal Reform: The Case of Pakistan and Family Law." *Yale Journal of Law and Feminism* 12: 287.
Mahmud, Tayyab. 1995. "Freedom of Religion and Religious Minorities in Pakistan: A Study of Judicial Practice." *Fordham International Law Journal* 19: 40.
Newberg, Paula R. 1995. *Judging the State: Courts and Constitutional Politics in Pakistan.* Cambridge: Cambridge University Press.
Shah, Nasim Hasan. 1999. *Essays and Addresses on Constitution, Law and Pakistan Legal System.* Lahore: Research Society of Pakistan.

PALAU

GEOGRAPHY

Palau (locally known as Belau) is an island nation located in the Micronesian region of the Pacific. It has four big islands and many small islands, with a total landmass of 500 square kilometers. The large islands are made of volcanic rock, while smaller ones are made of raised coral limestone. There are also some low-lying atolls in the group with huge reef enclosures. The islands have a beautiful tropical climate, with heavy rains from July to August and from December to January. From November to April, the northeast trade winds blow, while from May to June, the easterly winds predominate. Palauans are Micronesians, although there is an ethnic and linguistic mix within the group. The estimated population in 1998 was 18,110 people, but many Palauans live overseas, especially in Guam.

POLITICAL HISTORY

For hundreds of years, Palau was governed by traditional leaders and regulated by indigenous customs. During the eighteenth and nineteenth centuries, these traditional political establishments were drastically changed. The islands saw four waves of imperial powers. In 1885, during the European scramble for the Pacific, Germany disputed with Spain over the control of the Caroline Islands (which then included Palau). The dispute was submitted to Pope Leo XIII, who determined that Spain should have sovereignty over the Carolines (including Palau). The Spaniards ruled Palau for about fifteen years. In 1899, however, Spain had to sell Palau back to its former disputant (Germany) after Spain was defeated by the Americans in the Spanish-American War. Palauan customs and traditions were then subjected to German rule and ideologies. In 1914, Germany relinquished its hold on Palau and tossed it to the Japanese. In an attempt to consolidate the administration of protected territories, the recently formed League of Nations mandated Palau to Japan as class C. Japan, now secured with the formal recognition of its mandate, made Palau its administrative center for Micronesia and initiated mining, plantation agriculture, and commercial fishing in Palau. The large migration of Japanese into Palau again radically changed Palauan culture. After World War II, Palau was to see yet another colonial master—the United States. Japan had been defeated in the war, and together with that went its control over Palau. The United States became the new superpower after World War II and acquired Palau (and other Micronesian states) for their strategic locations. In 1947, under a trusteeship agreement, the United Nations authorized the United States to administer Palau, the Federated States of Micronesia, Northern Mariana Islands, and Marshall Islands as the "Trust Territory of the Pacific Islands." For the next two decades, Micronesia was governed under this arrangement. In 1965, the Congress of Micronesia was formed, a body made up of leaders from all the Micronesian territories under the Trust Territories of the Pacific Islands to decide the future of those territories. In 1969, the United States began negotiating with the Congress of Micronesia on the political future of the territory, and in 1981, through a referendum, Palau adopted a constitution and became a republic. One year later, in 1982, all the U.S. trust territories signed a Compact of Free Association with the United States. The compact gives autonomy to the former trust states and substantial economic assistance, as well as defense and technical services. Initially, Palau didn't ratify the compact because it provided the U.S. with the option to operate nuclear vessels in Palauan territory, a clause that was inconsistent with the Palau Constitution. In October 1994, however, after much legal wrangling, Palau endorsed the Compact of Free Association

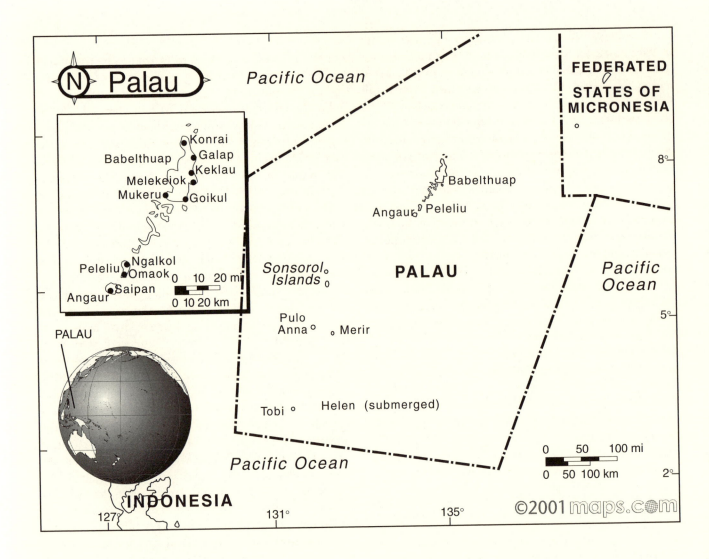

with the United States. According to the compact, the United States has military access to Palauan waters and can operate two military bases in the islands. The locally drafted Constitution of the Republic of Palau entered into effect on January 1, 1981. In December 1994, Palau became a member of the United Nations, and in 1997, it was admitted into the International Monetary Fund.

SOURCES OF LAW

Palau Constitution

An important source of law is the Constitution of Palau. As in most of the countries in the South Pacific, the constitution is the supreme law of the land. Any law that is inconsistent with the constitution will be void to the extent of the inconsistency. Article 14 provides for the amendment of the constitution, which may be done if proposed by (1) a constitutional convention, (2) a popular initiative signed by 25 percent of the voters, or (3) a resolution adopted by at least three-fourths of the members of the Olbiil Era Kelulau (the Palauan legislature).

An amendment will be adopted if, during a general election, a simple majority supports it.

Legislation

In Palau, all legislation and subsidiary legislation is codified in the Palau National Code. The code was compiled in 1985, and since its first publication, two supplements have been issued. The code is a compilation of all the laws applicable in Palau, which includes laws of the local Palau District Code and the Trust Territory Code, as well as laws made by the Olbiil Era Kelulau. Additionally, Section 30 of the code gives effect to the UN Trusteeship Agreement and the laws of the United States that are applicable to Palau. The code is divided into titles according to subject and includes all matters of criminal and civil law. In a situation in which laws conflict, the legislation overrides all other laws except the Constitution of Palau.

Common Law

A third source of law in Palau is common law. As in all the other countries having free association with the United States, common law in the Palauan context refers to the rules of common law as expressed in the restatements prepared by the America Law Institute or as applied in the United States or the courts in Palau. In that regard, Palau (and the other former trust territories) differ from the rest of the South Pacific states that define common law to be the common law existing in England before those countries acquired independence. Common law is abrogated if inconsistent with the constitution or statutes (legislation and subsidiary legislation).

Custom

Custom is yet another source of law in Palau. Other South Pacific jurisdictions make a clear statement about the application and weight of custom, but Palau's constitution and code each take a different approach in this regard. Article 5 of the constitution purports to make "statutes and traditional law . . . equally authoritative," but the code (Title 1, Section 302) resolves conflicts in favor of written law. Unfortunately, the courts have never resolved the difference between the constitution and the code. Customary law has been applied to questions of landownership, disputes over traditional money, and claims to the title of chief. However, the same customary law has been rejected as a defense in criminal cases and intentional torts. In the final analysis, custom is subject to written law.

THE KEY GOVERNMENT STRUCTURES

Head of State

Article 8 of the Palau Constitution provides for the office of the president and vests it with the executive authority, which means the president is both chief of state and head of government. This arrangement differs from that of Pacific countries with a Westminster model, in which the prime minister is head of government. Any Palauan citizen who is at least thirty-five years old and who has resided in Palau for the five years immediately preceding the election is eligible to become president or vice president. The president is elected for a four-year term and may not serve for more than two consecutive terms. If the office of the president is vacant with less than 180 days remaining in the term, the vice president succeeds the president for the remainder of the term. If the remaining term is more than 180 days, a special election is held. The president may be impeached for treason, bribery, or other serious crimes by a vote of at least two-thirds of the members of the Olbiil Era Kelulau (Parliament). The president may also be removed from office by a referendum.

The constitution gives the president the power and duty to, inter alia, enforce the law of the land, conduct negotiations with foreign nations and make treaties with the advice and consent of the legislature, appoint ambassadors, appoint judges, propose the budget, and represent the government in legal actions.

Cabinet

Under the president, the executive branch also consists of a cabinet. The members of the cabinet must not be members of the legislature. In this respect, Palau is different from other Pacific states whose cabinets are composed of members of the legislature. The ministers are appointed by the president on the advice of the Senate (the upper house of Olbiil Era Kelulau). The ministers are responsible for the day-to-day functioning of their ministries. The constitution also establishes the Council of Chiefs composed of one traditional chief from each of the states, which advise the president on traditional laws and custom.

Legislature

Article 9 of the constitution vests the legislative power in the Olbiil Era Kelulau, which is made up of two houses—the lower house (House of Delegates) and the upper house (the Senate). The House of Delegates consists of one delegate elected from each of Palau's sixteen states. By contrast, senators are selected by the Congressional Reapportionment Commission. As of 2001, there were eighteen senators. Members of either house must be citizens at least twenty-five years of age and must have been resident in Palau for at least five years preceding the election. Pursuant to Article 9, the Olbiil Era Kelulau has power to make laws to:

- Collect government revenue
- Regulate commerce
- Regulate natural resources
- Regulate immigration
- Provide a monetary and banking system and national currency
- Impeach the president
- Delegate authority to the states
- Provide for the general welfare, peace, and security
- Enact other necessary laws

As in other jurisdictions, a law is first presented as a bill in the Olbiil Era Kelulau. It must be approved by both houses and signed by the president in order to become law. The president may veto a bill, but this veto may be overruled by a vote of two-thirds of the members in either house. When the bill is passed as an act, it is then published in the national gazette.

Judiciary

The Palauan judiciary consists of a Supreme Court, a National Court, and inferior courts of limited jurisdiction. Article 10 of the constitution vests the judicial power of Palau in the judiciary. The judicial power extends to all matters in law and equity and all persons physically within Palau.

Supreme Court

This is the highest appellate court in the country. The Supreme Court is divided into the Trial Division and the Appellate Division. The Trial Division has original and exclusive jurisdiction over all matters affecting ambassadors, other public ministers and consuls, admiralty and maritime cases, and cases in which the national government or a state government is a party. Any matter brought before the Trial Division is usually heard by one justice. If any party is not satisfied with the decision of the Trial Division, the decision can be appealed to the Appellate Division of the Supreme Court. Appeals are normally heard by three justices. To become a justice of the Supreme Court, a lawyer must have been admitted to practice law before the highest court of the state in which he or she seeks to be admitted. Prior to such appointment, the person must also have practiced in that state for at least five years.

National Court

The National Court hears any case that does not fall within the jurisdiction of the Supreme Court. Matters heard by the National Court include those dealing with land and interests in land. The National Court usually sits with one presiding judge. The requirement for admittance of justices for the National Court is the same as that for the Supreme Court.

Court of Common Pleas

This is a court with limited jurisdiction. The Court of Common Pleas hears all civil cases in which the amount claimed does not exceed U.S.$100. The court, however, does not hear cases involving title to or an interest in the land (such cases are reserved for the National Court). In certain circumstances, the Court of Common Pleas may hear claims up to U.S.$2,000 or five years of imprisonment or both. A judge of the Court of Common Pleas must have been a judge in the District Courts of the Trust Territory, an attorney or trial assistant licensed to practice before the Courts of the Trust Territories or the Courts of Palau, or a Palauan with wide knowledge of custom.

THE CIVIL LAW AND PROCEDURE

As in other common law jurisdictions, the civil law in Palau regulates activities that are not criminal in nature, including matters relating to revenue law, administrative law, tort law, welfare law, property law, wills and succession, company law, commercial law, contract law, and labor law. Title 14 of the Palau National Code additionally provides that a person may sue where his or her rights are affected in the following circumstances:

- Transaction of any business within Palau
- The operation of a motor vehicle within Palau

Structure of Palauan Courts

Palauan Supreme Court	
Appellate Jurisdiction	Trial Jurisdiction

National Court

Court of Common Pleas

- The operation of a vessel within the territorial waters or airspace of Palau
- The commission of a tort
- Contracting to insure any person, property, or risk within Palau at a time of contracting
- The ownership, use, or possession of property within Palau
- Entering into a contract
- Acting within Palau as an officer of any corporation
- Acting as administrator of an estate
- Causing injury to person or property within Palau
- Living in a marital relationship within Palau

The Courts of the Republic of Palau Rules of Civil Procedure, promulgated by the Supreme Court under Article 10 of the constitution, also provides for procedural rights. Accordingly, the court may give actual or constructive notice to the parties. Additionally, all civil actions must be commenced in the National Court or the Court of Common Pleas. The title also provides that certain actions against the republic (such as erroneously collected tax) must be initiated in the Trial Court of the Supreme Court. Section 1101 of Title 14 also provides that where two parties agree to an "amicable settlement" on their rights, this agreement shall be reduced to writing, and it will assume the force of a judgment. Finally, the Courts of the Republic are bound by the rules of evidence, promulgated by the Supreme Court pursuant to Article 10 of the constitution. Where any of these rights are violated, a case can be set aside. In civil cases, the burden of proof rests with the plaintiff; the civil standard of proof—preponderance of evidence—also applies.

THE CRIMINAL LAW AND PROCEDURE

In Palau, as in all other Pacific Islands, criminal law is prescribed by statute. This is provided in Title 17 of the Palau National Code. Crimes are either felonies (punishable by one year of imprisonment) or misdemeanors (all other offenses). Certain people are excused from criminal proceedings, such as the insane and minors under the age of ten. Children from the ages of ten to eighteen are presumed incapable until proven otherwise (rebuttable presumption). The National Code spells out the following as crimes: abortion, arson, assault and battery, bigamy, bribery, burglary, conspiracy, rioting, drunk and disorderly behavior in public, nuisance, obstruction of justice, perjury, robbery, sex crimes, and trespass. Furthermore, the private ownership of firearms and ammunitions is also illegal. Sentencing is also governed by Title 17 and must consider the customs of the people, evidence of good and bad character, and prior criminal record. Depending on the crime, the judge may order imprisonment, fine, or forfeiture; alternatively, the judge may suspend the sentence or place a person on probation. As in any other common law jurisdictions, criminal proceedings in Palau are initiated by the state, and the level of proof is "beyond reasonable doubt."

Phillip Tagini

See also Common Law; Customary Law

References and further reading

Douglas, Norman, and Ngaire Douglas. 1989. *Pacific Islands Yearbook*. North Ryde, New South Wales: Angus and Robertson.
Ntumy, M., ed. 1993. *South Pacific Islands Legal Systems*. Honolulu: University of Hawai'i Press.
U.S. Department of State. "Background Note: Palau." http:// www.state.gov/r/pa/bgn/index.cfm?docid=1840 (accessed January 9, 2002).

PALESTINE

COUNTRY INFORMATION

In the wake of the initial stages of the peace process with Israel, the Palestinian Authority, though not yet recognized by the international community as a state, gained autonomous control over the noncontiguous territories of the Gaza Strip and certain parts of the West Bank. These regions are part of what used to be known as Palestine, a political-geographic entity that emerged after the collapse of the Ottoman Empire in World War I, located on the eastern shore of the Mediterranean, south of Lebanon, west of Jordan, and northeast of Egypt. For many centuries a crossroads between Africa, Europe, and Asia, Palestine formed part of the Ottoman Empire following the Turkish conquest in 1516.

The Gaza Strip and the West Bank differ considerably in geography, population, and access to other societies. The Gaza Strip occupies a small sliver of territory (only 144 square miles) along the Mediterranean coastline, bordered by Israel in the northeast and southeast and by Egypt in the southwest. The West Bank, which does not share the coastline of the Mediterranean, sits, in part, on the western edge of the Dead Sea and is much larger (approximately 2,300 square miles). Israel surrounds the West Bank in the west, north, and south, and Jordan borders it on the east. The West Bank has had much more open access to Jordan and Israel, whereas the Gaza Strip is a functionally gated, isolated territory.

The population in Gaza and the West Bank is approximately 2.8 million. Islam is the religion of nearly 97 percent of the Palestinian people; however, approximately 50,000 Palestinian people (3 percent) practice Christianity. The demographic growth rate of 3.7 percent, which would double the population within twenty years, is among the highest in the world. Unemployment remains high, with under 50 percent of the working-age population participating in the labor market. In Gaza, the figure is under 40 percent. Women continue to play a limited role in the workforce, at a rate of 11 percent in the West Bank and 3–4 percent in Gaza. The gross national product per capita is approximately $1,800.

LEGAL HISTORY

For many generations, foreign control and occupation deprived the Palestinian people of the opportunity to develop their own functioning legal order. They were dominated by the Ottoman Empire from the sixteenth century until World War I. The legal and judicial systems of the Palestinian Authority have been greatly influenced by the reception of the French Napoleonic Codes under Turkish rule, as well as Islamic law under the 1877 Civil Code (the Majelle). Between the two world wars, the territories were held under British authority. From 1948 until 1967, Egypt controlled Gaza, and Jordan absorbed the West Bank. Egypt had minimal influence over Gaza's British mandate system, in contrast to the greater Jordanian influence in the West Bank during the same period. Because Jordan's legal system bears more similarity to continental European models, the West Bank system has fewer British characteristics. Finally, the Israeli government occupied both Gaza and the West Bank after the 1967 war until transitional self-rule was initiated in 1993. A series of military orders added yet another layer of law to the mix of Palestinian legal sources. In sum, the structure of the courts and legal process mainly follows a continental European civil law model.

With these historical overlays of control up to the initiation of the peace process in 1993, the Palestinians inherited two separate legal systems, each with weak institutional frameworks and resources, demoralized professions, poorly functioning legal processes, and an outdated substantive law based on overlapping and inconsistent legal sources.

IMPACT OF THE PEACE PROCESS

The Israeli-Palestinian peace process has consisted of an exchange of recognitions (Israel's recognition of the Palestinian Liberation Organization [PLO] as representative of the Palestinian people and the PLO's recognition of Israel's right to exist in peace and security), phased withdrawal of

Israeli troops, and the establishment of an interim Palestinian self-governing authority (the Palestinian National Authority). However, to date, the incomplete transfer of authority and control from Israel to the Palestinian National Authority, which continues to lack the full attributes of a state, has restricted its ability to gain control over land and water, as well as access to cross-border exchanges of goods, services, and capital. It has also inhibited the rapid transformation of a unified legal and judicial system.

THE LEGAL SYSTEM

On January 20, 1996, the Palestinian people held their first democratic elections. They elected eighty-eight members of the Palestinian Legal Council and a president (Yassir Arafat) of the Executive Authority. The Executive Authority—composed of the head of the council, ministers, and department chiefs selected from within the council, and others—is responsible for the exercise of executive power, though in practice, the real decision-making power has rested with President Arafat. The Palestinian Legislative Council passed a draft Basic Law in April 1997; however, without explanation, President Arafat has not signed it.

The Oslo Accords also allocated justice functions to an independent judiciary; however, the judiciary has not been able to effectuate its review of executive authority. The Palestinian legal systems stem from numerous sources of law that reflect the historical layers of Islamic, Ottoman, British, Jordanian (West Bank), Egyptian (Gaza), and Israeli influence. This multiplicity of legal sources, when combined with the lack of published legal texts and judicial decisions within Gaza and the West Bank, creates confusion as to which authorities control in a given case. This frustrates consistent and timely adjudication and produces gaps between the written law and the actual practice of law. Finally, Palestinian substantive and procedural law lacks uniformity, causing conflicts between Gazan and West Bank legal precepts.

Despite the halting nature of the peace process, the transitional period of Palestinian state building has begun to have an effect on the legal disunity caused by overlapping legal sources, a weak judiciary, and poorly trained and organized legal professionals.

THE STRUCTURE OF COURTS

Generally, the court systems in Gaza and the West Bank have maintained many of their British mandate features, while simultaneously developing into a unified system. Approximately seventy judges serve the courts of Gaza and the West Bank, with the chief justice located in Gaza. Single-judge Magistrates' Courts serve as tribunals of original jurisdiction for small cases. Multijudge District Courts hear larger matters. Appeals courts hear appeals from both levels, and the High Court sits as the highest court of appeals. As of 1994, the High Court in Gaza had jurisdiction over all territory under the Palestinian Authority; however, in 1999, the president formed a new High Court in Ramallah and appointed a new chief justice. Specialized courts for tax and local government, as well as for election disputes, have been reinstituted. In 1995, a single attorney general was appointed.

The competence of the courts is differentiated vertically, as follows.

Magistrates' Courts

The Magistrates' Court, in which a single judge sits, has the power to hear three main categories of cases: (1) civil cases with a value of less than JD20,000 (approximately U.S.$28,500), (2) land cases regardless of value, and (3) criminal cases involving minor offenses and misdemeanors. The magistrates also act as investigating authorities in felony cases. The Magistrates' Courts are evenly distributed throughout the territories.

District Courts

District Courts sit in three-judge panels, with special exceptions for one-judge decisions. A District Court has the power to act as (1) a court of appeal in appeals from the Magistrates' Courts, (2) a court of original jurisdiction in civil cases for claims in value exceeding JD20,000 (approximately U.S.$28,500), and (3) an appellate court for minor offenses and misdemeanors heard in the Magistrates' Courts and as a court of first instance for all felonies. There are three District Courts in the West Bank and two in Gaza.

High Courts

The High Court is the general court of appeal for judgments from the District Courts. It also serves as an administrative court for disputes arising from administrative decisions by the executive authority (for example, decrees or ministerial decisions). The High Court serves as the primary authority to ensure the implementation of laws and the reconciliation of contradictory laws.

Judicial Independence

Efforts to create judicial independence have encountered many obstacles. Judicial selection criteria and procedures have not been determined (for example, years of experience, professional reputation), and they continue to be controlled by the president. Judges suffer poor working conditions and low compensation.

Judges have been forced to resign or dismissed for issuing judgments disfavored by the government. Furthermore, Palestinian Authority officials have refused to implement judicial decisions. A new law on the independence of the judiciary, which would create a Supreme Judicial

Legal Structure of Palestine Courts

High Courts
(Gaza and West Bank)
Appellate and Original Administrative Jurisdiction

District Courts
Original Civil and Criminal Jurisdiction
Appellate Jurisdiction from Magistrate Courts

Magistrate Courts
Original Jurisdiction for Small Civil Claims
and Nonfelony Criminal Offenses

Council with responsibility for hiring, transfer, promotion, and discipline, was passed by the council in 1998, but it is still awaiting presidential ratification. Budgetary and administrative control over the judiciary continues to rest with the Ministry of Justice.

Demand for Adjudication and Continued Paucity of Resources

The peace process brought with it a new demand for public adjudication, and some reports indicate that the number of court cases per year has nearly tripled, with a staggering estimate of over 200,000 pending cases in 2000. The Palestinian National Authority has not increased the supply of judicial services to meet this crushing demand. The courts, in their current condition, are generally impoverished and dilapidated in terms of both human and physical resources. Judicial salaries are low, vacancies are high, and the backlogs are growing. Delays are now estimated to be three to five years from filing to final judgment.

The courts are also in great need of physical resources, such as courtrooms; judicial chambers or offices; libraries with published laws, decisions, and scholarly commentaries; efficient docketing and filing systems; computers; microfiche; office equipment; and other supplies, including paper, which ran out in a Jenin court in 1999. Increases in court utilization will continue to produce severe backlog and delay if these resource needs are not addressed.

The Police

Although training has increased markedly, the Palestinian police are still in need of forensic technology, investigative training, and criminal laboratories. For example, the police do not have any movable laboratory technology for drug testing, fingerprinting, photographic evidence, and so forth. As a consequence, investigations often rely almost entirely on statements taken while a defendant is detained, thus forcing reliance on confessions.

Bar Associations

During occupation, the two bar associations of the West Bank and the Gaza Strip maintained separate identities and had no effective authority to certify and regulate lawyers. A major ongoing effort to unify these groups has yet to be authorized. In the absence of a public defenders' office or any other legal aid program, the bar has not been able to provide an institutional response to meet the need for legal services to the indigent. Statutory formulas for attorneys' fees reduce incentives for zealous and effective advocacy, and they may actually encourage delay. Efforts to develop a unified bar association were boosted by a 1997 agreement. In 1999, a law was passed to unify the bar associations and provide for bylaws; however, the geographic restrictions on intra-Authority travel between the West Bank and Gaza have precluded effective unification.

Access to Legal Education

Prior to 1991, there were no Palestinian law schools. Now, there are four law faculties within the West Bank and Gaza. Al Azhar University School of Law, established in 1991 and 1992 in Gaza, has twelve faculty members and offers a B.A. in law to 1,500 students. Al Quds University School of Law, established in 1991 and 1992 in East Jerusalem, has 12 faculty members and offers a B.A. in law to 450 students, an M.A. in law to 25 students, and an M.A. in judicial studies to 2 students. An Najah National University School of Law, established in 1994 and 1995 in Nablus, has 9 faculty members and offers a B.A. in law to 450 students. Bir Zeit University Institute of Law, established in 1993, has 2 full-time faculty members and in 1996 began to offer classes toward an M.A. in law. In 2000–2001, twenty-five students were enrolled.

SPECIALIZED BODIES

Alternative Dispute Resolution

Palestinians traditionally utilized varied forms of community mediation or conciliation (*sulha*), especially in times when the courts could not be trusted as impartial. The *intifada* period experienced a rise in these mechanisms in order to avoid the Israeli-controlled courts. In the post-Oslo period, Palestinians turned first to the police and security forces to resolve their disputes. Over time, they established legal departments to handle these disputes. These departments were extended to the local governorates. Additionally, the Palestinian National Authority has appointed mediators to deal with disputes between families and tribes. Alternatives for business disputes remain underdeveloped. A new arbitration law passed in 2000 offers a first step toward enhancement of the legal framework for alternative dispute resolution; however, it is too early to tell whether institutional implementation will be sufficient to realize its aims.

Security Courts

One of the most controversial developments in the Palestinian Authority is the establishment of security courts to monitor and control dissent and attacks on the emerging state. The Palestinian Authority established these courts in April 1995, after two suicide bombings that killed seven Israeli soldiers and one civilian in the Gaza Strip, under the 1945 Emergency Regulations of the British mandate law. Five military officers were appointed as judges, and three officers were assigned as prosecutors. The president initiates cases, which are heard nearly instantaneously. Many die in detention prior to their hearings. These tribunals are conducted at all hours of the night, frequently only for a few minutes per case, typically without any representation for the accused, and almost always resulting in conviction. Each of the four people sentenced to death in 1999, including one who was executed, were tried by security or military courts. Furthermore, the security forces tend to ignore judicial decisions that serve to hold the state accountable for alleged human rights violations. For example, despite a recent order by the High Court to release fifty-two detainees, apparently only four have been released. Since 1998, the security court jurisdiction has been extended to a broader list of crimes, and this has resulted in a bifurcation of the Supreme State Security Court, which continues to serve the president's wishes, and the State Security Court, which more closely resembles the regular courts.

CONCLUSION

Historical occupation and failures of the peace process have undermined the development of a strong, integrated economy, as well as a stable civil society. Economic, political, and social problems within the territories have mounted significant obstacles to the restoration and modernization of legal processes in Gaza and the West Bank. Furthermore, the internal conflicts with the Palestinian Authority have also frustrated cooperation and collaboration among the judiciary, the private bar, arbitrators, mediators, and civic institutions representing various social and commercial interests in Gaza and the West Bank. Finally, the current violent conflict with Israel has exacerbated each of these systemic problems and significantly impedes the development of a legal order based on the rule of law.

Hiram E. Chodosh
Sharhabeel Al Zaeem

See also Alternative Dispute Resolution; Civil Law; Egypt; Human Rights Law; Islamic Law; Israel; Jordan; Judicial Independence; Ottoman Empire

References and further reading
Chodosh, Hiram E., and Stephen A. Mayo. 1997. "The Palestinian Legal Study: Consensus and Assessment of the New Palestinian Legal System." *Harvard International Law Journal* 38: 375.
Ciment, James. 1997. *Conflict and Crisis in the Post–Cold War World—Palestine/Israel: The Long Conflict.* New York: Facts on File.
Frish, Hillel. 1998. *Countdown to Statehood—Palestinian State Formation in the West Bank and Gaza.* Albany: State University of New York Press.
Robinson, Glenn E. 1997. *Building a Palestinian State: The Incomplete Revolution.* Bloomington and Indianapolis: Indiana University Press.
Sayigh, Yezid, and Khalil Shiaki. 1999. *Strengthening Palestinian Public Institutions.* New York: Council on Foreign Relations.
Shapira, Amos, and Mala Tabory. 1999. *New Political Entities in Public and Private International Law, with Special Reference to the Palestinian Entity.* The Hague: Kluwer Law International.
"Symposium: The Legal Foundations for Peace and Prosperity in the Middle East." 1999 and 2000. *Case Western Reserve Journal of International Law* 31, nos. 2–3 (1999); *Case Western Reserve Journal of International Law* 32, no. 2.
Watson, Geoffrey R. 2000. *The Oslo Accords: International Law and the Israeli-Palestinian Peace Agreements.* Oxford: Oxford University Press.

PANAMA

GENERAL INFORMATION

The Republic of Panama is located in the Western Hemisphere and borders the Caribbean Sea to the north, the Pacific Ocean to the south, Colombia to the east, and Costa Rica to the west. With Costa Rica, Panama forms an isthmus between Central America and South America that is 80 kilometers wide in its narrower section. The republic has an area of 77,082 square kilometers, being mountainous toward the Caribbean coast, with rolling hills and extensive savannas toward the Pacific. The country's population of 2.7 million speaks Spanish as the official language. However, English is widely spoken and understood in the urban centers. Various native languages exist, such as Kuna and Ngobe-Bugle. Minority urban groups speak Italian, French, Greek, Cantonese Chinese, and Hindi, among others, giving the capital of Panama City a heterogeneous character. No official census is kept about ethnic groups, but unofficial estimates state the population to be around 14 percent black, 10 percent white, and 6 percent Amerindian, with the majority, 70 percent, being of mixed racial groups known as mestizo. Some 85 percent of the population is Catholic, as the National Constitution acknowledges. Some 15 percent is Protestant, and small Jewish, Moslem, and Hindi congregations coexist.

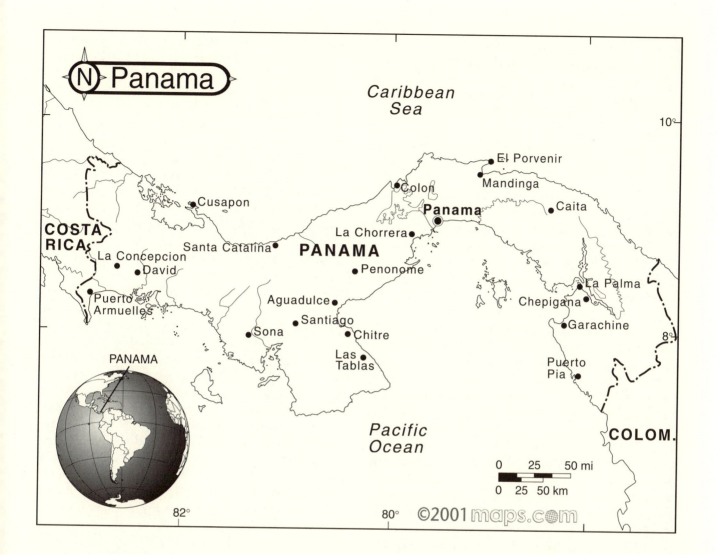

Panama invests a great part of the national budget in education. Its private and public schools are under the supervision of the Ministry of Education. The school system is organized in primary and secondary levels of six years each, as well as higher education or university. Eleven universities exist, with substantial enrollment. The University of Panama and the Technological University are state-run, while the Universidad Santa María la Antigua and others (including the Panama campuses of Florida State University and other U.S. institutions) are private.

The climate of Panama is tropical, and the temperature is virtually uniform throughout the year. The nights are generally fresh. The average temperature is of 27° C. The country has two seasons: the rainy season (May through January) and the dry season (January through May).

The economy is fully dollarized, with the local Balboa and the U.S. dollar being currencies of legal tender. The constitution forbids the enactment of laws providing for a currency of compulsory tender, which has preserved the freedom from currency restrictions. This fact has made the country different from most of its neighbors, as the economy is composed of 75 percent services, 16 percent industries, and 10 percent agricultural activities. The rate of inflation is no more than 1.5 percent, and the official rate of unemployment is 11 percent. Major international markets for its exports of bananas, products refined from oil, shrimp, and sugar are the United States, Germany, and Sweden. Services to foreign customers are an important source of revenue that makes up for the substantial imports, mostly from the United States and Japan.

HISTORY

While human settlements have existed in Panama from prehistoric times (around 12,000 B.C.E.), the lack of any written records has forced scholars to rely on archaeological findings to elaborate a history of pre-Columbian peoples of the Isthmus.

The prevalent theory about organized human groups points to a southward migration of Meso-American peoples in the twelfth century as the source of Amerindian organizations in the Isthmus. Unlike the empires of the Incas or the city-states of Meso-America, political organizations in Panama did not rise above the village, headed by autocratic chieftains, sometimes ruling with the advice of councils of elders. A body of customs emerged in each village, regulating aspects of family life as well as crimes against life. The minimal information currently available on the customary law of those days is that collected by Spanish chroniclers that lived then among the Amerindian tribes.

The arrival in 1501 of Spanish troops resulted in the conquest of the Isthmus and the imposition of Spanish laws. A special body of laws was enacted for application in the American colonies and the Philippines, codified in the Recopilación de Leyes de Indias y Filipinas, published in 1680. The compilation has nine volumes, 218 titles, and more than six thousand laws covering all aspects of legislation in the Spanish colonies overseas. As the character of Spanish presence changed from that of a military campaign to a colonial, territorial expansion, the Isthmus was subject throughout three centuries to territorial institutions such as the governorship, the viceroyalty, and the Audiencia.

The governorship was a military, political, and judicial institution, called Castilla de Oro and later, in 1513, Veraguas, which included Panama. The viceroyalty was a jurisdiction where political and administrative powers of the king were exercised by a lieutenant appointed by each king. As the importance of Panama decreased, it became part of the viceroyalty of New Granada in 1718, until independence in 1821. These entities governed along with the Audiencia—an entity with political, administrative, and judicial duties. It also exercised judicial review of decisions taken by governors and viceroys. The Panama Audiencia was created in 1535 and operated intermittently throughout the colonial period.

Panama declared its independence in 1821 and joined the Gran Colombia—a confederation also formed by Colombia, Venezuela, and Ecuador. A presidential decree of 1825 provided that Spanish laws in force in the colonies up to 1808 would be a source of law supplementary to the Colombian laws enacted. These Colombian laws eventually were enacted by autocratic executive and subordinate legislative powers in Bogotá. During that period, several attempts to have the Isthmus secede ensued. An exception was a brief period between 1863 and 1885 when Colombia was a federal entity of which Panama was a state called the Sovereign State of the Isthmus with a state constitution and assembly. The state assembly enacted a Civil and an Administrative Code for Panama that replaced Spanish laws in most cases, and even served as a model for other Colombian states. The enactment in 1873 of the national Colombian Civil Code finally abrogated the Spanish law, along with all state constitutions and codes.

The fifth secession attempt, in 1903, finally succeeded in creating the Republic of Panama, which by 1904 had approved a constitution with a laissez-faire orientation, a product of the century just ended. A Codifying Commission submitted to the legislature in 1916 drafts of the Civil, Commerce, Criminal, Judicial, Mining, and Tax Codes, which were enacted in 1917 along with an Administrative Code.

A common law area subsisted in the Panama Canal Zone, a Panamanian territory under U.S. jurisdiction pursuant to the 1904 Panama Canal treaties. Canal Zone courts applied U.S. federal law, as dictated in the Panama Canal title of the U.S. Code and executive orders, until their abrogation by new treaties in 1979.

The Constitutions of 1941 and 1946 granted social rights and the duties of the welfare state the rank of constitutional guarantees. Eventually, a Labor and a Health Code were approved, and the Tax Code was replaced by a more progressive version. These socializing trends were abruptly derailed in 1968, when a military coup d'état against the civilian regime led to a suspension of most freedoms, the abrogation of all political parties, and the removal of most judicial civil servants. A new constitution, approved in 1972 by a single-party legislature, appeared to expand on most social rights but reserved the appointment of cabinet ministers and Supreme Court justices to the sole discretion of the chief of staff of the National Guard. Constitutional amendments in 1983 removed that reserve and most authoritarian provisions, leading to increasing restoration of the rule of law. In the following two years the Criminal, Judicial, and Mining Codes were replaced by more modern versions.

LEGAL CONCEPTS

The Republic of Panama is a sovereign and independent state. Its government is centralized, republican, democratic, and representative, composed of a president, two vice presidents, and twelve ministers of state that make up the executive branch; the Legislative Assembly, with seventy-two legislators integrating the legislative branch; and nine magistrates that head the judicial branch. These three powers are the ones that govern the country.

The civil law system is applied by the judicial system, by which judges are not bound by judicial precedent in their decisions. Judges rely on the constitution, followed by codes, laws, and regulations as the direct source of law. Only three identical decisions by the full Supreme Court have a rank of mere "probable doctrine." In the absence of express legal provisions applicable to a subject matter, general principles of law as stated in scholarly publications (and in commerce law, local customs if practiced by five or more merchants who testify to that fact) serve as an indirect source of law.

The constitution and procedural laws have provisions from which Panamanian jurists have determined the main concepts or principles that guide the legal system. A chapter of the constitution is devoted to individual freedoms, providing safeguards against arbitrary detention or punishment. Article 20 of the constitution provides that no discrimination shall exist by reason of birth, race, sex, or religion, and that foreigners and nationals are equal before the law. This equality is also applicable to the acts and appearances of parties before the judicial entities. Another constitutional guarantee provides that nobody shall be judged other than by a competent authority for violations of the previously enacted law. This rule of law principle is also extended to the imposition of fines or any other decisions that any public official takes with regard to citizens or their properties. Constitutional provisions that have been criticized abroad are the powers granted to high-ranking officials to order a detention without due process for up to twenty-four hours and the imprisonment penalties for libel that results in "offenses to the honor."

Another chapter of the constitution provides principles for the actions of the judiciary. The constitutional principle of judicial independence provides that judges are independent in their acts and are subject to nothing more than the constitution and the laws (Article 207).

The 1984 Judicial Code, based on provisions in force in Colombia, expanded on the scope of the constitutional guarantees as applied in the procedural area. These principles are those of contradiction or bilateral character (whereby parties are granted all the opportunities for their defense [or actions] as provided under the law), publicity (whereby proceedings are public [except when open only to the parties involved because of reasons of morality] and secret proceedings are prohibited), procedural economy (whereby procedures must be conducted pursuant to the law but also in a manner that brings results promptly and with the use of fewer resources), res judicata, double instance (whereby decisions are subject to review by a superior judicial entity), and congruence (whereby the award rendered should not exceed or be different from that which is requested by the parties). An important principle of valuation of evidence is that the sound judgment (*sana crítica*) of the judge, based on his technical knowledge and previous experience, is the standard whereby evidence is valuated. However, the judge does not have a proactive approach under the procedural truth principle, whereby the evidence provided by the parties is the only evidence to be admitted by the judge, instead of the material truth.

According to the Fraser Institute, the Panama legal structure and its impact on property rights received a ranking in 1997 of 6.9 out of 10. Aspects such as security of private ownership rights were ranked 7.2, while viability of contracts and rule of law received rankings of 6.6 and 7.0, respectively. In 1997, Panama's rating was 8.3, up from 6.9 in 1990. Its ranking rose from thirtieth in 1990 to fourteenth in 1997. In spite of these negative factors that reduce the trust of investors, Panama has the best economic freedom rating in Central America, being ranked fourteenth in the world.

CURRENT STRUCTURE

On a national level, Panama has executive, legislative, and judicial branches. The executive branch is formed by the president—elected in general elections for a five-year term—who appoints at his or her discretion cabinet ministers and the directors of several regulatory entities. The branch has some entities with duties related to the legal system, such as the Ministry of Government and Justice, which includes several entities such as the Public Registry, in charge of registering deeds and property transfers; the Public Force, in charge of national defense and police duties; and the Directorate of Correction, in charge of penitentiaries. Other entities are the Ministry of Economy and Finance, which imposes fines for tax infringements (and its Customs Tribunal imposes imprisonment penalties for customs fraud); the Ministry of Labor and Labor Development, which provides dispute resolution on labor claims (and its Boards of Conciliation and Decision hear cases for unjustified termination); the Commission of Free Competition and Consumer Affairs, which provides dispute resolution in consumer disputes and files actions ex officio in anticompetitive matters; and the Regulatory Entity of Public Services, which provides dispute resolution in disputes between public utilities and their users and hears cases for violations of telecommunications laws.

The legislative branch is formed by the Legislative Assembly, elected by popular vote. It enacts laws but hears cases during impeachment proceedings only.

The judicial branch is headed by the Supreme Court of Justice, formed by nine justices. They jointly hear constitutionality cases, while groups of three justices form four sections: Civil, Criminal, Contentious-Administrative (judicial review of administrative cases, appeal of labor courts), and General Affairs, each with its specialized caseload. Civil Superior Justice Tribunals act as appellate courts, while civil circuit and municipal judges try cases above and below U.S.$1,000, respectively. Courts of special jurisdiction are the family courts, which try family law cases, and the single Admiralty Court, which deals with admiralty cases arising from incidents in ships sailing the Panama Canal and Panamanian waters, or on board ships flying the Panamanian flag wherever they are located.

In the criminal jurisdiction, criminal circuit and municipal judges try cases with imprisonment terms above and below two years, respectively. Their decisions are appealed before Criminal Superior Justice Tribunals and may be subject to extraordinary review by the Criminal Section of the Supreme Court. A Public Defender's Office is of recent creation and is meant to provide counsel to defendants indicted.

A special labor jurisdiction has superior justice tribunals as appellate courts, and sectional judges who hear cases. Extraordinary review of their decisions is exercised by the Contentious-Administrative Section of the Supreme Court, in the absence of the Labor Section provided under the Labor Code.

The Public Ministry is formed by the attorney ("procurador") general of the nation and the solicitor (also called "procurador") general of the administration. The attorney general works along with lower district attorneys (*Fiscales de Distrito*), circuit attorneys (*Fiscales de Circuit*), and municipal attorneys (*Personeros*), who prosecute criminal cases before criminal courts. The Technical Judicial Police is the investigative department of the Public Ministry. Scholars debate as to which of the branches the Public Ministry belongs, since it is not subordinate to any of the heads of the branches.

On a local level, municipalities have their equivalent of the three branches of power. Each municipality is led by a mayor, who enforces ordinances enacted by a municipal council of community representatives (*Representantes de Corregimientos*)—all of whom are elected for five-year terms in general elections. The mayor appoints justices of the peace (*Corregidores*), who assist in enforcing ordinances in each *Corregimiento*. *Corregidores* deal with most minor offenses, as they have a presence in each of the more than five hundred *Corregimiento* communities. Their decisions are subject to appeal before the mayor of the relevant municipality, and to judicial review by the Contentious-Administrative Section of the Supreme Court.

SPECIALIZED JUDICIAL BODIES

The Electoral Tribunal is a court separate from the other branches of government. Its three magistrates are appointed by the Assembly for ten-year terms not concurrent with the presidential term or with each other's terms. The tribunal keeps birth and marriage records, serves as the electoral office, and also tries cases for violation of electoral laws. The electoral attorney (*Fiscal*) takes cases to them for trial.

The people's defender, or ombudsman, investigates complaints from citizens about abuses by government officials and can call for the officials' sanction or removal. The ombudsman is appointed by the Assembly for a five-year term not concurrent with the presidential term.

A special district attorney (*Fiscal Especial*) was created in 1990 to prosecute crimes against the nation. It prosecuted several cases of human rights violations by the military of pre-1990 governments. However, cases were tried before traditional criminal courts, and acts of alleged coercion against juries preceded the acquittals of some.

Some nongovernmental organizations have acted as human rights groups to gather complaints of violations or abuses by the Panamanian or U.S. military between 1968 and 1990. The twenty-year statute of limitations for further prosecution of pre-1980 violations and the uncovering of human remains at a former Panamanian military air base triggered the appointment by the president of an ad hoc truth commission in 2001. The commission has the duty of gathering information about complaints of human rights violations by the Panamanian military, and its mandate has a specific exclusion from exercising judicial duties. Despite budgetary constraints, the commission has compiled a list of more than a hundred disappearances allegedly related to the Panamanian military.

STAFFING

The top positions in the judiciary require a number of years' experience as an accredited attorney-at-law (or a position that requires a law degree), and that the candidate be at least thirty years of age, be in full exercise of political or civil rights, and have Panamanian citizenship by birth. The main positions with tenure requirements are seen in the figure.

The cabinet retains discretion in the selection of its appointments, while lower positions are subject to the Civil Service law that was enacted in 1991 to cover judicial branch employees. This law is not applicable to the appointment of Supreme Court justices and their assistants. The "judicial service" is meant to ensure the filling of positions with competitive candidates on a nonpolitical basis, through the merit-based system. Judicial branch statistics indicate that out of 2,382 judicial employees in 1996, 1,382 were appointed through the judicial service selection system.

Accreditation as attorney-at-law is granted to all Panamanian citizens that earn a law degree from a Panamanian law school (or a law school from a Spanish-speaking country recognized by the University of Panama) and apply to the General Affairs Section of the Supreme Court. Graduates from nonrecognized foreign law schools must comply with a thesis requirement in Panama. Membership in a Panamanian bar association is a requirement to litigate.

There is no training requirement for court administrative personnel, so a Judicial School was created with assistance from the U.S. Agency for International Development in 1993. Some seven thousand judicial and administrative servants have received training courses at the school.

IMPACT

The law in Panama has acted mostly as an instrument of centralized (and in the past authoritarian) regimes, rather than as a means for peaceful resolution of disputes between

Structure of Panamanian Courts

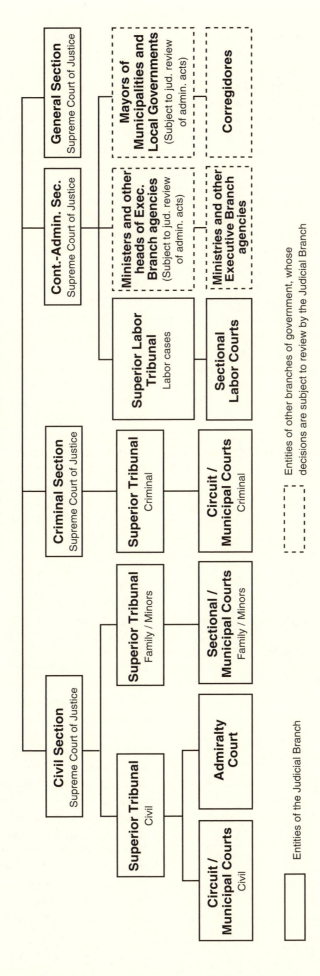

individuals. In that sense, the law has a profound impact on everyday public and private affairs, especially among the ever-growing urban population. Since the opening of the trans-isthmian railroad in 1855, the position of Panama as a trade center has resulted in a prolific production of legal treatises and legislation by local jurists geared toward civil and business law. However, pressures from changing party-oriented political administrations, as well as kinship and social links typical of a small population, have, in a decreasing manner, affected the independence of the judiciary and the perception of its proper administration of justice.

Negative political factors in the administration of justice have been addressed through legal reforms or have been lessened by the evolution of the local community. This has led to the realization that nonpolitical factors, such as overloaded dockets, excessive bureaucratic proceedings, lack of training and equipment, and budgetary deficiencies continue to affect the administration of justice and its ability to give the law the role it is meant to have. The visible forms of these effects are the duration of cases and the fact that more than half of the jail population is made up of detainees awaiting a hearing. The most recent administrations, with financing and training from the United States and the European Union foreign aid entities, have continued implementing projects to reverse this trend.

Alvaro Aguilar-Alfu

See also Civil Law; Colombia; Indigenous and Folk Legal Systems; Magistrates—Civil Law Systems; Napoleonic Code; Native American Law, Traditional; Roman Law; Spain

References and further reading
Arosemena, Justo. *Panama y nuestra America*. UNAM, 1981.
Barsallo, Pedro. 1998. *Derecho Procesal I*. Panamá: Universidad de Panamá.
Bureau of Democracy, Human Rights, and Labor, U.S. Department of State. *1999 Country Reports on Human Rights Practices—Panama,* February 25, 2000. http://www.state.gov/g/drl/rls/hrrpt/1999/index.cfm?docid=396 (accessed November 20, 2000).
Corte Suprema de Justicia. 1998. "Organo judicial." http://www.sinfo.net/orgjup/organo.htm (accessed November 20, 2000).
Diaz, Laurentino. 1979. *Sociedad y Derecho Prehispanicos Americanos*. Panama: Editorial La Antigua.
Difernan, Bonifacio. n.d. *Curso de derecho civil Panameño*. Vol. I. Panama: Editorial La Antigua.
Fraser Institute. "Economic Freedom of the World 2000." http:// www.fraserinstitute.ca/publications/books/econ_free_2000/section_11/panama.html, http://www.fraserinstitute.ca/publications/books/econ_free_2000/section_12/panama.html (accessed April 5, 2001).
Hernandez, Guillermo. 1969. *El derecho en Indias y en su Metropoli*. Bogotá: Editorial Temis.

PAPUA NEW GUINEA

COUNTRY INFORMATION

Papua New Guinea comprises the eastern half of New Guinea, the world's second largest island. It has a total land area of 463,000 square kilometers and a sea area of 3.12 million square kilometers. There are also a number of smaller islands to the east of the mainland, the largest of which are Bougainville, New Britain, and New Ireland. The country's topography is extremely varied, incorporating the imposing mountains and high valleys of the central Highlands ranges, vast tracts of lowland swamps, and numerous low-lying islands and scattered atolls. Papua New Guinea shares a land border with Indonesia to the west, and sea borders with Australia to the south and the Solomon Islands to the east. The climate is tropical and, in coastal areas, generally hot, humid, and wet, subject to local variations.

The indigenous peoples are predominantly Melanesian. Prior to colonial incursion in the late nineteenth century, the inhabitants led a subsistence lifestyle using rudimentary agricultural, hunting, and fishing techniques. The largest permanent political units typically comprised 200–300 persons living together in one or more villages, or dispersed in hamlets and homesteads. In the more densely populated Highlands, such groups were generally about a thousand in number, rising to several thousand in places. Traditional societies were organized around principles of kinship, marriage, and descent, and these continue to play an important role in contemporary social relations.

Papua New Guinea remains one of the most culturally diverse countries in the world. Approximately 800 languages are spoken among a total population of 4.6 million people. English, Tok Pisin (Pidgin), and Motu (the lingua franca of the Papua region) are the official languages. Melanesian cultures have proved remarkably resilient and adaptable in the face of rapid and pervasive change. The spectrum of Papua New Guinea society now ranges from traditional village-based life dependent on subsistence and small cash-crop agriculture to modern urban life in the growing cities of Port Moresby (the national capital), Lae, Madang, Wewak, and Mount Hagen. Some 85 percent of the population still derive their livelihood from agriculture, while 15 percent live in urban areas. Christianity is the official religion.

Papua New Guinea (PNG) is richly endowed with natural resources including timber, marine resources, agricultural land, oil, gas, copper, and other minerals. Despite this, economic growth has consistently fallen short of expectations. While classified as a low-middle-income country, PNG's main social indicators are closer to those of low-income countries, and urban and rural poverty has grown significantly in recent years. Life ex-

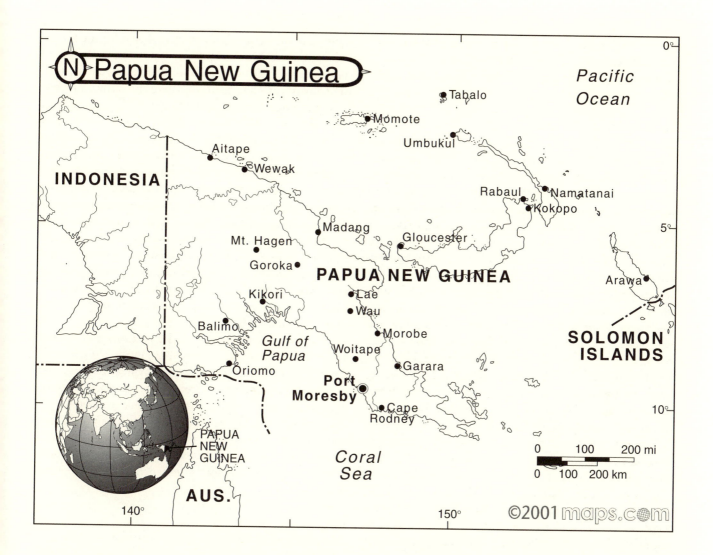

pectancy and adult literacy rates are substantially below those in neighboring countries in the South Pacific and Southeast Asia. The infant mortality rate, crude birth and death rates, and the fertility rate are all above the average of neighboring countries. Corruption, political instability, and lawlessness are major areas of concern.

The national legal system is based on an Anglo-Australian common law system established originally under the colonial administration. In practice, the formal legal system exists alongside a vibrant informal system built around customary beliefs and institutions as adapted to recent change.

HISTORY

Precontact

The early inhabitants of New Guinea migrated from Asia about 50,000 years ago. Traditional communities were largely self-contained. Intergroup warfare was endemic in many places. Social relations were essentially kinship relations, with each individual's rights and obligations flowing from membership of the extended family. Reciprocity

was an integral feature of Melanesian morality. Patterns of inheritance to land, special knowledge, and personal property could be either patrilineal or, as in many coastal and island societies, matrilineal. Men were dominant, even in matrilineal societies. Leadership status was typically achieved rather than inherited. The Melanesian *big man* built his reputation by manipulating material resources and social relationships.

Each society developed means for settling disputes between its members. These usually varied according to the status of the parties concerned and the relationships between them. Where parties had to continue to live together, emphasis was on restoring relations between them. Compensation or the exchange of gifts was a common form of redress in such cases. Where there was no morally binding relationship between the parties, as between strangers or members of rival groups, retaliation or payback was more likely. Retaliation, in turn, could lead to intergroup warfare.

Portuguese and Spanish navigators recorded the first European sightings of New Guinea in the sixteenth century. Although colonial intervention did not occur until the late nineteenth century, an assortment of seafarers, missionaries, traders, gold prospectors, and foreign adventurers began visiting coastal and island areas in the 1830s.

British New Guinea (Papua)

Responding to Germany's annexation of northeast New Guinea in 1884 and pressure from the Australian colonies, the British declared a protectorate over the southeast of the island in the same year. Constitutional uncertainty about the status of the protectorate led to British New Guinea being annexed as a full colony in 1888, prior to its transfer to Australia and renaming as Papua in 1905. English imperial acts applied after annexation. A local Legislative Council was also established, which enacted the Courts and Laws Adopting Ordinance 1888. This adopted, subject to qualifications, the laws of the British colony of Queensland. In 1898, English law was made the basic law. English law comprised English statutes in force in Queensland on September 17, 1888, and the rules of English common law and equity applying from time to time. When the territory was transferred to Australia, the Papua Act 1905 provided for the continuation of laws previously in force.

German New Guinea

The German imperial government annexed the northeastern portion of New Guinea in 1884. Between 1885 and 1899, the German New Guinea Company administered the colony under a charter from the imperial government. German law applied and the company also had legislative powers over all matters excepting those reserved by the imperial government. In 1899, the imperial government assumed direct control. Between 1914 and 1921, New Guinea was occupied by an Australian military force and German law continued to apply. In 1921, New Guinea became a mandated Territory of the League of Nations under Australian administration. The Laws Repeal and Adopting Ordinance 1921 replaced German law with English law, comprising English statutes applying in Queensland on May 9, 1921, and English common law applying on the same date.

Papua and New Guinea

Papua and New Guinea were administered separately until World War II. In addition to laws introduced from Australia and England, the legislative councils in each territory could enact their own laws. From 1942 an Australian military administration jointly administered areas not under Japanese occupation. The United Nations agreed to joint administration after the war and this was formalized in the Papua and New Guinea Act 1949.

For most of the colonial period, indigenous contact with the introduced system was more likely to be with the system of native administration than with the formal judicial system. Native regulations applying exclusively to indigenes were introduced in both territories and administered by special courts presided over by district officers. A single judge in the district court or Supreme Court heard the most serious criminal cases. The civil jurisdiction of the courts was largely taken up with the regulation of the commercial activities of the expatriate community. Melanesian custom was never accorded the status of law. In New Guinea, the Laws Repeal and Adopting Ordinance 1921–1923 provided for limited recognition of custom. No similar statute existed for Papua, although the courts did occasionally recognize custom and were required to do so where customary land rights were involved. The Native Customs (Recognition) 1963 made more elaborate provision for the recognition and application of custom, primarily as a mitigating factor in criminal cases.

A period of institutional modernization from the late 1950s led to the gradual dismantling of the old system of native administration and its replacement with a modern, centralized system of justice. Under growing international and domestic pressure, Australia belatedly prepared Papua New Guinea for independence. A process of rapid localization of administrative positions began. In 1973, Australia granted Papua New Guinea internal self-government, followed by full independence on September 16, 1975.

Papua New Guinea

The absence of a unifying struggle for independence, in combination with PNG's unique social diversity, meant that there was little sense of shared identity among citizens of the new country. While most Papua New Guineans welcomed independence, there were many, particularly in the less developed Highlands, who viewed its timing as premature. For the first generation of national leaders, and their successors in recent years, binding the country's disparate communities into an effective political and ideological unit presents a formidable challenge.

The most pressing tasks facing PNG in 1975 related to the need to secure the resources necessary for national development, on the one hand, and the need to respond to emergent law and order problems, on the other. On the first issue, Papua New Guinea's major source of revenue at independence was an annual grant from Australia, accounting for over 40 percent of public expenditure. The constitution set economic self-reliance as one of the national goals. In the long term, this meant reducing reliance on Australian budgetary support by developing alternative sources of revenue. As well as expanding existing agricultural exports, such as coffee, cocoa, and copra, this meant exploring opportunities for mineral exploitation.

On the issue of law and order, decolonization was accompanied by the emergence of serious social conflict. This manifested itself in micronationalist movements in some of the more developed regions, notably Bougainville, the Gazelle Peninsula, and parts of Papua; the growth of urban street crime; and the revival of intergroup warfare in parts of the Highlands. Secessionist tensions on Bougainville had their origins in a long history of government neglect, made worse by Bougainville's relative geographic isolation. The immediate catalyst was the start of construction of the Panguna copper mine in 1969 in the face of determined local opposition. While successfully defused by the first national government, led by Prime Minister Michael Somare, the conflict was to reemerge in the late 1980s.

Urban crime rates began to increase in the late 1960s. Juvenile gangs appeared against a background of urban growth. The earlier abolition of colonial restrictions over indigenous movement had opened up the towns, formerly the preserve of the European elite, to migration from rural areas. Concerns about law and order in the towns and some rural areas have since grown, as aggravated by the availability of modern firearms, lack of legitimate economic opportunities, urban drift, the erosion of traditional constraints, and the relative weakness of state controls. The revival of intergroup fighting in parts of the Highlands was viewed by many as symptomatic of the withdrawal of state from local levels.

For the majority of Papua New Guineans who continue to live in rural villages, the introduced system of law is culturally, and often geographically, remote. Allegiances to tribes, clans, and subclans remain strong. Collective responsibility is a social fact in most communities and generates tensions with the principles of individual responsibility underlying the modern legal system. Customary law and practice, as adapted to the forces of modernization, continue to wield considerable influence in most villages.

Given the weakness of local markets, national development policies have aimed at attracting foreign investment. Lack of alternative sources of revenue and the discovery of sizable new reserves have led to a growing dependence on the mineral and petroleum sector. In the decade after independence, approximately one-quarter of internally generated revenue came from the Panguna mine on Bougainville. By 1989, this single mine accounted for nearly 10 percent of the country's gross domestic product. In 1988, an armed rebellion was launched by local Panguna landowners angry about the distribution of royalties and the environmental damage caused by the mine. This rebellion closed the mine and escalated rapidly into a secessionist war between members of the self-styled Bougainville Revolutionary Army and PNG security forces. The Bougainville War lasted for nine years and caused enormous suffering to the people of Bougainville, as well as having a major impact on the national economy. A protracted peace process began in mid-1997 and, while a final settlement remains elusive, the armed conflict has now ceased. The Bougainville conflict highlights the fragile and contested nature of nationhood in postcolonial Papua New Guinea.

LEGAL CONCEPTS

Papua New Guinea's autochthonous National Constitution is the supreme law and establishes the system of government and law. Section 9 of the constitution identifies the sources of law as follows:

- The National Constitution;
- Organic Laws;
- Acts of Parliament;
- Acts of Provincial Legislatures;
- Subordinate Legislation;
- Emergency Regulations;
- Laws made under or adopted by the National Constitution;
- The Underlying Law.

Organic Laws are special constitutional laws made by the National Parliament as Organic Laws under special authorization of the constitution (sec. 12). An Organic Law must not be inconsistent with the constitution and has the same authority as the constitution. The provisions on provincial government were introduced initially in response to secessionist tensions in Bougainville in the early 1970s. Dissatisfaction with the ability of provincial governments to deliver services led to a major reform of the system in 1995. The Organic Law on Provincial and Local Level Government created provincial assemblies and local-level governments and these are now gradually assuming a number of the national government's responsibilities. There are currently nineteen provinces: Central, East New Britain, East Sepik, Eastern Highlands, Enga, Gulf, Madang, Manus, Milne Bay, Morobe, New Ireland, North Solomons, Oro, Sandaun, Simbu, Southern Highlands, West New Britain, Western, and Western Highlands.

The Underlying Law is the unwritten law to be applied on any matter where there is no legislation. Section 20(1) of the constitution provides that an act of Parliament shall declare and provide for the development of the underlying law. Such an act was only introduced in 2000 (see below). Schedule 2.1 of the constitution provides that "custom is adopted, and shall be applied and enforced, as part of the underlying law" except in respect of any custom that is, and to the extent that it is, inconsistent with a constitutional law or statute, or repugnant to the general principles of humanity.

By Schedule 2.2, the adopted common law and equity of England (applying immediately before the date of independence on September 16, 1975) are also made part of the Underlying Law unless inconsistent with the constitution or a statute, or inapplicable and inappropriate to the circumstances of the country from time to time, or inconsistent with custom as adopted under Schedule 2.1.

Under Schedule 2.3, where a court is dealing with a matter "where there appears to be no rule of law that is applicable or appropriate to the circumstances of the country," then the court, and in particular, the Supreme Court and the national court, are duty-bound to formulate an appropriate rule as part of the underlying law, having regard to:

- The National Goals and Directive Principles;
- The Basic Rights set out in Division III.3 of the National Constitution;
- Analogies from statutes and custom;
- Legislation and cases of countries with a similar legal system;
- Relevant Papua New Guinean decisions; and
- The circumstances of the country from time to time.

The National Goals and Directive Principles, which are nonjusticiable, are a statement of the basic philosophy of the founders of the constitution. Every person and organization is to be guided by these directives. In summary, these are:

- Integral human development;
- Equity and participation;
- National sovereignty and self-reliance;
- Conservation of natural resources and the environment;
- The promotion of Papua New Guinean ways.

The elaborate constitutional scheme envisages an important role for Melanesian custom in the postindependence legal order. In practice, progress toward fulfilling these early aspirations has been relatively disappointing. Parliament has often been blamed for its failure to enact relevant enabling legislation as prescribed in the constitution. This situation has been remedied recently with the enactment of the Underlying Law 2000. Others have criticized the constitutional scheme, pointing to the nonjusticiable character of the National Goals and Directive Principles, the wholesale adoption of preindependence laws, the subordinate role of the underlying law in the constitutional scheme, and the reluctance of lawyers to introduce custom into legal arguments.

A Law Reform Commission was established under the constitution "to assist in the development of an indigenous jurisprudence." While the commission produced many reports in the 1970s and 1980s, relatively few of its recommendations have been enacted. Over the past ten years, the commission has been marginalized progressively as a result of lack of funds, effective leadership, and political commitment.

Sections 32–37 and 42–56 of the constitution provide for basic rights and freedoms. By and large, these are rights and liberties that existed under common law. Four basic rights are recognized:

- The right to freedom;
- The right to life;
- The right to freedom from inhuman treatment; and
- The right to protection from the law (secs. 32, 35, 36, and 37).

A guaranteed right or freedom may be enforced by any person who has an interest in the enforcement of the right or by someone acting on his/her behalf. The courts have generally reinforced these basic rights, regardless of government pressure. In fact, in recent times the courts have ordered government officials to make payments in settlement of claims against the government and have held these individuals responsible.

Sections 26–31 of the constitution and the Organic Law on the Duties and Responsibilities of Leadership provide a code of conduct (the Leadership Code) for those holding public office. The Ombudsman Commission, established by the constitution, investigates and prosecutes breaches of the Leadership Code. Many parliamentarians have resigned or been removed from office as a result of investigations. The commission can also receive and investigate complaints about any conduct on the part of any state service or a member of a state service, any government body, or officer or employee of a government body, or any other body referred to it (sec. 13 of the Organic Law on the Ombudsman Commission and sec. 219 of the constitution).

Section 99 of the constitution defines the national government as consisting of three principal organs:

- The National Parliament, which is a single-chamber elective legislature subject to constitutional laws, and with unlimited powers of law making. There are currently 109 members of Parliament. A member of Parliament holds office for five years, the official life of Parliament. Parliament must, however, be dissolved and a general election called if, during the last twelve months of its life, a successful vote of no confidence is brought against the prime minister, or if the prime minister has raised a vote of no confidence and is defeated. Parliament can dissolve itself at any time by an absolute majority vote. Numerous motions of no confidence have been introduced since independence and several of these have been successful. The use of this procedure has created great instability. In 1991, Parliament amended the constitution, extending the period following an election during which a no-confidence motion is prohibited from six months to eighteen months.

- The National Executive Council (NEC), comprising cabinet ministers and headed by the prime minister. The NEC is responsible for the executive government of the country. NEC ministers are, under section 141 of the constitution, "collectively answerable to the people through the Parliament, for the proper carrying out of the executive government of Papua New Guinea and for all things done by or under the National Executive."
- The National Judicial System exercises "the judicial authority of the people" (sec. 158) and "shall give paramount consideration to the dispensation of justice" in interpreting the law. Sections 160 and 163 establish, respectively, the Supreme Court and the national court. Acts of Parliament establish the district courts, local land courts, and the village courts.

The Constitution establishes an essentially Westminster system of government. The head of state is Queen Elizabeth II, represented in Papua New Guinea by a governor-general. The powers of the head of state are limited and can only be exercised with advice of the NEC. Political parties are numerous but the party system is not well developed. In practice, the government is usually formed by a loose coalition of parties.

CURRENT COURT SYSTEM STRUCTURE

The Supreme Court

Under section 18 of the constitution, the Supreme Court exercises an original jurisdiction in any matter relating to the interpretation or application of a provision of constitutional law. Section 19 also confers an advisory jurisdiction on the Court. On an application by one of the prescribed authorities, the Supreme Court can give its opinion on a question concerning the interpretation or application of a provision of a constitutional law, including questions relating to the validity of a law. The Supreme Court has an appellate jurisdiction as the final court of appeal in Papua New Guinea. When hearing an appeal, the Supreme Court is normally constituted of three judges. While the Court is based in the national capital, Port Moresby, it occasionally sits in regional centers. The Supreme Court also has a power of judicial review that is particularly relevant to the enforcement of the basic rights under the constitution.

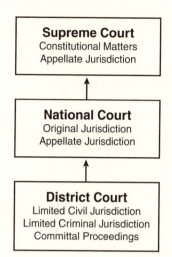

Legal Structure of Papua New Guinea Courts

Supreme Court
Constitutional Matters
Appellate Jurisdiction

National Court
Original Jurisdiction
Appellate Jurisdiction

District Court
Limited Civil Jurisdiction
Limited Criminal Jurisdiction
Committal Proceedings

The National Court

The national court has an unlimited original jurisdiction in criminal and civil matters. It has an inherent power to review the exercise of judicial authority by inferior courts or tribunals and powers to enforce the constitutional laws except when the Supreme Court is exercising these powers. The national court also has jurisdiction to hear appeals from the local and district courts. A single judge presides and there is now a resident national court judge in most provincial capitals. Appeals from the national court are heard by the Supreme Court.

The District Court

The district court is presided over by a single magistrate. It has a criminal jurisdiction over summary offenses, committal hearings, and certain indictable offenses (Schedule 2 of the Criminal Code Act). The court also has civil jurisdiction to hear personal claims not exceeding Papua New Guinea Kina (PGK)10,000 and certain other specified matters (e.g., custody and maintenance, village court appeals, land dispute settlements, adultery and enticement).

Other Courts

The Coroners Court

Magistrates are coroners for the purposes of the Coroners Act. They sit as the coroners court when they receive reports of deaths, fires, or missing persons and conduct an inquest or inquiry.

The Land Court

A magistrate of the district court sits as the local land court under the Land Disputes Settlement Act and hears disputes relating to land boundaries or ownership and use of customary land. A decision of a local land court may be reviewed by, or taken on appeal to, the provincial land court. The provincial land court is presided over by a principal magistrate, who is normally resident in the provincial center.

The Children's Court

A district court magistrate sits as the children's court when the accused in a criminal case is a child between the ages of seven and sixteen years old.

The Tax Court

A district court magistrate sits as the tax court when hearing tax prosecutions or claims for unpaid taxes. The commissioner for Inland Revenue is the only party that can bring proceedings before a tax court.

The Military Court

A national court judge or a principal magistrate of the district court can sit as the military court under the Defense Act to hear charges against, or appeals under, this Act and the Code of Military Conduct.

The Village Court

The village courts are not part of the national judicial system. They are the only courts that apply and enforce customary laws and practices to disputes. The rationale is to provide an accessible forum for dealing with minor disputes and infractions and one that is responsive to local needs and expectations. There are no formal and strict requirements of evidence and standards of proof. No procedural distinction is made between criminal and civil matters. Village courts are presided over by village court magistrates appointed from village leaders and are assisted by peace officers and court clerks. A village court area consists of between 2,500 and 10,000 people and may cover five or six villages. These courts also operate in the urban centers. There are currently 1,082 village courts covering approximately 84 percent of the country. The Village Courts Act emphasizes mediation, compromise, and compensation. A village court can award compensation up to PGK1,000 or order a person to do work for the aggrieved party for up to twelve weeks. It can hear a range of minor offenses specified in the Village Courts Regulations. The court cannot impose a sentence of imprisonment in the first instance but it has limited powers of imprisonment in respect of a person who fails to appear before it or who fails to pay a fine or perform community work. District courts can review, and hear appeals against, village court decisions.

The Informal Sector

In rural areas, where most of the population lives, minor disputes are still dealt with mainly by informal means. These vary significantly but are likely to include a range of self-help strategies: negotiation or mediation by kin, traditional leaders, or church officials; village moots; or the decisions of local *komitis*. The effectiveness of these informal processes is largely a consequence of the small size and social cohesion of village communities. They are likely to be less effective in urban settings given the higher level of cultural heterogeneity, the availability of formal remedies, and the more pervasive impact of Western influences. Modernization has, of course, affected even the most isolated rural communities and older methods of dispute resolution have been weakened in most places. A number of NGOs are active in conflict-resolution training among rural and urban communities. The Papua New Guinea government's recently endorsed National Law and Justice Policy prioritizes the strengthening of community-based conflict prevention and reduction.

STAFFING

The courts, and the superior courts in particular, are often lauded as one of the success stories of the postindependence period. There are growing signs, however, that the generic problem of lack of resources is having an impact at even the highest judicial levels. An expanding caseload has placed great pressure on the court system and led to lengthy delays in court proceedings. National court judges currently sit as Supreme Court judges although there is a proposal to move toward a separate Supreme Court. Full-time citizen judges are appointed for a ten-year period, after which their appointment may be renewed or extended. Full-time noncitizen judges are appointed for a three-year term, which may be extended or renewed. Acting judges are appointed up to a twelve-month period. There are currently eighteen judges. Finding suitably qualified applicants to sit as judges has long been a problem.

Lack of resources, including training and support services, has been an even greater challenge for the magistracy and staff of the inferior courts. The district court consists of magistrates of the Magisterial Service. These include the chief magistrate, two deputy chief magistrates, principal magistrates, and magistrates of the Magisterial Service. Most magistrates are appointed on a permanent basis. The exceptions are the chief magistrate and the deputy chief magistrate who are appointed for a six-year period. Magistrates are now required to have a law degree. There are currently 130 district court magistrates. This works out at only 1 magistrate per 36,500 people and less than 1.5 per district. In some districts there are, in fact, no magistrates. The poor condition of court buildings and staff accommodation has affected the workings of these courts in many parts of the country.

Village court magistrates are not legally qualified but receive some basic training. The minister for Justice appoints them. There are currently 12,656 village court officials. Responsibility for the payment of allowances to village court officials was transferred from the national government to provincial and local-level governments under the Organic Law on Provincial and Local Level Government 1995. Provincial and local-level governments claim that when these functions were transferred, no actual funding was transferred with them. As a result, many village court officials have not been receiving their allowances. While some continue to work, others refuse to hear cases until they receive payment.

The Department of Justice and Attorney General has overall responsibility for the delivery of justice services. It also provides the state with legal advice and representation. It contains a number of components of the formal legal system including the public prosecutor, public solicitor, Parole Board, and Law Reform Commission. The department also administers the village courts, community corrections, probation, and land courts. It currently has a staff of 203 officials, of whom 81 are lawyers. One of the difficulties it faces is the brain drain among its legally qualified staff, with many joining private practices or becoming magistrates or lawyers. Another is that there are not enough competent lawyers to ensure that the necessary training and development of young lawyers occur. Lawyers entrusted with serious and legally challenging cases often do not have the necessary legal skills or experience to handle them. As a result, many cases are lost unnecessarily. In addition, there is a serious shortage of government lawyers in a number of specialist areas, such as constitutional law, resources, and legal drafting.

The Law School at the University of Papua New Guinea is the country's only law school. It too experiences difficulty in recruiting and retaining professionally competent staff, particularly in specialist fields and at senior levels. Like other government-funded institutions it all operates within severe financial constraints. After completing a four-year law degree, law graduates attend the Legal Training Institute for practical training prior to admission to the bar. The Legal Training Institute also has difficulty in recruiting and retaining suitably qualified staff.

IMPACT OF LAW

The PNG legal environment is characterized by a high level of pluralism. Introduced laws and legal institutions operate alongside indigenous regulatory systems based on customary law and practice. There is often a distinct lack of articulation between the two systems, although the village courts provide an important exception. The constitution envisaged a far greater degree of indigenization of law and legal institutions than has happened in practice. Formal legal processes remain remote and expensive for most ordinary Papua New Guineans and, in recent years,

there has been a revival of older indigenous traditions for dealing with conflicts and disputes. While some of these appear to work well, others generate further conflict. The formal system, like other areas of government, suffers from chronic underresourcing and a growing risk of politicization and these have undoubtedly diminished its impact. The more fundamental challenge, as recognized in the new National Law and Justice Policy, is to build on existing community structures for dealing with local conflicts and to develop appropriate linkages between the formal and informal sectors of justice. It is clear that this area of reform is a long-term task but one that is essential to the development of the rule of law in this complex and rapidly changing country.

Sinclair Dinnen

See also Australia; Constitutional Law; Criminal Law; Customary Law; Human Rights Law; Indigenous and Folk Legal Systems; Legal Pluralism; Trial Courts

References and further reading

Brunton, Brian, and Duncan Colquhoun-Kerr. 1985. *The Annotated Constitution of Papua New Guinea.* Port Moresby: Papua New Guinea Press.

Chalmers, D. R. C., D. Weisbrot, and W. J. Andrew. 1985. *Criminal Law and Practice of Papua New Guinea.* Sydney: The Law Book Company Limited.

Dinnen, Sinclair. 2001. *Law and Order in a Weak State— Crime and Politics in Papua New Guinea.* Honolulu: University of Hawai'i Press.

Fitzpatrick, Peter. 1980. *Law and State in Papua New Guinea.* London: Academic Press.

Gordon, Robert J., and Mervyn Meggitt. 1985. *Law and Order in the New Guinea Highlands.* Hanover, NH: University Press of New England.

Government of PNG. 1999. The National Law and Justice Policy and Plan of Action. Port Moresby: GoPNG.

Government of PNG/United Nations Development Program. 1999. Papua New Guinea Human Development Report 1998. Hong Kong: GoPNG and UNDP.

Strathern, Marilyn. 1972. *Official and Unofficial Courts: Legal Assumptions and Expectations in a Highlands Community.* Port Moresby: New Guinea Research Unit Bulletin 47.

PARAGUAY

GEOGRAPHY

Paraguay sits in the southeastern section of South America. Wedged between three larger neighbors, it has suffered from invasion and war and found itself isolated from much of the world. To its north and northeast is Brazil, its largest neighbor and the one most involved in Paraguay's internal politics. To its north and west sits Bolivia, another landlocked country with an unstable government. To its south and west is Argentina.

Comprising some 406,750 square kilometers, Paraguay is a medium-sized country in South America. It is divided

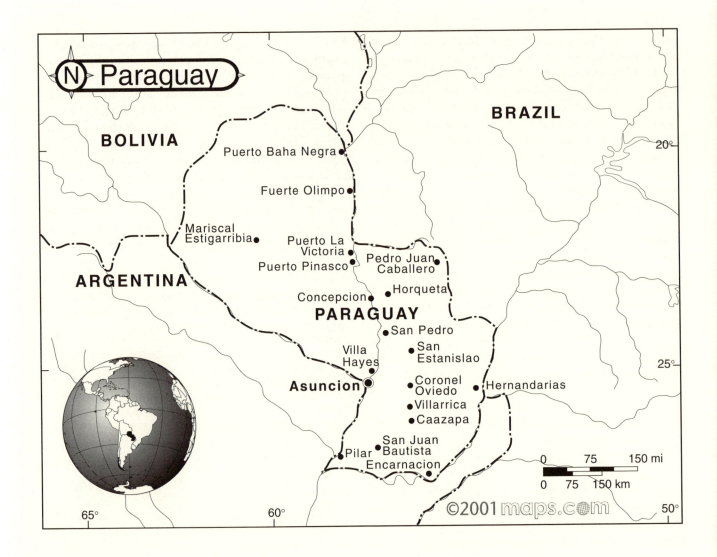

by the Paraguay River from north to south. The mountainous and hilly portion of the country along the Brazilian border is where the country's larger rivers find their source. The northern half of Paraguay is lowland and known as the Gran Chaco. This region was taken from Bolivia during the Chaco War of 1932–1935.

Paraguay's largest city is the capital, Asunción, located on the Paraguay River along the Argentinean border. Two of the country's largest cities are Encarnación, located on the banks of the Rio Parcana River, which borders Argentina in the extreme south of Paraguay, and Concepción, on the Paraguay River in the middle of the country.

Paraguay has suffered from economic problems throughout its history, which can be attributed to the fact it has lacked a seaport for over a century, has been surrounded by hostile neighbors, and has suffered from poor governmental policies. A lack of natural resources also prevents Paraguay from exporting to developed countries. Its small population, approximately 5.75 million people in 2000, has made it the target of invasion by its larger and more populous neighbors. During the last half of the nineteenth century, Paraguay was devastated by

war and dictatorship and appears to have never completely recovered from that period.

Paraguay's geography and location have been a major factor in its historical development. Its isolation in South America and its proximity to larger neighbors have limited the ability of Paraguay to develop a sound political and economic system.

HISTORY

Paraguay began as a Spanish colony, settled starting in 1537. Unlike many of the other South American colonies, Paraguay had little gold or silver, making it less valuable to the Spanish. Without those natural resources, Paraguay was able to obtain independence from Spain more quickly than the other colonies. In 1811, it became one of the first independent states in Latin America.

But freedom from Spain did not mean freedom at home. A series of civilian dictators came to run the country, beginning in 1816. José de Francia ruled as dictator for life until 1840. His policy of economic isolation prevented goods and people from crossing the country's borders. From his death in 1840 until 1871, two men, Carlos López and his son Francisco López, ruled Paraguay. The Lópezes brought the country out of its isolation but almost destroyed Paraguay by going to war against its larger neighbors Argentina and Brazil. The 1865–1870 War of the Triple Alliance saw Paraguay battle Argentina, Brazil, and Uruguay for control of territory. Paraguay was able to mobilize nearly its entire male population and hold off its combined enemies for nearly five years. Hundreds of thousands were killed, including two-thirds of the entire Paraguayan male population. Upon losing the war, Paraguay was forced to surrender its outlet to the sea to Argentina and Brazil. The military occupation by Brazil also saw the creation of a two-party system, with the Colorado Party supported by Brazil and the Liberal Party opposing Brazilian influence in the country.

The Liberal Party controlled Paraguay prior to World War II but lost its hold after the Chaco War of 1932–1935. This war saw Paraguay expand its northern territory by battling Bolivia, but the lack of a clear-cut military victory led to a military coup and the rise of Higinio Morinigo, who became the military dictator, starting in 1940. Morinigo maintained close ties with the German Nazi Party, and these ties continued even after the German defeat in 1945, when many former Nazi officials sought safety in Paraguay. Morinigo was himself replaced by another civilian dictator, Federico Chavez, who ruled Paraguay until the 1954 coup.

The main political and military figure in Paraguay during the last half of the twentieth century was Alfredo Stroessner. The general was the military leader from 1954 until 1989, when he was overthrown in a military coup. During those thirty-five years, known as the Stronato, Paraguay achieved political and economic stability. Mindful of his larger neighbors Argentina and Brazil, Stroessner guided the country between foreign enemies and internal opposition.

At the same time, most independent governmental institutions, such as the legislature and the courts, wilted under Stroessner's one-man rule. He was able to outlast much of his opposition, surrendering power only with old age.

The post-Stroessner government saw friction between the military and the civilian government. The new constitution was written in 1992, and the Colorado and Liberal Parties traded political power. In 1999, the sitting vice president was assassinated, and there was suspicion that the president was responsible. In 2000, there was an attempted military coup that failed but produced political repression by the government. These events point to the weakness of Paraguay's democracy and the difficulty of enforcing the rule of law.

LEGAL CONCEPTS

Paraguay operates under a civil law system. Because it was a Spanish colony, Paraguay initially adopted Spanish law, but upon independence, the new government composed a law code based on the Napoleonic Code. It was replaced by the Argentinean code during the latter half of the nineteenth century. But after the wars and other disputes, the Paraguayan government created its own legal code, written in 1914 and used for most of the twentieth century. In 2000, a new commercial, civil, and criminal code was enacted, updating the laws and improving procedures. The codes increased the number of protections for criminal defendants, including the possibility of government-provided counsel. Juries are not used in Paraguay. Instead, in many cases, the judge receives written reports from both sides and can issue a verdict in a single hearing.

The right to appeal can include arguments that the law was incorrectly applied or that the trial or the law violated the constitution. The constitution protects basic liberties including speech, religious practice, and ownership of property. It also sets the rules for how trials will be conducted. The courts are given the role of ruling on whether government has violated those rights and can exercise the power of judicial review and declare a law unconstitutional and thus void.

During the Stroessner period and during the rule of many of his predecessors, the courts and the rule of law were ignored and the constitutions treated as providing suggestions rather than commands. After Stroessner, the new government's political instability has prevented it from creating the rule of law. The assassinations and attempted coups have led to political repression and continuing limits on constitutional rights. As institutions in a country that has no tradition of an independent judiciary, the Paraguayan courts must struggle to assert their authority over the executive and legislative branches of government.

STRUCTURE

During most of Paraguay's history, the courts have been the weakest and most ignored institution of government. During the Stroessner regime, the courts rarely stepped out of their boundaries to challenge the government or protect the rights of citizens. The end of Stroessner's power and the writing of a new constitution in 1992 changed the role and authority granted the courts. The new judiciary, at least on paper, was to be free of government control or influence and to have broad powers to act as a check on government.

Chapter 3 of the 1992 Constitution begins by stating that the courts in Paraguay are to operate separately from the president and the legislature. Article 249 guarantees the courts at least 3 percent of the national budget, ensuring their funding cannot be cut or eliminated. Article 251 establishes a five-year term for all lower court and appeals court judges and prohibits removal of a judge during that term of office.

Legal Structure of Paraguay Courts

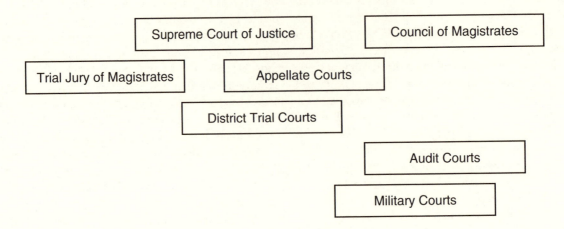

The constitution also creates the basic structure of the judiciary. Chapter 3 specifically mentions a Supreme Court of Justice and a Council of Magistrates and lists their powers and duties. It also grants the national legislature the power to create all lower courts in the country.

At the lowest level of Paraguay's judiciary are four types of courts, each with a special jurisdiction. These district courts include commercial and civil courts, criminal courts, labor courts, and juvenile courts. These courts operate within Paraguay's major cities, including the capital, and larger towns and regional centers. At the local and village levels, justice of the peace courts hear the entire range of issues involving minor disputes. Major criminal cases and civil trials involving large sums of money are heard in the district courts.

The decisions of these courts can be appealed to one of the five different appellate courts in Asunción. The five appellate panels hear civil and commercial, criminal, labor, administrative, and juvenile appeals. These courts decide only whether the lower court properly applied the law and if the trial was legal under Paraguayan law. In most cases, the appellate court operates as the final appeal for those who lose in the trial courts.

The highest court in Paraguay is the Supreme Court of Justice. Composed of nine justices, the Supreme Court hears appeals based on the law and claims that constitutional rights have been violated by the government. These constitutional claims can be heard only by the Supreme Court, and its decisions in constitutional cases cannot be overridden by any other court or by the executive or legislative branch. When faced with a constitutional case, the Supreme Court breaks into its constitutional chamber and determines whether a law is void.

In addition to its legal duties, the Supreme Court oversees how other judges operate in Paraguay. The constitution allows the Supreme Court to suspend lower court judges accused of violating the law. It also oversees jails and prisons to ensure that minimal living conditions are maintained for criminals.

The justices are appointed to a lifetime term that ends at the mandatory retirement age of seventy-five. Although judges can be removed for illegal acts, the difficulty in doing so has prevented any wholesale change in membership.

Although the Supreme Court is not a new institution in Paraguay, the 1992 Constitution does provide it with broad power to strike down laws. During the Stroessner regime, the court never struck down a law and rarely challenged the legality of a government action. This tradition of a weak judiciary in Paraguay continues even under the new constitution.

SPECIAL COURTS

The major special court in Paraguay is the Council of Magistrates, which does not issue legal rulings but is involved in the appointment of Supreme Court and lower court judges. The council is composed of a single Supreme Court justice; a member of the executive branch; a senator; and two attorneys and two law professors, one from the national university, the other from a private university. All members must be at least thirty-five years of age and have ten years of legal experience. The members of the council serve a three-year nonrenewable term.

The national government also operates audit courts. The judges in those courts can audit the finances of any government agency and determine if government funds were properly spent.

Another special court, the Trial Jury for Magistrates, works closely with the Supreme Court in determining whether a judge has violated the law. Composed of appeals and trial court judges, this court hears charges made against a sitting judge and can request that the Supreme Court suspend the judge. The decision of the Trial Jury for Magistrates can be used to impeach and remove a guilty judge.

Another set of special courts, the military courts, saw their importance decline with the removal of Stroessner and the creation of a constitutional system. From 1954 to 1989, the military courts heard cases involving civilians accused of challenging the government. With the formulation of the 1992 Constitution, military courts were relegated to a minor role, and their decisions could be appealed to and overruled by the Supreme Court of Justice.

SELECTION AND STAFFING

The history of authoritarian presidents in Paraguay, wielding unrestricted appointment power over judges, prompted the framers of the 1992 Constitution to remove the power to appoint from the executive branch. The Council of Magistrates presents three candidates to the Senate and the president. One of the three candidates is chosen and confirmed for the office. All lower court vacancies are filled using the same method.

The council's role in appointing judges is intended to limit political influence over judges and prevent the president from packing the judiciary with his or her supporters. Merit, experience, and recognition in the legal community are the criteria used by the council in choosing its nominees for the courts.

Paraguay has two major universities, the National University and the Catholic University, both in Asunción. Both universities have law schools that prepare students based on the Roman and French models of the law. With the creation of a new democracy in the country, the number of law students in these schools has increased, and the Paraguayan government has had little difficulty in finding properly trained lawyers to fill its court vacancies.

IMPACT

The end of the Stroessner regime in Paraguay saw the formation of a democratic government in the country. The 1992 Constitution promised a court system free of political influence and powerful enough to prevent government from abusing individual rights. The courts have the power of judicial review, and the selection of judges has been removed from the president's control, but a powerful judiciary has yet to develop. The most powerful court, the Supreme Court of Justice, has yet to exert its power and has been unable to check the president when he or she has used military and political crises to suspend the constitutional guarantees of free speech and press. Although the basic outline of a democratic society and an independent judiciary in Paraguay exists, without a more assertive and powerful judiciary, many of the promises of the 1992 Constitution will not be fulfilled.

Douglas Clouatre

See also Appellate Courts; Argentina; Brazil; Civil Law; Constitutional Review; The Spanish Empire and the Laws of the Indies

References and further reading
Crow, John. 1992. *The Epic of Latin America.* Berkeley: University of California Press.
Farcau, Bruce. 1996. *The Chaco War: Bolivia and Paraguay 1932–1935.* Westport, CT: Praeger.
Hanratty, Dennis, and Sandra Meditz. 1990. *Paraguay: A Country Study.* Washington, DC: Library of Congress.
Kelly, Robert. 1998. *Country Review: Paraguay 1998/1999.* New York: Commercial Data International.
Lambert, Peter, and Andrew Nickson, eds. 1997. *A Transition to Democracy in Paraguay.* New York: St. Martin's Press.
Lewis, Paul. 1980. *Paraguay under Stroessner.* Chapel Hill: University of North Carolina Press.
Morrison, Marion. 2000. *Paraguay.* Philadelphia: Chelsea House Publishers.
Roett, Riordan, and Richard Sacks. 1991. *Paraguay: The Personalist Legacy.* Boulder, CO: Westview Press.
Turner, Brian. 1993. *Community Politics and Peasant-State Relations in Paraguay.* New York: University Press of America.
Whigham, Thomas. 2001. *The Paraguayan War.* Omaha: University of Nebraska Press.

PARALEGAL

WHAT IT IS

Paralegal is the term used to describe an individual who engages in legal work but is not educated or licensed as a lawyer. In the United States and Canada, the term *paralegal* is used interchangeably with the term *legal assistant.* In other countries they may be known as legal executives, legal specialists, law managers, or law clerks. However, the term *law clerk* is often used to describe a new lawyer in training or in an apprenticeship. There are two national paralegal organizations in the United States, the National Federation of Paralegal Associations and the National Association of Legal Assistants.

Most paralegals in the United States work under the direct supervision of an attorney. Without attorney supervision, the paralegal runs the risk of engaging in the unauthorized practice of law, which is a crime in most states. However, in recent years there has been an increase in the number of independent paralegals who perform legal services without the direct supervision of a lawyer. The 1995 report of the American Bar Association, Commission on Nonlawyer Practice recognized that "nonlawyers, both as paralegals accountable to lawyers and in other roles permitted by law, have become an important part of the delivery of legal services and that their expertise and dedication to the system have led to improvements in public access to affordable legal services" (10).

In reality, all countries have positions that are filled by

persons who have legal training but are not licensed as lawyers. The term *paralegal* in a more general sense applies to any paraprofessional in a society who performs law-related tasks. The issue becomes whether the country requires, through licensing or some other form of regulation, that these tasks be assigned exclusively to an individual trained as a lawyer. Tax accountants, mediators, insurance claim adjusters, and even law enforcement officers, when determining if a law has been violated, are all individuals who to a certain extent are practicing law. Although protecting the public through licensing is a legitimate governmental function, this licensing should recognize that there are many legal activities that may be effectively performed by nonlawyers with specialized skills.

A paralegal often has specialized legal education or training. In the United States, paralegal education is provided by a variety of academic institutions, which include certificate programs offered by private educational providers, two-year associate of art degrees offered by community colleges, and university degrees offered by paralegal or legal studies programs. Slightly more than half of the practicing paralegals in the United States have earned a bachelor's degree. Many paralegals have moved from legal secretarial positions to paralegal positions as a result of in-service training and experience.

In continental European, Latin American, and other civil law countries, the position of the notary has developed to undertake many important law tasks. Notaries are highly trained individuals who prepare documents such as deeds, contracts, and articles of incorporation. They are licensed and regulated by the government, and in many countries their training is as extensive as the training provided to lawyers. They ensure not only that the documents are prepared properly but that they are recorded in the proper manner. They should not be confused with notaries in the United States, who primarily verify the accuracy of signatures but do not have the training or the legal authority to provide the services of a civil law notary.

The citizen advice bureau that has developed in the United Kingdom and Australia is another example of an organization that provides legal services primarily through the use of nonlawyers. Advice bureaus are private organizations that receive public and private funding. They exist in virtually every community in the United Kingdom. Some may be little more than a room in a library that contains brochures and other written materials, whereas others are large organizations. They are staffed primarily with volunteers on a part-time basis, but some have large paid staffs as well as volunteers and may even have a lawyer or solicitor on the payroll. They provide advice on a variety of legal subjects from landlord-tenant relations to marital dissolution, child custody, and government benefits programs. If a case is complex, a referral may be made to a lawyer, but in most situations a nonlawyer provides the advice. In the United States, an organization that openly gave legal advice would in all likelihood be confronted with charges that it was engaging in the unauthorized practice of law.

HISTORY

The term *paralegal* was first used in the mid-1960s to describe individuals used by the Office of Economic Opportunity, Legal Services Program in the effort to bring legal aid to poor communities as a part of the War on Poverty. These paralegals were either individuals from the poor community or individuals who received special in-service training. They were used primarily to do outreach, interview potential clients, and assist clients in selected areas of the law, such as family law or government benefits.

The benefits of using paralegals were soon recognized by the private bar and by other government organizations. The American Bar Association established a Standing Committee on Legal Assistants in 1968. In these early days of paralegal use, many legal secretaries became paralegals through training or experience. However, by the mid-1970s, a variety of educational institutions were developing paralegal education programs, and the American Bar Association began a program of approving these educational institutions.

The use of paralegals has continued to expand. According to the Department of Labor, the paralegal profession was the fastest-growing profession in the United States in the 1980s. In 2000, there were 130,000 paralegals in the United States, and it is estimated that there will be 189,000 paralegals by the year 2006.

The increased use of paralegals, in some measure, is a response to the growth of government and government programs. The history of citizen advice bureaus in the United Kingdom is an example of such response. Advice bureaus were created as an emergency measure in World War II to help people receive wartime assistance from private and government sources. A large percentage of the workload of these bureaus continues to be assisting people in obtaining government benefits and in securing government approval and licenses.

MAJOR VARIANTS

The manner in which law-related work is assigned varies from country to country. Factors such as what is considered a legal matter, the extent and nature of legal training, the political power of lawyers, and whether a written work is produced play a role in determining whether a task is assigned to a fully trained professional lawyer or a paraprofessional paralegal in any given country.

A critical variable in determining whether work is assigned to a paralegal is how the society defines a legal matter. Generally, this decision is related to what institution is assigned the task of dealing with the matter. If issues are resolved in courts or institutions that follow a formal courtlike procedure, then it is more likely that a fully trained lawyer will be involved. However, if the matter is handled by some type of informal dispute resolution mechanism, then it is more likely that a paralegal will be involved.

Another variable is the extent to which the general population is trained in law. In Europe and many civil law countries, knowledge of law and legal institutions is more widespread. Law and legal studies are considered a major component of an undergraduate education. In the United States, law is primarily taught in specialized graduate-level law schools. The lack of general knowledge of law by the population results in more matters being assigned to lawyers. The United States has more lawyers than other countries not only because it treats more matters as legal disputes but because it does not have as many other individuals with the knowledge to address the matters. As issues become more complex and less routine, there is a tendency to turn to someone with greater knowledge and understanding. If other alternatives do not exist, these matters will be assigned to the fully trained professional lawyer.

A third variable is the extent to which the dominant profession, lawyers, controls the subprofession, paralegals. In the United States lawyers have considerable political power, which they use to protect their professional status. Consequently, there is a high degree of emphasis placed upon the unauthorized practice of law. In many other countries, there is a greater willingness to allow others not as fully trained in the law to undertake law-related work.

A fourth variable is whether the matter can be handled by advice only, or whether some form of document must be prepared. Generally, there is more of a willingness to allow paraprofessional involvement if the issue can be limited to advice. The inability to regulate advice-only situations and the fact that the advice given is often specialized and routine and can be supervised through an administrative hierarchy may explain why this variable exists.

SIGNIFICANCE

The use of paralegals and other paraprofessionals in the delivery of legal services is likely to increase in the future. As society becomes more complex, individuals who have a significant level of legal training but not necessarily the complete training of a lawyer will be needed. There will continue to be a need to develop institutions that can provide quality legal services at a price that is reasonable. For example, in California, the position of "legal documents assistant" has been authorized by statute. Although not as highly trained as the civil law notary, these are individuals with paralegal training who are authorized to help individuals complete standardized form contracts and other legal documents for a fee. The task of completing such documents is sufficiently routine that requiring the services of a fully trained lawyer would not be cost-efficient.

Additionally, as the role of government increases and there is a greater demand for government services and regulation, there will be an increased amount of legal activity in a society, which will require persons with knowledge of the law and processes of government. Many of the tasks will be routine or specialized. Individuals with paralegal training will be able to undertake this type of work, particularly if they work in an organization where their work is supervised to ensure that the public is receiving appropriate legal services.

Finally, the major changes that have occurred in information technology will continue to lead to changes in the manner in which law-related work is divided between professionals and paraprofessionals. One of the criteria of being a professional is that there is a body of knowledge that is understood and accessible only by individuals with the professional training. Legal information about both the substance and the process of the law is now readily available to any individual with sufficient training to access it through available information systems. Paralegals who specialize in limited areas of law often are more familiar with the legal issues in that area than generally trained attorneys. In an era of information availability and specialization, the trend toward the greater use of paralegals is likely to continue.

Ironically, in the future, having specialized knowledge in one area may not be as important to the definition of being considered a professional as having sufficient knowledge in a variety of areas that will allow for analysis of the information. Undoubtedly, individuals will continue to need to know what their legal rights and responsibilities are, legal transactions will continue to occur, and disputes will arise. There will continue to be a need for individuals trained in the law to assist persons with legal problems, but choices will have to be made as to whether that individual must have the professional training of a lawyer or whether some other form of legal education is more appropriate.

Frank Kopecky

See also Citizens Advice Bureaux; Law Clerks; Lay Judiciaries; Legal Education; Notaries

References and further reading

American Bar Association, Commission on NonLawyer Practice. 1995. *Nonlawyer Activity in Law Related Situations: A Report with Recommendations.* Chicago: American Bar Association.
Kritzer, Herbert M. 1998. *Legal Advocacy: Lawyers and Non-lawyers at Work.* Ann Arbor: University of Michigan Press.
Louisiana Notary Association, "The Role of the Notary in the Civil Law Tradition: Alejandro M. Garro," http://www. lna.org/l_esprit/garro.htm (cited February 20, 2001).

Malavet, Pedro A. "Counsel for the Situation: The Latin American Notary, a Historical and Comparative Model." *Hastings International and Comparative Law Review* 19: 389–488.

National Association of Citizen Advice Bureaux. "Homepage," http://www.nacab.org.uk/ (cited February 20, 2001).

Schneeman, Angela. 2000. *Paralegal Careers.* Albany, NY: West Legal Studies.

PARLIAMENTARY SUPREMACY

PARLIAMENTARY SUPREMACY IN ENGLAND

Parliamentary supremacy, sometimes called parliamentary sovereignty, originated and is found in its purest form in England. Parliamentary supremacy means that Parliament, rather than a written constitution or court interpretations of law, is the supreme, ultimate source of law. Under parliamentary supremacy, Parliament has the final say as to what it can do. It can change any law and any definition of rights that it chooses. Parliament alone, not courts, has the final say as to what is or is not lawful. There are no fundamental constitutional laws that Parliament cannot change, other than the doctrine of parliamentary sovereignty itself. Parliament has the right to make or unmake any law whatsoever, and no person or body is recognized by the law of England as having a right to override or set aside the legislation of Parliament. Moreover, under parliamentary supremacy, Parliament cannot bind successor parliaments. A statute cannot be protected from repeal, and a later parliament can always undo the act of a previous parliament, whatever words the previous act contains to prevent its own repeal. In the event of a conflict between a statute and some other kind of law, custom, or moral principle, the statute must always prevail.

Parliamentary supremacy has been described as the most fundamental, keystone element in the English legal system; it also has been described as a noble lie, as an ugly Victorian monument, and as having a hypnotic effect on legal perceptions. The value placed on parliamentary supremacy in the English political system resulted from a centuries-long, hard-won battle by Parliament to limit the abuse of power by the monarch. However, the legal concept of parliamentary supremacy is a relatively recent invention, originating in 1885 by Albert Venn Dicey and developed by him into a hegemonic political and legal theory in the late nineteenth and early twentieth centuries. Before 1871, parliamentary supremacy was rarely mentioned in court cases.

This doctrine reflects the commonplace notion that in a democracy, the legislature should always be free to change its mind by majority vote. The omnipotence of Parliament and the will of the people through their elected representatives are created anew every time it meets; therefore, efforts to place limits on the power of successor parliaments must not be permitted. No special rules relating to the amount of parliamentary support a bill must have in order to become a law, other than a majority vote, can be forced on successor parliaments. Therefore, a parliament cannot define laws as basic, containing, for example, fundamental rights, and force successor parliaments to change or amend them by supermajorities or complex amending processes. If any parliament could bind its successors by requiring supramajority voting or agreement by bodies other than Parliament, then parliamentary supremacy in its purest form would be nullified. The principle that no other body can deny the supremacy of Parliament means that neither the courts of England nor international courts have the power to declare an act of Parliament invalid and that they may not impose their will as to what rights are lawful without the assent in law of Parliament.

Under parliamentary supremacy as found in England, there is no power of constitutional review in which courts can invalidate an act of Parliament, nor is there a written constitution to be interpreted by courts. This means that Parliament is legally competent to legislate on any issue at all. There are only political, not legal, constraints on its power to write laws. Parliament can overrule any judicial decision. Judges do not have the authority to rule on the constitutional validity of an act of Parliament or engage in a wide-ranging interpretation of statutes.

Courts are to interpret of the words of the statute as written by Parliament, not divine the intent of Parliament. English courts must look at the actual language of an act; they cannot look at extrinsic documents, such as committee reports, to discover the "intent" of Parliament. However, in *Pepper v. Hart* (1992), the Law Lords in the House of Lords, the highest court in England, held that where the language of a statute is unclear, a court can turn to the public record of the Parliament's debate to find a clear and unambiguous statement from a sponsor of the legislation as to what the provision was intended to mean.

Courts have no authority to judge statutes invalid for violating either moral or legal principles. That is, judges in England do not have the power to invalidate statutes because they are in conflict with what they view as natural rights or implied fundamental rights. Moreover, there is no need for Parliament to be explicit about its intention to overrule prior legislation: a later statute that is inconsistent with one of its predecessors is automatically construed as having overturned the earlier act. Thus, the doctrine of parliamentary supremacy demands that the constitutionality of legislation cannot be questioned by British courts; a judge may not strike legislation down, irrespective of the draconian way in which it may impinge upon basic moral or political values. In rare, extraordinary cases, a court may choose to disobey a law on the grounds that the legal authority to obey is overridden by a moral duty to disobey. However, if Parliament seeks to enforce its will, parliamentary supremacy means that the will of Parliament is supreme.

England does not have a written constitution that lists and limits the powers of government bodies or the fundamental rights of its citizens. Without a constitution and the concept of fundamental rights, which courts can interpret in ways that limit the power of Parliament to pass ordinary legislation, the will of Parliament in England is truly supreme. Unlike in the United States, there is no requirement that fundamental rights or the powers of Parliament or the executive are limited and can only be changed by supermajority voting in Parliament or complex amending procedures. Parliamentary supremacy rejects the U.S. notion that the political power of bodies in government is limited and that fundamental rights and values must be ranked in order of their importance; the more important the value, the more difficult it should be for citizens to amend such values. In the United States, the most important values are those contained in the constitution, as interpreted by judges and justices of the Supreme Court, who may declare as unconstitutional laws that violate such values. In England, the courts' role is to ensure that Parliament's will is respected; judicial review is not constitutional law review.

At one level, parliamentary supremacy is not formally concerned with Parliament as a political institution because it is essentially a legal concept. However, even Dicey, the father of the concept, acknowledged that politics placed limits on the supremacy of Parliament. Dicey realized that no government would promote legislation that it felt would so antagonize the electorate that it would be voted out of office in the next election. By viewing parliamentary supremacy as a legal concept, Dicey was emphasizing that the concept centered on the relationship between courts and Parliament and that courts must obey the will of Parliament.

Today, critics view Dicey's doctrine of parliamentary supremacy as abandoning the traditional common law understanding that law making was subject to fundamental legal principles and replacing it with an undeserved faith in Parliament as a democratic lawmaker. In addition, domestic and international forces challenge these assumptions. No longer is there a political consensus that Parliament should be unlimited in its power. Also, with the large number of votes that the parties in power have held since the 1970s, the ability of Parliament and the will of the people to check the government in power is severely limited.

A CHALLENGE TO PARLIAMENTARY SUPREMACY: ENGLAND JOINS THE EUROPEAN UNION

Thus, Dicey's concept of parliamentary sovereignty was unrealistic. Not only was the concept to be viewed as primarily legal in nature, but it also had a far too simplified vision of the separation of law and politics. This problem is most clear if we look at the challenge to parliamentary sovereignty caused by England joining the European Economic Community (later the European Union) in 1973 and the passage of the Human Rights Act in 1998, which incorporated the European Convention on Human Rights into English law.

The European Court of Justice interprets European economic, social, and governance directives; the European Court of Human Rights has authority over human rights and interprets the European Convention on Human Rights. So the presence of the convention and European Union social and economic directives and the availability of these European Union courts have meant that England is under political and moral pressure to limit the will of Parliament when it is in conflict with European Union norms. The convention sets up new standards for individual rights, standards through which judges now may be more willing to enter doctrinal areas that were off-limits to them.

Although each day one reads about English cases being brought to these European courts, with some cases resulting in a clear finding of England's violation of convention rights or economic and social directives, one can overstate the impact of European Union court cases on the doctrine of parliamentary supremacy. European Union courts and the convention itself are very deferential to the views and needs of their member nations. Governments may be viewed by the European Court of Human Rights as not in violation of the convention by reasons of national security, because of the need for political peace and stability, and out of respect for a nation's moral and religious values. Moreover, its takes many years and much money to sustain suits before these courts.

Because the power of judicial review is so weak under the doctrine of parliamentary supremacy and because Parliament determines the nature of constitutional rights, cases decided by European Union and English courts under the "incorporated" European Convention on Human Rights are not self-executing. Parliament must write legislation to incorporate into English law the individual rights that are defined in the decisions of the European Court of Human Rights. Moreover, until a specific law is passed that accepts the principles of the court decision based on convention principles, the law, which has been discredited by European and English courts as in violation of the Convention on Human Rights, continues in effect.

Most important, Parliament and English courts have never rejected the principle of parliamentary supremacy. A government in power in the future could choose to reject any European Union directive or rights principle in the convention, as defined by the European Court of Human Rights. Moreover, under the doctrine of parliamentary supremacy, the incorporation of the European Convention on Human Rights into English law did not mean it was embedded into English law, to be directly applied by English or European Union courts. Embedding the individual rights defined in court cases into English law only occurs when Parliament acts to specifically do so in legislation.

Finally, many scholars argue that the concept of parliamentary supremacy could be changed or modified, since it is a man-made rule. It could be modified so Parliament could bind future parliaments. Yet such a modification would have to be agreed to by future prime ministers and governments, who traditionally have favored the principle of parliamentary supremacy so that they will have full power to act when they are victorious at the polls.

PARLIAMENTARY SUPREMACY AND INDIVIDUAL RIGHTS AROUND THE WORLD

Another way to understand parliamentary supremacy is to see it in operation in less pure forms in nations that honor the principle of parliamentary supremacy but, unlike England, may have a written constitution, a bill of rights, and a constitutional court with the power of constitutional judicial review to invalidate or limit the will of Parliament. Most of these nations are members of the British Commonwealth, former colonies that have accepted English principles of law and governance to some degree. These include Australia, New Zealand, and Canada. Other nations that follow the doctrine of parliamentary supremacy include Israel, the Netherlands, and Switzerland. More generally, around the world there has been a decline in the principle of parliamentary supremacy, an increase in the number of nations with written constitutions that include bills of rights that are superordinate to ordinary legislation, and a significant increase in the number of nations with constitutional courts with wide-ranging powers of judicial review. To see the relationship of parliamentary supremacy to law and politics in nations that have rejected England's pure form of the doctrine, I will discuss the doctrine of parliamentary supremacy in New Zealand, Australia, and Israel. Can a nation be committed to a principle of parliamentary supremacy but, unlike England, have a written constitution, a belief in fundamental rights above ordinary legislation, or a strong constitutional court with the power of judicial review?

New Zealand

Of all the major Commonwealth nations, New Zealand continues to most resemble England. It has no written constitution or bill of rights. Its General Assembly can alter constitutional or fundamental law as it would regular law. The General Assembly came to have plenary, unlimited, legislative, and constituent power in 1947, although unlike in Canada, no formal legal separation from England and its Parliament has occurred. There have been calls for a written constitution with a bill of rights to be enforced by a strong constitutional court. However, in 1990, New Zealand chose to pass the Bill of Rights Act as ordinary legislation rather than to entrench a bill of rights modeled on the Canadian Charter of Rights and Freedoms, which requires amendment by more than a simple majority vote in the legislature.

The passage of the Bill of Rights Act has signaled a changed constitutional emphasis. New Zealand courts are now more activist in the regulation of bureaucracy and public power. The act is engendering a wider acceptance of constitutional rights among citizens, police, politicians, judges, and the legal profession and academy. It has intensified rights inquiries by courts and the application of common law in rights cases; it is viewed as similar to the 1960 Canadian Bill of Rights Act, which Canada replaced in 1982 with the Charter of Rights and Freedoms. However, without the entrenchment of human rights in a bill of rights, New Zealand courts do not feel they can go beyond the words of an act signed by the governor-general when they interpret legislation. Nor do they feel that they can define implied fundamental rights. New Zealand could entrench a bill of rights; that is up to the political will of the people and is not formally limited by the parliamentary supremacy of the English Parliament.

Australia

Australian lawyers, like most Commonwealth lawyers, were never taught to question the Dicey doctrine of parliamentary supremacy. Despite this, an England-like concept of parliamentary supremacy has never governed the operation of the constitutional system in Australia. Interest in legislative supremacy is marginalized because of the extent of the federal division of powers in Australia between the central government and its states. In Australia, the national legislature, named the Commonwealth Parliament, is supreme but not absolutely supreme when compared to England, which has unlimited legal authority. The Australian Commonwealth Parliament is guaranteed only a superior claim against any other legislative body claiming legislative competence to act.

Unlike in England, there is a written constitution in Australia that divides up powers among the central Parliament and the legislatures of the states. The legal limitations that delineate the boundaries of the powers of Australian parliaments are precisely what deny the Commonwealth Parliament absolute supremacy. State parliaments may have different legislative procedures and rights. However, states in Australia are subject to limitations on their powers that are set by the Australian Commonwealth Constitution. In some areas, states are not permitted to legislate; in other areas, state legislatures and the Australian Commonwealth Parliament have concurrent legislative power. However, Australian Commonwealth law prevails when it is in conflict with state law.

Most importantly, the Australian Commonwealth Constitution includes several explicitly stated rights: compensation for compulsory acquisition of property, trial by jury, freedom of religion, and equal application of law. In addition, since 1992, the Australian High Court has sought to expand individual rights by discerning a right to freedom of political speech as implicit in the nature of the constitution.

Although the Australian Commonwealth Parliament has supreme legislative authority, that power is not absolute, given the national and state constitutions and High Court interpretations. The Commonwealth Constitution brokers the synthesis between legislative supremacy and judicial interpretations of what a rule of law requires. Therefore, parliamentary supremacy is present in Australia but in a qualified form. Moreover, in Australia, there is the purported discovery of implied fundamental rights found in the constitution. The High Court has allowed this process to continue in practice while choosing to refuse to explore parliamentary supremacy as a legal concept. Ironically, Australia has a less dominant judiciary than Israel, even though Israel has no written constitution.

Israel

Most emerging democratic states in eastern Europe, Africa, and Asia have chosen to base their democracies on written constitutions with bills of rights, not on the principle of parliamentary supremacy. However, in 1948, Israel accepted the concept of parliamentary supremacy and chose not to include a written constitution or a bill of rights in its system of governance. No political consensus on the language of a constitution could be reached because religious parties objected to drafting a constitution that makes reference to the people, not to religious values, as the ultimate source of sovereignty and legitimacy, and secular parties did not want a constitution to make reference to divided authority between religious and secular institutions. As waves of immigrants came to Israel and governments needed to maintain coalitions of both secular and religious parties, political leaders did not want to freeze a dynamic political process into a rigid mold. Moreover, leaders feared that too much power

would be granted the government if a constitution was made during the nation's struggle for physical survival.

Between 1948 and 1992, there was a Supreme Court but no written constitution and no bill of rights. The Supreme Court had no formal power to engage in judicial review. The Israeli parliament, the Knesset, could change any constitutional principle or right by simple majority and did so at times to meet problems that prime ministers had in forming governing coalitions or to avoid government crises as political parties threatened to leave governing coalitions.

However, in these years, the Israeli Supreme Court became a much stronger and independent body than in England, New Zealand, or Australia, even though technically it did not have the power to rule on the constitutionality of acts of the Knesset. The Supreme Court used international law, Jewish law, and rights principles in the Israeli Declaration of Independence and in common law to make judgments about individual rights.

Even without a written constitution and with the doctrine of parliamentary supremacy in place, there were few areas in which the Israeli Supreme Court did not engage in judicial review. It overturned decisions by the government to build settlements. It said there was a right to freedom of speech, banned censorship in the arts, reduced the effects of military censorship on news reporting, supported the right of reporters not to disclose sources, and found a campaign finance law in violation of the basic law's principle of equality in elections. It overturned decisions of the religious Grand Rabbinical Court, which had refused women the right to divorce and immigrant status if they had converted to Judaism in a Reform U.S. synagogue, and ordered the inclusion of women in religious councils.

In 1992, there was a more formal recognition by the Knesset of the Supreme Court power of judicial review. In 1992, the Knesset passed three basic laws concerning freedom of occupation, the government, and human dignity and liberty. By stating that for the Knesset to change a basic law, there must be an absolute voting majority of all members of the Knesset and not just a majority of those present and voting, the Knesset made it more difficult for it to overturn basic law. Moreover, courts now had the power to review whether new legislation violated rights protected by basic laws, such as the rights of human dignity, life, property, and freedom of occupation. Since 1992, a constitutional dialogue has grown to such a degree that the fear of Israeli Supreme Court invalidation of legislation affects the writing of laws and results in less arbitrary government decisions.

Israel has accepted, to a far greater degree than England, New Zealand, and Australia, that fundamental moral principles as interpreted by courts may limit politics and legislatures, that basic laws have primacy over ordinary legislation, and that the Israeli Supreme Court has a quite forceful power of judicial review, although it is still possible that the Supreme Court's power of judicial review can be reined in by the Knesset. The Israeli situation suggests that a nation can continue to support the legal doctrine of parliamentary supremacy and also have a Supreme Court with very aggressive power of judicial review if there is the political will to do so. It also suggests that a strong power of judicial review can exist even without a written constitution or a bill of rights, which are viewed as fundamental laws that are above and limit ordinary legislation and cannot be changed except by extraordinary supermajorities in the legislature or complex processes of amendment.

This comparison suggests that the doctrine of parliamentary supremacy itself is only one factor, among many factors legal, historical, political, and socioeconomic in nature, that explains the power of courts and legislatures to define public policy and individual rights. It also suggests that it is possible for a nation to continue to formally accept the doctrine of parliamentary supremacy but reduce the actual supremacy of a legislature over defining the power of government and individual rights without formally disestablishing the doctrine or establishing a written constitution and a bill of rights. Finally, the comparison suggests that there could be a significant change in the power of courts and Parliament in England without a written constitution, a bill of rights, and the specific rejection of the doctrine of parliamentary supremacy, if there is a political will to do so.

Ronald C. Kahn

See also Australia; Canada; Common Law; Constitutional Law; Constitutional Review; Constitutionalism; England and Wales; European Court and Commission on Human Rights; European Court of Justice; Israel; Judicial Independence; Judicial Review; Natural Law; New Zealand; United Kingdom

References and further reading
Craig, P. P. 1990. *Public Law and Democracy in the United Kingdom and the United States.* Oxford: Oxford University Press.
Epp, Charles R. 1998. *The Rights Revolution: Lawyers, Activists, and Supreme Courts in Comparative Perspective.* Chicago: University of Chicago Press.
Hirschl, Ron. 2000. "The Political Origins of Judicial Empowerment through Constitutionalization: Lessons from Four Constitutional Revolutions." *Law and Social Inquiry* 25, no. 1: 91–147.
Hofnung, Menachem. 1996. "The Unintended Consequences of Unplanned Constitutional Reform: Constitutional Politics in Israel." *The American Journal of Comparative Law* 44: 585–604.
Joseph, Phillip A. 1999. "The New Zealand Bill of Rights Experience." Pp. 283–317 in *Promoting Human Rights through Bills of Rights: Comparative Perspectives.* Edited by Phillip Alston. Oxford: Oxford University Press.
Kinley, David. 1994. "Constitutional Brokerage in Australia: Constitutions and the Doctrines of Parliamentary Supremacy and the Rule of Law." *Federal Law Review* 22: 194–204.
Kritzer, Herbert M. 1996. "Courts, Justice, and Politics in England." Pp. 81–176 in *Courts, Law and Politics in Comparative Perspective.* Edited by Herbert Jacob, Erhard Blankenburg, Herbert M. Kritzer, Doris Marie Provine, and Joseph Sanders. New Haven: Yale University Press.
Loveland, Ian. 2000. *Constitutional Law: A Critical Introduction.* 2d ed. London: Butterworths.
Markesinis, Basil S., ed. 1998. *The Impact of the Human Rights Bill on English Law.* Oxford: Oxford University Press.
Shapira, Amos. 1983. "Judicial Review without a Constitution: The Israeli Paradox." *Temple Law Quarterly* 56: 405–461.

PENNSYLVANIA

GENERAL INFORMATION

Pennsylvania is called the Keystone State because of its key role in the economic, social, and political development of the United States. One of the original thirteen colonies, Pennsylvania is surrounded by the states of New York, New Jersey, Delaware, Maryland, West Virginia, and Maryland. The total land area of Pennsylvania is approximately 44,000 square miles, and its average width is 285 miles from east to west and 156 miles from north to south. The natural boundaries of Pennsylvania are the Delaware River in the southeast and Lake Erie in the northwest corner of the state. On March 4, 1681, a charter granted to William Penn by King Charles II of England established the remaining borders of Pennsylvania. Penn, before settling Pennsylvania, bought the claims of the Indians. Although there is debate regarding its validity, it is believed that in 1682 Penn and the settlers signed a "Great Treaty" with the natives of that land, paying them a fair value for its use. The primary settlers in Pennsylvania were English Quakers, but large numbers of Germans and Scotch-Irish also settled there. After the Civil War, a new wave of immigration brought Swedes, Finns, Russians, Ukrainians, Jews, and other peoples from Scandinavia and eastern Europe. In 1940, the Commonwealth of Pennsylvania was the second most populous state in the nation, but by 2000 its rank had dropped to fifth, and the median age had become higher than that of any state except Florida. The reasons for this trend go back to the Industrial Revolution of the nineteenth century; the strong economy of Pennsylvania was founded on steel and iron. Andrew Carnegie, Henry Frick, Andrew Mellon, Charles Schwab, and other leaders of the industry concentrated iron and steel production in western Pennsylvania. Pittsburgh, a frontier outpost in colonial times, grew to be known as the "steel city." In the twentieth century Pennsylvania also led the nation in the industries of lumber, petroleum, natural gas, and coal. Ironically, Pennsylvania's early ascendance in these venues presents an obstacle to the continued vitality of the state in the twenty-first century. Heavy capital investment in aging industrial plants, mills, and equipment poses a liability to the state as it rushes to attract high-tech industry and arrest the outmigration of its younger population.

EVOLUTION AND HISTORY

The state's founder had a profound influence on the evolution of Pennsylvania's legal system. William Penn arrived in America by a circuitous route. The son of the British admiral Sir William Penn, the junior Penn was born into an elite social position and benefited from the best education. While at Oxford University in the 1660s, Penn was exposed to the teachings of George Fox, the founder of the Quaker religion. Quakers were distinct from other Christians in their assertion that individuals possessed the spiritual capacity to communicate directly with God. The democratic leveling implicit in this claim ran counter to the teachings of the established Anglican church and threatened the order of the state. The offense to the political and religious culture of the time provoked routine violence against Quakers who espoused these views.

Penn's attraction to Quaker ideals led to his expulsion from Oxford and his later arrest for addressing a Quaker meeting, an event depicted in a mural in the governor's reception room in the Pennsylvania state capitol building. The New World offered a safe haven for Penn, who settled a debt owed to King Charles II by Penn's late father by asking the king to grant him land in America by charter. The Charter of Pennsylvania was signed on March 4, 1681. It established the state, named for Penn's father, and assured the people of Pennsylvania of the protection of English laws.

The Quaker background of William Penn influenced the basis of law in the state of Pennsylvania. In 1862 he drew up a Frame of Government for the colony in which he outlined his Quaker ideals. In October 1862, the first Assembly united the Delaware counties with Pennsylvania, adopted a naturalization act, and, on December 7, adopted the Great Law, a humanitarian code that became the fundamental basis of Pennsylvania law and that guaranteed libery of conscience. Penn's democratic ideals led him to reject the principle of one-man rule. This limitation on centralized political power is a theme that pervades Penn's *Frame of Government of Pennsylvania* and *Laws Agreed Upon,* which share the common theme of the rule of the people as a source of governmental authority. Toward the end of the reign of Charles II of England, Penn returned to England. His accomplishments during this visit included the suppression of piracy, the granting of a charter to Philadelphia, and the issuance of the *Charter of Privileges,* a guarantee of religious freedom, all of which served as precursors to the concept of fundamental rights protected both in the Constitution of the United States and in the several state constitutions.

The antilegalism of Quaker ideology shaped the way disputes were resolved in Pennsylvania. The early Quaker settlers employed mediation, arbitration, and reconciliation and resorted to the legal system only when other means failed. Pennsylvania's first arbitration statute was adopted in 1705. It allowed litigants to submit disputes to arbitration voluntarily. In 1810, arbitration was made compulsory if one of the parties requested it. These provisions were incorporated in the subsequent statute of 1836, which dealt with the issue of arbitration. In 1951, the legislature amended the 1836 statute to allow the Common Pleas Court to order compulsory arbitration in all cases involving a dispute over an amount less than $1,000.

Quaker tenets allowed a plethora of religious sects to flourish in Pennsylvania. Most German settlers belonged to the Lutheran and Reformed churches; the Mennonites, Amish, and German Baptist Brethren also found freedom to worship there. The rich diversity of religious sects owed largely to Penn's principles and the freedom of expression that prevailed in the early commonwealth. Later, those same principles helped draw Jews and Orthodox Christian Slavs from Eastern Europe.

This cultural and religious diversity created the context for a vibrant intellectual life. Pennsylvania was a leader in law and medicine; the first hospital, first library, and first insurance company in the United States were established in Philadelphia. Because the American Revolution had urban origins, Philadelphia represented the center of resistance, taking a stand against the Stamp Act and supporting Boston in opposition to the Intolerable Acts in 1774. On the eve of the Revolution, Pennsylvania was the third largest British colony in population and provided leadership for the evolution of a nation. Yet despite this prominence, political changes within Pennsylvania prompted extralegal committees to take over the reins of government and call for a state convention in July 1776. The new constitution, adopted on September 28, 1776, provided a legislature of one house and a supreme executive council instead of a governor. In 1790, the constitution was rewritten to add a second legislative house and create the basis for a strong governor. In 1838, a convention was again called to revise state laws and draft a new constitution, this time resulting in a reduction of the governor's power and an increase in the number of elective offices. And in 1968, nearly a hundred years after another constitutional revision in 1874, the present constitution of Pennsylvania was drafted.

Because of its Quaker origins, in the nation's early years Pennsylvania spearheaded the organized effort to oppose slavery. Pennsylvania's role in the antislavery movement is marked by a state statute against kidnapping that was passed in 1788 and made illegal the practice in which slave speculators (slavers) purchased the rights to runaway slaves and then resold them at a profit. The Pennsylvania state statute was a precursor to the Fugitive Slave Act of 1826, which prevented the return to their owners of slaves who had fled to free states. Pennsylvania also played an important part in establishing the so-called underground railroad to help slaves in the South escape to freedom in the North.

The growth of industry in Pennsylvania in the nineteenth century also made the state a leader in the growth of labor unions. The Iron Molders Union under William H. Sylvis in 1859 epitomized the spirit of organized labor in Pennsylvania. Sylvis saw that unions would have to organize nationally if they were going to be effective. Similarly, the Knights of Labor and the American Federation of Labor made the Commonwealth of Pennsylvania the site of some of the largest strikes (1879 and 1881) in the history of the American labor. Ironically, however, the steel industry was not unionized until the late 1930s. After World War II, labor strikes erupted. The infamous steel strikes of 1952 and 1959–1960 resulted in the intervention of Presidents Harry S. Truman and Dwight D. Eisenhower. President Truman seized the steel industry when companies rejected the Wage Stabilization Board's recommendations. An eight-week strike followed when the Supreme Court found the president's actions unconstitutional. And while the recession of the 1970s undermined the vitality of the labor unions in the steel industry, unionization of other workers has continued on.

The origins of the Pennsylvanian judiciary are complex. Some of the courts were based upon the ideas of the Duke of York, while others were established by William Penn. Notably, the courts were run locally by nonlawyers and operated on a part-time basis. Because the overriding authority for colonial legislation rested with the Crown in London, attempts to establish a final court of appeal in Pennsylvania were delayed. In 1722, the Judiciary Act at last created the Pennsylvania Supreme Court. This court met twice a year in Philadelphia and traveled the circuit during the interim. The bill also created the Court of Common Pleas in Philadelphia, Bucks, and Chester Counties. Between 1790 and 1850, constitutional changes and the demands of an increasing workload effected changes in the jurisdiction and tenure of the judiciary. In 1895 the Pennsylvania General Assembly established the Superior Court to hear appeals from certain decisions of the courts of common pleas. The Superior Court is often the final arbiter of legal disputes in Pennsylvania. Although the Supreme Court may grant a petition for an appeal from a decision of the Superior Court, in most cases such petitions are denied.

CURRENT STRUCTURE

The state constitution of 1968 gave the Pennsylvania judiciary its current form. The Unified Judicial System includes the Supreme Court, Superior Court, and Commonwealth Court, the courts of common pleas, the Philadelphia municipal court, the Pittsburgh Magistrates' Court, the Philadelphia traffic court, and district justice. The Supreme Court is Pennsylvania's highest court, the court of last resort, and supervises all other state courts. In 1980, as caseloads increased, the legislature responded by reducing the mandated jurisdiction of the Supreme Court and expanding that of the Superior Court.

The Pennsylvania Supreme Court has four specific jurisdictions: original, appellate, discretionary, and extraordinary. Its original jurisdiction includes writs of mandamus, issues prohibited from other courts; writs of habeas corpus, in cases involving the denial of due process; and quo warranto writs, lawsuits challenging the right of an individual to hold public office. In 1980, the legislature approved a modification of the Supreme Court's mandated jurisdiction. The Pennsylvania Supreme Court exercises its discretion in accepting or rejecting most appellate cases that originate in the commonwealth courts or in appeals from final orders from the common pleas courts. The Supreme Court exercises original jurisdiction over issues arising in the various entities under its purview, including the Legislative Reapportionment Commission, the Court of Judicial Discipline, the Minor Judiciary Education Board, the Pennsylvania Board of Law Examiners, and the Disciplinary Board of the Supreme Court. Finally, the Supreme Court exercises extraordinary jurisdiction, on its own or by its direction, over issues of immediate public importance. This jurisdiction is also referred to as king's bench power.

The Superior Court, by order of the Pennsylvania general assembly in 1895, hears appeals from certain decisions of the courts of common pleas. In limited circumstances, the Superior Court exercises original jurisdiction. The matters triggering original jurisdiction include applications made by the attorney general and district attorneys under the Wiretapping and Electronic Surveillance Control Act. The Superior Court is often the de facto final appeal, for the Supreme Court exercises discretion in accepting appeals.

The subject matter of appeals includes child custody, visitation, adoption, divorce and support, criminal cases, wills and estates, property disputes, contractual breaches, and personal injury. Judges of the Superior Court are also responsible for hearing applications made by the attorney general and district attorneys.

The Commonwealth Court was created by an amendment to the state constitution in 1968. The court has both appellate and original jurisdiction. The original jurisdiction is triggered when claims are brought against the commonwealth or an officer of the government. Other instances of original jurisdiction include matters falling under the election code and any civil actions brought by the commonwealth.

Legal Structure of Pennsylvania Courts

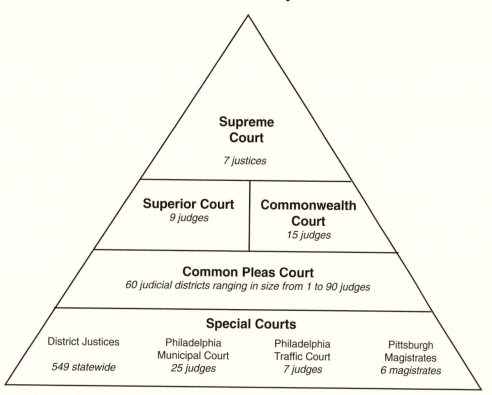

The Commonweath Court hears appeals from county courts of common pleas and state administrative agencies in such matters as zoning, taxation, civil service, negligence involving state or local government, and eminent domain. From state administrative agencies, the Commonwealth Court hears appeals in matters involving workers' and unemployment compensation, environmental issues, welfare claims, and public utility rate disputes.

The courts of common pleas are Pennsylvania's courts of general trial jurisdiction. Since the state constitution of 1776, the common pleas courts have enjoyed constitutional status. Prior to the 1968 constitution, there were also the courts of oyer and terminer and general jail delivery, quarter sessions of the peace, and orphans' courts, all of which were incorporated in 1968 into the existing common pleas courts. There are 60 judicial districts that are generally organized geographically; each district has from 1 to 95 judges. Common pleas courts exercise original jurisdiction over judgments received from special courts presided over by district justices, also called minor courts. The courts of common pleas also hear appeals from specific state and most local government agencies.

The special courts of Pennsylvania are the points of access to the legal system for most Pennsylvania citizens. These courts are also called minor courts. District justices preside over district courts in all counties except Philadelphia. In these minor courts, justices consider nonjury civil matters not exceeding $8,000 and nonjury criminal

matters not involving delinquent acts. These justices may also issue arrest warrants and preside over preliminary arraignments. The minor courts also consider traffic and ordinance violations. Notably, district justices are not required to be lawyers, but nonlawyers wishing to serve as district justices must take a class and pass an examination.

The Philadelphia municipal court is Pennsylvania's only court of record at the minor court level. The jurisdiction of this minor court is in most ways the same as that of the other special courts in Pennsylvania, but its jurisdiction includes all criminal offenses except summary traffic offenses that may result in less than five years' imprisonment. This court may also issue judgment in civil matters under $10,000. All its justices must be lawyers.

In the Philadelphia traffic court, seven justices deal with all traffic and ordinance violations. The justices of this court need not be lawyers, but nonlawyers must complete a course and pass an examination. The governor appoints the president of this court.

Pittsburgh has six separate Magistrates' Courts. These justices are appointed by the mayor of Pittsburgh to four-year terms. They preside over preliminary hearings and arraignments for violations within the city. They also consider traffic and ordinance violations brought by the Pittsburgh police.

The administration of the Pennsylvania courts is established under the commonwealth's 1968 constitution. The Supreme Court exercises general supervisory and

administrative authority and appoints a court administrator, who heads the administrative offices of Pennsylvania courts. There are eight operational units of the administrative offices, four in Philadelphia and four in
Mechanicsburg. These units include court management,
research, legal and judicial services, financial systems,
payroll, human resources, the Judicial Computer Project,
data processing, and communications/legislative affairs.

NOTABLE FEATURES
OF THE PENNSYLVANIA LEGAL SYSTEM

In its 1776 constitution Pennsylvania is designated as
both a commonwealth and a state. Although the distinction between the two terms has no legal significance, official references to Pennsylvania and its legal processes use
the term *commonwealth.*

The antilegalism of Quaker ideology meant that Pennsylvania gained more experience with arbitration than
did most parts of the country. However, despite the early
trend toward arbitration in Pennsylvania, the system of
resolving disputes eventually fell under judicial supervision. Over time, arbitration ceased to be independent in
Pennsylvania and instead became an accepted component of the state court system.

The sentencing structure in Pennsylvania allows the
potential for a misdemeanor to receive a longer sentence
than a felony. Felonies are divided into three degrees. A
felony of the first degree is fixed by the court at not more
than twenty years; a felony of the second degree, not
more than ten years; and a felony of the third degree, not
more than seven years. A misdemeanor, on the other
hand, receives a definite term fixed by the court: five
years in the case of a misdemeanor of the first degree, two
years in the case of a misdemeanor of the second degree,
and one year in the case of a misdemeanor of the third
degree.

STAFFING

All justices and judges, except for district justices and
Philadelphia Traffic Court judges, must be members of
the bar of the Pennsylvania Supreme Court. All justices
and judges, except for special court judges, are elected to
ten-year terms.

District justices and judges of Philadelphia's municipal
and traffic courts are elected to terms of six years. The
mayor appoints judges of Pittsburgh Magistrates' Court
with the advice and consent of the Pittsburgh city council. All such judges shall not be of the same political party.

Except for the Pittsburgh magistrates, judges and district justices are elected for a regular term of office at the
municipal election. Judges and justices may serve an unlimited number of terms. At the end of each term, a judicial officer may file a declaration of candidacy for retention election with the secretary of the commonwealth.

If a judicial officer files a declaration, the name is submitted to the electors without party designation, as a separate judicial question or in a separate column at the municipal election preceding the expiration of the judge's
term of office. If a majority is against retention, the vacancy is filled by appointment. A vacancy in the office of
judge or district justice is filled by appointment by the
governor with the advice and consent of two-thirds of the
senate, in the case of judges, or a simple majority of senators, in the case of district justices. The appointed officer serves for a term ending on the first Monday of January following the next municipal election more than ten
months after the vacancy occurs or for the remainder of
the unexpired term, whichever is less. This appointed judicial officer may then file for a retention election.

The mandatory retirement age for judges is seventy.
Retired judges may, however, serve the Commonwealth
Court as senior judges to ease the backlog of cases.

The Superior Court was originally composed of seven
judges, but in 1978 the Supreme Court ordered it to construct panels of three judges composed of a Supreme
Court justice, a Superior Court judge, and a common
pleas judge. Each panel would constitute a quorum and
represent the position of the entire Superior Court. In
1979 the Pennsylvania Constitution was amended to
allow the Superior Court to be enlarged to fifteen seats.

Pennsylvania has seven law schools: at Dickinson College, in Carlisle; at Duquesne University, in Pittsburgh; at
the University of Pennsylvania, in Philadelphia; at the
University of Pittsburgh, in Pittsburgh; at Temple University, in Philadelphia; at Villanova University, in Villanova; and at Widener College, in Harrisburg. Starting
salaries at Pennsylvania law firms are generally lower than
the national average for the small and mid-sized firms
(from two to fifty lawyers) and the largest firms (over 250
attorneys). Pennsylvania has 60,000 attorneys serving 12
million residents, approximately one lawyer for every 200
people. The proportion of attorneys in Pennsylvania continues to exceed the nation's. One of every 218 Pennsyl-
vanians is licensed to practice law, compared to one of
every 295 Americans nationwide. Some 39 percent of
Pennsylvania lawyers, about 22,000, are in private practice. Of these, almost 40 percent, about 8,000, are solo
practitioners. Roughly one-quarter (24.9 percent) of
lawyers in Pennsylvania are women.

Candidates for membership in the bar of Pennsylvania
must, in addition to passing a written examination, meet
certain requirements relating to character and prior conduct. They must file a written application including
background information pertaining to reputation, education, and employment. The Pennsylvania Board of Law
Examiners recommends individuals to the practice of law
in the state. This process includes reviewing admission
applications and considering applications from attorneys

in other states seeking admittance to the bar without sitting for the examination. As to lawyers who have been disbarred on account of professional misconduct, Pennsylvania has the highest readmission rate, 86 percent, of any of the large states.

Lisa Nelson

See also Appellate Courts; Constitutional Review; Judicial Review; Legal Education; United States—Federal System; United States—State Systems

References and further reading
Administration Office of Pennsylvania. 1998. "Annual Report 1998." http://www.courts.state.pa.us/Index/Aopc/AnnualReport/annual98/ann98toc.asp.
Albert, William. 2000. "A Consumer View of Pennsylvania Legal Practice: Learning from our Mistakes." *Pennsylvania Bar Association Quarterly* 70 (April): 71–81.
Curran, Barbara, and Carla N. Carson. 1991. *The U.S. Legal Profession in the 1990s.* American Bar Foundation.
FindLaw. N.d. Report on Pennsylvania law schools. http://stu.findlaw.com/schools/pennsylvania.html.
Loyd, William H. 1986 [1910]. *The Early Courts of Pennsylvania.* University of Pennsylvania Law School Series, no. 2. Littleton, CO: F. B. Rothman.
Matthews-Giba, F. 2000. "Religious Dimensions of Mediation." *Fordham Urban Law Journal* 27 (June): 1695.
Nash, Gary. 1966. "The Framing of Government in Pennsylvania: Ideas in Contact with Reality." *William and Mary Quarterly* 3 (April): 183–209.
Nejelski, Paul, and Andrew Zeldin. 1983. "Court-Annexed Arbitration in the Federal Courts: The Philadelphia Story." *Maryland Law Review* 27: 787.
Owen, Ireland. 1973. "Ethnic and Religious Dimensions in Pennsylvania Politics, 1778–1779." *William and Mary Quarterly* 3 (July): 423–448.
Rowe, G. S. 2000. *Embattled Bench: The Pennsylvania Supreme Court and the Forging of a Democratic Society, 1684–1809.* Newark: University of Delaware Press.
Thompson, Anne Marie. 1996. "Profiles of Pennsylvania Law Schools: A Guide to Where Lawyers Come From." *Pennsylvania Lawyer* 18 (February): 12.

PERU

COUNTRY INFORMATION

Peru is located on the northern Pacific coast of South America, bordered by Ecuador, Colombia, Brazil, Bolivia, and Chile. Its territory of roughly 1.3 million square kilometers is divided into three regions: the more economically developed arid coast; the mountainous highlands, the traditional seat of the pre-Columbian civilizations; and the Eastern tropical lowlands, which have a relatively sparse population and make up roughly two-thirds of the landmass. The country's 26.6 million inhabitants (1999 estimate) include a mixture of European, Amerindian, Asian, and African ancestries; Amerindians and mestizos (mixed European and Amerindian) constitute 42 and 37

percent, respectively. Racial classifications, as in many parts of Latin America, are as much culturally as genetically based; an Indian who moves to the city or enters the modern economy, speaks Spanish, and adopts Western clothing becomes a mestizo. While movement in the other direction is less common, it occurred in the colonial period during times of economic hardship, and today, some mestizos are reasserting their indigenous heritage.

For much of its independent history, Peru has been characterized by a boom-and-bust development, driven by the rise and fall of one or another raw material export. This has made it extremely vulnerable to fluctuations in world prices and to climatic and other natural disasters. It also contributes to the extremely unequal distribution of income. Despite the economic improvements of the late twentieth century, almost 50 percent of the population lives below the poverty line. Poverty is most prevalent among indigenous groups in the rural highlands, but migration from the countryside has created large slums in the major urban areas.

As of 1997, the gross domestic product (GDP) composition by sector was 7 percent agriculture, 37 percent industry and mining, and 56 percent services. Current major exports are: minerals (copper, zinc, lead, refined silver), fishmeal, crude petroleum and its by-products, coffee, and cotton. Unemployment is estimated at 8.2 percent; underemployment may be several times that figure. Direct state participation in the economy has declined rapidly since the 1970s, when state expenditures reached 25 percent of the GDP, and most key industries and services were state-controlled. Cutbacks in government employment and a massive privatization program under the administration of President Alberto Fujimori accelerated the transition to a market economy, as well as eliminating the hyperinflation of the late 1980s, restoring positive growth rates, and attracting foreign investment.

HISTORY

Long before the arrival of the Spanish colonizers, Peru was the center of a series of dynamic and complex Amerindian civilizations. By the late fifteenth century, the most recent of these, the Incas, had conquered an empire that extended into what is now Ecuador to the north and to the northern reaches of modern Chile. Beset by internal conflicts, the Incas quickly fell to the Spaniards, who replaced them as the masters of the subjugated peoples. Disease and harsh working conditions rapidly decimated the indigenous population, encouraging the adoption of still harsher policies to ensure access to the native workforce. Individual colonists received legal claim to much of the inhabited territory, thereby enhancing their control over the supply of labor. However, the Spaniards established their major settlements on the coast, creating a new capital, Lima. This facilitated communication with the

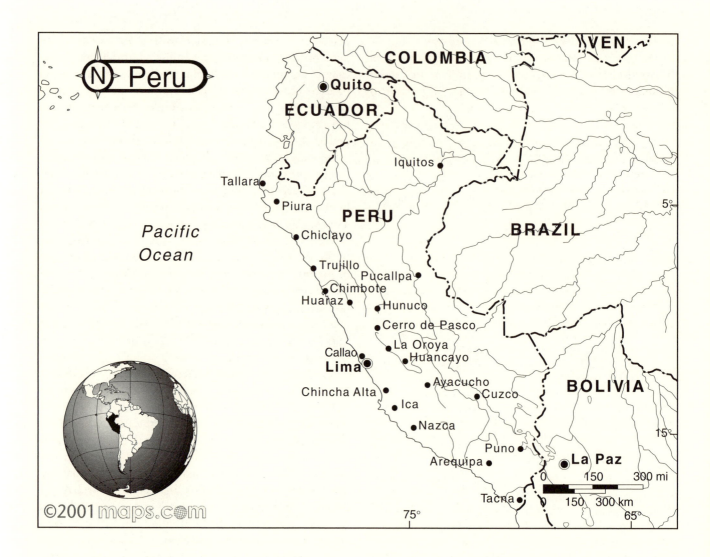

Map labels:

Peru

N | Peru

COLOMBIA
VEN
Quito
ECUADOR
Iquitos
Tallara
5°
Piura
PERU
Pacific
Ocean
Chiclayo
Trujillo
Pucallpa
BRAZIL
Chimbote
Huaraz
Hunuco
Cerro de Pasco
La Oroya
Callao
Huancayo
Lima
Ayacucho
BOLIVIA
Chincha Alta
Cuzco
Ica
Nazca
Puno
15°
Arequipa
La Paz
0   150   300 mi
0   150   300 km
Tacna
75°
65°

©2001 maps.com

---

outside world but weakened contacts with the traditional highlands, forcing a dependence on intermediaries, indirect controls, and parallel institutions to link the old and new population centers. Thus, while the Spanish brought their legal institutions with them, outside the urban areas, traditional practices and the will of the local *cacique* (boss), either the large landowner or his resident manager, were the effective law until well into the present century.

Peru, one of Spain's most valuable viceroyalties, came to independence reluctantly in 1824. Civil wars and irregular transfers of government persisted until the 1870s, when Peruvians elected their first civilian president. From 1895 to 1919, the country enjoyed an unprecedented period of peaceful civilian rule and rapid and diversified economic growth. Increasing social tensions brought the eleven-year dictatorship of August Leguia (from 1919 to 1930), who curtailed political opposition, opened the country to foreign investment, and ran up the foreign debt with massive infrastructure projects. Leguia also introduced progressive legislation to protect urban workers and professed an interest in the welfare of the Indian majority. Some of these principles were enacted in the new

Constitution of 1920, which also introduced periodic ratifications for seated judges. Through this mechanism and his control of Supreme Court appointments, Leguia kept the judiciary compliant to his will.

Rampant corruption and the worldwide depression brought Leguia's ouster and over thirty years of alternating elected and de facto governments, backed by an alliance of the military, the new urban elites, and the traditional large landowners. Urban elites benefited in that economic growth was largely centered on the coast. Government remained small and noninterventionist, but it did finance the military and provide employment for a significant portion of a small but expanding middle class. Meanwhile, the landowners controlled the highlands and the votes (and livelihood) of the rural population. They were, however, the weakest link in the system, and the source of mounting pressures from a rural workforce that could no longer survive without access to land or gainful employment. The period saw the slow growth of the judicial organization and the adoption of new substantive and procedural codes, inspired by the latest European models. However, the impact of these changes was largely limited to modern (that is, urban and coastal) Peru. In the hinterlands, less formal practices continued to prevail. Yet this did not prevent indigenous communities from attempting to access the courts, especially for land disputes with each other or with large holders. Their growing frustrations with slow, formalistic, and often biased justice would eventually lead to more direct action in the form of land invasions and escalating migrations to Lima and other urban areas. Both developments made it increasingly difficult for modern Peru to ignore the situation in the rest of the country.

An eventual breakdown was heralded by a brief but radical military government (from 1962 to 1963). Fernando Belaunde, the president elected in the latter year, represented a last effort to work improvements within the old system. Belaunde attempted a land reform, called for a program of economic and political decentralization, and encouraged broader political participation. His efforts came too late. In 1968, a military coup initiated a "revolutionary government" based on state control of the economy, expropriation of all large landholdings and key industries, and a new form of political participation, without the benefit of the traditional parties or institutions. Although the courts were not initial targets of the revolutionaries, their refusal to back the government changed the plan. Beginning in 1969, the military conducted several irregular purges of the judiciary, eliminated the Ministry of Justice and nascent Public Ministry, introduced a judicial council to vet and select judges, created new agrarian and labor courts outside the ordinary court structure, and, based on their 1975 Supreme Court appointments, turned the judiciary over to the "New Law" group, which immediately announced a still more radical restructuring.

The New Law group's reign was short-lived: Most of their plans went straight to the judicial archives. By the mid-1970s, political and economic mismanagement and corruption had taken their toll, precipitating an internal coup by a more conservative military faction and a gradual return to civilian government. What was returned was far different from what the military inherited in 1968. Escalating unrest and unmet popular expectations, an overextended state, opportunistic politicians, and rampant corruption characterized the next two and a half elected civilian administrations and precipitated the *autogolpe* (self-coup) of President Alberto Fujimori in April 1992. Still, during the twelve years of constitutional democracy, the judiciary experienced further changes. The 1979 Constitution allowed the civilian government entering in 1980 to conduct its own special judicial purge; reinstated the Ministry of Justice and Public Ministry, the latter as a semiautonomous body responsible for criminal prosecution (although not investigation, which remained with an instructional judge); reduced the judi-

cial council's role to vetting judicial candidates for final selection by the executive; and created the separate Constitutional Court. The special agrarian and labor courts were gradually reabsorbed into the ordinary court system.

It took Fujimori and his military backers only a few years to undo much of the military's work. A massive privatization campaign eliminated most of the state-owned enterprises and the bureaucratic structure established to run them. The two major ills, hyperinflation and terrorism, were defeated by 1992, and a constitution, approved by referendum in 1993, consolidated the new rules of the game. Peru's economy, in steady collapse since the mid-1970s, was once again growing, and foreign investment had returned; poverty remained rampant, but it was pushed below the 50 percent mark. Unfortunately, these advances were made by short-circuiting and further undermining democratic processes and institutions. The legislative and judicial branches were the most prominent victims, but even the executive branch suffered. Much of its budget and the most effective agencies were concentrated in the Ministry of the Presidency or the Ministry of the Economy. Having accomplished what he had promised, the president and his military allies were also reluctant to step down. In a move in apparent violation of his own constitution, Fujimori was elected for a third term in April 2000. Six months later, a scandal involving Vladimiro Montesinos, his principal adviser and the alleged power behind the throne, precipitated Montesinos's flight, Fujimori's self-imposed exile in Japan, and the transfer of effective power to a transitional government. New elections were held in April 2001. Following a runoff in June, Alejandro Toledo was proclaimed president.

LEGAL CONCEPTS

Peru is a unitary republic; its twenty-four departments and one "constitutional province" are mere administrative divisions, all law is national (although municipal governments may issue regulations), and the major justice sector institutions are nationally based. Since 1969, there have been various attempts to create a smaller number of regional governments, but so far, they have met with little success. All recent constitutions have recognized three principal branches of government, with a series of other entities (Public Ministry, Human Rights Ombudsman, Electoral Board, Comptroller) accorded semi-independent status. While the current government, like its predecessors, features a strong presidency, this is a matter as much of political practice as of constitutional dictate.

Officially, Peru's constitution is the supreme law of the land. International treaties are incorporated automatically as ordinary law, but those affecting constitutional provisions require constitutional amendments. Excepting these cases and those affecting human rights, national sovereignty, national defense, or state financial obligations, the president may ratify the treaty without prior congressional approval. Many governments have chosen to ignore inconvenient constitutional provisions or used their exceptional powers to waive them temporarily. Contrary to regional trends, the 1993 Constitution conspicuously reduces the social and economic rights accumulated over the prior decades, simplifies government structure (for example, replacing the bicameral legislature with a smaller, unicameral body), limits government intervention in the economy, and consciously adopts a market framework. It also is unusual in its reduced length, due in large part to the elimination (or reservation for secondary law) of detailed descriptions of the internal organization and procedures of many public organizations.

The three most recent constitutions do coincide in their guarantee of basic political rights—including due process, property, privacy, and freedom of speech, religion, the press, movement, and assembly. However, the president's ability to declare exceptional states allows him to waive some of these rights, across the board or in specific regions of the country. After 1993, his ability to do so has been aided by a more easily controlled unicameral legislature, its 120 members elected (under transitory dispositions) from a single national district. The three constitutions also declare the independent status of the judicial branch of government, and in the 1979 version, the judiciary was guaranteed 2 percent of the national budget. Other sector organizations given constitutional status include the National Magistrates Council, the Judicial Academy, the Public Ministry, the Constitutional Court, the Ministry of Justice, and the National Police.

Peru inherited a civil code tradition from the Spanish, and in a history of further modifications, it has always looked first to Europe for models. Major procedural and substantive codes can usually be traced to European examples, as can such recent innovations as the Judicial Council, Judicial Academy, and Constitutional Court. Over the past few decades, this process has produced efforts to abandon the inquisitorial criminal justice system, to introduce oral trials in all proceedings, and to increase the role of various alternative mechanisms. However, an early emphasis on the separation of powers and provisions for judicial review is clearly influenced by the United States. Needless to say, Peru also has a strong tradition of partial implementation of its legal frameworks. Still, it was among the first in the region to establish an independent Public Ministry (1982), and by 1940, it was already conducting oral trials (still based, however, on the case file, or *expediente,* assembled by an instructional judge).

Peru was also early in establishing mechanisms for protesting the violation of constitutional rights. Prior to 1979, this was accomplished through a writ of habeas corpus, most often used for illegal detention but theoretically of far greater applicability. The 1979 Constitution introduced the writ of *amparo* to cover all rights but that of individual liberty, leaving habeas corpus for the latter. The 1993 Constitution added the writs of *habeas data* (for release of information managed by a public entity) and compliance (against a public agency's act of omission). Both constitutions provide several means for entering a protest against an unconstitutional law or regulation, some of which were never attempted in practice. Under both the 1979 and 1993 Constitutions, the review of constitutionality is reserved for the Constitutional Court or tribunal, and while it has been exercised, legislation introduced in 1996 (requiring agreement of six of the seven justices to declare a law unconstitutional) seems designed to reduce the recourse to a minimum. Individual judges are still constitutionally empowered to refuse to apply an unconstitutional law; the recent experience of those who have followed this mandate is not positive.

Over the past century, Peru's constitutions and secondary law have grappled with the dilemma of how to deal with the large and traditionally exploited indigenous population. The 1924 Criminal Code promised special detention centers for Indians convicted of crimes, in the belief that they could not bear the same responsibility as other citizens. The military's agrarian and labor courts were provided with abbreviated procedures and instructed to ensure that their clients (the rural and urban poor) were adequately apprised of their rights and defended against predatory elites. The military also gave Quechua and Aymara the status of official languages (along with Spanish); the current constitution accepts the first officially and recognizes the second. Peru's 4,000 lay justices of the peace are chosen on the basis of their local standing and expected to make their decisions in accord with both local custom and national law. The 1979 Constitution promised to protect indigenous culture, but only the 1993 document provides for indigenous communities to retain their own systems for resolving conflicts, as long as they did not contradict universal human rights standards.

CURRENT STRUCTURE

Since late 1969, the structure of the justice sector has undergone substantial change, and more appears in store. In fact, some of the most questionable innovations (the executive commissions and the transitory courts) have been eliminated. In December 2000, a Transitory Commission was named to evaluate the changes introduced during the Fujimori period and repeal those considered in violation of the constitution. Meanwhile, the Constitutional Court, the governing bodies of the judiciary and the Public Ministry, and the Judicial Council have had their full constitutional powers restored. Several of their members, as well as other judges and *fiscales* (prosecutors) with close ties to the Fujimori regime, have been removed, and some, including two former attorneys general, now face criminal charges.

Despite the use of judicial misbehavior as a pretext for this "self-coup," President Fujimori's judicial reform measures have themselves been criticized for circumventing legal and even constitutional guarantees. In 1991 and 1992 (just prior to the self-coup), the legislature approved several new laws affecting judicial organization and procedures. The new Civil Procedures and Criminal Codes were allowed to go into effect, but the accompanying Criminal Procedures Code, after repeated modifications, has only entered partially. A new Organic Law for the Judiciary was also substantially modified. The first change, quickly following on the de facto government's temporary closure of the courts, reduced Supreme Court membership from the new thirty-one justices to eighteen. The government also closed the Constitutional Court and conducted further massive purges of both the judiciary and the Public Ministry, replacing redundant employees with provisional judges and *fiscales*. Provisional appointees to the Supreme Court raised its membership to the former level, but with their removal in 2001, the number dropped to twelve.

The 1993 Constitution is the basis for the current organization. It reinstated the Constitutional Tribunal and National Magistrates Council, expanding the latter's powers to selecting as well vetting both judges and *fiscales*. Two significant changes were a provision for the election of justices of the peace and the recognition of indigenous law. The government dragged its feet on implementation: The council and tribunal, along with the newly created Human Rights Ombudsman office (Defensor del Pueblo), only became operational in 1996. The first elections of justices of the peace were held in 1999, but the provision on indigenous law has yet to be put into effect. Law 26648 of November 1995 created the Executive Commission to replace the Supreme Court's internal governance body (the Executive Council, composed of the chief justice, three other justices, and a representative of the bar associations). The commission was headed by an executive secretary, chosen by the government and charged with overseeing an emergency period of judicial reform. A similar body was later created for the Public Ministry, headed by a former *fiscal de la nacion* (attorney general), distinguished by her unconditional loyalty to President Fujimori. Law 26623 (June 1996) provided for the creation of the Judicial Coordinating Council to supersede the commission. However, it was never fully implemented, and, until their elimination in late 2000, effective power remained with the two commissions.

The emergency reform had further effects on the sector's structure. In addition to changes in staffing (see the later discussion), it created a series of transitory courts, some of them as part of a backlog reduction program and others to attend to special concerns of the government. These latter "specialized" transitory courts (drugs, tax crimes) were especially susceptible to political control. Clashes between the reformers and the National Magistrates Council over the council's constitutional mandate to manage the judicial career (that is, selecting and disciplining or removing judges) led to the restriction of the council's powers and resignation of its members. Similar clashes with the government itself brought the dismissal of three of the seven members of the Constitutional Tribunal. While both bodies still existed, they were virtually inoperative. Additional changes altered the internal structure of individual courts, created itinerant appellate bodies, modified the structures and powers of Supreme Court dependencies (for example, the Office of Judicial Control), and gave the Judicial Academy responsibility for evaluating judges, under the direction of the commission.

As regards the judiciary itself, the current structure retains the basic divisions visible throughout the twentieth century. It is headed by a Supreme Court, until recently deprived of its former role of judicial governance but retaining its specialized appellate functions. As people elsewhere in Latin America, Peruvians have attempted to transform the Supreme Court from a third-instance trial court to one focused on the review of legal issues (*casacion*). Current caseloads suggest only partial success. There is a second level of Superior Courts with both appellate and trial functions and a lower level of trial courts, now called *juzgados especializados*. At a still lower level are the lawyer (*jueces de paz letrados*) and lay (*jueces de paz*) justices of the peace. Both see minor civil and criminal cases, as defined by the size of the claim or the likely penalty. The country is divided into twenty-seven judicial districts, each headed by a Superior Court, which like the Supreme Court is divided into panels (*salas*) specialized by functional jurisdiction. The usual divisions are criminal, civil, family, labor, constitutional (Supreme Court only), and administrative. In smaller districts, both Superior Court panels and the lower trial courts may combine specializations. Lima's Superior Court has the most complex organization, with seventeen panels, divided by both material and type of proceedings, and a similarly complex division extends to its trial courts.

The Public Ministry's divisions mirror those of the court—except that there is no counterpart to the *jueces de paz*. Most members handle criminal or criminal and civil matters (in mixed jurisdictions). Some also attend (with no major role) purely civil cases. *Fiscales* do not represent the state in cases of interest to it. This role is played by a separate set of *procuradores,* or in-house lawyers hired by state agencies, and, in theory, directed by the Ministry of Justice. Traditionally, members of the Public Ministry were expected to represent society's interests and ensure compliance with legal procedures. It was only in 1982 that

Legal Structure of Peru Courts

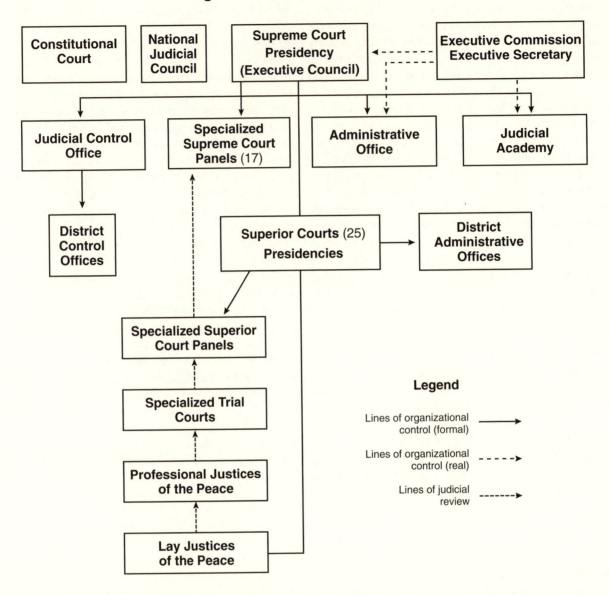

they received organizational independence from the judiciary. With the gradual move to a more adversarial system, the *fiscales* now oversee investigations and criminal prosecution. In theory this should also mean a more active role for defense counsel, but despite the indigent status of most criminal defendants, for most of its history Peru's public defense system retained an extraordinarily traditional and very ineffective structure. Under the Fujimori government, it was composed of only fifty lawyers assigned to individual courts and appointed and paid by the Ministry of Justice. There was no separate office to oversee their work, set policies, and supervise performance. The ministry has since increased the number to 260 and introduced an organizational structure. The ministry also runs twenty-three legal service clinics in Lima and a few provincial cities, providing legal advice to poor clients.

SPECIALIZED JUDICIAL BODIES

Peru has always had judicial bodies located outside the ordinary court system. The first of these are the military courts, the importance and jurisdiction of which fluctuate across administrations. During the height of the Fujimori antiterrorist campaign (between 1992 and 1995), these courts were especially well known for their faceless judges, responsible for trying most terrorist cases (especially after the ordinary court system proved incapable of setting up its own faceless courts). The military judges' ability to try civilians has been under debate since at least 1969. In theory, the Supreme Court has the final word in assigning jurisdiction, but justices have been susceptible to government pressure on this matter.

Over its history, Peru has also had a series of administrative or other special tribunals outside the ordinary court systems. Currently, the most important are the tax courts under the Tax Superintendency, although those accused of criminal tax evasion have their cases seen by specialized judges or panels of the ordinary court system. A brief experiment with drug courts (in 1996 and 1997) was also superseded by the referral of these cases to a specialized Supreme Court panel. The judiciary is currently reviewing these arrangements as the specialized panels and judges are suspected of numerous abuses. The Fujimori administration promoted other mechanisms for resolving conflicts that might go to the judiciary—the most successful of these is undoubtedly the National Institute for Defense of Competition and Intellectual Property (INDECOPI), which deals with consumer complaints, bankruptcy, patents, and competition law, relying extensively on mediation. An arbitration law, passed in 1992, has also encouraged the use of that device by businesses. The Chamber of Commerce has one of the most important services and has heard up to seventy-four cases (contesting a total of $52,549,370) annually. The government has also created a series of special offices (Demunas, Ombudsmen for Children and Adolescents) to oversee cases involving minors; they rely extensively on mediation. Finally, a recent law makes some kind of mediation, judicially annexed or independent, compulsory prior to submission to the judiciary of most types of civil cases. It currently affects only Lima and three other departments but is expected to soon have national coverage.

Without question, the most successful and popular recent innovation is the human rights ombudsman, *defensor del pueblo*. While the ombudsman's office cannot issue binding rulings, it can investigate alleged government abuses, including those of the courts themselves, and either recommend further action or negotiate a solution with the parties. A prohibition on its entering military installations is a serious impediment to efforts to exert control over the armed forces. One of the Defensoria's most important activities was reviewing the cases of prisoners held or sentenced for terrorism and securing presidential pardons for almost 500. Even with five field offices, the Defensoria's capacity is limited, and it must choose cases carefully. Thus, while it was a thorn in the government's side, it was a small one, perhaps explaining its amazing independence; of the 60,000 citizen complaints it has handled since September, 1996, 20,000 were directed against state agencies.

STAFFING

For a country of its geographic characteristics and population, Peru has always had relatively few judges. As of 2001, the professional judiciary numbered roughly 1,500, with an additional 4,600 lay justices of the peace. The Public Ministry has about 1,000 *fiscales*. Excepting the lay justices of the peace, this represents an increase of roughly 50 percent over the pre-1990 numbers. The lay justices of the peace considerably improve the coverage, but they work only part-time, are not legally trained, and receive no salaries for their labors. Reliable statistics on filing rates and caseloads are not available, but even with backlog-reduction programs, the number carried from one year to another continues to rise. Figures released by the Executive Commission show all Superior Courts handling 1,088,685 active cases in 1996 and 1,781,861 in 1999, with carryovers of 682,502 and 772,683, respectively.

The most serious concern, however, regards the status of the judges and *fiscales*. Following the Fujimori purges, most of these officials (an estimated 80 percent at present) have either provisional or *suplente* (substitute) status. A provisional appointee is a tenured judge who has been assigned to a position higher than his or her actual grade; a *suplente* is a lawyer hired to fill a vacancy but not enjoying tenure. Both categories were supposed to be temporary, but many incumbents have been in these posts for years. It is widely believed that their situation increased their vulnerability to political pressures and corruption, as well as discouraging broader recruitment. Even with recent salary increases, judicial positions are usually not the first choice of practicing lawyers. A comparison of the backgrounds of the seated bench with those holding positions prior to 1992 indicates that the only major difference is greater youth and less experience.

Since January 2001, the newly reactivated Judicial Council has begun to attack the problem of regularizing all appointments. The first two steps were to return all provisional judges and *fiscales* to their official positions and to ratify (evaluate) the 364 tenured officials with seven years or more in their current postings. The ratifications produced 144 dismissals. The larger task, that of filling all positions held by *suplentes*, began in late 2001. Three new Supreme Court justices and one assistant attorney general (*fiscal supremo*) were selected in a nationwide competition. A second competition to fill the remaining 1,890 positions was scheduled for April 2002. The legal requirement that all candidates first pass a training program organized by the Judicial Academy was temporarily waived to avoid additional delays. For a country that had made a practice of reform by judicial purge, this was an unprecedented undertaking, albeit politically unavoidable.

A further major change worked by the Fujimori program affected the support personnel assigned to individual courtrooms. As the former incumbents were a major source of inefficiency and corruption, the reformers introduced a program of early, compensated retirement and sought to replace them with specially trained (and better paid) recent law graduates. In the Lima courts and in other urban centers, the replacement has been almost total. In addition to special training, court personnel are differently organized. A major innovation is the "corporate" courtroom, featuring the use of pooled or shared staff by several judges. This and related changes were believed to lessen the chances for bribe taking by administrative staff. In this and other areas (e.g., delay reduction), the new mechanisms were less successful than promised, in part because of subsequent neglect. Many of the specially trained staff either never took courtroom jobs or left soon after, discouraged by low salaries, limited opportunities for advancement, and a division of labor that left them doing most of the judges' work, a traditional practice that has now been legalized.

Virtually no attention has been paid to another kind of personnel, the private bar. Admission to legal practice requires only a law degree and membership in one of the country's several bar associations. There are no examinations, except what each law faculty may require, and the thirty-three universities offering law degrees vary widely in quality. A national survey from 1997 indicated there were 34,127 practicing attorneys and a nearly equivalent number of law students, many of whom perform some legal work. While bar associations function as effective lobbies, they exercise little control over their members' performance. The largest (29,000 members) and most prestigious, the Lima Bar Association, is said to sanction an average of five members a year.

IMPACT

For at least the past 30 years, Peru's justice system has been criticized for its inefficiency, inefficacy, inaccessibility, and lack of neutrality. It may have been guilty on all these counts before, but its limited reach and lower public expectations discouraged complaints. However, a more complex society, with more conflicts and a greater need for predictable, timely, relevant, and authoritative decisions, has made the judiciary's shortcomings all too visible. Given Peru's recent growth rates, one cannot say the judiciary impeded economic performance, but it certainly made no active contribution. In fact, as currently constituted, the courts seem most in danger of being perceived as irrelevant, or as marginal obstacles for those who cannot find a way to avoid dealing with them.

Surveys taken just after the *autogolpe* indicated a 92 percent public approval rate for the intervention of the judiciary. Despite the addition of judges and courts, new laws, and programs to increase efficiency and reduce backlogs, recent polls do not show much improvement. Ironically, while many respondents indicate a reluctance to use the formal system, a growing caseload makes congestion and delay a chronic problem. The addition of alternative mechanisms has reduced some pressure and apparently pleased many clients. It may also decrease interest in reforming the courts themselves. Given the demoralization and discredited image of the current bench,

handing them full responsibility for self-improvement might not, however, be a viable alternative unless they can somehow find a way to work with their strongest critics, the growing number of independent jurists and civic interest groups who are the most active proponents of a new reform effort.

Linn Hammergren

See also Alternative Dispute Resolution; Appellate Courts; Arbitration; Constitutional Review; Habeas Corpus, Writ of; Human Rights Law; Indigenous and Folk Legal Systems; Inquisitorial Procedure; Judicial Review; Lay Judiciaries; Legal Aid; Legal Education; Mediation; Prosecuting Authorities; Trial Courts

References and further reading
Comision Andina de Juristas. 1996. *Region Andina, 1995: Modernizacion e inestablidad*. Lima.
De Belaunde, Javier. 1998. "Justice, Legality, and Judicial Reform." Pp. 173–191 in *Fujimori's Peru: The Political Economy*. Edited by John Crabtree and Jim Thomas. London: Institute of Latin American Studies.
Hammergren, Linn. 1998. *The Politics of Justice and Justice Reform in Latin America: Peru in Comparative Perspective*. Boulder, CO: Westview.
Lawyers Committee for Human Rights. 2000. "Building on Quicksand: The Collapse of the World Bank's Judicial Reform Project in Peru." New York.
Ledesma Narvaez, Marianella. 1999. *Jueces y reforma judicial*. Lima: Gaceta Juridica.
Leon Pastor, Ricardo. 1996. *Diagnostico de la cultura judicial peruana*. Lima: Academia de la Magistratura.
Ortiz de Zevallos, Gabriel, and Pierina Pollarolo, eds. 2000. *Reforma del poder judicial*. Lima: Instituto Apoyo.
Pasara, Luis. 1982. *Jueces, justicia, y poder en el Peru*. Lima: CEDYS.
Youngers, Coletta A. 2000. *Deconstructing Democracy: Peru under President Alberto Fujimori*. Washington, DC: Washington Office on Latin America.

PHILIPPINES

GENERAL INFORMATION

Some seventy-one hundred islands compose the nation known as the Philippines. Close to seventy million people inhabit the 300,000 square kilometers of the archipelago. The country is divided into seventy-two provinces within twelve major regions (Illocos, Cagayan Valley, and Central Luzon in the north; Southern Tagalog, Bicol, and the Western, Central, and Eastern Visayas in the center; and Western, Northern, Southern, and Central Mindanao in the south). More than half the population resides in the northern region of Luzon, which includes the capital area of Manila. Approximately 25 percent of the population lives in the central Visayas, and 21 percent in the southern province of Mindanao. Some 91 percent of the population is Christian Malay, 4 per-

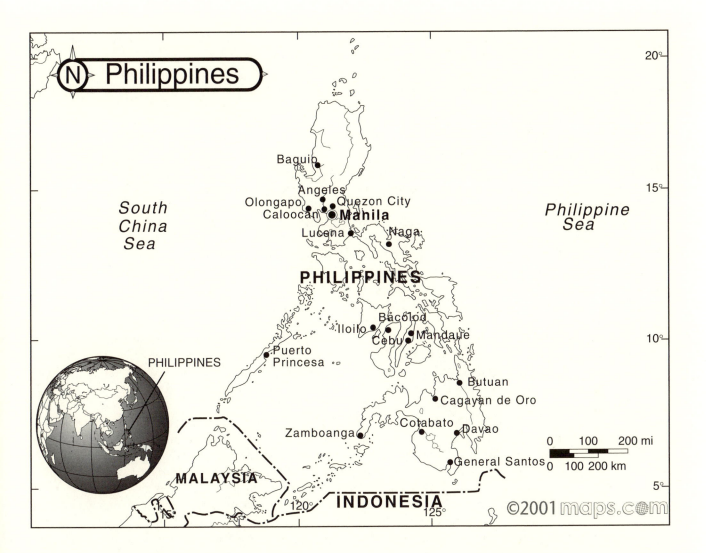

cent Muslim Malay, and close to 1 percent Chinese. Another 3 percent of the population is composed of various tribal groups. The predominant religion is Roman Catholicism (over 80 percent). Iglesia ni Kristo and other Protestant denominations compose approximately 9 percent, another 5 percent are Muslim, and the remaining population is distributed among a variety of Buddhist, Daoist, and other religions. The life expectancy for women is sixty-nine years, and sixty-four years for men.

While both English and Tagalog are the official languages, some eleven languages and eighty-seven dialects are used throughout the islands. About half of the population lives below the poverty line. As of 1997, the unemployment rate was 8.7 percent, the Gross Domestic Product was $3,200 per capita, and the GDP's real growth rate was approximately 5.1 percent (CIA World Factbook 1998). The climate is tropical, and the monsoon occurs in the northeast from December to February and in the southwest from May to October. The country's location in Southeast Asia has made the Philippines of particular strategic interest to the United States as a global midway point.

HISTORY

The first inhabitants of the islands, the Negritos, are presumed to have arrived via land bridges more than thirty thousand years ago. Subsequent Malay populations arriving by water scattered over the islands. These settlers formed *barangays*, or small communities, headed by a *datu*, or chief. These *barangays* were the basic social structure and exist today as well. By 1500, Indonesian settlers brought their Islamic faith with them and spread throughout the southern region of the country. While Muslims established their own political structures around the territorial states, the majority of the population remained in the *barangay* settlements.

On March 16, 1521, Ferdinand Magellan reached Cebu and claimed the land for Charles I of Spain; he was killed by a local chief one month later. Subsequent expeditions established Spanish domination, with its capital in Manila. The islands were named after Philip II, who ruled Spain from 1556 to 1598. The loosely structured spiritual beliefs of the indigenous populations were replaced in the sixteenth and seventeenth centuries with Catholicism, one of the primary objectives of Spanish colonization. With only the short intervention of British rule from 1762 to 1778, Spain utilized the Philippines both for its exports—indigo, tea, silk, opium poppies, and tobacco—and as a trading post with Mexico.

During Spanish rule both major and minor trial courts existed under the aegis of the Royal Decree of May 1583, supplanted by the Royal Decree of 1595. The superior courts consisted of the Audiencia Territorial de Manila, the Audiencia de lo Criminal de Cebua, and the Audiencia de lo Criminal de Cigan. Minor courts were composed of the courts of first instance, as well as justice of the peace courts. The Spanish Civil Code supplanted the indigenous legal rules of the *barangays* whenever the two come into conflict. Although a judicial body, the Audience also exercised executive powers in the absence of the Spanish governor and served as advisor to the government. The Supreme Court of Spain maintained appellate jurisdiction over all legal matters (Supreme Court of the Philippines 2000, 1–2).

In conjunction with its Cuban confrontation in 1898, the United States seized Manila Bay, destroying the Spanish fleet in May of that year. Filipinos joined American troops to defeat the Spanish, and a prearranged surrender occurred in August 1898. Filipinos had hoped that the U.S. presence would be short-lived; they were quickly disappointed. Two days after the faux battle and subsequent surrender, General Merritt, the military leader of the U.S. troops, established a military government that allowed those local municipal, property, and penal laws not in conflict with military objectives to remain in force, but under the administration of the officers appointed by the military government (Supreme Court of the Philippines 2000, 3). Although Filipino revolutionaries would battle the military expedition forces for some three years, they would ultimately fail in their bid for independence.

In May 1899 the military governor reconvened the Audiencia Territorial de Manila, or the Supreme Court of Manila. The court maintained its previous jurisdiction over the subsequently reconvened courts of first instance and the justice of the peace courts in June of that year. Don Cayetano Arellano was appointed president of the Supreme Court, and a mixture of Filipinos and Americans were appointed as associate justices. Despite the title of "court," these bodies were little more than extensions of the military government (Cruz Paño and Martinez 1989, 5–6). A constitution was passed in 1899 paralleling its U.S. counterpart, including a representative assembly, a judiciary, and a president with unlimited four-year terms.

Civil government was established by President McKinley on June 11, 1901, considered the formal beginning of the Philippine legal system. Congress ratified these actions in 1902. Judicial power was vested in a Supreme Court, courts of first instance, justice of the peace courts, and other such courts to be established subsequently as necessary.

The Supreme Court of the United States had appellate jurisdiction over all actions, cases, or proceedings in which the constitution, statute, treaty, title, right, or privilege of the United States was involved, or where the value in the controversy exceeded $25,000.

The Supreme Court was composed of a chief justice and six associate judges. The Supreme Court sat en banc, but five judges constituted a quorum. American appointees dominated the Filipino Supreme Court. From 1901 to 1925, twenty Americans were appointed to the high court, while only eleven Filipinos were appointed during the same period (ibid., 4). In 1935, Philippine citizenship became a requirement, eliminating the capacity of Americans to serve in the courts.

The Supreme Court had original jurisdiction to issue writs of mandamus, certiorari, prohibition, habeas corpus, and quo warranto, as well as to decide other disputes brought before it as provided by law. The court held appellate jurisdiction over all actions and special proceedings from the lower courts and tribunals over which it had jurisdiction.

The courts of first instance had both original and appellate jurisdiction over the justice of the peace courts that were established in every municipality and had jurisdiction over misdemeanors and minor criminal and civil cases. These municipal courts were also established in the non-Christian provinces and worked in conjunction with the tribal ward courts. While the jurisdictions of the two courts were concurrent, the tribal ward courts heard minor civil and criminal actions in which any of the parties in interest was a member of a non-Christian tribe. The governor and secretary were justices of the tribal ward courts, and the sentences of the tribal ward courts were appealable to a court of first instance. Those cases not appealed could still be modified by the provincial governor after a review of the case (ibid., 12).

Every province maintained at least one court of first instance, the trial court of record. One or more judges were named to each district; four additional "judges-at-large" were assigned to various districts by the Secretary of Finance and Justice (a judicial administrator to the chief executive or civil governor) as deemed necessary—for example, in cases of vacancies or absences. Judges were required to have been practicing attorneys or to have held the lawyer's diploma for at least five years, to hold membership in the Philippine Bar, and, as of 1935, to be a Philippine citizen.

Service of notices and execution of orders, as well as the maintenance of courtroom order, was delegated to sheriffs and clerks of court. The city police were responsible for criminal arrests and detentions. Individuals accused of crimes were represented by both public defenders and private counsel. Although assessors—laypersons who assist in trials—were adopted in some provinces, they were not used in the non-Christian areas (ibid., 13–14).

Under the tutelage of the Americans, the Roman law transplanted by the Spanish was integrated with the common law tradition of the United States. Although the early efforts of the revolutionaries had failed, Filipino desire for independence had not waned. Those desires were partially fulfilled with the passage of the independence bill for the Philippines, formally known as the Tydings-McDuffie Act, on March 24, 1934. A constitution was drafted, approved by the president and the Filipino voters in 1936. The Tydings-McDuffie Act mandated a bill of rights as well as continued trade relations for five years. The U.S. Supreme Court maintained appellate review of all court decisions emanating from the archipelago throughout the commonwealth period (Grossholtz 1964, 26–29).

During the commonwealth period, the transitional ten years from the declaration of independence to Philippine autonomy, Japanese forces arrived in 1941, easily defeating the scant American and Filipino troops. The returning American forces had to contend not only with the Japanese forces and the Filipino collaborators, but also with the emerging power of the communist-organized Hukbo ng Bayan Laban sa Hapon ("Peoples' Army to Fight the Japanese"), or the Huks, who continue to battle for control to this day. After regaining control of the Philippines, the United States began efforts to rehabilitate the Philippine economy and the American role in it. On July 4, 1946, the Philippines became an independent republic (ibid., 31–33).

With the minor interruption of the Japanese occupation, the courts continued operation as they had since their creation under the auspices of the United States, but they no longer were responsible to the United States. Indeed, the postwar Philippine Supreme Court emerged as a powerful institution with a reputation for independence and integrity. The court enjoyed both the power of judicial review as well as broad jurisdiction over a number of important economic, political, and social issues (Tate and Haynie 1993). It was considered one of the most powerful and politically respected appellate courts in existence (Becker 1970; Wurfel 1964). Although corruption plagued the newly independent republic, the court was considered largely above the machinations of the other branches and bureaucracies, and it was important in establishing the legitimacy of the rule of law.

Then came Marcos and his declaration of martial law in September 1972, which laid the groundwork for his "constitutional authoritarianism," a process that over time would politicize the courts. While economic woes and the ongoing struggle with the Huks were used as rationalizations for the declaration, without it Marcos could not have sought an additional third term as presi-

dent. Following the declaration of martial law, Marcos disbanded Congress; detained oppositionists; suspended the rights of habeas corpus, speech, press, and assembly; and imposed strict censorship requirements, essentially abandoning all pretense of democratic processes with one exception: the capacity of the courts to review his actions. This review, which was also included in the 1973 Constitution that Marcos engineered, rarely hindered Marcos, since his previous eight years in office provided ample time to pack the courts; ultimately he appointed thirty-two justices to the Supreme Court during his twenty years in office (Haynie 1998; Tate and Haynie 1994). Eventually the court began to reverse its earlier acquiescence and ruled against Marcos in a number of challenges. For example, the court ruled that authorities must show a clear and present danger of a substantive evil to deny a permit (*Reyes v. Bagatsing,* 125 SCRA 553); the government was prohibited from summarily closing a radio station without demonstrating a clear and present danger (*Eastern Broadcasting Corp. v. Dans,* 137 SCRA 628); the court nullified the closure of a newspaper critical of Marcos (*Burgos v. Chief of Staff,* 133 SCRA 800); military officers were prohibited from intimidating members of the media (*Babst v. National Intelligence Board,* 132 SCRA 316); individuals could not be criminally indicted for political discussions (*Salonga v. Pano,* 134 SCRA 438); among others (Cruz Paño and Martinez 1989, 46–47). Despite these decisions, the reputation and prestige of the legal system and the Supreme Court decreased dramatically. Not only were the prestige and popularity of the Supreme Court declining precipitously but so were Marcos's, as evidenced by his electoral defeat in the so-called snap elections, called quickly to limit the capacity of the opposition to organize effectively. Despite the limited time span, voters elected Corazon Aquino, the wife of slain political hero Benigno Aquino, though Marcos refused to accept defeat. Only after the relatively peaceful People's Power Revolution did Marcos take refuge, fleeing in U.S. helicopters.

Aquino's rise to power was followed by the passage of a new constitution in 1987. President Aquino's election has been followed by two peaceful transitions. The first was to President Fidel Ramos in 1992. Ramos served as deputy chief of staff of the armed forces under Marcos, but he threw critical support to Aquino during the 1986 revolt. He served as Aquino's defense secretary and had her backing during the 1992 election. Following the constitutionally mandated single term of six years, Ramos was succeeded by Joseph Estrada in 1998. After a rancorous and ultimately interrupted impeachment proceeding on alleged corruption in the Estrada administration, Vice President Gloria Macapagal Arroyo, daughter of Diasdado Macapagal, Philippine president from 1961 to 1965, was sworn in as the new president in January 2001.

The Supreme Court issued a resolution in an administrative matter that authorized the chief justice to administer the oath of office to Arroyo. The resolution did not make any finding on the vacancy of the office of president or the validity or legality of Arroyo's oath, but it was interpreted as the court's legitimizing her ascension, transforming the ouster of Estrada into a case of perceived constitutional succession rather than an extralegal expulsion. After military support collapsed, Estrada vacated the presidential palace peacefully but maintained that he was the duly elected president. The elections and ascensions of these individuals typify the personality-driven electoral process in the Philippines. Parties are malleable constructs dependent upon the candidates who head them, and they have little or no continuity in substance or structure. While all four post-Marcos leaders have faced political instability and constitutional and economic challenges, the emerging democracy has persisted.

COURT STRUCTURE

The current Philippines legal system is composed of an integrated judiciary. The lowest trial courts consist of metropolitan trial courts, municipal trial courts in cities, and municipal circuit trial courts. These courts decide cases of limited jurisdiction, including violations of city or municipal ordinances and offenses whose punishments do not exceed six years' punishment, in civil cases not to exceed P100,000 (P200,000 in metro Manila). Above municipal courts are the regional trial courts of general jurisdiction for criminal and civil cases whose punishments or values are above those permitted in the metropolitan or municipal courts. Cases decided by the metropolitan or municipal courts can be appealed to the regional trial courts. Above the trial courts are the intermediate courts of appeal, which review cases appealed from the regional trial courts. Intermediate courts of appeal may review questions of both fact and law. Cases heard initially by the regional trial courts can be appealed as a matter of right. Those cases appealed to the courts of appeal that were initially heard in the municipal courts and subsequently decided by the regional trial courts are accepted upon discretion.

The Supreme Court sits at the apex of the judicial system and theoretically hears only questions of law. It exercises appellate review over the regional trial courts and the courts of appeal. Appeals to the Supreme Court are not a matter of right, with the exception of criminal cases whose sentences include death or life imprisonment. The Supreme Court also has authority to issue extraordinary writs, including certiorari, prohibition, mandamus, habeas corpus, injunction, and contempt, among others.

The Supreme Court is composed of a chief justice and fourteen associate justices. Although it may sit en banc, it does so on rare occasions. Panels of three, five, or seven members are determined at the discretion of the court to hear appeals. Justices serve during good behavior until the age of seventy and enjoy salary protection. Lower court judges must be natural-born citizens and members of the Philippine Bar. In addition, justices of the Supreme Court must be at least forty years of age and must have served as a judge in the lower courts or have been a practicing attorney in the Philippines for at least fifteen years. The 1987 Constitution alters the method of selection of judges and justices. It establishes a Judicial and Bar Council (JBC) composed of the secretary of justice, one senator, one member of Congress, an academic, a member of the private sector, a representative of the Integrated Bar of the Philippines, one retired justice, and the chief justice of the Supreme Court. This body reviews potential candidates for the bench and provides at least three nominees to the president, who must select one of the three to fill a vacancy or reject them all. Previously, appointments to the bench were made by the president and approved by a constitutional body, the Commission on Appointments. Appointment via the JBC is supposed to lessen the political nature of the appointment process, which had always been used as a reward system. Little has changed with the JBC, however. The president is influential in the composition of the council, and the JBC is now perceived as facilitating the appointment of those individuals loyal to the president (Haynie 1998).

The court is also responsible for the administration of the judiciary, as well as the supervision of the Integrated Bar of the Philippines (IBP). The rules of court as promulgated by the Supreme Court of the Philippines require that any individual who desires to practice law must be a citizen at least twenty-one years of age, of good moral character, free from charges of moral turpitude, and must have passed the bar examination given by the Supreme Court. In order to sit for the bar examination, applicants must have successfully completed a four-year specified law curriculum in an accredited university. More than fifty law schools exist throughout the country. Between thirty-five hundred and forty-five hundred individuals sit for the bar examination annually. Of those, anywhere from six hundred to fifteen hundred are admitted to the bar each year. The legal profession was integrated into a corporate body on January 16, 1973. The IBP, with forty-five thousand members, maintains legal aid and human rights projects. Continuing education and training programs have been developed for those individuals subsequently appointed to the bench or to other positions within the justice system. For example, the National Prosecution Service Legal Education and Training Program was developed to increase the professionalization of the work of prosecutors throughout the country. Similarly, mandatory orientation programs exist for

Legal Structure of Phillippine Courts

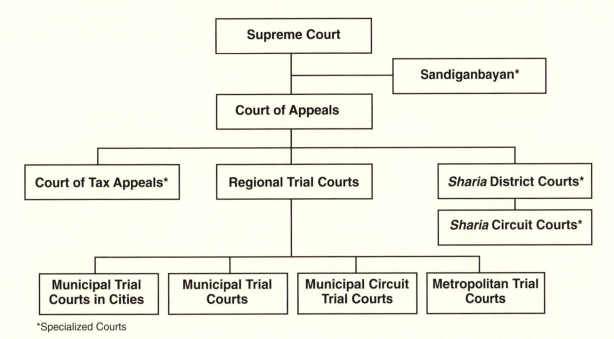

*Specialized Courts

newly appointed judges, and the Supreme Court requires continuing education for sitting judges.

SPECIALIZED COURTS AND TRIBUNALS

The Court of Tax Appeals exercises exclusive jurisdiction over decisions of the commissioner of Internal Revenue, the commissioner of customs, and the provincial or city boards of assessment appeals. Decisions of the Court of Tax Appeals are directly reviewable by the Supreme Court.

The Sandiganbayan, the Graft Court, has authority to try and decide cases involving violations of the Anti-Graft and Corrupt Practices Act, such as bribery or other felonies committed by public officials in relation to their office. Decisions of the Sandiganbayan are appealable to the Supreme Court.

The *sharia* circuit courts and *sharia* district courts exercise limited jurisdiction over Muslim populations in Mindanao, where the Muslim codes on personal law are enforced. The *sharia* courts have exclusive jurisdiction over a number of personal and family laws, including custody, guardianship, paternity, and the distribution, disposition, and settlement of estates. Decisions of the *sharia* circuit courts are appealable to the *sharia* district courts. Decisions of the *sharia* district courts are appealable to the Court of Appeals and ultimately the Supreme Court over certain constitutionally defined areas.

A number of administrative tribunals or commissions have authority to decide certain categories of cases, and they are referred to as quasi-courts, or quasi-judicial agencies. These include constitutional creatures such as the

Civil Service Commission, the Commission on Elections, and the Commission on Audit. The decisions of these commissions are directly appealable to the Supreme Court. Other quasi-courts created by statute include the National Labor Relations Commission, the Department of Agrarian Reform, the Insurance Commission, and the Land Registration Authority. Decisions of these courts are appealable to the Court of Appeals (see figure).

CONSTITUTIONAL FRAMEWORK

The 1987 Philippine Constitution, modeled after its U.S. counterpart, similarly establishes three separate branches of government. The executive branch is headed by a president and vice president elected separately to one six-year term. Because they are elected separately, they need not be of the same party. Indeed, in 1998 Joseph Estrada of the Struggle for the Nationalist Filipino Masses (LAMMP) was elected president while Gloria Macapagal-Arroyo, backed by the People's Power–National Union of Christian Democrats (*Lakas*-NUCD), was elected vice president. The bicameral legislative branch is composed of a 24-member Senate elected at large and a 260-member House of Representatives elected from designated districts. Members of the Senate may serve a maximum of two six-year terms, members of the House of Representatives a maximum of three three-year terms. The judiciary is composed of a 15-member Supreme Court, which hears cases in three divisions of five members each (Banks and Muller 1999, 777–780).

The constitution provides an extensive bill of rights,

which includes all of the protections found in the U.S. Bill of Rights as well as some additional protections. For example, the constitution protects not just speech but also expression; not just protection from unwarranted searches and seizures but also protection of the "liberty of the abode"; protections for labor; for contracts; for "political beliefs and aspirations"; and protection against "physical, psychological, or degrading punishment against any prisoner or detainee or the use of substandard or inadequate penal facilities under subhuman conditions." Article VIII of the constitution requires the government to regulate property and working conditions to maximally promote "social justice and human rights." Although the death penalty was outlawed under the 1987 Constitution, it was reinstated in 1993 for thirteen crimes, including kidnapping, murder, rape, piracy, treason, and plundering the treasury. While the rhetoric is impressive, delivering on the promises of the 1987 Constitution has proved difficult (ibid., 776).

While the legal system remained largely unaltered under the 1987 Constitution, the perceived allegiance of the courts to the Marcos regime fueled efforts to strengthen the independence of the legal system, and the Supreme Court in particular. The Supreme Court is given administrative supervision of the lower courts, judges, employees, and the discipline of the bar. Previously, the Justice Department was responsible for the administration of the judiciary. The constitution also expands the already broad jurisdiction of the courts to include "grave abuse of discretion" or "lack or excess of jurisdiction on the part of any branch or instrumentality of Government." Since the court has no discretionary control of its docket, and given the generally litigious nature of Filipino society, there are few issues that do not ultimately reach the court.

The strengthening of the court was accompanied by a concomitant increase in power. And with this increasing power came increasing scrutiny of the court by the press (Haynie 1998). The court enjoyed a surge in its popularity and perceived legitimacy immediately following the 1986 revolution. Under the leadership of Chief Justice Teehankee, considered a protagonist of Marcos in the latter years of his rule, the court was extremely popular. A survey of the Makati Business Club, an association of business executives asked to rate the performance of government agencies, placed the court at the top. However, a series of scandals plagued the courts in the late 1990s (under Chief Justice Andres Narvasa), including bribery among the lower-court judges, the unfettered access of retired justices (hired by prominent firms) to sitting members of the Supreme Court, the winning party to a case authoring a Supreme Court opinion, and manipulation of the writers of a majority opinion to achieve a particular outcome. As a result, a decade after Marcos's de-

parture, a similar survey by the Makati Business Club ranked the court nineteen of thirty-two bodies, below the military and labor departments. The court system generally ranked thirty of the thirty-two, not even able to rate higher than garbage collection (ibid.). The furor surrounding allegations of corruption has lessened under the current guidance of Chief Justice Hilario Davide.

Stacia L. Haynie

See also Civil Law; Common Law; Constitutional Law; Islamic Law; Judicial Independence; Judicial Review

References and further reading
Banks, Arthur S., and Thomas C. Muller. 1999. *Political Handbook of the World: 1999*. Binghamton, NY: CSA Publications.
Becker, Theodore L. 1970. *Comparative Judicial Politics: The Political Functioning of Courts*. Chicago: Rand McNally.
Cruz Paño, E., and D. T. Martinez. 1989. *Justice and Freedom: The Supreme Court Story—from Arellano to Fernan*. Manila: Philippine Supreme Court.
Grossholtz, Jean. 1964. *Politics in the Philippines*. Boston: Little, Brown.
Haynie, Stacia L. 1998. "Politicization of the Judiciary: The Philippines Supreme Court and the Post Marcos Era." *Asian Studies Review* 22: 459–473.
Haynie, Stacia L., and C. Neal Tate. 2000. "Comparative Judicial Politics in the Year 2000 and the Role of Research Collaboration between Indigenous and American Scholars." Paper presented at the annual meeting of the American Political Science Association.
Supreme Court of the Philippines. 2000. "A Brief History." http://www.supremecourt.gov.ph/.
Tate, C. Neal, and Stacia L. Haynie. 1993. "Authoritarianism and the Functions of Courts: A Time Series Analysis of the Philippine Supreme Court." *Law and Society Review* 27: 201–234.
———. 1994. "The Philippine Supreme Court under Authoritarian and Democratic Rule: The Perceptions of the Justices." *Asian Profile* 22: 209–226.
World Fact Book. 1998. Washington, DC: Central Intelligence Agency, Superintendent of Documents. U.S. G.P.O. Distributor.
Wurfel, David. 1964. "The Philippines." Pp. 679–769 in *Governments and Politics of Southeast Asia*. Edited by G. McTurnin Kahin. Ithaca, NY: Cornell University Press.

PLEA BARGAINING

WHAT IT IS

The entry of a plea of guilty by a defendant in a criminal case is, as a judicial confession, regarded as the highest form of proof, thereby permitting the court to move directly to the sentencing stage. A guilty plea of itself has no other necessary consequences. By contrast, plea bargaining is a feature of criminal justice systems in which a formal or informal agreement is entered into, usually by the prosecutor and defense lawyer but sometimes involving the judge, under which, in return for a plea of guilty, the sentence that would otherwise be imposed on conviction following trial will be replaced by a lesser sentence.

Plea bargaining has been identified as a practice both in lower courts where crimes of the less serious variety are dealt with as well as in higher courts, which handle more serious criminal infractions. Although plea bargaining is conventionally associated with Anglo-American legal systems, being prevalent in countries such as Australia, Canada, England, South Africa, and the United States of America, it is now emerging as a prominent part of criminal justice in countries that have, or have historically enjoyed, an inquisitorial tradition, such as Germany, Italy, and Poland.

HISTORICAL BACKGROUND

There is no agreement among experts as to the precise origins of and reasons for the emergence of plea bargaining. The fact that, at some point in the nineteenth-century United States, trial by jury was replaced by guilty pleas is well documented in the research literature. By the end of the nineteenth century, cities such as Boston, Chicago, New York, and Philadelphia had substantial guilty plea rates, and their criminal courts were organized to reward those who cooperated in their own conviction so that one observer was famously to write in 1928 of the "vanishing jury."

Commentators have offered several general explanations to account for the systemic reliance on guilty pleas. For some, plea bargaining emerged when the growth in caseload began to overwhelm the capacity of the courts to handle the daily business, and courtroom actors were compelled to rationalize justice through cost-efficient methods of disposition. For others, the explanation lies less in increases in caseload and more in increases in case complexity, as methods of proof became more formal and time-consuming because of the elaboration of safeguards for defendants that began to be put in place during the last part of the nineteenth century.

The most popular explanation, however, locates the rise in systemic guilty pleas in the gradual replacement of an amateur courtroom work group by a new class of lawyers and judges who brought to the task of decision making an innovative professionalism that simplified the cumbersome and inefficient work practices that had hitherto characterized courts. In this understanding, there never was a "golden age" of jury trial: in a system run by amateurs, justice was rough and ready, and the jury was valued because of the democratic element it introduced rather than because it offered precision in its verdicts. This changed, however, with the emergence of professional police forces beginning in the mid-nineteenth century. Under this view, the "new" police, utilizing scientific means of detection, transformed the quality of evidence available to the prosecution so as to ensure its reliability.

As this happened, there emerged a new professional group of lawyers skilled in evaluating evidence, who were able to rationally sort cases. In this way, "dead-bang" cases in which evidence of guilt was overwhelming and a guilty plea appropriate could be distinguished scientifically from those that had triable issues and accordingly deserved the expenditure of official time and resources.

More recent scholarship has undermined, if not destroyed, the central tenets of the traditional explanations. The depiction of pre–plea bargain courtrooms as theaters of the amateur has no empirical basis: instead, it is clear that they were sites in which a barristerial class of lawyers practiced before trained judges. There is no foundation for the view that policing changed in significant ways at the time of the emergence of plea bargaining, and the forensic advances claimed to have enhanced police investigations are clearly inventions of the twentieth century. The argument that the transformation from trials to guilty pleas was a function of the professionalization of law practice, to make any sense, would have to have occurred through an evolutionary process spanning the best part of a century; yet it is common ground that the change from jury trials to guilty pleas was abrupt, with systemic reliance on guilty pleas overwhelming trials within little more than a decade in some areas. Nor is there any empirical support for the view that guilty pleas were a response to case pressure.

Setting aside the lack of empirical grounding, the central problem with traditional explanations is that they have tried to isolate events within the courtroom from the political and social environment within which courts operate. Recent scholarship has, by contrast, sought to link changed practices in the court to the wider political economy and, in particular, to the changing relationship between the individual and the state. What appears to have happened is that the criminal process became transformed from a private dispute between individuals to one in which the state assumed a clear interest in both process and outcome. With concerns over cost-effectiveness and efficiency, the state came to see crime in aggregate terms as it evolved an interest in the management of social groupings thought to pose a particular threat to public order and decency. As this occurred, ownership of cases passed from the private prosecutor to publicly elected prosecutors and centrally organized police, who perfected the methods for achieving rapid dispositions through a system of inducements to plead guilty that were offered to classes of defendants.

MAJOR VARIANTS

Plea bargaining can take many forms. Commentators have traditionally distinguished between *explicit* and *implicit* bargaining. Explicit bargaining occurs where there are discussions or negotiations over plea or sentence or over the facts that will be laid before the court as the basis for sentence. The prosecution may, for example, accept the defendant's plea to only some counts in a multiple-count indictment. There might be an offer by the prosecutor to recommend a reduced sentence or a promise by the judge to impose a lesser sentence in return for a guilty plea.

Alternatively, in the absence of a direct sentence promise, all the parties may conduct discussions or undertake acts with the implicit understanding or knowledge that there will be a reduced sentence. Thus, a defendant charged with robbery may enter a plea of guilty to theft with the agreement of the prosecutor or judge in the secure knowledge that the sentence will be reduced. The same result may be achieved in jurisdictions where the sentencing practice of the court is so well known that a lesser sentence for a guilty plea is effectively judicial policy.

Additionally, the prosecution may use a range of other discretions in order to secure the cooperation of the defendant in the guilty plea process. An example that is widely relied upon by state officials is to agree to present the "facts" to the court in a way that lessens the seriousness of the crime or the defendant's role in it, for example, by omitting aggravating factors such as the use of a weapon or by telling the court, contrary to what really happened, that the defendant was cooperative with the police and showed immediate and genuine remorse.

There are also variations in the openness with which criminal justice systems engage with plea bargaining. In the United States, at least since the second half of the twentieth century, courts and prosecutors have tended to treat the idea of plea bargaining as an item of public property, to be advocated as a common good even if individual deals or precise mechanics are less openly discussed. By contrast, English courts have not wanted to come out of the closet, with the result that in that country, there is the hypocrisy of public denunciation accompanied by secret practice.

Other countries, such as Austria, Germany, and Sweden, have also had difficulty in admitting the practice of plea bargaining because it is considered to be in violation of the legality principle, which mandates prosecution of every reported transgression of the law. In some countries, however, compromise agreements of one sort or another are increasingly to be found in formal law and procedure, as with the Italian system of *patteggiamento,* the Spanish *conformidad,* and related variants in Bulgaria, the Czech Republic, Poland, and Slovenia.

SIGNIFICANCE

Lying behind these variants is the understanding that the guilty plea no longer need be seen as a purely voluntary act of the defendant but rather as a decision in which the state has a legitimate interest. This attitude both drama-tizes the significance of the transformatory effect of plea bargaining and underscores potential weaknesses.

It is incontestable that a system of plea bargaining poses central challenges to criminal justice as a system. In conventional understandings, whether in accusatorial or inquisitorial systems, the protections and safeguards against one major type of system failure, the wrongful conviction of the innocent, operate in advance of verdict through procedural and evidentiary prophylactic rules. Plea bargaining, by contrast, can effectively bypass those protective mechanisms and thereby increase the risk of system failure.

For some, plea bargaining also potentially offends against the other system risk, namely, the wrongful acquittal of the guilty, because it encourages convictions for offenses that are less serious than might actually have been committed by the guilty party. Indeed, some argue that from a sentencing perspective, plea bargaining can never result in justice: innocent defendants get more than they deserve; guilty defendants get less than they deserve; and no one actually gets what he or she deserves.

This unintended consequence has led commentators to put wider questions about the theory and practice of plea bargaining and how to fit it into traditional understandings of criminal justice and the respective rights and responsibilities of the parties. Should, for example, a prosecutor offer a lesser plea when the prosecutor is fully aware that the case would fail at trial because key witnesses have failed to appear or are unwilling to testify in the way earlier intimated? Can a defense lawyer place pressure upon the defendant to plead guilty and forgo trial under any circumstances without breathing life into a practice that he or she might otherwise find distasteful? Because of their position in the courtroom hierarchy, can judges enter the arena of bargaining without being seen to overwhelm the independent decision making of all the other parties? Is it possible to reconcile the professional ethical responsibilities of a lawyer with private agreements that result in the lawyer having to make statements in court that may contradict the truth? What involvement, if any, should the complainant/victim have in the striking of a deal? And should all plea bargain agreements be honored even when the sentencer forms the view that the offense committed deserves greater punishment than that which was the agreed basis of the bargain?

Whatever these concerns and whatever its precise historical origin, the spread to plea bargaining in both common law and civil law jurisdictions continues unabated because of its perceived positive attributes. These lie principally in savings of time and resources and the removal of risk and unpredictability that accompanies any trial.

Mike McConville

See also Adversarial Systems; Criminal Procedures; England and Wales

References and further reading

Alschuler, Albert. 1979. "Plea Bargaining and Its History." *Law and Society Review* 13: 211–246.

Blumberg, Abraham. 1967. *Criminal Justice.* Chicago: Quadrangle Books.

Feeley, Malcolm. 1997. "Legal Complexity and the Transformation of the Criminal Process: The Origins of Plea Bargaining." *Israeli Law Review* 31, nos. 1–3: 183–222.

Fisher, George. 2000. "Plea Bargaining's Triumph." *Yale Law Journal* 109, no. 5: 857–1082.

Friedman, Lawrence, and Robert Percival. 1981. *The Roots of Justice: Crime and Punishment in Alameda County.* Chapel Hill: University of North Carolina Press.

Langbein, John. 1979. "Land without Plea Bargaining: How the Germans Do It." *Michigan Law Review* 78: 204–255.

McConville, Mike, and Chester Mirsky. 1995. "The Rise of Guilty Pleas: The Court of General Sessions, New York, 1800–1865." *Journal of Law and Society* 22, no. 4: 443–474.

POLAND

COUNTRY INFORMATION

Poland is a country located in the heart of central Europe between the Baltic Sea on the north and the Carpathian Mountains on the south. The capital, Warsaw, is situated in central Poland. The country, with an area of 312,683 square kilometers (120,725 square miles), is a little bit smaller than New Mexico. It has land boundaries on the east with Belarus, Lithuania, Russia, and Ukraine, with the Czech Republic and Slovakia on the south, and with Germany on the west. The country is located within an east-west plain extending from Central Europe to the Ural Mountains. Southern Poland has, however, very picturesque mountains, the most beautiful of which are the Tatras, with the highest point in Poland, Rysy, at 2,499 meters. Poland's moderate climate produces relatively severe winters and mild summers with a lot of precipitation. In winter, average temperatures in Warsaw range from 23° to 30° F; in summer, to 63° to 80° F. During the winter, the temperature in the mountains may drop below 40° F and in summer, in central Poland, it may exceed 100° F.

With the population of 38,608,929 (estimated July 1999), Poland is religiously and ethnically more homogeneous than the other East Central European new democracies. Ethnic Poles make up about 97.6 percent of the population; the small ethnic minority groups are Germans, Ukrainians, Byelorussians, Lithuanians, Czechs, Slovaks, and Jews. Poland is a predominantly Roman Catholic country (95 percent) with smaller Eastern Orthodox, Protestant, Jewish, and Muslim minorities. Since the fall of communism Poland has successfully progressed economically, showing a steady growth of GDP over

5 percent. Poland's biggest problem still remains agriculture. Farmers, once protected by socialism, had recently to face high taxes, falling prices of agricultural goods, and rising prices of fertilizers, fuel, and machinery. Restructuring and privatization of sensitive industrial sectors are another urgent problem for the country. The country's legal system is deeply rooted in the civil law traditions. Polish is the official language of the republic.

HISTORY

Almost since the beginning of its political existence, Poland has been part of the Christian cultural world. The Christianization of Poland in 966 not only converted the country to Christianity but also established a church administration, bringing Poland into the Roman family of civilization. Its geopolitical location exposed Poland to incessant attacks from Germany and Russia and raids of barbarian neighbors like the Mongols, Lithuanians, and Prussians. By the eleventh century, as a result of struggles with these neighbors, Poland's international position was established, along with a significant expansion in the authority of the Polish rulers. In the fourteenth century the prestige of the king grew abroad, and the state became one of the most powerful members of the European community.

This process enhanced the privileged position of the gentry, who had become conscious of their military and social importance. The considerable privileges acquired by the gentry, while limiting the king's power, culminated in the establishment of a unique political structure, the Commonwealth of the Gentry. During the second half of the sixteenth century, Poles began to elect their kings, and Polish nobles reached the height of their political influence. The competition for power between magnates and gentry contributed to the anarchy often associated by historians with the political situation in the Polish state during the rule of the Saxon dynasty (1697–1763). At the end of the seventeenth century and during the eighteenth century, the internal crisis in Poland contributed to the decay of the Polish international position, which chronologically coincided with the process of establishing absolute political systems in neighboring Russia, Prussia, and Austria. Poland's neighbors were interested in keeping Poland in a state of anarchy, which could justify plans to partition off Polish territories.

The idea that the Polish political system was in need of reform resulted in the adoption of Poland's first (and the first European) written constitution, of May 3, 1791. The constitution introduced a system that featured some attributes of parliamentary government. Under Russian pressure, the constitution was, however, abolished by the rebel confederation in 1792 and was followed by the partition of Poland of January 23, 1793. In 1794, Poland tried to end Russian tutelage. The national insurrection

led by Tadeusz Kosciuszko, the hero of the American Revolution, was, however, unsuccessful and was followed by the next partition (third) of Poland, which eliminated the Polish state. Most Polish territories were incorporated into Austria, Prussia, or Russia.

Two successive constitutions were granted to the Polish territories by the foreign emperors and show small links to the Constitution of 1791. In July 1807, the short-lived Constitution of 1807 was granted by Napoleon to the Grand Duchy of Warsaw, which was established by him in the part of the territories carved out of the Prussian segment of Poland. After the fall of Napoleon, the new Constitution of the Kingdom of Poland of 1815 was granted by Russian Tsar Alexander I. It was proclaimed as the most liberal constitution in the world but, in fact, the Russian absolutist administrators of the Polish provinces treated it as a mere declaration whose provisions were manipulated, avoided, and violated at whim. The kingdom was a country with a constitution but without a constitutional order. After the two unsuccessful uprisings of 1830 and 1863 the autonomy of the kingdom was further suppressed, and in official documents the name of the province was changed to "the Country at the Vistula River."

An independent Polish state was reestablished after World War I. The new constitution was adopted in 1921. In May 1926, the political ferment in the country resulted in the coup d'état led by Marshal Jozef Pilsudzki. The law of August 2, 1926, enhanced the executive power of the president. The influence of the opposition parties dwindled and the power was taken over by the "colonels," the higher officers of the army, who were clearly in control of the government after Pilsudzki's death in 1935. In April 23, 1935, the new constitution was adopted. The 1935 Constitution marked a distinct evolution of the system toward an authoritarian government.

World War II and more than five years of Nazi occupation exposed the Polish nation to oppression and systematic destruction of human rights. Poles and particularly Polish Jews were victims of the program of mass extermination, kidnapping in the streets, and public executions. The Polish government-in-exile was established in France and transferred later to London. At the same time, the Polish Committee of National Liberation, organized under Soviet protection, announced the land reform that provided for the expropriation of larger landowners, the nationalization of industry, and the transfer of authority into the hands of the working masses. Communism brought to Poland the control of society by a single party, which was represented as a mass organization but was in fact an elitist structure. The Communist Party was conceived as a ruling structure and monolithic vanguard of the proletariat for which both democracy and human rights were nothing but a cliché. The Polish Constitution of 1952 shared a common core with all socialist constitutions. It exposed the citizens' duties and elaborated on economic and social rights. The constitution did not provide for judicial control of the observance of fundamental constitutional rights, which seemed to conflict with fundamental assumptions of socialist jurisprudence.

Economic collapse, ideological crisis, and moral degeneration of the ruling communist elite set in motion a process of irreversible disintegration of the communist system. In the beginning of the 1980s, the process resulted in the establishment in Poland of Solidarity, the first independent trade union under a communist regime. The activity of the union culminated with the imposition of martial law on December 13, 1981, and finally led to the so-called Polish peaceful revolution of the late 1980s. The Communist Party agreed to open the roundtable negotiations with Solidarity in February 1989. The roundtable accords resulted in new elections in June 1989, which gave Solidarity clear dominance in the newly elected senate where the union captured ninety-nine of one hundred seats. Solidarity also won 35 percent (or 161) of the seats open to opposition candidates in the Seym (Polish main legislative chamber). The electoral success of legalized Solidarity contributed to the Communist Party's removal from its leading role in state affairs and finally to the elevation of Solidarity's leader, Lech Walesa, to president in new direct elections at the end of 1990.

After the fall of communism, Poland amended the 1952 Constitution and the constitutional committees began working on drafts of the new constitutional act. In 1992, the Small/Interim Constitution was adopted. It was expected that the constitution would soon be supplemented with a new bill of rights. The process of constitution making was, however, hampered by frequent changes of the governments and finally the dissolution of the Parliament in May 1993. In the second half of 1995, the drafters' attention was diverted from constitutional work and centered on the forthcoming presidential campaign. In a close vote, Aleksander Kwasniewski, a minister in the last communist Polish government and leader of the Social Democratic Party that had been assembled from remnants of communist organizations in 1990, took the presidency from Walesa. The process of constitution drafting was completed in 1997, when Poland adopted an entirely new and fully developed constitution.

LEGAL CONCEPTS

The 1997 Constitution describes Poland as a democratic republic with a unitary organization of the state, respecting the rule of law and the principles of social justice. The purpose of the constitutional description of the state as "democratic" is (1) to make people as a whole a subject of sovereignty (art. 4, sec. 1), (2) to state that people manifest their will in a variety of ways and that the principle of political pluralism is fundamental to an efficiently functioning constitutional government (arts. 11, 120), and (3) to express that government of the people and by the people means both representative government and some elements of direct democracy (art. 4, sec. 2). The concept of social justice (art. 2) means that the government is "for the people" in the sense that it respects the idea of civic society, which subordinates the state to societal interests. The idea of "social market economy" (art. 20) means persistent widespread support for a role played by the state in the distribution of wealth and in mitigating excessive injustices of the system based on free competition.

The concept of the rule of law or the legal state, as provided for in articles 2 and 7, also contains several essential elements. First, it assumes that the state operates within the clear framework of hierarchically arranged legal acts, with basic laws recognized as the apex of the legal system (art. 8, sec. 1). Second, the idea of the state of law is identified with the legality or submission of the state to the law; it means that the organs of public authority function on the basis of, and within the limits of, the law (art. 7). Third, the state of law provides for constitutional guarantees of the law's observance. The most important of them is the concept of limited government as embodied by the division of powers and checks and balances (art. 10). The constitutional state of law also guarantees respect for international law (art. 9) and provides extended protection for human rights in the form of judicial review of the legality of administrative actions and of the constitutionality of statutes, international agreements, and executive orders (arts. 188, 184).

The 1997 Constitution has a separate chapter on the sources of law (Chapter III). The constitution distinguishes between the sources of law that are universally binding in the entire republic (enactments of local law) and those that are binding only within the organizational units of the issuing organ. The first are the constitution, laws (statutes), ratified international agreements, and regulations (art. 87, sec. 1); the second are all legal acts issued by territorial organs of power (art. 87, sec. 2); in the third group, the constitution lists only resolutions of the Council of Ministers and orders of the prime minister (art. 93, sec. 1). The constitution clearly declares principles of the supremacy of the constitution (art. 8, sec. 1) and primacy of the statutory law. The first principle means that the constitution is the highest law of the republic; the second means that the executive regulations shall be issued "on the basis of specific authorization contained in, and for the purpose of implementation of, statutes by the organs specified in the Constitution" (art. 92, sec. 1).

The relevant provisions of the 1997 Constitution of Poland on the relations between the statutes and international agreements are quite elaborate and complicated. The constitution grants the right to ratify and renounce international agreements to the president of the republic (art. 133, sec. 1). It distinguishes between international agreements that require the prior consent of the laws for ratification and those that are ratified without consent. The consent requires the vote of two-thirds of both chambers in the presence of at least half of the deputies and senators. The consent can also be granted by a nationwide referendum (arts. 88, 89, 90, secs. 2, 3). Self-executing agreements are directly applicable after their promulgation; other agreements become a part of domestic law after the adoption of implementing laws (art. 91, sec. 1). The Polish Constitution confirms that ratified international agreements are a source of domestic law, but their rank in the hierarchy of the laws varies. Article 91, section 2 states that, in case of conflict, an international agreement ratified upon prior statutory consent takes precedence over statutes. The placement, after the statutes, of the other agreements in the list of the sources of law (art. 87) indicates the intention of the drafters to give them a subordinate status in relation to the statutory law, although higher than the acts of substatutory character.

The 1997 Constitution dropped all provisions of the constitutional preamble and confirmed a bicameral structure for the legislative body, but a reduced role of the president, who is now described as "the supreme representative of the Republic of Poland" and "the guarantor of the continuity of State authority" (art. 126, sec. 1).

First, the 1997 Constitution makes the president "a representative of the State in foreign affairs" (art. 133, sec. 1), but deprives him of the right of "general supervision in the field of international relations" reserved for him by article 32 of the 1992 Constitution. Under the 1997 Constitution, the Council of Ministers "exercises general control in the field of relations with other States and international organizations" (art. 146, sec. 4/9) and "concludes international agreements requiring ratification as well as accept and renounce other international agreements" (art. 146, sec. 4/10).

Second, the 1997 Constitution maintains the procedure of the 1992 Constitution in accordance with which the right to nominate a prime minister would pass back and forth from the president to the main legislative chamber, the Seym (arts. 154, 155). It provides, however, that after the third unsuccessful attempt to get the support of an appropriate majority of the Seym for the presidential appointee, the president must dissolve the chamber and order a new election (art. 155). The right of the president to appoint an interim government was dropped. Under the 1997 Constitution, the president has discretion to dissolve the parliament if it failed to adopt the state budget within four months from the submission of the bill to the Seym (art. 225).

Third, the 1997 Constitution maintained the "constructive vote of no-confidence" (art. 158) but dropped the provision of the 1992 Constitution on the regular vote of no-confidence. It means that the Seym, differently than in the Small Constitution, cannot just dismiss the government by the vote of "negative" majority of the opposition without a simultaneous and successful action to elect a new prime minister (art. 158). A subsequent motion of the same kind may be submitted no sooner than after the end of three months from the day of the previous motion, with the exception of the situation when the first motion was signed by at least 115 deputies (art. 158, sec. 2).

Fourth, under the 1992 Constitution, the Seym could authorize the Council of Ministers to issue regulations, which had the force of statute (art. 23). The 1997 Constitution reserves the legislative power exclusively for the parliament (art. 10, sec. 2). The only exception authorizes the president to issue decrees having force of law during a period of martial law (art. 234, sec. 1); such decrees must be approved by the Seym at its next sitting.

Fifth, the Seym has exclusive power to control the activity of the government (art. 95, sec. 2). The presidential prerogative to give opinion on nominations of ministers of Foreign and Internal Affairs and minister of National Defense was dropped by the 1997 Constitution. The president may still convene and preside over the meetings of the Cabinet Council but this body does not have the competence of the Council of Ministers (art. 141, secs. 1, 2). The authority of the prime minister as an independent organ of the state was confirmed and the 1997 Constitution extended his power to represent, coordinate, and control the work of the Council of Ministers (art. 148).

Sixth, the president can send the bill back to the Seym but the 1997 Constitution requires only a three-fifths majority of the chamber and the presence of at least half of the total number of deputies to overrule the presidential veto (art. 122, sec. 5).

The principles of electoral laws provided by the Constitution are implemented in several statutory laws. The main electoral law, the 1993 Statute on Elections to Seym, was amended on May 1, 2001. It provided that the elections to the Seym are based on principles of "general, direct, equal, proportional elections, by secret ballot" (art. 1, sec. 1). The Seym is elected for a four-year term of office. Three hundred ninety-one deputies were elected from the electoral lists in multiseat electoral districts and sixty-nine deputies from nationwide lists (art. 2). The new electoral law of 2001 eliminated the nationwide list.

The voters have only one vote, and choose one of the lists but indicate their preferences for individual candidates by marking those candidates' names on the list (art. 39, sec. 2). Votes used to be distributed to parties according to the d'Hondt system, which provides that the number of votes given to particular lists is divided by numerical figures (1, 2, 3, 4, etc.) and the seats were allocated to the parties according to the highest results. The seats were given to the candidates on the list who received the highest voter support (arts. 111–118). The seats from the nationwide lists were distributed through the d'Hondt system but they were given to the candidates at the top of the lists, excepting those who already received seats from the district lists (art. 119, sec. 1). The system of nationwide lists effectively guaranteed the election of unpopular party leaders not elected from the district lists. If a seat in the Seym becomes vacant, the Speaker of the Chamber (art. 132) fills it. In 2001 this system was changed. The nationwide list was dropped and the d'Hondt system was replaced by the Sainte-Lague formula. This system uses only odd divisors (1, 3, 5, 7 . . .), which increases the chances of smaller parties.

There are significant differences between the electoral systems of the Polish Seym and Senate. The 1997 Constitution (art. 97, sec. 2) states that the elections to the Senate are "general, direct and based on secret ballot." They are not equal because two (or more) senatorial seats are allocated to the electoral districts regardless of their population. The elections are not proportional either because the voters choose particular candidates not from party lists. The elections of 100 senators to this chamber are based on the plurality system. The two candidates with the highest number of votes receive seats in the two-seat districts and three candidates get the seats in three-seat districts. The senators are elected for four-year terms. If a senatorial seat is vacant, the Senate makes a decision about supplementary elections within six months (art. 20, sec. 1).

Presidential elections are "general, equal, direct and based on secret ballot" (arts. 2–6). The elections are called by the Speaker of the Seym no later than three months before the end of the tenure of the current president (art. 7). The president is elected for five years (art. 8, sec. a) from the candidates selected and registered by social and political organizations and the citizens, and must be supported by the signatures of at least 100,000 of the voters (art. 40, sec. 1). If none of the candidates receives an absolute majority, the second round of the elections is held (fourteen days after the first ballot) in which the two candidates who received the highest number of votes and did not withdraw their candidatures participate. If one of the candidates dies, withdraws, or becomes ineligible for election, the next individual from the list with the highest number of first-round votes participates in the second round (art. 8b, secs. 2, 4). A plurality suffices to be elected in the second round.

COURTS, TRIBUNALS, AND INSTITUTIONS PROTECTING HUMAN RIGHTS

Article 175 of the 1997 Constitution provides that the administration of justice in Poland is implemented by two categories of courts: courts of general jurisdiction and special courts. Within the first category, the constitutions mention only the Supreme Court with a supervisory power and common courts of general jurisdiction. The special courts are administrative courts and military courts. The Supreme Court also supervises the military courts (art. 183). The administrative courts are not subject to supervision by the Supreme Court; a separate judicial organ, the Chief Administrative Court, exercises control over their performance. Extraordinary courts and summary procedures may be established in Poland only during war (art. 175, sec. 2). Judicial power is separate and independent (art. 173).

The common courts in Poland are district courts, regional courts, and courts of appeals. The common courts exercise jurisdiction in all matters except those reserved for other courts, those falling within the jurisdiction of the Supreme Court and special courts. Article 176, section 1 of the 1997 Constitution guarantees at least a two-instance court system, which is to be established within a period of five years.

In fact, the recent Polish system used in the courts of general jurisdiction provides for three-stage proceedings. The parties may challenge the decisions of the courts of first instance in appellate procedure and the decisions of the courts of second instance are subject to cassation. The appealing party must establish some grounds of appellate review, which are infringement of the material law, infringement of the procedural requirements, or discovery of new facts or new evidence. Cassations are exclusively on the law and the cassational court may either confirm the challenged judgment or reverse and remand the case to the intermediate appellate court. The regional courts hear appeals from the decisions of the district courts and they serve also as the courts of first instance in more serious criminal and civil cases listed by the appropriate statutory laws. Courts of appeals hear appeals from the decisions of the regional courts working as the courts of first instance and cassations from the appellate decisions of these courts; cassations from the decisions of the courts of appeals fall in the jurisdiction of the Supreme Court.

Structure of Polish Courts

SPECIAL COURTS		THE COURTS OF GENERAL JURISDICTION	
Chief Administrative Court (not subject to supervision of the Supreme Court)	**Military Courts** (under supervision of the Supreme Court)	**The Supreme Court**	**The Common Courts** (Courts of Appeals, Regional Courts, District Courts)
SPECIAL TRIBUNALS			
CONSTITUTIONAL TRIBUNAL		**TRIBUNAL OF STATE**	

COURTS OF GENERAL JURISDICTION			
SUPREME COURT CHAMBERS			
ADMINISTRATION	**LABOR AND SOCIAL INSURANCE**	**CIVIL**	**CRIMINAL AND MILITARY**

COURTS OF APPEALS		
President	General Assembly	Appellate Chamber

REGIONAL COURTS		
President	General Assembly	Appellate Chamber

DISTRICT COURTS

The Supreme Court has four chambers: administration, labor, and social insurance chamber; civil chamber; criminal chamber; and military chamber. The Court is composed of the first president, presidents, and judges whose number is determined by the president of the republic upon request of the National Council of Judiciary. Judges of the Supreme Court are appointed on the motion of the National Council of Judiciary. The president of the Court is appointed for a six-year term by the president of the republic from candidates proposed by all judges of the Supreme Court. Judges of the Supreme Court may recall the president of the Court on the motion of the president of the republic who himself appoints and recalls all other presidents of the Court. The single organs of the district courts are their presidents; the organs of the regional and appellate courts are the president, the general assembly of the judges, and the appellate chamber. The presidents of all common courts are appointed by the minister of Justice based on the opinion of the judges of the relevant courts.

The National Council of Judiciary established in Poland in 1989 is an organ responsible for the protection of judicial independence. It is composed of the first president of the Supreme Court; the minister of Justice; the president of the Chief Administrative Court; one member appointed by the president of the republic; fifteen judges chosen by the judges of the Supreme Court, common courts, and special courts; four members chosen by the Seym from its deputies; and two members chosen by the Senate from the senators. The members of the council are selected for four years.

Poland had a tradition of administrative adjudication that dates back to the interwar period when the Polish constitution of March 7, 1921, announced the establishment of the Supreme Administrative Tribunal (SAT) and local administrative courts. After World War II, the SAT became inoperable and some of its functions relating to the system of social insurance were taken over by the Tribunal of Social Security. The 1952 Constitution did not provide for administrative courts. In the late 1960s and 1970s the attitude toward the judicial review of administrative decisions began to change and finally on January 31, 1980, the Polish parliament adopted the new statute amending the Code of Administrative Procedure and providing for establishment of the Chief Administrative Court in Warsaw and in some local administrative districts. The 1997 Constitution finally constitutionalized the status of the Chief Administrative Court. Until the year 2002 the Court will be only an organ with cassational jurisdiction reviewing the complaints on administrative decisions. The complaints can be submitted by any applicants showing a legal interest after the exhaustion of all administrative remedies. Five years after the adoption of the 1997 Constitution, the administrative review will become a two-stage proceeding. The Court operates in Warsaw and in special districts covering several administrative units (voivodships).

On March 26, 1982, Poland became the first country in the Soviet bloc to amend its 1952 Constitution and add article 33A on the Constitutional Tribunal. The tribunal was, however, not established until the adoption of the statute on the Constitutional Tribunal on April 29, 1985. By doing so, Poland established a precedent that has been followed by virtually all new European democracies until quite recently.

In comparison with previous regulations, the Constitution of 1997 significantly changed the scope of the tribunal's jurisdiction. The main role of the tribunal is to rule on the conformity of laws and international agreements with the constitution, and on the conformity of substatutory laws with the constitution, ratified international agreements, and statutes. In the past, the rulings of the tribunal on the constitutionality of statutes were subject to the confirmation of the Seym, which could overrule the decision of the tribunal with a two-thirds majority. The 1997 Constitution states that the judgments of the tribunal are final (art. 190), excepting only the rulings on the nonconformity of laws adopted before the constitution came into force; these rulings will be subject to the confirmation of the Seym for two years after the day the constitution entered into force (art. 239). The constitution does not grant the tribunal the power to issue any binding interpretations of the constitution; this function has been vested in the Supreme Court. The tribunal also does not review the laws adopted by local administrative organs—this power was reserved for the Chief Administrative Court. Another change is the introduction of the right of the individual to complain about constitutional infringements. The tribunal is composed of fifteen judges appointed by the Seym for nine years from the candidates nominated by at least fifty deputies or the presidium of the Seym. The resolution of the Seym requires a majority of the vote with at least half of the deputies present.

The Constitution of 1997 also guarantees that everyone has the right to appeal to the Commissioner for Citizens' Rights (art. 80), for assistance in the protection of their freedoms and rights. An ombudsman's position was established in Poland by statute on June 15, 1987, and was constitutionalized by an amendment of April 7, 1989. In accordance with the implementing law of August 24, 1991, the Commissioner became an independent organ of the state. The 1997 Constitution states that the Commissioner is appointed by the Seym for five years, with the consent of the Senate (art. 209). In this sense, the Commissioner is independent politically (art. 209, sec. 3) and is only "accountable to the Seym in accordance with principles specified by law" (art. 212). The Commissioner cannot be held criminally responsible or deprived of freedom without prior consent of the Seym (art. 211). Polish law provides that the Commissioner is an organ with supervisory and investigative functions. He/she informs the parliament about the effectiveness of the constitutional protection of rights and freedoms and can petition the Constitutional Tribunal to review the laws, but cannot make decisions about the merits of the case.

The Tribunal of State is a constitutional organ established to decide in impeachment proceedings against the highest officials of the state. Within the scope of jurisdiction of the tribunal are the cases involving constitutional accountability and mixed constitutional and criminal responsibility of the president of the republic; the prime minister, ministers, or persons granted powers of management over a ministry; the presidents of the National Bank; the Supreme Chamber of Control; members of the National Council of Radio Broadcasting and Television, the commander-in-chief of the armed forces; and deputies and senators. The regular criminal cases against the president of the republic also fall within the jurisdiction of the tribunal. The president of the Supreme Court is ex officio chairperson of the tribunal. The Seym elects two deputy chairpersons and sixteen members of the tribunal. They cannot hold the position of deputy or senator and at least half of the members should have the judicial qualifications.

A private dispute resolution system was poorly working in socialist Poland. In 1989, however, the state renounced Moscow's 1972 convention on arbitration between the state-owned enterprises of the countries of the Soviet bloc. The reconstructed arbitration court, established at the Polish Chamber of Commerce, extended its jurisdiction on the disputes between the private parties. It signed agreements with the American Arbitration Association and the Arbitral Center of the Federal Economic Chamber in Vienna. In accordance with the recent civil procedure the parties may select a forum for all civil law disputes with the exception of those related to labor and family issues. If the parties do not decide differently, three arbitrators hear the routine disputes. The parties to the private dispute resolution system may ask the courts of general jurisdiction for the enforcement of the decision of the arbitrators.

STAFFING

Poland has thirteen state-sponsored law schools offering programs at the undergraduate level. The graduates, after five years of study, are placed for three years of practical training in the courts or apprenticeship programs organized by the state procurators, associations of attorneys or notaries. The entrance exams for all programs of practical training are comprehensive and competitive, and usually not more than 10 percent of the applicants are admitted.

The judges appointed must be Polish citizens of unblemished character, graduates of the law schools, at least twenty-six years old, who completed practical training for judges or procurators and passed comprehensive examinations concluding the apprenticeship, and worked for at least one year of a probationary period in a court or procurator's office. The requirements regarding a practical training and probationary period do not apply to practicing attorneys, legal advisors, and notaries with more than three years of legal practice, professors, or persons with an academic degree of habilitated doctor (highest scholarly degree) working at the Polish law schools, Polish Academy of Science, or other research institutions. The judges of the appellate courts have to work for five years as judges of the lower courts. The judges of the Supreme Court have to distinguish themselves by their knowledge and professional experience, work for at least ten years as legal professionals, or hold professorial degrees or habilitations from Polish law schools; the same requirements are applicable to judges of the Chief Administrative Court who in addition have to be at least thirty-five years old. Judges of the Constitutional Tribunal have to possess qualifications required by the judges of the Supreme Court or the Chief Administrative Court.

Only the constitution and laws (art. 178) bind the Polish judges, and several provisions fitting generally recognized standards of protection guarantee their independence. First, they are appointed by the president for an indefinite period (art. 179) on the motion of the National Council of Judiciary, which safeguards the independence of the courts and judiciary. The judges are irremovable through the regular administrative process (art. 180). They can be removed or suspended from office or moved to another branch or position only on the basis of the court decision (art. 180, secs. 1–2). The way in which they can be retired will be specified by the new law (art. 180, secs. 3, 4). Second, the judges are guaranteed judicial immunity; they cannot "without prior consent granted by a court be held criminally responsible nor deprived of freedom" (art. 181). Third, the constitution requires that the judges will be politically neutral and will not belong to a political party or trade union or perform public activities incompatible with the principles of independence (art. 178, sec. 3). Fourth, the judges are

guaranteed appropriate conditions of work and "remuneration consistent with the dignity of their office and the scope of their duties" (art. 179, sec. 2).

Public prosecutors in Poland are civil law servants whose functioning is regulated by the Statute on Procuratura of June 20, 1985, amended several times, most recently in 1990, 1993, and 1996. The organs of Procuratura are units of appellate, regional, and district procuraturas, and National Procuratura. The Chief Officer of Procuratura is Procurator General. As the Procuratura is accountable to the government, the Procurator General also serves as the minister of Justice. One of his deputies is National Procurator, the chief officer of the National Procuratura. The hierarchical structure of Procuratura is equivalent to the structure of the Polish courts. The military units of Procuratura are accountable also to the Procurator General; the Chief Military Procurator is one of the deputies of the Procurator General. The procurators have to be at least twenty-six years old and professionally be as qualified as judges; their immunity is the same as judges.

Private legal practitioners work in Poland as attorneys (adwokat), legal advisors (radca prawny), and notaries (notariusz). The attorneys are organized in Adwokatura, the association of all practicing advocates. The organs of Adwokatura are the National Convention of Adwokatura, National Council of Advocates, Higher Disciplinary Court, and Higher Appellate Commission. The local associations of advocates are composed of chambers of advocates (izby adwokackie). Advocates must have the same qualifications as judges or procurators, but they need either to complete a special, three-year-long apprenticeship for advocates, pass the bar exam, or work for three years as judges, procurators, notaries, or legal advisors. The legal advisors are fully qualified legal practitioners who may represent clients in civil courts but do not have the right of audience in criminal courts. There is a tendency in Poland to merge the advocates with legal advisors. Notaries have the same qualifications as other legal practitioners in Poland but they need to complete a special period of articles for notaries. They are practitioners of considerable importance who draft important legal documents, such as wills, corporate charters, conveyances, and contracts; authenticate instruments' signatures; and certify documents that may have evidentiary effect (the same as original documents) in the courts.

Poland's political culture is the result of this country's being suspended somewhere between its socialist legacy and Western traditions. With all the remarkable changes in Poland, the feeling of "suspension in the transitory period" results in some confusing beliefs and emotions toward the West and some irrational longing for the communist "equality in misery." Blending and mixing of models became a style, a significant feature of constitutional culture that this country shares with other East Central European democracies. It has to be noted, however, that the public mood in Poland is quickly changing. The media's reports, disputes, and everyday explorations of public reactions contributed to a higher feeling of participation in the process of policymaking among Poles than among those in other countries in this region. It may be the most significant effect of the "democratization" of political life in Poland.

Rett R. Ludwikowski

See also Administrative Tribunals; Appellate Courts; Arbitration; Civil Law; Constitutional Review; Judicial Independence; Judicial Selection, Methods of; Legal Education; Russia; Soviet System

References and further reading
Biskupski, M. B., and James S. Pula. 1993. *Poland and Europe: Historical Dimensions.* New York: Columbia University Press.
Brzezinski, Mark. 1998. *The Struggle for Constitutionalism in Poland.* Oxford: St Antony's College.
First Polish Economic Guide. 2000. Warsaw: Common Europe Publications.
Fiszman, Samuel. 1997. *Constitution and Reform in Eighteenth-Century Poland.* Bloomington: Indiana University Press.
Gieysztor, Aleksander, Stefan Kieniewicz, Emanuel Rostworowski, Janusz Tazbir, and Henryk Wereszycki. 1968. *History of Poland.* Warsaw: Polish Scientific Publishers.
Ludwikowski, Rett R. 1991. *Continuity and Change in Poland.* Washington, DC: CUA Press.
———. 1996. *Constitution-Making in the Region of Former Soviet Dominance.* Durham, NC; London: Duke University Press.
Ludwikowski, Rett R., and William F. Fox, Jr. 1993. *The Beginning of the Constitutional Era.* Washington, DC: CUA Press.
Mojak, Ryszard, ed. 2000. *Ustroj konstytucyjny Rzeczypospolitej Polskiej* [Constitutional System of the Polish Republic]. Lublin: University of M. Curie-Sklodowska.
Polish Constitutional Law. The Constitution and Selected Statutory Materials. 2000. Warsaw: Chancellery of the Sejm.
Sarnecki, Pawel, ed. 1999. *Prawo konstytucyjne Rzeczypospolitej Polskiej* [Constitutional Law of the Polish Republic]. Warsaw: C. H. Beck.
Thompson, Kenneth W., and Rett R. Ludwikowski. 1991. *Constitutionalism and Human Rights: America, Poland, and France.* Lanham, MD: University Press of America, for the Miller Center, University of Virginia.
Wyrzykowski, Miroslaw, ed. 1999. *Constitutional Studies.* Warsaw: Institute of Public Affairs.

PORTUGAL

GENERAL INFORMATION

Situated in southwest Europe (southwestern tip of the Iberian Peninsula), Portugal is one of the more ancient countries in Europe, with its frontiers definitively constituted in the thirteenth century. Its area is 92,075 square kilometers, distributed across its continental region (88,944 square kilometers) and its islands, Madeira and Azores. Today the population of Portugal reaches about 11 million people, including a growing number of citizens of Black African descent, who are immigrating from the former colonies. The country displays a great variety of geographical features, but we can roughly divide it in a southern region, consisting of lowlands, and a northern one, where 90 percent of the area lies above 1,300 feet. Another major division is that which defines an interior region, poorer and less populated, and a littoral one, where the great cities are located (including Lisbon, the capital) and where the population is concentrated. Portugal has been a member of the European Union since 1986.

LAW HISTORY

Portugal was part of the Roman province of Hispania. Here the Roman civil law, being influenced by local legal traditions, gave origin to a vulgarized Roman law. This law survived in the law of the Visigoths, the German people who replaced Roman authorities in the Peninsula, about the middle of the fifth century B.C.E. Visigothic law was codified, but the everyday life went on, ruled by unwritten legal rules. Moors invaded Iberia in 711, but the Christian Reconquista expelled them and almost obliterated the influence of the Islamic law.

In 1140, Portugal was established as an independent kingdom. By the time of independence, its inhabitants lived in autonomous communities, ruled by their own norms. Until the thirteenth century, royal statutes were not very important. Another legal order was the canon law.

From the thirteenth century onward, Roman law became the European common law, by influence of the work of the Italian glossators and commentators. Portugal was strongly influenced by this new common law. From the fifteenth century on, royal legislation acquired a growing importance, the first codifications of Portuguese law being published at this time (1446, 1514–1521, 1603).

In medieval and modern times, the coexistence of various legal systems created a situation of legal pluralism, where the common law jurists aimed to rule the jurisdiction of each legal system (the church, the kingdom, the municipal, and others). Because of this pluralism, and in order to establish the supremacy of royal law, the kings tried to give a hierarchy to the legal orders existing within the kingdom. This hierarchy was not always similar to the one proposed by the common law jurists, a fact that gave rise to numerous judicial disputes. Nevertheless, the law of the kingdom was not the law most often applied, not only because it didn't cover a number of matters covered by the common law doctrine, but also because local customs were still applied by "rustic judges."

After the mid-eighteenth century, rationalism and voluntarism of modern natural law introduced important changes: a statute of 1769 reformed the system of sources of Portuguese law, reasserting the primacy of royal statute law, as well as the merely subsidiary value of Roman law. Common law doctrine ceased to be applicable. The value of canon law, jurisprudence, and custom was restricted. Political and economic matters began to be ruled by the law of the "Christian, enlightened and civilized Nations."

Portuguese constitutions of the liberal monarchy (1820–1910) consecrated civil rights, national sovereignty, a representative system, division of powers, monarchical government, and restrictive electoral rights. We can characterize them according to their proximity to two models. One of them asserts the primacy of national sovereignty, the broadening of electoral rights, the supremacy of Parliament, and unicameralism. To this model belongs the first liberal constitution (1822–1823; 1836–1838). The other model was characterized by conservatism, the *monarchical principle,* restricted electoral rights, weakened parliamentarism, and bicameralism. To this model belongs the Constitutional Charter (1826),

which embodied the permanent liberal-conservative compromise until 1910.

In 1910, the monarchy was overthrown by a Republican revolution and a new constitution organized a lay democratic republican regime. A pure parliamentary structure was installed, and the electoral system was democratized.

In 1926, a military movement instituted the dictatorship that brought Antonio Salazar to the government. A new constitution was approved in 1933. Reacting against the parliamentary system of the former regime, this was a strongly presidential model. Reacting also against the former individualistic philosophy, it installed a corporatist regime, with a corporative chamber. Although recognizing fundamental rights, the constitution severely restricted their efficiency, submitting them to the restrictions of the ordinary (even governmental) law.

Concerning ordinary law, codification developed quite late in Portugal. The ancient regime's legislation remained in force into the nineteenth century, along with foreign law, namely the French Civil Code of 1804. In 1832, a set of decrees adapted justice, civil, and fiscal administration to the principles of a liberal state. Administrative reform was the first step to embody a new model of state, according to more or less centralized patterns. It was only during the republic that the administrative principle of decentralization was firmly established. During Salazar's regime a centralized conception was reinstalled, which only came to an end with the democratic revolution of 1974.

In private law, the first branch to be codified was commercial law (1833). Penal law was the object of three codes (1837, 1852, and 1886). Justice was reorganized in 1837, suffering several other reforms thereafter. The civil code, the most relevant codification of private common law, appeared in 1867, marked by an underlying individualistic philosophy. All these codes show influences of foreign codes, but in all of them innovation is combined with tradition.

At the beginning of the twentieth century, new legislation on labor matters echoed developments in Portuguese capitalism. Only in the 1930s, with Salazar's corporatism and the ideas of state interventionism, did a new economic law arise, similar to those of the contemporary Providence States (welfare states). At the same time private law received some strokes of conservatism (restriction of divorce for Catholics) and anti-individualism. Much of these elements disappeared from the new legal system established after the democratic revolution in 1974.

LEGAL CONCEPTS

The Portuguese legal system is one in the civil law tradition and is normally classified as a Roman-Germanic legal system. The highest law of the legal order is the constitution, which sets up the basic legal, economic, and political framework of the state. The Constitution of the Portuguese Republic was approved in 1976 after the democratic revolution of 1974. Its original text was embedded with some of the revolutionary ideals that marked the complex period that followed the 1974 peaceful revolution. As a consequence, the original constitutional text is a compromise between those wanting to establish in Portugal a traditional Western liberal democracy and those wanting to promote the establishment of a socialist society. The latter reflected itself in many of the economic and social rights granted by the constitution and in its programmatic social character supported in a constitutional economic model that promoted public planning and ownership of the main sectors of economic activity. Most of these provisions have now disappeared from the constitutional text following several constitutional amendments. The socialist rhetoric is preserved in the preamble of the constitution but its text now reflects the adoption of a model of market economy and liberal democracy found in the rule of law.

The constitution establishes a semipresidential system but there has been a tendency to reinforce the powers of the Parliament (Assembleia da Republica) and the government at the expense of those of the president. The government exercises the executive function and the Parliament is responsible for legislation. However, it is common for the Parliament to delegate many legislative acts in the government. This "subordination" of the Parliament to the government has been reinforced by the tendency to have majoritarian or quasi-majoritarian governments since the 1980s and by the circumstance that the electoral system (proportional representation in regional electoral circles) does not allow the members of Parliament much independence from their parties. The president has no executive powers and is increasingly seen as an arbiter of the political system. The president's political veto is seldom used and can be overcome by a special vote of the Parliament. Although Parliament appoints the prime minister and the other members of government (after a proposal of the prime minister), this appointment is largely bound to the election results and reflects the majority in the Parliament. The present text of the constitution has also limited the conditions under which the president can exonerate the government. According to Article 195, paragraph 2 of the constitution, that can only take place when necessary to guarantee the regular functioning of the democratic institutions. The president, however, still holds the power to dissolve the Parliament.

Article 6 of the constitution defines Portugal as a unitary state. Although the constitution also affirms the autonomy of the regions of Azores and Madeira, the predominant view appears to be that the existence of these two regions does not change the characterization of the state as unitary. The establishment of the autonomous regions was the only unanimously approved provision of the constitution and it marked a rupture with a long-term period of centralized government. The same purpose was intended with the anticipation in the constitutional text of the future creation of administrative regions, which were also given direct democratic legitimacy through the partial election of its regional assemblies. However, the establishment of these regions in the mainland was successively postponed until recently when, in light of an amendment made to the constitution, the creation of the administrative regions was subject to a national referendum. The result of the referendum sanctioned the political status quo and opposed the creation of any administrative regions in mainland Portugal.

The constitution regulates four general areas of the political and administrative autonomy of the regions: legislative and administrative powers (where they may legislate subject to several conditions); financial and budgetary autonomy; political organization of the regions (institutions, decision making, and so on); and overseeing by the state and safeguarding of national interest. Most powers given to the regions are dependent upon or to be developed by the central state (mainly, the national Parliament). In some important areas the constitution does not grant powers directly to the regions but authorizes the National Parliament to delegate those powers to the regions. Powers directly given to the regions are generally concurrent with national powers and potential conflicts of competence are constitutionally solved by granting priority to the central state in those areas of concurrent powers. There is no area of reserved legislative competencies for the regions. But budgetary autonomy is constitutionally protected (as well as the right to receive tax income collected in the region).

As a result of the referendum that defeated the proposal aiming at creating new autonomous regions throughout the state, the main form of local power continues to be boroughs or counties. The mayor and the other members of the local executive are elected but their powers are relatively limited. They have limited regulatory local powers. Their funding comes from the central government and from local tax revenue (these taxes are created and mostly regulated by Parliament). Their main executive functions have been extended in recent years and include local transportation and public works, housing, tourism, and education (in limited respects).

The constitution includes a very broad and sophisticated catalog of fundamental rights, including political rights and freedoms, and economic, social, and cultural rights. Many of these rights are simply of a programmatic nature. The constitution's bill of rights still includes many workers' rights. An important element of the Portuguese Constitution with regard to political rights and freedoms protection is that it expressly states its horizontal effect (they are binding on both public and private actors). However, in practice, the direct applicability of such rights to private actors is limited and usually dependent on legislative acts. It must also be recalled that Portugal is party to the European Convention of Human Rights and Freedoms and that this constitutes a further net of protection of fundamental rights to which individuals can appeal in the Portuguese legal order.

The main source of law in the Portuguese legal system is statutory law. There is also an important tradition of codification, which currently exists in several codes, such as the civil code, penal code, commercial and company code, civil procedure code, and the penal procedure code. Chapter 1 of the civil code describes the traditional system of sources of law in the Portuguese legal system but is now, in part, outdated. As stated, the dominant source of law is statutory law, which also occupies the primary position in the legal hierarchy (subject only to constitutional norms). Article 112 of the constitution refers the different types of normative acts (statutory law) in the Portuguese legal order and the hierarchy among them.

There are other sources of law accepted in the legal system, such as case law (*jurisprudência*) and doctrine. Both these sources of law are usually classified as indirect or instrumental sources of law (*fontes mediatas*). Customary norms are seldom accepted and applied and, even in those limited cases, they are applied via reference of statutory law. Portuguese legal order does not confer the value of binding precedent to judicial decisions. However, in practice, judicial decisions have a great persuasive value and often courts tend to maintain a coherent and stable line of case law.

The status of international law is regulated in Article 8 of the constitution, which incorporates international customary and conventional norms into the Portuguese legal order, granting them direct effect. The position of those international norms in the legal hierarchy of the Portuguese legal system is not peaceful but there is a tendency to consider that they occupy a superior position to ordinary legislation and that they are only subordinate to constitutional norms. In this sense, the Portuguese Constitution appears to adopt a monism of international law with the exception of constitutional norms themselves. The same constitutional provision also recognizes the supremacy and direct effect of European Union law.

Legal interpretation and methodology tend to be rather formalistic. It is common for legal arguments and/or judicial decisions to be presented in a traditional syllogistic form. The civil code, in its Chapter 2, addresses the principles and techniques of interpretation and application of the law referring to the literal element, the historical intent, the telos of the norm, and its systematic and coherent interpretation. The balance between these different elements is, as in any other legal order, the subject of many doctrinal debates. A peculiar aspect of Portuguese judicial decisions is that they tend to be long and often cite doctrinal works and not only case law.

CURRENT COURT STRUCTURE AND JUDICIAL PROCESSES

The general organization and architecture of the judicial system are set up in the constitution. The highest court of the judicial system is the constitutional court, first introduced in a constitutional amendment of 1982. However, such a position in the judicial system is not formally recognized to preserve a symbolic parity between the constitutional court and the Supreme Court with the highest appeals court of the common judicial branch (the Supreme Court of Justice, which was for many years the highest court of the land). The structure of Portuguese courts is highly complex and even confusing. Broadly, one can highlight two main categories of courts: specialized and common courts. The first comprises the constitutional court, administrative and tax courts, the court of auditors, and military courts. Their jurisdiction is limited to those

Legal Structure of Portugal Courts

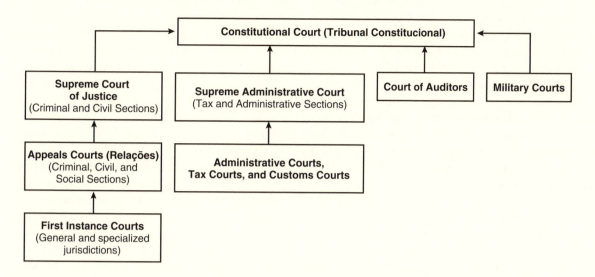

specialized branches of the law. Common courts exercise jurisdiction over private and criminal law disputes.

The basic statute regulating the organization of common courts is Law no. 3/99 (Lei de Organização e Funcionamento dos Tribunais Judiciais). But there are also a code of civil procedure and a code of criminal procedure of relevance in this area. The code of civil procedure suffered its last substantial amendment in 1996 but continues to be frequently revised. The code of criminal procedure was last amended in 1998. As has been stated, the common courts have generalized jurisdiction in private law and criminal matters. However, within common courts, there are courts of first instance with specific competences in certain areas (for example, criminal cases). Appeals courts and the Supreme Court also have specialized sections corresponding to those areas. There are three levels of jurisdiction in the common courts' judicial system: courts of first instance (generally the Tribunais de Comarca), courts of second instance (Tribunais da Relação), and the Supreme Court of Justice (Supremo Tribunal de Justiça). The constitution and the civil procedure court also established a conflicts court to decide conflicts of jurisdiction between the administrative and common courts. In great part to deal with the overwhelming amount of litigation straining the resources of the judiciary, there are a growing number of arbitration courts that are legally recognized and settle small consumer and commercial disputes. However, these are courts of voluntary jurisdiction (some minor exceptions are allowed by Articles 1525–1528 of the civil procedure code). There have been debates on whether to subject particular types of consumer and commercial litigation to mandatory arbitration courts or other informal forums of dispute resolution. However, no such steps have been taken so far and, for some, subjecting certain legal disputes to the mandatory jurisdiction of nonjudicial bodies as arbitration courts would violate the constitutional provision that reserves the settlement of legal disputes to state courts. To address the same problem of excessive workload in the courts, a recent amendment to the civil procedure code has established a very simplified form of civil procedure for certain types of credit disputes (corresponding to litigation arising from mass contracts regarding public utilities, banking, and so on). This simplified form may dispense the intervention of a judge.

Contrary to civil procedure, criminal prosecution is a monopoly of the state exercised by the Public Prosecution Office (the Ministério Público, which is headed by the Procurador Geral da République). Only the Ministério Público has legitimacy to start a criminal process, although it may be procedurally supported by particulars in the quality of *Assistentes* that are mainly conceived as cooperating with the Ministério Público. The latter can, however, have an important independent role in producing or requesting evidence to the court or in appealing from the decisions of the Ministério Público (for example, appealing from a decision not to proceed with criminal prosecution). It must also be stated that the prosecution of some crimes by the Ministério Público depends on the lodging of a complaint by the person that has suffered the crime. These are called semipublic crimes, to be distinguished from public crimes whose prosecution is mandatory to the Ministério Público, and do not depend upon a private complaint. The Ministério Público directs all investigations of suspected crimes, coordinating the different police departments. Several acts of the investigation, however, require a judicial decision. After the Ministério Público decides to criminally prosecute a suspect, the latter can ask for an intermediary procedural stage of judicial character called *instrução*. In this stage further evidence can be produced by both parties and the process of inquiry is directed by the *juiz de instrução* (a judge). It is this judge that takes the decision on whether to proceed or not to a final judgment on the basis of reasonable expectations of guilt. Depending on the presumed crimes, the final judgment may take place before a single judge or a collective court of judges. In either case there is a right of appeal. The Portuguese criminal process does not authorize judgment by juries except, in some instances, at the request of the accused themselves.

The constitutional court is given very broad powers of constitutional review. The Portuguese Constitution established a very comprehensive system of constitutional judicial review that allows for several types of judicial actions to be brought to the court. The first type is called "preventive concentrated constitutional review" and grants to the president the possibility to request from the court an ex-ante constitutional review of laws that have been approved and sent to the president for promulgation before they enter into effect. In limited cases regarding regional legislation this possibility is also open to the regional ministers (representatives of the State Sovereignty on the Autonomous Regions of Madeira and Azores). The judgment of the court is binding on the president. With the reduction (in political practice and in law) of the president's powers of political veto over legislation, this constitutional form of action has become, in some respects, the main political tool of the president to express his opposition to certain legislative acts. The second form of constitutional judicial action is "ex-post abstract concentrated constitutional review," which grants to several public entities the possibility to raise before the court in abstract an issue of constitutionality regarding any norm independently of any specific conflict. The action can be brought to the court by, among other entities, the president, the prime minister, the ombudsman, the attorney general, and members of Parliament constituting at least 10 percent of the total members. The last form of constitutional judicial action is the broadest and corresponds to the traditional form of diffuse constitutional judicial review. It grants the right of appeal to the constitutional court of any decision by any other court of the judicial system that either refused to apply a certain norm on the basis of its unconstitutionality or applied a norm whose unconstitutionality has been raised by any of the litigants. Apart from its fundamental task of constitutional judicial review the constitutional court has also been given some other specialized functions regarding electoral law, the financing and operation of the political system, and the review of norms with regard to international law and special legislative acts of higher ranking. Some of these competencies do not result from

the constitution but are set up in Law 28/82 of November 15 (as amended by subsequent laws), which regulates the statute of the constitutional court.

Finally, it must be recalled that the Portuguese legal courts system can no longer be seen in isolation from the legal and judicial system of the European Union. Both the European Court of Justice and the European Court of First Instance already exercise jurisdiction over broad areas of the national legal order. At the same time, Portuguese courts are also the courts of first instance in the application of EU law. The main mechanism of cooperation and connection between the national and European courts is Article 234 of the EC Treaty (*see* European Court of Justice). Here it is only important to stress that Portuguese courts have generally recognized and accepted the supremacy and direct effect of EU legal norms in their national legal order. However, at the same time, Portuguese courts have been one of the EU national judicial systems that have made fewer references for a preliminary ruling to the European Court of Justice (seven, compared with Austria's fifty-six in 1999). The constitutional court has been very cautious in addressing the status of EU law with regard to national constitutional law (the *kompetenz-kompetenz* question) in parallel with the usual reaction of national constitutional courts throughout the Union. On the other hand, it has recognized the supremacy and direct effect of EU law over national infraconstitutional norms and, contrary to other European national constitutional courts, it has admitted (though it has never practiced it) the possibility of requesting a ruling itself from the European Court of Justice on a question regarding the interpretation and application of EU law.

STAFFING

The university law degree is organized as a five-year program in almost all law schools. The only exception to this system is the curriculum of the Faculdade de Direito da Universidade Nova de Lisboa, which is organized as a credits system following a model similar to that in place in American law schools. However, even in this law school the number of credits required is set so that, in practice, a student would normally need at least five years of study. There are public and private law schools. The fees of public universities are very low, but admission is subject to *numerus clausus*. As a consequence, private universities (with the exception of Universidade Católica) have normally been aimed at providing education to those left out of the public system and are usually understaffed in terms of faculty members. The largest faculties are those of the Faculdade de Direito da Universidade de Coimbra (the oldest law school), Faculdade de Direito da Universidade de Lisboa, Faculdade de Direito da Universidade Nova de Lisboa, and Faculdade de Direito da Universidade Católica. The first three are all public law schools.

The possession of the legal degree (*Licenciatura*) is not in itself sufficient to have access to the legal profession. Attorneys need to be members of the bar association (Ordem dos Advogados), and for this they first need to pass the so far relatively accessible exam and to have a training period of eighteen months under the supervision of a senior attorney. Most people holding a law degree undergo a training period but many then move on to different professions. In 1999 there were 17,637 practicing attorneys and 4,652 people enrolled in the training period. These numbers present an enormous rise in recent years mainly due to the increased number of law degrees offered by private universities. This steep increase in the number of practicing lawyers gives Portugal one of the highest numbers of attorneys per capita (165 per 100,000 inhabitants) among European countries. This distinction, together with many criticisms of the quality of some of the law degrees offered, has raised calls for increased scrutiny of the access of holders of law degrees to the Ordem dos Advogados.

Access to the judiciary and the Public Prosecution Office is dependent on complementary studies that are undertaken in common at a professional public school called Centro de Estudos Judiciários. These studies take two years and are complemented and followed by training periods in different courts or in the Public Prosecution Office. The judiciary profession is under the supervision and control of the Conselho Superior de Magistratura, which, among other things, appoints the judges, reviews their careers, and exercises disciplinary powers. The Conselho Superior de Magistratura is composed by judges and other independent personalities and is presided over by the president of the Supremo Tribunal de Justiça. In 1998, there were a total of 1,364 judges in office (13 per 100,000 inhabitants). At the same time there were 982 public prosecutors (11 per 100,000 inhabitants). It must be said that, in Portugal, the public prosecutors have functions that go beyond criminal actions, including acting as attorneys for the state and protecting certain diffuse interests.

IMPACT OF LAW

It has become common in Portugal to say that the justice system is in crisis. The crisis of the justice system is one of the main topics of public discourse in politics, in the media, and in public opinion. One of the main reasons for the perception of such a crisis lies in the extensive delays in the provision of justice by the judicial process, which is, in part, a consequence of the explosion of litigation that took place in Portugal in the 1980s and 1990s. The average time for a judicial process in Portugal is fifteen months. In criminal cases it extends up to seventeen months (excluding prejudgment proceedings). The consequence of the high number of judicial

processes burdening the courts, coupled with the long time that a judicial process normally takes, is a very high number of pending cases. In 1998 there were more than a million cases pending only in the common courts. In the same judicial branch, there were 731,057 (736 per 1,000 inhabitants) proceedings started in that year and 619,529 (6,208 per 1,000 inhabitants) concluded. This means that the tendency is for the number of pending cases to grow. The average number of processes allocated to a judge is 802. If the participants in litigation processes tend to be fairly spread between individual actors and corporate and institutional actors, processes started by the latter tend to be decided in a shorter period of time. This pattern corresponds to the lower information and transaction costs to which institutional and corporate actors are subject and is fairly typical of a judicial model based on a market economy and the rule of law.

The perception of a crisis in the justice system has spilled over to the criminal justice system. Much is due to the fact that, under Portuguese law, criminal prosecution is forfeited if not completed in a certain period of time. Many high-profile cases of criminal prosecution were forfeited in this way due to complex criminal investigations coupled with technicalities that prevented the suspension of the forfeit period. This has had a great impact on the media and public opinion. As a consequence, the public has a generalized perception of impunity with regard to many such cases (several of them related to forms of public corruption). This extends into an overall distrust of the criminal system, with some claims that the Portuguese legal system provides excessive guarantees to the rights of the accused and that courts are "soft on crime." There is a growing tension between, on the one side, the dominant legal thinking that reflects the Portuguese tradition of low penalties and the vision of criminal law as directed toward the social rehabilitation of individuals and, on the other side, growing public appeals for a stronger fight against crime expressing itself less in protective criminal procedure and more in punitive law. In any event, Portugal is still a country with a low crime rate. There were around 330,000 crimes in 1998 reported to the different police branches but most of these crimes were of a nonviolent nature. The number of crimes against people reported to the Polícia Judiciária (the most serious crimes) was 2,141.

Cristina Nogueira da Silva
Miguel Poiares Maduro

See also Angola; Brazil; Cape Verde; Civil Law; European Court of Justice; Mozambique; Roman Law; São Tomé and Príncipe; Small Claims Courts
References and further reading
Albuquerque, Martim, and Ruy Albuquerque. 1986. *História do direito Português*. Lisboa: Faculdade de Direito de Lisboa.
Almeida, Carlos Ferreira de. 1998. *Introdução ao direito comparado*. 2d ed. Coimbra: Almedina.

Barreto, António. 2000. *A Situação Social em Portugal,* vol. 2. Lisboa: ICS.

Barreto, António, ed. 2000. *Justiça em crise? Crises da justiça.* Lisboa: Dom Quixote.

Canotilho, Joaquim J. Gomes. 2000. *Direito constitucional,* Coimbra: Almedina.

Hespanha, António Manuel. 1988. "Notas do tradutor." In *Introdução histórica ao direito.* Edited by J. Gilissen. Lisboa: Gulbenkian.

Ministério da Justiça. 1998. GEP, Estatísticas da Justiça, Lisboa.

Santos, Boaventura Sousa, Maria Manuel Leitão Marques, and João e Lopes Ferreira Pedroso. *Os tribunais nas sociedades contemporâneas: O caso Português.* Porto: Edições Afrontamento.

Silva, Nuno Espinosa Gomes da. 1992. *História do direito Português.* Lisboa: Gulbenkian.

PRINCE EDWARD ISLAND

GENERAL INFORMATION

In 1770 an unpaid assistant justice of the Supreme Court of Nova Scotia, John Duport, was named chief justice of the newly minted colony of St. John's Island (renamed "Prince Edward Island" in 1799). As chief justice, Duport was now entitled to pay. Unfortunately, the government of Governor Walter Patterson was unable to collect quit-rents—a form of taxation—owed by the "proprietors" (each of whom owned twenty thousand–acre townships on the island). Consequently, Duport's pay was meager and sporadic. Lacking other means of support, he died of malnutrition in May 1774.

His successor, Peter Stewart, a brother of one of the proprietors, was appointed chief justice in 1775, but, owing to hostilities between Britain and some of its other North American colonies, his commission did not arrive until July 1776, with the result that the island was effectively for two years without a chief justice. Not that the situation improved when the commission finally appeared. The law administered on St. John's Island was the common law of Great Britain, but Stewart, a Scot, was educated in Scots' Law, a branch of the great Roman Law tree. This defect in legal knowledge was matched by a considerable lack of scruple, and decisions from the two decades when Stewart sat on the bench must be accounted "fascinating."

Given these less than auspicious beginnings, the legal system of Prince Edward Island really had no direction to move but up.

"THE ISLAND"

Taking into account the size of its population and its small landmass, Prince Edward Island should probably be a county of Nova Scotia. That was the original intention. The island was annexed to Nova Scotia by the Royal Proclamation of 1763, issued after the Treaty of Paris ceded, among other territories, the former Îsle St. Jean to England. However, pressure from "the proprietors"—creditors of the Crown and military officers owed back pay, who were awarded twenty thousand–acre townships in lieu of payment by a lottery held on July 23, 1767—convinced the king's council to endorse a political separation of the island from Nova Scotia, effective June 28, 1769. The continued maintenance of this distinct colonial status explains Prince Edward Island's distinct constitutional status, today, as the smallest of Canada's ten provinces.

Prince Edward Island is a scimitar-shaped landmass lying in the Gulf of St. Lawrence, just off the northern coasts of New Brunswick and Nova Scotia. It is 139 miles (224 kilometers) long and varies from 4 to 40 miles (6 to 64 kilometers) in width. Slightly more than half of the land is in agricultural production and, indeed, agriculture is the largest industry in the province. In recent decades, the island has been marketed as a vacation destination, and tourism now represents the second largest business sector, with the fishery, formerly number two, taking up third place. However, a substantial portion of the island's gross provincial product—something approaching 40 percent of gross revenues—actually derives from "transfer" and "equalization" payments injected into the economy by the federal government. Not surprisingly, there is a thriving public sector and large civil service.

"THE CRADLE OF CONFEDERATION": PRINCE EDWARD ISLAND AND THE CANADIAN CONFEDERATION

In September 1864, delegates from Nova Scotia, New Brunswick, and Prince Edward Island were to meet in Charlottetown, the capital of Prince Edward Island, to discuss a plan to unite those three provinces into a single political unit. This meeting was effectively "crashed" by a delegation from the United Province of Canada (now Ontario and Quebec), who came with a proposal to create a larger federation of provinces. This proposal was adopted in principle by all the delegations, with the ultimate result that the country of Canada came into being three years later on July 1, 1867. Thus Prince Edward Island in general (and the city of Charlottetown in particular) is known as "the Cradle of Confederation."

"Cradle" though it may have been, P.E.I., through its delegation, disagreed on certain key points with other provincial delegations during the succeeding constitutional discussions and debates, and the province declined to enter the Canadian Confederation in 1867. Only after suffering serious financial loss occasioned by the building of a railway did Prince Edward Island resume negotiations for admission into the confederation. It became a province of Canada in 1873.

One of the sticking points for P.E.I. in 1864 had been the nature of the Canadian upper house, the Senate. Curiously enough, when the island entered confederation in 1873, the Senate seats it was accorded became the basis for the province's current unique constitutional status. Prince Edward Island was given four seats, only two less than the far more populous province of British Columbia. But what is more significant is the impact on the island's representation in the Canadian House of Commons. Section 51A of the Constitution Act of 1867, as amended, provides that a province shall not have fewer seats in the House of Commons than it has in the Senate. Thus the 138,000 people of P.E.I. are represented by four members of Parliament. This is anomalous. The city of St. Catharines, Ontario, for example, has a population of 106,000 but is entitled to only one MP. The fundamental democratic principle of representation by population takes a unique constitutional twist in the case of Prince Edward Island.

LAW-MAKING

This unique constitutional status aside, Prince Edward Island differs little from the other nine Canadian provinces in its law making and in the administration of justice. Laws are made by the Legislative Assembly. As is the case with other Canadian provinces, the Assembly is unicameral. However, until comparatively recently, it was unicameral with a twist.

P.E.I., like other provinces, originally had an upper house, the Legislative Council, and a lower, the Assembly, modeled on the "lower" House of Commons and "upper" House of Lords of the British Parliament. In the 1880s, many provinces discarded their upper houses. In the face of this popular trend, Prince Edward Island hesitated and then compromised. The Legislative Council would disappear as a separate chamber, but not the legislative councilors. They would join the assemblymen in a single chamber, but keep their status, with the result that, until the election of 1996, every constituency on the island voted for a councilor and an assemblyman.

Otherwise, the nature of government and the practices and procedures of the Legislative Assembly derive, in large outline, from the pattern provided by the British "Mother of Parliaments" at Westminster. (Unfortunately, the political "culture," which elects members of the legislature, is still the ward boss/patronage kind of system that has disappeared in many other places.)

THE BENCH AND THE BAR

Prince Edward Island is likewise far from unique in the administration of justice. Like all other provinces and territories of Canada, its courts are part of an essentially unitary system (as compared with the dual federal/state court systems of the United States, for example), in which the

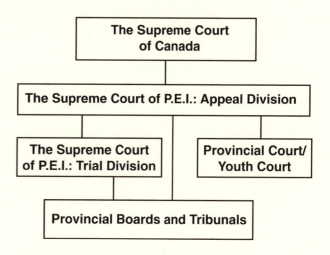

Legal Structure of Prince Edward Island Courts

highest court of appeal for the province is the Supreme Court of Canada. Like all other provinces and territories, P.E.I. has a two-tiered court system: a superior court in two divisions—the Supreme Court, whose judges are appointed by the federal government under S. 96 of the Constitution Act of 1867—and a "specialist" Provincial Court, the judges of which are appointed by the province. There is also a provincial Youth Court, staffed by the judges of the Provincial Court. Unlike many provinces, the P.E.I. Provincial Court deals only with criminal matters and provincial regulatory offenses, and the Youth Court administers criminal law within the limits set by the Young Offenders Act of Canada.

As has been the case with many other common law legal systems, the jurisdiction of the Supreme Court of Prince Edward Island has been effectively diminished by the transferring of certain subject areas to the jurisdiction of statutory administrative boards and tribunals. For example, landlord and tenant matters are dealt with by the Island Regulatory and Appeals Commission (IRAC), a powerful—possibly overly powerful—omnibus board that also regulates matters as diverse as rural land use and the price of gasoline. Decisions of boards of this type are subject to judicial review by the Trial Division of the Supreme Court or, in some instances, are subject to direct appeal to the Appeal Division.

The Trial Division of the Supreme Court of P.E.I. is administered by its own chief justice, and the Appeal Division likewise has a chief justice, who is also the chief justice of the province. The Appeal Division is of recent vintage. Until 1987, appeals were heard by the court sitting en banc—that is, judges of a single-layered Supreme Court, other than the judge who heard the matter at trial, sitting as a group to hear the appeal.

Like other courts in the common law world, the manner of proceeding is adversarial, an essentially irrational process that is founded on the belief that a "battle" between contesting parties in front of an "impartial" umpire (the judge) will somehow produce a result that is true and just.

As is the case with many, if not most, courts in the common law world, the P.E.I. Supreme Court has a "fused" jurisdiction of law and equity; that is, it administers justice according to the principles—"law"—developed by the so-called common law courts (Common Pleas, King's Bench, Exchequer Court) in England, and according to the principles and practices of equity as developed in the British Court of Chancery.

This was not always the case, and, indeed, the fusion is of relatively recent vintage. The current court is a lineal descendant of a court that predated the creation of the Canadian Confederation. The Constitution Act of 1867 effectively recognized the existing courts of the four provinces that made up the original confederation, as opposed to creating new bodies. That same recognition extended to the existing Supreme Court of Prince Edward Island when it joined the confederation in 1873.

The superior court of Prince Edward Island was titled the "Supreme Court" from the time of its founding. Governor Walter Patterson's instructions authorized him to establish courts of law for St. John's Island (as well as a House of Assembly, among other things). He did so almost immediately upon his arrival, with the result that John Duport, as already mentioned, became chief justice in 1770, three years before the first sitting of the Assembly.

The Supreme Court of St. John's Island was modeled on the Supreme Court of Nova Scotia. Like that court, the Supreme Court of St. John's Island was a court of law, not a court of equity, as that was understood in the British tradition. (The reason for this lies in the British separation of "law," administered by the so-called courts of common law, and "equity," administered by the chancellor.) In British colonies, the office of chancellor belonged, in the opinion of the law officers of the Crown, to the person who held the "great seal" of the colony—namely, the governor.

The result was that, effectively, there were two courts administering justice in St. John's (later Prince Edward) Island. Both might be involved in the same matter, if an issue of equity arose, as was the situation in one celebrated case, *Bowley v. Cambridge,* which started in the Supreme Court in 1794 (as *Cambridge v. Bowley*) and finished in Chancery in 1841, having four times been appealed to what was then the court of appeal for the colony, the Royal Privy Council in England.

Legislation fused the common law courts and Chancery into a single High Court in England in the 1880s, and Canadian provinces generally followed suit.

The exception (as it had been to some extent in the instance of abolishing legislative councils) was Prince Edward Island. Until 1975, P.E.I. maintained a separate Chancery Court with a single judge sitting as chancellor.

Judges of the Supreme Court of Prince Edward Island—five justices of the Trial Division, three justices of Appeal—are drawn from the complement of lawyers practicing at the bar of Prince Edward Island (as required by SS. 97 and 98 of the Constitution Act of 1867); they must have at least ten years' total practice at any provincial bar (S. 3 of the Judges Act). As is generally the case in Canada, there is no specific training for the position of judge.

Likewise, judges of the Provincial Court are drawn from the provincial bar and must have been in practice for five years. The Provincial Court of Prince Edward Island is, effectively, a successor institution to what were formerly Magistrates' Courts, presided over by lay justices of the peace. Like all other Canadian provinces, P.E.I. has professionalized this jurisdiction by appointing lawyers to the bench—though, as already mentioned, unlike many provinces, the jurisdiction of the P.E.I. Provincial Court's three judges extends to criminal matters only.

Lawyers practicing on Prince Edward Island fall under the jurisdiction of the Law Society of Prince Edward Island. All applicants for membership in the society and call to the bar must have completed a bachelor of laws (LL.B.) program (equivalent to the juris doctor in the United States). As in other Canadian provinces, a period of "articles" is required (twelve months' apprenticeship), part of which is a seven-week "bar course." While maintaining this bar course as a requirement, the Law Society apparently lacks the resources to mount the course itself, with the result that articling students must attend, at considerable expense, the course offered by the Nova Scotia Barristers' Society in Halifax, Nova Scotia.

Upon completing all requirements, the candidate is called to the bar—literally presented by his or her principal to one of the justices of the Supreme Court, who administers the barrister's oath. Since the bar of Prince Edward Island is small, these "calls" are individual (as compared with the province of Ontario, for example, where hundreds may be called at the same time). A lawyer is called as "barrister, solicitor, *and* attorney" (unlike many other provincial jurisdictions in the British legal tradition, where lawyers are "barristers and solicitors" only).

CONCLUSION

Nearly two and a half centuries after its inelegant start, the legal system of Prince Edward Island is structured like that of other Canadian provincial systems and, though small in size, carries on the same functions. The bar and bench share the same professional characteristics as their fellows in other provinces. The system has come a long way from the days of John Duport and Peter Stewart, but this is not to say that an ideal state has been reached. Like other legal systems in the common law world, the system found in P.E.I. is characterized by the retention of the essentially irrational adversary system, and, like many other systems of law generally, it is characterized by inaccessibility arising from costs. It would seem that, in those particulars, it still has a long way to go.

David M. Bulger

See also Administrative Law; Adversarial Systems; Alternative Dispute Resolution; Barristers; Canada; Civil Procedure; Constitutional Law; Constitutionalism; Criminal Law; Criminal Procedures; England and Wales; Equity; Federalism; Human Rights Law; Law Clerks; Lay Judiciaries; New Brunswick; Nova Scotia; Privy Council; Quebec; Scotland; Solicitors; Trial Courts

References and further reading
Baar, Carl. 1988. "The Structure and Personnel of the Canadian Judiciary." Pp. 53–82 in *The Political Role of Law Courts in Democracies*. Rev. ed. Edited by Holland and Waltman. London and Basingstoke: Macmillan.
Bolger, Francis W. P., ed. 1973. *Canada's Smallest Province*. Halifax: Nimbus Publishing.
Bulger, David M. 1998. "'Mr. Cambridge Is Anxious That It Should Not Be Supposed That He Has Any Desire to Procrastinate a Final Decision . . .' *Bowley v. Cambridge*: A Colonial Jarndyce and Jarndyce." Paper presented at Canadian Legal History Conference, "Exploring Canada's Legal Past," Toronto.
Bumsted, J. M. 1992. "The Bench of Early Prince Edward Island, 1769–1824." Paper presented at Learned Societies Conference, Charlottetown.
Greco, Clara. 1990. "The Superior Court Judiciary of Nova Scotia, 1754–1900: A Collective Biography." P. 42 in *Essays in the History of Canadian Law*. Vol. III. Edited by Philip Girard and Jim Phillips. Toronto: Osgoode Society.
Holman, H. T. 1992. "The Profits of the Profession of Law Will Not Maintain a Gentleman: The Bar of Prince Edward Island 1769–1853." Paper presented at Learned Societies Conference, Charlottetown.

PRIVATE LAW

Private law is that body of law that governs claims for relief brought by one private party against another. In this context, a party is "private" in that he or she is not an agent or representative of any governmental entity but an individual acting in his or her own personal interest. This is in contrast to the bodies of law that purport to articulate the interests of a larger public, which include criminal law, constitutional law, or laws concerning political or governmental conduct. Modern private law covers suits for torts (wrongful acts committed by one person that harm another), breach of contract, and property law, as well as a host of special subcategories. Between them, it is understood that the categories of private law should define the circumstances under which an individual may appeal to public institutions for the validation of a private interest. As a result, an examination of the system of private law in a legal system reveals a great deal about the kinds of interests that are deemed worthy of public protection in that system.

The alternative to private law is public law, meaning the body of law that governs matters of governmental or constitutional concern. The line dividing private from public law has varied across history and geography, but some general characteristics that are typical of private law regimes can be delineated. Private law tends to be precedent-driven, judge-made law. This description is true not only in common law systems such as the United States and Britain but also in the code-based systems common in European countries. Since private law determines the outcome of specific disputes between individuals, it is necessarily much more specific to a particular set of facts. So, for example, a criminal law need only define conduct that is to be prohibited; by contrast, private law doctrines of breach of contract have to account for myriad variations in the phrasing of contracts, the manner of their execution, and a nearly infinite set of possible fact-scenarios. Thus even in code-based systems there is room for a range of variations that invites and ultimately requires judges to supply detailed formulations specific to their cases. In a legal system that recognizes the concept of "precedent," the accretion of these decisions invariably leads to a situation in which private law becomes a separate, more or less autonomous system of legal doctrines that stand on their own.

The recognition of a separate body of private law begins with the Roman system of civil law. In Roman law, "public law" meant criminal law, the application and enforcement of rules and state sanctions for their violation. Private law, or *civiliter,* consisted of *in rem* (property) and *in personam* (personal) actions. Criminal law was public in that it reflected an act of the state and in that the outcome would be a judgment designed to punish the wrongdoer. Civil law was private in that it governed complaints brought by private individuals against other individuals, and the outcome would be a judgment designed to remedy the harm that the plaintiff had suffered. The same words and the basic distinctions that they represent were brought into English law beginning in the thirteenth century, but some of the particular differentiating features dropped out. In early English law, the distinction between private and public law was largely a distinction based on procedures rather than on the substance of the underlying facts of the case or the remedy that the court might enforce. The distinction was made between "common pleas" and "pleas to the crown" (to this day, many local courts are called "courts of common pleas" in both England and United States). The remedies that were available under the two categories were not clearly distinct, as all common law actions in those days had a penal aspect. Tort law, in particular, was a category of private law that seemed to straddle the traditional Roman distinctions. To sue someone in "trespass" in early modern England, the most common and broadly defined of the early pleas, looks to modern eyes a good deal like a criminal prosecution. The complaint would say that the defendant had committed his or her acts "with force of arms" and "against the king's peace." The person sued would be arrested and, if found guilty, would be held in prison until the judgment was satisfied. This bit of early English history points to an important point about private law generally: within different legal systems, "private law" may have a more or less "public" aspect, both in terms of the involvement of the machinery of the state in enforcement and in terms of the ways in which private law doctrines can become instruments of public policy.

In the eighteenth century, William Blackstone's commentaries on the common law reiterated the Roman categories of private law and included a separate chapter discussing "injuries proceeding from, or affecting, the Crown." The discussion of this last category continued the blurring between private and public law, when it spoke of "injuries, or private wrongs, that may be offered by one subject to another, all of which are redressed by the command and authority of the king." In addition, Blackstone continued to call for a fine to accompany any civil judgment, "for his wilful delay of justice in not immediately obeying the king's writ by rendering the plaintiff his due." Despite these elements, however, by that time it was generally the case that public law and private law were sharply differentiated by the remedies provided, a basis for distinction that would become more clear with the abolition of debtor's prison. The focus on differences in remedies as the hallmark of the separation between civil and criminal law continued in the U.S. tradition. At the same time, the blurring of the two categories also continued, as with the inclusion of punitive damages in certain private actions—damages that mixed punitive elements with the idea of "make whole" compensation—and, by the latter part of the nineteenth century, with the increasingly prominent role of state legislatures in promulgating rules for the adjudication of private law cases. To see the significance of the legislative role, however, we need to look outside England for the experience of Europe.

Like English law, the private law of other European nations—notably France, Germany, Italy, the Netherlands, and Belgium—began with inherited Roman codes, which were grafted onto existing local customs. There were two basic contrasts between the European and English experiences, however. First, prior to the nineteenth century, European nations' systems of private law were far less uniform than was that of England. In the twelfth century, Henry II announced that England would be governed by a "common law," a single national system governing private claims as well as public edicts, and despite the persistence of significant local variations, Henry's proclamation defined the essential shape of English legal development thereafter. Initially, "common" law had referred to matters of sufficient public import that they should be nationally uniform, but by the time of Blackstone, the idea of a single system of private as well as public common law was well established.

By contrast, in Europe before the 1800s, the idea of a national system of private law was barely known at all. Instead, what prevailed was a combination of local legal custom and *jus commune,* a combination of inherited Roman and canonical principles whose proponents argued was applicable throughout Western society. Thus there was local private law and universal private law but not a clear category of national private law. In the 1800s, however, the form of European private law underwent a profound transformation with the introduction of the idea of "codification." The first and most important of these codifications of private law systems occurred in France under Napoleon, in 1804. The French codifiers did not conceive of themselves as replacing the combination of customary and Roman law with an entirely new, government-designed system. To the contrary, they viewed their project as the preservation and organization of the existing system of laws, which they took to be expressions of their nation's historical path of development. With time, said Jean Portalis, the leading member of the drafting committee, "codes make themselves; strictly speaking nobody makes them." Objectors insisted that codification violated the idea of law as a historical expression of common wisdom rather than as a set of positive, political calculations. In other words, the objection was that private law was fundamentally different from public questions of policy. In England, the idea of codification never took hold because of the success of the bar in making these sorts of objections. At the other extreme were German writers who argued that codification ought to replace historical tradition entirely. Christian von Wolff, influenced by Baruch Spinoza and Gottfried Leibniz, thought of law as a "scientific" endeavor whose universal principles could be deduced from known axioms in the manner of geometry. As Wolff put it in 1754, "all obligations are deduced from human nature in a universal system."

The French approach marked a middle path, deliberately leaving judges enough freedom to adapt rules to particular cases. It is for this reason that in civil law countries, private law remains a function of judicial interpretation to this day. Wolff's thought was immensely influential in Germany, and the German code adopted in 1900 was far more theoretically oriented and represented a far sharper departure from existing customs than the more positivist, case-by-case rules of the French Civil Code. Wolff's approach can be seen today in the German concept of *Begriffsjurisprudenz,* a jurisprudence based on logic. The difference goes directly to the difference in the conception of the relationship between private and public law. As van Caenegem puts it, "in Germanic lands the citizens were the product of the law, whereas in France the law was the product of the citizens, for there the law derived not from a sovereign but from the volonte generale ('common will')" (1992, 126). European private law doctrines are uniformly code-based, civil law systems with Roman and customary roots, but they display varying degrees of French historicism and German deductivism.

The U.S. pattern of development has been different from those of England, Germany, or France, although it has connections to all of them. The United States has followed a basically historicist tradition, strongly grounded in the English approach. In the United States, however, more than in most other places, it is useful to speak of private law as one of three categories: private law, public law, and political or constitutional law. In his 1864 "Introduction to Municipal Law," John Norton Pomeroy distinguishes between private and political law and puts criminal law in the private law category. The point was not that Pomeroy did not see a role for the state in enforcing and formulating criminal law but rather that he was observing a different distinction, between laws that served a public policy purpose and those that merely regulated individual conduct. This observation reflects a basic difference between public and private law, but the location of that difference is at the points at which various systems diverge. Public law, in this understanding, is a deliberate intervention in historical development, an act of a legislature designed to produce some desirable social outcome based on a plan of action. Private law, by contrast, reflects social relations at the level of individuals and is therefore to a much greater degree understood as an articulation of the reality of those relations rather than a prescription for a desirable direction of future development. To a deductivist, by contrast, there is no such sharp difference, so that broad conceptual distinctions between public and private law are difficult to describe.

The other difference between historicist and deductivist approaches to codification led to continuing differences in the governing conception of the relationship between courts and legislatures in the formulation of private law doctrines. Deductivists, who believe that private law derives from universal, natural law precepts, and "realists," who deny the distinction between private and public law and conceive of all laws as political or economic measures, are more likely to look to legislatures as the source of fixed rules. Both of these tendencies, for example, can be seen at work in the efforts to formulate rules applicable throughout the European Union on questions of private law, such as the rules for employment. By contrast, historicists tend to give more power to courts and judges, as institutions uniquely empowered with the ability to express the consciousness of a "people."

As the reference to employment indicates, however, in historicist systems there is a constant tendency for legislatures to assume a role in the formulation of private law rules, a pattern exemplified by the historical experience of the United States, where national constitutional principles and state-specific policy preferences are both frequently the basis for legislative adjustments to private law rules. Conversely, it is equally the case that courts adjudicating private law claims may become caught up in questions of public policy. In the U.S. case, again, constitutional principles represent the point at which claims of private rights act as checks on the public capacities of governments. In a different way, the modern tendency toward mass lawsuits—most recently against tobacco companies but earlier against polluters, drug companies, auto manufacturers, and many others—has made U.S. private law one of the most powerful regulatory forces in the system of national governance. Companies in Germany conduct themselves in accordance with statutes and are generally not susceptible to suits for private damages when they violate those rules. In the United States, by contrast, companies must conduct themselves so as to avoid liability in common law courts for private lawsuits. To a great extent, this demonstrates the supremacy of private law over public regulation in the U.S. system of jurisprudence.

Howard Schweber

See also Civil Law; Common Law; Commercial Law (International Aspects); Contract Law; Customary Law; Law and Society Movement; Public Law; Tort Law

References and further reading

Baker, John H. 1990. *An Introduction to English Legal History.* Boston: Butterworths.
Berman, Harold J. 1983. *Law and Revolution: The Formation of the Western Legal Tradition.* Cambridge, MA: Harvard University Press.
Blackstone, William. 1979. *Commentaries on the Laws of England.* 4 vols. Chicago: University of Chicago Press.
Friedman, Lawrence M. 1985. *A History of American Law.* 2d ed. New York: Simon and Schuster.
Hoeflich, Michael H. 1997. *Roman and Civil Law and the Development of Anglo-American Jurisprudence in the Nineteenth Century.* Athens: University of Georgia Press.
van Caenegem, R. C. 1992. *An Historical Introduction to Private Law.* Translated by D. E. L. Johnston. Cambridge: Cambridge University Press.

PRIVY COUNCIL

DEFINITION

The Judicial Committee of the Privy Council was created by statute in 1833 to function as the final appeals court to review civil and criminal cases for certain Commonwealth countries and the Channel Islands (Jersey and Guernsey) and the Isle of Man in the United Kingdom (Privy Council Office, January 16, 2001). Other appellate jurisdictions added were those from prize courts, admiralty courts, and ecclesiastical cases, such as divorce. Cases referred from various medical boards have been added to the Judicial Committee's jurisdiction, as has the responsibility under the 1998 devolution statutes to decide whether the governments of Wales, Scotland, and Northern Ireland act properly according to the enabling legislation.

The Judicial Committees of the Privy Council and the House of Lords, which are separate from each other, constitute final appellate authorities for different parts of the English courts. The Judicial Committee within the House of Lords serves as the final appeals court for the United Kingdom. That of the Privy Council is as previously described (Swinfen 1987). The House of Lords hears civil and criminal appeals from England, Wales, and Northern Ireland and civil appeals from Scotland. The Judicial Committee constitutes one of several Privy Council committees. In general, the Privy Council Office is the administrative office for the cabinet. Current and previous cabinet members and lords retain the title of "P.C." for life.

HISTORY

Originally, the Privy Council functioned as the sovereign's private council. Before the fifteenth century, the council was mainly concerned not with common law issues but those of foreign merchants and trade, with either "actions in which the common law failed to provide adequate remedies" or matters "touching on the King's own interests" (Curzon 1979, 176). Under the reign of Henry VII in the fifteenth and sixteenth centuries, the council was given more power to act as a Crown arbitrator (Curzon 1979, 177).

By the sixteenth century, the King's Council was disaggregated into the Privy Council, Courts of Chancery, Star Chamber, and High Commission. The judicial function of the Privy Council is said to rest on the "ancient prerogative of the Sovereign as the fountain of justice throughout the dominions" (Privy Council Office, June 5, 2001). Within the judicial branch, the Chancery Court was independent from both the King's Council and the common law. The King's counselor, at the Chancery Court's head, issued writs and heard proceedings against the Crown (Curzon 1979, 104–105). The

Star Chamber, separated from the Privy Council in 1540, administered criminal law. The High Commission existed to enforce the state's religious policy (Curzon 1979, 158, 177–181). It could excommunicate, fine, and imprison citizens.

Following the English civil war, in 1641 the Privy Council was stripped of much of its power by parliamentarians and lawyers angry at its basis in royal prerogative power, its political actions, and power over common law. That year, Parliament abolished the Star Chamber, High Commission, and all Privy Council functions except the appellate jurisdiction over the Channel Islands and overseas dominions (Swinfen 1987, 3). Colonial charters granted after 1660 generally included the Crown's right to hear appeals from these colonies. Although appeals technically came to the king or queen as the source of justice, they would be referred to the Privy Council. Short-term committees of the Privy Council were appointed to hear overseas appeals until 1679, at which time this jurisdiction was moved to the Board of Trade. In 1696, the responsible body became the "Committees of Appeals," which were ad hoc committees appointed for each case (Swinfen 1987, 3–4). This system existed until the early 1830s, becoming increasingly inefficient during the period of the empire's greatest expansion. Chief complaints included judicial incompetence (judges appointed to each committee happened to be whoever was available on a particular day), that a system of inconsistent legal norms was developing throughout the colonies with different legal systems, and that appeals were not only expensive but becoming backlogged for up to one year (Swinfen 1987, 3–5).

These complaints were all answered by the passage of the 1833 Judicial Committee Act. The person behind this movement was Henry Brougham, lord chancellor from 1831 to 1834, who is credited with "having created the Judicial Committee almost singlehandedly" (Swinfen 1987, 3 n. 7). Brougham's proposal involved the appointment of judges drawn from a regular bar. It immediately included twenty privy councilors who had held or did hold high judicial offices, such as past or present lords president of the Privy Council and the chief justices of the Courts of King's Bench and Common Pleas. The lord chancellor and master of the rolls (both ex officio judges from the Court of Appeal) were to sit on the committee. Privy councilors who were not lawyers were excluded (Howell 1979, 122–123). The act also added retired colonial or Indian judges so as to provide judges familiar with various types of colonial law. Another provision was to raise the quorum from three to four and stipulate that the proceedings would be run by a "presiding judge acting as deputy to the Lord President of the Council" (Swinfen 1987, 7). Finally, the position of registrar was created to cover administrative functions of the Judicial

Committee, since regular meetings of the committee were to be scheduled (Swinfen 1987, 6–7). However, not all eligible members attended Judicial Committee meetings; ten of the original twenty privy councilors eligible "never attended a single sitting" (Howell 1979, 122).

At the time, the jurisdiction of the Judicial Committee included appeals "from the forty-four colonies and plantations, East India Company territories, the Channel Islands and Isle of Man, Malta, Gibraltar and the Ionian Islands" (Swinfen 1987, 7). The Privy Council Appeals Act of 1832 had already added English maritime jurisdiction and some ecclesiastical cases, which became Judicial Committee cases in 1833. The 1833 Judicial Committee Act also included a "special reference" section for matters to go to the Judicial Committee "on any . . . other matters" as the king shall see fit (Swinfen 1987, 7).

The new Judicial Committee was initially so efficient that the appeals backlog was cleared by 1844 (Swinfen 1987, 8). However, satisfaction with the committee began to wane within thirty years of its creation. Australia and Canada argued that in appealing to the Judicial Committee, dominions were inferior to the rest of the United Kingdom, whose appeals went to the House of Lords. This complaint began the "larger debate on constitutional relationships" within the British Empire, where colonies and dominions argued that they could never become fully sovereign unless the final right of appeal changed to their indigenous supreme courts (Swinfen 1987, 9).

By the late 1850s, Judicial Committee appeals were again in arrears. A sudden increase in the number of cases occurred in transferring the powers and territories of the East India Company to the Crown in 1858, and appeals from India by 1867 numerically equaled all the rest of the cases heard by the Judicial Committee that year (Howell 1979, 112). However, a reduction in ecclesiastical cases, particularly those the committee tended to hear, took place after the creation of probate and divorce courts in 1858. From that time on, cases regarding the "discipline or doctrines of the Church of England" fell to an average of 2.2 cases per year until the late 1880s and to an average of 1 per year one century later (Howell 1979, 119; Privy Council Office, June 5, 2001).

It became clear that judges singularly dedicated to Judicial Committee work needed to be appointed. In the Judicial Committee Act of 1871, a provision established the appointment of four salaried judges to the committee, two of whom had to have served as English superior court judges and two of whom had to have served as chief justice of an Indian superior court (Howell 1979, 67). In combination with the Judicial Committee Act of 1833, the act of 1871 was one of the most important acts governing the Judicial Committee.

The high point of the Judicial Committee's jurisdiction was undoubtedly during the height of the British Empire and into the twentieth century, from about the late 1860s through 1930. By sitting five days per week year-round (as opposed to the House of Lords, which held court four days per week, six months per year) and with the appointment of full-time Judicial Committee judges in 1871, the Judicial Committee could dispose of cases more efficiently and again reduced the backlog (Howell 1979, 221). In the late 1860s, there were 302 appeals combined to the Judicial Committee, with the largest single category being those from India, one-third that number originating from the rest of the colonies combined, and the Admiralty Courts' cases coming in third (Howell 1979, 110, Table I). This pattern continued into the early 1870s, with 304 cases, although the number of Indian cases dropped (still the largest number) and the other colonies' increased from fifty-five to eighty-five, as did the admiralty cases (Howell 1979, 110). Also interesting is the geographic shift in colonial appeals in the nineteenth century. The West Indies constituted the largest proportion of appeals through the mid-nineteenth century. After that, the number of appeals from the "prospering Australasian and North American colonies" increased (Howell 1979, 111).

By 1931 and the passage of the Statute of Westminster, British dominions were able to withdraw their appeals procedure from the Judicial Committee and vest it in their own supreme courts. It also established the convention that the British Parliament's legislation would no longer supersede that of the dominions when there was a conflict. Canada, which had been agitating for this change since the 1870s, was the first to end its criminal appeals to the committee in 1933, followed by civil ones in 1949 (Swinfen 1987, 27).

CURRENT RESPONSIBILITIES

The committee's scope has narrowed since World War II. Although it heard more than 300 cases annually in the early 1870s, it currently hears about 65–75 cases per year, mainly on discretionary "appeals by leave" (Privy Council Office, January 16, 2001). Appeals by leave are usually either those in criminal cases from the local Court of Appeal, in civil disputes over a certain amount, and by "special leave of her Majesty in Council," again usually in criminal cases but possibly in civil cases in which the appellant could not comply with local procedure (Privy Council Office, June 5, 2001). These procedures cover the Commonwealth-affiliated countries of Anguilla, Antigua and Barbuda, Bahamas, Barbados, Belize, Bermuda, British Antarctic Territory, British Indian Ocean Territory, British Virgin Islands, Cayman Islands, Falkland Islands, Gibraltar, Grenada, Jamaica, Montserrat, New Zealand, St. Christopher and Nevis, St. Helena, St. Lucia, Saint Vincent and Grenadines, the Turks and

Caicos, Tuvalu, and Akrotiri in Cyprus (Privy Council Office, June 5, 2001).

The independent republics of Trinidad and Tobago, Dominica, Kiribati, and Mauritius within the Commonwealth have chosen to retain their procedure of direct appeal to the Judicial Committee. Appeals also come from the Arches Court of Canterbury (ecclesiastical cases); from Prize Courts; and under the House of Commons Disqualification Act, the Court of Admiralty and the disciplinary committees of medical practitioners, dentists, opticians, veterinary surgeons, osteopaths, and chiropractors (Privy Council Office, June 5, 2001). The islands in the United Kingdom covered by this mechanism (Channel and Man) start their appeals to the sovereign, who refers them to the Judicial Committee. Finally, appeals may be made from the House of Lords. Under the devolution issue, questions arising from legislation of either the Scottish Parliament or the Northern Ireland Assembly are sent to the Judicial Committee as a court of first instance (Privy Council Office, June 5, 2001).

From 1985 to 1994, there were 214 total appeals to the Privy Council out of 163 appeals decided after a hearing, the majority (102 cases) upheld the local Court of Appeal, and the rest reversed the previous judgment (Bryan 1998, 186). In the three most recent years, the highest category of appeals has been from the overseas territories, and the second most numerous from medical boards, excluding dentists. The Judicial Committee is described as mainly concerned with "executive acts of a formal nature" (Curzon 1979, 178).

COMPOSITION

Those who are eligible for the Judicial Committee include the following: privy councilors (current and former) who are lawyers, lords who are also lawyers, English judges who currently sit or have sat on superior courts in England, judges in analogous positions in Commonwealth countries, and Episcopal privy councilors or deputies (Swinfen 1987, 189, 201–202, 228). The number required to sit is five judges for appeals and three for other matters (Privy Council Office, June 5, 2001).

PROCEDURES

Similar to the House of Lords, the Judiciary Committee does not fit within the hierarchy of English courts, but rather the two arch over that framework. It does not operate on the stare decisis (adherence to precedent) principle. The committee may hear different cases concurrently by sitting in multiple divisions.

Unlike decisions in the House of Lords, which take effect immediately, those of the Judicial Committee, which are written, only take effect after the Crown concurs and the decision is embodied in an Order in Council. Another difference from the lords' procedure is that the Judicial Committee produces two documents, including one descriptive assessment for the sovereign in council and a "fuller document read out in open court giving the Committee's decision" (Swinfen 1987, 19). Although dissents are recorded, they are not allowed to be made public, unlike the lords' chamber (Swinfen 1987, 19). The lack of published Judicial Committee dissents was intended to minimize disputes in the ecclesiastical, rather than the imperial, purview (Swinfen 1987, 222). The procedure was changed to publishing dissents in 1966, which was thought to be related mainly to Australian interests (and its chief justice). They wanted Commonwealth judges to play a larger role on the Judicial Committee but would not do so if dissenting opinions were silenced. This 1966 Order in Council was approved by all Commonwealth countries (Swinfen 1987, 240).

CURRENT ISSUES

Currently, the largest number of appeals to the committee is criminal cases from the Commonwealth Caribbean (Privy Council Office, June 5, 2001). In criminal cases, especially involving the death penalty, the Judicial Committee has established a record of commuting such judgments from the Caribbean. In 1993, the committee ruled that after convicted murderers had spent more than five years on death row, that in itself constituted "cruel and unusual punishment" and that sentences should be commuted to life imprisonment (Howe 2000, 22). In 1992, after Trinidad and Tobago executed nine men in less than a week, the Judicial Committee commuted many death sentences to life, including those of seven men on death row in Jamaica (Howe 2000, 22). The attorneys general of the Commonwealth countries issued unanimous statements to abolish the Judicial Committee appeals. On the one hand, Caribbean law officers argue for the need to stop the "rising tide of violence and drug trafficking" and for sovereignty in criminal law. On the other hand, English civil rights attorneys believe that Judicial Committee jurisdiction should remain, since it appropriately revisits the Caribbean judgments where all legal challenges have not been exhausted. In February 2001, eleven of the CARICOM members (excluding Dominica, St. Vincent and the Grenadines, and Montserrat) signed an agreement to establish a Caribbean Court of Justice. It will be based in Trinidad and will start with a U.S. funding base of $21 million. The Jamaican Bar Association, however, reflecting the position of many of the CARICOM bar associations, is challenging the court's establishment until it is permanently entrenched in all members' constitutions. The court must be ratified by at least three CARICOM nations at the July 2001 annual summit and is said to be unlikely to sit before 2003.

The other area of current publicity for the Judicial Committee is its interpretation of the 1998 devolution statutes, involving mostly criminal cases. The first such case on which the Judicial Committee ruled, in July 2000, involved Chapter 46, Schedule 6 of the 1998 Scotland Act, in this instance, whether the Scottish lord advocate had acted correctly in a case. Since he was indicted for murder in Scotland, the plaintiff appealed, claiming that since the lord advocate had acted improperly in trying the case in Scotland, where there was much pretrial publicity about the case, it had become a "devolution issue" and thus the Judicial Committee's jurisdiction. The Judicial Committee's response was that the lord justice general in Scotland had done everything possible to "warn the jurors of the danger of partiality. . . ." Therefore, the appeal was dismissed (*Montgomery v. HM Advocate,* 2000).

In general, the role and shape of the Judicial Committee after 1833 and of the Privy Council before it have mirrored the development of royal rule and the British Empire and the changing conditions of both. Much of the committee's Caribbean jurisdiction is likely to be removed. Interestingly, it will continue to play a role in the United Kingdom, long denied to it but added on through the 1998 devolution statutes.

Melissa Haussman

See also Appellate Courts; Capital Punishment; Channel Islands; Human Rights Law; United Kingdom

References and further reading
Bryan, Roget. 1998. "Toward the Development of a Caribbean Jurisprudence: The Case for Establishing a Caribbean Court of Appeal." *Journal of Transnational Law and Policy* 7: 181–214.
Cownie, Fiona, and Anthony Bradney. 1996. *English Legal System in Context.* London: Butterworths.
Curzon, L. B. 1979. *English Legal History.* 2d ed. Estover, Plymouth, UK: Macdonald and Evans.
Howe, Darcus. 2000. "The Privy Council Halts Caribbean Hangings." *New Statesman* 129, no. 4508: 22.
Howell, P. A. 1979. *The Judicial Committee of the Privy Council, 1833–1876: Its Origins, Structure, and Development.* Cambridge, England: Cambridge University Press.
Privy Council Office, Judicial Committee, "The Judicial Committee of the Privy Council." http://www.privy-council.org.uk/judicial-committee/index.htm (cited January 16, 2001, and June 5, 2001)
Quicklaw. http://www.quicklaw.org.
Swinfen, David B. 1987. *Imperial Appeal: The Debate on the Appeal to the Privy Council. 1833–1986.* Wolfeboro, NH: Manchester University Press.
"Vestige of Empire." 1998. *Reed Business Information Ltd. Estates Gazette,* 125–127.

PRO SE CASES

DEFINITION

Pro se is a Latin-derived legal term that translates to "for oneself," "on one's behalf," or "without a lawyer" (Black 1990, 1221). In legal language, *Black's Law Dictionary* defines *pro se* as "one who represents oneself in a court proceeding with the assistance of a lawyer or attorney" (Black 1990, 1221). Other common legal terms that are synonymous with *pro se* are *pro persona, in propria persona,* and *self-representation.* Self-representation in legal proceedings has been considered by some to be the right of an individual to defend himself or herself against the legal action of a state or other person. Pro se representation has also come to be a problem or concern in some legal systems if the individual is deemed to be less powerful or have less knowledge than his or her adversary in proceedings such as courts and trials.

APPLICABILITY

Self-representation is applicable to a variety of world legal systems as well as by the type of law within some systems. The representation of clients is considered a necessity in legal systems in which the system is quite formalistic and laden with complex rules and procedures (for example, the U.S. adversary system). In other legal systems, representation of accused criminals or civil clients is not mandated or is debated because the legal system is based on judicial discovery of facts (for example, civil systems in France, Germany, and Japan). In addition, the type of law within systems, such as criminal and civil or domestic law, may contribute to variation in terms of whether an individual is self-represented or is represented by an attorney. For instance, in some legal systems, routine disputes such as divorces or small claims are often afforded very informal tribunals in which efficiency may predominate over due process (a small claims courts in the United States and common law systems such as that in Great Britain).

The use of pro se representation also varies by the type of law being applied. Thus, in the criminal context, if a person is accused of a crime, the sanctions applied if he or she is found responsible for that crime can range from being deprived of property to even death. In civil or domestic legal matters, the dispute, though serious, may not have the same magnitude of outcome to the individual. For example, in a divorce case in the United States, an individual may represent himself or herself when the stakes of the case are small or when agreement has been reached between the two parties. At the most serious, an individual may face a legal action where his or her property and personal privacy are at stake. In some legal systems, the type of law, then, has led to variation in the choice to represent oneself and also in the rules governing pro se representation. Indigent status, in some countries, is one example. In certain legal systems, indigents are afforded a state-supported attorney in criminal proceedings in which the legal consequences can be high. In Great Britain, legal aid pays for most criminal proceedings, whether large or small. However, in personal plight cases such as civil and domestic matters, individuals may be left to choose the type of legal representation that they can afford, turn to charitable legal aid, or represent themselves pro se.

Some examples of world legal structures further enlighten us about the variation of self-representation with legal institutions and the type of legal dispute. For instances, in Islamic-based legal systems, legal procedures and administration are often similar to those in common or socialist legal systems. However, the law is based on the fundamental religious teachings of Islam. In Islamic law, pro se representation depends more on the political institutions of the given country employing the law than on the type of law itself. In an inquisitorial system, the judge adopts the approach of being both an arbiter and an investigator. In such a system, pro se representation may be common in that the judge is there to find fact as well as rule on evidence. Consequently, the protection of being represented by an attorney may be viewed as less important than in an adversarial system, where training in the law makes a difference as to whether an individual wins or loses. In adversarial systems, pro se representation is often considered a right, but it is also often discouraged by the necessity of representation. In an adversarial proceeding, the accused and the prosecutor each make use of legal precedents and statutes to persuade the arbiter in a battle of arguments. Thus, there is more concern that an individual without training in the law may not be able to effectively compete in such an environment.

The U.S. System

In the U.S. adversarial system of law, the competitive nature of both the process and the litigants has established a constitutional right to have representation in felony criminal cases. However, no such right exists for civil law litigants. In civil matters, legal representation is often based on the ability to pay, the availability of charitable legal services, or whether an attorney may take a case on a contingency fee basis. Judicial systems around the world include or have been reformed to include more informal tribunals for small claims cases and methods of alternative dispute resolution, such as mediation and arbitration. These types of tribunals or procedures allow a litigant the opportunity for representation by attorneys, but they are designed to make the process informal and simple enough procedurally to be efficient and to not necessitate representation.

The United Kingdom

In common law countries such as the United Kingdom, self-representation is, indeed, an issue but primarily in civil matters. In criminal matters in England, the accused is entitled to legal counsel in courts that handle minor cases (the Magistrates' Courts) and in courts that handle more serious cases (the Crown Court). As in the U.S. setting, defendants must pay for their legal services; however, almost all criminal representation is paid for by legal aid. In Magistrates' Courts, for instance, legal aid pays for a "duty solicitor" to be present to assist defendants. In civil matters in the British system, some have argued that even the least formal courts, such as administrative tribunals and county courts, have become more legalistic. As such, parties who are not represented may have problems in civil matters due to the complexity of the law. Additionally, because the legal profession of the United Kingdom is divided into solicitors and barristers, litigants may have to pay for two different lawyers—a solicitor to prepare the case and a barrister to later litigate the case at trial. Therefore, money can become an even greater barrier to legal access than in the U.S. setting and lead to pro se litigants. However, the United Kingdom places few restrictions on the unauthorized practice of law, so individuals may turn to others for legal advice in personal plight cases.

France

In civil law systems such as that in France, the judiciary is not a coequal branch of government. In fact, the courts play a lesser role in protecting individual rights in the French system of law. For example, criminal matters in France do not come with a presumption of innocence, and police investigation is given priority over the citizen's rights. However, this does not extend to representation where access to legal services is state regulated and is less controversial. In France, free legal counsel, in the form of the services of an *advocat,* is offered to people who are charged with crimes. There are also state-regulated rates for common legal services such as handling disputes between individuals and disputes against businesses. Other legal procedures, such as administrative tribunals used to hear workplace disputes and other small disputes, are informal and do not necessitate legal representation. In such hearings, most disputants are pro se.

Germany

Also a civil-based system, the legal system in Germany uses the inquisitorial style of court that does not have a jury. Under this process, the judge prepares a decision on the basis of the evidence in the case file. Unlike in adversarial systems, this makes it unnecessary for the defense to prepare an inquiry in case of a surprise from the other side. As in France, the rights of the accused are fewer than in adversarial legal systems. In fact, in Germany, there is no recognized right to legal representation for those defendants who cannot pay. Individuals are free to pay for legal representation, but in minor cases, most choose to represent themselves. In serious felony cases that are heard in district courts, attorneys are typically assigned to defendants. In local courts, the prosecutor may assign an attorney if the potential penalty is imprisonment of five years or longer or if a defendant has been detained for longer than three months. As in other countries, civil law matters in Germany are increasingly diverted from courts to informal alternatives. In addition, in the German system, civil matters are often investigated by the judge in an inquisitorial fashion for both sides of the dispute. Therefore, self-representation is common but is not necessitated by the German legal system. Indeed, as in France, it may be advantageous to *not* be represented because a judge may compensate for the lack of experience and aid the unrepresented client who is facing another person armed with an attorney. Again as in France, legal aid does exist in Germany, but it is generally spent on divorce cases, which make up much of the German caseload. Many middle-class people protect themselves against legal costs by buying legal insurance.

VARIATIONS

The major variations of pro se representation include the petitioning of or access to tribunals or courts and involvement within the process of tribunals or courts. Additionally, the meaning of pro se representation varies somewhat according to the type of law in action, including whether the action is civil or criminal. In the case of petitioning, some legal systems require showing harm or standing to receive entry into a proceeding for legal relief.

The ability to petition pro se can be said to affirm the basic right of an individual, regardless of economic or social status, to have the opportunity to seek the aid or protection of the law. One example, in the United States and other common law countries, is the ability to petition or appeal to a court as a pauper, or *in forma pauperis,* which allows access to individuals who cannot afford to pay the costs of courts. In addition, another common pro se action by individuals who are detained by law is the petition of habeas corpus. In adversarial and common law legal systems, individuals bring such a petition to ask a judge to inquire as to the legality of a loss of personal liberty, such as imprisonment, without cause or without due process. In the United States and the United Kingdom, individuals often hire representation to prepare and file a case. In the United Kingdom, this is the job of a solicitor.

Pro se representation is also important within a formal legal process such as a tribunal or court. On one hand, individuals may be given the right or choice to participate in such proceedings by themselves and despite their financial circumstances. On the other hand, in adversarial

legal systems, there is a consideration that one disputant may have more resources or be armed with the legal skills to negotiate what are often complex legal procedures. In such systems as adversarial and common law–based systems, the lack of involvement of an attorney on one's behalf can greatly enhance the chances of losing. The right of an individual to have legal counsel if he or she is declared indigent was, in fact, recognized in U.S. courts as a necessity in criminal proceedings, in which the state has the ability, with counsel, to deprive a person of his or her individual rights. Other legal systems, such as those in Great Britain and France, however, generally make provisions for representation in felony criminal cases. Nonetheless, in civil matters, common law and adversarial systems may not provide attorneys to indigents, and self-representation may be the only option for them in court proceedings. Another issue of concern to pro se representation can be the mental fitness of individuals to represent themselves when their freedom or property is at stake. If individuals have a mental defect, then they may be declared unfit to represent themselves in some legal systems, such as the U.S. system. Thus, balancing the right or choice of an individual to represent himself or herself in legal proceedings is often weighed against the consequences of such representation.

It is much more common to represent oneself in informal or alternative dispute resolution forums, such as mediation, arbitration, and negotiation. These procedures are often used by judicial systems to make the process less costly to litigants and to the justice system. For example, mediation in U.S. neighborhood justice centers encourages individuals to represent themselves in order to promote resolutions of disputes that are of their own making and that are less constrained by formal law. However, self-representation in such tribunals can be problematic, as well. Studies of arbitration in the English system have found that parties may be uninformed about the complex questions of law that can arise in arbitration. These parties may use up a lot of the system's time in order to work out these complexities with an uninformed party.

EVOLUTION AND CHANGE

Two trends in law have been recognized in many legal systems: the growth in the number of individuals who choose to represent themselves and the reform of legal institutions to accommodate and provide greater access to individuals who wish to be heard by courts and tribunals.

In the United States and the United Kingdom, studies have shown that pro se litigation is on the rise and is more prevalent in domestic actions and other small civil cases. In addition, there have been movements in a number of countries to bureaucratize court systems in order to provide better service and administration. A portion of this bureaucratization has involved providing small claims courts that make the legal process simple and efficient as well as improving access to courts by making proceedings less costly to disputants. Some of these systems, such as those in the United States and Great Britain, present these forums in such a fashion as to make it less necessary for legal representation. However, one study of small claims courts in England and Wales has suggested that attorneys are still very much involved in these procedures (Baldwin 1997, 78). These reforms were similar to options that were already available in other civil law–based systems such as those seen in Germany and France.

These trends have led to further questions about the costs and outcomes of pro se representation to litigants (as well as to courts). For litigants, the cost of pro se representation can be greatly reduced by avoiding the expense of hiring an attorney to represent them or for the state to provide aid in the individuals' defense. In fact, in some civil law countries without juries, judges have been said to compensate on behalf of pro se clients facing litigants who are represented. Self-representation, then, may be advantageous to some clients. There has also been a recent movement among pro se litigants in the United States to organize and provide information to others who wish to proceed with self-representation (for example, the American Pro Se Association and the Utopia Society). Nonetheless, self-representation can be costly for individuals if they are not adequately prepared or are discriminated against by legal systems.

Even though some legal systems recognize that self-representation is an individual right, pro se representation can be costly for the courts. For instance, studies in the United States have documented the concern of judges and court administrators about the increasing number of people who enter the legal system alone. Since in some systems they must abide by the same rules as all others in court, mistakes can hinder the delivery of justice. In addition, some systems require that aid be given to those who make procedural errors if the errors impinge on the legal rights of others. Therefore, pro se litigants may take up valuable court time and add to administrative expenses by delaying proceedings and using resources of the courts to have procedures explained. One interesting example of this in the United Kingdom involves the "vexatious litigant"—the self-represented litigant who files suit after suit, some or all of which may even be frivolous. In such circumstances in England, if a litigant is found to be vexatious, then he or she is required to obtain leave of the court before initiating a court action. Because of such problems in U.S. courts, scholars and organizations such as the American Judicature Society have lobbied for more court funding to aid pro se litigants (as occurs in Great Britain) without violating the impartiality of the adversarial process by requiring judges to provide such assistance.

An additional trend relates to recent questions by scholars about whether pro se representation by individuals without economic wealth, knowledge, and skill benefits those with more wealth, knowledge, and skills. Some argue that increasing the ease with which individuals can represent themselves actually benefits the state, corporations, and wealthy individuals who can afford representation or have more knowledge of legal procedures as repeat players. This concern is not exclusive to adversarial proceedings. In other systems, such as inquisitorial types, individuals who represent themselves may be at the mercy of the state that runs the inquisition. For example, in France and Germany, the rights of the accused are given much less weight than the need to fight crime. The same criticism has been leveled by some scholars at alternative dispute resolution forums such as mediation; they argue that individuals who are less "armed" for conflict will be coerced into agreements that benefit the more powerful party in the mediation or negotiation. Thus, some would suggest that legal systems should do more to protect individuals, for example, by granting them an attorney.

Roger E. Hartley

See also Barristers; Legal Aid; Legal Professionals—Civil Law Traditions; Mediation; Small Claims Courts; Solicitors

References and further reading

Baldwin, John. 1997. *Small Claims in County Courts in England and Wales.* Oxford: Clarendon Press.
Black, Henry Campbell, ed. 1990. *Black's Law Dictionary.* 6th ed. St. Paul, MN: West Publishing.
Gilfrich, Nathalie, Richard Granant, Michael Millemann, and Frank Broccolina. 1997. "Law Students Assist Pro Se Litigants in Maryland." *Judicature* 81: 82–84.
Goldschmidt, Jona. 1998. "How Are Courts Handling Pro Se Litigants?" *Judicature* 82: 13–22.
———. 1998. *Meeting the Challenge of Pro Se Litigation: A Report and Guidebook for Judges and Court Managers.* Chicago: American Judicature Society.
Jacob, Herbert J., Erhard Blankenburg, Herbert M. Kritzer, Doris Marie Provine, and Joseph Sanders. 1996. *Courts, Law, and Politics in Comparative Perspective.* New Haven, CT, and London: Yale University Press.
Whelan, Christopher J., ed. 1990. *Small Claims Courts: A Comparative Study.* Oxford: Clarendon Press.

PROBATE/SUCCESSION LAW

Probate or succession law is the set of rules and principles governing the orderly transmission of property at death.

APPLICABILITY

Succession law pertains to the transmission of privately held, inheritable property, which generally includes any economic interest in real or personal property but in modern societies excludes personal rights such as tenure or elected office. Every society has rules about succession, but the right to choose how to devolve property at death—also known as the right of testation—is a statutory right given by (and theoretically taken away by) legislative bodies.

Every major legal system today has rules to facilitate the transfer of property at death. The two primary systems for purposes of succession law are the civil law system and the Anglo-American, or common law, system. The civil law rules of succession derive ultimately from concepts of Roman law. The common law rules of succession were established in four early English statutes: the Statute of Uses (1536), the Statute of Wills (1540), the Statute of Frauds (1677), and the Wills Act (1837). In the United States, succession is a matter of state law and thus varies from state to state. All states follow the basic common law system, except for Louisiana, which uses civil law. In a few countries, including India and Pakistan, succession is governed by religious rather than local or national law.

VARIATIONS

Both the civil law and the common law systems of succession are based on the basic principle that individuals have the right to decide how their property will be distributed at death. Those wishes must be expressed through a formal document called a will, which complies with rather strict, formalistic rules. Both systems impose some restrictions on the right of testation in order to protect surviving family members or societal interests. And for individuals who do not express their wishes, or do so inadequately, both systems provide a default (intestate) scheme of succession. Although the similarities are greater than the differences, there are some important variations in succession law between civil law and common law, which will be treated in three categories: testate succession, intestate succession, and estate administration.

Testate Succession

Testate succession is the system for transferring property at death through a will.

Execution of Wills

Anglo-American law recognizes three types of wills: attested, holographic, and nuncupative. A valid attested will is a written document executed with specified formalities, namely the signature of the testator followed by the attestation of two disinterested witnesses who observed the testator sign or acknowledge his signature. A holographic will, valid in only one-third of U.S. states, is a will entirely in the handwriting of the testator, signed by the testator (but not any witnesses), and dated. A few states permit soldiers and sailors in active combat, individuals suffering a last illness, or others in similar dire circumstances to make a nuncupative, or oral will, which is valid for only a few months. Joint wills—wills executed by spouses having a common testamentary plan—are generally valid, as are contracts to make wills. The power to write a will is limited to those individuals of sound mind and a requisite age (usually eighteen). Wills must be executed without fraud, duress, or undue influence in order to be valid.

Civil law jurisdictions also recognize the holographic will, provided it is dated and signed by the testator, as well as notarial and mystic wills. A notarial will, similar to the common law attested will, is one executed in the presence of a notary and two witnesses. In civil law countries, the notary has an authority of law unknown in common law jurisdictions. A mystic will is a secret will that is drawn up and signed by the testator and then delivered in a sealed envelope to a notary in the presence of two witnesses. Civil law also permits oral wills for servicemen and -women on active duty, those on a sea voyage, and those suffering from an epidemic. Like the U.S. nuncupative will, such wills are valid for only a short period after the special circumstances have ceased and generally are effective only to convey personal property. Many testators in civil law countries deposit their wills with notaries for safekeeping. Most civil law jurisdictions other than France recognize joint wills and inheritance contracts. Testamentary capacity in civil law means the same thing as it does in Anglo-American law, requiring sound mind and a minimum age, though the civil law generally grants limited rights of testation to minors over age sixteen. Wills executed under undue influence, fraud, or mistake are invalid.

In both civil law and common law jurisdictions, wills are ambulatory; they can be revoked during the lifetime of the testator by a physical act, by execution of a new will, or by express written revocation.

Restrictions on Testation

No legal system permits a truly unfettered right of testation. Most jurisdictions give some measure of protection against disinheritance to a surviving spouse; civil law jurisdictions protect children and sometimes parents as well. Most jurisdictions also limit the degree to which the "dead hand" can control property.

Most civil law countries retain the concept of forced heirship. Regardless of what a testator's will may provide, the surviving spouse, children, and sometimes other close relatives are generally entitled to a certain portion of the estate. The reserved portion ranges from one-third to three-fourths of a decedent's estate. Germany, for example, gives a compulsory share both to the surviving spouse and to descendants, and Switzerland has a forced heirship for descendants, parents, siblings, and the surviving spouse.

Anglo-American law does not recognize forced heirship for children. England and the United States take different approaches to protecting the surviving spouse. In England, New Zealand, and Australia, the judge overseeing a decedent's estate has discretion to make a reasonable financial provision from the estate to support specified categories of dependents, including the surviving spouse, children (legal or de facto), a former spouse who has not remarried, and any other person who was wholly supported by the decedent at the time of her death. The amount of the provision is based on need.

U.S. states take one of two approaches to protecting the surviving spouse. Eight states have a community property regime, in which the surviving spouse is entitled to one-half of the property accumulated during the marriage. The surviving spouse is not entitled, however, to any portion of the decedent spouse's one-half of the community property or his separate property. In the remaining states, there is no community property (each spouse has title to his or her own property), but the surviving spouse is entitled to a statutory share of the decedent spouse's estate. The spouse has the option to take what she is given under her spouse's will or elect against the will and take a forced share—typically one-third—of his estate instead. Unlike the English system, neither U.S. approach is discretionary or expressly based on need, but both instead implement a partnership theory of marriage that gives the surviving spouse her share of that partnership when the marriage ends.

There is no provision in U.S. law similar to either forced heirship (except in Louisiana) or the English family protection. The only protection for children is against unintentional disinheritance; some states require testators to expressly disinherit their children; others give a mandatory share to pretermitted children—those born after the execution of a parent's will.

The other primary restrictions on testation relate to the duration of trusts. The trust is a basic institution of Anglo-American property law. It is a fiduciary relationship in which a trustee holds title and possession of certain property for the benefit of one or more beneficiaries. The central feature of the U.S. trust is a division between legal and equitable ownership; the beneficiary holds the former, and the trustee holds the latter. A trust can be created by the grantor during his lifetime by declaration or trust instrument or at death by will. By creating testamentary trusts instead of granting outright bequests of property, the grantor can impose greater control over the use of the assets after his death. Too great control, however, is considered contrary to a free economy and the commitment to the alienability of property. Thus, Anglo-American jurisdictions use the rule against perpetuities to restrict the duration of trusts. Essentially, though the rules are very technical, trusts cannot last longer than the "lives in being" at the time of the trust's creation plus twenty-one years. This often works out, in fact, to be about a century.

The basic concept of the trust is not present in civil law. Civil law has nothing comparable to the division of title between the trustee and the beneficiary or the creation of a future interest that ripens upon termination of prior interests. Today, some civil law countries permit private trusts of relatively short duration, say, thirty years. Other civil law countries permit certain kinds of trusts, such as family foundations for the support and education of its members (Swiss) and trusts for the masses (Spanish).

Estate taxes, which confiscate a portion of very large estates, place an additional limit on the freedom of testation. "Unnatural" wills (those that disinherit family members in favor of strangers or unusual beneficiaries) are legal but are vulnerable to challenge under the guise of undue influence, fraud, or mistake; ambiguities are sometimes resolved in favor of normal succession. The availability of jury trials in U.S. will contests gives greater force to such expectations.

Intestate Succession
Intestate succession is the system for transferring property when an individual dies without a will or with a will that disposes of only part of her estate. It is essentially a default, state-mandated scheme of inheritance. All such default systems reflect a collective judgment about appropriate or normal succession and thus try to emulate what the average testator would (or should) have done had she written a will. All intestate schemes protect the surviving spouse and children. Common to all systems are the exclusion of unrelated individuals, the preference of near relatives to more distant ones and descendants to ancestors or collateral relatives, and an inflexibility that does not permit consideration of the actual circumstances of any particular family. (The English system flexibly provides for the family first before resorting to the rigid rules of intestate succession.) The variations in intestate succession laws relate to the order of succession, the allocation of shares to heirs, and the eligibility of particular heirs to inherit.

Under Anglo-American law, a share for the surviving spouse is parceled out first. This share is typically larger than the elective share (the share given against the express wishes of the decedent spouse) and in many jurisdictions comprises the entire estate. The treatment of the spouse under civil law varies. In France, for example, the surviving spouse is granted a usufruct—a right to use and live off the income of a portion of the decedent's estate (typically one-fourth) during her life. In Germany, however, the surviving spouse takes an outright share. Switzerland and Turkey give the surviving spouse a choice between a usufruct and one-half of the decedent's estate outright.

The remainder of the estate, if any, goes to descendants. Direct descendants (children, grandchildren, and so on) and descendants of parents (brothers and sisters) inherit by representation, that is, children take their deceased parent's share. The size of that share may be calculated using a per capita method (by the head) or a per stirpes method (by the "stocks" or family line). As a general matter, if there are any living descendants, ancestors and collateral relatives will not take.

If there are no living descendants, there are two methods for determining who takes and in what share. Under the civil law method, the heirs are determined by counting degrees of kinship. To determine the degree, a court will count the number of generations from the intestate up to a common ancestor and down to the prospective heir. The nearest generation takes to the exclusion of more distant generations (i.e., a relative in the fourth degree takes over a relative in the fifth degree). Under the Parentelic method (which is used in some civil law jurisdictions, including Germany), heirs are determined by counting lines of kinship. Direct descendants of the intestate are first-line relatives, descendants of the intestate's parents are second-line collaterals, and so on. In this system, heirs in the closest line take to the exclusion of heirs in more distant lines. Children of deceased heirs in the closest line generally take by representation. Variations exist as to when inheritance rights cut off. Many jurisdictions do not permit relatives beyond the third line (descendants of grandparents) or the sixth degree to inherit.

Both civil and common law jurisdictions generally deny inheritance to stepchildren, an heir who has murdered the decedent, or any kin who predecease him. Adopted, nonmarital, and conceived but unborn children, however, can typically inherit. Some countries favor whole-bloods over half-bloods. Neither civil law nor common law countries today distinguish between sexes with regard to inheritance rights or recognize primogeniture.

Estate Administration
Important to both testate and intestate succession is the process by which decedents' estates are administered. In this area, there are significant differences between common law and civil law systems.

Common Law Estate Administration
Under Anglo-American law, an estate must go through a formal, legal process prior to being distributed. Most jurisdictions have specialized courts to deal with probate, sometimes called orphans' or surrogates' courts. If an individual dies testate, his will must go through probate, and literally be "proved" as a validly executed last will. Central to probate is the appointment of a personal representative called an executor—usually someone named in the will—to oversee administration of the estate. The court will issue letters testamentary to the executor, which gives her title to the estate's assets and authority to

take whatever steps are necessary to distribute the estate according to the decedent's will. Creditors and potential claimants are notified that the estate is in probate and given an opportunity to contest the validity of the will or the planned distribution of assets. The executor files an inventory listing the probate assets of the estate (those to be transmitted via the will), and after all potential challenges to the will, forced shares, or creditor claims are satisfied or dismissed, the executor will distribute the assets under court supervision.

When an individual dies without a will, the process is similar. Once notified of the decedent's death, the court will appoint a personal representative called an administrator to oversee distribution of the intestate's assets according to the governing statute of descent and distribution. The court will issue letters of administration to give the administrator the same authority as an executor.

Civil Law Estate Administration
Civil law estate administration differs from the common law in two principal respects. The principle of universal succession applies when one heir succeeds to the entire estate or multiple heirs take undivided portions of the entire estate. When universal succession applies, title to the estate vests immediately upon death in the heirs; they have the right and opportunity to administer the estate. Most jurisdictions today give the universal successor the opportunity to accept or reject the estate, usually with the benefit of inventory. If the successor accepts, he then becomes liable for all debts of the estate even if they exceed the assets. Beneficiaries who get only a portion of the estate, such as a specific piece of property or a sum of money, are not vested with title upon the death of the testator but instead receive ownership only upon delivery of the assets.

Most civil law jurisdictions do not have any institution comparable to probate or any courts designed to deal specifically with inheritance. (Germany does have a court equivalent to a U.S. probate court that issues a certificate of inheritance.) Testators can appoint an executor to pay out legacies, settle the estate, defend the validity of the will, or sell property to satisfy bequests, but the executor does not receive title to the estate, as that has passed directly to the heirs. As a general matter, the heirs are in charge of administration. Court will occasionally supervise the administration of an estate (under the auspices of an "official liquidation" in Switzerland or an "estate watcher" in Germany), particularly if there are creditors whose rights may be compromised by unsupervised distribution.

EVOLUTION AND CHANGE
There are three significant areas of evolution in succession law. First, there is a notable trend against formalism

in the execution of wills. Regardless of the applicable legal system, testators have traditionally been forced to express their testamentary wishes through a highly formalized procedure under which a single mistake can invalidate a will and force the estate to pass through intestacy. Courts and legislatures are gradually relaxing these requirements in order to give greater effect to testator intent. Second, testate and intestate succession rules have broadened to accommodate nontraditional families. Distinctions between legitimate and illegitimate children and relatives of the whole- and half-blood have begun to disappear, and the rights of a surviving spouse have been influenced by the reality of multiple, sequential marriages and blended families. Finally, there has been a marked increase in the availability of will substitutes, devices such as living, life insurance, and bank account trusts, that operate to pass property outside of a will.

Joanna L. Grossman

See also Civil Law; Common Law; Australia; England and Wales; France; Germany; Italy; Juries; Louisiana; New Zealand; Roman Law; United States—State Systems

References and further reading
Browder, Olin L., Jr. 1969. "Recent Patterns of Testate Succession in the United States and England." *Michigan Law Review* 67: 1303.
Chester, Ronald. 1982. *Inheritance, Wealth, and Society.* Bloomington: Indiana University Press.
Friedman, Lawrence M. 1966. "The Law of the Living, the Law of the Dead: Property, Succession, and Society." *Wisconsin Law Review* 1966: 340–378.
McKnight, Joseph W. 1996. "Spanish Legitim in the United States—Its Survival and Decline." *American Journal of Comparative Law* 44: 75–107.
Pelletier, George A., Jr., and Michael Roy Sonnenreich. 1966. "A Comparative Analysis of Civil Law Succession." *Villanova Law Review* 11: 323–356.
Shapo, Helene S. 1993. "'A Tale of Two Systems': Anglo-American Problems in the Modernization of Inheritance Legislation." *Tennessee Law Review* 60: 707–781.
Sussman, Marvin B., Judith N. Cates, and David T. Smith. 1970. *The Family and Inheritance.* New York: Russell Sage Foundation.

PROSECUTING AUTHORITIES

WHAT THEY ARE

Every modern state has some actor in the governmental process who is responsible for representing the interests of the state in the justice system. Although ordinarily this function is fulfilled by a public official called a prosecutor, a procurator, a district attorney, or an attorney general, occasionally it is carried out by the police, judges, or even private attorneys or citizens. The chief function of the prosecuting authority is to institute legal proceedings against a person accused of a crime or other breach of the law. Prosecutors often participate in pretrial investigations of criminal activity and almost always bring the charges against accused individuals, matching their alleged criminal conduct with the criminal codes of the state. In addition, prosecutors represent the interests of the government in the actual trial proceedings, although their importance in this process varies widely depending upon the nature of the legal system.

Prosecuting authorities can be located in either the executive branch of government (where they often also have responsibility for overseeing the general administration of the justice system at the national level) or within the judicial branch (where their role tends to be more limited to pretrial investigative and charging decisions). In most countries, prosecutors tend to be in career civil service positions.

HISTORICAL BACKGROUND

The role of prosecutor has evolved over time from one that was purely private to one that is largely public. This evolution has paralleled the larger changes that have occurred in legal systems. Once informal norms enforced within communities, law became increasingly formalized as societies became more diverse and complex. Today, virtually every government has some public actors with the responsibility of bringing charges against those who violate society's rules, and in most systems the state has a monopoly on this power.

Early in Western legal history, injured persons were responsible for seeking community sanctions against the people who wronged them. For a much longer time, Muslim law recognized the right of the family to seek prosecution for murder of one of its members. In many Asian legal cultures, the influence of Confucian thought, with its emphasis on duty, harmony, stability, and community, discouraged the development of extensive formal justice systems. Instead, these cultures sought more informal ways to bring the values of the community to bear on deviants. But as criminal law developed, especially in civil law systems where the state imposed elaborate codes of law to regulate behavior, the public interest in enforcing these codes became more evident. In European civil law systems, this move began very intentionally in the eighteenth century. The notion of private justice and vengeance was replaced by the idea that the state should be responsible for bringing charges because it had an interest in and was also injured by violations of the codes. Additionally, public prosecution made the criminal justice process more open and theoretically less arbitrary than the more secret process of private prosecution.

In common law systems, the role of a public prosecutor is more recent. For example, in Great Britain it was 1985 before the Crown Prosecution Service was created. Prior to that time, the police hired local attorneys in private practice to act on their behalf in prosecutions. Shop owners who wanted to bring charges against shoplifters had to bear the cost of hiring a private attorney to act as a prosecutor on their behalf. This delay in making prosecution public is attributed to the adversarial nature of most common law systems, where the injured and the accused are engaged in a "duel" of sorts before an impartial judge. The public role that seemed most necessary was the judge, not the prosecutor.

MAJOR VARIANTS

Prosecuting authorities have in common their responsibility for representing the interests of the state in the criminal justice process. The most significant variations include (1) the nature of the legal system within which they operate and the implications of those differences for their recruitment to office, (2) the degree of independence they have from other political actors and the difficulty of dealing with cases that involve allegations of wrongdoing by these actors, and (3) the amount of discretion they exercise in carrying out their duties.

Prosecutorial power varies between civil law and common law systems. Civil law systems are characterized by extensive legal codes enacted by legislatures that establish general rules and principles of law, as opposed to common law systems where much of the law is developed incrementally through judicial decisions in individual cases. These differences have significant implications for the training, recruitment, and influence of the prosecutor.

In most civil law systems (Europe, Latin America, and Francophone Africa), judges and prosecutors are trained at universities in special law programs that focus on the legal science of learning the key concepts and principles embodied in the legal codes of the country. Upon completion of their education and usually successful performance on an exam, they choose a career civil service path that leads them to the judiciary. Most often in these systems, prosecutors are considered to be part of the judicial branch of government, and prosecution may be a step toward becoming a judge. Judges are often key actors in the pretrial investigation and may be responsible for creating the initial dossier that contains the results of their interrogation of witnesses and the defendants. In many Latin American countries, use of prosecutors is a relatively new development. Traditionally, police and judges have had the primary responsibility for prosecuting functions. In Germany, prosecutors are part of the court system but have the primary responsibility for pretrial investigation and charging. In civil law systems, judges are much more active during the trial, taking the lead in asking questions. Prosecutors and defense attorneys play a much more subordinate role than they do in adversarial processes found in common law systems.

In most common law systems (Great Britain and its former colonies), those exercising prosecuting authority play a more active role in trial proceedings. Because these systems tend to be adversarial in nature, the judge plays a more passive and impartial role, whereas the attorneys represent the two sides in the contest of the trial. The investigative process is located outside the judiciary, usually with the police and, where there is a public prosecutor's office, with oversight and involvement of the prosecutor. Consequently, prosecutors are more partisan in the sense that they are charged with trying to persuade the judge (and in some cases, the jury) that their version of the facts is the correct one. Their skill at developing the case and presenting the evidence can have a significant impact on the outcome of the trial.

Recruitment of prosecutors varies in common law systems. The Crown Prosecution Service is made up of career civil servants, as are the public prosecutors in South Africa. In the United States, prosecutors are part of the executive branch of government. The federal Department of Justice is made up of both career prosecutors and political appointees. U.S. attorney's offices are overseen by political appointees but staffed by career prosecutors. The United States is unusual in that so many of its prosecuting attorneys are elected. Among the fifty states, forty-three of the attorneys general are elected. Most chief prosecutors at the local government level (usually called district attorneys) are also directly elected. Staff attorneys for these offices are hired by the district attorney. Prosecutor's jobs are often seen as stepping-stones to political careers in other areas.

In some common law countries, the decision of whether to prosecute may be located in persons other than a public prosecutor. In England, solicitors in private practice may be hired by the police or by private individuals to bring suits. Although the Crown Prosecution Service now exists to carry out this public function, it is still the case that police usually institute criminal proceedings and independent barristers must be hired to argue cases at any level above Magistrates' Courts. In South Africa, private prosecutions are permitted in some limited circumstances when a private party feels that the attorney general has wrongly refused to prosecute.

No prosecutors are completely independent from the political process, and so all of them face the difficulty of upholding the rule of law in the face of political pressure, especially where public corruption is involved. The ability to resist such pressure varies widely between countries and depends upon characteristics of the legal tradition and the political system. In the United States, where prosecutors are most clearly political actors, their executive branch placement makes it difficult for them to act independently when dealing with allegations of misconduct against the executive. This problem has led to the use of special prosecutors, brought in from the outside to investigate high-profile political cases. In European civil law systems, where prosecutors are part of the independent judiciary, there is the appearance of freedom to act, but because the judicial role is generally considered subordinate to parliamentary supremacy, prosecutors are very cautious about challenging the politically powerful. In France, the combination of state control of the legal profession and the fact that judges and prosecutors are state civil servants results in little public confidence in their ability to take on public corruption cases. Japanese prosecutors operate with a considerable degree of independence from the political process. Nonetheless, the hierarchical structure of the prosecution service and the principle of prosecutorial unity that drives it mean that politicians at the top of the Ministry of Justice can keep line prosecutors from pursuing public corruption cases against the party in power.

In many political systems where the notion of law being independent from politics is less firmly rooted in tradition, prosecutors face even greater pressures. The most powerful examples of public prosecutors' offices in Latin America, the Mexican Procuraduria General de la Republica and the Panamanian Public Ministry, are considered by many observers to be central sources of corruption in these justice systems. In many Latin American and African countries with strong presidential models of government, control of the judicial branch has been considered to be the legitimate province of political victors and use of the apparatus of the justice system a legitimate way to maintain control and punish rivals. In China, several levels of procuracies have carried out the prosecutorial function, but these offices have always been essentially agents of the party apparatus. During the Cultural Revolution, the expertise of lawyers in the procuracies was considered dangerous, and these offices were closed down and replaced by informal people's tribunals.

Finally, prosecutors have varying amounts of discretion to make investigative and charging decisions. Prosecutors in the United States seem to have the most discretion because courts have ruled that the exercise of that discretion is not subject to review by courts, largely for separation of powers reasons. In addition, because so many prosecuting authorities are elected, especially at the state and local levels, they have a great deal of autonomy to act. Prosecutors in South Africa also have considerable discretion in making judgments about whether to pursue prosecution. In most civil law systems, however, the discretion of prosecutors is much more restrained. German prosecutors have statutory constraints imposed upon their discretion and in most cases are not permitted to dismiss a case that has merit. In Japan, line prosecutors must have their decisions cleared by several levels of the justice hierarchy.

Despite the restraints placed on prosecuting discretion, all legal systems are faced with the problem of managing a caseload that inevitably exceeds the resources allocated for that purpose. As a consequence, all systems must devise a mechanism for diverting some significant portion of the caseload from the courts. In systems where prosecutors are relatively autonomous and exercise substantial discretion, plea bargaining is the chosen method for efficient case disposition. In the United States, for example, almost 90 percent of cases are disposed of through negotiated pleas prior to trial. In Japan, plea bargaining is frowned upon, but extensive use is made of the confession as a way of disposing of a case before trial. Defendants who confess and show remorse are given lighter punishments. In Germany, prosecutors can dispose of minor offenses by giving defendants the option of paying retribution or giving money to charity.

SIGNIFICANCE

Prosecuting authorities exercise a critical power of the modern state. They have the ability to bring the full force of the state's criminal justice apparatus to bear on individuals accused of violating the society's rules. Their power to act without interference from other actors varies widely, but all of them face the problem of balancing the interests of justice with those of the politically powerful. Prosecutors are embedded in their unique legal cultures, and their career paths, degree of independence, and amount of decision-making discretion are reflections of the larger values of the legal and political systems within which they operate. The social value placed on democracy, the rule of law, and individual rights all shape the way in which prosecutors exercise their power.

Katy Harriger

See also Adversarial Systems; Barristers; Civil Law; Common Law; Criminal Law; Criminal Procedures; Government Legal Departments; Plea Bargaining; Solicitors; Trial Courts

References and further reading

Dreyer, June Teufel. 2000. *China's Political System: Modernization and Tradition.* 3d ed. Addison-Wesley Longman.

Ehrmann, Henry W. 1976. *Comparative Legal Cultures.* Englewood Cliffs, NJ: Prentice-Hall.

Glendon, Mary Ann, Michael Wallace Gordon, and Paolo G. Carozza. 1999. *Comparative Legal Traditions in a Nutshell.* 2d ed. St. Paul, MN: West Group.

Hammergren, Linn A. 1998. *The Politics of Justice and Justice Reform in Latin America: The Peruvian Case in Comparative Perspective.* Boulder, CO: Westview Press.

Jacob, Herbert, Erhard Blankenberg, Herbert M. Kritzer, Doris Marie Provine, and Joseph Sanders. 1996. *Courts, Law, and Politics in Comparative Perspective.* New Haven, CT: Yale University Press.

Johnson, David T. 1998. "The Organization of Prosecution and the Possibility of Order." *Law and Society Review* 32, no. 2: 247–308.

Neubauer, David W. 1998. *American Courts and the Criminal Justice System.* 6th ed. Pacific Grove, CA: Brooks-Cole.

van Wyk, Dawid, John Dugard, Berties de Villiers, and
Dennis Davis. 1995. *Rights and Constitutionalism: The New
South African Legal Order.* Oxford: Clarendon Press.

PROTECTION OF SOCIETY

Protecting society from individuals who refuse to live by society's laws underlies the correctional philosophy of incapacitation. As a correctional goal, incapacitation is a strategy for crime control that involves isolating an offender from the community to prevent further crime. Significant variation exists across the globe in terms of protecting society through the use of incapacitative strategies. These differences have little to do with the actual threat crime poses to society but rather can be attributed to differences in public attitudes toward offenders, sentencing policies, the existence of alternatives to incarceration, and the extent to which citizens are afforded civil liberties.

As a result of the growing disillusionment with efforts to rehabilitate or deter offenders, coupled with increasing crime rates, the United States embraced the idea of using its correctional system to incapacitate offenders beginning in the 1970s. The idea itself, however, is nothing new; it can be traced back to primitive times when offenders were "banished" from society. Banishment was in effect "civil" death but usually ended in the physical death of the offender. A significant number of the early American settlers had been banished from England and transported to the colonies. Banishment would eventually be replaced by imprisonment and capital punishment.

During the 1820s, the penitentiary would emerge as the centerpiece of the U.S. correctional system. Based on the belief that institutions had the ability to change behavior, incarceration as a criminal sanction was intended to reform criminal offenders. Although physically secure and located in remote areas, early prisons were not for the purpose of protecting society from the inmates but rather for protecting inmates from the corrupting influences of society. Today, efforts to incapacitate offenders attempt to protect the community in one of three ways—detaining suspects in jail prior to trial, isolating convicted offenders in prison, and putting convicted offenders to death.

PREVENTIVE DETENTION

Historically, defendants suspected of a crime who were considered to be a flight risk would be held in a temporary holding facility to ensure their appearance at trial. More recently, judges have started denying bail to defendants who are believed to pose a threat to society. The idea is known as preventive detention. All states and the federal government currently allow judges to refuse bail to certain classes of defendants who, because of the seri-

ousness of their current offense or because of their prior record, are likely to commit additional crimes while out on bail. The U.S. Supreme Court upheld the constitutionality of preventive detention for adults as well as for juvenile offenders. The extent to which preventive detention protects society depends upon whether a significant amount of the crime that occurs in society is committed by offenders who have been released into the community pending their trial dates. Data from the National Pretrial Reporting Program suggest that *only* 6 percent of all defendants released before trial were convicted of a new felony offense before their scheduled trial date (Walker 1998). Property offenders are more likely to commit a new criminal offense while out on bail, and judges typically do not consider property offenders dangerous enough to warrant the use of preventive detention.

In many developing countries, including Bangladesh, Ecuador, Uganda, and Nigeria, pretrial detainees constitute a *majority* of the prison population. Further, the length of detention is considerably long. Suspects are frequently held in detention for longer periods than the actual sentence received. Article 9, section 3 of the International Covenant on Civil and Political Rights asserts that pretrial detention should be narrowly reserved for offenders who pose a flight risk or constitute a clear and serious threat to the community. Countries with significant pretrial detention populations are often lacking in explicit criteria to determine eligibility or exclude particular defendants because of the nature of their crimes. Without the civil liberties to protect individuals who have merely been suspected of a crime, many individuals are held for long periods without just cause.

IMPRISONMENT

Imprisonment is the most common type of incapacitation strategy used in the United States. Two approaches are employed: collective (also referred to as gross) and selective incapacitation. Collective incapacitation attempts to reduce crime through the imprisonment of a large number of offenders. The more offenders behind bars, the safer society will be from those offenders. For the past thirty years, U.S. prison populations have continuously increased. The number of inmates behind bars increased 650 percent between 1968 and 1997. During this past decade, more than 400 new prisons were constructed. The United States currently leads the world in terms of incarceration rates, with 3.1 percent of the U.S. population being under some type of correctional supervision. The cost of protecting society through incarceration is high, with average prison expenditures totaling $400 billion annually. Correctional expenditures top many state budgets.

Proponents of collective incapacitation recognize that the cost of incarceration is high but believe it is well worth the cost to society. In 1987, Edwin Zedlewski released a report titled "Making Confinement Decisions." The report was a cost-benefit analysis that revealed that imprisonment actually saves money. Zedlewski determined that crime cost society approximately $100 billion annually (this includes criminal justice expenditures, victim losses, property damage, etc.). Using inmate information collected by the Rand Corporation, he estimated that each offender commits an average of 187 crimes a year, with an average cost per crime of $2,300. The cost of keeping an offender behind bars is about $25,000, but this represents a savings of $405,100 ($2,300 x 187 = $430,100 – $25,000) per year. Zedlewski's assumptions and his report have since been the subject of continuous criticism. There is debate among scholars, but most agree that the average offender commits fewer than twenty crimes per year—*not* 187 (Zimring and Hawkins 1995).

Estimates of crime reduction resulting from the use of incarceration rest on three questionable assumptions: first, that offenders share the same risk of being apprehended, convicted, and incarcerated. There is considerable variation between property crimes and crimes committed against a person in terms of clearance rates, the decision to file charges, and whom judges are likely to send to prison. Second, those making these estimates assume that the criminal activities of those sent to prison will not be replaced by those of other offenders. Crime displacement is especially common for drug crimes and auto theft. Third, they assume that the experience of being in prison will have no effect on an offender's behavior once released. In other words, offenders are not being rehabilitated while in prison, and the prison experience is not deterring offenders from returning.

Locking up large numbers of offenders can be an effective way to reduce crime, but the question becomes, how many offenders does a society have to put behind bars before it can expect to see a significant reduction in the overall crime rate? The difficulty stems from a lack of empirical research demonstrating a clear, direct relationship between incarceration and crime. Incapacitation proponents argue that increases in incapacitation will reduce crime, but some of our largest crime waves occurred when incarceration rates were very high. The national decline in crime rates from 1991 to 1998 has been attributed in part to the increased use of incarceration (prison populations grew by 47 percent during this time). However, states with the largest increases in incarceration experienced on average smaller declines in crime than states with lower rates of incarceration. It is estimated that prison populations would have to increase anywhere from 10 to 20 percent to produce a 1 percent reduction in the crime rate.

In furtherance of efforts to incapacitate offenders, all states as well as the federal government have adopted mandatory sentencing policies. Mandatory sentences impose mandatory imprisonment for certain crimes or mandatory minimum prison terms or both. Mandatory sentences involve legislative efforts to curtail judicial discretion during the sentencing phase of the criminal justice process. Research reveals that mandatory sentences have little, if any, impact on crime. In reality, mandatory sentencing increases the prosecuting attorney's discretion in charging. Prosecutors frequently use the threat of a mandatory prison term as a way to encourage defendants to plead guilty to a lesser charge. When mandatory sentences are imposed, they tend to result in unnecessarily harsh prison sentences, leading many, including the American Bar Association, to recommend that mandatory prison terms be abolished.

Given how expensive collective incapacitation has proven to be, efforts to incapacitate offenders changed somewhat in the 1980s. Selective incapacitation involves identifying the high-rate offender or "career criminal" and imposing lengthy prison terms only for these offenders. Research by Marvin Wolfgang and associates (1972) at the University of Pennsylvania revealed that a small number of offenders are responsible for the majority of crime in society. Selective incapacitation promises a savings over collective incapacitation as well as a reduction in crime by targeting these chronic recidivists. In 1982, the Rand Corporation put forth a sentencing structure that would reduce robbery by 15 percent while at the same time reducing prison populations by 5 percent (with collective incapacitation, prison populations would have to increase 25 percent to reduce crime by 5 percent). The problem with the Rand formula lies in the ability of the decision makers in the criminal justice system to predict future criminal behavior. Prior criminal records are weak indicators of future behavior. Prediction efforts typically result in more, not fewer, offenders being sent to prison.

Three strikes legislation became very popular in the 1990s. The first law was passed in the state of Washington, and several states as well as the federal government followed suit. Variations in the actual application of three strikes laws are found between states, but typically the laws impose a mandatory prison term of twenty-five years to life for repeat offenders. What constitutes a strike will also differ. In some states, all three offenses must be serious felonies, whereas in others, drug offenses and juvenile crimes count as strikes against a defendant. Evaluations of three strikes laws revealed decreases in crime after the laws went into effect, but larger decreases in crime occurred in states without these laws, suggesting that something other than the increased use of incarceration is responsible for declining crime rates (many criminologists attribute the national decline in crime rates to a decline in the proportion of crime-prone individuals in society aged fourteen to twenty-four). Three strikes legislation is contributing to an already overcrowded prison system, and prisons are experiencing rapid increases in the number of geriatric inmates.

Incarceration rates outside the United States dwindle in comparison. Five percent of the world's population resides in the United States; however, one in four incarcerated individuals is in the United States. The rate of incarceration in the United States is five to eight times higher than in Canada and most European nations. Russia and South Africa also have high rates of incarceration, but Iceland, Japan, and India have some of the lowest rates (Sentencing Project 1997). Crime rates alone cannot explain the differences across countries. In Russia, for example, offenders are more likely to be incarcerated for minor offenses and for longer time periods. Prison sentences in the United States are on average twice those of France. Public attitudes toward offenders and the criminal justice system best explain variations in sentencing severity. Individuals in countries with large disparities in wealth (like the United States) typically display more punitive attitudes toward offenders, compared to individuals who live in countries with more advanced social welfare programs. In addition, the current "war on drugs" policy initiative in the United States has significantly increased its prison population by increasing the number of drug offenders being sent to prison for long periods of time. From 1980 to 1997, there was a 1,040 percent increase in imprisoned drug offenders, compared to an 82 percent increase in violent offenders (Justice Policy Institute 2000). The United States has chosen imprisonment as its primary response to the drug problem, but many European countries as well as Australia view substance abuse from a medical model perspective and offer more in the way of treatment to offenders.

CAPITAL PUNISHMENT

Finally, the use of capital punishment is considered to be a way to *permanently* incapacitate an offender, thereby protecting society from any future criminal behavior. Capital punishment was historically the most common method of punishment used by society. It is more commonly supported from a retribution or deterrence argument. Executions were always held in public to send a message to potential offenders. The last public execution in the United States was in 1936. There are approximately 3,500 U.S. inmates currently under a sentence of death. Less than 100 inmates are actually put to death in any given year.

From an incapacitation standpoint, capital punishment offers little in terms of protecting society. Thirteen states do not have death penalty statutes, and over one-half of the executions in 1999 occurred in only three states. In the United States, capital punishment is reserved for a narrow class of homicide offenses (and the rare offense of treason), and research suggests that homicide offenders have some of the lowest recidivism rates of all offenders. Fewer than 1 percent commit another homicide, and only 4.5 percent commit another violent crime (Potter 2000). Capital punishment is also a very expensive criminal sanction, costing *more* than incarceration. The average execution costs $3.2 million, six times the amount needed to house an inmate for life.

More than half the countries in the world have either abolished capital punishment or do not currently execute offenders. The United States ranks third in terms of total executions, falling behind China and the Democratic Republic of Congo. Even countries with punitive attitudes toward punishment *and* high incarceration rates have abolished capital punishment. Russia and South Africa have recently suspended the use of capital punishment.

Amy Thistlethwaite

See also Capital Punishment; General Deterrence; Incarceration; Rehabilitation; Retribution

References and further reading

Gainsborough, Jenni, and Marc Mauer. 2000. *Diminishing Returns: Crime and Incarceration in the 1990s.* Washington, DC: Sentencing Project.
Justice Policy Institute. 2000. *Poor Prescription: The Costs of Imprisoning Drug Offenders in the US.* Washington, DC: Justice Policy Institute.
Potter, Gary W. 2000. "Cost, Deterrence, Incapacitation, Brutalization and the Death Penalty: The Scientific Evidence." *The Advocate* 22, no. 1: 24–29.
Sentencing Project. 1997. *Americans behind Bars: U.S. and International Use of Incarceration.* Washington, DC: Sentencing Project.
Visher, Christy A. 1987. "Incapacitation and Crime Control: Does a 'Lock 'Em Up' Strategy Reduce Crime?" *Justice Quarterly* 4, no. 4: 513–543.
Walker, Samuel. 1998. *Sense and Nonsense about Crime and Drugs: A Policy Guide.* 4th ed. Belmont, CA: Wadsworth Publishing.
Wolfgang, Marvin, Robert M. Figlio, and Thorsten Sellin. 1972. *Delinquency in a Birth Cohort.* Chicago: University of Chicago Press.
Zedlewski, Edwin. 1987. "Making Confinement Decisions." Research in Brief publication. Washington, DC: National Institute of Justice, U.S. Department of Justice.
Zimring, Franklin E., and Gordon Hawkins. 1995. *Incapacitation: Penal Confinement and the Restraint on Crime.* New York: Oxford University Press.

PUBLIC LAW

Public law has two related but distinct meanings. First and most important, it describes those areas of law that directly involve the state as a legal actor—constitutional, administrative, and criminal law. In this meaning, public law is contrasted with private law, which describes those areas of law in which the state is not directly or primarily a party—contracts, torts, probate, family law, and so forth. Second, public law is a technical term that refers to laws of general application, as opposed to private or special laws, which concern only a small class or group (perhaps even a single individual).

The distinction between public law, as laws defining the state or governing the state in its relations with citizens, and private law, as laws governing the relations among citizens, is increasingly ambiguous. Although it defines civil code systems, the distinction is much less important in common law countries. Further, while the distinction has been important historically in various kinds of social science research, its utility is now widely questioned.

The differentiation of public and private aspects of law has its roots in Roman law. It became increasingly important during the nineteenth century, as modern regulatory states became the dominant model of political organization. Ironically (but not surprisingly), this period also marked the most significant erosion of the utility of the public/private law distinction: Scholars became most interested in defining what was public and what was private at precisely the moment that the expanding power and scope of the state began to make the distinction less and less clear.

Because of its origins in Roman law, the public/private distinction has historically been strongest in European countries, where the Roman law provided the template for later codes. Conversely, because Roman law had relatively little impact on England during the medieval and early modern eras, legal systems based on English common law do not place much importance on the public/private distinction. Some scholars argue that the history of English feudal land law, in which property rights and political rights were inextricably linked, is fundamentally incompatible with the conceptual division of law into public and private realms.

As John Merryman (1968) points out, this significant difference in the importance of the public/private dichotomy suggests that the distinction is not fundamental to law itself, as has been argued historically, but is instead local to the history and sociology of particular legal systems. From this perspective, the public/private distinction is ideological, articulating a belief that there are some aspects of community life that are not—and should not be—regulated by the state, such as property rights, freedom of contract, and family law.

One of the problems with the concept of public law is defining exactly what the distinction is between public and private matters. There are several axes of differentiation that offer partial divisions between public and private law, although none of the criteria is able to offer a definitive separation.

A basic distinction between public and private is based on the identities of the parties in a legal matter. If the matter is between two citizens, rather than between the citizen and the state or one of its subsidiaries, the matter is considered to be private. But this distinction can be blurred by statutory recognition of provisions such as *qui tam* actions, which allow private parties to act on behalf of and thereby enforce general public interests by filing civil suits in which the plaintiff sues for the state, as well as for him- or herself.

A closely related mode of differentiation is based on subject matter. Law relating to aspects of individual and private life that do not concern the broader public or a specific interaction with the state, such as contracts, family law, and wills, could be considered private law matters. But even these matters are increasingly subject to state regulation.

Venue also offers a possibility for differentiating between public and private. This can be interpreted quite broadly to say that all matters adjudicated and enforced through the judicial system of a state are inherently public because they involve the enforcement mechanisms of the state, leaving little that would fall under the private law heading. Allowing for a slightly more nuanced definition, one could define public/private by the specific type of court involved. For example, public and private law distinctions are explicit in civil code systems, where separate courts handle public and civil law matters. Even in common law countries, there is some institutional division of labor, with specialized courts for family law, bankruptcy, and some kinds of administrative law.

In the United States, the growth of arbitration and mediation, and other forms of "alternative dispute resolution" (ADR), beginning in the 1970s, might be viewed as an attempt to extend either the public or private venues of law. One view suggests that the growth of court-ordered or statutorily required ("appended") arbitration and ADR makes private law actions a part of public policy. In contrast, one could also consider the move by private businesses, such as major credit card companies, automobile dealerships, and national franchises, to write arbitration and ADR provisions into their contracts with employees and consumers as a reclaiming of a private law sphere. Requiring that disputes be resolved initially (or exclusively) through arbitration or ADR effectively removes private law matters from the courts and carves out a space for individuals to resolve issues in a truly nonpublic setting.

An additional criterion acknowledges the ever-present involvement of the state in all things legal and thus bases its determination of public or private law on the passive/active disposition of adjudication. In the more passive private model, the judge or law in question is supposed to be a neutral arbiter, ensuring fairness of process and limiting analysis and statements to questions concerning rules governing the proceeding and general situation. In the public law model, the judge is vested not only with ensuring procedural fairness but also with determining issues of fact and determining a just outcome.

Public policy concerns may also play a role in distinguishing the public and private functions of law. Public law tends to be more general, may involve multiple parties or interests, is more likely to be prospective, and, in some cases, encourages judicial remedies that go beyond monetary damage awards. Private law, which is often retrospectively concerned with resolving specific disputes about past conduct between identifiable parties, rarely has public policy implications. The public's main interest in the resolution of such disputes is that they be settled peaceably by fair procedures. In this regard, both public and private matters can arise out of a single transaction. This is most easily recognized with personal injuries arising from crimes, where the state has an interest in proscribing and punishing behavior that violates community order and where criminal actions create specific victims who seek restitution for loss or grievances. The same would be true of class-action lawsuits by workers claiming back pay and damages for alleged discrimination by employers under statutory procedures.

There are three main critiques that suggest that the distinction between private and public law is not always a useful one and that the true nature of modern law is almost entirely public. First, "private" lawsuits and class-action litigation have developed to a point where civil legal actions are no longer limited to disputes between private parties about private rights. Instead, civil suits increasingly have implications for public policy. Second, the lives of citizens are regulated as much by "private" laws as they are by public laws. Thus, any attempt to understand the political life of a society through a study of its legal culture must include both the public and private aspects of law.

Third, it is difficult to clearly delimit public from private law because government intervention and codification have progressed to the point that there are very few, if any, areas of life that are not affected by the legal framework of the state. Even if a matter concerns a predominately private relationship, the modern state has statutes and regulations that govern and enforce the legal concerns of these private functions. Thus, while the matter itself could be classified as private, it is from a public entity or statutory authority that one takes one's starting point for determining its appropriate legal form, and it is on state actors that one relies for the enforcement of "private" actions such as divorce settlements, contracts, and wills.

Public law is thus a broad concept with evolving and sometimes confusing meaning and significance. The distinction between public and private law is most useful within the context of civil code systems, where it articulates a definitive ideological and practice-oriented split within the legal system of a country. It is much less useful in countries with a common law tradition. Retention of a broad public/private law distinction by social scientists and legal scholars for both civil code and common law countries, without differentiation, is therefore problematic at best.

Joel B. Grossman
Erin Ackerman

See also Alternative Dispute Resolution; Civil Law; Common Law; Private Law; Roman Law

References and further reading

Chayes, Abram. 1976. "The Role of the Judge in Public Law Litigation." *Harvard Law Review* 89: 1281–1316.
Kreml, William P. 1997. *The Constitutional Divide: The Private and Public Sectors in American Law.* Columbia: University of South Carolina Press.
Merryman, John Henry. 1968. "The Public-Private Law Distinction in European and American Law." *Emory Journal of Public Law* 17: 3–19.
Nicholas, Barry. 1962. *An Introduction to Roman Law.* Oxford: Oxford University Press.
Shapiro, Martin. 1972. "From Public Law to Public Policy or the 'Public' in 'Public Law.'" *P.S.* 5: 410–418.

PUERTO RICO

GENERAL INFORMATION

Puerto Rico, along with the adjacent islands of Culebra, Vieques, and Mona, are part of over 2,200 islands that belong to the United States, but are not a part of the nation (*Torres v. Sablan*, 2000). Puerto Rico is located in the easternmost area of the Greater Antilles, and it is surrounded by the Atlantic Ocean to the north and the Caribbean Sea to the south. The island is roughly 110 by 35 miles in size. It has a population of close to 4 million people, including both U.S. citizens and transient populations from the surrounding Caribbean islands. For the most part the residents of the island are Spanish-speaking U.S. citizens of Hispanic and Afro-Antillean heritage.

Puerto Rico is a major producer and exporter of manufactured goods, pharmaceuticals, and advanced technological equipment. The island's gross domestic product (GDP) exceeds $48 million with a per capita income of $12,212. While this per capita income is the highest in Latin America, it is one of the lowest in the United States. The services sector, including tourism, comprises 37 percent of the GDP. The island boasts that its rum production comprises 83 percent of the rum that is sold in the U.S. mainland.

HISTORY

Diplomatic and commercial relations between the United States and Puerto Rico date back to the early 1820s. In the late 1880s some U.S. policymakers expressed interest in

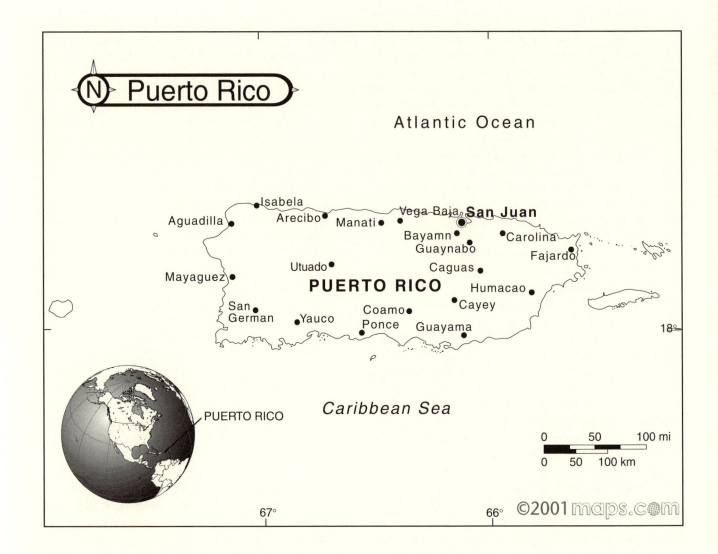

Puerto Rico

Atlantic Ocean

Aguadilla • Isabela • Arecibo • Manati • Vega Baja **San Juan**
Bayamn • Carolina
Guaynabo • Fajardo
Utuado • Caguas
Mayaguez • **PUERTO RICO** • Humacao
San German • Coamo • Cayey
Yauco • Ponce • Guayama

18°

PUERTO RICO

Caribbean Sea

| 0 | 50 | 100 mi |
| 0 | 50 | 100 km |

©2001 maps.com

67° 66°

the annexation of new markets like Cuba, Hawai'i, the Philippines, and Puerto Rico. The War of 1898 served as a catalyst for the acquisition of these island territories. To be sure, after the battles in Cuba, Gen. Nelson A. Miles moved to conquer Puerto Rico. On July 25, 1898, the Spanish forces formally surrendered the island to General Miles, and Puerto Rico became a possession of the United States. This date marked the beginning of a two-year military government that set the subsequent legal basis for the legal system that currently governs the island.

The formal surrender of Spain and the cession of Puerto Rico to the United States were ratified in the Treaty of Paris of 1898 (30 Stat. 1754). This treaty established the legal foundations for the relationship between Puerto Rico and the United States. Article 9 was the most controversial provision of the treaty because it made the inhabitants of the island nationals of Puerto Rico. More importantly, under the tenets of this article, the U.S. Congress would determine the civil and political rights of the inhabitants of the island.

Between 1898 and 1900, Puerto Rico was governed by a succession of generals under the supervision of the pres-

ident of the United States. They were authorized to develop a temporary or provisional government under the provisions of a series of presidential mandates or general orders. The last of these rulers, Brig. Gen. George W. Davis, created a U.S. provisional court and restructured the island's legal system. He also provided the blueprints for the civil government that would replace him the following year.

The Foraker Act of 1901 (Ch. 191, 31 Stat. 77) replaced the military regime and provided a civil government for the island. This law represented a departure from the previous territorial policy, and it represented the first experiment in U.S. imperial legislation. Unlike the previous practice of extending the Constitution to the territories, the Foraker Act gave Congress plenary power to govern the island as a colonial dependency. One of the more important provisions of this organic act was the imposition of a 15 percent duty on merchandise exported and imported to and from the United States (sec. 3). In addition, the residents of the island became Puerto Rican citizens (sec. 7). The act also replaced the provisional court with a federal district court under the appellate jurisdiction of the Supreme Court (sec. 34). The act did not include a bill of rights for the protection of the citizens of the island.

The Foraker Act was institutionalized by the Supreme Court in a series of decisions known as the *Insular Cases* (1901–1922). These rulings laid the foundations for the legal relationship with the U.S. and all the colonial dependencies acquired subsequently. The main theory underpinning this policy was established in *Downes v. Bidwell* (1901). In this case, the Court established that Puerto Rico was an unincorporated territory. This meant that the island *belonged* to the United States, but was not a *part* of the nation. This new status allowed lawmakers to treat Puerto Rico as a foreign nation for constitutional purposes and as domestic for international concerns.

Until the transfer of sovereignty to the United States, which brought the Anglo-American common law system, Puerto Rico used the Spanish civil code. The character of the courts was rapidly transformed from a Hispanic and colonial to a North American model. Under the Spanish regime the courts relied on Spanish and continental European practices of correcting errors committed in the interpretation of the law by the lower courts. The Anglo-American legal system, however, transformed the courts into an appellate system akin to those existing in the states of the Union at the time.

The legal system also experienced important changes in the area of substantive due process. For example, the reigning public law was replaced by North American structural and legislative models that relied on rules of evidence and procedure that were in line with the adversarial and oral character of the common law system. The integration resulted in the development of a mixed system of law that retained some aspects of the civil law tradition (codification) while simultaneously embracing a common law jurisprudence and a precedent system.

In 1917 the Jones Act (31 Stat. 1132) naturalized and extended U.S. citizenship to the residents of Puerto Rico. This act provided the first bill of rights for the residents of the island. In addition, this organic act inserted Puerto Rico in the First Circuit Court of Appeals.

In 1922, the Supreme Court reaffirmed the theory of unincorporation that had been laid out in the *Downes* opinion. In *Balzac v. People of Puerto Rico* (1922) the Court ruled that U.S. citizens residing in Puerto Rico were not entitled to a trial by jury in criminal cases because the Constitution did not extend fully to the territories that were not part of the nation. The Court did note that U.S. citizens residing on the island were entitled to some fundamental protections, but it refused to define which rights were encompassed in this definition. During the years following this decision, the island experienced political turmoil resulting in the demand for the clarification of the island's status and a call for increased self-government.

In 1947 Congress authorized the election of a governor (P.L. 362), and in 1950 it permitted Puerto Rico to draft its own constitution (P.L. 81-600, Ch. 446, 64 Stat. 319). In 1952, President Harry S. Truman signed a congressional joint resolution (H.J. Res. 430) that approved the Constitution of Puerto Rico. Under the provisions of this constitution, Puerto Rico became a "Free-Associated-State," which was translated into the word *commonwealth*. This new status represented a compromise between a legal compact, akin to the Autonomic Charter of 1897, and full constitutional status within the nation. The Puerto Rican constitution had been modeled after the U.S. Constitution and United Nations Declaration of Human Rights. In 1953, the UN General Assembly adopted Resolution 748 (VIII), which recognized the new self-governing status of Puerto Rico. However, Puerto Ricans continued to debate the island's future because of the ambiguous nature of the commonwealth status.

At the time of this writing there were three political parties representing three positions, namely an annexationist, an autonomous, and an independence ideology. More importantly, the Supreme Court continues to treat Puerto Rico as an unincorporated territory.

CURRENT STRUCTURE

Legal Profession and Legal Training
Created on June 27, 1840, the Colegio de Abogados (College of Attorneys) is the oldest legal professional institution in existence in Puerto Rico. This is the equivalent to the state bar association in the United States. Any attorney who wishes to practice law on the island must be a member of this institution. Currently there are 9,828 active members, of which 6,334 are public notaries. Puerto Rico has four law schools, namely the Escuela de Derecho, Universidad de Puerto Rico (San Juan); Escuela de Derecho, Universidad Interamericana de Puerto Rico (San Juan); Escuela de Derecho, Pontificia Universidad Católica (Ponce); and Escuela de Derecho Eugenio Maria de Hostos (Humacao) (nonaccredited).

Legal Aid and Criminal Defense Services
There are various institutions in Puerto Rico that provide legal representation to indigent defendants. The legal clinics of the three accredited law schools provide legal assistance on civil, penal, and juvenile cases. The Society for Legal Assistance provides legal assistance for defendants in criminal cases. Servicios Legales de Puerto Rico and PRO-BONO, INC. provide legal assistance in civil and juvenile cases. In addition, there are two special programs that provide support in civil cases, Programa de Ayuda Legal del Municipio de San Juan, and the Special Project for Victims of Domestic Violence.

Administrative Hearings

Government agencies generally provide an administrative forum where individuals can seek redress for their grievances and other personal claims. Generally, the organic law that organizes the agency also provides for the creation of procedures for administrative hearings. With few exceptions, appeals resulting from administrative rulings are heard in the circuit court of appeals. There are at least two interagency administrative agencies that evaluate, adjudicate, and review lower administrative decisions. These are the Junta de Apelaciones del Sistema de Administración de Personal (JASAP), and the Junta de Apelaciones sobre Construcciones y Lotificaciones. These agencies generally follow the same rules of procedure as any administrative agency in the U.S.

JUDICIAL SYSTEM

The adoption of the Puerto Rican constitution in 1952 transformed the judiciary structure in important ways. Article 5 created a General Court of Justice, with jurisdiction over the whole island, composed of a Supreme Court and those lower courts created by the Legislative Assembly. Currently the General Court of Justice is composed of a Supreme Court, a circuit court of appeals, and a trial court or court of first instance. The constitution further established that the courts would constitute a unified system for administrative, functioning, and jurisdictional purposes. The judicial system in Puerto Rico is structured in the following manner:

Alternative Dispute Resolution

The judiciary has established a Center for Conflict Resolution as a mechanism to solve disputes outside of the courts. The center provides a trained professional, free of charge, to help individuals resolve particular disputes. The types of cases that this center services include child custody, child support, complaints regarding animals, domestic disputes, conflicts between neighbors, some contract disputes, and other cases involving social relations.

Court of First Instance

The court of first instance is composed of superior and municipal tribunals. For administrative purposes, the court is divided into thirteen judicial regions, which in turn cover seventy-eight municipalities on the island. Each region has a superior court section.

The court of first instance hears both criminal and civil cases. The civil jurisdiction hears cases regarding the following: family law, labor law, successions, constitutional law, administrative law, corporate law, torts and contracts, damages and injuries, special and extraordinary actions, proceedings to enforce administrative decisions, and any other civil matter.

Legal Structure of Puerto Rico Courts

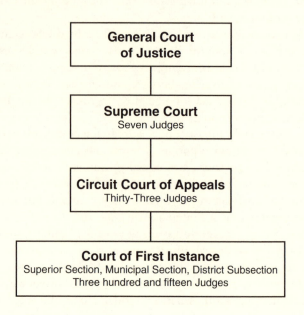

General Court of Justice

Supreme Court
Seven Judges

Circuit Court of Appeals
Thirty-Three Judges

Court of First Instance
Superior Section, Municipal Section, District Subsection
Three hundred and fifteen Judges

Circuit Court of Appeals

The circuit court of appeals was created in 1995 to review sentences and rulings from the court of first instance. It is an intermediate court between the trial courts and the Puerto Rican Supreme Court. The court also reviews all final rulings and/or decisions from administrative agencies.

This court is managed by two judges, which have the responsibilities of an administrator and an auxiliary administrator. The court is divided into eleven panels, each composed of three judges. The chief justice of the Supreme Court determines the composition and distribution of each territorial panel. The judges are regularly rotated so that each has an opportunity to serve in every territorial jurisdiction during her term in office.

The court of appeals exercises its appellate function in four areas of law. As an appellate court, this court hears appeals from the court of first instance rulings, both criminal and civil. Through a certiorari procedure, the court has the power to revise all interlocutory resolutions dictated by the lower courts. This power is further extended to hear resolutions relating to autonomous municipalities, and determinations and/or orders from the State Electoral Commission. The court can also revise all lower rulings, rules, orders, and administrative resolutions. Finally, the court is empowered to expedite rights of habeas corpus and mandamus.

The Supreme Court

The Puerto Rican Supreme Court is the court of last instance on the island. The Court also claims to be the ultimate interpreter of the Puerto Rican constitution and its laws.

Article 5, sec. 4 of the Puerto Rican Constitution established that the Supreme Court would operate under the rules of its own adoption. This court can hold both divided and bench hearings. In addition, Supreme Court tribunals are composed of no less than three judges. A majority of the sitting judges must agree in order to declare a law unconstitutional. The Supreme Court's rulings and opinions become a source of law and precedent as established by the doctrine of stare decisis in the Anglo-American tradition of common law.

The Court has original jurisdiction in mandamus, habeas corpus, quo warranto, injunctions, and all others determined by law. The Court has appellate jurisdiction and certiorari over all rulings emanating from the lower courts. It is also charged with all cases involving the constitutionality of a Puerto Rican law. The Court is empowered to revise any government action. It should be noted that the Puerto Rican Supreme Court has extensive rule-making powers. The island's constitution has granted the Court the power to adopt rules of evidence, civil and criminal procedure, as well as to adopt rules for the administration of the lower courts. Finally, the Court has adopted Canons of Professional Ethics and Judicial Ethics under its powers to regulate the Puerto Rican legal profession.

JUDICIAL SELECTION AND STAFFING

The governor, with the advice and consent of the Senate, appoints judges in the general court of justice. Superior Court justices serve for a term of twelve years, while municipal court judges serve for eight years. The court of appeals is composed of thirty-three judges. They are appointed for a term of sixteen years.

The Supreme Court is composed of a chief justice and six associate justices. Although the justices of the Court are appointed for life, they are required to retire on their seventieth birthday. The number of judges sitting on the bench can only be changed upon the request of the Court.

FEDERAL COURTS

There are two federal courts that exercise jurisdiction in Puerto Rico, the U.S. bankruptcy court and the district court of Puerto Rico. Both courts are part of the First Circuit Court of Appeals. The bankruptcy court has three sitting judges, while the district court has ten. All judges are selected in accordance with federal procedures. It should be noted that the current chief judge for the First Circuit Court of Appeals, Juan R. Torruella, is one of three Puerto Rican judges sitting in the federal courts of appeals.

In the past there has been some tension between the federal and Puerto Rican courts over the district courts' practice of hearing cases involving Puerto Rican law. These tensions have been especially exacerbated by the district court's practice of making policy decisions by extending its jurisdiction and ruling on local controversial political issues along partisan lines.

Charles R. Venator Santiago

See also Civil Law; Common Law; United States—Federal System

References and further reading

Balzac v. People of Puerto Rico. 1922. 258 U.S. 298.

Delgado Cintrón, Carmelo. 1988. *Derecho y colonialismo: La trayectoria histórica del derecho puertorriqueño, ensayos.* Rio Piedras: Editorial Edil, Inc.

Downes v. Bidwell. 1901. 182 U.S. 244.

Graffam, Richard. 1986. "The Federal Courts' Interpretation of Puerto Rican Law: Whose Law Is It, Anyway?" *Revista del Colegio de Abogados* 47: 111.

"Judiciary of Puerto Rico." http://www.tribunalpr.org/ (accessed November 25, 2001).

López Baralt, José. 1999. *The Policy of the United States Towards Its Territories with Special Reference to Puerto Rico.* Rio Piedras: Editorial de la Universidad de Puerto Rico.

Rivera Ramos, Efrén. 2001. *The Legal Construction of Identity: The Judicial and Social Legacy of American Colonialism in Puerto Rico.* Washington, DC: American Psychological Association.

Serrano Geyls, Raúl. 1997. *Derecho constitucional de Estados Unidos y Puerto Rico,* 2 vols. 2d ed. San Juan: Programa de educación jurídica continua Universidad Interamericana de Puerto Rico.

Silvestrini, Blanca G., and María Dolores Luque de Sánchez. 1992. *Historia de Puerto Rico: Trayectoria de un pueblo.* San Juan: Ediciones Cultural Panamericana, Inc.

Torres v. Sablan. 2000. 68 USLW 3178.

Torruella, Juan R. 1988. *The Supreme Court and Puerto Rico: The Doctrine of Separate and Unequal.* Rio Piedras: Editorial de la Universidad de Puerto Rico.

Trías Monge, José. 1988. *El sistema judicial de Puerto Rico.* 2d ed. Rio Piedras: Editorial de la Universidad de Puerto Rico.

———. 1997. *Puerto Rico: The Trials of the Oldest Colony in the World.* New Haven: Yale University Press.

United States General Accounting Office. 1991. *U.S. Insular Areas: Applicability of Relevant Provisions of the U.S. Constitution,* GAO/HRD-91–18 June 1991. Washington DC: Government Printing Office.

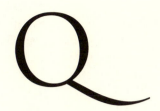

QADI (QAZI) COURTS

The term *qadi court* (alternatively *sharia court*) refers to a court in which a Muslim judge decides cases in accordance with Islamic law. The qadi (in English transliteration, cadi, kazi, or kadi) is a Muslim judge, although the Arabic term *qadi* is not an exact equivalent of the English term *judge*. In Muslim history, the qadi was a government official who, in addition to his judicial activities, might perform other official duties. Qadi courts originally exercised jurisdiction in both civil and criminal matters and were not clearly distinguished from other courts.

Beginning in the colonial period, qadi courts came to be distinguished as special courts for the application of Islamic laws relating to Muslim personal status (about marriage, divorce, inheritance, and endowments). These special courts were, however, gradually abolished when Muslim personal laws had been codified. In a few countries, qadi courts continued to operate with restricted jurisdiction as *sharia* courts. In recent years, *sharia* courts have been reestablished in some Muslim countries, and their jurisdiction has been expanded. What follows is a general description of the institution of qadi in Islamic legal theory and an overview of the history of the qadi courts in Muslim history.

THEORY

Muslim jurists developed a distinct genre of literature, known as *adab al-qadi* (the qadi code of ethics), in which they explained and clarified the standards for the administration of Islamic justice. In these texts, they discussed the significance of the qadiship, the prerequisites for holding office, the appointment and dismissal of qadis, and the laws of procedure (one also finds chapters on *adab al-qadi* in Islamic legal works).

In theory, the caliph is the source of the executive power, which he may delegate to other officials, including the qadi. The qadi is required to be of good character, and he or she is expected to have mastered Islamic legal texts and to be competent to deduce laws from these texts. As a rule, the qadi is male, but some jurists approve of the appointment of a female qadi. The caliph or his delegated agent may appoint a qadi. In view of continuity of law and order in society, Muslim jurists also consider valid this appointment by a Muslim rebel or by a non-Muslim ruler. The appointment should take place in the presence of at least two witnesses and is contractual in nature. The appointing authority may limit the jurisdiction of a qadi or depose him at any time.

In theory, the jurisdiction of a qadi court includes both civil and criminal matters, but the qadi's competence in criminal matters was increasingly limited by the development of the *shurta* (police) and *mazalim* (complaint) courts (see below). The development of various schools in Islamic law in the ninth century led to a diversity of its application in qadi courts. A qadi's letter of appointment sometimes specified the law school that he should follow in reaching his judgment. Because the inhabitants of certain cities and regions often were adherents of more than one school, the delegating authority appointed qadis who represented each school.

The qadi court normally consists of a single judge, who is encouraged to consult with jurists who are sometimes attached to his court (called *mushawar* in Spain and North Africa). The qadi might also consult with a *mufti,* that is, a distinguished student of Islamic law who gives his expert opinion (*fatwa*) in response to a request from a qadi, from state authorities, or from the people in general. The muftiship was sometimes an official position. Whereas the judgment of a qadi is legally binding, the opinion of a *mufti* is not. The *mufti* clarifies a point of law; the qadi applies the law to the facts of the case, although he may base his decision on local custom as well.

The qadi court consists of a secretary (*amin* or *katib*), a guard (*haras*), an official who executes the punishment (*jalwaz*), and a warden (*sajjan*). Professional witnesses (*shahids* or *udul*) play an important role in the qadi court. In addition to giving testimony, these witnesses serve as notaries. Although there were no lawyers (the *muhami,* or lawyer, is a modern development), men knowledgeable in the law often served as agents (*wakil*) for litigants; alternatively, litigants came to court armed with a *fatwa* solicited from an independent *mufti*.

Islamic procedural law operates on the principle of "freedom from liability" (*bara'at al-dhimma*). Any accused person is presumed to be innocent until proven guilty. Similarly, no claim can be awarded unless the plaintiff produces a legal proof. The qadi begins a case by deciding which party bears the burden of proof; generally, it is the party that brings the claim to court. During the initial hearing, however, the burden of proof may shift one or more times between the parties. Every time that one of the litigants makes a claim (*da'wa*), he or she becomes the plaintiff. If the other party denies it, the claimant (not necessarily the party that initiated the lawsuit) must prove its claim.

A claim can be established on the strength of the testimony of two witnesses who are Muslims, adults, and men of integrity. Women may serve as witnesses in cases in which male witnesses are unavailable; normally two female witnesses are required to support one male witness. In cases where women are in a better position to testify to the truth of a matter (e.g., the establishment of virginity), the testimony of female witnesses alone is sufficient. In civil cases, one witness is regarded as sufficient proof, on the condition that the claimant agrees to swear a solemn oath. Written documents have no probative value unless certified by two witnesses. Circumstantial evidence is rarely acceptable in a limited number of cases (e.g., in murder cases in which eyewitnesses are unavailable). If a claimant proves his claim, the qadi issues a judgment in his favor; if not, he holds in favor of the defendant.

The qadi's judgment is final and binding upon the litigants. Although the issuing qadi may not reverse his own judgment, all his judgments are subject to review by his successor; if a successor judge discovers a mistake of law, he has the power to overturn an earlier decision.

HISTORICAL DEVELOPMENT

Muslim historians generally trace the roots of the qadiship to the Qur'an, which speaks directly about the judicial function of the Prophet Muhammad (see Qur'an 4:65,105; 5:42, 48–49; 24:48, 51). The Qur'an used the term *hukm* (decision, judgment), which recalls the *hakam*, or tribal arbitrator of pre-Islamic times. Whereas the *hakam* did not have the authority to enforce his decisions, the Prophet Muhammad did: he was the leader of the *umma* who had signed agreements with most tribes throughout Arabia. The caliphs inherited Muhammad's judicial function, and the first caliphs served as judges. With the expansion of the caliphate, it became customary to appoint qadis in the capital and major cities. The qadi of the army post (*qadi al-jund, qadi 'askar,* or *qadi lashkar*) played an important role in the newly conquered territories. During the Umayyad period (661–750 C.E.), the qadi was responsible for the administration of justice as well as for the maintenance of public order. In the Abbasid period (750–1258), the caliphs assigned duty of the maintenance of law and order to other officials and gave them relevant judicial powers. Harun al-Rashid (r. 786–809) was the first to give the title "chief qadi" (*qadi*

al-qudat) to the qadi of the capital, who had general authority for the administration of justice; he was also responsible for the nomination, control, and dismissal of qadis and other judicial officials. The chief qadi did not have authority, however, over special courts or agents, for example, police, the market inspector (*muhtasib*), or the court of complaints (*mazalim*). These courts, headed by state officials, followed a summary procedure in which oath played a vital role. For instance, a claimant might support his claim by taking oath, and the accused might take an oath of denial.

Until the rise of the Fatimids in Egypt (909–1171), there was only one *qadi al-qudat* in Islam: in Baghdad, capital of the Abbasids. He was often described as the chief qadi of the caliphate. Later, when the Fatimids in Egypt and Umayyads in Spain (al-Andalus) broke away from Baghdad, they appointed their own chief qadis. The chief qadi in Cordoba was called *qadi al-jama'a* (the qadi of the community). The Umayyad caliph in al-Andalus, Abd al-Rahman (755–788), gave the title *qadi al-jama'a* to his military qadi (*qadi al-jund*) in order to declare his independence from the Abbasids in Baghdad.

The Fatimids established their own chief qadi in Cairo. Whereas the Abbasid chief qadi exercised his authority in the name of the caliph, the Fatimid chief qadi did so in his own name. Under the Mamluks in Egypt (1250–1517), the chief qadi in the capital delegated his authority to chief qadis in major cities, so that there were a number of chief qadis throughout the realm. The Mamluks also recognized the practical need to appoint a chief qadi for each law school. As the Ottomans favored the Hanafi school of Islamic law, in the Ottoman provinces, there was usually one Hanafi qadi in each town who followed the Hanafi school. He had three deputy qadis belonging to other schools of Islamic law.

The qadi courts were the mainstay of the Muslim judicial systems in the Mughal Empire (1526–1857) and the Ottoman Empire (1280–1924). But they were not the only courts to enforce law and order. In addition to fiscal, administrative, and military courts, guilds, local rural institutions, and the heads of non-Muslim communities settled disputes. Qadis in the capital and in major cities had more powers than other qadis and could delegate their jurisdiction to others.

The qadi courts were, nevertheless, in a precarious position under the Muslim emperors in the sixteenth century. Their authority was derived from the delegated power from the emperor; as custodians of *sharia*, however, they also had a measure of independence. During the frequent power struggles between the center and provinces in this period, qadi courts stood out as symbols of the central power. At the same time, powerful rulers issued laws, known as *Qanun,* not always strictly adhering to *sharia* laws. Under the Ottomans, major reforms in the judicial system in the sixteenth century generally aimed at the further restriction of the jurisdiction of qadis. In the nineteenth century, the emergence of the notion of the sovereign state led to a major reform of the Ottoman legal system. A new court system, the *nizamiyya*, took over large areas of jurisdiction from the qadi courts. New administrative departments were created. The qadi courts came to be known in some countries as "*sharia* courts," and the notion of *sharia* was reduced to personal status laws.

The European colonial powers also introduced changes in the qadi courts. In India, the British created courts headed by a common law judge, who was assisted by a Muhammadan (Muslim) law officer attached to the court. This person is designated variably in the documents of the period as Moulawi, Kazi, or Mufti and more commonly Kazi in the later acts (e.g., "The Kazis Act, 1880, Act No. XII of 1880"). Because Islamic law was still applicable and the common law judges were not conversant with that law, the qadi advised the judge on points of law. Later, when application of Islamic law was limited to matters of personal status (and as English translations of Islamic legal texts became increasingly available), the qadiship was abolished.

QADI COURTS TODAY

After independence, colonial legal systems continued to operate in Muslim countries. Although laws of personal status were largely based on *sharia,* there were no qadi courts to apply them. Between 1950 and 1970, these laws underwent further reforms. Qadi courts, known as *sharia* courts, existed in some areas but more as a continuation of precolonial traditions. In the twentieth century, Muslim countries have dealt with the institution variably. In a few countries (e.g., in Turkey and Tunisia), *sharia* courts were abolished as Islamic law ceased to apply. Qadi courts ceased to exist independently in most Muslim countries as they were either merged into the national court system (e.g., in Egypt, Libya, and Yemen), which continued to apply Islamic law side by side with Western laws, or as they were made subordinate to the national court system (e.g., in Syria, Indonesia, Morocco, Nigeria, India, etc.). In some countries (e.g., in Malaysia, Pakistan, Lebanon, Jordan) *sharia* courts continue as special courts separate from other courts. In some countries like Saudi Arabia, qadi courts function separately but have general and residual jurisdiction. Generally, in a number of Muslim countries where local courts (e.g., area courts in Nigeria) or courts of first instance still function as qadi courts, they have exposed the modern judicial system to serious criticism. Compared to other courts, the qadi courts are less bureaucratic, less expensive, and less tardy. Their closeness to ordinary lives of the people provides more opportunities to the ordinary people to participate in the process of justice. Nevertheless, since judgments of these qadis are subject to appeal, scrutiny, and revision by higher courts, the qadis are under pressure. However, some recent studies have found a close link between this popular view of justice at the qadi courts and the movements demanding Islamization of laws. Consequently, some Muslim countries (e.g., Iran, the Sudan, and Afghanistan) have unified the civil courts under the general jurisdiction of *sharia,* while others (e.g., Pakistan and Malaysia) have moved toward an expanded jurisdiction of *sharia* in their judicial system.

MAJOR VARIANTS

In Islamic history, several variants of the qadi courts appeared. I shall mention only one of them. The court of complaint (*nazar al-mazalim*) was a special court introduced during the Abbasid period. This court was the responsibility of the caliph, governor, or delegated authority. The mazalim court was composed of a qadi, guard, jurists, secretaries, and notaries. This court heard complaints against the abuse of official powers. The procedural law of the mazalim court allowed for the use of coercion and for the introduction of evidence not acceptable in qadi courts. This court had the power to compel parties or witnesses to appear before it, a power that the qadi did not possess. Because mazalim courts were largely concerned with administrative issues, they became increasingly bureaucratic, reaching a climax in this regard under the Mamluks in Egypt. Presentation of the petition, channels of administration of these petitions, and procedures were increasingly formalized.

Muhammad Khalid Masud

See also Egypt; Islamic Law; Nigeria; Ottoman Empire
References and further reading
Christelow, Allan. 1995. "Mahkama." Pp. 22–23 in *Oxford Encyclopedia of the Modern Islamic World,* vol. 3. Edited by J. L. Esposito. New York: Oxford University Press.
Jackson, Sherman A. 1996. *Islamic Law and the State: The Constitutional Jurisprudence of Shihab al-Din al-Qarafi.* Leiden: E. J. Brill.
Mallat, Chibli. 1993. *Constitutional Law in the Middle East: The Emergence of Judicial Power.* London: School of Oriental and African Studies, University of London.
al-Mawardi (d. 1058), Abi al-Hasan 'Ali ibn Muhammad ibn Habib. 1971–1972. *Adab al-Qadi.* Edited by Muhyi Hilal al-Sarhan. Baghdad: Ri'asat Diwan al-Awqaf.
Powers, D. S. 1992. "On Judicial Review in Islamic Law." *Law and Society Review* 26, no. 2: 315–341.
Rosen, Lawrence. 2000. *The Justice of Islam: Comparative Perspectives on Islamic Law and Society.* Oxford: Oxford University Press.
Schacht, J., H. Inalcik, C. V. Findley, A. K. S. Lambton, A. Layish, and D. S. Lev. 1991. "Mahkama." Pp. 1–44 in *The Encyclopaedia of Islam,* vol. 6. Edited by C. E. Bosworth, E. van Donzel, B. Lewis, W. P. Heinrichs, and Ch. Pellat. Leiden: E. J. Brill.

QATAR

GEOGRAPHY

Jutting out as a peninsula from the northwest reaches of the Arabian Peninsula, the independent state of Qatar covers approximately 10,300 square kilometers of land. Most of Qatar is desert, with low hills and little vegetation. There are no mountain ranges or navigable waterways in the country.

Qatar's geographic position places it in a strategic portion of the Persian Gulf. At the northern end of the gulf, it witnessed firsthand the instabilities brought about by the Iranian revolution and the subsequent Iran-Iraq and Persian Gulf Wars. While the politically unstable gulf lies to its north, Qatar has a land border to the south. It is connected to the Arabian Peninsula, with boundaries to Saudi Arabia and the United Arab Emirates. The border with the emirate is disputed in regard to the waterway known as the Khawr al Udayd. A further dispute exists between Qatar and the nearby island nation of Bahrain over control of the Hawar Islands just off the western coast of Qatar.

Qatar is a mix of indigenous people and a variety of immigrants. Approximately one-quarter of the population of the country is of Qatari origins, and only 40 percent is of Arab descent. The remainder of the population is composed of Baluchis from nearby Pakistan or Iranians. While this mix would be expected to create societal and political problems, Qatar has maintained a stable government and society. This can be attributed, in part, to the oilfields that provide a considerable income to the people and the nation.

Qatar's small size and even smaller population have made it vulnerable to external forces throughout its history. This has compelled its people to find a larger power that can protect the nation from others, a strategy Qatar continues to follow in modern times.

HISTORY

Qatar has a brief history as a separate state on the Arabian Peninsula. It was first conquered and held by the Persian Empire, which controlled much of the Persian Gulf until it was conquered itself by Alexander the Great. His death and the splitting of his empire allowed Qatar to continue as a region filled with nomadic tribes. Most of the inhabitants of the region were Bedouins who foraged the area from the Arabian deserts. Before the development of any state, the Bedouins controlled the area according to their patterns of living. The Bada were nomads who moved their herds through the interior of the region. The *hadar*, or settlers, populated the coastal areas, including Doha on the coast. The ability of these tribes to use their form of desert law to settle disputes was hampered by the arrival of Islam. Suddenly, the informal approach to set-tling disputes was replaced by *sharia* (Islamic law) as developed in the eleventh century. The Hanbali school of Islam enforced strict interpretation of the law, using only the works of Muhammad including the Qur'an and the Sunnah.

The arrival of the Portuguese placed Qatar under the control of its first European colonial power. The Portuguese sought trade with India and the Far East and used its colonies along the Persian Gulf to serve as safe ports of calls for its trading ships. This control continued through the sixteenth and the seventeenth centuries until the arrival of the British. The English, though, were unable to hold Qatar after the invasion by a nearby powerful empire.

The Ottoman Empire was next to rule the region, but during the nineteenth and twentieth centuries, as Ottoman power disintegrated, local authority began to reassert itself. A religiously based movement, Wahhabism, developed in Qatar, which led to new political leadership. Wahhabism supported the purification of Islam and the removal of desert law as the basis for court decisions regarding the area. One of the main supporters of this movement was the Al Thani tribe. In 1878, the tribe became dominant, and its ruling family controlled the peninsula area and the trading port of Doha.

The start of World War I saw the Ottomans fighting the British in much of the Middle East. By 1916, Great Britain had acquired control of the gulf region, occupying ports and cities along the Arabian Peninsula. It signed a treaty with the Al-Thani rulers in which Qatar pledged not to grant territory or basing rights to any country other than Britain, while the British promised to protect Qatar from its external enemies and allow the Al-Thani family to run the country's internal affairs. After the war, the British established naval bases in cities such as Muscat, Abu Dhabi, and Manama in the Gulf. Much like Kuwait and Oman, which maintained a thoroughly separate identity under British authority, the Al-Thani family was allowed to control native Qataris using their own legal system and legal traditions. At the same time, the British established a separate set of governing institutions, including courts, for their citizens. It was a tradition that would continue once Qatar was granted its independence.

Because of its small size and tiny population, Qatar had few resources available for its own defense. Initially, this forced the ruling family to maintain close ties and a series of defense treaties with the British. Qatar became more than a backwater populated with nomadic tribespeople when it was found to hold considerable oil reserves. Initially controlled by the British, oil production began in the 1940s and became an almost entirely Qatari concern by the 1970s. Qatar gained control of its natural resources after the British began pulling out of bases in

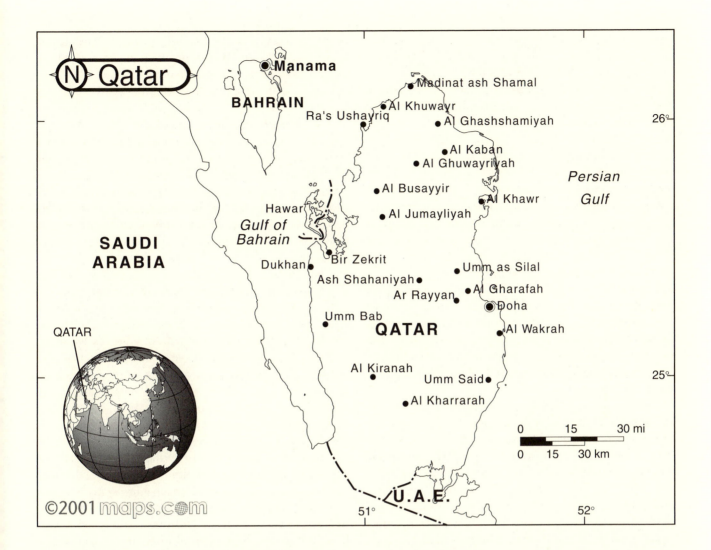

the gulf in 1971. A provisional constitution was ratified, along with independence for Qatar, on September 1, 1970.

At this time, the Al Thani family ruled the country, having done so during several decades of British involvement. Control of the government and broad power was tightly held within the family, and succession has occurred not after the death of the ruling sheikh but with a decision of the family members to make a change in leadership. The first shift in power came in 1972 when Kalifah Al Thani deposed his cousin Ahmad. The change was sudden but nonviolent and was apparently the result of agreement in the family that oil revenues were being wasted and that the economic development of the country was moving too slowly. A similar change in leadership came in 1995 with the overthrow of Khalifah by his son. Once again, the change was sudden and unexpected to outside observers but peaceful and bloodless. The result of the change was a shift in policy as Qatar became more open, weakening the strictures of Islamic law placed on the behavior of individual Qataris.

The 1995 change in government was followed in 1996 by an attempted coup, intended to overthrow the newly installed emir. The emir's brother headed the attempt, which was quickly put down. A trial followed in which several leaders were sentenced to death, but those sentences were commuted by the emir. Once political stability was reestablished in the country, the new emir embarked on a liberalization program to open Qatari society. New decrees lessened the reach of censorship of the media. The Qatari satellite television station became active in discussing the politics of the region. Qatari citizens also saw some previous Islamic-based restrictions on their behavior lifted by the emir. Those changes made Qatar the one place on the Arabian Peninsula where alcohol was publicly served and consumed.

The country also began a process of allowing local democracy. In 1999, there were municipal elections in which women were allowed to vote, and most Qataris were allowed to choose their local leaders. While there are no immediate plans to hold national elections or to create an elected parliament, it is assumed that the new constitution will include some type of representative body at the national level. The Qatari government also adopted a policy during the 1990s of maintaining close military and diplomatic ties with the United States. It signed a defense agreement allowing up to 2,000 U.S. troops to be stationed in Qatar. This leaning in favor of the United States was likely a response to the military threats posed by Iraq and Iran.

By the turn of the twenty-first century, Qatar remained a politically stable country. The ruling Al-Thani family proved able to provide positive changes in Qatar while holding on to their monarchical control. The country has also begun to move away from the strict interpretation of *sharia* that was becoming more popular in many Middle Eastern countries.

LEGAL CONCEPTS

Since the 1979 Iranian Islamic Revolution, one of the difficulties facing Qatar and its government has involved the competing demands of the traditional *sharia* system of law and the need for a civil law regime that will allow the economy to grow and also protect individual rights. These conflicting legal systems have always been a part of Qatar's history.

The origin of the law in Qatar can be traced back to the so-called desert law of the region. The nomadic tribes of the area developed customs to handle such thorny issues as water rights, dowries, and property ownership. These customs were advanced orally and enforced using informal tribal courts. The head of each tribe, the sheikh, was given the final say in implementing or commuting a particular sentence. Customary law, though, came under attack with the rise of Islam. Muslim judges, or *qadis* (*qazis*), were given the task of deciding disputes based on the written works of the religion—specifically, the Qur'an and the Sunnah—or using their interpretive powers, the *ra'ay*. But the Islamic system found it was dependent on local tribal judges to handle cases as Muslim power expanded throughout the Middle East. Many of these judges were unfamiliar with the details of Islamic law. The result was a hybrid system in many regions, including Qatar, where customs were used along with Islamic law to decide disputes. As a consequence, the meaning of Islamic law differed widely from region to region, and at times, rulings appeared to follow custom more than the teachings of Muhammad.

Even with the dilution of Islamic law throughout its area of control, *sharia* remained dominant in the region of Qatar during is occupation by the Ottoman Empire. It was only with the arrival of the British in 1916, after sweeping the Turks from the Persian Gulf region, that any significant changes occurred in the law. The British adhered to the policy of English common law being applied to its citizens living within its colonial possessions. This led to the development of a dual judicial system, one where traditional *sharia* operated for the indigenous people and common law for British citizens. The system continued when the British departed and the Al-Thani family began to rule Qatar as a monarchy.

Qatar's absolute monarchy and the absence of a written constitution limit its judiciary's power to protect individual liberties against government intrusion. With the law based on executive decrees issued by the emir, the courts can only determine if an individual is in violation of those decrees. There is no opportunity for judges to compare government decrees with those societal values expressed in a constitution. For this reason, the main struggle within the judiciary is not whether judges can challenge governmental power—they cannot—but rather whether *sharia* will be replaced by a more Western and secular law.

Islamic groups within the country favor strict adherence to *sharia* and its values, while supporting the development of a fundamentalist state not unlike Iran's. The government, though, has rejected this view, refused to establish an Islamic republic, and allowed secular and Western law to become a greater part of the Qatari legal system.

STRUCTURE OF THE COURTS

The legacy of a dual legal system had become as much of a tradition in Qatar as a strict adherence to *sharia* law. Through a series of decrees beginning in 1971, the government balanced the need for a civil law system acceptable to the country's large number of migrants with the desire for maintaining the traditional *sharia* courts and law to fend off the criticisms from its fundamentalist critics.

Sharia courts, dating back several centuries, had provided justice to Qatar before there were any established legal systems. Their continuation was a necessity for the Al-Thani regime. The *sharia* system, while based on religious law and with courts manned by religiously trained judges, remains under the tight control of the Qatari government. The Qatari Ministry of Endowment and Political Affairs oversees the administration of the courts and the training and appointment of judges.

The lowest court in the *sharia* system, the Court of First Instance or Petty Sharia Court, has several divisions with control over specific issues. The Penal Division hears criminal cases, with a variety of civil divisions including marital affairs, legacies, and legal authentication. These represent the civil jurisdiction of the *sharia* courts or the types of cases they can decide. Each of the courts has a single judge sitting in judgment, specializing in its area of the law and not serving in any of the other divisions.

Litigants seeking to appeal a trial court opinion do so in the *Sharia* Court of Appeals. The court has two division, one that hears criminal appeals, the other civil appeals. A three-judge panel sits on each court, which serves as the final court of record in any dispute. The *Sharia* Appeals Court also has special jurisdiction over cases involving the death penalty, including death by stoning—as is allowed under *sharia* law—or any penalty involving amputation of limbs. In many of these cases, if the sentence is upheld by the court, the emir of Qatar grants a commutation. This policy extends to the death sentences handed down against those who mounted a coup against the government in 1996.

Additional judicial agencies operate under the ministry on behalf of the courts. The Technical and Administrative Office maintains all records for the courts, the statistics of cases, and a law library for research purposes. The Execution Office is given the task of enforcing judicial decisions including civil awards for a plaintiff.

The Ministry of Endowment and Political Affairs also includes some agencies formed to advance Islamic teachings and law. One such agency, the Hajj Affairs Committee, organizes and regulates Qatari citizens in their *hajj,* or pilgrimage, to Mecca in Saudi Arabia. The committee is responsible for ensuring that the caravan companies taking the pilgrims do not cheat them. The government is also known to provide monetary grants for pilgrims unable to pay for the *hajj* themselves.

The Zakat Fund aids Muslims in performing another traditional task required under *sharia* law, that is, donating part of their income to the poor. While the Zakat, or tithe, is required of practicing Muslims under *sharia* law, the fund emphasizes voluntary participation. Another agency, the Department of Islamic Affairs, has a more powerful enforcement arm. While the department's goal sounds ordinary—spreading Islamic values and culture throughout the country—it has sweeping powers to carry out this duty. One involves censorship of the print media, television, and cable systems for anything considered derogatory or offensive toward Islam. The department staff considered them and had the right to pull any material based on their judgment. Under the new emir and since 1995, much of this censorship has ended, though the department can still ban news condemning Islam or the government.

Separate from the *sharia* system and with a different subject matter and duties, the Adlea courts are answerable to the Ministry of Justice. The Adlea courts, used mainly by non-Muslims, have separate criminal and civil divisions. The Petty Penal Courts decide most felony and all misdemeanor criminal cases. The Grand Penal Court hears appeals from the petty court and conducts trials in serious criminal cases, including homicide cases. The Adlea system also has a civil division, with three areas covering property disputes, civil disputes, and personal status or family law matters. Decisions by these courts can be appealed to the Adlea Court of Appeals, which serves as the final appeals court for the system. These courts are available to Muslims but are completely relied on by non-Muslims because they use Western law created by the emir's decrees.

The dual judicial systems are different not only in the type of law they follow but also in the different procedures they use. *Sharia* courts tend to be more informal in their approach. Litigants do not use counsel to argue their sides, though counsel may be present to provide legal advice to the litigant. Because of the lack of many of the formal procedures found in Western courts, the *sharia* courts conduct shorter trials. In addition, the trials are not open to the public or the press, though immediate family members are allowed to witness the proceedings.

The Adlea courts practice the procedures found in most Western courtrooms. Common law and written law are the bases of rulings. Counsel is used by both sides, and procedures such as questioning witnesses, ensuring protection against self-incrimination, and acquiring evidence legally are followed. For these reasons, non-Muslims use the Adlea courts, while many native Qataris have begun to take their disputes to these courts.

The dual nature of the Qatari court system does provide an advantage to citizens of the country. In civil cases, a citizen of Qatar who files a suit against a non-Muslim can choose to have his or her case heard in *sharia* court, where the law and tradition are alien to the non-Muslim. Without the aid of a trained counsel, the non-Muslim litigant has difficulty in mounting a proper defense.

Yet, as Qatar's number of immigrants rises and native Qataris are exposed to Western legal procedures, the Adlea courts have seen their caseloads rise dramatically. Muslims have sought out the secular courts to decide cases they would have once brought to *sharia* courts.

SPECIALIZED COURTS

There are only two specialized courts within Qatar's judicial system and only one functioning in a judicial role. The labor courts handle commercial cases within a Western legal framework. These courts were created because of the difficulties presented by *sharia* law when handling commercial disputes. Because there are limited legal protections for workers within Qatar, there are few cases involving labor rights or the formation of unions. The number and scope of cases coming before the labor courts increased dramatically during the 1990s as both Muslims and non-Muslims took their claims to the judges.

State Security Courts are the other type of specialized courts within the system. Used primarily in handling cases involving threats to the government or secret material that could not be heard in open court, the state security courts would not follow many of the procedures found in the Adlea courts and would hold closed hearings. Possibly for these reasons, the courts have not been used recently. They were not even used for the trial of the 1996 coup plotters.

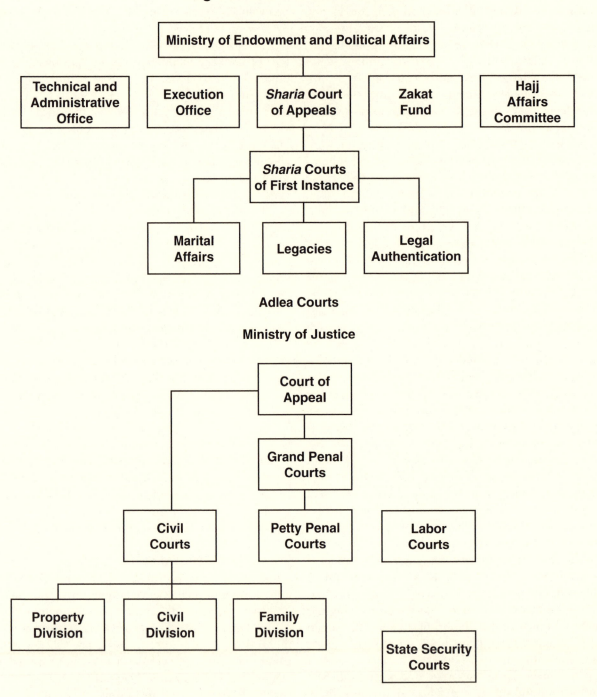

Legal Structure of Qatar Courts

Ministry of Endowment and Political Affairs

Technical and Administrative Office | Execution Office | *Sharia* Court of Appeals | Zakat Fund | Hajj Affairs Committee

Sharia Courts of First Instance

Marital Affairs | Legacies | Legal Authentication

Adlea Courts

Ministry of Justice

Court of Appeal

Grand Penal Courts

Civil Courts | Petty Penal Courts | Labor Courts

Property Division | Civil Division | Family Division

State Security Courts

Though technically still in existence, the state security courts are likely to die out from lack of use.

LEGAL TRAINING

Qatar's oil wealth has allowed the nation to create an elementary-, secondary-, and university-level educational system that is free to all Qatari citizens. This has advanced literacy and overall education levels within Qatar. Yet in the area of legal training, the country has lacked a method for producing judges or lawyers able to practice

in Adlea courts. Instead, the government has emphasized traditional Islamic teachings, with the result that most non-Muslims have formed private schools.

The major educational institution, the University of Qatar, has a college program for training students in *sharia* law. The Faculty of Sharia Law and Islamic Studies produces graduates who receive Bachelor's of Law and Shari'a degrees. There is no comparable training in Western law. For this reason, Qatari students seeking a degree in Western law must attend universities in other Persian

Gulf states, Europe, or the United States. With legal training for the Adlea courts lacking, Qatar has found itself dependent on noncitizens to act as judges in the Adlea courts. This problem is becoming less severe as the number of indigenous judges begins to increase, but the squeeze on legal training has squeezed the judiciary.

The presence of foreign judges has also made the judiciary dependent on the government. Judges who issue unpopular opinions can have their visas revoked and be deported by the government. Appointment of judges is also controlled by the ministry under which the judicial system serves. The Ministry of Justice determines who will serve in the courts in the Adlea system, while the Ministry of Endowment and Islamic Affairs chooses *sharia* judges.

This approach may appear to decentralize appointment powers, except that all ministers, including the prime minister, are appointed by the emir of Qatar and serve at his pleasure. Judicial appointments will reflect the preferences of the emir and will likely not run counter to his governing philosophy.

IMPACT

Qatar is an example of a functioning dual system of justice. As an Islamic country in a Muslim-dominated region, Qatar has maintained its *sharia* system of law while recognizing that the centuries-old system is not appropriate in many modern legal disputes. Influenced by the British colonial system, Qatar allows a Western judicial structure to function and, in many cases, compete with the traditional system. The two sets of courts also serve the political role of allowing the country to modernize its institutions and the law while at the same time continuing to respect the country's Islamic heritage. This has reduced the pressure on the government from those seeking to establish a type of Islamic republic, as found in neighboring Iran.

The Adlea courts serve as a partially independent institution within a monarchical government. While the emir of the country exercises influence over the Adlea judges—including the power to deport them if they are foreign nationals—he has less authority in overseeing the enforcement of the laws.

Yet Qatar's judiciary, whether the *sharia* courts or the Adlea courts, is constrained by the lack of a written constitution and the monarchy that controls the levers of government power. Political power is reserved solely and exercised completely by the emir. Judges are expected to apply the law as handed down by the emir but are forbidden to create law through their judgments. This limits the protection that courts can provide to the Qatari population. Without a permanent written constitution, Qatari judges are dependent on the emir's decrees to establish the law they must enforce. Yet even with these

limits, the Qatari judiciary has been able to maintain a system that applies two sets of laws while maintaining a level of justice for most citizens of the country.

Douglas Clouatre

See also Civil Law; Islamic Law; Qadi (Qazi) Courts; Saudi Arabia
References and further reading
Anscombe, Frederick. 1997. *The Ottoman Gulf.* New York: Columbia University Press.
Caiger-Smith, Martin. 1986. *Qatar.* New York: Stacy International Press.
Crystal, Jill. 1995. *Oil and Politics in the Gulf.* New York: Columbia University Press.
Hakima, Ahman Abu. 1995. *Eastern Arabia Qatar.* New York: International Book Publishing.
Kelly, Robert, ed. 1999. *Qatar, Country Review.* New York: Country Watch.
Metz, Helen. 1994. *Persian Gulf States.* Washington, DC: Library of Congress.
Othman, Nassar. 1984. *With Their Bare Hands: The Story of Oil Industry in Qatar.* London: Longman Group.
Zahlen, Rosemarie Said, and Roger Owen. 1999. *The Making of the Modern Gulf States.* Self-published.

QUEBEC

GENERAL INFORMATION

Quebec is the largest of Canada's ten provinces. Situated between Ontario and the Maritimes, north of New England, it has an area of 594,860 square miles (more than 1,500,000 square kilometers) and a population of 7 million inhabitants, more than 82 percent of whom speak French as a first language. Quebec City is its capital city, and Montreal, Canada's second-largest urban center, is its multicultural metropolis.

Quebec's natural resources are varied and numerous: iron ore, copper, and gold are among the main minerals extracted. The head offices of Alcan Aluminum Limited, one of the world's largest aluminum producers, are in Montreal. Electric power, which was nationalized in 1963, is clearly one of Quebec's most obvious objects of pride; Hydro-Quebec is Canada's largest electricity producer and even exports electricity to the United States. Forestry is still one of the primary exploited resources of the land, while agriculture, Quebec's traditional calling, is concentrated along the rich soils of the valley of the St. Lawrence River. The Montreal region has seen a spectacular development in industry in the last decades. For instance, Bombardier Corporation, originally the first manufacturer of snowmobiles, is today the world's third-largest aircraft manufacturer in the world.

What makes the Province of Quebec unique, however, is the fact that it is mostly French-speaking and that its private law is based on a civil code. It is a civil law juridiction, although it can also be classified as a mixed jurisdiction. In order to have a better understanding of Quebec's uniqueness, it is necessary to consider its history.

EVOLUTION AND HISTORY

The Province of Quebec was originally the greater part of New France, a French settlement and colony on the land that was discovered by Jacques Cartier in 1534 and claimed on behalf of the king of France. The French were thereafter defeated by the English, and the land came under the English Crown in 1763. In 1774, the Quebec Act allowed the local inhabitants to keep their French customs, and only the English public and criminal sections of the common law were introduced.

In 1866, the Civil Code of Lower Canada (as the Province of Quebec was known then) was enacted in the two official languages, French and English. It was based essentially on the French Civil Code of 1804, or the Code Napoléon, and the former French customary law, with a few legal concepts or norms arising out of the common law.

In 1867, the British North America Act was passed by the imperial Parliament in Westminster, and it is still the basis of the Constitution of Canada. This act provided for a federal state composed of New Brunswick, Nova Scotia, and Upper Canada and Lower Canada, later to become Ontario and Quebec, respectively.

Until 1960, the Province of Quebec remained a mostly French-speaking, rural, and Catholic part of Canada, proud of its roots and culture. It has known an accelerated evolution since then, the main landmark of which is the coming to power, in 1976, of the Parti Québecois, a separatist political party whose main goal is the accession of Quebec to sovereignty as an independant state. The people of Quebec voted no in two referendums on the matter, first in 1980 and then in 1995 (when 49.9 percent nevertheless voted yes). Other steps have been taken, as well, to distinguish Quebec from the rest of Canada: Since 1977, Bill 101 has made French the only official language in Quebec (in an officially bilingual Canada).

CURRENT STRUCTURE

Within the jurisdictional powers allotted by the Canadian Constitution, statutes are voted by the National Assembly (as the monocameral legislature is called). The administration of justice in the province is specifically within the jurisdiction of the provincial government. Parallel to the federal minister of justice, the Quebec minister of justice sees to this as attorney general for the Province of Quebec. The judicial system is roughly modeled on the English judiciary.

Criminal Courts

At the lowest level, presided over by part-time judges (outside of Montreal), municipal courts deal with petty offenses. Their jurisdiction, however, is not limited to municipal or traffic regulations; it covers some matters included in the federal Criminal Code, as well.

Most criminal offenses are tried without a jury by a judge of the Quebec Court, criminal division. When a trial by jury is chosen by the accused (or provided for by law), the judge is a member of the Superior Court. In that case appeals, on matters of law, are heard by the Court of Appeal and, ultimately, by leave (i.e., at the court's discretion) most of the time, by the Supreme Court of Canada.

Civil Courts

The Superior Court is the court of original general jurisdiction. The Court of Quebec, civil division, has jurisdiction over matters specified by the Code of Civil Procedure and various statutes, more especially in suits wherein the sum claimed or the value of the thing demanded is less than $30,000. Within the Court of Quebec, a small claims division hears cases for the recovery of sums of $3,000 and less.

Appeals from judgments of the Superior Court go to the Court of Appeal (with twenty judges), which sits in Montreal and also in Quebec City. Appeals from the Court of Quebec are scarce and are allowed only on leave.

The Supreme Court of Canada

At the summit of the judicial hierarchy towers the Supreme Court of Canada. It is not only the court of last resort for matters involving federal statutes (such as the Canadian Criminal Code) and constitutional issues but also (unlike the U.S. Supreme Court) the court of last resort for each of the ten provinces. Appeals are allowed on leave. There is a constitutional requirement that, among the nine Supreme Court justices, three must come from the Province of Quebec.

LEGAL PROFESSIONS

All judges are former lawyers of at least ten years' standing. Legal education is the prerogative of the six law faculties of Quebec, McGill Law School being the only English-speaking one (though most courses are also given in French). After three years of studies, the students obtain their law degrees and choose between becoming a member of the Quebec bar and a member of the Chamber of Notaries, both of which require exams and a clerkship.

Notaries (some 3,000 in number) are a distinctive feature of the Quebec legal system. They have nothing to do with the common law notaries public. Rather, they are full-fledged jurists who cannot argue cases in court but can give legal advice and are responsible for authenticating and certifying private deeds such as marriage contracts, wills, or hypothecs (mortgages); they are akin to the notaries prevailing in continental Europe and South America.

Legal Structure of Quebec Courts

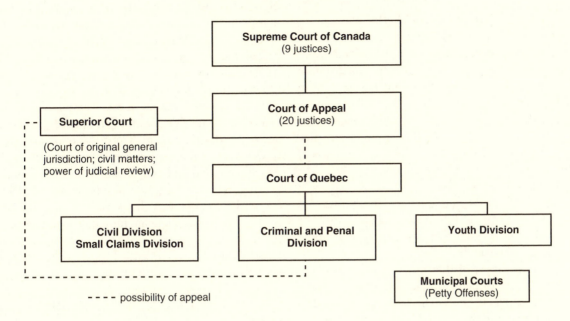

Judges of the superior courts (Superior Court, Court of Appeal, Supreme Court of Canada) are appointed by the federal government and hold office until retirement. Judges of the lower courts (municipal courts and the Court of Quebec) are appointed by the Quebec government and also hold office until retirement. The chief justice of Quebec is the chief justice of the Court of Appeal.

There are over 18,000 members of the bar of Quebec. The bar itself ensures discipline among its members. At the head of the Quebec bar and representing it is the *bâtonnier* (president of the bar), who is elected by his or her peers on an annual basis.

SPECIFICITY OF THE QUEBEC LEGAL SYSTEM

The Quebec legal system is a distant cousin of the Louisiana legal system. Its basis is a civil code making use of the concepts, vocabulary, and legal reasoning of the French Civil Code. On January 15, 1994, the new Quebec Civil Code replaced the 1866 Civil Code of Lower Canada. Its preliminary provision states that the Civil Code of Quebec, in harmony with the Quebec Charter of Human Rights and Freedoms and the general principles of law, governs persons, relations between persons, and property. The Civil Code comprises a body of rules that, in all matters within the letter, spirit, or object of its provisions, lays down the *jus commune* (common law), expressly or by implication. In these matters, the code is the foundation of all other laws, although other laws may complement the code or make exceptions to it. The Civil Code of Quebec comprises ten books:

• Book 1: Persons

• Book 2: The Family
• Book 3: Successions
• Book 4: Property
• Book 5: Obligations
• Book 6: Prior Claims and Hypothecs
• Book 7: Evidence
• Book 8: Prescription
• Book 9: Publication of Rights
• Book 10: Private International Law

The common law as such is not part of Quebec private law, although some common law institutions, such as the trust or movable sureties, have been adapted and included in the new code. However, other fields, such as administration law, municipal law, most parts of corporation law, and provincial criminal law, stem from the common law and can be classified as part of the common law system. It is usually said that Quebec is a mixed jurisdiction; its jurists are equally familiar with the civil law and the common law systems.

Adrian Popovici

See also Canada; Civil Law; France; Louisiana

References and further reading
Baudouin, Jean-Louis. 1991–1992. "Reflections on the Process of Recodification of the Quebec Civil Code." *Tulane Civil Law Forum* 6 and 7: 283.
Brierly, John E. C., and Roderick A. Macdonald, eds. 1993. *Quebec Civil Law: An Introduction to Quebec Private Law.* Toronto: Edmond Montgomery.
Valcke, Catherine. 1996. "Quebec Civil Law and Canadian Federalisms." *Yale Journal of International Law* 21: 67.

QUEENSLAND

GENERAL INFORMATION

Queensland is the second largest and the third most populous of the six states that constitute the federal Commonwealth of Australia. It is situated in the northeastern corner of the Australian continent, and has an area of 1,727,200 square kilometers (22.5 percent of the continent), a coastline of 7,400 kilometers, and a population of 3,216,500. The capital city of Queensland is Brisbane, which is Australia's third largest city, with a population of 1,520,596. Queensland has in recent decades been the fastest growing of the six states.

Although its climate, geography, and economy have distinctive characteristics, Queensland shares with the other Australian states a relatively homogenous cultural, legal, and political character.

Geographically, most of the state is divided into the western plains, eastern highlands, and an eastern coastal strip. The prevailing climate ranges from semitropical in the south to tropical in the north. Near-desert conditions prevail in the southwest, whereas monsoonal rainfall is characteristic of the northern coast. Protracted droughts are common in the west, often with severe economic consequences.

In contrast to New South Wales and Victoria, and similarly to Western Australia, much of the Queensland economy is pastoral, agricultural, and mining, with relatively fewer manufacturing and service industries. Another important aspect of the Queensland economy is the growing tourist industry.

Although approximately half of the Queensland population is concentrated in the southeast corner of the state, the Queensland population is relatively more decentralized than the other mainland states. Important regional centers include the Gold Coast, Ipswich, Toowoomba, Maryborough, Bundaberg, Rockhampton, Mackay, Townsville, Cairns, and Mount Isa. This relative decentralization has contributed to some of the unique features of Queensland politics. Moreover, unlike other capital cities like Sydney and Melbourne, Brisbane does not have substantial ethnic communities.

EVOLUTION AND HISTORY

The British settlement of what is now Queensland began with the establishment of a penal station in Moreton Bay (now Brisbane) in 1824. In 1842, the station was closed, and the district was opened up to free settlement. As part of the colony of New South Wales, Moreton Bay was erected into a legislative district that elected representatives to the New South Wales legislature.

By Letters Patent of 1859 the settlement was converted into a separate colony under the name of Queensland. An Order in Council of 1859 provided for a structure of government similar to New South Wales, including an elected Legislative Assembly, a Legislative Council nominated by the governor, and a responsible ministry. With British settlement, as much of the common law of England and English statutory law as was applicable to the circumstances of the colony became part of its law. Queensland retains a common law system.

In 1865, the Colonial Laws Validity Act (UK) confirmed the capacity of the Queensland Parliament to amend the Queensland Constitution. In 1867, the Queensland Parliament enacted a Constitution Act, which reenacted and consolidated the various provisions relating to the Constitution of Queensland. In 1922, the Queensland Parliament abolished its Legislative Council. In 1986, the United Kingdom Parliament enacted the Australia Act, by which it abdicated its capacity to legislate for Queensland and ended appeals from the Queensland Supreme Court to the Privy Council.

CURRENT STRUCTURE

Queensland has a representative, parliamentary system of government.

The Queensland Constitution is contained in a number of Imperial and Queensland statutes, principally the Constitution Act of 1867. The Legal, Constitutional, and Administrative Review Committee of the Queensland Legislative Assembly has recently recommended the consolidation of the Queensland Constitution.

Legislative power is vested in the Parliament of Queensland, which consists of eighty-nine members representing single-member electorates. Unlike the other Australian states, the Queensland Parliament is unicameral, consisting only of the queen and a lower house called the Legislative Assembly. The Legislative Assembly is elected by Queensland voters, and members of the assembly hold their seats for a maximum of three years or until the assembly is dissolved by the state governor. Voting is compulsory. There is a universal adult franchise.

The powers of the Queensland Parliament are plenary, but are subject to the Constitution of the Commonwealth of Australia. The Queensland Parliament has full power to amend the state constitution. However, it can only alter the composition and powers of the Parliament, or affect the office and certain powers of the governor after such proposals are approved at a referendum.

Executive power is vested in the queen, who is represented in Queensland by the state governor. The governor is appointed by the queen on the advice of the premier. The premier is appointed by the governor on the basis that the governor is satisfied that the premier has the confidence of Parliament and is able to guarantee supply. Ministers of state are appointed by the governor on the advice of the premier. The governor as a matter of convention exercises the ordinary executive powers of government on the advice of the premier and cabinet. Consequently, real control over the government rests with the cabinet. The Queensland Constitution elliptically refers to the operation of this system of responsible government by referring to officers "liable to retire on political grounds." It also gives the legislature control over government expenditure, thus enabling it to force the resignation of a ministry that no longer has the support of a majority of its members.

In 2001, Queensland had eighteen cabinet ministers. Each minister has a portfolio through which the various state government departments and statutory authorities are administered. The cabinet meets regularly to determine government policy. All ministers take collective responsibility for and publicly support decisions made by the cabinet. They are also individually responsible for their separate departments.

Each government department is generally headed by a chief executive, accountable to the responsible minister. The government departments include premier and cabinet, Treasury, Education, Aboriginal Affairs, Attorney General and Justice, Communication and Information, Local Government and Planning, Emergency Services, Employment, Training and Industrial Relations, Environment and Heritage and Natural Resources, Equity and Fair Trading, Families, Youth and Community Care and Disability Services, Health, Mines and Energy and Regional Development, Police and Corrective Services, Primary Industries and Rural Communities, Public Works and Housing, State Development and Trade, Tourism and Racing, and Transport and Main Roads.

There are a number of other important public bodies in Queensland. The Criminal Justice Commission monitors, reviews, and initiates reform of the administration of criminal justice in Queensland. The Queensland Crime Commission specially investigates organized crime and pedophilia. The Ombudsman's Office investigates and reviews the fairness and legality of administrative actions and decisions taken by state government departments, local governments, and public authorities. The Electoral Commission of Queensland administers Queensland electoral laws. The Queensland Audit Office undertakes an independent, external audit of all Queensland public sector entities. The Public Service Commissioner monitors and reviews the management of the Queensland public service. The Information Commissioner undertakes an independent external investigation and review of certain kinds of decisions of ministers and government agencies.

Judicial power in Queensland is vested in the state Supreme Court, district courts, and Magistrates' Courts. The Supreme Court is the highest court in the Queensland court system. It consists of the chief justice and two divisions, the trial division and the court of appeal. The

Legal Structure of Queensland Courts

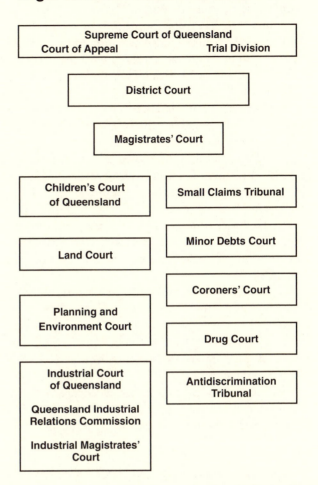

Supreme Court hears serious criminal offences, civil disputes where the amount in dispute is more than $250,000, and administrative law matters. It sits permanently in Brisbane, Cairns, Rockhampton, and Townsville, and as a circuit court in other towns. The court of appeal hears appeals from the trial division of the Supreme Court. Such appeals are by rehearing as of right, although the hearing is based on the transcript of evidence at trial and a written outline of argument, supplemented by full oral argument.

The district courts hears serious criminal cases such as rape and armed robbery, civil disputes where the amount in dispute is between $50,000 and $250,000, and appeals against some decisions of Magistrates' Courts. District court judges are permanently stationed in or visit twenty-nine towns in Queensland, as well as Brisbane.

Magistrates' Courts deal with less serious offenses, civil cases where the amount in dispute is up to $50,000, and decide whether to commit persons accused of serious offenses to trial in the higher courts. There are eighty-two magistrates' courthouses in Queensland, presided over by stipendiary magistrates. (Only barristers or solicitors can be appointed as stipendiary magistrates.) Magistrates also preside as the Small Claims Tribunal, the small debts court, and the coroners' court.

Criminal matters in the Supreme Court and district court are heard before a judge and jury. Most civil matters are heard by a judge alone, although either party may elect that the matter be tried by a judge and jury except in motor vehicle and work accident cases. There is provision for the referral of matters to alternative dispute resolution, such as mediation and case appraisal. Legal aid is available to financially disadvantaged persons.

Queensland has also established a children's court, a Land and Resources Tribunal (which deals with issues relating to native title, resource development, and land management), a land court (which largely hears appeals against land valuations), and a planning and environment court (which determines appeals from town planning decisions of local government authorities and other matters).

The Local Government Act provides for the local government of cities, towns, and shires.

STAFFING
Judges of the Supreme Court and district court and stipendiary magistrates are appointed by the governor in council, on the advice of the attorney general, in consultation with the cabinet. The legal profession is divided between barristers and solicitors at the point of admission.

RELATIONSHIP TO NATIONAL SYSTEM
The government of Queensland is constitutionally independent of the federal government. However, the federal government exercises some influence over state policy through financial incentives.

Under the state constitution, the Queensland Parliament has power to legislate generally for the peace, order, and good government of the state, but shares this power in respect of certain matters that also lie with the legislative power of the federal Parliament under the federal constitution. So long as federal legislation strictly relates to such matters, state legislation inconsistent with federal legislation is inoperative to the extent of the inconsistency.

The people of Queensland are represented in the federal Senate by twelve senators (equally with the people of the other states) and in the federal House of Representatives by twenty-six representatives (in proportion to the population of the state).

The High Court of Australia has jurisdiction to hear appeals in all matters from the Supreme Court of Queensland. State supreme courts are empowered to exercise federal jurisdiction by federal laws passed under the federal constitution.

Nicholas Aroney

See also Australia; Common Law; Federalism; New South Wales; Privy Council; South Australia; Tasmania; Victoria, State of; Western Australia

References and further reading

Davis, Solomon Rufus, ed. 1960. *The Government of the Australian States.* London: Longmans, Green and Co., Ltd.

Hughes, Colin Anfield. 1980. *The Government of Queensland.* St. Lucia: University of Queensland Press.

Lumb, Richard Darrell. 1992. *The Constitutions of the Australian States.* 5th ed. St. Lucia: University of Queensland Press.

Queensland Government Internet Resources. http://www.qld. gov.au/ (accessed May 10, 2001).

Webster's Encyclopedia of Australia. 1998. "Queensland." Sydney: Webster Publishing.

R

REHABILITATION

DEFINITION

Rehabilitation is one of the four major philosophies of punishment employed within correctional systems to compel people to act in a manner consistent with society's laws and norms. The three other philosophies are retribution, deterrence, and incapacitation. Rehabilitation strives to change lawbreakers into law abiders. It does so by targeting an array of psychological and social factors that contributed to an offender's criminality or caused an offender to violate the law.

APPLICABILITY

Rehabilitation programs are used to "treat" offenders by educating or training them to become productive and law-abiding citizens. A variety of treatment programs are commonly offered throughout prisons in the United States. They include educational programs, work programs, life-skills training programs, and vocational training programs. The underlying theme of these treatment programs is that they attempt to teach inmates the skills they need to be productive citizens outside prison. For instance, life-skills training programs teach skills such as how to apply and interview for a job, manage money, parent, and obtain a driver's license. Other types of rehabilitation programs attempt to change the underlying "causes" of an offender's criminality. Examples of these types of programs include individual counseling, group counseling, drug abuse programs, and sex offender treatment programs.

Not all rehabilitation programs occur within prisons. Many offenders receive treatment while they are under some type of community supervision, such as probation or parole. Examples of this type of community treatment include drug and alcohol counseling, domestic violence counseling, sex offender counseling, family counseling, vocational and employment counseling, and life-skills education.

EVOLUTION AND CHANGE

The Rise and Fall of Rehabilitation in the United States
Prior to the creation of the penitentiary in the 1820s, of-

fenders were either punished publicly within the community or executed. Incarceration, which was infrequently used, existed to detain offenders awaiting trial, not as a means of reforming offenders or correcting their behaviors.

During the 1820s, a radical switch occurred involving the use of institutionalization—within penitentiaries—as a sanction for offenders. Penitentiaries developed based on the public's fear that family disruption and lack of order in a person's life were the sources of crime. The penitentiary—deeply rooted in Christian beliefs—introduced rehabilitation as a core penal philosophy. The founders believed that the orderly environment in the penitentiary would have the power to transform the moral character of inmates so that they would reject criminal behavior and become productive members of society. To accomplish this goal, criminals had to be housed in penitentiaries that segregated them from society.

During the Civil War period, two key problems with the penitentiary system became apparent. First, penitentiaries suffered from overcrowding that led officials to focus on maintaining custody and control rather than providing a rehabilitative environment. Second, there were inconsistencies between the determinate sentencing philosophy that based sentences on the severity of the offense and the rehabilitative ideal. Determinate sentences prescribe a specific length of time for which offenders are to be incarcerated, as opposed to open-ended, indeterminate sentences. Rehabilitative goals can best be achieved with indeterminate sentences, in which changes in an offender's attitudes, rather than the passage of time, determine when an offender is released.

In 1870, reformers attending the National Congress on Penitentiary and Reformatory Discipline recognized these problems and devised a "new penology" that advocated the use of indeterminate sentences. The new penologists provided a process of tailoring sentences to individuals: a merit-based system that allowed inmates to earn greater degrees of privileges within penal institutions that progressively led to their release from the institution.

During the middle of the Progressive era, namely, the first two decades of the 1900s, the next generation of reformers adopted the concept of "individualized treatment."

This concept rested on three interrelated principles. First, individuals commit crimes for different reasons. Thus, the nature of the offender, rather than the offense, should shape sentencing decisions. Second, criminal acts were caused by individual psychological or social factors, or both. Therefore, crime reduction could best be achieved by "treating" the conditions that made a person commit a crime. Third, offenders should remain under probation and parole supervision, where officers could supervise and counsel them in the community until they were rehabilitated.

The core ideas of the modern rehabilitative ideal—the belief in offender treatment, the indeterminate sentence, and the individualization of correctional intervention—led to a host of correctional reforms. These reforms included presentence reports that assisted judges in deciding which treatment option best suited an offender, probation and parole supervision in the community, parole boards to decide when an offender was "cured" and ready to return to the community, and the formation of a separate juvenile justice system.

Rehabilitation was the dominant U.S. correctional philosophy until it came under severe attack from two fronts during the late 1960s and early 1970s. The first attack came from within the political arena. Conservatives considered rehabilitation efforts too soft on offenders. Liberals—the traditional defenders of rehabilitation—joined the antitreatment crusade. They argued that the unbounded discretion that individualized treatment offered criminal justice personnel could lead to corruption and abuse. For different reasons, conservatives and liberals reached an odd consensus: rehabilitation was responsible for the ills that characterized the criminal justice system. The second attack (and final blow) came from within academia. Robert Martinson (1974) conducted a literature review of 231 studies evaluating treatment programs to determine whether rehabilitation programs reduced offender recidivism. His results suggesting that treatment has "no appreciable effects on recidivism" were interpreted by some as showing that "nothing works" in rehabilitation (25). He argued that it was most likely that rehabilitation was ineffective and that prisons should pursue the penal philosophy of deterrence rather than rehabilitation. His claims were accepted by many criminologists who opposed rehabilitation as being coercive and unjust.

The attacks on rehabilitation were consequential. Unlike in the Civil War period, when reformers looked for alternative rehabilitation programs that could be effective, Martinson ushered in an era of penal reform when reformers looked to two crime control approaches: deterrence and incapacitation. Even Martinson's (1979) own recantation of the "nothing works" doctrine, based on updated evaluation data, fell on deaf ears.

Although rehabilitation did not vanish from the policy arena, during the 1980s its influence waned and it was replaced by a more punitive movement in corrections. This movement placed the penal philosophies of retribution, deterrence, and incapacitation in the forefront of the correctional system through "get tough" reforms that provided lengthy mandatory sentences for offenders. To accommodate crowded prisons brought about by longer mandatory sentences, "intermediate sanctions" such as boot camps, intensive probation supervision, home confinement, and electronic monitoring became popular means to deter offenders. There is virtually no evidence that these interventions have succeeded in deterring offenders from engaging in future crimes (see Cullen and Gendreau 2000). Still, politicians have favored more punitive programs based on their perceptions of public opinion. Evidence does suggest, however, that the public may favor rehabilitation more than politicians think.

Public Opinion toward Rehabilitation

Public opinion research in the United States, England, and Canada suggests that although their general feelings about criminals are punitive, the public favors rehabilitation as a goal of the system. In the United States, when respondents to a survey are given detailed information about an offender or an offense and a range of punishment options, they tend to be less punitive. Likewise, findings from the British Crime Survey (BCS) revealed that "when given adequate information about the range of legal punishments available, the public is less likely to endorse the use of imprisonment" (Hough and Roberts 1999, 23). In Canada, although the public supports the notion that offenders can be punished while remaining in the community, the public wants the conditions of community sentences to have an impact on the offender's lifestyle (Sanders and Roberts 2000).

Other research within the United States suggests four major conclusions—in addition to their desire to balance rehabilitative aims with their punitiveness—about the American public's view toward rehabilitation. First, rehabilitation competes with other goals as the preferred purpose of punishing offenders. At the very least, Americans rank rehabilitation as an "important" goal that should be pursued in conjunction with more punitive goals. Second, although there is support for rehabilitating adult offenders, there is even stronger support for rehabilitating juvenile delinquents. Third, there seems to be less support for rehabilitating chronic and violent offenders, but Americans also do not want the correctional system simply to inflict pain or warehouse offenders. They want the system to pursue the goal of trying to make offenders less criminal through rehabilitation. Finally, there is some evidence that since the 1960s, support for rehabilitation has declined, but contrary results exist, and the degree of the trend is highly disputed. Even so, rehabilitation remains widely endorsed by Americans as an important function of the correctional system (see Cullen, Fisher, and Applegate 2000).

VARIATIONS IN CURRENT PUNISHMENT POLICIES

Canadian psychologists have been innovative in determining what works in correctional rehabilitation through the development of behavioral and cognitive-behavioral treatment programs. These programs are based on principles that meta-analyses have identified as being able to reduce recidivism by up to 30 percent in the United States, Canada, and European countries (Andrews et al. 1990; Lipsey and Wilson 1998; Redondo, Sanchez-Meca, and Garrido 1999).

Though not in the forefront of any nation's correctional system, rehabilitation programs have been implemented in the following countries: the United States, Canada, Great Britain, the Netherlands, Sweden, Spain, and Germany. For example, similar to the United States, Great Britain offers a diverse array of treatment programs, including behavioral therapy, psychotherapy, school education and education materials, therapeutic communities, and cognitive-behavioral programs. Although other countries have also adopted treatment programs, they are more limited in the treatment modality used. For example, in the Netherlands, cognitive-behavioral and behavioral treatment programs have been used, whereas in Sweden, psychotherapy and therapeutic community programs have been adopted (see Redondo, Sanchez-Meca, and Garrido 1999).

These innovations in punishment, coupled with the "something works" results from meta-analyses of treatment programs and the similarity in public opinions from different countries, suggest that a new era of punishment is not beyond reach. The state, researchers, and the public are recognizing that rehabilitation should not be ignored, because of how it can benefit society by improving offenders' lives and changing their behaviors.

Bonnie S. Fisher
Shannon A. Santana
Sharon Levrant Miceli

See also General Deterrence; Incarceration; Retribution

References and further reading

Andrews, D. A., Ivan Zinger, Robert D. Hoge, James Bonta, Paul Gendreau, and Francis T. Cullen. 1990. "Does Correctional Treatment Work? A Clinically Relevant and Psychologically Informed Meta-Analysis." *Criminology* 28: 369–404.
Cullen, Francis T., Bonnie S. Fisher, and Brandon K. Applegate. 2000. "Public Opinion about Punishment and Corrections." Pp. 1–79 in *Crime and Justice: A Review of Research.* Edited by Michael Tonry. Chicago: University of Chicago Press.
Cullen, Francis T., and Paul Gendreau. 2000. "Assessing Correctional Rehabilitation: Policy, Practice, and Prospects." Pp. 109–175 in *Policies, Processes and Decisions of the Criminal Justice System,* vol. 3. Edited by Julie Horney. U.S. Department of Justice, Office of Justice Programs, National Institute of Justice.
Hough, Mike, and Julian V. Roberts. 1999. "Sentencing Trends in Britain." *Punishment and Society* 1, no. 1: 11–26.
Lipsey, Mark W., and David B. Wilson. 1998. "Effective Intervention for Serious Juvenile Offenders." Pp. 313–345 in *Serious and Violent Juvenile Offenders: Risk Factors and Successful Interventions.* Edited by Rolf Loeber and David P. Farrington. Thousand Oaks, CA: Sage Publications.
Martinson, Robert. 1974. "What Works?—Questions and Answers about Prison Reform." *The Public Interest* 35 (Spring): 22–54.
———. 1979. "New Findings, New Views: A Note of Caution Regarding Sentencing Reform." *Hofstra Law Review* 7: 243–258.
Redondo, Santiago, Julio Sanchez-Meca, and Vicente Garrido. 1999. "The Influence of Treatment Programmes on the Recidivism of Juvenile and Adult Offenders: A European Meta-Analytic Review." *Psychology, Crime and Law* 5: 251–278.
Sanders, Trevor, and Julian V. Roberts. 2000. "Public Attitudes toward Conditional Sentencing: Results of a National Survey." *Canadian Journal of Behavioural Science* 32, no. 4: 199–207.

RETRIBUTION

DEFINITION

As a practice of sentencing convicted criminals, "retribution" is the infliction of harsh treatment on an offender in proportion to the harm inflicted by the offender on society. The legal application of the term is sometimes confused with revenge, although the two terms reflect different processes. *Revenge* is punishment inflicted on an offender by the person who was actually harmed, thereby satisfying an emotional need (the restoration of pride) within the person wronged. Punishment inflicted on an offender by a passionate victim can lead to punishments that are excessive relative to the actual crimes committed. By contrast, retribution involves punishment administered dispassionately by persons with legal authority for the purpose of condemning an offender's actions. There is no interest on the part of the state in the actual or predicted consequences of the punishment. Retribution simply reflects the idea that persons who inflict "pain" on society by violating legally prescribed rules will have pain inflicted on themselves by society. In this context, society is viewed as the victim of any crime. Regardless of the number of victims involved, any act that violates a legal rule advocated by all citizens is symbolically an act that victimizes all members of a society. When punishment is imposed on an offender by the state, the state is acting as the voice of the people in condemning the offender. Removing punishment from the hands of the emotional victim permits greater equity across offenders convicted of the same crimes, at least in theory. This practice is compatible with the goal of general deterrence, because consistency in punishment allows citizens to understand exactly what can happen to them if they choose to engage in criminal behavior.

APPLICABILITY

Retribution is one of the oldest sentencing practices adopted by legal systems around the world, predated only by punishments that were excessive relative to the severity of criminal acts (such as the "blood feuds" of hunting and gathering societies, in which members of a victim's family would kill the offender and his family). Even the act of publicly stoning a criminal in ancient Athens was based on the notion that each stone thrown by a citizen symbolized a "missile of guilt" cast onto the offender as condemnation for the harm inflicted upon society.

Retributive punishments are generally no longer physical in nature. It is recognized around the world today that exact retribution is not feasible because of an inability to objectively measure the actual harm inflicted by a crime. Considering that some crimes can inflict physical, emotional, and economic pain on an individual (not to mention the pains inflicted on a victim's family), it is impossible to gauge these harms in order to derive punishments of equal weight. The expansion of written laws further complicates the task by multiplying such calculations literally hundreds of times. For these reasons, the idea of retribution has evolved into a practice whereby punishments are graded according to how legal statutes define gradations of offense seriousness. For example, in the United States, one of the differences between felony assault and misdemeanor assault involves the use of a weapon (posing a greater threat to personal safety). Convicted felons may be sentenced to multiple years in prison, whereas convicted misdemeanants will most often serve less than one year in jail or a term of probation. This practice preserves the original notion that punishment should be proportionate to the offense, but there is no way to judge whether a fixed term of incarceration causes the same "amount" of pain for the offender as the pain endured by the victim. Even capital punishment does not reflect absolute punishment, because the method of execution is not intended to be as physically painful as a homicide might have been to the victim, yet the "wait for death" may exact more psychological pain on offenders and their families (see Van den Haag and Conrad [1978] for a detailed debate over the symbolic and utilitarian functions of capital punishment).

Also common to all industrial societies today is the use of incarceration for the purpose of retribution. Sentences of incarceration can be graded in length according to the severity of the offense, thus facilitating the goal of proportionality in punishment. Capital punishment is also a method of retribution (as well as incapacitation), although its use has declined significantly around the world, with a few exceptions such as the United States. Monetary fines, also common around the world, are sometimes referred to as being "retributive" in nature because the amount is usually graded in proportion to the severity of the offense. However, a fine reflects more a penalty than a punishment, in that individuals who can afford to do so can simply pay for the "right" to break the law.

Most industrial nations no longer inflict physical pain on an offender for the purpose of retribution. With the exception of some Third World countries, even capital punishment is not intended to be physically painful, beyond the pain that may be felt as a consequence of natural death (hence the reason that it is not deemed "cruel and unusual" punishment in the United States). Instead, retribution has come to be understood as punishment intended to deprive an individual of the personal freedoms enjoyed by citizens who abide by societal rules (for example, liberty and autonomy). Physical pains that are endured by incarcerated offenders, such as those resulting from victimization by other inmates, are not "intended" by the state. Also common to all legal systems today, retribution can be imposed only after establishing that the person was responsible for his actions, although the definition of "responsibility" varies across cultures.

VARIATIONS

Despite the fact that most legal systems adopt similar definitions of *retribution,* and similar means of achieving it, there is some disagreement among legal scholars regarding the factors that should be considered in determining a proportionate punishment. Although there is general agreement that the severity of the harm inflicted should play the dominant role in shaping the severity of a punishment, there is variation in perceptions regarding (1) specific offense severity, (2) whether the culpability of the offender should also be considered, and (3) whether an offender's history of criminal behavior should be considered.

Regarding offense severity, certain crimes may pose more or less harm depending on cultural (and individual) norms. For example, government officials with more egalitarian notions of justice will define sex crimes against women as more severe in more egalitarian cultures. Even in the United States we see differences across states in how rape is conceptualized; some jurisdictions still do not define the act of forced sex by a spouse as a felony crime. Such differences create variation across states in how individuals who have engaged in the same crimes are punished, even though they have all engaged in the same acts and have been punished under state sentencing guidelines that were developed under a retributive framework.

Considerations of offender culpability and prior record are relevant to a debate over whether punishment should address only the crime or the criminal as well. Both culpability and prior record reflect aspects of the criminal, because one must recognize the individual's state of mind in determining responsibility for the action (culpability), as well as the individual's previous history of criminal behavior (prior record). The purist would argue that only the crime should be considered for retributive punishment, since the punishment symbolizes the harm inflicted on society by the act itself. On the other hand, wrapped up in notions of offense seriousness is the blameworthiness of offenders, since the two often go hand in hand (that is, the most heinous acts of violence are most often planned). Similarly, a history of criminality merely adds to an offender's level of culpability for the current offense by demonstrating a pattern of similar behavior. This last perspective is a useful justification for punishing first-time offenders less severely than repeat offenders who have committed the same crime, since the absence of a criminal history introduces doubt concerning factual guilt. The argument can be made that any legal system is subject to errors in decision making, and grading punishments by prior record is consistent with the notion that each repeated offense simply increases the likelihood that a guilty verdict is justified (see Von Hirsch [1976] for a discussion of punishing crimes versus criminals under retribution).

EVOLUTION AND CHANGE

Although retribution is one of the oldest punishment philosophies, retributive punishments were historically less common than the use of excessive punishments prior to the 1700s. The absence of written laws and corresponding punishments, lack of formality in case processing, limited or nonexistent resources for detecting crimes and collecting evidence, and a reliance on religious (versus scientific) explanations for deviant behavior all contributed to disproportionately severe sanctions relative to the crimes committed (see Johnson and Wolfe [1996] for a historical overview). Not until the 1700s did retribution begin to take hold as a dominant practice throughout the world, mainly as a consequence of philosophical debates beginning in the 1600s regarding the state of crime control in western Europe at that time. Questions regarding definitions of "justice," lack of separation between church and state, the need for consistency in punishment, and the fallibility of criminal procedure contributed to a focus on matching the severity of punishment to the severity of a crime. Appealing to moral sentiment, philosophers such as Montesquieu, Voltaire, and Beccaria provided compelling arguments as to the need for proportionate pun-

ishments in order to achieve the utilitarian goal of general deterrence. Perhaps the most compelling argument was provided by Beccaria, who noted that if an equally harsh sanction exists for two crimes that injure society to varying degrees, there is nothing to deter individuals from engaging in the more serious crime if it generates greater rewards to the offender (see the translation of Beccaria's arguments by Paolucci [1963]). Although Beccaria's focus was ultimately general deterrence, retribution was seen as the means to achieving that goal. Similar arguments are used today in order to justify the idea that the death penalty should not be used for crimes other than homicide, since criminals would benefit more by killing their victims in order to eliminate witnesses and avoid capital punishment.

Although advancements in technology and scientific thought have brought changes to sentencing philosophies since the 1700s (for example, the focus on rehabilitation for juvenile offenders and some adult offenders, and a greater use of incarceration for the purpose of incapacitation), retribution persists as one of the defining principles of "justice" across legal systems. The major distinctions between the original retributivists and the "neoretributivists" of today include the first group's sole focus on punishing the crime rather than the criminal. This distinction is understandable, however, in light of subsequent recognitions that (1) not everyone in society is guided by free will, and (2) any system of fact-finding is subject to a certain likelihood of error.

John Wooldredge

See also General Deterrence; Incarceration

References and further reading
Barton, Charles. 1999. *Getting Even*. Chicago: Open Court.
Beccaria, Cesare. 1963. *On Crimes and Their Punishments*. Translated by H. Paolucci. Englewood Cliffs, NJ: Prentice-Hall.
Johnson, Herbert, and Nancy Wolfe. 1996. *History of Criminal Justice*. Cincinnati, OH: Anderson.
Newman, Graeme. 1985. *Punishment Response*. New York: Macmillan.
Van den Haag, Ernest, and John P. Conrad. 1978. *The Death Penalty: A Debate*. New York: Plenum Press.
Von Hirsch, Andrew. 1976. *Doing Justice: The Choice of Punishments*. Boston: Northeastern University Press.

RHODE ISLAND

GENERAL INFORMATION

Rhode Island is one of the six New England states. It borders Massachusetts to the north and east, Connecticut to the west, and the Atlantic Ocean primarily to the south. It is the smallest of the fifty states in area, measuring only 48 miles long and 37 miles wide. The population, approaching 1.5 million, is forty-third in rank, but it is one of the most densely populated states in the country.

Practically the birthplace of the Industrial Revolution, Rhode Island was long known for its textile mills and factories. The same year that Rhode Island endorsed the U.S. Constitution, Samuel Slater started a textile factory in the town of Pawtucket. Powerful mercantile interests came to dominate the state. With a high proportion of blue-collar workers and self-employed businessmen, Rhode Island has never had a significant managerial class. It has been characterized as the closest of any state in the country to an industrialized city-state. The state's capital is Providence, the only significant urban metropolitan area in Rhode Island.

The state has a tradition of autonomy that is symbolized by the statue of the Independent Man that sits atop the capitol dome. Rhode Island was first of the thirteen colonies to declare independence from Great Britain, doing so two months before the issuing of the national Declaration of Independence, and was the last of the original colonies to sign the Constitution. Roger Williams, who fled the Massachusetts Bay Colony in 1636, hoped that the new settlement he named Providence would be "a shelter for persons distressed of conscience." Rhode Island soon became a haven for Quakers, who were persecuted in Massachusetts and Connecticut. The Rhode Island legislature later enacted a law protecting Jews in liberty of conscience.

CONSTITUTIONAL HISTORY

In 1663 Rhode Island petitioned King George II for a new charter for the colony. The petition expressed a commitment to "a lively experiment" based on "full liberty in religious commitments." Strangely, the charter's rules of governance remained the fundamental law of the state long after the American Revolution. Although Rhode Island was the first colony to renounce all allegiance to King George III, the state did not adopt its own constitution until 1842 when, prompted by a civic insurrection known as the Dorr Rebellion, it finally provided universal male suffrage. The Rhode Island constitution adopted some features of the U.S. Constitution, but it also retained features securing legislative dominance over the other branches of government.

There was not another constitutional convention in Rhode Island for more than one hundred years. The limited, predetermined question for the constitutional convention of 1944 involved exempting members of the armed forces from voting registration requirements. Just seven years later, there was another constitutional convention, to consider eight proposed amendments. The voters approved six but rejected increases in legislative pay and life tenure for supreme and superior court judges. Lifetime tenure for judges failed again in 1955

when put before the voters after another limited constitutional convention.

In November 1964, voters approved the call for an unlimited constitutional convention—the first since 1843. The convention lasted almost five years and ended in a resounding rejection by the electorate of all the proposals. Analyzing the entire convention process, Cornwell and Goodman (1969, 80) concluded that "there do not appear to be any simple answers to the question of how to succeed at constitutional reform." There was another limited constitutional convention in 1973, whereby eighteen-year-olds were granted the right to vote. The electorate rejected four-year terms for statewide offices. Another constitutional convention in 1986 produced fourteen proposed amendments. The voters approved eight, including the creation of an Ethics Commission to establish campaign finance rules and establish a code of ethics for public officials. The Ethics Commission would become the focus of a continuing controversy over the separation of powers in Rhode Island government that continues today.

POLITICAL CORRUPTION

The long history of political corruption in the state is summed up in a 1905 national magazine article entitled "Rhode Island, a State for Sale." From the Civil War until the mid-1930s, Rhode Island was controlled by the boss-ridden and often corrupt Republican Party. The Democrats seized control of the state government in 1935. On January 1, 1935, the General Assembly engineered a complete purge of the Republican-controlled Supreme Court, declaring all five seats vacant and appointing five new justices. The purge was disguised as voluntary resignations provided in exchange for generous lifetime pensions.

On January 1, 1946, the Rhode Island Supreme Court decided the outcome of the gubernatorial election after a scandalous controversy that came to be known as "the long count." The incumbent Democratic governor, who appeared to have won the popular vote on Election Day, then seemed to have lost after the absentee ballots were counted. The governor proceeded to challenge the constitutionality of the absentee ballot law, which had been enacted during his administration. The Rhode Island Supreme Court eventually threw out the absentee ballots and on Inauguration Day, while both would-be governors stood by at the statehouse, declared the Democratic incumbent the victor.

January 1, 1991, became another infamous day in Rhode Island history when the newly elected governor was forced to declare a bank holiday, closing all of the credit unions in the state, following the collapse of the privately funded deposition insurance system. The credit unions collapsed through a combination of corruption and mismanagement. The corruption uncovered in the

Legal Structure of Rhode Island Courts

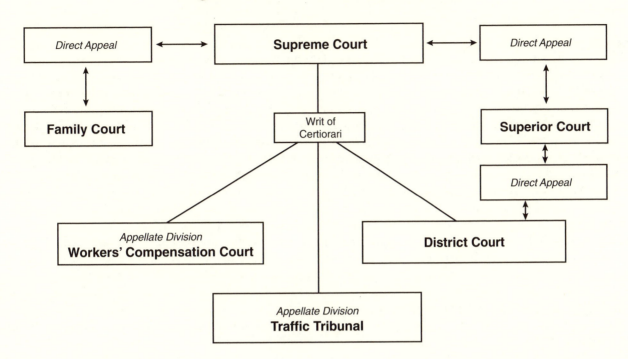

aftermath of this crisis eventually resulted in the successful prosecution of the previous governor, Edward DiPrete.

During the 1980s and 1990s, two consecutive chief justices resigned from the Rhode Island Supreme Court under the threat of impeachment. Chief Justice Joseph A. Bevilacqua resigned in 1986. The previous year, the Commission on Judicial Tenure and Discipline had found that Bevilacqua had brought his office into serious disrepute by associating with known members of organized crime. After a public censure by the commission, the General Assembly asked the court for an advisory opinion on their power to declare the office vacant. The apparent precedent was the Democrats' 1935 purge of the entire Supreme Court. But since those justices had technically resigned, the purge's legality had never been formally challenged. In 1986 the Rhode Island Supreme Court advised the General Assembly that the "Joint Resolution to Vacate the Judgeship of the Chief Justice" was not constitutional. Accordingly, formal impeachment proceedings, provided for by the state constitution, were later initiated, and the chief justice resigned.

His replacement, Thomas Faye, resigned as chief justice in 1993, along with his handpicked state court administrator, a former Speaker of the House, after the *Providence Journal* published a series of articles (for which it later won a Pulitzer Prize) that disclosed widespread corruption in their management of the Rhode Island court system. A similar investigative report in 1998 exposed serious problems with the traffic court.

CURRENT STRUCTURE

There are thirty-nine cities and towns in Rhode Island, as well as five counties, although there is no meaningful level of county government in the state. The right of cities and towns to have home rule charters was added to the state constitution in 1951. Rhode Island has a statewide, unified court system. The three primary courts are district courts, superior courts, and the Supreme Court. There is no intermediary court of appeal in Rhode Island. There are also three state-funded specialized courts: family court, workers' compensation court, and administrative adjudication court, commonly known as traffic court.

District Courts

District courts have limited jurisdiction in civil and criminal matters. They handle misdemeanors, along with initial appearances in felony cases. If a defendant invokes the right to trial by jury, the case is transferred to a superior court. District courts also hear appeals by administrative agencies and general civil disputes up to $10,000.

Superior Courts

Superior courts are the trial courts of general jurisdiction in Rhode Island. They have original jurisdiction over all felony cases, and they hear appeals of misdemeanors. The civil jurisdiction encompasses civil disputes beyond the jurisdictional limit in district court, equity proceedings, probate appeals, zoning appeals, and condemnation proceedings. Habeas corpus cases (in which a prisoner challenges the legality of imprisonment) are also heard in superior court.

Supreme Court

The Rhode Island Supreme Court is the state's only appellate court. It is responsible for regulating admission to the Rhode Island bar and disciplining its members. The Supreme Court has five members. The chief justice has authority over the judicial budget and appoints the state court administrator. The Supreme Court is authorized to issue advisory opinions on request from the legislative or executive branch.

The Office of the Attorney General handles all felony prosecutions in the state. Rhode Island does not have local district attorneys. City and town solicitors handle misdemeanors. The attorney general is elected, and in 1994 the term of office was increased to four years from two.

NOTABLE FEATURES OF THE LEGAL SYSTEM

Separation of Powers

The most unusual feature of the Rhode Island legal system is the supremacy of the legislative branch, which stands in contradiction to the traditional separation of powers in the United States. In 1997, the Ethics Commission adopted a regulation barring the long-standing tradition that members of the General Assembly may serve on state boards and commissions. That regulation was eventually invalidated by the Rhode Island Supreme Court. In 2000, the court also affirmed the denial of an injunction sought by the governor to limit legislative control of the Lottery Commission, a majority of whose members are appointed by the House Speaker and the Senate Majority Leader. In 1999, the legislatively appointed members outvoted the other members in a controversial decision, opposed by the governor, to expand the use of video slot machines. The court's decision upholding Rhode Island's unique system of government caused various reform groups to place a nonbinding question on the ballot, asking Rhode Islanders whether they wanted a constitutional convention "to expressly establish that Rhode Island government consists of separate and co-equal" branches of government. The nonbinding measure was approved by a wide margin in November 2000, but nothing has happened (or is likely to), because those in power are opposed to changing the system.

Judicial Selection

In 1994, Rhode Island became the only state in the last twenty years to move toward selection of judges on the basis of merit. Voters approved a constitutional amendment providing for a new method of selecting Supreme Court justices, eliminating legislative selection through a Grand Committee of the House and Senate in joint session. (Superior court judges were originally selected by the Grand Committee, but the system was eventually replaced by gubernatorial selection.) Under the new system, which originated in the General Assembly as a constitutional amendment to be put before the voters, the legislative branch retains considerable influence over the process. Nominations originate from a judicial nominating commission consisting of nine members. Although the governor enjoys full discretion in appointing four members—three attorneys and one non-attorney—the governor's choice for the five remaining members is restricted to people nominated by various officers of the General Assembly. Also setting Rhode Island's version of merit selection apart from that of other states is the lack of any specific requirement of nonpartisanship and provisions to ensure representation of both political parties.

The judicial selection commission holds hearings to assess the qualifications of various candidates and submits a list of three to five names to the governor, who selects all lower court judges, subject to Senate confirmation. Unlike virtually all other merit selection states, there is a separate, politicized process for the selection of Supreme Court justices. The process begins with the forwarding of a list of names to the governor. But instead of Senate confirmation, these nominees are subject to approval in the House and the Senate. If either body rejects the nominee, the process begins anew.

The experience in 1997 suggests that Supreme Court nominations remain subject to political manipulation by the General Assembly. In what has been dubbed the Tuesday Night Massacre, the General Assembly rejected a Supreme Court nomination by the governor without any apparent reason connected to merit. (The nominee went on to become a successful U.S. attorney for Rhode Island.) The governor then sent the name of someone with close ties to the General Assembly. She was approved without incident.

Such machinations have increased in the lower state courts, where the number of magistrates has grown since 1990 from two to fifteen. Magistrates have many similar powers to judges. They set bail, hear pretrial motions and arraignments, and rule on evidence. Magistrates receive lifetime appointments and have salaries in line with those of judges. But they are not subject to the judicial merit selection system. Instead, the chief judges of the respective courts dole out these appointments. In 2001, there were four magistrates in the Superior Court, six in the Family Court, two in the District Court, and three in the Traffic Tribunal. Former legislators hold many of these positions. In 2000, a magistrate position in the Superior Court was filled by the wife of the speaker of the House, raising further questions about the extent to which judicial selection is nonpartisan.

Although the judicial selection process in Rhode Island is infused with politics, a countervailing feature that promotes judicial independence is that judges have lifetime tenure. Massachusetts and New Hampshire are the only other states that have long provided the same lifetime guarantee that all federal judges have. Lifetime tenure is ensured by statute in Rhode Island. Voters have rejected amendments on several occasions that would make this provision a matter of constitutional law.

LEGAL EDUCATION AND THE LEGAL PROFESSION

In 2000, there were 4,465 practicing attorneys in Rhode Island, and the state ranked eighth nationally in the number of attorneys per thousand residents. Attorneys are required to earn a law degree and pass the state bar examination before practicing in the state. There was no law school in Rhode Island until 1992, when one was founded at Roger Williams University in Providence. The school soon earned full accreditation from the American Bar Association and in 1997 was rededicated as the Ralph R. Papitto School of Law.

RELATIONSHIP TO NATIONAL SYSTEM

There is one federal district court for Rhode Island. Cases are appealed from it to the Second Circuit Court of Appeals in Boston and ultimately to the U.S. Supreme Court, which can also hear appeals from the state Supreme Court.

Two landmark U.S. Supreme Court cases on the separation of church and state originated in Rhode Island. In *Lynch v. Donnelly* (1984), popularly known as the Pawtucket Crèche case, a sharply divided court held that the city of Pawtucket, in displaying a Christmas crèche at the town hall, had not violated the First Amendment's Establishment Clause. In *Lee v. Weisman* (1994), the court, again divided, held that including benedictions by clergy at public school graduation ceremonies—a regular practice in Providence—violated the Establishment Clause. Although Rhode Island is the most Roman Catholic state in the country, the benediction at issue in this case, invoked at Nathan Bishop Middle School, was delivered by a rabbi.

There have also been two noteworthy civil rights cases in federal district court in Rhode Island. One has resulted in oversight of the state prison for almost twenty years. The other case, *Cohen v. Brown University* (1995), broke new ground in gender equity in college sports.

Ross E. Cheit

See also Massachusetts; United States—Federal System; United States—State Systems

References and further reading

Conley, Patrick T. 1977. *Democracy in Decline: Rhode Island's Constitutional Development, 1776–1841.* Providence: Rhode Island Historical Society.
Cornwell, Elmer, and Jay S. Goodman. 1969. *The Politics of the Rhode Island Constitutional Convention.* New York: National Municipal League.
McLoughlin, William. 1986. *Rhode Island: A History.* New York: W. W. Norton.
Moakley, Maureen, and Elmer Cornwell. 2001. *Rhode Island Politics and Government.* Lincoln: University of Nebraska Press.
Steffens, Lincoln. 1905. "Rhode Island, a State for Sale." *McClure's* 24 (February): 330–353.
Terrace, Rachel. 1988. "The 'Tuesday Night Massacre': Judicial Selection in Rhode Island and the Nomination of Margaret Curran." *Comparative State Politics* 19:1–22.

ROMAN LAW

HISTORY

Traditionally the origin of the Roman legal system is dated to the composition of what has become known as the Twelve Tables, a brief set of laws of the fourth or fifth century B.C.E. Scholars believe that these laws reflect some borrowing from earlier Greek law as well as the agrarian condition of Rome of that period. During this earliest period of Roman law there was an intermingling of law and religion and the Roman priesthood exercised numerous legal functions. The next succeeding period, which reached to the end of the republic, was one marked by the increasing importance of Hellenistic philosophy as well as the gradual decline in importance of priests in the legal system and the rising importance of the Roman elite. During the republic, in particular, major strides in the law were accomplished and Roman legal oratory, particularly in the person of Marcus Tullius Cicero, achieved heights it would never see again. It is with the shift in Roman government from the republic to the principate under the Emperor Augustus, however, that what has become known as the classical period of Roman law truly begins. It is during this period that the greatest of the Roman jurists, those whose works would later be enshrined in Justinian's *Digest*, lived and worked. During this classical period the full majesty of the Roman legal system was worked out in the writings of the jurists. It was during this period as well that the final form of the basis of much of Roman jurisprudence, the *Edictum Perpetuum*, was achieved. It was also during this period that the traditional form of Roman juristic reasoning, which marks all Roman legal analysis for the next millennium, was established.

The classical period of Roman law is generally deemed to have ended with the accession of the Emperor Diocletian to the imperial throne at the end of the third century C.E. From this point on, Roman government became far more autocratic and Roman law became the province of imperial bureaucrats to a large extent. It is for this reason that this period of Roman law is often referred to as the bureaucratic period of Roman law. Between the accession of Diocletian and the completion of the publication of the Emperor Justinian's codification in 534 C.E., the Roman Empire was transformed from the dominant political and military force in both the East and West with its capital at Rome to a much more restricted state with an Eastern focus centered at Constantinople. During these centuries, the imperial court became the primary source of Roman law and the legal production of the imperial bureaucracy, particularly in the form of rescripts (letters from the emperor or his servants), multiplied. This, and the increasing fragmentation of the empire, led to near chaos. To combat this the Emperor Theodosius II proposed a massive legal codification, which resulted in the promulgation of the *Theodosian Code,* a compilation of imperial laws and rescripts, in 438 C.E. A century later the Emperor Justinian appointed a group of jurists led by Tribonian to revise and expand upon Theodosius II's work. This resulted in the publication between 529 and 534 of the *Digest,* a compilation of juristic writings of the classical period; the *Code,* a revision of the Theodosian Code; the *Institutes,* a school textbook based on a second-century text of the jurist Gaius; and the *Novels,* a second compilation of imperial laws.

From the end of Justinian's reign until the end of the eleventh century, Roman law continued to have some influence in the West, mainly through canon law and, to varying degrees, through the various barbarian codes, but its first great period of influence and creativity was over. The second great period in the history of Roman law began in the late eleventh century with the rediscovery of the *Digest* and the revival of scientific jurisprudence in the West. This revival of interest in Roman law led to a great educational movement in which Roman law became one of the primary subjects for university-level instruction from the eleventh until the sixteenth centuries. It was during this period that many of the newly emerging nation-states based their legal systems on Roman law or a combination of Roman and customary law. It was during this period as well that some of the greatest Roman juristic works of the Middle Ages were produced, including the Accursian *Gloss,* the commentaries of Baldus and Bartolus, as well as many others. During this period from the end of the eleventh century until the beginning of the sixteenth century, Roman law was, in many respects, the *jus commune* (common law) of Western Europe and, as such, was once again a living legal system.

By the sixteenth century, however, because of changing legal, political, and intellectual conditions, Roman law came to play a much reduced role in the legal life of Europe. To a large extent, Roman law continued to be influential as a source of modern law, but it ceased to be a living legal system and its study became, throughout most of Europe, an academic subject. As an influential source of law, it remained important and a whole class of legal systems, known as civil law systems, were so defined because of their dependence upon Roman law and Roman legal models. But by the very act of distinguishing between Roman law and civil law, Roman law's role was diminished. By the nineteenth century, particularly in Germany, Roman law was studied largely from the historical perspective by academics rather than as a practical subject by practicing lawyers. It was during this period, however, that Roman law studies as an academic field made great advances through the work of scholars and jurists such as Friedrich Karl von Savigny, Anthon Thibaut, Theodor Mommsen, and Paul Krieger. Through the work of these scholars many classical and postclassical Roman texts were brought to light and modern, scientific editions were produced.

There has been renewed interest in Roman law from both the academic and the practical perspectives in the late twentieth and early twenty-first centuries. As economic and political unification has become a strong force in Europe, the desire for legal uniformity, if not unification, has grown apace. Many European jurists, led by Prof. Reinhard Zimmerman in Germany and Prof. Manlio Bellomo in Italy, have argued for a renewed reliance on Roman law as a source for a new common law of Europe. As a result, general interest in Roman law has once again been on the increase and it is possible that Roman law may well experience another renaissance in Europe during the twenty-first century.

CHARACTER

It is somewhat difficult to make general characterizations about Roman law since it is a legal system that has existed and evolved over 2,000 years and flourished throughout a third of the known world. However, there are certain very broad attributes of Roman law upon which most scholars and lawyers can agree.

Since the middle of the bureaucratic period of Roman legal history, when imperial efforts at codification began to bear fruit in the Theodosian and Justinian codifications, Roman law has been marked by and praised for its systematic character. The Romans had a genius for organization, in government, architecture, and, of course, in law. For most of its history Roman law has been held up as a model of organizational structure. Most notably, Justinian's *Institutes,* designed to be an elementary textbook for the late Roman law schools, has been used as a model of organization and arrangement for more than a millennium by Rome's successor states. Indeed, credit for the very idea of codification is often given to Theodosius II and Justinian, and such codes as the Visigothic Code of the seventh century, the Prussian Code of the eighteenth century, the Napoleonic Code of the early nineteenth century, and the German BGB of the late nineteenth and early twentieth centuries owe their existence, in part at least, to the late Roman codification projects.

A second attribute of Roman law is that of terminological precision. Roman legal vocabulary achieved a high level of clarity and precision, a level seldom reached by successor legal systems. Much modern legal terminology comes from Roman law. Thus, a key concept in French contract law, *cause,* is directly derived from the Roman legal term and concept *causa.* In both French and German law we speak of *obligation,* a term and concept directly derived from the Roman legal term *obligatio.* One could cite thousands of such terms as examples. Indeed, scholars of Anglo-American common law have often compared the language of the common law unfavorably to that of the civil law systems derived from Roman law. John Austin, for instance, one of the greatest of English nineteenth-century jurists and author of *The Province of Jurisprudence Determined,* saw in Roman law a cause for what he perceived to be the obscurity of common law language and proposed to import Roman legal terms into the common law to improve and clarify it.

A third important attribute of Roman law is its practicality and sophistication. Roman law as a system developed in the historical context of a great military and commercial empire. As a result Roman law was the first legal system that was forced to deal with a host of complex social and commercial problems, such as conflict-of-laws problems. This meant that Roman legal sources were particularly useful to European states in the early modern and modern period as these states began to encounter similar types of problems that required legal solutions. Instead of starting from the beginning, legislators, lawyers, and judges in these European states were able to turn to the Roman sources for inspiration and models.

Roman legal discourse was also characterized by a series of ideas and attitudes that have played an important role in Western jurisprudence. Professor Fritz Schulz, in his classic book *Principles of Roman Law,* identified ten such ideas: isolation, abstraction, simplicity, tradition, nation, liberty, authority, humanity, fidelity, and security. Each of these legal principles embodied in Roman law played an important role not only in Roman law itself, but also in the development of all those legal systems that were influenced by Roman law and that continue to be so today. Many concepts central to modern legal systems, such as individual rights, the separation of legal and nonlegal rules, and the instrumental conception of law as a guardian of liberty and security, derive directly from Roman law.

Many of the aspects noted above about Roman law in general are illustrated in the way Roman law handled specific substantive areas. The Roman law of contract, for instance, was extremely pragmatic and changed over time. It began as a highly formalistic subject but, as Roman so-ciety became more sophisticated and the scope of Roman commerce increased, Roman law developed apace. Roman law developed a series of contract doctrines covering such areas as hire, purchase, and gratuitous transfer. Roman contract law avoided the cumbersome notion of consideration, which has so burdened the common law, however. Indeed, the Romans understood contract law to be part of a greater whole, that of obligations, which also included delict, that part of Roman law closest to the common law subject of torts. Here, too, the law of delict was marked by a level of pragmatism and sophistication far in advance of other contemporary systems.

Roman family law, particularly in those areas that impacted the maintenance and transfer of wealth, was highly developed. The Romans had sophisticated and often complex rules on succession, both testamentary and intestate. The Roman law of marriage developed over the centuries and moved from a highly patriarchal model to one that gave eventually significant rights to women, particularly as to certain property. Divorce was common in Roman society and the laws reflected this fact. Much the same was true of adoption. Roman property law, in particular, reflected the needs of a wealthy, international society. For instance, modern riparian law, both in civil and common law jurisdictions, is closely derived from Roman law. The modern law of condominium ownership is also essentially Roman law.

DIFFUSION

The history of the spread of Roman law and Roman legal ideas over the past 2,000 years is remarkable. What started as the legal system of a small city-state expanded eventually into a legal system in force from the easternmost reaches of Europe to the British Isles, from the edge of the Baltic to North Africa. At the height of the empire, Roman law was the legal system in force throughout the Western world. In 212 C.E. the Roman state granted citizenship to virtually all of its subjects and, thereby, made Roman law applicable to millions of individuals. At the same time, the Romans also were tolerant of foreign systems and accorded a degree of autonomy to those populations that wished to maintain their own legal systems, such as the Jews.

After the decline of Roman political and military power, Roman law remained in force, in Greek translation, throughout the Byzantine Empire and was also applied to various populations in the West through codes such as the Lex Romana Burgundionum. Thus, its geographical diffusion remained great even after Rome's political decline. With the renaissance of Roman legal studies in the late eleventh century, Roman law again became a powerful force throughout Western Europe and remained as such until the rise of national states and national laws in the sixteenth century.

During the later eighteenth and early nineteenth centuries, Roman law moved across the Atlantic Ocean and began to influence the development of law in the United States. For a short period there was some discussion of replacing the common law with Roman law in the new American republic, but this movement failed. Roman law greatly influenced several areas of American law, however. Commercial law, the law of wills, admiralty, and the laws relating to waterways were all derived, in part, from Roman legal models. Further, important jurisprudential movements in the United States, particularly the movement for codification of American law, were inspired by Roman law.

At the dawn of the twenty-first century Roman law is still studied throughout Europe and the United States. It is studied as a model legal system. It is studied as a source for sophisticated legal rules and concepts. It is studied as a model of legal reasoning and jurisprudence. After more than 2,000 years, Roman law remains alive and well.

M. H. Hoeflich

See also Civil Law; Germany; Lousiana; Napoleonic Code
References and further reading
Bellomo, Manlio. 1995. *The Common Legal Past of Europe.* Washington, DC: Catholic University of America Press.
Hoeflich, M. H. 1997. *Roman and Civil Law and the Development of Anglo-American Jurisprudence.* Athens: University of Georgia Press.
Robinson, Olivia F. 1997. *The Sources of Roman Law: Problems and Methods for Ancient Historians.* London: Routledge.
Schulz, Fritz. 1936. *Principles of Roman Law.* Translated by M. Wolff. Oxford: Clarendon Press.
———. 1953. *History of Roman Legal Science.* Oxford: Clarendon Press.
Stein, Peter. 1988. *The Character and Influence of the Roman Civil Law: Historical Essays.* London/Ronceverte, WV: Hambledon Press.
———. 1999. *Roman Law in European History.* New York: Cambridge University Press.
Watson, Alan. 1981. *The Making of the Civil Law.* Cambridge, MA: Harvard University Press.
———. 1995. *The Spirit of Roman Law.* Athens: University of Georgia Press.

ROMANIA

COUNTRY INFORMATION

Romania is located in the southeastern corner of Central Europe, to the north of the Balkan Peninsula. Most of the country occupies the Danube River basin, with the Black Sea occupying much of Romania's eastern boundary, along with the Republic of Moldova and Ukraine. Romania is also bounded by Bulgaria to the south, Yugoslavia to the south and southwest, and Hungary to the west. Romania's land surface area is 238,391 square kilometers, which makes it the twelfth largest country in Europe. Romania is divided into roughly three geographical zones, each comprising approximately one-third of the country's surface area: the Carpathian Mountains, which run from east to west across the center of the country; foothills and plateaus on the northern and southern escarpments of the Carpathians; and flat plains, which run farther north and south of the mountains to the Danube River and then east to the Black Sea.

According to the 1992 census figures, there are about 23 million Romanians living in the country itself, with another 9 million dispersed in Europe and North America due to a steady flow of emigration over the last ten years. In terms of ethnic composition, 90 percent of the population self-identifies as ethnic Romanian, 7 percent as ethnic Hungarian, about 2 percent as Romani, with the remaining 1 percent composed of ethnic groups from many parts of the world.

After the fall of the Soviet Union and its satellites at the end of the 1980s and beginning of the 1990s, including Ceauşescu-led Romania, the Romanian economy was left with an outmoded industrial sector that was inefficient, badly organized, and structured for an obsolete geopolitical reality. After several years of political instability, the country embarked on a plan of macroeconomic reform on the way to a privatized market economy. As of the late 1990s, per capita GDP was U.S.$1,713, while the national GDP was at U.S.$38 billion. Major industries include the following: mining, timber, building materials, metallurgy, machinery, agriculture, oil production, and, increasingly, tourism.

Although, as will be seen below, the current Romanian legal system is the product of a long and complex history, in the broadest of terms we can say that it is a civil law system with features common to the other continental civil law countries whose legal systems were much influenced by early Roman law.

HISTORY

The current Republic of Romania is a nation with ancient origins. It is also a nation with a history of multiethnic hybridization that has impacted the past and current legal system to greater or lesser degrees. Ethnic Romanians are the descendants of the Dacians, who were a Thracian population that was finally subdued by the Roman Emperor Trajan in the third century B.C.E. After the fall of Roman influence in south-central Europe, the region composed of Romanians became subject to the rule of a dizzying number of foreign powers, including Ostrogoths, Slavs, and Tartars in the early years after the Roman collapse; the Magyar Empire, the Ottoman Turks, the Austro-Hungarian Empire; and, from the mid-eighteenth century to the last third of the nineteenth, the Imperial Russians. Although Romanians had an identity as an autonomous ethnic nation, they had never retained actual state auton-

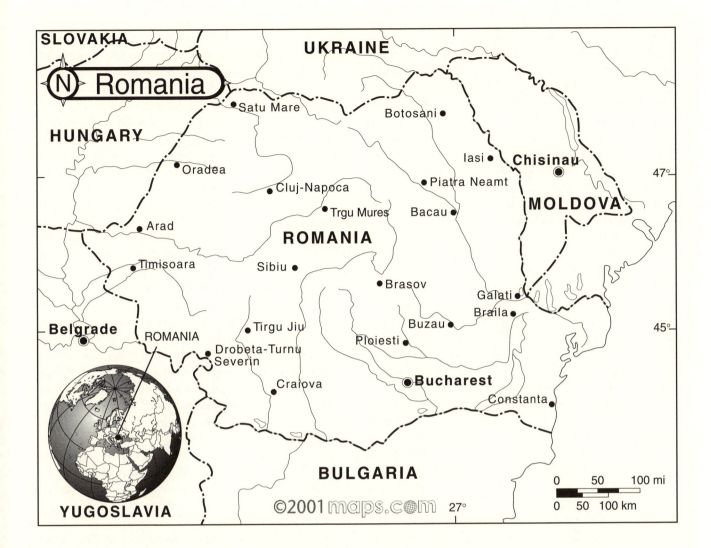

omy until 1878, when the Kingdom of Romania was guaranteed its independence during the Congress of Berlin. But it was not until the end of World War I that the ancient boundaries of ethnic Romania became contiguous in fact for the first time: Transylvania and Bukovina were awarded to Romania from defeated Austro-Hungary, while Bessarabia was returned by Russia.

After the rise of Nazi Germany, and especially after the fall of France in 1940, Romania was forced within the German sphere of influence through the Molotov-Ribbentrop Pact (1940). Romanian soldiers fought alongside Germans even though the area of Romania escaped the massive ground wars of the more northern Eastern Front and the entire Western Front. By 1947, after the defeat of the Axis Powers, the Romanian king was forced to abdicate and a communist republic was declared, which was firmly within the Soviet Union's sphere of control. Bessarabia, which had been occupied by the Russians during the war, was simply annexed to the Soviet Union, and eventually became the Soviet Socialist Republic of Moldavia.

During the 1960s, the People's Republic of Romania became increasingly isolated even in relation to other So-

viet Bloc countries because of the influence of Nicolae Ceauşescu. Although Ceauşescu was revered early on because of his Tito-like nationalist communism and personal charisma, he later became a hated symbol of the brutality of the Stalinist brand of totalitarianism that he admired and implemented. The Ceauşescu regime was finally overthrown in 1989 during a brief but bloody people's revolution (which unfolded quite differently than the various velvet revolutions in other parts of Eastern Europe), in which students, labor unionists, and rebellious elements of the army turned against Ceauşescu and the loyal members of the dreaded Securitate, the regime's secret police.

From 1989 to the present, Romania has struggled to make the transition to a market-oriented economy. This has been due most clearly to the persistence of corruption at all levels in society, a general inefficiency in bureaucratic structures, and, increasingly, the loss of crucial human capital, as a whole generation of young technically educated Romanians, no longer willing to wait for opportunities at home, emigrate to Western Europe and North America in search of well-paying jobs and more secure futures.

This brief account of Romania's history is necessary to understand the extraordinarily diverse nature of Romania's legal history and current legal system. Given its origins as a Roman province, it is not surprising that Romanian law has always shown the hallmarks of the classic civil law legal system: the constitution and statutes as the sole source of legal legitimacy; an investigative role for judges and an absence of an adversarial trial system; the absence of a jury; the lack of judge-made or case law; and a prominent role for legal scientists, who are called on to guide legislators in crafting legislation that is logically and legally consistent and socially desirable.

Despite this civil law heritage, Romanian legal history has been marked by the same extent of layering as we find in its political history. Most commentators trace the rise of Romania's modern legal history to the 1600s, when the first important regional codifications of laws were undertaken, the *Pravila lui Vasile Lupu* (1646), which was directed by Vasile Lupu, ruler of Moldavia, and the *Pravila lui Mateiu Basarab* (1652), which was undertaken by the Walachian prince Matei Basarab. These two compilations were important in that they, taken together, represented an attempt to create a unified Romanian law out of the many legal traditions that had been competing with each other in the region, including law derived from the Byzantine codes, canon law that was heavily influenced from the north and had been transmitted in Old Slavonic, the Roman law from the west, and, finally, the many disparate customary legal traditions that had always played a subtle role from pre-Roman times.

This process of intentional, but selective, legal syncretism—that is, the fusing of legal traditions, but from among primarily Byzantine, Russian, Roman, and local customary legal sources—continued from the seventeenth century until the mid-nineteenth century, after which it underwent a profound transformation during the time period of independence. During the nineteenth century, French language and culture had reached a level of prestige and influence in Romania among the elite, much as they did in Russia during this same epoch. Romanian intellectuals and scholars traveled to what was believed to be the center of enlightenment for education; they returned with models for political and legal reforms. Given this, it is not surprising that Romanian jurists turned to French legal codes for inspiration during this time of openness to Western ideas and practices.

Specifically, in many cases Romanian jurists simply translated French codes into Romanian and gave them official force. For example, the commercial code (1839), the penal code (1852), and the civil code (1864) were direct translations of the equivalent portions of the Code Napoléon. Nevertheless, this new and relatively sudden incorporation of French legal codes did not mean that the more organic preexisting legal structure was completely supplanted; rather, the older Byzantine-Russian-Roman-customary legal apparatus—which some commentators have referred to as a true case of legal pluralism—remained as a foundation upon which the French codes were overlaid.

During the years leading up to World War I, new territory was added to Romania, and this meant that Romanian law was forced, yet again, to incorporate different legal codes, in this case primarily those from Austria and Hungary. From the end of World War I to 1945, the Romanian legal system underwent a period of legal syncretism in some ways equal to the mid-nineteenth century. The goal of King Carol II and his ministers during this time was to create a consistent body of legislation in order to achieve stability for a country whose boundaries finally embraced what were believed to be the historically ethnic Romanian regions; it was felt that a coherent national law would bind this fragile geopolitical arrangement together in the face of a wider regional instability. The result was that by 1947, Romanian law was indeed well integrated if diverse: for example, French and Italian sources most heavily influenced Romanian contract law; German and Italian law influenced Romanian property law; and Romanian inheritance law resembled its German counterpart.

With the re-creation of Romania as a communist republic after the end of World War II, the legal system underwent a profound transformation. From the mid-seventeenth century to 1947—despite the periods of assimilation and legal pluralism—Romanian law was influenced by a fairly consistent guiding legal philosophy derived from proto-Enlightenment and Enlightenment sources: within this model, legislation was thought to be objective, neutral, and a reflection of timeless moral truths. But after 1947 a different legal philosophy was adopted in Romania, as it was in all the Soviet Bloc countries: the legal philosophy of Marxism-Leninism. The idea of law as a neutral, apolitical body of rules was rejected and replaced by a philosophy that saw law as a positive force for the reconstruction of a society in which one class, the bourgeois, had used the pretensions to an objective law to maintain economic inequality and class dominance.

Nevertheless, despite over forty years of socialist legislation, much of the presocialist Romanian law survived, which should hardly be surprising given Romania's long history of legal pluralism and eclecticism. Indeed, many commentators argue that socialist law did not replace the preexisting legal structures in Romania; rather, it was, much like earlier periods of legal assimilation, merely superimposed on a body of legislation that was the product of hundreds of years of selective incorporation and marked influence by Western European legal models.

From 1989 to 2001, Romanian law has undergone yet another period of important change. The socialist legal overlay has been largely removed, leaving the eclectic civil law foundation intact. What has been added has been a series of legal reforms intended to create an environment in Romania that is conducive to foreign capital investment, attractive to international lending institutions like the World Bank and the International Monetary Fund, and that meets the criteria—especially in areas like contract law and intellectual property protection—for European Union candidacy.

LEGAL CONCEPTS

As a legal system within the continental civil law tradition, the Romanian legal system resembles other countries' in that legal legitimacy resides exclusively in written statutes and the national constitution. This is a basic but important concept to underscore, especially for readers from common law jurisdictions, because the practical effect of this is to reduce the flexibility of judges during the resolution of disputes in court. Proponents of statute-based dispute resolution argue that it is fairer and less arbitrary than the case-by-case judge-made law found in common law systems. Nevertheless in Romania, as in other civil countries in recent years, legal scholars have argued for greater flexibility for judges because of what is perceived to be an unwanted effect of statute-based dispute resolution: results are often logically consistent but subjectively undesirable for the parties. Interestingly, this push for greater flexibility for judges in Romania as in other civil law countries is the mirror opposite of movements in common law jurisdictions, in which legal reformers have argued for less flexibility and increased codification in order to prevent results that are perceived as being arbitrary and without value as precedent.

Another legal concept specific to the Romanian legal system—though echoed in part in other former Soviet Bloc civil law countries—is the disproportionate strength of public prosecutors compared with lawyers and judges. Many commentators believe that this was an inevitable result of the 1947–1989 period because of the re-creation of Romanian law along Marxist-Leninist lines, and the general weakness of judges in light of the political use of law by the government. But even after 1989, the procuracy has remained relatively powerful—many would argue too powerful—because the 1991 National Constitution did not embrace the separation-of-powers principle as much as many would have liked, with the result that prosecutors remain a forceful arm of the judiciary rather than a branch of the executive, as many legal scholars would prefer.

CURRENT STRUCTURE

Romania's legal structure was most fundamentally changed after 1989 through Law no. 59 (1993), which modified the code of civil procedure. The judicial system

Structure of Romanian Courts

| Curtea Constitutionala (Constitutional Court) | Curtea Suprema de Justitie (Supreme Court of Justice) • Civil • Criminal • Military • Administrative |

Curti de Apel (Courts of Appeal)

Tribunale (Tribunals)

Judecatorii (Courts of First Instance)

is now hierarchically organized as follows: at the lowest level is the Judecatorii, or courts of first instance. These courts somewhat unusually have jurisdiction over all types of cases irrespective of content—civil, criminal, administrative, family, and commercial—as long as the value of the case is less than 10 million *lei*.

The next level in the judicial system is composed of the Tribunale, or tribunals. These courts act both as courts of appeal from judgments taken in the Judecatorii and as courts of first instance in certain circumstances, for example for civil cases with values greater than 150 million *lei*, commercial cases with values greater than 10 million *lei*, in cases involving commercial property rights, and for specified criminal cases. When acting as courts of appeal from judgments taken in the Judecatorii, appellate decisions cannot be appealed above the tribunals except where parties assert that a legal error has been made; in other words, judgments of the tribunals acting in their appellate capacity cannot be appealed for new findings of fact.

The third level moving up the judicial hierarchy in Romania is composed of Curti de Apel, or courts of appeal. These courts act as courts of appeal from judgments taken in tribunals acting as courts of first instance, and as courts of review from judgments on appeal from the tribunals acting as courts of appeal for cases that began in the Judecatorii. In special circumstances the Curti de Apel can act as courts of first instance.

The court of last resort in Romania is the Curtea Suprema de Justitie, or Supreme Court of Justice. Like courts of resort in other parts of Europe, the Romanian Supreme Court of Justice acts primarily as a court of appeal for judgments of the next highest courts of appeal, in this case the Curti de Apel. The Supreme Court of Justice has four sections: civil, criminal, military, and administrative. The judges of the Supreme Court of Justice are appointed by the president for terms of six years, and they may be reappointed after the first six years have expired.

SPECIALIZED JUDICIAL BODIES

The two most important specialized judicial bodies in Romania are the Curtea Constitutionala, or Constitutional Court, which was created after 1989, and the Higher Council of the Judiciary. The Romanian Supreme Court of Justice, unlike the Supreme Court of the United States, for example, does not have within its jurisdiction questions of legislative constitutionality. The Romanian court of last resort does decide whether lower courts applied legislation correctly in specific cases, but the Supreme Court of Justice cannot make determinations as to the correctness of the legislations itself in light of guiding constitutional doctrine; this job is delegated to the new Constitutional Court through Constitutional Article 144.

The role of the Constitutional Court is to decide whether acts of Parliament (from either the Chamber of Deputies or the Senate), presidential decrees, election procedures, and matters involving political parties are in compliance with the mandates of the national constitution. The court is composed of nine judges, who are appointed by the president (3), the Chamber of Deputies (3), and the Senate (3) for nine-year terms. Judges cannot hold any other public or private appointments during their term in office, except that of university professor. The first Constitutional Court judges were appointed in 1992.

The Higher Council of the Judiciary is composed of fifteen members, who are elected for terms of four years by the Chamber of Deputies and Senate sitting in joint session. Congress can elect to the Higher Council of the Judiciary members drawn from the ranks of the following: the Supreme Court of Justice, public prosecutors, and judges from the Court of Appeal for Bucharest. The Higher Council of the Judiciary has important legal functions, including the following: (1) it proposes for appointment at all levels judges, who—after appointment by the president of the republic—are guaranteed nonremovable tenures under the new national constitution; (2) it decides on the promotion, transfer, and suspension of judges who have already been appointed; and (3) at the request of the Ministry of Justice, it conducts research into problems affecting the administration of justice.

STAFFING

Both judges and lawyers in Romania receive the same foundational training. A lawyer in Romania is called an *avocat,* or advocate. In order to become an *avocat* one must first attend one of the accredited faculties of law in Romania for a course of four years. Traditionally these faculties were to be found within the major public universities, such as the Universities of Bucharest, Cluj, and Iaşi, but after 1989 there has been a proliferation of smaller, private universities that feature accredited law programs. During their course of study Romanian law students must take a wider variety of courses than those required of American law students, for example. In addition to courses in constitutional law, civil law, criminal law, and legal theory, Romanian law students must pass courses in sociology, political economy, criminology, human rights, and forensic pathology. Romanian law students are also required to take foreign language courses; in the past the most popular language was French, but after 1989 English has become the language of choice.

After graduating from an accredited law faculty, a Romanian law student must serve a two-year course of practical training under the supervision of a certified *avocat.* Only after this two-year apprenticeship may the Romanian law student sit for the bar examination, which, when passed, qualifies one as a licensed *avocat* able to practice law in Romania in all capacities.

After 1989 the bar became privatized in Romania. With privatization, the power of the traditional advocates' union diminished as competing bar associations came into being, especially after the rules of legal practice were changed in 1995. Currently the most important bar associations in Romania are the Uniunea Juriştilor Democraţi din România, or Democratic Lawyers' Union of Romania, and the Uniunea Avocaţilor din România, or Union of Romanian Advocates.

I should also mention that in Romania, as in other civil law countries, notaries play an indispensable role within the legal system. Indeed, lawyers and notaries public make up the two most important branches of the Romanian legal profession. Notaries' official stamps are necessary in order to give legal force to a variety of documents that are essential to any legal process, and they often work in informal association with a lawyer or associations of lawyers. According to the new Law of Public Notaries (1995), the normal route for appointment as notary public in Romania is to first graduate from a recognized course of notarial studies at a university. After this, candidates must sit for a nationwide notarial exam, which is administered by the Ministry of Justice. Open vacancies throughout Romania in the notarial profession are filled based on the results of this competitive exam. Notaries in Romania are organized into a union, the Uniunea Naţională a Notarilor Publici din Romania, or National Union of Romanian Public Notaries.

IMPACT

The Romanian legal system is currently at a crossroads. Because of the legacy of the political use of the legal system by the state during the 1947–1989 period, people in Romania came to view legal processes with mistrust and skepticism. But since 1989 the government has been trying to inculcate a new respect for law through substantive legal reforms. This new effort is the result of a desire to bring the Romanian legal system into compliance with European Union requirements for membership candidacy, create an environment conducive to attracting foreign capital investment, and, most importantly, establish a rule of law that works for people throughout society. Nevertheless, the formal legal reforms have not had, to date, the intended effects at the local level. Corruption and mistrust still characterize people's perceptions of legal processes at various levels, and Romania's record of attracting foreign investment has not been as extensive as legal and business leaders would hope. Despite this, Romania has made a concerted effort to reform its legal system in ways that could bear fruit in the near future.

Mark Goodale

See also Civil Law; Customary Law; Legal Pluralism; Legal Professionals—Civil Law Traditions; Magistrates—Civil Law Systems; Marxist Jurisprudence; Moldova; Napoleonic Code; Notaries; Roman Law; Soviet System

References and further reading
Ceterchi, I. 1987. *Istoria dreptului românesc.* Vol. 2, Part 2. Bucharest: Acadamiei Republicii Socialiste România.
Damant, B., and V. Lunceau. 1986. "Note on the History of Romania Law." *Journal of Legal History* 7: 99.
Gogeanu, P., and L. P. Marcu. 1981. *A Concise History of Romanian Law.* Bucharest: Scientific and Encyclopedic Publishing House.
Jacobini, H. B. 1987. *Romanian Public Law: Some Leading Internal Aspects.* Boulder, CO: East European Monographs.
Romania. 1989. *Monitorul official al României: Communicate, decrete-lege, decrete, hotărîri ale guvernului si alte acte* 1, no. 1 (December 22).
Stoicoiu, Virgiliu. 1964. *Legal Sources and Bibliography of Romania.* New York: Praeger.
Tismaneanu, Vladimir, and Gail Kligman, eds. 2001. "Romania after the 2000 Elections." Special edition, *East European Constitutional Review* 10, no. 1 (Winter).

RUSSIA

GENERAL INFORMATION

Following the dissolution of the Soviet Union in December 1991, the Russian Federation became a sovereign state with its own self-contained legal system. The Russian legal system, as it has evolved, represents an amalgamation of the influences of the preexisting Soviet and czarist legal systems and the legal systems of various Western liberal democracies. Without doubt, the civil law tradition constitutes the strongest influence.

The Russian Federation is the largest country in the world, with a total of 17,025,200 square kilometers spread out over the northern Eurasian landmass. Its population of approximately 147 million is concentrated in the European portion of the country. The majority of the population (approximately 80 percent) is ethnically Russian, though there are more than one hundred other ethnic groups represented throughout Russia. Russian is the official language. The Russian government continues to struggle with its policy regarding ethnic minorities, and in the decade following the breakup of the Soviet Union, the tolerance for ethnic diversity in terms of language and culture has increased, though discrimination remains a problem.

Russia is a federation of eighty-nine subjects (geographic units to which political-legal rights attach), including forty-nine regions (*oblasti*), twenty-one autonomous republics (*avtonomnye respubliki*), ten autonomous areas (*avtonomnye okrugy*), six territories (*krai*), two federal cities (Moscow and St. Petersburg), and one autonomous region (*avtonomnaya oblast'*). The relationship between the government of the Russian Federation and its subjects is governed by the constitution, as well as legislation and administrative regulations.

HISTORY

The legal system of the Russian Federation emerged out of the Soviet legal system, which, in turn, was the successor to the czarist legal system. For most of the Soviet era, law was used instrumentally by those in power to achieve their goals. During the mid-1980s, under the leadership of M. S. Gorbachev, reforms were undertaken that had a significant effect on the legal system. In particular, Gorbachev articulated the goal of moving toward a "rule-of-law-based state" (*pravovoe gosudarstvo*), in which all citizens would be treated equally before the law. Although not fully realized during his tenure, concrete changes were made that curtailed the influence of the Communist Party within the legal system. Among these changes were the introduction of competitive elections for the national legislature (which had the effect of opening up the legislative process) and a revised selection process for judges. The introduction of a constitutional tribunal with limited powers (the Constitutional Supervisory Committee of the USSR) signaled the acceptance of judicial review.

The reform of the Russian legal system accelerated with the emergence of the Russian Federation as a sovereign state in January 1992. The Yeltsin regime openly embraced the goals of moving toward a market democracy and set about to reform the existing legislative base and legal institutions so as to facilitate that transition. The process of adopting the legislation necessary for the evolution toward a market economy (including privatization) proved laborious and contentious, with a prolonged struggle for dominance between the legislative and executive branches. This struggle culminated in the so-called

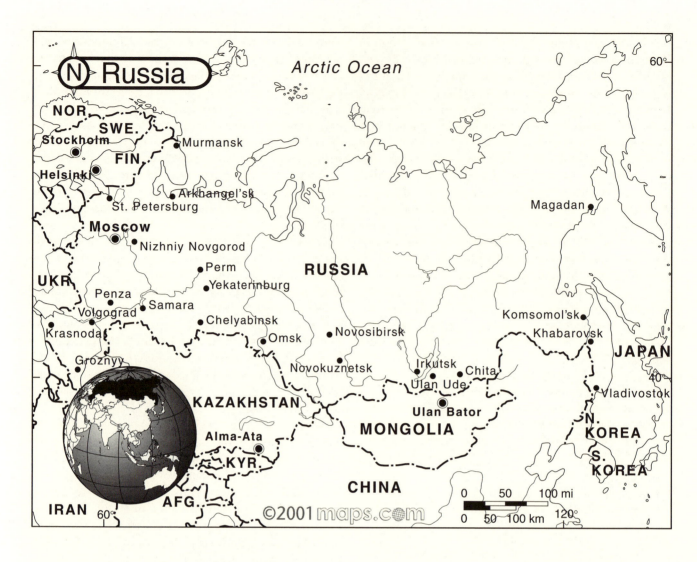

October Events, during which violence broke out when the legislature refused to accept the decision of then-president Yeltsin to dissolve it. In the wake of this crisis, a new constitution was adopted by referendum in December 1993. The cornerstone principles of socialist law, such as the guiding role of the Communist Party and the educative function of courts, were abandoned. Although the legacy of state socialism could not be eliminated overnight, the Russian government exhibited a strong desire to be seen as having a civil law legal system. All of the major codes were amended and most were completely redrafted. The 1990s witnessed an unprecedented flurry of legislative activity. Many of the changes were profound. For example, this new legislation endorsed basic market principles, such as private property, the profit incentive, the protection of shareholders' interests, and bankruptcy.

LEGAL CONCEPTS

The adherence to legal positivism, which persisted from the czarist legal system through the Soviet era, endures in post-Soviet Russia. The codes remain the primary source of law, though tempered by an increased willingness to recognize judicial interpretations as mediating influences. Judicial review has been institutionalized through the operation of the Constitutional Court. This court, along with the Russian Supreme Court and the Higher *Arbitrazh* Court, has been active in interpreting the codes, both in the context of cases and on their own initiative. The lower courts view these interpretations as binding, though whether they technically tie the hands of the lower courts is debatable.

Russian judicial process remains principally inquisitorial. In both civil and criminal settings, the judge continues to be the central figure. Typically the judge questions the witnesses first, and, although the litigants' counsel has the right to ask additional questions, the preemptive rights of the judge often result in counsel being marginalized. The 1993 Constitution grants citizens the right to an adversarial procedure. The procedural codes passed thereafter have declared that the litigants are responsible for assembling and presenting evidence supporting their claims. Yet observers in both the courts of general jurisdiction and the *arbitrazh* courts have commented that the day-to-day reality remains judge-centered and inquisitorial.

The problem of corruption within the legal system of Russia is a source of concern. As a consequence of their low salaries and the irregularity of wage payments in the 1990s, officials within the legal system are often assumed to be susceptible to bribes. Many Russian firms and individuals distrust the police and have engaged private security firms to protect themselves. The true extent of corruption is almost impossible to document, but the widespread belief in its pervasiveness has convinced some potential litigants that justice is elusive, has discouraged international investment, and has given rise to the common wisdom that it is impossible to do business legally in Russia.

As during the Soviet period, attitudes about law are disparate. The transition away from state socialism has brought a greater prominence to law within Russian society. In contrast to the Soviet period, when the Communist Party elite dictated the content of law, the law-making process has now become more contested. The popular media regularly reports on the ongoing debates on draft laws and publishes a wide variety of opinions. Even so, many ordinary Russians continue to regard law with cynicism, believing that law remains a tool that the state uses to impose its will on society. Contributing to this skepticism is a recognition that the Russian state routinely flouts the law in its interactions with individuals and businesses. That leaves ordinary citizens unconvinced of the legitimacy of the law. At the same time, the propensity to use legal institutions, such as the courts, has escalated in the decade following the breakup of the Soviet Union. Not only do Russians use the courts for family law and housing issues, as was true even during the Soviet era, but they are increasingly challenging state authority via the courts. This suggests that the legal culture of post-Soviet Russia may be in the middle of a profound shift.

CURRENT STRUCTURES

The judicial system of the Russian Federation is divided along jurisdictional grounds. The basic framework is outlined in the constitution and elaborated in laws detailing the procedural norms for each court.

Courts of General Jurisdiction

Most cases are heard by the courts of general jurisdiction. These courts have jurisdiction over all cases involving physical persons, including criminal cases, labor disputes, family law issues, housing disputes, and consumer complaints. This system is organized hierarchically. Most cases begin in the district courts, which are located in each rural or urban district. Cases can be appealed, though the names given to these appellate courts vary across the country. More serious civil and criminal cases are heard for the first time by these appellate courts. Depending on the subject matter and seriousness of the cases, they are heard either by a judge and two lay asses-

sors or by a three-judge panel. Military tribunals hear cases involving servicemen and certain crimes that raise national security concerns, as specified by legislation. The decisions of these tribunals can be appealed to appellate military courts. The court of last resort for military-related cases as well as all other cases within this system is the Supreme Court of the Russian Federation. As of 2001, there were more than fifteen thousand judges within the hierarchy of the courts of general jurisdiction.

The Supreme Court is made up of 111 judges, divided into three panels that focus on civil cases, criminal cases, and military matters (see figure). This court has two basic functions. Its primary task is to supervise the activities of the lower courts. As such, it reviews judgments of individual cases at the request of litigants. It also exercises supervisory review, which is initiated by the procurator general or the chairman or deputy chairmen of the Supreme Court. Its second function is to oversee the general development of judicial practice. To that end, it periodically issues guiding explanations of legislation that has been interpreted in contradictory fashion by lower courts and occasionally uses its right of legislative initiative to submit draft laws to the legislature.

The rules governing the operations of the courts of general jurisdiction are set forth in the procedural codes (civil, criminal, and military). The legislature has been working on revising these codes since the late 1980s. It has proven more difficult for the legislators to come to a consensus on the procedural law than on the underlying substantive law. The criminal procedure code has proven particularly perplexing, with reformers pushing for greater controls on the police and the procuracy, while others defend the status quo. Most criminal cases are heard by a judge and two lay assessors, though an experiment with jury trials for the most serious cases (especially, in practice, aggravated murders) has been under way in nine regions since 1993. Jury trials tend to be adversarial, with a more central role for lawyers than is the case in nonjury trials, in which the old-style inquisitorialism persists.

The procedural codes establish strict timetables for resolving civil and criminal cases. Civil cases are to be resolved within ten days of the commencement of the trial. In criminal cases, judges have fourteen days after receiving the case from the procurator to decide whether to proceed to trial, and they must proceed to trial within fourteen days thereafter. The popular news media is rife with accounts of delays in the courts of general jurisdiction. The reality, however, is more complicated. In comparative perspective, the Russian courts are not unduly sluggish, and the perception of high delay rates is due in no small part to the unrealistic deadlines established in the procedural codes. Criminal defendants are understandably disgruntled by the often lengthy pretrial investigation, during which most are detained by the state.

Legal Structure of Russian Courts

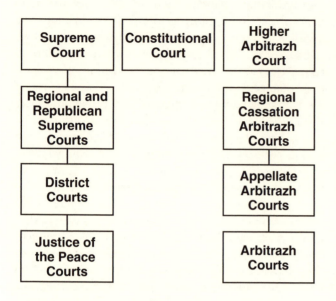

The living conditions for these pretrial detainees are horrific in many parts of Russia.

Those responsible for investigating alleged crimes are not considered neutral, but are part of the prosecutorial team. These investigators are keen to maintain a high rate of solved cases, which tends to bring an accusatorial bias into the criminal system. An effort was made to ameliorate this dilemma in 1990 by introducing a right to counsel for the accused within twenty-four hours of arrest, and allowing defense counsel to participate in the pretrial process at other key moments. The actual impact of this apparently significant reform has been undermined by the lack of competent defense counsel and by the persisting limits on the rights of such counsel.

In an effort to relieve the burden on trial courts and to get cases resolved more quickly, legislation was adopted in 1998 to create justice of the peace courts. These courts, which took their inspiration from an analogous czarist institution, will gradually assume responsibility for all administrative offenses: simple civil disputes and criminal cases that involve charges that could bring no more than two years' imprisonment. The decisions of these courts can be appealed to the district courts. Precisely how these justice of the peace courts will operate in practice is not yet entirely clear. Each subject of the Russian Federation has to make an independent decision about introducing these courts by passing legislation and making budgetary commitments. Legal officials anticipated that, by the end of 2001, approximately forty-five hundred justice of the peace courts would be operational.

Constitutional Court

The Constitutional Court was first established in 1991, and it was modeled on the German Federal Constitu-

tional Court. In the first few years of its existence, it became embroiled in a series of controversial and highly politicized cases that tended to undermine its effectiveness as an independent institution. In the clash between the executive and legislative branches that culminated in the dismissal of the legislature by President Yeltsin in September 1993, a majority of the Constitutional Court sided with the legislators. Yeltsin responded by suspending the activities of the court. The court was given new life, however, by the constitution that was approved by popular referendum in December 1993. In the subsequent legislation that laid out the powers of this court, an effort was made to limit its ability to become entangled in political questions.

The Constitutional Court consists of nineteen judges appointed by the president and confirmed by the upper house of the legislature (the Federation Council). The judges are divided into two panels of nine and ten judges, though they sit in plenary session when issuing advisory opinions and for certain other matters. In terms of their background, they diverge from the judges of the courts of the general jurisdiction and the *arbitrazh* courts. The judges of the Constitutional Court are drawn from the top ranks of legal scholars and come to the bench only after several decades of working in universities or research institutes.

The Constitutional Court has jurisdiction over four categories of cases. First, the court is charged with abstract review of the constitutionality of federal laws and other normative acts of the executive and legislative organs of power. Such claims may be initiated by the president, by any member of the legislature, by the government, the Supreme Court, the Higher *Arbitrazh* Court, the lower house of the legislature (the Duma), or by one-fifth of the members of the upper house of the legislature (the Federation Council). Second, the court hears cases involving concrete complaints of violations of constitutional rights by individuals and legal entities. The court also hears questions raising constitutional issues that are referred by the courts of general jurisdiction and the *arbitrazh* courts. There is no requirement that the complainant exhaust all other remedies before appealing to the Constitutional Court. Third, the court has jurisdiction over disputes between the subjects of the federation. Fourth, the court is required to respond to requests from organs of the executive or legislative branch for interpretations of various aspects of the constitution.

Arbitrazh Courts

Economic disputes involving economic entities are within the jurisdiction of the *arbitrazh* courts. These are the successor to the Soviet institution of state *arbitrazh*, which was an administrative agency charged with resolving disputes among state-owned enterprises. The legalization of private property and the introduction of new legal mechanisms for doing business, such as joint-stock companies and limited liability companies, exposed the limitations of state *arbitrazh*. In response, in 1991 the *arbitrazh* courts were created on the foundation of state *arbitrazh*. The decision makers, known as arbiters, were renamed judges, thereby enhancing their status. As of 2001, there were approximately twenty-five hundred judges within the *arbitrazh* court system. The *arbitrazh* courts have jurisdiction over three categories of cases: disputes between legal entities, disputes between legal entities and the state, and bankruptcy.

In their day-to-day operations, *arbitrazh* courts represent a hybrid of inquisitorial civil law procedures and the more informal norms of arbitration. Although the procedural code, adopted in 1995, calls for litigants to take responsibility for proving their claims, suggesting a move toward a more adversarial system, judges continue to dominate the proceedings. Evidence must be submitted in documentary form, though litigants may provide oral explanations. In the first decade of their existence, the docket of the *arbitrazh* courts has been dominated by debt-collection cases. Following the amendment of the bankruptcy law in 1998, bankruptcy petitions increased dramatically.

Each subject (or subunit) of the Russian Federation has an *arbitrazh* court. All cases originate at this trial level. Most cases are heard by a single judge, though exceptions are made for bankruptcy and cases involving the state as a party, which are heard by a three-judge panel. If either party is dissatisfied with the result at trial, they can appeal. The first level of appeal, known as the appellate instance, is a de novo review, heard by a three-judge panel. The procedural code establishes a strict timetable for processing cases, allowing two months at trial and one month on appeal. The second level of appeal, which is limited to legal error, is to the cassation courts. There are ten cassation courts, organized on a regional basis. The final and ultimate appeal for any *arbitrazh* case is to the Higher *Arbitrazh* Court. In addition to hearing appeals, this court has the right of abstract review and routinely issues interpretations of legislation and administrative regulations that are binding on the *arbitrazh* courts. At present, twenty-two judges sit on the Higher *Arbitrazh* Court.

Private Arbitration

With the consent of the parties, economic disputes may be submitted to private arbitration tribunals. The best known of these tribunals is the International Commercial Arbitration Court, which is located in Moscow and is affiliated with the Chamber of Commerce and Industry of the Russian Federation. There are private arbitration tribunals located in many other Russian cities. They are cre-

ated and thrive in locales in which the demand for dispute resolution services is high and where specialists are available to serve as arbiters. Those who serve as arbiters tend to be off-duty *arbitrazh* court judges, professors, or lawyers. Russian law mandates that the state court system enforce the decisions of private arbitration tribunals, if necessary. Russia has ratified the UN Convention on the Recognition and Enforcement of Foreign Arbitral Awards (the "New York Convention"). In practice, the Russian courts have a mixed record on enforcing arbitration awards, both domestic and foreign.

STAFFING

Legal Education

Students are admitted to the study of law after completion of secondary education. The popularity of legal education has grown dramatically in the post-Soviet era, and the number of institutions offering programs leading to a law degree has multiplied accordingly. Decisions about admission are based on the results of entry exams and the record in secondary school. Russian legal education is composed of five years of course work. Traditionally, lectures devoted to the codes have been the primary method of instruction, though recent years have brought more emphasis on judicial decisions. Beginning in the fourth year, students can specialize in preparation for careers in criminal or civil law.

Lawyers

Russia has a divided legal profession. The basic choices for graduates of law faculties are: trial lawyer (*advokat*), in-house lawyer for an enterprise (*iuriskonsul't*), prosecutor (*prokuror*), and judge (*sud'ya*). Each group has its own professional organization; there is no umbrella bar association that encompasses all these groups.

The opportunities available to lawyers have expanded in the wake of the Soviet Union. Those interested in working as private attorneys can practice on their own, join law firms, or work in-house for enterprises. During the Soviet era, private law firms were forbidden. Those interested in becoming trial lawyers had to join *kollegiya*, which were regulated by the Ministry of Justice. The number of *advokaty* was artificially limited, and admission to a *kollegiya* often depended on political connections. The primary function of *advokaty* was to defend those accused of crimes, though citizens had the right to request legal assistance on other matters. The *kollegiya* still exist in present-day Russia, though they no longer hold a monopoly on the provision of legal services to Russians. *Advokaty* may choose to join a *kollegiya*, to join a private law firm, or to create their own firm. The range of specialties is much broader. Although some firms continue to specialize in criminal defense work, a thriving business-law practice has also begun to develop, particularly in the larger cities.

Another option for lawyers is to work in-house for a specific company. Many Russian enterprises have legal departments staffed by lawyers, known as *iuriskonsul'ty*. Traditionally, in-house legal departments are dominated by women, which indicates the relatively low status of lawyers within enterprises. As a rule, management relies on the legal staff to provide technical advice about the legality of contracts, but does not seek advice from these in-house lawyers about the prudence of the underlying transaction. *Iuriskonsul'ty* represent their companies in both the courts of general jurisdiction and *arbitrazh* courts.

Procuracy

One potent legacy of the Soviet era is the procuracy, which is charged with supervising the operation of law throughout the country. The best known function of this agency is the prosecution of criminal defendants, but its jurisdiction extends to civil law as well. The procuracy is organized on a hierarchical basis, with offices in each of the subjects of the Russian Federation. It is headed by the procurator general, who is appointed by the president for a five-year term, subject to confirmation by the upper house of the legislature (the Federation Council). It is staffed by lawyers who enjoy broad discretion to bring claims in both courts of general jurisdiction and *arbitrazh* courts when such actions are deemed necessary to protect state and public interests.

Judges

The system of selecting judges has undergone dramatic changes since the Soviet era, when the Communist Party thoroughly dominated this process. The 1993 Constitution provides that judges be appointed by the president. Appointments to the three courts of last resort—the Constitutional Court, the Supreme Court, and the Higher *Arbitrazh* Court—must be confirmed by the Federation Council. Candidates for the Supreme Court and the Higher *Arbitrazh* Court tend to be drawn from the ranks of the professional judiciary. By contrast, the judges of the Constitutional Court are drawn from the top ranks of legal scholars and generally come to the bench only after several decades of working in universities or research institutes. All candidates must be at least forty years of age and have at least fifteen years' experience.

Appointments to lower courts are also made by the president, though with considerable input from others. Beginning in 1997, all candidates have had to be endorsed by a judicial qualification commission and confirmed by the regional legislature before having their names submitted to the Supreme Court or the Higher *Arbitrazh* Court (depending on the nature of the appointment) for approval. Only at that point are the candidates' names forwarded to the president. All candidates for the judiciary must be at least twenty-five years of age. They must also have completed higher legal education and have at least five years' experience. Because the courts are poorly funded and judges are held in relatively low esteem, it has proven difficult to recruit a sufficient number of new judges. As in other civil law systems, the Russian judiciary is structured along a civil service model in which becoming a judge is regarded as a career choice. The typical candidate for the courts of general jurisdiction is a woman who has graduated from a night school or obtained her degree through a correspondence program. The *arbitrazh* courts tend to recruit from the legal departments of industrial enterprises, because these lawyers have relevant experience.

As of 1992, the law required that all Russian judges be appointed with life tenure, with no mandatory retirement age. Prior to that, judges were appointed for ten-year terms. As those terms have expired, some of these judges have been reappointed with life tenure. Judges can be removed for cause by the judicial qualification commission, though that happens rarely.

Bailiffs

Both judges and litigants have long been dissatisfied with the process for enforcing judgments that are not satisfied voluntarily by the parties. Complaints have persisted that winning at trial was a hollow victory because of the difficulty and sometimes impossibility of collecting on the judgment. The responsibility for assisting in the enforcement of the judgments of the courts of general jurisdiction and the *arbitrazh* court resides with the bailiff (*sudebnye pristavy*) service. This institution was completely reformed in 1998, and it is now within the hierarchy of the Ministry of Justice. The powers of bailiffs to go after the assets of the loser at trial have been clarified and enhanced. The bulk of the requests for assistance directed to the bailiffs are generated by family law disputes—for example, alimony and child support. Only a small percentage of the bailiffs' work revolves around commercial disputes that originate in the *arbitrazh* courts. Whether the changes made to the bailiff service will have the desired result of making it easier to collect on judgments remains to be seen.

The 1999 reforms assigned a new function to the bailiff service. Bailiffs are now charged with providing security services to the courts. Those working in this branch of the bailiff service carry guns. Violence directed at judges by litigants dissatisfied with the outcome of cases in which they were involved was the impetus for creating armed bailiffs. Neither type of bailiff is required to have completed higher legal education.

Kathryn Hendley

See also Inquisitorial Procedure; Judicial Review; Judicial Selection, Methods of; Legal Professionals—Civil Law Traditions; Soviet System; Trial Courts

References and further reading
Butler, W. E. 1999. *Russian Law.* Oxford: Oxford University Press.
Danilenko, Gennady M., and William Burnham. 1999. *Law and Legal System of the Russian Federation.* Juris Publishing.
Ledeneva, Alena V., and Marina Kurkchiyan. 2000. *Economic Crime in Russia.* London: Kluwer Law International.
Maggs, Peter B., ed. and trans. 1997. *The Civil Code of the Russian Federation, Parts 1 and 2.* Moscow: International Centre for Financial and Economic Development.
Murrell, Peter, ed. 2001. *Assessing the Value of Law in Transition Economies.* Ann Arbor: University of Michigan Press.
Sachs, Jeffrey D., and Katharina Pistor, eds. 1997. *The Rule of Law and Economic Reform in Russia.* Boulder, CO: Westview Press.
Sharlet, Jeffrey D. 2001. *Constitutional Politics in Russia.* Armonk, NY: M. E. Sharpe.
Solomon, Peter H., Jr., and Todd S. Foglesong. 2000. *Courts and Transition in Russia.* Boulder, CO: Westview Press.

RWANDA

GENERAL INFORMATION

Rwanda is located between Uganda in the north, Tanzania in the east, Burundi in the south, and the Congo in the west. It has an area of 26,338 square kilometers and around 7,500,000 inhabitants. Rwandans are divided into three ethnic or social groups that have distinct cultures, languages, and social practices: the Hutu (85 percent), Tutsi (14 percent), and Twa (1 percent). The capital is Kigali. The official languages are Kinyarwanda, French, and English. The latter two are spoken by a small minority of the educated population.

Beginning in 1895, Rwanda was a German protectorate. The peace treaty signed at Versailles in 1919, and particularly a decision of the League of Nations in 1922, brought Rwandan territory under Belgian mandate.

The traditional indigenous administration was carried out by a hereditary king from the Tutsi clan of the Banyiginyas, which was overthrown in 1959. A republic was proclaimed in January 1961 and confirmed by referendum in September that year. The Hutu and the Tutsi clashed over ethnic differences. Some of the Tutsi were forced to leave the country and find refuge in neighboring countries.

The refugee issue was never addressed, with the effect that former refugees from the Ugandan army led an armed attack against the government of Rwanda in October 1990. Despite the Arusha peace accords in 1993, the death of President Habyarimana in April 1994 was followed by the genocide of the Tutsi and the massacre of Hutu opponents. This tragedy resulted in the death of more than a million people and a massive exodus of the surviving population to bordering countries.

In November 1994, the UN Security Council created an International Criminal Tribunal for Rwanda to judge the serious violations of international humanitarian rights committed in Rwanda and the neighboring countries between January 1 and December 31, 1994. Presently forty-four people are detained in Arusha and are being prosecuted for genocide and crimes against humanity. The tribunal applies Rwandan law to determine punishment and common law for procedures.

EVOLUTION OF A PLURALIST LEGAL SYSTEM

Legal pluralism is undoubtedly the most striking characteristic of Rwandan law. It originated during the period of Belgian administration and was instituted into law to permit an opening in society toward new rules. The population, which was more than 90 percent rural, continued to apply traditional laws that were better known, better understood, and still capable of governing social interactions. Leadership reverted to the magistrate, whose mission was to develop the traditional law in accordance with new exigencies and mentalities, with respect to universal public order and the laws (Lamy 1960).

Article 4 from the law of October 18, 1908, provided:

The unnaturalized indigenous citizens of [Congo] enjoy civil rights that are recognized by the colonial legislation and by their own customs so long as the latter are not contrary to the legislation nor to public order. (Law of October 18, 1908, from the Belgian Government of the Congo, October 19–20, 1908, 5887–5894. This law was rendered applicable to Ruanda-Urundi by virtue of Article 1 of the law of August 21, 1925, from the Ruanda-Urundi government)

Thus, unlike France, Belgium didn't impose its own civil code in Rwanda; it adopted a colonial code elaborated by an ad hoc commission that was assumed to be better suited to the desires of the local populace. In civil and commercial matters, the ordinance of the general administrator of the Congo of May 14, 1886, provided that "when the matter isn't foreseen by a decree, an order or an ordinance already promulgated, the disputes that fall under the purview of the tribunals of [Congo] will be judged according to local customs, general principles of the law and equity" (*Bulletin Officiel,* 1886, 188). In penal matters, only the imported law could apply, but the customary jurisdictions could try standard offenses and impose sentences of up to a month in penal servitude. Belgian authorities counted on the eventual decline of customary law resulting from sociocultural contacts and evolving practices.

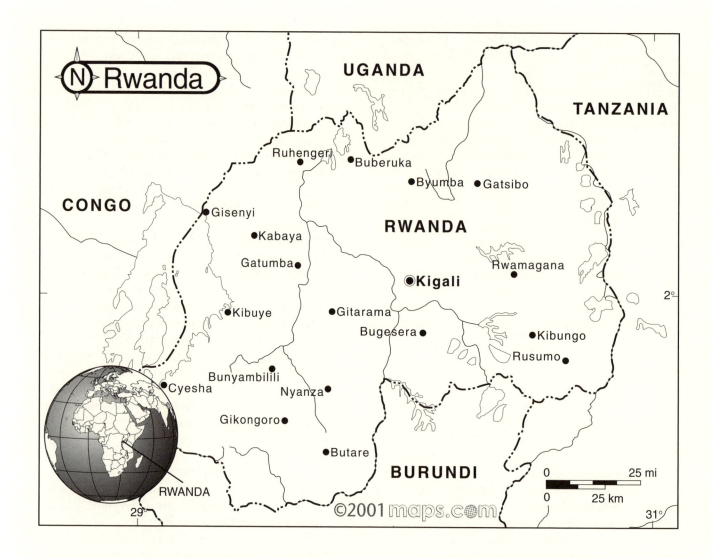

Rwandan law currently consists of traditional oral law and written law, principally of Roman-Germanic origin, containing rules issued from common law, which were introduced beginning in 1996, notably in the Law of August 30, 1996, governing the legal proceedings of genocidal crimes.

To avoid conflicts between applicable rules, the Rwandan Constitution sanctioned the enforcement of legal provisions from the period of Belgian rule and established the primacy of the constitution over the laws and of written law over traditional law. Article 98 of the Rwandan Constitution provides: "Customs remain applicable only in as much as they have not been replaced by a law and are not contrary in any way to the Constitution, the laws, the regulations, public order and proper standards."

This principle doesn't seem consistent in practice. As R. David has argued, populations continue to live according to their traditional way of life without caring about the body of artificial laws imposed by legislators (1973, 32). The practices of the populace correspond "to the economic needs, the religion, the standards of the people whose legal relationships it must govern" (Solus 1927, 232).

THE THREE LEGAL BRANCHES OF RWANDAN LAW

The Traditional Legal System

Customary Rwandan law consists of a group of continued practices, respected by the Rwandans as social necessities and considered by them as having binding force. Custom primarily influences family law, property law, and inheritances and gifts. Some principles based on custom are also found in arbitral decisions and in penal and commercial matters.

An Oral Legal System Derived from Common Practices

In general, traditional law is preceded by a long period of acceptance by the population concerned before being made compulsory. In fact, an element becomes a rule only inasmuch as feelings of obligation and constraint are likely to ensue. The public must be convinced that every other type of conduct goes against the commonly accepted rule and could lead to punishment. It is the manifestation of the desire for better societal organization that results in the adoption of a new rule.

The source of customary Rwandan law, however, is equally found in the decrees and rulings of traditional authorities, which were later prescribed as bills and applied by traditional jurisdictions. The decisions of traditional authorities, pronounced solemnly and publicly, were transmitted orally from generation to generation. Even if these decisions arose from an isolated incident, they were meant to correct or guide social behavior, to create new institutions, or to confirm existing, but noncompulsory, deeds. The decreed rule was integrated with the practices of the populace.

Many examples of decrees (*iteka*) introduced by decision of the king (*Mwami*) can be cited, notably the introduction of the five-day week, the keeping of the sacred fire in the court and the use of the drum emblem *Kalinga* as an ensign of the country, and the suspension of the contract of pastoral serfdom (*ubuhake*). The Belgian trusteeship forced the king of Rwanda to submit drafts of the decrees to the Supreme Council of the country before they were adopted.

Traditional law originated equally from decisions of the customary courts in Ruanda-Urundi and from instances in which courts of written law affected traditional law by creating new rules or forbidding traditional behavior (Sohier 1953). Several examples of decisions made this way can be noted, particularly the prohibition of marriage by abduction (1949), the grant of part of inheritances to girls (1954), and the prohibition of usurious interest, which was thought to undermine universal public order. These decisions were gradually adopted by the traditional courts in the same way that customary laws were brought about by the people's practices.

A Traditional Law with an Uncommon Philosophy
Unlike Western law, traditional law isn't a discipline distinct from religion, morality, and other mechanisms of social control. Traditional law differs from Western law in terms of its philosophy, creation, application, and purpose.

The rights of each person are determined according to the responsibilities that person assumes in the group. Moreover, these rights are not established definitively—the protection of the individual is sometimes superseded by the need to maintain group cohesion. The rule of law often bends before imperatives of collective security. The feeling of belonging to a group and the somewhat magic hold it has over each of its members attenuate individual claims to a certain extent.

Traditional law is conciliatory in essence. Rwandans fear the law, because it doesn't allow conflicts to be settled but instead maintains them. Thus bringing someone before the courts constitutes a serious injury to his social standing and to the position of his family, because it is interpreted as refusing the principle of conciliation. Instead of leading to social harmony, it crystallizes positions, and

gives each a right to assert himself against his social group, his family, or his state. It equally perpetuates the resentments of disputing parties by declaring a winner and a loser and by placing limitations on the damages that can be claimed.

Traditional law continues to change. It has evolved a lot, notably because of the introduction of Christianity, European education and culture, and the development of a new form of social advancement independent of birth status. Lemarchand perfectly summarizes this new situation in these terms:

> As long as the place of an individual in society was wholly determined by the strength, or vagaries, of a strictly personal relationship, one could hardly conceive of individual rights, only economy and concurrent growth of the cash nexus. With the spread of Christian ethics and the internalisation of egalitarian values, a new situation was engendered that brought about a reversal of conditional roles. As the stratification system became more fluid and diversified, as new social groupings emerged, status became increasingly dissociated from authority. For the old corporate categories of patrons and clients were substituted new social aggregates based on personal achievement; growing numbers of individuals came to be identified not only as patrons or clients but also as clerks, catechists, carpenters, innkeepers, traders, etc. (Lemarchand 1970, 127)

Customary law also governs property law. The system of appropriation, management, and development of rural lands remains subject to custom. The settlement of minor disagreements is not submitted to the tribunals but to the traditional Gacaca system, where the head of the family or a local wise man decides matters, relying on custom. These matters of inheritance, matrimonial estates, and gifts, regarding which the law was passed only in November 1999, continue to follow customary law in practice. The population prefers amicable solutions to legal battles, which are often slow and which risk incurring enmity.

The unification and codification of Rwandan law were part of the movement for global modernization, and the establishment of a uniform law was considered an important part of national integration. Legal pluralism, as created by colonial powers, was perceived as discriminatory because the same laws weren't applicable to all citizens. Europeans and naturalized citizens followed the written law, while the rest of the indigenous people followed their customary laws.

At the outset certain leaders wanted to introduce a truly national law, at the core of which elements of popular law would be retained and integrated, but the desire for modernization and a rupture with the past resulted in the pure and simple suppression of popular law and its replacement with a modern legal system.

Western-Inspired Laws

The laws currently in force are drawn principally from Belgian law, but since the seizure of power by native peoples of Uganda, common law has been progressively introduced, notably in legal proceedings. Hence the Law of August 30, 1996, related to the pursuit of genocidal offenses and crimes against humanity, and has introduced systems of guilty or not-guilty pleas, counterinterrogation of witnesses, and limited appeal.

The Law: Principal Source of Rwandan Rights

"The law governs all matters that relate to the letter or spirit of its provisions" (Civil Code, book I, article 3). Adopted rules were drawn from the Roman-Germanic legal family, notably from Belgian and French legislation in civil and criminal matters, and from common law since 1996.

The right to propose legislation belongs to the government, the president of the republic, and the deputies. Bills drawn up by the government and members of Parliament are submitted to the National Assembly, which debates and adopts them. Bills that are passed are then submitted to the Constitutional Court, one of the six branches of the Supreme Court, which rules on their constitutionality. A law that is declared to conform to the constitution is submitted to the president of the republic for signature and proclamation. A law declared unconstitutional is returned to the Parliament for a second examination. It also must return to the Constitutional Court for a new investigation. In principle, the laws are not retroactive—they apply only to future situations. (The law of September 30, 1996, relating to the repression of genocide was declared retroactive for crimes back to October 1, 1990. The crimes committed were so serious that the legislature considered it worth the exception.)

In civil law, the rights of individuals and families are regulated by the laws of October 27, 1988, and November 15, 1999 (Law No. 42/1988 of October 27, 1988, J.O., 1989, p. 9; and Law No. 22/99 of November 12, 1999, related to inheritances, matrimonial estates, and gifts ["libéralités"], J.O., no. 22 of November 15, 1999). The law of October 27 organizes matters of individuals and family relations: personal identification (name, domicile, residency, civil status); registration of family relationships (marriage, filiation, adoption, divorce); and declarations of unfitness. The law of November 15, 1999, relates to matrimonial estates, inheritances, and gifts. This law establishes the joint estate of married couples as a legal estate and determines temporary measures for people who haven't formally settled their estate. Rights of inheritance sanction the principle of bilineal

consanguinity, a principle unknown in Rwandan custom, and give women the right to inherit their husbands' estates. Property law and contract law are vestiges from Belgian rule. Written law applicable in urban areas recognizes property rights, but such areas cover only a tenth of the national territory. Traditional law governs real estate in rural areas but doesn't guarantee a veritable property right, and eviction of property holders in the general interest doesn't require the state to issue a formal expropriation.

The law governs all matters of public policy (revision of the fundamental law ["Loi fondamentale"] of May 6, 1995, J.O., 1995, p. 3). Fundamental law organizes institutions. It comprises the Constitution of June 10, 1991; the Arusha peace accords of August 4, 1993, the Declaration of the Rwandan Patriotic Front of July 17, 1994; and the accords treaty between political forces on the establishment of national institutions of November 24, 1994. Administrative matters are equally governed by different provisions organizing public services. Fiscal law governs all kinds of taxes: individual income and corporate income taxes, sales tax, the minimum personal contribution (*contribution personnelle minimum*), value-added tax, and so forth. Criminal matters are regulated entirely by written laws. They include the penal code (Decree-law No. 21/77 of August 18, 1977, related to penal code, J.O., 1978, p. 1), criminal procedure (Law of February 23, 1963, related to the Criminal Procedure Code, J.O., 1963, p. 98), and law related to pursuing offenses constituting crimes of genocide and crimes against humanity (Organic law ["Loi organique"] of August 30, 1996, organizing pursuit of crimes of genocide and crimes against humanity, J.O., 1996, p. 3). This legislation sets out criteria for determining offenses, organizes pursuit procedures in the courts and tribunals, and determines punishments and their execution. Labor law and social security are organized by a law.

Jurisprudential Source

The place of jurisprudence and doctrine among sources of Rwandan law is defined by the law: "In default of an applicable legal disposition, the judge will rule according to customary law, and in default of a custom, according to the rules that he would establish if he were to legislate an act. He follows the remedies consecrated by doctrine and jurisprudence" (Law of October 27, 1988, related to the preliminary title and first book in Civil Code, Article 3, paragraph 2).

But jurisprudence, understood as a group of rules issuing from constant and unanimous decisions of Rwandan courts, is little known. It is not impossible to encounter contradictory decisions made under the same jurisdiction in similar cases. Decisions are not published. The judgments of the Cassation Court (Cour de Cassation) from 1982 to 1990 are the only ones that have been published in a casebook. Some court and tribunal judgments were published in the *Rwandan Judicial Review* (*Revue Juridique du Rwanda*) between 1977 and 1994. (The Rwandan Judicial Review has been out of print since 1994. The law faculty started the *Scientific Review of Law* [*Revue Scientifique de Droit*], which has slowly become the same publication.) The role of jurisprudence is still negligible in sources of Rwandan law.

General Principles
General principles of law are equally a source of Rwandan law. But they are little known and infrequently utilized by law practitioners.

Doctrine
During the period of Belgian rule, several works and articles were published on colonial law and custom by the magistrates and officers of the Belgian colonial administration. At the time of independence, the Belgian administration had not trained a single jurist. Up until 1977, Rwanda counted fewer than ten bachelors of law educated in Belgium working in Rwandan institutions. The Rwandan Judicial Review published court decisions accompanied by analyses and commentaries, as well as articles on doctrine. Law practitioners equally referred to Belgian and French doctrine.

THE RWANDAN COURT SYSTEM

Jurisdictions of the Judiciary
The fundamental law establishes several principles to guarantee the proper functioning of justice. It recognizes the separation of powers: "[J]udiciary power is exercised by the courts and tribunals and other jurisdictions; it is independent of legislative and executive powers" (Arusha peace treaty, 1993, Protocole sur le partage du Pouvoir, Arts. 25 and 27; Constitution of June 10, 1991, Article 87). The Supreme Court is the guarantor of this independence. The status of judiciary personnel and that of the Supreme Council of Magistrates (Conseil Supérieur de la Magistrature) are defined in law.

In performing their duties, magistrates of the bench are independent of executive and legislative power. In sovereign fashion they evaluate cases that are submitted to them and decide their outcomes in total independence (Art. 37, Statut du personnel judiciaire). But the law does not sanction the principle of nomination for life, nor that of irremovability. Except for the magistrates holding high responsibilities in the Supreme Court, named by the government and Parliament, nomination is made by the Supreme Court in consultation with the Supreme Council of Magistrates. But political and other types of pressure can have influence.

Decisions are collegial. Dissenting opinions are unknown. The bench system is known exceptionally for issuing sentences of preventive detention and provisional decisions (*décision en référé*). All hearings and rulings are public. The right to defense is guaranteed, but only those who can afford a lawyer are defended. An order of lawyers was created in 1997; forty lawyers took the oath on August 30, 1997. The high number of people being tried prevents all from being assisted and defended. Only the right to be heard before final sentencing remains. The right of appeal is recognized within limits defined by law.

The judiciary structure (Code d'organisation et compétence judiciaires, 1980, J.O., no. 16, bis, p. 1, as modified to the current day) is made up of the following elements. A Supreme Court comprises six sections: the Court of Cassation, the Constitutional Court, the Audit Office, the Council of State, the Department of Courts and Tribunals, and the Department of Gacacan Courts.

The Court of Cassation reviews appeals against last-degree decisions, rulings of judges, and decisions in criminal matters for people who constitutionally have the privilege of jurisdiction. Appeals before convened Supreme Court sections may be filed against first-resort penal decisions from the Court of Cassation. The Audit Office presides over the accounts for all public services. The Department of Courts and Tribunals manages magistrates' careers: recruitment, promotions, and inspections of courts and tribunals. The Council of State rules on petitions for the annulment of administrative acts that contain illegal provisions, supervises the regularity of elections, and rules on institutional conflicts.

There are four appellate courts (Kigali, Ruhengeri, Nyabisindu, and Cyangugu). The Court of Cassation rules on appeals against first-resort decisions rendered by the courts of first instance, appeals of arbitrational sentences, and lawsuits for miscarriage of justice against magistrates from lower jurisdictions. It tries fiscal disputes to the first degree.

The country's twelve courts of first instance hear all civil suits that the law doesn't ascribe to other jurisdictions. They have a general authority. They notably rule on appeals against the decisions of canton tribunals, proceedings to enforce judgments rendered by judges, and legal instruments drawn by foreign authorities. In criminal matters, the court of first instance tries crimes and misdemeanors, appeals against the rulings of canton courts, and all actions that the law doesn't ascribe to another jurisdiction.

In civil matters, the canton court tries cases in which the value doesn't exceed 50,000 Rwandan francs, and cases related to unregistered buildings (on land subject to customary law) regardless of value. The canton court is unauthorized to rule on actions involving the state and those involving the legal competency of individuals, claims of an

Structure of Rwandan Courts

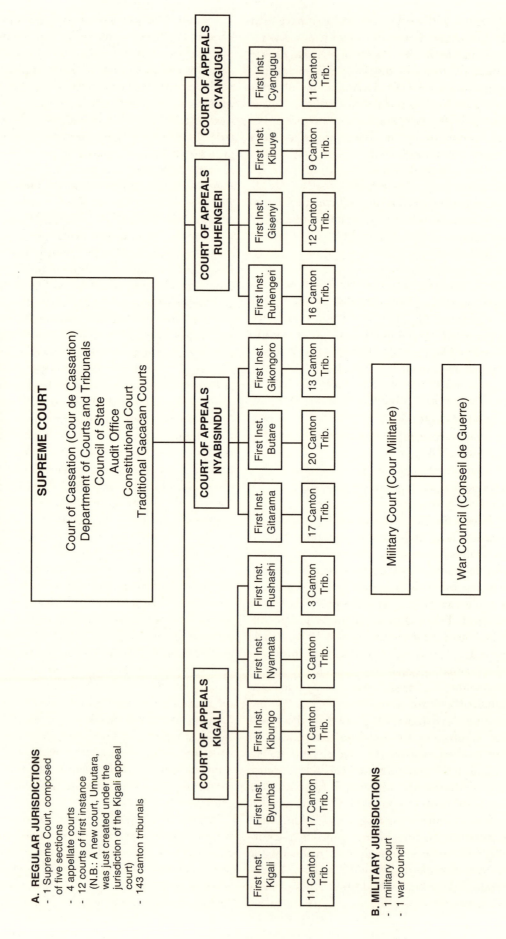

A. REGULAR JURISDICTIONS
- 1 Supreme Court, composed of five sections
- 4 appellate courts
- 12 courts of first instance (N.B.: A new court, Umutara, was just created under the jurisdiction of the Kigali appeal court)
- 143 canton tribunals

SUPREME COURT

Court of Cassation (Cour de Cassation)
Department of Courts and Tribunals
Council of State
Audit Office
Constitutional Court
Traditional Gacacan Courts

COURT OF APPEALS KIGALI

First Inst. Kigali — 11 Canton Trib.

First Inst. Byumba — 17 Canton Trib.

First Inst. Kibungo — 11 Canton Trib.

First Inst. Nyamata — 3 Canton Trib.

First Inst. Rushashi — 3 Canton Trib.

COURT OF APPEALS NYABISINDU

First Inst. Gitarama — 17 Canton Trib.

First Inst. Butare — 20 Canton Trib.

First Inst. Gikongoro — 13 Canton Trib.

COURT OF APPEALS RUHENGERI

First Inst. Ruhengeri — 16 Canton Trib.

First Inst. Gisenyi — 12 Canton Trib.

First Inst. Kibuye — 9 Canton Trib.

COURT OF APPEALS CYANGUGU

First Inst. Cyangugu — 11 Canton Trib.

B. MILITARY JURISDICTIONS
- 1 military court
- 1 war council

Military Court (Cour Militaire)

War Council (Conseil de Guerre)

indeterminate value, and actions in reparation of damages caused by an offense that isn't within its governance. There are 143 district tribunals. In criminal matters the canton court tries minor offenses and misdemeanors.

Military jurisdictions include the War Council and the military court. The War Council presides over all offenses committed by soldiers, noncommissioned officers, and officers up to the rank of captain. The military court tries in first-resort offenses committed on all national territory by superior officers from the major guard up. It equally tries appeals against judgments issued by the War Council. Suits against general officers are in the jursidiction of the Court of Cassation, which tries them in first resort.

The Department of the Public Prosecutor's Office (Ministère Public), directed by the attorney general (Ministère de la Justice), comprises a general office attached to the Supreme Court, four general offices in the four appellate courts, and twelve republic offices in the courts of first instance. An officer of the Criminal Investigation Department (Police Judiciaire) performs the functions of the public prosecutor in the canton courts. The public prosecutor for the military courts is overseen by the defense minister.

The Gacacan (or People's) Courts

The Gacacan courts represent an innovation. Rwanda has ten thousand courts. The term *Gacaca* stems from an old tradition of conciliatory justice central to families. It has been institutionalized to judge the crimes of genocide and crimes against humanity.

The law, passed on October 12, 2000, organizes the Gacacan courts. The public participates directly in the proceedings. Only suspects in the first category of criminals—that is, the planners and promoters of genocide—are judged in the first degree by the Court of First Instance. Other offenses related to crimes against humanity fall under the authority of popular jurisdiction. Some ten thousand new courts are going to be created, with nineteen judges each.

Organization and Procedures of the Gacaca

The Gacacan courts comprise four levels: cell, sector, district, and province. A Department of Gacacan Courts in the Supreme Court coordinates Gacacan activities and oversees their internal regulation.

Within a cell, the basic administrative unit comprising around fifty households, nineteen judges are elected from among those who are at least eighteen years old (Rwanda has some 9,104 cells). The electees form a coordinating committee composed of five people, who in turn elect a president and two secretaries who know how to read and write Kinyarwanda (the language spoken by all Rwandans). Educational background is not taken into consideration.

Each lower administrative level elects five more people to represent it in the assembly of the level directly above, who will constitute its seat. This is how the seats of sectors, districts, and provinces are constituted.

Jurisdiction of Gacacan Courts

Contrary to traditional Gacaca, the new courts judge in strict accordance with the law. They must hear witnesses, qualify offenses and definitively determine the category in which the accused should be classed, decide on the transfer of cases to relevant jurisdictions, and rule on offenses within their authority. Classification has consequences related to the penalties that are imposed.

The Gacacan courts are authorized to judge perpetrators, accessories or accomplices in murders or serious assaults leading to death, those guilty of serious assaults, and the perpetrators of attacks against property.

In principle, part of the punishment is spent in prison; the other part is spent in community service. People who are classified in the fourth category are sentenced only to remedy the damage caused. Judgments are in principle open to appeal before the court directly superior, except in cases in which the law excludes any possibility of appeal.

THE TRAINING OF JURISTS AND MAGISTRATES

To fill the void left by the death or exile of magistrates in 1994, a three-month training for future magistral candidates was administered by the Belgian association Réseau de Citoyens (Citizens' Network) in collaboration with the Belgian Justice Department. More than five hundred people were thus trained. The law department in the University of Rwanda trains jurists. Studies are based on the Belgian model. They involve general educational courses (philosophy, economics, sociology, accounting, history, theory of knowledge, English law, and so forth) and classes on Rwandan law and comparative law. Studies lead to a bachelor's degree in law. Graduates may enter directly into the magistrature, the bar or other public services as magistrates, or work as legal advisors.

THE ROLE OF THE LAW: A PROGRAMMATIC LAW

Recent codifications have unified the law, drawing from Western laws, customs, and international human rights conventions. Legal pluralism has resulted in imported law being imposed as common law and in traditional law being relegated to an auxiliary role, but certain traditional rules continue to hold sway in private law—hence creating a gap between the law of the people and the law of the legislator. Rwanda isn't a unique case in Africa. In many countries and many legal domains "the law acts as an ideal more than as an instrument of immediate transformation of the judicial order" (Alliot 1980).

Even if constitutional principles vouch for the independence of magistrates in performing their duties, their independence isn't entirely ensured. Their nomination is actually preceded by administrative selection by the executive power, which remains the sole master of the game. It is difficult to talk of independence of the magistrature without the guarantee of irremovability and nomination for life. Thus magistrates might have been imprisoned or stripped of their posts because they refused to follow orders given by administrative authorities or because they decided to give amnesty to those who were wrongly imprisoned.

The difference between popular practices and official actions might be explained by another conception of law, in the fundamental existence of two societies: one urban, another organized as a group for survival, by interests divided between public authorities and the population. Codification remains a lengthy process that requires a slow and profound maturation of thought, options that are sometimes transitory but that must mesh with the mentality of the people at the risk of becoming inapplicable. Faced with change, outside influence is necessary and inevitable. But it can be integrated only in stages.

Charles Ntampaka
Translated by Karna Hughes

References and further reading

Alliot, M. 1980. "Un droit nouveau est-il en train de naître en Afrique." Pp. 467–506 in *Dynamiques et finalités des droits africains: Actes du colloque de las Sorbonne.* Edited by Gérard Conac. Paris: Economica.

Bourgeois, R. 1954. *Banyarwanda et Barundi.* Vols. I and II. Tervuren: Institut Royal Colonial Belge.

David, René. 1973. *Les grands systèmes de droit contemporains.* Paris: Cinquième édition Dalloz.

Hooker, M. B. 1975. *Legal Pluralism: An Introduction to Colonial and Neo-Colonial Laws.* London: Oxford University Press.

Lamy, E. 1960. "Possibilités actuelles de codification du droit coutumier au Ruanda-Urundi." *Journal des Tribunaux d'Outre-mer* 11, no. 121 (July 15): 111–116.

Lemarchand, René. 1970. *Rwanda and Burundi.* London: Pall Mall Press.

Maquet, Jacques Jérôme Piérre. 1954. *Le Système des relations sociales dans le Rwanda ancien.* Tervuren: Institut Royal Colonial Belge.

Ntampaka, Charles, et al. 1994. "Family Law in Rwanda." Pp. 415–438 in *The International Survey of Family Law.* Edited by A. Bainham. The Hague: Martinus Nijhoff.

———. 1997. *La Répression du génocide en droit rwandais.* Bruxelles: Assepac.

———. 1998. *Codes usuels du Rwanda.* Bruxelles: Bruylant.

Reyntjens, Filip. 1985. *Pouvoir et droit au Rwanda: Droit public et évolution politique 1916–1973.* Tervuren, Belgium: Musée Royal de l'Afrique Centrale.

Sohier, Antoine. 1954. *Traité élémentaire de droit coutumier du Congo belge.* Bruxelles: F. Larcier.

Sohier, Jean. 1953. *Répertoire de jurisprudence du Congo belge et du Ruanda-Urundi jusqu'au 31 décembre 1953.* Bruxelles: Larcier.

Solus, Henry 1927. *Traité de la condition des indigènes en droit privé.* Paris: Sirey.

Vanderlinden, Jacques. 1972. *African Law Bibliography, 1947–1966.* Bruxelles: Presses Universitaires de Bruxelles.

———. 1983. *Les Systèmes juridiques africains.* Paris: P.U.F.